1998 Index of Economic Freedom

Bryan T. Johnson,
Kim R. Holmes,
and Melanie Kirkpatrick

The Heritage Foundation   THE WALL STREET JOURNAL.

BRYAN T. JOHNSON is a Policy Analyst at The Heritage Foundation.

KIM R. HOLMES is Vice President and Director of Foreign Policy and Defense Studies at The Heritage Foundation.

MELANIE KIRKPATRICK is Assistant Editor of *The Wall Street Journal* Editorial Page.

Robert L. Bartley is Editor of *The Wall Street Journal*.

William W. Beach is John M. Olin Senior Fellow in Economics at The Heritage Foundation.

Gareth Davis is a Research Assistant at The Heritage Foundation.

Brett D. Schaefer is Jay Kingham Fellow in International Regulatory Affairs at The Heritage Foundation.

L. Gordon Crovitz, based in Hong Kong, is Managing Director of Dow Jones Markets in Asia and Senior Dow Jones Representative in the region.

Layout and design by James V. Rutherford
Cover design and graphics by Thomas J. Timmons

ISBN 0–89195–244–6
ISSN 1095–7308

The Heritage Foundation
214 Massachusetts Avenue, N.E.
Washington, D.C. 20002
(202) 546-4400
http://www.heritage.org

The Wall Street Journal
Dow Jones & Company, Inc.
200 Liberty Street
New York, N.Y. 10281
(212) 416-2000
http://wsj.com

Table of Contents

Chapter 6:
The 1998 *Index of Economic Freedom*: The Countries 53
by Bryan T. Johnson

Acknowledgments

We would like to express our appreciation to several individuals at The Heritage Foundation who helped complete the fourth edition of the *Index of Economic Freedom*. We are grateful to the staffs of the Foreign Policy Studies and Domestic Policy Studies departments and the Asian Studies Center that participated in The Heritage Foundation's internal peer review process. The expertise of these analysts greatly enhanced the detailed analysis of the various countries included in this year's *Index*. The members of this group are Ariel Cohen, Senior Policy Analyst for Russian and Eurasian Affairs; Richard D. Fisher, Senior Policy Analyst for Asian Affairs; Robert P. O'Quinn, Policy Analyst for Asian Trade and Economics; James Phillips, Senior Policy Analyst for Middle East Affairs; James J. Przystup, Director of the Asian Studies Center; Brett D. Schaefer, Jay Kingham Fellow in International Regulatory Affairs; John P. Sweeney, Policy Analyst for Trade and Latin American Affairs; and Stephen J. Yates, Policy Analyst for China.

Kate Dwyer of the Foreign and Defense Policy Studies staff managed the data and the extensive research process. Kate was instrumental in contributing a substantial amount of research, crunching numbers, checking facts, and developing the charts and graphs. In addition, Yvette Campos and Simona Cremonini provided vital production support. Without their help we would not have met our deadlines.

We also would like to thank Janice A. Smith, Managing Editor, who was tasked with fine-tuning and editing the bulk of the book; Senior Editor Richard Odermatt; Director of Production

Services Ann Klucsarits; and the Heritage team that contributed so much to the final production of the book: Copy Editor William T. Poole, Editing and Publishing Associate James V. Rutherford, and Manager of Graphic Design Services Thomas J. Timmons. Their editorial and design skills were invaluable.

The maps in this edition were created by Thomas J. Timmons, who used a variety of source materials in developing both the regional and country maps: Cartesia Software's MapArt™, Mountain High Maps Frontiers™, and the CIA *World Factbook 1996*. He was responsible for formatting the charts and tables in this volume and also designed the *Index*'s cover.

Countless individuals serving with various accounting firms, businesses, research organizations, U.S. government agencies, embassies in Washington, and other organizations cooperated in providing us the data used in the *Index*. Their assistance is much appreciated. So, too, is the help of Heritage interns. In particular, Anne Crosmun, Nate Delemarre, and Lyndsay Nelson were extremely helpful in producing this edition of the *Index*. Like their predecessors in 1996, they did the legwork, cheerfully running down data throughout the humid Washington summer. We wish them the best in their new ventures.

We are grateful to Heritage Trustee Ambassador J. William Middendorf for encouraging us to undertake such a study of global economic freedom. Many other people within The Heritage Foundation generously have lent their expertise to our effort. We would like to express our appreciation to the many people who have enthusiastically praised the *Index of Economic Freedom*. We have been pleased indeed at how well the *Index* has been received. The support and encouragement of people worldwide has been important in inspiring us to produce this edition in cooperation with *The Wall Street Journal* Editorial Page. We hope this effort matches the expectations of all our supporters.

B.T.J.
K.R.H.
M.K.

Foreword

With the end of the Cold War, international events increasingly are defined not by wars or military formations but by economic events. Vivid imaginations have seen various juggernauts—the Arab sheiks, the Japanese multinationals, and now the Chinese masses—about to conquer the world not with bullets but with trade. Yet somehow, with the plunge in the oil price or the collapse of Japanese stocks, markets always seem to prevail.

Accordingly, more and more of the world has come to the conclusion that you can't fight the markets; you have to join them. The catchword of the new era is market opening—lowering of barriers to trade, abolition of restraints on the movement of capital, the privatization of enterprises the government previously deigned to run. If you allow the markets to work freely and openly, we now (or once again) see clearly, they will serve you with prosperity and progress.

Economic freedom, that is to say, bids to be the defining issue of a new era.

So *The Wall Street Journal* is glad once gain to join with The Heritage Foundation in publishing this year's edition of the *Index of Economic Freedom*. The ratings here provide a benchmark of economic freedom in more than 150 different countries. We hope and believe they will be useful to investors, to policymakers both international and domestic in these various countries, and indeed to anyone interested in the human condition.

No single measure, of course, can capture everything in an increasingly dynamic world economy. As this introduction is written, the financial headlines are about the currency crisis in Southeast Asia, a sharp reversal for countries that recently were "tigers." Argentina's bottom-rung rating on monetary policy accurately reflects its inflation over five years, but not its more recent success with an anti-inflationary currency board. Hong Kong's otherwise sterling rating is marred by a 2 in monetary policy, although with its dollar firmly anchored to the U.S. dollar, its measured inflation mostly represents constantly increasing prosperity among its citizens.

Yet current judgments need the historical benchmarks offered here. Whether Hong Kong will maintain its number-one rating after reversion to China is obviously no small question. Will Russia (number 104) really be eclipsed over coming years by China (number 120)? Or will we find that having put economic development ahead of political modernization, China still has before it the problems Russia is confronting now? Will the likely advent of a unified European currency be an impetus for a "fortress Europe" or a discipline on the welfare state? The ratings here will help us answer those large questions on a philosophical level, as on a practical level they will provide handy first impressions for investment decisions in different economies.

As I detailed in the introduction to last year's *Index*, the issue of economic freedom has been a preoccupation of *The Wall Street Journal* since its founding in 1889. Over that time, we have developed from a small financial sheet to an international network that embraces *The Wall Street Journal* in North America, *The Asian Wall Street Journal*, *The Wall Street Journal Europe*, *The Journal Americas* reprinted in newspapers throughout Latin America, and *The Wall Street Journal Interactive Edition*, which we believe to be the most successful paid site on the worldwide Internet.

Throughout this development, our editorial policy has always championed free people and free markets. Often over the past century, these ideas have been on the defensive, and it is remarkable to witness them reemerging and gaining the ascendancy as a new century approaches. We are delighted to join with The Heritage Foundation, another champion of the same ideals, to offer this volume celebrating—and we hope advancing—the cause of economic freedom throughout the world.

Robert L. Bartley
Editor
The Wall Street Journal
October 1997

Preface

As my colleagues at The Heritage Foundation and I travel the world to talk about the *Index of Economic Freedom,* we continually are impressed by the growing recognition on the part of many governments that economic freedom is a critically important ingredient of economic growth and prosperity. Governments around the world have been eager to receive a good score on the *Index,* not only because doing so signals acceptance into an advanced economics club, but also because they know foreign investors, market analysts, and economists increasingly look at economic freedom as a measure of an economy's general health and prospects for growth.

This linkage between economic freedom and prosperity has not always been so self-evident. It was not uncommon 20 or even 10 years ago to hear most Western economists and government policymakers argue that global poverty was largely the result of unequal global economic development, the West's plundering of natural resources, overpopulation, or even the failure of the West to share its wealth with the rest of the world. Of course, these views still hold sway in some places, but they no longer are as dominant as they once were. Instead, many more economists and policymakers hold the view today that the most important factors in determining long-range economic growth and prosperity are policies that reduce, as much as possible, governmental constraints on economic activity. They realize, in short, that the most important key to economic

prosperity is economic freedom.

The main purpose in publishing the annual *Index of Economic Freedom* has been to document and substantiate this key connection between economic freedom and economic prosperity. To achieve this goal, this fourth edition of the *Index* measures the impact of tax laws; tariffs; business regulations; government intervention in the economy; corruption in the judiciary, customs service, and bureaucracy; and a host of other economic environment factors on 156 countries around the world. Thus, the 1998 *Index of Economic Freedom* is the most comprehensive, concise, and up-to-date measurement of the world's economies ever published.

Since the *Index of Economic Freedom* was published as the first-ever study of economic freedom in 1994, other groups have published similar studies. For example, Freedom House published *World Survey of Economic Freedom* in 1996, and the Fraser Institute in Canada recently published *Economic Freedom of the World 1997*. We at The Heritage Foundation commend our colleagues at our sister institutions for taking on the challenge of expanding the understanding of the linkage between economic freedom and development and growth. We particularly commend Mike Walker of the Fraser Institute who, under the guiding spirit of Professor Milton Friedman, has done so much to advance the theoretical model. Jim Gwartney, a world-class economist at Florida State University, has devoted a considerable portion of his professional career over the past several years to defining, in a sophisticated way, these relationships. His pioneering work is helpful to all of the approaches of the different studies.

As happy as we are to see the appearance of these other studies, however, we believe The Heritage Foundation/Wall Street Journal 1998 *Index of Economic Freedom* remains unique. It employs a methodology that Heritage economists believe to be best-suited to understanding the relationship between the political, legal, and social environment on the one hand and economic well-being on the other. For example, unlike the Fraser study, the *Index* analyzes not only such factors as the rule of law and corruption in the judiciary and customs service, but also the impact of capital gains, value-added, and payroll taxes on economic activity. Moreover, instead of relying on a poll of economists to determine arbitrary weighting scales for its factors, we weigh all 10 economic factors of the economic environment equally. Our statistical analysis and, indeed, the analyses of many leading economists show that—at least at this point in the stage of research—specific weighting of different factors in the economic environment is not scientifically justifiable. It may be possible to do so in the future, and we commend efforts to study this problem further.

We take great care to ensure the comprehensiveness, integrity, and accuracy of our data and sources. The editors of the *Index* verify all data and information received from government sources with independent and internationally recognized sources. The main sources that were used for the *Index* are also the most objective sources available. This measure of transparency means that its data and scores are verifiable and replicable by independent scholars.

The 1998 *Index* has many other interesting features. Heritage economists William W. Beach and Gareth Davis provide a discussion of the crucial relationship between free trade and economic prosperity. They update their important finding from last year's *Index* that economic freedom is strongly related to economic growth. In addition, L. Gordon Crovitz of Dow Jones Markets discusses the usefulness of the *Index* as an investment tool, especially in Asia. And once again, Heritage analyst Bryan T. Johnson gives a critical assessment of the impact of U.S. foreign aid on economic development.

The most important new feature of the 1998 *Index* is a chapter presenting supplemental economic and social data on selected developed and developing countries. Brett D. Schaefer, Jay Kingham Fellow in International Regulatory Affairs at The Heritage Foundation, provides detailed information on members of the Organization for Economic Cooperation and Development, whose economies are the destination for most global foreign investment dollars. The chapter also includes data on the important developing economies of Brazil, India, Indonesia, the People's Republic of China, and Russia. The additional data in this chapter are important indicators or "signposts" to aid the investor.

The 1998 *Index of Economic Freedom* will foster many conclusions. But the most important is surely that government coercion and control over the entrepreneurial process are deadly forces when it comes to economic prosperity. Economies in which people are most free to work, accumulate earnings, and dispense those earnings as they see fit usually are also the most wealthy. By contrast, countries imposing the greatest amount of government control over their economies generally are also the poorest. This is a lesson that all countries—rich and poor, developed and underdeveloped—should heed if they wish to become (or remain, as the case may be) prosperous in the 21st century.

Edwin J. Feulner, Ph.D.
President
The Heritage Foundation
November 1997

Executive Summary

by Bryan T. Johnson, Kim R. Holmes, and Melanie Kirkpatrick

The concept of producing a user-friendly "index of economic freedom" as a tool for policymakers and investors was first discussed at The Heritage Foundation in the late 1980s. The goal then, as it is today, was to develop an index to measure empirically the level of economic freedom in countries around the world. To this end, a set of objective economic criteria was established; and since 1994, these criteria have been used to study and grade various countries for the annual publication of the *Index of Economic Freedom*. The *Index*, however, is more than just an empirical listing of scores; it is a careful analysis of the factors that contribute the most to the institutional setting for economic growth. And although many theories exist about the origins and causes of economic development, the findings of this study are conclusive: Countries that have the most economic freedom also have higher rates of economic growth and are more prosperous than those having less economic freedom.

The Heritage Foundation/Wall Street Journal 1998 *Index of Economic Freedom* measures how well 156 countries score on a list of 10 broad economic factors: The higher the score on a factor, the greater the level of government interference in the economy and the less economic freedom. A total of 50 independent economic variables were analyzed. These variables were grouped into the following 10 economic factors:

- Trade policy,
- Taxation,
- Government intervention in the economy,
- Monetary policy,
- Capital flows and foreign investment,
- Banking,
- Wage and price controls,
- Property rights,
- Regulation, and
- Black Market.

The methodology chapter explains these factors in detail. Taken cumulatively, the factors offer an empirical snapshot of a country's level of economic freedom. An objective analysis of these factors continues to demonstrate unequivocally that countries with the highest levels of economic freedom also have the highest living standards.

Similarly, countries with the lowest levels of economic freedom also have the lowest standards of living.

This year, the *Index* also offers a comparison of a country's 1998 score with its scores in previous editions. This comparison highlights an interesting phenomenon: Wealthy and economically free countries have been introducing new restrictions on economic freedom over time. These countries have begun to add welfare and other social programs that previously were not affordable. For example, after becoming economically "liberated," countries like Germany and France have fallen back down the scale of economic freedom, achieving lower scores than the newly emerging, free economies of Hong Kong and Singapore. Even though the economies of these so-called Asian tigers are growing and developing, they, too, may have begun to introduce post-industrial welfare and environmental policies that could restrict their economies in the future, albeit on a much smaller scale.

Scores in this fourth edition of the *Index* reflect this trend. Of the 10 highest-ranking countries in last year's edition, two received worse scores this year, seven remained the same, and only one improved its score. Bahrain and the Netherlands received worse scores because of increased restrictions on economic freedom. Bahrain increased its government regulations, and the Netherlands increased wage and price controls as well as government regulations. Future editions of the *Index* will continue to track this trend.

Six new countries are included in the study this year (55 have been added since the first edition). With these new countries, the *Index* offers its readers an even clearer vision of the world's most economically free and most repressed regions. And, as was true last year, most of the world's economies remain economically unfree. Of the 156 countries graded, 73 are mostly free or free, up from 72 last year, while 83 are mostly unfree or repressed, up from 78 last year. Of the top 10 freest countries, 4 are in North America or Europe, 4 are in Asia, 1 is in the Middle East, and 1 is in Latin America. Most of the world's freest economies are in North America and Europe, while most of the world's most economically repressed countries are in Africa and the Middle East. Asia has a mixture of free and unfree economies.

By region, many interesting developments have occurred since last year's edition. For example:

North America and Europe. In 1997, North America and Europe made the second greatest overall progress toward economic freedom. Of the 40 countries graded for the 1997 and 1998 editions of the *Index,* 15 (38 percent) achieved higher scores this year and 10 regressed. The region had the third lowest percentage of declining scores (25 percent), for a net increase of 13 percent. The United States is the most economically free country in North America, while Switzerland is the most economically free country in Europe. The economies of the United Kingdom, Ireland, Belgium, and Austria are the next most free. Former Marxist countries continue to make progress toward increasing economic freedom. The best examples are Estonia and the Czech Republic, both of which score well in the 1998 *Index*. These countries are following the models of Hong Kong and Singapore and promoting large economic growth rates by expanding economic freedom. Germany is the only country in Europe that has had declining scores every year since the first edition of the *Index*. The most recent cause of Germany's decline is an increase in banking restrictions and government regulations. Scores for both the Netherlands and Denmark have been worse three years in a row. Latvia and Lithuania both have marked three years of improving scores. Russia's score, which was worse in last year's edition than in the two previous editions, improved for this year's edition primarily because of reduced barriers to trade and reduced government intervention in the economy.

Latin America and the Caribbean. In 1997, this region made the greatest overall progress toward economic freedom. Of the 26 countries graded in this region, 12 (46 percent) improved their scores and 3 regressed for this year's edition of the *Index*. Latin America and the Caribbean also had the lowest percentage of declining scores (12 percent), for a net increase of 34 percent. The Bahamas is the most economically free country in Latin America and the Caribbean. Chile is the most economically free country in Central and South America, and Panama is the second most free economy, followed by El Salvador, Trinidad and Tobago, and Argentina. Mexico has made little progress and remains mostly unfree. Despite a rush of media reports on purported economic reform in Cuba, the facts show that Havana continues to pursue economically repressive policies. It remains the most economically unfree country in Latin America and one of the three most economically repressed countries in the world. In Central and South America, Chile, Panama, El Salvador, Argentina, Bolivia, Peru, Ecuador, Colombia, Nicaragua, and Venezuela all recorded better scores this year. Belize, Paraguay, and Guyana received lower scores. The rest remained the same.

Asia. Asia made modest progress toward economic freedom in 1997. The region made the third greatest progress overall. Of the 29 countries graded in the 1997 and 1998 editions of the *Index*, 10 (34 percent) improved their scores and 4 regressed. Asia also had the second lowest percentage of declining scores (14 percent), for a net increase of 20 percent. Three of the top five most free economies in the world are in Asia: Hong Kong, Singapore, and New Zealand. Australia, South Korea, and the Philippines all are in the top 50 and have improved over last year. Despite the enthusiasm of the investment community, Vietnam remains economically unfree, ranking sixth in a listing of the world's most economically repressed countries. It continues to suffer from corrupt border officials, an inadequate foreign investment law, and a legal system that offers little protection for private property. It has a centrally planned economy with a marginal, albeit growing, free market. India's score remains the same; so does Japan's, indicating that its spiraling economic recession has leveled off. China remains one of the most economically unfree countries in the world, although its score has improved over last year.

North Africa and the Middle East. Economic freedom in North Africa and the Middle East declined in 1997. Of the 17 countries graded, 3 (18 percent) improved their scores and 5 (29 percent) regressed. This region also had the lowest percentage of countries improving their scores, for a net decrease of 11 percent. Bahrain is the most economically free country in the Middle East and North Africa region, and it is the third freest economy in the world, although its overall score is worse this year than last year. Bahrain's high ranking is chiefly the result of a lack of taxation on personal income or corporate profits. Thus,

almost all income derived in Bahrain is tax-free. Bahrain also has one of the world's lowest levels of inflation, as well as a strong and efficient court system that upholds the rule of law. In the Middle East, the United Arab Emirates has the second most free economy, followed by Kuwait, Cyprus, and Oman. Although Israel improved its "mostly unfree" designation to "mostly free" by the second edition of the *Index,* it has not made any additional progress since then. In North Africa and the Middle East, Algeria, Egypt, Lebanon, and Pakistan have mostly unfree economies; Iran, Iraq, Libya, Syria, and Yemen have repressed economies. Egypt, Oman, and Syria achieved better overall scores this year. Overall scores for Bahrain, Jordan, Lebanon, Morocco, Pakistan, and Yemen, however, have worsened since last year's edition.

Sub-Saharan Africa. As a whole, sub-Saharan Africa remains the most economically unfree—and by far the poorest—area in the world. Of the 38 sub-Saharan African countries graded, none received a rating of free. Only 7 received a rating of mostly free, 25 were rated unfree, and 6 were rated repressed. Economic freedom in sub-Saharan Africa, in fact, declined in 1997; 11 countries (29 percent) received lower scores this year, while 9 (24 percent) improved their scores. This region also had a low percentage of improving scores, for a net decrease of 5 percent. The *Index* demonstrates quite clearly that sub-Saharan Africa's poverty is not the result of insufficient levels of foreign aid, weather patterns, or even internal strife; on a per capita basis, many sub-Saharan African countries are among those receiving the highest levels of economic assistance in the world. Rather, the main cause of poverty in sub-Saharan Africa is the lack of economic freedom embodied in policies these countries have imposed on themselves.

The findings of the *Index* regarding sub-Saharan Africa cast doubt on the assertion that economic growth can be achieved by huge transfers of wealth from the industrialized economies to the less-developed world. The people of Angola, Mozambique, Haiti, and Ukraine are not poor because wealthy people in the West do not share their riches. They are poor because their governments pursue destructive economic policies that depress free enterprise. Only when they increase the economic freedom of their citizens and unleash the phenomenal power of the free market will the poor countries of the world begin to achieve true prosperity and economic growth. Anything short of this is not only economically unwise, but inhumane.

The 1998 *Index of Economic Freedom* includes a chapter from *The Wall Street Journal* on the usefulness of the *Index* as an investment tool. Asia is the preeminent example here. Investors worried about the recent turmoil in Asian financial markets can take heart from the long-term trends identified in the *Index*. The impressive performance of so many Asian economies over the past decade has been based on openness to foreign investment, protection of property rights, relatively low levels of regulation, and investment in human capital. These strengths will become firm foundations as the region struggles to overcome structural problems in banking and real estate. Similarly, the *Index* can help investors spot developing countries elsewhere in the world whose economies are likely to grow the fastest.

The *Index* again includes a chapter by Heritage Foundation economists on the statistical connection between economic freedom and economic growth. The authors examine the economic benefits that flow from economic freedom and conclude that there is strong evidence, both from the emerging field of New Growth Theory and from statistical tests that they themselves have

conducted, linking the concepts measured in the *Index* to higher growth rates and greater prosperity. They conclude that introducing the sorts of reforms that would boost a country's score on the *Index* could well produce massive improvements in the living standards experienced by people in many of the poorest and most unfree economies.

Finally, a new chapter in the *Index* offers supplemental economic and social data that are important signposts for international investors. Most of these data are available only for a limited number of the world's economies. Thus, this information is provided solely to give additional information on issues relating to foreign investment. The chapter presents detailed information on member countries of the Organization for Economic Cooperation and Development (OECD), an organization that includes many of the world's most industrialized economies. OECD countries are the destination for the lion's share of global foreign investment. In addition, in recognition of the increasing importance of the developing world to investors, this chapter includes data on Brazil, India, Indonesia, the People's Republic of China, and Russia. The analysis of these data both underscores the importance of economic freedom to economic growth and provides international investors with supplemental information as a quick reference guide to the world's most important markets.

Global Distribution of Economic Freedom

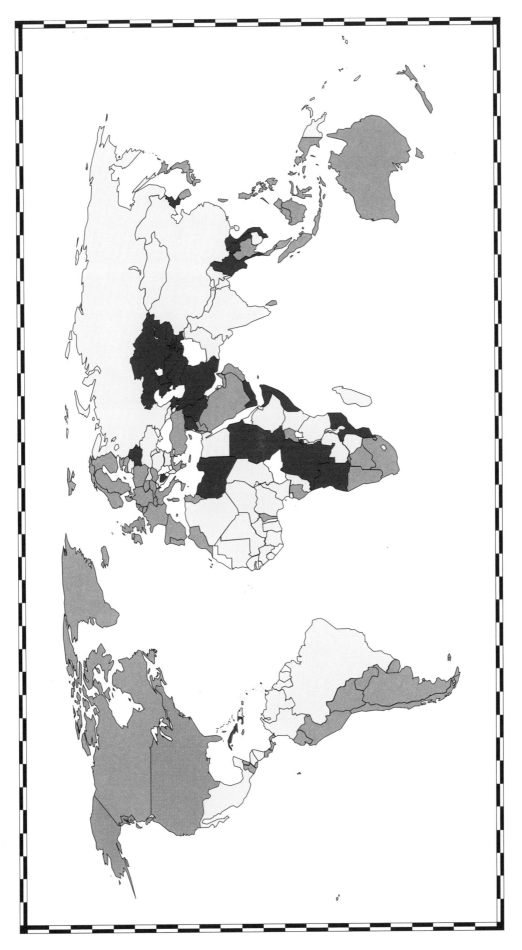

Free
Score: 1.00 to 1.99

Mostly Free
Score: 2.00 to 2.99

Mostly Unfree
Score: 3.00 to 3.99

Repressed
Score: 4.00 to 5.00

Not Ranked

Regional Rankings: Asia and the Pacific (32 Economies)

Regional Rank	World Rank		1998 Score	1997 Score	1996 Score	1995 Score
5	12	Australia	2.05	2.15	2.10	2.20
26	143	Azerbaijan	4.40	4.60	4.70	—
21	120	Bangladesh	3.75	3.70	3.65	3.90
18	96	Cambodia	3.35	3.55	—	—
21	120	China	3.75	3.80	3.80	3.80
16	85	Fiji	3.20	3.20	3.10	3.30
1	1	Hong Kong	1.25	1.25	1.25	1.25
20	117	India	3.70	3.70	3.75	3.70
13	62	Indonesia	2.85	2.85	2.85	3.35
5	12	Japan	2.05	2.05	2.05	1.95
24	136	Kazakstan	4.10	—	—	—
23	132	Kyrgyzstan	4.00	—	—	—
31	154	Laos	5.00	5.00	5.00	—
8	28	Malaysia	2.40	2.60	2.40	2.15
14	80	Mongolia	3.10	3.30	3.50	3.33
25	140	Myanmar (Burma)	4.30	4.30	4.30	—
19	102	Nepal	3.40	3.60	3.50	—
3	4	New Zealand	1.75	1.75	1.75	—
31	154	North Korea	5.00	5.00	5.00	5.00
16	85	Pakistan	3.20	3.10	3.05	3.15
15	83	Papua New Guinea	3.15	3.10	3.10	—
11	44	Philippines	2.65	2.80	2.90	3.30
2	2	Singapore	1.30	1.30	1.30	1.25
7	24	South Korea	2.30	2.45	2.30	2.15
10	32	Sri Lanka	2.45	2.45	2.65	2.80
4	7	Taiwan	1.95	1.95	1.95	1.95
26	143	Tajikistan	4.40	—	—	—
8	28	Thailand	2.40	2.30	2.30	2.30
28	145	Turkmenistan	4.50	—	—	—
29	146	Uzbekistan	4.55	—	—	—
30	147	Vietnam	4.70	4.70	4.70	4.70
12	53	Western Samoa	2.80	2.80	2.80	—

Economic Freedom in Asia and the Pacific

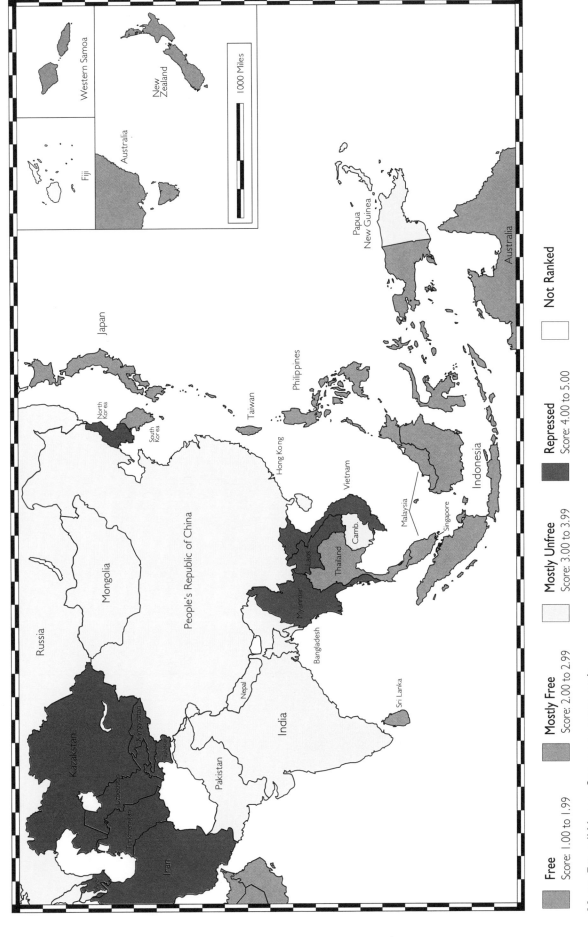

Free
Score: 1.00 to 1.99

Mostly Free
Score: 2.00 to 2.99

Mostly Unfree
Score: 3.00 to 3.99

Repressed
Score: 4.00 to 5.00

Not Ranked

Note: Fiji and Western Samoa are not to scale.

Regional Rankings: North America and Europe (42 Economies)

Regional Rank	World Rank		1998 Score	1997 Score	1996 Score	1995 Score
38	120	Albania	3.75	3.65	3.45	3.55
34	104	Armenia	3.45	3.45	3.75	–
8	17	Austria	2.15	2.15	2.05	2.05
41	135	Belarus	4.05	3.85	3.55	3.65
6	14	Belgium	2.10	2.10	2.10	–
42	152	Bosnia	4.80	–	–	–
36	114	Bulgaria	3.65	3.60	3.50	3.50
6	14	Canada	2.10	2.10	2.00	2.00
38	120	Croatia	3.75	3.70	3.70	–
21	39	Cyprus	2.60	2.60	2.60	–
10	20	Czech Republic	2.20	2.05	2.00	2.10
12	22	Denmark	2.25	2.05	1.95	–
8	17	Estonia	2.15	2.35	2.35	2.25
12	22	Finland	2.25	2.30	2.30	–
18	35	France	2.50	2.50	2.30	2.30
37	114	Georgia	3.65	3.85	3.85	–
14	24	Germany	2.30	2.20	2.10	2.00
26	66	Greece	2.90	2.85	2.80	2.80
26	66	Hungary	2.90	2.90	2.90	2.80
15	24	Iceland	2.30	2.50	–	–
5	10	Ireland	2.00	2.20	2.20	2.20
18	35	Italy	2.50	2.60	2.70	2.50
24	62	Latvia	2.85	2.95	3.05	–
29	74	Lithuania	3.00	3.10	3.50	–
3	7	Luxembourg	1.95	2.05	1.95	–
24	62	Malta	2.85	2.95	3.05	3.25
33	96	Moldova	3.35	3.35	3.45	4.10
10	20	Netherlands	2.20	2.00	1.85	–
16	27	Norway	2.35	2.45	2.45	–
28	67	Poland	2.95	3.15	3.05	3.25
21	39	Portugal	2.60	2.60	2.60	2.80
32	94	Romania	3.30	3.40	3.70	3.55
34	104	Russia	3.45	3.65	3.50	3.50
30	77	Slovak Republic	3.05	3.05	2.95	2.75
31	80	Slovenia	3.10	3.10	3.35	–
18	35	Spain	2.50	2.60	2.70	2.60
17	32	Sweden	2.45	2.45	2.55	2.65
1	5	Switzerland	1.90	1.90	1.80	–
23	53	Turkey	2.80	2.80	3.00	3.00
40	125	Ukraine	3.80	3.75	4.00	3.90
3	7	United Kingdom	1.95	1.95	1.95	1.95
1	5	United States	1.90	1.90	1.90	1.90

Economic Freedom in North America and Europe

Free
Score: 1.00 to 1.99

Mostly Free
Score: 2.00 to 2.99

Mostly Unfree
Score: 3.00 to 3.99

Repressed
Score: 4.00 to 5.00

Not Ranked

Regional Rankings: North Africa and the Middle East (18 Economies)

Regional Rank	World Rank		1998 Score	1997 Score	1996 Score	1995 Score
10	88	Algeria	3.25	3.25	3.25	3.15
1	3	Bahrain	1.70	1.60	1.70	1.60
13	103	Cape Verde	3.44	3.44	3.44	—
12	96	Egypt	3.35	3.45	3.45	3.50
16	147	Iran	4.70	4.70	4.70	—
18	153	Iraq	4.90	4.90	4.90	—
7	53	Israel	2.80	2.80	2.90	3.10
5	49	Jordan	2.75	2.70	2.80	2.90
3	28	Kuwait	2.40	2.40	2.40	—
10	88	Lebanon	3.25	2.95	2.95	—
16	147	Libya	4.70	4.70	4.70	—
9	69	Morocco	2.95	2.75	2.70	2.90
4	44	Oman	2.65	2.75	2.85	2.65
7	53	Saudi Arabia	2.80	2.80	2.90	—
14	132	Syria	4.00	4.20	4.20	—
5	49	Tunisia	2.75	2.75	2.65	2.85
2	14	United Arab Emirates	2.10	2.10	2.10	—
15	136	Yemen	4.10	3.90	3.75	3.75

Sub-Saharan Africa (37 Economies)

Regional Rank	World Rank		1998 Score	1997 Score	1996 Score	1995 Score
35	142	Angola	4.35	4.35	4.35	4.35
6	69	Benin	2.95	2.95	2.95	—
2	49	Botswana	2.75	2.85	2.80	3.05
19	107	Burkina Faso	3.50	3.50	3.70	—
30	129	Burundi	3.90	3.80	—	—
19	107	Cameroon	3.50	3.60	3.60	3.60
27	125	Chad	3.80	3.80	—	—
26	120	Congo	3.75	3.75	3.80	3.90
36	147	Congo (former Zaire)	4.70	4.20	4.20	—
12	85	Djibouti	3.20	3.00	—	—
24	117	Ethiopia	3.70	3.60	3.70	3.80
6	69	Gabon	2.95	2.95	3.05	3.06
22	112	Gambia	3.60	3.60		—
8	74	Ghana	3.00	3.20	3.20	3.30
13	88	Guinea	3.25	3.45	3.35	3.35
17	96	Ivory Coast	3.35	3.35	3.25	3.25
9	77	Kenya	3.05	3.05	3.05	3.05
19	107	Lesotho	3.50	3.65	3.65	—
17	96	Madagascar	3.35	3.25	3.35	3.50
23	114	Malawi	3.65	3.55	3.40	3.40
11	80	Mali	3.10	3.10	3.10	3.50
27	125	Mauritania	3.80	3.80	3.80	—
32	136	Mozambique	4.10	4.00	4.05	4.40
2	49	Namibia	2.75	2.95	—	—
24	117	Niger	3.70	3.70	3.70	—
16	94	Nigeria	3.30	3.20	3.25	3.15
34	140	Rwanda	4.30	4.20	—	—
13	88	Senegal	3.25	3.25	3.40	—
29	128	Sierra Leone	3.85	3.85	3.75	3.75
36	147	Somalia	4.70	4.70	4.70	—
5	66	South Africa	2.90	3.00	3.00	3.00
33	139	Sudan	4.20	4.20	4.10	4.22
1	47	Swaziland	2.70	2.80	2.90	2.90
13	88	Tanzania	3.25	3.25	3.45	3.50
4	53	Uganda	2.80	2.90	2.83	2.94
9	77	Zambia	3.05	2.85	2.95	3.05
30	129	Zimbabwe	3.90	3.70	3.70	3.50

Economic Freedom in Africa and the Middle East

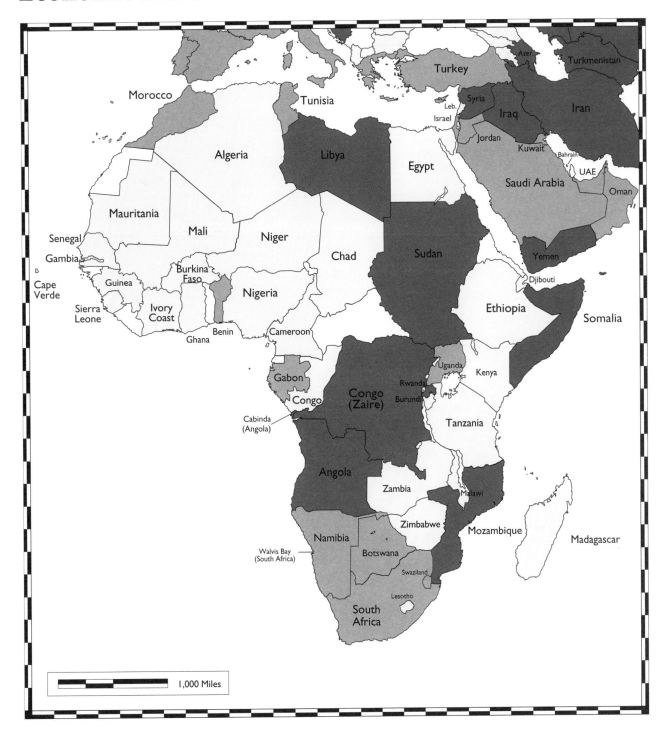

Free Score: 1.00 to 1.99	**Mostly Free** Score: 2.00 to 2.99	**Mostly Unfree** Score: 3.00 to 3.99	**Repressed** Score: 4.00 to 5.00	**Not Ranked**

Regional Rankings: Latin America and the Caribbean (27 Economies)

Regional Rank	World Rank		1998 Score	1997 Score	1996 Score	1995 Score
6	39	Argentina	2.60	2.65	2.65	2.85
1	10	Bahamas	2.00	2.00	2.00	2.10
6	39	Barbados	2.60	2.80	3.00	—
11	53	Belize	2.80	2.70	2.70	2.70
9	44	Bolivia	2.65	2.85	2.75	3.20
20	96	Brazil	3.35	3.35	3.45	3.30
2	17	Chile	2.15	2.25	2.45	2.50
17	74	Colombia	3.00	3.10	3.00	2.90
11	53	Costa Rica	2.80	2.80	2.80	2.90
27	154	Cuba	5.00	5.00	5.00	5.00
21	104	Dominican Republic	3.45	3.45	3.45	3.40
16	69	Ecuador	2.95	3.05	3.15	3.25
4	32	El Salvador	2.45	2.55	2.45	2.65
11	53	Guatemala	2.80	2.80	2.85	3.05
24	112	Guyana	3.60	3.50	3.35	—
26	132	Haiti	4.00	4.00	4.20	4.20
18	83	Honduras	3.15	3.15	3.15	3.15
6	39	Jamaica	2.60	2.60	2.70	2.80
19	88	Mexico	3.25	3.35	3.35	3.05
22	107	Nicaragua	3.50	3.60	3.60	3.90
3	28	Panama	2.40	2.50	2.40	2.70
15	62	Paraguay	2.85	2.75	2.65	2.75
11	53	Peru	2.80	2.90	3.00	3.40
25	129	Suriname	3.90	4.00	3.90	—
5	38	Trinidad and Tobago	2.55	2.55	2.50	—
10	47	Uruguay	2.70	2.70	2.80	2.90
22	107	Venezuela	3.50	3.60	3.50	3.00

Economic Freedom in South America

Venezuela

Guyana

Colombia

Surimane

Ecuador

Peru

Brazil

Bolivia

Paraguay

Chile

Argentina

Uruguay

1,000 Miles

Falkland Islands
(United Kingdom)

South Georgia Island
(United Kingdom)

	Free		Mostly Free		Mostly Unfree		Repressed		Not Ranked
	Score: 1.00 to 1.99		Score: 2.00 to 2.99		Score: 3.00 to 3.99		Score: 4.00 to 5.00		

Economic Freedom in Central America and the Caribbean

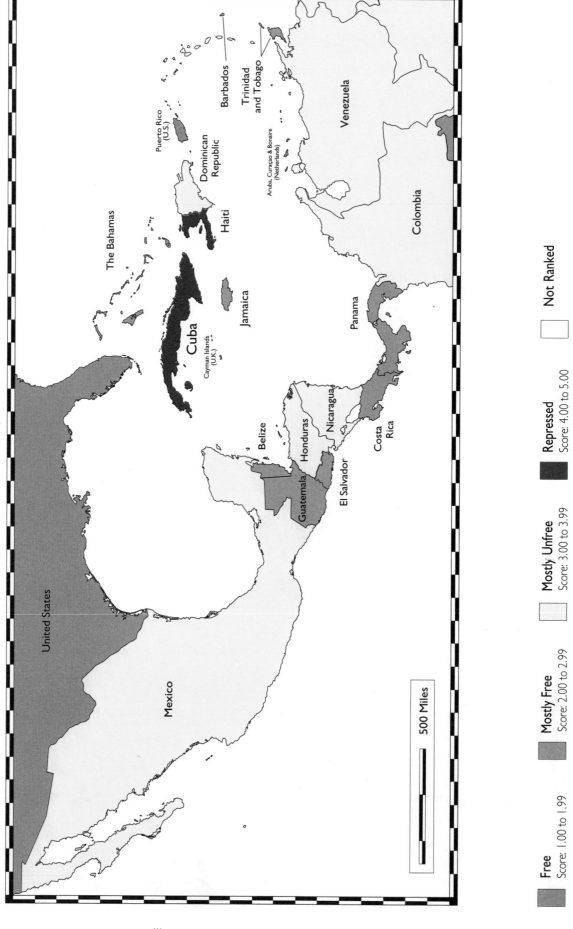

Free
Score: 1.00 to 1.99

Mostly Free
Score: 2.00 to 2.99

Mostly Unfree
Score: 3.00 to 3.99

Repressed
Score: 4.00 to 5.00

Not Ranked

500 Miles

United States

Mexico

The Bahamas

Cuba

Cayman Islands (U.K.)

Jamaica

Haiti

Dominican Republic

Puerto Rico (U.S.)

Barbados

Trinidad and Tobago

Aruba, Curaçao & Bonaire (Netherlands)

Venezuela

Colombia

Panama

Costa Rica

Nicaragua

Honduras

El Salvador

Guatemala

Belize

Index of Economic Freedom Rankings

Rank		1998 Score	1997 Score	1996 Score	1995 Score	Trade	Taxation	Government Intervention	Monetary Policy	Foreign Investment	Banking	Wage/Prices	Property Rights	Regulation	Black Market
1	Hong Kong	1.25	1.25	1.25	1.25	1	1.5	1	2	1	1	2	1	1	1
2	Singapore	1.30	1.30	1.30	1.25	1	3	1	1	1	2	1	1	1	1
3	Bahrain	1.70 -	1.60	1.70	1.60	2	1	3	1	2	2	2	1	2 -	1
4	New Zealand	1.75	1.75	1.75	—	2	3.5	2	1	2	2	2	1	2	1
5	Switzerland	1.90	1.90	1.80	—	2	3	3	1	2	2	2	1	3	1
5	United States	1.90	1.90	1.90	1.90	2	4	2	1	2	2	2	1	2	1
7	Luxembourg	1.95 +	2.05	1.95	—	2	3.5 +	3	1	2	2	2	1	2	1
7	Taiwan	1.95	1.95	1.95	1.95	2	2.5	2	1	3	3	2	1	2	1
7	United Kingdom	1.95	1.95	1.95	1.95	2	4.5	2	1	2	2	2	1	2	1
10	Bahamas	2.00	2.00	2.00	2.10	5	1	2	1	3	2	2	1	1	2
10	Ireland	2.00 +	2.20	2.20	2.20	2	5	2	1	2	2	2	1	2	+
12	Australia	2.05 +	2.15	2.10	2.20	2	4.5	3	1	2	3	2	1	3	+
12	Japan	2.05	2.05	2.05	1.95	2	4.5	1	1	3	3	2	1	2	1
14	Belgium	2.10	2.10	2.10	—	2	5	2	1	2	2	2	1	3	1
14	Canada	2.10	2.10	2.00	2.00	2	5	2	1	3	2	2	1	2	1
14	United Arab Emirates	2.10	2.10	2.10	—	2	1	3	2	4	3	3	1	2	1
17	Austria	2.15	2.15	2.05	2.05	2 +	4.5	3	1	2	2 -	2	1	3	1
17	Chile	2.15 +	2.25	2.45	2.50	2	3.5	1	3	2	3	2	1	2	2 +
17	Estonia	2.15 +	2.35	2.35	2.25	1 +	3.5	2	4	1	2	2	2	2	2 +
20	Czech Republic	2.20 -	2.05	2.00	2.10	2 -	4 -	2	2	2	2	2	2	2 -	3 +
20	Netherlands	2.20 -	2.00	1.85	—	2	5	3	1	2	2	3 -	1	3 -	1
22	Denmark	2.25 -	2.05	1.95	—	2	4.5	4	1	2	2	2 -	1	2	1
22	Finland	2.25 +	2.30	2.30	—	2	4.5 -	3	1	2	3	2 +	1	3	3 -
24	Germany	2.30 -	2.20	2.10	2.00	2	5	2 +	1	2	3 -	2	1	4	1
24	Iceland	2.30 +	2.50	—	—	2	4	3	2 +	2 +	3	2 +	1	3	1
24	South Korea	2.30 +	2.45	2.30	2.15	3	4 +	2	2	2 +	2	2	1	3	2
27	Norway	2.35 +	2.45	2.45	—	2 +	4.5	3	1	2	3	3	1	3	1
28	Kuwait	2.40	2.40	2.40	—	2	1	4	2	4	3	3	1	2	2
28	Malaysia	2.40 +	2.60	2.40	2.15	3 +	3	2	1	3	3	3	2	2	2
28	Panama	2.40 +	2.50	2.40	2.70	3 +	3	3	1	2	1	2	3	3	3
28	Thailand	2.40 -	2.30	2.30	2.30	3	3	2 -	1	2 +	3	3	2 -	3	2
32	El Salvador	2.45 +	2.55	2.45	2.65	3	2.5	1 +	3	2	2	2	3	3	3
32	Sri Lanka	2.45	2.45	2.65	2.80	3	3.5	2	2	3	3	1	3	2	3
32	Sweden	2.45	2.45	2.55	2.65	2	4.5	5	1	2	2	2	2	3	—
35	France	2.50	2.50	2.30	2.30	2	5	3	1	3	3	3	2	3	1
35	Italy	2.50 +	2.60	2.70	2.50	2 +	5	3	2	2	2	2	2	3	2
35	Spain	2.50 +	2.60	2.70	2.60	2	5	2	2	2	2 +	3	2	3	2
38	Trinidad and Tobago	2.55	2.55	2.50	—	5	4.5	2	2	1	2	2	1	3	3
39	Argentina	2.60 +	2.65	2.65	2.85	4	3 +	2	5	2	2	2	2	2	2

Note: Scores followed by a plus sign (+) have improved from last year. Those followed by a minus sign (-) have worsened.

Index of Economic Freedom Rankings

Rank		1998 Score	1997 Score	1996 Score	1995 Score	Trade	Taxation	Government Intervention	Monetary Policy	Foreign Investment	Banking	Wage/ Prices	Property Rights	Regulation	Black Market
39	Barbados	2.60 +	2.80	3.00	–	3 –	5	3	1	2	2	2	2 +	3	3
39	Cyprus	2.60	2.60	2.60	–	3	4	3	1	2	2	3	3	2	3
39	Jamaica	2.60	2.60	2.60	2.80	2	3	2	4	2	2	3	2	3	3
39	Portugal	2.60	2.60	2.60	2.80	2	5	3	2	2	3	2	2	3	2
44	Bolivia	2.65 +	2.85	2.75	3.20	2	2.5	3 +	3	2	2	1	3	4	4
44	Oman	2.65 +	2.75	2.85	2.65	2 –	3.5	4	1	3	4	3	2	2	2
44	Philippines	2.65 +	2.80	2.90	3.30	3 +	3.5 –	1	2	3	3	2	3	3	4
47	Swaziland	2.70 +	2.80	2.90	2.90	3 +	3	2	2	2	3	3	2	3	4
47	Uruguay	2.70	2.70	2.80	2.90	2	3	3	5	2	2	2	2	3	3
49	Botswana	2.75 +	2.85	2.80	3.05	3 +	2.5	4	2	3	2	2	2	3	4 –
49	Jordan	2.75 –	2.70	2.80	2.90	4	2.5 +	3 –	2	2	2	3	2	3	4
49	Namibia	2.75 +	2.95	–	–	4	3.5	4	2	2	2	2 +	2	3 +	3
49	Tunisia	2.75	2.75	2.65	2.85	5	3.5	3	2	2	2	2	3	2	3
53	Belize	2.80 –	2.70	2.70	2.70	5	4	2	1	2	3	2	3 –	3	3
53	Costa Rica	2.80	2.80	2.80	2.90	4	3	2	3	2	3	2	3	3	3
53	Guatemala	2.80	2.80	2.85	3.05	3	3	1	3	3	2	3	3	4	3
53	Israel	2.80	2.80	2.90	3.10	2	5	4	3	1	3	2	2	2	4
53	Peru	2.80 +	2.90	3.00	3.40	2 +	3	4 –	5	2	2	2	3	4	4
53	Saudi Arabia	2.80	2.80	2.90	–	4	3	4	1	4	2	2	1 –	2	2
53	Turkey	2.80	2.80	3.00	3.00	2 –	4 +	2	5	2	2	3	2	3	3
53	Uganda	2.80 +	2.90	2.83	2.94	5 –	4	2 +	5	2	3	1	2	2 +	2
53	Western Samoa	2.80	2.80	2.80	–	3	4	2	2	3	3	3	3	3	2
62	Indonesia	2.85	2.85	2.85	3.35	2	3.5	1	2	2	3	3	3	4	5
62	Latvia	2.85 +	2.95	3.05	–	2 +	2.5	3	5	2	2	2	3 –	3	4
62	Malta	2.85 +	2.95	3.05	3.25	4	3.5	2	1	2	3	4	2 +	3	4
62	Paraguay	2.85 –	2.75	2.65	2.75	2	2.5	2	4	1	2	3	4 –	3	5
66	Greece	2.90 –	2.85	2.80	2.80	2	4 –	3	3	2	4	2	2	3	3
66	Hungary	2.90	2.90	2.90	2.80	4	4	3	4	2	2	2	2	3	3
66	South Africa	2.90 +	3.00	3.00	3.00	4 +	4	3	3	2	2	2	3	2	3
69	Benin	2.95	2.95	2.95	–	4	3.5	3	3	3	3	3	3	3	3
69	Ecuador	2.95 +	3.05	3.15	3.25	3	2.5	1	5	2	3	2 +	3	4	4
69	Gabon	2.95	2.95	3.05	3.06	5	4.5	3	1	2	2	3	3	3	3
69	Morocco	2.95 –	2.75	2.70	2.90	5 –	3.5	3	1	2	3	3	3 –	3	3
69	Poland	2.95 +	3.15	3.05	3.25	2 +	3.5	3	5	2	3	3	2	3	3
74	Colombia	3.00 +	3.10	3.00	2.90	3 +	4	2	4	3	2	2	3	3	5
74	Ghana	3.00 +	3.20	3.20	3.30	3 +	3	3	4	3	3	2	3	4	2
74	Lithuania	3.00 +	3.10	3.50	–	1 +	3	3	5	2	3	3	3	3	4
77	Kenya	3.05	3.05	3.05	3.05	4	3.5	3	2	3	2	3	3	4	3
77	Slovak Republic	3.05	3.05	2.95	2.75	3 –	4.5	3	2 +	3	3	3	3	3	3

Note: Scores followed by a plus sign (+) have improved from last year. Those followed by a minus sign (–) have worsened.

Index of Economic Freedom Rankings

Rank		1998 Score	1997 Score	1996 Score	1995 Score	Trade	Taxation	Government Intervention	Monetary Policy	Foreign Investment	Banking	Wage/ Prices	Property Rights	Regulation	Black Market
77	Zambia	3.05 -	2.85	2.95	3.05	3 -	3.5	3 -	5	2	2	2	3	4	3
80	Mali	3.10	3.10	3.10	3.50	3	5	3	1	2	3	3	3	3	5
80	Mongolia	3.10 +	3.30	3.50	3.33	1 +	4	3	5	3	3	3	3	3	3
80	Slovenia	3.10	3.10	3.35	–	4	4	3	5 -	2 +	2	3	2 +	3	3
83	Honduras	3.15	3.15	3.15	3.15	4	3.5	1 +	3 -	3	3	3	3	4	4
83	Papua New Guinea	3.15 -	3.10	3.10	–	5	2.5 +	3	1	3	4	3	3	4 -	3
85	Djibouti	3.20	3.00	–	–	4	2	5 -	1	3	3	3	3	4	4
85	Fiji	3.20	3.20	3.10	3.30	5	3	3	1	3	3	3	3	4	4
85	Pakistan	3.20 -	3.10	3.05	3.15	5	4	3	2	2	3	3	3 -	4	3
88	Algeria	3.25	3.25	3.25	3.15	5	3.5	3	3	3	3	3	3	3	3
88	Guinea	3.25 +	3.45	3.35	3.35	3 +	4.5	3 -	3	3	2	2	4	4	4 +
88	Lebanon	3.25	2.95	2.95	–	5 -	2.5	2	5	3	2	2	3	3	5
88	Mexico	3.25 +	3.35	3.35	3.05	3	3.5	2 +	5	2	4	3	3	4	3
88	Senegal	3.25	3.25	3.40	–	4 +	4.5	3	1	3	3	4	3	3	3
88	Tanzania	3.25	3.25	3.45	3.50	3	3.5	3	4	3	3	2	3	4	4
94	Nigeria	3.30 -	3.20	3.25	3.15	5	3	2	5 -	2	4	2	3	4	3
94	Romania	3.30 +	3.40	3.70	3.55	2	5	3	5	2	3	2	4	3	3 +
96	Brazil	3.35	3.35	3.45	3.30	4	2.5	3	5	3	3	3	3	3	4
96	Cambodia	3.35 +	3.55	–	–	3 +	2.5	3 +	5 -	3	3	3	4	3	3
96	Egypt	3.35 +	3.45	3.45	3.50	5	4.5	3	3	3	2 +	3	3	4	4
96	Ivory Coast	3.35	3.35	3.25	3.25	5	3.5	3	1	3	3	3	4	3	4
96	Madagascar	3.35 -	3.25	3.35	3.50	5 -	3.5	2	3	4	4	2	3	3	4
96	Moldova	3.35	3.35	3.45	4.10	3	3.5	3	5	3	4	3	3	3	4
102	Nepal	3.40 +	3.60	3.50	–	3 +	3	2 +	2	4	4	4	3	4	5
103	Cape Verde	3.44	3.44	3.44	–	5	N/A	3	2	2	5	4	2	4	4
104	Armenia	3.45	3.45	3.75	–	2	3.5	3	5	4	3	3	3	4	4
104	Dominican Republic	3.45	3.45	3.45	3.40	5	2.5	2	5	3	3	2	4	4	4
104	Russia	3.45 +	3.65	3.50	3.50	4 +	3.5	3 +	5	3	2	3	3	4	4
107	Burkina Faso	3.50	3.50	3.70	–	5	4	3	1	2	4	4	3	4	5
107	Cameroon	3.50 +	3.60	3.60	3.60	5	4	2 +	1	3	4	3	4	4	5
107	Lesotho	3.50 +	3.65	3.65	–	3 +	4 +	3	3	3	4	4	3	4	4
107	Nicaragua	3.50 +	3.60	3.60	3.90	4 +	3	2	5	2	3	3	4	4	5
107	Venezuela	3.50 +	3.60	3.50	3.00	3 +	4	3	5	3	3	3	3	3	5
112	Gambia	3.60	3.60	3.40	–	4	4	3	2	4	4	4	2	4	5
112	Guyana	3.60 -	3.50	3.35	3.70	5 -	4	3	5	3	3	2	2	4	4
114	Bulgaria	3.65 -	3.60	3.50	3.50	4 -	4.5 +	3	5	3	3	3	3	4	4
114	Georgia	3.65 +	3.85	3.85	–	3	2.5	2 +	5	3	4	4	4	4	5
114	Malawi	3.65 -	3.55	3.40	3.40	5	4.5	3	4 -	3	3	3	3	3	4
117	Ethiopia	3.70	3.60	3.70	3.80	5 -	3	3	2	4	4	3	4	4	4

Note: Scores followed by a plus sign (+) have improved from last year. Those followed by a minus sign (-) have worsened.

Index of Economic Freedom Rankings

Rank		1998 Score	1997 Score	1996 Score	1995 Score	Trade	Taxation	Government Intervention	Monetary Policy	Foreign Investment	Banking	Wage/Prices	Property Rights	Regulation	Black Market
117	India	3.70	3.70	3.75	3.70	5	4	3	2	3	4	4	3	4	5
117	Niger	3.70	3.70	3.70	—	5	4	3	1	4	4	4	3	4	5
120	Albania	3.75 -	3.65	3.45	3.55	3	3.5	5	5	2	4	3	4 -	3	5
120	Bangladesh	3.75 -	3.70	3.65	3.90	5	3.5 +	3 -	2	3	3	4	4	5	5
120	China	3.75 +	3.80	3.80	3.80	5	3.5 +	5	3	3	3	3	4	4	4
120	Congo	3.75	3.75	3.80	3.90	5	4.5	3	1	4	4	3	4	4	5
120	Croatia	3.75 -	3.70	3.70	—	3	3.5 -	5	5	3	3	4	4	4	3
125	Chad	3.80	3.80	—	—	5	4	3	1	4	4	4	4	4	4
125	Mauritania	3.80	3.80	3.80	—	5	4	3	2	3	5	4	4	4	4
125	Ukraine	3.80 -	3.75	4.00	3.90	4	4 +	3	5	3	4	3	4 -	3	4
128	Sierra Leone	3.85	3.85	3.75	3.75	4	4.5	3	5	3	4	3	4	3	5
129	Burundi	3.90 -	3.80	3.75	—	5	4	3	2 -	4	4	3	4	4	5
129	Suriname	3.90 +	4.00	3.90	—	5	4 +	3	5	3	3	3	3	4	5
129	Zimbabwe	3.90 -	3.70	3.70	3.50	3	4	4 -	4	3	3	3	4 -	5	4
132	Haiti	4.00	4.00	4.20	4.20	4	3	3	3	4	4	4	5	5	5
132	Kyrgyzstan	4.00	4.20	—	—	4	4	3	5	3	4	4	4	4	5
132	Syria	4.00 +	4.20	4.20	—	5	5	3	3 +	4	5	4	4 -	2	5
135	Belarus	4.05 -	3.85	3.55	3.65	4 +	4.5	3	5	4	3	4 -	4 -	4 -	5
136	Kazakstan	4.10	—	4.00	—	4	4	3	5	4	4	4	4	4	5
136	Mozambique	4.10 -	4.00	4.05	4.40	5 -	4	3	5	4	3 +	3	4	5	5
136	Yemen	4.10 -	3.90	3.75	3.75	5	3	4	5	4 -	4	3	4	4	5
139	Sudan	4.20	4.20	4.10	4.22	5	5	3	5	4	4	4	4	4	4
140	Myanmar (Burma)	4.30	4.30	4.30	—	4	3	5	4	5	4	4	4	5	5
140	Rwanda	4.30 -	4.20	—	—	5	5	4	2 -	4	5	3	5	5	5
142	Angola	4.35	4.35	4.35	4.35	5	3.5	4	5	4	4	4	4	5	5
143	Azerbaijan	4.40 +	4.60	4.70	—	5	4	5	5	4 +	4	5	4	4	4 +
143	Tajikistan	4.40	—	—	—	5	5	4	5	4	4	4	4	4	5
145	Turkmenistan	4.50	—	—	—	5	5	4	5	4	5	4	4	4	5
146	Uzbekistan	4.55	—	—	—	5	4.5	4	5	4	5	4	4	5	5
147	Congo (former Zaire)	4.70 -	4.20	4.20	—	5 -	5	4 -	5	5 -	5 -	4	5 -	4	5
147	Iran	4.70	4.70	4.70	—	5	5	5	4	5	5	4	5	4	5
147	Libya	4.70	4.70	4.70	—	5	5	5	2	5	5	5	5	5	5
147	Somalia	4.70	4.70	4.70	—	5	5	5	5	4	4	3	5	5	5
147	Vietnam	4.70	4.70	4.70	4.70	5	5	5	5	4	5	4	5	5	5
152	Bosnia	4.80	—	—	—	5	5	5	5	4	5	5	5	4	5
153	Iraq	4.90	4.90	4.90	—	5	5	5	5	5	5	4	5	5	5
154	Cuba	5.00	5.00	5.00	5.00	5	5	5	5	5	5	5	5	5	5
154	Laos	5.00	5.00	5.00	5.00	5	5	5	5	5	5	5	5	5	5
154	North Korea	5.00	5.00	5.00	5.00	5	5	5	5	5	5	5	5	5	5

Note: Scores followed by a plus sign (+) have improved from last year. Those followed by a minus sign (-) have worsened.

The Institutional Setting of Economic Growth

by William W. Beach and Gareth Davis

To those struggling to be successful in business, it is well known that the rules of the government and customs of the community can influence the scope of business activity. Certain communities permit trade on holy days; others do not. Some governments encourage exchange with suppliers and customers in other countries; others raise barriers that prohibit international transactions. Workers and business owners in some countries face taxes that burden entrepreneurship so greatly that innovation withers; in other countries, governments levy just enough tax to support the judicial and protective functions needed by those who risk physical property and personal labor to create new products.

What ordinary business people have understood for countless generations is now working its way back into mainstream economics. After a long and relatively barren period, economists are paying full attention to the crucial role played by civil and political institutions in shaping economic activity. Academic and policy economists now ask questions about the institutional setting for economic growth—questions that remind historians of economic doctrine of problems that dominated the attention of the early classical economists like Adam Smith, David Ricardo, and John Stuart Mill. What set of rules and policies will best ensure a country's prosperity? What set of institutional arrangements most promotes economic growth? The modern economist's question about economic growth should be of concern to all citizens who care about their economic future: How can institutions and policies be changed so that higher levels of economic well-being and output are achieved?

Those who ask these types of questions can gain significant insight about how best to answer them by carefully studying The Heritage Foundation/Wall Street Journal 1998 *Index of Economic Freedom*. Not only does the *Index* clearly identify successful countries that can serve as models for achieving higher levels of economic performance, it also identifies the institutional arrangements that appear to be conducive to achieving superior levels of well-being and growth. As this chapter will demonstrate, the *Index* draws on a rich body of scholarship on economic growth that encompasses insights as old as Adam Smith's and as recent as the New Growth Theory of the 1990s. In short, the *Index of Economic Freedom* is more than an interesting annual snapshot of international progress toward freer markets and freer people; it also can be a road map to help reduce poverty and expand economic horizons around the world.

Importance of the Institutional Context for Economic Growth

Adam Smith, the 18th century Scottish philosopher and founder of modern economics, devoted the whole of his *Inquiry into the Nature and Causes of the Wealth of Nations* to a seemingly simple question: Why do some countries prosper while others do not?[1] For Smith and his many followers, the answer was obvious: All economic growth flourishes from the single root of creatively dividing labor in the production of desirable goods, and blossoms in a political environment that protects private property, free exchange, and the justly deserved fruits of labor. Countries will experience opulence and peace, Smith argued, once they create the institutions that encourage entrepreneurship and savings (the stock of capital upon which all production takes place). On the other hand, countries reap only poverty and despair when they discourage business and punish productive activities.

Subsequent generations of economists—in fact, nearly all major schools of economic thought since Smith—have begun their work with the same question: What is economic growth? And all these perspectives on economic life—from Alfred Marshall and Karl Marx to John Maynard Keynes and Friedrich Hayek—have emphasized the critical relationship between economic activity and its institutional setting when explaining the phenomenon of economic growth. Perhaps more important, much of the policymaking community and intellectually active public already recognizes that sustainable, long-term growth stems in some fashion from the synergy between freewheeling capitalism and the institutions that sustain the civil society.

Even so, experts and laymen alike differ on what is meant by economic growth and the nature of its mediating institutions. Is economic growth merely the expansion of an economy's size, or is it the extension of improved well-being to all of a country's citizens? Do a country's imperial designs executed in the name of economic growth count

at all in answering the basic question of what constitutes growth, or does growth in any meaningful sense occur only when peaceful domestic and international exchange leaves, as in David Ricardo's felicitous example, the English and the Portuguese both better off through trade in cloth and wine?[2]

Similarly, if government policy puts labor behind and capital ahead in the struggle for income shares, or strips capital owners of their property in the name of improved welfare for labor, is that really growth? Does public policy play any role at all in the long-term growth of an economy, or does economic expansion really stem only from changes in population and technology that are not related to public policy?

Considering these difficult questions, many of which are raised by experts on economic growth, is it any wonder that non-experts, from oil tycoons to short-order cooks, wonder what to believe? Nearly everyone lives in the massive currents of economic change, the swirl and rush of markets, the rise and tumble of great companies, and the ebb and flow of everyday working life. These are the economic rhythms that shape people's lives and punctuate their everyday work, and they leave precious little time for abstracting the big questions from the minutiae of living.

Although most people can sense that more income, more goods and services, and more economic opportunities promote economic growth, they, like many experts, puzzle over what ingredients are essential to facilitate that growth. They wonder about what public policies they should support, which politicians they should believe, and what they can do to ensure a bigger economy for their children and grandchildren.

It is on these questions that The Heritage Foundation/Wall Street Journal *Index of Economic Freedom* sheds much-needed light. The *Index* measures a country's degree of economic freedom using a composite score consisting of 10 elements, each of which forms a major part of that country's institutional setting. These 10 elements are trade policy, taxes, government consumption of economic output, monetary policy, capital flows and foreign investment policy, banking regulation, wage and price controls, protection of property rights, business regulation, and the strength of the black market. Each element is scored separately, with the average of all elements for a country constituting a rating of that country's level of economic freedom.

What does this year's *Index of Economic Freedom* suggest about a country's prospects for superior economic growth? This chapter takes two approaches to answering this question. First, many economists of the New Growth Theory[3] school believe that the institutional setting strongly influences the rate of economic growth. A review of recent developments in this new field of research supports the position that low *Index* (greater economic freedom) scores imply superior rates of economic growth. Second, statistical work conducted independently by The Heritage Foundation also links *Index* scores to economic growth.

A Short Primer on the Economics of Growth

From the 1960s to the mid-1980s, the dominant academic theory of what causes economic growth was the Solow Growth Model, named after Nobel Laureate Robert Solow. From both a factual and a policy viewpoint, this theory has performed poorly.

First, the theory offered meager advice to policymakers on how to generate economic growth. Solow argued that the only way a country could boost its level of growth was to save more and therefore accumulate physical capital. Even an increase in the rate of capital accumulation would bring only a one-time boost in income, however, and have only a short- or medium-term increase in economic growth rates. The long-run rate of economic growth (the "steady state" level) was determined by "technological innovation." This technological innovation was a mysterious force within Solow's model that could not be analyzed by economists or influenced by government policy. In the Solow model, to paraphrase the famous Cambridge economist Joan Robinson, technology (and hence growth) falls like manna from heaven.

Second, the major factual prediction of traditional growth theory (that poorer countries generally would grow faster and "converge" to the economic status of richer countries) has not been borne out in the real world.[4]

What Is the New Growth Theory?

In 1983, Professor Paul Romer, then at the University of Rochester, published a paper entitled "Increasing Returns and Long Run Growth."[5] Some 35 pages long and accessible only to those with a firm grasp of mathematics, this paper revolutionized the field of growth theory and led to the emergence of the New Growth Theory.

Romer argued that an initial increase in a society's productive capacity can feed on itself (because of what are known technically as *increasing returns*) to produce permanently higher rates of growth. This feedback effect stands in sharp contrast to the *decreasing returns* contained in the old theory, under which the growth effects of an increase in a society's productive capacity are only temporary. In other words, under the old theory of decreasing returns, policy changes would produce only a one-time boost to economic activity, after which the economy would return to its long-term growth rate. Under the new theory of increasing returns, however, it is possible to affect the long-term growth rate itself.

The old growth theory predicted that establishing sound policies would lead only to a one-time boost in income (and therefore only a transitory increase in economic growth rates). The theory of increasing returns, however, implies that instituting sensible policies can result in a GDP growth rate that is permanently higher. This means that the benefits of instituting wise economic policies (and the costs of pursuing misguided policies) are much greater than was thought to be the case under the old theories that assumed decreasing returns. In this model, introducing a "good" policy can create a virtuous circle of economic expansion that will feed on itself to bring about a permanent acceleration in the growth of prosperity. Likewise, "bad" policies can mean permanently lower growth rates and cost society more than earlier economists had thought possible.

Importance of Technology, Institutions, and Human Capital to Economic Growth. The New Growth Theory is sometimes referred to as *Endogenous Growth Theory* because key factors in economic growth (human capital, technology, innovation, and institutions) are now examined within and form an integral part of (that is, are "endogenous" to) this view of the world. No longer seen

Lessons from New Growth Theory

- **Accumulate capital.** Increasing the stock of physical capital available for each worker in the economy is one of the best ways to increase per capita income.

- **Keep government small.** Government spending consumes scarce resources that could be used for productive investment and distorts the incentives faced by individuals and firms. State ownership of capital stock means that the output from those productive assets will be lower than if they were in private hands.

- **Open the economy to foreign trade and investment.** New Growth Theory has uncovered many previously unknown gains from foreign trade and investment, including the faster and deeper diffusion of technology from abroad, an increase in competition that improves efficiency, and more rapid capital accumulation.

- **Respect property rights and the rule of law.** Without adequate protection for property rights and a secure political environment, individuals and firms will face severe disincentives to invest and engage in productive activities.

- **Do not burden the productive sector with government regulations and controls.** Regulations, mandates, and wage and price controls are a drag on economic growth. They raise the cost of producing goods and services and make innovation and invention more expensive. Government controls also increase the opportunities for gains from corruption and thus divert entrepreneurship from productive activities to nonproductive "rent-seeking" activities.

- **Invest in "human capital."** Education, which increases worker productivity, is very important to growth, according to many leading New Growth economists. In this context, it is important that education systems operate primarily to educate students rather than to serve the ends of "social justice" or of powerful political groups.

as mysterious and unfathomable, these factors are treated as concrete entities over which policymakers can exercise some influence, whether for good or for ill. The focus of Romer's original paper was technology. Other theorists, such as 1995 Nobel Laureate Robert Lucas, have examined the growth implications of human capital, institutions, and other factors. In the old growth theory, the only things for which its advocates could account were the accumulation of physical capital and population growth. None of the other factors that cause economic growth could be explained, predicted, or influenced by public policies.

Emphasis on Investigating the Causes of Economic Growth Using Statistical Tests. New Growth Economics extends beyond mere theory. Economists have been inspired by these new

theories to use statistical models. In the past eight years, a massive volume of econometric research has been carried out on explanations for the differences in growth rates across countries. This has been made possible by the recent emergence of internationally compatible and reliable long-run economic data for developing and developed countries. Even though this work is ongoing and in a state of relative infancy, several generalized findings have begun to emerge.

There is a striking correspondence between the elements of the *Index of Economic Freedom* and the key statistical findings of the New Growth Theory. New Growth economists show that high levels of growth are positively associated with (1) the level of private investment (especially in machinery); (2) "openness" to international trade and finance; (3) the educational attainment level of the population; and (4) the rule of law, political stability, and the protection of property rights. Economists in this field also associate slow or negative economic growth with hyperinflation, high levels of government consumption and taxation, and excessive regulation. The *Index* considers nearly all of these factors to be crucial in evaluating economic freedom across countries.

Above all, the New Growth Theory strongly suggests that public policies *do* matter. In a recent essay on why some countries enjoy better economic performance than others, Mancur Olson, one of the world's leading economic theorists, observes that "Those countries with the best policies and institutions achieve most of their potential, while other countries achieve only a tiny faction of their potential income."[6] Olson further notes that

> the large differences in per capita income across countries cannot be explained by differences in access to the world's stock of productive knowledge or to its capital markets, by differences in the ratio of population to land or natural resources, or by differences in the quality of marketable human capital or personal culture.... The only remaining plausible explanation is that the great differences in the wealth of nations are mainly due to differences in the quality of their institutions and economic policies.[7]

Statistical Relationship of the *Index* to Economic Growth

In addition to the strong support this scholarship affords the *Index* as an indicator of future economic performance, statistical tests performed by The Heritage Foundation further underscore the applicability of the *Index* to discussions of economic growth. Using one of the largest datasets designed for comparisons of inter-country growth,[8] Heritage analysts found statistically significant relationships both between the *Index* and country-by-country levels of economic development and between the *Index* and economic growth rates.

Chart 1.1 shows the type of relationship observed between economic growth and *Index* values. In Chart 1.1, the vertical axis contains the percentage change in real gross domestic product (GDP) per capita for 1995. The horizontal axis shows the *Index* values for 1995 based on data from the preceding year. This graph clearly shows a distinct association between lower *Index* numbers (freer economies) and higher levels of economic growth. In other words, this analysis strongly suggests that countries with free-market public policies grow faster than countries with repressed economies.[9]

Chart 1.2 demonstrates this correlation between economic freedom and economic growth as well by describing the average annual real per capita growth rate of countries in each *Index* category. Countries with repressed economies or mostly unfree economies in 1996 experienced negative per capita income growth on average over the period from 1980 to 1993. Free economies, and to a lesser extent mostly free economies, on average experienced positive real income growth.

Despite the limitations of these and other data used to explore the implications of policy changes on cross-country growth rates, numerous other eminent scholars have found similar and significant relationships between economic growth and government policies. For example, Robert Barro, a Harvard professor and contributing editor of *The Wall Street Journal*, found a strong positive relationship between growth rates and data that measure the degree to which a country rules itself by law as opposed to the whims and edicts of political strongmen. He also found that growth rates are better in those countries in which government consumes a lower share of GDP than they are in those countries in which government consumes higher percentages of GDP. Barro has determined that other policy and institutional or non-economic variables significantly related to growth include the rate of inflation, political rights, the fertility rate, years of secondary and higher education, and the initial level of GDP.[10]

Responding to the Critics

As the *Index of Economic Freedom* gains stature as a measure of relative economic freedom, it naturally has attracted the attention of critics as well as the commendations of many readers worldwide. The authors, economists, and editors of the *Index* are delighted, of course, by the increasing scrutiny

Chart 1.1

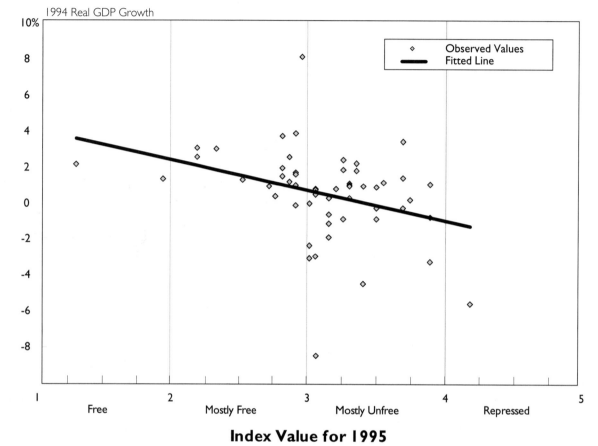

Relationship of Economic Growth to Index Values for 1995

1994 Real GDP Growth

Index Value for 1995

Free · Mostly Free · Mostly Unfree · Repressed

◊ Observed Values
━━ Fitted Line

Source: Michael Bruno, and William Easterly, "Inflation Crises and Long-Run Growth," *Journal of Monetary Economics,* forthcoming, 1997. These data are made available through the World Bank's Growth Project. They are available on the World Wide Web at: *http://www.worldbank.org/html/prdmg/grthweb/datasets.htm*

their work has received, and a number of criticisms made over the past year have resulted in additional explanation in this year's *Index*. The editors always review constructive criticisms seriously and use them, wherever possible, as the basis for improving future editions of the *Index*.

Two recent reviews, however, merit special commentary. The Fraser Institute and Bruce Scott of the Harvard Business School raised questions about last year's *Index of Economic Freedom* that reveal misunderstandings about our work, and a few words here may clarify our objectives for readers of this year's edition.[11]

The Fraser Institute, a long-time colleague in

the field of measuring relative degrees of economic freedom, regularly publishes its own scores of economic liberty. The Fraser Institute, however, focuses much more on measuring economic freedom in terms of economic outcomes rather than institutional inputs. Its method of scoring countries reflects this focus.

If the sole purpose of the Heritage Foundation/Wall Street Journal *Index of Economic Freedom* were to explain economic growth, the Fraser Institute's criticism would have some purchase. The *Index,* however, is devoted to describing important aspects of the institutional environment within which economic activity takes

Chart I 2

Long-Run Average Annual Per Capita Growth

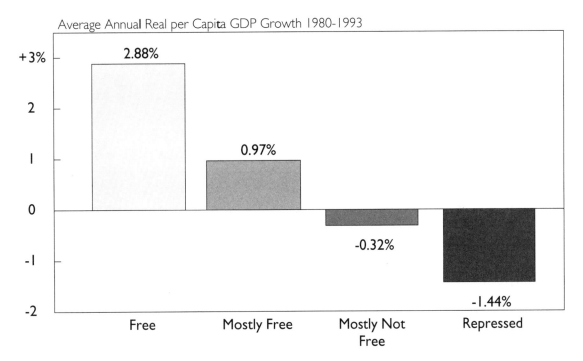

Average Annual Real per Capita GDP Growth 1980-1993

1997 Index of Economic Freedom Classification

Note: Per capita GDP growth is expressed in terms of Purchasing Power Parities.
Source: Heritage calculations based on Barro-Lee data described in Robert Barro and Xavier Sala-I-Martin, *Economic Growth,* 1995.

place. As this chapter notes, there doubtless is a strong connection between economic growth and economic freedom, but the growth rates of individual countries also are affected by many other factors, including the average age of the population, the historical size of the economy, weather, war, and pestilence. The *Index* attempts to affirm the truth that societies with high degrees of economic freedom also are societies with long-term, superior economic well-being. We believe that describing the economic world in terms of its institutional setting sheds more light on the reasons that some economies grow and others do not than would another deterministic, narrowly specified model of how economies grow.

Criticisms of last year's *Index* from Harvard University professor and economist Bruce Scott went well beyond methodological quibbles. Scott attacked the *Index* as a typical product of free-market conservatives who dismiss the key role of government, particularly in shaping economic activity and achieving high growth rates through programs that (1) force citizens to save and (2) coerce other economic behaviors that expand annual output. Professor Scott no doubt speaks for reconstructed central planners all over the world who today recognize the importance of markets but continue to insist on certain interventionist public policies to produce defined economic results. He is particularly interested in using the state to achieve a more apparent equality in the distribution of income.

The *Index,* of course, speaks for those who understand that free markets produce steadier and fairer economic progress than markets shaped by government edict. Not only does history show the central role of economic freedom in producing superior economic well-being and growing

Table 1.1

What Would it Mean for Congolese Living Standards if the Economic Growth Rate Increased?

If it grew as fast as . . .	Real GDP Growth Rate 1980-1993	Income Per Person After 10 Years	Income Per Person After 25 Years	Income Per Person After 50 Years
Congo	-1.0%	$525	$451	$347
OECD	2.1%	715	976	1,642
Hong Kong	5.4%	982	2,163	8,055
Singapore	6.1%	1,050	2,552	11,216
Botswana	6.2%	1,060	2,613	11,757
Thailand	6.4%	1,080	2,739	12,917
South Korea	8.2%	1,277	4,166	29,884

Note: All figures are in 1985 inflation-adjusted U.S. dollars.
Source: Heritage calculations based on data from 1994 World Bank *World Development Report* and Penn *World Tables* Version 5.5.

economies, it also shows that state intervention in private economic decision making nearly always reduces long-term well-being. Professor Scott simply is wrong in arguing that the *Index* ignores the state. The *Index* does recognize government's role in protecting free markets, principally through its judicial, monetary, and international functions. In fact, the *Index* may be viewed correctly as singularly devoted to examining government's role in economic affairs.

Unlike Professor Scott, who suggests that government can get the economy right by using its unique powers of coercion, the *Index* argues that "getting it right" largely means finding ways to assure that the power of the state in economic affairs will be reduced and government's energies redirected to supporting the institutional framework for economic freedom.

How Higher Growth Rates Affect Poor Countries

Enormous benefits would accrue for human welfare if countries solved the riddle of what causes economic growth. An indication of this can be obtained by taking the case of the former Zaire—now the Democratic Republic of Congo, one of the world's poorest and most destitute

countries—and seeing how much faster it would grow if its economy expanded at the long-term rates sustained by a diverse group of market-oriented economies.

In 1989, the latest year for which data are available, Zaire had a real, average income per capita of $580 in inflation-adjusted 1995 U.S. dollars—just under one-40th of per capita income in the United States. During the 1980s, real per capita income in Zaire declined at an average rate of just over 1 percent per annum.

Heritage economists analyzed what would happen to living standards in the Democratic Republic of Congo over the next 50 years if its economy were to grow at an annual rate of 2.1 percent. This percentage growth rate is equivalent to that achieved by countries in the Organization for Economic Cooperation and Development (OECD) during the 1980s, and actually better than the historical rates achieved by Zaire or, indeed, Third World countries in general. The results of this analysis were compared with what could happen if the Democratic Republic of Congo's policymakers implemented the market-orientated measures that would enable the country to sustain the long-term growth rates achieved by Hong Kong, South Korea, Singapore, Botswana, and Thailand over the period from 1980 to 1993.

Chart 1.3

The Democratic Republic of Congoís GDP per Capita Under Three Different Growth Scenarios

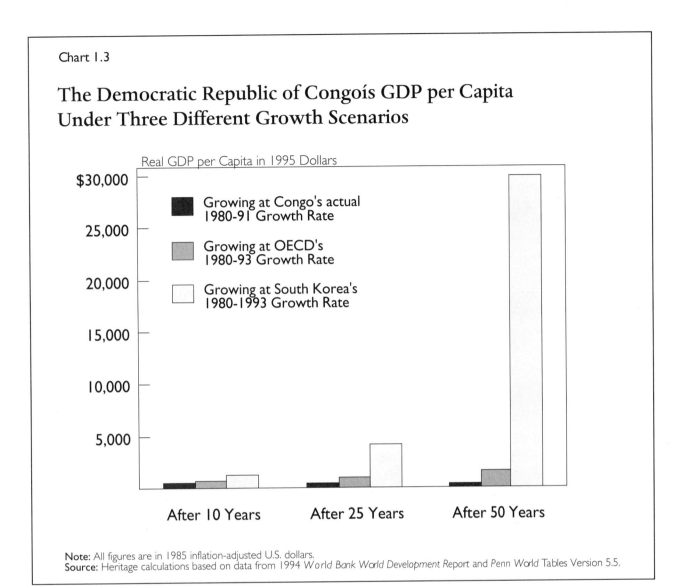

Real GDP per Capita in 1995 Dollars

Legend:
- Growing at Congo's actual 1980-91 Growth Rate
- Growing at OECD's 1980-93 Growth Rate
- Growing at South Korea's 1980-1993 Growth Rate

After 10 Years   After 25 Years   After 50 Years

Note: All figures are in 1985 inflation-adjusted U.S. dollars.
Source: Heritage calculations based on data from 1994 *World Bank World Development Report* and *Penn World* Tables Version 5.5.

As can be seen from Table 1.1, if the Democratic Republic of Congo's economy grew at a rate of only 2.1 percent, a decade's worth of growth would raise income levels by only 23 percent, from $580 to $715 per capita in real 1995 dollars—roughly the per capita income currently enjoyed by Uganda. And if the Democratic Republic of Congo's per capita income grew at 2.1 percent per annum for 50 years, real per capita income would reach only $1,642—roughly the same as the standard of living enjoyed by the Ivory Coast or Zimbabwe today.

By contrast, if the Democratic Republic of Congo adopted the policies necessary to attain the long-term growth rates of those countries listed in Table 1.1, it could escape poverty rapidly. If its growth rate rose to the same level as the long-term rate achieved by Singapore, Botswana, or

Thailand, its living standards within 25 years would approximate roughly those currently enjoyed by such countries as Morocco or El Salvador. Within 50 years, income levels in the Democratic Republic of Congo would be roughly equivalent to those currently enjoyed by Cyprus, Greece, or Portugal. Also within 50 years, even at the lower Hong Kong growth rate, the country would attain living standards equivalent to levels currently enjoyed by Malaysia or Hungary. And if the Democratic Republic of Congo sustained the growth rates achieved by South Korea, within 50 years its standard of living would well exceed that which is currently enjoyed by the United States.

At a mediocre growth rate of 2.1 percent, it would take the Democratic Republic of Congo almost 200 years to achieve the living standards currently enjoyed in the industrial world. The typical child born there in 1996, with a life expectancy of 46 years, would not be alive to experience these income levels.[12] If, however, the country achieved growth rates equivalent to those in Hong Kong, Singapore, Botswana, Thailand, or South Korea, this child would be likely to live long enough to enjoy living standards equivalent to those enjoyed today by some of the world's richer countries. When it is realized that the costs of flawed interventionist policies may not be merely mediocre growth rates, but rather stagnant or even declining incomes, the potential benefits from a market-orientated regime become even greater.

The growth rates necessary for the Democratic Republic of Congo to achieve these feats are well within reach. With the sorts of income levels that are produced by faster economic growth, more resources would be available for individuals to meet their own basic human wants and needs, such as food, housing, medical care, education, and other goods. The result would be large numbers of people who are healthier, better fed, and better educated, and who have more resources with which to improve their lives. The economic growth rates used in this analysis were achieved for a sustained period of time by a diverse group of countries ranging from Hong Kong to Thailand (with its formerly rice-based subsistence economy)

to the sub-Saharan African state of Botswana. What they all have in common are relatively high levels of economic freedom.[13]

Conclusion

What could happen in the Democratic Republic of Congo could occur also in scores of other countries caught in the grip of poverty and economic decline. In fact, any country willing to embrace the policies of economic freedom could produce the powerful effects of pro-growth economic policies. Although cultural and political factors (including the frequency of wars) will make each country's response somewhat different, it appears to be a universal truth that free trade, free markets, and free men and women create stronger economies and better lives than is possible with any other "mix" of public policies.

The *Index of Economic Freedom* points clearly to those policies that reduce want and increase life spans. This makes the *Index* more than an intellectual exercise. This chapter began with a discussion of Adam Smith and ended with the Democratic Republic of Congo. This progression might strike some as odd, but Adam Smith—whose economics lived squarely in the real world—certainly would understand.

Appendix:
Evidence from New Growth Economics
on Components of the *Index of Economic Freedom*

Evidence from the New Growth literature, combined with the work of earlier economists, supports the argument that the concepts measured by the *Index of Economic Freedom* are related to economic growth. That is, conclusions from New Growth Economics link differences in the rate of economic growth across countries to a number of policy variables, many of which the *Index* attempts to measure.

Econometric studies by economists at Harvard, the World Bank, and the Federal Reserve Bank have found that long-term growth rates rise as restraints on foreign trade and investment are lowered.[14] Calculations by Columbia economist Richard Baldwin have demonstrated that old models of growth tend to underestimate drastically the magnitude of gains from free trade.[15] A March 1996 cross-section/time series econometric analysis of over 120 countries by Columbia University economist Ann Harrison revealed a robust relationship between economic growth in developing countries and numerous measurements of the degree of openness to international trade and investment.[16] These results, which show a strong statistical link between free-trade policies and economic success, replicate the findings of a 1991 World Bank study of 95 developing countries over the period 1976–1986.[17]

The latest professional evidence also overwhelmingly supports the case that openness to international trade and foreign investment—not the reverse—causes economic growth. A recent National Bureau of Economic Research study by Berkeley economists Jeffrey Frankel, David Romer, and Teresa Cyrus clearly shows that, in a host of high-growth East Asian countries, the direction of causation has been from free trade and open investment policies to economic growth.[18]

Likewise, numerous cross-country studies have established that high levels of government spending will slow the long-term rate of economic growth.[19] An econometric model calibrated by Professors Robert King and Sergio Rebelo of the University of Rochester found that traditional growth models underestimate the negative growth effect of taxes by a magnitude of 40.[20]

Studies also have found links between inflation (particularly hyperinflation) and lower long-term GDP growth rates.[21] Recent statistical evidence also indicates the special importance of a strong, sophisticated, and unencumbered banking and financial system as a conduit for economic growth.[22]

Robert Barro of Harvard and Xavier Sala-I-Martin of Yale University have found a correlation between lower rates of growth and measures of the distortions caused by wage, price, and exchange controls and other forms of government regulation.[23] Economists also have succeeded recently in uncovering a robust empirical link between cross-country, long-term economic growth and the degree to which governments abide by the rule of law and respect and enforce property rights and contracts.[24]

After a decade of New Growth Economics, the scientific evidence is more persuasive than ever that the concepts measured in the *Index of Economic Freedom* indicate clearly the degree to which a country's current economic policies and institutions are friendly or unfriendly to economic growth.[25]

Notes

1. Adam Smith, *An Inquiry into the Nature and Causes of the Wealth of Nations,* Glasgow Edition, R. H. Campbell and A. S. Skinner, eds. (Oxford: Oxford University Press, 1976); published originally in 1776.

2. David Ricardo, *On the Principles of Political Economy and Taxation,* Third Edition, Piero Sraffa, ed. (Cambridge: Cambridge University Press, 1951); published originally in 1821. See especially Chapter 7, "On Foreign Trade," for Ricardo's discussion of how two economies can grow by trading commodities in which each has a comparative advantage.

3. For a brief review of the New Growth literature, see Appendix, "Evidence from New Growth Economics on Components of the *Index of Economic Freedom,*" *infra.*

4. Some economists have found evidence of convergence when they control for countries' differing savings rates, but this convergence has been very weak. In any case, the traditional model of growth has no explanation for what causes these international differences in savings rates, and therefore no policy prescriptions in this regard.

5. Published in *Journal of Political Economy,* Vol. 94 (1986), pp. 1002–1037.

6. Mancur Olson, Jr., "Big Bills Left on the Sidewalk: Why Some Nations Are Rich, and Others Are Poor," *Journal of Economic Perspectives,* Vol. 10 (Spring 1996), p. 6.

7. *Ibid.,* p. 19.

8. Michael Bruno and William Easterly, "Inflation Crises and Long-Run Growth," *Journal of Monetary Economics,* forthcoming 1997. These data are made available through the World Bank's Growth Project, available on the World Wide Web at *http://www.worldbank.org/html/prdmg/grthweb/datasets.htm.*

9. A number of qualifications must be made about the association contained in Chart 1.1. First, a number of factors outside the sphere of economic policy affect a country's growth rate: natural disasters, mineral discoveries, commodity price shifts, war, pestilence, and the policies of other countries, to name a few. A prudent use of the relationship illustrated above is valid, however; at the very least, it emphasizes a connection between economic performance and public policies. Second, only 56 countries out of 156 in the full *Index* are present in this analysis. Even so, the array of countries contained in Chart 1.1 is representative of the full set of countries scored in the 1995 *Index.*

10. Robert J. Barro, presentation to Heritage Foundation Roundtable on Economic Growth, June 26, 1996; copies available upon request from The Heritage Foundation. See also Robert J. Barro, "Economic Growth in a Cross-Section of Countries," *Quarterly Journal of Economics,* Vol. 106 (1991), pp. 407–443.

11. James D. Gwartney and Robert A. Lawson, *Economic Freedom of the World 1997* (Vancouver, Canada: Fraser Institute, 1997); and Bruce R. Scott, "How Do Economies Grow?" *Harvard Business Review,* May–June 1997, pp. 2–6.

12. Based on an estimate contained in the 1996 *CIA World Factbook.*

13. All of the high-growth nations mentioned here have relatively high levels of economic freedom. Among sub-Saharan African nations, Botswana had by far the best 1996 *Index of Economic Freedom* ranking and has enjoyed its economic success in a region ravaged by widespread declines in average income levels. Hong Kong and Singapore are the first and second most economically free countries in the 1997 *Index of Economic Freedom.* Thailand and South Korea (ranked 23 and 27, respectively, out of 150) also receive relatively good scores. The Democratic Republic of Congo (then Zaire) was ranked 136. Many commentators have argued that rapid population growth and "culture" bar such countries as the Democratic Republic of Congo from enjoying rapid income growth even if the proper policies are implemented. This is a fallacy. The societies mentioned in this analysis are very different from one another, and some in

the past were "diagnosed" as facing some of the same problems afflicting the Democratic Republic of Congo.

14. Ross Levine and David Renelt, "A Sensitivity Analysis of Cross-Country Growth Regressions," *American Economic Review,* Vol. 82 (1990), pp. 943–963; David Gould and Roy Ruffin, "What Determines Economic Growth?" *Economic Review,* Federal Reserve Bank of Dallas, 1993, pp. 25–40.

15. Richard Baldwin, "The Growth Effects of 1992," *Economic Policy,* November 1989, pp. 248–283.

16. Ann Harrison, "Openness and Growth: A Time-Series, Cross-Country Analysis for Developing Countries," *Journal of Development Economics,* Vol. 48, No. 2 (March 1996), pp. 419–447.

17. D. Dollar, "Outward Oriented Developing Economies Really Do Grow More Rapidly: Evidence from 95 LDCs, 1976–85," *Economic Development and Cultural Change,* Vol. 40, No. 3 (1991), pp. 523–544.

18. Jeffrey Frankel, David Romer, and Teresa Cyrus, "Trade and Growth in East Asian Countries: Cause and Effect," National Bureau of Economic Research *Working Paper* No. 5732, August 1, 1996.

19. Barro, "Economic Growth in a Cross-Section of Countries"; Barro and Xavier Sala-I-Martin, *Economic Growth* (New York: McGraw-Hill, 1995), p. 434; Daniel Landau, "Government and Economic Growth in the Lesser Developed Countries: An Empirical Study for 1960–80," *Economic Development and Cultural Change,* Vol. 35 (October 1986), p. 68; Michael Marlow, "Links Between Taxes and Economic Growth: Some Empirical Evidence," *Journal of Economic Growth,* Vol. 1, No. 4 (1986); Eric Engen and Jonathan Skinner, "Fiscal Policy and Economic Growth," National Bureau of Economic Research *Working Paper* No. 4223, 1992;

and Kevin Grier and Gordon Tullock, "An Empirical Analysis of Cross-National Economic Growth, 1951–80," *Journal of Monetary Economics,* Vol. 24 (1989), pp. 259–276.

20. Robert King and Sergio Rebelo, "Public Policy and Economic Growth: Developing Neoclassical Implications," *Journal of Political Economy,* Vol. 98 (1990).

21. For a full discussion of the evidence, see Kevin Dowd, "The Costs of Inflation and Disinflation," *Cato Journal,* Fall 1994. A 1993 panel and cross-sectional study by top MIT economist Stanley Fischer concludes that "high growth is not sustainable in the presence of high inflation." See Stanley Fischer, "The Role of Macroeconomic Factors in Growth," *Journal of Monetary Economics,* Vol. 32, No. 3 (1993), pp. 485–512.

22. Robert King and Ross Levine, "Finance, Entrepreneurship and Growth: Theory and Evidence," *Journal of Monetary Economics,* Vol. 32, No. 3 (December 1993), pp. 513–542; see also Robert King and Ross Levine, "Finance and Growth: Schumpeter Might Be Right," *Quarterly Journal of Economics,* Vol. 108, No. 3 (August 1993), pp. 717–737.

23. Barro and Sala-I-Martin, *Economic Growth,* pp. 434–435.

24. Steven Knack and Philip Keefer, "Institutional and Economic Performance: Cross-Country Tests Using Alternative Institutional Measures," *Economics and Politics,* Vol. 7 (1995), pp. 207–227, and Barro and Sala-I-Martin, *Economic Growth,* pp. 439–440.

25. An introduction to the latest ongoing scientific research into the process of economic growth may be found at Oxford University's *Economic Growth Resources Home Page,* located on the World Wide Web at *http://www.nuff.ox.ac.uk/Economics/Growth/.*

2

Economic Freedom and Foreign Aid

by Bryan T. Johnson

Foreign aid bureaucrats have argued for years that U.S. foreign assistance is vital to the economic well-being of less-developed countries. J. Brian Atwood, administrator of the U.S. Agency for International Development, which has responsibility for handing out most of the $14 billion U.S. foreign aid budget, even has suggested that the overall economic prosperity of the post–World War II era can be attributed largely to the Marshall Plan and successive foreign aid efforts.[1] Such claims, however, grossly exaggerate the benefits of development aid and ignore its many harmful effects. Not only has the U.S. foreign aid program failed to promote economic growth in less-developed countries, but many recipient countries are worse off today than they were before beginning to receive aid.

As the data presented in the *Index of Economic Freedom* will demonstrate, economic freedom is the single most important factor in creating the conditions for economic prosperity. Data presented in this chapter will show that, rather than help poor countries lift themselves out of poverty, U.S. development aid impedes economic growth as it damages fragile economies. Economic freedom, not development aid, is what matters most in achieving economic development.

Data in the *Index of Economic Freedom* will show as well that many long-term U.S. foreign aid recipients have unfree or repressed economies. No matter how much money the United States and other donors give to recipients like Tanzania, Sudan, and Ethiopia, economic development will not be forthcoming. Indeed, the countries scored

by the *Index* as having mostly unfree or repressed economies have yet to generate substantial levels of wealth. By comparison, countries ranked at the very top of the *Index* are among the richest in the world.

The data compiled and compared for the *Index* demonstrate clearly that poverty is caused largely by ill-conceived and repressive economic policies. Such factors as history, culture, war, and climate may influence a country's development, but the level of economic freedom is far and away the most important determinant in the long run. The data show that no amount of foreign aid can offset the effects of the conditions that exist in economically unfree economies. Some countries, in fact, have received U.S. foreign aid for over 50 years yet are no better off today than they were before.

A close look at the recipients of U.S. foreign aid and their economic performance over the past several decades supports these points:

- Of the 83 countries ranked as mostly unfree or repressed by the *Index,* 35 have received U.S. foreign aid for at least 35 years—many for as long as 53 years[2] (see Table 2.1);
- Of these 35 recipient countries, 25 are no better off today than they were in 1965; and
- Of these 25 recipients, 13 are poorer today than they were in 1965.

These facts raise several questions. If development aid is so important to economic growth, as Mr. Atwood claims, why are so many long-term recipients of foreign aid still so poor? If development aid is essential for economic growth and development, why are so many long-term recipients—over one-third, in fact—becoming poorer? And if development aid is essential to economic prosperity, why has there been so little progress by the countries that are the most dependent on foreign aid?

The answer to each of these questions is simple: Economic freedom, not aid, is the key to economic development. Consider the following examples (see Table 2.2):

1. **Haiti** has depended on U.S. foreign aid for 53 years, yet it is one of the world's poorest countries.[3] In 1965, Haiti's per capita gross domestic product (GDP) was $360; in 1995, it was even lower: $231.[4] During this time, Haiti received almost $1 billion in foreign aid from the United States alone, not including money that the United States spent on a military operation to "restore" democracy in Haiti in 1994.

2. **Nicaragua** has received over $800 million in foreign aid from the United States over the past 50 years. In 1965, Nicaragua's GDP per capita was $1,752. By 1995, it had shrunk to $816.

3. **Niger** has received over $500 million in U.S. foreign assistance over the past 38 years, but its per capita wealth fell by more than 55 percent from 1965 to 1995—from $617 to $275.

If the *Index of Economic Freedom* provides any insight into the economic development process, it is not to suggest which countries deserve economic development aid: No country does.[5] Rather, it is to show the general futility of providing economic development assistance in the first place. Although a well-intentioned foreign aid program may help a newly independent country pay for the development of a commercial code, for example, it is far more likely to hinder the country's economic development process. Foreign aid delays economic growth by prolonging the implementation of such much-needed reforms as privatization of state-owned industries and the lowering of taxes, tariffs, and other factors measured by the *Index* that have a demonstrable impact on economic growth. Until the less-developed countries adopt these free-market reforms, they will continue to be impoverished no matter how much foreign aid they receive.

Table 2.1

Economic Freedom and Economic Prosperity

	Index of Economic Freedom Score 1998	GDP per Capita 1965, Constant 1987 US$	GDP per Capita 1995, Constant 1987 US$	Increase in GDP per Capita 1965–1995	Years Receiving Aid
Free Countries					
Hong Kong	1.25	$2422	$11911	392%	—
Singapore	1.30	1685	13451	698	—
Taiwan †††	1.95	833	9020	983	—
Unfree Countries					
Colombia	3.00	690	1377	100%	53
Ghana	3.00	501	420	-16	41
Kenya	3.05	221	375	70	45
Zambia	3.05	478	257	-46	40
Mali	3.10	227	256	13	38
Honduras	3.15	746	904	21	53
Guinea *	3.25	386	404	5	40
Mexico	3.25	1136	1724	52	52
Senegal	3.25	752	661	-12	38
Tanzania	3.25	134	155	16	41
Nigeria	3.30	335	355	6	38
Egypt	3.35	300	726	142	46
Madagascar	3.35	320	199	-38	40
Nepal	3.40	151	206	36	47
Dominican Republic	3.45	372	838	125	46
Burkina Faso	3.50	180	258	44	38
Cameroon	3.50	618	727	18	39
Lesotho	3.50	126	354	181	38
Nicaragua	3.50	1752	816	-53	50
Gambia	3.60	225	274	22	41
Guyana	3.60	479	541	13	45
Malawi	3.65	113	146	29	43
Ethiopia **	3.70	187	154	-18	50
India	3.70	217	425	96	52
Niger	3.70	617	275	-55	38
Chad	3.80	202	178	-12	37
Mauritania	3.80	516	503	-3	39
Sierra Leone	3.85	137	171	25	44
Burundi	3.90	124	182	47	38
Haiti	4.00	360	231	-36	53
Sudan	4.20	806	**800**	-1	41
Myanmar (Burma)	4.30	210	**267**	27	37
Rwanda	4.30	229	198	-14	37
Somalia ††	4.70	111	115	3	42
Congo (former Zaire)†	4.70	282	153	-46	43

Note: Shaded countries experienced growth of less than 1% per year. Figures in **Bold** are from 1994.
   * First GDP/capita from 1986.   ** First GDP/capita from 1983.   ††† First GNP/capita from 1967,
   † Second GDP/capita from 1992.   †† Second GDP/capita from 1990.   second GNP/capita from 1994.

Sources: *World Data 1995 CD-ROM*, The World Bank, 1996; *Foreign Aid Reduction Act of 1995*, Committee on Foreign Relations; 1997 World Development Indicators CD-ROM, The World Bank, 1997; *Congressional Presentation: Summary Tables, Fiscal Year 1998*, U.S. Agency for International Development; Taiwan Figures from *The Republic of China Yearbook, 1996*, Government Information Office, Republic of China, p. 155.

Table 2.2

Long-Term Recipients of U.S. Foreign Aid and Their Economic Performance: 1965-1995

Years Receiving Aid		GDP per Capita 1965, Constant 1987 US$	GDP per Capita 1995, Constant 1987 US$	Increase in GDP per Capita 1965-1995
53	Bolivia	$682	$790	16%
53	Chile	1236	2532	105%
53	Colombia	690	1377	100%
53	Costa Rica	1128	1899	68%
53	Ecuador	626	1241	98%
53	El Salvador	913	1024	12%
53	Guatemala	690	898	30%
53	Haiti	360	231	-36%
53	Honduras	746	904	21%
53	Panama	1371	2434	78%
53	Peru	1126	1033	-8%
53	Philippines	464	630	36%
52	India	217	425	96%
52	Indonesia	189	720	281%
52	Mexico	1136	1724	52%
52	Turkey	834	1865	124%
52	Uruguay	434	2786	542%
51	Liberia †	627	495	-21%
50	Ethiopia **	187	154	-18%
50	Nicaragua	1752	816	-53%
49	Lebanon	-	-	-
49	Thailand	366	1843	404%
48	Israel	4654	10551	127%
48	Jordan **	2253	**1629**	-28%
47	Morocco	500	871	74%
47	Nepal	151	206	36%
46	Dominican Republic	372	838	125%
46	Egypt	300	726	142%
46	Tunisia	638	1436	125%
45	Guyana	479	541	13%
45	Kenya	221	375	70%
44	Afghanistan	-	-	-
44	Sierra Leone	137	171	25%

Years Receiving Aid		GDP per Capita 1965, Constant 1987 US$	GDP per Capita 1995, Constant 1987 US$	Increase in GDP per Capita 1965-1995
44	Sri Lanka	$213	$512	140%
43	Belize	830	2113	155%
43	Zaire ++	282	153	-46%
43	Jamaica	1272	1578	24%
43	Malawi	113	146	29%
42	Somalia +++	111	115	3%
42	Uganda **	452	557	23%
41	Gambia	225	274	22%
41	Ghana	501	420	-16%
41	Portugal	1849	5175	180%
41	Sudan	806	**800**	-1%
41	Tanzania	134	155	16%
40	Benin	346	**362**	5%
40	Guinea *	386	404	5%
40	Madagascar	320	199	-38%
40	Togo	366	327	-11%
40	Zambia	478	257	-46%
39	Cameroon	618	727	18%
39	Gabon	2798	3640	30%
39	Mauritania	516	503	-3%
39	Mauritius	968	2516	160%
38	Burkina Faso	180	258	44%
38	Burundi	124	182	47%
38	Central African Rep.	408	357	-12%
38	Lesotho	126	354	181%
38	Mali	227	256	13%
38	Niger	617	275	-55%
38	Nigeria	335	355	6%
38	Senegal	752	661	-12%
38	Seychelles	1918	**4965**	159%
38	Swaziland	478	800	67%
37	Chad	202	178	-12%
37	Myanmar/Burma	210	**267**	27%
37	Rwanda	229	198	-14%

Note: Shaded figures indicate countries whose per capita GDPs rose less than 1% per year. Figures in **Bold** are from 1994.
* First GDP/capita from 1986.   ** First GDP/capita from 1983.   ††† Second GDP/capita from 1990.
† Second GDP/capita from 1987.   †† Second GDP/capita from 1992.

Sources: *World Data 1995 CD-ROM,* The World Bank, 1996; *1997 World Development Indicators CD-ROM, The World Bank,* 1997; *Foreign Aid Reduction Act of 1995,* Committee on Foreign Relations; *Congressional Presentation: Summary Tables, Fiscal Year 1998,* U.S. Agency for International Development, 1997.

Notes

1. Remarks by AID Administrator J. Brian Atwood to Center for National Policy, Washington, D.C., December 14, 1994.

2. Some aid recipients in sub-Saharan Africa and elsewhere have at least doubled their wealth in the past 30 years. In 1965, for example, Lesotho's per capita GDP (in constant 1987 dollars) was $126; by 1995, its per capita wealth had reached $354. Nevertheless, Lesotho obviously remains an extremely poor country. The growth rates for Lesotho and other aid-dependent countries pale in comparison to those of the "Asian Tigers," most of which increased their wealth over 500 percent during the same period. Thus, foreign aid recipients that have doubled or even tripled their economic wealth since 1965 are still worse off than the Asian Tigers, which had much higher growth rates without receiving much foreign aid. The reason for the difference: free-market economic policies.

3. Figures include both military and economic assistance, although most assistance to less-developed countries has been in the form of economic aid. For example, of the $932.5 million in U.S. foreign aid that Haiti received from 1946 to 1990, $917.2 million was in the form of economic assistance. For more information, see *Foreign Operations, Export Financing, and Related Programs Appropriations Bill, 1994,* Report No. 103–142, U.S. Senate, September 14, 1993.

4. All figures are GDP per capita, expressed in constant 1987 dollars; from World Bank, *World Data 1997, CD–ROM,* Washington, D.C., 1997.

5. Some U.S. military and security aid may help secure U.S. foreign policy interests abroad. For example, programs like the International Military Education Training Program, which allows the U.S. military to train with foreign militaries, when used prudently may improve the ability of the United States to defend its national security interests. In addition, some humanitarian and disaster relief provides much-needed help to victims of earthquakes, mass floods, and other natural disasters.

3

Economic Freedom: Asian Lessons for the West

by L. Gordon Crovitz

A 19th century print of early Hong Kong that hangs in my office helps explain why this capitalist enclave of China ranks first in the 1998 *Index of Economic Freedom* for the fourth year in a row. A legend gives details of significant sites on the dramatic harbor and skyline. These notable places are not government offices or monuments, but instead include such highlights as "Jardine Matheson, and Co., estab. 1841," "Lane, Crawford, and Co., estab. 1850," and "Hongkong and Shanghai Bank." It is no surprise that a territory founded as an open trading port and administered to maximize economic opportunity for its people should do so well in the *Index*. Nor should it be a surprise that Hong Kong's neighbors in Asia have learned its lessons well enough to have together transformed their region from poverty to wealth in just a generation. Asia, the poorest part of the world following World War II, has been the fastest-growing part of the world for the past decade. It is also no surprise that this is the region with a disproportionate share of top rankings in the 1998 *Index*, including Hong Kong (number 1), Singapore (number 2), New Zealand (number 4), and Taiwan (number 7).

Can Asia retain its role as the engine for world economic growth? Medium- and even short-term investors can take heart from the long-term trends identified in the *Index*. The performance over the past generation of many of the economies in Asia, especially in Southeast Asia, has reflected steady improvements in economic freedom. In the 1998 *Index,* both Hong Kong and Singapore get perfect scores for free trade, lack of government intervention in the economy, openness to foreign investment, protection of property rights, low level of regulation, and the absence of a black market.

The underlying trends identified in the *Index* portend well for the ability of countries in Asia to overcome recent reminders that even here markets can go down as well as up. After a slowdown in exports in 1996—caused in large part by the growing success of low-cost China as an emerging world-class exporter—summer 1997 rocked the region's financial markets, with currency collapses in Indonesia (number 62), the Philippines (number 44), and Thailand and Malaysia (tied at number 28). But the factors underlying these rankings suggest that no one should count Asia out. The openness of many Asian countries to the discipline of foreign investment, their competitiveness fostered by liberalized domestic economies, and their focus on investment in human capital set them apart from developing countries in other parts of the world. These strengths will be firm foundations as the region tries to overcome structural problems highlighted by loose lending for real-estate development and consumer spending, with huge inflows of capital causing unjustified increases in asset prices and exposing banks to enormous bad risks.

In Southeast Asia, the gross national product of most countries is still expected to grow at an annual average rate of more than 6 percent for the next five years; this is more than twice the expected growth rate for the United States or Europe. It continues a regional trend that began in 1985 and within 10 years had doubled per capita income. This fast rate of growth has meant the region's nearly 2 billion people have had the fastest increase in wealth in the history of the world. As the *Index* rankings suggest, the high levels of economic freedom in Southeast Asia both reflect and reinforce values of personal responsibility, whether through the refusal of most governments in the region to create welfare states or through their reluctance to block the forces of domestic and foreign competition through restrictive trade practices.

But outside of Hong Kong and Singapore, the rapid growth of the Southeast Asian economies has revealed the same problem that has plagued Japan for several years: It threatens to outpace the creation of the institutions required to maintain modern economies. What this means is that the region needs even more disclosure and even more transparent markets in order to tolerate the huge influx of capital and investment.

In terms of strong institutions, Hong Kong is a role model for Asia and beyond. The currency crisis of 1997 was the latest reminder for Hong Kong's neighbors that the territory benefits enormously from its ability to stabilize its currency. In the 1997 *Index,* my colleague George

Melloan, deputy editor, international, of *The Wall Street Journal,* stressed that currency convertibility and stability are key ingredients for economic freedom. He quoted David Malpass, chief international economist at Bear, Stearns, as saying, "The most important thing to me about a country is whether I can buy a given amount of its currency for a dollar when I go into the country and get my dollar back for the same amount when I go out again." The importance of stable currencies became very clear in a year in which several currencies in the region, starting with the Thai baht, lost between 20 percent and 30 percent of their value relative to the U.S. dollar.

It is worth taking a moment to understand how the Hong Kong dollar peg differs from the pegs that broke in most of the rest of Asia during the summer of 1997. After World War II, the Hong Kong dollar was linked to Britain's pound sterling. This proved unsatisfactory during periods of British monetary instability, especially after a devaluation in the late 1960s. Hong Kong eventually broke its link to the pound, floating its dollar in 1974. But political unrest in China meant the Hong Kong dollar lost its value relative to the U.S. dollar, the leading trading currency. So in 1983, Hong Kong adopted a currency board approach, which anchored its dollar to the U.S. dollar at a rate of HK$7.8 to US$1. This link has remained ever since, with each Hong Kong dollar fully backed by the territory's U.S. dollar reserves. The supply of Hong Kong dollars has been determined solely by demand, with the nominal exchange rate remaining fixed.

Currency stability was one reason that even the return of Hong Kong to China (number 120) on July 1, 1997, went reasonably smoothly, although the abolition of the elected legislature and the passing of some retroactive laws were causes for concern. One key reason that Hong Kong could remain stable even as it became a special administrative region of China is clear from its top position in the *Index:* Economic freedom in Hong Kong is the highest in the world largely because of the limited role of government to do good or to do ill, regardless of whether sovereignty resides in London or in Beijing. The key to Hong Kong, then, is not so much what the government does as what the government restrains itself from doing. Although there is occasional talk of adopting an industrial policy or adding new limits to immigration, Hong Kong remains freer than any other economy in the world. The challenge for Beijing is to follow the maxim that the government that governs least governs best. This is a familiar concept in Hong Kong, but it is still radical in most places—including, of course, in Beijing.

During the hand-over period, the editorial pages of Dow Jones publications in the region recalled how Hong Kong developed its unmatched system for protecting economic freedoms. *The Asian Wall Street Journal* and *The Far Eastern Economic Review* reported that the tradition of small government was best personified by Sir John Cowperthwaite, who came to Hong Kong in 1945 as a colonial civil servant and served as financial secretary from 1961 to 1971. On the role of government in the economy, he applied the "theory of positive non-intervention," otherwise known as laissez-faire, and often made the case in memorable terms. For example:

- Arguing against government regulation: "In the long run, the aggregate of decisions of individual businessmen exercising individual judgment in a free economy, even if often mistaken, is less likely to be counteracted faster."
- Arguing against a subsidy to reduce the cost of water: "I see no reason why someone who is content with a cold shower should subsidize someone who is able to luxuriate in a deep hot bath, or why someone who waters a few plants on his windowsill should subsidize someone who waters his extensive lawns."
- Arguing against a tax increase: "Enterprise in Hong Kong has a good record of productive re-investment and I have a keen realization of the importance of not withdrawing capital from the private sector of the economy.... I am confident, however old-fashioned this may sound, that funds left in the hands of the public will come into the Exchequer with interest in the future when we need them."
- Arguing against keeping economic statistics, such as trade "deficits" or "surpluses": "We are in the happy position where the leverage exercised by government on the economy is so small that it is not necessary, nor even of any particular value, to have these figures available for the formation of policy."

Sir John also helped introduce Hong Kong to the world by explaining some 40 years ago how the then-small local economy worked to a visitor from the University of Chicago economics department. Nobel Prize winner Milton Friedman went on to cite Hong Kong as the model of economic freedom in his many books and articles. Mr. Friedman commented on the hand-over with a *Wall Street Journal* editorial page article headlined "If Only the U.S. Were as Free as Hong Kong." Mr. Friedman noted that, in Hong Kong, direct government spending is less than 15 percent of national income compared with 40 percent in the United States. Indirect government spending through regulations on individuals and businesses, he wrote, is negligible in Hong Kong but accounts for another 10 percent of national income in the United States. Most Hong Kong residents would agree that they get more for their 15 percent than U.S. residents get for their 50 percent in terms of excellent schools and roads, not to mention Hong Kong's excellent civil servants (the civil service pays private-sector wages and thus attracts top quality) and its predictable, independent, and efficient legal system (no one understands lawyer jokes here, where contingency fees are illegal and litigation is further discouraged by requiring the losing side to pay the winning side's legal bills).

The section on Hong Kong in the 1998 *Index* warns that calls for more welfare spending could reduce the territory's standing in future years. There was the unusual spectacle in the last years of British rule of officials in communist China attacking Hong Kong Governor Christopher Patten, the former leader of Britain's Conservative Party, for pursuing what they called "dangerous socialism" when he proposed increasing some areas of welfare spending in Hong Kong. In fact, most Hong Kong people have a healthy skepticism of welfare policies, preferring to continue to rely on strong families and high savings rates. Indeed, the first proposal submitted by the most popular political party, the Democratic Party, in the short-lived elected Legislative Council was a tax cut for business in order to boost employment. And it is striking that there is almost no call for redistribution of wealth in Hong Kong, where only about 60 percent of employed people pay any income taxes, with lower earners fully exempt. Hong Kong's flat tax is thus also very progressive. There is no soak-the-rich politicking even in a place in which the top income tax burden is 15 percent—probably because it is an article of faith among Hong Kong people that they or their children will have every opportunity to become wealthy themselves.

Even the number 2–ranked economy in the 1998 *Index,* Singapore, looks to the Hong Kong model, cutting taxes in recent years to become more competitive with its fellow trading city to the north. With about 20 percent of its work force made up of foreign workers, and with no minimum wage laws, Singapore has one of the world's freest labor markets—and unemployment in the 2 percent range. Singapore's approach to the media also reflects growing openness, with limits on foreign publications being slowly reduced and with official encouragement for Singaporeans to become active users of the Internet.

A healthy competition among Asian countries for economic advantage has led many countries in the region to view Hong Kong and Singapore as models. Malaysia, for example, made great efforts in the early 1990s to position Kuala Lumpur as an alternative financial center for the region by cutting taxes and regulations. The trend toward open financial markets was interrupted in late summer 1997, but the interruption is as interesting for how quickly it was reversed as for the interruption itself. After Thailand devalued its currency, Malaysia took unusual steps in a futile effort to isolate itself. The Kuala Lumpur Stock Exchange banned the short selling of 100 blue-chip stocks, Prime Minister Mahathir Mohamad announced a $20 billion fund that would be used to boost shares, and some officials hinted that traders who "sabotage" the economy by selling stock or the currency could be arrested under anti-subversion laws. But within a week, Dr. Mahathir backed off on the short selling and instead announced that the government would rein in public spending to increase confidence in the economy. He delayed

several big infrastructure projects, including a $5 billion dam, a new airport, and a one-mile-long shopping mall proposed to be built over a river in Kuala Lumpur.

Dr. Mahathir's high-profile attacks against George Soros and other currency traders attracted considerable international attention. Foreign investors were shocked by hearing the Malaysian prime minister call Mr. Soros a "moron" (despite Mr. Soros's explanation that his hedge fund was long, not short, the Malaysian ringgit) and by xenophobic attacks in Malaysia's media. But despite the official rhetoric, the government's swift reversal of its intervention policy was a reminder that economies that benefit from foreign investment risk instant and severe repercussions if they try to change the rules. In the meantime, Prime Minister Mahathir did attract some support for his criticism of the World Bank and the International Monetary Fund for encouraging countries to devalue their currencies.

Freedom is contagious, and the economic liberty that is prevalent in so much of the rest of Asia has even exerted pressure on China, where many government officials now recognize that the country has reached the stage of development that requires structural reform to protect property rights. One of China's periodic propaganda campaigns included an unusual focus in 1997: It urged a more open flow of financial information about the country's stock markets. "Quite a few companies think that the shareholding system is simply a way to raise money," said an editorial in the *People's Daily.* "They lack understanding of the rules of information disclosure, and the legal obligations to shareholders." In fact, the editorial noted, "The information disclosure of some listed companies is seriously inconsistent with facts." In Asia, this concern for the well-being of capitalist shareholders is known as socialism with Chinese characteristics.

4

Signposts for the Foreign Investor: Economic Indicators for OECD and Select Developing Countries

by Brett D. Schaefer

As the economies of the world become more interdependent, businesses are looking increasingly to foreign countries as profitable destinations for investment. Investors face the daunting task, however, of deciding which countries offer the most promise with the least risk. Not coincidentally, the amount of reliable information available on a certain country's economy goes hand in hand with the level of economic and political freedom in that country. Open economies have fewer restrictions on the flow of economic resources and information—a characteristic that makes both the country and the investor better able to adapt their decisions to economic changes. As a result, countries that embrace economic freedom become more stable and less risky as destinations for foreign investment dollars.

The *Index of Economic Freedom* offers businesses an objective comparison of the economic environment in 156 countries. All are judged by the same criteria, allowing businesses to decide which countries might best suit their goals. The *Index* also indicates policies that are likely to lead to future economic growth. For example, a study in Chapter 1 that examines the growth rates of real per capita gross domestic product (GDP) between 1980 and 1993 for 138 countries shows that policies supporting economic freedom correlate positively with increased economic growth. Countries ranked as economically free experienced an average annual per capita GDP growth rate of 2.88 percent for that period, while countries classified as economically repressed experienced a growth rate of -1.44 percent. The bottom line: Increases in per capita wealth correspond to increases in economic freedom.

Moreover, the analysis indicates that increased

economic freedom, as measured by the *Index,* improves the possibility of increased domestic consumption for exports and increased flows of foreign direct investment. This year, Heritage economists conducted statistical analyses to determine whether a relationship exists between the amount of exports to and foreign direct investment in certain countries and the levels of economic freedom in those countries.[1] The analysis shows conclusively that there is a statistically significant relationship. The results indicate that lower *Index* scores (indicating a higher level of economic freedom) are associated with greater amounts of U.S. exports and higher levels of U.S. direct foreign investment. Therefore, this analysis indicates that investors can use the *Index* as a guide when seeking comparatively low-risk, profitable destinations for capital and strong, stable markets for goods and services.

This chapter presents supplemental data on various developing and developed countries to aid investors. It primarily examines data on member countries of the Organization for Economic Cooperation and Development (OECD) because they are the destinations for the majority of global investment.[2] Developing countries, however, are of great interest to investors today. Investment growth in the developing countries currently is outpacing growth in the OECD countries. And investment in the developing world is flowing disproportionately to five countries referred to collectively as the "Big 5": Brazil, China, India, Indonesia, and Russia. The remarkable dominance of these countries led the World Bank to predict that the Big 5 will "fundamentally change the way the world does business."[3] For this reason, these countries were selected specifically from the large number of developing countries for closer examination. The following data present vital indicators or "signposts" that investors can use to determine where to invest in the future.

The data that follow are grouped into eight categories of economic indicators that are considered frequently by international investors. Four of the categories relate specifically to OECD countries, and four to the Big 5. Each category includes several distinct groups of data presented in tabular format with accompanying descriptions.[4] In many cases, the information is presented as a percentage of per capita GDP to aid in country comparisons.

Economic Indicators for OECD Countries

The leading economic indicators for OECD member countries fall within four general categories.

Category 1: Taxation

Taxation is an impediment to investment, affecting nearly all facets of potential investment. It influences decisions over where and how much to invest and what form that investment should take. Investors need to examine the differences in taxation between countries.

Tax Revenue: Includes net taxes on citizens and business activity within or at the borders. Also includes interest and penalties collected on nonpayments or late payments of taxes. In relation to GDP, taxation level is an impartial representation of the size of the state sector in the economy and its intrusion into the market.

Taxes on Income, Profit, and Capital Gains: Assessments on the reported or estimated net income of individuals, business profits, and capital gains (the difference between an asset's purchase and selling prices). Amount includes social security contributions after deductions and personal exemptions; internal government payments are excluded. Presented as a percentage of total government revenue, demonstrating government's reliance on this source of income. Heavy government reliance on income, profit, and capital gains discourages investment by reducing returns on investments.

Taxes on International Trade: Includes import and export duties, profits of export or import monopolies, and profits and taxes earned in foreign exchange transactions. Presented as a percentage of total government revenue, demonstrating reliance on this source of income.

Category 2: Government Interference in the Economy

Large-scale government interference in the economy is detrimental to growth and long-term economic health. Through confiscation and redirection of resources through taxation, governments exert tremendous influence over economic conditions in their respective economies. The size

Table 4.1

Taxation Data for OECD Countries

	1998 Index of Economic Freedom Score	Tax Revenues as a % of GDP, 1985-95 *	Taxes on Income, Profit, and Capital Gains as a % of Government Revenue, 1985-95 **	Taxes on International Trade as a % of Government Revenue, 1985-95 ***
New Zealand	1.75	32.84%	n/a	n/a
Switzerland	1.90	20.03	n/a	n/a
United States	1.90	18.21	51.11%	1.59%
Luxembourg	1.95	40.00	33.98	0.01
United Kingdom	1.95	32.74	37.91	0.08
Ireland	2.00	35.09	35.77	7.54
Australia	2.05	22.21	62.31	4.09
Japan	2.05	14.53	54.54	1.36
Belgium	2.10	43.13	33.07	0.06
Canada	2.10	18.02	51.55	3.61
Austria	2.15	32.29	18.14	1.52
Netherlands	2.20	44.36	29.71	0.00
Denmark	2.25	34.91	47.47	0.07
Finland	2.25	28.30	30.40	0.89
Germany	2.30	29.23	16.75	0.07
Iceland	2.30	24.25	15.65	9.38
Norway	2.35	32.93	17.56	0.51
Sweden	2.45	35.02	17.87	0.87
France	2.50	37.82	17.57	0.01
Italy	2.50	37.36	36.84	0.02
Spain	2.50	28.25	26.11	2.20
Portugal	2.60	28.80	21.79	2.24
Turkey	2.80	12.48	36.88	5.39
Greece	2.90	29.06	23.34	0.17
Mexico	3.25	14.86	28.26	4.05

Notes: * Data for New Zealand missing 1989. Data for Germany from 1991-95; Canada from 1985-92; Ireland, Japan, and Spain from 1985-93; Austria, Belgium, Finland, Greece, Iceland, Italy, Luxembourg, Mexico, Norway, Portugal, and Switzerland from 1985-94.

** Data for Australia, France, Greece, Iceland, Italy, and the United States from 1985-94; Austria and Japan from 1985-93, 1995; Canada, Ireland, Norway, and Portugal from 1985-92; the United Kingdom from 1985-93; Spain from 1985-92, 95; Mexico from 1985-90.

*** Data for Australia, France, Greece, Iceland, Italy, and the United States from 1985-94; Finland, Luxembourg, and the United Kingdom from 1985-93; Canada, Ireland, Norway, and Portugal from 1985-92. Data for Austria and Japan missing for 1994; Spain missing from 1993-94. n/a -- data unavailable.

Source: *1997 World Development Indicators*, The World Bank.

of government has a direct impact on all sectors of the economy and therefore should be considered carefully by investors before committing their resources.

Government Consumption: Includes all current expenditures on goods and services—as well as capital expenditures on national defense and security—by all levels of government, excluding most state-owned enterprises.

Government Expenditure: Includes current and capital expenditures that are not reimbursed, and excludes government lending, repayment to the government, or government acquisition of equity for public policy purposes.

Subsidies and Current Transfers: Includes all one-way current account transfers to private and public enterprises as well as costs incurred in departmental enterprise sales to the public.

Category 3: Key Economic Indicators

A number of factors affect the domestic economy and its relation to the global economy. Some influence economic stability and growth; others reflect the domestic economy's integration into, and its reliance on, the global trading system. Five characteristics of particular interest to investors are listed.

Trade: The sum of exports and imports of goods and services. The level of trade indirectly reflects domestic restrictions on trade—typically in inverse proportion to the level of trade. It also reflects the domestic economy's competitiveness on the global stage.

Gross Domestic Savings: Gross domestic savings are the difference between GDP and total consumption. Domestic saving represents a potential pool of capital for financing all types of productive economic activity and, as such, bolsters

Table 4.2

Government Interference in the Economy for OECD Countries

	1998 Index of Economic Freedom Score	Government Consumption as a % of GDP, 1985-95	Annual Growth Government Consumption, 1985-95	Government Expenditures as a % of GDP, 1985-95	Subsidies and Other Current Transfers as a % of Government Expenditures, 1985-95
New Zealand	1.75	16.1%	0.2%	39.7%	46.8%
Switzerland	1.90	13.6	2.2	25.3	58.1
United States	1.90	17.7	1.4	23.7	51.7
Luxembourg	1.95	13.1	2.6	41.2	65.9
United Kingdom	1.95	21.1	1.2	39.1	54.6
Ireland	2.00	16.1	1.4	44.7	57.0
Australia	2.05	17.8	3.0	26.2	62.5
Japan	2.05	9.3	2.0	18.4	53.3
Belgium	2.10	15.4	0.8	51.3	56.3
Canada	2.10	20.2	1.8	23.9	58.9
Austria	2.15	18.6	1.8	39.7	57.4
Netherlands	2.20	14.9	1.8	53.6	70.4
Denmark	2.25	25.4	1.1	41.1	60.8
Finland	2.25	21.7	1.4	35.3	69.0
Germany	2.30	19.8	n/a	32.9	57.1
Iceland	2.30	19.5	4.1	31.8	28.3
Norway	2.35	20.6	2.7	39.7	71.9
Sweden	2.45	27.1	0.9	43.9	70.8
France	2.50	18.9	2.3	44.5	64.2
Italy	2.50	16.9	1.1	49.2	56.2
Spain	2.50	15.8	4.4	34.6	55.7
Portugal	2.60	15.7	3.8	40.6	36.9
Turkey	2.80	9.3	3.8	19.7	26.7
Greece	2.90	19.7	1.6	51.6	35.6
Mexico	3.25	9.4	0.8	22.0	14.7

Source: The World Bank, *1997 World Development Indicators.*

stable economic growth. The domestic savings level also indicates whether a country's population possesses a positive impression of their country's economic prospects.

Interest Rate Spread: The interest rate charged by banks on loans minus the interest rate paid by commercial or similar banks for demand, time, or savings deposits. The interest rate spread indirectly represents confidence in the economy: Higher spreads indicate anticipation of inflation or similar government induced costs of doing business. Investors are also interested in the interest rate spread if they are likely to seek financing in the domestic economy.

Inflation: Based on a consumer price index calculated by the World Bank. Consumer price indices reflect fluctuations in the cost of acquiring a set basket of goods and services. Inflation measured by consumer price fluctuations is seldom reliable for inter-country comparisons, but offers insight into domestic economies. High rates of

inflation are undesirable.

Private Consumption: Based on the market value of all goods and services, including durable products (such as cars, washing machines, and home computers) purchased or received as income in kind by households and nonprofit institutions. Includes imputed rent for owner-occupied dwellings but excludes purchases of dwellings. Also includes any statistical discrepancy in the use of resources.

Category 4: Investment Data

Investment strengthens an economy by providing resources for new ventures, overhauling inventories and assets, and supporting current businesses. A strong economy attracts investment because of the opportunities for return on investment and profit. Investment trends, therefore, can serve as an indicator of economic stability and strength. In addition, the presence of other investments lends

Table 4.3

Economic Indicators for OECD Countries

	1998 Index of Economic Freedom Score	Trade as a % of GDP, 1995	Annual Growth in Exports of Goods and Services, 1990-95	Annual Growth in Imports of Goods and Services, 1990-95	Gross Domestic Savings as a % of GDP, 1990-95	Annual Interest Rate Spread, 1990-95	Consumer Price Inflation, 1990-95	Private Consumption as a % of GDP, 1990-95
New Zealand	1.75	62%	5.37%	6.71%	22.56%	4.22%	2.77%	61.49%
Switzerland	1.90	68	1.43	1.12	27.3	1.77	3.57	58.68
United States	1.90	24	7.63	8.31	15.26 *****	n/a	3.56	67.05
Luxembourg	1.95	184	3.01	3.62	25.57 *	2.12	2.99	61.09 *
United Kingdom	1.95	57	4.26	2.23	15.3 ***	1.95	4.4	63.64 *
Ireland	2.00	136	9.96	5.68	26.63	6.22	2.62	57.6
Australia	2.05	40	7.65	5.32	20.46	6.4 *	3.29	61.6
Japan	2.05	17	4.01	3.65	32.22	2.83	1.65	58.45
Belgium	2.10	143	4.68	4.48	22.88	5.63	2.63	62.35
Canada	2.10	71	8.27	6.53	19.2	1.2	2.71	60
Austria	2.15	77	3.86	5.1	26.19	n/a	3.21	55.35
Netherlands	2.20	99	4.14	3.61	26.1	6.83	2.62	59.46
Denmark	2.25	64	3.78	2.78	21.76	5.27	2.05	52.66
Finland	2.25	68	7.37	1.3	21.79	4.53	2.79	55.35
Germany	2.30	46	n/a	n/a	22.65 **	5.93	3.11	57.59
Iceland	2.30	70	1.15	-0.04	18.6	6.53	5.55	61.18
Norway	2.35	71	5.77	3.11	26.43 ***	4.05	2.61	52.62 ***
Sweden	2.45	77	5.56	2.78	18.85	6.53	5.3	53.8
France	2.50	43	4.53	3.53	20.8	4.75	2.48	60.09
Italy	2.50	49	8.08	4.91	20.75	6.75	5.31	62.06
Spain	2.50	47	8.93	6.6	20.75	3.45	5.48	62.65
Portugal	2.60	66	4.84	7.17	18.00 ****	6.87	8.31	65.00 ****
Turkey	2.80	45	7.81	13.76	21	n/a	77	67.85
Greece	2.90	57	4.87	8.76	8.75	8.47	15.05	71.74
Mexico	3.25	48	7.38	7.26	19.48	n/a	19.47	70.59

Notes: * Data from 1990-91.   ** Data from 1991-95.   *** Data from 1990-91, 1995.   **** Data from 1995.   ***** Data from 1990-93.
Source: The World Bank, 1997 World Development Indicators.

an air of stability to an economy and indicates that profitable opportunities exist.

Direct Investment Inflows: Indicates new real capital or financial assets invested, with a minimum of 10 percent equity ownership, in the domestic economy by foreign individuals or firms.

Direct Investment Outflows: Indicates new real capital or financial assets invested in foreign economies by individuals or firms.

Direct Investment Position: A measure of the net value of direct investment. Presented as a percentage change in value over time for both inflows and outflows. Significant changes in the flows reflect investor confidence in the domestic economy.

Gross Domestic Investment: Includes outlays to increase fixed assets (such as improvements in property, industrial capital, infrastructure, or buildings) and net changes in inventories.

Economic Indicators for the Big 5 Developing Countries

The second four economic indicators apply to the Big 5 developing countries, as follows:

Category 1: Investment Data

Investment data for developing countries generally are not as accurate or readily available as they are for OECD countries. The manner and type of investment also are different. For example, OECD countries typically are donating development assistance, not receiving it. As a result, different groups of investment data are examined for the Big 5 countries. The table presents data on six different aspects of investment:

Investment: Net total investment in the economy.

Net Private Capital Flows: Includes all private flows as well as debt flows from commercial bank lending, bonds, and other private credit sources.

Table 4.4

Investment Data for OECD Countries

	1998 Index of Economic Freedom Score	Overall Increase in Direct Investment Inflows as a % of GDP, 1985-95	Overall Increase in Direct Investment Outflows as a % of GDP, 1985-95	Overall Increase in Inward Direct Investment Position, 1984-94	Overall Increase in Outward Direct Investment Position, 1984-94	Gross Domestic Investment as a % of GDP, 1990-95*
New Zealand	1.75	3.67%	1.7%	n/a	n/a	20.44%
Switzerland	1.90	-0.42	-0.95	n/a	n/a	24.16
United States	1.90	0.56	1.07	205.26%	193.61%	16.23
Luxembourg	1.95	2.26	3.36	n/a	n/a	25.73
United Kingdom	1.95	1.45	1.29	336.50	222.86	16.92
Ireland	2.00	2.79	n/a	n/a	n/a	16.01
Australia	2.05	0.42	-0.17	223.53	405.54	20.93
Japan	2.05	n/a	-0.04	357.67	627.40	30.42
Belgium	2.10	2.26	3.36	597.50	807.83	18.66
Canada	2.10	1.54	-0.09	71.89	153.74	19.15
Austria	2.15	-0.03	0.34	426.58	1516.61	25.74
Netherlands	2.20	1.39	1.05	423.60	258.19	20.83
Denmark	2.25	2.22	1.25	n/a	n/a	15.63
Finland	2.25	0.52	0.55	537.98	1023.58	18.63
Germany	2.30	0.29	0.71	835.41	672.00	22.27
Iceland	2.30	-0.59	n/a	n/a	n/a	16.75
Norway	2.35	1.58	-0.25	n/a	n/a	19.55
Sweden	2.45	5.5	2.61	n/a	n/a	16.26
France	2.50	0.45	0.27	n/a	n/a	19.40
Italy	2.50	0.19	0.1	408.39	496.45	18.86
Spain	2.50	0.07	0.48	1061.26	614.06	22.34
Portugal	2.60	-0.53	0.55	n/a	n/a	28.00
Turkey	2.80	0.4	n/a	n/a	n/a	24.24
Greece	2.90	-0.18	n/a	n/a	n/a	19.17
Mexico	3.25	0.6	n/a	n/a	n/a	22.11

Note: * Data for Luxembourg from 1990-91; Norway and the United Kingdom from 1990-91, 1995; Portugal from 1995; and the United States from 1990-93.
Sources: The World Bank, *1997 World Development Indicators on CD-ROM*; The Organization for Economic Cooperation and Development, *International Direct Investment Statistics Yearbook, 1997*.

Also includes foreign direct and portfolio equity investment.

Portfolio Investment: Includes the sum of country funds, depository receipts, direct foreign purchases of shares, and foreign-held bonds. Portfolio bond includes privately held bonds, both publicly guaranteed and non-guaranteed.

Official Development Assistance: Includes all disbursements of technical cooperation and assistance, loans, and grants (with a grant element of more than 25 percent) made bilaterally or through multilateral development agencies on concessional terms to promote economic development and welfare. High levels generally indicate a repressed economy and governmental resistance to market reform.

Foreign Direct Investment: A net figure of foreign acquisitions of 10 percent or more of voting stock in a business. Includes long- and short-term capital listed in the national balance of payments, equity investment, and reinvestment of earnings.

Gross Domestic Investment: Includes outlays to increase fixed assets, such as improvements in property, industrial capital, infrastructure, buildings, and net changes in inventories. High domestic investment indicates a commitment to maintain and improve domestic infrastructure (a key element for growth) as well as confidence in the economy by domestic businesses that increase inventories.

Category 2: Currency Stability

Investors often must use local currencies. If currencies lose value rapidly or fluctuate wildly, investors may suffer great losses. A strong currency indicates a healthy economy. A weak or declining currency raises import prices, deters foreign investment, lowers living standards, and undermines business confidence. Investors place a high value on currency stability.[5] Three methods of measuring currency stability are provided:

Table 4.5

Investment Data for the Big 5 Developing Countries

	1998 Index of Economic Freedom Score	Investment as a % of GDP, 1995	Annual Increase in Net Private Capital Flows, 1990-95	Annual Increase in Portfolio Investment (Bonds plus Equity), 1990-95	Official Development Assistance as a % of GNP, 1990-95	Annual Net Inflows of Foreign Direct Investment as a % of GDP, 1990-95	Gross Domestic Investment as a % of GDP, 1990-95
Indonesia	2.85	38%	130.2%	184.57%	1.29%	1.35%	31.9%
Brazil	3.35	22	176.38	335.19	0.03	0.44	20.63
Russia	3.45	25	922.6	n/a	0.38	0.19	30.48
India	3.70	25	31.37	1352.33	0.75	0.15	23.5
China	3.75	40	54.8	391.75	0.62	3.76	38.22

Source: The World Bank, *1997 World Development Indicators on CD-ROM*; International Finance Corporation, Emerging Markets Factbook 1997.

Table 4.6

Currency Stability for the Big 5 Developing Countries

	1998 Index of Economic Freedom Score	Annual Inflation Rate, 1990-95	Monetary Supply (M2) as a % of GDP, 1995	Annual Growth In Monetary Supply (M2), 1990-95	Annual Change in Value of Currency vs. the U.S. Dollar, 1990-96
Indonesia	2.85	8.69%	38.68%**	18.62% ***	-3.69%
Brazil	3.35	1547.83	26.14	1,272.42	-62.73
Russia *	3.45	460.36	11.58	165.28 ****	-42.91
India	3.70	10.18	46.03	16.70	-10.14
China	3.75	2.05	92.4	32.96	-6.63

Notes: * Data from 1994-96. Average annual change in value vs. the U.S. dollar from 1992-96.   ** Data from 1992.   *** Data from 1990-92.   **** Data from 1993-95.
Sources: The World Bank, *1997 World Development Indicators on CD-ROM*; International Monetary Fund, International Financial Statistics, June 1997.

Inflation: Based on a consumer price index calculated by the World Bank. Consumer price indices reflect fluctuations in the cost of acquiring a set basket of goods and services. Inflation measured by consumer price fluctuations is seldom reliable for inter-country comparisons, but can offer insight into domestic economies. High rates of inflation are undesirable.

Monetary Supply: Includes the amount of paper money outside banks, private demand deposits, current savings, and private foreign currency deposits. Presented both as an annual growth figure from 1990 to 1995 and as a percent of GDP in 1995. The amount of money in circulation has a direct impact on the value of a currency. Countries often instigate inflation by printing currency in excess of demand (growth in the economy or acquisition by foreign holders). This grouping is commonly referred to as "M2" by economists. Although growth in M2 is a necessary byproduct of economic growth and currency strength, it must correspond with economic

growth. Rapid growth in M2 more often is a sign of poor economic management.

Exchange Rate versus the Dollar: Value fluctuations against the dollar are useful because most international transactions and contracts are valued in dollar terms. The stability of the dollar makes it a convenient benchmark against which to measure other currencies.

Category 3: Stock Market Performance

Many investments require the long-term commitment of resources. Investors may be unwilling to allocate capital to lengthy ventures, particularly in risky developing countries. Stock markets provide investors with an opportunity for short-term investments, allowing assets to be acquired quickly and abandoned just as quickly. They also provide vitally needed capital for long-term investments. Spurred by broad-based market liberalization, developing country stock markets in particular have grown in recent years. Three indicators are

Table 4.7

Stock Market Performance for the Big 5 Developing Countries

	1998 Index of Economic Freedom Score	Market Capitalization in 1996, (US$ billions)	Annual Growth in Market Capitalization, 1990-1996	Number of Domestic Companies Listed, 1996	Annual Growth in the Number of Domestic Companies Listed, 1990-96	World Value Traded, 1996 (US$ billions)	Annual Growth in World Value Traded, 1990-96
Indonesia	2.85	$91.016	59.27%	253	12.6%	$32.142	52.58%
Brazil	3.35	216.990	67.05	551	-0.87	112.108	79.45
Russia	3.45	37.230	2235.3	73	63.28	2.958	304.81
India	3.70	122.605	22.82	8,800	6.11	109.448	112.27
China	3.75	113.755	219.36	540	132.11	256.008	517.63

Notes: Russia market capitalization data from 1991-96, world value traded from 1994-96, number of listed companies from 1991-96. China data from 1991-96.
Source: International Finance Corporation, *Emerging Markets Factbook 1997*.

Table 4.8

Demographic Trends for the Big 5 Developing Countries

	1998 Index of Economic Freedom Score	Population, 1995 (millions)	Urban Population, 1995	Labor Force as a % of Population, 1990	Labor Force in the Industrial Sector, 1990	Life Expectancy, 1995 (years)	Literacy Rate, 1994
Indonesia	2.85	193	34%	44	14%	64	83.2%
Brazil	3.35	159	78	44	23	67	82.7
Russia	3.45	148	73	52	42	65	98.7
India	3.70	929	27	43	16	62	51.2
China	3.75	1,200	30	59	15	69	80.9

Sources: United Nations Development Programme, *1997 Human Development Report*; The World Bank, *1997 World Bank Atlas*.

listed in this category, in performance between 1990 and 1996 and the 1996 value for perspective.

Market Capitalization: The price of the share multiplied by the number of shares outstanding. This represents the overall size and value of the stock market.

Number of Domestic Companies Listed: The number of companies that have offered and traded shares publicly on the market. The number of companies typically indicates the sophistication and breadth of the market in the local economy.

World Value Traded: The value traded refers to the total value of shares traded globally.

Category 4: Demographic Trends

The importance of population as a source of labor and as a market for goods and services cannot be overstated. Aspects of population that affect the labor force are presented. Level of education, for example, affects the efficiency of the work force, while increasing urbanization and distribution of employment define the size of the available labor force. Developed countries share such traits as low population growth, high literacy and educational achievement, better health with longer life spans, and predominantly urban populations. The populations of developing countries, however, have a broader range of characteristics that are quite different from those of developed countries. Therefore, six sets of demographic data that may be of particular interest to investors are presented on the Big 5.

Population: The 1995 estimated population. Population levels reveal the size of potential domestic markets and labor forces.

Urban Population: The percentage of the total population living in areas considered urban in that country. Advantages in investing in urban areas include access to shipping, resources, and labor.

Labor Force: The percentage of the population economically active, including both the employed and unemployed. This category includes people who have the potential to supply labor for production.

Labor Force in the Industrial Sector: The percentage of the labor force involved in the industrial sector. Provides insight into both the overall employment structure and the level of industrialization. Opportunities for investment in the industrial sector in developing countries include relatively cheaper labor, looser environmental regulations, and opportunities to purchase former state industries.

Life Expectancy: The number of years an infant can be expected to live under the health conditions of the year of his or her birth. Directly reflects the general population's level of health. Healthy populations are more productive, have fewer absences due to illness, are more efficient, and remain in the work force longer.

Literacy Rate: The percentage of the adult population (age 15 and above) that is functionally literate. Literacy is an indirect indicator of education; greater levels of education generally make it easier for workers to learn new skills and be more productive.

Notes

1. U.S. exports and foreign direct investment position were chosen because the United States is the world's largest exporter and source of investment. A description of the methodology used in this analysis is available upon request.

2. The member countries of the OECD are Australia, Austria, Belgium, Canada, Denmark, Finland, France, Germany, Greece, Iceland, Ireland, Italy, Japan, Luxembourg, Mexico, the Netherlands, New Zealand, Norway, Portugal, Spain, Sweden, Switzerland, Turkey, the United Kingdom, and the United States.

3. Richard Lawrence, "'Big 5' Developing Nations Seen Destined for Greatness," *Journal of Commerce,* September 10, 1997, p. 2A.

4. Descriptions based on definitions provided by source materials. Tables 4.1–4.7 contain columns of percentage-change data for 5- or 10-year periods. These data are average percentage changes for these time periods. Technical explanations of these calculations are available upon request.

5. A weakening currency does benefit some foreign investors, however. Those producing goods for export may realize an advantage because it will increase their international competitiveness. Most exporters rely on imports of finished goods, and the costs of these will rise if currency is weak.

5

Methodology: Factors of the *Index* of *Economic Freedom*

by Bryan T. Johnson

Since 1995, the *Index of Economic Freedom* has offered the international community an in-depth examination of the factors that contribute most directly to a country's level of economic freedom and prosperity. As the first-ever-published comprehensive study of economic freedom in 1995, the *Index* defined the method by which economic freedom and growth could be measured in such vastly different places as Hong Kong and Cuba, and in every country in between. Today, other studies are available that analyze such issues as trade or government intervention in the economy.[1] The *Index* remains the only annual study, however, that also analyzes such critical economic determinants as:

- **Corruption** in the judiciary, customs service, and government bureaucracy;
- **Nontariff barriers** such as import bans and quotas, strict labeling and licensing requirements, and burdensome health, safety, and environmental regulations;
- **Taxation** such as capital gains, value-added, and payroll taxes;
- **Rule of law,** efficiency within the judiciary, and the ability to enforce contracts;
- **Regulatory burdens** on business;
- **Restrictions on banks** regarding financial services, such as selling securities and insurance;
- **Labor market regulations,** such as established work weeks and mandatory separation pay; and
- **Black market activities,** including smuggling, piracy of intellectual property rights, and black market labor and provision of services.

Analyzing economic freedom on an annual basis is important. It permits the immediate inclusion of the most recent data available on a country-by-country basis. Not surprisingly, changes in government policy occur at an alarming rate in most less-developed countries. Some countries of the former Soviet Union, for example, make major economic policy reversals on an almost daily basis. Studies that are not published annually rely on information that may be grossly out of date by the time it is analyzed and published. Consequently, such studies cannot track yearly trends for individual countries in important economic determinants like trade policy and regulation. Only the *Index of Economic Freedom* enables readers to see how such recent changes may affect a country's overall level of economic freedom. For this fourth edition, six new countries—Kazakstan, Kyrgyzstan, Tajikistan, Turkmenistan, and Uzbekistan, all of which used to be part of the Soviet Union, and Bosnia-Herzegovina, formerly part of communist Yugoslavia—have been added, bringing the total number of countries studied to 156.

Measuring Economic Freedom

The concept of economic freedom has been the subject of intense debate for centuries, but particularly since the 18th century and the emergence of the modern field of economics. The dictionary defines *freedom* as the "absence of necessity, coercion, or constraint on choice or action" and *economic* as "of, relating to, or based on the production, distribution, and consumption of goods and services."[2] Although leading economists and political theorists only now are reaching consensus on this important concept, economic freedom can be defined as the absence of government coercion or constraint on the production, distribution, or consumption of goods and services.

Governments have placed various constraints on economic activity throughout history, and some of these constraints have been greater than others. Generally, these constraints can be measured. Because economic freedom is the degree to which individuals are free to produce, distribute, and consume goods and services, one way to measure it is to study the number of constraints a government has imposed. Government policies and conditions that either maximize or restrict personal economic choices can be examined objectively.

The purpose of the *Index of Economic Freedom* is to go one step further and explain the reason that some countries are rich today while others remain poor, even after years of development assistance from the international community. To do this, the *Index* has studied 50 independent economic variables important to economic freedom to rate the level of economic freedom in each country. The variables fall into 10 broad categories, or "factors," of economic freedom: trade policy, taxation, government intervention in the economy, monetary policy, foreign investment, banking, wage and price controls, property rights, regulation, and black market activity. (These factors and their respective variables will be discussed more fully later in this chapter.)

Inputs vs. Outputs. Most *Index* factors should be considered as inputs in the economic freedom equation. In other words, they are factors that measure the governmental policies that either maximize or restrict economic freedom. Such factors as trade policy and monetary policy do not represent outputs in the economic freedom equation.[3] That is, they do not measure the results or consequences of policies that are economically free or unfree as other studies do.[4] Instead, such factors as trade policy and monetary policy measure the specific restriction on economic activity. Thus, it is an input. Studies that measure outputs often focus more on explaining the changes in economic growth rates than on understanding and describing the political, economic, and social environment necessary for economic activity. They measure economic freedom by looking at such outputs as the ability of a country's citizens to put their money in overseas bank accounts, or the difference between a country's official currency exchange rate and its black market exchange rate. These elements are not inputs in determining economic freedom; they are not governmental policies. Instead, they are behavioral adaptations to a government's policies, or outputs by people and companies.

Attempting to measure economic freedom by analyzing outputs confuses context with content. The *Index of Economic Freedom* ranks the relative degree to which countries achieve economic freedom; in other words, it indicates the best context (or set of institutional inputs) for economic growth. Heritage analysts believe that the activity from analyzing such inputs will lead more readily to superior levels of economic prosperity than economic activity that takes place in less free environments.

Weighting. The *Index of Economic Freedom* treats the 10 factors as equally important to the level of economic freedom in any country. Thus, to determine an overall score, the factors are weighted equally. This approach is the fairest and most scientifically sound at this stage of research. Although other studies maintain that certain components are more important than others, they do not provide sufficient scientific support for their conclusions.[5] Rather than utilize scientific methods or statistics, they base their findings on opinion polls of economists. Opinion surveys are interesting, but they cannot be considered an objective or scientifically adequate way to determine the relative weight of each economic factor.

The authors and editors of The Heritage Foundation/Wall Street Journal 1998 *Index of Economic Freedom* do not believe it is possible at this stage of academic research to know with a high degree of certainty which factors are more important than others. What *is* known is that, for a country to achieve long-term growth and economic well-being, it must perform well in all the factors evaluated in the *Index*'s methodology.

Heritage economists will continue to develop a statistical and scientifically supportable method for determining which factors play a larger role in economic freedom and how much weight each one deserves in relation to the others. Once such statistical relationships have been established and reviewed by leading economists, they will be incorporated in the grading process for future editions of the *Index*. Until that time, however, the authors of the *Index* believe the most objective way to grade economic freedom is to weigh all factors of economic freedom equally.

The Grading Scale. Each country in the *Index* has been given an overall economic freedom score based on the average of the 10 individual factor scores. Each factor was scored according to a grading scale unique for that factor. The scales run from 1 to 5: a score of 1 signifies a variable that is the most conducive to economic freedom, while a score of 5 signifies one that is the least conducive. In other words, factors rated with a 1 are variables of mostly free economies, and factors rated with a 5 are variables of least free economies. In addition, each score is followed by a plus sign (+), a minus sign (−), or "Stable." This additional information indicates, respectively, whether the factor of economic freedom is improving, is getting worse, or has stayed the same compared with the country's score last year. Finally, the factors are

added and averaged, and an overall score is assigned and used to rank the countries.

The four broad rankings of economic freedom for the countries are:

- **Free:** Countries with an average overall score of 1.99 or less.
- **Mostly free:** Countries with an average overall score of 2.00 to 2.99.
- **Mostly not free:** Countries with an average overall score of 3.00 to 3.99.
- **Repressed:** Countries with an average overall score of 4.00 or higher.

Previous Scores. The *Index of Economic Freedom* includes a comprehensive listing of the 156 countries with their scores for each of the 10 factors. This year, the country listings include 1995, 1996, 1997, and 1998 overall scores. With only a cursory glance, one can discern how rapidly a country has been increasing or reducing its level of economic freedom, or whether it has stayed the same over time.

Transparency. Because the *Index* is based on scientific methodology, it is both transparent and capable of analyzing a wide variety of data. The discussions that follow in this chapter explain the reason that the factor is an important element of economic freedom, how the five levels of economic freedom are broken down and scored for that factor, and what sources were used for its analysis. Thus, scoring is straightforward. If a country's banking system has a score of 3, it has most of the characteristics spelled out on pages 45–46 as level 3: There is heavy government influence on its banks, government owns or operates some of its banks, the government maintains strict control of credit, and there are significant barriers to the formation of domestic banks. Similarly, a country receiving a score of 5 in trade policy has an average tariff rate of at least 20 percent or very high nontariff barriers that, for all practical purposes, close its markets to imports (see pages 38–39, Trade Policy).

A country must meet most, but not necessarily all, conditions specified for each grade level of a factor. In the banking factor, a country would rate a grade of 2 (which is better than a grade of 3) if its banking system has only some government limits on financial services and deposit insurance and minor barriers to new bank formation. It would receive a 4 (which is worse than a 3) if its banking system is in transition, its banks are tightly controlled by the government, there is some corruption present, or domestic bank formation is virtually nonexistent.

Sources. The primary sources used to determine how a country meets the criteria for each *Index* factor are listed. The analysis relies heavily on these sources. Additional sources for data that are critical to a country's score also are documented. For example, a statement about the level of corruption in a country's customs service would be followed with a supporting quote from a reliable source. There are innumerable lesser sources of information, including conversations with government officials and visits to Internet sites. Because it would be cumbersome to cite all the sources for every single variable of each factor, specific endnotes are reserved for the most important information used to establish a score or score change.

A Summary of the Factor Variables

To grade each country for the *Index,* some 50 independent variables are examined to determine the overall level of economic freedom. Information pertaining to all 50 independent factors was collected and used to determine which of the five grades established for each of the 10 factors most closely applies to the country. Even though all of the variables are analyzed, not all receive an individual score or specific mention in the text. For example, it is not necessary to mention the cases in which corruption is virtually nonexistent in a country's judiciary. This variable is mentioned only when corruption in the judiciary is a documented problem. Consequently, instead of grading each of the 50 variables for each of the 156 countries individually, the *Index* divides the 50 variables into the 10 broad factors of economic freedom. Although all of the 50 variables are analyzed, grades are provided only for the 10 broad factors of economic freedom. Such a system keeps the *Index* at a manageable length.

The independent variables are summarized in the callout box in the descriptions of each factor.

The Factors of Economic Freedom

Factor #1: Trade Policy

Trade policy is a key factor in measuring economic freedom. The degree to which government hinders the free flow of foreign commerce has a direct bearing on a country's economic growth. Trade policy also is an important factor in the industrialization of developing economies. International trade enables a country's industries to maximize production by allowing them to import raw materials and foreign goods and services that are cheaper than those produced at home. It also offers access to the world market, which can lead to greater wealth.

Methodology. For trade policy, a score is given based on a country's average tariff rate—the higher the rate, the worse (or higher) the score. Whenever average tariff rates are not available, the average rate is determined by calculating the revenue raised from tariffs and duties as a percentage of total imports.

Variables of Factor #1: Trade Policy

- Average tariff rate
- Nontariff barriers
- Corruption in the customs service

Tariffs are not the only barriers to trade, however. Many countries increasingly impose import quotas, licensing requirements, and other mandates to restrict imports. These are referred to as nontariff barriers. Such nontariff barriers are examined; if they exist in sufficient quantity, a country's score based solely on tariff rates is given an additional point on the scale (representing decreased economic freedom). The trade analysis also considers corruption within the customs service. This is an important consideration because, even though countries may have lower published tariff rates and no official nontariff barriers, their customs officials may be corrupt and require bribes to allow products entry into their ports. Or there may be instances in which

Trade Policy Grading Scale

Score	Levels of Protectionism	Criteria
1	Very low	Average tariff rate of less than 4 percent and/or very low nontariff barriers.
2	Low	Average tariff rate of 5 percent to 9 percent and/or low nontariff barriers.
3	Moderate	Average tariff rate of 10 percent to 14 percent and/or moderate nontariff barriers.
4	High	Average tariff rate of 15 percent to 19 percent and/or high nontariff barriers.
5	Very high	Average tariff rate of 20 percent and higher and/or very high nontariff barriers that virtually close the market to imports.

customs officials steal the goods for themselves. These circumstances are analyzed and documented whenever possible.

Sources. For each country, unless otherwise noted, the following sources are used in determining scores for trade policy: Arrowhead International, *World Trade and Customs Directory,* Spring 1997; Economist Intelligence Unit, *EIU Country Reports* and *Investing, Licensing and Trading Conditions Abroad (ILT Reports);* International Monetary Fund, *Government Finance Statistics Yearbook* and *International Financial Statistics Yearbook;* United States Trade Representative, *1997 National Trade Estimate Report on Foreign Trade Barriers;* U.S. Department of Commerce, *Country Commercial Guides,* 1997; U.S. Department of State, *Country Reports on Economic Policy and Trade Practices,* 1997; and various official government publications.

Factor #2: Taxation

Taxes are a key factor in measuring economic freedom. All taxes are harmful to economic activity because a tax essentially is a government-imposed disincentive to perform the activity being taxed. For this reason, exorbitant taxes slow economic growth. When analyzing taxation, taxes on corporate profits, income, and other significant activities are measured.

Methodology. Two types of taxation are

scored: income taxes and corporate taxes. First, each country is scored based on these two major types of taxation, which many economists agree have the most negative economic impact on individuals. These scores then are averaged to achieve a single taxation score. Finally, other taxes, such as value-added taxes, sales taxes, payroll

Variables of Factor #2: Taxation

- Top income tax rate
- Tax rate that applies to the average income level
- Top corporate tax rate
- Other taxes

taxes, and state and local taxes are examined. If they exist in sufficient quantity, the taxation score is moved one-half point higher on the scale, representing the relative impact of these other taxes on individual economic freedom. This one-half-point increase signifies decreased economic freedom.

It should be noted that the author of the *Index* methodology also considered using the level of tax

Income Tax Grading Scale

This scale lists a score from 1 through 5. The higher the score, the higher the tax rate. In each case, the highest level that applies to a country becomes that country's score.

Score	Tax Rates	Criteria
1	Very low taxes	No taxes on income, or a flat tax rate on income of 10 percent or less.
2	Low taxes	A top tax rate of 25 percent or below, or a flat income tax between 10 percent and 20 percent, or a top rate of 40 percent or below and a tax on average income below 10 percent.
3	Moderate taxes	A top tax rate of 35 percent or below, or a tax on average income below 15 percent.
4	High taxes	A top income tax rate of 36 percent to 50 percent, or an average tax level between 15 percent and 20 percent, and a tax structure not fully developed by the government or in a state of disarray.
5	Very high taxes	A top rate above 50 percent and a tax on average income between 20 percent and 25 percent, or a tax rate on average income of 25 percent or above regardless of the top rate, or a tax system through which the government confiscates most economic output resulting from government ownership of most economic activity.

revenues as a percentage of the economy, based on the assumption that the higher the percentage, the lower the economic freedom. According to this assumption, taxes are higher when they equal a higher percentage of the overall economy. After this approach had been examined, however, it was deemed to be inaccurate and misleading.[6] Tax revenue data usually are several years old by the time they are published, whereas tax rate and tax bracket data are published yearly and are therefore current for the year in which the *Index* is published. By analyzing tax data based on rates and brackets, the author includes the most up-to-date information in each edition.

Moreover, not only are the tax revenue data out of date by the time they are published, they also can be inaccurate. For example, the main source of tax revenue data available in a worldwide publication is the International Monetary Fund's (IMF) *Government Financial Statistics*. The data are unreliable, however, because many of the less-developed countries listed in this publication are recipients of IMF loans. A conflict of interest exists for many IMF recipient countries between supplying reliable data for this survey and making their economies look better to attract additional aid. These figures therefore should be viewed with some skepticism.

There are other reasons to avoid using tax revenues as a percentage of gross domestic product (GDP) when measuring a country's tax structure. For example, when a country cuts taxes, revenues eventually increase in most cases as a result of increased economic activity. Thus, the percentage of tax revenues to the overall economy may increase more rapidly than GDP. This lag time can cause distortions in the measurements: Tax revenues may increase, which could be taken

Corporate Tax Grading Scale

The second type of tax analyzed for each country is its corporate tax. Each country is scored according to a sliding scale based on corporate tax rates.

Score	Tax Rates	Criteria
1	Very low taxes	Limited or no taxes are imposed on corporate profits.
2	Low taxes	Flat corporate tax of less than 25 percent, or a progressive top tax of less than 25 percent.
3	Moderate taxes	A progressive corporate tax system with top rate of between 26 percent and 35 percent, or a flat tax system with tax levels above 25 percent.
4	High taxes	A progressive corporate tax system with a top rate of between 36 percent and 45 percent, and a tax structure not fully developed by the government or in a state of disarray.
5	Very high taxes	A cumbersome progressive tax system with top corporate tax rates of more than 46 percent, or a tax system in which the government confiscates most economic output resulting from government ownership of most economic activity.

to mean that taxes also have increased; in reality, however, revenues increased because taxes were cut. Measuring tax revenues as a percentage of the economy initially could "penalize" countries that cut their taxes. Likewise, when taxes are increased, revenues usually drop. Revenues as a percentage of the economy may drop initially as well. Although it is true that, as taxes go up, the economy may slow or shrink faster than the falling revenues, it also is true that the effect is not immediate. Measuring taxation this way could "reward" countries that increase taxes.

The best way to measure a country's tax structure is to examine its tax rates, especially those that apply to the average taxpayer. This method, employed by the *Index,* allows Heritage economists to account for an increase, or a decrease, in economic freedom immediately as countries reduce or raise their taxation rates.

Sources. For each country, unless otherwise noted, the following sources are used for information on taxation: Economist Intelligence Unit, *ILT Reports;* Ernst & Young, *1997 Worldwide Executive Tax Guide and Directory* and *1997 Worldwide Corporate Tax Guide and Directory;* U.S. Department of Commerce, *Country Commercial Guides,* 1997, and reports available through STAT–USA; and various official government publications.

Income taxes. Some countries have relatively high top income tax rates, but these rates apply to very few people. For example, Japan has a top income tax rate of 50 percent, but the income levels upon which it is levied are so large that very few people fall into this bracket. The tax rate that applies to the average Japanese taxpayer is much lower. To measure taxation policy accurately, it is necessary to examine not only the top income tax rate, but also the rate that applies to the average taxpayer. To discover the average income tax rate, a country's per capita GDP is used.[7] Each country then is scored on (1) its top tax rate and (2) the tax rate that applies to the average income.

Government Intervention Grading Scale

Score	Level of Government Intervention in the Economy	Criteria
1	Very low	Less than 10 percent of GDP; virtually no government-owned enterprises.
2	Low	11 percent to 25 percent of GDP; a few government-owned enterprises, like the postal service; aggressive privatization program in place.
3	Moderate	26 percent to 35 percent of GDP; several government-owned enterprises like telecommunications, some banks, and energy production; stalled or limited privatization program.
4	High	36 percent to 45 percent of GDP; many government-owned enterprises like transportation, goods distributors, and manufacturing companies.
5	Very high	46 percent or more of GDP; mostly government-owned industries; few private companies.

Factor #3: Government Intervention in the Economy

The greater the degree to which the government intrudes in an economy, the less individuals are free to engage in their own economic activities. By taking government consumption as a percentage of GDP, one can begin to determine the level of government intervention in the economy. The higher the rate of government consumption as a percentage of GDP, the higher the *Index* score and, hence, the lower the level of economic freedom.

Methodology. Measuring government consumption as a percentage of GDP reveals only an approximation of the government's role in a country's economy.[8] In the United States, for example, the federal budget is about 24 percent of GDP. This figure includes servicing the federal budget deficit and transfer payments through entitlements like Medicaid. For most less-developed countries, government consumption figures do not include funds spent on servicing the budget deficit and some transfer payments. Although government consumption figures probably understate total government intervention in the economy, they are useful as a starting point in

> **Variables of Factor #3: Government Intervention in the Economy**
>
> - Government consumption as a percentage of the economy
> - Government ownership of businesses and industries
> - Economic output produced by the government

gauging the degree of government intervention.

The next step in scoring government consumption is to determine the size of the state-owned sector of a country's economy. If a country has many state-owned enterprises, or if a large portion of its GDP is produced by the state-owned sector, it is scored one point higher on the scale, signifying decreased economic freedom. The state of any privatization programs also is examined. If a country has a state-owned sector that is being privatized aggressively, this is noted. This puts into context any statements made about the size of the

Monetary Policy Grading Scale

Score	Inflation Rate	Criteria
1	Very low	Below 6 percent.
2	Low	Between 7 percent and 13 percent.
3	Moderate	Between 14 percent and 20 percent.
4	High	Between 21 percent and 30 percent.
5	Very high	Over 30 percent.

state-owned sector. If the privatization program has stalled, however, or one is not in place, that too is mentioned.

Sources. For each country, unless otherwise noted, the following sources are used for information on government intervention in the economy: U.S. Department of State and U.S. Department of Commerce, various reports; Economist Intelligence Unit, *EIU Country Reports;* and World Bank, *World Development Indicators on CD–ROM 1997.*

Factor #4: Monetary Policy

The value of a country's currency is based largely on its monetary policy. When a government maintains a tight monetary policy—that is, the supply of currency does not exceed the demand—individuals have the economic freedom to engage in productive and profitable economic activities. If the government maintains a loose monetary policy—that is, it supplies more currency than the demand requires—the currency loses its value and individuals are less free to engage in productive and profitable economic activities. The best way to measure monetary policy is to analyze the inflation rate over a period of time because it is more difficult to maintain low stable inflation rates over a long period of time than over a short one. The inflation rate is linked directly with the government's ability to manage the money supply in the economy.

Methodology. The main criterion for this factor is a country's average inflation rate. Countries with high rates of inflation have a loose monetary policy and are graded higher because they have less economic freedom than countries with lower inflation rates. Countries with low rates of inflation have a tight monetary policy and are graded lower because they have more economic freedom.

Countries of the former Soviet Union pose a unique problem in determining average inflation rates. Because these countries had command economies, annual inflation rate averages from 1985 to 1995 are misleading. Without a market-based system, the state can hold prices constant. Therefore, countries of the former Soviet Union are graded solely on an estimated average inflation rate since 1992. Although these figures are high, especially because of the recent transformation of their economies to a market-based system, they are more accurate reflections of current conditions than are figures based on the Soviet era.

Variables of Factor #4: Monetary Policy

- Average inflation rate from 1985 to 1995
- Average inflation rate for 1996 (informational purposes only)

Moreover, measuring inflation on a historical basis may understate the current economic conditions within certain countries. If, for example, a country had high rates of inflation in the early 1980s but low rates today, the average rate of inflation might still be quite high. In these instances, it is important to include information giving the most current inflation rate figures available. These figures appear at the end of the Monetary Policy section for each country. For

Capital Flows and Foreign Investment Grading Scale

Score	Barriers to Foreign Investment	Criteria
1	Very low	Open and impartial treatment of foreign investment; accessible foreign investment code.
2	Low	Restrictions on investments like utilities, companies vital to national security, and natural resources; limited, efficient approval process.
3	Moderate	Restrictions on many investments, but official policy that conforms to established foreign investment code; bureaucratic approval process.
4	High	Investment permitted on a case-by-case basis; possible presence of bureaucratic approval process and corruption.
5	Very high	Government that seeks actively to prevent foreign investment; rampant corruption.

purposes of grading monetary policy, however, they are used only to determine whether inflation is going down, increasing, or staying even with historical levels.

Sources. Unless otherwise noted, the main source for data on monetary policy is *The World Bank World Atlas 1997.* Inflation figures for countries without an average inflation rate, or for countries of the former Soviet Union, come from Economist Intelligence Unit, *EIU Country Reports* and *ILT Reports,* and U.S. Department of State, *1997 Country Reports on Economic Policy and Trade Practices.* For some countries, the average rate of inflation is not available. In other cases, consumer price inflation or only retail inflation rates are used.

Factor #5: Capital Flows and Foreign Investment Policy

Foreign investment provides funds for economic expansion. Foreign investors supply the capital domestic investors need to start or expand their businesses. Restrictions on foreign investment limit the inflow of capital and thus hamper economic freedom. By contrast, little or no restriction of foreign investment maximizes economic freedom and thus increases the flow of investments. For this

Variables of Factor #5: Capital Flows and Foreign Investment

- Foreign investment code
- Restrictions on foreign ownership of business
- Restrictions on the industries and companies open to foreign investors
- Restrictions and performance requirements on foreign companies
- Foreigner ownership of land
- Equal treatment under the law for both foreign and domestic companies
- Restrictions on the repatriation of earnings
- Availability of local financing for foreign companies

category, the more restrictions a country imposes on foreign investment, the lower the level of economic freedom and the higher the score.

Banking Grading Scale

Score	Restrictions on Banks	Criteria
1	Very low	Very few restrictions on foreign banks; banks can engage in all types of financial services; government controls few, if any, commercial banks; no government deposit insurance.
2	Low	Few limits on foreign banks; country may maintain some limits on financial services and have interstate banking restrictions and deposit insurance; domestic bank formation may face some barriers.
3	Moderate	Heavy influence on banks by government; government owns or operates some banks; strict government control of credit; domestic bank formation may face significant barriers.
4	High	Banking system in transition; banks tightly controlled by government; possible corruption; domestic bank formation virtually nonexistent.
5	Very High	Financial institutions in chaos; banks operate on primitive basis; most credit goes only to state-owned enterprises; corruption rampant.

Methodology. Each country's policies toward foreign investment are scrutinized in order to determine its overall investment climate. The factor examines such variables as the extent to which foreign ownership limits domestic industries; the presence of a foreign investment code that defines the country's investment laws and procedures; whether the government encourages foreign investment through fair and equitable treatment of investors; whether foreign corporations are treated the same as domestic corporations under the law; and whether specific industries are closed to foreign investment. This analysis helps develop an overall description of the investment climate in the country for this *Index*. Each country then is graded on its investment climate.

Sources. For each country, unless otherwise noted, the following sources are used for data on capital flows and foreign investment policy: Economist Intelligence Unit, *ILT Reports;* United States Trade Representative, *1997 National Trade Estimate Report on Foreign Trade Barriers;* U.S. Department of Commerce, *Country Commercial*

Guides, 1997; U.S. Department of State, *Country Reports on Economic Policy and Trade Practices;* and official government publications of the respective countries.

Factor #6: Banking

In most countries, banks provide the economy with the financial means to operate. They lend money to start businesses; provide services such as real estate, insurance, and securities investments; and furnish a safe place for individuals to store their earnings. The more government controls banks, the less free they are to engage in these activities. The consequence of heavy regulation of banks is restricted economic freedom. Therefore, the more a government restricts its banking sector, the higher its score and the lower its economic freedom.

Methodology. This factor is scored by determining the openness of a country's banking system: specifically, whether foreign banks are able to operate freely; how difficult it is to open

Wage and Price Controls Grading Scale

Score	Wage and Price Controls	Criteria
1	Very low	Wages and prices determined by the market; no minimum wage.
2	Low	Most prices determined by supply and demand, although some prices determined by the government or such monopolies as utilities; may or may not have minimum wage laws.
3	Moderate	Mixture of market forces and government-determined wages and prices, or heavy government control of either prices or wages.
4	High	Rationing, wage and price controls on most jobs and items.
5	Very high	Wages and prices almost completely controlled by the government.

domestic banks; how heavily regulated the banking system is; and whether banks are free to provide customers with insurance, sell real estate, and invest in securities. This analysis is used to develop a description of the country's banking climate. The *Index's* banking factor measures the relative openness of a country's banking system.

Variables of Factor #6: Banking

- Government ownership of banks
- Restrictions on the ability of foreign banks to open branches and subsidiaries
- Government influence over the allocation of credit
- Government regulations, such as deposit insurance
- Freedom to offer all types of financial services, such as buying and selling real estate, securities, and insurance policies

Sources. For each country, unless otherwise noted, the following sources are used for data on

banking: Economist Intelligence Unit, *EIU Country Reports* and *ILT Reports;* U.S. Department of Commerce, *Country Commercial Guides,* 1997, and National Trade Data Bank of the United States; U.S. Department of State, *1997 Country Reports on Economic Policy and Trade Practices;* official government publications of the respective countries; and the World Bank.

Factor #7: Wage and Price Controls

A free economy is one that allows individual businesses to set not only the prices on the goods

Variables of Factor #7: Wage and Price Controls

- Minimum wage laws
- Freedom to set prices privately without government influence
- Government price controls
- The extent to which government price controls are used
- Government subsidies to businesses that affect prices

Property Rights Grading Scale

Score	Protection of Private Property	Criteria
1	Very high	Private property guaranteed by the government, and efficient court system enforces contracts; justice system punishes those who unlawfully confiscate private property; expropriation unlikely.
2	High	Private property guaranteed by the government, but enforcement lax; expropriation unlikely.
3	Moderate	Government recognizes some private property rights, such as land, but property can be nationalized; expropriation possible; judiciary may be influenced by other branches of government.
4	Low	Property ownership limited to personal items with little legal protection; communal property the rule; expropriation likely, and government does not protect private property adequately; judiciary subject to influence from other branches of government; possible corruption within judicial process; legal system has collapsed.
5	Very low	Private property outlawed; almost all property belongs to the state; expropriation certain, or country so corrupt and chaotic that property protection is nonexistent.

and services they sell, but also the wages they pay to the workers they employ. Some governments mandate wage and price controls. By doing so, they restrict economic activity and curtail economic freedom. Therefore, the more a government intervenes and controls prices and wages, the higher its *Index* score and the lower its economic freedom.

Methodology. This factor is scored by the extent to which a country allows the market or the government set wages and prices. Specifically, it looks at which products have prices set by the government, whether the government controls such things as utilities, and whether the government has a minimum wage policy or sets other wages. The factor's scale measures the relative degree of government control over wages and prices. A "very low" score of 1 represents wages

and prices that are set almost completely by the market, whereas a "very high" score of 5 means wages and prices are set almost completely by the government.

Sources. For each country, unless otherwise noted, the following sources are used for data on wage and price controls: Economist Intelligence Unit, *ILT Reports;* U.S. Department of Commerce, *Country Commercial Guides,* 1997; U.S. Department of State, *1997 Country Reports on Economic Policy and Trade Practices;* and the World Bank.

Factor #8: Property Rights

The ability to accumulate private property is the main motivating force in a market economy, and the rule of law is vital to a fully functioning, efficient market economy. This factor examines the extent to which the government protects private property and how safe private property is from expropriation. The less protection private property receives, the higher the score and the lower the economic freedom.

Variables of Factor #8: Property Rights

- Freedom from government influence over the judicial system
- Commercial code defining contracts
- Sanctioning of foreign arbitration of contract disputes
- Government expropriation of property
- Corruption within the judiciary
- Delays in receiving judicial decisions
- Legally granted and protected private property

Methodology. The degree to which private property is a guaranteed right in the country is scored. So too is the extent to which the government protects—and enforces laws that protect—private property. The probability that the state will expropriate private property also is examined. In addition, this factor analyzes the independence of the judiciary, the existence of corruption within the judiciary, and the ability of individuals and businesses to enforce contracts. The less legal protection of private property, the higher the score. Similarly, the greater the chances of government expropriation of private property, the higher the score.

Sources. For each country, unless otherwise noted, the following sources are used for information on property rights: Economist Intelligence Unit, *ILT Reports;* U.S. Department of Commerce, National Trade Data Bank of the United States and *Country Commercial Guides,* 1997; U.S. Department of State, *Country Reports on Human Rights Practices for 1996;* and the World Bank.

Factor #9: Regulation

In many less-developed economies, obtaining a business license to sell goods or services is nearly impossible. Regulations and restrictions make it difficult for entrepreneurs to create new businesses. In some cases, government officials frown on any private-sector initiative and may even make them illegal. Although there are many regulations that hinder business, the most important are associated with licensing new companies and businesses. In some countries, such as the United States, obtaining a business license is as simple as mailing in a registration form with a minimal fee. In others, especially in sub-Saharan Africa and parts of South America, obtaining a business license requires endless trips to a government building and countless bribes, and may take up to a year.

Variables of Factor #9: Regulation

- Licensing requirements to operate a business
- Ease of obtaining a business license
- Corruption within the bureaucracy
- Labor regulations, such as established work weeks, paid vacations, and maternity leave, as well as selected labor regulations
- Environmental, consumer safety, and worker health regulations
- Regulations that impose a burden on business

Once a business is open, government regulation does not always subside. In some cases, it increases. Some countries apply their regulations haphazardly. For example, an environmental regulation may be used to shut down one business but not another. Business owners are uncertain about which regulations must be obeyed. Moreover, the existence of many regulations can support corruption as confused and harassed business owners try to work around the red tape.

Regulation Grading Scale

Score	Levels of Regulation	Criteria
1	Very low	Existing regulations straightforward and applied uniformly to all businesses; regulations not much of a burden for business; corruption nearly nonexistent.
2	Low	Simple licensing procedures; existing regulations relatively straightforward and applied uniformly most of the time, but still burdensome in some instances; corruption, although possible, rare and not a problem.
3	Moderate	Existing regulations may be applied haphazardly and in some instances are not even published by the government; complicated licensing procedure; regulations impose substantial burden on business; significant state-owned sector; corruption present and poses some minor strain on businesses.
4	High	Government-set production quotas and some state planning; major barriers to opening a business; complicated licensing process; very high fees; bribes sometimes necessary; corruption present and burdensome; regulations impose a great burden on business.
5	Very high	Government discourages the creation of new businesses; corruption rampant; regulations applied randomly.

Methodology. This factor measures how easy or difficult it is to open and operate a business. The more regulations on business, the harder it is to open one. It also examines the degree of corruption and whether regulations are applied uniformly to all businesses. Another consideration is whether the country has state planning agencies that set production limits and quotas. The scale establishes a set of conditions for each of the five possible grades. These conditions include such items as the extent of government corruption, how uniformly regulations are applied, and the extent to which regulations impose a burden on business. At one end of the scale is the "very low" score of 1, at which corruption is nonexistent and regulations are minimal and applied uniformly. At the other end of the scale is the "very high" score of 5, at which corruption is rampant, regulations are applied randomly, and the general level of regulation is very high. A country need only meet a majority of the conditions in each score to receive that score.

Sources. For each country, unless otherwise noted, the following sources are used for data on regulation: U.S. Department of Commerce, National Trade Data Bank of the United States and *Country Commercial Guides,* 1997; and official government publications of the respective countries.

Factor #10: Black Market

Black markets are a direct result of government intervention in the market. A black market activity—the only kind of output measured in the *Index*—is one that the government has outlawed. Although there are many activities that even the most civil of societies will outlaw, such as illicit drugs and prostitution, governments frequently limit individual liberty by outlawing others, such

Black Market Grading Scale

Score	Black Market Activity	Criteria
1	Very low	Very low level of black market activity; economies are free markets with black markets in such things as drugs and weapons.
2	Low	Low level of black market activity; economies may have some black market involvement in labor or pirating of intellectual property.
3	Moderate	Moderate level of black market activity; countries may have some black market activities in the labor, agriculture, and transportation sectors, and moderate levels of piracy in intellectual property.
4	High	High level of black market activity; countries may have substantial levels of black market activity in such areas as labor, pirated intellectual property, and smuggled consumer goods, and in such services as transportation, electricity, and telecommunications.
5	Very high	Very high level of black market activity; countries have black markets that are larger than their formal economies.

as private transportation and construction services. Furthermore, government regulation or restriction in one area may create the need for a black market in another. For example, a country with high barriers to trade may have laws that protect its domestic market and prevent the import of foreign goods. Yet these barriers create incentives for smuggling, and a black market often is created for the barred products. In addition, governments that do not have strong property rights protection for items like intellectual property, or that do not enforce existing laws, encourage piracy and theft in these sectors.

For purposes of the *Index,* the larger the black market is in a particular country, the lower the country's level of economic freedom. The more prevalent these activities are, the worse the country's score. Conversely, the smaller the black market, the higher the country's level of economic freedom. The less prevalent these activities are, the better its score.

Methodology. This factor considers the extent to which black market activities occur. Although

Variables of Factor #10: Black Market

- Smuggling
- Piracy of intellectual property in the black market
- Agricultural production supplied on the black market
- Manufacturing supplied on the black market
- Services supplied on the black market
- Transportation supplied on the black market
- Labor supplied on the black market

information on the size of black markets in less-developed countries is difficult to find, it has become more readily available. Information can be found on the extent of smuggling in a country, the level of piracy of intellectual property, and the level of black market labor. When information is available on these issues, it is used to determine the extent to which black market activities occur. The presence or absence of these types of activities is used to estimate the level of activity that occurs in the black market. The higher the black market activity, the higher a country's score and the lower its level of economic freedom. As newer data become available, it may become possible to document the percentage of black market activity in a country's overall economy.

Although this factor measures black market activity in the production, distribution, or consumption of goods and services, it does not measure such things as black market exchange rates, gambling, illegal narcotics, illegal arms, prostitution, or related activities. Such activities are very difficult to quantify with objectivity.

Sources. For this factor, unless otherwise noted, the following sources are used for information on black market activities: U.S. Department of Commerce, *Country Commercial Guide,* 1997; U.S. Department of State, *Country Reports on Economic Policy and Trade Practices;* official U.S. government cables supplied by the U.S. Department of Commerce and U.S. Department of State, available through the National Trade Data Bank; and official government publications of the respective countries.

Notes

1. See also James D. Gwartney and Robert A. Lawson, *Economic Freedom of the World 1997* (Vancouver, Canada: Fraser Institute, 1997), and Richard E. Messick, *World Survey of Economic Freedom: 1995–1996* (New Brunswick, N.J.: Transaction Publishers, 1996).

2. *Webster's Ninth New Collegiate Dictionary* (Springfield, Mass.: Merriam Webster, Inc., 1997).

3. The black market factor is the only one that measures outputs in the *Index.* Black market activities are a direct result of government restrictions on economic freedom, so the black market factor serves to supplement the others, allowing the author to provide a more detailed analysis of the level of economic freedom in each country measured.

4. For example, see Gwartney and Lawson, *Economic Freedom of the World 1997.*

5. *Ibid.*

6. The author did rely on this approach, however, when information on tax rates was not available. These instances are noted.

7. Because these figures were readily available, this method allowed the author to generate the average income level for nearly all countries.

8. GDP is used in most cases. When only gross national product (GNP) figures were available, this is so stated.

6

The 1998 *Index of Economic Freedom: The Countries*

by Bryan T. Johnson

This section is a compilation of countries, each graded in all 10 factors of the *Index of Economic Freedom*. Each country receives a 1 through 5 score for all 10 factors. Those scores then are averaged to get the final *Index of Economic Freedom* score. Countries with a score between 1 and 2 have the freest economies. Countries with a score around 3 are less free. Countries with a score near 4 are over-regulated and need significant economic reforms to achieve even the most basic increases in economic growth. Those with the score of 5 are the most economically oppressed countries.

Albania   3.75

| 1997 Score: **3.65** | 1996 Score: **3.45** | 1995 Score: **3.55** |

Trade	3	Banking	4
Taxation	3.5	Wages and Prices	3
Government Intervention	5	Property Rights	4
Monetary Policy	5	Regulation	3
Foreign Investment	2	Black Market	5

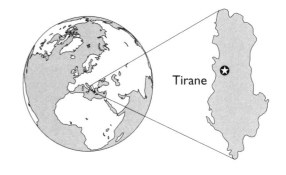

Tirane

Albania gained its independence from the Ottoman Empire in 1912, but the struggle for independence resulted in the loss of about half its territory in southeastern Europe and 40 percent of its people to neighboring Greece and Serbia. During World War I, much of the country was destroyed. After the war, it was an independent state ruled by a monarch. But even though King Zog sought economic self-sufficiency, Albania became increasingly dependent on Benito Mussolini's Italy, which occupied parts of the country in 1939. The Albanian Communist Party was formed in 1941; after World War II, Albania became one of the world's most oppressive communist states. The communist regime was deposed in 1991, and President Sali Berisha was elected in 1992 and reelected in 1996. A recent pyramid investment scheme scandal, however, enabled the Socialist Party to regain control of the legislature amid widespread violence. In July 1997, Berisha resigned from office and the Socialist Party won the parliamentary elections, regaining power. Albania has been plagued by violence, rampant organized crime, and the collapse of its law enforcement system. There also has been an increase in corruption within the judiciary. As a result, this year's overall score is 0.1 point worse than last year's.

TRADE POLICY
Score: 3–Stable (moderate level of protectionism)

Albania's tariffs range from 7 percent to 40 percent, although most products enter at a rate of 10 percent to 15 percent. Import licenses are not required.

TAXATION
Score–Income taxation: 2–Stable (low tax rates)
Score–Corporate taxation: 3–Stable (moderate tax rates)
Final Taxation Score: 3.5–Stable (high tax rates)

Albania has a top income tax rate of 24 percent[1] and a top corporate tax rate of 30 percent. It also has a small business tax, a social contributions tax, and a turnover tax.

GOVERNMENT INTERVENTION IN THE ECONOMY
Score: 5–Stable (very high level)

The public sector generates about 50 percent of Albania's GDP.[2] The country has made significant progress in privatizing some industries like agriculture, however, and this could lead to less government intervention in the economy in the future.

MONETARY POLICY
Score: 5–Stable (very high level of inflation)

Inflation has been very high, but dropped from 226 percent in 1992 to 31 percent in 1993. The rate of inflation fell below 20 percent in 1994 but increased to 22 percent in 1995. In 1996, it fell to 12 percent. Although there are not enough data to develop an average inflation rate from 1985 to 1994, it is possible to estimate an average rate from 1992 to 1996: well over 30 percent.

1	Hong Kong	1.25		77	Zambia	3.05
2	Singapore	1.30		80	Mali	3.10
3	Bahrain	1.70		80	Mongolia	3.10
4	New Zealand	1.75		80	Slovenia	3.10
5	Switzerland	1.90		83	Honduras	3.15
5	United States	1.90		83	Papua New Guinea	3.15
7	Luxembourg	1.95		85	Djibouti	3.20
7	Taiwan	1.95		85	Fiji	3.20
7	United Kingdom	1.95		85	Pakistan	3.20
10	Bahamas	2.00		88	Algeria	3.25
10	Ireland	2.00		88	Guinea	3.25
12	Australia	2.05		88	Lebanon	3.25
12	Japan	2.05		88	Mexico	3.25
14	Belgium	2.10		88	Senegal	3.25
14	Canada	2.10		88	Tanzania	3.25
14	United Arab Emirates	2.10		94	Nigeria	3.30
17	Austria	2.15		94	Romania	3.30
17	Chile	2.15		96	Brazil	3.35
17	Estonia	2.15		96	Cambodia	3.35
20	Czech Republic	2.20		96	Egypt	3.35
20	Netherlands	2.20		96	Ivory Coast	3.35
22	Denmark	2.25		96	Madagascar	3.35
22	Finland	2.25		96	Moldova	3.35
24	Germany	2.30		102	Nepal	3.40
24	Iceland	2.30		103	Cape Verde	3.44
24	South Korea	2.30		104	Armenia	3.45
27	Norway	2.35		104	Dominican Republic	3.45
28	Kuwait	2.40		104	Russia	3.45
28	Malaysia	2.40		107	Burkina Faso	3.50
28	Panama	2.40		107	Cameroon	3.50
28	Thailand	2.40		107	Lesotho	3.50
32	El Salvador	2.45		107	Nicaragua	3.50
32	Sri Lanka	2.45		107	Venezuela	3.50
32	Sweden	2.45		112	Gambia	3.60
35	France	2.50		112	Guyana	3.60
35	Italy	2.50		114	Bulgaria	3.65
35	Spain	2.50		114	Georgia	3.65
38	Trinidad and Tobago	2.55		114	Malawi	3.65
39	Argentina	2.60		117	Ethiopia	3.70
39	Barbados	2.60		117	India	3.70
39	Cyprus	2.60		117	Niger	3.70
39	Jamaica	2.60		120	Albania	3.75
39	Portugal	2.60		120	Bangladesh	3.75
44	Bolivia	2.65		120	China (PRC)	3.75
44	Oman	2.65		120	Congo	3.75
44	Philippines	2.65		120	Croatia	3.75
47	Swaziland	2.70		125	Chad	3.80
47	Uruguay	2.70		125	Mauritania	3.80
49	Botswana	2.75		125	Ukraine	3.80
49	Jordan	2.75		128	Sierra Leone	3.85
49	Namibia	2.75		129	Burundi	3.90
49	Tunisia	2.75		129	Suriname	3.90
53	Belize	2.80		129	Zimbabwe	3.90
53	Costa Rica	2.80		132	Haiti	4.00
53	Guatemala	2.80		132	Kyrgyzstan	4.00
53	Israel	2.80		132	Syria	4.00
53	Peru	2.80		135	Belarus	4.05
53	Saudi Arabia	2.80		136	Kazakstan	4.10
53	Turkey	2.80		136	Mozambique	4.10
53	Uganda	2.80		136	Yemen	4.10
53	Western Samoa	2.80		139	Sudan	4.20
62	Indonesia	2.85		140	Myanmar	4.30
62	Latvia	2.85		140	Rwanda	4.30
62	Malta	2.85		142	Angola	4.35
62	Paraguay	2.85		143	Azerbaijan	4.40
66	Greece	2.90		143	Tajikistan	4.40
66	Hungary	2.90		145	Turkmenistan	4.50
66	South Africa	2.90		146	Uzbekistan	4.55
69	Benin	2.95		147	Congo/Zaire	4.70
69	Ecuador	2.95		147	Iran	4.70
69	Gabon	2.95		147	Libya	4.70
69	Morocco	2.95		147	Somalia	4.70
69	Poland	2.95		147	Vietnam	4.70
74	Colombia	3.00		152	Bosnia	4.80
74	Ghana	3.00		153	Iraq	4.90
74	Lithuania	3.00		154	Cuba	5.00
77	Kenya	3.05		154	Laos	5.00
77	Slovak Republic	3.05		154	North Korea	5.00

Mostly Unfree

Capital Flows and Foreign Investment
Score: 2–Stable (low barriers)

Albania has moved quickly to open its borders to desperately needed foreign capital and has passed laws forbidding state expropriation of foreign property. Foreign firms and domestic firms are treated equally under the law. No sectors are closed to foreign investment. Political instability, however, will work against foreign investment until order is reinstated.[3]

Banking
Score: 4–Stable (high level of restrictions)

Although Albania has made significant strides in replacing the communist central bank and providing avenues for implementing a competitive market-driven system, the financial system is still not fully private. Albania's financial system consists of seven major banks: four state-owned banks, two joint ventures between state-owned banks and private banks, and only one bank that is fully private. The failure of an illegal pyramid investment scheme has curtailed many financial sector operations severely, hurling the industry into a financial crisis.

Wage and Price Controls
Score: 3–Stable (moderate level)

Albania has a minimum wage. Although the government officially has ended price controls, most prices are set by the huge state-owned sector of the economy, which still receives government subsidies. These state-owned enterprises often are able to control prices because they can undercut prices determined by the market.

Property Rights
Score: 4– (low level of protection)

Even though the government has made some strides in privatization, the private sector remains small compared with the size of public holdings. In addition, the court system is not sufficiently developed to handle a growing caseload of property disputes. Recent reports on the court system point to increasing corruption. According to the U.S. Department of State, for example, "The judicial branch remains subject to strong executive pressure and corruption."[4] As a result, this year's property rights score is one point worse than last year's.

Regulation
Score: 3–Stable (moderate level)

Albania has made some progress in streamlining its bureaucracy. Nevertheless, the bureaucracy has been unable to adapt to the emerging private sector. It remains large and inefficient.

Black Market
Score: 5–Stable (very high level of activity)

Albania's legal market may be growing, but many consumers and entrepreneurs still find it easier and more profitable to deal in the black market. Taxi and bus transportation are provided by black marketeers. Smugglers have discovered that the scarcities caused by high tariffs on auto parts present ample opportunity for profit on the black market. Moreover, many agricultural items continue to be provided by black marketeers. According to the U.S. Department of Commerce, "Customs tax evasion also results in Albanian import statistics that undercount the true quantity/value of imported poultry by almost half. Black market sales of perishable food items have also presented problems for the Albanian Food Inspection Service."[5]

Notes

1. Information with which to determine the tax on the average income level is not available.
2. Budgetary figures are not available for Albania. Therefore, it is not possible to generate a government consumption figure. Albania's grade is based strictly on the fact that 50 percent of GDP is generated by the public sector.
3. Most barriers to investment are the result of political instability, and thus are not measurable. Such issues as rule of law, however, are taken into account in the other factors like property rights. Overall, Albania maintains low barriers to investment.
4. U.S. Department of State, "Albania Country Report on Human Rights Practices for 1996," 1997.
5. U.S. Department of Commerce, *Country Commercial Guide,* 1996.

Algeria   3.25

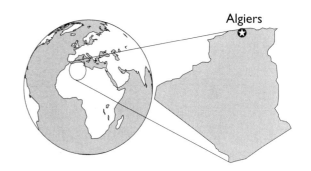

Algiers

| 1997 Score: **3.25** | 1996 Score: **3.25** | 1995 Score: **3.15** |

Trade	5	Banking	3
Taxation	3.5	Wages and Prices	3
Government Intervention	3	Property Rights	3
Monetary Policy	3	Regulation	3
Foreign Investment	3	Black Market	3

Algeria has had a state-controlled socialist economy since gaining its independence from France in 1962. Years of government mismanagement coupled with low oil prices in the mid-1980s led to anti-government riots in 1988. In 1989, Algeria adopted a new constitution that ended one-party rule and called for multiparty elections, but the elections were canceled in January 1992 after the results of the first round of voting made it clear that the radical Islamic Salvation Front would take control. This precipitated a rebellion by Islamic radicals against the military-backed government. Since 1992, more than 50,000 Algerians have been killed in a brutal civil war. Although Islamic terrorists have targeted foreigners in an effort to cut Algeria's economic links to the outside world and fuel discontent, the militants appear to have lost strength in recent months. In this uncertain climate, economic growth has been negligible over the past several years. Under pressure from the international financial community, the government has made a commitment to economic liberalization, but the pursuit of economic reform has been erratic.

TRADE POLICY
Score: 5–Stable (very high level of protectionism)

The government reformed its tariff schedule in 1992, cutting the top rate from 120 percent to 60 percent and reducing the number of categories. Importers also must pay two other taxes, adding a combined 17 percent to 90 percent to the cost of imports. Algeria's average tariff rate is about 22.9 percent.[1] The importation of some 70 goods, including textiles and shoes, is banned.

TAXATION
Score–Income taxation: 3–Stable (moderate tax rates)
Score –Corporate taxation: 3–Stable (moderate tax rates)
Final Taxation Score: 3.5–Stable (high tax rates)

Algeria's top income tax rate is 50 percent. There is no tax on average income. Income earned by foreigners is taxed at a flat 20 percent; in the past, the rate has been as high as 70 percent. The corporate tax rate is 50 percent for business profits and 20 percent for earnings that are reinvested. Tax breaks are available for companies locating in poorer areas. Algeria also maintains a value-added tax of 21 percent.

GOVERNMENT INTERVENTION IN THE ECONOMY
Score: 3–Stable (moderate level)

State-controlled enterprises dominate most commerce and industry. Private-sector involvement is increasing slowly. Government consumes 16 percent of Algeria's GDP.[2] Algeria's state sector is large, accounting for some 60 percent of national production. An announced privatization effort has made little progress, and opposition to it is mounting.

1	Hong Kong	1.25
2	Singapore	1.30
3	Bahrain	1.70
4	New Zealand	1.75
5	Switzerland	1.90
5	United States	1.90
7	Luxembourg	1.95
7	Taiwan	1.95
7	United Kingdom	1.95
10	Bahamas	2.00
10	Ireland	2.00
12	Australia	2.05
12	Japan	2.05
14	Belgium	2.10
14	Canada	2.10
14	United Arab Emirates	2.10
17	Austria	2.15
17	Chile	2.15
17	Estonia	2.15
20	Czech Republic	2.20
20	Netherlands	2.20
22	Denmark	2.25
22	Finland	2.25
24	Germany	2.30
24	Iceland	2.30
24	South Korea	2.30
27	Norway	2.35
28	Kuwait	2.40
28	Malaysia	2.40
28	Panama	2.40
28	Thailand	2.40
32	El Salvador	2.45
32	Sri Lanka	2.45
32	Sweden	2.45
35	France	2.50
35	Italy	2.50
35	Spain	2.50
38	Trinidad and Tobago	2.55
39	Argentina	2.60
39	Barbados	2.60
39	Cyprus	2.60
39	Jamaica	2.60
39	Portugal	2.60
44	Bolivia	2.65
44	Oman	2.65
44	Philippines	2.65
47	Swaziland	2.70
47	Uruguay	2.70
49	Botswana	2.75
49	Jordan	2.75
49	Namibia	2.75
49	Tunisia	2.75
53	Belize	2.80
53	Costa Rica	2.80
53	Guatemala	2.80
53	Israel	2.80
53	Peru	2.80
53	Saudi Arabia	2.80
53	Turkey	2.80
53	Uganda	2.80
53	Western Samoa	2.80
62	Indonesia	2.85
62	Latvia	2.85
62	Malta	2.85
62	Paraguay	2.85
66	Greece	2.90
66	Hungary	2.90
66	South Africa	2.90
69	Benin	2.95
69	Ecuador	2.95
69	Gabon	2.95
69	Morocco	2.95
69	Poland	2.95
74	Colombia	3.00
74	Ghana	3.00
74	Lithuania	3.00
77	Kenya	3.05
77	Slovak Republic	3.05

77	Zambia	3.05
80	Mali	3.10
80	Mongolia	3.10
80	Slovenia	3.10
83	Honduras	3.15
83	Papua New Guinea	3.15
85	Djibouti	3.20
85	Fiji	3.20
85	Pakistan	3.20
88	Algeria	3.25
88	Guinea	3.25
88	Lebanon	3.25
88	Mexico	3.25
88	Senegal	3.25
88	Tanzania	3.25
94	Nigeria	3.30
94	Romania	3.30
96	Brazil	3.35
96	Cambodia	3.35
96	Egypt	3.35
96	Ivory Coast	3.35
96	Madagascar	3.35
96	Moldova	3.35
102	Nepal	3.40
103	Cape Verde	3.44
104	Armenia	3.45
104	Dominican Republic	3.45
104	Russia	3.45
107	Burkina Faso	3.50
107	Cameroon	3.50
107	Lesotho	3.50
107	Nicaragua	3.50
107	Venezuela	3.50
112	Gambia	3.60
112	Guyana	3.60
114	Bulgaria	3.65
114	Georgia	3.65
114	Malawi	3.65
117	Ethiopia	3.70
117	India	3.70
117	Niger	3.70
120	Albania	3.75
120	Bangladesh	3.75
120	China (PRC)	3.75
120	Congo	3.75
120	Croatia	3.75
125	Chad	3.80
125	Mauritania	3.80
125	Ukraine	3.80
128	Sierra Leone	3.85
129	Burundi	3.90
129	Suriname	3.90
129	Zimbabwe	3.90
132	Haiti	4.00
132	Kyrgyzstan	4.00
132	Syria	4.00
135	Belarus	4.05
136	Kazakstan	4.10
136	Mozambique	4.10
136	Yemen	4.10
139	Sudan	4.20
140	Myanmar	4.30
140	Rwanda	4.30
142	Angola	4.35
143	Azerbaijan	4.40
143	Tajikistan	4.40
145	Turkmenistan	4.50
146	Uzbekistan	4.55
147	Congo/Zaire	4.70
147	Iran	4.70
147	Libya	4.70
147	Somalia	4.70
147	Vietnam	4.70
152	Bosnia	4.80
153	Iraq	4.90
154	Cuba	5.00
154	Laos	5.00
154	North Korea	5.00

Mostly Unfree

MONETARY POLICY
Score: 3–Stable (moderate level of inflation)

Algeria's average annual rate of inflation between 1985 and 1995 was 23.1 percent. Inflation was estimated at 20 percent for 1996.

CAPITAL FLOWS AND FOREIGN INVESTMENT
Score: 3–Stable (moderate barriers)

Algeria's 1993 investment code does not distinguish between foreign and domestic investment. It includes incentives for foreign investors, but the wording is vague. Laws governing oil and natural gas exploration have been liberalized, resulting in greater foreign investment. The large role played by state enterprises limits investment opportunities, and it is not uncommon for foreign investors to spend two years negotiating with government officials who have been charged with overseeing investments. Radical Islamic groups attacked and killed several foreign oil workers in 1995 and continue to pose a threat to all foreigners.

BANKING
Score: 3–Stable (moderate level of restrictions)

Algeria has liberalized its heavily state-controlled banking sector. Foreign banks may establish operations in Algeria but must maintain the same level of capital as Algerian banks. The central bank assumes nonperforming commercial loans made by five state banks, many of which are carried by state-controlled enterprises.

WAGE AND PRICE CONTROLS
Score: 3–Stable (moderate level)

The government controls the profit margins and sales of medicine, school supplies, tobacco, sugar, coffee, and vegetable oil. There has been, however, substantial progress toward eliminating price controls. In 1994, 89 percent of the prices of goods considered in the consumer price index were freely determined; in 1989, the figure was 10 percent. The government's widespread participation in the economy, however, limits pricing competition. Subsidies on food items continue, although many were reduced in 1995. Algeria has a minimum wage.

PROPERTY RIGHTS
Score: 3–Stable (moderate level of protection)

Government expropriation is unlikely in Algeria. Collective farms recently have been parceled and made into lease properties, a modest advance for property rights. Overall, private property is reasonably well protected. According to the U.S. Department of State, however, "Although the Constitution provides for an independent judiciary, recent executive branch decrees have restricted some of the judiciary's authority."[3] The biggest threats to private property remain terrorist attacks and the confiscation of property by Islamic militants as they continue their struggle against the government.

REGULATION
Score: 3–Stable (moderate level)

Algeria's relatively few private-sector enterprises must contend with burdensome regulations. Workers cannot be dismissed easily; the norm is employment for life. This represents a considerable burden on foreign companies and the private sector. Setting up a business is fairly straightforward, and there has been some lessening of the difficulties encountered in hiring expatriate workers.

BLACK MARKET
Score: 3–Stable (moderate level of activity)

Subsidies on foodstuffs have led to the smuggling of goods into neighboring countries. There is considerable smuggling of high-tariff electronics and textiles. Algeria has advanced, efficient laws protecting such intellectual property rights. Enforcement is strict.

NOTES

1. World Bank, "Open Economies Work Better," *Policy Research Working Paper* No. 1636, 1996.
2. World Bank, *World Development Report 1997*.
3. U.S. Department of State, "Algeria Country Report on Human Rights Practices for 1996," 1997.

Angola

4.35

Luanda

1997 Score: **4.35**	1996 Score: **4.35**	1995 Score: **4.35**

Trade	5	Banking	4
Taxation	3.5	Wages and Prices	4
Government Intervention	4	Property Rights	4
Monetary Policy	5	Regulation	5
Foreign Investment	4	Black Market	5

Angola went to war with colonial power Portugal in 1961 and finally won its independence in 1975. The government adopted a socialist economic system and maintained close ties with Cuba and the Soviet Union. Since 1975, Angola has been embroiled almost continually in civil war, including a 20-year conflict between the government and the National Union for the Total Independence of Angola (UNITA) that has left the country economically devastated and unable to take advantage of its considerable natural resources, which include oil, diamonds, and numerous minable ores. A peace agreement signed in late 1994 opened the door to a renewed United Nations peacekeeping mission, which is still present. Recently, tensions have been rising between the government of President Jose-Eduardo dos Santos and UNITA leader Jonas Savimbi, and renewed conflict may erupt. Economic liberalization efforts launched since 1991 have had modest impact, with GDP growth averaging 9.7 percent from 1994 to 1996, primarily because of increased production in the petroleum sector. Considerable opposition to economic liberalization continues inside the government.

TRADE POLICY
Score: 5–Stable (very high level of protectionism)

Angola's market is virtually closed. The average tariff rate is about 30 percent, and the market is highly protected by a wall of trade quotas and import licenses that are required for all imports. Corruption in the customs services hampers foreign imports, and politically well-connected firms continue to dominate trade. According to the U.S. Department of Commerce, "State owned firms in some service industries have in the recent past attempted to keep out foreign competition, sometimes with success."[1]

TAXATION
Score–Income taxation: 2–Stable (low tax rates)
Score–Corporate taxation: 4–Stable (high tax rates)
Final Taxation Score: 3.5–Stable (high tax rates)

Angola's top marginal income tax rate is 40 percent. For the average income level, the rate is 4 percent. Angola also has a top corporate tax rate of 40 percent, a 40 percent tax on capital gains, and a 7 percent social contributions tax.

GOVERNMENT INTERVENTION IN THE ECONOMY
Score: 4–Stable (high level)

Government consumes 33.9 percent of Angola's GDP. Progress with privatization has been minimal, and the government continues to control most economic sectors.

1	Hong Kong	1.25		77	Zambia	3.05
2	Singapore	1.30		80	Mali	3.10
3	Bahrain	1.70		80	Mongolia	3.10
4	New Zealand	1.75		80	Slovenia	3.10
5	Switzerland	1.90		83	Honduras	3.15
5	United States	1.90		83	Papua New Guinea	3.15
7	Luxembourg	1.95		85	Djibouti	3.20
7	Taiwan	1.95		85	Fiji	3.20
7	United Kingdom	1.95		85	Pakistan	3.20
10	Bahamas	2.00		88	Algeria	3.25
10	Ireland	2.00		88	Guinea	3.25
12	Australia	2.05		88	Lebanon	3.25
12	Japan	2.05		88	Mexico	3.25
14	Belgium	2.10		88	Senegal	3.25
14	Canada	2.10		88	Tanzania	3.25
14	United Arab Emirates	2.10		94	Nigeria	3.30
17	Austria	2.15		94	Romania	3.30
17	Chile	2.15		96	Brazil	3.35
17	Estonia	2.15		96	Cambodia	3.35
20	Czech Republic	2.20		96	Egypt	3.35
20	Netherlands	2.20		96	Ivory Coast	3.35
22	Denmark	2.25		96	Madagascar	3.35
22	Finland	2.25		96	Moldova	3.35
24	Germany	2.30		102	Nepal	3.40
24	Iceland	2.30		103	Cape Verde	3.44
24	South Korea	2.30		104	Armenia	3.45
27	Norway	2.35		104	Dominican Republic	3.45
28	Kuwait	2.40		104	Russia	3.45
28	Malaysia	2.40		107	Burkina Faso	3.50
28	Panama	2.40		107	Cameroon	3.50
28	Thailand	2.40		107	Lesotho	3.50
32	El Salvador	2.45		107	Nicaragua	3.50
32	Sri Lanka	2.45		107	Venezuela	3.50
32	Sweden	2.45		112	Gambia	3.60
35	France	2.50		112	Guyana	3.60
35	Italy	2.50		114	Bulgaria	3.65
35	Spain	2.50		114	Georgia	3.65
38	Trinidad and Tobago	2.55		114	Malawi	3.65
39	Argentina	2.60		117	Ethiopia	3.70
39	Barbados	2.60		117	India	3.70
39	Cyprus	2.60		117	Niger	3.70
39	Jamaica	2.60		120	Albania	3.75
39	Portugal	2.60		120	Bangladesh	3.75
44	Bolivia	2.65		120	China (PRC)	3.75
44	Oman	2.65		120	Congo	3.75
44	Philippines	2.65		120	Croatia	3.75
47	Swaziland	2.70		125	Chad	3.80
47	Uruguay	2.70		125	Mauritania	3.80
49	Botswana	2.75		125	Ukraine	3.80
49	Jordan	2.75		128	Sierra Leone	3.85
49	Namibia	2.75		129	Burundi	3.90
49	Tunisia	2.75		129	Suriname	3.90
53	Belize	2.80		129	Zimbabwe	3.90
53	Costa Rica	2.80		132	Haiti	4.00
53	Guatemala	2.80		132	Kyrgyzstan	4.00
53	Israel	2.80		132	Syria	4.00
53	Peru	2.80		135	Belarus	4.05
53	Saudi Arabia	2.80		136	Kazakstan	4.10
53	Turkey	2.80		136	Mozambique	4.10
53	Uganda	2.80		136	Yemen	4.10
53	Western Samoa	2.80		139	Sudan	4.20
62	Indonesia	2.85		140	Myanmar	4.30
62	Latvia	2.85		140	Rwanda	4.30
62	Malta	2.85		142	Angola	4.35
62	Paraguay	2.85		143	Azerbaijan	4.40
66	Greece	2.90		143	Tajikistan	4.40
66	Hungary	2.90		145	Turkmenistan	4.50
66	South Africa	2.90		146	Uzbekistan	4.55
69	Benin	2.95		147	Congo/Zaire	4.70
69	Ecuador	2.95		147	Iran	4.70
69	Gabon	2.95		147	Libya	4.70
69	Morocco	2.95		147	Somalia	4.70
69	Poland	2.95		147	Vietnam	4.70
74	Colombia	3.00		152	Bosnia	4.80
74	Ghana	3.00		153	Iraq	4.90
74	Lithuania	3.00		154	Cuba	5.00
77	Kenya	3.05		154	Laos	5.00
77	Slovak Republic	3.05		154	North Korea	5.00

Repressed

MONETARY POLICY
Score: 5–Stable (very high level of inflation)

Inflation has reached astronomical levels in Angola. The average inflation rate from 1985 to 1995 was 169.5 percent; in 1995, the inflation rate was 2,800 percent.

CAPITAL FLOWS AND FOREIGN INVESTMENT
Score: 4–Stable (high barriers)

Angola is effectively closed to most foreign investment. The economic and political crisis serves to deter foreign investment, which is prohibited in several sectors. Red tape and corruption plague the investment-approval bureaucracy. All investments are approved on a case-by-case basis. Although there has been some easing of investment restrictions, several proposed projects languish because of government roadblocks. The U.S. Department of Commerce reports that "Foreign investment remains prohibited or limited in defense, law and order, banking, public telecommunications, energy, media, education, health and transport."[2]

BANKING
Score: 4–Stable (high level of restrictions)

Banks are controlled mainly by the government. Despite recent attempts to allow foreign investment in banks, little progress has been made.

WAGE AND PRICE CONTROLS
Score: 4–Stable (high level)

Price controls have been lifted on some items but remain on many goods and services. The Ministry of Labor and Social Security sets wages and benefits. Petroleum price subsidies were eliminated recently, but large subsidies remain on a broad array of services, including transportation and telecommunications.

PROPERTY RIGHTS
Score: 4–Stable (low level of protection)

The government has few means to protect private property, and expropriation is likely. Corruption and bureaucratic inefficiency are still pervasive. According to the U.S. Department of State, "Travel within Angola remains unsafe due to the presence of bandits, undisciplined police and troops...."[3] In addition, "The Constitution provides for an independent judiciary, but in practice the court system lacked the means, experience, and training to be truly independent from the influence of the President.... The judicial system was largely destroyed during the civil war and during 1996 did not function in large areas of the country."[4]

REGULATION
Score: 5–Stable (very high level)

Government regulations are a severe hindrance to business. Labor regulations are particularly onerous. Corruption and bureaucratic red tape have created an environment in which legal businesses find it nearly impossible to operate. According to the U.S. Department of Commerce, "Administrative chaos, corruption, hyperinflation, and war have vitiated normal economic activity and attempts at reform."[5] The U.S. Department of State reports that "Foreign nationals, especially independent entrepreneurs, are subject to arbitrary detention and/or deportation by immigration and police authorities."[6]

BLACK MARKET
Score: 5–Stable (very high level of activity)

A significant share of Angola's economic output goes through the black market. The government has been cracking down on "parallel economic activities," but both medicine and food are sold on the black market, and there is considerable smuggling of goods. An illegal diamond trade also exists. The civil war, too, has boosted black market activity. According to the U.S. Department of Commerce, "To date, Angola has not adhered to any of the principal international intellectual property rights conventions."[7]

NOTES

1. U.S. Department of Commerce, *Country Commercial Guide,* 1996.
2. *Ibid.*
3. U.S. Department of State, "Angola—Travel Warning," *Market Research Reports,* April 18, 1997.
4. U.S. Department of State, "Angola Country Report on Human Rights Practices for 1996," 1997.
5. U.S. Department of Commerce, *Country Commercial Guide,* 1996.
6. U.S. Department of State, "Angola—Travel Warning," April 18, 1997.
7. U.S. Department of Commerce, *Country Commercial Guide,* 1996.

Argentina   2.60

1997 Score: **2.65**	1996 Score: **2.65**	1995 Score: **2.85**

Trade	4	Banking	2
Taxation	3	Wages and Prices	2
Government Intervention	2	Property Rights	2
Monetary Policy	5	Regulation	2
Foreign Investment	2	Black Market	2

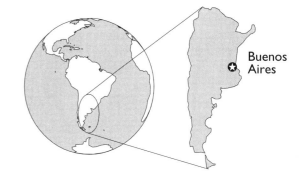

Buenos
Aires

By the 1930s, Argentina had become the world's fourth richest country. Its standard of living just before World War II was equal to those of the United States and much of Europe. Following the war, however, the government introduced a series of social and economic policies that sent the economy into a spiraling decline. It then retreated into a foreign policy of isolationism that lasted until 1989. In 1990, under the leadership of President Carlos Menem, Argentina began a free-market revival that has increased economic freedom. As a result, inflation has stabilized and the economy is growing. From 1991 to 1994, the economy grew by an average of 8 percent annually. Although economic growth slowed to 2 percent in 1996, Menem's economic liberalization policies have helped reverse a trend of economic stagnation. The tax rate on the average income is lower than last year. Thus, Argentina's overall score now is 0.05 point better.

TRADE POLICY

Score: 4–Stable (high level of protectionism)

Argentina's average tariff rate is about 10 percent. Some nontariff barriers remain in the country's rapidly opening market. For example, faced with the global proliferation of antidumping laws and duties, especially U.S. duties on Argentine exports to the United States, Argentina responded by enforcing its antidumping laws more aggressively. The result was higher duties on some items like textile products. There also are trade quotas for some imported automobiles. According to the U.S. Department of State, "Customs procedures are cumbersome and time consuming, thus raising the cost for importers."[1] Recently, in an attempt to address complaints of corruption within the customs bureau, Argentina appointed a new director of customs who has pledged to wipe out corruption.

TAX POLICY

Score–Income taxation: 2+ (low tax rates)
Score–Corporate taxation: 3–Stable (moderate tax rates)
Final Taxation Score: 3+ (moderate tax rates)

Argentina has reduced its tax rates to stimulate the economy. The top income tax rate is 30 percent, and the rate for the GDP per capita level is 6 percent, down from 11 percent last year. As a result, Argentina's tax score is half a point better than last year. The top marginal corporate tax rate is 33 percent, up from 30 percent last year. Argentina also maintains a 33 percent capital gains tax and a 10.5 percent to 27 percent value-added tax.

GOVERNMENT INTERVENTION IN THE ECONOMY

Score: 2–Stable (low level)

The government consumes about 15 percent of Argentina's GDP. Argentina has undertaken a massive privatization program that is open to both foreign and domestic investors. Even some nuclear power plants are being privatized partially. If completed, this privatization program will reduce government

1	Hong Kong	1.25		77	Zambia	3.05
2	Singapore	1.30		80	Mali	3.10
3	Bahrain	1.70		80	Mongolia	3.10
4	New Zealand	1.75		80	Slovenia	3.10
5	Switzerland	1.90		83	Honduras	3.15
5	United States	1.90		83	Papua New Guinea	3.15
7	Luxembourg	1.95		85	Djibouti	3.20
7	Taiwan	1.95		85	Fiji	3.20
7	United Kingdom	1.95		85	Pakistan	3.20
10	Bahamas	2.00		88	Algeria	3.25
10	Ireland	2.00		88	Guinea	3.25
12	Australia	2.05		88	Lebanon	3.25
12	Japan	2.05		88	Mexico	3.25
14	Belgium	2.10		88	Senegal	3.25
14	Canada	2.10		88	Tanzania	3.25
14	United Arab Emirates	2.10		94	Nigeria	3.30
17	Austria	2.15		94	Romania	3.30
17	Chile	2.15		96	Brazil	3.35
17	Estonia	2.15		96	Cambodia	3.35
20	Czech Republic	2.20		96	Egypt	3.35
20	Netherlands	2.20		96	Ivory Coast	3.35
22	Denmark	2.25		96	Madagascar	3.35
22	Finland	2.25		96	Moldova	3.35
24	Germany	2.30		102	Nepal	3.40
24	Iceland	2.30		103	Cape Verde	3.44
24	South Korea	2.30		104	Armenia	3.45
27	Norway	2.35		104	Dominican Republic	3.45
28	Kuwait	2.40		104	Russia	3.45
28	Malaysia	2.40		107	Burkina Faso	3.50
28	Panama	2.40		107	Cameroon	3.50
28	Thailand	2.40		107	Lesotho	3.50
32	El Salvador	2.45		107	Nicaragua	3.50
32	Sri Lanka	2.45		107	Venezuela	3.50
32	Sweden	2.45		112	Gambia	3.60
35	France	2.50		112	Guyana	3.60
35	Italy	2.50		114	Bulgaria	3.65
35	Spain	2.50		114	Georgia	3.65
38	Trinidad and Tobago	2.55		114	Malawi	3.65
39	Argentina	2.60		117	Ethiopia	3.70
39	Barbados	2.60		117	India	3.70
39	Cyprus	2.60		117	Niger	3.70
39	Jamaica	2.60		120	Albania	3.75
39	Portugal	2.60		120	Bangladesh	3.75
44	Bolivia	2.65		120	China (PRC)	3.75
44	Oman	2.65		120	Congo	3.75
44	Philippines	2.65		120	Croatia	3.75
47	Swaziland	2.70		125	Chad	3.80
47	Uruguay	2.70		125	Mauritania	3.80
49	Botswana	2.75		125	Ukraine	3.80
49	Jordan	2.75		128	Sierra Leone	3.85
49	Namibia	2.75		129	Burundi	3.90
49	Tunisia	2.75		129	Suriname	3.90
53	Belize	2.80		129	Zimbabwe	3.90
53	Costa Rica	2.80		132	Haiti	4.00
53	Guatemala	2.80		132	Kyrgyzstan	4.00
53	Israel	2.80		132	Syria	4.00
53	Peru	2.80		135	Belarus	4.05
53	Saudi Arabia	2.80		136	Kazakstan	4.10
53	Turkey	2.80		136	Mozambique	4.10
53	Uganda	2.80		136	Yemen	4.10
53	Western Samoa	2.80		139	Sudan	4.20
62	Indonesia	2.85		140	Myanmar	4.30
62	Latvia	2.85		140	Rwanda	4.30
62	Malta	2.85		142	Angola	4.35
62	Paraguay	2.85		143	Azerbaijan	4.40
66	Greece	2.90		143	Tajikistan	4.40
66	Hungary	2.90		145	Turkmenistan	4.50
66	South Africa	2.90		146	Uzbekistan	4.55
69	Benin	2.95		147	Congo/Zaire	4.70
69	Ecuador	2.95		147	Iran	4.70
69	Gabon	2.95		147	Libya	4.70
69	Morocco	2.95		147	Somalia	4.70
69	Poland	2.95		147	Vietnam	4.70
74	Colombia	3.00		152	Bosnia	4.80
74	Ghana	3.00		153	Iraq	4.90
74	Lithuania	3.00		154	Cuba	5.00
77	Kenya	3.05		154	Laos	5.00
77	Slovak Republic	3.05		154	North Korea	5.00

Mostly Free

involvement in the economy and expand opportunities for investors significantly. Argentina also is privatizing its pension fund, much as Chile has done.

MONETARY POLICY
Score: 5–Stable (very high level of inflation)

From 1985 to 1995, Argentina's average annual rate of inflation was 255.4 percent. In 1996, it was around 0.4 percent. These lower figures demonstrate Argentina's commitment to reducing inflation and pursuing sound monetary policies. If these trends continue, Argentina's average inflation rate can be expected to decrease over time.

CAPITAL FLOWS AND FOREIGN INVESTMENT
Score: 2–Stable (low barriers)

There are few investment barriers in Argentina. Firms do not need to gain permission from the government to invest, most local companies may be wholly owned by foreign investors, and no permission is needed to own investment shares in the local stock exchange. These policies have resulted in a significant foreign corporate presence. Foreign investment is prohibited only in the ship-building, fishing, insurance, and nuclear power–generation industries.

BANKING
Score: 2–Stable (low level of restrictions)

Argentina's banking system is becoming more competitive because of privatization. As banks became profit-driven, they streamlined and modernized their business practices. The government recently reduced most barriers to foreign banking. There no longer are any distinctions between foreign and domestic banks, and both types are treated equally.

WAGE AND PRICE CONTROLS
Score: 2–Stable (low level)

Under the leadership of President Menem, the government has liberalized prices. Today, no major items are subject to price controls, and most wages are determined by the market. The government fixes wages for public-sector employees, however, and there is a minimum wage.

PROPERTY RIGHTS
Score: 2–Stable (high level of protection)

Private property is secure in Argentina, and the likelihood of property expropriation is low. Court protection of private property, however, can be weak. According to the U.S. Department of State, the Argentine court systems can be subject to political "influence."[2]

REGULATION
Score: 2–Stable (low level)

Argentina has reduced cumbersome registration requirements. Thus, opening a business is generally easy. Existing regulations are relatively straightforward and, in general, are applied uniformly.

BLACK MARKET
Score: 2–Stable (low level of activity)

In the past, most of Argentina's GDP was produced in the black market. As Argentina's market has become more integrated into the world economy, however, black market activity has shrunk to the point that it now is minimal. The government recently passed new laws extending the protection of intellectual property rights to pharmaceuticals and computer software.

NOTES
1. U.S. Department of State, *Country Reports on Economic Policy and Trade Practices,* 1997, p. 201.
2. U.S. Department of State, "Argentina Country Report on Human Rights Practices for 1996," 1997.

Armenia   3.45

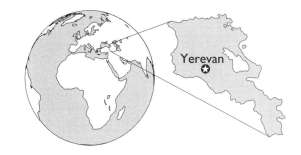
Yerevan

1997 Score: **3.45**	1996 Score: **3.75**	1995 Score: **n/a**

Trade	2	Banking	3
Taxation	3.5	Wages and Prices	3
Government Intervention	3	Property Rights	3
Monetary Policy	5	Regulation	4
Foreign Investment	4	Black Market	4

Armenia was an independent country from 1918 until 1922, when it was incorporated into the Soviet Union. Before 1918, it had been divided between the Russian and Ottoman Empires. Armenia became independent once again in September 1991. Since that time, it has attempted to shed its centrally planned, communist economy and adopt a system based on free markets. The move toward a free market, however, has been hindered by political instability, an entrenched bureaucracy, a war with neighboring Azerbaijan over the enclave of Nagorno-Karabakh, trade embargoes imposed by Azerbaijan and Turkey, and civil unrest in neighboring Georgia. Interruptions in supplies of fuel, natural gas, and electricity also have damaged the economy. Armenia held new elections in 1996, but many observers have questioned the validity of the outcome. Re-elected President Levon Ter-Petrosian has been striving to reestablish the government's credibility.

Trade Policy
Score: 2–Stable (low level of protectionism)

Armenia has an average tariff rate of less than 5 percent. It maintains nontariff barriers in the form of licensing requirements for several products, including some pharmaceuticals.

Taxation
Score–Income taxation: 3–Stable (moderate tax rates)
Score–Corporate taxation: 3–Stable (moderate tax rates)
Final Taxation Score: 3.5–Stable (high tax rates)

Armenia has a top income tax rate of 30 percent. The tax on the average income level is 12 percent to 15 percent. The top marginal corporate tax rate is 30 percent. Armenia also maintains a 20 percent value-added tax.

Government Intervention in the Economy
Score: 3–Stable (moderate level)

The government consumes about 13 percent of Armenia's GDP.[1] Moreover, there is a substantial state-owned sector, and the war with Azerbaijan consumes considerable resources.

Monetary Policy
Score: 5–Stable (very high level of inflation)

Armenia has been plagued by high inflation rates: 729 percent in 1992, 3,732 percent in 1993, 2,331 percent in 1994, 26 percent in 1995, and 214 percent in 1996. Since gaining its independence, Armenia has had an average annual inflation rate well above 500 percent.

1	Hong Kong	1.25		77	Zambia	3.05
2	Singapore	1.30		80	Mali	3.10
3	Bahrain	1.70		80	Mongolia	3.10
4	New Zealand	1.75		80	Slovenia	3.10
5	Switzerland	1.90		83	Honduras	3.15
5	United States	1.90		83	Papua New Guinea	3.15
7	Luxembourg	1.95		85	Djibouti	3.20
7	Taiwan	1.95		85	Fiji	3.20
7	United Kingdom	1.95		85	Pakistan	3.20
10	Bahamas	2.00		88	Algeria	3.25
10	Ireland	2.00		88	Guinea	3.25
12	Australia	2.05		88	Lebanon	3.25
12	Japan	2.05		88	Mexico	3.25
14	Belgium	2.10		88	Senegal	3.25
14	Canada	2.10		88	Tanzania	3.25
14	United Arab Emirates	2.10		94	Nigeria	3.30
17	Austria	2.15		94	Romania	3.30
17	Chile	2.15		96	Brazil	3.35
17	Estonia	2.15		96	Cambodia	3.35
20	Czech Republic	2.20		96	Egypt	3.35
20	Netherlands	2.20		96	Ivory Coast	3.35
22	Denmark	2.25		96	Madagascar	3.35
22	Finland	2.25		96	Moldova	3.35
24	Germany	2.30		102	Nepal	3.40
24	Iceland	2.30		103	Cape Verde	3.44
24	South Korea	2.30		104	Armenia	3.45
27	Norway	2.35		104	Dominican Republic	3.45
28	Kuwait	2.40		104	Russia	3.45
28	Malaysia	2.40		107	Burkina Faso	3.50
28	Panama	2.40		107	Cameroon	3.50
28	Thailand	2.40		107	Lesotho	3.50
32	El Salvador	2.45		107	Nicaragua	3.50
32	Sri Lanka	2.45		107	Venezuela	3.50
32	Sweden	2.45		112	Gambia	3.60
35	France	2.50		112	Guyana	3.60
35	Italy	2.50		114	Bulgaria	3.65
35	Spain	2.50		114	Georgia	3.65
38	Trinidad and Tobago	2.55		114	Malawi	3.65
39	Argentina	2.60		117	Ethiopia	3.70
39	Barbados	2.60		117	India	3.70
39	Cyprus	2.60		117	Niger	3.70
39	Jamaica	2.60		120	Albania	3.75
39	Portugal	2.60		120	Bangladesh	3.75
44	Bolivia	2.65		120	China (PRC)	3.75
44	Oman	2.65		120	Congo	3.75
44	Philippines	2.65		120	Croatia	3.75
47	Swaziland	2.70		125	Chad	3.80
47	Uruguay	2.70		125	Mauritania	3.80
49	Botswana	2.75		125	Ukraine	3.80
49	Jordan	2.75		128	Sierra Leone	3.85
49	Namibia	2.75		129	Burundi	3.90
49	Tunisia	2.75		129	Suriname	3.90
53	Belize	2.80		129	Zimbabwe	3.90
53	Costa Rica	2.80		132	Haiti	4.00
53	Guatemala	2.80		132	Kyrgyzstan	4.00
53	Israel	2.80		132	Syria	4.00
53	Peru	2.80		135	Belarus	4.05
53	Saudi Arabia	2.80		136	Kazakstan	4.10
53	Turkey	2.80		136	Mozambique	4.10
53	Uganda	2.80		136	Yemen	4.10
53	Western Samoa	2.80		139	Sudan	4.20
62	Indonesia	2.85		140	Myanmar	4.30
62	Latvia	2.85		140	Rwanda	4.30
62	Malta	2.85		142	Angola	4.35
62	Paraguay	2.85		143	Azerbaijan	4.40
66	Greece	2.90		143	Tajikistan	4.40
66	Hungary	2.90		145	Turkmenistan	4.50
66	South Africa	2.90		146	Uzbekistan	4.55
69	Benin	2.95		147	Congo/Zaire	4.70
69	Ecuador	2.95		147	Iran	4.70
69	Gabon	2.95		147	Libya	4.70
69	Morocco	2.95		147	Somalia	4.70
69	Poland	2.95		147	Vietnam	4.70
74	Colombia	3.00		152	Bosnia	4.80
74	Ghana	3.00		153	Iraq	4.90
74	Lithuania	3.00		154	Cuba	5.00
77	Kenya	3.05		154	Laos	5.00
77	Slovak Republic	3.05		154	North Korea	5.00

Mostly Unfree

CAPITAL FLOWS AND FOREIGN INVESTMENT
Score: 4–Stable (high barriers)

There are few official restrictions on investment in Armenia, and investors are welcome in most industries. There are, however, many informal but substantial barriers to investment, including a slow privatization process, inadequate infrastructure, and inefficient banking and court systems.

BANKING
Score: 3–Stable (moderate level of restrictions)

The banking system in Armenia is becoming more efficient, and there are now over 40 private banks. These banks offer few services and inadequate lending potential to the private sector (see Capital Flows and Foreign Investment), however, and the government still owns and operates several banks.

WAGE AND PRICE CONTROLS
Score: 3–Stable (moderate level)

Most prices are set by the market. Price controls on rent, electricity, and public transportation remain in effect, however.

PROPERTY RIGHTS
Score: 3–Stable (moderate level of protection)

Private property is guaranteed by law in Armenia. Neither legal enforcement nor the judicial system, however, provides adequate protection. "According to the Foreign Investment Law," reports the U.S. Department of Commerce, "all disputes that may arise between a foreign investor and the Republic of Armenia must be settled in the Armenian courts."[2] This restricts the ability of property owners, especially foreign investors, to receive an impartial hearing. Moreover, the judiciary is not entirely independent. According to the U.S. Department of State, "The Constitution provides for an independent judiciary; however, in practice judges are subject to political pressure from both the executive and legislature."[3] By global standards, however, Armenia provides a moderate level of protection of private property.

REGULATION
Score: 4–Stable (high level)

It is becoming easier to establish a business in Armenia. A corrupt bureaucracy, however, often applies the regulations haphazardly. According to the U.S. Department of Commerce, "The government's impressive progress in economic reform has not yet eliminated many of the problems faced by traders and investors in other NIS: difficult bureaucrats, tax transparency, corruption and inefficiency."[4]

BLACK MARKET
Score: 4–Stable (high level of activity)

Some black market activity is found in the transportation and labor sectors of the economy. Because of trade embargoes, many goods (including foodstuffs) are smuggled, primarily from Iran. In addition, Armenia does not provide sufficient protection of intellectual property, and piracy is rampant. According to the Office of the U.S. Trade Representative, "Pirated copies of U.S. video, audio, software, and books are widely available."[5]

NOTES

1. World Bank, *World Development Report 1997.*
2. U.S. Department of Commerce, *Country Commercial Guide,* 1997.
3. U.S. Department of State, "Armenia Country Report on Human Rights Practices for 1996," 1997.
4. U.S. Department of Commerce, *Country Commercial Guide,* 1997.
5. Office of the U.S. Trade Representative, *1997 National Trade Estimate on Foreign Trade Barriers.*

Australia   2.05

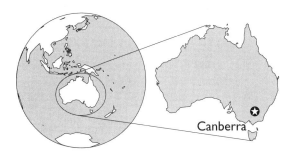

Canberra

Trade	2	Banking	1
Taxation	4.5	Wages and Prices	2
Government Intervention	3	Property Rights	1
Monetary Policy	1	Regulation	3
Foreign Investment	2	Black Market	1

In 1901, six self-governing British colonies federated to form the Commonwealth of Australia. The country became fully independent in 1932. Throughout most of its history, Australia maintained high trade barriers to promote industrialization, shunned trade with its Asian neighbors, and based wages and working conditions on principles of social justice rather than market conditions. With the election of a Labor Party government in 1983, it began to deregulate financial markets, remove substantial trade barriers, improve ties with Asia, and privatize many federally owned firms. Today, Australia is a leading force seeking trade liberalization in the World Trade Organization and the emerging Asia Pacific Economic Cooperation (APEC) forum. The Liberal-National Coalition government, headed by John Howard, was elected on March 2, 1996, and pledged to defederalize Australia's labor market and reduce the swelling budget deficit—not by raising taxes, but by cutting spending. The first year's budget did curtail spending, and the government seems near its goal of reaching a budget surplus within three years. Australia's black market activities have been curtailed significantly, resulting in a 0.1-point improvement in its overall score this year.

TRADE POLICY
Score: 2–Stable (low level of protectionism)

Australia has an average tariff rate of 2.8 percent. It maintains nontariff barriers in the form of strict import licenses for certain automobiles, textiles, clothing, and footwear.

TAXATION
Score–Income taxation: 4–Stable (high tax rates)
Score–Corporate taxation: 4–Stable (high tax rates)
Final Taxation Score: 4.5–Stable (very high tax rates)

Australia's top income tax rate is 47 percent; the average income level is taxed at a rate of 20 percent. The top corporate tax rate is 36 percent, up from 33 percent in 1995. Australia has a 12 percent to 45 percent wholesale sales tax. Capital gains, after adjustment for inflation, are taxed at the same rate as other personal or corporate income.

GOVERNMENT INTERVENTION IN THE ECONOMY
Score: 3–Stable (moderate level)

The government consumes 16.5 percent of Australia's GDP. State-owned enterprises still exist in such industries as telecommunications, utilities, and railways. The Howard government, however, privatized some shares in a federally owned telecommunications firm in 1996, and the state of Victoria privatized its state-owned electricity generation, distribution, and transmission system.

1	Hong Kong	1.25		77	Zambia	3.05
2	Singapore	1.30		80	Mali	3.10
3	Bahrain	1.70		80	Mongolia	3.10
4	New Zealand	1.75		80	Slovenia	3.10
5	Switzerland	1.90		83	Honduras	3.15
5	United States	1.90		83	Papua New Guinea	3.15
7	Luxembourg	1.95		85	Djibouti	3.20
7	Taiwan	1.95		85	Fiji	3.20
7	United Kingdom	1.95		85	Pakistan	3.20
10	Bahamas	2.00		88	Algeria	3.25
10	Ireland	2.00		88	Guinea	3.25
12	Australia	2.05		88	Lebanon	3.25
12	Japan	2.05		88	Mexico	3.25
14	Belgium	2.10		88	Senegal	3.25
14	Canada	2.10		88	Tanzania	3.25
14	United Arab Emirates	2.10		94	Nigeria	3.30
17	Austria	2.15		94	Romania	3.30
17	Chile	2.15		96	Brazil	3.35
17	Estonia	2.15		96	Cambodia	3.35
20	Czech Republic	2.20		96	Egypt	3.35
20	Netherlands	2.20		96	Ivory Coast	3.35
22	Denmark	2.25		96	Madagascar	3.35
22	Finland	2.25		96	Moldova	3.35
24	Germany	2.30		102	Nepal	3.40
24	Iceland	2.30		103	Cape Verde	3.44
24	South Korea	2.30		104	Armenia	3.45
27	Norway	2.35		104	Dominican Republic	3.45
28	Kuwait	2.40		104	Russia	3.45
28	Malaysia	2.40		107	Burkina Faso	3.50
28	Panama	2.40		107	Cameroon	3.50
28	Thailand	2.40		107	Lesotho	3.50
32	El Salvador	2.45		107	Nicaragua	3.50
32	Sri Lanka	2.45		107	Venezuela	3.50
32	Sweden	2.45		112	Gambia	3.60
35	France	2.50		112	Guyana	3.60
35	Italy	2.50		114	Bulgaria	3.65
35	Spain	2.50		114	Georgia	3.65
38	Trinidad and Tobago	2.55		114	Malawi	3.65
39	Argentina	2.60		117	Ethiopia	3.70
39	Barbados	2.60		117	India	3.70
39	Cyprus	2.60		117	Niger	3.70
39	Jamaica	2.60		120	Albania	3.75
39	Portugal	2.60		120	Bangladesh	3.75
44	Bolivia	2.65		120	China (PRC)	3.75
44	Oman	2.65		120	Congo	3.75
44	Philippines	2.65		120	Croatia	3.75
47	Swaziland	2.70		125	Chad	3.80
47	Uruguay	2.70		125	Mauritania	3.80
49	Botswana	2.75		125	Ukraine	3.80
49	Jordan	2.75		128	Sierra Leone	3.85
49	Namibia	2.75		129	Burundi	3.90
49	Tunisia	2.75		129	Suriname	3.90
53	Belize	2.80		129	Zimbabwe	3.90
53	Costa Rica	2.80		132	Haiti	4.00
53	Guatemala	2.80		132	Kyrgyzstan	4.00
53	Israel	2.80		132	Syria	4.00
53	Peru	2.80		135	Belarus	4.05
53	Saudi Arabia	2.80		136	Kazakstan	4.10
53	Turkey	2.80		136	Mozambique	4.10
53	Uganda	2.80		136	Yemen	4.10
53	Western Samoa	2.80		139	Sudan	4.20
62	Indonesia	2.85		140	Myanmar	4.30
62	Latvia	2.85		140	Rwanda	4.30
62	Malta	2.85		142	Angola	4.35
62	Paraguay	2.85		143	Azerbaijan	4.40
66	Greece	2.90		143	Tajikistan	4.40
66	Hungary	2.90		145	Turkmenistan	4.50
66	South Africa	2.90		146	Uzbekistan	4.55
69	Benin	2.95		147	Congo/Zaire	4.70
69	Ecuador	2.95		147	Iran	4.70
69	Gabon	2.95		147	Libya	4.70
69	Morocco	2.95		147	Somalia	4.70
69	Poland	2.95		147	Vietnam	4.70
74	Colombia	3.00		152	Bosnia	4.80
74	Ghana	3.00		153	Iraq	4.90
74	Lithuania	3.00		154	Cuba	5.00
77	Kenya	3.05		154	Laos	5.00
77	Slovak Republic	3.05		154	North Korea	5.00

Mostly Free

MONETARY POLICY
Score: 1–Stable (very low level of inflation)

From 1985 to 1995, inflation in Australia averaged 3.7 percent annually. In 1996, the inflation rate was just 2.6 percent.

CAPITAL FLOWS AND FOREIGN INVESTMENT
Score: 2–Stable (low barriers)

Australia has opened its economy to foreign investment. It provides equal treatment for domestic and foreign firms and has opened particular service industries, such as insurance and accounting, to some foreign participation.

BANKING
Score: 1–Stable (very low level of restrictions)

Banks in Australia are relatively free from intrusive government control. Foreigners are allowed to establish wholly owned institutions or branches. The banking system, once dominated by a few banks, has been deregulated substantially. In 1985, Australia allowed foreign banks to enter the market, and over 30 foreign banks have obtained banking licenses thus far.

WAGE AND PRICE CONTROLS
Score: 2–Stable (low level)

Minimum wages and working conditions are determined through a mandatory and centralized arbitration process involving labor, government, and business. Most wages and almost all prices, however, are determined by the market.

PROPERTY RIGHTS
Score: 1–Stable (very high level of protection)

Property is very secure in Australia, which has an efficient legal and judicial system that enforces contracts and settles disputes. Government expropriation is very unlikely.

REGULATION
Score: 3–Stable (moderate level)

Some regulations are cumbersome, especially those affecting labor, occupational safety and health standards, and the environment.

BLACK MARKET
Score: 1+ (very low level of activity)

Australia's black market activity is negligible. Intellectual property rights laws are well-enforced, and piracy in recorded music, film, and computer software has been reduced significantly. Thus, this year's score is one point better than last year's.

Austria   2.15

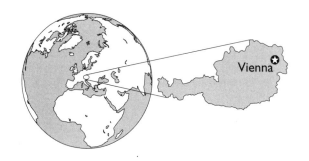

1997 Score: **2.15**	1996 Score: **2.05**	1995 Score: **2.05**

Trade	2	Banking	2
Taxation	4.5	Wages and Prices	2
Government Intervention	3	Property Rights	1
Monetary Policy	1	Regulation	3
Foreign Investment	2	Black Market	1

Austria has long played an important role in Europe's history and culture. Following World War I, the government intervened deeply in the economy, causing a massive economic recession in the 1930s. After World War II, Austria was occupied by U.S. and Soviet troops; in 1955, it became an independent neutral country. Although ruled mainly by socialist parties since that time, Austria has pursued some free-market policies that have helped it maintain a relatively high standard of living. Austria became a member of the European Union in 1995. Since then, most economic changes have been designed to bring the economy into alignment with EU standards. Over time, Austria has lowered its barriers to trade, but it also has failed to privatize one of its largest banks. As a result, its overall score is the same as last year's.

TRADE POLICY
Score: 2+ (low level of protectionism)

When Austria entered the EU in 1995, 63 percent of its tariffs were lowered and some 31 percent were increased. "Although Austria has reduced its customs duties in recent years," reports the Economist Intelligence Unit, "import tariffs at an average of 10.7 percent are higher than the EU average of 7.3 percent."[1] Sixty percent of all products from non-EU countries, however, enter without any tariff. Thus, weighted to take into account duty-free imports, Austria's average tariff rate is much lower: about 3.3 percent. Austria has nontariff barriers common to other EU members, as well as additional certification requirements for some electronic goods that may restrict imports. Because Austria's average tariff rate is lower, its trade policy score is one point better this year.

TAXATION
Score–Income taxation: 5–Stable (very high tax rates)
Score–Corporate taxation: 3–Stable (moderate tax rates)
Final Taxation Score: 4.5–Stable (very high tax rates)

Austria has a top income tax rate of 50 percent, and the average income level is taxed at a rate of 32 percent. The top corporate tax rate is 34 percent. Austria also imposes several other taxes, including a 34 percent capital gains tax, a 20 percent value-added tax, and a 3.5 percent real estate tax.

GOVERNMENT INTERVENTION IN THE ECONOMY
Score: 3–Stable (moderate level)

Austria's government consumes 19 percent of GDP. There is a large state-owned industrial sector, however, and a recent privatization program is slowing. One-third of the work force is employed in the public sector. The government either owns outright or has controlling stakes in Austrian Radio and Television, Austrian Airlines, postal services, and long-distance busing. Nevertheless, government involvement in the economy is relatively moderate by global standards.

1	Hong Kong	1.25	77	Zambia	3.05
2	Singapore	1.30	80	Mali	3.10
3	Bahrain	1.70	80	Mongolia	3.10
4	New Zealand	1.75	80	Slovenia	3.10
5	Switzerland	1.90	83	Honduras	3.15
5	United States	1.90	83	Papua New Guinea	3.15
7	Luxembourg	1.95	85	Djibouti	3.20
7	Taiwan	1.95	85	Fiji	3.20
7	United Kingdom	1.95	85	Pakistan	3.20
10	Bahamas	2.00	88	Algeria	3.25
10	Ireland	2.00	88	Guinea	3.25
12	Australia	2.05	88	Lebanon	3.25
12	Japan	2.05	88	Mexico	3.25
14	Belgium	2.10	88	Senegal	3.25
14	Canada	2.10	88	Tanzania	3.25
14	United Arab Emirates	2.10	94	Nigeria	3.30
17	Austria	2.15	94	Romania	3.30
17	Chile	2.15	96	Brazil	3.35
17	Estonia	2.15	96	Cambodia	3.35
20	Czech Republic	2.20	96	Egypt	3.35
20	Netherlands	2.20	96	Ivory Coast	3.35
22	Denmark	2.25	96	Madagascar	3.35
22	Finland	2.25	96	Moldova	3.35
24	Germany	2.30	102	Nepal	3.40
24	Iceland	2.30	103	Cape Verde	3.44
24	South Korea	2.30	104	Armenia	3.45
27	Norway	2.35	104	Dominican Republic	3.45
28	Kuwait	2.40	104	Russia	3.45
28	Malaysia	2.40	107	Burkina Faso	3.50
28	Panama	2.40	107	Cameroon	3.50
28	Thailand	2.40	107	Lesotho	3.50
32	El Salvador	2.45	107	Nicaragua	3.50
32	Sri Lanka	2.45	107	Venezuela	3.50
32	Sweden	2.45	112	Gambia	3.60
35	France	2.50	112	Guyana	3.60
35	Italy	2.50	114	Bulgaria	3.65
35	Spain	2.50	114	Georgia	3.65
38	Trinidad and Tobago	2.55	114	Malawi	3.65
39	Argentina	2.60	117	Ethiopia	3.70
39	Barbados	2.60	117	India	3.70
39	Cyprus	2.60	117	Niger	3.70
39	Jamaica	2.60	120	Albania	3.75
39	Portugal	2.60	120	Bangladesh	3.75
44	Bolivia	2.65	120	China (PRC)	3.75
44	Oman	2.65	120	Congo	3.75
44	Philippines	2.65	120	Croatia	3.75
47	Swaziland	2.70	125	Chad	3.80
47	Uruguay	2.70	125	Mauritania	3.80
49	Botswana	2.75	125	Ukraine	3.80
49	Jordan	2.75	128	Sierra Leone	3.85
49	Namibia	2.75	129	Burundi	3.90
49	Tunisia	2.75	129	Suriname	3.90
53	Belize	2.80	129	Zimbabwe	3.90
53	Costa Rica	2.80	132	Haiti	4.00
53	Guatemala	2.80	132	Kyrgyzstan	4.00
53	Israel	2.80	132	Syria	4.00
53	Peru	2.80	135	Belarus	4.05
53	Saudi Arabia	2.80	136	Kazakstan	4.10
53	Turkey	2.80	136	Mozambique	4.10
53	Uganda	2.80	136	Yemen	4.10
53	Western Samoa	2.80	139	Sudan	4.20
62	Indonesia	2.85	140	Myanmar	4.30
62	Latvia	2.85	140	Rwanda	4.30
62	Malta	2.85	142	Angola	4.35
62	Paraguay	2.85	143	Azerbaijan	4.40
66	Greece	2.90	143	Tajikistan	4.40
66	Hungary	2.90	145	Turkmenistan	4.50
66	South Africa	2.90	146	Uzbekistan	4.55
69	Benin	2.95	147	Congo/Zaire	4.70
69	Ecuador	2.95	147	Iran	4.70
69	Gabon	2.95	147	Libya	4.70
69	Morocco	2.95	147	Somalia	4.70
69	Poland	2.95	147	Vietnam	4.70
74	Ghana	3.00	152	Bosnia	4.80
74	Colombia	3.00	153	Iraq	4.90
74	Lithuania	3.00	154	Cuba	5.00
77	Kenya	3.05	154	Laos	5.00
77	Slovak Republic	3.05	154	North Korea	5.00

Mostly Free

MONETARY POLICY
Score: 1–Stable (very low level of inflation)

Austria had an average annual inflation rate of 3.2 percent from 1985 to 1995. Inflation was about 2 percent in 1996.

CAPITAL FLOWS AND FOREIGN INVESTMENT
Score: 2–Stable (low barriers)

Austria depends heavily on foreign investment and welcomes it openly. There are few restrictions, although foreign investors at times must deal with slow bureaucratic procedures to gain approval for new operations.

BANKING
Score: 2– (low level of restrictions)

Foreign banks can operate in Austria so long as they have prior government approval. Austrian banks are permitted to engage in all kinds of services, including the underwriting of loans and the brokering of securities and mutual funds. They may own subsidiaries that underwrite and sell insurance policies, and are allowed to invest in, develop, and manage real estate ventures. After six years, however, Austria failed to privatize one of its largest banks, Creditanstalt, and instead sold it to Bank Austria, which is controlled mainly by the government. This is a major setback for Austria's banking sector, which had been moving toward increased independence from government. As a result, Austria's banking score this year is one point worse than it was last year.

WAGE AND PRICE CONTROLS
Score: 2–Stable (low level)

Most wages and prices are set by the market. Austrian businesses voluntarily cooperate with the government, however, to set prices. Thus, prices are not completely free. Some price controls are still in effect on rail travel, telecommunications, and some energy. Austria maintains a minimum wage.

PROPERTY RIGHTS
Score: 1–Stable (very high level of protection)

Property is very secure in Austria, which has an efficient and well-established legal system that respects and protects private property and contractual agreements.

REGULATION
Score: 3–Stable (moderate level)

Although Austria experienced long periods of economic growth after World War II, it also allowed the state to become involved in regulating the economy. A growing environmental movement threatens to shackle many Austrian businesses with burdensome regulations. Competitiveness is hindered further by extensive worker health and safety standards. According to the U.S. Department of Commerce, "Terms of employment are closely regulated by law in Austria. Working hours, minimum vacation time, maternity leave, juvenile work allowances, statutory separation notice, protection against dismissal, and the right to severance payment are all secured by law."[2] Nevertheless, by global standards, Austria's economy is only moderately regulated.

BLACK MARKET
Score: 1–Stable (very low level of activity)

Austria's black market is relatively small to nonexistent. Goods and services move fairly freely across the border, limiting the incentives for smuggling. The government passed legislation in 1995 to protect many types of intellectual property, including satellite broadcasting and cable television. There is still some piracy of video cassettes and computer software, although these activities are minuscule when compared with the size of Austria's economy.

NOTES

1. Economist Intelligence Unit, *ILT Reports: Austria,* August 1996, updated February 1997.
2. U.S. Department of Commerce, *Country Commercial Guide,* 1997.

Azerbaijan 4.40

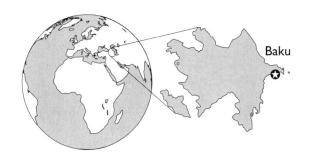

Baku

	1997 Score: **4.60**	1996 Score: **4.70**	1995 Score: **n/a**

Trade	5	Banking	4
Taxation	4	Wages and Prices	5
Government Intervention	5	Property Rights	4
Monetary Policy	5	Regulation	4
Foreign Investment	4	Black Market	4

Iran ceded the territory of Turkic-speaking, predominantly Shiite Azerbaijan to Russia in 1813 and 1828. Azerbaijan gained its independence from Russia in 1918 and then was conquered by the Soviet Union in 1920. In 1989, Azerbaijan claimed its sovereignty from the Soviet Union; by 1991, it had become fully independent. Since then, the government (currently led by Haydar Aliyev) has embarked on a course of gradual reform, the success of which is threatened by a well-entrenched bureaucracy. The discovery of significant oil deposits on the shelf of the Caspian Sea (deposits larger than those of the North Sea) has attracted the attention of foreign investors, and several Western-led consortia are about to begin work on oil fields. During the past year, the government passed two new laws to protect intellectual property rights and allow some foreign ownership of land. It also is stepping up privatization. As a result, Azerbaijan's overall score is 0.2 point better this year.

TRADE POLICY
Score: 5–Stable (very high level of protectionism)

In January 1997, the government passed a new law establishing a uniform tariff rate of 15 percent. This is still high by global standards, and significant nontariff barriers still exist. According to the U.S. Department of Commerce, "Companies often face problems in getting goods through customs due to officials who delay in hope of receiving bribes."[1]

TAXATION
Score—Income taxation: 4+ (high tax rates)
Score—Corporate taxation: 3–Stable (moderate tax rates)
Final Taxation Score: 4–Stable (high tax rates)

Azerbaijan's top income tax rate is 40 percent, down from 55 percent in 1996. The tax on the average income level is 15 percent. The top marginal corporate tax rate is 35 percent. Azerbaijan also maintains a 20 percent value-added tax.

GOVERNMENT INTERVENTION IN THE ECONOMY
Score: 5–Stable (very high level)

Azerbaijan is privatizing its large state-owned sector. The economy remains dominated by large state enterprises, however, particularly in the agricultural sector.[2]

MONETARY POLICY
Score: 5–Stable (very high level of inflation)

Azerbaijan has made tremendous progress in reducing inflation, which declined from rates as high as 616 percent in 1992, 1,130 percent in 1993, 1,664 percent in 1994, and 411 percent in 1995 to 19.9 percent in 1996. Nevertheless, the rate of inflation remains very high by global standards.

1	Hong Kong	1.25
2	Singapore	1.30
3	Bahrain	1.70
4	New Zealand	1.75
5	Switzerland	1.90
5	United States	1.90
7	Luxembourg	1.95
7	Taiwan	1.95
7	United Kingdom	1.95
10	Bahamas	2.00
10	Ireland	2.00
12	Australia	2.05
12	Japan	2.05
14	Belgium	2.10
14	Canada	2.10
14	United Arab Emirates	2.10
17	Austria	2.15
17	Chile	2.15
17	Estonia	2.15
20	Czech Republic	2.20
20	Netherlands	2.20
22	Denmark	2.25
22	Finland	2.25
24	Germany	2.30
24	Iceland	2.30
24	South Korea	2.30
27	Norway	2.35
28	Kuwait	2.40
28	Malaysia	2.40
28	Panama	2.40
28	Thailand	2.40
32	El Salvador	2.45
32	Sri Lanka	2.45
32	Sweden	2.45
35	France	2.50
35	Italy	2.50
35	Spain	2.50
38	Trinidad and Tobago	2.55
39	Argentina	2.60
39	Barbados	2.60
39	Cyprus	2.60
39	Jamaica	2.60
39	Portugal	2.60
44	Bolivia	2.65
44	Oman	2.65
44	Philippines	2.65
47	Swaziland	2.70
47	Uruguay	2.70
49	Botswana	2.75
49	Jordan	2.75
49	Namibia	2.75
49	Tunisia	2.75
53	Belize	2.80
53	Costa Rica	2.80
53	Guatemala	2.80
53	Israel	2.80
53	Peru	2.80
53	Saudi Arabia	2.80
53	Turkey	2.80
53	Uganda	2.80
53	Western Samoa	2.80
62	Indonesia	2.85
62	Latvia	2.85
62	Malta	2.85
62	Paraguay	2.85
66	Greece	2.90
66	Hungary	2.90
66	South Africa	2.90
69	Benin	2.95
69	Ecuador	2.95
69	Gabon	2.95
69	Morocco	2.95
69	Poland	2.95
74	Colombia	3.00
74	Ghana	3.00
74	Lithuania	3.00
77	Kenya	3.05
77	Slovak Republic	3.05
77	Zambia	3.05
80	Mali	3.10
80	Mongolia	3.10
80	Slovenia	3.10
83	Honduras	3.15
83	Papua New Guinea	3.15
85	Djibouti	3.20
85	Fiji	3.20
85	Pakistan	3.20
88	Algeria	3.25
88	Guinea	3.25
88	Lebanon	3.25
88	Mexico	3.25
88	Senegal	3.25
88	Tanzania	3.25
94	Nigeria	3.30
94	Romania	3.30
96	Brazil	3.35
96	Egypt	3.35
96	Ivory Coast	3.35
96	Madagascar	3.35
96	Moldova	3.35
102	Nepal	3.40
103	Cape Verde	3.44
104	Armenia	3.45
104	Dominican Republic	3.45
104	Russia	3.45
107	Burkina Faso	3.50
107	Cameroon	3.50
107	Lesotho	3.50
107	Nicaragua	3.50
107	Venezuela	3.50
112	Gambia	3.60
112	Guyana	3.60
114	Bulgaria	3.65
114	Georgia	3.65
114	Malawi	3.65
117	Ethiopia	3.70
117	India	3.70
117	Niger	3.70
120	Albania	3.75
120	Bangladesh	3.75
120	China (PRC)	3.75
120	Congo	3.75
120	Croatia	3.75
125	Chad	3.80
125	Mauritania	3.80
125	Ukraine	3.80
128	Sierra Leone	3.85
129	Burundi	3.90
129	Suriname	3.90
129	Zimbabwe	3.90
132	Haiti	4.00
132	Kyrgyzstan	4.00
132	Syria	4.00
135	Belarus	4.05
136	Kazakstan	4.10
136	Mozambique	4.10
136	Yemen	4.10
139	Sudan	4.20
140	Myanmar	4.30
140	Rwanda	4.30
142	Angola	4.35
143	Azerbaijan	4.40
143	Tajikistan	4.40
145	Turkmenistan	4.50
146	Uzbekistan	4.55
147	Congo/Zaire	4.70
147	Iran	4.70
147	Libya	4.70
147	Somalia	4.70
147	Vietnam	4.70
152	Bosnia	4.80
153	Iraq	4.90
154	Cuba	5.00
154	Laos	5.00
154	North Korea	5.00

Repressed

Capital Flows and Foreign Investment
Score: 4+ (high barriers)

Although the government wants to increase foreign investment, relatively little non-petroleum investment has been forthcoming, chiefly because of an ineffective legal environment, an untrained and corrupt bureaucracy, and a weak infrastructure. Moreover, nearly all foreign investment must be approved by the government, and ownership of land was forbidden until recently. In addition, as the U.S. Department of Commerce reports, "There are significant challenges facing non-oil investors in Azerbaijan. These include: the problems of economic transition, slowness of the privatization process, lack of transparency in tax and other government economic policies, and corruption."[3] The government has reduced most formal barriers to investment, however, and in July 1996 removed one of the last formal barriers to investment by passing a law that allows private ownership of land by foreign corporations. As a result, Azerbaijan's score this year has improved by one point over last year.

Banking
Score: 4–Stable (high level of restrictions)

The banking system is in disarray. The government owns most banks in whole or in part, and many are insolvent. Although there are some foreign banks, few have the ability or the capital to operate without government involvement.

Wage and Price Controls
Score: 5–Stable (very high level)

Wages and prices are controlled by government ministries and the large state-owned sector. According to the U.S. Department of Commerce, "Several key commodities, including bread, natural gas and gasoline, remain under price controls. While the government raises these controlled prices periodically, they remain artificially low, and shortages of these goods occur along with corruption and black market activity."[4]

Property Rights
Score: 4–Stable (low level of protection)

Private property in Azerbaijan is not sufficiently protected by the legal system. Until recently, foreigners could own land, and government expropriation was possible, but property rights still are not protected. The U.S. Department of Commerce reports that "The Azeri judicial system is not independent of political and financial influences. Corruption is a major problem."[5]

Regulation
Score: 4–Stable (moderate level)

Establishing a business can be a tedious and time-consuming procedure that requires individuals to overcome numerous bureaucratic barriers. Some private businesses are opening in the retail sector, but racketeering and corruption are widespread. However, Azerbaijan is developing a formalized process by which businesses will be able to register and obtain licenses. According to the U.S. Department of Commerce, "The lack of a Western-style commercial law framework is a major problem. There are no effective means for enforcing property or commercial rights.... Corruption is endemic in Azerbaijan although most pervasive in areas of government procurement and the regulatory system."[6]

Black Market
Score: 4+ (high level of activity)

Smuggling is rampant. Because bartered trade is the norm, substantial underground economies exist in the trading of all kinds of goods. Azerbaijan has passed a new intellectual property rights law protecting copyrights, trademarks, and patents, however, and some black market activity has been curtailed in this area. As a result, this year's score is one point better than last year's.

Notes

1. U.S. Department of Commerce, "Azerbaijan–Investment Climate," *Market Research Reports*, Washington, D.C., August 12, 1996.
2. Government consumption rates are not available.
3. U.S. Department of Commerce, "Azerbaijan–Investment Climate," August 12, 1996.
4. U.S. Department of Commerce, *Country Commercial Guide*, 1996.
5. U.S. Department of Commerce, "Azerbaijan–Investment Climate," August 12, 1996.
6. *Ibid.*

The Bahamas 2.00

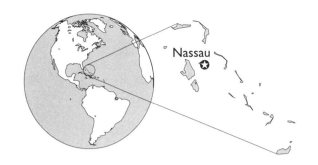

Nassau

1997 Score: **2.00**	1996 Score: **2.00**	1995 Score: **2.10**

Trade	5	Banking	2
Taxation	1	Wages and Prices	2
Government Intervention	2	Property Rights	1
Monetary Policy	1	Regulation	1
Foreign Investment	3	Black Market	2

The Bahamas includes about 700 islands, of which only 30 are inhabited. The country is a member of the British Commonwealth and has a parliamentary democracy. Its biggest industry is tourism. With a few notable exceptions, the economy is essentially free from government control. The government recently passed a new foreign investment code, opening its borders to more investment.

TRADE POLICY
Score: 5–Stable (very high level of protectionism)

Import duties are a main source of revenue for the Bahamian government, and tariff rates are very high. The general rate of duty charges on imports is 32.8 percent. There are no other significant barriers to trade.

TAXATION
Score–Income taxation: 1–Stable (very low tax rates)
Score–Corporate taxation: 1–Stable (very low tax rates)
Final Taxation Score: 1–Stable (very low tax rates)

The Bahamas has no income tax, no corporate income tax, no capital gains tax, and no value-added tax.

GOVERNMENT INTERVENTION IN THE ECONOMY
Score: 2–Stable (low level)

The government consumes 12.8 percent of the Bahamas' GDP and plays only a limited role in the economy.

MONETARY POLICY
Score: 1–Stable (very low level of inflation)

From 1985 to 1995, the average annual rate of inflation in the Bahamas was 3.2 percent. In 1996, the inflation rate was only 1.6 percent.

CAPITAL FLOWS AND FOREIGN INVESTMENT
Score: 3–Stable (moderate barriers)

The Bahamas has passed a new foreign investment law and seeks increased foreign investment. The government will restrict foreign investment, however, in areas that compete directly with Bahamian-owned businesses, such as construction and restaurants (except gourmet and ethnic restaurants). It does this by preventing foreign companies from obtaining business licenses and by imposing other requirements in areas where Bahamian businesses already exist.

BANKING
Score: 2–Stable (low level of restrictions)

The Bahamas is one of the financial centers of the Caribbean. The government seeks to attract foreign banks, and the financial sector is extremely open to foreigners.

1	Hong Kong	1.25	77	Zambia	3.05
2	Singapore	1.30	80	Mali	3.10
3	Bahrain	1.70	80	Mongolia	3.10
4	New Zealand	1.75	80	Slovenia	3.10
5	Switzerland	1.90	83	Honduras	3.15
5	United States	1.90	83	Papua New Guinea	3.15
7	Luxembourg	1.95	85	Djibouti	3.20
7	Taiwan	1.95	85	Fiji	3.20
7	United Kingdom	1.95	85	Pakistan	3.20
10	Bahamas	2.00	88	Algeria	3.25
10	Ireland	2.00	88	Guinea	3.25
12	Australia	2.05	88	Lebanon	3.25
12	Japan	2.05	88	Mexico	3.25
14	Belgium	2.10	88	Senegal	3.25
14	Canada	2.10	88	Tanzania	3.25
14	United Arab Emirates	2.10	94	Nigeria	3.30
17	Austria	2.15	94	Romania	3.30
17	Chile	2.15	96	Brazil	3.35
17	Estonia	2.15	96	Cambodia	3.35
20	Czech Republic	2.20	96	Egypt	3.35
20	Netherlands	2.20	96	Ivory Coast	3.35
22	Denmark	2.25	96	Madagascar	3.35
22	Finland	2.25	96	Moldova	3.35
24	Germany	2.30	102	Nepal	3.40
24	Iceland	2.30	103	Cape Verde	3.44
24	South Korea	2.30	104	Armenia	3.45
27	Norway	2.35	104	Dominican Republic	3.45
28	Kuwait	2.40	104	Russia	3.45
28	Malaysia	2.40	107	Burkina Faso	3.50
28	Panama	2.40	107	Cameroon	3.50
28	Thailand	2.40	107	Lesotho	3.50
32	El Salvador	2.45	107	Nicaragua	3.50
32	Sri Lanka	2.45	107	Venezuela	3.50
32	Sweden	2.45	112	Gambia	3.60
35	France	2.50	112	Guyana	3.60
35	Italy	2.50	114	Bulgaria	3.65
35	Spain	2.50	114	Georgia	3.65
38	Trinidad and Tobago	2.55	114	Malawi	3.65
39	Argentina	2.60	117	Ethiopia	3.70
39	Barbados	2.60	117	India	3.70
39	Cyprus	2.60	117	Niger	3.70
39	Jamaica	2.60	120	Albania	3.75
39	Portugal	2.60	120	Bangladesh	3.75
44	Bolivia	2.65	120	China (PRC)	3.75
44	Oman	2.65	120	Congo	3.75
44	Philippines	2.65	120	Croatia	3.75
47	Swaziland	2.70	125	Chad	3.80
47	Uruguay	2.70	125	Mauritania	3.80
49	Botswana	2.75	125	Ukraine	3.80
49	Jordan	2.75	128	Sierra Leone	3.85
49	Namibia	2.75	129	Burundi	3.90
49	Tunisia	2.75	129	Suriname	3.90
53	Belize	2.80	129	Zimbabwe	3.90
53	Costa Rica	2.80	132	Haiti	4.00
53	Guatemala	2.80	132	Kyrgyzstan	4.00
53	Israel	2.80	132	Syria	4.00
53	Peru	2.80	135	Belarus	4.05
53	Saudi Arabia	2.80	136	Kazakstan	4.10
53	Turkey	2.80	136	Mozambique	4.10
53	Uganda	2.80	136	Yemen	4.10
53	Western Samoa	2.80	139	Sudan	4.20
62	Indonesia	2.85	140	Myanmar	4.30
62	Latvia	2.85	140	Rwanda	4.30
62	Malta	2.85	142	Angola	4.35
62	Paraguay	2.85	143	Azerbaijan	4.40
66	Greece	2.90	143	Tajikistan	4.40
66	Hungary	2.90	145	Turkmenistan	4.50
66	South Africa	2.90	146	Uzbekistan	4.55
69	Benin	2.95	147	Congo/Zaire	4.70
69	Ecuador	2.95	147	Iran	4.70
69	Gabon	2.95	147	Libya	4.70
69	Morocco	2.95	147	Somalia	4.70
69	Poland	2.95	147	Vietnam	4.70
74	Colombia	3.00	152	Bosnia	4.80
74	Ghana	3.00	153	Iraq	4.90
74	Lithuania	3.00	154	Cuba	5.00
77	Kenya	3.05	154	Laos	5.00
77	Slovak Republic	3.05	154	North Korea	5.00

Mostly Free

WAGE AND PRICE CONTROLS
Score: 2–Stable (low level)

The Bahamas maintains some price controls on such items as automobiles, auto parts, flour, gasoline, public transportation, and utilities, but wages are determined mainly by the market. There is no minimum wage, although the government plans to introduce one soon.

PROPERTY RIGHTS
Score: 1–Stable (very high level of protection)

Private property is easy to acquire and protect in the Bahamas, which has an advanced and efficient legal system based on English common law. The Bahamian government never has expropriated private property and is very unlikely to do so in the future.

REGULATION
Score: 1–Stable (very low level)

Regulation is virtually nonexistent in the Bahamas; the government follows a hands-off approach to business. There are no specific requirements for establishing a business, and English common law is used to enforce contracts. In addition, profits are not taxed, and businesses are free from burdensome regulation.

BLACK MARKET
Score: 2–Stable (low level of activity)

The black market in the Bahamas, like that in most developed countries, focuses on guns and drugs. Gambling is legalized. Because the government outlaws few things and businesses are free to operate as they see fit, the black market is very small, although high trade barriers encourage smuggling in such areas as auto parts and electronics. According to the U.S. Department of State, "Although local intellectual property laws exist, enforcement is generally weak."[1] Thus, there is a growing black market in such materials as pirated compact disks and videocassettes, although this increase is not substantial enough to warrant a change in score at this time.

NOTE
1. U.S. Department of State, *Country Reports on Economic Policy and Trade Practices*, 1997, p. 206.

Bahrain   1.70

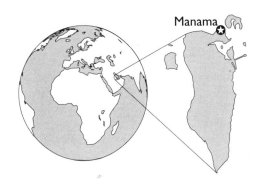

1997 Score: **1.60**	1996 Score: **1.70**	1995 Score: **1.60**

Trade	2	Banking	2
Taxation	1	Wages and Prices	2
Government Intervention	3	Property Rights	1
Monetary Policy	1	Regulation	2
Foreign Investment	2	Black Market	1

Bahrain declared its independence from Great Britain in 1971 and became a member of the United Nations and the Arab League. It has maintained a vibrant free-market economic system. The principal export is oil; but because oil reserves are expected to last only 20 more years, the government is pursuing ways to diversify and modernize the economy. Government spending has been reduced. Since December 1994, Bahrain has been troubled by civil disturbances, arson attacks, and occasional bombings by disaffected members of the Shia community. The Shiites—about two-thirds of the population—suffer from high unemployment rates and claim religious discrimination by the Sunni-dominated government. Domestic disturbances have lessened since the June 1996 arrest of 44 people involved in an Iranian-inspired plot to overthrow the government. Due to an increase in reports of corruption, Bahrain's overall score this year is 0.1 point worse than last year.

TRADE POLICY
Score: 2–Stable (low level of protectionism)

With an average tariff rate of 3.3 percent, Bahrain has few barriers to trade. The government maintains strict labeling requirements on imported products, however. This practice limits imports because exporters do not wish to spend the extra money to meet these requirements.

TAXATION
Score–Income taxation: 1–Stable (very low tax rates)
Score–Corporate taxation: 1–Stable (very low tax rates)
Final Taxation Score: 1–Stable (very low tax rates)

Bahrain has no taxes on income or corporate profits. There is no capital gains tax or value-added tax.

GOVERNMENT INTERVENTION IN THE ECONOMY
Score: 3–Stable (moderate level)

The government consumes 33.3 percent of Bahrain's GDP. It also owns significant portions of some industries, including oil, which contributes most of the country's GDP. Industrial and service companies have been privatized within the past year. According to the U.S. Department of Commerce, "The Government of Bahrain has set out to make the country into the Singapore or Hong Kong of the Gulf, and hopefully, of the whole Middle East plus South Asia."[1]

MONETARY POLICY
Score: 1–Stable (very low level of inflation)

The average annual inflation rate from 1985 to 1995 was 0.4 percent. In 1996, inflation fell to -0.2 percent, and prices actually decreased.

1	Hong Kong	1.25	77	Zambia	3.05
2	Singapore	1.30	80	Mali	3.10
3	Bahrain	1.70	80	Mongolia	3.10
4	New Zealand	1.75	80	Slovenia	3.10
5	Switzerland	1.90	83	Honduras	3.15
5	United States	1.90	83	Papua New Guinea	3.15
7	Luxembourg	1.95	85	Djibouti	3.20
7	Taiwan	1.95	85	Fiji	3.20
7	United Kingdom	1.95	85	Pakistan	3.20
10	Bahamas	2.00	88	Algeria	3.25
10	Ireland	2.00	88	Guinea	3.25
12	Australia	2.05	88	Lebanon	3.25
12	Japan	2.05	88	Mexico	3.25
14	Belgium	2.10	88	Senegal	3.25
14	Canada	2.10	88	Tanzania	3.25
14	United Arab Emirates	2.10	94	Nigeria	3.30
17	Austria	2.15	94	Romania	3.30
17	Chile	2.15	96	Brazil	3.35
17	Estonia	2.15	96	Cambodia	3.35
20	Czech Republic	2.20	96	Egypt	3.35
20	Netherlands	2.20	96	Ivory Coast	3.35
22	Denmark	2.25	96	Madagascar	3.35
22	Finland	2.25	96	Moldova	3.35
24	Germany	2.30	102	Nepal	3.40
24	Iceland	2.30	103	Cape Verde	3.44
24	South Korea	2.30	104	Armenia	3.45
27	Norway	2.35	104	Dominican Republic	3.45
28	Kuwait	2.40	104	Russia	3.45
28	Malaysia	2.40	107	Burkina Faso	3.50
28	Panama	2.40	107	Cameroon	3.50
28	Thailand	2.40	107	Lesotho	3.50
32	El Salvador	2.45	107	Nicaragua	3.50
32	Sri Lanka	2.45	107	Venezuela	3.50
32	Sweden	2.45	112	Gambia	3.60
35	France	2.50	112	Guyana	3.60
35	Italy	2.50	114	Bulgaria	3.65
35	Spain	2.50	114	Georgia	3.65
38	Trinidad and Tobago	2.55	114	Malawi	3.65
39	Argentina	2.60	117	Ethiopia	3.70
39	Barbados	2.60	117	India	3.70
39	Cyprus	2.60	117	Niger	3.70
39	Jamaica	2.60	120	Albania	3.75
39	Portugal	2.60	120	Bangladesh	3.75
44	Bolivia	2.65	120	China (PRC)	3.75
44	Oman	2.65	120	Congo	3.75
44	Philippines	2.65	120	Croatia	3.75
47	Swaziland	2.70	125	Chad	3.80
47	Uruguay	2.70	125	Mauritania	3.80
49	Botswana	2.75	125	Ukraine	3.80
49	Jordan	2.75	128	Sierra Leone	3.85
49	Namibia	2.75	129	Burundi	3.90
49	Tunisia	2.75	129	Suriname	3.90
53	Belize	2.80	129	Zimbabwe	3.90
53	Costa Rica	2.80	132	Haiti	4.00
53	Guatemala	2.80	132	Kyrgyzstan	4.00
53	Israel	2.80	132	Syria	4.00
53	Peru	2.80	135	Belarus	4.05
53	Saudi Arabia	2.80	136	Kazakstan	4.10
53	Turkey	2.80	136	Mozambique	4.10
53	Uganda	2.80	136	Yemen	4.10
53	Western Samoa	2.80	139	Sudan	4.20
62	Indonesia	2.85	140	Myanmar	4.30
62	Latvia	2.85	140	Rwanda	4.30
62	Malta	2.85	142	Angola	4.35
62	Paraguay	2.85	143	Azerbaijan	4.40
66	Greece	2.90	143	Tajikistan	4.40
66	Hungary	2.90	145	Turkmenistan	4.50
66	South Africa	2.90	146	Uzbekistan	4.55
69	Benin	2.95	147	Congo/Zaire	4.70
69	Ecuador	2.95	147	Iran	4.70
69	Gabon	2.95	147	Libya	4.70
69	Morocco	2.95	147	Somalia	4.70
69	Poland	2.95	147	Vietnam	4.70
74	Colombia	3.00	152	Bosnia	4.80
74	Ghana	3.00	153	Iraq	4.90
74	Lithuania	3.00	154	Cuba	5.00
77	Kenya	3.05	154	Laos	5.00
77	Slovak Republic	3.05	154	North Korea	5.00

Free (marker at left of upper portion of the ranking list)

CAPITAL FLOWS AND FOREIGN INVESTMENT
Score: 2–Stable (low barriers)

Bahrain maintains few barriers to foreign investment and has no foreign investment law, preferring to rely on various commercial codes. There are no ownership requirements on new industrial investments, and foreigners now may own non-industrial companies in whole (although they may not purchase or own land).

BANKING
Score: 2–Stable (low level of restrictions)

Over the past 20 years, Bahrain has established itself as a financial center for the Persian Gulf region and the Arab world. "As of the beginning of 1996," reports the U.S. Department of Commerce, "there were 19 full commercial banks, two specialized banks, 41 representative offices, 28 investment banks, six foreign exchange and money brokers, and 27 money-changing companies registered in Bahrain."[2] The government has made it easy to establish a bank, both by streamlining the paperwork process and by placing few, if any, restrictions and requirements on new banks. Foreign banks are welcome.

WAGE AND PRICE CONTROLS
Score: 2–Stable (low level)

The market sets most wages and prices in Bahrain. Price controls remain only on some basic foodstuffs, such as bread. Importers of certain goods must pay a 5 percent fee to a local agent, and this increases the cost of these goods. Several other price controls have been removed. Bahrain has a minimum wage.

PROPERTY RIGHTS
Score: 1–Stable (very high level of protection)

Property is secure in Bahrain, and expropriation remains unlikely. According to the U.S. Department of Commerce, "The Bahraini legal system adequately protects and facilitates acquisition and disposition of other property rights."[3]

REGULATION
Score: 2– (low level)

Bahrain's bureaucracy is efficient and unobtrusive, and businesses are free to operate as they see fit. Bahrain has a fast-track business application process under which companies can be registered and licensed within seven days, with most registered and licensed within only five days. Environmental and occupational health and safety regulations are not burdensome. Despite the existence of anticorruption laws, the U.S. Department of Commerce reports that "Corruption is sometimes part of doing business in Bahrain [and] is most pervasive in government procurement."[4] For this reason, Bahrain's score is one point worse this year. There is scant evidence, however, that corruption is prevalent throughout the economy or that bribery is widespread.

BLACK MARKET
Score: 1–Stable (very low level of activity)

Bahrain has virtually no black market. With few barriers to imports, smuggling is not a problem. There is almost no black market in pirated intellectual property, although the U.S. Department of State recently has documented some piracy of audio and visual recordings. The total cost of this piracy is not known, but it represents only a small fraction of Bahrain's overall economy.

NOTES
1. U.S. Department of Commerce, *Country Commercial Guide,* 1996.
2. U.S. Department of Commerce, *Country Commercial Guide,* 1997.
3. U.S. Department of Commerce, *Country Commercial Guide,* 1996.
4. U.S. Department of Commerce, *Country Commercial Guide,* 1997.

Bangladesh 3.75

1997 Score: **3.70**	1996 Score: **3.65**	1995 Score: **3.90**

Trade	5	Banking	3
Taxation	3.5	Wages and Prices	4
Government Intervention	3	Property Rights	4
Monetary Policy	2	Regulation	5
Foreign Investment	3	Black Market	5

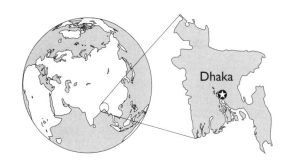

Dhaka

Bangladesh seceded from Pakistan in 1971, and since then has experienced several coups. One of the world's most densely populated countries, Bangladesh has struggled to produce and import enough food to feed its people. Some 60 percent of the labor force is engaged in agriculture. Bangladesh has received massive infusions of foreign aid, much of which has been squandered on underused buildings, roads, and bridges. In 1991, the government embarked on a path of economic reform. But even though it has reduced some taxes, its privatization program has stalled, leaving many enterprises in government hands. As a result, Bangladesh's overall score this year is 0.05 point worse than it was last year.

TRADE POLICY
Score: 5–Stable (very high level of protectionism)

Bangladesh's average tariff rate is 50 percent, up from 40 percent in 1992. According to the U.S. Department of State, "Customs procedures are lengthy and burdensome, and further complicated by corruption."[1]

TAXATION
Score–Income taxation: 2–Stable (low tax rates)
Score–Corporate taxation: 4+ (high tax rates)
Final Taxation Score: 3.5+ (high tax rates)

The top marginal income tax rate in Bangladesh is 25 percent, down from 50 percent in 1991. The tax on the average income level is 0 percent. The top corporate tax rate is 45 percent, down from 47.5 percent. As a result, this year's score has improved one-half point over last year's. Bangladesh also has a 15 percent value-added tax.

GOVERNMENT INTERVENTION IN THE ECONOMY
Score: 3– (moderate level)

The government consumes 13.7 percent of Bangladesh's GDP, up from 6.3 percent in 1980. As a result, Bangladesh's score is a full point worse than it was last year. Privatization has been slowed by opposition from many state-owned industries. According to the U.S. Department of State, "The state's presence in the economy continues to be large, and money-losing state enterprises have been a chronic drain on the treasury."[2] By global standards, however, government intervention in the economy is moderate.

MONETARY POLICY
Score: 2–Stable (low level of inflation)

Bangladesh's average annual rate of inflation from 1985 to 1995 was 6.4 percent. The inflation rate in 1996 was 6.5 percent.

1	Hong Kong	1.25		77	Zambia	3.05
2	Singapore	1.30		80	Mali	3.10
3	Bahrain	1.70		80	Mongolia	3.10
4	New Zealand	1.75		80	Slovenia	3.10
5	Switzerland	1.90		83	Honduras	3.15
5	United States	1.90		83	Papua New Guinea	3.15
7	Luxembourg	1.95		85	Djibouti	3.20
7	Taiwan	1.95		85	Fiji	3.20
7	United Kingdom	1.95		85	Pakistan	3.20
10	Bahamas	2.00		88	Algeria	3.25
10	Ireland	2.00		88	Guinea	3.25
12	Australia	2.05		88	Lebanon	3.25
12	Japan	2.05		88	Mexico	3.25
14	Belgium	2.10		88	Senegal	3.25
14	Canada	2.10		88	Tanzania	3.25
14	United Arab Emirates	2.10		94	Nigeria	3.30
17	Austria	2.15		94	Romania	3.30
17	Chile	2.15		96	Brazil	3.35
17	Estonia	2.15		96	Cambodia	3.35
20	Czech Republic	2.20		96	Egypt	3.35
20	Netherlands	2.20		96	Ivory Coast	3.35
22	Denmark	2.25		96	Madagascar	3.35
22	Finland	2.25		96	Moldova	3.35
24	Germany	2.30		102	Nepal	3.40
24	Iceland	2.30		103	Cape Verde	3.44
24	South Korea	2.30		104	Armenia	3.45
27	Norway	2.35		104	Dominican Republic	3.45
28	Kuwait	2.40		104	Russia	3.45
28	Malaysia	2.40		107	Burkina Faso	3.50
28	Panama	2.40		107	Cameroon	3.50
28	Thailand	2.40		107	Lesotho	3.50
32	El Salvador	2.45		107	Nicaragua	3.50
32	Sri Lanka	2.45		107	Venezuela	3.50
32	Sweden	2.45		112	Gambia	3.60
35	France	2.50		112	Guyana	3.60
35	Italy	2.50		114	Bulgaria	3.65
35	Spain	2.50		114	Georgia	3.65
38	Trinidad and Tobago	2.55		114	Malawi	3.65
39	Argentina	2.60		117	Ethiopia	3.70
39	Barbados	2.60		117	India	3.70
39	Cyprus	2.60		117	Niger	3.70
39	Jamaica	2.60		120	Albania	3.75
39	Portugal	2.60		120	Bangladesh	3.75
44	Bolivia	2.65		120	China (PRC)	3.75
44	Oman	2.65		120	Congo	3.75
44	Philippines	2.65		120	Croatia	3.75
47	Swaziland	2.70		125	Chad	3.80
47	Uruguay	2.70		125	Mauritania	3.80
49	Botswana	2.75		125	Ukraine	3.80
49	Jordan	2.75		128	Sierra Leone	3.85
49	Namibia	2.75		129	Burundi	3.90
49	Tunisia	2.75		129	Suriname	3.90
53	Belize	2.80		129	Zimbabwe	3.90
53	Costa Rica	2.80		132	Haiti	4.00
53	Guatemala	2.80		132	Kyrgyzstan	4.00
53	Israel	2.80		132	Syria	4.00
53	Peru	2.80		135	Belarus	4.05
53	Saudi Arabia	2.80		136	Kazakstan	4.10
53	Turkey	2.80		136	Mozambique	4.10
53	Uganda	2.80		136	Yemen	4.10
53	Western Samoa	2.80		139	Sudan	4.20
62	Indonesia	2.85		140	Myanmar	4.30
62	Latvia	2.85		140	Rwanda	4.30
62	Malta	2.85		142	Angola	4.35
62	Paraguay	2.85		143	Azerbaijan	4.40
66	Greece	2.90		143	Tajikistan	4.40
66	Hungary	2.90		145	Turkmenistan	4.50
66	South Africa	2.90		146	Uzbekistan	4.55
69	Benin	2.95		147	Congo/Zaire	4.70
69	Ecuador	2.95		147	Iran	4.70
69	Gabon	2.95		147	Libya	4.70
69	Morocco	2.95		147	Somalia	4.70
69	Poland	2.95		147	Vietnam	4.70
74	Colombia	3.00		152	Bosnia	4.80
74	Ghana	3.00		153	Iraq	4.90
74	Lithuania	3.00		154	Cuba	5.00
77	Kenya	3.05		154	Laos	5.00
77	Slovak Republic	3.05		154	North Korea	5.00

Mostly Unfree

CAPITAL FLOWS AND FOREIGN INVESTMENT
Score: 3–Stable (moderate barriers)

Some industries, like power generation, forestry, telecommunications, air transportation, railways, and mining, are closed to foreign investment. Nevertheless, Bangladesh has made modest efforts to attract foreign investment. Foreign and domestic investors now enjoy equal treatment.

BANKING
Score: 3–Stable (moderate level of restrictions)

The government has initiated reforms that limit its control of the banking system, although the central bank still restricts some types of lending. Although some reforms are aimed at increasing access to banking services for poor people, parts of the system are chaotic and corrupt. The state still owns some banks: of the 23 commercial banks operating in Bangladesh, for example, 14 are privately owned and 9 are state-owned.

WAGE AND PRICE CONTROLS
Score: 4–Stable (high)

Some price reform has been accomplished, but prices in Bangladesh continue to be influenced by large state-owned and state-subsidized industrial sectors, such as textile production and jute and sugar processing. Heavy government subsidies affect prices negatively.

PROPERTY RIGHTS
Score: 4–Stable (low level of protection)

Even though private property is guaranteed by law, the U.S. Department of Commerce reports that "The country's legal system is outdated and undermanned, leading to long delays in resolving cases. A large and recalcitrant bureaucracy often views its role more as controlling commercial activity than stimulating it. Corruption is endemic."[3]

REGULATION
Score: 5–Stable (very high)

Bangladesh's largest regulatory problems are corruption and outdated business laws that do not protect private contracts. "Foreigners often find that the implementing ministries still require licenses and permissions which were supposedly done away with," says the U.S. Department of Commerce. "Added to these difficulties are such problems as slow government decisionmaking, corruption, labor militancy, an uncertain law and order situation, poor infrastructure, inadequate commercial laws and courts, and policy instability (i.e., policies being altered at the behest of special interests)."[4]

BLACK MARKET
Score: 5–Stable (very high level of activity)

According to the U.S. Department of State, "Bangladesh has outdated intellectual property rights (IPR) laws, and an unwieldy system of registering and enforcing [IPR]. Intellectual property infringement is common particularly of pharmaceuticals products and audio and video cassettes."[5] There remains much smuggling of textiles across Bangladesh's borders.

NOTES

1. U.S. Department of State, *Country Reports on Economic Policy and Trade Practices,* 1997, p. 378.
2. *Ibid.*
3. U.S. Department of Commerce, *Country Commercial Guide,* 1997.
4. *Ibid.*
5. U.S. Department of State, *Country Reports on Economic Policy and Trade Practices,* 1997, p. 378.

Barbados

2.60

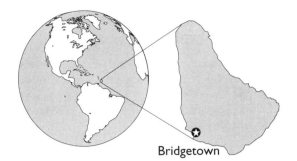

Bridgetown

1997 Score: **2.80**	1996 Score: **3.00**	1995 Score: **n/a**

Trade	3	Banking	2
Taxation	5	Wages and Prices	2
Government Intervention	3	Property Rights	2
Monetary Policy	1	Regulation	3
Foreign Investment	2	Black Market	3

Barbados, a former British colony with a parliamentary democracy, has few natural resources and must import much of what it consumes, including energy, food, and most consumer goods. The country has a fairly large public sector. Recent reforms, however, have sought to open the economy to more foreign investment, trade, and competition. Since 1990, Barbados has achieved significant reform in specific areas of the economy. It recently lowered some barriers to trade, reformed its banking system, allowed more foreign investment, and slashed price controls. Thus, its overall score this year is 0.2 point better than last year.

TRADE POLICY
Score: 3+ (high level of protectionism)

Barbados is a member of the Caribbean Community and has brought its tariffs in line with the rest of the region. The average tariff rate is about 11.5 percent,[1] and most nontariff barriers have been removed. As a result, this year's trade policy score is one point better than last year's.

TAXATION
Score–Income taxation: 5–Stable (very high tax rates)
Score–Corporate taxation: 4–Stable (high tax rates)
Final Taxation Score: 5–Stable (very high tax rates)

Barbados has a top income tax rate of 40 percent; the tax on the average income level is 25 percent. The top marginal corporate tax rate is 40 percent. There also is a value-added tax of 7.5 percent to 15 percent.

GOVERNMENT INTERVENTION IN THE ECONOMY
Score: 3–Stable (moderate level)

The government consumes about 20 percent of Barbados's GDP, and the public sector is rather large. According to the U.S. Department of Commerce, "Successive Barbadian governments have used indicative planning, in keeping with the existence of (and desire for) a mixed economy. Indicative planning is designed to enable governments to plan and implement developmental activity in partnership and collaboration with the private sector.... In short, the Government has, and likely will continue to have, a large role in Barbados' economy."[2] By global standards, however, the government intervenes only moderately in the economy.

MONETARY POLICY
Score: 1–Stable (very low level of inflation)

From 1985 to 1995, the average rate of inflation was 2.5 percent. In 1996, the inflation rate was 1.9 percent.

1	Hong Kong	1.25
2	Singapore	1.30
3	Bahrain	1.70
4	New Zealand	1.75
5	Switzerland	1.90
5	United States	1.90
7	Luxembourg	1.95
7	Taiwan	1.95
7	United Kingdom	1.95
10	Bahamas	2.00
10	Ireland	2.00
12	Australia	2.05
12	Japan	2.05
14	Belgium	2.10
14	Canada	2.10
14	United Arab Emirates	2.10
17	Austria	2.15
17	Chile	2.15
17	Estonia	2.15
20	Czech Republic	2.20
20	Netherlands	2.20
22	Denmark	2.25
22	Finland	2.25
24	Germany	2.30
24	Iceland	2.30
24	South Korea	2.30
27	Norway	2.35
28	Kuwait	2.40
28	Malaysia	2.40
28	Panama	2.40
28	Thailand	2.40
32	El Salvador	2.45
32	Sri Lanka	2.45
32	Sweden	2.45
35	France	2.50
35	Italy	2.50
35	Spain	2.50
38	Trinidad and Tobago	2.55
39	Argentina	2.60
39	Barbados	2.60
39	Cyprus	2.60
39	Jamaica	2.60
39	Portugal	2.60
44	Bolivia	2.65
44	Oman	2.65
44	Philippines	2.65
47	Swaziland	2.70
47	Uruguay	2.70
49	Botswana	2.75
49	Jordan	2.75
49	Namibia	2.75
49	Tunisia	2.75
53	Belize	2.80
53	Costa Rica	2.80
53	Guatemala	2.80
53	Israel	2.80
53	Peru	2.80
53	Saudi Arabia	2.80
53	Turkey	2.80
53	Uganda	2.80
53	Western Samoa	2.80
62	Indonesia	2.85
62	Latvia	2.85
62	Malta	2.85
62	Paraguay	2.85
66	Greece	2.90
66	Hungary	2.90
66	South Africa	2.90
69	Benin	2.95
69	Ecuador	2.95
69	Gabon	2.95
69	Morocco	2.95
69	Poland	2.95
74	Colombia	3.00
74	Ghana	3.00
74	Lithuania	3.00
77	Kenya	3.05
77	Slovak Republic	3.05

77	Zambia	3.05
80	Mali	3.10
80	Mongolia	3.10
80	Slovenia	3.10
83	Honduras	3.15
83	Papua New Guinea	3.15
85	Djibouti	3.20
85	Fiji	3.20
85	Pakistan	3.20
88	Algeria	3.25
88	Guinea	3.25
88	Lebanon	3.25
88	Mexico	3.25
88	Senegal	3.25
88	Tanzania	3.25
94	Nigeria	3.30
94	Romania	3.30
96	Brazil	3.35
96	Cambodia	3.35
96	Egypt	3.35
96	Ivory Coast	3.35
96	Madagascar	3.35
96	Moldova	3.35
102	Nepal	3.40
103	Cape Verde	3.44
104	Armenia	3.45
104	Dominican Republic	3.45
104	Russia	3.45
107	Burkina Faso	3.50
107	Cameroon	3.50
107	Lesotho	3.50
107	Nicaragua	3.50
107	Venezuela	3.50
112	Gambia	3.60
112	Guyana	3.60
114	Bulgaria	3.65
114	Georgia	3.65
114	Malawi	3.65
117	Ethiopia	3.70
117	India	3.70
117	Niger	3.70
120	Albania	3.75
120	Bangladesh	3.75
120	China (PRC)	3.75
120	Congo	3.75
120	Croatia	3.75
125	Chad	3.80
125	Mauritania	3.80
125	Ukraine	3.80
128	Sierra Leone	3.85
129	Burundi	3.90
129	Suriname	3.90
129	Zimbabwe	3.90
132	Haiti	4.00
132	Kyrgyzstan	4.00
132	Syria	4.00
135	Belarus	4.05
136	Kazakstan	4.10
136	Mozambique	4.10
136	Yemen	4.10
139	Sudan	4.20
140	Myanmar	4.30
140	Rwanda	4.30
142	Angola	4.35
143	Azerbaijan	4.40
143	Tajikistan	4.40
145	Turkmenistan	4.50
146	Uzbekistan	4.55
147	Congo/Zaire	4.70
147	Iran	4.70
147	Libya	4.70
147	Somalia	4.70
147	Vietnam	4.70
152	Bosnia	4.80
153	Iraq	4.90
154	Cuba	5.00
154	Laos	5.00
154	North Korea	5.00

Mostly Free

CAPITAL FLOWS AND FOREIGN INVESTMENT
Score: 2–Stable (low barriers)

Barbados permits 100 percent foreign ownership of enterprises and treats domestic and foreign firms equally. There are few restrictions on investment. Prior government approval is needed for investment in utilities, broadcasting, banking, and insurance.

BANKING
Score: 2–Stable (low level of restrictions)

The banking system is fairly open to competition. Some foreign banks already operate in Barbados, but government approval is needed for foreign investment in banks.

WAGE AND PRICE CONTROLS
Score: 2–Stable (low level)

Wages and prices are set mainly by the market. The government, however, continues to set prices on some goods and services (for example, some household appliances and food staples).[3]

PROPERTY RIGHTS
Score: 2+ (low level of protection)

Private property in Barbados is a legal right. The legal tradition is based on British common law, and courts operate independently, although there are some delays.[4]

REGULATION
Score: 3–Stable (moderate level)

Establishing a business in Barbados is simple if the business does not compete directly with the large state-owned sector. Some newer regulations, like the environmental "green tax," hinder business formation and raise costs for consumers.

BLACK MARKET
Score: 3–Stable (moderate level of activity)

According to the U.S. Department of Commerce, "There have been no recent court challenges or settlements for patent, trademark, or copyright infringements, although infringement is commonplace in certain sub-sectors of the economy (e.g., rentals and sales of films on videocassettes, tee-shirt production of unlicensed copyrighted images, unlicensed use of trademarks as store names, software piracy, satellite signal piracy)."[5] The U.S. Department of State notes that "The major problem is illegal copying from promotional tapes provided by movie distributors or from U.S. hotel 'pay-per-view' movies and shows or from satellite transmissions."[6] By global standards, this represents only a moderate level of black market activity.

NOTES

1. Based on total taxes on international trade as a percentage of total imports. The author considered tax revenues garnished from import duties as well as stamp duties applied by customs on imports. From "Economic and Financial Statistics," Central Bank of Barbados, Bridgetown, Barbados, April 1997.
2. U.S. Department of Commerce, *Country Commercial Guide,* 1996.
3. U.S. Department of State, *Country Reports on Economic Policy and Trade Practices,* 1996, p. 328.
4. Data for 1997, unlike those for 1996, do not identify problems with the legal enforcement of trademarks.
5. U.S. Department of Commerce, National Trade Data Bank, 1996.
6. U.S. Department of State, *Country Reports on Economic Policy and Trade Practices,* 1996, p. 331.

Belarus 4.05

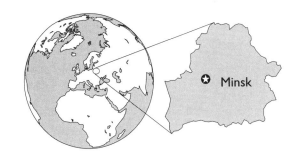

Minsk

1997 Score: **3.85**	1996 Score: **3.55**	1995 Score: **3.65**

Trade	4	Banking	3
Taxation	4.5	Wages and Prices	4
Government Intervention	3	Property Rights	4
Monetary Policy	5	Regulation	4
Foreign Investment	4	Black Market	5

Belarus had one of the highest income levels of all the republics of the former Soviet Union, but the collapse of the Soviet empire left its heavily industrialized economy in shambles. Market reforms have been halfhearted at best, and there are signs of a possible socialist resurgence under President Oleksandr Lukashenka. The size of the economy has shrunk. The government has reduced formal barriers to trade, especially with Russia, but price controls and regulation of business have increased, and protection of private property has decreased. As a result, this year's overall score is 0.2 point worse than last year's.

TRADE POLICY
Score: 4+ (high level of protectionism)

The average tariff rate in Belarus was under 3 percent in 1995,[1] down from 11 percent in 1992. In 1995, Belarus and Russia entered a customs union, the effective result of which has been to eliminate tariffs on goods shipped between the two countries. As a condition of this arrangement, however, Belarus also raised its tariffs on all imported goods not originating in Russia; these tariffs, which had ranged from 5 percent to 10 percent, now range from 20 percent to 40 percent. Thus, the average tariff rate is closer to Russia's 11 percent, down from 17 percent in 1994. As a result, Belarus's trade policy score is one point better this year than it was last year. Nontariff barriers include heavy user fees on imports and some currency requirements on businesses trying to import raw materials.

TAXATION
Score–Income taxation: 5–Stable (very high tax rates)
Score–Corporate taxation: 3–Stable (moderate tax rates)
Final Taxation Score: 4.5–Stable (very high tax rates)

Income taxes in Belarus are among Europe's highest. The top income tax rate is 60 percent, and the average income level is taxed at 37 percent. The top corporate income tax rate is 30 percent, but can be as high as 80 percent for income earned in auctions and through leases. Belarus also has a value-added tax of 20 percent.

GOVERNMENT INTERVENTION IN THE ECONOMY
Score: 3–Stable (moderate level)

The government dominates Belarus's economy, consuming about 22 percent of GDP. Privatization has been halted and even reversed in some cases. Most enterprises still are state-owned. But by global standards, the level of government intervention in the economy is moderate.

MONETARY POLICY
Score: 5–Stable (very high level of inflation)

Belarus has chronically high inflation rates: 2,096 percent in 1993, 2,059 percent in 1994, 709 percent in 1995, and 52 percent in 1996.[2]

1	Hong Kong	1.25	77	Zambia	3.05
2	Singapore	1.30	80	Mali	3.10
3	Bahrain	1.70	80	Mongolia	3.10
4	New Zealand	1.75	80	Slovenia	3.10
5	Switzerland	1.90	83	Honduras	3.15
5	United States	1.90	83	Papua New Guinea	3.15
7	Luxembourg	1.95	85	Djibouti	3.20
7	Taiwan	1.95	85	Fiji	3.20
7	United Kingdom	1.95	85	Pakistan	3.20
10	Bahamas	2.00	88	Algeria	3.25
10	Ireland	2.00	88	Guinea	3.25
12	Australia	2.05	88	Lebanon	3.25
12	Japan	2.05	88	Mexico	3.25
14	Belgium	2.10	88	Senegal	3.25
14	Canada	2.10	88	Tanzania	3.25
14	United Arab Emirates	2.10	94	Nigeria	3.30
17	Austria	2.15	94	Romania	3.30
17	Chile	2.15	96	Brazil	3.35
17	Estonia	2.15	96	Cambodia	3.35
20	Czech Republic	2.20	96	Egypt	3.35
20	Netherlands	2.20	96	Ivory Coast	3.35
22	Denmark	2.25	96	Madagascar	3.35
22	Finland	2.25	96	Moldova	3.35
24	Germany	2.30	102	Nepal	3.40
24	Iceland	2.30	103	Cape Verde	3.44
24	South Korea	2.30	104	Armenia	3.45
27	Norway	2.35	104	Dominican Republic	3.45
28	Kuwait	2.40	104	Russia	3.45
28	Malaysia	2.40	107	Burkina Faso	3.50
28	Panama	2.40	107	Cameroon	3.50
28	Thailand	2.40	107	Lesotho	3.50
32	El Salvador	2.45	107	Nicaragua	3.50
32	Sri Lanka	2.45	107	Venezuela	3.50
32	Sweden	2.45	112	Gambia	3.60
35	France	2.50	112	Guyana	3.60
35	Italy	2.50	114	Bulgaria	3.65
35	Spain	2.50	114	Georgia	3.65
38	Trinidad and Tobago	2.55	114	Malawi	3.65
39	Argentina	2.60	117	Ethiopia	3.70
39	Barbados	2.60	117	India	3.70
39	Cyprus	2.60	117	Niger	3.70
39	Jamaica	2.60	120	Albania	3.75
39	Portugal	2.60	120	Bangladesh	3.75
44	Bolivia	2.65	120	China (PRC)	3.75
44	Oman	2.65	120	Congo	3.75
44	Philippines	2.65	120	Croatia	3.75
47	Swaziland	2.70	125	Chad	3.80
47	Uruguay	2.70	125	Mauritania	3.80
49	Botswana	2.75	125	Ukraine	3.80
49	Jordan	2.75	128	Sierra Leone	3.85
49	Namibia	2.75	129	Burundi	3.90
49	Tunisia	2.75	129	Suriname	3.90
53	Belize	2.80	129	Zimbabwe	3.90
53	Costa Rica	2.80	132	Haiti	4.00
53	Guatemala	2.80	132	Kyrgyzstan	4.00
53	Israel	2.80	132	Syria	4.00
53	Peru	2.80	135	Belarus	4.05
53	Saudi Arabia	2.80	136	Kazakstan	4.10
53	Turkey	2.80	136	Mozambique	4.10
53	Uganda	2.80	136	Yemen	4.10
53	Western Samoa	2.80	139	Sudan	4.20
62	Indonesia	2.85	140	Myanmar	4.30
62	Latvia	2.85	140	Rwanda	4.30
62	Malta	2.85	142	Angola	4.35
62	Paraguay	2.85	143	Azerbaijan	4.40
66	Greece	2.90	143	Tajikistan	4.40
66	Hungary	2.90	145	Turkmenistan	4.50
66	South Africa	2.90	146	Uzbekistan	4.55
69	Benin	2.95	147	Congo/Zaire	4.70
69	Ecuador	2.95	147	Iran	4.70
69	Gabon	2.95	147	Libya	4.70
69	Morocco	2.95	147	Somalia	4.70
69	Poland	2.95	147	Vietnam	4.70
74	Colombia	3.00	152	Bosnia	4.80
74	Ghana	3.00	153	Iraq	4.90
74	Lithuania	3.00	154	Cuba	5.00
77	Kenya	3.05	154	Laos	5.00
77	Slovak Republic	3.05	154	North Korea	5.00

Repressed

CAPITAL FLOWS AND FOREIGN INVESTMENT
Score: 4–Stable (high barriers)

Foreign investment in Belarus is hindered by political instability, anti-Western sentiment, inefficient bureaucracy, corruption, and lack of privatization. Foreigners are not permitted to own land. The Office of the U.S. Trade Representative reports that "Significant informal barriers to investment exist, notably an unstable, unpredictable business climate."[3]

BANKING
Score: 3–Stable (moderate level of restrictions)

Banking is one area in which Belarus outpaces most of its former communist neighbors. In 1994, the government abolished most commercial banking regulations. The result was a boom in small banks. Belarus has over 44 commercial banks, one of which has as many as 20 branches, but the government still influences the country's largest banks. According to the U.S. Department of Commerce, "To date, most of the commercial banks in Belarus, including the four specialized banks, are largely owned by groups of state enterprises which exert powerful influence over their bank's operations and enjoy privileged treatment in their banking activities."[4]

WAGE AND PRICE CONTROLS
Score: 4– (high level)

Recent evidence indicates that price controls, shortages, and rationing of certain items are on the rise. According to the U.S. Department of Commerce, "The state continues to be the largest operator in virtually every sphere of economic activity. Certain prices are set at illogical levels, leading to shortages (particularly of eggs and butter) or apparently unintentional bargains."[5] As a result, this year's score is one point worse than last year's.

PROPERTY RIGHTS
Score: 4– (high level of protection)

The legal system in Belarus does not protect private property in full, and the inefficient court system does not enforce contracts with consistency. The U.S. Department of State characterizes the judiciary as "not independent" and "largely unable to act as a check on the executive branch and its agents."[6] Thus, Belarus's score is one point worse this year.

REGULATION
Score: 4– (high level)

There is corruption in Belarus, and regulations are not always applied evenly. Moreover, there are signs that the government is increasing the regulatory burden on business. According to the U.S. Department of Commerce, "There is very little understanding among GOB [government of Belarus] officials that businesses require a stable business environment to make plans.... Businesses also complain about tax officials who appear frequently and apply different laws each time they appear. These officials can enforce their decisions by unilaterally attaching funds to bank accounts. Resort to the courts is a theoretical possibility, but time-consuming, and tax authorities allegedly ignore court decisions if they disagree."[7] As a result, this year's score is one point worse than last year's.

BLACK MARKET
Score: 5–Stable (very high level of activity)

Belarus's black market, which was large even when the country was a part of the Soviet Union, has increased in size because of the slow pace of economic reform. Black market activity includes the smuggling of consumer goods, the provision of transportation and other services, and violations of intellectual property rights, such as the pirating of audio and video productions and software.

NOTES

1. Based on taxes raised from international trade taken as a percentage of imports in 1995. World Bank, "Statistical Handbook 1996, States of the Former USSR."
2. Based on the consumer price index.
3. Office of the United States Trade Representative, *1997 National Trade Estimate Report on Foreign Trade Barriers.*
4. U.S. Department of Commerce, *Country Commercial Guide, 1997.*
5. U.S. Department of Commerce, "Recent Commercial Developments in Belarus," May 26, 1997.
6. U.S. Department of State, "Belarus Country Report on Human Rights Practices for 1996," 1997.
7. U.S. Department of Commerce, "Recent Commercial Developments in Belarus," May 26, 1997.

Belgium   2.10

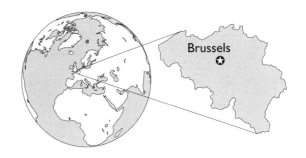

Brussels

1997 Score: **2.10**	1996 Score: **2.10**	1995 Score: **n/a**

Trade	2	Banking	2
Taxation	5	Wages and Prices	2
Government Intervention	2	Property Rights	1
Monetary Policy	1	Regulation	3
Foreign Investment	2	Black Market	1

Belgium officially became independent of the Netherlands in 1839. The country was occupied by Germany during both World War I and World War II, and its monarchy fell victim to internal political strife immediately following World War II. Civil unrest between the French-speaking Walloons and the Flemings during the late 1960s led to the collapse of the government in 1968. In the 1970s, a socialist regime gained power and expanded the government's authority over the economy. In the 1990s, however, the government has implemented limited economic reforms.

TRADE POLICY
Score: 2–Stable (low level of protectionism)

The average tariff rate is 3.6 percent. As a member of the European Union, Belgium maintains nontariff barriers (such as government restrictions on trade in the telecommunications industry) that are common among EU members. The government has taken limited action to open portions of its telecommunications sector to foreign competition. For example, although the government maintains the majority share of the country's public telephone operator, Belgacom, a consortium of foreign companies now owns the other 49 percent.

TAXATION
Score–Income taxation: 5–Stable (very high tax rates)
Score–Corporate taxation: 4–Stable (high tax rates)
Final Taxation Score: 5–Stable (very high tax rates)

Belgium's top income tax rate is 55 percent; the average taxpayer is in the 35 percent bracket. The top marginal corporate tax rate is 40 percent. Belgium also maintains a 40 percent capital gains tax and a 21 percent value-added tax.

GOVERNMENT INTERVENTION IN THE ECONOMY
Score: 2–Stable (low level)

The government consumes 14.8 percent of Belgium's GDP. Unlike some of its neighbors, Belgium has made significant progress in privatization; the government currently is selling portions of its telecommunications, mail, energy, and transportation services.

MONETARY POLICY
Score: 1–Stable (very low level of inflation)

From 1985 to 1995, Belgium's average rate of inflation was 3.1 percent. In 1996, the inflation rate was about 2.1 percent.

CAPITAL FLOWS AND FOREIGN INVESTMENT
Score: 2–Stable (low barriers)

Belgium's foreign investment climate is one of the best in Europe. Foreign and domestic firms are treated equally, and there are no restrictions on foreign

1	Hong Kong	1.25
2	Singapore	1.30
3	Bahrain	1.70
4	New Zealand	1.75
5	Switzerland	1.90
5	United States	1.90
7	Luxembourg	1.95
7	Taiwan	1.95
7	United Kingdom	1.95
10	Bahamas	2.00
10	Ireland	2.00
12	Australia	2.05
12	Japan	2.05
14	Belgium	2.10
14	Canada	2.10
14	United Arab Emirates	2.10
17	Austria	2.15
17	Chile	2.15
17	Estonia	2.15
20	Czech Republic	2.20
20	Netherlands	2.20
22	Finland	2.25
22	Denmark	2.25
24	Germany	2.30
24	Iceland	2.30
24	South Korea	2.30
27	Norway	2.35
28	Kuwait	2.40
28	Malaysia	2.40
28	Panama	2.40
28	Thailand	2.40
32	El Salvador	2.45
32	Sri Lanka	2.45
32	Sweden	2.45
35	France	2.50
35	Italy	2.50
35	Spain	2.50
38	Trinidad and Tobago	2.55
39	Argentina	2.60
39	Barbados	2.60
39	Cyprus	2.60
39	Jamaica	2.60
39	Portugal	2.60
44	Bolivia	2.65
44	Oman	2.65
44	Philippines	2.65
47	Swaziland	2.70
47	Uruguay	2.70
49	Botswana	2.75
49	Jordan	2.75
49	Namibia	2.75
49	Tunisia	2.75
53	Belize	2.80
53	Costa Rica	2.80
53	Guatemala	2.80
53	Israel	2.80
53	Peru	2.80
53	Saudi Arabia	2.80
53	Turkey	2.80
53	Uganda	2.80
53	Western Samoa	2.80
62	Indonesia	2.85
62	Latvia	2.85
62	Malta	2.85
62	Paraguay	2.85
66	Greece	2.90
66	Hungary	2.90
66	South Africa	2.90
69	Benin	2.95
69	Ecuador	2.95
69	Gabon	2.95
69	Morocco	2.95
69	Poland	2.95
74	Colombia	3.00
74	Ghana	3.00
74	Lithuania	3.00
77	Kenya	3.05
77	Slovak Republic	3.05

Mostly Free

77	Zambia	3.05
80	Mali	3.10
80	Mongolia	3.10
80	Slovenia	3.10
83	Honduras	3.15
83	Papua New Guinea	3.15
85	Djibouti	3.20
85	Fiji	3.20
85	Pakistan	3.20
88	Algeria	3.25
88	Guinea	3.25
88	Lebanon	3.25
88	Mexico	3.25
88	Senegal	3.25
88	Tanzania	3.25
94	Nigeria	3.30
94	Romania	3.30
96	Brazil	3.35
96	Cambodia	3.35
96	Egypt	3.35
96	Ivory Coast	3.35
96	Madagascar	3.35
96	Moldova	3.35
102	Nepal	3.40
103	Cape Verde	3.44
104	Armenia	3.45
104	Dominican Republic	3.45
104	Russia	3.45
107	Burkina Faso	3.50
107	Cameroon	3.50
107	Lesotho	3.50
107	Nicaragua	3.50
107	Venezuela	3.50
112	Gambia	3.60
112	Guyana	3.60
114	Bulgaria	3.65
114	Georgia	3.65
114	Malawi	3.65
117	Ethiopia	3.70
117	India	3.70
117	Niger	3.70
120	Albania	3.75
120	Bangladesh	3.75
120	China (PRC)	3.75
120	Congo	3.75
120	Croatia	3.75
123	Chad	3.80
125	Mauritania	3.80
125	Ukraine	3.80
128	Sierra Leone	3.85
129	Burundi	3.90
129	Suriname	3.90
129	Zimbabwe	3.90
132	Haiti	4.00
132	Kyrgyzstan	4.00
132	Syria	4.00
135	Belarus	4.05
136	Kazakstan	4.10
136	Mozambique	4.10
136	Yemen	4.10
139	Sudan	4.20
140	Myanmar	4.30
140	Rwanda	4.30
142	Angola	4.35
143	Azerbaijan	4.40
143	Tajikistan	4.40
145	Turkmenistan	4.50
146	Uzbekistan	4.55
147	Congo/Zaire	4.70
147	Iran	4.70
147	Libya	4.70
147	Somalia	4.70
147	Vietnam	4.70
152	Bosnia	4.80
153	Iraq	4.90
154	Cuba	5.00
154	Laos	5.00
154	North Korea	5.00

investment that do not apply to domestic investment as well, except in industries vital to national defense.

BANKING
Score: 2–Stable (low level of restrictions)

Foreign banks are allowed to operate in Belgium and are subject to relatively few restrictions. The domestic banking system often is tightly regulated by the government, but even here progress is being made toward greater freedom.

WAGE AND PRICE CONTROLS
Score: 2–Stable (low level)

Belgium's market determines most wages and prices. But both state ownership of some industries and a massive program of government subsidies affect pricing in many areas, such as electricity and agricultural products. Some price controls remain on household rent and certain pharmaceuticals. Belgium also maintains a minimum wage.

PROPERTY RIGHTS
Score: 1–Stable (very high level of protection)

Private property generally is safe from government expropriation in Belgium. The legal and judicial system is like that of any other advanced industrial state.

REGULATION
Score: 3–Stable (moderate level)

Establishing a business in Belgium can be easy if the business does not compete directly with government-owned industries (such as some utilities), and regulations are applied evenly in most cases. Belgium requires generous worker benefits, and regulations are making it more difficult for some companies to survive. According to the U.S. Department of State, "Some U.S. retailers, including Toys 'R' Us, have experienced considerable difficulties in obtaining permits for outlets in Belgium. Current legislation is designed to protect small shopkeepers, and its application is not transparent."[1] But by global standards, the level of regulation is moderate.

BLACK MARKET
Score: 1–Stable (very low level of activity)

Belgium's black market is negligible. According to U.S. Department of State estimates, some 20 percent of the videocassette and compact disc market, and some 48 percent of all software, involves pirated material.[2] This is small when compared with the size of Belgium's economy.

NOTES

1. U.S. Department of State, *Country Reports on Economic Policy and Trade Practices,* 1997, p. 93.
2. *Ibid.,* p. 94.

Belize

2.80

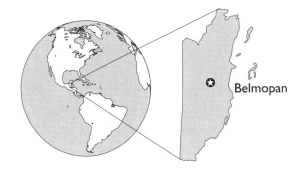

Belmopan

1997 Score: **2.70**	1996 Score: **2.70**	1995 Score: **2.70**

Trade	5	Banking	3
Taxation	4	Wages and Prices	2
Government Intervention	2	Property Rights	3
Monetary Policy	1	Regulation	3
Foreign Investment	2	Black Market	3

Belize has achieved significant economic gains since the early 1980s, when its main export (sugarcane) was hit by disease and the economy stagnated. Sound economic policies and favorable trade conditions in Latin and North America, the recipients of many of its exports, have led to extremely high rates of economic growth. Recent evidence of increasing government influence on the judicial process causes Belize's overall score this year to be 0.1 point worse than it was last year.

TRADE POLICY
Score: 5–Stable (very high level of protectionism)

Trade is a primary source of revenue for the government. Tariffs average almost 26 percent.[1] The government requires licenses for imports of 26 different products, including citrus, flour, meats, jams and jellies, pepper sauce, pasta, matches, and peanut butter.[2]

TAXATION
Score–Income taxation: 4–Stable (high tax rates)
Score–Corporate taxation: 3–Stable (moderate tax rates)
Final Taxation Score: 4–Stable (high tax rates)

Belize's top marginal income tax rate is 45 percent, and the average income level is taxed at 15 percent. The corporate income tax rate is a flat 35 percent. Belize has a social contributions tax.

GOVERNMENT INTERVENTION IN THE ECONOMY
Score: 2–Stable (low level)

The government consumes 16.1 percent of Belize's GDP.

MONETARY POLICY
Score: 1–Stable (very low level of inflation)

From 1985 to 1995, the average annual rate of inflation in Belize was 3.5 percent. In 1996, it was 6.8 percent.

CAPITAL FLOWS AND FOREIGN INVESTMENT
Score: 2–Stable (low barriers)

Although Belize generally is open to foreign investment and has an established investment code, foreign investment is not permitted in a variety of industries and economic activities, including accounting, beekeeping, commercial fishing, insurance, legal services, merchandising and distribution, real estate, sugarcane production, and transportation.

1	Hong Kong	1.25	77	Zambia	3.05
2	Singapore	1.30	80	Mali	3.10
3	Bahrain	1.70	80	Mongolia	3.10
4	New Zealand	1.75	80	Slovenia	3.10
5	Switzerland	1.90	83	Honduras	3.15
5	United States	1.90	83	Papua New Guinea	3.15
7	Luxembourg	1.95	85	Djibouti	3.20
7	Taiwan	1.95	85	Fiji	3.20
7	United Kingdom	1.95	85	Pakistan	3.20
10	Bahamas	2.00	88	Algeria	3.25
10	Ireland	2.00	88	Guinea	3.25
12	Australia	2.05	88	Lebanon	3.25
12	Japan	2.05	88	Mexico	3.25
14	Belgium	2.10	88	Senegal	3.25
14	Canada	2.10	88	Tanzania	3.25
14	United Arab Emirates	2.10	94	Nigeria	3.30
17	Austria	2.15	94	Romania	3.30
17	Chile	2.15	96	Brazil	3.35
17	Estonia	2.15	96	Cambodia	3.35
20	Czech Republic	2.20	96	Egypt	3.35
20	Netherlands	2.20	96	Ivory Coast	3.35
22	Denmark	2.25	96	Madagascar	3.35
22	Finland	2.25	96	Moldova	3.35
24	Germany	2.30	102	Nepal	3.40
24	Iceland	2.30	103	Cape Verde	3.44
24	South Korea	2.30	104	Armenia	3.45
27	Norway	2.35	104	Dominican Republic	3.45
28	Kuwait	2.40	104	Russia	3.45
28	Malaysia	2.40	107	Burkina Faso	3.50
28	Panama	2.40	107	Cameroon	3.50
28	Thailand	2.40	107	Lesotho	3.50
32	El Salvador	2.45	107	Nicaragua	3.50
32	Sri Lanka	2.45	107	Venezuela	3.50
32	Sweden	2.45	112	Gambia	3.60
35	France	2.50	112	Guyana	3.60
35	Italy	2.50	114	Bulgaria	3.65
35	Spain	2.50	114	Georgia	3.65
38	Trinidad and Tobago	2.55	114	Malawi	3.65
39	Argentina	2.60	117	Ethiopia	3.70
39	Barbados	2.60	117	India	3.70
39	Cyprus	2.60	117	Niger	3.70
39	Jamaica	2.60	120	Albania	3.75
39	Portugal	2.60	120	Bangladesh	3.75
44	Bolivia	2.65	120	China (PRC)	3.75
44	Oman	2.65	120	Congo	3.75
44	Philippines	2.65	120	Croatia	3.75
47	Swaziland	2.70	125	Chad	3.80
47	Uruguay	2.70	125	Mauritania	3.80
49	Botswana	2.75	125	Ukraine	3.80
49	Jordan	2.75	128	Sierra Leone	3.85
49	Namibia	2.75	129	Burundi	3.90
49	Tunisia	2.75	129	Suriname	3.90
53	Belize	2.80	129	Zimbabwe	3.90
53	Costa Rica	2.80	132	Haiti	4.00
53	Guatemala	2.80	132	Kyrgyzstan	4.00
53	Israel	2.80	132	Syria	4.00
53	Peru	2.80	135	Belarus	4.05
53	Saudi Arabia	2.80	136	Kazakstan	4.10
53	Turkey	2.80	136	Mozambique	4.10
53	Uganda	2.80	136	Yemen	4.10
53	Western Samoa	2.80	139	Sudan	4.20
62	Indonesia	2.85	140	Myanmar	4.30
62	Latvia	2.85	140	Rwanda	4.30
62	Malta	2.85	142	Angola	4.35
62	Paraguay	2.85	143	Azerbaijan	4.40
66	Greece	2.90	143	Tajikistan	4.40
66	Hungary	2.90	145	Turkmenistan	4.50
66	South Africa	2.90	146	Uzbekistan	4.55
69	Benin	2.95	147	Congo/Zaire	4.70
69	Ecuador	2.95	147	Iran	4.70
69	Gabon	2.95	147	Libya	4.70
69	Morocco	2.95	147	Somalia	4.70
69	Poland	2.95	147	Vietnam	4.70
74	Colombia	3.00	152	Bosnia	4.80
74	Ghana	3.00	153	Iraq	4.90
74	Lithuania	3.00	154	Cuba	5.00
77	Kenya	3.05	154	Laos	5.00
77	Slovak Republic	3.05	154	North Korea	5.00

Mostly Free

BANKING
Score: 3–Stable (moderate level of restrictions)

Bank loans in Belize are closely regulated, and banks are under tight government control. Recently promulgated regulations have increased government oversight of some banks. Foreigners need official permission to operate, and government restrictions on the formation of new banks limit competition.

WAGE AND PRICE CONTROLS
Score: 2–Stable (low level)

The market sets most wages and prices, but there are price controls on some foodstuffs. Belize maintains a minimum wage.

PROPERTY RIGHTS
Score: 3– (moderate level of protection)

The chances for expropriation remain remote, and the court system is adequate. According to the U.S. Department of State, however, there is "political influence on the judiciary."[3] As a result, this year's property rights score is one point worse than last year's.[4]

REGULATION
Score: 3–Stable (moderate level)

Some regulations, like health and safety standards, can be onerous, especially for smaller companies. Regulations often are applied haphazardly, and obtaining a business license can be complicated. According to the U.S. Department of Commerce, "Corruption remains a problem in Belize."[5]

BLACK MARKET
Score: 3–Stable (moderate level of activity)

Black market activity takes many forms in Belize. Some construction, transportation, and other cash transactions are carried out primarily in the black market; and although the government is updating its copyright laws and other laws pertaining to intellectual property, there is a growing black market in pirated trademarks and prerecorded music and video tapes.

NOTES

1. Based on total revenue from taxes on international transactions as a percentage of total imports.
2. These rates are for the 1994 taxable year, the most recent for which data are available. See Deloitte & Touche Tohmatsu International, "Taxation in Central and South America," New York, N.Y., 1994.
3. U.S. Department of State, "Belize Country Report on Human Rights Practices for 1996," 1997.
4. The score in this factor has changed from 2 in 1997 to 3 in 1998. Previously unavailable data provide a more accurate understanding of the country's performance; see U.S. Department of State, "Belize Country Report on Human Rights Practices for 1996," 1997. The methodology for this factor remains the same.
5. U.S. Department of Commerce, *Country Commercial Guide,* 1997.

Benin   2.95

| 1997 Score: **2.95** | 1996 Score: **2.95** | 1995 Score: **n/a** |

Trade	4	Banking	3
Taxation	3.5	Wages and Prices	3
Government Intervention	3	Property Rights	3
Monetary Policy	1	Regulation	3
Foreign Investment	3	Black Market	3

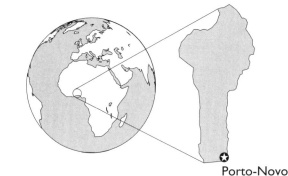

Porto-Novo

The Republic of Benin gained its independence from France in 1960 as Dahomey. In 1975, it was renamed by a Marxist government that had seized power in a 1972 coup. Free elections were held in 1991 following the adoption of a new constitution in 1990, which established a unitary republic. Benin currently has one of Africa's more vibrant democracies. Its old dictator, Mathieu Kerekou, was elected president in 1996. Two decades of Marxism had devastated Benin's economy, which is based primarily on agriculture, mining, and regional trade, and Benin's people ranked among the world's 25 poorest in 1995. But economic liberalization policies initiated in 1989 have led to consistent economic growth, averaging 4.8 percent between 1992 and 1996. Benin maintains close political and economic ties with France, including membership in the French Franc Zone.

TRADE POLICY
Score: 4–Stable (high level of protectionism)

Benin has been liberalizing its trade policies. The tariff structure was simplified in 1993, but the average tariff rate is still 20.2 percent.[1] Import licensing controls were removed in 1993, and overall tariff rates were reduced in 1994. Thus, the average tariff rate probably is much less than 20 percent. There are few, if any, nontariff barriers.

TAXATION
Score–Income taxation: 3–Stable (moderate tax rates)
Score–Corporate taxation: 3–Stable (moderate tax rates)
Final Taxation Score: 3.5–Stable (high tax rates)

Benin's top income tax rate is 35 percent.[2] The corporate tax recently was reduced from 48 percent to 38 percent. An 18 percent value-added tax covering most goods was introduced in 1991.

GOVERNMENT INTERVENTION IN THE ECONOMY
Score: 3–Stable (moderate level)

The government consumes about 11.4 percent of Benin's GDP. There has been significant progress with privatization and liquidation of state-owned enterprises over the past several years, but some 30 enterprises remain in state hands. Further privatization is planned.

MONETARY POLICY
Score: 1–Stable (very low level of inflation)

From 1985 to 1995, Benin's average rate of inflation was 2.9 percent. In 1996, however, it was 5.75 percent.

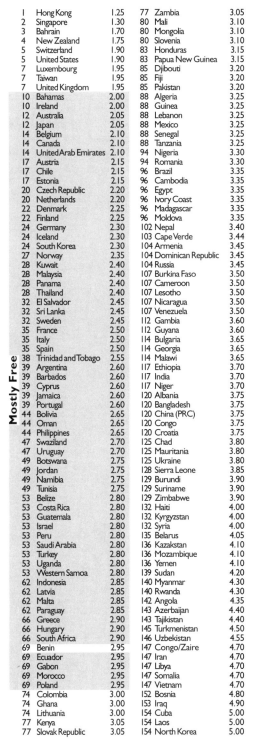

1	Hong Kong	1.25		77	Zambia	3.05
2	Singapore	1.30		80	Mali	3.10
3	Bahrain	1.70		80	Mongolia	3.10
4	New Zealand	1.75		80	Slovenia	3.10
5	Switzerland	1.90		83	Honduras	3.15
5	United States	1.90		83	Papua New Guinea	3.15
7	Luxembourg	1.95		85	Djibouti	3.20
7	Taiwan	1.95		85	Fiji	3.20
7	United Kingdom	1.95		85	Pakistan	3.20
10	Bahamas	2.00		88	Algeria	3.25
10	Ireland	2.00		88	Guinea	3.25
12	Australia	2.05		88	Lebanon	3.25
12	Japan	2.05		88	Mexico	3.25
14	Belgium	2.10		88	Senegal	3.25
14	Canada	2.10		88	Tanzania	3.25
14	United Arab Emirates	2.10		94	Nigeria	3.30
17	Austria	2.15		94	Romania	3.30
17	Chile	2.15		96	Brazil	3.35
17	Estonia	2.15		96	Cambodia	3.35
20	Czech Republic	2.20		96	Egypt	3.35
20	Netherlands	2.20		96	Ivory Coast	3.35
22	Denmark	2.25		96	Madagascar	3.35
22	Finland	2.25		96	Moldova	3.35
24	Germany	2.30		102	Nepal	3.40
24	Iceland	2.30		103	Cape Verde	3.44
24	South Korea	2.30		104	Armenia	3.45
27	Norway	2.35		104	Dominican Republic	3.45
28	Kuwait	2.40		104	Russia	3.45
28	Malaysia	2.40		107	Burkina Faso	3.50
28	Panama	2.40		107	Cameroon	3.50
28	Thailand	2.40		107	Lesotho	3.50
32	El Salvador	2.45		107	Nicaragua	3.50
32	Sri Lanka	2.45		107	Venezuela	3.50
32	Sweden	2.45		112	Gambia	3.60
35	France	2.50		112	Guyana	3.60
35	Italy	2.50		114	Bulgaria	3.65
35	Spain	2.50		114	Georgia	3.65
38	Trinidad and Tobago	2.55		114	Malawi	3.65
39	Argentina	2.60		117	Ethiopia	3.70
39	Barbados	2.60		117	India	3.70
39	Cyprus	2.60		117	Niger	3.70
39	Jamaica	2.60		120	Albania	3.75
39	Portugal	2.60		120	Bangladesh	3.75
44	Bolivia	2.65		120	China (PRC)	3.75
44	Oman	2.65		120	Congo	3.75
44	Philippines	2.65		120	Croatia	3.75
47	Swaziland	2.70		125	Chad	3.80
47	Uruguay	2.70		125	Mauritania	3.80
49	Botswana	2.75		125	Ukraine	3.80
49	Jordan	2.75		128	Sierra Leone	3.85
49	Namibia	2.75		129	Burundi	3.90
49	Tunisia	2.75		129	Suriname	3.90
53	Belize	2.80		129	Zimbabwe	3.90
53	Costa Rica	2.80		132	Haiti	4.00
53	Guatemala	2.80		132	Kyrgyzstan	4.00
53	Israel	2.80		132	Syria	4.00
53	Peru	2.80		135	Belarus	4.05
53	Saudi Arabia	2.80		136	Kazakstan	4.10
53	Turkey	2.80		136	Mozambique	4.10
53	Uganda	2.80		136	Yemen	4.10
53	Western Samoa	2.80		139	Sudan	4.20
62	Indonesia	2.85		140	Myanmar	4.30
62	Latvia	2.85		140	Rwanda	4.30
62	Malta	2.85		142	Angola	4.35
62	Paraguay	2.85		143	Azerbaijan	4.40
66	Greece	2.90		143	Tajikistan	4.40
66	Hungary	2.90		146	Turkmenistan	4.50
66	South Africa	2.90		146	Uzbekistan	4.55
69	Benin	2.95		147	Congo/Zaire	4.70
69	Ecuador	2.95		147	Iran	4.70
69	Gabon	2.95		147	Libya	4.70
69	Morocco	2.95		147	Somalia	4.70
69	Poland	2.95		147	Vietnam	4.70
74	Colombia	3.00		152	Bosnia	4.80
74	Ghana	3.00		153	Iraq	4.90
74	Lithuania	3.00		154	Cuba	5.00
77	Kenya	3.05		154	Laos	5.00
77	Slovak Republic	3.05		154	North Korea	5.00

Mostly Free

CAPITAL FLOWS AND FOREIGN INVESTMENT
Score: 3–Stable (moderate level)

Benin has improved its foreign investment climate considerably over the past few years. Investment incentives have been established, foreign investment has increased, and a one-stop foreign investment approval center is being planned. In the meantime, foreign investors must contend with numerous hurdles imposed by inefficient bureaucracies subject to corruption. The mining, energy, water, forestry, transport, and communications sectors remain under state control.

BANKING
Score: 3–Stable (moderate level of restrictions)

The banking sector collapsed in the late 1980s. Several state-controlled banks became bankrupt and subsequently were liquidated. Today, five private banks operate in Benin. The government remains involved in providing agricultural credit, and interest rates are dictated by the Central Bank of West Africa. New banks must meet minimum capital and other requirements.

WAGE AND PRICE CONTROLS
Score: 3–Stable (moderate level)

Although Benin's elaborate price control scheme has been dismantled, price controls on several foodstuffs have been reimposed in an effort to combat inflation. There are price controls on cement, medicine, school equipment, electricity, and water, as well as a producer price for cotton, the country's largest export commodity. There is a minimum wage, and the government plays a significant role in guiding private-sector wage negotiations.

PROPERTY RIGHTS
Score: 3–Stable (moderate level of protection)

Private property is legal, but two decades of Marxist rule left Benin's court and legal system in disarray.

REGULATION
Score: 3–Stable (moderate level)

Benin's government has recognized the need to simplify business licensing procedures and to revise the labor code to allow employers more flexibility in hiring and firing. The government recently reduced the licensing tax.

BLACK MARKET
Score: 3–Stable (moderate level of activity)

The reimposition of price controls on several products has led to the establishment of surveillance teams to combat smuggling.

NOTES

1. 1996 World Bank figure based on 1994 data; see World Bank, *African Development Figures 1996*.
2. The tax on the average income level is not available; therefore, Benin's income tax score is based solely on the top rate.

Bolivia

2.65

1997 Score: **2.85**	1996 Score: **2.75**	1995 Score: **3.20**

Trade	2	Banking	2
Taxation	2.5	Wages and Prices	1
Government Intervention	3	Property Rights	3
Monetary Policy	3	Regulation	4
Foreign Investment	2	Black Market	4

Bolivia is a constitutional democracy with an economy that is beginning to experience substantial gains. Even so, it still continues to lag behind many of its neighbors in overall economic freedom. The government recently reformed the banking sector by selling state-owned banks, and it also has reduced inflation. The success of the Sanchez de Lozada government's economic reform plan is the result of lower government spending, reduced barriers to trade and investment, and the privatization of large sections of the economy. A presidential election was held in June 1997, and President Hugo Banzer of the Nationalist Democratic Alliance has pledged to continue Bolivia's economic liberalization. Because government spending levels have decreased steadily over the past several years, Bolivia's overall score is 0.2 point better than it was last year.

TRADE POLICY
Score: 2–Stable (low level of protectionism)

In 1990, the government reduced the average tariff rate from 16 percent to 10 percent on all but capital goods, which has a rate of 5 percent. The average tariff rate is 5.12 percent.[1] There are few, if any, nontariff barriers.

TAXATION
Score–Income taxation: 2–Stable (low tax rates)
Score–Corporate taxation: 2–Stable (low tax rates)
Final Taxation Score: 2.5–Stable (moderate tax rates)

Bolivia has a flat income tax of 13 percent and a top corporate tax rate of 25 percent. It also has a 13 percent value-added tax and a variety of other transaction and property taxes.

GOVERNMENT INTERVENTION IN THE ECONOMY
Score: 3+ (moderate level)

The government consumption rate in Bolivia is 13 percent, and total government spending accounts for some 40 percent of GDP,[2] largely because of the country's state-owned industries. Privatization has helped reduce spending, however, and overall government consumption and spending as a percentage of the economy have been decreasing steadily. As a result, Bolivia's score this year is one point better than last year.

MONETARY POLICY
Score: 3–Stable (moderate level of inflation)

From 1985 to 1995, the average rate of inflation was 18.5 percent; in 1996, the rate was 12.4 percent.

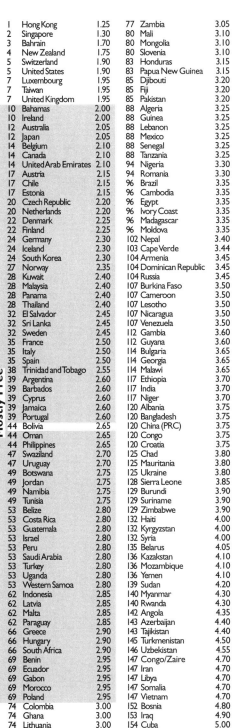

1	Hong Kong	1.25	77	Zambia	3.05
2	Singapore	1.30	80	Mali	3.10
3	Bahrain	1.70	80	Mongolia	3.10
4	New Zealand	1.75	80	Slovenia	3.10
5	Switzerland	1.90	83	Honduras	3.15
5	United States	1.90	83	Papua New Guinea	3.15
7	Luxembourg	1.95	85	Djibouti	3.20
7	Taiwan	1.95	85	Fiji	3.20
7	United Kingdom	1.95	85	Pakistan	3.20
10	Bahamas	2.00	88	Algeria	3.25
10	Ireland	2.00	88	Guinea	3.25
12	Australia	2.05	88	Lebanon	3.25
12	Japan	2.05	88	Mexico	3.25
14	Belgium	2.10	88	Senegal	3.25
14	Canada	2.10	88	Tanzania	3.25
14	United Arab Emirates	2.10	94	Nigeria	3.30
17	Austria	2.15	94	Romania	3.30
17	Chile	2.15	96	Brazil	3.35
17	Estonia	2.15	96	Cambodia	3.35
20	Czech Republic	2.20	96	Egypt	3.35
20	Netherlands	2.20	96	Ivory Coast	3.35
22	Denmark	2.25	96	Madagascar	3.35
22	Finland	2.25	96	Moldova	3.35
24	Germany	2.30	102	Nepal	3.40
24	Iceland	2.30	103	Cape Verde	3.44
24	South Korea	2.30	104	Armenia	3.45
27	Norway	2.35	104	Dominican Republic	3.45
28	Kuwait	2.40	104	Russia	3.45
28	Malaysia	2.40	107	Burkina Faso	3.50
28	Panama	2.40	107	Cameroon	3.50
28	Thailand	2.40	107	Lesotho	3.50
32	El Salvador	2.45	107	Nicaragua	3.50
32	Sri Lanka	2.45	107	Venezuela	3.50
32	Sweden	2.45	112	Gambia	3.60
35	France	2.50	112	Guyana	3.60
35	Italy	2.50	114	Bulgaria	3.65
35	Spain	2.50	114	Georgia	3.65
38	Trinidad and Tobago	2.55	114	Malawi	3.65
39	Argentina	2.60	117	Ethiopia	3.70
39	Barbados	2.60	117	India	3.70
39	Cyprus	2.60	117	Niger	3.70
39	Jamaica	2.60	120	Albania	3.75
39	Portugal	2.60	120	Bangladesh	3.75
44	Bolivia	2.65	120	China (PRC)	3.75
44	Oman	2.65	120	Congo	3.75
44	Philippines	2.65	120	Croatia	3.75
47	Swaziland	2.70	125	Chad	3.80
47	Uruguay	2.70	125	Mauritania	3.80
49	Botswana	2.75	125	Ukraine	3.80
49	Jordan	2.75	128	Sierra Leone	3.85
49	Namibia	2.75	129	Burundi	3.90
49	Tunisia	2.75	129	Suriname	3.90
53	Belize	2.80	129	Zimbabwe	3.90
53	Costa Rica	2.80	132	Haiti	4.00
53	Guatemala	2.80	132	Kyrgyzstan	4.00
53	Israel	2.80	132	Syria	4.00
53	Peru	2.80	135	Belarus	4.05
53	Saudi Arabia	2.80	136	Kazakstan	4.10
53	Turkey	2.80	136	Mozambique	4.10
53	Uganda	2.80	136	Yemen	4.10
53	Western Samoa	2.80	139	Sudan	4.20
62	Indonesia	2.85	140	Myanmar	4.30
62	Latvia	2.85	140	Rwanda	4.30
62	Malta	2.85	142	Angola	4.35
62	Paraguay	2.85	143	Azerbaijan	4.40
66	Greece	2.90	143	Tajikistan	4.40
66	Hungary	2.90	145	Turkmenistan	4.50
66	South Africa	2.90	146	Uzbekistan	4.55
69	Benin	2.95	147	Congo/Zaire	4.70
69	Ecuador	2.95	147	Iran	4.70
69	Gabon	2.95	147	Libya	4.70
69	Morocco	2.95	147	Somalia	4.70
69	Poland	2.95	147	Vietnam	4.70
74	Colombia	3.00	152	Bosnia	4.80
74	Ghana	3.00	153	Iraq	4.90
74	Lithuania	3.00	154	Cuba	5.00
77	Kenya	3.05	154	Laos	5.00
77	Slovak Republic	3.05	154	North Korea	5.00

Mostly Free

CAPITAL FLOWS AND FOREIGN INVESTMENT
Score: 2–Stable (low barriers)

Bolivia encourages foreign investment. Few restrictions remain, and those that apply to the petroleum and mining industries are minimal.

BANKING
Score: 2–Stable (low level of restrictions)

Bolivia's banking system has been reformed. Government-owned banks no longer exist. The banking industry is composed primarily of 18 institutions, of which 13 are private domestic banks and the rest are foreign-owned.

WAGE AND PRICE CONTROLS
Score: 1–Stable (very low level)

There are few price controls in Bolivia, although the government still reserves the right to limit the prices of foodstuffs. Wages and prices are being set more freely as more state-owned companies are privatized. There are no minimum wage laws.

PROPERTY RIGHTS
Score: 3–Stable (moderate level of protection)

Legal protection of private property in Bolivia is lax. Large property owners are particularly vulnerable because property can be seized without just compensation and "taxed" by corrupt government officials. According to the U.S. Department of State, "The judiciary, while independent, is corrupt and inefficient."[3] But by global standards, private property protection is moderate because the legal system is functional and communal property is not the rule.

REGULATION
Score: 4–Stable (high level)

Bolivia's economy often is regulated through haphazardly applied government requirements on business, and even though the government maintains no occupational or environmental regulations, there are many complaints of corruption. The government has begun a crackdown on corruption, but the effects are not visible yet.

BLACK MARKET
Score: 4–Stable (high level of activity)

Some estimates place Bolivia's black market at about 30 percent of GDP. This share is being reduced, however. Piracy of intellectual property is widespread: Piracy in motion pictures, sound recordings, computer software, and books, for example, cost U.S. companies over $42 million in Bolivia during 1995.

NOTES

1. Based on revenues gained from taxes on international trade as a percentage of total imports.
2. The government consumption rate is from World Bank, *World Development Report 1997*. Total government spending, based on current 1996 dollars, is from U.S. Department of Commerce, *Country Commercial Guide*, 1997.
3. U.S. Department of State, "Bolivia Country Report on Human Rights Practices for 1996," 1997.

Bosnia and Herzegovina

4.80

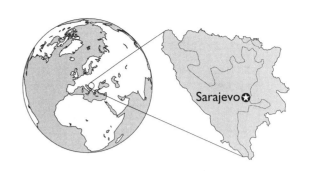

Sarajevo ⊙

1997 Score: **n/a**	1996 Score: **n/a**	1995 Score: **n/a**

Trade	5	Banking	5
Taxation	5	Wages and Prices	4
Government Intervention	5	Property Rights	5
Monetary Policy	5	Regulation	5
Foreign Investment	4	Black Market	5

The collapse of Yugoslavia in 1990 and 1991 created four independent countries, including Bosnia and Herzegovina. In 1992, the government of Bosnia and Herzegovina held a referendum on independence; the Bosnian Serbs, supported by nearby Serbia, responded with armed resistance, seeking to divide Bosnia largely along ethnic lines, with Serbian regions joining Serbia. Industrial production collapsed, and both inflation and unemployment skyrocketed. In 1994, Muslims and Croats in Bosnia reached a ceasefire and signed an accord to create a Muslim–Croat confederation; the Serbs, however, controlled over 70 percent of the country, and fighting continued. A negotiated peace among the Serbs, Muslims, and Croats finally was achieved in Dayton, Ohio, in 1995, and an international peacekeeping force of 60,000 troops organized by the North Atlantic Treaty Organization entered the country later that year. The Dayton settlement calls for a multi-ethnic confederated state consisting of two administrative units: the Muslim–Croat Federation and the Serbian Republika Srpska. Elections for central and local political offices were held in September 1996.

TRADE POLICY
Score: 5–Stable (very high level of protectionism)

The governments of Bosnia and Herzegovina have yet to establish fully functioning customs systems, and procedures that do exist are fraught with corruption. Official tariff rates generally average 13 percent for the Muslim–Croat Federation and 28 percent for the Republika Srpska.

TAXATION
Score–Income taxation: 5–Stable (very high tax rates)
Score–Corporate taxation: 5–Stable (very high tax rates)
Final Taxation Score: 5–Stable (very high tax rates)

The top income tax rate generally is 35 percent, and the top corporate tax rate is 30 percent. There also are many other taxes, such as a 20 percent capital gains tax. Local and federal government entities are only beginning to establish tax administration offices, so tax collection is haphazard and applied arbitrarily. Much taxation still takes the form of government confiscation of goods produced by what little economic activity has occurred. Therefore, the true rates are very high.

GOVERNMENT INTERVENTION IN THE ECONOMY
Score: 5–Stable (very high level)

Government consumes almost all current GDP in Bosnia and Herzegovina. With most economic output still going to the military, most revenue is spent before it is collected. Government continues to control most of the enterprises that were confiscated during the war and have yet to be given back to their rightful owners.

1	Hong Kong	1.25	
2	Singapore	1.30	
3	Bahrain	1.70	
4	New Zealand	1.75	
5	Switzerland	1.90	
5	United States	1.90	
7	Luxembourg	1.95	
7	Taiwan	1.95	
7	United Kingdom	1.95	
10	Bahamas	2.00	
10	Ireland	2.00	
12	Australia	2.05	
12	Japan	2.05	
14	Belgium	2.10	
14	Canada	2.10	
14	United Arab Emirates	2.10	
17	Austria	2.15	
17	Chile	2.15	
17	Estonia	2.15	
20	Czech Republic	2.20	
20	Netherlands	2.20	
22	Denmark	2.25	
22	Finland	2.25	
24	Germany	2.30	
24	Iceland	2.30	
24	South Korea	2.30	
27	Norway	2.35	
28	Kuwait	2.40	
28	Malaysia	2.40	
28	Panama	2.40	
28	Thailand	2.40	
32	El Salvador	2.45	
32	Sri Lanka	2.45	
32	Sweden	2.45	
35	France	2.50	
35	Italy	2.50	
35	Spain	2.50	
38	Trinidad and Tobago	2.55	
39	Argentina	2.60	
39	Barbados	2.60	
39	Cyprus	2.60	
39	Jamaica	2.60	
39	Portugal	2.60	
44	Bolivia	2.65	
44	Oman	2.65	
44	Philippines	2.65	
47	Swaziland	2.70	
47	Uruguay	2.70	
49	Botswana	2.75	
49	Jordan	2.75	
49	Namibia	2.75	
49	Tunisia	2.75	
53	Belize	2.80	
53	Costa Rica	2.80	
53	Guatemala	2.80	
53	Israel	2.80	
53	Peru	2.80	
53	Saudi Arabia	2.80	
53	Turkey	2.80	
53	Uganda	2.80	
53	Western Samoa	2.80	
62	Indonesia	2.85	
62	Latvia	2.85	
62	Malta	2.85	
62	Paraguay	2.85	
66	Greece	2.90	
66	Hungary	2.90	
66	South Africa	2.90	
69	Benin	2.95	
69	Ecuador	2.95	
69	Gabon	2.95	
69	Morocco	2.95	
69	Poland	2.95	
74	Colombia	3.00	
74	Ghana	3.00	
74	Lithuania	3.00	
77	Kenya	3.05	
77	Slovak Republic	3.05	

77	Zambia	3.05	
80	Mali	3.10	
80	Mongolia	3.10	
80	Slovenia	3.10	
83	Honduras	3.15	
83	Papua New Guinea	3.15	
85	Djibouti	3.20	
85	Fiji	3.20	
85	Pakistan	3.20	
88	Algeria	3.25	
88	Guinea	3.25	
88	Lebanon	3.25	
88	Mexico	3.25	
88	Senegal	3.25	
88	Tanzania	3.25	
94	Nigeria	3.30	
94	Romania	3.30	
96	Brazil	3.35	
96	Cambodia	3.35	
96	Egypt	3.35	
96	Ivory Coast	3.35	
96	Madagascar	3.35	
96	Moldova	3.35	
102	Nepal	3.40	
103	Cape Verde	3.44	
104	Armenia	3.45	
104	Dominican Republic	3.45	
104	Russia	3.45	
107	Burkina Faso	3.50	
107	Cameroon	3.50	
107	Lesotho	3.50	
107	Nicaragua	3.50	
107	Venezuela	3.50	
112	Gambia	3.60	
112	Guyana	3.60	
114	Bulgaria	3.65	
114	Georgia	3.65	
114	Malawi	3.65	
117	Ethiopia	3.70	
117	India	3.70	
117	Niger	3.70	
120	Albania	3.75	
120	Bangladesh	3.75	
120	China (PRC)	3.75	
120	Congo	3.75	
120	Croatia	3.75	
125	Chad	3.80	
125	Mauritania	3.80	
125	Sierra Leone	3.80	
128	Sierra Leone	3.85	
129	Burundi	3.90	
129	Suriname	3.90	
129	Zimbabwe	3.90	
132	Haiti	4.00	
132	Kyrgyzstan	4.00	
132	Syria	4.00	
135	Belarus	4.05	
136	Kazakstan	4.10	
136	Mozambique	4.10	
136	Yemen	4.10	
139	Sudan	4.20	
140	Myanmar	4.30	
140	Rwanda	4.30	
142	Angola	4.35	
143	Azerbaijan	4.40	
143	Tajikistan	4.40	
145	Turkmenistan	4.50	
146	Uzbekistan	4.55	
147	Congo/Zaire	4.70	
147	Iran	4.70	
147	Libya	4.70	
147	Somalia	4.70	
147	Vietnam	4.70	
152	Bosnia	4.80	
153	Iraq	4.90	
154	Cuba	5.00	
154	Laos	5.00	
154	North Korea	5.00	

Repressed

MONETARY POLICY
Score: 5–Stable (very high level of inflation)

Inflation is chronic. Although official statistics do not exist, most accounts of the monetary situation describe a system with rapidly increasing prices. Although a monetary system has yet to be established to control the printing of money and the supply of currency, the new constitution calls for the creation of a single central bank that would issue currency for the Federation and the Republika Srpska. For the first six years, the central bank would function as a currency board, pegging the value of the currency to a yet-to-be-determined foreign currency. If enacted, this should reduce inflation significantly.

CAPITAL FLOWS AND FOREIGN INVESTMENT
Score: 4–Stable (high barriers)

The current foreign investment code allows for investment in most areas of the economy. In practice, however, investments are allowed on a case-by-case basis. There are restrictions on investment in land, energy, transportation, telecommunications, forestry, public information, and utilities.

BANKING
Score: 5–Stable (very high level of restrictions)

The banking system is in complete disarray. The government owns most banks and controls most financial assets.

WAGE AND PRICE CONTROLS
Score: 4–Stable (high level)

The market alone does not set wages and prices. Price controls continue on public utilities, transportation, and items produced by the state-owned sector. There also are minimum wage laws.

PROPERTY RIGHTS
Score: 5–Stable (very low level of protection)

Private property is not safe in Bosnia and Herzegovina. According to the U.S. Department of State, "The Constitution provides for an independent judiciary, extends the judiciary's independence to the investigative division of the criminal justice system, and establishes a judicial police force that reports directly to the courts. However, the provisions have not yet been implemented, and the executive appears to exercise authority over the judiciary."[1]

REGULATION
Score: 5–Stable (very high level)

Corruption is widespread within many arms of the government, and existing regulations are applied haphazardly. Most regulatory functions and implementation are left to local governments, creating inconsistency and arbitrary enforcement.

BLACK MARKET
Score: 5–Stable (very high level of activity)

Almost all economic output is produced in the black market. According to the U.S. Department of Commerce, "[A]n estimated two-thirds of the labor force is unemployed or working in the informal sector."[2]

NOTES

1. U.S. Department of State, "Bosnia and Herzegovina Country Report on Human Rights Practices for 1996," 1997.
2. U.S. Department of Commerce, "Bosnia-Herzegovina: Annual Report on Prospects for Economic and Social Growth," 1997.

Botswana   2.75

| 1997 Score: **2.85** | 1996 Score: **2.80** | 1995 Score: **3.05** |

Trade	3	Banking	2
Taxation	2.5	Wages and Prices	2
Government Intervention	4	Property Rights	2
Monetary Policy	2	Regulation	3
Foreign Investment	3	Black Market	4

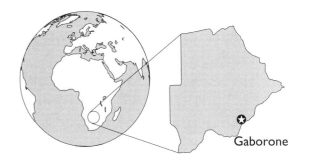

Gaborone

Botswana became a British protectorate in 1885 and gained its independence in 1966. One of the few African countries to experience continuous civilian rule since becoming independent, Botswana operates as a multiparty unitary republic. In the 1980s, led by the mining sector, annual economic growth rates neared 10 percent. This growth has slowed over the past few years, but the economy remains one of the most vibrant in Africa. Being landlocked, Botswana depends on neighboring countries for access to international markets. It is a member of the Southern African Customs Union (SACU), whose member countries accounted for 78 percent of its imports and 14 percent of its exports in 1994. The government has made significant progress in cutting taxes, reforming the banking sector, and curbing the black market. It has further reduced barriers to trade, but also has experienced an increase in black market activity. Botswana's overall score this year is 0.1 point better than it was last year.

TRADE POLICY
Score: 3+ (moderate level of protectionism)

Botswana is part of SACU with South Africa, Lesotho, Swaziland, and Namibia.[1] Its average tariff rate is less than 12 percent, down from around 30 percent in 1992, and there are few, if any, nontariff barriers. As a result, this year's trade score is one point better than last year's.

TAXATION
Score–Income taxation: 2–Stable (low tax rates)
Score–Corporate taxation: 2–Stable (low tax rates)
Final Taxation Score: 2.5–Stable (moderate tax rates)

Botswana recently cut taxes and now has one of southern Africa's lower tax burdens. The top marginal income tax rate is 30 percent, and the average income level is taxed at 0 percent. Botswana also has a 25 percent corporate income tax,[2] a 25 percent capital gains tax, a 10 percent sales tax, and a 12.5 percent tax on such transfers as inheritance.

GOVERNMENT INTERVENTION IN THE ECONOMY
Score: 4–Stable (high level)

Government consumes 28.9 percent of Botswana's GDP, down from 34.9 percent in 1995. The state sector owns a sizable portion of the country's enterprises.

MONETARY POLICY
Score: 2–Stable (low level of inflation)

From 1985 to 1995, Botswana's average annual rate of inflation was 11.6 percent; in 1996, the rate of inflation was 10.1 percent.

1	Hong Kong	1.25	77	Zambia	3.05
2	Singapore	1.30	80	Mali	3.10
3	Bahrain	1.70	80	Mongolia	3.10
4	New Zealand	1.75	80	Slovenia	3.10
5	Switzerland	1.90	83	Honduras	3.15
5	United States	1.90	83	Papua New Guinea	3.15
7	Luxembourg	1.95	85	Djibouti	3.20
7	Taiwan	1.95	85	Fiji	3.20
7	United Kingdom	1.95	85	Pakistan	3.20
10	Bahamas	2.00	88	Algeria	3.25
10	Ireland	2.00	88	Guinea	3.25
12	Australia	2.05	88	Lebanon	3.25
12	Japan	2.05	88	Mexico	3.25
14	Belgium	2.10	88	Senegal	3.25
14	Canada	2.10	88	Tanzania	3.25
14	United Arab Emirates	2.10	94	Nigeria	3.30
17	Austria	2.15	94	Romania	3.30
17	Chile	2.15	96	Brazil	3.35
17	Estonia	2.15	96	Cambodia	3.35
20	Czech Republic	2.20	96	Egypt	3.35
20	Netherlands	2.20	96	Ivory Coast	3.35
22	Denmark	2.25	96	Madagascar	3.35
22	Finland	2.25	96	Moldova	3.35
24	Germany	2.30	102	Nepal	3.40
24	Iceland	2.30	103	Cape Verde	3.44
24	South Korea	2.30	104	Armenia	3.45
27	Norway	2.35	104	Dominican Republic	3.45
28	Kuwait	2.40	104	Russia	3.45
28	Malaysia	2.40	107	Burkina Faso	3.50
28	Panama	2.40	107	Cameroon	3.50
28	Thailand	2.40	107	Lesotho	3.50
32	El Salvador	2.45	107	Nicaragua	3.50
32	Sri Lanka	2.45	107	Venezuela	3.50
32	Sweden	2.45	112	Gambia	3.60
35	France	2.50	112	Guyana	3.60
35	Italy	2.50	114	Bulgaria	3.65
35	Spain	2.50	114	Georgia	3.65
38	Trinidad and Tobago	2.55	114	Malawi	3.65
39	Argentina	2.60	117	Ethiopia	3.70
39	Barbados	2.60	117	India	3.70
39	Cyprus	2.60	117	Niger	3.70
39	Jamaica	2.60	120	Albania	3.75
39	Portugal	2.60	120	Bangladesh	3.75
44	Bolivia	2.65	120	China (PRC)	3.75
44	Oman	2.65	120	Congo	3.75
44	Philippines	2.65	120	Croatia	3.75
47	Swaziland	2.70	125	Chad	3.80
47	Uruguay	2.70	125	Mauritania	3.80
49	Botswana	2.75	125	Ukraine	3.80
49	Jordan	2.75	128	Sierra Leone	3.85
49	Namibia	2.75	129	Burundi	3.90
49	Tunisia	2.75	129	Suriname	3.90
53	Belize	2.80	129	Zimbabwe	3.90
53	Costa Rica	2.80	132	Haiti	4.00
53	Guatemala	2.80	132	Kyrgyzstan	4.00
53	Israel	2.80	132	Syria	4.00
53	Peru	2.80	135	Belarus	4.05
53	Saudi Arabia	2.80	136	Kazakstan	4.10
53	Turkey	2.80	136	Mozambique	4.10
53	Uganda	2.80	136	Yemen	4.10
53	Western Samoa	2.80	139	Sudan	4.20
62	Indonesia	2.85	140	Myanmar	4.30
62	Latvia	2.85	140	Rwanda	4.30
62	Malta	2.85	142	Angola	4.35
62	Paraguay	2.85	143	Azerbaijan	4.40
66	Greece	2.90	143	Tajikistan	4.40
66	Hungary	2.90	145	Turkmenistan	4.50
66	South Africa	2.90	146	Uzbekistan	4.55
69	Benin	2.95	147	Congo/Zaire	4.70
69	Ecuador	2.95	147	Iran	4.70
69	Gabon	2.95	147	Libya	4.70
69	Morocco	2.95	147	Somalia	4.70
69	Poland	2.95	147	Vietnam	4.70
74	Colombia	3.00	152	Bosnia	4.80
74	Ghana	3.00	153	Iraq	4.90
74	Lithuania	3.00	154	Cuba	5.00
77	Kenya	3.05	154	Laos	5.00
77	Slovak Republic	3.05	154	North Korea	5.00

Mostly Free

CAPITAL FLOWS AND FOREIGN INVESTMENT
Score: 3–Stable (moderate barriers)

Some sectors, including most utilities, some smaller retail stores, and some restaurants and bars, are closed to private investment. The requirement that licenses be obtained for expatriate employees can be cumbersome. Botswana permits 100 percent foreign ownership.

BANKING
Score: 2–Stable (low level of restrictions)

Botswana's banking system is both competitive and advanced compared with those of most other African states, and three new foreign-controlled commercial banks have been established. The government, however, plays a significant regulatory role.

WAGE AND PRICE CONTROLS
Score: 2–Stable (low level)

Price controls have been eliminated, but some agriculture prices are established through negotiated agreements with the government.

PROPERTY RIGHTS
Score: 2–Stable (high level of protection)

Property is relatively safe in Botswana, and there is little history of expropriation. Because of financial constraints, however, the court system does not operate efficiently in all cases. According to the U.S. Department of State, "In many instances the judicial system did not provide timely fair trials due to a serious backlog of cases."[3]

REGULATION
Score: 3–Stable (moderate level)

Government bureaucracy often is burdensome. A business license is relatively easy to obtain, but the bureaucracy plays a significant role in running the economy. The government regulates the length of the work week, maternity leave, and standards for hiring and firing. According to the U.S. Department of Commerce, "Low-level governmental corruption exists in Botswana."[4] There is no evidence, however, that this includes bribery. The government recently established an oversight agency to root out corrupt bureaucrats, and has stepped up its efforts to prosecute them. Thus, regulation is moderate by global standards.

BLACK MARKET
Score: 4– (high level of activity)

The elimination of price controls has diminished the level of black market activity, but according to the U.S. Department of Commerce, "Copyright protection is virtually nonexistent in Botswana. The pirating of videos, software, and television programming for local consumption is common."[5] The government recognizes this problem and is working to establish copyright laws and their enforcement, but new statistics show there is a growing informal economy. According to the U.S. Department of State, "Over 50 percent of the population is employed in the informal sector."[6] As a result, Botswana's black market score this year is one point worse than last year.

NOTES
1. The Southern African Customs Union has a common external tariff of 12 percent.
2. The basic corporate tax rate is 15 percent, although some companies are assessed an additional 10 percent.
3. U.S. Department of State, "Botswana Country Report on Human Rights Practices for 1996," 1997.
4. U.S. Department of Commerce, *Country Commercial Guide,* 1997.
5. *Ibid.*
6. U.S. Department of State, "Botswana Country Report on Human Rights Practices for 1996," 1997.

Brazil   3.35

| 1997 Score: **3.35** | 1996 Score: **3.45** | 1995 Score: **3.30** |

Trade	4	Banking	3
Taxation	2.5	Wages and Prices	3
Government Intervention	3	Property Rights	3
Monetary Policy	5	Regulation	3
Foreign Investment	3	Black Market	4

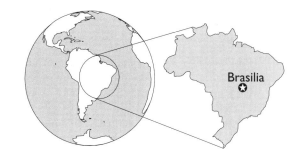

Brasilia ✪

Brazil, once a colony of Portugal, is the largest country in Latin America. Under President Fernando Collor de Mello, who was impeached in 1992, Brazil reduced trade barriers, privatized state-owned enterprises, controlled inflation, and maintained a tight monetary policy. Collor's successor, President Itamar Franco, stalled economic reforms, raised taxes, and increased government control of credit. Current President Fernando Henrique Cardoso has reduced Brazil's tax and tariff rates and has privatized many state-owned businesses. Under Cardoso, Brazil also has launched an ambitious package of trade and economic reforms and has become a leading force for hemispheric trade liberalization.

TRADE POLICY
Score: 4–Stable (high level of protectionism)

Brazil's average tariff rate is 13.6 percent.[1] It also has import licenses and other duties. "Import licenses are now used primarily for statistical purposes and generally are issued automatically within 5 days," reports the U.S. Department of State. "However, obtaining an import license can occasionally still be difficult."[2]

TAXATION
Score–Income taxation: 2–Stable (low tax rates)
Score–Corporate taxation: 2–Stable (low tax rates)
Final Taxation Score: 2.5–Stable (moderate tax rates)

Brazil's top income tax rate is 25 percent, down from 35 percent in 1995. The government determines tax brackets based on a "fiscal unit of reference" that allows it to determine an individual's annual income after factoring in a year's worth of inflation. Theoretically, the government obtains the maximum amount of revenue from income that continuously is losing its value because of inflation. The tax on the average income is 0 percent, and the maximum corporate tax rate is 15 percent, down from 25 percent in 1995. Brazil also has a capital gains tax of 15 percent, a top federal value-added tax of 365.6 percent, a state value-added tax of 7 percent to 25 percent, and a maximum municipal service tax of 10 percent.

GOVERNMENT INTERVENTION IN THE ECONOMY
Score: 3–Stable (moderate level)

Government consumes 15.2 percent of Brazil's GDP. Its privatization program has not reduced the extent of government intervention significantly. The government still owns companies in the petroleum, electricity, mining, railways, and banking sectors, although it gradually is selling some of these assets to private investors.

MONETARY POLICY
Score: 5–Stable (very high level of inflation)

From 1985 to 1995, the annual rate of inflation was 873.8 percent. The government cracked down on inflation in mid-1994, so that the rate decreased to about 16.5 percent in 1996.[3]

1	Hong Kong	1.25	77	Zambia	3.05
2	Singapore	1.30	80	Mali	3.10
3	Bahrain	1.70	80	Mongolia	3.10
4	New Zealand	1.75	80	Slovenia	3.10
5	Switzerland	1.90	83	Honduras	3.15
5	United States	1.90	83	Papua New Guinea	3.15
7	Luxembourg	1.95	85	Djibouti	3.20
7	Taiwan	1.95	85	Fiji	3.20
7	United Kingdom	1.95	85	Pakistan	3.20
10	Bahamas	2.00	88	Algeria	3.25
10	Ireland	2.00	88	Guinea	3.25
12	Australia	2.05	88	Lebanon	3.25
12	Japan	2.05	88	Mexico	3.25
14	Belgium	2.10	88	Senegal	3.25
14	Canada	2.10	88	Tanzania	3.25
14	United Arab Emirates	2.10	94	Nigeria	3.30
17	Austria	2.15	94	Romania	3.30
17	Chile	2.15	96	Brazil	3.35
17	Estonia	2.15	96	Cambodia	3.35
20	Czech Republic	2.20	96	Egypt	3.35
20	Netherlands	2.20	96	Ivory Coast	3.35
22	Denmark	2.25	96	Madagascar	3.35
22	Finland	2.25	96	Moldova	3.35
24	Germany	2.30	102	Nepal	3.40
24	Iceland	2.30	103	Cape Verde	3.44
24	South Korea	2.30	104	Armenia	3.45
27	Norway	2.35	104	Dominican Republic	3.45
28	Kuwait	2.40	104	Russia	3.45
28	Malaysia	2.40	107	Burkina Faso	3.50
28	Panama	2.40	107	Cameroon	3.50
28	Thailand	2.40	107	Lesotho	3.50
32	El Salvador	2.45	107	Nicaragua	3.50
32	Sri Lanka	2.45	107	Venezuela	3.50
32	Sweden	2.45	112	Gambia	3.60
35	France	2.50	112	Guyana	3.60
35	Italy	2.50	114	Bulgaria	3.65
35	Spain	2.50	114	Georgia	3.65
38	Trinidad and Tobago	2.55	114	Malawi	3.65
39	Argentina	2.60	117	Ethiopia	3.70
39	Barbados	2.60	117	India	3.70
39	Cyprus	2.60	117	Niger	3.70
39	Jamaica	2.60	120	Albania	3.75
39	Portugal	2.60	120	Bangladesh	3.75
44	Bolivia	2.65	120	China (PRC)	3.75
44	Oman	2.65	120	Congo	3.75
44	Philippines	2.65	120	Croatia	3.75
47	Swaziland	2.70	125	Chad	3.80
47	Uruguay	2.70	125	Mauritania	3.80
49	Botswana	2.75	125	Ukraine	3.80
49	Jordan	2.75	128	Sierra Leone	3.85
49	Namibia	2.75	129	Burundi	3.90
49	Tunisia	2.75	129	Suriname	3.90
53	Belize	2.80	129	Zimbabwe	3.90
53	Costa Rica	2.80	132	Haiti	4.00
53	Guatemala	2.80	132	Kyrgyzstan	4.00
53	Israel	2.80	132	Syria	4.00
53	Peru	2.80	135	Belarus	4.05
53	Saudi Arabia	2.80	136	Kazakstan	4.10
53	Turkey	2.80	136	Mozambique	4.10
53	Uganda	2.80	136	Yemen	4.10
53	Western Samoa	2.80	139	Sudan	4.20
62	Indonesia	2.85	140	Myanmar	4.30
62	Latvia	2.85	140	Rwanda	4.30
62	Malta	2.85	142	Angola	4.35
62	Paraguay	2.85	143	Azerbaijan	4.40
66	Greece	2.90	143	Tajikistan	4.40
66	Hungary	2.90	145	Turkmenistan	4.50
66	South Africa	2.90	146	Uzbekistan	4.55
69	Benin	2.95	147	Congo/Zaire	4.70
69	Ecuador	2.95	147	Iran	4.70
69	Gabon	2.95	147	Libya	4.70
69	Morocco	2.95	147	Somalia	4.70
69	Poland	2.95	147	Vietnam	4.70
74	Colombia	3.00	152	Bosnia	4.80
74	Ghana	3.00	153	Iraq	4.90
74	Lithuania	3.00	154	Cuba	5.00
77	Kenya	3.05	154	Laos	5.00
77	Slovak Republic	3.05	154	North Korea	5.00

Mostly Unfree

CAPITAL FLOWS AND FOREIGN INVESTMENT
Score: 3–Stable (moderate barriers)

Restrictions on investment in the service industries can be high. The ability of foreigners to invest in petroleum, banking, insurance, and mining is limited, and other forms of investment (for example, in transportation, utilities, media, real estate, and shipping) are prohibited. Brazil's Congress recently passed a new foreign investment law, however, that allows equal treatment for domestic and foreign firms and opens the overall economy to increased foreign investment.

BANKING
Score: 3–Stable (moderate level of restrictions)

Most banks are restricted in their ability to add branches or do business with state-owned companies. Private banks, both foreign and domestic, must compete with a substantial number of state-owned banks.

WAGE AND PRICE CONTROLS
Score: 3–Stable (moderate level)

Brazil has a long history of wage and price controls. It last froze prices in 1990 but has been easing controls gradually since that time. Price controls remain in effect on a variety of goods and services, however, including some foodstuffs, and many prices of products manufactured by state-owned companies also are controlled.

PROPERTY RIGHTS
Score: 3–Stable (moderate level of protection)

There is little chance that private property belonging to foreign investors will be expropriated in Brazil, where a number of major multinational corporations operate and the government is trying to attract additional foreign investment. The court system often is inefficient. According to the U.S. Department of State, "The judiciary has a large case backlog and is often unable to ensure the right to a fair trial. Justice is slow and often unreliable, especially in rural areas where powerful landowners use violence to settle land disputes and influence the local judiciary."[4]

REGULATION
Score: 3–Stable (moderate level)

Government regulation has begun to fall from its previously high level, and is now moderate by global standards. But environmental, health, consumer, labor, financial, and other regulations still restrain business activity, and they frequently are not applied evenly or consistently. "Although some administrative improvements have been made in recent years," reports the U.S. Department of Commerce, "the Brazilian legal and regulatory system is far from transparent. The government has historically exercised considerable control over private business through extensive and frequently changing regulations."[5]

BLACK MARKET
Score: 4–Stable (high level of activity)

Black market activity is increasing. According to the Office of the U.S. Trade Representative, the "new [intellectual property rights] law improves many aspects of Brazil's industrial property regime, but some problems remain."[6] There is significant pirating of patented and copyrighted materials. The U.S. Department of Commerce also reports a growing black market in labor: as much as 35 percent of the country's GDP is produced by such black market activities.[7]

NOTES

1. Office of the United States Trade Representative, *1997 National Trade Estimate Report on Foreign Trade Barriers.*
2. U.S. Department of State, *Country Reports on Economic Policy and Trade Practices,* 1997, p. 217.
3. Based on the consumer price index.
4. U.S. Department of State, "Brazil Country Report on Human Rights Practices for 1996," 1997.
5. U.S. Department of Commerce, *Country Commercial Guide,* 1997.
6. U.S. Department of State, *Country Reports on Economic Policy and Trade Practices,* 1997, pp. 213–219.
7. U.S. Department of Commerce, "Brazil–Sao Paulo Informal Market," *Market Research Reports,* November 1, 1996.

Bulgaria

3.65

Trade	4	Banking	3
Taxation	4.5	Wages and Prices	3
Government Intervention	3	Property Rights	3
Monetary Policy	5	Regulation	4
Foreign Investment	3	Black Market	4

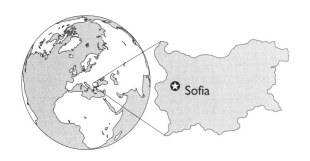

⊗ Sofia

Bulgaria began to move away from communism after the fall of the Berlin Wall in 1989, finally succeeding in 1991. Pressure to slow the pace of economic reform is growing because of economic hardship, and a substantial slowdown followed the 1994 elections, which returned a neocommunist majority to parliament and brought in a cabinet controlled by former members of the Communist Party. But popular discontent swept the neocommunists out of power in the presidential and parliamentary elections of 1997. Although Bulgaria remains behind the Czech Republic, Hungary, and Poland in economic reforms, it has made progress in restoring land to its original owners and in privatizing small businesses, primarily in the trade and services sectors. Major privatization and liberalization initiatives are under way, although recent evidence indicates that tariffs are higher than previously thought. Bulgaria's overall score this year is 0.05 point worse than it was last year.

TRADE POLICY

Score: 4– (high level of protectionism)

Bulgaria's average tariff rate is 17.97 percent.[1] Neither the Office of the U.S. Trade Representative nor the U.S. Department of State reports any nontariff barriers.

TAXATION

Score–Income taxation: 4+ (high tax rates)
Score–Corporate taxation: 4–Stable (high tax rates)
Final Taxation Score: 4.5+ (very high tax rates)

Bulgaria's top income tax rate is 50 percent. The average income level is taxed at 20 percent, down from 33 percent last year, and the top corporate tax rate is 36 percent, down from 40 percent last year. This year's taxation score is one-half point better than last year's. Bulgaria also has a 22 percent value-added tax.

GOVERNMENT INTERVENTION IN THE ECONOMY

Score: 3–Stable (moderate level)

Government consumption of Bulgaria's GDP is 15 percent and falling.[2] Some smaller businesses have been privatized, but most large state-owned industries have yet to be sold to the private sector. According to the U.S. Department of State, "The privatization process is often non-transparent and major deals are frequently accompanied by controversy."[3]

MONETARY POLICY

Score: 5–Stable (very high level of inflation)

The rate of inflation was between 110 percent and 120 percent in 1994. It fell to 35 percent in 1995 but then jumped back up to 123 percent in 1996. Bulgaria recently adopted a currency board that has pegged its local currency to the German mark. This limits the government's ability to finance budget deficits by printing money, and may result in lower rates of inflation in the future.

1	Hong Kong	1.25		77	Zambia	3.05
2	Singapore	1.30		80	Mali	3.10
3	Bahrain	1.70		80	Mongolia	3.10
4	New Zealand	1.75		80	Slovenia	3.10
5	Switzerland	1.90		83	Honduras	3.15
5	United States	1.90		83	Papua New Guinea	3.15
7	Luxembourg	1.95		85	Djibouti	3.20
7	Taiwan	1.95		85	Fiji	3.20
7	United Kingdom	1.95		85	Pakistan	3.20
10	Bahamas	2.00		88	Algeria	3.25
10	Ireland	2.00		88	Guinea	3.25
12	Australia	2.05		88	Lebanon	3.25
12	Japan	2.05		88	Mexico	3.25
14	Belgium	2.10		88	Senegal	3.25
14	Canada	2.10		88	Tanzania	3.25
14	United Arab Emirates	2.10		94	Nigeria	3.30
17	Austria	2.15		94	Romania	3.30
17	Chile	2.15		96	Brazil	3.35
17	Estonia	2.15		96	Cambodia	3.35
20	Czech Republic	2.20		96	Egypt	3.35
20	Netherlands	2.20		96	Ivory Coast	3.35
22	Denmark	2.25		96	Madagascar	3.35
22	Finland	2.25		96	Moldova	3.35
24	Germany	2.30		102	Nepal	3.40
24	Iceland	2.30		103	Cape Verde	3.44
24	South Korea	2.30		104	Armenia	3.45
27	Norway	2.35		104	Dominican Republic	3.45
28	Kuwait	2.40		104	Russia	3.45
28	Malaysia	2.40		107	Burkina Faso	3.50
28	Panama	2.40		107	Cameroon	3.50
28	Thailand	2.40		107	Lesotho	3.50
32	El Salvador	2.45		107	Nicaragua	3.50
32	Sri Lanka	2.45		107	Venezuela	3.50
32	Sweden	2.45		112	Gambia	3.60
35	France	2.50		112	Guyana	3.60
35	Italy	2.50		114	Bulgaria	3.65
35	Spain	2.50		114	Georgia	3.65
38	Trinidad and Tobago	2.55		114	Malawi	3.65
39	Argentina	2.60		117	Ethiopia	3.70
39	Barbados	2.60		117	India	3.70
39	Cyprus	2.60		117	Niger	3.70
39	Jamaica	2.60		120	Albania	3.75
39	Portugal	2.60		120	Bangladesh	3.75
44	Bolivia	2.65		120	China (PRC)	3.75
44	Oman	2.65		120	Congo	3.75
44	Philippines	2.65		120	Croatia	3.75
47	Swaziland	2.70		125	Chad	3.80
47	Uruguay	2.70		125	Mauritania	3.80
49	Botswana	2.75		125	Ukraine	3.80
49	Jordan	2.75		128	Sierra Leone	3.85
49	Namibia	2.75		129	Burundi	3.90
49	Tunisia	2.75		129	Suriname	3.90
53	Belize	2.80		129	Zimbabwe	3.90
53	Costa Rica	2.80		132	Haiti	4.00
53	Guatemala	2.80		132	Kyrgyzstan	4.00
53	Israel	2.80		132	Syria	4.00
53	Peru	2.80		135	Belarus	4.05
53	Saudi Arabia	2.80		136	Kazakstan	4.10
53	Turkey	2.80		136	Mozambique	4.10
53	Uganda	2.80		136	Yemen	4.10
53	Western Samoa	2.80		139	Sudan	4.20
62	Indonesia	2.85		140	Myanmar	4.30
62	Latvia	2.85		140	Rwanda	4.30
62	Malta	2.85		142	Angola	4.35
62	Paraguay	2.85		143	Azerbaijan	4.40
66	Greece	2.90		143	Tajikistan	4.40
66	Hungary	2.90		145	Turkmenistan	4.50
66	South Africa	2.90		146	Uzbekistan	4.55
69	Benin	2.95		147	Congo/Zaire	4.70
69	Ecuador	2.95		147	Iran	4.70
69	Gabon	2.95		147	Libya	4.70
69	Morocco	2.95		147	Somalia	4.70
69	Poland	2.95		147	Vietnam	4.70
74	Colombia	3.00		152	Bosnia	4.80
74	Ghana	3.00		153	Iraq	4.90
74	Lithuania	3.00		154	Cuba	5.00
77	Kenya	3.05		154	Laos	5.00
77	Slovak Republic	3.05		154	North Korea	5.00

Mostly Unfree

CAPITAL FLOWS AND FOREIGN INVESTMENT
Score: 3–Stable (moderate)

Bulgaria has a nonrestrictive foreign investment code and claims foreign investment is welcome. Tax incentives are offered in some cases, there are no restrictions on foreign ownership, and requirements for local content of goods and services produced in Bulgaria have been eliminated. A well-entrenched bureaucracy remains the most significant obstacle to foreign investment, which until recently also was discouraged by the large state-owned sector and weak infrastructure. Some Western companies have complained of a growing demand for bribes and kickbacks. According to the U.S. Department of State, "U.S. firms complain that the inflexible or rigid enforcement of tax and other regulations inhibits investment plans."[4] By global standards, Bulgaria subscribes to an established foreign investment code, and its restrictions on foreign investment are considered moderate.

BANKING
Score: 3–Stable (moderate level of restrictions)

Foreign participation in Bulgarian banks requires permission from the government, which still owns seven large banks that hold most of the country's industrial assets. A law postponing debt payments to private Western commercial banks has hindered the willingness of foreign banks to move into Bulgaria. A few banks from the Netherlands, Austria, and Greece have set up branches nevertheless.

WAGE AND PRICE CONTROLS
Score: 3–Stable (moderate level)

Despite attempts to adopt a free market, Bulgaria still has a mixed economy. Government-owned corporations supply subsidized raw materials to companies, thereby affecting the end prices of goods and services. Several items (mainly electricity, heating, domestic coal, postal services, and tobacco products) remain subject to price controls. Bulgaria has a minimum wage.

PROPERTY RIGHTS
Score: 3–Stable (moderate level of protection)

Private property has gained greater protection from a legal code and an increasingly efficient legal system. There is a lack of progress, however, in both land privatization and the protection of real estate ownership. According to the U.S. Department of State, "The judicial system is independent but continues to struggle with structural and staffing problems."[5]

REGULATION
Score: 4–Stable (high level)

Bureaucrats held over from the communist era impose a significant burden on businesses. According to the U.S. Department of Commerce, "Racketeering and corruption are reportedly escalating. Among some state-owned companies, assets have been siphoned-off by unscrupulous management as the enterprises await privatization."[6] Licenses occasionally require a bribe, and many businesses complain of an arbitrary bureaucracy that applies regulations haphazardly. This confusion often results in conflicting information from different government agencies.

BLACK MARKET
Score: 4–Stable (high level of activity)

Because economic reforms have yet to establish themselves fully, Bulgaria's black market still involves many activities like construction, transportation, and food production. The government estimates that as much as one-third of the active labor force is engaged in the black market. Even though Bulgaria maintains laws to protect intellectual property, enforcement is lax, and there is substantial black market activity in such pirated materials as computer software and prerecorded music and video.

NOTES

1. The score in this factor has changed from 3 in 1997 to 4 in 1998. Previously unavailable data provide a more accurate understanding of the country's performance. This average tariff rate is based on official statistics from Bulgaria's government. The methodology for this factor remains the same.
2. World Bank, *World Development Report 1997*.
3. U.S. Department of State, *Country Reports on Economic Policy and Trade Practices*, 1997, p. 98.
4. *Ibid.*
5. U.S. Department of State, "Bulgaria Country Report on Human Rights Practices for 1996," 1997.
6. U.S. Department of Commerce, *Country Commercial Guide*, 1997.

Burkina Faso   3.50

Ouagadougou

| 1997 Score: **3.50** | 1996 Score: **3.70** | 1995 Score: **n/a** |

Trade	5	Banking	4
Taxation	4	Wages and Prices	4
Government Intervention	3	Property Rights	3
Monetary Policy	1	Regulation	4
Foreign Investment	2	Black Market	5

Burkina Faso, formerly Upper Volta, gained its independence from France in 1960. Over 80 percent of this landlocked country's population depends on subsistence agriculture; and because it must import nearly all its consumer goods, capital goods, and fuel, the country has a chronic trade deficit. Although the government instituted a significant economic reform program in 1991 outlining its plans to limit government spending and privatize several state-owned industries, many restrictions on economic freedom continue, and there has been little progress.

TRADE POLICY
Score: 5–Stable (very high level of protectionism)

Among other taxes, Burkina Faso imposes a 5 percent customs fee, a variable import duty, a variable value-added tax, a 4 percent statistical tax (an administrative fee), a 1 percent solidarity tax, and a 1 percent tax to support government enforcement of trade laws. All these taxes bring the average tariff rate to over 15 percent of an imported item's value. Burkina Faso also maintains some import bans and quotas.

TAXATION
Score–Income taxation: 3–Stable (moderate tax rates)
Score–Corporate taxation: 4–Stable (high tax rates)
Final Taxation Score: 4–Stable (high tax rates)

Burkina Faso has a top income tax rate of 35 percent and a top marginal corporate tax rate of 45 percent. It also maintains a 25 percent capital gains tax as well as real estate and other taxes.

GOVERNMENT INTERVENTION IN THE ECONOMY
Score: 3–Stable (moderate level)

Government consumes about 14.5 percent of Burkina Faso's GDP. There is a significant public sector.

MONETARY POLICY
Score: 1–Stable (very low level of inflation)

Burkina Faso had an average inflation rate of 2.5 percent from 1985 to 1995. The inflation rate for 1996 is unavailable.

CAPITAL FLOWS AND FOREIGN INVESTMENT
Score: 2–Stable (low barriers)

There are few restrictions on investment in Burkina Faso. In 1992, the government adopted a new investment code that treats foreign and domestic firms equally. Some tax incentives are granted. Corruption remains a problem, however.

1	Hong Kong	1.25		77	Zambia	3.05
2	Singapore	1.30		80	Mali	3.10
3	Bahrain	1.70		80	Mongolia	3.10
4	New Zealand	1.75		80	Slovenia	3.10
5	Switzerland	1.90		83	Honduras	3.15
5	United States	1.90		83	Papua New Guinea	3.15
7	Luxembourg	1.95		85	Djibouti	3.20
7	Taiwan	1.95		85	Fiji	3.20
7	United Kingdom	1.95		85	Pakistan	3.20
10	Bahamas	2.00		88	Algeria	3.25
10	Ireland	2.00		88	Guinea	3.25
12	Australia	2.05		88	Lebanon	3.25
12	Japan	2.05		88	Mexico	3.25
14	Belgium	2.10		88	Senegal	3.25
14	Canada	2.10		88	Tanzania	3.25
14	United Arab Emirates	2.10		94	Nigeria	3.30
17	Austria	2.15		94	Romania	3.30
17	Chile	2.15		96	Brazil	3.35
17	Estonia	2.15		96	Cambodia	3.35
20	Czech Republic	2.20		96	Egypt	3.35
20	Netherlands	2.20		96	Ivory Coast	3.35
22	Denmark	2.25		96	Madagascar	3.35
22	Finland	2.25		96	Moldova	3.35
24	Germany	2.30		102	Nepal	3.40
24	Iceland	2.30		103	Cape Verde	3.44
24	South Korea	2.30		104	Armenia	3.45
27	Norway	2.35		104	Dominican Republic	3.45
28	Kuwait	2.40		104	Russia	3.45
28	Malaysia	2.40		107	Burkina Faso	3.50
28	Panama	2.40		107	Cameroon	3.50
28	Thailand	2.40		107	Lesotho	3.50
32	El Salvador	2.45		107	Nicaragua	3.50
32	Sri Lanka	2.45		107	Venezuela	3.50
32	Sweden	2.45		112	Gambia	3.60
35	France	2.50		112	Guyana	3.60
35	Italy	2.50		114	Bulgaria	3.65
35	Spain	2.50		114	Georgia	3.65
38	Trinidad and Tobago	2.55		114	Malawi	3.65
39	Argentina	2.60		117	Ethiopia	3.70
39	Barbados	2.60		117	India	3.70
39	Cyprus	2.60		117	Niger	3.70
39	Jamaica	2.60		120	Albania	3.75
39	Portugal	2.60		120	Bangladesh	3.75
44	Bolivia	2.65		120	China (PRC)	3.75
44	Oman	2.65		120	Congo	3.75
44	Philippines	2.65		120	Croatia	3.75
47	Swaziland	2.70		125	Chad	3.80
47	Uruguay	2.70		125	Mauritania	3.80
49	Botswana	2.75		125	Ukraine	3.80
49	Jordan	2.75		128	Sierra Leone	3.85
49	Namibia	2.75		129	Burundi	3.90
49	Tunisia	2.75		129	Suriname	3.90
53	Belize	2.80		129	Zimbabwe	3.90
53	Costa Rica	2.80		132	Haiti	4.00
53	Guatemala	2.80		132	Kyrgyzstan	4.00
53	Israel	2.80		132	Syria	4.00
53	Peru	2.80		135	Belarus	4.05
53	Saudi Arabia	2.80		136	Kazakstan	4.10
53	Turkey	2.80		136	Mozambique	4.10
53	Uganda	2.80		136	Yemen	4.10
53	Western Samoa	2.80		139	Sudan	4.20
62	Indonesia	2.85		140	Myanmar	4.30
62	Latvia	2.85		140	Rwanda	4.30
62	Malta	2.85		142	Angola	4.35
62	Paraguay	2.85		143	Azerbaijan	4.40
66	Greece	2.90		143	Tajikistan	4.40
66	Hungary	2.90		145	Turkmenistan	4.50
66	South Africa	2.90		146	Uzbekistan	4.55
69	Benin	2.95		147	Congo/Zaire	4.70
69	Ecuador	2.95		147	Iran	4.70
69	Gabon	2.95		147	Libya	4.70
69	Morocco	2.95		147	Somalia	4.70
69	Poland	2.95		147	Vietnam	4.70
74	Colombia	3.00		152	Bosnia	4.80
74	Ghana	3.00		153	Iraq	4.90
74	Lithuania	3.00		154	Cuba	5.00
77	Kenya	3.05		154	Laos	5.00
77	Slovak Republic	3.05		154	North Korea	5.00

Mostly Unfree

BANKING
Score: 4–Stable (high level of restrictions)

The government heavily regulates and controls the banking system through direct ownership of many banks. There are plans, however, to privatize some of these banks.

WAGE AND PRICE CONTROLS
Score: 4–Stable (high level)

Wages and prices in Burkina Faso are affected mainly by significant government involvement in the economy. The government continues to subsidize many domestically produced products.

PROPERTY RIGHTS
Score: 3–Stable (moderate level of protection)

Private property in Burkina Faso is subject to government expropriation, and some cases can take years to resolve. The U.S. Department of Commerce reports that "Burkina Faso has a legal system which protects and facilitates acquisition and disposition of all property rights, including intellectual property."[1] According to the U.S. Department of State, "The Constitution provides for an independent judiciary; however, in practice it is subject to executive branch influence."[2]

REGULATION
Score: 4–Stable (high level)

Establishing a business in Burkina Faso can be difficult if the business intends to compete with a state-owned company. Regulations can be applied unevenly and inconsistently.

BLACK MARKET
Score: 5–Stable (very high level of activity)

The black market in Burkina Faso, by some estimates, comprises almost half the formal economy. According to the U.S. Department of Commerce, "The tertiary sector, contributing about 41 percent in value added to the economy, is poised for growth. This sector is dominated by the so-called 'informal sector' (70 percent)."[3]

NOTES

1. U.S. Department of Commerce, *Country Commercial Guide,* 1997.
2. U.S. Department of State, "Burkina Faso Country Report on Human Rights Practices for 1996," 1997.
3. *Ibid.*

Burundi   3.90

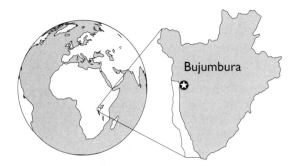

Bujumbura

1997 Score: **3.80**	1996 Score: **n/a**	1995 Score: **n/a**

Trade	5	Banking	4
Taxation	4	Wages and Prices	4
Government Intervention	3	Property Rights	4
Monetary Policy	2	Regulation	4
Foreign Investment	4	Black Market	5

Burundi gained its independence from a Belgian-administered United Nations trusteeship in 1962. The economy is primarily agricultural, with over 80 percent of the population engaged in subsistence farming. After gaining its independence, Burundi was one of the poorest countries in sub-Saharan Africa and quickly became embroiled in civil unrest and political instability. Today, the government is trying to attract foreign investment. It struggles to develop a market system, but this is secondary to establishing a stable political system. There was a coup d'état in 1996, and ethnic tension and violence continue. Economic growth has averaged about -9.0 percent from 1993 to 1995, and per capita GNP was estimated to be only $160 in 1995. The rate of inflation also is on the rise. As a result, Burundi's overall score this year is 0.1 point worse than it was last year.

Trade Policy
Score: 5–Stable (very high level of protectionism)

Burundi's average tariff rate was 60 percent from 1990 to 1993, but the most significant barriers to trade remain ethnic conflict and unstable borders. "In light of continuing ethnic/political tensions," reports the U.S. Department of Commerce, "all areas of the country are potentially unstable. Politically motivated urban terrorism is a threat in Bujumbura, where land mines have exploded in a number of areas frequented by Americans. Sporadic violence also remains a problem in the interior where large numbers of displaced persons are encamped or in hiding."[1]

Taxation
Score–Income taxation: 4–Stable (high tax rates)
Score–Corporate taxation: 4–Stable (high tax rates)
Final Taxation Score: 4–Stable (high tax rates)

Tax revenue as a percentage of GDP has averaged over 20 percent since 1990.[2] Tax evasion is pervasive, indicating that the actual tax burden is quite high.

Government Intervention in the Economy
Score: 3–Stable (moderate level)

Government consumes about 12 percent of Burundi's GDP,[3] and the public sector generates most GDP overall. Burundi also has a large number of state-owned companies.

Monetary Policy
Score: 2– (low level of inflation)

Burundi's inflation rate in 1995 was over 6 percent, up from an average annual rate of 5.2 percent from 1985 to 1994. As a result, Burundi's score is one point worse this year. Inflation rates were not available for 1996.

1	Hong Kong	1.25	77	Zambia	3.05
2	Singapore	1.30	80	Mali	3.10
3	Bahrain	1.70	80	Mongolia	3.10
4	New Zealand	1.75	80	Slovenia	3.10
5	Switzerland	1.90	83	Honduras	3.15
5	United States	1.90	83	Papua New Guinea	3.15
7	Luxembourg	1.95	85	Djibouti	3.20
7	Taiwan	1.95	85	Fiji	3.20
7	United Kingdom	1.95	85	Pakistan	3.20
10	Bahamas	2.00	88	Algeria	3.25
10	Ireland	2.00	88	Guinea	3.25
12	Australia	2.05	88	Lebanon	3.25
12	Japan	2.05	88	Mexico	3.25
14	Belgium	2.10	88	Senegal	3.25
14	Canada	2.10	88	Tanzania	3.25
14	United Arab Emirates	2.10	94	Nigeria	3.30
17	Austria	2.15	94	Romania	3.30
17	Chile	2.15	96	Brazil	3.35
17	Estonia	2.15	96	Cambodia	3.35
20	Czech Republic	2.20	96	Egypt	3.35
20	Netherlands	2.20	96	Ivory Coast	3.35
22	Denmark	2.25	96	Madagascar	3.35
22	Finland	2.25	96	Moldova	3.35
24	Germany	2.30	102	Nepal	3.40
24	Iceland	2.30	103	Cape Verde	3.44
24	South Korea	2.30	104	Armenia	3.45
27	Norway	2.35	104	Dominican Republic	3.45
28	Kuwait	2.40	104	Russia	3.45
28	Malaysia	2.40	107	Burkina Faso	3.50
28	Panama	2.40	107	Cameroon	3.50
28	Thailand	2.40	107	Lesotho	3.50
32	El Salvador	2.45	107	Nicaragua	3.50
32	Sri Lanka	2.45	107	Venezuela	3.50
32	Sweden	2.45	112	Gambia	3.60
35	France	2.50	112	Guyana	3.60
35	Italy	2.50	114	Bulgaria	3.65
35	Spain	2.50	114	Georgia	3.65
38	Trinidad and Tobago	2.55	114	Malawi	3.65
39	Argentina	2.60	117	Ethiopia	3.70
39	Barbados	2.60	117	India	3.70
39	Cyprus	2.60	117	Niger	3.70
39	Jamaica	2.60	120	Albania	3.75
39	Portugal	2.60	120	Bangladesh	3.75
44	Bolivia	2.65	120	China (PRC)	3.75
44	Oman	2.65	120	Congo	3.75
44	Philippines	2.65	120	Croatia	3.75
47	Swaziland	2.70	125	Chad	3.80
47	Uruguay	2.70	125	Mauritania	3.80
49	Botswana	2.75	125	Ukraine	3.80
49	Jordan	2.75	128	Sierra Leone	3.85
49	Namibia	2.75	129	Burundi	3.90
49	Tunisia	2.75	129	Suriname	3.90
53	Belize	2.80	129	Zimbabwe	3.90
53	Costa Rica	2.80	132	Haiti	4.00
53	Guatemala	2.80	132	Kyrgyzstan	4.00
53	Israel	2.80	132	Syria	4.00
53	Peru	2.80	135	Belarus	4.05
53	Saudi Arabia	2.80	136	Kazakstan	4.10
53	Turkey	2.80	136	Mozambique	4.10
53	Uganda	2.80	136	Yemen	4.10
53	Western Samoa	2.80	139	Sudan	4.20
62	Indonesia	2.85	140	Myanmar	4.30
62	Latvia	2.85	140	Rwanda	4.30
62	Malta	2.85	142	Angola	4.35
62	Paraguay	2.85	143	Azerbaijan	4.40
66	Greece	2.90	143	Tajikistan	4.40
66	Hungary	2.90	145	Turkmenistan	4.50
66	South Africa	2.90	146	Uzbekistan	4.55
69	Benin	2.95	147	Congo/Zaire	4.70
69	Ecuador	2.95	147	Iran	4.70
69	Gabon	2.95	147	Libya	4.70
69	Morocco	2.95	147	Somalia	4.70
69	Poland	2.95	147	Vietnam	4.70
74	Colombia	3.00	152	Bosnia	4.80
74	Ghana	3.00	153	Iraq	4.90
74	Lithuania	3.00	154	Cuba	5.00
77	Kenya	3.05	154	Laos	5.00
77	Slovak Republic	3.05	154	North Korea	5.00

Mostly Unfree

CAPITAL FLOWS AND FOREIGN INVESTMENT
Score: 4–Stable (high barriers)

Burundi treats domestic and foreign firms equally and actively seeks investment. But it remains a country in turmoil. The most significant barriers to investment remain underdeveloped financial institutions, unsafe conditions, and insecure borders.

BANKING
Score: 4–Stable (high level of restrictions)

The banking system is heavily controlled by the government and is severely underdeveloped.

WAGE AND PRICE CONTROLS
Score: 4–Stable (high level)

Wages and prices in Burundi are affected by a large public sector, import substitution policies, and government subsidies.

PROPERTY RIGHTS
Score: 4–Stable (low level of protection)

Private property in Burundi is subject to government expropriation and armed bandits. The government is attempting to privatize many state-owned enterprises, but crime and theft remain problems. According to the U.S. Department of State, "The decree of September 13 provides for an independent judiciary, but in practice the judiciary is dominated by Tutsis.... Besides the frequent lack of counsel...other major shortcomings in the legal system include a lack of adequate resources and trained personnel, and an outmoded legal code."[4]

REGULATION
Score: 4–Stable (high level)

Establishing a business in Burundi is difficult because of a massive and corrupt bureaucracy. Bribery sometimes is present, as is embezzlement by government officials.

BLACK MARKET
Score: 5–Stable (very high level of activity)

Burundi's black market is larger than the formal market and growing. Most of this activity occurs in smuggled consumer goods, labor, and pirated intellectual property.

NOTES

1. U.S. Department of Commerce, "Burundi, Travel Conditions," *Market Research Reports*, April 15, 1997.
2. Tax rates for Burundi were not available; therefore, the author relies on total tax revenues as a percentage of the overall economy.
3. World Bank, *World Development Report 1997*.
4. U.S. Department of State, "Burundi Country Report on Human Rights Practices for 1996," 1997.

Cambodia 3.35

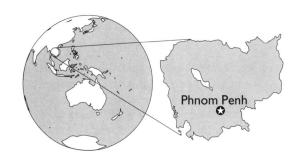
Phnom Penh

1997 Score: **3.55**	1996 Score: **n/a**	1995 Score: **n/a**

Trade	3	Banking	3
Taxation	2.5	Wages and Prices	3
Government Intervention	3	Property Rights	4
Monetary Policy	5	Regulation	4
Foreign Investment	3	Black Market	3

Since 1945, Cambodia has been ruled by France, a Cambodian monarch, and a military regime. After the United States ended its military and economic aid, the Khmer Rouge took power and killed over 1 million people. In 1979, Vietnam invaded Cambodia and installed its puppet Cambodia People's Party (CPP) in Phnom Penh. The CPP was opposed by remnants of the Khmer Rouge and Western-backed noncommunist factions in a war that continued until the 1991 Paris Peace Agreement, which called for a transitional government to be run by the United Nations until elections could be held in 1993. The 1993 elections saw the defeat of the CPP by the royalist party of Prince Ranariddh, but the CPP managed to force a coalition government on Ranariddh. This government was overthrown by a coup d'état in 1997. Before the coup, some progress had been made. As a result, Cambodia's overall score this year is 0.2 point better than it was last year.

TRADE POLICY
Score: 3+ (moderate level of protectionism)

Cambodia's average tariff is 8.5 percent.[1] Import licenses have been abolished for most items but remain in effect for pharmaceuticals.

TAXATION
Score–Income taxation: 2–Stable (low tax rates)
Score–Corporate taxation: 2–Stable (low tax rates)
Final Taxation Score: 2.5–Stable (moderate tax rates)

Cambodia's top marginal income tax rate is 20 percent;[2] its top corporate income tax rate is also 20 percent. Cambodia also has a 4 percent sales tax as well as other taxes.

GOVERNMENT INTERVENTION IN THE ECONOMY
Score: 3+ (moderate level)

The government consumes 20 percent of Cambodia's GDP.[3] The government sector also produces most of the country's GDP.

MONETARY POLICY
Score: 5– (very high level of inflation)

Between 1985 and 1995, Cambodia's average annual rate of inflation was 70.5 percent.[4] In 1996, the inflation rate was 10 percent.

CAPITAL FLOWS AND FOREIGN INVESTMENT
Score: 3–Stable (moderate barriers)

For the most part, Cambodia welcomes foreign investment. It treats foreign and domestic firms equally and has an established foreign investment code. Most foreign investments still must be approved by the government, however.

1	Hong Kong	1.25	77	Zambia	3.05
2	Singapore	1.30	80	Mali	3.10
3	Bahrain	1.70	80	Mongolia	3.10
4	New Zealand	1.75	80	Slovenia	3.10
5	Switzerland	1.90	83	Honduras	3.15
5	United States	1.90	83	Papua New Guinea	3.15
7	Luxembourg	1.95	85	Djibouti	3.20
7	Taiwan	1.95	85	Fiji	3.20
7	United Kingdom	1.95	85	Pakistan	3.20
10	Bahamas	2.00	88	Algeria	3.25
10	Ireland	2.00	88	Guinea	3.25
12	Australia	2.05	88	Lebanon	3.25
12	Japan	2.05	88	Mexico	3.25
14	Belgium	2.10	88	Senegal	3.25
14	Canada	2.10	88	Tanzania	3.25
14	United Arab Emirates	2.10	94	Nigeria	3.30
17	Austria	2.15	94	Romania	3.30
17	Chile	2.15	96	Brazil	3.35
17	Estonia	2.15	96	Cambodia	3.35
20	Czech Republic	2.20	96	Egypt	3.35
20	Netherlands	2.20	96	Ivory Coast	3.35
22	Denmark	2.25	96	Madagascar	3.35
22	Finland	2.25	96	Moldova	3.35
24	Germany	2.30	102	Nepal	3.40
24	Iceland	2.30	103	Cape Verde	3.44
24	South Korea	2.30	104	Armenia	3.45
27	Norway	2.35	104	Dominican Republic	3.45
28	Kuwait	2.40	104	Russia	3.45
28	Malaysia	2.40	107	Burkina Faso	3.50
28	Panama	2.40	107	Cameroon	3.50
28	Thailand	2.40	107	Lesotho	3.50
32	El Salvador	2.45	107	Nicaragua	3.50
32	Sri Lanka	2.45	107	Venezuela	3.50
32	Sweden	2.45	112	Gambia	3.60
35	France	2.50	112	Guyana	3.60
35	Italy	2.50	114	Bulgaria	3.65
35	Spain	2.50	114	Georgia	3.65
38	Trinidad and Tobago	2.55	114	Malawi	3.65
39	Argentina	2.60	117	Ethiopia	3.70
39	Barbados	2.60	117	India	3.70
39	Cyprus	2.60	117	Niger	3.70
39	Jamaica	2.60	120	Albania	3.75
39	Portugal	2.60	120	Bangladesh	3.75
44	Bolivia	2.65	120	China (PRC)	3.75
44	Oman	2.65	120	Congo	3.75
44	Philippines	2.65	120	Croatia	3.75
47	Swaziland	2.70	125	Chad	3.80
47	Uruguay	2.70	125	Mauritania	3.80
49	Botswana	2.75	125	Ukraine	3.80
49	Jordan	2.75	128	Sierra Leone	3.85
49	Namibia	2.75	129	Burundi	3.90
49	Tunisia	2.75	129	Suriname	3.90
53	Belize	2.80	129	Zimbabwe	3.90
53	Costa Rica	2.80	132	Haiti	4.00
53	Guatemala	2.80	132	Kyrgyzstan	4.00
53	Israel	2.80	132	Syria	4.00
53	Peru	2.80	135	Belarus	4.05
53	Saudi Arabia	2.80	136	Kazakstan	4.10
53	Turkey	2.80	136	Mozambique	4.10
53	Uganda	2.80	136	Yemen	4.10
53	Western Samoa	2.80	139	Sudan	4.20
62	Indonesia	2.85	140	Myanmar	4.30
62	Latvia	2.85	140	Rwanda	4.30
62	Malta	2.85	142	Angola	4.35
62	Paraguay	2.85	143	Azerbaijan	4.40
66	Greece	2.90	143	Tajikistan	4.40
66	Hungary	2.90	145	Turkmenistan	4.50
66	South Africa	2.90	146	Uzbekistan	4.55
69	Benin	2.95	147	Congo/Zaire	4.70
69	Ecuador	2.95	147	Iran	4.70
69	Gabon	2.95	147	Libya	4.70
69	Morocco	2.95	147	Somalia	4.70
69	Poland	2.95	147	Vietnam	4.70
74	Colombia	3.00	152	Bosnia	4.80
74	Ghana	3.00	153	Iraq	4.90
74	Lithuania	3.00	154	Cuba	5.00
77	Kenya	3.05	154	Laos	5.00
77	Slovak Republic	3.05	154	North Korea	5.00

Mostly Unfree

BANKING
Score: 3–Stable (moderate level of restrictions)

Cambodia's banking system remains under government influence. There are 2 major state-owned banks and 17 private banks, but the government has plans to privatize its state-owned banks. By global standards, Cambodia's restrictions on banking are moderate.

WAGE AND PRICE CONTROLS
Score: 3–Stable (moderate level)

Most wages and prices are determined by the market. There are some controls on such items as foodstuffs and some energy products. Companies in Cambodia's large state-owned sector receive subsidies that allow them to offer goods and services at artificially low prices.

PROPERTY RIGHTS
Score: 4–Stable (low level of protection)

Cambodia's legal system does not protect private property effectively. "Cambodia's court system is weak," reports the U.S. Department of Commerce. "Judges have been trained either for a short period at home or under other systems of law, have little access to published Cambodian law and, because paid a minimal salary (USD20/month), are susceptible to corruption."[5]

REGULATION
Score: 4–Stable (high level)

Government corruption in Cambodia remains pervasive and often manifests itself in bribes, kickbacks, and payoffs. The bureaucracy is cumbersome and inefficient, making it difficult to open businesses and keep them open.

BLACK MARKET
Score: 3–Stable (moderate level of activity)

Most of Cambodia's black market activity occurs in labor and pirated intellectual property.

NOTES

1. Based on taxes on international trade as a percentage of total imports. The score in this factor has changed from 5 in 1997 to 3 in 1998. Previously unavailable data provide a more accurate understanding of the country's performance. The average tariff rate is from Kingdom of Cambodia, "Financial Law 1997—Annex 3," December 23, 1996. The methodology for this factor remains the same.
2. The tax on the average income level was unavailable. Therefore, Cambodia's score is based solely on the top rate.
3. The score in this factor has changed from 4 in 1997 to 3 in 1998. Previously unavailable data provide a more accurate understanding of the country's performance. The government consumption rate is from Kingdom of Cambodia, "Financial Law 1997—Annex 3," December 23, 1996. The methodology for this factor remains the same.
4. The score in this factor has changed from 4 in 1997 to 5 in 1998. Previously unavailable data provide a more accurate understanding of the country's performance. The average rate of inflation is from World Bank, *World Atlas 1997;* previously, this source had not included this information. The methodology for this factor remains the same.
5. U.S. Department of Commerce, *Country Commercial Guide,* 1997.

Cameroon   3.50

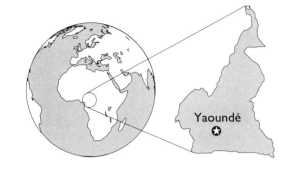

Yaoundé

1997 Score: **3.60**	1996 Score: **3.60**	1995 Score: **3.60**

Trade	5	Banking	4
Taxation	4	Wages and Prices	3
Government Intervention	2	Property Rights	4
Monetary Policy	1	Regulation	4
Foreign Investment	3	Black Market	5

Cameroon gained its independence from a French-administered United Nations trusteeship in 1960. A one-party state was established, and political repression followed. The government legalized opposition parties in 1990, spurred by increasing domestic and international pressure for democratization, and it held elections in 1992. These elections were widely criticized by international observers as flawed. President Paul Biya promised elections in 1997, but has used strong-arm tactics to bolster his chances for reelection and stifle the democratic process. The United States has responded by closing its aid mission. Despite its considerable resources, Cameroon has suffered negative GDP growth from 1987 to 1994. The economy grew in 1995 and 1996, however, possibly because of several instances of privatization and a reduction in government consumption of economic output. As a result, Cameroon's overall score is 0.1 point better this year.

TRADE POLICY
Score: 5–Stable (very high level of protectionism)

Cameroon's average tariff rate is around 28 percent.[1] Almost 40 percent of total government revenue is raised through tariffs, and countervailing and antidumping duties are used to protect inefficient domestic industries. According to the U.S. Department of Commerce, "Customs fraud is endemic in Cameroon and protracted negotiations with customs officers over the value of imported goods are common."[2]

TAXATION
Score–Income taxation: 3–Stable (moderate tax rates)
Score–Corporate taxation: 4–Stable (high tax rates)
Final Taxation Score: 4–Stable (high tax rates)

Cameroon's top income tax rate is 60 percent;[3] but the tax rate on the average income level is 0 percent. The top corporate tax rate is 38.5 percent. Cameroon also has a 38.5 percent capital gains tax and an 18.7 percent turnover tax.

GOVERNMENT INTERVENTION IN THE ECONOMY
Score: 2+ (low level)

The government consumes 9 percent of Cameroon's GDP, down from almost 12 percent.[4] As a result, this year's government intervention score is one point better than last year's. The public sector remains large, however, and privatization has been sluggish and plagued with scandal. The government continues to own enterprises in airline industry, shipping, railroads, and investment funds.

MONETARY POLICY
Score: 1–Stable (very low level of inflation)

From 1985 to 1995, Cameroon's average annual rate of inflation was 2 percent. In 1996, inflation ran around 6 percent.

1	Hong Kong	1.25
2	Singapore	1.30
3	Bahrain	1.70
4	New Zealand	1.75
5	Switzerland	1.90
5	United States	1.90
7	Luxembourg	1.95
7	Taiwan	1.95
7	United Kingdom	1.95
10	Bahamas	2.00
10	Ireland	2.00
12	Australia	2.05
12	Japan	2.05
14	Belgium	2.10
14	Canada	2.10
14	United Arab Emirates	2.10
17	Austria	2.15
17	Chile	2.15
17	Estonia	2.15
20	Czech Republic	2.20
20	Netherlands	2.20
22	Denmark	2.25
22	Finland	2.25
24	Germany	2.30
24	Iceland	2.30
24	South Korea	2.30
27	Norway	2.35
28	Kuwait	2.40
28	Malaysia	2.40
28	Panama	2.40
28	Thailand	2.40
32	El Salvador	2.45
32	Sri Lanka	2.45
32	Sweden	2.45
35	France	2.50
35	Italy	2.50
35	Spain	2.50
38	Trinidad and Tobago	2.55
39	Argentina	2.60
39	Barbados	2.60
39	Cyprus	2.60
39	Jamaica	2.60
39	Portugal	2.60
44	Bolivia	2.65
44	Oman	2.65
44	Philippines	2.65
47	Swaziland	2.70
47	Uruguay	2.70
49	Botswana	2.75
49	Jordan	2.75
49	Namibia	2.75
49	Tunisia	2.75
53	Belize	2.80
53	Costa Rica	2.80
53	Guatemala	2.80
53	Israel	2.80
53	Peru	2.80
53	Saudi Arabia	2.80
53	Turkey	2.80
53	Uganda	2.80
53	Western Samoa	2.80
62	Indonesia	2.85
62	Latvia	2.85
62	Malta	2.85
62	Paraguay	2.85
66	Greece	2.90
66	Hungary	2.90
66	South Africa	2.90
69	Benin	2.95
69	Ecuador	2.95
69	Gabon	2.95
69	Morocco	2.95
69	Poland	2.95
74	Colombia	3.00
74	Ghana	3.00
74	Lithuania	3.00
77	Kenya	3.05
77	Slovak Republic	3.05

77	Zambia	3.05
80	Mali	3.10
80	Mongolia	3.10
80	Slovenia	3.10
83	Honduras	3.15
83	Papua New Guinea	3.15
85	Djibouti	3.20
85	Fiji	3.20
85	Pakistan	3.20
88	Algeria	3.25
88	Guinea	3.25
88	Lebanon	3.25
88	Mexico	3.25
88	Senegal	3.25
88	Tanzania	3.25
94	Nigeria	3.30
94	Romania	3.30
96	Brazil	3.35
96	Cambodia	3.35
96	Egypt	3.35
96	Ivory Coast	3.35
96	Madagascar	3.35
96	Moldova	3.35
102	Nepal	3.40
103	Cape Verde	3.44
104	Armenia	3.45
104	Dominican Republic	3.45
104	Russia	3.45
107	Burkina Faso	3.50
107	Cameroon	3.50
107	Lesotho	3.50
107	Nicaragua	3.50
107	Venezuela	3.50
112	Gambia	3.60
112	Guyana	3.60
114	Bulgaria	3.65
114	Georgia	3.65
114	Malawi	3.65
117	Ethiopia	3.70
117	India	3.70
117	Niger	3.70
120	Albania	3.75
120	Bangladesh	3.75
120	China (PRC)	3.75
120	Congo	3.75
120	Croatia	3.75
125	Chad	3.80
125	Mauritania	3.80
125	Ukraine	3.80
128	Sierra Leone	3.85
129	Burundi	3.90
129	Suriname	3.90
129	Zimbabwe	3.90
132	Haiti	4.00
132	Kyrgyzstan	4.00
132	Syria	4.00
135	Belarus	4.05
136	Kazakhstan	4.10
136	Mozambique	4.10
136	Yemen	4.10
139	Sudan	4.20
140	Myanmar	4.30
140	Rwanda	4.30
142	Angola	4.35
143	Azerbaijan	4.40
143	Tajikistan	4.40
145	Turkmenistan	4.50
146	Uzbekistan	4.55
147	Congo/Zaire	4.70
147	Iran	4.70
147	Libya	4.70
147	Somalia	4.70
147	Vietnam	4.70
152	Bosnia	4.80
153	Iraq	4.90
154	Cuba	5.00
154	Laos	5.00
154	North Korea	5.00

Mostly Unfree

CAPITAL FLOWS AND FOREIGN INVESTMENT
Score: 3–Stable (moderate barriers)

Cameroon is open to foreign investment in most industries, but it remains partial to investments from France and, in some cases, blocks investment from other countries. Its corrupt bureaucracy and unstable legal institutions provide little comfort. Investment is approved on a case-by-case basis. Foreign direct investment is declining because of deteriorating economic conditions. "Cameroon's policies, as defined in law, contain all necessary elements of an open investment regime," reports the U.S. Department of Commerce. "However, current practice does not permit a fair, transparent and impartial implementation of the country's laws and policies."[5]

BANKING
Score: 4–Stable (high level of restrictions)

The banking sector is in crisis. Several state-owned banks are near collapse, and several French banks are reducing their presence. Banks in Cameroon have been influenced heavily by the state and by France. Interest rates, for example, are controlled by the government and often do not reflect market conditions. There also is a domestic banking industry. According to the U.S. Department of Commerce, "The government's role in the troubled banking system has been reduced considerably since 1989 by a series of structural and legal reforms. It remains a major shareholder in most banks and still has considerable influence over the banking sector."[6]

WAGE AND PRICE CONTROLS
Score: 3–Stable (moderate level)

The government controls prices on some items, both by owning and operating enterprises and by officially dictating the prices of some goods that are produced by private firms and farms. There also is corruption in the price control bureaucracy. Price controls are imposed on pharmaceuticals, petroleum products, and goods and services provided by public monopolies. The market, however, still determines most prices. Thus, by global standards, Cameroon has a moderate level of wage and price controls.

PROPERTY RIGHTS
Score: 4–Stable (low level of protection)

Private property, although legal, is not entirely safe in Cameroon. A corrupt government and an uncertain legal environment can result in the confiscation of private property. According to the U.S. Department of Commerce, "Cameroon's revised judiciary is considerably influenced by the Executive Branch."[7]

REGULATION
Score: 4–Stable (high level)

According to the U.S. Department of Commerce, "Corruption and a dysfunctional judicial system severely disrupt Cameroon's economy and society."[8] Existing regulations are applied unevenly and impose a huge burden on businesses. Establishing a business is a complicated procedure, and it is difficult to hire expatriate employees.

BLACK MARKET
Score: 5–Stable (very high level of activity)

Cameroon's black market is nearly as large as its legal market. Smugglers regularly bring in beef and other food products to circumvent the government's often high duties on agricultural products.

NOTES

1. Based on total taxes on international trade as a percentage of total imports.
2. U.S. Department of Commerce, *Country Commercial Guide, 1997*.
3. Some estimates place the top income tax rate at 66 percent.
4. World Bank, *World Development Report 1997*.
5. U.S. Department of Commerce, *Country Commercial Guide, 1997*.
6. *Ibid.*
7. *Ibid.*
8. *Ibid.*

Canada

2.10

1997 Score: **2.10**	1996 Score: **2.00**	1995 Score: **2.00**

Trade	2	Banking	2
Taxation	5	Wages and Prices	2
Government Intervention	2	Property Rights	1
Monetary Policy	1	Regulation	2
Foreign Investment	3	Black Market	1

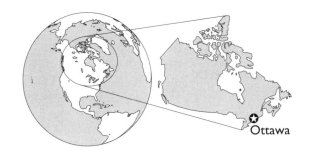

Ottawa

Canada, a self-governing dominion within the British Empire, became fully independent in 1932. Today, it has the world's seventh-largest market economy and is moving away from many of its formerly interventionist economic policies. In 1992, for example, Alberta elected Conservative Premier Ralph Klein on a platform of spending cuts and deregulation. In 1995, Ontario elected Conservative Premier Mike Harris, who pledged to cut provincial income taxes 30 percent, balance the budget, and reduce regulations; he already has accomplished most of these goals. By 1996, even Quebec had joined this trend. New Parti Quebeçois Premier Lucien Bouchard proposed sharp spending reductions and a deregulation program, and has implemented many of the cuts in spending. On the federal level, Liberal Prime Minister Jean Chretien is curbing government spending to reduce Ottawa's budget deficit. On June 2, 1997, Canada held a national election in which Chretien's Liberal Party won by a narrow majority. The Liberal Party has pledged to continue economic liberalization and work toward a balanced budget by 1999. This election, however, demonstrated the growing distance between Quebec and the rest of Canada, making another referendum on secession likely by the year 2000.

TRADE POLICY
Score: 2–Stable (low level of protectionism)

Canada, a party to the North American Free Trade Agreement (NAFTA) along with the United States and Mexico, generally supports free trade. In 1996, it negotiated bilateral NAFTA-like free trade agreements with Chile and Israel, and its average tariff rate is just over 4 percent.[1] Canada also maintains trade barriers, however, against such products as dairy, poultry, eggs, fresh fruit and vegetables, potatoes, processed horticultural products, and live swine.

TAXATION
Score–Income taxation: 4–Stable (high tax rates)
Score–Corporate taxation: 5–Stable (very high tax rates)
Final Taxation Score: 5–Stable (very high tax rates)

Canada's top marginal income tax rate is 52.92 percent,[2] with the average income taxed at 17 percent. The top marginal corporate tax rate is 46.12 percent.[3] Canada also has a 21.84 percent capital gains tax and a 7 percent value-added tax (called the Goods and Services Tax).

GOVERNMENT INTERVENTION IN THE ECONOMY
Score: 2–Stable (low level)

Government consumes 19.4 percent of Canada's GDP. Since 1984, it has undertaken substantial privatization. Canada's provinces also are privatizing provincially owned firms, especially utilities.

1	Hong Kong	1.25	77	Zambia	3.05
2	Singapore	1.30	80	Mali	3.10
3	Bahrain	1.70	80	Mongolia	3.10
4	New Zealand	1.75	80	Slovenia	3.10
5	Switzerland	1.90	83	Honduras	3.15
5	United States	1.90	83	Papua New Guinea	3.15
7	Luxembourg	1.95	85	Djibouti	3.20
7	Taiwan	1.95	85	Fiji	3.20
7	United Kingdom	1.95	85	Pakistan	3.20
10	Bahamas	2.00	88	Algeria	3.25
10	Ireland	2.00	88	Guinea	3.25
12	Australia	2.05	88	Lebanon	3.25
12	Japan	2.05	88	Mexico	3.25
14	Belgium	2.10	88	Senegal	3.25
14	Canada	2.10	88	Tanzania	3.25
14	United Arab Emirates	2.10	94	Nigeria	3.30
17	Austria	2.15	94	Romania	3.30
17	Chile	2.15	96	Brazil	3.35
17	Estonia	2.15	96	Cambodia	3.35
20	Czech Republic	2.20	96	Egypt	3.35
20	Netherlands	2.20	96	Ivory Coast	3.35
22	Denmark	2.25	96	Madagascar	3.35
22	Finland	2.25	96	Moldova	3.35
24	Germany	2.30	102	Nepal	3.40
24	Iceland	2.30	103	Cape Verde	3.44
24	South Korea	2.30	104	Armenia	3.45
27	Norway	2.35	104	Dominican Republic	3.45
28	Kuwait	2.40	104	Russia	3.45
28	Malaysia	2.40	107	Burkina Faso	3.50
28	Panama	2.40	107	Cameroon	3.50
28	Thailand	2.40	107	Lesotho	3.50
32	El Salvador	2.45	107	Nicaragua	3.50
32	Sri Lanka	2.45	107	Venezuela	3.50
32	Sweden	2.45	112	Gambia	3.60
35	France	2.50	112	Guyana	3.60
35	Italy	2.50	114	Bulgaria	3.65
35	Spain	2.50	114	Georgia	3.65
38	Trinidad and Tobago	2.55	114	Malawi	3.65
39	Argentina	2.60	117	Ethiopia	3.70
39	Barbados	2.60	117	India	3.70
39	Cyprus	2.60	117	Niger	3.70
39	Jamaica	2.60	120	Albania	3.75
39	Portugal	2.60	120	Bangladesh	3.75
44	Bolivia	2.65	120	China (PRC)	3.75
44	Oman	2.65	120	Congo	3.75
44	Philippines	2.65	120	Croatia	3.75
47	Swaziland	2.70	125	Chad	3.80
47	Uruguay	2.70	125	Mauritania	3.80
49	Botswana	2.75	125	Ukraine	3.80
49	Jordan	2.75	128	Sierra Leone	3.85
49	Namibia	2.75	129	Burundi	3.90
49	Tunisia	2.75	129	Suriname	3.90
53	Belize	2.80	129	Zimbabwe	3.90
53	Costa Rica	2.80	132	Haiti	4.00
53	Guatemala	2.80	132	Kyrgyzstan	4.00
53	Israel	2.80	132	Syria	4.00
53	Peru	2.80	135	Belarus	4.05
53	Saudi Arabia	2.80	136	Kazakstan	4.10
53	Turkey	2.80	136	Mozambique	4.10
53	Uganda	2.80	136	Yemen	4.10
53	Western Samoa	2.80	139	Sudan	4.20
62	Indonesia	2.85	140	Myanmar	4.30
62	Latvia	2.85	140	Rwanda	4.30
62	Malta	2.85	142	Angola	4.35
62	Paraguay	2.85	143	Azerbaijan	4.40
66	Greece	2.90	143	Tajikistan	4.40
66	Hungary	2.90	145	Turkmenistan	4.50
66	South Africa	2.90	146	Uzbekistan	4.55
69	Benin	2.95	147	Congo/Zaire	4.70
69	Ecuador	2.95	147	Iran	4.70
69	Gabon	2.95	147	Libya	4.70
69	Morocco	2.95	147	Somalia	4.70
69	Poland	2.95	147	Vietnam	4.70
74	Colombia	3.00	152	Bosnia	4.80
74	Ghana	3.00	153	Iraq	4.90
74	Lithuania	3.00	154	Cuba	5.00
77	Kenya	3.05	154	Laos	5.00
77	Slovak Republic	3.05	154	North Korea	5.00

Mostly Free

Monetary Policy
Score: 1–Stable (very low level of inflation)

The Bank of Canada sets monetary policy. The average annual rate of inflation from 1985 to 1995 was 2.9 percent. Today, the inflation rate is about 1.6 percent per year.

Capital Flows and Foreign Investment
Score: 3–Stable (moderate barriers)

Canada maintains several restrictions on investment. The Investment Canada Act, for example, requires the government to review each foreign investment to determine whether there is a "net benefit to Canada." Although most such investments are approved, the act often is used to restrict foreign investment in energy, publishing, telecommunications, broadcasting, and cable television.

Banking
Score: 2–Stable (low level of restrictions)

Canada has a private financial system with some restrictions. In mid-1992, the government implemented a financial sector reform package that increased competition among banks, trust companies, and insurance companies. The Canadian banking system, however, prohibits entry by foreign-owned branches.

Wage and Price Controls
Score: 2–Stable (low level)

Most prices in Canada are set by the market without government involvement. Some notable exceptions include government-owned utilities, the health care system, and such agricultural goods as eggs, poultry, and dairy products.

Property Rights
Score: 1–Stable (very high level of protection)

Private property is a fundamental principle of Canada's economy. The legal and judicial system affords adequate protection.

Regulation
Score: 2–Stable (low level)

It is relatively easy to establish a business in Canada. Each business must be registered in its province (except in New Brunswick, which does not require registration). Canada does not have a single, uniform internal market, and regulations differ from province to province. The various provincial governments are seeking agreements that would establish common regulatory policies.

Black Market
Score: 1–Stable (very low level of activity)

Canada's black market is confined to the sale of goods and services considered harmful to public safety: weapons, drugs, and stolen merchandise. High taxes on alcohol and cigarettes encourage some smuggling of these products.

Notes

1. This rate does not take into account the large amount of trade that occurs between the United States and Canada, most of which is at reduced rates or duty-free due to the U.S.–Canada Free Trade Agreement. When this is taken into account, the average tariff rate is only 2.4 percent.
2. This is a combined rate for 1996 in Ontario, which consists of a 31.32 percent federal tax and a 21.87 percent provincial tax. It is included here because both federal and provincial taxes are collected at the federal level. Thus, for all intents and purposes, the two tax rates are combined into one overall tax rate. Ontario is used because this is the rate reported in *The Worldwide Executive Tax Guide and Directory,* 1997 edition (New York, N.Y.: Ernst & Young, 1997). Other provinces may have higher or lower taxes, but the average for Canada is about 53 percent.
3. This rate includes both federal and provincial rates and was provided by *Worldwide Corporate Tax Guide and Directory,* 1997 edition (New York, N.Y.: Ernst & Young, 1997).

Cape Verde   3.44

| 1997 Score: **3.44** | 1996 Score: **3.44** | 1995 Score: **n/a** |

Trade	5	Banking	5
Taxation	n/a	Wages and Prices	4
Government Intervention	3	Property Rights	2
Monetary Policy	2	Regulation	4
Foreign Investment	2	Black Market	4

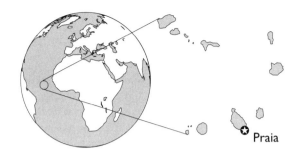
Praia

Cape Verde gained its independence from Portugal in 1975. It maintains close ties with Portugal, its principal trading partner, and is considering associating the value of its currency with Portugal's. Cape Verde has few natural resources and is highly dependent on imports. Although the country has a market-based economy, the government maintains many restrictions on economic activity. Cape Verde typically is able to produce only 15 percent of its food requirements and therefore relies heavily on international food aid.

TRADE POLICY

Score: 5–Stable (very high level of protectionism)

Cape Verde's tariff rates range from 5 percent to 50 percent; the average rate is about 20 percent. Imports are subject to a 7 percent tax on top of the tariff, in addition to a 5 percent to 20 percent consumption tax. Nontariff barriers include strict import licenses and documentation requirements.

TAXATION

Score–Income taxation: Not Scored
Score–Corporate taxation: Not Scored
Final Taxation Score: Not Scored

Tax information for Cape Verde is not available.

GOVERNMENT INTERVENTION IN THE ECONOMY

Score: 3–Stable (moderate level)

Government consumes about 18 percent of Cape Verde's GDP. The country has a significant state-owned sector.

MONETARY POLICY

Score: 2–Stable (low level of inflation)

Cape Verde had an average inflation rate of 7.2 percent from 1985 to 1995. The inflation rate for 1996 is not available.

CAPITAL FLOWS AND FOREIGN INVESTMENT

Score: 2–Stable (low barriers)

Nearly all sectors of the economy are now open to investment, but some restrictions remain. For example, delays often occur when revenue is converted to another currency and sent to the investor's home country, and the approval process for some investments can be slow.

1	Hong Kong	1.25	77	Zambia	3.05
2	Singapore	1.30	80	Mali	3.10
3	Bahrain	1.70	80	Mongolia	3.10
4	New Zealand	1.75	80	Slovenia	3.10
5	Switzerland	1.90	83	Honduras	3.15
5	United States	1.90	83	Papua New Guinea	3.15
7	Luxembourg	1.95	85	Djibouti	3.20
7	Taiwan	1.95	85	Fiji	3.20
7	United Kingdom	1.95	85	Pakistan	3.20
10	Bahamas	2.00	88	Algeria	3.25
10	Ireland	2.00	88	Guinea	3.25
12	Australia	2.05	88	Lebanon	3.25
12	Japan	2.05	88	Mexico	3.25
14	Belgium	2.10	88	Senegal	3.25
14	Canada	2.10	88	Tanzania	3.25
14	United Arab Emirates	2.10	94	Nigeria	3.30
17	Austria	2.15	94	Romania	3.30
17	Chile	2.15	96	Brazil	3.35
17	Estonia	2.15	96	Cambodia	3.35
20	Czech Republic	2.20	96	Egypt	3.35
20	Netherlands	2.20	96	Ivory Coast	3.35
22	Denmark	2.25	96	Madagascar	3.35
22	Finland	2.25	96	Moldova	3.35
24	Germany	2.30	102	Nepal	3.40
24	Iceland	2.30	103	Cape Verde	3.44
24	South Korea	2.30	104	Armenia	3.45
27	Norway	2.35	104	Dominican Republic	3.45
28	Kuwait	2.40	104	Russia	3.45
28	Malaysia	2.40	107	Burkina Faso	3.50
28	Panama	2.40	107	Cameroon	3.50
28	Thailand	2.40	107	Lesotho	3.50
32	El Salvador	2.45	107	Nicaragua	3.50
32	Sri Lanka	2.45	107	Venezuela	3.50
32	Sweden	2.45	112	Gambia	3.60
35	France	2.50	112	Guyana	3.60
35	Italy	2.50	114	Bulgaria	3.65
35	Spain	2.50	114	Georgia	3.65
38	Trinidad and Tobago	2.55	114	Malawi	3.65
39	Argentina	2.60	117	Ethiopia	3.70
39	Barbados	2.60	117	India	3.70
39	Cyprus	2.60	117	Niger	3.70
39	Jamaica	2.60	120	Albania	3.75
39	Portugal	2.60	120	Bangladesh	3.75
44	Bolivia	2.65	120	China (PRC)	3.75
44	Oman	2.65	120	Congo	3.75
44	Philippines	2.65	120	Croatia	3.75
47	Swaziland	2.70	125	Chad	3.80
47	Uruguay	2.70	125	Mauritania	3.80
49	Botswana	2.75	125	Ukraine	3.80
49	Jordan	2.75	128	Sierra Leone	3.85
49	Namibia	2.75	129	Burundi	3.90
49	Tunisia	2.75	129	Suriname	3.90
53	Belize	2.80	129	Zimbabwe	3.90
53	Costa Rica	2.80	132	Haiti	4.00
53	Guatemala	2.80	132	Kyrgyzstan	4.00
53	Israel	2.80	132	Syria	4.00
53	Peru	2.80	135	Belarus	4.05
53	Saudi Arabia	2.80	136	Kazakstan	4.10
53	Turkey	2.80	136	Mozambique	4.10
53	Uganda	2.80	136	Yemen	4.10
53	Western Samoa	2.80	139	Sudan	4.20
62	Indonesia	2.85	140	Myanmar	4.30
62	Latvia	2.85	140	Rwanda	4.30
62	Malta	2.85	142	Angola	4.35
62	Paraguay	2.85	143	Azerbaijan	4.40
66	Greece	2.90	143	Tajikistan	4.40
66	Hungary	2.90	145	Turkmenistan	4.50
66	South Africa	2.90	146	Uzbekistan	4.55
69	Benin	2.95	147	Congo/Zaire	4.70
69	Ecuador	2.95	147	Iran	4.70
69	Gabon	2.95	147	Libya	4.70
69	Morocco	2.95	147	Somalia	4.70
69	Poland	2.95	147	Vietnam	4.70
74	Colombia	3.00	152	Bosnia	4.80
74	Ghana	3.00	153	Iraq	4.90
74	Lithuania	3.00	154	Cuba	5.00
77	Kenya	3.05	154	Laos	5.00
77	Slovak Republic	3.05	154	North Korea	5.00

Mostly Unfree

BANKING
Score: 5–Stable (very high level of restrictions)

Cape Verde's banking system is underdeveloped. According to the U.S. Department of Commerce, "Financial services to the private sector are limited, with the result that the existing system is considered inadequate to efficiently and effectively satisfy the private sector's needs for credit."[1] There is no stock market and no capital market, and banking accounting systems, although clear, are not always consistent with international norms. The government owns most banks.

WAGE AND PRICE CONTROLS
Score: 4–Stable (high level)

Wages and prices in Cape Verde are affected by the large public sector and the transfer of government subsidies to those institutions.

PROPERTY RIGHTS
Score: 2–Stable (high level of protection)

Private property is guaranteed in Cape Verde, whose legal and judicial system is based on English law. Property can be expropriated, however, if such action is deemed to be in the national interest. According to the U.S. Department of State, "The Constitution provides for the right to a fair trial. A judiciary independent of the executive branch generally provides due process."[2]

REGULATION
Score: 4–Stable (high level)

Establishing a business can be cumbersome if the business competes with Cape Verde's state-owned sector. Regulations are applied evenly in most cases, but some corruption and a growing domestic monopoly in certain industries make it difficult to open new businesses.

BLACK MARKET
Score: 4–Stable (high level of activity)

Cape Verde has a growing and pervasive black market, mainly in consumer goods, luxury items, and Western books, video and audio cassettes, and movies.

NOTES
1. U.S. Department of Commerce, *Country Commercial Guide,* 1996.
2. U.S. Department of State, "Cape Verde Country Report on Human Rights Practices for 1996," 1997.

Chad
3.80

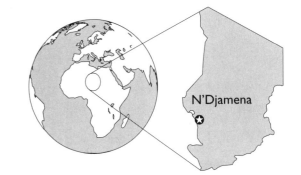

N'Djamena

| 1997 Score: **3.80** | 1996 Score: **n/a** | 1995 Score: **n/a** |

Trade	5	Banking	4
Taxation	4	Wages and Prices	4
Government Intervention	3	Property Rights	4
Monetary Policy	1	Regulation	4
Foreign Investment	4	Black Market	5

Chad gained its independence from France in 1960. Its economy is primarily agricultural, with more than 80 percent of the population engaged in subsistence farming and fishing. After independence, it became one of the poorest and least politically cohesive of the former colonies, experiencing constant civil unrest and political instability. The World Bank and the International Monetary Fund by and large dictate economic policy because Chad remains extremely dependent on foreign aid. Despite an economic liberalization agenda, little progress has been made, and prospects for growth are dim. Economic growth averaged only 2.8 percent from 1990 to 1996, and per capita GNP remains below $200.

TRADE POLICY
Score: 5–Stable (very high level of protectionism)

Chad's average tariff rate is 9.89 percent,[1] but the most significant deterrent to trade remains an unsafe and non-navigable road system. "Roads are in poor condition and dangerous," reports the U.S. Department of State. "No emergency services exist. Travelers on roads in all areas of the country are subject to attacks by armed bandits."[2]

TAXATION
Score–Income taxation: 4–Stable (high tax rates)
Score–Corporate taxation: 4–Stable (high tax rates)
Final Taxation Score: 4–Stable (high tax rates)

Chad's tax system changes constantly, and evasion is endemic. The main form of taxation is government expropriation of agricultural crops and goods produced by merchants. Such action—by government officials as well as armed bandits—is common at the local level.[3]

GOVERNMENT INTERVENTION IN THE ECONOMY
Score: 3–Stable (moderate level)

Government consumes about 17 percent of Chad's GDP, most of which is generated by the public sector. Many companies are state-owned.

MONETARY POLICY
Score: 1–Stable (very low level of inflation)

Chad's average annual rate of inflation from 1985 to 1995 was 3.1 percent. No figure was available for 1996.

CAPITAL FLOWS AND FOREIGN INVESTMENT
Score: 4–Stable (high barriers)

Even though Chad provides equal treatment for domestic and foreign firms, its international reputation for hostility to foreign investment and its conflict with Libya remain the biggest impediments to foreign investment. According to the U.S. Department of Commerce, "The effects of the war on foreign investment

1	Hong Kong	1.25	77	Zambia	3.05
2	Singapore	1.30	80	Mali	3.10
3	Bahrain	1.70	80	Mongolia	3.10
4	New Zealand	1.75	80	Slovenia	3.10
5	Switzerland	1.90	83	Honduras	3.15
5	United States	1.90	83	Papua New Guinea	3.15
7	Luxembourg	1.95	85	Djibouti	3.20
7	Taiwan	1.95	85	Fiji	3.20
7	United Kingdom	1.95	85	Pakistan	3.20
10	Bahamas	2.00	88	Algeria	3.25
10	Ireland	2.00	88	Guinea	3.25
12	Australia	2.05	88	Lebanon	3.25
12	Japan	2.05	88	Mexico	3.25
14	Belgium	2.10	88	Senegal	3.25
14	Canada	2.10	88	Tanzania	3.25
14	United Arab Emirates	2.10	94	Nigeria	3.30
17	Austria	2.15	94	Romania	3.30
17	Chile	2.15	96	Brazil	3.35
17	Estonia	2.15	96	Cambodia	3.35
20	Czech Republic	2.20	96	Egypt	3.35
20	Netherlands	2.20	96	Ivory Coast	3.35
22	Denmark	2.25	96	Madagascar	3.35
22	Finland	2.25	96	Moldova	3.35
24	Germany	2.30	102	Nepal	3.40
24	Iceland	2.30	103	Cape Verde	3.44
24	South Korea	2.30	104	Armenia	3.45
27	Norway	2.35	104	Dominican Republic	3.45
28	Kuwait	2.40	104	Russia	3.45
28	Malaysia	2.40	107	Burkina Faso	3.50
28	Panama	2.40	107	Cameroon	3.50
28	Thailand	2.40	107	Lesotho	3.50
32	El Salvador	2.45	107	Nicaragua	3.50
32	Sri Lanka	2.45	107	Venezuela	3.50
32	Sweden	2.45	112	Gambia	3.60
35	France	2.50	112	Guyana	3.60
35	Italy	2.50	114	Bulgaria	3.65
35	Spain	2.50	114	Georgia	3.65
38	Trinidad and Tobago	2.55	114	Malawi	3.65
39	Argentina	2.60	117	Ethiopia	3.70
39	Barbados	2.60	117	India	3.70
39	Cyprus	2.60	117	Niger	3.70
39	Jamaica	2.60	120	Albania	3.75
39	Portugal	2.60	120	Bangladesh	3.75
44	Bolivia	2.65	120	China (PRC)	3.75
44	Oman	2.65	120	Congo	3.75
44	Philippines	2.65	120	Croatia	3.75
47	Swaziland	2.70	125	Chad	3.80
47	Uruguay	2.70	125	Mauritania	3.80
49	Botswana	2.75	125	Ukraine	3.80
49	Jordan	2.75	128	Sierra Leone	3.85
49	Namibia	2.75	129	Burundi	3.90
49	Tunisia	2.75	129	Suriname	3.90
53	Belize	2.80	129	Zimbabwe	3.90
53	Costa Rica	2.80	132	Haiti	4.00
53	Guatemala	2.80	132	Kyrgyzstan	4.00
53	Israel	2.80	132	Syria	4.00
53	Peru	2.80	135	Belarus	4.05
53	Saudi Arabia	2.80	136	Kazakstan	4.10
53	Turkey	2.80	136	Mozambique	4.10
53	Uganda	2.80	136	Yemen	4.10
53	Western Samoa	2.80	139	Sudan	4.20
62	Indonesia	2.85	140	Myanmar	4.30
62	Latvia	2.85	140	Rwanda	4.30
62	Malta	2.85	142	Angola	4.35
62	Paraguay	2.85	143	Azerbaijan	4.40
66	Greece	2.90	143	Tajikistan	4.40
66	Hungary	2.90	145	Turkmenistan	4.50
66	South Africa	2.90	146	Uzbekistan	4.55
69	Benin	2.95	147	Congo/Zaire	4.70
69	Ecuador	2.95	147	Iran	4.70
69	Gabon	2.95	147	Libya	4.70
69	Morocco	2.95	147	Somalia	4.70
69	Poland	2.95	147	Vietnam	4.70
74	Colombia	3.00	152	Bosnia	4.80
74	Ghana	3.00	153	Iraq	4.90
74	Lithuania	3.00	154	Cuba	5.00
77	Kenya	3.05	154	Laos	5.00
77	Slovak Republic	3.05	154	North Korea	5.00

Mostly Unfree

are still felt today, as investors who left Chad between 1979–82 have only recently begun to regain confidence in the country's future."[4] Problems include a strict investment review process, a hostile state-owned sector, corruption, and a cumbersome bureaucracy.

BANKING
Score: 4–Stable (high level of restrictions)

The banking system in Chad is heavily controlled by the government, although some recent progress has been made on increasing foreign investment in this area.

WAGE AND PRICE CONTROLS
Score: 4–Stable (high level)

Wages and prices in Chad are affected by the large public sector, import substitution policies, and government subsidies.

PROPERTY RIGHTS
Score: 4–Stable (low level of protection)

Private property is subject to government expropriation in Chad, although there are few recent examples of nationalization. The government is attempting to privatize many state-owned enterprises, but crime and theft remain problems. According to the U.S. Department of State, "The judicial system remained ineffective and subject to government interference, unable to provide citizens with prompt trials."[5]

REGULATION
Score: 4–Stable (high level)

Establishing a business is difficult because of Chad's massive and corrupt government bureaucracy. Bribery is sometimes present, as is embezzlement by those government officials who collect fees. Regulations often are applied haphazardly.

BLACK MARKET
Score: 5–Stable (very high level of activity)

Chad's black market is larger than its formal market, and growing. Most activity occurs in smuggled consumer goods, labor, and pirated intellectual property.

NOTES

1. Based on taxation on international trade as a percentage of total imports.
2. U.S. Department of State Travel Advisory, 1997.
3. Tax rate information is not available.
4. U.S. Department of Commerce, National Trade Data Bank, and Economic Bulletin Board, products of STAT–USA.
5. U.S. Department of State, "Chad Country Report on Human Rights Practices for 1996," 1997.

Chile 2.15

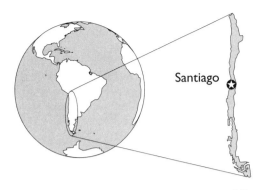

Santiago

1997 Score: **2.25**	1996 Score: **2.45**	1995 Score: **2.50**

Trade	2	Banking	3
Taxation	3.5	Wages and Prices	2
Government Intervention	1	Property Rights	1
Monetary Policy	3	Regulation	2
Foreign Investment	2	Black Market	2

Since 1960, most economic success stories have come from Asia, but Chile is an excellent example of a Latin American country enjoying economic success. A massive economic transformation during the 1980s created some of the fastest economic growth in the Western hemisphere and led Chile to adopt a series of political reforms that culminated in democratic elections in 1989. Chile's constitution defines and protects individual liberties, and President Eduardo Frei is continuing the country's free-market course. Recent, strengthened enforcement of intellectual property rights laws already has reduced black market activity in that area. As a result, Chile's overall score this year is 0.1 point better than it was last year.

TRADE POLICY
Score: 2–Stable (low level of protectionism)

International trade is the cornerstone of Chile's economy. The government maintains a flat tariff rate of 11 percent on most products; because Chile has opened its borders to many of its neighbors and many items enter duty-free, the average tariff rate is less than 6 percent. Chile has removed most of its nontariff barriers.

TAXATION
Score–Income taxation: 4–Stable (high tax rates)
Score–Corporate taxation: 2–Stable (low tax rates)
Final Taxation Score: 3.5–Stable (high tax rates)

Chile's top income tax rate is 45 percent; the average taxpayer is in the 10 percent bracket. The top corporate income tax rate is 15 percent. Chile maintains a 15 percent capital gains tax and an 18 percent value-added tax.

GOVERNMENT INTERVENTION IN THE ECONOMY
Score: 1–Stable (very low level)

Chile is an example of how reduced government intervention produces solid economic growth. Government consumes 8.8 percent of Chile's GDP; the country has achieved this low rate by permitting private enterprises to supply such "public" services as education, pension funds, social security, and some utilities.[1] Chile's social security system, for example, is privately owned and operated.

MONETARY POLICY
Score: 3–Stable (moderate level of inflation)

Chile's average annual rate of inflation from 1985 to 1995 was 17.9 percent. In 1996, the inflation rate was 7.4 percent.

1	Hong Kong	1.25	77	Zambia	3.05
2	Singapore	1.30	80	Mali	3.10
3	Bahrain	1.70	80	Mongolia	3.10
4	New Zealand	1.75	80	Slovenia	3.10
5	Switzerland	1.90	83	Honduras	3.15
5	United States	1.90	83	Papua New Guinea	3.15
7	Luxembourg	1.95	85	Djibouti	3.20
7	Taiwan	1.95	85	Fiji	3.20
7	United Kingdom	1.95	85	Pakistan	3.20
10	Bahamas	2.00	88	Algeria	3.25
10	Ireland	2.00	88	Guinea	3.25
12	Australia	2.05	88	Lebanon	3.25
12	Japan	2.05	88	Mexico	3.25
14	Belgium	2.10	88	Senegal	3.25
14	Canada	2.10	88	Tanzania	3.25
14	United Arab Emirates	2.10	94	Nigeria	3.30
17	Austria	2.15	94	Romania	3.30
17	Chile	2.15	96	Brazil	3.35
17	Estonia	2.15	96	Cambodia	3.35
20	Czech Republic	2.20	96	Egypt	3.35
20	Netherlands	2.20	96	Ivory Coast	3.35
22	Denmark	2.25	96	Madagascar	3.35
22	Finland	2.25	96	Moldova	3.35
24	Germany	2.30	102	Nepal	3.40
24	Iceland	2.30	103	Cape Verde	3.44
24	South Korea	2.30	104	Armenia	3.45
27	Norway	2.35	104	Dominican Republic	3.45
28	Kuwait	2.40	104	Russia	3.45
28	Malaysia	2.40	107	Burkina Faso	3.50
28	Panama	2.40	107	Cameroon	3.50
28	Thailand	2.40	107	Lesotho	3.50
32	El Salvador	2.45	107	Nicaragua	3.50
32	Sri Lanka	2.45	107	Venezuela	3.50
32	Sweden	2.45	112	Gambia	3.60
35	France	2.50	112	Guyana	3.60
35	Italy	2.50	114	Bulgaria	3.65
35	Spain	2.50	114	Georgia	3.65
38	Trinidad and Tobago	2.55	114	Malawi	3.65
39	Argentina	2.60	117	Ethiopia	3.70
39	Barbados	2.60	117	India	3.70
39	Cyprus	2.60	117	Niger	3.70
39	Jamaica	2.60	120	Albania	3.75
39	Portugal	2.60	120	Bangladesh	3.75
44	Bolivia	2.65	120	China (PRC)	3.75
44	Oman	2.65	120	Congo	3.75
44	Philippines	2.65	120	Croatia	3.75
47	Swaziland	2.70	125	Chad	3.80
47	Uruguay	2.70	125	Mauritania	3.80
49	Botswana	2.75	125	Ukraine	3.80
49	Jordan	2.75	128	Sierra Leone	3.85
49	Namibia	2.75	129	Burundi	3.90
49	Tunisia	2.75	129	Suriname	3.90
53	Belize	2.80	129	Zimbabwe	3.90
53	Costa Rica	2.80	132	Haiti	4.00
53	Guatemala	2.80	132	Kyrgyzstan	4.00
53	Israel	2.80	132	Syria	4.00
53	Peru	2.80	135	Belarus	4.05
53	Saudi Arabia	2.80	136	Kazakstan	4.10
53	Turkey	2.80	136	Mozambique	4.10
53	Uganda	2.80	136	Yemen	4.10
53	Western Samoa	2.80	139	Sudan	4.20
62	Indonesia	2.85	140	Myanmar	4.30
62	Latvia	2.85	140	Rwanda	4.30
62	Malta	2.85	142	Angola	4.35
62	Paraguay	2.85	143	Azerbaijan	4.40
66	Greece	2.90	143	Tajikistan	4.40
66	Hungary	2.90	145	Turkmenistan	4.50
66	South Africa	2.90	146	Uzbekistan	4.55
69	Benin	2.95	147	Congo/Zaire	4.70
69	Ecuador	2.95	147	Iran	4.70
69	Gabon	2.95	147	Libya	4.70
69	Morocco	2.95	147	Somalia	4.70
69	Poland	2.95	147	Vietnam	4.70
74	Colombia	3.00	152	Bosnia	4.80
74	Ghana	3.00	153	Iraq	4.90
74	Lithuania	3.00	154	Cuba	5.00
77	Kenya	3.05	154	Laos	5.00
77	Slovak Republic	3.05	154	North Korea	5.00

Mostly Free

CAPITAL FLOWS AND FOREIGN INVESTMENT
Score: 2–Stable (low barriers)

Chile aims to attract foreign investors by granting them quick government approval in some industries. But even though Chile has reformed its foreign investment code to attract investment, some barriers still exist. For example, all foreign investors must secure permission from the government's Foreign Investment Committee (although this rarely proves to be a barrier), and the government restricts investment in the fishing, maritime transport, and oil and gas industries.

BANKING
Score: 3–Stable (moderate level of restrictions)

Although Chile's banking system is relatively free of government corruption, it is not fully competitive and market-oriented. The government requires a license for foreign banks, and all licenses have been frozen. Despite plans to consider further banking reform by the end of 1997, no major liberalization had been achieved as of the time this book was published; as a practical matter, therefore, new foreign banks are not allowed. Domestic banks, especially those in the lending business, often find themselves in competition with state-owned banks, which distorts market operations. A state-operated agency provides subsidized loans to the public and private sectors, but the 40 percent default rate has swallowed up lending capital and skewed the banking system with bad loans. Banks may not engage in insurance, real estate, or investment services.

WAGE AND PRICE CONTROLS
Score: 2–Stable (low level)

Chile's pricing policy is determined mainly by the market, although there are some exceptions, such as prices for urban and public transport and some utilities. Minimum wages, hours worked, and safety regulations are controlled by the government, but most price controls have been removed.

PROPERTY RIGHTS
Score: 1–Stable (very high level of protection)

Private property is gaining increasing protection from the Chilean government through greater efficiency in the court system and legal institutions. Chile has had a comprehensive program of privatization since the early 1980s, and it continues today. The likelihood of private property expropriation is very low.

REGULATION
Score: 2–Stable (low level)

Government regulation in Chile runs from nonexistent in some areas to overbearing in others, but opening a business is far easier than in many other Latin American countries. Regulations are moderate, although some can be burdensome for private businesses. The Ministry of Public Health, for example, regulates the production, storage, distribution, sale, and import of all food and drug products.

BLACK MARKET
Score: 2+ (low level of activity)

Like most other countries in Latin America, Chile has a black market. Piracy of intellectual property is decreasing, but the large black market business in this area continues. As much as 65 percent of computer software is pirated, and there still is a large black market in pirated pharmaceuticals from the United States. According to the U.S. Department of State, "Chilean authorities have taken aggressive enforcement measures against video, video game, audio, and computer software pirates in recent years, and piracy has declined in each of these areas."[2] As a result, Chile's score is one point better this year.

NOTES

1. Cristian V. Larroulet, ed., *The Chilean Experience: Private Solutions to Public Problems,* Instituto Libertad y Desarrollo and Center for International Private Enterprise, 1991.
2. U.S. Department of State, *Country Reports on Economic Policy and Trade Practices,* 1997, p. 228.

China, People's Republic of 3.75

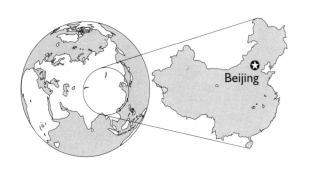

Beijing

1997 Score: **3.80**	1996 Score: **3.80**	1995 Score: **3.80**

Trade	5	Banking	3
Taxation	3.5	Wages and Prices	3
Government Intervention	5	Property Rights	4
Monetary Policy	3	Regulation	4
Foreign Investment	3	Black Market	4

Although often criticized for its human rights abuses and communist political system, the People's Republic of China is more open and advanced economically today than it was just two decades ago. Despite some twists and turns, economic reforms have remained on track, expanding since they began in the late 1970s. Economic growth reached 13.5 percent in 1993 and now is running at 9.7 percent. Several pockets within the Chinese economy have performed well over the past several years and can be credited with causing most of the country's economic growth. The government continues to own over 118,000 companies, and a majority of these are losing money. State-owned enterprises employ almost two-thirds of the 170 million–strong urban workforce. Many foreign investors realize they severely underestimated the difficulties of doing business in a country striving to achieve the inherently contradictory goal of a "socialist market economy." Foreign investment is falling for the first time this decade and is expected to be more than $12 billion less in 1997 than it was in 1996. Even so, China remains the largest destination for foreign investment in Asia. Tax rates that apply to the average income are lower than they were last year. As a result, China's overall score is 0.05 point better this year.

TRADE POLICY
Score: 5–Stable (very high level of protectionism)

China's average tariff rate is 23 percent. In an effort to support its bid for accession to the World Trade Organization, China has announced that it will reduce its average tariff rate to 15 percent by the year 2000. According to the Office of the U.S. Trade Representative, "U.S. and other foreign businesses selling goods into China also complain about China's lack of uniformity in customs valuation practices. Different ports of entry may charge significantly different duty rates on the same products."[1] Some tariffs are coming down, and over the next two years China will phase out tariff exemptions on capital equipment imported by foreign investors. Nontariff barriers include "import licenses, import quotas, and other import controls."[2]

TAXATION
Score–Income taxation: 3+ (moderate tax rates)
Score–Corporate taxation: 3–Stable (moderate tax rates)
Final Taxation Score: 3.5+ (high tax rates)

China's top marginal income tax rate is 45 percent; the average income level is taxed at 5 percent, down from the previous 15 percent. Consequently, China's overall tax score is one-half point better this year. The top corporate tax rate is 30 percent. China has a 33 percent capital gains tax, a 17 percent value-added tax, and a 3 percent to 20 percent business tax.

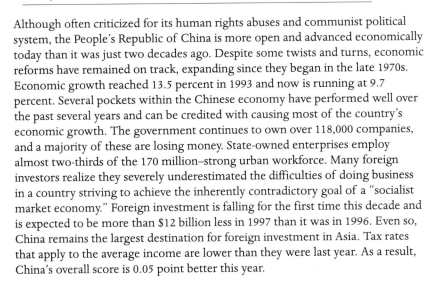

1	Hong Kong	1.25	77	Zambia	3.05
2	Singapore	1.30	80	Mali	3.10
3	Bahrain	1.70	80	Mongolia	3.10
4	New Zealand	1.75	80	Slovenia	3.10
5	Switzerland	1.90	83	Honduras	3.15
5	United States	1.90	83	Papua New Guinea	3.15
7	Luxembourg	1.95	85	Djibouti	3.20
7	Taiwan	1.95	85	Fiji	3.20
7	United Kingdom	1.95	85	Pakistan	3.20
10	Bahamas	2.00	88	Algeria	3.25
10	Ireland	2.00	88	Guinea	3.25
12	Australia	2.05	88	Lebanon	3.25
12	Japan	2.05	88	Mexico	3.25
14	Belgium	2.10	88	Senegal	3.25
14	Canada	2.10	88	Tanzania	3.25
14	United Arab Emirates	2.10	94	Nigeria	3.30
17	Austria	2.15	94	Romania	3.30
17	Chile	2.15	96	Brazil	3.35
17	Estonia	2.15	96	Cambodia	3.35
20	Czech Republic	2.20	96	Egypt	3.35
20	Netherlands	2.20	96	Ivory Coast	3.35
22	Denmark	2.25	96	Madagascar	3.35
22	Finland	2.25	96	Moldova	3.35
24	Germany	2.30	102	Nepal	3.40
24	Iceland	2.30	103	Cape Verde	3.44
24	South Korea	2.30	104	Armenia	3.45
27	Norway	2.35	104	Dominican Republic	3.45
28	Kuwait	2.40	104	Russia	3.45
28	Malaysia	2.40	107	Burkina Faso	3.50
28	Panama	2.40	107	Cameroon	3.50
28	Thailand	2.40	107	Lesotho	3.50
32	El Salvador	2.45	107	Nicaragua	3.50
32	Sri Lanka	2.45	107	Venezuela	3.50
32	Sweden	2.45	112	Gambia	3.60
35	France	2.50	112	Guyana	3.60
35	Italy	2.50	114	Bulgaria	3.65
35	Spain	2.50	114	Georgia	3.65
38	Trinidad and Tobago	2.55	114	Malawi	3.65
39	Argentina	2.60	117	Ethiopia	3.70
39	Barbados	2.60	117	India	3.70
39	Cyprus	2.60	117	Niger	3.70
39	Jamaica	2.60	120	Albania	3.75
39	Portugal	2.60	120	Bangladesh	3.75
44	Bolivia	2.65	120	China (PRC)	3.75
44	Oman	2.65	120	Congo	3.75
44	Philippines	2.65	120	Croatia	3.75
47	Swaziland	2.70	125	Chad	3.80
47	Uruguay	2.70	125	Mauritania	3.80
49	Botswana	2.75	125	Ukraine	3.80
49	Jordan	2.75	128	Sierra Leone	3.85
49	Namibia	2.75	129	Burundi	3.90
49	Tunisia	2.75	129	Suriname	3.90
53	Belize	2.80	129	Zimbabwe	3.90
53	Costa Rica	2.80	132	Haiti	4.00
53	Guatemala	2.80	132	Kyrgyzstan	4.00
53	Israel	2.80	132	Syria	4.00
53	Peru	2.80	135	Belarus	4.05
53	Saudi Arabia	2.80	136	Kazakstan	4.10
53	Turkey	2.80	136	Mozambique	4.10
53	Uganda	2.80	136	Yemen	4.10
53	Western Samoa	2.80	139	Sudan	4.20
62	Indonesia	2.85	140	Myanmar	4.30
62	Latvia	2.85	140	Rwanda	4.30
62	Malta	2.85	142	Angola	4.35
62	Paraguay	2.85	143	Azerbaijan	4.40
66	Greece	2.90	143	Tajikistan	4.40
66	Hungary	2.90	145	Turkmenistan	4.50
66	South Africa	2.90	146	Uzbekistan	4.55
69	Benin	2.95	147	Congo/Zaire	4.70
69	Ecuador	2.95	147	Iran	4.70
69	Gabon	2.95	147	Libya	4.70
69	Morocco	2.95	147	Somalia	4.70
69	Poland	2.95	147	Vietnam	4.70
74	Colombia	3.00	152	Bosnia	4.80
74	Ghana	3.00	153	Iraq	4.90
74	Lithuania	3.00	154	Cuba	5.00
77	Kenya	3.05	154	Laos	5.00
77	Slovak Republic	3.05	154	North Korea	5.00

Mostly Unfree

GOVERNMENT INTERVENTION IN THE ECONOMY
Score: 5–Stable (very high level)

The World Bank reports that government consumes only 12 percent of China's GDP, up from 8.3 percent in 1980.[3] These figures severely understate the level of government intervention in the economy, however, primarily because official government consumption rates do not include education and social welfare expenditures made by state-owned enterprises in China. In most countries, these expenditures are included in official consumption figures. Although officially designated state-owned enterprises produce only 34 percent of industrial output, this figure rises to 75 percent if joint venture companies with partial government ownership and local government cooperatives are included. Therefore, by global standards, government intervention in China's economy remains very high.

MONETARY POLICY
Score: 3–Stable (moderate level of inflation)

As a command economy, China's annual rate of inflation averaged only 9.5 percent from 1985 to 1995. Government subsidies and price controls, however, may depress the inflation rate artificially. If this is taken into account, the average yearly rate of inflation during this period probably would have been higher than 13 percent, which is moderate by global standards.

CAPITAL FLOWS AND FOREIGN INVESTMENT
Score: 3–Stable (moderate barriers)

China always has maintained barriers to foreign investment. The government uses foreign investment policy to prevent foreign companies from competing with some state-owned industries while directing them toward other state-owned enterprises, such as power, telecommunications, aviation, and information technologies. According to the U.S. Department of State, "Multiple time consuming approval procedures adversely affect establishment of investments. Depending on the locality, investments above $30 million require national as well as local approval. Export requirements, local content requirements, and foreign exchange balancing requirements detract from China's investment climate.... China does not provide national treatment to foreign investors on establishment or operation of investments. In some key areas, such as input costs, foreign investors are often treated less favorably than Chinese firms. Foreign investors may not own land in China."[4] China's special foreign investment zones in the south, however, give it a somewhat better score.

BANKING
Score: 3–Stable (moderate level of restrictions)

China controls its financial sector through four large state-owned commercial banks and one state-owned insurance company. Most of these firms are insolvent. Since 1988, however, the government has allowed some private

domestic and foreign banks to engage in financial activity. Thus, by global standards, China's restrictions on banking are moderate.

WAGE AND PRICE CONTROLS
Score: 3–Stable (moderate level)

China has a history of price controls. After the 1993 recession, the government imposed controls on the prices of such items as foodstuffs and utilities. Controls on the prices of foodstuffs were removed recently, but the production of items in some areas remains centrally planned by the government. China also has a minimum wage.

PROPERTY RIGHTS
Score: 4–Stable (low level of protection)

Because China remains a communist system, most property remains in government hands. The government is privatizing some major industries and moving some state-owned assets into private hands. Nevertheless, private property is still far from common, and the court system is both inefficient and far from impartial. According to the U.S. Department of State, "Officials state that China's judiciary is independent but acknowledge that it is subject to the Communist Party's policy guidance.... Corruption and conflicts of interest also affect judicial decision making."[5]

REGULATION
Score: 4–Stable (high level)

In an attempt to boost the private sector, the Chinese bureaucracy sometimes does not enforce cumbersome regulations. China still has a state planning agency that makes significant business and economic decisions, and this central planning results in high levels of regulation. Corruption also is a problem. According to the U.S. Department of Commerce, "Based on surveys reported in the western media and on the general views expressed by foreign business people and lawyers in China, U.S. firms do consider corruption in China a hindrance to foreign direct investment. Corruption probably exists to some degree in all sectors of the Chinese economy."[6]

BLACK MARKET
Score: 4–Stable (high level of activity)

Because of existing trade restrictions and central economic planning, the black market in China is rather large. There is extensive smuggling, both of automobiles from Hong Kong and of consumer electronic products like televisions and videocassette recorders. According to the U.S. Department of Commerce, "High duties on imported brands have given rise to smuggling. Restrictions on importation, distribution and foreign participation have also created a huge amount of illegal trade. Industry experts estimate that less than 5 percent of imported alcohol enters China legally. The remainder is brought in cheaply through corrupt customs officials in southern ports or by boat from Hong Kong."[7]

The U.S. Department of Commerce further reports that "Due to the strong demand for pork variety meats and the prohibition on its importation, smuggling of frozen pork variety meats is rampant in China."[8]

NOTES

1. Office of the United States Trade Representative, *1997 National Trade Estimate Report on Foreign Trade Barriers.*
2. *Ibid.*
3. World Bank, *World Bank Development Report 1997.*
4. U.S. Department of State, *Country Reports on Economic Policy and Trade Practices,* 1997, p. 28.
5. U.S. Department of State, "China Country Report on Human Rights Practices for 1996," 1997.
6. U.S. Department of Commerce, *Country Commercial Guide,* 1997.
7. U.S. Department of Commerce, "China—Daily Briefing," *Market Research Reports,* March 11, 1997.
8. U.S. Department of Commerce, "China; Livestock; Frozen Pork Wholesale Market in Shanghai; Voluntary Report," *Agworld Attaché Reports,* 1996.

China, Republic of (Taiwan)   1.95

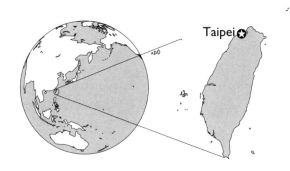

Taipei

Trade	2	Banking	3
Taxation	2.5	Wages and Prices	2
Government Intervention	2	Property Rights	1
Monetary Policy	1	Regulation	2
Foreign Investment	3	Black Market	1

The Republic of China on Taiwan (ROC) has one of the world's fastest-growing economies. In the late 1950s, mired in conflict with mainland China, Taiwan was held back by an inefficient and over-regulated economy. In the late 1960s, however, the government began to reform the economy. It guaranteed private property and set up a legal system to protect it, reformed the banking and financial sectors, stabilized taxes, gave public lands to private individuals, and allowed the free market to expand. These policies launched Taiwan, one of Asia's famous "tigers," into the industrialized world.[1] Today, annual economic growth is around 6 percent. The ROC also has developed a functional democracy and conducted successful multiparty elections in both the legislative and executive branches of government. Bipartisan proposals made at the December 1996 National Development Conference should improve Taiwan's international competitiveness by furthering deregulation and opening its market to foreign competition, although recent populist calls by the opposition party for broader social welfare programs, government investment in infrastructure, and other forms of welfare statism could undermine this progress.

TRADE POLICY
Score: 2–Stable (low level of protectionism)

Taiwan's average tariff rate is only 4 percent. There are, however, rather high barriers to the importation of agricultural goods like chicken, meat, peanuts, and pork; tariffs on these goods can reach 50 percent. Taiwan's rather inefficient distribution system adds to the price of many products, making imports noncompetitive.

TAXATION
Score–Income taxation: 2–Stable (low tax rates)
Score–Corporate taxation: 2–Stable (low tax rates)
Final Taxation Score: 2.5–Stable (moderate tax rates)

Taiwan's top income tax rate is 40 percent, and the average income level is taxed at 6 percent. The maximum corporate tax rate is 25 percent. Taiwan also has a 25 percent capital gains tax and a 5 percent value-added tax.

GOVERNMENT INTERVENTION IN THE ECONOMY
Score: 2–Stable (low level)

Government consumes 14.2 percent of Taiwan's GDP. The state continues to privatize the remaining public companies.

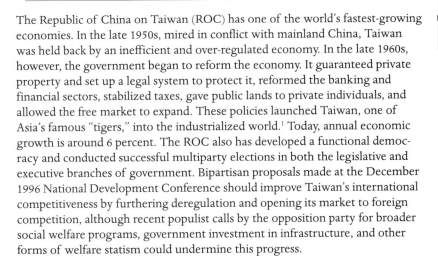

Free	1	Hong Kong	1.25	77	Zambia	3.05
	2	Singapore	1.30	80	Mali	3.10
	3	Bahrain	1.70	80	Mongolia	3.10
	4	New Zealand	1.75	80	Slovenia	3.10
	5	Switzerland	1.90	83	Honduras	3.15
	5	United States	1.90	83	Papua New Guinea	3.15
	7	Luxembourg	1.95	85	Djibouti	3.20
	7	China (ROC)	1.95	85	Fiji	3.20
	7	United Kingdom	1.95	85	Pakistan	3.20
	10	Bahamas	2.00	88	Algeria	3.25
	10	Ireland	2.00	88	Guinea	3.25
	12	Australia	2.05	88	Lebanon	3.25
	12	Japan	2.05	88	Mexico	3.25
	14	Belgium	2.10	88	Senegal	3.25
	14	Canada	2.10	88	Tanzania	3.25
	14	United Arab Emirates	2.10	94	Nigeria	3.30
	17	Austria	2.15	94	Romania	3.30
	17	Chile	2.15	96	Brazil	3.35
	17	Estonia	2.15	96	Cambodia	3.35
	20	Czech Republic	2.20	96	Egypt	3.35
	20	Netherlands	2.20	96	Ivory Coast	3.35
	22	Denmark	2.25	96	Madagascar	3.35
	22	Finland	2.25	96	Moldova	3.35
	24	Germany	2.30	102	Nepal	3.40
	24	Iceland	2.30	103	Cape Verde	3.44
	24	South Korea	2.30	104	Armenia	3.45
	27	Norway	2.35	104	Dominican Republic	3.45
	28	Kuwait	2.40	104	Russia	3.45
	28	Malaysia	2.40	107	Burkina Faso	3.50
	28	Panama	2.40	107	Cameroon	3.50
	28	Thailand	2.40	107	Lesotho	3.50
	32	El Salvador	2.45	107	Nicaragua	3.50
	32	Sri Lanka	2.45	107	Venezuela	3.50
	32	Sweden	2.45	112	Gambia	3.60
	35	France	2.50	112	Guyana	3.60
	35	Italy	2.50	114	Bulgaria	3.65
	35	Spain	2.50	114	Georgia	3.65
	38	Trinidad and Tobago	2.55	114	Malawi	3.65
	39	Argentina	2.60	117	Ethiopia	3.70
	39	Barbados	2.60	117	India	3.70
	39	Cyprus	2.60	117	Niger	3.70
	39	Jamaica	2.60	120	Albania	3.75
	39	Portugal	2.60	120	Bangladesh	3.75
	44	Bolivia	2.65	120	China (PRC)	3.75
	44	Oman	2.65	120	Congo	3.75
	44	Philippines	2.65	120	Croatia	3.75
	47	Swaziland	2.70	125	Chad	3.80
	47	Uruguay	2.70	125	Mauritania	3.80
	49	Botswana	2.75	125	Ukraine	3.80
	49	Jordan	2.75	128	Sierra Leone	3.85
	49	Namibia	2.75	129	Burundi	3.90
	49	Tunisia	2.75	129	Suriname	3.90
	53	Belize	2.80	129	Zimbabwe	3.90
	53	Costa Rica	2.80	132	Haiti	4.00
	53	Guatemala	2.80	132	Kyrgyzstan	4.00
	53	Israel	2.80	132	Syria	4.00
	53	Peru	2.80	135	Belarus	4.05
	53	Saudi Arabia	2.80	136	Kazakstan	4.10
	53	Turkey	2.80	136	Mozambique	4.10
	53	Uganda	2.80	136	Yemen	4.10
	53	Western Samoa	2.80	139	Sudan	4.20
	62	Indonesia	2.85	140	Myanmar	4.30
	62	Latvia	2.85	140	Rwanda	4.30
	62	Malta	2.85	142	Angola	4.35
	62	Paraguay	2.85	143	Azerbaijan	4.40
	66	Greece	2.90	143	Tajikistan	4.40
	66	Hungary	2.90	145	Turkmenistan	4.50
	66	South Africa	2.90	146	Uzbekistan	4.55
	69	Benin	2.95	147	Congo/Zaire	4.70
	69	Ecuador	2.95	147	Iran	4.70
	69	Gabon	2.95	147	Libya	4.70
	69	Morocco	2.95	147	Somalia	4.70
	69	Poland	2.95	147	Vietnam	4.70
	74	Colombia	3.00	152	Bosnia	4.80
	74	Ghana	3.00	153	Iraq	4.90
	74	Lithuania	3.00	154	Cuba	5.00
	77	Kenya	3.05	154	Laos	5.00
	77	Slovak Republic	3.05	154	North Korea	5.00

MONETARY POLICY
Score: 1–Stable (very low level of inflation)

Taiwan's average annual rate of inflation during the 1980s was less than 2 percent.[2] From 1990 to 1994, the inflation rate was only 3.8 percent; in 1995, it was 4.3 percent; for 1996, it was 3.1 percent.

CAPITAL FLOWS AND FOREIGN INVESTMENT
Score: 3–Stable (moderate barriers)

Foreign investment has been a major concern of Taiwan's government officials. For the first half of 1995, reforms caused investment to rise 57 percent compared with 1994. Foreign investment in agriculture, cable television, cigarette manufacturing, housing construction, liquor production, and the refining of petroleum is still banned, however, and foreign ownership of mining and shipping is limited.

BANKING
Score: 3–Stable (moderate level of restrictions)

Privatization of the country's commercial banks has yet to be implemented in full. In addition, there still are some restrictions on the opening of new banks. Nevertheless, banks are competitive and serve as an important source of capital for Taiwan's expanding economy.

WAGE AND PRICE CONTROLS
Score: 2–Stable (low level)

Taiwan maintains a minimum wage policy and requires equal pay for men and women. Prices are monitored regularly by the Commodity Price Supervisory Board, which is composed of members of the Ministry of Finance, the Ministry of Economic Affairs, the Agricultural Commission, and the Ministry of Communications, although it does not have the power to set prices directly.

PROPERTY RIGHTS
Score: 1–Stable (very high level of protection)

Property rights are fully protected in Taiwan. The judiciary is efficient and independent of overt government influence.

REGULATION
Score: 2–Stable (low level)

Even though the government has established some moderately burdensome regulations, entrepreneurs can open a business in Taiwan with little difficulty. Most regulations are applied openly and evenly, and pose only a minor burden. By global standards, the level of regulation is low.

BLACK MARKET
Score: 1–Stable (very low level of activity)

Because Taiwan has a free economy, its black market is very small. Taiwan has developed an advanced and efficient intellectual property rights protection law, consistent with the World Trade Organization. Although there is some trade in pirated material, it is minuscule in comparison with the size of the economy overall.

NOTES

1. Lawrence J. Lau and Lawrence R. Klein, *Models of Development: A Comparative Study of Economic Growth in South Korea and Taiwan* (San Francisco, Cal.: ICS Press, 1990).
2. *Ibid.*, p. 187.

Colombia
3.00

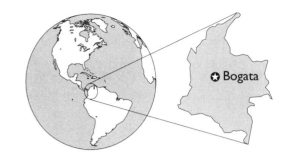
○ Bogata

1997 Score: **3.10**	1996 Score: **3.00**	1995 Score: **2.90**

Trade	3	Banking	2
Taxation	4	Wages and Prices	2
Government Intervention	2	Property Rights	3
Monetary Policy	4	Regulation	3
Foreign Investment	2	Black Market	5

Colombia's political system has come under growing pressure in recent years as drug traffickers have increased their influence within the government, corrupting executive, legislative, and judicial institutions. After several years of economic stability and growth because of free-market reforms first applied in 1990 by President Cesar Gaviria, the economy has been slowing since the end of 1994. This is due primarily to drug scandals involving current President Ernesto Samper and several current and former cabinet members. Samper has called for increased government spending on social welfare programs that also could jeopardize Colombia's recent economic gains. The level of government intervention in the economy has increased, and the Samper government has imposed more burdensome regulations. Colombia recently reduced its level of protectionism, and this improves its overall score by 0.1 point over last year's score.

TRADE POLICY
Score: 3+ (low level of protectionism)

Colombia has an average tariff rate of 12 percent, down from 35.5 percent in 1990,[1] and maintains many nontariff barriers. Recent trade agreements between Colombia and other South American countries, however, have reduced the average tariff rate significantly. Taking these agreements into account, Colombia's average tariff rate is closer to 6.34 percent. Thus, this year's trade score is one point better than last year's. Colombia still requires importers to obtain licenses for dairy, poultry, and other products.

TAXATION
Score–Income taxation: 4–Stable (high tax rates)
Score–Corporate taxation: 3–Stable (moderate tax rates)
Final Taxation Score: 4–Stable (high tax rates)

Colombia's top income tax rate is 30 percent,[2] and the average income level is taxed at less than 5 percent. Many of these taxpayers are not required to fill out a tax return.[3] The government is cracking down on tax fraud, and more collections are being made than ever before. The top corporate tax rate is 35 percent, up from 30 percent in 1995. Colombia also has a 35 percent capital gains tax and a 16 percent value-added tax.

GOVERNMENT INTERVENTION IN THE ECONOMY
Score: 2–Stable (low level)

Government consumes 13.4 percent of Colombia's GDP. According to the Economist Intelligence Unit, the "weight of the state in the economy has been growing steadily in recent years. Total public outlays are estimated at 46 percent of GDP in 1995, 6 percentage points above the level at the start of the decade. Samper's Social Leap assumes that this proportion will grow to 51 percent by 1998, as he takes a more interventionist approach to economic policy."[4] Nevertheless, Colombia has undertaken significant privatization. Since 1991, it has privatized ports, railroads, and cellular telephone services, as well as a number of chemical, agro-industrial, fishing, and gasoline companies and banks. This program has stalled recently.

1	Hong Kong	1.25	77	Zambia	3.05
2	Singapore	1.30	80	Mali	3.10
3	Bahrain	1.70	80	Mongolia	3.10
4	New Zealand	1.75	80	Slovenia	3.10
5	Switzerland	1.90	83	Honduras	3.15
5	United States	1.90	83	Papua New Guinea	3.15
7	Luxembourg	1.95	85	Djibouti	3.20
7	Taiwan	1.95	85	Fiji	3.20
7	United Kingdom	1.95	85	Pakistan	3.20
10	Bahamas	2.00	88	Algeria	3.25
10	Ireland	2.00	88	Guinea	3.25
12	Australia	2.05	88	Lebanon	3.25
12	Japan	2.05	88	Mexico	3.25
14	Belgium	2.10	88	Senegal	3.25
14	Canada	2.10	88	Tanzania	3.25
14	United Arab Emirates	2.10	94	Nigeria	3.30
17	Austria	2.15	94	Romania	3.30
17	Chile	2.15	96	Brazil	3.35
17	Estonia	2.15	96	Cambodia	3.35
20	Czech Republic	2.20	96	Egypt	3.35
20	Netherlands	2.20	96	Ivory Coast	3.35
22	Denmark	2.25	96	Madagascar	3.35
22	Finland	2.25	96	Moldova	3.35
24	Germany	2.30	102	Nepal	3.40
24	Iceland	2.30	103	Cape Verde	3.44
24	South Korea	2.30	104	Armenia	3.45
27	Norway	2.35	104	Dominican Republic	3.45
28	Kuwait	2.40	104	Russia	3.45
28	Malaysia	2.40	107	Burkina Faso	3.50
28	Panama	2.40	107	Cameroon	3.50
28	Thailand	2.40	107	Lesotho	3.50
32	El Salvador	2.45	107	Nicaragua	3.50
32	Sri Lanka	2.45	107	Venezuela	3.50
32	Sweden	2.45	112	Gambia	3.60
35	France	2.50	112	Guyana	3.60
35	Italy	2.50	114	Bulgaria	3.65
35	Spain	2.50	114	Georgia	3.65
38	Trinidad and Tobago	2.55	114	Malawi	3.65
39	Argentina	2.60	117	Ethiopia	3.70
39	Barbados	2.60	117	India	3.70
39	Cyprus	2.60	117	Niger	3.70
39	Jamaica	2.60	120	Albania	3.75
39	Portugal	2.60	120	Bangladesh	3.75
44	Bolivia	2.65	120	China (PRC)	3.75
44	Oman	2.65	120	Congo	3.75
44	Philippines	2.65	120	Croatia	3.75
47	Swaziland	2.70	125	Chad	3.80
47	Uruguay	2.70	125	Mauritania	3.80
49	Botswana	2.75	125	Ukraine	3.80
49	Jordan	2.75	128	Sierra Leone	3.85
49	Namibia	2.75	129	Burundi	3.90
49	Tunisia	2.75	129	Suriname	3.90
53	Belize	2.80	129	Zimbabwe	3.90
53	Costa Rica	2.80	132	Haiti	4.00
53	Guatemala	2.80	132	Kyrgyzstan	4.00
53	Israel	2.80	132	Syria	4.00
53	Peru	2.80	135	Belarus	4.05
53	Saudi Arabia	2.80	136	Kazakstan	4.10
53	Turkey	2.80	136	Mozambique	4.10
53	Uganda	2.80	136	Yemen	4.10
53	Western Samoa	2.80	139	Sudan	4.20
62	Indonesia	2.85	140	Myanmar	4.30
62	Latvia	2.85	140	Rwanda	4.30
62	Malta	2.85	142	Angola	4.35
62	Paraguay	2.85	143	Azerbaijan	4.40
66	Greece	2.90	143	Tajikistan	4.40
66	Hungary	2.90	145	Turkmenistan	4.50
66	South Africa	2.90	146	Uzbekistan	4.55
69	Benin	2.95	147	Congo/Zaire	4.70
69	Ecuador	2.95	147	Iran	4.70
69	Gabon	2.95	147	Libya	4.70
69	Morocco	2.95	147	Somalia	4.70
69	Poland	2.95	147	Vietnam	4.70
74	Colombia	3.00	152	Bosnia	4.80
74	Ghana	3.00	153	Iraq	4.90
74	Lithuania	3.00	154	Cuba	5.00
77	Kenya	3.05	154	Laos	5.00
77	Slovak Republic	3.05	154	North Korea	5.00

Mostly Unfree

MONETARY POLICY
Score: 4–Stable (high level of inflation)

From 1985 to 1995, Colombia's average rate of inflation was 25.2 percent. Since that time, the inflation rate has remained stable at around 18 percent.

CAPITAL FLOWS AND FOREIGN INVESTMENT
Score: 2–Stable (low barriers)

Colombia permits 100 percent foreign ownership in almost all sectors of its economy. The exceptions are in national security and hazardous waste industries. Permission is needed for investments in the public service, water, waste, and transportation industries, or for large investments in mining and petroleum enterprises. A simple registration and licensing process is required for all investments.

BANKING
Score: 2–Stable (low level of restrictions)

Foreign banks have complete access to credit and the entire Colombian financial system, and almost all credit is directed by the private sector. "Foreign investors experience no discrimination in access to local credit," reports the U.S. Department of Commerce. "While the Colombian government still directs credit to some areas (notably agriculture) credit is for the most part allocated by the private financial market. Credit subsidies were phased out with the establishment of FINAGRO, a state-owned agricultural credit intermediary."[5] Colombia has yet to achieve a completely free banking system, however. Domestic banks may sell securities, insurance policies, and investment services.

WAGE AND PRICE CONTROLS
Score: 2–Stable (low level)

Colombia's pricing policy is one of the most free-market in Latin America. According to the Economist Intelligence Unit, "Price controls apply only to a few pharmaceutical products, petroleum derivatives, gas, some petrochemicals, several basic consumer goods, school books, school tuition, residential rents and certain services (e.g., bus fares, utilities, and airline fares)."[6] Thus, the market sets most prices. Colombia also maintains a minimum wage.

PROPERTY RIGHTS
Score: 3–Stable (moderate level of protection)

The most significant threats to private property in Colombia are the violence created by the drug cartels and the government's attempt to distribute wealth more equally. Private property generally is protected, and the government is privatizing state-owned enterprises. The legal system is not always efficient, however. "The Colombian judicial system continues to be clogged and cumbersome," reports the U.S. Department of Commerce, "although its reform and streamlining are stated goals of the Samper administration."[7] According to the U.S. Department of State, "The judiciary is severely overburdened, and has a huge case backlog estimated at over 1 million cases."[8]

REGULATION
Score: 3–Stable (moderate level)

Colombia has a free-market economy, and the government tends to exercise minimal control of the private sector. Obtaining a business license is not difficult; there is a limited registration process, and the government tends to allow businesses to operate as they see fit. A growing environmental movement is causing increased regulation of business, however, and corruption within the Colombian bureaucracy is growing.

BLACK MARKET
Score: 5–Stable (very high level of activity)

The drug trade makes Colombia's black market very large. There also is a growing black market in pirated intellectual property, mainly because of lagging legal protection of intellectual property rights. "Despite significant improvement in 1993 and 1994 in the area of intellectual property rights," reports the Office of the U.S. Trade Representative, "Colombia does not yet provide adequate and effective protection.... U.S. industry estimates that video cassette piracy continues to represent 75 percent of the video market, sound recording piracy has soared to 66 percent of the market, and business software piracy has dropped slightly to 67 percent of the market."[9]

NOTES

1. Office of the United States Trade Representative, *National Trade Estimate Report on Foreign Trade Barriers, 1997.*
2. Colombia's top marginal income tax rate is 55 percent: a top tax rate of 30 percent plus a 25 percent tax penalty for making more than a specific level of income. The 25 percent tax payment becomes a deduction on the following year's taxes, however. Thus, only the top rate of 30 percent was used in grading this factor.
3. For purposes of grading, the 5 percent figure was used.
4. Economist Intelligence Unit, *ILT Reports, Colombia, 1997,* p. 7.
5. U.S. Department of Commerce, *Country Commercial Guide, 1997.*
6. Economist Intelligence Unit, *ILT Reports, Colombia, 1997,* p. 21.
7. *Ibid.*
8. U.S. Department of State, "Colombia Country Report on Human Rights Practices for 1996," 1997.
9. Office of the United States Trade Representative, *National Trade Estimate Report on Foreign Trade Barriers, 1997.*

Congo, Democratic Republic of (formerly Zaire)

4.70

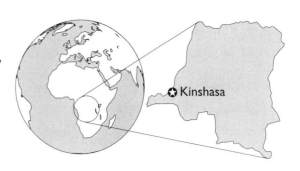

⊛ Kinshasa

1997 Score: **4.20**   1996 Score: **4.20**   1995 Score: **n/a**

Trade	5	Banking	5
Taxation	5	Wages and Prices	4
Government Intervention	4	Property Rights	5
Monetary Policy	5	Regulation	4
Foreign Investment	5	Black Market	5

In May 1997, Zaire became known as the Democratic Republic of Congo.[1] It gained its independence from Belgium in 1960 and quickly fell into turmoil as various regionally based and superpower-backed factions fought for control. A largely futile United Nations peacekeeping operation took place in what then was called the Congo. In 1965, Mobutu Sese Seko seized control of the central government, changed the country's name to Zaire, and began decades of repression, forcing the people to live under a strict government-controlled economy. In May 1997, after years of relatively minor rebel activity, Zaire's government and Mobutu were overthrown by rebel leader Laurent Kabila. Three days after Mobutu had been ousted, Kabila proclaimed himself president of the renamed Democratic Republic of Congo. Kabila has promised to focus on "social market" issues: schools, roads, and health care. After promising not to extend a state takeover of the economy, Kabila's rebels nationalized one of Congo's major railways. But even though Kabila has established a government and appointed ministers to his cabinet, the government remains a shambles. Sporadic fighting continues, most economic activity has ceased, and most members of the bureaucracy are not receiving paychecks. As Kabila seeks aid from Western countries and from international aid agencies, his government is accused of slaughtering thousands of Rwandan refugees and arbitrarily arresting those who oppose the new government. In addition, the government has increased its barriers to trade and foreign investment, its intervention in the economy, and its restrictions on banking. Thus, this year's score for the Democratic Republic of Congo is 0.5 point worse than last year's score for Zaire.

TRADE POLICY
Score: 5– (very high level of protectionism)

The recent change of government has decreased the movement of goods across the border severely. Corruption is rampant in what remains of the customs bureau as customs officials seek to confiscate imports arbitrarily or solicit bribes from importers to release goods. According to the U.S. Department of State, "As of early June 1997, customs and immigration services have not been fully re-established in Kinshasa."[2] As a result, Congo's trade score is one point worse this year.

TAXATION
Score - Income taxation: 5–Stable (very high tax rates)
Score - Corporate taxation: 5–Stable (very high tax rates)
Final Taxation Score: 5–Stable (very high tax rates)

Zaire had a top income tax rate of 45 percent and a top marginal corporate tax rate of 50 percent. The new government has yet to establish a system to collect and enforce taxes, and the result is arbitrary government raids on civilians and

1	Hong Kong	1.25		77	Zambia	3.05
2	Singapore	1.30		80	Mali	3.10
3	Bahrain	1.70		80	Mongolia	3.10
4	New Zealand	1.75		80	Slovenia	3.10
5	Switzerland	1.90		83	Honduras	3.15
5	United States	1.90		83	Papua New Guinea	3.15
7	Luxembourg	1.95		85	Djibouti	3.20
7	Taiwan	1.95		85	Fiji	3.20
7	United Kingdom	1.95		85	Pakistan	3.20
10	Bahamas	2.00		88	Algeria	3.25
10	Ireland	2.00		88	Guinea	3.25
12	Australia	2.05		88	Lebanon	3.25
12	Japan	2.05		88	Mexico	3.25
14	Belgium	2.10		88	Senegal	3.25
14	Canada	2.10		88	Tanzania	3.25
14	United Arab Emirates	2.10		94	Nigeria	3.30
17	Austria	2.15		94	Romania	3.30
17	Chile	2.15		96	Brazil	3.35
17	Estonia	2.15		96	Cambodia	3.35
20	Czech Republic	2.20		96	Egypt	3.35
20	Netherlands	2.20		96	Ivory Coast	3.35
22	Denmark	2.25		96	Madagascar	3.35
22	Finland	2.25		96	Moldova	3.35
24	Germany	2.30		102	Nepal	3.40
24	Iceland	2.30		103	Cape Verde	3.44
24	South Korea	2.30		104	Armenia	3.45
27	Norway	2.35		104	Dominican Republic	3.45
28	Kuwait	2.40		104	Russia	3.45
28	Malaysia	2.40		107	Burkina Faso	3.50
28	Panama	2.40		107	Cameroon	3.50
28	Thailand	2.40		107	Lesotho	3.50
32	El Salvador	2.45		107	Nicaragua	3.50
32	Sri Lanka	2.45		107	Venezuela	3.50
32	Sweden	2.45		112	Gambia	3.60
35	France	2.50		112	Guyana	3.60
35	Italy	2.50		114	Bulgaria	3.65
35	Spain	2.50		114	Georgia	3.65
38	Trinidad and Tobago	2.55		114	Malawi	3.65
39	Argentina	2.60		117	Ethiopia	3.70
39	Barbados	2.60		117	India	3.70
39	Cyprus	2.60		117	Niger	3.70
39	Jamaica	2.60		120	Albania	3.75
39	Portugal	2.60		120	Bangladesh	3.75
44	Bolivia	2.65		120	China (PRC)	3.75
44	Oman	2.65		120	Congo	3.75
44	Philippines	2.65		120	Croatia	3.75
47	Swaziland	2.70		125	Chad	3.80
47	Uruguay	2.70		125	Mauritania	3.80
49	Botswana	2.75		125	Ukraine	3.80
49	Jordan	2.75		128	Sierra Leone	3.85
49	Namibia	2.75		129	Burundi	3.90
49	Tunisia	2.75		129	Suriname	3.90
53	Belize	2.80		129	Zimbabwe	3.90
53	Costa Rica	2.80		132	Haiti	4.00
53	Guatemala	2.80		132	Kyrgyzstan	4.00
53	Israel	2.80		132	Syria	4.00
53	Peru	2.80		135	Belarus	4.05
53	Saudi Arabia	2.80		136	Kazakstan	4.10
53	Turkey	2.80		136	Mozambique	4.10
53	Uganda	2.80		136	Yemen	4.10
53	Western Samoa	2.80		139	Sudan	4.20
62	Indonesia	2.85		140	Myanmar	4.30
62	Latvia	2.85		140	Rwanda	4.30
62	Malta	2.85		142	Angola	4.35
62	Paraguay	2.85		143	Azerbaijan	4.40
66	Greece	2.90		143	Tajikistan	4.40
66	Hungary	2.90		145	Turkmenistan	4.50
66	South Africa	2.90		146	Uzbekistan	4.55
69	Benin	2.95		147	Congo/Zaire	4.70
69	Ecuador	2.95		147	Iran	4.70
69	Gabon	2.95		147	Libya	4.70
69	Morocco	2.95		147	Somalia	4.70
69	Poland	2.95		147	Vietnam	4.70
74	Colombia	3.00		152	Bosnia	4.80
74	Ghana	3.00		153	Iraq	4.90
74	Lithuania	3.00		154	Cuba	5.00
77	Kenya	3.05		154	Laos	5.00
77	Slovak Republic	3.05		154	North Korea	5.00

Repressed

businesses to collect revenue. The breakdown of civil order has given rise to looting and banditry by Congo's citizens, former Mobutu government officials, and Kabila's rebels.

GOVERNMENT INTERVENTION IN THE ECONOMY
Score: 4– (high level)

Congo's government is in disarray. Most civil servants have not been paid since the takeover, and major roads and bridges are being overtaken by jungle. Because most economic activity has ceased, rebel forces now consume most of the country's economic output for their own purposes. As a consequence, Congo's government intervention score is one point worse this year.

MONETARY POLICY
Score: 5–Stable (very high level of inflation)

Zaire historically had high average annual rates of inflation: over 2,000 percent from 1985 to 1993 and 5,000 percent in 1994. Today, control over Congo's money supply is uncertain.

CAPITAL FLOWS AND FOREIGN INVESTMENT
Score: 5– (very high barriers)

Before the rebel takeover, Zaire's economy had been opening slowly to foreign investment. Although the new rebel government has publicly said it seeks to attract foreign investment and ensure the rights of current foreign investors, its actions prove otherwise. The breaking of a contract for the private operation of Congo's main railway led to nationalization by Kabila's troops. Foreign investment has subsided to a trickle. It is not clear whether the former Zairian commercial code and foreign investment code still apply. As a result, this year's score is one point worse than last year's.

BANKING
Score: 5– (very high level of restrictions)

Congo's banking score this year is one point worse than it was last year. The banking system has collapsed, and even though some small banks have tried to reopen for business, they remain hampered by an indeterminable and unreliable money supply. The Central Bank has been able to conduct some financial activity, restoring the Congolese franc some 23 years after it was supplanted by Zaire's currency, but the franc has yet to be put into circulation.

WAGE AND PRICE CONTROLS
Score: 4–Stable (high level)

Because of the chaos in Congo, there is little official control over prices and wages. Most economic transactions are conducted as barter arrangements, and traditional market pricing mechanisms have ceased to exist, although market prices still apply for some goods in various rural parts of the country.

PROPERTY RIGHTS
Score: 5– (very low level of protection)

Private property is not secure because of corruption and recent instances of government expropriation, including that of Congo's largest railway. This expropriation broke a contract between a private firm and the former Mobutu government. As a result, Congo's score in this factor is one point worse than last year. According to the U.S. Department of State, "The new government forces are still in a formative state and have not yet taken full control of the country. There are continued reports of pillaging, vehicle thefts, carjackings, and extrajudicial violent settlements of accounts in some parts of Kinshasa, as well as ethnic tensions and continued military operations elsewhere in the country."[3]

REGULATION
Score: 4–Stable (high level)

Kabila's troops have yet to establish the rule of law. The remaining businesses are harassed by corrupt bandits, former government officials, and renegade military personnel seeking bribes, kickbacks, and loot.

BLACK MARKET
Score: 5–Stable (very high level of activity)

Almost all economic activity is conducted in the black market.

NOTES

1. For purposes of this study, the Democratic Republic of Congo is identified by its former name of Zaire whenever historical events before May 1997 are discussed.
2. U.S. Department of State Travel Advisory, 1997.
3. *Ibid.*

Congo, Republic of

3.75

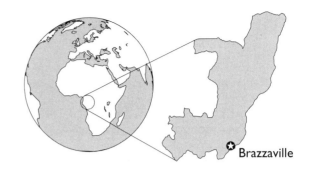

Brazzaville

1997 Score: **3.75**	1996 Score: **3.80**	1995 Score: **3.90**

Trade	5	Banking	4
Taxation	4.5	Wages and Prices	3
Government Intervention	3	Property Rights	4
Monetary Policy	1	Regulation	4
Foreign Investment	4	Black Market	5

Since receiving its independence from France in 1960, Congo has endured one-party rule, Marxist economic policies, political repression, and frequent military coups. In 1990, Marxism was abandoned and political parties were legalized. The country changed its name to the Republic of the Congo in 1991 and held multiparty elections in 1992. Congo's democracy, however, is fragile: The elections spawned riots and civil unrest in 1993 and 1994, and conflict has erupted recently between forces loyal to President Pascal Lissouba and those loyal to opposing militia leader and former President Denis Sassou Nguesso. There has been little progress toward fundamental democratic reform, and market reforms have been negligible. The state plays a leading role in the stagnating economy, and GDP growth has averaged only 1.1 percent from 1992 to 1996.

TRADE POLICY
Score: 5–Stable (very high level of protectionism)

Congo's average tariff rate is over 30 percent. In the early 1980s, it was 8.6 percent. The most significant nontariff barriers to trade still are red tape, an inefficient customs service, and outright theft of imported goods by government officials.

TAXATION
Score–Income taxation: 4–Stable (high tax rates)
Score–Corporate taxation: 4–Stable (high tax rates)
Final Taxation Score: 4.5–Stable (very high tax rates)

Congo's top income tax rate is 50 percent, and the average income level is taxed at 15 percent. The top corporate tax is 45 percent. Congo also has a 45 percent capital gains tax and a 17.85 percent goods and services tax.

GOVERNMENT INTERVENTION IN THE ECONOMY
Score: 3–Stable (moderate level)

Government consumes 20.6 percent of Congo's GDP, and the state-owned sector is extremely large. A privatization effort has yielded minimal results.

MONETARY POLICY
Score: 1–Stable (very low level of inflation)

Congo's average annual rate of inflation from 1985 to 1995 was 2.2 percent. In 1996, inflation ran at an estimated 3 percent.

1	Hong Kong	1.25	77	Zambia	3.05
2	Singapore	1.30	80	Mali	3.10
3	Bahrain	1.70	80	Mongolia	3.10
4	New Zealand	1.75	80	Slovenia	3.10
5	Switzerland	1.90	83	Honduras	3.15
5	United States	1.90	83	Papua New Guinea	3.15
7	Luxembourg	1.95	85	Djibouti	3.20
7	Taiwan	1.95	85	Fiji	3.20
7	United Kingdom	1.95	85	Pakistan	3.20
10	Bahamas	2.00	88	Algeria	3.25
10	Ireland	2.00	88	Guinea	3.25
12	Australia	2.05	88	Lebanon	3.25
12	Japan	2.05	88	Mexico	3.25
14	Belgium	2.10	88	Senegal	3.25
14	Canada	2.10	88	Tanzania	3.25
14	United Arab Emirates	2.10	94	Nigeria	3.30
17	Austria	2.15	94	Romania	3.30
17	Chile	2.15	96	Brazil	3.35
17	Estonia	2.15	96	Cambodia	3.35
20	Czech Republic	2.20	96	Egypt	3.35
20	Netherlands	2.20	96	Ivory Coast	3.35
22	Denmark	2.25	96	Madagascar	3.35
22	Finland	2.25	96	Moldova	3.35
24	Germany	2.30	102	Nepal	3.40
24	Iceland	2.30	103	Cape Verde	3.44
24	South Korea	2.30	104	Armenia	3.45
27	Norway	2.35	104	Dominican Republic	3.45
28	Kuwait	2.40	104	Russia	3.45
28	Malaysia	2.40	107	Burkina Faso	3.50
28	Panama	2.40	107	Cameroon	3.50
28	Thailand	2.40	107	Lesotho	3.50
32	El Salvador	2.45	107	Nicaragua	3.50
32	Sri Lanka	2.45	107	Venezuela	3.50
32	Sweden	2.45	112	Gambia	3.60
35	France	2.50	112	Guyana	3.60
35	Italy	2.50	114	Bulgaria	3.65
35	Spain	2.50	114	Georgia	3.65
38	Trinidad and Tobago	2.55	114	Malawi	3.65
39	Argentina	2.60	117	Ethiopia	3.70
39	Barbados	2.60	117	India	3.70
39	Cyprus	2.60	117	Niger	3.70
39	Jamaica	2.60	120	Albania	3.75
39	Portugal	2.60	120	Bangladesh	3.75
44	Bolivia	2.65	120	China (PRC)	3.75
44	Oman	2.65	120	Congo	3.75
44	Philippines	2.65	120	Croatia	3.75
47	Swaziland	2.70	125	Chad	3.80
47	Uruguay	2.70	125	Mauritania	3.80
49	Botswana	2.75	125	Nigeria	3.80
49	Jordan	2.75	128	Sierra Leone	3.85
49	Namibia	2.75	129	Burundi	3.90
49	Tunisia	2.75	129	Suriname	3.90
53	Belize	2.80	129	Zimbabwe	3.90
53	Costa Rica	2.80	132	Haiti	4.00
53	Guatemala	2.80	132	Kyrgyzstan	4.00
53	Israel	2.80	132	Syria	4.00
53	Peru	2.80	135	Belarus	4.05
53	Saudi Arabia	2.80	136	Kazakstan	4.10
53	Turkey	2.80	136	Mozambique	4.10
53	Uganda	2.80	136	Yemen	4.10
53	Western Samoa	2.80	139	Sudan	4.20
62	Indonesia	2.85	140	Myanmar	4.30
62	Latvia	2.85	140	Rwanda	4.30
62	Malta	2.85	142	Angola	4.35
62	Paraguay	2.85	143	Azerbaijan	4.40
66	Greece	2.90	143	Tajikistan	4.40
66	Hungary	2.90	146	Turkmenistan	4.50
66	South Africa	2.90	146	Uzbekistan	4.55
69	Benin	2.95	147	Congo/Zaire	4.70
69	Ecuador	2.95	147	Iran	4.70
69	Gabon	2.95	147	Libya	4.70
69	Morocco	2.95	147	Somalia	4.70
69	Poland	2.95	147	Vietnam	4.70
74	Colombia	3.00	152	Bosnia	4.80
74	Ghana	3.00	153	Iraq	4.90
74	Lithuania	3.00	154	Cuba	5.00
77	Kenya	3.05	154	Laos	5.00
77	Slovak Republic	3.05	154	North Korea	5.00

Mostly Unfree

CAPITAL FLOWS AND FOREIGN INVESTMENT
Score: 4–Stable (high barriers)

Foreign investment is ruled by a government code that has yet to be implemented in full. Foreign investors face hostile government bureaucrats and labor conditions, and many labor unions remain under the influence of Marxist ideology, making it nearly impossible to do business. French vested interests also work against foreign investment. Consequently, new foreign investment is virtually nonexistent outside the petroleum and retail sectors. The government has established a "one-stop shop" in an effort to attract foreign investors.

BANKING
Score: 4–Stable (high level of restrictions)

Banks remain under the control or influence of corrupt government officials, and hostile labor conditions limit foreign banks' ability to operate. The government claims that it may sell state banks to foreign investors. According to the U.S. Department of Commerce, "The Congolese banking sector is all but moribund.... There is a network of credit unions and a rural credit association but lending levels for both these institutions is minimal."[1]

WAGE AND PRICE CONTROLS
Score: 3–Stable (moderate level)

Prices are controlled through large state-owned companies, which also are subsidized by the government. There is a minimum wage.

PROPERTY RIGHTS
Score: 4–Stable (low level of protection)

Government expropriation of property remains possible. An insufficient judicial and legal framework means little government protection of private property. Although the courts are supposed to be independent, most are not. According to the U.S. Department of Commerce, "Judicial independence is a new concept and the courts are not yet able to effectively enforce property and contractual rights. There have been recent allegations of government interference in the courts.... The judicial system currently is not capable of securing land, building, and mortgage rights."[2]

REGULATION
Score: 4–Stable (high level)

Government regulators are corrupt, often requiring bribes. Regulations, in addition to being burdensome, are enforced haphazardly, and labor laws favor militant unions at the expense of employers. "Although the government has recently enacted measures to decrease bureaucratic red-tape," reports the U.S. Department of Commerce, "administrative procedures remain extremely time-consuming.... Corruption takes numerous forms and runs a gamut from a government official requesting a beer in return for a service to an apartment in France."[3]

BLACK MARKET
Score: 5–Stable (very high level of activity)

Congo's black market is large. Corruption among customs officials creates a market for the smuggling of all types of goods, and high tariffs encourage the smuggling of many foodstuffs. There is a considerable trade in illegal arms.

NOTES

1. U.S. Department of Commerce, *Country Commercial Guide,* 1997.
2. *Ibid.*
3. *Ibid.*

Costa Rica 2.80

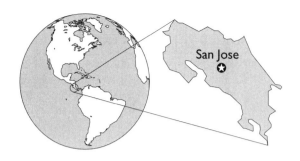

1997 Score: **2.80**	1996 Score: **2.80**	1995 Score: **2.90**

Trade	4	Banking	3
Taxation	3	Wages and Prices	2
Government Intervention	2	Property Rights	3
Monetary Policy	3	Regulation	3
Foreign Investment	2	Black Market	3

Costa Rica declared its independence from Spain in 1821. Foreign aid has decreased drastically since the end of the Cold War, and trade between the United States and Costa Rica is growing. The United States remains the country's largest trading partner. Costa Rica's economic growth has resulted primarily from increased trade and economic reforms. Inflation is on the rise again, however, despite recent gains in the government's efforts to reduce it, and some economic reforms have slowed.

Trade Policy
Score: 4–Stable (high level of protectionism)

Although Costa Rica has been moving toward greater openness, it remains a rather difficult market to penetrate. The average tariff rate is 11 percent, and customs procedures are cumbersome and plagued with inefficiency. Many companies are forced to hire a customs specialist just to get their products across the border. There are significant nontariff barriers as well.

Taxation
Score–Income taxation: 2–Stable (low tax rates)
Score–Corporate taxation: 3–Stable (moderate tax rates)
Final Taxation Score: 3–Stable (moderate tax rates)

Costa Rica's top marginal income tax rate is 25 percent, and the tax on the average income is about 10 percent. The top corporate income tax rate is 30 percent. Costa Rica also has a 15 percent sales tax.

Government Intervention in the Economy
Score: 2–Stable (low level)

Government consumes about 16.8 percent of Costa Rica's GDP.

Monetary Policy
Score: 3–Stable (high level of inflation)

Costa Rica's rate of inflation from 1985 to 1995 was 18.5 percent. The rate for 1996 was 13.9 percent.

Capital Flows and Foreign Investment
Score: 2–Stable (low barriers)

Costa Rica offers one of the best investment climates in Central America. There are no repatriation requirements, foreigners are allowed to take out all their profits, and the government offers a widening group of incentives, including tax holidays for some specific investments. Costa Rica does not discriminate against foreign investors; they are treated the same as local investors. Some restrictions remain on utilities and services, and investment in these areas is barred.

Mostly Free

1	Hong Kong	1.25	77	Zambia	3.05
2	Singapore	1.30	80	Mali	3.10
3	Bahrain	1.70	80	Mongolia	3.10
4	New Zealand	1.75	80	Slovenia	3.10
5	Switzerland	1.90	83	Honduras	3.15
5	United States	1.90	83	Papua New Guinea	3.15
7	Luxembourg	1.95	85	Djibouti	3.20
7	Taiwan	1.95	85	Fiji	3.20
7	United Kingdom	1.95	85	Pakistan	3.20
10	Bahamas	2.00	88	Algeria	3.25
10	Ireland	2.00	88	Guinea	3.25
12	Australia	2.05	88	Lebanon	3.25
12	Japan	2.05	88	Mexico	3.25
14	Belgium	2.10	88	Senegal	3.25
14	Canada	2.10	88	Tanzania	3.25
14	United Arab Emirates	2.10	94	Nigeria	3.30
17	Austria	2.15	94	Romania	3.30
17	Chile	2.15	96	Brazil	3.35
17	Estonia	2.15	96	Cambodia	3.35
20	Czech Republic	2.20	96	Egypt	3.35
20	Netherlands	2.20	96	Ivory Coast	3.35
22	Denmark	2.25	96	Madagascar	3.35
22	Finland	2.25	96	Moldova	3.35
24	Germany	2.30	102	Nepal	3.40
24	Iceland	2.30	103	Cape Verde	3.44
24	South Korea	2.30	104	Armenia	3.45
27	Norway	2.35	104	Dominican Republic	3.45
28	Kuwait	2.40	104	Russia	3.45
28	Malaysia	2.40	107	Burkina Faso	3.50
28	Panama	2.40	107	Cameroon	3.50
28	Thailand	2.40	107	Lesotho	3.50
32	El Salvador	2.45	107	Nicaragua	3.50
32	Sri Lanka	2.45	107	Venezuela	3.50
32	Sweden	2.45	112	Gambia	3.60
35	France	2.50	112	Guyana	3.60
35	Italy	2.50	114	Bulgaria	3.65
35	Spain	2.50	114	Georgia	3.65
38	Trinidad and Tobago	2.55	114	Malawi	3.65
39	Argentina	2.60	117	Ethiopia	3.70
39	Barbados	2.60	117	India	3.70
39	Cyprus	2.60	117	Niger	3.70
39	Jamaica	2.60	120	Albania	3.75
39	Portugal	2.60	120	Bangladesh	3.75
44	Bolivia	2.65	120	China (PRC)	3.75
44	Oman	2.65	120	Congo	3.75
44	Philippines	2.65	120	Croatia	3.75
47	Swaziland	2.70	125	Chad	3.80
47	Uruguay	2.70	125	Mauritania	3.80
49	Botswana	2.75	125	Ukraine	3.80
49	Jordan	2.75	128	Sierra Leone	3.85
49	Namibia	2.75	129	Burundi	3.90
49	Tunisia	2.75	129	Suriname	3.90
53	Belize	2.80	129	Zimbabwe	3.90
53	Costa Rica	2.80	132	Haiti	4.00
53	Guatemala	2.80	132	Kyrgyzstan	4.00
53	Israel	2.80	132	Syria	4.00
53	Peru	2.80	135	Belarus	4.05
53	Saudi Arabia	2.80	136	Kazakstan	4.10
53	Turkey	2.80	136	Mozambique	4.10
53	Uganda	2.80	136	Yemen	4.10
53	Western Samoa	2.80	139	Sudan	4.20
62	Indonesia	2.85	140	Myanmar	4.30
62	Latvia	2.85	140	Rwanda	4.30
62	Malta	2.85	142	Angola	4.35
62	Paraguay	2.85	143	Azerbaijan	4.40
66	Greece	2.90	143	Tajikistan	4.40
66	Hungary	2.90	145	Turkmenistan	4.50
66	South Africa	2.90	146	Uzbekistan	4.55
69	Benin	2.95	147	Congo/Zaire	4.70
69	Ecuador	2.95	147	Iran	4.70
69	Gabon	2.95	147	Libya	4.70
69	Morocco	2.95	147	Somalia	4.70
69	Poland	2.95	147	Vietnam	4.70
74	Colombia	3.00	152	Bosnia	4.80
74	Ghana	3.00	153	Iraq	4.90
74	Lithuania	3.00	154	Cuba	5.00
77	Kenya	3.05	154	Laos	5.00
77	Slovak Republic	3.05	154	North Korea	5.00

BANKING
Score: 3–Stable (moderate level of restrictions)

Foreigners are prevented from engaging in some banking services, such as checking and savings. Banking competition is generally free and open in Costa Rica, although banks are not permitted to sell insurance policies and other services. The banking sector is mainly dominated by four state-owned banks.

WAGE AND PRICE CONTROLS
Score: 2–Stable (low level)

The market sets most wages and prices. Most price controls have been eliminated, except for those on a few basic foodstuffs. Costa Rica maintains a minimum wage.

PROPERTY RIGHTS
Score: 3–Stable (moderate level of protection)

Private property is not entirely safe in Costa Rica. Expropriation remains a threat, and the owner rarely receives market value when property is taken. In many cases, the government offers no compensation. Some U.S. property rights claims date back 25 years. Domestic property owners could lose their land to growing numbers of squatters who band together to expropriate property and are becoming increasingly violent. The legal system has been unable to deal with this situation.

REGULATION
Score: 3–Stable (moderate level)

There are few major barriers to opening a business in Costa Rica. Regulations are easily understood and, for the most part, equally applied. There is scant evidence of corruption or bribery. Some regulations (for example, regulations requiring environmental impact studies) are moderately burdensome, and the government requires private companies to grant vacations, holidays, overtime, and social insurance.

BLACK MARKET
Score: 3–Stable (moderate level of activity)

Some construction, telephone installation, and transportation is performed in the black market. Intellectual property rights laws, although sufficient, are not enforced adequately. Thus, piracy in computer software, audio recordings, and video tapes remains a problem in Costa Rica.

Croatia   3.75

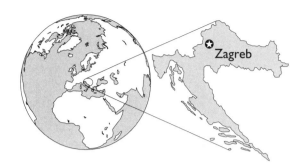

Zagreb

1997 Score: **3.70**	1996 Score: **3.70**	1995 Score: **n/a**

Trade	3	Banking	3
Taxation	3.5	Wages and Prices	4
Government Intervention	5	Property Rights	4
Monetary Policy	5	Regulation	4
Foreign Investment	3	Black Market	3

The collapse of Yugoslavia in 1990 and 1991 led to the creation of four independent countries, including Croatia. Since 1991, Croatia has been involved in a civil war that has ravaged its economy—now only about half the size it was in 1990. The war, with its flow of dispossessed refugees, continues to strain the country. The government was forced to focus on military operations instead of instituting necessary economic reforms. Some 25 percent to 30 percent of the country's agricultural capacity has been decimated. Croatia recently raised taxes; as a result, its overall score is 0.05 point worse this year.

TRADE POLICY
Score: 3–Stable (moderate level of protectionism)

Croatia's average tariff rate is about 12.1 percent.[1] Nontariff barriers include strict testing and certification requirements for some foods, pharmaceuticals, and electronics.

TAXATION
Score–Income taxation: 3–Stable (moderate tax rates)
Score–Corporate taxation: 3– (moderate tax rates)
Final Taxation Score: 3.5– (high tax rates)

Croatia's top income tax rate is 35 percent; the average taxpayer finds himself in the 25 percent bracket. The top marginal corporate tax rate is 35 percent, up from 25 percent last year. As a result, this year's taxation score is one point worse than last year's. Croatia also imposes a host of other taxes, including a 2.5 percent to 20 percent goods and services tax and a sales tax.

GOVERNMENT INTERVENTION IN THE ECONOMY
Score: 5–Stable (very high level)

Government consumes about 45 percent of Croatia's GDP,[2] much of which is generated by state-owned and -subsidized companies.

MONETARY POLICY
Score: 5–Stable (very high level)

Chronic inflation has plagued Croatia until very recently. In 1992, retail inflation alone was 669 percent; in 1993, it was 1,517 percent. In 1994, Croatia's inflation rate was 98 percent. In 1995, it fell to 2 percent; and in 1996, it was 3.6 percent. Overall, however, Croatia has had very high levels of inflation since 1992.

CAPITAL FLOWS AND FOREIGN INVESTMENT
Score: 3–Stable (moderate barriers)

Croatia encourages foreign investment. It gives foreign companies national treatment, making them equal to domestic firms under the law. Foreign investors are not allowed, however, to establish a fully owned company in the military-industrial, rail or air transport, insurance, publishing, or the mass media

1	Hong Kong	1.25	77	Zambia	3.05
2	Singapore	1.30	80	Mali	3.10
3	Bahrain	1.70	80	Mongolia	3.10
4	New Zealand	1.75	80	Slovenia	3.10
5	Switzerland	1.90	83	Honduras	3.15
5	United States	1.90	83	Papua New Guinea	3.15
7	Luxembourg	1.95	85	Djibouti	3.20
7	Taiwan	1.95	85	Fiji	3.20
7	United Kingdom	1.95	85	Pakistan	3.20
10	Bahamas	2.00	88	Algeria	3.25
10	Ireland	2.00	88	Guinea	3.25
12	Australia	2.05	88	Lebanon	3.25
12	Japan	2.05	88	Mexico	3.25
14	Belgium	2.10	88	Senegal	3.25
14	Canada	2.10	88	Tanzania	3.25
14	United Arab Emirates	2.10	94	Nigeria	3.30
17	Austria	2.15	94	Romania	3.30
17	Chile	2.15	96	Brazil	3.35
17	Estonia	2.15	96	Cambodia	3.35
20	Czech Republic	2.20	96	Egypt	3.35
20	Netherlands	2.20	96	Ivory Coast	3.35
22	Denmark	2.25	96	Madagascar	3.35
22	Finland	2.25	96	Moldova	3.35
24	Germany	2.30	102	Nepal	3.40
24	Iceland	2.30	103	Cape Verde	3.44
24	South Korea	2.30	104	Armenia	3.45
27	Norway	2.35	104	Dominican Republic	3.45
28	Kuwait	2.40	104	Russia	3.45
28	Malaysia	2.40	107	Burkina Faso	3.50
28	Panama	2.40	107	Cameroon	3.50
28	Thailand	2.40	107	Lesotho	3.50
32	El Salvador	2.45	107	Nicaragua	3.50
32	Sri Lanka	2.45	107	Venezuela	3.50
32	Sweden	2.45	112	Gambia	3.60
35	France	2.50	112	Guyana	3.60
35	Italy	2.50	114	Bulgaria	3.65
35	Spain	2.50	114	Georgia	3.65
38	Trinidad and Tobago	2.55	114	Malawi	3.65
39	Argentina	2.60	117	Ethiopia	3.70
39	Barbados	2.60	117	India	3.70
39	Cyprus	2.60	117	Niger	3.70
39	Jamaica	2.60	120	Albania	3.75
39	Portugal	2.60	120	Bangladesh	3.75
44	Bolivia	2.65	120	China (PRC)	3.75
44	Oman	2.65	120	Congo	3.75
44	Philippines	2.65	120	Croatia	3.75
47	Swaziland	2.70	125	Chad	3.80
47	Uruguay	2.70	125	Mauritania	3.80
49	Botswana	2.75	125	Ukraine	3.80
49	Jordan	2.75	128	Sierra Leone	3.85
49	Namibia	2.75	129	Burundi	3.90
49	Tunisia	2.75	129	Suriname	3.90
53	Belize	2.80	129	Zimbabwe	3.90
53	Costa Rica	2.80	132	Haiti	4.00
53	Guatemala	2.80	132	Kyrgyzstan	4.00
53	Israel	2.80	132	Syria	4.00
53	Peru	2.80	135	Belarus	4.05
53	Saudi Arabia	2.80	136	Kazakstan	4.10
53	Turkey	2.80	136	Mozambique	4.10
53	Uganda	2.80	136	Yemen	4.10
53	Western Samoa	2.80	139	Sudan	4.20
62	Indonesia	2.85	140	Myanmar	4.30
62	Latvia	2.85	140	Rwanda	4.30
62	Malta	2.85	142	Angola	4.35
62	Paraguay	2.85	143	Azerbaijan	4.40
66	Greece	2.90	143	Tajikistan	4.40
66	Hungary	2.90	145	Turkmenistan	4.50
66	South Africa	2.90	146	Uzbekistan	4.55
69	Benin	2.95	147	Congo/Zaire	4.70
69	Ecuador	2.95	147	Iran	4.70
69	Gabon	2.95	147	Libya	4.70
69	Morocco	2.95	147	Somalia	4.70
69	Poland	2.95	147	Vietnam	4.70
74	Colombia	3.00	152	Bosnia	4.80
74	Ghana	3.00	153	Iraq	4.90
74	Lithuania	3.00	154	Cuba	5.00
77	Kenya	3.05	154	Laos	5.00
77	Slovak Republic	3.05	154	North Korea	5.00

Mostly Unfree

sectors. The most formidable deterrents to foreign investment are political and civil unrest and an underdeveloped infrastructure.

BANKING
Score: 3–Stable (moderate level of restrictions)

The government regulates Croatia's banking system heavily. Permission is required for foreign banks to open branches, and banks may not engage in such nonbank services as selling insurance. The government continues to own many banks, either outright or through other state-owned companies, which are major shareholders in many banks.

WAGE AND PRICE CONTROLS
Score: 4–Stable (high level)

Wages and prices are not set entirely by the free market. Croatia continues to harbor a large public sector that controls prices and wages on many items. The government also extends large subsidies and price payments to farmers.

PROPERTY RIGHTS
Score: 4–Stable (low level of protection)

Property in Croatia is generally free from expropriation, but it is unclear whether this will continue to be the case. A significant increase in political or civil unrest, for example, could increase the risk of expropriation. In addition, the court system is cumbersome and inefficient. According to the U.S. Department of Commerce, "As Croatian courts face a tremendous backlog, partly due to lack of judges, settlement of commercial disputes is often a matter of years. In October 1995, there were more than a million cases pending in Croatian courts."[3]

REGULATION
Score: 4–Stable (high level)

Croatia's bureaucracy, like the bureaucracies of many other post-communist regimes, remains entrenched. Privatization of public firms is often opposed by ex-party officials and bureaucrats, and there is corruption.

BLACK MARKET
Score: 3–Stable (moderate level of activity)

Croatia has a black market, primarily in labor services; the black market provides, for example, some transportation and construction services. The government has managed to stamp out other black market activity, however, particularly in pirated intellectual property. A copyright law passed in 1993 provides stiff penalties for trafficking in pirated video and music recordings, as well as in related materials. Over the past several years, Croatia has enforced these laws vigorously, partly to attract foreign investment.

NOTES
1. Based on total taxes on international trade as a percentage of total imports.
2. This figure includes central government spending, spending on health and pension plans, and local government spending. From *Croatia* (London: Smith New Court, 1995).
3. U.S. Department of Commerce, *Country Commercial Guide*, 1997.

Cuba   5.00

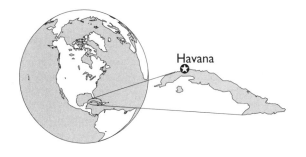

Havana

| 1997 Score: **5.00** | 1996 Score: **5.00** | 1995 Score: **5.00** |

Trade	5	Banking	5
Taxation	5	Wages and Prices	5
Government Intervention	5	Property Rights	5
Monetary Policy	5	Regulation	5
Foreign Investment	5	Black Market	5

Cuba's economy—one of the world's most repressed, centralized, and government-planned—is rife with corruption and graft. Despite various news reports about Cuba's move toward a free market, there is a nearly complete lack of legal and private economic activity. Individual economic freedom is virtually nonexistent. Although some forms of foreign investment are permitted, Cuba's constitution still outlaws foreign ownership of private property. In 1995, President Bill Clinton signed the Helms–Burton Act, passed by Congress to protect the property of Americans stolen by the regime of Fidel Castro in 1959. Cuba remains one of the world's poorest countries, primarily because of its lack of economic freedom.

TRADE POLICY
Score: 5–Stable (very high level of protectionism)

The Castro government inspects and approves all imports. In many cases, customs officials confiscate imports (especially scarce goods, like electronics) for their own use; such corruption enjoys official sanction. As a result, the government's trade barriers effectively bar most imports. Perhaps the biggest impediment to trade is Cuba's obsession with protecting its borders; this makes it nearly impossible for merchant ships to bring imports into the country. According to the U.S. Department of State, "Entering Cuban territory, territorial waters or airspace without prior authorization from the Cuban government may result in arrest or other enforcement action by Cuban authorities for violation of Cuban law. Any vessel or aircraft that enters the 12-mile limit off the coast of Cuba would be inside Cuban territorial waters or airspace and thus subject to the jurisdiction of the Cuban government. If persons enter Cuban territorial waters or airspace without prior permission, they may place themselves and others at serious personal risk."[1]

TAXATION
Score–Income taxation: 5–Stable (very high tax rates)
Score–Corporate taxation: 5–Stable (very high tax rates)
Final Taxation Score: 5–Stable (very high tax rates)

Because the government controls Cuba's entire economy, it essentially confiscates the proceeds of all economic activity. Because the government owns the fruits of almost all such activity, the rate of taxation approaches 100 percent.

GOVERNMENT INTERVENTION IN THE ECONOMY
Score: 5–Stable (very high level)

Although Castro permits some private (albeit highly restricted) economic activity, the means of production and most of the profits gained remain entirely in the hands of the state. Cuba's government owns and runs most of the country's economy.

1	Hong Kong	1.25		77	Zambia	3.05
2	Singapore	1.30		80	Mali	3.10
3	Bahrain	1.70		80	Mongolia	3.10
4	New Zealand	1.75		80	Slovenia	3.10
5	Switzerland	1.90		83	Honduras	3.15
5	United States	1.90		83	Papua New Guinea	3.15
7	Luxembourg	1.95		85	Djibouti	3.20
7	Taiwan	1.95		85	Fiji	3.20
7	United Kingdom	1.95		85	Pakistan	3.20
10	Bahamas	2.00		88	Algeria	3.25
10	Ireland	2.00		88	Guinea	3.25
12	Australia	2.05		88	Lebanon	3.25
12	Japan	2.05		88	Mexico	3.25
14	Belgium	2.10		88	Senegal	3.25
14	Canada	2.10		88	Tanzania	3.25
14	United Arab Emirates	2.10		94	Nigeria	3.30
17	Austria	2.15		94	Romania	3.30
17	Chile	2.15		96	Brazil	3.35
17	Estonia	2.15		96	Cambodia	3.35
20	Czech Republic	2.20		96	Egypt	3.35
20	Netherlands	2.20		96	Ivory Coast	3.35
22	Denmark	2.25		96	Madagascar	3.35
22	Finland	2.25		96	Moldova	3.35
24	Germany	2.30		102	Nepal	3.40
24	Iceland	2.30		103	Cape Verde	3.44
24	South Korea	2.30		104	Armenia	3.45
27	Norway	2.35		104	Dominican Republic	3.45
28	Kuwait	2.40		104	Russia	3.45
28	Malaysia	2.40		107	Burkina Faso	3.50
28	Panama	2.40		107	Cameroon	3.50
28	Thailand	2.40		107	Lesotho	3.50
32	El Salvador	2.45		107	Nicaragua	3.50
32	Sri Lanka	2.45		107	Venezuela	3.50
32	Sweden	2.45		112	Gambia	3.60
35	France	2.50		112	Guyana	3.60
35	Italy	2.50		114	Bulgaria	3.65
35	Spain	2.50		114	Georgia	3.65
38	Trinidad and Tobago	2.55		114	Malawi	3.65
39	Argentina	2.60		117	Ethiopia	3.70
39	Barbados	2.60		117	India	3.70
39	Cyprus	2.60		117	Niger	3.70
39	Jamaica	2.60		120	Albania	3.75
39	Portugal	2.60		120	Bangladesh	3.75
44	Bolivia	2.65		120	China (PRC)	3.75
44	Oman	2.65		120	Congo	3.75
44	Philippines	2.65		120	Croatia	3.75
47	Swaziland	2.70		125	Chad	3.80
47	Uruguay	2.70		125	Mauritania	3.80
49	Botswana	2.75		125	Ukraine	3.80
49	Jordan	2.75		128	Sierra Leone	3.85
49	Namibia	2.75		129	Burundi	3.90
49	Tunisia	2.75		129	Suriname	3.90
53	Belize	2.80		129	Zimbabwe	3.90
53	Costa Rica	2.80		132	Haiti	4.00
53	Guatemala	2.80		132	Kyrgyzstan	4.00
53	Israel	2.80		132	Syria	4.00
53	Peru	2.80		136	Belarus	4.05
53	Saudi Arabia	2.80		136	Kazakstan	4.10
53	Turkey	2.80		136	Mozambique	4.10
53	Uganda	2.80		136	Yemen	4.10
53	Western Samoa	2.80		139	Sudan	4.20
62	Indonesia	2.85		140	Myanmar	4.30
62	Latvia	2.85		140	Rwanda	4.30
62	Malta	2.85		142	Angola	4.35
62	Paraguay	2.85		143	Azerbaijan	4.40
66	Greece	2.90		143	Tajikistan	4.40
66	Hungary	2.90		145	Turkmenistan	4.50
66	South Africa	2.90		146	Uzbekistan	4.55
69	Benin	2.95		147	Congo/Zaire	4.70
69	Ecuador	2.95		147	Iran	4.70
69	Gabon	2.95		147	Libya	4.70
69	Morocco	2.95		147	Somalia	4.70
69	Poland	2.95		147	Vietnam	4.70
74	Colombia	3.00		152	Bosnia	4.80
74	Ghana	3.00		153	Iraq	4.90
74	Lithuania	3.00		154	Cuba	5.00
77	Kenya	3.05		154	Laos	5.00
77	Slovak Republic	3.05		154	North Korea	5.00

Repressed

MONETARY POLICY
Score: 5–Stable (very high level of inflation)

The government claims that inflation does not exist in Cuba. This is fiction. If price controls were lifted and the true value of the currency were measured, inflation would be extremely high. The official prices of goods may be low because they are controlled and subsidized by the state, but the tremendous scarcity of goods and services attests to their real value. In short, Cuba's currency is worthless. It is not convertible on the international market.

CAPITAL FLOWS AND FOREIGN INVESTMENT
Score: 5–Stable (very high barriers)

Some foreign investment is permitted in Cuba. In September 1995, the government moved to allow foreigners—in exceptional cases—to control a majority share in some joint-venture operations. To say that Cuba has liberalized its foreign investment code, however, is misleading. Cuba's constitution still outlaws all foreign ownership of property and forbids any Cuban citizens from participating in joint ventures with foreigners. It is still illegal to hire Cubans directly. Foreign employers must pay the wages due their employees directly to the Cuban government, in hard currency. The government then pays the workers in Cuban pesos at a fraction of the value—sometimes less than 10 percent—of what the foreign business gives the government. Furthermore, although the new foreign investment law provides additional protection against expropriation, all arbitration must take place in corrupt, government-run ministries that afford the investor little protection. Thus, even though Cuba's government does not seek actively to prevent foreign investment, its constitution, economy, and corrupt legal and government institutions have the same effect. According to the U.S. Department of State, "Crimes against foreigners continue to increase. Foreigners are prime targets for purse snatchings, pickpocketing and thefts from hotel rooms, beaches, historic sites and other attractions."[2]

BANKING
Score: 5–Stable (very high level of restrictions)

Banks in Cuba are owned and operated by the government and heavily influenced by the state-owned central bank. There is no free-market competition in this industry.

WAGE AND PRICE CONTROLS
Score: 5–Stable (very high level)

Cuba's government sets virtually all wages and prices.

PROPERTY RIGHTS
Score: 5–Stable (very low level of protection)

Cuba outlaws private property. Some individuals are allowed to operate self-employed businesses, but the government can confiscate all earnings from these activities if the individuals are deemed "unduly wealthy." Corrupt government and police officials often confiscate the money arbitrarily, especially if it is hard currency. There is no enforcement of contracts, and many European and Canadian investors have found that their investments can be renationalized and sold again to other uninformed investors. This has been particularly true in the hotel industry. Moreover, Cuba does not allow international arbitration of disputes, its court system is strongly influenced by the government, and corruption is rampant. According to the U.S. Department of State, "President Castro exercises control over all aspects of Cuban life through the Communist Party and its affiliated mass organizations, the government bureaucracy, and the state security apparatus.... The party controls all government positions, including judicial offices."[3]

REGULATION
Score: 5–Stable (very high level)

The Cuban government regulates the entire economy by owning and operating the means of production. Corrupt government officials and police routinely require those who are engaged in the few private-sector activities that are permitted to pay bribes or provide services free of charge.

BLACK MARKET
Score: 5–Stable (very high level of activity)

Cuba's black market is larger than its legal economy. As might be expected in a command economy, even basic economic activities—including the sale of milk and bread, transportation services, and housing—are performed in the black market. Smuggling is another big business; in addition to its importance as a major hub for illegal drugs entering the United States, Cuba has substantial smuggling of consumer goods.

NOTES
1. U.S. Department of State Travel Advisory, 1996.
2. *Ibid*.
3. U.S. Department of State, "Cuba Country Report on Human Rights Practices for 1996," 1997.

Cyprus   2.60

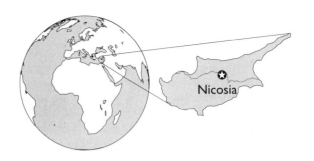

Nicosia

| 1997 Score: **2.60** | 1996 Score: **2.60** | 1995 Score: **n/a** |

Trade	3	Banking	2
Taxation	4	Wages and Prices	3
Government Intervention	3	Property Rights	3
Monetary Policy	1	Regulation	2
Foreign Investment	2	Black Market	3

Cyprus gained its independence from Great Britain in 1960. Tensions between Greek Cypriots and the Turkish Cypriot minority led to intercommunal strife in 1963 and 1967. In 1974, Greek Cypriot military officers, supported by the military junta in Athens, staged a coup and sought unity with Greece. Turkey responded by dispatching troops to protect the Turkish minority. Today, the Cypriot government controls 59 percent of the island; the "Turkish Republic of Northern Cyprus," recognized only by Turkey, controls 37 percent, supported by 30,000 Turkish troops; and the United Nations, which is promoting negotiations to establish a federal, bicommunal republic, maintains peacekeeping forces in a buffer zone that comprises the remaining 4 percent. At the July 1997 summit of the North Atlantic Treaty Organization in Madrid, Greece and Turkey agreed not to use force or the threat of force over quarrels in the Aegean Sea. Two rounds of United Nations–sponsored direct talks on a comprehensive Cyprus settlement were held in the United States in July 1997 and in Switzerland in August 1997, but much remains to be negotiated.

TRADE POLICY
Score: 3–Stable (moderate level of protectionism)

The average tariff rate in Cyprus is 6.9 percent.[1] Nontariff barriers include licensing requirements and strict inspections.

TAXATION
Score–Income taxation: 5–Stable (very high tax rates)
Score–Corporate taxation: 2–Stable (low tax rates)
Final Taxation Score: 4–Stable (high tax rates)

Cyprus has a top income tax rate of 40 percent; the average taxpayer finds himself in the 30 percent bracket. The top marginal corporate tax rate is 25 percent. Cyprus also has a 20 percent capital gains tax and an 8 percent value-added tax.

GOVERNMENT INTERVENTION IN THE ECONOMY
Score: 3–Stable (moderate level)

Government consumes 16.8 percent of Cyprus's GDP and continues to play a large role in many companies. For example, it owns and operates the telecommunications industry.

MONETARY POLICY
Score: 1–Stable (very low level of inflation)

The average annual rate of inflation from 1985 to 1995 was 4.2 percent. In 1996, the inflation rate was 3 percent.

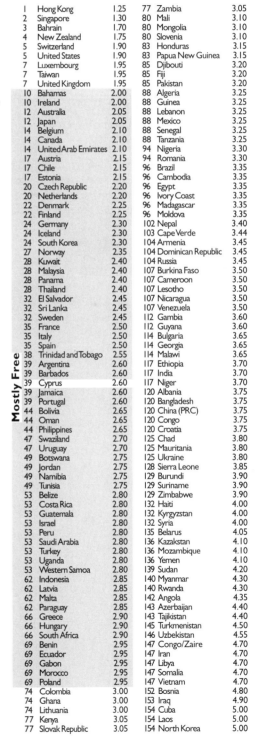

1	Hong Kong	1.25
2	Singapore	1.30
3	Bahrain	1.70
4	New Zealand	1.75
5	Switzerland	1.90
5	United States	1.90
7	Luxembourg	1.95
7	Taiwan	1.95
7	United Kingdom	1.95
10	Bahamas	2.00
10	Ireland	2.00
12	Australia	2.05
12	Japan	2.05
14	Belgium	2.10
14	Canada	2.10
14	United Arab Emirates	2.10
17	Austria	2.15
17	Chile	2.15
17	Estonia	2.15
20	Czech Republic	2.20
20	Netherlands	2.20
22	Denmark	2.25
22	Finland	2.25
24	Germany	2.30
24	Iceland	2.30
24	South Korea	2.30
27	Norway	2.35
28	Kuwait	2.40
28	Malaysia	2.40
28	Panama	2.40
28	Thailand	2.40
32	El Salvador	2.45
32	Sri Lanka	2.45
32	Sweden	2.45
35	France	2.50
35	Italy	2.50
35	Spain	2.50
38	Trinidad and Tobago	2.55
39	Argentina	2.60
39	Barbados	2.60
39	Cyprus	2.60
39	Jamaica	2.60
39	Portugal	2.60
44	Bolivia	2.65
44	Oman	2.65
44	Philippines	2.65
47	Swaziland	2.70
47	Uruguay	2.70
49	Botswana	2.75
49	Jordan	2.75
49	Namibia	2.75
49	Tunisia	2.75
53	Belize	2.80
53	Costa Rica	2.80
53	Guatemala	2.80
53	Israel	2.80
53	Peru	2.80
53	Saudi Arabia	2.80
53	Turkey	2.80
53	Uganda	2.80
53	Western Samoa	2.80
62	Indonesia	2.85
62	Latvia	2.85
62	Malta	2.85
62	Paraguay	2.85
66	Greece	2.90
66	Hungary	2.90
66	South Africa	2.90
69	Benin	2.95
69	Ecuador	2.95
69	Gabon	2.95
69	Morocco	2.95
69	Poland	2.95
74	Colombia	3.00
74	Ghana	3.00
74	Lithuania	3.00
77	Kenya	3.05
77	Slovak Republic	3.05
77	Zambia	3.05
80	Mali	3.10
80	Mongolia	3.10
80	Slovenia	3.10
83	Honduras	3.15
83	Papua New Guinea	3.15
85	Djibouti	3.20
85	Fiji	3.20
85	Pakistan	3.20
88	Algeria	3.25
88	Guinea	3.25
88	Lebanon	3.25
88	Mexico	3.25
88	Senegal	3.25
88	Tanzania	3.25
94	Nigeria	3.30
94	Romania	3.30
96	Brazil	3.35
96	Cambodia	3.35
96	Egypt	3.35
96	Ivory Coast	3.35
96	Madagascar	3.35
96	Moldova	3.35
102	Nepal	3.40
103	Cape Verde	3.44
104	Armenia	3.45
104	Dominican Republic	3.45
104	Russia	3.45
107	Burkina Faso	3.50
107	Cameroon	3.50
107	Lesotho	3.50
107	Nicaragua	3.50
107	Venezuela	3.50
112	Gambia	3.60
112	Guyana	3.60
114	Bulgaria	3.65
114	Georgia	3.65
114	Malawi	3.65
117	Ethiopia	3.70
117	India	3.70
117	Niger	3.70
120	Albania	3.75
120	Bangladesh	3.75
120	China (PRC)	3.75
120	Congo	3.75
120	Croatia	3.75
125	Chad	3.80
125	Mauritania	3.80
125	Ukraine	3.80
128	Sierra Leone	3.85
129	Burundi	3.90
129	Suriname	3.90
129	Zimbabwe	3.90
132	Haiti	4.00
132	Kyrgyzstan	4.00
132	Syria	4.00
135	Belarus	4.05
136	Kazakstan	4.10
136	Mozambique	4.10
136	Yemen	4.10
139	Sudan	4.20
140	Myanmar	4.30
140	Rwanda	4.30
142	Angola	4.35
143	Azerbaijan	4.40
143	Tajikistan	4.40
145	Turkmenistan	4.50
146	Uzbekistan	4.55
147	Congo/Zaire	4.70
147	Iran	4.70
147	Libya	4.70
147	Somalia	4.70
147	Vietnam	4.70
152	Bosnia	4.80
153	Iraq	4.90
154	Cuba	5.00
154	Laos	5.00
154	North Korea	5.00

Mostly Free

CAPITAL FLOWS AND FOREIGN INVESTMENT
Score: 2–Stable (low barriers)

Most of the few restrictions on foreign investment in Cyprus are imposed in areas vital to national security. The government requires an approval process for some investments; but even though this may cause some delays, there is little evidence it serves to hinder investment. The government recently streamlined regulations concerning foreign investment, opening entire new sectors to investors.

BANKING
Score: 2–Stable (low level of restrictions)

The banking system in Cyprus is open and competitive. There are more than 28 foreign banks.

WAGE AND PRICE CONTROLS
Score: 3–Stable (moderate level)

The market principally sets wages and prices. The government plays a large role in setting wages for Cyprus's state-owned companies, however, and controls some prices, particularly in the state-owned telecommunications industry and through large subsidies to the agricultural sector.

PROPERTY RIGHTS
Score: 3–Stable (moderate level of protection)

Private property in Cyprus is protected from government expropriation. Even though some legal enforcement is lax, expropriation is unlikely.

REGULATION
Score: 2–Stable (low level)

Establishing a business is relatively easy in Cyprus. Regulations are applied evenly in most cases, although some (such as worker health and safety laws) are burdensome. Corruption is nearly nonexistent, but the bureaucracy often is inefficient and laden with red tape.

BLACK MARKET
Score: 3–Stable (moderate level of activity)

There is some smuggling of pirated video and audio cassettes, as well as copied books and other materials.

NOTE
1. Based on total tax revenues on international trade as a percentage of total imports.

Czech Republic   2.20

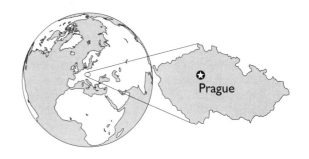
Prague

Trade	2	Banking	1
Taxation	4	Wages and Prices	2
Government Intervention	2	Property Rights	2
Monetary Policy	2	Regulation	2
Foreign Investment	2	Black Market	3

The Czech Republic became independent in January 1993 after separating from the Slovak Republic. Since the breakup of the Warsaw Pact in 1989, it has pursued economic liberalization, trading mainly with countries of the former Soviet Union and the European Union (EU); more than half its foreign trade now is with EU countries, especially Germany. One of the leading free-market reformers among Europe's former communist states, the Czech Republic recently reelected Prime Minister Vaclav Klaus, who is responsible for much of the country's economic reform to date and remains dedicated to seeking further reform. In May 1997, because of international currency traders who believed it was overvalued, the Czech currency plummeted in value against the German mark and the U.S. dollar. Despite attempts by the Central Bank to maintain the currency by raising interest rates, its value has continued to drop, and annual economic growth has dropped to about 3 percent from 5 percent in 1995. These developments could lead the government to restrict economic freedom. For example, the government recently increased its use of nontariff trade barriers. There also are signs of emerging corruption, but enforcement against black market activities has reduced piracy of intellectual property rights. Overall, the Czech Republic's score this year is 0.15 point worse than it was last year.

TRADE POLICY
Score: 2– (low level of protectionism)

The Czech Republic has one of Europe's most open markets. The average tariff rate is about 3.8 percent, although tariffs on some products can run as high as 70 percent. As a result of the Uruguay Round of the General Agreement on Tariffs and Trade, the government has been prompted to impose some minor nontariff barriers, primarily restrictions on imported textiles and apparel, quotas, and seasonal tariffs on some agricultural goods. In an attempt to curb its mounting trade deficit, the government required importers of some food and consumer goods to place 20 percent of the import value in interest-bearing accounts for 180 days, thereby discouraging imports for these items. Thus, this year's overall score is one point worse than last year's.

TAXATION
Score–Income taxation: 4– (high tax rates)
Score–Corporate taxation: 4–Stable (high tax rates)
Final Taxation Score: 4– (high tax rates)

The Czech Republic's top marginal income tax rate is 40 percent, and the tax on the average income level has increased from 0 percent in 1996 to about 17 percent.[1] The top marginal corporate income tax rate is 39 percent. The Czech Republic also has a 39 percent capital gains tax, a 22 percent value-added tax, and a real estate transfer tax. As a result, its taxation score is one point worse this year.

1	Hong Kong	1.25	77	Zambia	3.05
2	Singapore	1.30	80	Mali	3.10
3	Bahrain	1.70	80	Mongolia	3.10
4	New Zealand	1.75	80	Slovenia	3.10
5	Switzerland	1.90	83	Honduras	3.15
5	United States	1.90	83	Papua New Guinea	3.15
7	Luxembourg	1.95	85	Djibouti	3.20
7	Taiwan	1.95	85	Fiji	3.20
7	United Kingdom	1.95	85	Pakistan	3.20
10	Bahamas	2.00	88	Algeria	3.25
10	Ireland	2.00	88	Guinea	3.25
12	Australia	2.05	88	Lebanon	3.25
12	Japan	2.05	88	Mexico	3.25
14	Belgium	2.10	88	Senegal	3.25
14	Canada	2.10	88	Tanzania	3.25
14	United Arab Emirates	2.10	94	Nigeria	3.30
17	Austria	2.15	94	Romania	3.30
17	Chile	2.15	96	Brazil	3.35
17	Estonia	2.15	96	Cambodia	3.35
20	Czech Republic	2.20	96	Egypt	3.35
20	Netherlands	2.20	96	Ivory Coast	3.35
22	Denmark	2.25	96	Madagascar	3.35
22	Finland	2.25	96	Moldova	3.35
24	Germany	2.30	102	Nepal	3.40
24	Iceland	2.30	103	Cape Verde	3.44
24	South Korea	2.30	104	Armenia	3.45
27	Norway	2.35	104	Dominican Republic	3.45
28	Kuwait	2.40	104	Russia	3.45
28	Malaysia	2.40	107	Burkina Faso	3.50
28	Panama	2.40	107	Cameroon	3.50
28	Thailand	2.40	107	Lesotho	3.50
32	El Salvador	2.45	107	Nicaragua	3.50
32	Sri Lanka	2.45	107	Venezuela	3.50
32	Sweden	2.45	112	Gambia	3.60
35	France	2.50	112	Guyana	3.60
35	Italy	2.50	114	Bulgaria	3.65
35	Spain	2.50	114	Georgia	3.65
38	Trinidad and Tobago	2.55	114	Malawi	3.65
39	Argentina	2.60	117	Ethiopia	3.70
39	Barbados	2.60	117	India	3.70
39	Cyprus	2.60	117	Niger	3.70
39	Jamaica	2.60	120	Albania	3.75
39	Portugal	2.60	120	Bangladesh	3.75
44	Bolivia	2.65	120	China (PRC)	3.75
44	Oman	2.65	120	Congo	3.75
44	Philippines	2.65	120	Croatia	3.75
47	Swaziland	2.70	125	Chad	3.80
47	Uruguay	2.70	125	Mauritania	3.80
49	Botswana	2.75	125	Ukraine	3.80
49	Jordan	2.75	128	Sierra Leone	3.85
49	Namibia	2.75	129	Burundi	3.90
49	Tunisia	2.75	129	Suriname	3.90
53	Belize	2.80	129	Zimbabwe	3.90
53	Costa Rica	2.80	132	Haiti	4.00
53	Guatemala	2.80	132	Kyrgyzstan	4.00
53	Israel	2.80	132	Syria	4.00
53	Peru	2.80	135	Belarus	4.05
53	Saudi Arabia	2.80	136	Kazakstan	4.10
53	Turkey	2.80	136	Mozambique	4.10
53	Uganda	2.80	136	Yemen	4.10
53	Western Samoa	2.80	139	Sudan	4.20
62	Indonesia	2.85	140	Myanmar	4.30
62	Latvia	2.85	140	Rwanda	4.30
62	Malta	2.85	142	Angola	4.35
62	Paraguay	2.85	143	Azerbaijan	4.40
66	Greece	2.90	143	Tajikistan	4.40
66	Hungary	2.90	145	Turkmenistan	4.50
66	South Africa	2.90	146	Uzbekistan	4.55
69	Benin	2.95	147	Congo/Zaire	4.70
69	Ecuador	2.95	147	Iran	4.70
69	Gabon	2.95	147	Libya	4.70
69	Morocco	2.95	147	Somalia	4.70
69	Poland	2.95	147	Vietnam	4.70
74	Colombia	3.00	152	Bosnia	4.80
74	Ghana	3.00	153	Iraq	4.90
74	Lithuania	3.00	154	Cuba	5.00
77	Kenya	3.05	154	Laos	5.00
77	Slovak Republic	3.05	154	North Korea	5.00

Mostly Free

GOVERNMENT INTERVENTION IN THE ECONOMY
Score: 2–Stable (low level)

Of all the countries that used to make up the Soviet bloc, the Czech Republic has one of the freest economies. The government has been consuming about 21 percent of GDP since the first half of 1996.

MONETARY POLICY
Score: 2–Stable (low level of inflation)

The Czech Republic has pursued an anti-inflationary monetary policy since 1992 and, according to the U.S. Department of State, has one of the world's most stable currencies.[2] When international currency traders recently lost confidence in the Czech currency, however, it lost value, and inflation now is moving back up again. The rate of inflation was 10 percent in 1992, 20.8 percent in 1993, 10 percent in 1994, 9 percent in 1995, and 8.8 percent in 1996—an average of about 12 percent. In 1997, it is expected to be about 10 percent.

CAPITAL FLOWS AND FOREIGN INVESTMENT
Score: 2–Stable (low barriers)

With the exception of defense-related industries, all sectors of the economy are open to foreign investment. The Czech Republic attracts more foreign investment per capita than any other country in Central and Eastern Europe, although that level has been declining in recent years.

BANKING
Score: 1–Stable (very low level of restrictions)

Competition in the Czech Republic's banking system is increasing, and there are few, if any, barriers to opening either a foreign or domestic bank. Banks also are open to foreign participation; a foreign bank may establish a wholly owned bank, buy into an existing bank, or open a branch. Private Czech banks are allowed to sell securities and make some investments.

WAGE AND PRICE CONTROLS
Score: 2–Stable (low level)

The market sets most wages and prices. The prices of many utilities, the price of rail and bus transport, and rent paid on government-owned housing remain controlled, however. The Czech Republic maintains minimum wage standards.

PROPERTY RIGHTS
Score: 2–Stable (high level of protection)

Private property receives a high level of protection in the Czech Republic, and expropriation is highly unlikely. Neither a complete system of law, however, nor an efficient court system that fully protects property has been created.

REGULATION
Score: 2– (low level)

The Czech Republic imposes few regulations on businesses, and most companies do not need a license to begin operation. The government is planning additional reductions in its regulation of business activity. But increased economic activity has brought a growth in bureaucratic procedures and some minor signs of corruption. According to the U.S. Department of State, "American business people often cite a convoluted—or in some cases corrupt—bureaucratic system at both national and local levels which can act as an impediment to market access."[3] The Czech Republic's regulation score this year is one point worse than last year.

BLACK MARKET
Score: 3+ (moderate level of activity)

Some goods and services still are supplied on the black market, but recent legislation to combat piracy of intellectual property, combined with increased enforcement, has reduced the piracy of prerecorded video cassettes and computer software significantly. Any remaining activity represents only a moderate portion of the total economy. The Czech Republic's black market score this year is one point better than last year.

NOTES

1. Based on an average income in local currency of 136,309 koruna. The tax on the first 84,000 koruna is 15 percent; the remainder is taxed at 20 percent, for a total tax of 23,061 koruna, or about 17 percent of the average income level.
2. U.S. Department of State, *Country Reports on Economic Policy and Trade Practices,* 1997, pp. 101–106.
3. *Ibid.,* p. 104.

Denmark   2.25

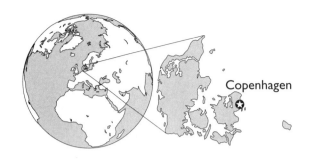

Copenhagen

1997 Score: **2.05**	1996 Score: **1.95**	1995 Score: **n/a**

Trade	2	Banking	2
Taxation	4.5	Wages and Prices	1
Government Intervention	4	Property Rights	1
Monetary Policy	1	Regulation	2
Foreign Investment	2	Black Market	3

Denmark, a constitutional monarchy since 1849, remained neutral during World War I but was invaded and occupied by Nazi Germany during World War II. Following the war, Denmark focused on rebuilding its industries. Although the Danes voted to stay out of the European Union (EU) in 1992, they voted to join in 1993 after the EU made changes in its social charter to meet Danish objections. Denmark's extremely high taxes have created an increase in black market labor. Employees try to get paid "under the table" to avoid paying taxes. This has caused Denmark's overall score to decrease by 0.2 point this year.

TRADE POLICY
Score: 2–Stable (low level of protectionism)

Although its average tariff rate is 3.6 percent, Denmark maintains trade restrictions common to other EU members (for example, in financial services, credit cards, insurance, and legal services). Because standards apply to all members, however, Denmark has led the fight within the EU to reduce nontariff barriers to imports.

TAXATION
Score–Income taxation: 5–Stable (very high tax rates)
Score–Corporate taxation: 3–Stable (moderate tax rates)
Final Taxation Score: 4.5–Stable (very high tax rates)

Denmark's top income tax rate is 60 percent; the tax on the average income level is 42 percent. The top marginal corporate tax rate is 34 percent. Denmark also has a 34 percent capital gains tax and a 25 percent value-added tax.

GOVERNMENT INTERVENTION IN THE ECONOMY
Score: 4–Stable (high level)

Government consumes about 26 percent of Denmark's GDP, but this probably understates the extent to which it consumes economic output. Denmark's government, unlike those of other countries, pays most unemployment benefits and other welfare bills. This social policy is good for the business community, which does not have to pay for those benefits, but negatively affects the rest of the economy, forcing tax rates to increase. Denmark's public sector is a net debtor and it continues to lose money each year.

MONETARY POLICY
Score: 1–Stable (very low level of inflation)

Denmark's average rate of inflation from 1985 to 1995 was 2.8 percent. In 1996, the inflation rate was 2.1 percent, where it remains today.

1	Hong Kong	1.25	77	Zambia	3.05
2	Singapore	1.30	80	Mali	3.10
3	Bahrain	1.70	80	Mongolia	3.10
4	New Zealand	1.75	80	Slovenia	3.10
5	Switzerland	1.90	83	Honduras	3.15
5	United States	1.90	83	Papua New Guinea	3.15
7	Luxembourg	1.95	85	Djibouti	3.20
7	Taiwan	1.95	85	Fiji	3.20
7	United Kingdom	1.95	85	Pakistan	3.20
10	Bahamas	2.00	88	Algeria	3.25
10	Ireland	2.00	88	Guinea	3.25
12	Australia	2.05	88	Lebanon	3.25
12	Japan	2.05	88	Mexico	3.25
14	Belgium	2.10	88	Senegal	3.25
14	Canada	2.10	88	Tanzania	3.25
14	United Arab Emirates	2.10	94	Nigeria	3.30
17	Austria	2.15	94	Romania	3.30
17	Chile	2.15	96	Brazil	3.35
17	Estonia	2.15	96	Cambodia	3.35
20	Czech Republic	2.20	96	Egypt	3.35
20	Netherlands	2.20	96	Ivory Coast	3.35
22	Denmark	2.25	96	Madagascar	3.35
22	Finland	2.25	96	Moldova	3.35
24	Germany	2.30	102	Nepal	3.40
24	Iceland	2.30	103	Cape Verde	3.44
24	South Korea	2.30	104	Armenia	3.45
27	Norway	2.35	104	Dominican Republic	3.45
28	Kuwait	2.40	104	Russia	3.45
28	Malaysia	2.40	107	Burkina Faso	3.50
28	Panama	2.40	107	Cameroon	3.50
28	Thailand	2.40	107	Lesotho	3.50
32	El Salvador	2.45	107	Nicaragua	3.50
32	Sri Lanka	2.45	107	Venezuela	3.50
32	Sweden	2.45	112	Gambia	3.60
35	France	2.50	112	Guyana	3.60
35	Italy	2.50	114	Bulgaria	3.65
35	Spain	2.50	114	Georgia	3.65
38	Trinidad and Tobago	2.55	114	Malawi	3.65
39	Argentina	2.60	117	Ethiopia	3.70
39	Barbados	2.60	117	India	3.70
39	Cyprus	2.60	117	Niger	3.70
39	Jamaica	2.60	120	Albania	3.75
39	Portugal	2.60	120	Bangladesh	3.75
44	Bolivia	2.65	120	China (PRC)	3.75
44	Oman	2.65	120	Congo	3.75
44	Philippines	2.65	120	Croatia	3.75
47	Swaziland	2.70	125	Chad	3.80
47	Uruguay	2.70	125	Mauritania	3.80
49	Botswana	2.75	125	Ukraine	3.80
49	Jordan	2.75	128	Sierra Leone	3.85
49	Namibia	2.75	129	Burundi	3.90
49	Tunisia	2.75	129	Suriname	3.90
53	Belize	2.80	129	Zimbabwe	3.90
53	Costa Rica	2.80	132	Haiti	4.00
53	Guatemala	2.80	132	Kyrgyzstan	4.00
53	Israel	2.80	132	Syria	4.00
53	Peru	2.80	135	Belarus	4.05
53	Saudi Arabia	2.80	136	Kazakstan	4.10
53	Turkey	2.80	136	Mozambique	4.10
53	Uganda	2.80	136	Yemen	4.10
53	Western Samoa	2.80	139	Sudan	4.20
62	Indonesia	2.85	140	Myanmar	4.30
62	Latvia	2.85	140	Rwanda	4.30
62	Malta	2.85	142	Angola	4.35
62	Paraguay	2.85	143	Azerbaijan	4.40
66	Greece	2.90	143	Tajikistan	4.40
66	Hungary	2.90	145	Turkmenistan	4.50
66	South Africa	2.90	146	Uzbekistan	4.55
69	Benin	2.95	147	Congo/Zaire	4.70
69	Ecuador	2.95	147	Iran	4.70
69	Gabon	2.95	147	Libya	4.70
69	Morocco	2.95	147	Somalia	4.70
69	Poland	2.95	147	Vietnam	4.70
74	Colombia	3.00	152	Bosnia	4.80
74	Ghana	3.00	153	Iraq	4.90
74	Lithuania	3.00	154	Cuba	5.00
77	Kenya	3.05	154	Laos	5.00
77	Slovak Republic	3.05	154	North Korea	5.00

Mostly Free

Capital Flows and Foreign Investment
Score: 2–Stable (low barriers)

There are few restrictions on investments in Denmark. Notable exceptions are the hydrocarbon exploration, arms production, aircraft, and maritime industries.

Banking
Score: 2–Stable (low level of restrictions)

Denmark's banking system is open to foreign investment and largely independent of the government. The law allows banks to engage in securities and insurance services, but there are restrictions on real estate activities.

Wage and Price Controls
Score: 1–Stable (very low level)

The market sets wages and prices in Denmark. There is no minimum wage.

Property Rights
Score: 1–Stable (very high level of protection)

Private property in Denmark is safe from government expropriation. The legal and judicial system is efficient.

Regulation
Score: 2–Stable (low level)

Establishing a business in Denmark is a simple process. Regulations are applied evenly in most cases, although such regulations as safety and health standards make it more difficult for some businesses to keep their doors open.

Black Market
Score: 3– (moderate level of activity)

An underground economy has developed in Denmark, primarily in labor. The tax system, the rates of which currently are among the highest in the world, may encourage workers to accept payments "under the table." According to the U.S. Department of State, "[M]any Danes believe the tax system needs further overhaul to improve incentives for work and investment and to reduce the underground economy, which may account for as much as 10 percent of GDP."[1] As a result, Denmark's black market score is two points worse this year. Moreover, even though Denmark has very strong intellectual property rights (IPR) laws and a long history of strictly enforcing these laws, there are signs of increased black market activity in pirated copyrighted materials, primarily computer software. In May 1997, the United States complained to the World Trade Organization that Denmark has failed to meet the stipulations of international agreements on IPR protection. These activities, however, represent only a moderate portion of Denmark's overall economy.

Note

1. The score in this factor has changed from 1 in 1997 to 3 in 1998. Previously unavailable data provide a more accurate understanding of the country's performance. The black market rate is from U.S. Department of State, *Country Reports on Economic Policy and Trade Practices,* 1997, p. 108. The methodology for this factor remains the same.

Djibouti, Republic of

3.20

| 1997 Score: **3.00** | 1996 Score: **n/a** | 1995 Score: **n/a** |

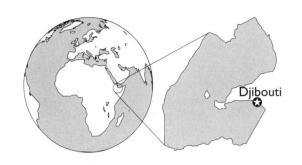

Trade	4
Taxation	2
Government Intervention	5
Monetary Policy	1
Foreign Investment	3

Banking	3
Wages and Prices	3
Property Rights	3
Regulation	4
Black Market	4

The Republic of Djibouti won its independence from France on June 27, 1977, although France still maintains a military presence. During the 1980s, Djibouti focused on maintaining political order and avoiding civil unrest. In 1991, crisis finally erupted and led to increased civil unrest and calls for multiparty democratic elections. As a result, long-term economic planning has been supplanted by short-term crisis management and undermined by political fragmentation, and the country has made little progress in developing sustainable levels of economic growth. From 1992 to 1995, economic growth averaged -1.7 percent. In addition, the government's rate of consumption has increased. Thus, Djibouti's overall score this year is 0.2 point worse than it was last year.

TRADE POLICY
Score: 4–Stable (high level of protectionism)

The most significant barriers to imports in Djibouti are corruption in the customs service, inadequate infrastructure to bring products into the country, and poor banking and financial services. Djibouti lies in the crucial maritime shipping lanes between the Mediterranean Sea and the Indian Ocean. With its ports so strategically located, the regime feels some pressure to liberalize its trade laws.

TAXATION
Score–Income taxation: 2–Stable (low tax rates)
Score–Corporate taxation: 2–Stable (low tax rates)
Final Taxation Score: 2–Stable (low tax rates)

Djibouti has a top income tax rate of 20 percent, a top corporate tax rate of 20 percent, and a capital gains tax of 20 percent. It also imposes other taxes.

GOVERNMENT INTERVENTION IN THE ECONOMY
Score: 5– (very high level)

Government consumes 36 percent of Djibouti's GDP.[1] As a result, its government intervention score is two points worse than last year. Moreover, much of the country's GDP is produced by the state, which continues to own large sections of the transportation industry, including some ports, airports, and maritime shipping.

MONETARY POLICY
Score: 1–Stable (very low level of inflation)

Djibouti has maintained the value of its currency over a considerable period of time. The average annual rate of inflation from 1985 to 1994 was 4.4 percent. No data are available for 1996.

1	Hong Kong	1.25	77	Zambia	3.05
2	Singapore	1.30	80	Mali	3.10
3	Bahrain	1.70	80	Mongolia	3.10
4	New Zealand	1.75	80	Slovenia	3.10
5	Switzerland	1.90	83	Honduras	3.15
5	United States	1.90	83	Papua New Guinea	3.15
7	Luxembourg	1.95	85	Djibouti	3.20
7	Taiwan	1.95	85	Fiji	3.20
7	United Kingdom	1.95	85	Pakistan	3.20
10	Bahamas	2.00	88	Algeria	3.25
10	Ireland	2.00	88	Guinea	3.25
12	Australia	2.05	88	Lebanon	3.25
12	Japan	2.05	88	Mexico	3.25
14	Belgium	2.10	88	Senegal	3.25
14	Canada	2.10	88	Tanzania	3.25
14	United Arab Emirates	2.10	94	Nigeria	3.30
17	Austria	2.15	94	Romania	3.30
17	Chile	2.15	96	Brazil	3.35
17	Estonia	2.15	96	Cambodia	3.35
20	Czech Republic	2.20	96	Egypt	3.35
20	Netherlands	2.20	96	Ivory Coast	3.35
22	Denmark	2.25	96	Madagascar	3.35
22	Finland	2.25	96	Moldova	3.35
24	Germany	2.30	102	Nepal	3.40
24	Iceland	2.30	103	Cape Verde	3.44
24	South Korea	2.30	104	Armenia	3.45
27	Norway	2.35	104	Dominican Republic	3.45
28	Kuwait	2.40	104	Russia	3.45
28	Malaysia	2.40	107	Burkina Faso	3.50
28	Panama	2.40	107	Cameroon	3.50
28	Thailand	2.40	107	Lesotho	3.50
32	El Salvador	2.45	107	Nicaragua	3.50
32	Sri Lanka	2.45	107	Venezuela	3.50
32	Sweden	2.45	112	Gambia	3.60
35	France	2.50	112	Guyana	3.60
35	Italy	2.50	114	Bulgaria	3.65
35	Spain	2.50	114	Georgia	3.65
38	Trinidad and Tobago	2.55	114	Malawi	3.65
39	Argentina	2.60	117	Ethiopia	3.70
39	Barbados	2.60	117	India	3.70
39	Cyprus	2.60	117	Niger	3.70
39	Jamaica	2.60	120	Albania	3.75
39	Portugal	2.60	120	Bangladesh	3.75
44	Bolivia	2.65	120	China (PRC)	3.75
44	Oman	2.65	120	Congo	3.75
44	Philippines	2.65	120	Croatia	3.75
47	Swaziland	2.70	125	Chad	3.80
47	Uruguay	2.70	125	Mauritania	3.80
49	Botswana	2.75	125	Ukraine	3.80
49	Jordan	2.75	128	Sierra Leone	3.85
49	Namibia	2.75	129	Burundi	3.90
49	Tunisia	2.75	129	Suriname	3.90
53	Belize	2.80	129	Zimbabwe	3.90
53	Costa Rica	2.80	132	Haiti	4.00
53	Guatemala	2.80	132	Kyrgyzstan	4.00
53	Israel	2.80	132	Syria	4.00
53	Peru	2.80	135	Belarus	4.05
53	Saudi Arabia	2.80	136	Kazakstan	4.10
53	Turkey	2.80	136	Mozambique	4.10
53	Uganda	2.80	136	Yemen	4.10
53	Western Samoa	2.80	139	Sudan	4.20
62	Indonesia	2.85	140	Myanmar	4.30
62	Latvia	2.85	140	Rwanda	4.30
62	Malta	2.85	142	Angola	4.35
62	Paraguay	2.85	143	Azerbaijan	4.40
66	Greece	2.90	143	Tajikistan	4.40
66	Hungary	2.90	145	Turkmenistan	4.50
66	South Africa	2.90	146	Uzbekistan	4.55
69	Benin	2.95	147	Congo/Zaire	4.70
69	Ecuador	2.95	147	Iran	4.70
69	Gabon	2.95	147	Libya	4.70
69	Morocco	2.95	147	Somalia	4.70
69	Poland	2.95	147	Vietnam	4.70
74	Colombia	3.00	152	Bosnia	4.80
74	Ghana	3.00	153	Iraq	4.90
74	Lithuania	3.00	154	Cuba	5.00
77	Kenya	3.05	154	Laos	5.00
77	Slovak Republic	3.05	154	North Korea	5.00

Mostly Unfree

Capital Flows and Foreign Investment
Score: 3–Stable (moderate barriers)

Djibouti is open to foreign investment. Investments must be reviewed by the government, however, and some sectors—mainly in areas the government has determined are vital to national security—are closed.

Banking
Score: 3–Stable (moderate level of restrictions)

The banking system is very open and competitive. According to the U.S. Department of Commerce, "Djibouti has one of the most liberal economic regimes in Africa, with almost unrestricted banking and commerce sectors."[2] The most significant problem, however, is the lack of sufficient capital to finance economic expansion. The government controls capital.

Wage and Price Controls
Score: 3–Stable (moderate level)

The market principally sets wages and prices for most products. The government, however, controls prices on electricity and transportation services.

Property Rights
Score: 3–Stable (moderate level of protection)

Private property is a respected right in Djibouti, although the courts often are overburdened and the enforcement of contracts can be both time-consuming and cumbersome. According to the U.S. Department of State, there is evidence that Djibouti's judiciary is not entirely free from government influence.[3]

Regulation
Score: 4–Stable (high level)

Government corruption is a burden on business, and bribes often are necessary in Djibouti. Health and safety regulations also add to the cost of doing business.

Black Market
Score: 4–Stable (high level of activity)

Much of Djibouti's economic activity, especially trade in pirated trademarks and computer software, occurs in the black market. Laws protecting intellectual property are not enforced in full.

Notes

1. The score in this factor has changed from 3 in 1997 to 5 in 1998. Previously unavailable data provide a more accurate understanding of the government's consumption of GDP. The methodology for this factor remains the same.
2. U.S. Department of Commerce, National Trade Data Bank and Economic Bulletin Board, products of STAT–USA.
3. U.S. Department of State, "Djibouti Country Report on Human Rights Practices for 1996," 1997.

Dominican Republic 3.45

Trade	5	
Taxation	2.5	
Government Intervention	2	
Monetary Policy	5	
Foreign Investment	3	
Banking	3	
Wages and Prices	2	
Property Rights	4	
Regulation	4	
Black Market	4	

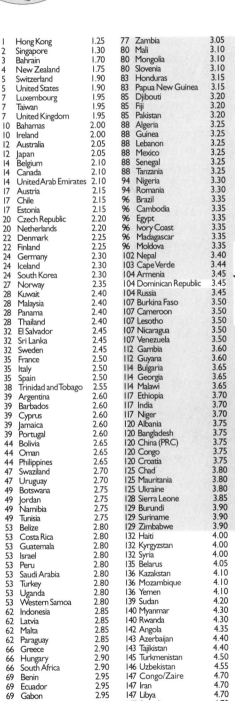

Santo Domingo

Since winning its independence from Spain in 1865, the Dominican Republic has developed a large agricultural industry. The government has intervened often in this and other industries. In the 1980s, the country suffered a major economic crisis when bad weather coupled with socialist economic policies ruined its agricultural production. Since 1990, the government has been trying to reform the economy. But even though it has made significant progress in reducing inflation, reforming its investment laws, and reducing its barriers to trade, substantial restrictions on economic freedom remain in effect, particularly in the areas of trade policy and monetary policy.

TRADE POLICY
Score: 5–Stable (very high level of protectionism)

The Dominican Republic's average tariff rate is 16.4 percent.[1] Nontariff barriers include arbitrary customs clearance procedures and a burdensome licensing requirement for selected imports. According to the U.S. Department of State, "Arbitrary customs clearance procedures sometimes cause problems for business. The use of 'negotiated fee' practices to gain faster customs clearance continues to put some U.S. firms at a competitive disadvantage in the Dominican market. U.S. firms must comply with the provisions of the U.S. Foreign Corrupt Practices Act. Customs officials routinely reject invoice prices for computing duties and customs fees and use higher figures."[2]

TAXATION
Score–Income taxation: 2–Stable (low tax rates)
Score–Corporate taxation: 2–Stable (low tax rates)
Final Taxation Score: 2.5–Stable (moderate tax rates)

The Dominican Republic's marginal top income tax rate is 25 percent; the tax on the average income level is 0 percent. The top corporate tax rate is 25 percent. The Dominican Republic also has a 25 percent capital gains tax and an 8 percent value-added tax.

GOVERNMENT INTERVENTION IN THE ECONOMY
Score: 2–Stable (low level)

The government consumes about 4 percent of the Dominican Republic's GDP.[3] The state-owned sector, however, is large. According to the U.S. Department of Commerce, "The Dominican government has traditionally played a large role in the country's economic life. The government is the owner of all public utilities (except telecommunications), an insurance company, the country's largest bank, and factories producing a variety of items.... The Dominican government has not yet embraced privatization.... The large government presence in the economy and a web of complicated regulations means that many economic decisions are politicized and businesspersons spend time 'lobbying' the government."[4] Nevertheless, because of its low level of consumption as a percentage of the total economy, the government's intervention in the economy is low by global standards.

1	Hong Kong	1.25
2	Singapore	1.30
3	Bahrain	1.70
4	New Zealand	1.75
5	Switzerland	1.90
5	United States	1.90
7	Luxembourg	1.95
7	Taiwan	1.95
7	United Kingdom	1.95
10	Bahamas	2.00
10	Ireland	2.00
12	Australia	2.05
12	Japan	2.05
14	Belgium	2.10
14	Canada	2.10
14	United Arab Emirates	2.10
17	Austria	2.15
17	Chile	2.15
17	Estonia	2.15
20	Czech Republic	2.20
20	Netherlands	2.20
22	Denmark	2.25
22	Finland	2.25
24	Germany	2.30
24	Iceland	2.30
24	South Korea	2.30
27	Norway	2.35
28	Kuwait	2.40
28	Malaysia	2.40
28	Panama	2.40
28	Thailand	2.40
32	El Salvador	2.45
32	Sri Lanka	2.45
32	Sweden	2.45
35	France	2.50
35	Italy	2.50
35	Spain	2.50
38	Trinidad and Tobago	2.55
39	Argentina	2.60
39	Barbados	2.60
39	Cyprus	2.60
39	Jamaica	2.60
39	Portugal	2.60
44	Bolivia	2.65
44	Oman	2.65
44	Philippines	2.65
47	Swaziland	2.70
47	Uruguay	2.70
49	Botswana	2.75
49	Jordan	2.75
49	Namibia	2.75
49	Tunisia	2.75
53	Belize	2.80
53	Costa Rica	2.80
53	Guatemala	2.80
53	Israel	2.80
53	Peru	2.80
53	Saudi Arabia	2.80
53	Turkey	2.80
53	Uganda	2.80
53	Western Samoa	2.80
62	Indonesia	2.85
62	Latvia	2.85
62	Malta	2.85
62	Paraguay	2.85
66	Greece	2.90
66	Hungary	2.90
66	South Africa	2.90
69	Benin	2.95
69	Ecuador	2.95
69	Gabon	2.95
69	Morocco	2.95
69	Poland	2.95
74	Colombia	3.00
74	Ghana	3.00
74	Lithuania	3.00
77	Kenya	3.05
77	Slovak Republic	3.05
77	Zambia	3.05
80	Mali	3.10
80	Mongolia	3.10
80	Slovenia	3.10
83	Honduras	3.15
83	Papua New Guinea	3.15
85	Djibouti	3.20
85	Fiji	3.20
85	Pakistan	3.20
88	Algeria	3.25
88	Guinea	3.25
88	Lebanon	3.25
88	Mexico	3.25
88	Senegal	3.25
88	Tanzania	3.25
94	Nigeria	3.30
94	Romania	3.30
96	Brazil	3.35
96	Cambodia	3.35
96	Egypt	3.35
96	Ivory Coast	3.35
96	Madagascar	3.35
96	Moldova	3.35
102	Nepal	3.40
103	Cape Verde	3.44
104	Armenia	3.45
104	Dominican Republic	3.45
104	Russia	3.45
107	Burkina Faso	3.50
107	Cameroon	3.50
107	Lesotho	3.50
107	Nicaragua	3.50
107	Venezuela	3.50
112	Gambia	3.60
112	Guyana	3.60
114	Bulgaria	3.65
114	Georgia	3.65
114	Malawi	3.65
117	Ethiopia	3.70
117	India	3.70
117	Niger	3.70
120	Albania	3.75
120	Bangladesh	3.75
120	China (PRC)	3.75
120	Congo	3.75
120	Croatia	3.75
125	Chad	3.80
125	Mauritania	3.80
125	Ukraine	3.80
128	Sierra Leone	3.85
129	Burundi	3.90
129	Suriname	3.90
129	Zimbabwe	3.90
132	Haiti	4.00
132	Kyrgyzstan	4.00
132	Syria	4.00
135	Belarus	4.05
136	Kazakhstan	4.10
136	Mozambique	4.10
136	Yemen	4.10
139	Sudan	4.20
140	Myanmar	4.30
140	Rwanda	4.30
142	Angola	4.35
143	Azerbaijan	4.40
143	Tajikistan	4.40
145	Turkmenistan	4.50
146	Uzbekistan	4.55
147	Congo/Zaire	4.70
147	Iran	4.70
147	Libya	4.70
147	Somalia	4.70
147	Vietnam	4.70
152	Bosnia	4.80
153	Iraq	4.90
154	Cuba	5.00
154	Laos	5.00
154	North Korea	5.00

Mostly Unfree

MONETARY POLICY
Score: 5–Stable (very high level of inflation)

Although the Dominican Republic reduced inflation to only 3.96 percent in 1996, its annual rate of inflation from 1985 to 1995 was a very high 26.3 percent.

CAPITAL FLOWS AND FOREIGN INVESTMENT
Score: 3–Stable (moderate barriers)

The government has made significant progress in removing most barriers to foreign investment. In the past, the U.S. Department of Commerce and the Office of the United States Trade Representative (USTR) have reported many informal barriers to foreign investment. Their 1997 reports, however, make no specific mention of these barriers. According to the USTR, "The December 1995 investment law is designed to remove barriers to investment and to provide equal access for foreign investors to all sectors of the economy, except toxic waste disposal, public health and environment, and defense, for which express presidential authorization is required."[5] The U.S. Department of State does note, however, the existence of continuing barriers to foreign investment: It "must receive approval from the Foreign Investment Directorate of the Central Bank to qualify for repatriation of profits.... Foreign employees may not exceed 20 percent of a firm's work force. This is not applicable when foreign employees only perform managerial or administrative functions.... [E]xpropriation standards (e.g., in the 'public interest') do not appear to be consistent with international law standards.... The Dominican Republic does not recognize the general right of investors to binding international arbitration."[6] Nevertheless, by global standards, restrictions on foreign investment remain moderate.

BANKING
Score: 3–Stable (moderate level of restrictions)

According to the USTR, "Until recently, foreign participation in the financial services sector was restricted by law. The 1995 foreign investment law, and financial-monetary code now before the Dominican Congress, permit foreign participation in the financial services sector. However, the practical impact of these provisions is not clear. There is no secondary securities market in the Dominican Republic so questions of brokerage services and securities underwriting, trading, etc., do not arise."[7] State-owned banks continue to play a vital role in the financial system, controlling almost one-third of all assets. Because of the lack of financial services like securities underwriting and trading, the continued government control of financial resources, and the lack of an assessment of financial-sector liberalization policies now being enacted, the Dominican Republic's banking score remains the same as last year.

WAGE AND PRICE CONTROLS
Score: 2–Stable (low level)

Most wages and prices are set by the market. The only exceptions are controls on sugar, beans, and propane gas.

PROPERTY RIGHTS
Score: 4–Stable (low level of protection)

The court system is inefficient; corruption and bureaucratic red tape run high; and the government can expropriate property. The U.S. Department of State explains, "Although the Constitution stipulates an independent judiciary... interference from other public and private entities, including the executive branch, substantially undermines judicial independence.... The autonomy of the judiciary remains in question.... The judicial system is plagued by chronic delays [and t]here are also perennial accusations of corruption."[8]

REGULATION
Score: 4–Stable (high level)

Regulations are not applied evenly or honestly, and corruption and red tape impose significant burdens. According to the U.S. Department of Commerce, "Dominican and foreign business leaders complain of judicial and administrative corruption, and some persons have charged that corruption affects the settlement of business disputes."[9]

BLACK MARKET
Score: 4–Stable (high level of activity)

The Dominican Republic has a high level of black market activity, particularly in labor services. Competition for workers is so intense that many legal labor regulations are ignored. There also is no regard for the protection of intellectual property. According to the U.S. Department of State, "Although the Dominican Republic is a signatory to the Paris Convention and the Universal Copyright Convention, and in 1991 became a member of the World Intellectual Property Organization, the lack of a strong regulatory environment results in inadequate protection of intellectual property rights.... In general, copyright laws are adequate, but...enforcement is weak, resulting in widespread piracy."[10]

NOTES

1. Based on total taxes on international trade as a percentage of total imports.
2. U.S. Department of State, *Country Reports on Economic Policy and Trade Practices,* 1997, p. 244.
3. World Bank, *World Development Report, 1997.*
4. U.S. Department of Commerce, *Country Commercial Guide,* 1997.
5. Office of the USTR, *1997 National Trade Estimate Report on Foreign Trade Barriers.*
6. U.S. Department of State, *Country Reports on Economic Policy and Trade Practices,* 1997, p. 244.
7. Office of the USTR, *1997 National Trade Estimate Report on Foreign Trade Barriers.*
8. U.S. Department of State, "Dominican Republic Country Report on Human Rights Practices for 1996," 1997.
9. U.S. Department of Commerce, *Country Commercial Guide,* 1997.
10. U.S. Department of State, *Country Reports on Economic Policy and Trade Practices,* 1996, p. 370.

Ecuador   2.95

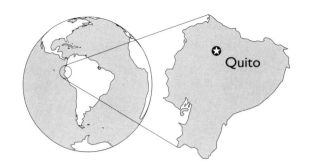

1997 Score: **3.05**	1996 Score: **3.15**	1995 Score: **3.25**

Trade	3	Banking	3
Taxation	2.5	Wages and Prices	2
Government Intervention	1	Property Rights	3
Monetary Policy	5	Regulation	4
Foreign Investment	2	Black Market	4

Ecuador gained its independence from Spain in 1830 and was plagued by instability and dictatorship for most of the following century. Today, its economy is based primarily on oil and bananas. During the oil boom of the late 1970s and early 1980s, the government used the increased wealth to subsidize businesses and raise the overall share of government consumption of the economy. After 1981, oil prices plummeted and the oil-based economy began to decline. Since the early 1990s, Ecuador has tried to carry out reforms that would reduce the level of state intervention in the economy, but results have been mixed. A new president, Abdala Bucaram, was elected in July 1996, but Congress removed him from office and replaced him with Fabian Alarcon. New elections will be held in August 1998. The government recently reduced some price controls. As a result, Ecuador's overall score this year is 0.1 point better than last year.

Trade Policy
Score: 3–Stable (moderate level of protectionism)

Ecuador's average tariff rate is 9 percent. Importers must obtain import licenses, and this can delay the movement of goods into the country. The government has made some progress in reforming cumbersome customs procedures. According to the U.S. Department of State, "Customs procedures can be difficult, but they are not normally used to discriminate against U.S. products. The government has appeared to backtrack on the customs reform program that was designed to reduce corruption and improve efficiency in the customs service and thereby eliminate a major constraint on trade."[1]

Taxation
Score–Income taxation: 2–Stable (low tax rates)
Score–Corporate taxation: 2–Stable (low tax rates)
Final Taxation Score: 2.5–Stable (moderate tax rates)

Ecuador's top marginal income tax rate is 25 percent, and the average income level is taxed at 0 percent. The top tax rate on corporate profits is 25 percent. Ecuador also has a 10 percent value-added tax.

Government Intervention in the Economy
Score: 1–Stable (very low level)

Government consumes only 9.1 percent of Ecuador's GDP. This may seem very low, considering that the government employs 25 percent of the workforce and state-owned firms dominate many industries, but the vast majority of firms are privately owned. The state-owned sector contributes less than 8 percent of GDP.

Monetary Policy
Score: 5–Stable (very high level of inflation)

Ecuador's main monetary goal has been to stabilize inflation by controlling the money supply. From 1985 to 1995, the average annual rate of inflation was 45.5 percent. In 1996, the inflation rate was 24.4 percent.

1	Hong Kong	1.25	77	Zambia	3.05
2	Singapore	1.30	80	Mali	3.10
3	Bahrain	1.70	80	Mongolia	3.10
4	New Zealand	1.75	80	Slovenia	3.10
5	Switzerland	1.90	83	Honduras	3.15
5	United States	1.90	83	Papua New Guinea	3.15
7	Luxembourg	1.95	85	Djibouti	3.20
7	Taiwan	1.95	85	Fiji	3.20
7	United Kingdom	1.95	85	Pakistan	3.20
10	Bahamas	2.00	88	Algeria	3.25
10	Ireland	2.00	88	Guinea	3.25
12	Australia	2.05	88	Lebanon	3.25
12	Japan	2.05	88	Mexico	3.25
14	Belgium	2.10	88	Senegal	3.25
14	Canada	2.10	88	Tanzania	3.25
14	United Arab Emirates	2.10	94	Nigeria	3.30
17	Austria	2.15	94	Romania	3.30
17	Chile	2.15	96	Brazil	3.35
17	Estonia	2.15	96	Cambodia	3.35
20	Czech Republic	2.20	96	Egypt	3.35
20	Netherlands	2.20	96	Ivory Coast	3.35
22	Denmark	2.25	96	Madagascar	3.35
22	Finland	2.25	96	Moldova	3.35
24	Germany	2.30	102	Nepal	3.40
24	Iceland	2.30	103	Cape Verde	3.44
24	South Korea	2.30	104	Armenia	3.45
27	Norway	2.35	104	Dominican Republic	3.45
28	Kuwait	2.40	104	Russia	3.45
28	Malaysia	2.40	107	Burkina Faso	3.50
28	Panama	2.40	107	Cameroon	3.50
28	Thailand	2.40	107	Lesotho	3.50
32	El Salvador	2.45	107	Nicaragua	3.50
32	Sri Lanka	2.45	107	Venezuela	3.50
32	Sweden	2.45	112	Gambia	3.60
35	France	2.50	112	Guyana	3.60
35	Italy	2.50	114	Bulgaria	3.65
35	Spain	2.50	114	Georgia	3.65
38	Trinidad and Tobago	2.55	114	Malawi	3.65
39	Argentina	2.60	117	Ethiopia	3.70
39	Barbados	2.60	117	India	3.70
39	Cyprus	2.60	117	Niger	3.70
39	Jamaica	2.60	120	Albania	3.75
39	Portugal	2.60	120	Bangladesh	3.75
44	Bolivia	2.65	120	China (PRC)	3.75
44	Oman	2.65	120	Congo	3.75
44	Philippines	2.65	120	Croatia	3.75
47	Swaziland	2.70	125	Chad	3.80
47	Uruguay	2.70	125	Mauritania	3.80
49	Botswana	2.75	125	Ukraine	3.80
49	Jordan	2.75	128	Sierra Leone	3.85
49	Namibia	2.75	129	Burundi	3.90
49	Tunisia	2.75	129	Suriname	3.90
53	Belize	2.80	129	Zimbabwe	3.90
53	Costa Rica	2.80	132	Haiti	4.00
53	Guatemala	2.80	132	Kyrgyzstan	4.00
53	Israel	2.80	132	Syria	4.00
53	Peru	2.80	135	Belarus	4.05
53	Saudi Arabia	2.80	136	Kazakstan	4.10
53	Turkey	2.80	136	Mozambique	4.10
53	Uganda	2.80	136	Yemen	4.10
53	Western Samoa	2.80	139	Sudan	4.20
62	Indonesia	2.85	140	Myanmar	4.30
62	Jamaica	2.85	140	Rwanda	4.30
62	Malta	2.85	142	Angola	4.35
62	Paraguay	2.85	143	Azerbaijan	4.40
66	Greece	2.90	143	Tajikistan	4.40
66	Hungary	2.90	145	Turkmenistan	4.50
66	South Africa	2.90	146	Uzbekistan	4.55
69	Benin	2.95	147	Congo/Zaire	4.70
69	**Ecuador**	**2.95**	147	Iran	4.70
69	Gabon	2.95	147	Libya	4.70
69	Morocco	2.95	147	Somalia	4.70
69	Poland	2.95	147	Vietnam	4.70
74	Colombia	3.00	152	Bosnia	4.80
74	Ghana	3.00	153	Iraq	4.90
74	Lithuania	3.00	154	Cuba	5.00
77	Kenya	3.05	154	Laos	5.00
77	Slovak Republic	3.05	154	North Korea	5.00

Mostly Free

CAPITAL FLOWS AND FOREIGN INVESTMENT
Score: 2–Stable (low barriers)

Ecuador's government has been liberalizing its foreign investment policies since 1990. Most investors are free to invest in almost any industry, except for such strategic industries as mining and state-owned enterprises.

BANKING
Score: 3–Stable (moderate level of restrictions)

Ecuador has more private banks than most of its neighbors. Domestically owned banks are relatively competitive with foreign banks; however, these privately owned banks must compete with state-owned development banks that provide a variety of subsidized loans to farmers, ranchers, and small businessmen.

WAGE AND PRICE CONTROLS
Score: 2+ (low level)

Although there are fewer price controls today than there were several years ago, the government still sets prices on such items as natural gas and electricity. The reduction in the number of price controls causes Ecuador's score to improve by one point this year. Ecuador maintains a minimum wage policy.

PROPERTY RIGHTS
Score: 3–Stable (moderate level of protection)

Ecuador's wide disparities in wealth increase the chances that property might be expropriated and redistributed to the poor. According to the U.S. Department of Commerce, "A cumbersome legal system can make it somewhat difficult to enforce property and concession rights, particularly in the agriculture and mining sectors."[2] In 1994, the government passed a new agriculture law to uphold the rights of rural landowners, but corruption still plagues the legal framework, making it unnecessarily difficult to enforce property rights.

REGULATION
Score: 4–Stable (high level)

The Superintendency of Companies, the Superintendency of Banks and Insurance Companies, and the Ecuadorian Standards Institute are Ecuador's primary regulatory bodies. Corruption causes these and other agencies to enforce regulations haphazardly.

BLACK MARKET
Score: 4–Stable (high level of activity)

Because of bureaucratic inefficiency and corruption, many entrepreneurs resort to Ecuador's black market. The government has reduced many trade tariffs on items that were being sold as contraband. According to the U.S. Department of State, however, "Copyright infringement occurs and there is widespread local trade in pirated audio and video recordings, as well as computer software."[3]

NOTES

1. U.S. Department of State, *Country Reports on Economic Policy and Trade Practices*, 1997, p. 249.
2. U.S. Department of Commerce, *Country Commercial Guide*, 1997.
3. U.S. Department of State, *Country Reports on Economic Policy and Trade Practices*, 1997, p. 250.

Egypt   3.35

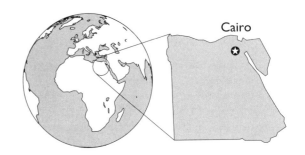
Cairo

1997 Score: **3.45**	1996 Score: **3.45**	1995 Score: **3.50**

Trade	5	Banking	2
Taxation	4.5	Wages and Prices	3
Government Intervention	3	Property Rights	3
Monetary Policy	3	Regulation	4
Foreign Investment	3	Black Market	3

Egypt gained its independence from the United Kingdom in 1922. Today, it is a social democracy ruled by President Hosni Mubarak. It also is the second-largest annual recipient of U.S. foreign aid. In 1991, the government launched a desperately needed market liberalization program; but despite attempts to remove the state from the market, little progress has been made in privatizing Egypt's massive and inefficient public sector. Little has been done to reform and reduce the size of the bureaucracy, either. Egypt has made some progress in lowering extremely high tariffs and establishing more fiscal discipline, however, and has removed some restrictions on the establishment of foreign banks. As a result, its overall score this year is 0.1 point better than it was last year.

TRADE POLICY
Score: 5–Stable (very high level of protectionism)

Despite progress over the past several years in liberalizing its trade policy, Egypt remains one of the world's most heavily protected markets, with an exceptionally high average tariff rate of 19.7 percent.[1] Import bans now apply only to textiles and apparels, although the government must eliminate them eventually as part of the World Trade Organization agreement. Import licenses no longer are required.

TAXATION
Score–Income taxation: 4–Stable (high tax rates)
Score–Corporate taxation: 4–Stable (high tax rates)
Final Taxation Score: 4.5–Stable (very high tax rates)

In 1993, Egypt lowered its top income tax rate from 65 percent to 48 percent, where it remains today. The tax on the average income level is 20 percent, and corporate income is taxed at a rate of 40 percent. Egypt also has a 40 percent capital gains tax, a sales tax, and a social insurance tax.

GOVERNMENT INTERVENTION IN THE ECONOMY
Score: 3–Stable (moderate level)

The government consumes 11.1 percent of Egypt's GDP.[2] With plans for wide-scale privatization proceeding at a slow pace, the large and inefficient state sector still accounts for some 70 percent of industrial production.

MONETARY POLICY
Score: 3–Stable (moderate level of inflation)

Egypt's average annual rate of inflation from 1985 to 1995 was 15.7 percent. The estimated rate for 1996 was 7.2 percent.

1	Hong Kong	1.25	77	Zambia	3.05
2	Singapore	1.30	80	Mali	3.10
3	Bahrain	1.70	80	Mongolia	3.10
4	New Zealand	1.75	80	Slovenia	3.10
5	Switzerland	1.90	83	Honduras	3.15
5	United States	1.90	83	Papua New Guinea	3.15
7	Luxembourg	1.95	85	Djibouti	3.20
7	Taiwan	1.95	85	Fiji	3.20
7	United Kingdom	1.95	85	Pakistan	3.20
10	Bahamas	2.00	88	Algeria	3.25
10	Ireland	2.00	88	Guinea	3.25
12	Australia	2.05	88	Lebanon	3.25
12	Japan	2.05	88	Mexico	3.25
14	Belgium	2.10	88	Senegal	3.25
14	Canada	2.10	88	Tanzania	3.25
14	United Arab Emirates	2.10	94	Nigeria	3.30
17	Austria	2.15	94	Romania	3.30
17	Chile	2.15	96	Brazil	3.35
17	Estonia	2.15	96	Cambodia	3.35
20	Czech Republic	2.20	96	Egypt	3.35
20	Netherlands	2.20	96	Ivory Coast	3.35
22	Denmark	2.25	96	Madagascar	3.35
22	Finland	2.25	96	Moldova	3.35
24	Germany	2.30	102	Nepal	3.40
24	Iceland	2.30	103	Cape Verde	3.44
24	South Korea	2.30	104	Armenia	3.45
27	Norway	2.35	104	Dominican Republic	3.45
28	Kuwait	2.40	104	Russia	3.45
28	Malaysia	2.40	107	Burkina Faso	3.50
28	Panama	2.40	107	Cameroon	3.50
28	Thailand	2.40	107	Lesotho	3.50
32	El Salvador	2.45	107	Nicaragua	3.50
32	Sri Lanka	2.45	107	Venezuela	3.50
32	Sweden	2.45	112	Gambia	3.60
35	France	2.50	112	Guyana	3.60
35	Italy	2.50	114	Bulgaria	3.65
35	Spain	2.50	114	Georgia	3.65
38	Trinidad and Tobago	2.55	114	Malawi	3.65
39	Argentina	2.60	117	Ethiopia	3.70
39	Barbados	2.60	117	India	3.70
39	Cyprus	2.60	117	Niger	3.70
39	Jamaica	2.60	120	Albania	3.75
39	Portugal	2.60	120	Bangladesh	3.75
44	Bolivia	2.65	120	China (PRC)	3.75
44	Oman	2.65	120	Congo	3.75
44	Philippines	2.65	120	Croatia	3.75
47	Swaziland	2.70	125	Chad	3.80
47	Uruguay	2.70	125	Mauritania	3.80
49	Botswana	2.75	125	Ukraine	3.80
49	Jordan	2.75	128	Sierra Leone	3.85
49	Namibia	2.75	129	Burundi	3.90
49	Tunisia	2.75	129	Suriname	3.90
53	Belize	2.80	129	Zimbabwe	3.90
53	Costa Rica	2.80	132	Haiti	4.00
53	Guatemala	2.80	132	Kyrgyzstan	4.00
53	Israel	2.80	132	Syria	4.00
53	Peru	2.80	135	Belarus	4.05
53	Saudi Arabia	2.80	136	Kazakhstan	4.10
53	Turkey	2.80	136	Mozambique	4.10
53	Uganda	2.80	136	Yemen	4.10
53	Western Samoa	2.80	139	Sudan	4.20
62	Indonesia	2.85	140	Myanmar	4.30
62	Latvia	2.85	140	Rwanda	4.30
62	Malta	2.85	142	Angola	4.35
62	Paraguay	2.85	143	Azerbaijan	4.40
66	Greece	2.90	143	Tajikistan	4.40
66	Hungary	2.90	145	Turkmenistan	4.50
66	South Africa	2.90	146	Uzbekistan	4.55
69	Benin	2.95	147	Congo/Zaire	4.70
69	Ecuador	2.95	147	Iran	4.70
69	Gabon	2.95	147	Libya	4.70
69	Morocco	2.95	147	Somalia	4.70
69	Poland	2.95	147	Vietnam	4.70
74	Colombia	3.00	152	Bosnia	4.80
74	Ghana	3.00	153	Iraq	4.90
74	Lithuania	3.00	154	Cuba	5.00
77	Kenya	3.05	154	Laos	5.00
77	Slovak Republic	3.05	154	North Korea	5.00

Mostly Unfree

CAPITAL FLOWS AND FOREIGN INVESTMENT
Score: 3–Stable (moderate barriers)

Egypt's government has established business zones free of customs duties, sales taxes, and other taxes. Despite these improvements, however, a cumbersome bureaucracy continues to frustrate foreign investment. Foreign investors occasionally face official discrimination, particularly when their proposals threaten public-sector interests. In practice, 100 percent foreign ownership, although legally permitted in most sectors, is rarely approved. Most foreigners, particularly non-Arabs, are likely to find themselves excluded from Egypt's still-embryonic privatization process. Foreigners are prohibited from owning agricultural land.

BANKING
Score: 2+ (low level of restrictions)

Egypt's banking industry is dominated by four large commercial banks, several of which are being privatized. Over 20 foreign banks operate branches in Egypt, and there are plans for further privatization of the banking sector. In June 1996, Egypt passed a new banking law allowing for 100 percent foreign ownership of Egyptian banks. As a result, its score is one point better this year.

WAGE AND PRICE CONTROLS
Score: 3–Stable (moderate level)

Price controls have been removed on most products, with the notable exceptions of pharmaceutical products, sugar, edible oils, and cigarettes. Basic foods and transportation are subsidized, although not as much as in recent years. The existence of a massive public sector limits the private sector's ability to set wages and prices. The government limits the amount of profit earned on some imported goods and also is involved in setting wages. There is a minimum wage.

PROPERTY RIGHTS
Score: 3–Stable (moderate level of protection)

Egypt's privatization effort has bogged down. Although private property is protected by the constitution, the judiciary is inefficient. "In some instances," according to the U.S. Department of Commerce, "Government entities refuse for years to accept contractual requirements to arbitrate even if arbitration is explicitly written into the contract. Local lawyers insist, however, that the recalcitrant party cannot prevent indefinitely the initiation of arbitration. It requires time, sometimes numerous court proceedings which in many cases average five years to reach primary court decision, and sometimes numerous appeals to senior Government officials. Legal appeal procedures can extend court cases to 15 years or longer."[3]

REGULATION
Score: 4–Stable (high level)

Corruption is endemic and bribery is the norm in Egypt's bureaucracy, which is massive and inefficient. The business environment is over-regulated, with managers spending an estimated 30 percent of their time handling bureaucratic paperwork, and the labor market is heavily regulated as well. According to the U.S. Department of Commerce, "Red tape remains a key business impediment in Egypt, including a multiplicity of regulations and regulatory agencies, delays in clearing goods through customs, arbitrary decision making, high market entry transaction costs, and an unresponsive commercial court system."[4]

BLACK MARKET
Score: 3–Stable (moderate level of activity)

With its long commitment to a command economy, and with economic reform proceeding at a slow pace, Egypt retains a large black market. According to the U.S. Department of Commerce, "No reliable data exist on Egypt's large informal sector, which may account for 30% of economic activity and serves as the employer of last resort for poor Egyptians."[5] Even though most goods are available in shops, substantial trade restrictions encourage smuggling.

NOTES
1. Based on total taxes on international trade as a percentage of total imports.
2. World Bank, *World Development Report, 1996.*
3. U.S. Department of Commerce, *Country Commercial Guide,* 1997.
4. *Ibid.*
5. *Ibid.*

El Salvador   2.45

| 1997 Score: **2.55** | 1996 Score: **2.45** | 1995 Score: **2.65** |

Trade	3	Banking	2
Taxation	2.5	Wages and Prices	2
Government Intervention	1	Property Rights	3
Monetary Policy	3	Regulation	3
Foreign Investment	2	Black Market	3

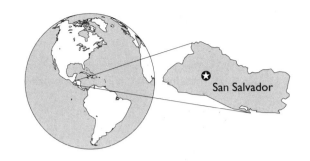

San Salvador

El Salvador suffered a terrible civil war in the 1980s. Despite massive infusions of foreign aid, El Salvador's economy grew by an average of only 2 percent per year from 1982 to 1989. Once the government began to implement market reforms, and after peace was established in 1991, the economy slowly began to recover, growing 3.4 percent in 1990, 3.5 percent in 1991, 4.8 percent in 1992, 7.4 percent in 1993, 6 percent in 1994, 5.5 percent in 1995, and 9.8 percent in 1996. Under President Alfredo Cristiani, the government abolished price controls, slashed import tariffs, privatized most of the financial system, and followed a relatively tight monetary policy. Although some problems remain, the economy is growing and shows signs of increasing prosperity. President Armando Calderon Sol has maintained Cristiani's reforms. The government recently achieved sweeping reform of the country's telecommunications industry, thus reducing overall government intervention in the economy. As a result, El Salvador's overall score this year is 0.1 point better than last year.

TRADE POLICY
Score: 3–Stable (moderate level of protectionism)

El Salvador recently slashed tariff rates and probably will continue to cut them through 1999. It now has an average tariff rate of 7 percent. Many nontariff barriers also have been removed, but arbitrary sanitation requirements on poultry imports, as well as some nontariff restrictions on selected agricultural imports, continue.

TAXATION
Score–Income taxation: 2–Stable (low tax rates)
Score–Corporate taxation: 2–Stable (low tax rates)
Final Taxation Score: 2.5–Stable (moderate tax rates)

El Salvador's top marginal income tax rate is 30 percent;[1] the rate for the average income level is 0 percent. The top corporate income tax rate is 25 percent. El Salvador also has a 13 percent value-added tax.

GOVERNMENT INTERVENTION IN THE ECONOMY
Score: 1+ (very low level)

Government consumes 7.8 percent of El Salvador's GDP, down from 14 percent in 1980. Recently passed legislation makes the country's telecommunications industry one of the most competitive in the world. Other privatization programs are nearly complete, and the government's role in the economy has been reduced significantly. As a result, El Salvador's government intervention score is one point better this year.

MONETARY POLICY
Score: 3–Stable (moderate level of inflation)

El Salvador's average annual rate of inflation from 1985 to 1995 was 14.7 percent. In 1996, the inflation rate was 9.8 percent.

	1	Hong Kong	1.25		77	Zambia	3.05
	2	Singapore	1.30		80	Mali	3.10
	3	Bahrain	1.70		80	Mongolia	3.10
	4	New Zealand	1.75		80	Slovenia	3.10
	5	Switzerland	1.90		83	Honduras	3.15
	5	United States	1.90		83	Papua New Guinea	3.15
	7	Luxembourg	1.95		85	Djibouti	3.20
	7	Taiwan	1.95		85	Fiji	3.20
	7	United Kingdom	1.95		85	Pakistan	3.20
	10	Bahamas	2.00		88	Algeria	3.25
	10	Ireland	2.00		88	Guinea	3.25
	12	Australia	2.05		88	Lebanon	3.25
	12	Japan	2.05		88	Mexico	3.25
	14	Belgium	2.10		88	Senegal	3.25
	14	Canada	2.10		88	Tanzania	3.25
	14	United Arab Emirates	2.10		94	Nigeria	3.30
	17	Austria	2.15		94	Romania	3.30
	17	Chile	2.15		96	Brazil	3.35
	17	Estonia	2.15		96	Cambodia	3.35
	20	Czech Republic	2.20		96	Egypt	3.35
	20	Netherlands	2.20		96	Ivory Coast	3.35
	22	Denmark	2.25		96	Madagascar	3.35
	22	Finland	2.25		96	Moldova	3.35
	24	Germany	2.30		102	Nepal	3.40
	24	Iceland	2.30		103	Cape Verde	3.44
	24	South Korea	2.30		104	Armenia	3.45
	27	Norway	2.35		104	Dominican Republic	3.45
	28	Kuwait	2.40		104	Russia	3.45
	28	Malaysia	2.40		107	Burkina Faso	3.50
	28	Panama	2.40		107	Cameroon	3.50
	28	Thailand	2.40		107	Lesotho	3.50
	32	El Salvador	2.45		107	Nicaragua	3.50
	32	Sri Lanka	2.45		107	Venezuela	3.50
	32	Sweden	2.45		112	Gambia	3.60
	35	France	2.50		112	Guyana	3.60
	35	Italy	2.50		114	Bulgaria	3.65
	35	Spain	2.50		114	Georgia	3.65
	38	Trinidad and Tobago	2.55		114	Malawi	3.65
	39	Argentina	2.60		117	Ethiopia	3.70
	39	Barbados	2.60		117	India	3.70
	39	Cyprus	2.60		117	Niger	3.70
	39	Jamaica	2.60		120	Albania	3.75
	39	Portugal	2.60		120	Bangladesh	3.75
	44	Bolivia	2.65		120	China (PRC)	3.75
	44	Oman	2.65		120	Congo	3.75
	44	Philippines	2.65		120	Croatia	3.75
	47	Swaziland	2.70		125	Chad	3.80
	47	Uruguay	2.70		125	Mauritania	3.80
	49	Botswana	2.75		125	Ukraine	3.80
	49	Jordan	2.75		128	Sierra Leone	3.85
	49	Namibia	2.75		129	Burundi	3.90
	49	Tunisia	2.75		129	Suriname	3.90
	53	Belize	2.80		129	Zimbabwe	3.90
	53	Costa Rica	2.80		132	Haiti	4.00
	53	Guatemala	2.80		132	Kyrgyzstan	4.00
	53	Israel	2.80		132	Syria	4.00
	53	Peru	2.80		135	Belarus	4.05
	53	Saudi Arabia	2.80		136	Kazakstan	4.10
	53	Turkey	2.80		136	Mozambique	4.10
	53	Uganda	2.80		136	Yemen	4.10
	53	Western Samoa	2.80		139	Sudan	4.20
	62	Indonesia	2.85		140	Myanmar	4.30
	62	Latvia	2.85		140	Rwanda	4.30
	62	Malta	2.85		142	Angola	4.35
	62	Paraguay	2.85		143	Azerbaijan	4.40
	66	Greece	2.90		143	Tajikistan	4.40
	66	Hungary	2.90		145	Turkmenistan	4.50
	66	South Africa	2.90		146	Uzbekistan	4.55
	69	Benin	2.95		147	Congo/Zaire	4.70
	69	Ecuador	2.95		147	Iran	4.70
	69	Gabon	2.95		147	Libya	4.70
	69	Morocco	2.95		147	Somalia	4.70
	69	Poland	2.95		147	Vietnam	4.70
	74	Colombia	3.00		152	Bosnia	4.80
	74	Ghana	3.00		153	Iraq	4.90
	74	Lithuania	3.00		154	Cuba	5.00
	77	Kenya	3.05		154	Laos	5.00
	77	Slovak Republic	3.05		154	North Korea	5.00

Mostly Free

CAPITAL FLOWS AND FOREIGN INVESTMENT
Score: 2–Stable (low barriers)

Foreigners may invest in almost any enterprise except electricity, which remains in government hands.

BANKING
Score: 2–Stable (low level of restrictions)

Foreign banks are permitted to operate in El Salvador as if they were domestic banks. All restrictions on foreign banks have been removed, and most local and foreign banks are allowed to compete in offering a wide range of financial services.

WAGE AND PRICE CONTROLS
Score: 2–Stable (low level)

The government has eliminated price controls on some 240 goods, although they remain in effect for bus fares and utilities. El Salvador has a minimum wage.

PROPERTY RIGHTS
Score: 3–Stable (moderate level of protection)

The government has undertaken a massive privatization program and is returning banks, hotels, and other enterprises to the private sector. But even though private property is guaranteed by law, the country lacks efficient legal protection of property; according to the U.S. Department of State, "The judiciary is inefficient and subject to corruption."[2] By global standards, however, the protection of private property in El Salvador is moderate.

REGULATION
Score: 3–Stable (moderate level)

Because price controls have been abolished, the government maintains little regulatory control over most businesses. Corruption remains a problem, however.

BLACK MARKET
Score: 3–Stable (moderate level of activity)

Some labor, such as construction, is provided by the black market. El Salvador's intellectual property laws suffer from a lack of enforcement, as well as from an inefficient bureaucracy.

NOTES
1. The effective tax rate may not exceed 25 percent of taxable income.
2. U.S. Department of State, "El Salvador Country Report on Human Rights Practices for 1996," 1997.

Estonia   2.15

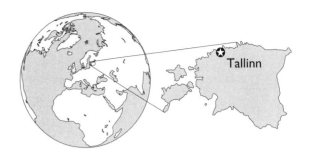

1997 Score: **2.35**	1996 Score: **2.35**	1995 Score: **2.25**

Trade	1	Banking	2
Taxation	3.5	Wages and Prices	2
Government Intervention	2	Property Rights	2
Monetary Policy	4	Regulation	2
Foreign Investment	1	Black Market	2

Estonia gained its independence in 1918, but it was forcibly annexed in 1940 by the Soviet Union. The most Western-oriented country of the former Soviet Union, with a clear Scandinavian and North European orientation, it has associate membership in the European Union and is applying for full membership. Of all the former Soviet republics, Estonia has been the most successful in reforming its economy. The government has undertaken a massive program of privatization, including the selling of many state-owned enterprises, and has established its own national currency, the kroon, which is both stable and convertible. The inflation rate has fallen dramatically, and trade with the West has grown 500 percent since 1991. Estonia has reduced its taxes on imports significantly, and recent crackdowns on pirated intellectual property have brought about a substantial reduction in black market activity. Thus, Estonia's overall score this year is 0.2 point better than it was last year.

TRADE POLICY
Score: 1+ (very low level of protectionism)

Estonia's average tariff rate is approximately 1 percent.[1] There are few, if any, nontariff barriers, and tariffs have been reduced. Thus, its trade score is one point better this year.

TAXATION
Score–Income taxation: 3–Stable (moderate tax rates)
Score–Corporate taxation: 3–Stable (moderate tax rates)
Final Taxation Score: 3.5–Stable (high tax rates)

Estonia has a flat income tax rate of 26 percent and a top corporate tax rate of 26 percent. It also has a 26 percent capital gains tax, an 18 percent value-added tax, a 20 percent social security tax, a 13 percent social insurance tax, and a 1 percent land tax.

GOVERNMENT INTERVENTION IN THE ECONOMY
Score: 2–Stable (low level)

Government consumes 23.4 percent of Estonia's GDP, up from 16 percent in 1995.

MONETARY POLICY
Score: 4–Stable (high level of inflation)

Although inflation is historically high in Estonia because of the 1992 monetary crisis in the former Soviet Union, it has dropped dramatically over the past two years. In 1992, the annual rate of inflation was 1,009 percent. In 1993, it fell to about 26 percent; in 1994, it rose to 40 percent; in 1995, it fell to about 29 percent; and in 1996, it fell again to about 23 percent. Overall, the average rate of inflation since 1992 has remained high.

1	Hong Kong	1.25	77	Zambia	3.05
2	Singapore	1.30	80	Mali	3.10
3	Bahrain	1.70	80	Mongolia	3.10
4	New Zealand	1.75	80	Slovenia	3.10
5	Switzerland	1.90	83	Honduras	3.15
5	United States	1.90	83	Papua New Guinea	3.15
7	Luxembourg	1.95	85	Djibouti	3.20
7	Taiwan	1.95	85	Fiji	3.20
7	United Kingdom	1.95	85	Pakistan	3.20
10	Bahamas	2.00	88	Algeria	3.25
10	Ireland	2.00	88	Guinea	3.25
12	Australia	2.05	88	Lebanon	3.25
12	Japan	2.05	88	Mexico	3.25
14	Belgium	2.10	88	Senegal	3.25
14	Canada	2.10	88	Tanzania	3.25
14	United Arab Emirates	2.10	94	Nigeria	3.30
17	Austria	2.15	94	Romania	3.30
17	Chile	2.15	96	Brazil	3.35
17	Estonia	2.15	96	Cambodia	3.35
20	Czech Republic	2.20	96	Egypt	3.35
20	Netherlands	2.20	96	Ivory Coast	3.35
22	Denmark	2.25	96	Madagascar	3.35
22	Finland	2.25	96	Moldova	3.35
24	Germany	2.30	102	Nepal	3.40
24	Iceland	2.30	103	Cape Verde	3.44
24	South Korea	2.30	104	Armenia	3.45
27	Norway	2.35	104	Dominican Republic	3.45
28	Kuwait	2.40	104	Russia	3.45
28	Malaysia	2.40	107	Burkina Faso	3.50
28	Panama	2.40	107	Cameroon	3.50
28	Thailand	2.40	107	Lesotho	3.50
32	El Salvador	2.45	107	Nicaragua	3.50
32	Sri Lanka	2.45	107	Venezuela	3.50
32	Sweden	2.45	112	Gambia	3.60
35	France	2.50	112	Guyana	3.60
35	Italy	2.50	114	Bulgaria	3.65
35	Spain	2.50	114	Georgia	3.65
38	Trinidad and Tobago	2.55	114	Malawi	3.65
39	Argentina	2.60	117	Ethiopia	3.70
39	Barbados	2.60	117	India	3.70
39	Cyprus	2.60	117	Niger	3.70
39	Jamaica	2.60	120	Albania	3.75
39	Portugal	2.60	120	Bangladesh	3.75
44	Bolivia	2.65	120	China (PRC)	3.75
44	Oman	2.65	120	Congo	3.75
44	Philippines	2.65	120	Croatia	3.75
47	Swaziland	2.70	125	Chad	3.80
47	Uruguay	2.70	125	Mauritania	3.80
49	Botswana	2.75	125	Ukraine	3.80
49	Jordan	2.75	128	Sierra Leone	3.85
49	Namibia	2.75	129	Burundi	3.90
49	Tunisia	2.75	129	Suriname	3.90
53	Belize	2.80	129	Zimbabwe	3.90
53	Costa Rica	2.80	132	Haiti	4.00
53	Guatemala	2.80	132	Kyrgyzstan	4.00
53	Israel	2.80	132	Syria	4.00
53	Peru	2.80	135	Belarus	4.05
53	Saudi Arabia	2.80	136	Kazakstan	4.10
53	Turkey	2.80	136	Mozambique	4.10
53	Uganda	2.80	136	Yemen	4.10
53	Western Samoa	2.80	139	Sudan	4.20
62	Indonesia	2.85	140	Myanmar	4.30
62	Latvia	2.85	140	Rwanda	4.30
62	Malta	2.85	142	Angola	4.35
62	Paraguay	2.85	143	Azerbaijan	4.40
66	Greece	2.90	143	Tajikistan	4.40
66	Hungary	2.90	145	Turkmenistan	4.50
66	South Africa	2.90	146	Uzbekistan	4.55
69	Benin	2.95	147	Congo/Zaire	4.70
69	Ecuador	2.95	147	Iran	4.70
69	Gabon	2.95	147	Libya	4.70
69	Morocco	2.95	147	Somalia	4.70
69	Poland	2.95	147	Vietnam	4.70
74	Colombia	3.00	152	Bosnia	4.80
74	Ghana	3.00	153	Iraq	4.90
74	Lithuania	3.00	154	Cuba	5.00
77	Kenya	3.05	154	Laos	5.00
77	Slovak Republic	3.05	154	North Korea	5.00

Mostly Free

CAPITAL FLOWS AND FOREIGN INVESTMENT
Score: 1–Stable (very low barriers)

There are relatively few restrictions on foreign investors. Investments are permitted in all areas of industry, including some utilities, and all foreign investment ventures are granted "national treatment"; that is, they are treated the same as businesses owned by Estonians. There are no repatriation limitations that force investors to keep their capital in the country.

BANKING
Score: 2–Stable (low level of restrictions)

Banks in Estonia have been made more accessible to foreign operation, and private banks are growing. There still are some restrictions, however, on banks selling investments and securities.

WAGE AND PRICE CONTROLS
Score: 2–Stable (low level)

The government has removed price controls on 95 percent of goods and services in Estonia; the only remaining controls are on the prices of items such as electricity and energy-producing agents like shale. There is a minimum wage.

PROPERTY RIGHTS
Score: 2–Stable (high level of protection)

The likelihood of expropriation in Estonia is low, and the legal protection of private property is relatively high. The court system and enforcement of court awards may be slightly inefficient.

REGULATION
Score: 2–Stable (low level)

Some regulations are burdensome. For example, increased attention to health, safety, and the environment, as well as testing and standards, inhibit business creation. Obtaining a business license, however, is relatively easy and corruption-free.

BLACK MARKET
Score: 2+ (low level of activity)

Because of reduced barriers to trade and a limited regulatory environment, the black market is shrinking. There had been widespread piracy in video and audio tapes and compact disks, but a recent government crackdown has reduced some of this activity. In addition, port authorities have focused their efforts on corruption, with the payoff of a reduction in smuggling. As a result, Estonia's black market score is one point better than last year.

NOTE

1. Although Estonia levies no "tariffs" on imports, it does impose "procedural fees" and other import duties that act as tariffs. Thus, this figure was derived by taking Estonia's taxes raised from international trade in 1993 as a percentage of total imports.

Ethiopia

3.70

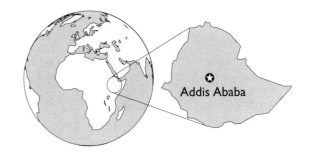
Addis Ababa

1997 Score: **3.60**   1996 Score: **3.70**   1995 Score: **3.80**

Trade	5	Banking	4
Taxation	4	Wages and Prices	3
Government Intervention	3	Property Rights	4
Monetary Policy	2	Regulation	4
Foreign Investment	4	Black Market	4

Years of civil war and Marxist economic policies have devastated Ethiopia, the second most populous country in sub-Saharan Africa—and one of the poorest, with an estimated per capita GDP of $120 in 1995. The Ethiopian People's Revolutionary Democratic Party seized power in 1991, having defeated the Marxist regime of Mengistu Haile Mariam. The transitional government of Prime Minister Meles Zenawi adopted a new constitution in December 1995. Democratic elections were held in 1995 but were boycotted by the major opposition parties. Zenawi's government favors a mixed economy and enjoys considerable support from foreign aid donors. The economy grew only 1.7 percent in 1993, when the province of Eritrea successfully declared its independence; GDP rose by 4.8 percent in 1994 and 7.7 percent in 1995. The level of trade protection, however, has increased. Thus, Ethiopia's overall score is 0.1 point worse than it was last year.

TRADE POLICY
Score: 5– (very high level of protectionism)

Although Ethiopia has liberalized trade somewhat, partly by eliminating the negative list of imports and lowering its maximum tariff to 80 percent, the average tariff rate is 16.36 percent, up from 13.5 percent last year.[1] Thus, its trade policy score is one point worse this year. The customs bureaucracy is cumbersome and inefficient, and delays in bringing goods into the country are not uncommon.

TAXATION
Score–Income taxation: 5–Stable (very high tax rates)
Score–Corporate taxation: 3–Stable (moderate tax rates)
Total Taxation Score: 4–Stable (high tax rates)

Ethiopia recently reduced taxes, but its top income tax rate remains over 50 percent, and the average income level is taxed at rates higher than 25 percent. The corporate tax rate is 50 percent.[2]

GOVERNMENT INTERVENTION IN THE ECONOMY
Score: 3–Stable (moderate level)

Government consumes 11 percent of Ethiopia's GDP, which is considerably lower than the 26.6 percent it consumed in 1990. The industrial sector is dominated by 15 public enterprises, and progress with planned privatization has been slow. State enterprises account for almost all manufacturing production.

MONETARY POLICY
Score: 2–Stable (low level of inflation)

Historically, Ethiopia's inflation rate has been low. The average annual rate of inflation from 1985 through 1995 was only 5.9 percent, although this was artificially low because Ethiopia was a communist country until 1991.

1	Hong Kong	1.25		77	Zambia	3.05
2	Singapore	1.30		80	Mali	3.10
3	Bahrain	1.70		80	Mongolia	3.10
4	New Zealand	1.75		80	Slovenia	3.10
5	Switzerland	1.90		83	Honduras	3.15
5	United States	1.90		83	Papua New Guinea	3.15
7	Luxembourg	1.95		85	Djibouti	3.20
7	Taiwan	1.95		85	Fiji	3.20
7	United Kingdom	1.95		85	Pakistan	3.20
10	Bahamas	2.00		88	Algeria	3.25
10	Ireland	2.00		88	Guinea	3.25
12	Australia	2.05		88	Lebanon	3.25
12	Japan	2.05		88	Mexico	3.25
14	Belgium	2.10		88	Senegal	3.25
14	Canada	2.10		88	Tanzania	3.25
14	United Arab Emirates	2.10		94	Nigeria	3.30
17	Austria	2.15		94	Romania	3.30
17	Chile	2.15		96	Brazil	3.35
17	Estonia	2.15		96	Cambodia	3.35
20	Czech Republic	2.20		96	Egypt	3.35
20	Netherlands	2.20		96	Ivory Coast	3.35
22	Denmark	2.25		96	Madagascar	3.35
22	Finland	2.25		96	Moldova	3.35
24	Germany	2.30		102	Nepal	3.40
24	Iceland	2.30		103	Cape Verde	3.44
24	South Korea	2.30		104	Armenia	3.45
27	Norway	2.35		104	Dominican Republic	3.45
28	Kuwait	2.40		104	Russia	3.45
28	Malaysia	2.40		107	Burkina Faso	3.50
28	Panama	2.40		107	Cameroon	3.50
28	Thailand	2.40		107	Lesotho	3.50
32	El Salvador	2.45		107	Nicaragua	3.50
32	Sri Lanka	2.45		107	Venezuela	3.50
32	Sweden	2.45		112	Gambia	3.60
35	France	2.50		112	Guyana	3.60
35	Italy	2.50		114	Bulgaria	3.65
35	Spain	2.50		114	Georgia	3.65
38	Trinidad and Tobago	2.55		114	Malawi	3.65
39	Argentina	2.60		117	Ethiopia	3.70
39	Barbados	2.60		117	India	3.70
39	Cyprus	2.60		117	Niger	3.70
39	Jamaica	2.60		120	Albania	3.75
39	Portugal	2.60		120	Bangladesh	3.75
44	Bolivia	2.65		120	China (PRC)	3.75
44	Oman	2.65		120	Congo	3.75
44	Philippines	2.65		120	Croatia	3.75
47	Swaziland	2.70		125	Chad	3.80
47	Uruguay	2.70		125	Mauritania	3.80
49	Botswana	2.75		125	Ukraine	3.80
49	Jordan	2.75		128	Sierra Leone	3.85
49	Namibia	2.75		129	Burundi	3.90
49	Tunisia	2.75		129	Suriname	3.90
53	Belize	2.80		129	Zimbabwe	3.90
53	Costa Rica	2.80		132	Haiti	4.00
53	Guatemala	2.80		132	Kyrgyzstan	4.00
53	Israel	2.80		132	Syria	4.00
53	Peru	2.80		135	Belarus	4.05
53	Saudi Arabia	2.80		136	Kazakstan	4.10
53	Turkey	2.80		136	Mozambique	4.10
53	Uganda	2.80		136	Yemen	4.10
53	Western Samoa	2.80		139	Sudan	4.20
62	Indonesia	2.85		140	Myanmar	4.30
62	Latvia	2.85		140	Rwanda	4.30
62	Malta	2.85		142	Angola	4.35
62	Paraguay	2.85		143	Azerbaijan	4.40
66	Greece	2.90		143	Tajikistan	4.40
66	Hungary	2.90		145	Turkmenistan	4.50
66	South Africa	2.90		146	Uzbekistan	4.55
69	Benin	2.95		147	Congo/Zaire	4.70
69	Ecuador	2.95		147	Iran	4.70
69	Gabon	2.95		147	Libya	4.70
69	Morocco	2.95		147	Somalia	4.70
69	Poland	2.95		147	Vietnam	4.70
74	Colombia	3.00		152	Bosnia	4.80
74	Ghana	3.00		153	Iraq	4.90
74	Lithuania	3.00		154	Cuba	5.00
77	Kenya	3.05		154	Laos	5.00
77	Slovak Republic	3.05		154	North Korea	5.00

Mostly Unfree

CAPITAL FLOWS AND FOREIGN INVESTMENT
Score: 4–Stable (high barriers)

The government of Prime Minister Zenawi has made modest progress in dismantling the hostile foreign investment climate created by the previous Marxist regime. Sectors remaining off-limits to private investment include the defense industry, large-scale electric power generation, and postal, telecommunications, financial, some export/import, and major transportation services. Ethiopians are granted priority for investment opportunities, and bureaucratic decision making is slow. Other impediments include a $500,000 minimum investment requirement and regulations designed to encourage Ethiopian participation in management. Although foreign investors can enjoy some tax incentives, little foreign investment has materialized.

BANKING
Score: 4–Stable (high level of restrictions)

The financial sector, nationalized in 1975, has been liberalized, and private investment in banking and insurance was permitted in 1994. The dominant Commercial Bank of Ethiopia and the Ethiopian Insurance Corporation remain under full state ownership. Private investment is limited to newly established bank and insurance operations, of which a few were established last year; the latter remain of marginal importance. Limits on banking and insurance ownership apply to individuals and families, and no foreign ownership of Ethiopian banks is permitted. Foreign banks may not operate in Ethiopia.

WAGE AND PRICE CONTROLS
Score: 3–Stable (moderate level)

Government-imposed price controls have been removed on all but a few products, although a slow and sometimes ineffective privatization program leaves large sections of the economy in government hands, often hindering price competition. State-owned retail and distribution companies, for example, reduce price and wage competition in these sectors because the government directly subsidizes their activities. Because many distribution companies are owned by the government, prices on all goods handled by these companies are affected negatively.

PROPERTY RIGHTS
Score: 4–Stable (low level of protection)

The Mengistu regime nationalized most industries and vast tracts of agricultural land, and the current government's failure to address adequately the status of rural land frustrates proposals for commercial agricultural development. Privatization of state farms is a long-term objective, but urban land will remain the property of the state, available to the private sector only through revocable long-term leases. Bureaucratic red tape and corruption further weaken property rights in Ethiopia. The judicial system remains subject to political influence and, according to the U.S. Department of State, "is weak and overburdened."[3] Property may be expropriated legally with compensation.

REGULATION
Score: 4–Stable (high level)

Impromptu police clearings of street stalls and other persecutions of merchants who threaten politically favored businesses are common. The business permit system is used to favor certain ethnic groups and is subject to corruption. Businesses targeted for government crackdowns include schools teaching computer skills, foreign languages, and typing. Ethiopia's regulatory regime greatly impedes legitimate business activity.

BLACK MARKET
Score: 4–Stable (high level of activity)

Many legitimate economic activities, especially retailing, are driven underground by repressive authorities. There is considerable smuggling of coffee, fruits and vegetables, cigarettes, alcohol, textiles, and electronics. Because Ethiopia has no legal protection of many intellectual property products—for example, there are no trademark or patent laws—piracy is rampant.

NOTES

1. Based on total taxes on international trade as a percentage of total imports.
2. Tax information from *Foreign Tax and Trade Briefs,* Matthew Bender and Co., Inc., June 1994.
3. U.S. Department of State, "Ethiopia Country Report on Human Right Practices for 1996," 1997.

Fiji

3.20

1997 Score: **3.20**	1996 Score: **3.10**	1995 Score: **3.30**

Trade	5	Banking	3
Taxation	3	Wages and Prices	3
Government Intervention	3	Property Rights	3
Monetary Policy	1	Regulation	4
Foreign Investment	3	Black Market	4

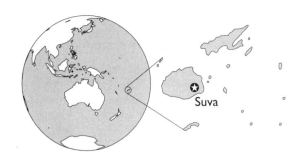

Suva

Fiji, a small island country in the South Pacific, gained its independence from Great Britain in 1970 and shortly thereafter developed a democratic constitution. During the 1980s, however, several military coups occurred. This political instability has prevented Fiji from adopting significant, long-lasting economic reform and achieving sustained economic growth, although the government has reduced taxes and cut its consumption of GDP.

TRADE POLICY
Score: 5–Stable (very high level of protectionism)

Fiji's average tariff rate is 13.34 percent.[1] Its many nontariff barriers include special licenses for powdered milk, butter, potatoes, rice, coffee, canned fish, lubricants, transformer and circuit breaker oils, cleansing oils, and hydraulic brake oils.

TAXATION
Score–Income taxation: 2–Stable (low tax rates)
Score–Corporate taxation: 3–Stable (moderate tax rates)
Final Taxation Score: 3–Stable (moderate tax rates)

Fiji's top income tax rate is 35 percent, down from 40 percent in 1995; the tax rate for the average income is 0 percent. The top corporate income tax rate is 35 percent. Fiji also has a 10 percent value-added tax and a social contributions tax ranging between 7 percent and 23 percent.

GOVERNMENT INTERVENTION IN THE ECONOMY
Score: 3–Stable (moderate level)

Government consumes 16.6 percent of Fiji's GDP. It also continues to own many companies in various industries, including banking.

MONETARY POLICY
Score: 1–Stable (very low level of inflation)

Fiji's average annual rate of inflation from 1985 to 1995 was 4.9 percent. In 1996, inflation was 3.3 percent.

CAPITAL FLOWS AND FOREIGN INVESTMENT
Score: 3–Stable (moderate barriers)

There are many restrictions on foreign investment in Fiji. Foreign investors are not permitted to buy into and gain a controlling share in any domestically owned business, and all investments must be approved by the government. Most foreign-owned enterprises are discouraged from seeking local financing. Fiji does conform to an established foreign investment code, however.

1	Hong Kong	1.25		77	Zambia	3.05
2	Singapore	1.30		80	Mali	3.10
3	Bahrain	1.70		80	Mongolia	3.10
4	New Zealand	1.75		80	Slovenia	3.10
5	Switzerland	1.90		83	Honduras	3.15
5	United States	1.90		83	Papua New Guinea	3.15
7	Luxembourg	1.95		85	Djibouti	3.20
7	Taiwan	1.95		85	Fiji	3.20
7	United Kingdom	1.95		85	Pakistan	3.20
10	Bahamas	2.00		88	Algeria	3.25
10	Ireland	2.00		88	Guinea	3.25
12	Australia	2.05		88	Lebanon	3.25
12	Japan	2.05		88	Mexico	3.25
14	Belgium	2.10		88	Senegal	3.25
14	Canada	2.10		88	Tanzania	3.25
14	United Arab Emirates	2.10		94	Nigeria	3.30
17	Austria	2.15		94	Romania	3.30
17	Chile	2.15		96	Brazil	3.35
17	Estonia	2.15		96	Cambodia	3.35
20	Czech Republic	2.20		96	Egypt	3.35
20	Netherlands	2.20		96	Ivory Coast	3.35
22	Denmark	2.25		96	Madagascar	3.35
22	Finland	2.25		96	Moldova	3.35
24	Germany	2.30		102	Nepal	3.40
24	Iceland	2.30		103	Cape Verde	3.44
24	South Korea	2.30		104	Armenia	3.45
27	Norway	2.35		104	Dominican Republic	3.45
28	Kuwait	2.40		104	Russia	3.45
28	Malaysia	2.40		107	Burkina Faso	3.50
28	Panama	2.40		107	Cameroon	3.50
28	Thailand	2.40		107	Lesotho	3.50
32	El Salvador	2.45		107	Nicaragua	3.50
32	Sri Lanka	2.45		107	Venezuela	3.50
32	Sweden	2.45		112	Gambia	3.60
35	France	2.50		112	Guyana	3.60
35	Italy	2.50		114	Bulgaria	3.65
35	Spain	2.50		114	Georgia	3.65
38	Trinidad and Tobago	2.55		114	Malawi	3.65
39	Argentina	2.60		117	Ethiopia	3.70
39	Barbados	2.60		117	India	3.70
39	Cyprus	2.60		117	Niger	3.70
39	Jamaica	2.60		120	Albania	3.75
39	Portugal	2.60		120	Bangladesh	3.75
44	Bolivia	2.65		120	China (PRC)	3.75
44	Oman	2.65		120	Congo	3.75
44	Philippines	2.65		120	Croatia	3.75
47	Swaziland	2.70		125	Chad	3.80
47	Uruguay	2.70		125	Mauritania	3.80
49	Botswana	2.75		125	Ukraine	3.80
49	Jordan	2.75		128	Sierra Leone	3.85
49	Namibia	2.75		129	Burundi	3.90
49	Tunisia	2.75		129	Suriname	3.90
53	Belize	2.80		129	Zimbabwe	3.90
53	Costa Rica	2.80		132	Haiti	4.00
53	Guatemala	2.80		132	Kyrgyzstan	4.00
53	Israel	2.80		132	Syria	4.00
53	Peru	2.80		135	Belarus	4.05
53	Saudi Arabia	2.80		136	Kazakstan	4.10
53	Turkey	2.80		136	Mozambique	4.10
53	Uganda	2.80		136	Yemen	4.10
53	Western Samoa	2.80		139	Sudan	4.20
62	Indonesia	2.85		140	Myanmar	4.30
62	Latvia	2.85		140	Rwanda	4.30
62	Malta	2.85		142	Angola	4.35
62	Paraguay	2.85		143	Azerbaijan	4.40
66	Greece	2.90		143	Tajikistan	4.40
66	Hungary	2.90		145	Turkmenistan	4.50
66	South Africa	2.90		146	Uzbekistan	4.55
69	Benin	2.95		147	Congo/Zaire	4.70
69	Ecuador	2.95		147	Iran	4.70
69	Gabon	2.95		147	Libya	4.70
69	Morocco	2.95		147	Somalia	4.70
69	Poland	2.95		147	Vietnam	4.70
74	Colombia	3.00		152	Bosnia	4.80
74	Ghana	3.00		153	Iraq	4.90
74	Lithuania	3.00		154	Cuba	5.00
77	Kenya	3.05		154	Laos	5.00
77	Slovak Republic	3.05		154	North Korea	5.00

Mostly Unfree

BANKING
Score: 3–Stable (moderate level of restrictions)

Fiji has few direct restrictions on banking. Although the government's ownership of banks inhibits competition, there is a growing private banking industry. Some local banks are encouraged not to lend to foreign-owned enterprises.

WAGE AND PRICE CONTROLS
Score: 3–Stable (moderate level)

Fiji maintains price controls on a select group of commodities and consumer goods. It also has a minimum wage.

PROPERTY RIGHTS
Score: 3–Stable (moderate level of protection)

Property expropriation in Fiji remains possible. According to the U.S. Department of State, "The judiciary is independent under the Constitution and in practice."[2] But the Economist Intelligence Unit reports that "Fijian lawyers have expressed concern about the administration of the higher court and magisterial court systems. Some judges have also criticized the long delays, procedural irregularities and the incompetence of court staff and even magistrates."[3]

REGULATION
Score: 4–Stable (high level)

Fiji's economy is heavily regulated, and many regulations are significantly burdensome. For example, the Prices and Incomes Board monitors the pricing and wage policies of Fiji's businesses. If the government determines that a business's price and wage policies violate its own established policies, it can shut down any business that fails to comply. There are persistent reports of corruption within Fiji's bureaucracy, particularly with respect to several government-owned financial institutions.[4]

BLACK MARKET
Score: 4–Stable (high level of activity)

Fiji's relatively closed market for imports creates a substantial black market in smuggled items. There is rampant piracy of such intellectual property as video and sound recordings and motion pictures.

NOTES

1. Based on total taxes on international trade as a percentage of total imports.
2. U.S. Department of State, "Fiji Report on Human Rights Practices for 1996," 1997.
3. Economist Intelligence Unit, *Country Report, Fiji,* 1997.
4. U.S. Department of Commerce, "Fiji Budget News," *Market Research Reports,* November 25, 1996.

Finland   2.25

1997 Score: **2.30**	1996 Score: **2.30**	1995 Score: **n/a**

Trade	2	Banking	3
Taxation	4.5	Wages and Prices	2
Government Intervention	3	Property Rights	1
Monetary Policy	1	Regulation	3
Foreign Investment	2	Black Market	1

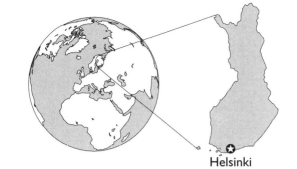

Helsinki

Once part of Sweden, Finland became an autonomous Grand Duchy under Russia's tsar from 1809 to 1917, and later an independent republic. During World War II, it fought both the Soviet Union and Germany. During the Cold War, it adopted a policy of neutrality between East and West. Finland has been ruled by coalition governments for most of the post–World War II period. During the 1990s, its economy was seriously weakened by increased restrictions on the free market. As a result of the economic depression in Russia (Finland's major trading partner) after the dissolution of the Soviet Union, Finland's economy shrank by 13 percent from 1990 to 1993. It began to recover in 1994 as a result of economic liberalization policies. In 1995, Finland joined the European Union (EU). The Finnish economy continues to recover and may reach annual growth rates of 4 percent over the next several years. Because of a reduction in wage and price controls, Finland's overall score is 0.05 point better this year.

TRADE POLICY
Score: 2–Stable (low level of protectionism)

Finland's average tariff rate is 5.9 percent, which is slightly higher than the average for members of the EU; its trade restrictions are the same as those of other EU members. Most nontariff barriers, including import licensing, have been eliminated.

TAXATION
Score–Income taxation: 5– (very high tax rates)
Score–Corporate taxation: 3–Stable (moderate tax rates)
Final Taxation Score: 4.5– (very high tax rates)

Finland's top income tax rate is 57 percent; the average taxpayer finds himself in the 27 percent bracket.[1] The top marginal corporate tax rate is 28 percent. The government also imposes many other taxes, including a 28 percent capital gains tax and a 22 percent value-added tax.

GOVERNMENT INTERVENTION IN THE ECONOMY
Score: 3–Stable (moderate level)

Government consumes 21.5 percent of Finland's GDP, and its presence in the economy is considerable. State-owned companies make up almost 19 percent of GDP, and the government owns shares in many Finnish companies. According to the U.S. Department of State, "four of Finland's ten largest companies are majority state-owned. The government is heavily involved in several key industrial sectors, including energy, forestry products, mining, and chemicals."[2]

MONETARY POLICY
Score: 1–Stable (very low level of inflation)

Finland's rate of inflation averaged 3.8 percent from 1985 to 1995. In 1996, inflation was less than 1 percent.

1	Hong Kong	1.25		77	Zambia	3.05
2	Singapore	1.30		80	Mali	3.10
3	Bahrain	1.70		80	Mongolia	3.10
4	New Zealand	1.75		80	Slovenia	3.10
5	Switzerland	1.90		83	Honduras	3.15
5	United States	1.90		83	Papua New Guinea	3.15
7	Luxembourg	1.95		85	Djibouti	3.20
7	Taiwan	1.95		85	Fiji	3.20
7	United Kingdom	1.95		85	Pakistan	3.20
10	Bahamas	2.00		88	Algeria	3.25
10	Ireland	2.00		88	Guinea	3.25
12	Australia	2.05		88	Lebanon	3.25
12	Japan	2.05		88	Mexico	3.25
14	Belgium	2.10		88	Senegal	3.25
14	Canada	2.10		88	Tanzania	3.25
14	United Arab Emirates	2.10		94	Nigeria	3.30
17	Austria	2.15		94	Romania	3.30
17	Chile	2.15		96	Brazil	3.35
17	Estonia	2.15		96	Cambodia	3.35
20	Czech Republic	2.20		96	Egypt	3.35
20	Netherlands	2.20		96	Ivory Coast	3.35
22	Denmark	2.25		96	Madagascar	3.35
22	Finland	2.25		96	Moldova	3.35
24	Germany	2.30		102	Nepal	3.40
24	Iceland	2.30		103	Cape Verde	3.44
24	South Korea	2.30		104	Armenia	3.45
27	Norway	2.35		104	Dominican Republic	3.45
28	Kuwait	2.40		104	Russia	3.45
28	Malaysia	2.40		107	Burkina Faso	3.50
28	Panama	2.40		107	Cameroon	3.50
28	Thailand	2.40		107	Lesotho	3.50
32	El Salvador	2.45		107	Nicaragua	3.50
32	Sri Lanka	2.45		107	Venezuela	3.50
32	Sweden	2.45		112	Gambia	3.60
35	France	2.50		112	Guyana	3.60
35	Italy	2.50		114	Bulgaria	3.65
35	Spain	2.50		114	Georgia	3.65
38	Trinidad and Tobago	2.55		114	Malawi	3.65
39	Argentina	2.60		117	Ethiopia	3.70
39	Barbados	2.60		117	India	3.70
39	Cyprus	2.60		117	Niger	3.70
39	Jamaica	2.60		120	Albania	3.75
39	Portugal	2.60		120	Bangladesh	3.75
44	Bolivia	2.65		120	China (PRC)	3.75
44	Oman	2.65		120	Congo	3.75
44	Philippines	2.65		120	Croatia	3.75
47	Swaziland	2.70		125	Chad	3.80
47	Uruguay	2.70		125	Mauritania	3.80
49	Botswana	2.75		125	Ukraine	3.80
49	Jordan	2.75		128	Sierra Leone	3.85
49	Namibia	2.75		129	Burundi	3.90
49	Tunisia	2.75		129	Suriname	3.90
53	Belize	2.80		129	Zimbabwe	3.90
53	Costa Rica	2.80		132	Haiti	4.00
53	Guatemala	2.80		132	Kyrgyzstan	4.00
53	Israel	2.80		132	Syria	4.00
53	Peru	2.80		135	Belarus	4.05
53	Saudi Arabia	2.80		136	Kazakstan	4.10
53	Turkey	2.80		136	Mozambique	4.10
53	Uganda	2.80		136	Yemen	4.10
53	Western Samoa	2.80		139	Sudan	4.20
62	Indonesia	2.85		140	Myanmar	4.30
62	Latvia	2.85		140	Rwanda	4.30
62	Malta	2.85		142	Angola	4.35
62	Paraguay	2.85		143	Azerbaijan	4.40
66	Greece	2.90		143	Tajikistan	4.40
66	Hungary	2.90		145	Turkmenistan	4.50
66	South Africa	2.90		146	Uzbekistan	4.55
69	Benin	2.95		147	Congo/Zaire	4.70
69	Ecuador	2.95		147	Iran	4.70
69	Gabon	2.95		147	Libya	4.70
69	Morocco	2.95		147	Somalia	4.70
69	Poland	2.95		147	Vietnam	4.70
74	Colombia	3.00		152	Bosnia	4.80
74	Ghana	3.00		153	Iraq	4.90
74	Lithuania	3.00		154	Cuba	5.00
77	Kenya	3.05		154	Laos	5.00
77	Slovak Republic	3.05		154	North Korea	5.00

Mostly Free

CAPITAL FLOWS AND FOREIGN INVESTMENT
Score: 2–Stable (low barriers)

Finland welcomes foreign investment, although there are some restrictions on investments in areas related to national security, transportation, and mining.

BANKING
Score: 3–Stable (moderate level of restrictions)

Finland's banking system generally is in line with the rest of the EU. Even though the government continues to own (or has ownership stakes in) banks that compete with private banks, it also allows foreign banks to compete. Finnish banks may engage in some financial services, such as the buying and selling of securities.

WAGE AND PRICE CONTROLS
Score: 2+ (low level)

Finland's market sets wages and prices, but the government can control prices through massive transfers of subsidies to such sectors as agriculture and manufacturing. It also can control the prices of some pharmaceuticals through its medical reimbursement programs; drugs subject to government reimbursement must abide by government-established pricing standards. Because these pricing policies generally are in line with EU directives and have been diminishing, Finland's score in wage and price controls is one point better this year.

PROPERTY RIGHTS
Score: 1–Stable (very high level of protection)

Private property is safe in Finland. The legal and judicial system is efficient, and there is no history of government expropriation.

REGULATION
Score: 3–Stable (moderate level)

Establishing a business in Finland is a simple process. Regulations are applied evenly in most cases, although increased regulation, primarily in financial services, is making it more difficult to acquire the capital needed to expand or open new businesses. Finland still maintains onerous health, safety, and employment requirements. According to the U.S. Department of State, "Finland's health and safety laws are among the strictest in the world."[3]

BLACK MARKET
Score: 1–Stable (very low level of activity)

Finland's black market is negligible. Laws protecting intellectual property are very strong, and the levels of computer software and prerecorded music and video piracy are among the world's lowest.

NOTES

1. Ernst & Young's 1997 *Worldwide Executive Tax Guide and Directory* reports that Finland's top income tax rate is 57 percent: the top rate of 39 percent plus an 18 percent municipal and church tax. This is the first year that Ernst & Young has reported the top rate to be 57 percent. See "Tax Cost Planner Modules: Global Expatriate Management System, 1995–96," *Worldwide Executive Tax Guide and Directory,* 1997 edition (New York, N.Y.: Ernst & Young, 1997). For purposes of scoring Finland's income tax rate, Heritage analysts used the 57 percent level. Previously unavailable data provide a more accurate understanding of the country's performance. Consequently, the income taxation score changed from 4 in 1997 to 5 in 1998, and the final taxation score changed from 4 in 1997 to 4.5 in 1998. The methodology for this factor remains the same. This is consistent with other measures that indicate that the tax burden in Finland has been increasing. Measured by tax revenues as a percentage of GDP, for example, Finland's tax burden was 46.5 percent in 1995 and 48.4 percent in 1996.
2. U.S. Department of State, *Country Reports on Economic Policy and Trade Practices,* 1997, p. 113.
3. *Ibid.,* p. 116.

France   2.50

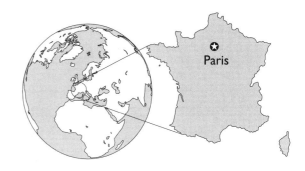

Paris

1997 Score: **2.50**	1996 Score: **2.30**	1995 Score: **2.30**

Trade	2	Banking	3
Taxation	5	Wages and Prices	3
Government Intervention	3	Property Rights	2
Monetary Policy	1	Regulation	2
Foreign Investment	3	Black Market	1

France is a founding member of the European Union (EU) and has the world's fourth largest industrialized economy. Although essentially a free market, it has had a history of centralized administrative control over many parts of its economy. After being elected president in May 1995, Jacques Chirac appointed Alain Juppe as premier to lead a center-right coalition of the Rally for the Republic and the Union for a Democratic France in the National Assembly. Juppe's government took some cautious steps toward economic liberalization, but its major focus was on reducing France's budget deficit through spending cuts and tax increases in order to meet Maastricht Treaty criteria for budget deficits and government debt and to qualify for the monetary union. Consequently, little progress was made toward reviving France's moribund economy or reducing unemployment. In June 1997, voters rejected the center-right coalition and returned a leftist majority composed of the Socialist, Communist, and Green Parties. Chirac was forced to appoint the Socialist Party's Lionel Jospin as premier. Shelving the timid liberalization plans of the Juppe government, Jospin has increased public spending and raised taxes on business and the wealthy. These steps backward could cause France's score to worsen next year.

TRADE POLICY

Score: 2–Stable (low level of protectionism)

Because France is a member of the EU, its trade policy is the same as those of other EU members. Imports are subject to the common EU external tariff of 3.6 percent. Even though economic integration has reduced some trade barriers, however, it has raised others. Particularly affected are electronics, audio-visual products, telecommunications equipment, medical and veterinary equipment, and agricultural products.

TAXATION

Score–Income taxation: 5–Stable (very high tax rates)
Score–Corporate taxation: 4–Stable (high tax rates)
Final Taxation Score: 5–Stable (very high tax rates)

France's top rate of income tax is 56.8 percent; the rate for the average income is 35 percent. The corporate tax is 33.33 percent. France also has a capital gains tax of 19 percent to 33.33 percent, a value-added tax of 20.6 percent, a business activity tax of up to 20 percent, and a social contributions tax of 16 percent to 45 percent.

GOVERNMENT INTERVENTION IN THE ECONOMY

Score: 3–Stable (moderate level)

Government consumes 19.3 percent of France's GDP. It also has monopoly control over several parts of the economy, such as energy generation and supply, rail transportation, postal services, telecommunications, and tobacco production and distribution. Attempts to privatize some of these and other industries have failed. State-owned companies dominate various industrial sectors, skewing pricing and adding inefficiency to the entire economy. Some of these companies

1	Hong Kong	1.25	77	Zambia	3.05
2	Singapore	1.30	80	Mali	3.10
3	Bahrain	1.70	80	Mongolia	3.10
4	New Zealand	1.75	80	Slovenia	3.10
5	Switzerland	1.90	83	Honduras	3.15
5	United States	1.90	83	Papua New Guinea	3.15
7	Luxembourg	1.95	85	Djibouti	3.20
7	Taiwan	1.95	85	Fiji	3.20
7	United Kingdom	1.95	85	Pakistan	3.20
10	Bahamas	2.00	88	Algeria	3.25
10	Ireland	2.00	88	Guinea	3.25
12	Australia	2.05	88	Lebanon	3.25
12	Japan	2.05	88	Mexico	3.25
14	Belgium	2.10	88	Senegal	3.25
14	Canada	2.10	88	Tanzania	3.25
14	United Arab Emirates	2.10	94	Nigeria	3.30
17	Austria	2.15	94	Romania	3.30
17	Chile	2.15	96	Brazil	3.35
17	Estonia	2.15	96	Cambodia	3.35
20	Czech Republic	2.20	96	Egypt	3.35
20	Netherlands	2.20	96	Ivory Coast	3.35
22	Denmark	2.25	96	Madagascar	3.35
22	Finland	2.25	96	Moldova	3.35
24	Germany	2.30	102	Nepal	3.40
24	Iceland	2.30	103	Cape Verde	3.44
24	South Korea	2.30	104	Armenia	3.45
27	Norway	2.35	104	Dominican Republic	3.45
28	Kuwait	2.40	104	Russia	3.45
28	Malaysia	2.40	107	Burkina Faso	3.50
28	Panama	2.40	107	Cameroon	3.50
28	Thailand	2.40	107	Lesotho	3.50
32	El Salvador	2.45	107	Nicaragua	3.50
32	Sri Lanka	2.45	107	Venezuela	3.50
32	Sweden	2.45	112	Gambia	3.60
35	France	2.50	112	Guyana	3.60
35	Italy	2.50	114	Bulgaria	3.65
35	Spain	2.50	114	Georgia	3.65
38	Trinidad and Tobago	2.55	114	Malawi	3.65
39	Argentina	2.60	117	Ethiopia	3.70
39	Barbados	2.60	117	India	3.70
39	Cyprus	2.60	117	Niger	3.70
39	Jamaica	2.60	120	Albania	3.75
39	Portugal	2.60	120	Bangladesh	3.75
44	Bolivia	2.65	120	China (PRC)	3.75
44	Oman	2.65	120	Congo	3.75
44	Philippines	2.65	120	Croatia	3.75
47	Swaziland	2.70	125	Chad	3.80
47	Uruguay	2.70	125	Mauritania	3.80
49	Botswana	2.75	125	Ukraine	3.80
49	Jordan	2.75	128	Sierra Leone	3.85
49	Namibia	2.75	129	Burundi	3.90
49	Tunisia	2.75	129	Suriname	3.90
53	Belize	2.80	129	Zimbabwe	3.90
53	Costa Rica	2.80	132	Haiti	4.00
53	Guatemala	2.80	132	Kyrgyzstan	4.00
53	Israel	2.80	132	Syria	4.00
53	Peru	2.80	135	Belarus	4.05
53	Saudi Arabia	2.80	136	Kazakstan	4.10
53	Turkey	2.80	136	Mozambique	4.10
53	Uganda	2.80	136	Yemen	4.10
53	Western Samoa	2.80	139	Sudan	4.20
62	Indonesia	2.85	140	Myanmar	4.30
62	Latvia	2.85	140	Rwanda	4.30
62	Malta	2.85	142	Angola	4.35
62	Paraguay	2.85	143	Azerbaijan	4.40
66	Greece	2.90	143	Tajikistan	4.40
66	Hungary	2.90	145	Turkmenistan	4.50
66	South Africa	2.90	146	Uzbekistan	4.55
69	Benin	2.95	147	Congo/Zaire	4.70
69	Ecuador	2.95	147	Iran	4.70
69	Gabon	2.95	147	Libya	4.70
69	Morocco	2.95	147	Somalia	4.70
69	Poland	2.95	147	Vietnam	4.70
74	Colombia	3.00	152	Bosnia	4.80
74	Ghana	3.00	153	Iraq	4.90
74	Lithuania	3.00	154	Cuba	5.00
77	Kenya	3.05	154	Laos	5.00
77	Slovak Republic	3.05	154	North Korea	5.00

Mostly Free

are found in such basic industries as iron and steel, aluminum, coal mining, aerospace, nuclear energy, and many forms of transportation (except trucking).

MONETARY POLICY
Score: 1–Stable (very low level of inflation)

France's average annual rate of inflation from 1985 to 1995 was 2.8 percent. In 1996, inflation was 2 percent.

CAPITAL FLOWS AND FOREIGN INVESTMENT
Score: 3–Stable (moderate barriers)

Although much of France's investment policy is determined by directives established by the EU, the government does restrict investments in ways that go beyond these directives, although it recently removed some of them. Investors from outside the EU, for example, used to be required to secure approval from the Ministry of Economics before buying a French business, and the ministry occasionally used this screening process to block some investments. This approval process has been eliminated for the most part, but France still discriminates against investors from non-EU members when their investments are aimed at industries owned by investors from other EU members. According to the U.S. Department of State, "[T]he French state has a very old tradition of extensive control of business and the economy, and firms controlled by non-EU nationals may be denied national treatment in the following sectors: agriculture, road transport, publishing, telecommunications, and tourism."[1]

BANKING
Score: 3–Stable (moderate level of restrictions)

The government controls one of France's largest banks, Credit Lyonnais, severely reducing the availability of credit. Nevertheless, foreign investors are finding it easier to invest in French financial services and to open banks. The government may entertain the notion of a partial privatization of Credit Lyonnais sometime in the future, but for now remains firmly committed to state ownership. Currently, the bank is declaring millions of dollars in losses, and a government bailout worth over $760 million was in the works at the time this edition went to press.

WAGE AND PRICE CONTROLS
Score: 3–Stable (moderate level)

France has a long history of legalized monopolies in such areas as telecommunications, public infrastructure, electricity, and rail transportation. In 1987, the government removed price controls, and most prices now are set by the market. Products still subject to price controls are pharmaceuticals, books, agricultural products, and electricity. France has a minimum wage, and some wages are controlled by the government.

PROPERTY RIGHTS
Score: 2–Stable (high level of protection)

Property rights are uniform throughout France, and enforcement is adequate. There are some impediments, however, to acquiring property. The country's constitution states that any company defined as a national public service or natural monopoly must pass into state ownership. It also allows the state to nationalize companies that fall into this category. Both in practice and by global standards, however, the level of property protection is high.

REGULATION
Score: 2–Stable (low level)

Reforms established by the EU have made it easier to open a business in France. Obtaining a business license is relatively easy, although some hurdles still must be overcome. A company must obtain a registration number from the district commercial court, and a copy of its lease and other documentation must accompany the application. The government has helped to streamline this cumbersome process by incorporating all the registration requirements into one office.

BLACK MARKET
Score: 1–Stable (very low level of activity)

The principal areas of black market activity in France are gambling and the buying and selling of illegal weapons, drugs, and stolen merchandise.

NOTE
1. U.S. Department of State, *Country Reports on Economic Policy and Trade Practices*, 1997, p. 119.

Gabon 2.95

1997 Score: **2.95**	1996 Score: **3.05**	1995 Score: **3.06**

Trade	5	Banking	2
Taxation	4.5	Wages and Prices	3
Government Intervention	3	Property Rights	3
Monetary Policy	1	Regulation	3
Foreign Investment	2	Black Market	3

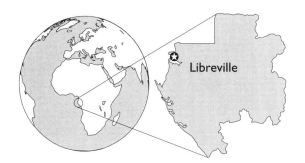
Libreville

Gabon gained its independence from France in 1960. Due to generous deposits of oil and such valuable minerals as uranium and manganese, and to its small population of about 1.4 million, Gabon is one of the most prosperous countries in sub-Saharan Africa. Per capita GDP was nearly $3,500 in 1995. Gabon maintains close ties with France, including membership in the French Franc Zone, giving it a measure of economic and political stability that is unusual in Africa. Although a number of political parties exist, the Parti democratique gabonais (PDG) is unquestionably in control. Led by President Omar Bongo, the PDG won 100 of Parliament's 120 seats in recent elections, and it dominates the newly founded Senate. Economic liberalization has been moving very slowly, and the economy remains dominated by the government and presidential cronies.

TRADE POLICY
Score: 5–Stable (very high level of protectionism)

Gabon's average tariff rate is a high 32.54 percent, and the tariff on electronics and vehicles is particularly high. There are quantitative import restrictions on sugar, vegetable oil, soap, mineral water, and cement; rice and wheat are subject to import licenses. The customs process is slow and cumbersome, and fraud is a problem.[1] Import bans on mineral water, cement, soap, and other items have been lifted.

TAXATION
Score–Income taxation: 5–Stable (very high tax rates)
Score–Corporate taxation: 3–Stable (moderate tax rates)
Final Taxation Score: 4.5–Stable (very high tax rates)

The highest tax bracket in Gabon is 60.5 percent;[2] the tax on the average income level is 15 percent. The corporate tax rate is 40 percent, and companies must pay 5 percent of their pretax profits into the Gabonese Investment Fund. Gabon also has a 40 percent capital gains tax and an 18 percent value-added tax. The latter was introduced in 1995 to replace other taxes, including the business turnover tax. Small and medium businesses routinely receive tax holidays.

GOVERNMENT INTERVENTION IN THE ECONOMY
Score: 3–Stable (moderate level)

Government consumes 12.6 percent of Gabon's GDP, and the public sector remains bloated despite retrenchment efforts. Although some state-owned enterprises have been liquidated, there has been little privatization of larger state-owned companies.

MONETARY POLICY
Score: 1–Stable (very low level of inflation)

Gabon's average annual rate of inflation between 1985 and 1995 was 4.8 percent. Under the Franc Zone Mechanism, Gabon exercises only limited control over its monetary policies. The Bank of France exerts tight control over the money supply. Inflation currently runs at some 5 percent.

1	Hong Kong	1.25	77	Zambia	3.05
2	Singapore	1.30	80	Mali	3.10
3	Bahrain	1.70	80	Mongolia	3.10
4	New Zealand	1.75	80	Slovenia	3.10
5	Switzerland	1.90	83	Honduras	3.15
5	United States	1.90	83	Papua New Guinea	3.15
7	Luxembourg	1.95	85	Djibouti	3.20
7	Taiwan	1.95	85	Fiji	3.20
7	United Kingdom	1.95	85	Pakistan	3.20
10	Bahamas	2.00	88	Algeria	3.25
10	Ireland	2.00	88	Guinea	3.25
12	Australia	2.05	88	Lebanon	3.25
12	Japan	2.05	88	Mexico	3.25
14	Belgium	2.10	88	Senegal	3.25
14	Canada	2.10	88	Tanzania	3.25
14	United Arab Emirates	2.10	94	Nigeria	3.30
17	Austria	2.15	94	Romania	3.30
17	Chile	2.15	96	Brazil	3.35
17	Estonia	2.15	96	Cambodia	3.35
20	Czech Republic	2.20	96	Egypt	3.35
20	Netherlands	2.20	96	Ivory Coast	3.35
22	Denmark	2.25	96	Madagascar	3.35
22	Finland	2.25	96	Moldova	3.35
24	Germany	2.30	102	Nepal	3.40
24	Iceland	2.30	103	Cape Verde	3.44
24	South Korea	2.30	104	Armenia	3.45
27	Norway	2.35	104	Dominican Republic	3.45
28	Kuwait	2.40	104	Russia	3.45
28	Malaysia	2.40	107	Burkina Faso	3.50
28	Panama	2.40	107	Cameroon	3.50
28	Thailand	2.40	107	Lesotho	3.50
32	El Salvador	2.45	107	Nicaragua	3.50
32	Sri Lanka	2.45	107	Venezuela	3.50
32	Sweden	2.45	112	Gambia	3.60
35	France	2.50	112	Guyana	3.60
35	Italy	2.50	114	Bulgaria	3.65
35	Spain	2.50	114	Georgia	3.65
38	Trinidad and Tobago	2.55	114	Malawi	3.65
39	Argentina	2.60	117	Ethiopia	3.70
39	Barbados	2.60	117	India	3.70
39	Cyprus	2.60	117	Niger	3.70
39	Jamaica	2.60	120	Albania	3.75
39	Portugal	2.60	120	Bangladesh	3.75
44	Bolivia	2.65	120	China (PRC)	3.75
44	Oman	2.65	120	Congo	3.75
44	Philippines	2.65	120	Croatia	3.75
47	Swaziland	2.70	125	Chad	3.80
47	Uruguay	2.70	125	Mauritania	3.80
49	Botswana	2.75	125	Ukraine	3.80
49	Jordan	2.75	128	Sierra Leone	3.85
49	Namibia	2.75	129	Burundi	3.90
49	Tunisia	2.75	129	Suriname	3.90
53	Belize	2.80	129	Zimbabwe	3.90
53	Costa Rica	2.80	132	Haiti	4.00
53	Guatemala	2.80	132	Kyrgyzstan	4.00
53	Israel	2.80	132	Syria	4.00
53	Peru	2.80	135	Belarus	4.05
53	Saudi Arabia	2.80	136	Kazakstan	4.10
53	Turkey	2.80	136	Mozambique	4.10
53	Uganda	2.80	136	Yemen	4.10
53	Western Samoa	2.80	139	Sudan	4.20
62	Indonesia	2.85	140	Myanmar	4.30
62	Latvia	2.85	140	Rwanda	4.30
62	Malta	2.85	142	Angola	4.35
62	Paraguay	2.85	143	Azerbaijan	4.40
66	Greece	2.90	143	Tajikistan	4.40
66	Hungary	2.90	145	Turkmenistan	4.50
66	South Africa	2.90	146	Uzbekistan	4.55
69	Benin	2.95	147	Congo/Zaire	4.70
69	Ecuador	2.95	147	Iran	4.70
69	Gabon	2.95	147	Libya	4.70
69	Morocco	2.95	147	Somalia	4.70
69	Poland	2.95	147	Vietnam	4.70
74	Colombia	3.00	152	Bosnia	4.80
74	Ghana	3.00	153	Iraq	4.90
74	Lithuania	3.00	154	Cuba	5.00
77	Kenya	3.05	154	Laos	5.00
77	Slovak Republic	3.05	154	North Korea	5.00

Mostly Free

CAPITAL FLOWS AND FOREIGN INVESTMENT
Score: 2–Stable (low barriers)

A 1989 rewrite of the investment code liberalized conditions for foreign businesses. Government participation in investment no longer is required. A requirement that all private companies established in Gabon contribute 10 percent of their shares to the government was repealed in 1994. Foreign investors face only minimal restrictions in most areas, and the government has allowed foreign-owned operations to compete with local businesses. Very few areas are off-limits to foreign investors, but the government dominates the most lucrative sectors of the marketplace. Foreign investors encounter protracted delays in the investment approval process. There are no free trade zones in Gabon, but tax holidays for certain investors are available.

BANKING
Score: 2–Stable (low level of restrictions)

The government exercises little control over Gabon's sophisticated banking system, composed primarily of competitive foreign banks. According to the U.S. Department of Commerce, "The local banking system, dominated by French and other foreign banks, is relatively sophisticated and offers most corporate banking services, or can procure them in Europe."[3]

WAGE AND PRICE CONTROLS
Score: 3–Stable (moderate level)

Price controls are imposed on 17 goods and most services, including insurance and construction. A relatively high minimum wage has attracted many unskilled immigrants from neighboring African countries. The minimum wage for non-Gabonese is 80 percent of what Gabonese workers must be paid.

PROPERTY RIGHTS
Score: 3–Stable (moderate level of protection)

Expropriation of foreign property in Gabon is not likely. There have been charges, however, that government officials use coercion to obtain control of successful businesses. Property also is threatened by ethnic clashes, by a lack of democratic progress, and by the growing resentment of foreign business. According to the U.S. Department of State, "The judiciary is independent but remains vulnerable to government manipulation."[4]

REGULATION
Score: 3–Stable (moderate level)

Although the bureaucracy is generally effective, lengthy delays in the processing of some business investments and expansions are common, corruption is present, and regulations make the business environment increasingly complicated. The success of Gabonese enterprises depends largely on their political connections. A "Gabonization" program instituted in 1992 forces employers to decrease the number of foreigners in their workforce. This has led to inefficiency.

BLACK MARKET
Score: 3–Stable (moderate level of activity)

The level of government control of and influence over economic activity in Gabon encourages black market activity, and high tariffs on luxury goods and automobiles encourage smuggling.

NOTES

1. U.S. Department of State, *Country Reports on Economic Policy and Trade Practices,* 1997, p. 8.
2. Includes a 5.5 percent supplementary tax.
3. U.S. Department of Commerce, *Country Commercial Guide,* 1996.
4. U.S. Department of State, "Gabon Country Report on Human Rights Practices for 1996," 1997.

The Gambia   3.60

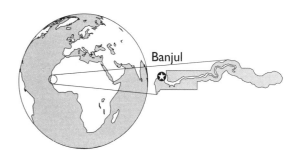
Banjul

Trade	4	Banking	4
Taxation	4	Wages and Prices	4
Government Intervention	3	Property Rights	2
Monetary Policy	2	Regulation	4
Foreign Investment	4	Black Market	5

The Gambia gained its independence from Great Britain in 1965 and established a multiparty system with elections every five years. Until the government was overthrown in 1994 in a military coup led by Colonel Yahyah Jammeh, the country had been ruled continuously by President Dawda Kairaba Jawara, who had been reelected five times. In September 1996, the Gambia held elections in which Colonel Jammeh became president; the U.S. Department of State referred to these elections as neither free nor fair.[1] Colonel Jammeh has promised to weed out corruption and strengthen legal institutions. He also has vowed to increase efforts to deregulate the economy, introduce a stock exchange, and establish export processing zones. These pledges may come to fruition in the future, but little progress has been made so far. In 1994, agriculture made up 23 percent of GDP; industry produced another 12 percent of GDP.

TRADE POLICY
Score: 4–Stable (high level of protectionism)

The Gambia's average tariff rate is 13.5 percent. Import bans apply mainly to over-the-counter medicines.

TAXATION
Score–Income taxation: 4–Stable (high tax rates)
Score–Corporate taxation: 4–Stable (high tax rates)
Final Taxation Score: 4–Stable (high tax rates)

Total government revenues represent about 23 percent of the Gambia's GDP. This is higher than comparable figures for most other countries in sub-Saharan Africa.[2]

GOVERNMENT INTERVENTION IN THE ECONOMY
Score: 3–Stable (moderate level)

Government consumes about 18 percent of the Gambia's GDP, most of which is generated by the public sector. Many companies are government-owned.

MONETARY POLICY
Score: 2–Stable (low level of inflation)

The Gambia's average annual rate of inflation from 1985 to 1995 was 10.3 percent. In 1996, the inflation rate was 1 percent.

CAPITAL FLOWS AND FOREIGN INVESTMENT
Score: 4–Stable (high barriers)

The Gambia provides equal treatment for domestic and foreign firms and actively seeks foreign investment. Investments must be approved, however, by the government on a case-by-case basis.

1	Hong Kong	1.25	77	Zambia	3.05
2	Singapore	1.30	80	Mali	3.10
3	Bahrain	1.70	80	Mongolia	3.10
4	New Zealand	1.75	80	Slovenia	3.10
5	Switzerland	1.90	83	Honduras	3.15
5	United States	1.90	83	Papua New Guinea	3.15
7	Luxembourg	1.95	85	Djibouti	3.20
7	Taiwan	1.95	85	Fiji	3.20
7	United Kingdom	1.95	85	Pakistan	3.20
10	Bahamas	2.00	88	Algeria	3.25
10	Ireland	2.00	88	Guinea	3.25
12	Australia	2.05	88	Lebanon	3.25
12	Japan	2.05	88	Mexico	3.25
14	Belgium	2.10	88	Senegal	3.25
14	Canada	2.10	88	Tanzania	3.25
14	United Arab Emirates	2.10	94	Nigeria	3.30
17	Austria	2.15	94	Romania	3.30
17	Chile	2.15	96	Brazil	3.35
17	Estonia	2.15	96	Cambodia	3.35
20	Czech Republic	2.20	96	Egypt	3.35
20	Netherlands	2.20	96	Ivory Coast	3.35
22	Denmark	2.25	96	Madagascar	3.35
22	Finland	2.25	96	Moldova	3.35
24	Germany	2.30	102	Nepal	3.40
24	Iceland	2.30	103	Cape Verde	3.44
24	South Korea	2.30	104	Armenia	3.45
27	Norway	2.35	104	Dominican Republic	3.45
28	Kuwait	2.40	104	Russia	3.45
28	Malaysia	2.40	107	Burkina Faso	3.50
28	Panama	2.40	107	Cameroon	3.50
28	Thailand	2.40	107	Lesotho	3.50
32	El Salvador	2.45	107	Nicaragua	3.50
32	Sri Lanka	2.45	107	Venezuela	3.50
32	Sweden	2.45	112	Gambia	3.60
35	France	2.50	112	Guyana	3.60
35	Italy	2.50	114	Bulgaria	3.65
35	Spain	2.50	114	Georgia	3.65
38	Trinidad and Tobago	2.55	114	Malawi	3.65
39	Argentina	2.60	117	Ethiopia	3.70
39	Barbados	2.60	117	India	3.70
39	Cyprus	2.60	117	Niger	3.70
39	Jamaica	2.60	120	Albania	3.75
39	Portugal	2.60	120	Bangladesh	3.75
44	Bolivia	2.65	120	China (PRC)	3.75
44	Oman	2.65	120	Congo	3.75
44	Philippines	2.65	120	Croatia	3.75
47	Swaziland	2.70	125	Chad	3.80
47	Uruguay	2.70	125	Mauritania	3.80
49	Botswana	2.75	125	Ukraine	3.80
49	Jordan	2.75	128	Sierra Leone	3.85
49	Namibia	2.75	129	Burundi	3.90
49	Tunisia	2.75	129	Suriname	3.90
53	Belize	2.80	129	Zimbabwe	3.90
53	Costa Rica	2.80	132	Haiti	4.00
53	Guatemala	2.80	132	Kyrgyzstan	4.00
53	Israel	2.80	132	Syria	4.00
53	Peru	2.80	135	Belarus	4.05
53	Saudi Arabia	2.80	136	Kazakstan	4.10
53	Turkey	2.80	136	Mozambique	4.10
53	Uganda	2.80	136	Yemen	4.10
53	Western Samoa	2.80	139	Sudan	4.20
62	Indonesia	2.85	140	Myanmar	4.30
62	Latvia	2.85	140	Rwanda	4.30
62	Malta	2.85	142	Angola	4.35
62	Paraguay	2.85	143	Azerbaijan	4.40
66	Greece	2.90	143	Tajikistan	4.40
66	Hungary	2.90	145	Turkmenistan	4.50
66	South Africa	2.90	146	Uzbekistan	4.55
69	Benin	2.95	147	Congo/Zaire	4.70
69	Ecuador	2.95	147	Iran	4.70
69	Gabon	2.95	147	Libya	4.70
69	Morocco	2.95	147	Somalia	4.70
69	Poland	2.95	147	Vietnam	4.70
74	Colombia	3.00	152	Bosnia	4.80
74	Ghana	3.00	153	Iraq	4.90
74	Lithuania	3.00	154	Cuba	5.00
77	Kenya	3.05	154	Laos	5.00
77	Slovak Republic	3.05	154	North Korea	5.00

Mostly Unfree

BANKING
Score: 4–Stable (high level of restrictions)

The banking system in the Gambia is heavily controlled by the government and severely underdeveloped.

WAGE AND PRICE CONTROLS
Score: 4–Stable (high level)

Wages and prices in the Gambia sometimes are affected significantly by the large public sector, through heavy government subsidies that influence prices, and by import substitution policies.

PROPERTY RIGHTS
Score: 2–Stable (high level of protection)

The legal system in the Gambia is efficient, fair, and independent. It also is overburdened at times, however, with a backlog of unresolved cases, and judgments can take several years.

REGULATION
Score: 4–Stable (high level)

Establishing a business in the Gambia can be difficult because of corruption in the government bureaucracy. Bribery and embezzlement are prevalent among the government officials who are responsible for collecting fees.

BLACK MARKET
Score: 5–Stable (very high level of activity)

The Gambia's black market is large. Most of this activity occurs in smuggled consumer goods, labor, and pirated intellectual property.

NOTES

1. U.S. Department of State, "The Gambia Country Report on Human Rights Practices for 1996," 1997.
2. Tax information is not available for the Gambia.

Georgia   3.65

1997 Score: **3.85**		1996 Score: **3.85**		1995 Score: **n/a**

Trade	3	Banking	4
Taxation	2.5	Wages and Prices	4
Government Intervention	2	Property Rights	4
Monetary Policy	5	Regulation	4
Foreign Investment	3	Black Market	5

Georgia was independent from 1918 until 1921, at which time it was conquered by the Soviet Union. It has a developed agricultural sector that includes citrus production, as well as resorts, light industry, and some high-tech enterprises. Ethnic unrest and two civil wars since becoming independent again in 1991 have hampered the development of a free market. The country has been plagued by hyperinflation and by declines in industry and manufacturing. The government of President Eduard Shevardnadze has achieved an economic turnaround by applying responsible economic policies. For example, Georgia has privatized many state-owned industries, opened its market to imports and foreign investment, and established a commercial code. Government spending as a percentage of the economy is shrinking. As a result, Georgia's overall score is 0.2 point better this year.

TRADE POLICY
Score: 3–Stable (moderate level of protectionism)

According to the U.S. Department of Commerce, "Import duties on most goods are set at 12 percent. Under the terms of the new customs law which came into effect January 1, 1997, capital goods, spare parts and goods intended for manufacturing are subject to a 5 percent tariff."[1] When these lower rates are taken into account, Georgia has an average tariff rate of about 8 percent. There are no import bans, but some government licenses are required for particular goods like medical equipment. Georgia also maintains import quotas.

TAXATION
Score–Income taxation: 2–Stable (low tax rates)
Score–Corporate taxation: 2–Stable (low tax rates)
Final Taxation Score: 2.5–Stable (moderate tax rates)

Georgia's top income tax rate is 20 percent; the average taxpayer finds himself in the 15 percent bracket. The top marginal corporate tax rate is 20 percent. Georgia also has several other taxes, including a 20 percent value-added tax. Tax collection is hampered by an inefficient bureaucracy.

GOVERNMENT INTERVENTION IN THE ECONOMY
Score: 2+ (low level)

Government consumes over 7 percent of Georgia's GDP, down from 30 percent in 1992. As a result, Georgia's score in this category has improved by two points this year. The state-owned sector accounts for most GDP. But because the government's consumption figure has fallen significantly, its level of intervention in the economy is low by global standards.

MONETARY POLICY
Score: 5–Stable (very high level of inflation)

Georgia suffers from chronic inflation; for example, from 1993 to 1994, prices increased roughly 60 percent a month. In 1996, inflation fell to 48 percent for the year. But by global standards this rate remains very high.

1	Hong Kong	1.25		77	Zambia	3.05
2	Singapore	1.30		80	Mali	3.10
3	Bahrain	1.70		80	Mongolia	3.10
4	New Zealand	1.75		80	Slovenia	3.10
5	Switzerland	1.90		83	Honduras	3.15
5	United States	1.90		83	Papua New Guinea	3.15
7	Luxembourg	1.95		85	Djibouti	3.20
7	Taiwan	1.95		85	Fiji	3.20
7	United Kingdom	1.95		85	Pakistan	3.20
10	Bahamas	2.00		88	Algeria	3.25
10	Ireland	2.00		88	Guinea	3.25
12	Australia	2.05		88	Lebanon	3.25
12	Japan	2.05		88	Mexico	3.25
14	Belgium	2.10		88	Senegal	3.25
14	Canada	2.10		88	Tanzania	3.25
14	United Arab Emirates	2.10		94	Nigeria	3.30
17	Austria	2.15		94	Romania	3.30
17	Chile	2.15		96	Brazil	3.35
17	Estonia	2.15		96	Cambodia	3.35
20	Czech Republic	2.20		96	Egypt	3.35
20	Netherlands	2.20		96	Ivory Coast	3.35
22	Denmark	2.25		96	Madagascar	3.35
22	Finland	2.25		96	Moldova	3.35
24	Germany	2.30		102	Nepal	3.40
24	Iceland	2.30		103	Cape Verde	3.44
24	South Korea	2.30		104	Armenia	3.45
27	Norway	2.35		104	Dominican Republic	3.45
28	Kuwait	2.40		104	Russia	3.45
28	Malaysia	2.40		107	Burkina Faso	3.50
28	Panama	2.40		107	Cameroon	3.50
28	Thailand	2.40		107	Lesotho	3.50
32	El Salvador	2.45		107	Nicaragua	3.50
32	Sri Lanka	2.45		107	Venezuela	3.50
32	Sweden	2.45		112	Gambia	3.60
35	France	2.50		112	Guyana	3.60
35	Italy	2.50		114	Bulgaria	3.65
35	Spain	2.50		114	Georgia	3.65
38	Trinidad and Tobago	2.55		114	Malawi	3.65
39	Argentina	2.60		117	Ethiopia	3.70
39	Barbados	2.60		117	India	3.70
39	Cyprus	2.60		117	Niger	3.70
39	Jamaica	2.60		120	Albania	3.75
39	Portugal	2.60		120	Bangladesh	3.75
44	Bolivia	2.65		120	China (PRC)	3.75
44	Oman	2.65		120	Congo	3.75
44	Philippines	2.65		120	Croatia	3.75
47	Swaziland	2.70		125	Chad	3.80
47	Uruguay	2.70		125	Mauritania	3.80
49	Botswana	2.75		125	Ukraine	3.80
49	Jordan	2.75		128	Sierra Leone	3.85
49	Namibia	2.75		129	Burundi	3.90
49	Tunisia	2.75		129	Suriname	3.90
53	Belize	2.80		129	Zimbabwe	3.90
53	Costa Rica	2.80		132	Haiti	4.00
53	Guatemala	2.80		132	Kyrgyzstan	4.00
53	Israel	2.80		132	Syria	4.00
53	Peru	2.80		135	Belarus	4.05
53	Saudi Arabia	2.80		136	Kazakhstan	4.10
53	Turkey	2.80		136	Mozambique	4.10
53	Uganda	2.80		136	Yemen	4.10
53	Western Samoa	2.80		139	Sudan	4.20
62	Indonesia	2.85		140	Myanmar	4.30
62	Latvia	2.85		140	Rwanda	4.30
62	Malta	2.85		142	Angola	4.35
62	Paraguay	2.85		143	Azerbaijan	4.40
66	Greece	2.90		143	Tajikistan	4.40
66	Hungary	2.90		145	Turkmenistan	4.50
66	South Africa	2.90		146	Uzbekistan	4.55
69	Benin	2.95		147	Congo/Zaire	4.70
69	Ecuador	2.95		147	Iran	4.70
69	Gabon	2.95		147	Libya	4.70
69	Morocco	2.95		147	Somalia	4.70
69	Poland	2.95		147	Vietnam	4.70
74	Colombia	3.00		152	Bosnia	4.80
74	Ghana	3.00		153	Iraq	4.90
74	Lithuania	3.00		154	Cuba	5.00
77	Kenya	3.05		154	Laos	5.00
77	Slovak Republic	3.05		154	North Korea	5.00

Mostly Unfree

CAPITAL FLOWS AND FOREIGN INVESTMENT
Score: 3–Stable (moderate barriers)

Georgia places few official restrictions on investment. Most industries are open to foreign investment, although a lack of legal protection, an inefficient and bloated bureaucracy, and the collapse of many state-owned businesses are problems. Laws concerning private ownership of land can be confusing and unclear.

BANKING
Score: 4–Stable (high level of restrictions)

The banking system in Georgia is a shambles. The government has a heavy hand in controlling the domestic banking system, and many state-owned banks are inefficient and led by officials who lack common business knowledge. According to the U.S. Department of Commerce, "Georgian law does permit the free flow of financial resources. But in practice, the flow is restrained because of poor and unreliable interbank communication (regular banking transactions within Georgia can take several days)."[2]

WAGE AND PRICE CONTROLS
Score: 4–Stable (high level)

The government sill sets some wages and prices. Government subsidies to state-owned industries cause goods to be sold at artificially low prices, and the government establishes prices for electricity, bread, and some municipal services.

PROPERTY RIGHTS
Score: 4–Stable (low level of protection)

The lack of effective government control over parts of Georgia's territory hampers the protection of private property. As yet, there is neither a fully functioning court system nor a legal environment conducive to the protection of private property. According to the U.S. Department of State, "The Constitution provides for an independent judiciary. Prior to adoption of the Constitution, the courts were often influenced by pressure from the executive branch. This pattern continues with judicial authorities frequently deferring to the executive branch, particularly at lower levels of the court system."[3]

REGULATION
Score: 4–Stable (high level)

Establishing a business in Georgia often is difficult, especially if the business is to compete directly with a state-owned company. Regulations generally are applied unevenly, and corruption frequently is present. The U.S. Department of Commerce identifies the "high level of crime and corruption" and "remnants of central planning and bureaucracy" as additional deterrents.[4]

BLACK MARKET
Score: 5–Stable (very high level of activity)

Some estimates indicate that Georgia's black market is equal in size to its formal market. It includes such activities as the sale of pirated computer software, compact disks, and videos, as well as labor. Smuggling from neighboring Turkey, Russia, Armenia, and Azerbaijan also is prevalent.

NOTES
1. U.S. Department of Commerce, "Georgia: Economic and Trade Overview," May 26, 1997.
2. *Ibid.*
3. U.S. Department of State, "Georgia Country Report on Human Rights Practices for 1996," 1997.
4. U.S. Department of Commerce, *Country Commercial Guide,* 1997.

Germany

2.30

1997 Score: **2.20**   1996 Score: **2.10**   1995 Score: **2.00**

Trade	2	Banking	3
Taxation	5	Wages and Prices	2
Government Intervention	2	Property Rights	1
Monetary Policy	1	Regulation	4
Foreign Investment	2	Black Market	1

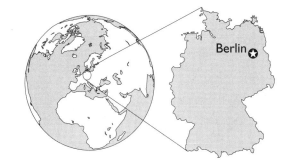

Berlin

Germany is the largest economic power in the European Union (EU). Since the reunification of West and East Germany, however, the country has experienced unemployment of around 10 percent per year. To ease the pain of reunification, the government increased social spending, which accounts for some 48 percent of total government expenditure.[1] Now that unemployment has leveled off at around 11 percent, the government is considering several deregulatory and tax-cutting measures to stimulate the economy. At the same time, the pace of privatization has slowed. Although Germany recently decreased its level of government intervention by renewing efforts to privatize major sections of its economy, a rise in government influence over private banks and an increase in bribery and kickbacks to government officials cause its overall score to be 0.1 point worse this year.

TRADE POLICY

Score: 2–Stable (low level of protectionism)

Germany's average tariff rate is about 2.8 percent. Nontariff barriers include overbearing consumer regulations on the labeling and testing of products. According to the U.S. Department of State, "Germany's regulations and bureaucratic procedures can prove a baffling maze, blunting the enthusiasm of U.S. exporters.... [G]overnment regulations offer a degree of protection to German suppliers."[2] But by global standards Germany's level of protectionism is low.

TAXATION

Score–Income taxation: 5–Stable (very high tax rates)
Score–Corporate taxation: 4–Stable (high tax rates)
Final Taxation Score: 5–Stable (very high tax rates)

Germany's taxes remain among the highest in both the industrialized world and the EU. The top income tax bracket is 53 percent,[3] and the tax on the average income level is over 35 percent. The top corporate tax rate is 45 percent, but corporations also pay a 7.5 percent "surcharge" tax, and municipality taxes on profits can increase the total corporate tax rate to over 70 percent. Germany also has a 45 percent capital gains tax, a 15 percent value-added tax, and land, property, and real estate taxes.

GOVERNMENT INTERVENTION IN THE ECONOMY

Score: 2+ (low level)

Government consumes 19.7 percent of Germany's GDP. After reunification, the government extended its generous social welfare system to the former East Germany. It also expanded subsidies for private investment. These expenditures have increased the government's role in the economy. The government also continues to be involved through local and state government regulations. Attempts to privatize certain sections of the economy stalled in 1995, but progress resumed in 1996. Most of the telecommunications network has been privatized or is being privatized. The government also plans partial privatization of the postal system (although a government monopoly is likely on letters of up

1	Hong Kong	1.25	77	Zambia	3.05
2	Singapore	1.30	80	Mali	3.10
3	Bahrain	1.70	80	Mongolia	3.10
4	New Zealand	1.75	80	Slovenia	3.10
5	Switzerland	1.90	83	Honduras	3.15
5	United States	1.90	83	Papua New Guinea	3.15
7	Luxembourg	1.95	85	Djibouti	3.20
7	Taiwan	1.95	85	Fiji	3.20
7	United Kingdom	1.95	85	Pakistan	3.20
10	Bahamas	2.00	88	Algeria	3.25
10	Ireland	2.00	88	Guinea	3.25
12	Australia	2.05	88	Lebanon	3.25
12	Japan	2.05	88	Mexico	3.25
14	Belgium	2.10	88	Senegal	3.25
14	Canada	2.10	88	Tanzania	3.25
14	United Arab Emirates	2.10	94	Nigeria	3.30
17	Austria	2.15	94	Romania	3.30
17	Chile	2.15	96	Brazil	3.35
17	Estonia	2.15	96	Cambodia	3.35
20	Czech Republic	2.20	96	Egypt	3.35
20	Netherlands	2.20	96	Ivory Coast	3.35
22	Denmark	2.25	96	Madagascar	3.35
22	Finland	2.25	96	Moldova	3.35
24	Germany	2.30	102	Nepal	3.40
24	Iceland	2.30	103	Cape Verde	3.44
24	South Korea	2.30	104	Armenia	3.45
27	Norway	2.35	104	Dominican Republic	3.45
28	Kuwait	2.40	104	Russia	3.45
28	Malaysia	2.40	107	Burkina Faso	3.50
28	Panama	2.40	107	Cameroon	3.50
28	Thailand	2.40	107	Lesotho	3.50
32	El Salvador	2.45	107	Nicaragua	3.50
32	Sri Lanka	2.45	107	Venezuela	3.50
32	Sweden	2.45	112	Gambia	3.60
35	France	2.50	112	Guyana	3.60
35	Italy	2.50	114	Bulgaria	3.65
35	Spain	2.50	114	Georgia	3.65
38	Trinidad and Tobago	2.55	114	Malawi	3.65
39	Argentina	2.60	117	Ethiopia	3.70
39	Barbados	2.60	117	India	3.70
39	Cyprus	2.60	117	Niger	3.70
39	Jamaica	2.60	120	Albania	3.75
39	Portugal	2.60	120	Bangladesh	3.75
44	Bolivia	2.65	120	China (PRC)	3.75
44	Oman	2.65	120	Congo	3.75
44	Philippines	2.65	120	Croatia	3.75
47	Swaziland	2.70	125	Chad	3.80
47	Uruguay	2.70	125	Mauritania	3.80
49	Botswana	2.75	125	Ukraine	3.80
49	Jordan	2.75	128	Sierra Leone	3.85
49	Namibia	2.75	129	Burundi	3.90
49	Tunisia	2.75	129	Suriname	3.90
53	Belize	2.80	129	Zimbabwe	3.90
53	Costa Rica	2.80	132	Haiti	4.00
53	Guatemala	2.80	132	Kyrgyzstan	4.00
53	Israel	2.80	132	Syria	4.00
53	Peru	2.80	135	Belarus	4.05
53	Saudi Arabia	2.80	136	Kazakstan	4.10
53	Turkey	2.80	136	Mozambique	4.10
53	Uganda	2.80	136	Yemen	4.10
53	Western Samoa	2.80	139	Sudan	4.20
62	Indonesia	2.85	140	Myanmar	4.30
62	Latvia	2.85	140	Rwanda	4.30
62	Malta	2.85	142	Angola	4.35
62	Paraguay	2.85	143	Azerbaijan	4.40
66	Greece	2.90	143	Tajikistan	4.40
66	Hungary	2.90	145	Turkmenistan	4.50
66	South Africa	2.90	146	Uzbekistan	4.55
69	Benin	2.95	147	Congo/Zaire	4.70
69	Ecuador	2.95	147	Iran	4.70
69	Gabon	2.95	147	Libya	4.70
69	Morocco	2.95	147	Somalia	4.70
69	Poland	2.95	147	Vietnam	4.70
74	Colombia	3.00	152	Bosnia	4.80
74	Ghana	3.00	153	Iraq	4.90
74	Lithuania	3.00	154	Cuba	5.00
77	Kenya	3.05	154	Laos	5.00
77	Slovak Republic	3.05	154	North Korea	5.00

Mostly Free

to 100 grams). Thus, Germany's government intervention score is one point better this year, even though the government still owns significant portions of the transportation industry, mainly air and rail transport.

MONETARY POLICY
Score: 1–Stable (very low level of inflation)

Germany's rate of inflation has been among the world's lowest: an average of 2.8 percent annually from 1985 to 1995, and 1.5 percent in 1996.

CAPITAL FLOWS AND FOREIGN INVESTMENT
Score: 2–Stable (low barriers)

Germany welcomes foreign investment and is one of the few countries to impose no permanent currency or administrative controls on foreign investments. Some government regulations, such as those regulating monopolies and competition, can present barriers to investment, however.

BANKING
Score: 3– (moderate level of restrictions)

Germany is a world financial center and banking powerhouse, but there are signs that government-owned banks are using their leverage and access to government funds to crowd out competition from private banks. A group of major privately owned banks recently objected to an injection of government funds into several publicly owned banks. The private banks, arguing that this move unfairly restricts competition, brought a complaint to the European Commission in Brussels. As a result of the government's support of the publicly owned banks, Germany's banking score is one point worse this year.

WAGE AND PRICE CONTROLS
Score: 2–Stable (low level)

Germany's free enterprise system is based on market-set prices and wages. Even though the market by and large determines wages, the government still maintains a Federal Cartel Office to monitor prices of specific goods and services. With the exception of rents and some agricultural goods, there are virtually no price controls in Germany.

PROPERTY RIGHTS
Score: 1–Stable (very high level of protection)

Germany's economy, based on the private ownership of property, is undergoing extensive privatization, especially in the former East Germany. The government is pursuing privatization of state-owned property, and the chances of expropriation are virtually nonexistent. The court system provides a very high level of property protection; it is efficient and available for all types of dispute resolution.

REGULATION
Score: 4– (high level)

Establishing a business in Germany is relatively easy, and there are few or no barriers: New businesses must notify the local economic supervisory office, which supplies them with a certificate. Laws on employment, product safety, and the environment, however, impose some burdens. The government also mandates certain social benefits, such as occupational safety and health insurance. The U.S. Department of State reports that Germany has a "regulatory system which discourages new entrants especially in the services sector."[4] According to an article in *The Wall Street Journal*, bribes and kickbacks to government bureaucrats are on the rise. Some estimates put the total cost of these bribes and kickbacks at about $30 billion a year, and these costs are added mainly to contracts for construction and manufacturing.[5] As a result, Germany's regulation score is one point worse this year.

BLACK MARKET
Score: 1–Stable (very low level of activity)

Black markets in Germany involve such illegal activities as drugs and guns. Prostitution is legal, as are some forms of gambling. Germany's protection of intellectual property is among the best in the world, leaving only a negligible black market in pirated materials.

NOTES

1. See Lawrence T. Di Rita and Bryan T. Johnson, "An Agenda for Leadership: The G–7 Summit in Naples," Heritage Foundation *Talking Points*, July 5, 1994.
2. U.S. Department of State, *Country Reports on Economic Policy and Trade Practices*, 1997, p. 124.
3. Some economists argue that Germany's actual tax rates are much higher. Some middle-income Germans have reported paying well above 70 percent of their income. For purposes of the *Index*, however, the official published top income tax rate of 53 percent has been used. For more information, see *Worldwide Executive Tax Guide and Directory*, 1997 edition (New York, N.Y.: Ernst &Young, 1997).
4. U.S. Department of State, *Country Reports on Economic Policy and Trade Practices*, 1997, p. 123.
5. "Germany Says Business Bribes on the Rise," *The Wall Street Journal*, April 14, 1997.

Ghana   3.00

| 1997 Score: **3.20** | 1996 Score: **3.20** | 1995 Score: **3.30** |

Trade	3	Banking	3
Taxation	3	Wages and Prices	2
Government Intervention	3	Property Rights	3
Monetary Policy	4	Regulation	4
Foreign Investment	3	Black Market	2

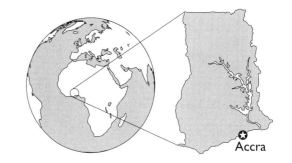

Accra

Ghana gained its independence from Great Britain in 1957, and Prime Minister Kwame Nkrumah quickly transformed it into a one-party socialist state. Flight Lieutenant J. J. Rawlings, who seized power though a military coup in 1981, legalized political parties, won Ghana's presidential election in 1992, and was reelected in December 1996. Although the elections were declared free and transparent by international observers, political tensions are rising because of concerns over the government's allegedly undemocratic practices. An economic liberalization program begun by Rawlings has improved what was a collapsing socialist economy. GDP has grown an average of 4.3 percent from 1992 to 1996, and the government has reduced tariffs and other trade barriers. As a result, Ghana's overall score this year is 0.2 point better than last year. The government also has lost fiscal discipline, however; the money supply has ballooned to pay for government wage increases and subsidies to inefficient state enterprises.

TRADE POLICY

Score: 3+ (moderate level of protectionism)

Ghana's average tariff rate is 11.66 percent.[1] The government has eliminated import licenses and quotas, and significant nontariff barriers no longer exist. Thus, Ghana's trade score is one point better this year than it was last year.

TAXATION

Score–Income taxation: 2–Stable (low tax rates)

Score–Corporate taxation: 3–Stable (moderate tax rates)

Final Taxation Score: 3–Stable (moderate tax rates)

Ghana has a progressive income tax system with a top bracket of 35 percent; the average taxpayer falls within the 5 percent bracket. The government taxes corporate profits at a top rate of 35 percent. Ghana also has a 5 percent capital gains tax and a gift tax that ranges from 0 percent to 15 percent.

GOVERNMENT INTERVENTION IN THE ECONOMY

Score: 3–Stable (moderate level)

Government consumes 11.7 percent of Ghana's GDP, and state-owned enterprises dominate many sectors, including the petroleum, steel, diamond, timber marketing, retail, and construction industries. Ghana's public sector continues to be one of the largest in sub-Saharan Africa. Organized labor generally opposes the government's privatization program, which has stalled.

MONETARY POLICY

Score: 4–Stable (high level of inflation)

Ghana's average rate of inflation from 1985 to 1995 was 28.4 percent. In 1996, inflation was 30 percent.

1	Hong Kong	1.25	77	Zambia	3.05
2	Singapore	1.30	80	Mali	3.10
3	Bahrain	1.70	80	Mongolia	3.10
4	New Zealand	1.75	80	Slovenia	3.10
5	Switzerland	1.90	83	Honduras	3.15
5	United States	1.90	83	Papua New Guinea	3.15
7	Luxembourg	1.95	85	Djibouti	3.20
7	Taiwan	1.95	85	Fiji	3.20
7	United Kingdom	1.95	85	Pakistan	3.20
10	Bahamas	2.00	88	Algeria	3.25
10	Ireland	2.00	88	Guinea	3.25
12	Australia	2.05	88	Lebanon	3.25
12	Japan	2.05	88	Mexico	3.25
14	Belgium	2.10	88	Senegal	3.25
14	Canada	2.10	88	Tanzania	3.25
14	United Arab Emirates	2.10	94	Nigeria	3.30
17	Austria	2.15	94	Romania	3.30
17	Chile	2.15	96	Brazil	3.35
17	Estonia	2.15	96	Cambodia	3.35
20	Czech Republic	2.20	96	Egypt	3.35
20	Netherlands	2.20	96	Ivory Coast	3.35
22	Denmark	2.25	96	Madagascar	3.35
22	Finland	2.25	96	Moldova	3.35
24	Germany	2.30	102	Nepal	3.40
24	Iceland	2.30	103	Cape Verde	3.44
24	South Korea	2.30	104	Armenia	3.45
27	Norway	2.35	104	Dominican Republic	3.45
28	Kuwait	2.40	104	Russia	3.45
28	Malaysia	2.40	107	Burkina Faso	3.50
28	Panama	2.40	107	Cameroon	3.50
28	Thailand	2.40	107	Lesotho	3.50
32	El Salvador	2.45	107	Nicaragua	3.50
32	Sri Lanka	2.45	107	Venezuela	3.50
32	Sweden	2.45	112	Gambia	3.60
35	France	2.50	112	Guyana	3.60
35	Italy	2.50	114	Bulgaria	3.65
35	Spain	2.50	114	Georgia	3.65
38	Trinidad and Tobago	2.55	114	Malawi	3.65
39	Argentina	2.60	117	Ethiopia	3.70
39	Barbados	2.60	117	India	3.70
39	Cyprus	2.60	117	Niger	3.70
39	Jamaica	2.60	120	Albania	3.75
39	Portugal	2.60	120	Bangladesh	3.75
44	Bolivia	2.65	120	China (PRC)	3.75
44	Oman	2.65	120	Congo	3.75
44	Philippines	2.65	120	Croatia	3.75
47	Swaziland	2.70	125	Chad	3.80
47	Uruguay	2.70	125	Mauritania	3.80
49	Botswana	2.75	125	Ukraine	3.80
49	Jordan	2.75	128	Sierra Leone	3.85
49	Namibia	2.75	129	Burundi	3.90
49	Tunisia	2.75	129	Suriname	3.90
53	Belize	2.80	129	Zimbabwe	3.90
53	Costa Rica	2.80	132	Haiti	4.00
53	Guatemala	2.80	132	Kyrgyzstan	4.00
53	Israel	2.80	132	Syria	4.00
53	Peru	2.80	135	Belarus	4.05
53	Saudi Arabia	2.80	136	Kazakhstan	4.10
53	Turkey	2.80	136	Mozambique	4.10
53	Uganda	2.80	136	Yemen	4.10
53	Western Samoa	2.80	139	Sudan	4.20
62	Indonesia	2.85	140	Myanmar	4.30
62	Latvia	2.85	140	Rwanda	4.30
62	Malta	2.85	142	Angola	4.35
62	Paraguay	2.85	143	Azerbaijan	4.40
66	Greece	2.90	143	Tajikistan	4.40
66	Hungary	2.90	145	Turkmenistan	4.50
66	South Africa	2.90	146	Uzbekistan	4.55
69	Benin	2.95	147	Congo/Zaire	4.70
69	Ecuador	2.95	147	Iran	4.70
69	Gabon	2.95	147	Libya	4.70
69	Morocco	2.95	147	Somalia	4.70
69	Poland	2.95	147	Vietnam	4.70
74	Colombia	3.00	152	Bosnia	4.80
74	Ghana	3.00	153	Iraq	4.90
74	Lithuania	3.00	154	Cuba	5.00
77	Kenya	3.05	154	Laos	5.00
77	Slovak Republic	3.05	154	North Korea	5.00

Mostly Unfree

CAPITAL FLOWS AND FOREIGN INVESTMENT
Score: 3–Stable (moderate barriers)

In 1992, the government developed a new investment code that eased restrictions on private-sector investment in Ghana, but restrictions on foreign investment remain in place. Some economic activities are closed to foreign investors or subject to a high minimum investment, and wholly owned foreign firms must meet a $200,000 investment minimum. Foreign investors may not engage in petty trading, taxi services, lotteries, and certain services like beauty salons and barber shops. An inefficient and corrupt bureaucracy creates considerable barriers to potential foreign investment. According to the Office of the United States Trade Representative, "The residual effects of a drastically overregulated economy and lack of transparency in government operations create an element of risk for potential investors. Bureaucratic inertia is sometimes a problem in government ministries, and administrative approvals often take longer than they should. Entrenched local interests sometimes have the ability to derail or delay new entrants, and securing government approvals may depend on an applicant's contacts."[2]

BANKING
Score: 3–Stable (moderate level of restrictions)

Five private commercial and investment banks are chartered in Ghana, and there is considerable competition among them. The Central Bank has abolished interest rate controls, but the bank otherwise maintains tight control over financial activities. There is a government monopoly on personal insurance. Several state-owned banks are being divested from government control. The Central Bank is influenced heavily by the government, however, and public-sector borrowing crowds out that by the private sector.

WAGE AND PRICE CONTROLS
Score: 2–Stable (low level)

Although employers and workers generally are encouraged to negotiate wages and working conditions, Ghana has a minimum wage. The government maintains some food subsidies.

PROPERTY RIGHTS
Score: 3–Stable (moderate level of protection)

Ghana's investment code guarantees private property against expropriation, so seizure remains unlikely. Domestically owned property is less secure than foreign-owned property; during the past several years, there have been cases of arbitrary seizure of domestic commercial property. There is no central land registry. According to the U.S. Department of State, "Inadequate resources and a system vulnerable to political influence compromised the integrity of the overburdened judicial system."[3] By global standards, however, Ghana's protection of private property is moderate.

REGULATION
Score: 4–Stable (high level)

Private-sector investors face a burdensome licensing process, and regulations require foreign firms to hire local employees. Additional problems include the need to gain bureaucratic approval for acquiring and selling land. Bureaucratic inertia and politically inspired administrative judgments reduce competition among domestic firms.

BLACK MARKET
Score: 2–Stable (low level of activity)

The dismantling of price controls has reduced the number of Ghana's once-legion "economic criminals" and removed a large incentive to engage in black market activity. There is little piracy of intellectual property.[4]

NOTES

1. Based on total taxes on international trade as a percentage of total imports.
2. Office of the United State Trade Representative, *1997 National Trade Estimate Report on Foreign Trade Barriers.*
3. U.S. Department of State, "Ghana Country Report on Human Rights Practices for 1996," 1997.
4. U.S. Department of State, *Country Reports on Economic Policy and Trade Practices,* 1997, pp. 1–5.

Greece   2.90

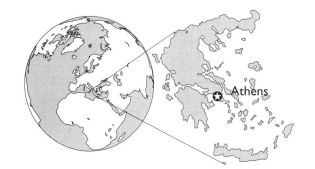

| 1997 Score: **2.85** | 1996 Score: **2.80** | 1995 Score: **2.80** |

Trade	2	Banking	4
Taxation	4	Wages and Prices	3
Government Intervention	3	Property Rights	2
Monetary Policy	3	Regulation	3
Foreign Investment	2	Black Market	3

Greece won its independence from the Ottoman Empire in 1829 and established a monarchy in 1833. From 1941 until 1944, during World War II, it was occupied by Nazi Germany. In 1946, a Soviet-backed communist attempt to take over the country led to a bloody civil war. Greece emerged from this ordeal as a pro-Western democracy and joined the North Atlantic Treaty Organization in 1952. It also has been involved in a bitter standoff with Turkey over the island of Cyprus. Since joining the European Union (EU) in 1981, Greece has worked to bring its economy in line with those of other European democracies. In September 1996, the voters reelected a Parliament with a Panhellenic Socialist Party majority, led by Prime Minister Constatinos Simitis. Because taxes on income recently have increased, Greece's overall score is 0.05 point worse this year.

TRADE POLICY
Score: 2–Stable (low level of protectionism)

Greece has an average tariff rate of 3.6 percent. As a member of the EU, it must conform to that organization's trade standards and practices. In addition to common EU trade restrictions, it maintains nationality requirements on a variety of services, such as those provided by lawyers, architects, and accountants. These restrictions have a severe effect on imported services.

TAXATION
Score–Income taxation: 3– (moderate tax rates)
Score–Corporate taxation: 4–Stable (high tax rates)
Final Taxation Score: 4– (high tax rates)

Greece's top income tax rate is 45 percent, and the rate for the average income level has increased to 15 percent. As a result, its tax score is one-half point worse this year. The top corporate income tax is 40 percent. Greece also has a 35 percent capital gains tax and an 18 percent value-added tax.

GOVERNMENT INTERVENTION IN THE ECONOMY
Score: 3–Stable (moderate level)

Government consumes 14.6 percent of Greece's GDP, but that rate is falling. State-owned industries still make up a significant portion of the economy, however—about 40 percent of GDP.

MONETARY POLICY
Score: 3–Stable (moderate level of inflation)

From 1985 to 1995, Greece's average annual rate of inflation was 15.1 percent. In 1996, the rate of inflation decreased to 8.5 percent.

1	Hong Kong	1.25		77	Zambia	3.05
2	Singapore	1.30		80	Mali	3.10
3	Bahrain	1.70		80	Mongolia	3.10
4	New Zealand	1.75		80	Slovenia	3.10
5	Switzerland	1.90		83	Honduras	3.15
5	United States	1.90		83	Papua New Guinea	3.15
7	Luxembourg	1.95		85	Djibouti	3.20
7	Taiwan	1.95		85	Fiji	3.20
7	United Kingdom	1.95		85	Pakistan	3.20
10	Bahamas	2.00		88	Algeria	3.25
10	Ireland	2.00		88	Guinea	3.25
12	Australia	2.05		88	Lebanon	3.25
12	Japan	2.05		88	Mexico	3.25
14	Belgium	2.10		88	Senegal	3.25
14	Canada	2.10		88	Tanzania	3.25
14	United Arab Emirates	2.10		94	Nigeria	3.30
17	Austria	2.15		94	Romania	3.30
17	Chile	2.15		96	Brazil	3.35
17	Estonia	2.15		96	Cambodia	3.35
20	Czech Republic	2.20		96	Egypt	3.35
20	Netherlands	2.20		96	Ivory Coast	3.35
22	Denmark	2.25		96	Madagascar	3.35
22	Finland	2.25		96	Moldova	3.35
24	Germany	2.30		102	Nepal	3.40
24	Iceland	2.30		103	Cape Verde	3.44
24	South Korea	2.30		104	Armenia	3.45
27	Norway	2.35		104	Dominican Republic	3.45
28	Kuwait	2.40		104	Russia	3.45
28	Malaysia	2.40		107	Burkina Faso	3.50
28	Panama	2.40		107	Cameroon	3.50
28	Thailand	2.40		107	Lesotho	3.50
32	El Salvador	2.45		107	Nicaragua	3.50
32	Sri Lanka	2.45		107	Venezuela	3.50
32	Sweden	2.45		112	Gambia	3.60
35	France	2.50		112	Guyana	3.60
35	Italy	2.50		114	Bulgaria	3.65
35	Spain	2.50		114	Georgia	3.65
38	Trinidad and Tobago	2.55		114	Malawi	3.65
39	Argentina	2.60		117	Ethiopia	3.70
39	Barbados	2.60		117	India	3.70
39	Cyprus	2.60		117	Niger	3.70
39	Jamaica	2.60		120	Albania	3.75
39	Portugal	2.60		120	Bangladesh	3.75
44	Bolivia	2.65		120	China (PRC)	3.75
44	Oman	2.65		120	Congo	3.75
44	Philippines	2.65		120	Croatia	3.75
47	Swaziland	2.70		125	Chad	3.80
47	Uruguay	2.70		125	Mauritania	3.80
49	Botswana	2.75		125	Ukraine	3.80
49	Jordan	2.75		128	Sierra Leone	3.85
49	Namibia	2.75		129	Burundi	3.90
49	Tunisia	2.75		129	Suriname	3.90
53	Belize	2.80		129	Zimbabwe	3.90
53	Costa Rica	2.80		132	Haiti	4.00
53	Guatemala	2.80		132	Kyrgyzstan	4.00
53	Israel	2.80		132	Syria	4.00
53	Peru	2.80		135	Belarus	4.05
53	Saudi Arabia	2.80		136	Kazakstan	4.10
53	Turkey	2.80		136	Mozambique	4.10
53	Uganda	2.80		136	Yemen	4.10
53	Western Samoa	2.80		139	Sudan	4.20
62	Indonesia	2.85		140	Myanmar	4.30
62	Latvia	2.85		140	Rwanda	4.30
62	Malta	2.85		142	Angola	4.35
62	Paraguay	2.85		143	Azerbaijan	4.40
66	Greece	2.90		143	Tajikistan	4.40
66	Hungary	2.90		145	Turkmenistan	4.50
66	South Africa	2.90		146	Uzbekistan	4.55
69	Benin	2.95		147	Congo/Zaire	4.70
69	Ecuador	2.95		147	Iran	4.70
69	Gabon	2.95		147	Libya	4.70
69	Morocco	2.95		147	Somalia	4.70
69	Poland	2.95		147	Vietnam	4.70
74	Colombia	3.00		152	Bosnia	4.80
74	Ghana	3.00		153	Iraq	4.90
74	Lithuania	3.00		154	Cuba	5.00
77	Kenya	3.05		154	Laos	5.00
77	Slovak Republic	3.05		154	North Korea	5.00

Mostly Free

CAPITAL FLOWS AND FOREIGN INVESTMENT
Score: 2–Stable (low barriers)

Greece has an open foreign investment code that invites many investments. There are some restrictions, however, especially with regard to banks, that require prior government approval and rarely result in 100 percent foreign ownership.

BANKING
Score: 4–Stable (high level of restrictions)

The government still owns a significant number of banks. State-owned banks control 73 percent of all deposits and loans.

WAGE AND PRICE CONTROLS
Score: 3–Stable (moderate level)

The government sets some prices, including those for bread, freight charges, motor vehicle insurance, pharmaceuticals, and telephone service. The government also controls the price of fuel.

PROPERTY RIGHTS
Score: 2–Stable (high level of protection)

Property expropriation is unlikely in Greece. Property receives adequate protection from the courts.

REGULATION
Factor Score: 3–Stable (moderate level)

Greece's government is highly bureaucratic, and many regulations are burdensome. According to the U.S. Department of Commerce, "The [regulatory] process is not transparent due to overlapping laws and confusion in their application. Foreign companies consider the complexity of government regulations and procedures to be the greatest impediment to operating in Greece."[1]

BLACK MARKET
Score: 3–Stable (moderate level of activity)

Greece is a popular place for smuggling, especially that of recorded music and videos. According to the U.S. Department of State, "Despite Greece's legal framework for and voiced commitment to copyright protection, piracy of copyrighted material remains widespread."[2]

NOTES

1.   U.S. Department of Commerce, *Country Commercial Guide,* 1997.
2.   U.S. Department of State, *Country Reports on Economic Policy and Trade Practices,* 1997, p. 129.

Guatemala 2.80

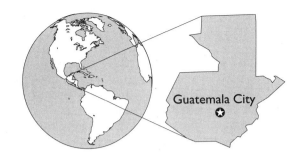

Guatemala City

1997 Score: **2.80**	1996 Score: **2.85**	1995 Score: **3.05**

Trade	3	Banking	2
Taxation	3	Wages and Prices	3
Government Intervention	1	Property Rights	3
Monetary Policy	3	Regulation	4
Foreign Investment	3	Black Market	3

After gaining its independence from Spain in 1821, Guatemala underwent decades of civil unrest and war. In 1985, a democratically elected government began to reduce the state's role in economic life. This process has faltered in the 1990s, leaving the country with a reform-resistant legislature. Despite an uncertain future, the private sector has managed to flourish. The government sector accounts for only 6 percent of GDP. President Alvaro Arzu was elected in January 1996 and, shortly after his inauguration, nominated several business leaders to cabinet-level and other government positions. Arzu's government is pursuing a new economic liberalization program.

TRADE POLICY

Score: 3–Stable (moderate level of protectionism)

Guatemala's average tariff rate is 8 percent.[1] Nontariff barriers include arbitrary application of customs procedures and red tape in the customs agency. There are some restrictions on poultry imports.

TAXATION

Score–Income taxation: 3–Stable (moderate tax rates)
Score–Corporate taxation: 2–Stable (low tax rates)
Final Taxation Score: 3–Stable (moderate tax rates)

Guatemala's top tax rate is 30 percent, up from 25 percent in 1995, and the average income level is taxed at 15 percent. The top corporate income tax is 30 percent. Guatemala also has a 15 percent capital gains tax, a 10 percent value-added tax, and a land tax.

GOVERNMENT INTERVENTION IN THE ECONOMY

Score: 1–Stable (very low level)

Government consumes 5.9 percent of Guatemala's GDP. The only remaining state-owned sectors to be privatized are telecommunications, electricity, and railways.

MONETARY POLICY

Score: 3–Stable (moderate level of inflation)

From 1985 to 1995, Guatemala's average annual rate of inflation was 18.6 percent. In 1996, inflation was 11.1 percent.

CAPITAL FLOWS AND FOREIGN INVESTMENT

Score: 3–Stable (moderate barriers)

Foreign investment in Guatemala is relatively welcome, although restrictions are imposed on investment in utilities and such domestic industries as fishing, mining, and forestry. Investments in banks, auditing, and insurance services also are subject to some restrictions.

1	Hong Kong	1.25	77	Zambia	3.05
2	Singapore	1.30	80	Mali	3.10
3	Bahrain	1.70	80	Mongolia	3.10
4	New Zealand	1.75	80	Slovenia	3.10
5	Switzerland	1.90	83	Honduras	3.15
5	United States	1.90	83	Papua New Guinea	3.15
7	Luxembourg	1.95	85	Djibouti	3.20
7	Taiwan	1.95	85	Fiji	3.20
7	United Kingdom	1.95	85	Pakistan	3.20
10	Bahamas	2.00	88	Algeria	3.25
10	Ireland	2.00	88	Guinea	3.25
12	Australia	2.05	88	Lebanon	3.25
12	Japan	2.05	88	Mexico	3.25
14	Belgium	2.10	88	Senegal	3.25
14	Canada	2.10	88	Tanzania	3.25
14	United Arab Emirates	2.10	94	Nigeria	3.30
17	Austria	2.15	94	Romania	3.30
17	Chile	2.15	96	Brazil	3.35
17	Estonia	2.15	96	Cambodia	3.35
20	Czech Republic	2.20	96	Egypt	3.35
20	Netherlands	2.20	96	Ivory Coast	3.35
22	Denmark	2.25	96	Madagascar	3.35
22	Finland	2.25	96	Moldova	3.35
24	Germany	2.30	102	Nepal	3.40
24	Iceland	2.30	103	Cape Verde	3.44
24	South Korea	2.30	104	Armenia	3.45
27	Norway	2.35	104	Dominican Republic	3.45
28	Kuwait	2.40	104	Russia	3.45
28	Malaysia	2.40	107	Burkina Faso	3.50
28	Panama	2.40	107	Cameroon	3.50
28	Thailand	2.40	107	Lesotho	3.50
32	El Salvador	2.45	107	Nicaragua	3.50
32	Sri Lanka	2.45	107	Venezuela	3.50
32	Sweden	2.45	112	Gambia	3.60
35	France	2.50	112	Guyana	3.60
35	Italy	2.50	114	Bulgaria	3.65
35	Spain	2.50	114	Georgia	3.65
38	Trinidad and Tobago	2.55	114	Malawi	3.65
39	Argentina	2.60	117	Ethiopia	3.70
39	Barbados	2.60	117	India	3.70
39	Cyprus	2.60	117	Niger	3.70
39	Jamaica	2.60	120	Albania	3.75
39	Portugal	2.60	120	Bangladesh	3.75
44	Bolivia	2.65	120	China (PRC)	3.75
44	Oman	2.65	120	Congo	3.75
44	Philippines	2.65	120	Croatia	3.75
47	Swaziland	2.70	125	Chad	3.80
47	Uruguay	2.70	125	Mauritania	3.80
49	Botswana	2.75	125	Ukraine	3.80
49	Jordan	2.75	128	Sierra Leone	3.85
49	Namibia	2.75	129	Burundi	3.90
49	Tunisia	2.75	129	Suriname	3.90
53	Belize	2.80	129	Zimbabwe	3.90
53	Costa Rica	2.80	132	Haiti	4.00
53	Guatemala	2.80	132	Kyrgyzstan	4.00
53	Israel	2.80	132	Syria	4.00
53	Peru	2.80	135	Belarus	4.05
53	Saudi Arabia	2.80	136	Kazakstan	4.10
53	Turkey	2.80	136	Mozambique	4.10
53	Uganda	2.80	136	Yemen	4.10
53	Western Samoa	2.80	139	Sudan	4.20
62	Indonesia	2.85	140	Myanmar	4.30
62	Latvia	2.85	140	Rwanda	4.30
62	Malta	2.85	142	Angola	4.35
62	Paraguay	2.85	143	Azerbaijan	4.40
66	Greece	2.90	143	Tajikistan	4.40
66	Hungary	2.90	145	Turkmenistan	4.50
66	South Africa	2.90	146	Uzbekistan	4.55
69	Benin	2.95	147	Congo/Zaire	4.70
69	Ecuador	2.95	147	Iran	4.70
69	Gabon	2.95	147	Libya	4.70
69	Morocco	2.95	147	Somalia	4.70
69	Poland	2.95	147	Vietnam	4.70
74	Colombia	3.00	152	Bosnia	4.80
74	Ghana	3.00	153	Iraq	4.90
74	Lithuania	3.00	154	Cuba	5.00
77	Kenya	3.05	154	Laos	5.00
77	Slovak Republic	3.05	154	North Korea	5.00

Mostly Free

BANKING
Score: 2–Stable (low level of restrictions)

The government recently liberalized the banking sector to allow for more foreign participation. There are 33 foreign banks in Guatemala, up from 21 in 1993. According to the U.S. Department of Commerce, "Government intervention in the financial sector is limited to implementation of monetary policy and to prudential regulation of the banks, investment firms, bonded warehouses and exchange houses. Credit is not rationed or otherwise directed by the government."[2]

WAGE AND PRICE CONTROLS
Score: 3–Stable (moderate level)

Guatemala has a minimum wage law. The government imposes no official price controls but does use "price bands" for some agricultural goods. A price band defines the price level of a given product; if the price rises above this level, the government may step in to impose a lower price. The effect, therefore, quite often is to control prices.

PROPERTY RIGHTS
Score: 3–Stable (moderate level of protection)

Property is not subject to expropriation in Guatemala, and none has been expropriated since the 1950s. The dispute settlement system often is cumbersome. According to the U.S. Department of Commerce, "On paper, Guatemalan procedures do not differ significantly from those of the United States. In practice, however, Guatemalan procedures are less transparent and more time-consuming."[3]

REGULATION
Score: 4–Stable (high level)

Guatemala's regulations are ambiguous, interpreted by bureaucrats who apply them arbitrarily. "Bureaucratic hurdles are common for both domestic and foreign companies wishing to operate in Guatemala," reports the U.S. Department of Commerce. "Not infrequently, companies are subject to ambiguous requirements, applied inconsistently by different government agencies. Regulations—where they exist—often contain few explicit criteria for the government decision maker, creating uncertainty. Public participation in the promulgation of regulations is rare and there is no consistent judicial review of administrative rule making."[4] Corruption also is present.[5]

BLACK MARKET
Score: 3–Stable (moderate level of activity)

Guatemala provides no effective protection for intellectual property, so there is black market activity in this area. "Guatemalan law does not provide for sufficient protection against counterfeiters nor does it afford adequate protection for internationally famous trademarks," reports the U.S. Department of Commerce. "The right to exclusive use of a trademark, for instance, is granted to whomever happens to file first to register the trademark. There is no requirement for use nor any cancellation process for nonusage. As a result, foreign firms whose trademark has been registered by another party in Guatemala have often had to pay royalties to that party."[6]

NOTES
1. Based on total taxes on international trade as a percentage of total imports.
2. U.S. Department of Commerce, *Country Commercial Guide,* 1997.
3. *Ibid.*
4. *Ibid.*
5. *Ibid.*
6. *Ibid.*

Guinea

3.25

Trade	3	Banking	2
Taxation	4.5	Wages and Prices	2
Government Intervention	3	Property Rights	4
Monetary Policy	3	Regulation	4
Foreign Investment	3	Black Market	4

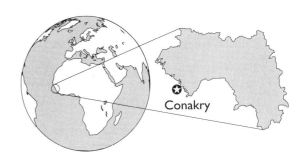

Conakry

Guinea was colonized by France in 1891 and gained its independence in 1958, after which the new government took control of the economy and established a socialist state. Despite abundant natural resources, including bauxite, diamonds, and gold, Guinea's state-controlled economy stagnated. In 1984, General Lansana Conté seized power and initiated an economic liberalization program. Progress, while slow, led to improved GDP growth of 4 percent from 1987 to 1995. A new constitution adopted in 1990 allowed for limited political and economic reforms. Opposition parties were legalized in 1992, and a widely questioned presidential vote was held in 1993, electing the former dictator, Conté. In an attempt to speed up the reform process, President Conté recently invited Sidya Toure from the Ivory Coast to be prime minister and implement economic reforms. Foreign aid donors have been disappointed with the slow progress of economic reform but continue to provide considerable aid. The government has reduced barriers to trade and restricted black market activities. Government spending, however, has increased and has raised Guinea's overall consumption of GDP. Guinea's overall score still is 0.2 point better this year.

TRADE POLICY
Score: 3+ (moderate level of protectionism)

Guinea's average tariff rate is about 8 percent.[1] Licenses are required for "restricted goods" like cement, rice, wheat flour, and other agricultural products. Some imports require special authorization from the Central Bank.

TAXATION
Score–Income taxation: 5–Stable (very high tax rates)
Score–Corporate taxation: 3–Stable (moderate tax rates)
Final Taxation Score: 4.5–Stable (very high tax rates)

Guinea's top income tax rate is 40 percent; the average income level is taxed at 25 percent. The top corporate tax rate is 35 percent. Guinea also has a 35 percent capital gains tax and an 18 percent value-added tax.

GOVERNMENT INTERVENTION IN THE ECONOMY
Score: 3– (moderate level)

Government consumes 11.1 percent of Guinea's GDP, up from 9 percent in 1995; its government intervention score is one point worse this year as a result. In an attempt to downsize a swollen government, Guinea plans to privatize schools and return doctors to the private sector by ending the state-supplied health care system. The pace of privatization has been slow, and Guinea still has a large state-owned sector.

MONETARY POLICY
Score: 3–Stable (moderate level of inflation)

From 1985 to 1995, Guinea's average annual rate of inflation was 16.8 percent. In 1996, the inflation rate fell to about 6 percent.

1	Hong Kong	1.25	77	Zambia	3.05
2	Singapore	1.30	80	Mali	3.10
3	Bahrain	1.70	80	Mongolia	3.10
4	New Zealand	1.75	80	Slovenia	3.10
5	Switzerland	1.90	83	Honduras	3.15
5	United States	1.90	83	Papua New Guinea	3.15
7	Luxembourg	1.95	85	Djibouti	3.20
7	Taiwan	1.95	85	Fiji	3.20
7	United Kingdom	1.95	85	Pakistan	3.20
10	Bahamas	2.00	88	Algeria	3.25
10	Ireland	2.00	88	Guinea	3.25
12	Australia	2.05	88	Lebanon	3.25
12	Japan	2.05	88	Mexico	3.25
14	Belgium	2.10	88	Senegal	3.25
14	Canada	2.10	88	Tanzania	3.25
14	United Arab Emirates	2.10	94	Nigeria	3.30
17	Austria	2.15	94	Romania	3.30
17	Chile	2.15	96	Brazil	3.35
17	Estonia	2.15	96	Cambodia	3.35
20	Czech Republic	2.20	96	Egypt	3.35
20	Netherlands	2.20	96	Ivory Coast	3.35
22	Denmark	2.25	96	Madagascar	3.35
22	Finland	2.25	96	Moldova	3.35
24	Germany	2.30	102	Nepal	3.40
24	Iceland	2.30	103	Cape Verde	3.44
24	South Korea	2.30	104	Armenia	3.45
27	Norway	2.35	104	Dominican Republic	3.45
28	Kuwait	2.40	104	Russia	3.45
28	Malaysia	2.40	107	Burkina Faso	3.50
28	Panama	2.40	107	Cameroon	3.50
28	Thailand	2.40	107	Lesotho	3.50
32	El Salvador	2.45	107	Nicaragua	3.50
32	Sri Lanka	2.45	107	Venezuela	3.50
32	Sweden	2.45	112	Gambia	3.60
35	France	2.50	112	Guyana	3.60
35	Italy	2.50	114	Bulgaria	3.65
35	Spain	2.50	114	Georgia	3.65
38	Trinidad and Tobago	2.55	114	Malawi	3.65
39	Argentina	2.60	117	Ethiopia	3.70
39	Barbados	2.60	117	India	3.70
39	Cyprus	2.60	117	Niger	3.70
39	Jamaica	2.60	120	Albania	3.75
39	Portugal	2.60	120	Bangladesh	3.75
44	Bolivia	2.65	120	China (PRC)	3.75
44	Oman	2.65	120	Congo	3.75
44	Philippines	2.65	120	Croatia	3.75
47	Swaziland	2.70	125	Chad	3.80
47	Uruguay	2.70	125	Mauritania	3.80
49	Botswana	2.75	125	Ukraine	3.80
49	Jordan	2.75	128	Sierra Leone	3.85
49	Namibia	2.75	129	Burundi	3.90
49	Tunisia	2.75	129	Suriname	3.90
53	Belize	2.80	129	Zimbabwe	3.90
53	Costa Rica	2.80	132	Haiti	4.00
53	Guatemala	2.80	132	Kyrgyzstan	4.00
53	Israel	2.80	132	Syria	4.00
53	Peru	2.80	135	Belarus	4.05
53	Saudi Arabia	2.80	136	Kazakstan	4.10
53	Turkey	2.80	136	Mozambique	4.10
53	Uganda	2.80	136	Yemen	4.10
53	Western Samoa	2.80	139	Sudan	4.20
62	Indonesia	2.85	140	Myanmar	4.30
62	Latvia	2.85	140	Rwanda	4.30
62	Malta	2.85	142	Angola	4.35
62	Paraguay	2.85	143	Azerbaijan	4.40
66	Greece	2.90	143	Tajikistan	4.40
66	Hungary	2.90	145	Turkmenistan	4.50
66	South Africa	2.90	146	Uzbekistan	4.55
69	Benin	2.95	147	Congo/Zaire	4.70
69	Ecuador	2.95	147	Iran	4.70
69	Gabon	2.95	147	Libya	4.70
69	Morocco	2.95	147	Somalia	4.70
69	Poland	2.95	147	Vietnam	4.70
74	Colombia	3.00	152	Bosnia	4.80
74	Ghana	3.00	153	Iraq	4.90
74	Lithuania	3.00	154	Cuba	5.00
77	Kenya	3.05	154	Laos	5.00
77	Slovak Republic	3.05	154	North Korea	5.00

Mostly Unfree

CAPITAL FLOWS AND FOREIGN INVESTMENT
Score: 3–Stable (moderate barriers)

Guinea has been opening its economy to foreign investment since 1990 and has adopted an investment code based on a system used by Ivory Coast that allows investment in many industrial sectors. In 1992, the government began to allow 100 percent private participation in the mining sector, and the telecommunications sector was opened partially to private participation. New investment is screened carefully, and there are some restrictions on repatriation of capital.

BANKING
Score: 2–Stable (low level of restrictions)

There are few restrictions on banks in Guinea. Most are in private hands as a result of a massive privatization of the banking industry in the late 1980s and early 1990s. Foreign banks are welcome, and six commercial banks currently are operating. The government is considering legislation to tighten lending regulations, raise reserve requirements, and tighten borrower qualifications.

WAGE AND PRICE CONTROLS
Score: 2–Stable (low level)

Price controls have been removed on most items but remain on fuel, taxis, and bus fares. The Ministry of Trade reserves the right to introduce emergency price control measures. There is no minimum wage.

PROPERTY RIGHTS
Score: 4–Stable (low level of protection)

Property is not completely secure in Guinea. Government corruption, an inefficient judiciary, and poor law enforcement all prevent full legal protection. Crime continues to be a threat. The land tenure system established in 1992 has not been administered successfully, and the government has "reclaimed" properties that Guineans had acquired previously through privatization. According to the U.S. Department of State, "The judiciary is subject to executive branch influence, particularly in politically sensitive cases."[2]

REGULATION
Score: 4–Stable (high level)

Although the government has taken steps to end its interference in private business, a huge bureaucracy remains an impediment to free enterprise. Registering a business is relatively easy, but corruption exists, and the most straightforward business transaction can be problematic. An employer's right to hire and fire is severely constrained, and regulations can be manipulated to advance the personal interests of the regulators. Hiring expatriate workers is not as difficult as it is in many other African countries, however.

BLACK MARKET
Score: 4+ (high level of activity)

Guinea has a large black market, especially in luxury goods (which otherwise would face a 40 percent tariff rate). The U.S. Department of Commerce reports, however, that the country is a member of the Universal Copyright Organization, and pirating of materials does not seem to be a problem. Thus, Guinea's score in this category is one point better than it was last year.

NOTES

1. The score in this factor has changed from 5 in 1997 to 3 in 1998. Previously unavailable data provide a more accurate understanding of the country's performance. The average tariff rate is from World Bank, "Open Economies Work Better," *Policy Research Working Paper* No. 1636, 1996. The methodology for this factor remains the same.
2. U.S. Department of State, "Guinea Country Report on Human Rights Practices for 1996," 1997.

Guyana   3.60

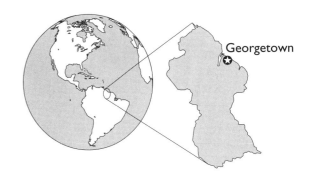

Georgetown

| 1997 Score: **3.50** | 1996 Score: **3.35** | 1995 Score: **n/a** |

Trade	5	Banking	3
Taxation	4	Wages and Prices	2
Government Intervention	3	Property Rights	3
Monetary Policy	5	Regulation	4
Foreign Investment	3	Black Market	4

Since winning its independence from the United Kingdom in 1966, Guyana has followed a mainly socialist economic course and today is among the world's poorest countries. The government is controlled by the People's Progressive Party. Past economic policies seriously impeded economic growth, but since 1992 the government has made sweeping reforms aimed at attracting foreign investment by relying on the free market. Recently, Guyana reduced its government consumption of GDP by limiting the size of its public sector, reforming its banking industry, and cutting back on some black market activities. The privatization program has slowed, however, and the government has failed to sell off significant sectors of the economy. As a result of slightly higher tariff rates, Guyana's overall score this year is 0.1 point worse than it was last year.

TRADE POLICY

Score: 5– (very high level of protectionism)

Despite an easing of formal barriers to trade, Guyana's tariffs still range from 0 percent to 40 percent. The average tariff is about 17 percent.[1] Government paperwork, corruption, and informal obstacles remain substantial barriers to trade. Import licenses are required for fruit, meat, and poultry.

TAXATION

Score–Income taxation: 3–Stable (moderate tax rates)
Score–Corporate taxation: 4–Stable (high tax rates)
Final Taxation Score: 4–Stable (high tax rates)

Guyana's tax on income is a flat 33.3 percent, and its top corporate tax rate is 45 percent.[2] Guyana also has a 20 percent capital gains tax and a property tax.

GOVERNMENT INTERVENTION IN THE ECONOMY

Score: 3–Stable (moderate level)

The central government consumes about 12.8 percent of Guyana's GDP. Its privatization program has not met investors' expectations. The government remains heavily involved in banking, such utilities as electrical and energy generation, transportation, and some agriculture sectors.

MONETARY POLICY

Score: 5–Stable (very high level of inflation)

Guyana's average annual rate of inflation from 1985 to 1995 was 51.1 percent. In 1996, the inflation rate was 4.5 percent.

CAPITAL FLOWS AND FOREIGN INVESTMENT

Score: 3–Stable (moderate barriers)

There are few restrictions on foreign investment in Guyana, although investors are concerned about civil unrest, crime, and corruption. According to the U.S. Department of Commerce, "After years of a state-dominated economy, the

1	Hong Kong	1.25	77	Zambia	3.05
2	Singapore	1.30	80	Mali	3.10
3	Bahrain	1.70	80	Mongolia	3.10
4	New Zealand	1.75	80	Slovenia	3.10
5	Switzerland	1.90	83	Honduras	3.15
5	United States	1.90	83	Papua New Guinea	3.15
7	Luxembourg	1.95	85	Djibouti	3.20
7	Taiwan	1.95	85	Fiji	3.20
7	United Kingdom	1.95	85	Pakistan	3.20
10	Bahamas	2.00	88	Algeria	3.25
10	Ireland	2.00	88	Guinea	3.25
12	Australia	2.05	88	Lebanon	3.25
12	Japan	2.05	88	Mexico	3.25
14	Belgium	2.10	88	Senegal	3.25
14	Canada	2.10	88	Tanzania	3.25
14	United Arab Emirates	2.10	94	Nigeria	3.30
17	Austria	2.15	94	Romania	3.30
17	Chile	2.15	96	Brazil	3.35
17	Estonia	2.15	96	Cambodia	3.35
20	Czech Republic	2.20	96	Egypt	3.35
20	Netherlands	2.20	96	Ivory Coast	3.35
22	Denmark	2.25	96	Madagascar	3.35
22	Finland	2.25	96	Moldova	3.35
24	Germany	2.30	102	Nepal	3.40
24	Iceland	2.30	103	Cape Verde	3.44
24	South Korea	2.30	104	Armenia	3.45
27	Norway	2.35	104	Dominican Republic	3.45
28	Kuwait	2.40	104	Russia	3.45
28	Malaysia	2.40	107	Burkina Faso	3.50
28	Panama	2.40	107	Cameroon	3.50
28	Thailand	2.40	107	Lesotho	3.50
32	El Salvador	2.45	107	Nicaragua	3.50
32	Sri Lanka	2.45	107	Venezuela	3.50
32	Sweden	2.45	112	Gambia	3.60
35	France	2.50	112	Guyana	3.60
35	Italy	2.50	114	Bulgaria	3.65
35	Spain	2.50	114	Georgia	3.65
38	Trinidad and Tobago	2.55	114	Malawi	3.65
39	Argentina	2.60	117	Ethiopia	3.70
39	Barbados	2.60	117	India	3.70
39	Cyprus	2.60	117	Niger	3.70
39	Jamaica	2.60	120	Albania	3.75
39	Portugal	2.60	120	Bangladesh	3.75
44	Bolivia	2.65	120	China (PRC)	3.75
44	Oman	2.65	120	Congo	3.75
44	Philippines	2.65	120	Croatia	3.75
47	Swaziland	2.70	125	Chad	3.80
47	Uruguay	2.70	125	Mauritania	3.80
49	Botswana	2.75	125	Ukraine	3.80
49	Jordan	2.75	128	Sierra Leone	3.85
49	Namibia	2.75	129	Burundi	3.90
49	Tunisia	2.75	129	Suriname	3.90
53	Belize	2.80	129	Zimbabwe	3.90
53	Costa Rica	2.80	132	Haiti	4.00
53	Guatemala	2.80	132	Kyrgyzstan	4.00
53	Israel	2.80	132	Syria	4.00
53	Peru	2.80	135	Belarus	4.05
53	Saudi Arabia	2.80	136	Kazakhstan	4.10
53	Turkey	2.80	136	Mozambique	4.10
53	Uganda	2.80	136	Yemen	4.10
53	Western Samoa	2.80	139	Sudan	4.20
62	Indonesia	2.85	140	Myanmar	4.30
62	Latvia	2.85	140	Rwanda	4.30
62	Malta	2.85	142	Angola	4.35
62	Paraguay	2.85	143	Azerbaijan	4.40
66	Greece	2.90	143	Tajikistan	4.40
66	Hungary	2.90	145	Turkmenistan	4.50
66	South Africa	2.90	146	Uzbekistan	4.55
69	Benin	2.95	147	Congo/Zaire	4.70
69	Ecuador	2.95	147	Iran	4.70
69	Gabon	2.95	147	Libya	4.70
69	Morocco	2.95	147	Somalia	4.70
69	Poland	2.95	147	Vietnam	4.70
74	Colombia	3.00	152	Bosnia	4.80
74	Ghana	3.00	153	Iraq	4.90
74	Lithuania	3.00	154	Cuba	5.00
77	Kenya	3.05	154	Laos	5.00
77	Slovak Republic	3.05	154	North Korea	5.00

Mostly Unfree

mechanisms for private investment, domestic or foreign, are still evolving."[3]

BANKING
Score: 3–Stable (moderate level of restrictions)

Guyana's banking system is becoming more competitive. The government still owns portions of some banks, but there are plans to privatize these holdings. According to the U.S. Department of Commerce, "Any foreign borrower applying to borrow [over 2 million in local currency] must be given permission by the Minister of Finance."[4]

WAGE AND PRICE CONTROLS
Score: 2–Stable (low level)

Guyana maintains a minimum wage and price controls on electricity rates.

PROPERTY RIGHTS
Score: 3–Stable (moderate level of protection)

Private property is guaranteed and receives legal protection, but several Western firms are engaged in legal battles with the government over contracts, and the judicial system often is slow and inefficient. According to the U.S. Department of State, "There is a constitutionally independent, albeit somewhat inefficient, judiciary."[5]

REGULATION
Score: 4–Stable (high level)

Some sectors of the economy, such as utilities and other state-owned industries, are highly regulated, and corruption often hinders the ability of companies in these sectors to do business. The U.S. Department of Commerce reports that "Attempts to reform bureaucratic procedures have not succeeded in limiting red tape: for example, businesses find that clearing shipments through customs is a long, tedious, and contentious process."[6]

BLACK MARKET
Score: 4–Stable (very high level of activity)

Guyana has a rather large black market, mainly because of trademark and copyright infringement and the massive pirating of video, audio recordings, and computer software. According to the U.S. Department of Commerce, "[T]here is so far essentially no enforcement of laws regarding intellectual property rights. Patent and trademark infringement are also common. Pirating of TV satellite signals is widespread and takes place with impunity."[7]

NOTES

1. The score in this factor has changed from 4 in 1997 to 5 in 1998. Previously unavailable data provide a more accurate understanding of the country's performance. The average tariff rate is from World Bank, "Open Economies Work Better," *Policy Research Working Paper* No. 1636, 1996. The methodology for this factor remains the same.
2. This rate applies to profits of commercial companies.
3. U.S. Department of Commerce, *Country Commercial Guide,* 1997.
4. *Ibid.*
5. U.S. Department of State, "Guyana Country Report on Human Rights Practices for 1996," 1997.
6. U.S. Department of Commerce, *Country Commercial Guide,* 1997.
7. *Ibid.*

Haiti

4.00

Trade	4	Banking	4
Taxation	3	Wages and Prices	4
Government Intervention	3	Property Rights	5
Monetary Policy	3	Regulation	5
Foreign Investment	4	Black Market	5

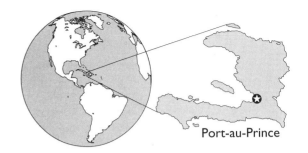

Port-au-Prince

Haiti has little economic freedom, and its current president, Rene Preval, is no advocate of free markets. Former leader Jean-Bertrand Aristide remains the country's most powerful and influential political figure. Following his ouster by military coup in September 1991, Haiti was isolated economically and subjected to a United Nations embargo. In October 1994, Aristide was returned to power after armed intervention by the United States; Preval was elected in 1995, but Haiti's economy has not improved. An inefficient, well-entrenched, and corrupt bureaucracy continues to hinder the development of free and open markets, and political violence could destroy the economy. Haiti remains plagued by outdated regulations, corruption, and an almost total absence of property rights.

TRADE POLICY
Score: 4–Stable (high level of protectionism)

Haiti has slashed tariffs to an average rate of 11.6 percent, but crime, corruption, and poor infrastructure make the Haitian market inaccessible to most imports. According to the U.S. Department of Commerce, "[C]orruption among customs officers does pose a problem in that petty bribes are sometimes necessary to clear shipments expeditiously. Some importers also reportedly negotiate customs duties with inspectors."[1]

TAXATION
Score–Income taxation: 3–Stable (moderate tax rates)
Score–Corporate taxation: 3–Stable (moderate tax rates)
Final Taxation Score: 3–Stable (high tax rates)

Haiti's top income tax rate is 30 percent, but the tax collection system is so poor that it is impossible to determine what rate applies to the average income. Tax evasion is massive, and direct taxes represent only 13 percent of total receipts.[2] The top corporate income tax rate is 35 percent.

GOVERNMENT INTERVENTION IN THE ECONOMY
Score: 3–Stable (moderate level)

Government consumes about 20 percent of Haiti's economic output, and a significant portion of GDP is produced by the state-owned sector. Preval wants to privatize many large state-owned enterprises, but this is being resisted by Aristide and the bureaucracy.

MONETARY POLICY
Score: 3–Stable (moderate level of inflation)

Haiti's average annual rate of inflation from 1985 to 1995 was 14.7 percent. In 1996, the inflation rate was about 17.1 percent.

1	Hong Kong	1.25	77	Zambia	3.05
2	Singapore	1.30	80	Mali	3.10
3	Bahrain	1.70	80	Mongolia	3.10
4	New Zealand	1.75	80	Slovenia	3.10
5	Switzerland	1.90	83	Honduras	3.15
5	United States	1.90	83	Papua New Guinea	3.15
7	Luxembourg	1.95	85	Djibouti	3.20
7	Taiwan	1.95	85	Fiji	3.20
7	United Kingdom	1.95	85	Pakistan	3.20
10	Bahamas	2.00	88	Algeria	3.25
10	Ireland	2.00	88	Guinea	3.25
12	Australia	2.05	88	Lebanon	3.25
12	Japan	2.05	88	Mexico	3.25
14	Belgium	2.10	88	Senegal	3.25
14	Canada	2.10	88	Tanzania	3.25
14	United Arab Emirates	2.10	94	Nigeria	3.30
17	Austria	2.15	94	Romania	3.30
17	Chile	2.15	96	Brazil	3.35
17	Estonia	2.15	96	Cambodia	3.35
20	Czech Republic	2.20	96	Egypt	3.35
20	Netherlands	2.20	96	Ivory Coast	3.35
22	Denmark	2.25	96	Madagascar	3.35
22	Finland	2.25	96	Moldova	3.35
24	Germany	2.30	102	Nepal	3.40
24	Iceland	2.30	103	Cape Verde	3.44
24	South Korea	2.30	104	Armenia	3.45
27	Norway	2.35	104	Dominican Republic	3.45
28	Kuwait	2.40	104	Russia	3.45
28	Malaysia	2.40	107	Burkina Faso	3.50
28	Panama	2.40	107	Cameroon	3.50
28	Thailand	2.40	107	Lesotho	3.50
32	El Salvador	2.45	107	Nicaragua	3.50
32	Sri Lanka	2.45	107	Venezuela	3.50
32	Sweden	2.45	112	Gambia	3.60
35	France	2.50	112	Guyana	3.60
35	Italy	2.50	114	Bulgaria	3.65
35	Spain	2.50	114	Georgia	3.65
38	Trinidad and Tobago	2.55	114	Malawi	3.65
39	Argentina	2.60	117	Ethiopia	3.70
39	Barbados	2.60	117	India	3.70
39	Cyprus	2.60	117	Niger	3.70
39	Jamaica	2.60	120	Albania	3.75
39	Portugal	2.60	120	Bangladesh	3.75
44	Bolivia	2.65	120	China (PRC)	3.75
44	Oman	2.65	120	Congo	3.75
44	Philippines	2.65	120	Croatia	3.75
47	Swaziland	2.70	125	Chad	3.80
47	Uruguay	2.70	125	Mauritania	3.80
49	Botswana	2.75	125	Ukraine	3.80
49	Jordan	2.75	128	Sierra Leone	3.85
49	Namibia	2.75	129	Burundi	3.90
49	Tunisia	2.75	129	Suriname	3.90
53	Belize	2.80	129	Zimbabwe	3.90
53	Costa Rica	2.80	132	Haiti	4.00
53	Guatemala	2.80	132	Kyrgyzstan	4.00
53	Israel	2.80	132	Syria	4.00
53	Peru	2.80	135	Belarus	4.05
53	Saudi Arabia	2.80	136	Kazakstan	4.10
53	Turkey	2.80	136	Mozambique	4.10
53	Uganda	2.80	136	Yemen	4.10
53	Western Samoa	2.80	139	Sudan	4.20
62	Indonesia	2.85	140	Myanmar	4.30
62	Latvia	2.85	140	Rwanda	4.30
62	Malta	2.85	142	Angola	4.35
62	Paraguay	2.85	143	Azerbaijan	4.40
66	Greece	2.90	143	Tajikistan	4.40
66	Hungary	2.90	145	Turkmenistan	4.50
66	South Africa	2.90	146	Uzbekistan	4.55
69	Benin	2.95	147	Congo/Zaire	4.70
69	Ecuador	2.95	147	Iran	4.70
69	Gabon	2.95	147	Libya	4.70
69	Morocco	2.95	147	Somalia	4.70
69	Poland	2.95	147	Vietnam	4.70
74	Colombia	3.00	152	Bosnia	4.80
74	Ghana	3.00	153	Iraq	4.90
74	Lithuania	3.00	154	Cuba	5.00
77	Kenya	3.05	154	Laos	5.00
77	Slovak Republic	3.05	154	North Korea	5.00

Repressed

Capital Flows and Foreign Investment
Score: 4–Stable (high barriers)

Haiti has opened its market to foreign investment, providing equal treatment to domestic and foreign firms. Its investment laws remain outdated, however, and are not always enforced by the corrupt bureaucracy. According to the U.S. Department of Commerce, "The protection and guarantees which Haitian law extends to investors are severely compromised by weak enforcement mechanisms, a poor judicial system and an antiquated legal system."[3]

Banking
Score: 4–Stable (high level of restrictions)

Although Haiti now welcomes foreign banks and recent changes allow them to engage in a variety of financial services, the banking system remains underdeveloped and in disarray. "Under Haitian law," reports the U.S. Department of Commerce, "banks are neither required to comply with internationally recognized accounting standards, nor to be audited by internationally recognized accounting firms.... Access to credit is restricted by the difficulty in assessing client risk and the lack of legal remedies for the lender in the event of default. Lack of a civil register, the absence of proper titles and problems with creating security interests pose additional institutional problems. As a result, banks lend only to their most trusted and credit-worthy clients."[4]

Wage and Price Controls
Score: 4–Stable (high level)

With most of the economy a shambles, Haiti's government has attempted to eliminate its direct control of prices. It still directly controls prices on some items, however, including cement, gasoline, and a variety of staples like food, and indirectly controls prices on others. Under Aristide, the government established "communitarian" shops to provide basic goods. These shops, because they are subsidized by the government, depress prices for legitimate store operators and limit competition. Haiti has a minimum wage.

Property Rights
Score: 5–Stable (very low level of protection)

Private property enjoys little or no protection in Haiti. The judiciary is notoriously corrupt, and even though expropriation is unlikely, property remains subject to crime and thievery. Haiti's police force also is corrupt, and oppression of the country's people is routine. According to the U.S. Department of State, "The judicial system—while theoretically independent—remained weak and corrupt after decades of government interference and corruption."[5]

Regulation
Score: 5–Stable (very high level)

It is virtually impossible to open a business legally under Haitian law. "Haiti's commercial code," reports the U.S. Department of Commerce, "dates from 1826 and underwent its last significant revision in 1944.... Bureaucratic procedures are not uniform and frequently involve excess red tape.... Tax, labor, and health and safety laws and policies are theoretically universally applicable, but are not universally applied or observed.... Haitian law is different in a number of areas, including operation of the judicial system; organization and operation of the executive branch; publication of laws; regulations and official notices; establishment of companies; land tenure and real property law and procedures; bank and credit operations; insurance and pension regulation; accounting standards; civil status documentation; customs law and administration; international trade and investment promotion; foreign investment regime; regulation of market concentration and competition; and privatization."[6] Haiti is among the world's most government-regulated countries.

Black Market
Score: 5–Stable (very high level of activity)

Even before the embargo, price controls and other inefficient government policies had created a large black market. At that time, the black market was around 40 percent of GDP; today, it surpasses GDP. According to the U.S. Department of Commerce, "Smuggling remains a major problem, with the Rice Corporation of Haiti (a subsidiary of American Rice, Inc.) complaining that contraband rice accounts for more than 50 per cent of rice imports."[7]

Notes

1. U.S. Department of Commerce, *Country Commercial Guide*, 1997.
2. For this factor, Haiti was graded only on its top income tax rate.
3. U.S. Department of Commerce, *Country Commercial Guide*, 1997.
4. *Ibid.*
5. U.S. Department of State, "Haiti Country Report on Human Rights Practices for 1996," 1997.
6. U.S. Department of Commerce, *Country Commercial Guide*, 1997.
7. *Ibid.*

Honduras 3.15

Trade	4	Banking	3
Taxation	3.5	Wages and Prices	3
Government Intervention	1	Property Rights	3
Monetary Policy	3	Regulation	4
Foreign Investment	3	Black Market	4

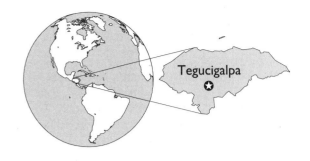

Tegucigalpa

Honduras declared its independence from Spain in 1821 and joined Costa Rica, El Salvador, Guatemala, and Nicaragua to form the Federal Republic of Central America, from which it withdrew in 1838. In the 1950s, the government introduced agrarian reforms, including the returning of many farms to private owners. This became the basis for its market system. The next several decades were characterized by military coups and civil unrest. "Despite abundant natural resources and substantial U.S. and multilateral economic assistance," reports the U.S. Department of State, "Honduras remains one of the poorest countries in the [Western] hemisphere."[1] Honduras recently cut government spending, thereby reducing its government consumption level, but inflation has been on the rise. Thus, its overall score has not changed.

TRADE POLICY
Score: 4–Stable (high level of protectionism)

Tariffs in Honduras range from 5 percent to 20 percent; the average tariff rate is about 11 percent. Nontariff barriers include strict labeling and sanitary requirements. According to the U.S. Department of State, "Honduras' customs administrative procedures are burdensome. There are extensive documentary requirements and red tape involving the payment of numerous import duties, customs surcharges, selective consumption taxes, consular fees and warehouse levies."[2]

TAXATION
Score–Income taxation: 2–Stable (low tax rates)
Score–Corporate taxation: 4–Stable (high tax rates)
Final Taxation Score: 3.5–Stable (high tax rates)

The top income tax rate in Honduras is 40 percent; no taxes are imposed on the average level of income. The top corporate tax rate is 40.25 percent. There also is a 40.25 percent capital gains tax, a 7 percent sales tax, and various local taxes.

GOVERNMENT INTERVENTION IN THE ECONOMY
Score: 1+ (very low level)

Honduras's government has reduced its consumption of GDP to 8.8 percent and has achieved significant privatization of state-owned enterprises and services. As a result, its score for this factor is one point better this year than it was last year. For example, Honduras has allowed several privately owned companies to open energy-generation plants and has removed these utilities from state ownership and control. The government also is privatizing some transportation services and airport services.

MONETARY POLICY
Score: 3– (moderate level of inflation)

From 1985 to 1995, the average annual rate of inflation in Honduras increased to 14.2 percent. In 1996, the inflation rate was 23.8 percent. As a result, the country's monetary policy score is one point worse this year.

1	Hong Kong	1.25	77	Zambia	3.05
2	Singapore	1.30	80	Mali	3.10
3	Bahrain	1.70	80	Mongolia	3.10
4	New Zealand	1.75	80	Slovenia	3.10
5	Switzerland	1.90	83	Honduras	3.15
5	United States	1.90	83	Papua New Guinea	3.15
7	Luxembourg	1.95	85	Djibouti	3.20
7	Taiwan	1.95	85	Fiji	3.20
7	United Kingdom	1.95	85	Pakistan	3.20
10	Bahamas	2.00	88	Algeria	3.25
10	Ireland	2.00	88	Guinea	3.25
12	Australia	2.05	88	Lebanon	3.25
12	Japan	2.05	88	Mexico	3.25
14	Belgium	2.10	88	Senegal	3.25
14	Canada	2.10	88	Tanzania	3.25
14	United Arab Emirates	2.10	94	Nigeria	3.30
17	Austria	2.15	94	Romania	3.30
17	Chile	2.15	96	Brazil	3.35
17	Estonia	2.15	96	Cambodia	3.35
20	Czech Republic	2.20	96	Egypt	3.35
20	Netherlands	2.20	96	Ivory Coast	3.35
22	Denmark	2.25	96	Madagascar	3.35
22	Finland	2.25	96	Moldova	3.35
24	Germany	2.30	102	Nepal	3.40
24	Iceland	2.30	103	Cape Verde	3.44
24	South Korea	2.30	104	Armenia	3.45
27	Norway	2.35	104	Dominican Republic	3.45
28	Kuwait	2.40	104	Russia	3.45
28	Malaysia	2.40	107	Burkina Faso	3.50
28	Panama	2.40	107	Cameroon	3.50
28	Thailand	2.40	107	Lesotho	3.50
32	El Salvador	2.45	107	Nicaragua	3.50
32	Sri Lanka	2.45	107	Venezuela	3.50
32	Sweden	2.45	112	Gambia	3.60
35	France	2.50	112	Guyana	3.60
35	Italy	2.50	114	Bulgaria	3.65
35	Spain	2.50	114	Georgia	3.65
38	Trinidad and Tobago	2.55	114	Malawi	3.65
39	Argentina	2.60	117	Ethiopia	3.70
39	Barbados	2.60	117	India	3.70
39	Cyprus	2.60	117	Niger	3.70
39	Jamaica	2.60	120	Albania	3.75
39	Portugal	2.60	120	Bangladesh	3.75
44	Bolivia	2.65	120	China (PRC)	3.75
44	Oman	2.65	120	Congo	3.75
44	Philippines	2.65	120	Croatia	3.75
47	Swaziland	2.70	125	Chad	3.80
47	Uruguay	2.70	125	Mauritania	3.80
49	Botswana	2.75	125	Ukraine	3.80
49	Jordan	2.75	128	Sierra Leone	3.85
49	Namibia	2.75	129	Burundi	3.90
49	Tunisia	2.75	129	Suriname	3.90
53	Belize	2.80	129	Zimbabwe	3.90
53	Costa Rica	2.80	132	Haiti	4.00
53	Guatemala	2.80	132	Kyrgyzstan	4.00
53	Israel	2.80	132	Syria	4.00
53	Peru	2.80	135	Belarus	4.05
53	Saudi Arabia	2.80	136	Kazakstan	4.10
53	Turkey	2.80	136	Mozambique	4.10
53	Uganda	2.80	136	Yemen	4.10
53	Western Samoa	2.80	139	Sudan	4.20
62	Indonesia	2.85	140	Myanmar	4.30
62	Latvia	2.85	140	Rwanda	4.30
62	Malta	2.85	142	Angola	4.35
62	Paraguay	2.85	143	Azerbaijan	4.40
66	Greece	2.90	143	Tajikistan	4.40
66	Hungary	2.90	145	Turkmenistan	4.50
66	South Africa	2.90	146	Uzbekistan	4.55
69	Benin	2.95	147	Congo/Zaire	4.70
69	Ecuador	2.95	147	Iran	4.70
69	Gabon	2.95	147	Libya	4.70
69	Morocco	2.95	147	Somalia	4.70
69	Poland	2.95	147	Vietnam	4.70
74	Colombia	3.00	152	Bosnia	4.80
74	Ghana	3.00	153	Iraq	4.90
74	Lithuania	3.00	154	Cuba	5.00
77	Kenya	3.05	154	Laos	5.00
77	Slovak Republic	3.05	154	North Korea	5.00

Mostly Unfree

CAPITAL FLOWS AND FOREIGN INVESTMENT
Score: 3–Stable (moderate barriers)

Honduras maintains some restrictions on foreign investment. Special state authorization must be obtained for investments in air transport, forestry, telecommunications, basic health services, fishing and aquaculture, exploration of "subsurface" resources, insurance and financial services, private education services, and agriculture and agro-industrial activities. The government requires that a majority of certain types of businesses be owned by Hondurans.

BANKING
Score: 3–Stable (moderate level of restrictions)

Foreigners must obtain government permission to engage in some types of banking services. Domestic banks are under the control of the government and the Central Bank, and are unduly influenced by Honduran business interests. According to the U.S. Department of Commerce, "Most [Honduran] banks are associated with powerful economic groups, and lend primarily to businesses owned by the group of which they are a part. The system has been criticized for permitting excessive amounts of unsecured lending to major stockholders or bank principals."[3]

WAGE AND PRICE CONTROLS
Score: 3–Stable (moderate level)

After years of eliminating price controls, Honduras imposed controls on the prices of 44 goods in 1993, including certain foodstuffs. The government still controls the prices of coffee, medicines, some housing rents, and petroleum products. Honduras has a minimum wage.

PROPERTY RIGHTS
Score: 3–Stable (moderate level of protection)

Expropriation remains possible in Honduras. The government does not protect property in full, corruption is a continuing problem, and those seeking legal recourse to protect their property frequently face an inefficient and ill-functioning court system. According to the U.S. Department of Commerce, "Honduras' lack of codified laws and the absence of the option for a jury trial result in a murky system of contradictory laws and regulations which sometimes frustrate international investors."[4]

REGULATION
Score: 4–Stable (high level)

Honduras's bureaucracy suffers from corruption and cronyism. According to the Office of the United States Trade Representative, "President Reina's 'moral revolution' has helped thwart corruption, although it remains a serious problem."[5] Regulations are applied unevenly, and often haphazardly.

BLACK MARKET
Score: 4–Stable (high level of activity)

Because Honduras maintains significant barriers to trade, its black market is rather large. Almost 50 percent of the labor force is supplied by the black market. Although Honduras has passed laws protecting intellectual property rights, piracy continues. According to the U.S. Department of State, "The piracy of books, sound and video recordings, compact discs, computer software, and television programs is widespread in Honduras."[6]

NOTES

1. U.S. Department of State, *Country Reports on Economic Policy and Trade Practices,* 1997, p. 265.
2. *Ibid.,* p. 267.
3. U.S. Department of Commerce, *Country Commercial Guide,* 1997.
4. *Ibid.*
5. Office of the United States Trade Representative, *1997 National Trade Estimate Report on Foreign Trade Barriers.*
6. U.S. Department of State, *Country Reports on Economic Policy and Trade Practices,* 1997, p. 268.

Hong Kong   1.25

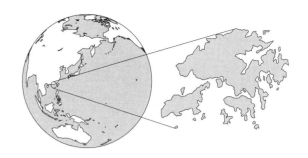

1997 Score: **1.25**   1996 Score: **1.25**   1995 Score: **1.25**

Trade	1	Banking	1
Taxation	1.5	Wages and Prices	2
Government Intervention	1	Property Rights	1
Monetary Policy	2	Regulation	1
Foreign Investment	1	Black Market	1

Hong Kong became a "special administrative region" (SAR) of the People's Republic of China on July 1, 1997. So far, there is little evidence that becoming part of China will alter Hong Kong's economic structure significantly. There continues to be little government interference in the marketplace; taxes remain low and predictable; increases in government spending are linked closely with economic growth; foreign trade still is free; and regulations, in addition to being transparent, continue to be applied both uniformly and consistently. For the fourth year in a row, Hong Kong is ranked first in the *Index of Economic Freedom*. In the waning days of Hong Kong's democratically elected Legislative Council, however, lawmakers passed a host of new social welfare laws and environmental regulations. The new legislature suspended the enactment of these laws until further review. As of this writing, some have been passed and some have not. Even if all should be enacted, however, it is too soon for their possible effects to be measured. They will be monitored closely for consideration in future editions of the *Index*.

TRADE POLICY
Score: 1–Stable (very low level of protectionism)

Hong Kong levies no import tariffs and is a duty-free port.[1] There are, in fact, very few barriers to imports in Hong Kong, which has one of the world's most accessible markets. It is a vital market for U.S. exports, and consumes U.S. manufactured and agricultural goods at a higher rate per capita than most of the world's other economies.

TAXATION
Score–Income taxation: 2–Stable (low tax rates)
Score–Corporate taxation: 1–Stable (very low tax rates)
Final Taxation Score: 1.5–Stable (low tax rates)

The top marginal personal income tax rate in Hong Kong is 20 percent;[2] the tax on the average income level is 2 percent. The corporate tax is a flat 16.5 percent.

GOVERNMENT INTERVENTION IN THE ECONOMY
Score: 1–Stable (very low level)

Even though Hong Kong's government has been criticized for increased spending on social welfare, government spending as a percentage of GDP continues to fall.[3] The government consumes about 5 percent of GDP, down from 8 percent in 1994.[4]

MONETARY POLICY
Score: 2–Stable (low level of inflation)

The Hong Kong dollar has been linked to the U.S. dollar since 1983. The rate of inflation has averaged 8.7 percent since 1985.

1	Hong Kong	1.25	77	Zambia	3.05
2	Singapore	1.30	80	Mali	3.10
3	Bahrain	1.70	80	Mongolia	3.10
4	New Zealand	1.75	80	Slovenia	3.10
5	Switzerland	1.90	83	Honduras	3.15
5	United States	1.90	83	Papua New Guinea	3.15
7	Luxembourg	1.95	85	Djibouti	3.20
7	Taiwan	1.95	85	Fiji	3.20
7	United Kingdom	1.95	85	Pakistan	3.20
10	Bahamas	2.00	88	Algeria	3.25
10	Ireland	2.00	88	Guinea	3.25
12	Australia	2.05	88	Lebanon	3.25
12	Japan	2.05	88	Mexico	3.25
14	Belgium	2.10	88	Senegal	3.25
14	Canada	2.10	88	Tanzania	3.25
14	United Arab Emirates	2.10	94	Nigeria	3.30
17	Austria	2.15	94	Romania	3.30
17	Chile	2.15	96	Brazil	3.35
17	Estonia	2.15	96	Cambodia	3.35
20	Czech Republic	2.20	96	Egypt	3.35
20	Netherlands	2.20	96	Ivory Coast	3.35
22	Denmark	2.25	96	Madagascar	3.35
22	Finland	2.25	96	Moldova	3.35
24	Germany	2.30	102	Nepal	3.40
24	Iceland	2.30	103	Cape Verde	3.44
24	South Korea	2.30	104	Armenia	3.45
27	Norway	2.35	104	Dominican Republic	3.45
28	Kuwait	2.40	104	Russia	3.45
28	Malaysia	2.40	107	Burkina Faso	3.50
28	Panama	2.40	107	Cameroon	3.50
28	Thailand	2.40	107	Lesotho	3.50
32	El Salvador	2.45	107	Nicaragua	3.50
32	Sri Lanka	2.45	107	Venezuela	3.50
32	Sweden	2.45	112	Gambia	3.60
35	France	2.50	112	Guyana	3.60
35	Italy	2.50	114	Bulgaria	3.65
35	Spain	2.50	114	Georgia	3.65
38	Trinidad and Tobago	2.55	114	Malawi	3.65
39	Argentina	2.60	117	Ethiopia	3.70
39	Barbados	2.60	117	India	3.70
39	Cyprus	2.60	117	Niger	3.70
39	Jamaica	2.60	120	Albania	3.75
39	Portugal	2.60	120	Bangladesh	3.75
44	Bolivia	2.65	120	China (PRC)	3.75
44	Oman	2.65	120	Congo	3.75
44	Philippines	2.65	120	Croatia	3.75
47	Swaziland	2.70	125	Chad	3.80
47	Uruguay	2.70	125	Mauritania	3.80
49	Botswana	2.75	125	Ukraine	3.80
49	Jordan	2.75	128	Sierra Leone	3.85
49	Namibia	2.75	129	Burundi	3.90
49	Tunisia	2.75	129	Suriname	3.90
53	Belize	2.80	129	Zimbabwe	3.90
53	Costa Rica	2.80	132	Haiti	4.00
53	Guatemala	2.80	132	Kyrgyzstan	4.00
53	Israel	2.80	132	Syria	4.00
53	Peru	2.80	135	Belarus	4.05
53	Saudi Arabia	2.80	136	Kazakstan	4.10
53	Turkey	2.80	136	Mozambique	4.10
53	Uganda	2.80	136	Yemen	4.10
53	Western Samoa	2.80	139	Sudan	4.20
62	Indonesia	2.85	140	Myanmar	4.30
62	Latvia	2.85	140	Rwanda	4.30
62	Malta	2.85	142	Angola	4.35
62	Paraguay	2.85	143	Azerbaijan	4.40
66	Greece	2.90	143	Tajikistan	4.40
66	Hungary	2.90	145	Turkmenistan	4.50
66	South Africa	2.90	146	Uzbekistan	4.55
69	Benin	2.95	147	Congo/Zaire	4.70
69	Ecuador	2.95	147	Iran	4.70
69	Gabon	2.95	147	Libya	4.70
69	Morocco	2.95	147	Somalia	4.70
69	Poland	2.95	147	Vietnam	4.70
74	Colombia	3.00	152	Bosnia	4.80
74	Ghana	3.00	153	Iraq	4.90
74	Lithuania	3.00	154	Cuba	5.00
77	Kenya	3.05	154	Laos	5.00
77	Slovak Republic	3.05	154	North Korea	5.00

Free (marker at left of table, rows 4–9)

Capital Flows and Foreign Investment
Score: 1–Stable (very low barriers)

Hong Kong's government encourages foreign investment and is one of the most receptive to investment in the world. There are no restrictions on foreign capital or investment, except in the media sector.

Banking
Score: 1–Stable (very low level of restrictions)

Hong Kong is a world banking center and one of the world's most stable banking environments. Banks are completely independent of the government. Foreign banks are free to operate with only limited restrictions on the number of automatic teller machines and branches.

Wage and Price Controls
Score: 2–Stable (low level)

Hong Kong's market largely sets wages and prices (the only exception pertains to certain telecommunications services). There are, however, price controls on rent, public transport, and electricity. The government has the power to enforce minimum wages, but has never done so.

Property Rights
Score: 1–Stable (very high level of protection)

Private property rights in Hong Kong are fully protected. The legal system to protect these rights is both highly efficient and effective. According to the U.S. Department of State, "The judicial and legal systems are organized according to principles of British constitutional law and legal precedent and provide for an independent judiciary."[5]

Regulation
Score: 1–Stable (very low level)

Hong Kong has a simple system to license businesses. The regulations imposed on business are few, not burdensome, and applied uniformly.[6] Hong Kong has refused to implement such regulations as antitrust or antidumping laws. The absence of both maximizes competition from domestic and foreign firms. The status of several new business regulations that initially were suspended by Hong Kong's new legislative body is not entirely certain as of this writing.

Black Market
Score: 1–Stable (very low level of activity)

The black market in Hong Kong is virtually nonexistent. There is no significant smuggling, and black market activity in pirated intellectual property is negligible.[7] According to the U.S. Department of State, "With respect to the legislative arena and international conventions, Hong Kong's [intellectual property] framework is world class."[8]

Notes

1. Minor import duties exist on alcoholic beverages, tobacco, and cosmetics.
2. The maximum tax rate is limited to the "standard rate" of 15 percent on total taxable income above $155,454. Therefore, because the maximum tax rate on the highest level of income is 15 percent, this percentage is used to grade Hong Kong's income tax score.
3. See "Biting the Invisible Hand," *Reason*, April 1996, p. 34.
4. "Hong Kong in Figures, 1996," Hong Kong government Internet site: *http://www.info.hk/cenststd/hkstat/hkinf/gdp/htm*.
5. U.S. Department of State, "Hong Kong Country Report on Human Rights Practices for 1996," 1997.
6. Although Hong Kong lacks antitrust laws, this does not restrain individual economic freedom; rather, it empowers consumers. With borders open to investment and trade, "malevolent monopolies" are impossible to sustain; competition is maximized by the absence of barriers to new entrants. In addition, "altruistic monopolies" provide consumers with goods and services of the highest quality at the cheapest price because competition from foreign investment or foreign trade would put them out of business. Rather than rely on government-imposed antitrust regulation, the government relies on a private-sector organization, the Hong Kong Consumer Council, to oversee businesses and regularly issue reports on business practices. If collusion among businesses is suspected and competition is hindered, the government may take action to break up the companies, as it did in 1994 when it moved to eliminate regulations on the banking industry in order to maximize competition.
7. Although some pirated intellectual property from the People's Republic of China finds its way into Hong Kong, the customs bureau is among the best in the world. As a result, most pirated material from the PRC is confiscated at the border. The amount of pirated material that does exist in Hong Kong is minuscule in comparison with the size of the economy, and the government is increasing its crackdown on pirated materials at the border. Although some pirated products remain for sale in Hong Kong, few are exported to other countries.
8. U.S. Department of State, *Country Reports on Economic Policy and Trade Practices*, 1997, p. 34.

Hungary   2.90

1997 Score: **2.90**   1996 Score: **2.90**   1995 Score: **2.80**

Trade	4	Banking	2
Taxation	4	Wages and Prices	2
Government Intervention	3	Property Rights	2
Monetary Policy	4	Regulation	3
Foreign Investment	2	Black Market	3

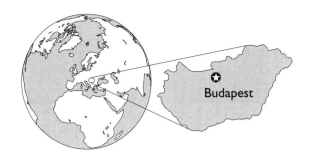

Budapest

Once part of the Austro–Hungarian Empire, Hungary was incorporated into the Soviet bloc after World War II. The government, which had practiced a type of reform communism, collapsed in 1989 and a democratically elected government introduced market reforms soon thereafter. Despite the Socialist victory in the 1994 elections, Hungary's economic policy of market reform has continued, and its political climate remains relatively stable. Hungary has an efficient system to protect intellectual property rights, weak labor unions, and a liberal foreign trade policy. It also has pursued an extensive program of privatization.

TRADE POLICY
Score: 4–Stable (high level of protectionism)

Hungary's average tariff rate is 12 percent. The government also maintains import quotas that mainly affect such consumer products as automobiles, clothing, leather footwear, and some foodstuffs. Other quotas, such as the one on agricultural products, have been replaced with tariffs.

TAXATION
Score–Income taxation: 5–Stable (very high tax rates)
Score–Corporate taxation: 2–Stable (low tax rates)
Final Taxation Score: 4–Stable (high tax rates)

Hungary's top income tax rate is 48 percent;[1] the average income level is taxed at 44 percent. The top corporate income tax rate is 18 percent (the government cut corporate taxes by half in 1995). Hungary also has an 18 percent capital gains tax, a 12 percent to 25 percent value-added tax, and various local taxes.

GOVERNMENT INTERVENTION IN THE ECONOMY
Score: 3–Stable (moderate level)

Government consumes 13.1 percent of Hungary's GDP, over 30 percent of which is generated by the public sector. The government remains heavily involved in energy, telecommunications, transportation, pharmaceuticals, and other areas. Privatization continues.

MONETARY POLICY
Score: 4–Stable (high level of inflation)

Hungary's annual rate of inflation was 23.6 percent in 1996, 28.2 percent in 1995, 18.8 percent in 1994, 22.5 percent in 1993, 23.0 percent in 1992, and 35 percent in 1991.[2] The average rate of inflation since the collapse of the communist regime has been about 25 percent.

CAPITAL FLOWS AND FOREIGN INVESTMENT
Score: 2–Stable (low barriers)

Hungary is very open to foreign investment and is leading the way on foreign investment reform, attracting most investment from the United States in the

1	Hong Kong	1.25	77	Zambia	3.05
2	Singapore	1.30	80	Mali	3.10
3	Bahrain	1.70	80	Mongolia	3.10
4	New Zealand	1.75	80	Slovenia	3.10
5	Switzerland	1.90	83	Honduras	3.15
5	United States	1.90	83	Papua New Guinea	3.15
7	Luxembourg	1.95	85	Djibouti	3.20
7	Taiwan	1.95	85	Fiji	3.20
7	United Kingdom	1.95	85	Pakistan	3.20
10	Bahamas	2.00	88	Algeria	3.25
10	Ireland	2.00	88	Guinea	3.25
12	Australia	2.05	88	Lebanon	3.25
12	Japan	2.05	88	Mexico	3.25
14	Belgium	2.10	88	Senegal	3.25
14	Canada	2.10	88	Tanzania	3.25
14	United Arab Emirates	2.10	94	Nigeria	3.30
17	Austria	2.15	94	Romania	3.30
17	Chile	2.15	96	Brazil	3.35
17	Estonia	2.15	96	Cambodia	3.35
20	Czech Republic	2.20	96	Egypt	3.35
20	Netherlands	2.20	96	Ivory Coast	3.35
22	Denmark	2.25	96	Madagascar	3.35
22	Finland	2.25	96	Moldova	3.35
24	Germany	2.30	102	Nepal	3.40
24	Iceland	2.30	103	Cape Verde	3.44
24	South Korea	2.30	104	Armenia	3.45
27	Norway	2.35	104	Dominican Republic	3.45
28	Kuwait	2.40	104	Russia	3.45
28	Malaysia	2.40	107	Burkina Faso	3.50
28	Panama	2.40	107	Cameroon	3.50
28	Thailand	2.40	107	Lesotho	3.50
32	El Salvador	2.45	107	Nicaragua	3.50
32	Sri Lanka	2.45	107	Venezuela	3.50
32	Sweden	2.45	112	Gambia	3.60
35	France	2.50	112	Guyana	3.60
35	Italy	2.50	114	Bulgaria	3.65
35	Spain	2.50	114	Georgia	3.65
38	Trinidad and Tobago	2.55	114	Malawi	3.65
39	Argentina	2.60	117	Ethiopia	3.70
39	Barbados	2.60	117	India	3.70
39	Cyprus	2.60	117	Niger	3.70
39	Jamaica	2.60	120	Albania	3.75
39	Portugal	2.60	120	Bangladesh	3.75
44	Bolivia	2.65	120	China (PRC)	3.75
44	Oman	2.65	120	Congo	3.75
44	Philippines	2.65	120	Croatia	3.75
47	Swaziland	2.70	125	Chad	3.80
47	Uruguay	2.70	125	Mauritania	3.80
49	Botswana	2.75	125	Ukraine	3.80
49	Jordan	2.75	128	Sierra Leone	3.85
49	Namibia	2.75	129	Burundi	3.90
49	Tunisia	2.75	129	Suriname	3.90
53	Belize	2.80	129	Zimbabwe	3.90
53	Costa Rica	2.80	132	Haiti	4.00
53	Guatemala	2.80	132	Kyrgyzstan	4.00
53	Israel	2.80	132	Syria	4.00
53	Peru	2.80	135	Belarus	4.05
53	Saudi Arabia	2.80	136	Kazakstan	4.10
53	Turkey	2.80	136	Mozambique	4.10
53	Uganda	2.80	136	Yemen	4.10
53	Western Samoa	2.80	139	Sudan	4.20
62	Indonesia	2.85	140	Myanmar	4.30
62	Latvia	2.85	140	Rwanda	4.30
62	Malta	2.85	142	Angola	4.35
62	Paraguay	2.85	143	Azerbaijan	4.40
66	Greece	2.90	143	Tajikistan	4.40
66	Hungary	2.90	145	Turkmenistan	4.50
66	South Africa	2.90	146	Uzbekistan	4.55
69	Benin	2.95	147	Congo/Zaire	4.70
69	Ecuador	2.95	147	Iran	4.70
69	Gabon	2.95	147	Libya	4.70
69	Morocco	2.95	147	Somalia	4.70
69	Poland	2.95	147	Vietnam	4.70
74	Colombia	3.00	152	Bosnia	4.80
74	Ghana	3.00	153	Iraq	4.90
74	Lithuania	3.00	154	Cuba	5.00
77	Kenya	3.05	154	Laos	5.00
77	Slovak Republic	3.05	154	North Korea	5.00

Mostly Free

region. Even though 100 percent ownership is guaranteed to foreign investors, the government sometimes opposes such ownership for newly privatized businesses. Once a foreign investor's business is located in Hungary, the law is applied evenly to both foreign and domestic firms.

BANKING
Score: 2–Stable (low level of restrictions)

Privatization of Hungary's banking industry is progressing. The government may not own more than 25 percent of a bank. The banking industry is becoming increasingly competitive, and banks are relatively free from burdensome government oversight.

WAGE AND PRICE CONTROLS
Score: 2–Stable (low level)

Hungary has eliminated most price controls. According to the U.S. Department of State, however, "[T]he prices for public transport, utilities such as gas, electricity and water, and vehicle fuel continue to be partially set by the state."[3] Hungary has a minimum wage.

PROPERTY RIGHTS
Score: 2–Stable (high level of protection)

There is little chance of property expropriation in Hungary. There have been no cases of government expropriation of foreign-owned assets since the 1950s, and private property is guaranteed by law. The legal system is at times corrupt, ineffective, and inefficient, but the U.S. Department of Commerce reports that it also "protects and facilitates the acquisition and disposition of property rights."[4]

REGULATION
Score: 3–Stable (moderate level)

Hungary has few regulations that burden business. A business license is required only for a few activities. New laws on consumer protection and the environment, however, are becoming burdensome. The environmental law, for example, imposes a "green tax" on certain businesses engaged in manufacturing such products as tires and refrigerators.

BLACK MARKET
Score: 3–Stable (moderate level of activity)

As Hungary moves closer to a free market, the level of black market activity is decreasing. According to the U.S. Department of Commerce, black market activity equals about one-third of the economy.[5] There is some infringement of intellectual property, and a significant black market exists in pirated materials, especially pharmaceuticals. By global standards, however, Hungary's black market is moderate in size.

NOTES
1. Economist Intelligence Unit, *ILT Reports, Hungary,* 1996.
2. Based on consumer price inflation; see *ibid.*
3. U.S. Department of State, *Country Reports on Economic Policy and Trade Practices,* 1996, p. 197.
4. U.S. Department of Commerce, *Country Commercial Guide,* 1997.
5. U.S. Department of Commerce, "Hungary: Investment Climate," *Market Research Reports,* September 17, 1996.

Iceland   2.30

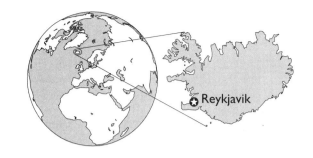

Reykjavik

1997 Score: **2.50**	1996 Score: **n/a**	1995 Score: **n/a**

Trade	2	Banking	3
Taxation	4	Wages and Prices	2
Government Intervention	3	Property Rights	1
Monetary Policy	2	Regulation	3
Foreign Investment	2	Black Market	1

Iceland, an island state in the North Atlantic Ocean, is the westernmost outpost of Europe. During the 1800s, it was primarily an agricultural and fishing country, and these industries produced substantial economic growth. By the 1900s, Iceland had an established industrial base. The country won its independence from Denmark in 1944. It has an advanced market economy and is a major export base for manufactured goods. Iceland recently decreased its rate of inflation and reduced some price controls. As a result, its overall score has improved 0.2 point this year.

TRADE POLICY
Score: 2–Stable (low level of protectionism)

Iceland's average tariff rate is about 1.89 percent.[1] Nontariff barriers continue in the form of quotas and some licensing requirements.

TAXATION
Score–Income taxation: 4–Stable (high tax rates)
Score–Corporate taxation: 3–Stable (moderate tax rates)
Final Taxation Score: 4–Stable (high tax rates)

Iceland has a flat income tax rate of 41.94 percent and a top marginal corporate tax rate of 33 percent. It also has a 33 percent capital gains tax and a 24.5 percent value-added tax.

GOVERNMENT INTERVENTION IN THE ECONOMY
Score: 3–Stable (moderate level)

Government consumes about 20.7 percent of Iceland's GDP, a substantial portion of which is produced by publicly owned companies.

MONETARY POLICY
Score: 2+ (low level of inflation)

Iceland's average rate of inflation fell to 11.8 percent from 1985 to 1995. In 1996, the inflation rate was below 2 percent. As a result, Iceland's score in this category is one point better this year.

CAPITAL FLOWS AND FOREIGN INVESTMENT
Score: 2–Stable (low barriers)

Iceland generally welcomes foreign investment, although the government still maintains some restrictions on foreign investment in fishing and primary fish processing, commercial banks, airlines, and industries considered vital to national security.

1	Hong Kong	1.25	77	Zambia	3.05
2	Singapore	1.30	80	Mali	3.10
3	Bahrain	1.70	80	Mongolia	3.10
4	New Zealand	1.75	80	Slovenia	3.10
5	Switzerland	1.90	83	Honduras	3.15
5	United States	1.90	83	Papua New Guinea	3.15
7	Luxembourg	1.95	85	Djibouti	3.20
7	Taiwan	1.95	85	Fiji	3.20
7	United Kingdom	1.95	85	Pakistan	3.20
10	Bahamas	2.00	88	Algeria	3.25
10	Ireland	2.00	88	Guinea	3.25
12	Australia	2.05	88	Lebanon	3.25
12	Japan	2.05	88	Mexico	3.25
14	Belgium	2.10	88	Senegal	3.25
14	Canada	2.10	88	Tanzania	3.25
14	United Arab Emirates	2.10	94	Nigeria	3.30
17	Austria	2.15	94	Romania	3.30
17	Chile	2.15	96	Brazil	3.35
17	Estonia	2.15	96	Cambodia	3.35
20	Czech Republic	2.20	96	Egypt	3.35
20	Netherlands	2.20	96	Ivory Coast	3.35
22	Denmark	2.25	96	Madagascar	3.35
22	Finland	2.25	96	Moldova	3.35
24	Germany	2.30	102	Nepal	3.40
24	Iceland	2.30	103	Cape Verde	3.44
24	South Korea	2.30	104	Armenia	3.45
27	Norway	2.35	104	Dominican Republic	3.45
28	Kuwait	2.40	104	Russia	3.45
28	Malaysia	2.40	107	Burkina Faso	3.50
28	Panama	2.40	107	Cameroon	3.50
28	Thailand	2.40	107	Lesotho	3.50
32	El Salvador	2.45	107	Nicaragua	3.50
32	Sri Lanka	2.45	107	Venezuela	3.50
32	Sweden	2.45	112	Gambia	3.60
35	France	2.50	112	Guyana	3.60
35	Italy	2.50	114	Bulgaria	3.65
35	Spain	2.50	114	Georgia	3.65
38	Trinidad and Tobago	2.55	114	Malawi	3.65
39	Argentina	2.60	117	Ethiopia	3.70
39	Barbados	2.60	117	India	3.70
39	Cyprus	2.60	117	Niger	3.70
39	Jamaica	2.60	120	Albania	3.75
39	Portugal	2.60	120	Bangladesh	3.75
44	Bolivia	2.65	120	China (PRC)	3.75
44	Oman	2.65	120	Congo	3.75
44	Philippines	2.65	120	Croatia	3.75
47	Swaziland	2.70	125	Chad	3.80
47	Uruguay	2.70	125	Mauritania	3.80
49	Botswana	2.75	125	Ukraine	3.80
49	Jordan	2.75	128	Sierra Leone	3.85
49	Namibia	2.75	129	Burundi	3.90
49	Tunisia	2.75	129	Suriname	3.90
53	Belize	2.80	129	Zimbabwe	3.90
53	Costa Rica	2.80	132	Haiti	4.00
53	Guatemala	2.80	132	Kyrgyzstan	4.00
53	Israel	2.80	132	Syria	4.00
53	Peru	2.80	135	Belarus	4.05
53	Saudi Arabia	2.80	136	Kazakstan	4.10
53	Turkey	2.80	136	Mozambique	4.10
53	Uganda	2.80	136	Yemen	4.10
53	Western Samoa	2.80	139	Sudan	4.20
62	Indonesia	2.85	140	Myanmar	4.30
62	Latvia	2.85	140	Rwanda	4.30
62	Malta	2.85	142	Angola	4.35
62	Paraguay	2.85	143	Azerbaijan	4.40
66	Greece	2.90	143	Tajikistan	4.40
66	Hungary	2.90	145	Turkmenistan	4.50
66	South Africa	2.90	145	Uzbekistan	4.55
69	Benin	2.95	147	Congo/Zaire	4.70
69	Ecuador	2.95	147	Iran	4.70
69	Gabon	2.95	147	Libya	4.70
69	Morocco	2.95	147	Somalia	4.70
69	Poland	2.95	147	Vietnam	4.70
74	Colombia	3.00	152	Bosnia	4.80
74	Ghana	3.00	153	Iraq	4.90
74	Lithuania	3.00	154	Cuba	5.00
77	Kenya	3.05	154	Laos	5.00
77	Slovak Republic	3.05	154	North Korea	5.00

Mostly Free

BANKING
Score: 3–Stable (moderate level of restrictions)

Although Iceland's banking system is becoming more liberalized, some banks still are state-owned. The government plans to privatize a few of these banks.

WAGE AND PRICE CONTROLS
Score: 2+ (low level)

The market sets most wages and prices in Iceland. The government has implemented policies that limit its impact on some prices. As a result, Iceland's wage and price controls score has improved by one point this year. The government can affect prices, however, through its use of various trade restrictions and production quotas in agriculture.

PROPERTY RIGHTS
Score: 1–Stable (very high level of protection)

Private property is safe from government confiscation. Iceland has an efficient and independent legal system.

REGULATION
Score: 3–Stable (moderate level)

Some of Iceland's economy—especially fishing, agriculture, and such service industries as telecommunications and the airlines—remains heavily regulated. Strict environmental laws also can add to the cost of doing business.

BLACK MARKET
Score: 1–Stable (very low level of activity)

Iceland has a very small black market and very strong and efficient laws regarding intellectual property rights. Piracy in these products is virtually nonexistent.

NOTE
1. Based on total government taxation of international transactions as a percentage of imports.

India   3.70

| 1997 Score: **3.70** | 1996 Score: **3.75** | 1995 Score: **3.70** |

Trade	5	Banking	4
Taxation	4	Wages and Prices	4
Government Intervention	3	Property Rights	3
Monetary Policy	2	Regulation	4
Foreign Investment	3	Black Market	5

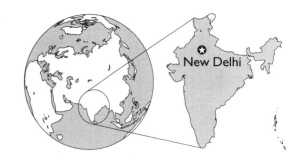

New Delhi

India gained its independence from Great Britain in 1947 and became a republic in 1950. Over the next four decades, the socialist-democratic government restricted economic growth by imposing exhaustive controls on production, prices, and employment; nationalizing industries; limiting competition through licensing; discouraging foreign investment; and raising tariffs and taxes. Following a foreign exchange crisis in 1991, the government under Prime Minister P. V. Narashima Rao began to liberalize the economy, accepting foreign investment and reducing barriers to trade. From 1990 to 1995, India's economy grew by an average of 4.6 percent. The government also has undergone frequent change during the past several years. Prime Minister H. D. Deve Gowda, who took office in June 1996 and headed a center-left coalition government, resigned in March 1997 after his government lost a parliamentary vote of confidence. External Affairs Minister I. K. Gujral became prime minister in April 1997. India's level of economic freedom has remained essentially the same as it was four years ago.

TRADE POLICY
Score: 5–Stable (very high level of protectionism)

India recently agreed to abolish all tariff and other trade restrictions on computers, telecommunications equipment, software, semiconductors, and printed circuit boards by the year 2000. The average tariff rate is 47.8 percent, up from 33.4 percent in 1991.[1] India also maintains a number of nontariff barriers.

TAXATION
Score–Income taxation: 3–Stable (moderate tax rates)
Score–Corporate taxation: 4–Stable (high tax rates)
Final Taxation Score: 4–Stable (high tax rates)

India's top income tax level is 40 percent; the tax on the average income level is 0 percent. The top corporate tax rate is 40 percent. India also has a 20 percent capital gains tax and both interest and sales taxes.

GOVERNMENT INTERVENTION IN THE ECONOMY
Score: 3–Stable (moderate level)

Government consumes 11 percent of India's GDP, a large portion of which is generated by state-owned enterprises. Privatization has slowed in recent years. Although shares of formerly state-owned firms such as Bharat Electronics and the Steel Authority of India now are traded on the Bombay stock exchange, the government retains managerial control.

MONETARY POLICY
Score: 2–Stable (low level of inflation)

From 1985 to 1995, India's average annual rate of inflation was 9.8 percent. In 1996, inflation reached 9 percent.

#	Country	Score	#	Country	Score
1	Hong Kong	1.25	77	Zambia	3.05
2	Singapore	1.30	80	Mali	3.10
3	Bahrain	1.70	80	Mongolia	3.10
4	New Zealand	1.75	80	Slovenia	3.10
5	Switzerland	1.90	83	Honduras	3.15
5	United States	1.90	83	Papua New Guinea	3.15
7	Luxembourg	1.95	85	Djibouti	3.20
7	Taiwan	1.95	85	Fiji	3.20
7	United Kingdom	1.95	85	Pakistan	3.20
10	Bahamas	2.00	88	Algeria	3.25
10	Ireland	2.00	88	Guinea	3.25
12	Australia	2.05	88	Lebanon	3.25
12	Japan	2.05	88	Mexico	3.25
14	Belgium	2.10	88	Senegal	3.25
14	Canada	2.10	88	Tanzania	3.25
14	United Arab Emirates	2.10	94	Nigeria	3.30
17	Austria	2.15	94	Romania	3.30
17	Chile	2.15	96	Brazil	3.35
17	Estonia	2.15	96	Cambodia	3.35
20	Czech Republic	2.20	96	Egypt	3.35
20	Netherlands	2.20	96	Ivory Coast	3.35
22	Denmark	2.25	96	Madagascar	3.35
22	Finland	2.25	96	Moldova	3.35
24	Germany	2.30	102	Nepal	3.40
24	Iceland	2.30	103	Cape Verde	3.44
24	South Korea	2.30	104	Armenia	3.45
27	Norway	2.35	104	Dominican Republic	3.45
28	Kuwait	2.40	104	Russia	3.45
28	Malaysia	2.40	107	Burkina Faso	3.50
28	Panama	2.40	107	Cameroon	3.50
28	Thailand	2.40	107	Lesotho	3.50
32	El Salvador	2.45	107	Nicaragua	3.50
32	Sri Lanka	2.45	107	Venezuela	3.50
32	Sweden	2.45	112	Gambia	3.60
35	France	2.50	112	Guyana	3.60
35	Italy	2.50	114	Bulgaria	3.65
35	Spain	2.50	114	Georgia	3.65
38	Trinidad and Tobago	2.55	114	Malawi	3.65
39	Argentina	2.60	117	Ethiopia	3.70
39	Barbados	2.60	117	India	3.70
39	Cyprus	2.60	117	Niger	3.70
39	Jamaica	2.60	120	Albania	3.75
39	Portugal	2.60	120	Bangladesh	3.75
44	Bolivia	2.65	120	China (PRC)	3.75
44	Oman	2.65	120	Congo	3.75
44	Philippines	2.65	120	Croatia	3.75
47	Swaziland	2.70	125	Chad	3.80
47	Uruguay	2.70	125	Mauritania	3.80
49	Botswana	2.75	125	Ukraine	3.80
49	Jordan	2.75	128	Sierra Leone	3.85
49	Namibia	2.75	129	Burundi	3.90
49	Tunisia	2.75	129	Suriname	3.90
53	Belize	2.80	129	Zimbabwe	3.90
53	Costa Rica	2.80	132	Haiti	4.00
53	Guatemala	2.80	132	Kyrgyzstan	4.00
53	Israel	2.80	132	Syria	4.00
53	Peru	2.80	135	Belarus	4.05
53	Saudi Arabia	2.80	136	Kazakstan	4.10
53	Turkey	2.80	136	Mozambique	4.10
53	Uganda	2.80	136	Yemen	4.10
53	Western Samoa	2.80	139	Sudan	4.20
62	Indonesia	2.85	140	Myanmar	4.30
62	Latvia	2.85	140	Rwanda	4.30
62	Malta	2.85	142	Angola	4.35
62	Paraguay	2.85	143	Azerbaijan	4.40
66	Greece	2.90	143	Tajikistan	4.40
66	Hungary	2.90	145	Turkmenistan	4.50
66	South Africa	2.90	146	Uzbekistan	4.55
69	Benin	2.95	147	Congo/Zaire	4.70
69	Ecuador	2.95	147	Iran	4.70
69	Gabon	2.95	147	Libya	4.70
69	Morocco	2.95	147	Somalia	4.70
69	Poland	2.95	147	Vietnam	4.70
74	Colombia	3.00	152	Bosnia	4.80
74	Ghana	3.00	153	Iraq	4.90
74	Lithuania	3.00	154	Cuba	5.00
77	Kenya	3.05	154	Laos	5.00
77	Slovak Republic	3.05	154	North Korea	5.00

Mostly Unfree

CAPITAL FLOWS AND FOREIGN INVESTMENT
Score: 3–Stable (moderate barriers)

India has reduced some barriers to foreign investment. Foreign investors, however, may not own 100 percent of an Indian concern without prior government approval, but there are few instances in which approval is not granted.

BANKING
Score: 4–Stable (high level of restrictions)

The government wields a heavy hand in controlling India's banking sector. According to the U.S. Department of Commerce, "All large Indian banks are nationalized, and all Indian financial institutions are in the public sector."[2] The government plans to permit only 5 licenses per year for foreign bank branches or extensions of current operations. Only 12 such licenses were granted from June 1993 to September 1994. The situation has not changed dramatically since then.

WAGE AND PRICE CONTROLS
Score: 4–Stable (high level)

Central and state governments still regulate the pricing of most essential products, including cereals, sugar, basic medicines, some energy, coal, and many industrial inputs. India has a minimum wage.

PROPERTY RIGHTS
Score: 3–Stable (moderate level of protection)

The massive gap between rich and poor leads to government policies that redistribute wealth, mainly through property expropriation. Even though India has an efficient court system, property remains at risk in rural areas because of long delays. According to the U.S. Department of State, "Case backlogs frequently lead to long procedural delays."[3]

REGULATION
Score: 4–Stable (high level)

India's economy is heavily regulated. The large public sector must meet all kinds of burdensome requirements, including restrictive licensing requirements, to remain open for business. In addition, the U.S. Department of Commerce reports that "U.S. firms have identified corruption as an obstacle to foreign direct investment. According to the embassy's 1995 investment survey, corruption was considered the third worst problem faced by U.S. firms in India after bureaucratic red tape and power shortages. Government procurement in particular has been subject to allegations of corruption, with telecom and power sectors especially prone to such charges."[4]

BLACK MARKET
Score: 5–Stable (very high level of activity)

India's huge tariffs make it very profitable to smuggle foreign goods into the country. Many goods are smuggled in from Myanmar (Burma). According to the U.S. Department of Commerce, "Local shopkeepers act as contact points for heavier smuggled goods, mostly teak and rice, and for Burmese gem stones."[5]

NOTES

1. Based on total taxes on international trade as a percentage of total imports.
2. U.S. Department of Commerce, *Country Commercial Guide,* 1997.
3. *Ibid.*
4. *Ibid.*
5. *Ibid.*

Indonesia 2.85

1997 Score: **2.85**	1996 Score: **2.85**	1995 Score: **3.35**

Trade	2	Banking	3
Taxation	3.5	Wages and Prices	3
Government Intervention	1	Property Rights	3
Monetary Policy	2	Regulation	4
Foreign Investment	2	Black Market	5

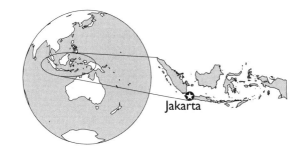

Jakarta

Indonesia gained its independence from the Netherlands in 1945. More recently, it has made significant progress toward economic liberalization. Although Indonesia has received rather large sums of foreign aid from the international community, the most significant impact on its economic prosperity has come from such policy reforms as cutting taxes, lowering barriers to trade, and opening the economy to foreign investment. Future challenges include responding to greater popular demand for political liberalization while managing a successful transition to a new government following that of President Suharto.

TRADE POLICY
Score: 2–Stable (low level of protectionism)

Indonesia's average tariff rate is 6 percent. There are strict licensing requirements on a number of products, including flour, sugar, and rice.

TAXATION
Score–Income taxation: 3–Stable (moderate tax rates)
Score–Corporate taxation: 3–Stable (moderate tax rates)
Final Taxation Score: 3.5–Stable (high tax rates)

Indonesia's top income tax rate is 30 percent, and the average income level is taxed at 10 percent. The top corporate income tax rate is 30 percent. Indonesia also has a 10 percent value-added tax and a sales tax.

GOVERNMENT INTERVENTION IN THE ECONOMY
Score: 1–Stable (very low level)

Government consumes 8.2 percent of Indonesia's GDP. According to the Economist Intelligence Unit, "The State continues to play a major role in Indonesian industry, though the government increasingly requires state firms to meet private-sector accounting and competitive standards. At the same time it is phasing out subsidies and a multitude of preferences, and making privatization a serious goal."[1] Thus, government consumption of the economy is minuscule.

MONETARY POLICY
Score: 2–Stable (low level of inflation)

Indonesia's average annual rate of inflation from 1985 to 1995 was 8.8 percent. In 1996, the inflation rate was 8.5 percent.

CAPITAL FLOWS AND FOREIGN INVESTMENT
Score: 2–Stable (low barriers)

Indonesia has reformed its foreign investment code. The government now allows 100 percent foreign ownership and has opened many sectors once closed to foreign investors, although foreign investment in some retail operations still is not permitted.

1	Hong Kong	1.25
2	Singapore	1.30
3	Bahrain	1.70
4	New Zealand	1.75
5	Switzerland	1.90
5	United States	1.90
7	Luxembourg	1.95
7	Taiwan	1.95
7	United Kingdom	1.95
10	Bahamas	2.00
10	Ireland	2.00
12	Australia	2.05
12	Japan	2.05
14	Belgium	2.10
14	Canada	2.10
14	United Arab Emirates	2.10
17	Austria	2.15
17	Chile	2.15
17	Estonia	2.15
20	Czech Republic	2.20
20	Netherlands	2.20
22	Denmark	2.25
22	Finland	2.25
24	Germany	2.30
24	Iceland	2.30
24	South Korea	2.30
27	Norway	2.35
28	Kuwait	2.40
28	Malaysia	2.40
28	Panama	2.40
28	Thailand	2.40
32	El Salvador	2.45
32	Sri Lanka	2.45
32	Sweden	2.45
35	France	2.50
35	Italy	2.50
35	Spain	2.50
38	Trinidad and Tobago	2.55
39	Argentina	2.60
39	Barbados	2.60
39	Cyprus	2.60
39	Jamaica	2.60
39	Portugal	2.60
44	Bolivia	2.65
44	Oman	2.65
44	Philippines	2.65
47	Swaziland	2.70
47	Uruguay	2.70
49	Botswana	2.75
49	Jordan	2.75
49	Namibia	2.75
49	Tunisia	2.75
53	Belize	2.80
53	Costa Rica	2.80
53	Guatemala	2.80
53	Israel	2.80
53	Peru	2.80
53	Saudi Arabia	2.80
53	Turkey	2.80
53	Uganda	2.80
53	Western Samoa	2.80
62	Indonesia	2.85
62	Latvia	2.85
62	Malta	2.85
62	Paraguay	2.85
66	Greece	2.90
66	Hungary	2.90
66	South Africa	2.90
69	Benin	2.95
69	Ecuador	2.95
69	Gabon	2.95
69	Morocco	2.95
69	Poland	2.95
74	Colombia	3.00
74	Ghana	3.00
74	Lithuania	3.00
77	Kenya	3.05
77	Slovak Republic	3.05
77	Zambia	3.05
80	Mali	3.10
80	Mongolia	3.10
80	Slovenia	3.10
83	Honduras	3.15
83	Papua New Guinea	3.15
85	Djibouti	3.20
85	Fiji	3.20
85	Pakistan	3.20
88	Algeria	3.25
88	Guinea	3.25
88	Lebanon	3.25
88	Mexico	3.25
88	Senegal	3.25
88	Tanzania	3.25
94	Nigeria	3.30
94	Romania	3.30
96	Brazil	3.35
96	Cambodia	3.35
96	Egypt	3.35
96	Ivory Coast	3.35
96	Madagascar	3.35
96	Moldova	3.35
102	Nepal	3.40
103	Cape Verde	3.44
104	Armenia	3.45
104	Dominican Republic	3.45
104	Russia	3.45
107	Burkina Faso	3.50
107	Cameroon	3.50
107	Lesotho	3.50
107	Nicaragua	3.50
107	Venezuela	3.50
112	Gambia	3.60
112	Guyana	3.60
114	Bulgaria	3.65
114	Georgia	3.65
114	Malawi	3.65
117	Ethiopia	3.70
117	India	3.70
117	Niger	3.70
120	Albania	3.75
120	Bangladesh	3.75
120	China (PRC)	3.75
120	Congo	3.75
120	Croatia	3.75
125	Chad	3.80
125	Mauritania	3.80
125	Ukraine	3.80
128	Sierra Leone	3.85
129	Burundi	3.90
129	Suriname	3.90
129	Zimbabwe	3.90
132	Haiti	4.00
132	Kyrgyzstan	4.00
132	Syria	4.00
135	Belarus	4.05
136	Kazakstan	4.10
136	Mozambique	4.10
136	Yemen	4.10
139	Sudan	4.20
140	Myanmar	4.30
140	Rwanda	4.30
142	Angola	4.35
143	Azerbaijan	4.40
143	Tajikistan	4.40
145	Turkmenistan	4.50
146	Uzbekistan	4.55
147	Congo/Zaire	4.70
147	Iran	4.70
147	Libya	4.70
147	Somalia	4.70
147	Vietnam	4.70
152	Bosnia	4.80
153	Iraq	4.90
154	Cuba	5.00
154	Laos	5.00
154	North Korea	5.00

Mostly Free

BANKING
Score: 3–Stable (moderate level of restrictions)

From 1969 until the late 1980s, foreign banks were prohibited from receiving a license. There have been some changes to allow more foreign bank participation, but foreign banks remain highly regulated. In many cases, they can operate only through joint ventures with Indonesian banks. Moreover, 100 percent foreign-owned banks are not permitted. Domestic banks have gained increased independence from the government.

WAGE AND PRICE CONTROLS
Score: 3–Stable (moderate level)

Most prices are set by the market, although the prices of many products, including sugar, soybeans, and rice, are controlled. According to the U.S. Department of State, "The government enforces a system of floor and ceiling prices for certain 'strategic' food products such as rice."[2] Indonesia has a minimum wage.

PROPERTY RIGHTS
Score: 3–Stable (moderate level of protection)

Indonesia's legal framework is based on Dutch commercial codes that have not been updated since colonial times. Court rulings can be arbitrary and inconsistent. According to the U.S. Department of Commerce, "Many foreign investors believe that the court system does not provide effective recourse for solving commercial disputes."[3]

REGULATION
Score: 4–Stable (high level)

Indonesia's regulatory environment is characterized by bribery, kickbacks, and other corruption. Many regulations are applied arbitrarily, and bribes may be necessary to receive an "exemption" from a government regulation. The U.S. Department of Commerce reports that corruption continues at some Indonesian port facilities in which bribes often are required to get some goods through customs. Moreover, "Despite major improvements in its economic environment, Indonesia continues to have a reputation as a difficult place to do business. The regulatory and legal environment can be tangled, confusing and time-consuming. In recent years, considerable attention has focused on the costs of corruption and influence-peddling."[4]

BLACK MARKET
Score: 5–Stable (very high level of activity)

Indonesia has a very large black market, mainly in labor and manufacturing. According to the U.S. Department of Commerce, "The informal sector in Indonesia is significant, with some estimates placing two thirds of the labor force in the sector."[5] Another cause of black market activity is the lack of protection for intellectual property. The U.S. government recently targeted Indonesia for intellectual property rights violations; and even though Indonesia's government has begun a swift crackdown on pirated copyrighted materials like video and audio tapes, pirated computer software remains rampant. Biotechnology products are not yet protected under Indonesian law, although they may be in the future.

NOTES

1. Economist Intelligence Unit, *ILT Reports, Indonesia,* 1997.
2. U.S. Department of State, *Country Reports on Economic Policy and Trade Practices,* 1996, p. 56.
3. U.S. Department of Commerce, *Country Commercial Guide,* 1997.
4. *Ibid.*
5. U.S. Department of Commerce, "Indonesia Labor Trends, 1992–94, Foreign Labor Trends," 1996; see also Ministry of Manpower, Republic of Indonesia, "Manpower and Employment Situation in Indonesia, 1992," p. 77.

Iran   4.70

| 1997 Score: **4.70** | 1996 Score: **4.70** | 1995 Score: **n/a** |

Trade	5	Banking	5
Taxation	5	Wages and Prices	4
Government Intervention	5	Property Rights	5
Monetary Policy	4	Regulation	4
Foreign Investment	5	Black Market	5

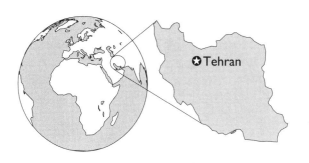

⊙ Tehran

Iran had one of the most advanced economies in the Middle East before the 1979 revolution, the 1980 to 1988 Iran–Iraq War, and widespread economic misman-agement crippled it. The country's radical Islamic leaders established an eco-nomic system that discouraged private enterprise and favored state-run enter-prises. As a result, most of the economy was nationalized. President Ali Akbar Rafsanjani had only limited success in pushing for economic liberalization during his two terms in office (1989–1997); a corrupt and intransigent bureaucracy allied with hard-line Islamic militants in Parliament fought these reforms. Iran's new president, Mohammed Khatami, campaigned in the May 1997 election in favor of limited economic and political reforms. Much of Iran's political power structure, however, including supreme leader Ayatollah Ali Khamenei and many members of Parliament, remain opposed to extensive economic reform.

TRADE POLICY

Score: 5–Stable (very high level of protectionism)

Iran controls imports through its exorbitant tariff rates, import bans, licensing, and a customs service that confiscates many goods that cross the border. The average tariff rate is about 15 percent, but once nontariff taxes are taken into account, the rate can increase to over 100 percent.[1] Many Western goods, especially those representing Western culture, are banned. Iran, imports little except for goods that the government deems vital—mainly raw materials, food, and medicine. According to the *Economist*, "Iranian industries are seldom self-sufficient, most of them depending on imported capital equipment. When imports are stopped or delayed by the need for permits and licenses, or shoot up in price because they have been smuggled in from Dubai, a business is reduced to a crawl."[2]

TAXATION

Score–Income taxation: 5–Stable (very high tax rates)
Score–Corporate taxation: 5–Stable (very high tax rates)
Final Taxation Score: 5–Stable (very high tax rates)

Iran's top income tax rate is 54 percent, and the average taxpayer is in the 35 percent bracket. The top marginal corporate tax rate is 54 percent. Iran also maintains many other taxes, including a 10 percent capital gains tax, a 3 percent municipality tax, and a social contributions tax.

GOVERNMENT INTERVENTION IN THE ECONOMY

Score: 5–Stable (very high level)

Government produces most of Iran's GDP. The private sector is discouraged, and the state owns the banking, petroleum, transportation, utilities, and mining sectors, although it plans to privatize portions of the banking sector. The public sector generates 86 percent of GDP; the remaining 14 percent is generated mainly by religious foundations called *bonyads,* which exist outside the govern-ment but get direct government capital support through subsidies.

1	Hong Kong	1.25	77	Zambia	3.05
2	Singapore	1.30	80	Mali	3.10
3	Bahrain	1.70	80	Mongolia	3.10
4	New Zealand	1.75	80	Slovenia	3.10
5	Switzerland	1.90	83	Honduras	3.15
5	United States	1.90	83	Papua New Guinea	3.15
7	Luxembourg	1.95	85	Djibouti	3.20
7	Taiwan	1.95	85	Fiji	3.20
7	United Kingdom	1.95	85	Pakistan	3.20
10	Bahamas	2.00	88	Algeria	3.25
10	Ireland	2.00	88	Guinea	3.25
12	Australia	2.05	88	Lebanon	3.25
12	Japan	2.05	88	Mexico	3.25
14	Belgium	2.10	88	Senegal	3.25
14	Canada	2.10	88	Tanzania	3.25
14	United Arab Emirates	2.10	94	Nigeria	3.30
17	Austria	2.15	94	Romania	3.30
17	Chile	2.15	96	Brazil	3.35
17	Estonia	2.15	96	Cambodia	3.35
20	Czech Republic	2.20	96	Egypt	3.35
20	Netherlands	2.20	96	Ivory Coast	3.35
22	Denmark	2.25	96	Madagascar	3.35
22	Finland	2.25	96	Moldova	3.35
24	Germany	2.30	102	Nepal	3.40
24	Iceland	2.30	103	Cape Verde	3.44
24	South Korea	2.30	104	Armenia	3.45
27	Norway	2.35	104	Dominican Republic	3.45
28	Kuwait	2.40	104	Russia	3.45
28	Malaysia	2.40	107	Burkina Faso	3.50
28	Panama	2.40	107	Cameroon	3.50
28	Thailand	2.40	107	Lesotho	3.50
32	El Salvador	2.45	107	Nicaragua	3.50
32	Sri Lanka	2.45	107	Venezuela	3.50
32	Sweden	2.45	112	Gambia	3.60
35	France	2.50	112	Guyana	3.60
35	Italy	2.50	114	Bulgaria	3.65
35	Spain	2.50	114	Georgia	3.65
38	Trinidad and Tobago	2.55	114	Malawi	3.65
39	Argentina	2.60	117	Ethiopia	3.70
39	Barbados	2.60	117	India	3.70
39	Cyprus	2.60	117	Niger	3.70
39	Jamaica	2.60	120	Albania	3.75
39	Portugal	2.60	120	Bangladesh	3.75
44	Bolivia	2.65	120	China (PRC)	3.75
44	Oman	2.65	120	Congo	3.75
44	Philippines	2.65	120	Croatia	3.75
47	Swaziland	2.70	125	Chad	3.80
47	Uruguay	2.70	125	Mauritania	3.80
49	Botswana	2.75	125	Ukraine	3.80
49	Jordan	2.75	128	Sierra Leone	3.85
49	Namibia	2.75	129	Burundi	3.90
49	Tunisia	2.75	129	Suriname	3.90
53	Belize	2.80	129	Zimbabwe	3.90
53	Costa Rica	2.80	132	Haiti	4.00
53	Guatemala	2.80	132	Kyrgyzstan	4.00
53	Israel	2.80	132	Syria	4.00
53	Peru	2.80	135	Belarus	4.05
53	Saudi Arabia	2.80	136	Kazakstan	4.10
53	Turkey	2.80	136	Mozambique	4.10
53	Uganda	2.80	136	Yemen	4.10
53	Western Samoa	2.80	139	Sudan	4.20
62	Indonesia	2.85	140	Myanmar	4.30
62	Latvia	2.85	140	Rwanda	4.30
62	Malta	2.85	142	Angola	4.35
62	Paraguay	2.85	143	Azerbaijan	4.40
66	Greece	2.90	143	Tajikistan	4.40
66	Hungary	2.90	145	Turkmenistan	4.50
66	South Africa	2.90	146	Uzbekistan	4.55
69	Benin	2.95	147	Congo/Zaire	4.70
69	Ecuador	2.95	147	Iran	4.70
69	Gabon	2.95	147	Libya	4.70
69	Morocco	2.95	147	Somalia	4.70
69	Poland	2.95	147	Vietnam	4.70
74	Colombia	3.00	152	Bosnia	4.80
74	Ghana	3.00	153	Iraq	4.90
74	Lithuania	3.00	154	Cuba	5.00
77	Kenya	3.05	154	Laos	5.00
77	Slovak Republic	3.05	154	North Korea	5.00

Repressed

MONETARY POLICY
Score: 4–Stable (high level of inflation)

Iran's average rate of inflation from 1985 to 1995 was 24.2 percent. In 1996, the inflation rate was about 30 percent.

CAPITAL FLOWS AND FOREIGN INVESTMENT
Score: 5–Stable (very high barriers)

Iran has removed some restrictions on foreign investment, but it is generally hostile to foreigners, especially non-Muslims. Foreign ownership is prohibited in banking, domestic trade, construction, and most defense-related industries. According to the *Economist*, "[T]he combination of a laborious bureaucracy and the need to hand out baksheesh [bribes] at every turn makes doing business in Iran...like coping with the combined bad habits of the old Soviet Union and the new Nigeria."[3]

BANKING
Score: 5–Stable (very high level of restrictions)

The banking system in Iran is completely government-owned.

WAGE AND PRICE CONTROLS
Score: 4–Stable (high level)

Wages and prices in Iran are controlled through the large public sector. Price controls apply to such items as gasoline, bread, electricity, and other essential goods and services.

PROPERTY RIGHTS
Score: 5–Stable (very low level of protection)

Iran's legal and judicial system is corrupt and inefficient. The government has confiscated huge amounts of private property—particularly property owned by supporters of the former Shah, political dissidents, or Westerners—and has outlawed private ownership of satellite dishes because people were using them to watch Western movies and television programs. According to the U.S. Department of State, "The traditional court system is not independent and is subject to government and religious influence."[4]

REGULATION
Score: 4–Stable (high level)

Establishing a business in Iran is discouraged. Regulations are applied unevenly in most cases, and corruption is rampant. According to the *Economist*, "[The] government...last year alone issued more than 250 regulations on imports and exports. Would-be investors say the problem is not so much that there are too many rules, but that the rules keep changing at the whim of ministers."[5]

BLACK MARKET
Score: 5–Stable (very high level of activity)

Because the government manages the level of imports into Iran, and because it maintains import bans on many consumer goods, smuggling is rampant. According to the *Economist*, "[I]mports [are] sharply restricted (although they can be smuggled in)."[6]

NOTES

1. The 15 percent average tariff rate is based on total revenues from tariffs as a percentage of total imports. According-ing to the World Bank, however, if total import charges for all products are taken into account, the rate increases to 100.9 percent. See World Bank, "Open Economies Work Better," *Policy Research Working Paper* No. 1636, August 1996.
2. "Hard Times," *Economist,* January 18, 1997, pp. 12–15.
3. *Ibid.*
4. U.S. Department of State, "Iran Country Report on Human Rights Practices for 1996," 1997.
5. "Hard Times."
6. *Ibid.*

Iraq

4.90

1997 Score: **4.90**	1996 Score: **4.90**	1995 Score: **n/a**

Trade	5	Banking	5
Taxation	5	Wages and Prices	5
Government Intervention	5	Property Rights	5
Monetary Policy	5	Regulation	4
Foreign Investment	5	Black Market	5

Iraq gained its independence from Great Britain in 1932. A military coup in 1958 replaced the Iraqi monarchy and ushered in a period of political instability. The Ba'ath Socialist Party, which came to power in a 1968 coup, nationalized large portions of the economy. Although Iraq's oil reserves are second only to Saudi Arabia's, its economy has been devastated by government mismanagement, the 1980–1988 war with Iran, the disastrous 1991 Persian Gulf War, and continuing United Nations economic sanctions. Iraq's government is dedicated to a socialist economic ideology and public ownership. Although some private-sector initiatives are permitted, the government regularly executes businessmen who charge excessive prices for scarce imported goods.

TRADE POLICY
Score: 5–Stable (very high level of protectionism)

Customs officials apply tariff rates arbitrarily. The government inspects and controls all imports, although there is considerable smuggling across most of Iraq's borders.

TAXATION
Score–Income taxation: 5–Stable (very high tax rates)
Score–Corporate taxation: 5–Stable (very high tax rates)
Final Taxation Score: 5–Stable (very high tax rates)

Taxes in Iraq generally take the form of confiscated property, much as they do in North Korea and Cuba. Farmers are permitted to grow their own crops, but much of the harvest is confiscated and rationed. Thus, Iraq has the equivalent of very high tax rates.

GOVERNMENT INTERVENTION IN THE ECONOMY
Score: 5–Stable (very high level)

Most economic output is produced by the government or performed in the black market, which the government is trying to restrict. There is little entrepreneurship; where it does occur, it often is subject to government extortion.

MONETARY POLICY
Score: 5–Stable (very high level of inflation)

Iraq's average rate of inflation from 1989 to 1993 was 53 percent. In 1994, the inflation rate was 60 percent. Rates for 1995 and 1996 are not available.

CAPITAL FLOWS AND FOREIGN INVESTMENT
Score: 5–Stable (very high barriers)

Even though Iraq has permitted some foreign investment, mainly to help it rebuild from the damage of the Persian Gulf War, it discourages such investment in most areas. Contracts are not guaranteed, and there is little recourse in the event their enforcement is needed. Investment is allowed only on a case-by-case basis.

1	Hong Kong	1.25	77	Zambia	3.05
2	Singapore	1.30	80	Mali	3.10
3	Bahrain	1.70	80	Mongolia	3.10
4	New Zealand	1.75	80	Slovenia	3.10
5	Switzerland	1.90	83	Honduras	3.15
5	United States	1.90	83	Papua New Guinea	3.15
7	Luxembourg	1.95	85	Djibouti	3.20
7	Taiwan	1.95	85	Fiji	3.20
7	United Kingdom	1.95	85	Pakistan	3.20
10	Bahamas	2.00	88	Algeria	3.25
10	Ireland	2.00	88	Guinea	3.25
12	Australia	2.05	88	Lebanon	3.25
12	Japan	2.05	88	Mexico	3.25
14	Belgium	2.10	88	Senegal	3.25
14	Canada	2.10	88	Tanzania	3.25
14	United Arab Emirates	2.10	94	Nigeria	3.30
17	Austria	2.15	94	Romania	3.30
17	Chile	2.15	96	Brazil	3.35
17	Estonia	2.15	96	Cambodia	3.35
20	Czech Republic	2.20	96	Egypt	3.35
20	Netherlands	2.20	96	Ivory Coast	3.35
22	Denmark	2.25	96	Madagascar	3.35
22	Finland	2.25	96	Moldova	3.35
24	Germany	2.30	102	Nepal	3.40
24	Iceland	2.30	103	Cape Verde	3.44
24	South Korea	2.30	104	Armenia	3.45
27	Norway	2.35	104	Dominican Republic	3.45
28	Kuwait	2.40	104	Russia	3.45
28	Malaysia	2.40	107	Burkina Faso	3.50
28	Panama	2.40	107	Cameroon	3.50
28	Thailand	2.40	107	Lesotho	3.50
32	El Salvador	2.45	107	Nicaragua	3.50
32	Sri Lanka	2.45	107	Venezuela	3.50
32	Sweden	2.45	112	Gambia	3.60
35	France	2.50	112	Guyana	3.60
35	Italy	2.50	114	Bulgaria	3.65
35	Spain	2.50	114	Georgia	3.65
38	Trinidad and Tobago	2.55	114	Malawi	3.65
39	Argentina	2.60	117	Ethiopia	3.70
39	Barbados	2.60	117	India	3.70
39	Cyprus	2.60	117	Niger	3.70
39	Jamaica	2.60	120	Albania	3.75
39	Portugal	2.60	120	Bangladesh	3.75
44	Bolivia	2.65	120	China (PRC)	3.75
44	Oman	2.65	120	Congo	3.75
44	Philippines	2.65	120	Croatia	3.75
47	Swaziland	2.70	125	Chad	3.80
47	Uruguay	2.70	125	Mauritania	3.80
49	Botswana	2.75	125	Ukraine	3.80
49	Jordan	2.75	128	Sierra Leone	3.85
49	Namibia	2.75	129	Burundi	3.90
49	Tunisia	2.75	129	Suriname	3.90
53	Belize	2.80	129	Zimbabwe	3.90
53	Costa Rica	2.80	132	Haiti	4.00
53	Guatemala	2.80	132	Kyrgyzstan	4.00
53	Israel	2.80	132	Syria	4.00
53	Peru	2.80	135	Belarus	4.05
53	Saudi Arabia	2.80	136	Kazakstan	4.10
53	Turkey	2.80	136	Mozambique	4.10
53	Uganda	2.80	136	Yemen	4.10
53	Western Samoa	2.80	139	Sudan	4.20
62	Indonesia	2.85	140	Myanmar	4.30
62	Latvia	2.85	140	Rwanda	4.30
62	Malta	2.85	142	Angola	4.35
62	Paraguay	2.85	143	Azerbaijan	4.40
66	Greece	2.90	143	Tajikistan	4.40
66	Hungary	2.90	145	Turkmenistan	4.50
66	South Africa	2.90	146	Uzbekistan	4.55
69	Benin	2.95	147	Congo/Zaire	4.70
69	Ecuador	2.95	147	Iran	4.70
69	Gabon	2.95	147	Libya	4.70
69	Morocco	2.95	147	Somalia	4.70
69	Poland	2.95	147	Vietnam	4.70
74	Colombia	3.00	152	Bosnia	4.80
74	Ghana	3.00	153	Iraq	4.90
74	Lithuania	3.00	154	Cuba	5.00
77	Kenya	3.05	154	Laos	5.00
77	Slovak Republic	3.05	154	North Korea	5.00

Repressed

BANKING
Score: 5–Stable (very high level of restrictions)

Although some private banks exist in Iraq, most are under the indirect and sometimes even direct control of the government. The banking system is in complete disarray.

WAGE AND PRICE CONTROLS
Score: 5–Stable (very high level)

Rationing is the norm in Iraq. The government confiscates most durable goods from producers in order to ration them. The regime does not allow private merchants to establish their own prices. It also regularly executes businessman who profit from the high prices charged for scarce and smuggled goods.

PROPERTY RIGHTS
Score: 5–Stable (very low level of protection)

Saddam Hussein's dictatorship does not respect private property. The legal and judicial system is corrupt and inefficient, and the state regularly confiscates private property. According to the U.S. Department of State, "The judiciary is not independent and is subject to presidential influence."[1]

REGULATION
Score: 4–Stable (high level)

Iraq executes government officials convicted of corruption. The bureaucracy is large and inefficient, however, and corruption remains rampant, particularly among Saddam Hussein's inner circle. Officially sanctioned extortion is increasing as the government seeks to force merchants to turn a larger portion of their products over to the state.

BLACK MARKET
Score: 5–Stable (very high level of activity)

Smuggling of all kinds of products is rampant in Iraq. According to the U.S. Department of Commerce, "Many consumer goods and basic necessities, including medicine, are available on the black market at highly inflated prices."[2] In an attempt to crack down on black market activity, the government has resorted to execution. The Department of Commerce also reports that "Capital punishment has been decreed for those smuggling cars and trucks from the country and harsh penalties have been levied on currency traders and 'profiteers.'"[3]

NOTES
1. U.S. Department of State, "Iraq Country Report on Human Rights Practices for 1996," 1997.
2. U.S. Department of Commerce, *Country Commercial Guide, 1996.*
3. *Ibid.*

Ireland   2.00

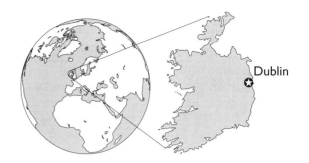

Dublin

1997 Score: **2.20**	1996 Score: **2.20**	1995 Score: **2.20**

Trade	2	Banking	2
Taxation	5	Wages and Prices	2
Government Intervention	2	Property Rights	1
Monetary Policy	1	Regulation	2
Foreign Investment	2	Black Market	1

Throughout much of its history, Ireland has been an agricultural country. Since the mid-1950s, however, it has become increasingly industrialized. Today, mining, manufacturing, construction, and public utilities account for about 37 percent of GDP; agriculture accounts for only 12 percent. Because of a largely open trade and investment environment during the late 1980s and early 1990s, Ireland became a base for the production of advanced consumer electronics. Many high-tech companies, both foreign and domestic, now operate in Ireland. Black market activity has been curtailed significantly over the past year. Parliamentary elections held in June 1997 brought to power a new coalition government of the Fianna Fail and the Progressive Democrats led by Prime Minister Bertie Ahern. The government has pledged to cut taxes. Ireland's overall score this year is 0.2 point better than it was last year.

TRADE POLICY
Score: 2–Stable (low level of protectionism)

As part of the European Union (EU), Ireland has an average tariff rate of 3.6 percent. It also maintains some of the EU's strictest plant and animal health standards, although there have been recent attempts to remove some of these restrictions, which often present barriers to the importation of such items as meat and vegetables.

TAXATION
Score–Income taxation: 5–Stable (very high tax rates)
Score–Corporate taxation: 4–Stable (high tax rates)
Final Taxation Score: 5–Stable (very high tax rates)

Ireland's top income tax rate is 48 percent, and the average income level is taxed at 27 percent. The top corporate income tax rate is 38 percent. Ireland also has a 40 percent capital gains tax and a 21 percent value-added tax. To attract high-tech companies, the government has instituted a top corporate tax of 10 percent on some companies involved in manufacturing, international finance, data processing, and research and development.

GOVERNMENT INTERVENTION IN THE ECONOMY
Score: 2–Stable (low level)

Government consumes about 16 percent of Ireland's GDP. It has sold most state-owned industries, including its iron and steel companies, which are among the world's largest. There are no prohibitions on private-sector involvement in any sector of the economy. State-owned industries are confined to such areas as energy production and telecommunications.

MONETARY POLICY
Score: 1–Stable (very low level of inflation)

Ireland's average annual rate of inflation from 1985 to 1995 was 2.5 percent. Inflation ran around 1.75 percent in 1996 and around 2 percent during the first half of 1997.

Mostly Free

1	Hong Kong	1.25		77	Zambia	3.05
2	Singapore	1.30		80	Mali	3.10
3	Bahrain	1.70		80	Mongolia	3.10
4	New Zealand	1.75		80	Slovenia	3.10
5	Switzerland	1.90		83	Honduras	3.15
5	United States	1.90		83	Papua New Guinea	3.15
7	Luxembourg	1.95		85	Djibouti	3.20
7	Taiwan	1.95		85	Fiji	3.20
7	United Kingdom	1.95		85	Pakistan	3.20
10	Bahamas	2.00		88	Algeria	3.25
10	Ireland	2.00		88	Guinea	3.25
12	Australia	2.05		88	Lebanon	3.25
12	Japan	2.05		88	Mexico	3.25
14	Belgium	2.10		88	Senegal	3.25
14	Canada	2.10		88	Tanzania	3.25
14	United Arab Emirates	2.10		94	Nigeria	3.30
17	Austria	2.15		94	Romania	3.30
17	Chile	2.15		96	Brazil	3.35
17	Estonia	2.15		96	Cambodia	3.35
20	Czech Republic	2.20		96	Egypt	3.35
20	Netherlands	2.20		96	Ivory Coast	3.35
22	Denmark	2.25		96	Madagascar	3.35
22	Finland	2.25		96	Moldova	3.35
24	Germany	2.30		102	Nepal	3.40
24	Iceland	2.30		103	Cape Verde	3.44
24	South Korea	2.30		104	Armenia	3.45
27	Norway	2.35		104	Dominican Republic	3.45
28	Kuwait	2.40		104	Russia	3.45
28	Malaysia	2.40		107	Burkina Faso	3.50
28	Panama	2.40		107	Cameroon	3.50
28	Thailand	2.40		107	Lesotho	3.50
32	El Salvador	2.45		107	Nicaragua	3.50
32	Sri Lanka	2.45		107	Venezuela	3.50
32	Sweden	2.45		112	Gambia	3.60
35	France	2.50		112	Guyana	3.60
35	Italy	2.50		114	Bulgaria	3.65
35	Spain	2.50		114	Georgia	3.65
38	Trinidad and Tobago	2.55		114	Malawi	3.65
39	Argentina	2.60		117	Ethiopia	3.70
39	Barbados	2.60		117	India	3.70
39	Cyprus	2.60		117	Niger	3.70
39	Jamaica	2.60		120	Albania	3.75
39	Portugal	2.60		120	Bangladesh	3.75
44	Bolivia	2.65		120	China (PRC)	3.75
44	Oman	2.65		120	Congo	3.75
44	Philippines	2.65		120	Croatia	3.75
47	Swaziland	2.70		125	Chad	3.80
47	Uruguay	2.70		125	Mauritania	3.80
49	Botswana	2.75		125	Ukraine	3.80
49	Jordan	2.75		128	Sierra Leone	3.85
49	Namibia	2.75		129	Burundi	3.90
49	Tunisia	2.75		129	Suriname	3.90
53	Belize	2.80		129	Zimbabwe	3.90
53	Costa Rica	2.80		132	Haiti	4.00
53	Guatemala	2.80		132	Kyrgyzstan	4.00
53	Israel	2.80		132	Syria	4.00
53	Peru	2.80		135	Belarus	4.05
53	Saudi Arabia	2.80		136	Kazakstan	4.10
53	Turkey	2.80		136	Mozambique	4.10
53	Uganda	2.80		136	Yemen	4.10
53	Western Samoa	2.80		139	Sudan	4.20
62	Indonesia	2.85		140	Myanmar	4.30
62	Latvia	2.85		140	Rwanda	4.30
62	Malta	2.85		142	Angola	4.35
62	Paraguay	2.85		143	Azerbaijan	4.40
66	Greece	2.90		143	Tajikistan	4.40
66	Hungary	2.90		145	Turkmenistan	4.50
66	South Africa	2.90		146	Uzbekistan	4.55
69	Benin	2.95		147	Congo/Zaire	4.70
69	Ecuador	2.95		147	Iran	4.70
69	Gabon	2.95		147	Libya	4.70
69	Morocco	2.95		147	Somalia	4.70
69	Poland	2.95		147	Vietnam	4.70
74	Colombia	3.00		152	Bosnia	4.80
74	Ghana	3.00		153	Iraq	4.90
74	Lithuania	3.00		154	Cuba	5.00
77	Kenya	3.05		154	Laos	5.00
77	Slovak Republic	3.05		154	North Korea	5.00

CAPITAL FLOWS AND FOREIGN INVESTMENT
Score: 2–Stable (low barriers)

Ireland welcomes foreign investment and offers such incentives as a guaranteed 10 percent maximum tax on investment profits for manufacturing companies. Foreigners may not invest, however, in sugar production, the production of electricity, or air and rail transport companies.

BANKING
Score: 2–Stable (low level of restrictions)

Ireland has a highly competitive and advanced banking and financial system. Foreign banks are welcome and are treated the same as domestic banks.

WAGE AND PRICE CONTROLS
Score: 2–Stable (low level)

Ireland has no price controls but does maintain a minimum wage.

PROPERTY RIGHTS
Score: 1–Stable (very high level of protection)

Property expropriation is very unlikely in Ireland. Property receives sufficient protection from the court system.

REGULATION
Score: 2–Stable (low level)

Regulations are applied uniformly in Ireland and are not substantially burdensome. The level of regulation has been increasing, however. The environmental movement is putting a great strain on business, especially on manufacturing companies, which must comply with stringent air quality laws. Some occupational health and safety laws also are burdensome.

BLACK MARKET
Score: 1+ (very low level of activity)

The level of black market activity in Ireland is minimal, although there is some piracy of computer software. Recently, the government curtailed the black market through a crackdown. Ireland's black market score is, therefore, two points better this year.

Israel   2.80

1997 Score: **2.80**	1996 Score: **2.90**	1995 Score: **3.10**

Trade	2	Banking	3
Taxation	5	Wages and Prices	2
Government Intervention	4	Property Rights	2
Monetary Policy	3	Regulation	2
Foreign Investment	1	Black Market	4

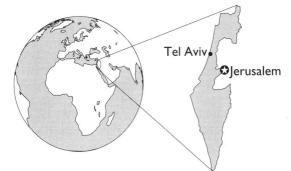

Tel Aviv
Jerusalem

Since gaining independence in 1948, Israel technically has been at war with most of its Arab neighbors. This has imposed a heavy defense burden that has been lightened only slightly by peace treaties with Egypt in 1979 and Jordan in 1994. Because of limited natural resources, Israel depends on imports of oil, grain, and raw materials. It usually posts current account deficits, which are caused by large transfer payments from abroad, as well as by foreign loans and foreign aid. A free trade area formed with the United States in 1985 has increased trade between the two countries. Israel's economy has a large state-controlled sector. Prime Minister Benjamin Netanyahu, elected in May 1996, called for economic liberalization and a gradual reduction of U.S. foreign aid. (Israel is the foremost recipient of U.S. foreign aid.) His economic reform program has proceeded at a slow pace, however.

TRADE POLICY
Score: 2–Stable (low level of protectionism)

Israel's average tariff rate is less than 2 percent. Nontariff barriers include import bans, strict product standards, and import quotas.

TAXATION
Score–Income taxation: 5–Stable (very high tax rates)
Score–Corporate taxation: 4–Stable (high tax rates)
Final Taxation Score: 5–Stable (very high tax rates)

Israel's top income tax level is 50 percent; the average income level is taxed at 30 percent. The top corporate tax rate is over 36 percent. Israel also has a 36 percent capital gains tax and a 17 percent value-added tax.

GOVERNMENT INTERVENTION IN THE ECONOMY
Score: 4–Stable (high level)

Government consumes 29.2 percent of Israel's GDP, primarily because of military expenditures and social welfare programs. According to the Economist Intelligence Unit, "The state bureaucracy and the public sector continue to play a considerable role in the Israeli economy."[1] The government continues to own large portions of the utilities, chemicals, airlines, and shipyard industries.

MONETARY POLICY
Score: 3–Stable (moderate level of inflation)

Israel's average annual rate of inflation from 1985 to 1995 was 17.1 percent. In 1996, consumer price inflation was 10.6 percent.

CAPITAL FLOWS AND FOREIGN INVESTMENT
Score: 1–Stable (very low barriers)

There are no significant barriers to foreign investment in Israel. The government permits 100 percent foreign ownership of businesses and offers such investment incentives as tax holidays.

1	Hong Kong	1.25	77	Zambia	3.05
2	Singapore	1.30	80	Mali	3.10
3	Bahrain	1.70	80	Mongolia	3.10
4	New Zealand	1.75	80	Slovenia	3.10
5	Switzerland	1.90	83	Honduras	3.15
5	United States	1.90	83	Papua New Guinea	3.15
7	Luxembourg	1.95	85	Djibouti	3.20
7	Taiwan	1.95	85	Fiji	3.20
7	United Kingdom	1.95	85	Pakistan	3.20
10	Bahamas	2.00	88	Algeria	3.25
10	Ireland	2.00	88	Guinea	3.25
12	Australia	2.05	88	Lebanon	3.25
12	Japan	2.05	88	Mexico	3.25
14	Belgium	2.10	88	Senegal	3.25
14	Canada	2.10	88	Tanzania	3.25
14	United Arab Emirates	2.10	94	Nigeria	3.30
17	Austria	2.15	94	Romania	3.30
17	Chile	2.15	96	Brazil	3.35
17	Estonia	2.15	96	Cambodia	3.35
20	Czech Republic	2.20	96	Egypt	3.35
20	Netherlands	2.20	96	Ivory Coast	3.35
22	Denmark	2.25	96	Madagascar	3.35
22	Finland	2.25	96	Moldova	3.35
24	Germany	2.30	102	Nepal	3.40
24	Iceland	2.30	103	Cape Verde	3.44
24	South Korea	2.30	104	Armenia	3.45
27	Norway	2.35	104	Dominican Republic	3.45
28	Kuwait	2.40	104	Russia	3.45
28	Malaysia	2.40	107	Burkina Faso	3.50
28	Panama	2.40	107	Cameroon	3.50
28	Thailand	2.40	107	Lesotho	3.50
32	El Salvador	2.45	107	Nicaragua	3.50
32	Sri Lanka	2.45	107	Venezuela	3.50
32	Sweden	2.45	112	Gambia	3.60
35	France	2.50	112	Guyana	3.60
35	Italy	2.50	114	Bulgaria	3.65
35	Spain	2.50	114	Georgia	3.65
38	Trinidad and Tobago	2.55	114	Malawi	3.65
39	Argentina	2.60	117	Ethiopia	3.70
39	Barbados	2.60	117	India	3.70
39	Cyprus	2.60	117	Niger	3.70
39	Jamaica	2.60	120	Albania	3.75
39	Portugal	2.60	120	Bangladesh	3.75
44	Bolivia	2.65	120	China (PRC)	3.75
44	Oman	2.65	120	Congo	3.75
44	Philippines	2.65	120	Croatia	3.75
47	Swaziland	2.70	125	Chad	3.80
47	Uruguay	2.70	125	Mauritania	3.80
49	Botswana	2.75	125	Ukraine	3.80
49	Jordan	2.75	128	Sierra Leone	3.85
49	Namibia	2.75	129	Burundi	3.90
49	Tunisia	2.75	129	Suriname	3.90
53	Belize	2.80	129	Zimbabwe	3.90
53	Costa Rica	2.80	132	Haiti	4.00
53	Guatemala	2.80	132	Kyrgyzstan	4.00
53	Israel	2.80	132	Syria	4.00
53	Peru	2.80	135	Belarus	4.05
53	Saudi Arabia	2.80	136	Kazakstan	4.10
53	Turkey	2.80	136	Mozambique	4.10
53	Uganda	2.80	136	Yemen	4.10
53	Western Samoa	2.80	139	Sudan	4.20
62	Indonesia	2.85	140	Myanmar	4.30
62	Latvia	2.85	140	Rwanda	4.30
62	Malta	2.85	142	Angola	4.35
62	Paraguay	2.85	143	Azerbaijan	4.40
66	Greece	2.90	143	Tajikistan	4.40
66	Hungary	2.90	145	Turkmenistan	4.50
66	South Africa	2.90	146	Uzbekistan	4.55
69	Benin	2.95	147	Congo/Zaire	4.70
69	Ecuador	2.95	147	Iran	4.70
69	Gabon	2.95	147	Libya	4.70
69	Morocco	2.95	147	Somalia	4.70
69	Poland	2.95	147	Vietnam	4.70
74	Colombia	3.00	152	Bosnia	4.80
74	Ghana	3.00	153	Iraq	4.90
74	Lithuania	3.00	154	Cuba	5.00
77	Kenya	3.05	154	Laos	5.00
77	Slovak Republic	3.05	154	North Korea	5.00

Mostly Free

BANKING
Score: 3–Stable (moderate level of restrictions)

Israel's government continues to sell shares of state-owned banks, but these banks remain highly centralized. A significant portion of the industry is manipulated by the government through regulations and controls. Banks are restricted from investing in real estate, insurance, and some other business activities.

WAGE AND PRICE CONTROLS
Score: 2–Stable (low level)

Although most price controls have been lifted, they remain in effect in a few areas, such as transportation. Israel has a minimum wage.

PROPERTY RIGHTS
Score: 2–Stable (high level of protection)

Expropriation of property is unlikely. "Israel has a modern legal system based on mandate and British case law," reports the U.S. Department of Commerce. "Effective means exist for enforcing property and contractual rights. Courts are independent; there is no government interference in the court system."[2]

REGULATION
Score: 2–Stable (low level)

Despite the central government's large role in the economy, Israel has an efficient bureaucracy that encourages business. Regulations are applied evenly and are not significantly burdensome.

BLACK MARKET
Score: 4–Stable (high level of activity)

Although the size of Israel's black market is shrinking, the level of nontariff barriers still encourages fairly extensive smuggling of some consumer goods. Smuggling of consumer electronics equipment, for example, is diminishing, but the black market in pirated videos and other forms of entertainment is substantial. According to the U.S. Department of State, "Cable, television, video, and software piracy is common in Israel. Israel currently has an antiquated copyright law which together with weak enforcement, has led to piracy in these industries."[3] Illegal showings of pirated U.S. movies and television programs and black market versions of U.S. music continue to flourish.

NOTES
1. Economist Intelligence Unit, *ILT Country Reports, Israel,* 1997.
2. U.S. Department of Commerce, *Country Commercial Guide,* 1997.
3. U.S. Department of State, *Country Reports on Economic Policy and Trade Practices,* 1997, p. 334.

Italy 2.50

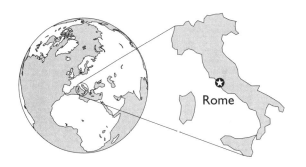

1997 Score: **2.60**	1996 Score: **2.70**	1995 Score: **2.50**

Trade	2	Banking	2
Taxation	5	Wages and Prices	2
Government Intervention	3	Property Rights	2
Monetary Policy	2	Regulation	3
Foreign Investment	2	Black Market	2

Italy was unified under a constitutional monarchy in March 1861. After World War I, it became a fascist dictatorship, but became a republic after World War II. A founding member of the European Union (EU), Italy is the world's fifth-largest economy and is one of the Group of Seven (G–7) advanced industrialized countries. Despite its large economy, Italy has pursued state-interventionist economic policies that have led to periods of deep economic recession and diminished economic freedom. Parliamentary elections in April 1996 failed to establish a majority in both chambers for any one party or coalition. As a result, Prime Minister Romano Prodi of the Olive Tree coalition has had difficulty achieving economic liberalization, although there has been some progress. Italy recently privatized many state-owned banks and reduced price controls. Black market activity, however, is on the rise. Italy has stamped out some corruption in the government procurement sector and in the customs bureau. As a result, its overall score is 0.1 point better this year.

Trade Policy
Score: 2+ (low level of protectionism)

As a member of the EU, Italy has an average tariff rate of 3.6 percent. Customs procedures, however, can be both strict and arbitrary, particularly with respect to agricultural goods, and this affects imports from all non-EU countries. "In Italy," reports the U.S. Department of State, "often non-transparent government procurement practices and previous problems with corruption have created obstacles to firms."[1] The State Department also reports that "rulings by individual local customs authorities can be arbitrary or incorrect, resulting in denial or delays of entry of U.S. exports into the country."[2] Recently, Italy began to crack down on corruption within the government procurement sector and in customs, making it easier for imports to enter the country. As a result, its trade score is one point better this year.

Taxation
Score–Income taxation: 5–Stable (very high tax rates)
Score–Corporate taxation: 4–Stable (high tax rates)
Final Taxation Score: 5–Stable (very high tax rates)

Italy's top income tax rate is 51 percent; the average income level is taxed at 34 percent. The top corporate income tax rate is 37 percent. Italy also has a 37 percent capital gains tax and a 19 percent value-added tax.[3]

Government Intervention in the Economy
Score: 3–Stable (moderate level)

Government consumes about 16.6 percent of Italy's GDP and is responsible for about 40 percent of all economic output. According to the U.S. Department of State, "The state plays an active role in the economy, not only in the formulation of macroeconomic policy and regulations, but also through state ownership of a number of large industrial and financial concerns."[4] The government owns the telephone utility, Telecom Italia, as well as energy utilities and transportation companies.

Mostly Free

1	Hong Kong	1.25	77	Zambia	3.05
2	Singapore	1.30	80	Mali	3.10
3	Bahrain	1.70	80	Mongolia	3.10
4	New Zealand	1.75	80	Slovenia	3.10
5	Switzerland	1.90	83	Honduras	3.15
5	United States	1.90	83	Papua New Guinea	3.15
7	Luxembourg	1.95	85	Djibouti	3.20
7	Taiwan	1.95	85	Fiji	3.20
7	United Kingdom	1.95	85	Pakistan	3.20
10	Bahamas	2.00	88	Algeria	3.25
10	Ireland	2.00	88	Guinea	3.25
12	Australia	2.05	88	Lebanon	3.25
12	Japan	2.05	88	Mexico	3.25
14	Belgium	2.10	88	Senegal	3.25
14	Canada	2.10	88	Tanzania	3.25
14	United Arab Emirates	2.10	94	Nigeria	3.30
17	Austria	2.15	94	Romania	3.30
17	Chile	2.15	96	Brazil	3.35
17	Estonia	2.15	96	Cambodia	3.35
20	Czech Republic	2.20	96	Egypt	3.35
20	Netherlands	2.20	96	Ivory Coast	3.35
22	Denmark	2.25	96	Madagascar	3.35
22	Finland	2.25	96	Moldova	3.35
24	Germany	2.30	102	Nepal	3.40
24	Iceland	2.30	103	Cape Verde	3.44
24	South Korea	2.30	104	Armenia	3.45
27	Norway	2.35	104	Dominican Republic	3.45
28	Kuwait	2.40	104	Russia	3.45
28	Malaysia	2.40	107	Burkina Faso	3.50
28	Panama	2.40	107	Cameroon	3.50
28	Thailand	2.40	107	Lesotho	3.50
32	El Salvador	2.45	107	Nicaragua	3.50
32	Sri Lanka	2.45	107	Venezuela	3.50
32	Sweden	2.45	112	Gambia	3.60
35	France	2.50	112	Guyana	3.60
35	Italy	2.50	114	Bulgaria	3.65
35	Spain	2.50	114	Georgia	3.65
38	Trinidad and Tobago	2.55	114	Malawi	3.65
39	Argentina	2.60	117	Ethiopia	3.70
39	Barbados	2.60	117	India	3.70
39	Cyprus	2.60	117	Niger	3.70
39	Jamaica	2.60	120	Albania	3.75
39	Portugal	2.60	120	Bangladesh	3.75
44	Bolivia	2.65	120	China (PRC)	3.75
44	Oman	2.65	120	Congo	3.75
44	Philippines	2.65	120	Croatia	3.75
47	Swaziland	2.70	125	Chad	3.80
47	Uruguay	2.70	125	Mauritania	3.80
49	Botswana	2.75	125	Ukraine	3.80
49	Jordan	2.75	128	Sierra Leone	3.85
49	Namibia	2.75	129	Burundi	3.90
49	Tunisia	2.75	129	Suriname	3.90
53	Belize	2.80	129	Zimbabwe	3.90
53	Costa Rica	2.80	132	Haiti	4.00
53	Guatemala	2.80	132	Kyrgyzstan	4.00
53	Israel	2.80	132	Syria	4.00
53	Peru	2.80	135	Belarus	4.05
53	Saudi Arabia	2.80	136	Kazakstan	4.10
53	Turkey	2.80	136	Mozambique	4.10
53	Uganda	2.80	136	Yemen	4.10
53	Western Samoa	2.80	139	Sudan	4.20
62	Indonesia	2.85	140	Myanmar	4.30
62	Latvia	2.85	140	Rwanda	4.30
62	Malta	2.85	142	Angola	4.35
62	Paraguay	2.85	143	Azerbaijan	4.40
66	Greece	2.90	143	Tajikistan	4.40
66	Hungary	2.90	145	Turkmenistan	4.50
66	South Africa	2.90	146	Uzbekistan	4.55
69	Benin	2.95	147	Congo/Zaire	4.70
69	Ecuador	2.95	147	Iran	4.70
69	Gabon	2.95	147	Libya	4.70
69	Morocco	2.95	147	Somalia	4.70
69	Poland	2.95	147	Vietnam	4.70
74	Colombia	3.00	152	Bosnia	4.80
74	Ghana	3.00	153	Iraq	4.90
74	Lithuania	3.00	154	Cuba	5.00
77	Kenya	3.05	154	Laos	5.00
77	Slovak Republic	3.05	154	North Korea	5.00

MONETARY POLICY
Score: 2–Stable (low level)

Italy's average annual rate of inflation from 1985 to 1995 was 6.0 percent. Inflation was 3.9 percent in 1996.

CAPITAL FLOWS AND FOREIGN INVESTMENT
Score: 2–Stable (low barriers)

As part of the EU, Italy generally welcomes foreign investment, mainly because of its importance in bringing new technologies into ailing industries. There are a few restrictions and bans on foreign investment in domestic air transport, aircraft manufacturing, and state monopolies. Industrial projects require a multitude of approvals and permits. Nevertheless, overall barriers to foreign investment are low by global standards.

BANKING
Score: 2–Stable (low level of restrictions)

Banks face some government restrictions and regulations, although Italy recently underwent some financial reform, including the privatization of several large banks.

WAGE AND PRICE CONTROLS
Score: 2–Stable (low level)

Although few direct price controls exist, the government does affect prices through state-owned and state-subsidized industries for which pricing policies are not determined by market forces. The government has abolished many of its price controls on pharmaceuticals and other products; and because many businesses have been privatized, it has much less control over prices now than it had a few years ago. Thus, Italy's wage and price controls today are low by global standards.

PROPERTY RIGHTS
Score: 2–Stable (high level of protection)

Property is safe from arbitrary government expropriation. Italy has an advanced legal system to protect property, although there are claims of corruption.

REGULATION
Score: 3–Stable (moderate level)

Despite recent government initiatives to eliminate cumbersome regulations that can be open to corruption, Italy's political crisis has led to the return of corruption. Although it is easy to open businesses, and bribes are no longer necessary, cumbersome laws regarding workers rights undermine the competitiveness of many Italian companies.

BLACK MARKET
Score: 2–Stable (low level of activity)

Italy's organized criminals are involved heavily in drugs and guns, but black market activity in smuggling, transportation services, and the construction industries is limited, and the government is making progress in stamping out some organized crime.[5] Italy recently enacted severe penalties for engaging in the piracy of protected intellectual property. Pirated computer software represented some 86 percent of the market in 1992; today, it represents less than 50 percent. Pirated video sales represent some 40 percent of the market. Compared with the size of Italy's economy, however, these activities are negligible.

NOTES

1. U.S. Department of State, *Country Reports on Economic Policy and Trade Practices,* 1997, p. 141.
2. *Ibid.*
3. It is important to point out that many Italians probably avoid paying taxes altogether.
4. U.S. Department of State, *Country Reports on Economic Policy and Trade Practices,* 1997, p. 139.
5. The methodology for this factor considers only black market activity that results from government restrictions on free enterprise. For a detailed explanation, see Chapter 4.

Ivory Coast   3.35

1997 Score: **3.35**		1996 Score: **3.25**		1995 Score: **3.25**

Trade	5	Banking	3
Taxation	3.5	Wages and Prices	3
Government Intervention	3	Property Rights	4
Monetary Policy	1	Regulation	4
Foreign Investment	3	Black Market	4

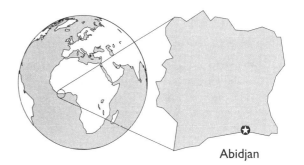

Abidjan

The Ivory Coast became a French colony in 1893 and was part of the Federation of French West Africa from 1904 to 1958. It gained its independence from France in 1960, although its cultural, economic, and military ties to Paris remain very close. Until his death in 1993, President Felix Houphouet-Boigny ruled the country with little regard for democracy. His successor, Henri Konan Bédié, has made modest strides in promoting political and economic reforms, which also are being pushed by foreign aid donors. The Ivory Coast embraced socialism upon gaining independence and remained committed to socialist economic policies into the 1990s. Growth in GDP averaged only 0.8 percent annually from 1990 to 1994, although it was strong in 1995 and 1996 (close to 7 percent) because of market reforms and a 1994 economy devaluation.

TRADE POLICY
Score: 5–Stable (very high level of protectionism)

The Ivory Coast has been reducing tariffs to some extent, but they remain high. The average tariff rate is 25.5 percent,[1] and there is a quota system for some goods. The government has a monopoly on rice imports and bans other imports, such as poultry products. There is extensive customs fraud.

TAXATION
Score–Income taxation: 3–Stable (moderate tax rates)
Score–Corporate taxation: 3–Stable (moderate tax rates)
Final Taxation Score: 3.5–Stable (high tax rates)

Taxes in the Ivory Coast are moderately high. The top income tax rate is 60 percent, and the average income is taxed at 10 percent. The top corporate income tax level is 35 percent. The Ivory Coast also has a 35 percent capital gains tax, a 20 percent value-added tax, and a turnover tax of from 10 percent to 25 percent on services and interest provided by banks and financial companies.

GOVERNMENT INTERVENTION IN THE ECONOMY
Score: 3–Stable (moderate level)

Government consumes 14.8 percent of the Ivory Coast's GDP, which is generated primarily by a significant state-owned sector. There has been some progress in privatization, including the sale of the country's largest rubber producer to a Belgian company.

MONETARY POLICY
Score: 1–Stable (very low level of inflation)

The Ivory Coast's average annual rate of inflation from 1985 to 1995 was 2.1 percent. In 1996, the rate of inflation was about 4.5 percent.

1	Hong Kong	1.25	77	Zambia	3.05
2	Singapore	1.30	80	Mali	3.10
3	Bahrain	1.70	80	Mongolia	3.10
4	New Zealand	1.75	80	Slovenia	3.10
5	Switzerland	1.90	83	Honduras	3.15
5	United States	1.90	83	Papua New Guinea	3.15
7	Luxembourg	1.95	85	Djibouti	3.20
7	Taiwan	1.95	85	Fiji	3.20
7	United Kingdom	1.95	85	Pakistan	3.20
10	Bahamas	2.00	88	Algeria	3.25
10	Ireland	2.00	88	Guinea	3.25
12	Australia	2.05	88	Lebanon	3.25
12	Japan	2.05	88	Mexico	3.25
14	Belgium	2.10	88	Senegal	3.25
14	Canada	2.10	88	Tanzania	3.25
14	United Arab Emirates	2.10	94	Nigeria	3.30
17	Austria	2.15	94	Romania	3.30
17	Chile	2.15	96	Brazil	3.35
17	Estonia	2.15	96	Cambodia	3.35
20	Czech Republic	2.20	96	Egypt	3.35
20	Netherlands	2.20	96	Ivory Coast	3.35
22	Denmark	2.25	96	Madagascar	3.35
22	Finland	2.25	96	Moldova	3.35
24	Germany	2.30	102	Nepal	3.40
24	Iceland	2.30	103	Cape Verde	3.44
24	South Korea	2.30	104	Armenia	3.45
27	Norway	2.35	104	Dominican Republic	3.45
28	Kuwait	2.40	104	Russia	3.45
28	Malaysia	2.40	107	Burkina Faso	3.50
28	Panama	2.40	107	Cameroon	3.50
28	Thailand	2.40	107	Lesotho	3.50
32	El Salvador	2.45	107	Nicaragua	3.50
32	Sri Lanka	2.45	107	Venezuela	3.50
32	Sweden	2.45	112	Gambia	3.60
35	France	2.50	112	Guyana	3.60
35	Italy	2.50	114	Bulgaria	3.65
35	Spain	2.50	114	Georgia	3.65
38	Trinidad and Tobago	2.55	114	Malawi	3.65
39	Argentina	2.60	117	Ethiopia	3.70
39	Barbados	2.60	117	India	3.70
39	Cyprus	2.60	117	Niger	3.70
39	Jamaica	2.60	120	Albania	3.75
39	Portugal	2.60	120	Bangladesh	3.75
44	Bolivia	2.65	120	China (PRC)	3.75
44	Oman	2.65	120	Congo	3.75
44	Philippines	2.65	120	Croatia	3.75
47	Swaziland	2.70	125	Chad	3.80
47	Uruguay	2.70	125	Mauritania	3.80
49	Botswana	2.75	125	Ukraine	3.80
49	Jordan	2.75	128	Sierra Leone	3.85
49	Namibia	2.75	129	Burundi	3.90
49	Tunisia	2.75	129	Suriname	3.90
53	Belize	2.80	129	Zimbabwe	3.90
53	Costa Rica	2.80	132	Haiti	4.00
53	Guatemala	2.80	132	Kyrgyzstan	4.00
53	Israel	2.80	132	Syria	4.00
53	Peru	2.80	135	Belarus	4.05
53	Saudi Arabia	2.80	136	Kazakstan	4.10
53	Turkey	2.80	136	Mozambique	4.10
53	Uganda	2.80	136	Yemen	4.10
53	Western Samoa	2.80	139	Sudan	4.20
62	Indonesia	2.85	140	Myanmar	4.30
62	Latvia	2.85	140	Rwanda	4.30
62	Malta	2.85	142	Angola	4.35
62	Paraguay	2.85	143	Azerbaijan	4.40
66	Greece	2.90	143	Tajikistan	4.40
66	Hungary	2.90	145	Turkmenistan	4.50
66	South Africa	2.90	146	Uzbekistan	4.55
69	Benin	2.95	147	Congo/Zaire	4.70
69	Ecuador	2.95	147	Iran	4.70
69	Gabon	2.95	147	Libya	4.70
69	Morocco	2.95	147	Somalia	4.70
69	Poland	2.95	147	Vietnam	4.70
74	Colombia	3.00	152	Bosnia	4.80
74	Ghana	3.00	153	Iraq	4.90
74	Lithuania	3.00	154	Cuba	5.00
77	Kenya	3.05	154	Laos	5.00
77	Slovak Republic	3.05	154	North Korea	5.00

Mostly Unfree

CAPITAL FLOWS AND FOREIGN INVESTMENT
Score: 3–Stable (moderate barriers)

The Ivory Coast recently developed a foreign investment code. Although there is little discrimination between domestic and foreign investors, proposals for total foreign ownership of assets are not approved in all cases, and some industries are off-limits to private investors. Foreign investors remain wary because of crime, corruption, an inefficient and abusive bureaucracy, and unstable legal protections.

BANKING
Score: 3–Stable (moderate level of restrictions)

The Ivory Coast is a member of the Communaute Financiere Africaine (CFA), a financial grouping of several African countries that base the value of their currency on the French franc, and its government exercises only moderate control of banking institutions, although it still owns shares in some banks. Ten commercial banks operate in the Ivory Coast.

WAGE AND PRICE CONTROLS
Score: 3–Stable (moderate level)

The government has made some progress toward liberalizing prices in the Ivory Coast. In 1994, however, price controls were imposed on 30 goods and services for three months in the wake of the CFA's devaluation of the franc.[2] State dominance of several sectors of the economy reduces price competition; the state both sets the producer price and engages in the marketing of coffee and cocoa exports. There also are price controls on wheat and rice. The Ivory Coast has a minimum wage law.

PROPERTY RIGHTS
Score: 4–Stable (low level of protection)

The Ivory Coast's court system, although much more efficient than in the past, is unable to protect private property adequately. According to the U.S. Department of Commerce, "Enforcement of contract rights can be a time consuming and expensive process. Not all cases are decided quickly, and some do not appear to be judged on their legal or contractual merits. This has led to a widely-held view within the business community that there are elements within the judiciary which can be corrupted."[3] Even when corruption is not present, the courts often disregard employment contracts and rule against businesses, regardless of the legal merits of the case. Thus, businesses often are at a legal disadvantage when being sued by their employees. According to the U.S. Department of Commerce, "The Ivorian courts have historically been viewed as favoring the employee in labor disputes."[4]

REGULATION
Score: 4–Stable (high level)

The Ivory Coast's bureaucracy is cumbersome, corrupt, and subject to political manipulation. Individuals sometimes find it difficult to complete the paperwork required to open a business. The government has tried—with very modest success—to reduce bureaucratic barriers by making it easier for businesses to conform to government regulations, but the private sector remains highly regulated. Labor legislation is more onerous than in many developed countries, and foreign companies are under increasing informal pressure to use local labor. Corruption also remains a problem. "Corruption is widely assumed to exist at all branches of the government," reports the U.S. Department of Commerce.[5]

BLACK MARKET
Score: 4–Stable (high level of activity)

The Ivory Coast's high trade barriers make the smuggling of many items, primarily consumer goods, a lucrative business. There is a growing black market in food aid, in addition to substantial activity in such pirated intellectual property as videos and computer software. According to the U.S. Department of Commerce, "Though in theory prohibited, counterfeit clothing, textiles, footwear, watches, and audio and video tapes can be found, particularly among street vendors and in local markets."[6]

NOTES

1. Based on total taxes on international trade as a percentage of total imports.
2. The CFA franc, a form of common currency, is used by African member countries that have agreed to peg their national currencies to a set value of the French franc.
3. U.S. Department of Commerce, *Country Commercial Guide,* 1997.
4. *Ibid.*
5. *Ibid.*
6. *Ibid.*

Jamaica   2.60

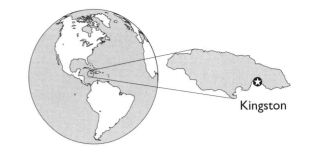

| 1997 Score: **2.60** | 1996 Score: **2.70** | 1995 Score: **2.80** |

Trade	2	Banking	2
Taxation	3	Wages and Prices	3
Government Intervention	2	Property Rights	2
Monetary Policy	4	Regulation	3
Foreign Investment	2	Black Market	3

Kingston

The Caribbean island country of Jamaica seldom adopts free-market approaches to economic policy. During the 1970s and part of the 1980s, the government was the primary player in the economy, and entrepreneurship was not encouraged. The country was well on its way toward developing a socialist economy. Until recently, the Jamaican economy was characterized by a high level of protectionism and government intervention. The government has opened the economy to foreign investments in the past several years, however, and has reduced both taxes and tariffs.

TRADE POLICY
Score: 2–Stable (low level of protectionism)

Jamaica's tariff rates range from 0 percent to 30 percent. The average tariff rate is 9 percent. There are no significant nontariff barriers. According to the U.S. Department of Commerce, "There have been some improvements as a result of the government of Jamaica's efforts to streamline customs procedures. In order to facilitate the movement of goods, the government simplified the documentation and clearance requirements for exporters. Computerization of the entire system is in progress."[1]

TAXATION
Score–Income taxation: 2–Stable (low tax rates)
Score–Corporate taxation: 3–Stable (moderate tax rates)
Final Taxation Score: 3–Stable (moderate tax rates)

Jamaica's top marginal income tax rate is 25 percent; the average income level also is taxed at 25 percent. The top marginal corporate tax rate is 33.33 percent. Jamaica also has a consumption tax of up to 15 percent.

GOVERNMENT INTERVENTION IN THE ECONOMY
Score: 2–Stable (low level)

Government consumes 12.5 percent of Jamaica's GDP, down from around 20 percent in 1980. In an effort to limit budget deficits and stimulate the private sector, the government has undertaken an aggressive program of privatization; for example, it is trying to privatize the railway system. This effort stalled recently when the government removed Jamaica's power company from the program because of opposition from workers and employees.[2]

MONETARY POLICY
Score: 4–Stable (high level of inflation)

Jamaica's average annual rate of inflation between 1985 and 1995 was 28.3 percent. The rate of inflation fell to 15.7 percent in 1996.

1	Hong Kong	1.25
2	Singapore	1.30
3	Bahrain	1.70
4	New Zealand	1.75
5	Switzerland	1.90
5	United States	1.90
7	Luxembourg	1.95
7	Taiwan	1.95
7	United Kingdom	1.95
10	Bahamas	2.00
10	Ireland	2.00
12	Australia	2.05
12	Japan	2.05
14	Belgium	2.10
14	Canada	2.10
14	United Arab Emirates	2.10
17	Austria	2.15
17	Chile	2.15
17	Estonia	2.15
20	Czech Republic	2.20
20	Netherlands	2.20
22	Denmark	2.25
22	Finland	2.25
24	Germany	2.30
24	Iceland	2.30
24	South Korea	2.30
27	Norway	2.35
28	Kuwait	2.40
28	Malaysia	2.40
28	Panama	2.40
28	Thailand	2.40
32	El Salvador	2.45
32	Sri Lanka	2.45
32	Sweden	2.45
35	France	2.50
35	Italy	2.50
35	Spain	2.50
38	Trinidad and Tobago	2.55
39	Argentina	2.60
39	Barbados	2.60
39	Cyprus	2.60
39	Jamaica	2.60
39	Portugal	2.60
44	Bolivia	2.65
44	Oman	2.65
44	Philippines	2.65
47	Swaziland	2.70
47	Uruguay	2.70
49	Botswana	2.75
49	Jordan	2.75
49	Namibia	2.75
49	Tunisia	2.75
53	Belize	2.80
53	Costa Rica	2.80
53	Guatemala	2.80
53	Israel	2.80
53	Peru	2.80
53	Saudi Arabia	2.80
53	Turkey	2.80
53	Uganda	2.80
53	Western Samoa	2.80
62	Indonesia	2.85
62	Latvia	2.85
62	Malta	2.85
62	Paraguay	2.85
66	Greece	2.90
66	Hungary	2.90
66	South Africa	2.90
69	Benin	2.95
69	Ecuador	2.95
69	Gabon	2.95
69	Morocco	2.95
69	Poland	2.95
74	Colombia	3.00
74	Ghana	3.00
74	Lithuania	3.00
77	Kenya	3.05
77	Slovak Republic	3.05

Mostly Free

77	Zambia	3.05
80	Mali	3.10
80	Mongolia	3.10
80	Slovenia	3.10
83	Honduras	3.15
83	Papua New Guinea	3.15
85	Djibouti	3.20
85	Fiji	3.20
85	Pakistan	3.20
88	Algeria	3.25
88	Guinea	3.25
88	Lebanon	3.25
88	Mexico	3.25
88	Senegal	3.25
88	Tanzania	3.25
94	Nigeria	3.30
94	Romania	3.30
96	Brazil	3.35
96	Cambodia	3.35
96	Egypt	3.35
96	Ivory Coast	3.35
96	Madagascar	3.35
96	Moldova	3.35
102	Nepal	3.40
103	Cape Verde	3.44
104	Armenia	3.45
104	Dominican Republic	3.45
104	Russia	3.45
107	Burkina Faso	3.50
107	Cameroon	3.50
107	Lesotho	3.50
107	Nicaragua	3.50
107	Venezuela	3.50
112	Gambia	3.60
112	Guyana	3.60
114	Bulgaria	3.65
114	Georgia	3.65
114	Malawi	3.65
117	Ethiopia	3.70
117	India	3.70
117	Niger	3.70
120	Albania	3.75
120	Bangladesh	3.75
120	China (PRC)	3.75
120	Congo	3.75
120	Croatia	3.75
125	Chad	3.80
125	Mauritania	3.80
125	Ukraine	3.80
128	Sierra Leone	3.85
129	Burundi	3.90
129	Suriname	3.90
129	Zimbabwe	3.90
132	Haiti	4.00
132	Kyrgyzstan	4.00
132	Syria	4.00
135	Belarus	4.05
136	Kazakstan	4.10
136	Mozambique	4.10
136	Yemen	4.10
139	Sudan	4.20
140	Myanmar	4.30
140	Rwanda	4.30
142	Angola	4.35
143	Azerbaijan	4.40
143	Tajikistan	4.40
145	Turkmenistan	4.50
146	Uzbekistan	4.55
147	Congo/Zaire	4.70
147	Iran	4.70
147	Libya	4.70
147	Somalia	4.70
147	Vietnam	4.70
152	Bosnia	4.80
153	Iraq	4.90
154	Cuba	5.00
154	Laos	5.00
154	North Korea	5.00

Capital Flows and Foreign Investment
Score: 2–Stable (low barriers)

Jamaica encourages foreign investment in nearly all areas. It also provides some incentives to investors who use Jamaican raw materials and supplies.

Banking
Score: 2–Stable (low level of restrictions)

Jamaica has a mixture of domestic and foreign banks. There are few direct restrictions on the formation of banks, and the government has reduced its control of the financial system.

Wage and Price Controls
Score: 3–Stable (moderate level)

Price controls remain on many items, including bus fares, water, electricity, telecommunications, and kerosene. Jamaica has a minimum wage law.

Property Rights
Score: 2–Stable (high level of protection)

The likelihood of expropriation in Jamaica is remote. Private property receives adequate protection.

Regulation
Score: 3–Stable (moderate level)

Most regulations are only moderately burdensome. Bribery and corruption exist in government, but they are minimal.

Black Market
Score: 3–Stable (moderate level of activity)

Smuggling is big business in Jamaica because prices remain high in many areas, such as consumer electronics. Pirated broadcasts, video tapes, and recorded music are found frequently on the black market. The U.S. Department of State reports that "Piracy of broadcast and prerecorded video cassettes for distribution in the domestic and regional market is widespread."[3]

Notes

1. U.S. Department of Commerce, *Country Commercial Guide*, 1997.
2. U.S. Department of State, *Country Reports on Economic Policy and Trade Practices*, 1997, p. 272.
3. *Ibid.*, p. 273.

Japan   2.05

1997 Score: **2.05**	1996 Score: **2.05**	1995 Score: **1.95**

Trade	2	Banking	3
Taxation	4.5	Wages and Prices	2
Government Intervention	1	Property Rights	1
Monetary Policy	1	Regulation	2
Foreign Investment	3	Black Market	1

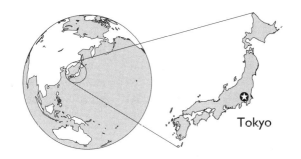

Tokyo

Since the end of World War II, Japan has had one of the world's fastest-growing economies. With its economy in ruins but democracy firmly in place by 1946, it eliminated most of the elements of its former statist economy and adopted the basics of a free-market system. These moves helped propel Japan's economy to its current level. The government, however, continues to impose controls on the economy, sometimes formally but often informally. Recent government mismanagement of the economy sent Japan into a dismal economic recession. The economy posted three straight years of less than 1 percent growth from 1993 to 1995 but now seems to be recovering, having posted a gain of almost 4 percent in 1996. This improvement has been achieved mainly through government stimulus of the economy and reduced regulation. Current Prime Minister Ryutaro Hashimoto has announced his government's commitment to a phased-in deregulation of Japan's financial services, which will begin in early 1998 and be completed over the subsequent several years. Japan's legislature, the Diet, already has begun to pass laws to implement the deregulation policies.

TRADE POLICY
Score: 2–Stable (low level of protectionism)

Many economists argue that Japan is very protectionist. Yet its average tariff rate is among the world's lowest: less than 3 percent, which is even lower than that of the United States. Tariffs have never been the problem they can be in less-developed countries, although Japan continues to be plagued with nontariff barriers, including government red tape, exclusionary private business practices, a fragmented distribution system, and a relatively unapproachable government bureaucracy. These may prove to be impediments to some imports, but Japan's market remains more accessible than those of most other countries. Therefore, by global standards, and especially when compared with countries like Bangladesh, India, and Yemen, Japan's trade barriers are relatively low. Since 1994, Japan has achieved several agreements with other countries, within the General Agreement on Tariffs and Trade and bilaterally with the United States, to reduce many nontariff barriers, including an import ban on rice.

TAXATION
Score–Income taxation: 4–Stable (high tax rates)
Score–Corporate taxation: 4–Stable (high tax rates)
Final Taxation Score: 4.5–Stable (very high tax rates)

Japan's top income tax rate is 50 percent; the tax on the average income level is 20 percent. The top marginal corporate tax rate is 37.5 percent. Japan also has prefectural and municipal taxes, an inhabitant's tax paid to the prefecture or municipality in which the company is located, a capital gains tax of 37.5 percent, and an enterprise tax of 6 percent to 12.6 percent. It recently raised its consumption tax from 3 percent to 5 percent.

1	Hong Kong	1.25	77	Zambia	3.05
2	Singapore	1.30	80	Mali	3.10
3	Bahrain	1.70	80	Mongolia	3.10
4	New Zealand	1.75	80	Slovenia	3.10
5	Switzerland	1.90	83	Honduras	3.15
5	United States	1.90	83	Papua New Guinea	3.15
7	Luxembourg	1.95	85	Djibouti	3.20
7	Taiwan	1.95	85	Fiji	3.20
7	United Kingdom	1.95	85	Pakistan	3.20
10	Bahamas	2.00	88	Algeria	3.25
10	Ireland	2.00	88	Guinea	3.25
12	Australia	2.05	88	Lebanon	3.25
12	Japan	2.05	88	Mexico	3.25
14	Belgium	2.10	88	Senegal	3.25
14	Canada	2.10	88	Tanzania	3.25
14	United Arab Emirates	2.10	94	Nigeria	3.30
17	Austria	2.15	94	Romania	3.30
17	Chile	2.15	96	Brazil	3.35
17	Estonia	2.15	96	Cambodia	3.35
20	Czech Republic	2.20	96	Egypt	3.35
20	Netherlands	2.20	96	Ivory Coast	3.35
22	Denmark	2.25	96	Madagascar	3.35
22	Finland	2.25	96	Moldova	3.35
24	Germany	2.30	102	Nepal	3.40
24	Iceland	2.30	103	Cape Verde	3.44
24	South Korea	2.30	104	Armenia	3.45
27	Norway	2.35	104	Dominican Republic	3.45
28	Kuwait	2.40	104	Russia	3.45
28	Malaysia	2.40	107	Burkina Faso	3.50
28	Panama	2.40	107	Cameroon	3.50
28	Thailand	2.40	107	Lesotho	3.50
32	El Salvador	2.45	107	Nicaragua	3.50
32	Sri Lanka	2.45	107	Venezuela	3.50
32	Sweden	2.45	112	Gambia	3.60
35	France	2.50	112	Guyana	3.60
35	Italy	2.50	114	Bulgaria	3.65
35	Spain	2.50	114	Georgia	3.65
38	Trinidad and Tobago	2.55	114	Malawi	3.65
39	Argentina	2.60	117	Ethiopia	3.70
39	Barbados	2.60	117	India	3.70
39	Cyprus	2.60	117	Niger	3.70
39	Jamaica	2.60	120	Albania	3.75
39	Portugal	2.60	120	Bangladesh	3.75
44	Bolivia	2.65	120	China (PRC)	3.75
44	Oman	2.65	120	Congo	3.75
44	Philippines	2.65	120	Croatia	3.75
47	Swaziland	2.70	125	Chad	3.80
47	Uruguay	2.70	125	Mauritania	3.80
49	Botswana	2.75	125	Ukraine	3.80
49	Jordan	2.75	128	Sierra Leone	3.85
49	Namibia	2.75	129	Burundi	3.90
49	Tunisia	2.75	129	Suriname	3.90
53	Belize	2.80	129	Zimbabwe	3.90
53	Costa Rica	2.80	132	Haiti	4.00
53	Guatemala	2.80	132	Kyrgyzstan	4.00
53	Israel	2.80	132	Syria	4.00
53	Peru	2.80	135	Belarus	4.05
53	Saudi Arabia	2.80	136	Kazakstan	4.10
53	Turkey	2.80	136	Mozambique	4.10
53	Uganda	2.80	136	Yemen	4.10
53	Western Samoa	2.80	139	Sudan	4.20
62	Indonesia	2.85	140	Myanmar	4.30
62	Latvia	2.85	140	Rwanda	4.30
62	Malta	2.85	142	Angola	4.35
62	Paraguay	2.85	143	Azerbaijan	4.40
66	Greece	2.90	143	Tajikistan	4.40
66	Hungary	2.90	145	Turkmenistan	4.50
66	South Africa	2.90	146	Uzbekistan	4.55
69	Benin	2.95	147	Congo/Zaire	4.70
69	Ecuador	2.95	147	Iran	4.70
69	Gabon	2.95	147	Libya	4.70
69	Morocco	2.95	147	Somalia	4.70
69	Poland	2.95	147	Vietnam	4.70
74	Colombia	3.00	152	Bosnia	4.80
74	Ghana	3.00	153	Iraq	4.90
74	Lithuania	3.00	154	Cuba	5.00
77	Kenya	3.05	154	Laos	5.00
77	Slovak Republic	3.05	154	North Korea	5.00

Mostly Free

GOVERNMENT INTERVENTION IN THE ECONOMY
Score: 1–Stable (very low level)

Government consumes 9.8 percent of Japan's GDP and has gone from granting extensive subsidies to opening up its market for some products, such as rice. Government expenditures have been kept lower than those of other countries because the United States has provided for Japan's defense. Even though Japan's economic recovery is based partially on increased government spending, that spending is declining as a percentage of GDP.

MONETARY POLICY
Score: 1–Stable (very low level of inflation)

Japan's annual rate of inflation averaged only 1.4 percent from 1985 to 1995. The rate of inflation rate was about 0.1 percent in 1996 and is expected to be about 0.2 percent for 1997.

CAPITAL FLOWS AND FOREIGN INVESTMENT
Score: 3–Stable (moderate barriers)

Japan's foreign investment procedures were overhauled in the early 1990s, eliminating the need to notify the government in advance of investment in all areas except agriculture, aircraft, atomic energy, fisheries, forestry, leather goods, oil and gas production, and space development. The close relationship between government and private businesses, however, continues to impede foreign investment because some businesses and government agencies collude to make it too costly.

BANKING
Score: 3–Stable (moderate level of restrictions)

The banking industry is very competitive in Japan. The government places few restrictions on Japanese banks and their ability to engage in a variety of services. Banks may underwrite, deal, and broker all kinds of securities through subsidiaries. This allows them to be more competitive. Japan maintains significant regulations on banks, however; it is difficult, for example, for banks to liquidate bad loans by selling them off to buyers at a discount, and banks may not list a loan as "in default" until it has been in arrears for at least six months (compared with only three months in the United States). These and other regulations make it difficult

to diversify risk and recoup losses on bad loans. The Japanese government also has imposed a host of new regulations to deal with a financial crisis and has agreed to bail out many failing financial institutions. Although the government plans to relax some of its recent regulations on the financial sector, little progress has been made.

WAGE AND PRICE CONTROLS
Score: 2–Stable (low level)

With the exception of rice, there are no price controls in Japan. Wages are set mainly by the market, although Japan also has a minimum wage.

PROPERTY RIGHTS
Score: 1–Stable (very high level of protection)

Japan has an efficient legal and court system that is able to protect property rights. Government expropriation is unlikely.

REGULATION
Score: 2–Stable (low level)

Although Japan's economy often is characterized as heavily regulated, most businesses enjoy a large amount of economic freedom. The process for opening a business has been made easier in the past several years. Even though some regulations may impose a burden on individuals, regulations on businesses are aimed at allowing them enough room to maximize profits; many either are not enforced or are not significantly burdensome. Japan rarely enforces its antitrust laws, allowing businesses to join forces without the threat of antimonopoly litigation from competitors. By global standards, the level of regulation is low.

BLACK MARKET
Score: 1–Stable (very low level of activity)

Japan's government has undertaken a large crackdown on such illegal activities as the buying and selling of guns and narcotics. Even though Japan has very strong protection for intellectual property rights, black market activity in pirated sound recording and computer software continues to some degree, and the government has increased its prosecution of those who violate such laws. These activities represent a minuscule portion of Japan's $4 trillion economy.

Jordan   2.75

| 1997 Score: **2.70** | 1996 Score: **2.80** | 1995 Score: **2.90** |

Trade	4	Banking	2
Taxation	2.5	Wages and Prices	3
Government Intervention	3	Property Rights	2
Monetary Policy	2	Regulation	3
Foreign Investment	2	Black Market	4

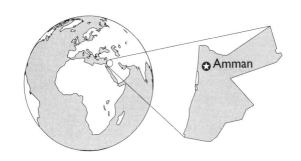

Jordan gained its independence from the United Kingdom in 1946, and King Hussein, the longest-ruling leader in the Middle East, has provided able political leadership since 1953. In 1988, King Hussein began a series of economic reforms to correct lagging growth rates. The king is attempting to reduce Jordan's budget deficit through controlled spending, reduced subsidies and tariffs, and lower taxes. The government still maintains many policies, however, that limit economic freedom and hinder economic growth. Jordan recently reduced taxes while increasing government intervention in the economy. Its overall score is 0.05 point worse this year.

TRADE POLICY
Score: 4–Stable (high level of protectionism)

Jordan's average tariff rate is 14.4 percent.[1] Taxes on items like automobiles are particularly high, ranging from 44 percent to 200 percent, and customs procedures are plagued by bureaucracy.

TAXATION
Score–Income taxation: 2+ (low tax rates)
Score–Corporate taxation: 3–Stable (moderate tax rates)
Final Taxation Score: 2.5+ (moderate tax rates)

The top marginal income tax rate in Jordan is 30 percent, down from 45 percent last year and 55 percent in 1995. Thus, Jordan's tax score is one point better this year. The average income level is taxed at a rate of 5 percent. The top corporate tax rate is 35 percent, down from 55 percent in 1996.

GOVERNMENT INTERVENTION IN THE ECONOMY
Score: 3– (moderate level)

Government consumes 23.1 percent of Jordan's GDP. Recent statistics demonstrate that nearly 50 percent of GDP is produced by government-owned companies and industries. As a result, Jordan's score is one point worse this year.[2]

MONETARY POLICY
Score: 2–Stable (low level of inflation)

Jordan's annual rate of inflation from 1985 to 1995 averaged 7.1 percent. In 1996, the inflation rate was 6 percent.

CAPITAL FLOWS AND FOREIGN INVESTMENT
Score: 2–Stable (low barriers)

Jordan maintains few restrictions on foreign investment. Industries deemed vital to national security, such as utilities, are not open to outside investors, and there are some ownership restrictions on trade and transportation industries.

1	Hong Kong	1.25	
2	Singapore	1.30	
3	Bahrain	1.70	
4	New Zealand	1.75	
5	Switzerland	1.90	
5	United States	1.90	
7	Luxembourg	1.95	
7	Taiwan	1.95	
7	United Kingdom	1.95	
10	Bahamas	2.00	
10	Ireland	2.00	
12	Australia	2.05	
12	Japan	2.05	
14	Belgium	2.10	
14	Canada	2.10	
14	United Arab Emirates	2.10	
17	Austria	2.15	
17	Chile	2.15	
17	Estonia	2.15	
20	Czech Republic	2.20	
20	Netherlands	2.20	
22	Denmark	2.25	
22	Finland	2.25	
24	Germany	2.30	
24	Iceland	2.30	
24	South Korea	2.30	
27	Norway	2.35	
28	Kuwait	2.40	
28	Malaysia	2.40	
28	Panama	2.40	
28	Thailand	2.40	
32	El Salvador	2.45	
32	Sri Lanka	2.45	
32	Sweden	2.45	
35	France	2.50	
35	Italy	2.50	
35	Spain	2.50	
38	Trinidad and Tobago	2.55	
39	Argentina	2.60	
39	Barbados	2.60	
39	Cyprus	2.60	
39	Jamaica	2.60	
39	Portugal	2.60	
44	Bolivia	2.65	
44	Oman	2.65	
44	Philippines	2.65	
47	Swaziland	2.70	
47	Uruguay	2.70	
49	Botswana	2.75	
49	Jordan	2.75	
49	Namibia	2.75	
49	Tunisia	2.75	
53	Belize	2.80	
53	Costa Rica	2.80	
53	Guatemala	2.80	
53	Israel	2.80	
53	Peru	2.80	
53	Saudi Arabia	2.80	
53	Turkey	2.80	
53	Uganda	2.80	
53	Western Samoa	2.80	
62	Indonesia	2.85	
62	Latvia	2.85	
62	Malta	2.85	
62	Paraguay	2.85	
66	Greece	2.90	
66	Hungary	2.90	
66	South Africa	2.90	
69	Benin	2.95	
69	Ecuador	2.95	
69	Gabon	2.95	
69	Morocco	2.95	
69	Poland	2.95	
74	Colombia	3.00	
74	Ghana	3.00	
74	Lithuania	3.00	
77	Kenya	3.05	
77	Slovak Republic	3.05	
77	Zambia	3.05	
80	Mali	3.10	
80	Mongolia	3.10	
80	Slovenia	3.10	
83	Honduras	3.15	
83	Papua New Guinea	3.15	
85	Djibouti	3.20	
85	Fiji	3.20	
85	Pakistan	3.20	
88	Algeria	3.25	
88	Guinea	3.25	
88	Lebanon	3.25	
88	Mexico	3.25	
88	Senegal	3.25	
88	Tanzania	3.25	
94	Nigeria	3.30	
94	Romania	3.30	
96	Brazil	3.35	
96	Cambodia	3.35	
96	Egypt	3.35	
96	Ivory Coast	3.35	
96	Madagascar	3.35	
96	Moldova	3.35	
102	Nepal	3.40	
103	Cape Verde	3.44	
104	Armenia	3.45	
104	Dominican Republic	3.45	
104	Russia	3.45	
107	Burkina Faso	3.50	
107	Cameroon	3.50	
107	Lesotho	3.50	
107	Nicaragua	3.50	
107	Venezuela	3.50	
112	Gambia	3.60	
112	Guyana	3.60	
114	Bulgaria	3.65	
114	Georgia	3.65	
114	Malawi	3.65	
117	Ethiopia	3.70	
117	India	3.70	
117	Niger	3.70	
120	Albania	3.75	
120	Bangladesh	3.75	
120	China (PRC)	3.75	
120	Congo	3.75	
120	Croatia	3.75	
125	Chad	3.80	
125	Mauritania	3.80	
125	Ukraine	3.80	
128	Sierra Leone	3.85	
129	Burundi	3.90	
129	Suriname	3.90	
129	Zimbabwe	3.90	
132	Haiti	4.00	
132	Kyrgyzstan	4.00	
132	Syria	4.00	
135	Belarus	4.05	
136	Kazakstan	4.10	
136	Mozambique	4.10	
136	Yemen	4.10	
139	Sudan	4.20	
140	Myanmar	4.30	
140	Rwanda	4.30	
142	Angola	4.35	
143	Azerbaijan	4.40	
143	Tajikistan	4.40	
145	Turkmenistan	4.50	
146	Uzbekistan	4.55	
147	Congo/Zaire	4.70	
147	Iran	4.70	
147	Libya	4.70	
147	Somalia	4.70	
147	Vietnam	4.70	
152	Bosnia	4.80	
153	Iraq	4.90	
154	Cuba	5.00	
154	Laos	5.00	
154	North Korea	5.00	

Mostly Free

BANKING
Score: 2–Stable (low level of restrictions)

Foreigners are allowed to invest in Jordanian banks. The government maintains some control over banks through strict reserve requirements.

WAGE AND PRICE CONTROLS
Score: 3–Stable (moderate level)

The government sets prices on such items as "non-strategic commodities," including automobile spare parts, construction materials, household cleaning materials, soft drinks, and some food and beverages served in restaurants. There is a minimum wage for specific trades.

PROPERTY RIGHTS
Score: 2–Stable (high level of protection)

Expropriation is unlikely in Jordan. Property receives adequate protection from legal institutions and the police force.

REGULATION
Score: 3–Stable (moderate level)

Jordan's regulatory environment is moderately bureaucratic and burdensome. Under a 1993 disabilities law, for example, many businesses are forced to retrofit their buildings to accommodate the hearing, sight, and physically disabled. This expense is proving to be a substantial burden on many businesses.

BLACK MARKET
Score: 4–Stable (high level of activity)

Because levels of trade protectionism are so high, smuggling is big business in Jordan. Computer software and related items provide significant business for black marketeers. According to the U.S. Department of State, "The practice of pirating audio and video tapes for commercial purposes is widespread, with the government making no effort to intervene. Pirated books are sold in Jordan though few, if any, are published within the country."[3]

NOTES

1. Based on International Monetary Fund statistics for taxes on international transactions as a percentage of total imports; from International Monetary Fund, *Government Financial Statistics,* 1996.
2. The score in this factor has changed from 2 in 1997 to 3 in 1998. Previously unavailable data provide a more accurate understanding of the country's performance in this factor. The methodology for this factor remains the same.
3. U.S. Department of State, *Country Reports on Economic Policy and Trade Practices,* 1997, p. 340.

Kazakstan

4.10

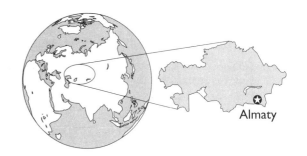

Almaty

Trade	4	Banking	4
Taxation	4	Wages and Prices	4
Government Intervention	3	Property Rights	4
Monetary Policy	5	Regulation	4
Foreign Investment	4	Black Market	5

Kazakstan became an autonomous republic of the Soviet Union in 1920 but was incorporated into the union in 1936. During some 70 years of Soviet rule, Moscow used part of Kazakstan as a penal colony. Its railways and mining quarries were built largely by prison labor. In the early stages of the Cold War, Josef Stalin used some areas of Kazakstan as a nuclear test center, turning parts of the country into lethal, radioactive deserts. Under Nikita Khrushchev, the Soviet Union built Baikonur, its major space center, in Kazakstan. Since gaining its independence in 1991, Kazakstan has moved to adopt the fundamentals of a market-based economy. Economic development, however, remains hindered by a quasi-authoritarian regime and an intransigent bureaucracy plagued with corruption.

TRADE POLICY
Score: 4–Stable (high level of protectionism)

The average tariff rate for Kazakstan is about 12 percent. One nontariff barrier is the presence of corrupt customs officials who often confiscate imports and exports. According to the U.S. Department of Commerce, "Kazakstan's customs system is often an obstacle to doing business, particularly because customs duties are not consistently and fully levied on all trade."[1]

TAXATION
Score–Income taxation: 4–Stable (high tax rates)
Score–Corporate taxation: 3–Stable (moderate tax rates)
Final Taxation Score: 4–Stable (high tax rates)

Kazakstan's top income tax rate is 40 percent.[2] The top marginal corporate tax rate is 30 percent. Kazakstan also has a 30 percent capital gains tax, a 20 percent value-added tax, and a 2 percent to 25 percent payroll tax.

GOVERNMENT INTERVENTION IN THE ECONOMY
Score: 3–Stable (moderate level)

Kazakstan is privatizing its large state-owned sector, although the economy remains dominated by big state enterprises, particularly in the agricultural sector. According to the U.S. Department of Commerce, "The government of Kazakstan remains an equity partner in a wide variety of parastatals—from banks to agriculture joint stock companies."[3] Government consumption as a percentage of GDP, however, is 15 percent. Thus, government intervention in the economy of Kazakstan is moderate by global standards.

MONETARY POLICY
Score: 5–Stable (very high level of inflation)

Kazakstan has been plagued by hyperinflation. Although projected to be less than 30 percent in 1996, the rate of inflation was 60.3 percent in 1995, 1,171 percent in 1994, and 1,758 percent in 1993. Thus, even though greatly reduced recently, inflation remains very high, both historically and by global standards.

1	Hong Kong	1.25	77	Zambia	3.05
2	Singapore	1.30	80	Mali	3.10
3	Bahrain	1.70	80	Mongolia	3.10
4	New Zealand	1.75	80	Slovenia	3.10
5	Switzerland	1.90	83	Honduras	3.15
5	United States	1.90	83	Papua New Guinea	3.15
7	Luxembourg	1.95	85	Djibouti	3.20
7	Taiwan	1.95	85	Fiji	3.20
7	United Kingdom	1.95	85	Pakistan	3.20
10	Bahamas	2.00	88	Algeria	3.25
10	Ireland	2.00	88	Guinea	3.25
12	Australia	2.05	88	Lebanon	3.25
12	Japan	2.05	88	Mexico	3.25
14	Belgium	2.10	88	Senegal	3.25
14	Canada	2.10	88	Tanzania	3.25
14	United Arab Emirates	2.10	94	Nigeria	3.30
17	Austria	2.15	94	Romania	3.30
17	Chile	2.15	96	Brazil	3.35
17	Estonia	2.15	96	Cambodia	3.35
20	Czech Republic	2.20	96	Egypt	3.35
20	Netherlands	2.20	96	Ivory Coast	3.35
22	Denmark	2.25	96	Madagascar	3.35
22	Finland	2.25	96	Moldova	3.35
24	Germany	2.30	102	Nepal	3.40
24	Iceland	2.30	103	Cape Verde	3.44
24	South Korea	2.30	104	Armenia	3.45
27	Norway	2.35	104	Dominican Republic	3.45
28	Kuwait	2.40	104	Russia	3.45
28	Malaysia	2.40	107	Burkina Faso	3.50
28	Panama	2.40	107	Cameroon	3.50
28	Thailand	2.40	107	Lesotho	3.50
32	El Salvador	2.45	107	Nicaragua	3.50
32	Sri Lanka	2.45	107	Venezuela	3.50
32	Sweden	2.45	112	Gambia	3.60
35	France	2.50	112	Guyana	3.60
35	Italy	2.50	114	Bulgaria	3.65
35	Spain	2.50	114	Georgia	3.65
38	Trinidad and Tobago	2.55	114	Malawi	3.65
39	Argentina	2.60	117	Ethiopia	3.70
39	Barbados	2.60	117	India	3.70
39	Cyprus	2.60	117	Niger	3.70
39	Jamaica	2.60	120	Albania	3.75
39	Portugal	2.60	120	Bangladesh	3.75
44	Bolivia	2.65	120	China (PRC)	3.75
44	Oman	2.65	120	Congo	3.75
44	Philippines	2.65	120	Croatia	3.75
47	Swaziland	2.70	125	Chad	3.80
47	Uruguay	2.70	125	Mauritania	3.80
49	Botswana	2.75	125	Ukraine	3.80
49	Jordan	2.75	128	Sierra Leone	3.85
49	Namibia	2.75	129	Burundi	3.90
49	Tunisia	2.75	129	Suriname	3.90
53	Belize	2.80	129	Zimbabwe	3.90
53	Costa Rica	2.80	132	Haiti	4.00
53	Guatemala	2.80	132	Kyrgyzstan	4.00
53	Israel	2.80	132	Syria	4.00
53	Peru	2.80	135	Belarus	4.05
53	Saudi Arabia	2.80	136	Kazakstan	4.10
53	Turkey	2.80	136	Mozambique	4.10
53	Uganda	2.80	136	Yemen	4.10
53	Western Samoa	2.80	139	Sudan	4.20
62	Indonesia	2.85	140	Myanmar	4.30
62	Latvia	2.85	140	Rwanda	4.30
62	Malta	2.85	142	Angola	4.35
62	Paraguay	2.85	143	Azerbaijan	4.40
66	Greece	2.90	143	Tajikistan	4.40
66	Hungary	2.90	145	Turkmenistan	4.50
66	South Africa	2.90	146	Uzbekistan	4.55
69	Benin	2.95	147	Congo/Zaire	4.70
69	Ecuador	2.95	147	Iran	4.70
69	Gabon	2.95	147	Libya	4.70
69	Morocco	2.95	147	Somalia	4.70
69	Poland	2.95	147	Vietnam	4.70
74	Colombia	3.00	152	Bosnia	4.80
74	Ghana	3.00	153	Iraq	4.90
74	Lithuania	3.00	154	Cuba	5.00
77	Kenya	3.05	154	Laos	5.00
77	Slovak Republic	3.05	154	North Korea	5.00

Repressed

CAPITAL FLOWS AND FOREIGN INVESTMENT
Score: 4–Stable (high barriers)

Even though the government wants to promote and increase foreign investment, it still maintains some barriers. Despite improvement in the investment laws, much of the foreign investment entering the country still is screened by the government. According to the U.S. Department of Commerce, "Foreign investment proposals are screened by host government officials, sometimes at the highest level. Although the government has promised that tendering will be done in an open and fair manner, there continue to be complaints that the tendering process is not always transparent and fair."[4] Corruption within the foreign investment approval process also remains a problem. "Although the government of Kazakstan publicizes its commitment to economic reform," reports the U.S. Department of Commerce, "corruption at all levels of the government remains an obstacle to foreign investment."[5]

BANKING
Score: 4–Stable (high level of restrictions)

As the U.S. Department of Commerce reports, "The banking system in Kazakstan is a system in transition, in the midst of a difficult phase of consolidation, increased competition and adaptation to international standards."[6] The government continues to own many banks and controls most assets of the financial systems.

WAGE AND PRICE CONTROLS
Score: 4–Stable (high level)

Powerful state-owned industries control wages and prices in Kazakstan. Price controls continue on such items as agricultural products, transportation, and utilities.

PROPERTY RIGHTS
Score: 4–Stable (low level of protection)

Kazakstan's legal system does not provide sufficient protection for private property. Legal reform is a major priority of the government, but the judiciary remains weak and corrupt. According to the U.S. Department of State, "The judiciary remained under the control of the President and the executive branch. The lack of an independent judiciary made it difficult to root out corruption, which is pervasive throughout the government."[7]

REGULATION
Score: 4–Stable (high level)

Establishing a business in Kazakstan is a tedious and time-consuming procedure that requires individuals to overcome numerous bureaucratic barriers. Although a 1995 business licensing decree established the legal framework for providing business licenses, its implementation has been severely inadequate. According to the U.S. Department of Commerce, "A subsequent [business license] implementing regulation (Resolution 1894) appears to identify 28 separate licensing bodies issuing licenses for more than 235 activities that require licensing.... This has led to confusion among businesses and government officials alike, particularly since in many cases the procedures and qualification requirements for issuing these licenses do not exist. For example, government inspectors are reported to have threatened businesses with fines and shut-downs for not having licenses that are, in most instances, legally impossible to obtain."[8] Government corruption also remains a problem. The U.S. Department of Commerce reports that "The Kazakstani Criminal Code contains special articles on penalties for accepting and giving bribes. Corruption is a problem in Kazakstan. U.S. firms and other foreign companies consider corruption an obstacle to investment. There have been no significant prosecutions for corruption."[9]

BLACK MARKET
Score: 5–Stable (very high level of activity)

Smuggling is rampant in Kazakstan; in fact, most imports are smuggled into the country. According to the U.S. Department of Commerce, "As reported by the Chairman of the Custom Committee, approximately 80 percent of imported goods to Kazakstan are smuggled."[10] Despite the existence of laws protecting intellectual property rights, significant piracy in computer software continues.

NOTES
1. U.S. Department of Commerce, "Kazakstan, Economic Overview," *Market Research Reports*, August 1996.
2. The tax on the average income level is not available. Therefore, Kazakstan is graded strictly on its top income tax rates.
3. U.S. Department of Commerce, *Country Commercial Guide*, 1997.
4. *Ibid.*
5. U.S. Department of Commerce, "Kazakstan, Economic Overview," August 1996.
6. U.S. Department of Commerce, *Country Commercial Guide*, 1997.
7. U.S. Department of State, "Kazakstan Country Report on Human Rights Practices for 1996," 1997.
8. U.S. Department of Commerce, *Country Commercial Guide*, 1997.
9. *Ibid.*
10. U.S. Department of Commerce, "Kazakhstan; Tobacco Annual 1997," *Annual Report, Agworld Attaché Reports*, 1997.

Kenya

3.05

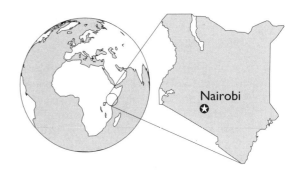

Nairobi

1997 Score: **3.05**		1996 Score: **3.05**		1995 Score: **3.05**	
Trade	4	Banking	2
Taxation	3.5	Wages and Prices	3
Government Intervention	3	Property Rights	3
Monetary Policy	2	Regulation	4
Foreign Investment	3	Black Market	3

Kenya gained its independence from Great Britain in 1963. A long period of one-party rule ended in 1991 with the legalization of opposition political parties through a constitutional amendment. Political freedoms, however, remain fairly constricted, and the economy—once one of Africa's freest and most prosperous—has deteriorated rapidly because of government corruption and mismanagement. Economic growth averaged less than 2.5 percent from 1992 to 1996, and per capita GNP was only $280 in 1995. Over the past several years, the government of President Daniel arap Moi has been in frequent conflict with Western donors and international financial institutions over Kenya's level of corruption and lack of economic reform. This conflict caused the International Monetary Fund and the World Bank to withhold credit to Kenya in July 1997, contingent upon implementation of anticorruption measures. Kenya also is plagued with serious ethnic conflict.

TRADE POLICY
Score: 4–Stable (high level of protectionism)

Kenya's average tariff rate is 12.22 percent.[1] In 1993, import licenses were abolished for most goods. According to the U.S. Department of State, "Customs procedures are overly detailed and rigidly implemented with resulting delays in clearing both imports and exports."[2] Some imports, including dairy products, are banned.

TAXATION
Score—Income taxation: 3–Stable (moderate tax rates)
Score–Corporate taxation: 3–Stable (moderate tax rates)
Total Taxation Score: 3.5–Stable (high tax rates)

Kenya's top income tax rate is 32.5 percent; the average income is taxed at approximately 10 percent. The top corporate income tax is 32.5 percent. Kenya also has a value-added tax that ranges from 8 percent to 15 percent.

GOVERNMENT INTERVENTION IN THE ECONOMY
Score: 3–Stable (moderate level)

Government consumes 15 percent of Kenya's GDP. It also plans to privatize over 100 state-owned companies, although at least 31 will be kept under state control. To date, little progress has been made in privatization.

MONETARY POLICY
Score: 2–Stable (low level of inflation)

Kenya's average annual rate of inflation between 1985 and 1995 was 13 percent. The inflation rate in 1996 was approximately 9 percent.

1	Hong Kong	1.25	77	Zambia	3.05
2	Singapore	1.30	80	Mali	3.10
3	Bahrain	1.70	80	Mongolia	3.10
4	New Zealand	1.75	80	Slovenia	3.10
5	Switzerland	1.90	83	Honduras	3.15
5	United States	1.90	83	Papua New Guinea	3.15
7	Luxembourg	1.95	85	Djibouti	3.20
7	Taiwan	1.95	85	Fiji	3.20
7	United Kingdom	1.95	85	Pakistan	3.20
10	Bahamas	2.00	88	Algeria	3.25
10	Ireland	2.00	88	Guinea	3.25
12	Australia	2.05	88	Lebanon	3.25
12	Japan	2.05	88	Mexico	3.25
14	Belgium	2.10	88	Senegal	3.25
14	Canada	2.10	88	Tanzania	3.25
14	United Arab Emirates	2.10	94	Nigeria	3.30
17	Austria	2.15	94	Romania	3.30
17	Chile	2.15	96	Brazil	3.35
17	Estonia	2.15	96	Cambodia	3.35
20	Czech Republic	2.20	96	Egypt	3.35
20	Netherlands	2.20	96	Ivory Coast	3.35
22	Denmark	2.25	96	Madagascar	3.35
22	Finland	2.25	96	Moldova	3.35
24	Germany	2.30	102	Nepal	3.40
24	Iceland	2.30	103	Cape Verde	3.44
24	South Korea	2.30	104	Armenia	3.45
27	Norway	2.35	104	Dominican Republic	3.45
28	Kuwait	2.40	104	Russia	3.45
28	Malaysia	2.40	107	Burkina Faso	3.50
28	Panama	2.40	107	Cameroon	3.50
28	Thailand	2.40	107	Lesotho	3.50
32	El Salvador	2.45	107	Nicaragua	3.50
32	Sri Lanka	2.45	107	Venezuela	3.50
32	Sweden	2.45	112	Gambia	3.60
35	France	2.50	112	Guyana	3.60
35	Italy	2.50	114	Bulgaria	3.65
35	Spain	2.50	114	Georgia	3.65
38	Trinidad and Tobago	2.55	114	Malawi	3.65
39	Argentina	2.60	117	Ethiopia	3.70
39	Barbados	2.60	117	India	3.70
39	Cyprus	2.60	117	Niger	3.70
39	Jamaica	2.60	120	Albania	3.75
39	Portugal	2.60	120	Bangladesh	3.75
44	Bolivia	2.65	120	China (PRC)	3.75
44	Oman	2.65	120	Congo	3.75
44	Philippines	2.65	120	Croatia	3.75
47	Swaziland	2.70	125	Chad	3.80
47	Uruguay	2.70	125	Mauritania	3.80
49	Botswana	2.75	125	Ukraine	3.80
49	Jordan	2.75	128	Sierra Leone	3.85
49	Namibia	2.75	129	Burundi	3.90
49	Tunisia	2.75	129	Suriname	3.90
53	Belize	2.80	129	Zimbabwe	3.90
53	Costa Rica	2.80	132	Haiti	4.00
53	Guatemala	2.80	132	Kyrgyzstan	4.00
53	Israel	2.80	132	Syria	4.00
53	Peru	2.80	135	Belarus	4.05
53	Saudi Arabia	2.80	136	Kazakstan	4.10
53	Turkey	2.80	136	Mozambique	4.10
53	Uganda	2.80	136	Yemen	4.10
53	Western Samoa	2.80	139	Sudan	4.20
62	Indonesia	2.85	140	Myanmar	4.30
62	Latvia	2.85	140	Rwanda	4.30
62	Malta	2.85	142	Angola	4.35
62	Paraguay	2.85	143	Azerbaijan	4.40
66	Greece	2.90	143	Tajikistan	4.40
66	Hungary	2.90	145	Turkmenistan	4.50
66	South Africa	2.90	146	Uzbekistan	4.55
69	Benin	2.95	147	Congo/Zaire	4.70
69	Ecuador	2.95	147	Iran	4.70
69	Gabon	2.95	147	Libya	4.70
69	Morocco	2.95	147	Somalia	4.70
69	Poland	2.95	147	Vietnam	4.70
74	Colombia	3.00	152	Bosnia	4.80
74	Ghana	3.00	153	Iraq	4.90
74	Lithuania	3.00	154	Cuba	5.00
77	Kenya	3.05	154	Laos	5.00
77	Slovak Republic	3.05	154	North Korea	5.00

Mostly Unfree

CAPITAL FLOWS AND FOREIGN INVESTMENT
Score: 3–Stable (moderate barriers)

Kenya permits complete foreign ownership of some enterprises, and most sectors are open to foreign participation. The government also has suggested that foreigners would be acceptable buyers of state-owned enterprises slated for privatization, although enterprises on the Kenyan Stock Exchange, which previously were limited to 20 percent foreign participation, are limited to 40 percent foreign participation. Export Promotion Zones offering tax breaks have been established; but because investment proposals are approved on a case-by-case basis and the procedures for obtaining government approval are burdensome, arbitrary, and often corrupt, foreign investment is declining. President Moi has been railing against foreign investment, and presidential approval is required for foreign acquisition of agricultural land. The government does not permit foreign investment in insurance or in government-sanctioned monopolies.

BANKING
Score: 2–Stable (low level of restrictions)

Two state-controlled banks make loans to state-owned industries. The National Bank of Kenya has been privatized in part. Lending levels for agriculture are mandated, and commercial banks are required to store a percentage of their deposits with the Central Bank. Kenya also has deregulated its banking industry, however. The U.S. Department of Commerce reports that "The financial sector, particularly banking, has been liberalized.... [M]ost banks are privately owned and operated."[3]

WAGE AND PRICE CONTROLS
Score: 3–Stable (moderate level)

The government has lifted price controls in almost every sector of Kenya's economy. The pricing of petroleum products has been freed, too. Some agricultural products, however, including coffee, must be sold through monopolistic government marketing boards. Monopolies, many of them government-sanctioned, control approximately half the Kenyan market, reducing price competition. Most wages are negotiated, although Kenya has a minimum wage.

PROPERTY RIGHTS
Score: 3–Stable (moderate level of protection)

Property in Kenya is constitutionally protected from compulsory state takeover. In the exceptional case of expropriation, owners receive compensation, albeit in local currency. In some cases, foreign investors have been deported and business licenses arbitrarily revoked. According to the U.S. Department of State, "Although the Constitution provides for an independent judiciary, it is subject to executive branch influence in practice."[4]

REGULATION
Score: 4–Stable (high level)

Companies are registered with relative ease, although some have found their operating licenses arbitrarily suspended. Businesses are required to file monthly reports on their activities, and it is difficult to terminate employees. To reduce unemployment, the government pressures firms to use labor-intensive methods of production instead of technology, and companies often find themselves overstaffed and facing excessively high payroll demands. Some progress has been made in cracking down on governmental corruption, but the U.S. Department of Commerce reports that "Public institutions are poorly managed and corruption remains widespread."[5]

BLACK MARKET
Score: 3–Stable (moderate level of activity)

The government's monopoly on the distribution of some agricultural products in Kenya encourages illegal trading, and the heavy regulation of business likewise encourages "illegal" commerce in many items. There is significant piracy of stolen intellectual property. According to the Office of the United States Trade Representative, "Pirated sound recordings are common, and virtually all videos available in shops are unlicensed."[6] These activities, however, affect Kenya's $6.6 billion economy only moderately.

NOTES

1. Based on taxation revenue on international trade as a percentage of total imports.
2. U.S. Department of State, *Country Reports on Economic Policy and Trade Practices,* 1996, p. 17.
3. U.S. Department of Commerce, "Kenya Economic Trends," *Market Research Reports,* March 14, 1997.
4. U.S. Department of State, "Kenya Country Report on Human Rights Practices for 1996," 1997.
5. U.S. Department of Commerce, "Kenya Economic Trends," March 14, 1997.
6. Office of the United States Trade Representative, *1997 National Trade Estimate Report on Foreign Trade Barriers.*

Korea, Democratic People's Republic of (North Korea)

5.00

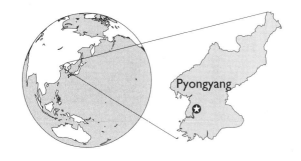

Pyongyang

| 1997 Score: **5.00** | 1996 Score: **5.00** | 1995 Score: **5.00** |

Trade	5	Banking	5
Taxation	5	Wages and Prices	5
Government Intervention	5	Property Rights	5
Monetary Policy	5	Regulation	5
Foreign Investment	5	Black Market	5

North Korea is one of the world's most economically repressed countries. Its economy is controlled by the central government, few entrepreneurial activities are legal, and little economic growth has occurred over the past decade. Although some signs point toward eventual economic liberalization, there is scant evidence that North Korea is heading down the economic path taken by the People's Republic of China. The country currently is facing a severe food shortage that will put increasing strain on its already weak economy. North Korea's economic problems are structural and long-term in nature, and overcoming them will require fundamental market-oriented reform.

TRADE POLICY
Score: 5–Stable (very high level of protectionism)

The government controls and inspects all imports into and exports from North Korea. There is an effective ban on many imports from Western countries. North Korea is essentially closed to trade, except for imports manufactured in South Korea.

TAXATION
Score–Income taxation: 5–Stable (very high tax rates)
Score–Corporate taxation: 5–Stable (very high tax rates)
Final Taxation Score: 5–Stable (very high tax rates)

Because North Korea is a communist state, the government owns all property. The government confiscates all economic output, resulting in real tax rates of 100 percent.

GOVERNMENT INTERVENTION IN THE ECONOMY
Score: 5–Stable (very high level)

North Korea has a command economy in which the government owns all property and sets production levels on most products. State-owned industries account for nearly all GDP.

MONETARY POLICY
Score: 5–Stable (very high level of inflation)

As a communist state, North Korea does not admit officially to having inflation. But even though the official prices of goods may be low because they are controlled and subsidized by the state, the tremendous scarcity of goods and

1	Hong Kong	1.25	77	Zambia	3.05
2	Singapore	1.30	80	Mali	3.10
3	Bahrain	1.70	80	Mongolia	3.10
4	New Zealand	1.75	80	Slovenia	3.10
5	Switzerland	1.90	83	Honduras	3.15
5	United States	1.90	83	Papua New Guinea	3.15
7	Luxembourg	1.95	85	Djibouti	3.20
7	Taiwan	1.95	85	Fiji	3.20
7	United Kingdom	1.95	85	Pakistan	3.20
10	Bahamas	2.00	88	Algeria	3.25
10	Ireland	2.00	88	Guinea	3.25
12	Australia	2.05	88	Lebanon	3.25
12	Japan	2.05	88	Mexico	3.25
14	Belgium	2.10	88	Senegal	3.25
14	Canada	2.10	88	Tanzania	3.25
14	United Arab Emirates	2.10	94	Nigeria	3.30
17	Austria	2.15	94	Romania	3.30
17	Chile	2.15	96	Brazil	3.35
17	Estonia	2.15	96	Cambodia	3.35
20	Czech Republic	2.20	96	Egypt	3.35
20	Netherlands	2.20	96	Ivory Coast	3.35
22	Denmark	2.25	96	Madagascar	3.35
22	Finland	2.25	96	Moldova	3.35
24	Germany	2.30	102	Nepal	3.40
24	Iceland	2.30	103	Cape Verde	3.44
24	South Korea	2.30	104	Armenia	3.45
27	Norway	2.35	104	Dominican Republic	3.45
28	Kuwait	2.40	104	Russia	3.45
28	Malaysia	2.40	107	Burkina Faso	3.50
28	Panama	2.40	107	Cameroon	3.50
28	Thailand	2.40	107	Lesotho	3.50
32	El Salvador	2.45	107	Nicaragua	3.50
32	Sri Lanka	2.45	107	Venezuela	3.50
32	Sweden	2.45	112	Gambia	3.60
35	France	2.50	112	Guyana	3.60
35	Italy	2.50	114	Bulgaria	3.65
35	Spain	2.50	114	Georgia	3.65
38	Trinidad and Tobago	2.55	114	Malawi	3.65
39	Argentina	2.60	117	Ethiopia	3.70
39	Barbados	2.60	117	India	3.70
39	Cyprus	2.60	117	Niger	3.70
39	Jamaica	2.60	120	Albania	3.75
39	Portugal	2.60	120	Bangladesh	3.75
44	Bolivia	2.65	120	China (PRC)	3.75
44	Oman	2.65	120	Congo	3.75
44	Philippines	2.65	120	Croatia	3.75
47	Swaziland	2.70	125	Chad	3.80
47	Uruguay	2.70	125	Mauritania	3.80
49	Botswana	2.75	125	Ukraine	3.80
49	Jordan	2.75	128	Sierra Leone	3.85
49	Namibia	2.75	129	Burundi	3.90
49	Tunisia	2.75	129	Suriname	3.90
53	Belize	2.80	129	Zimbabwe	3.90
53	Costa Rica	2.80	132	Haiti	4.00
53	Guatemala	2.80	132	Kyrgyzstan	4.00
53	Israel	2.80	132	Syria	4.00
53	Peru	2.80	135	Belarus	4.05
53	Saudi Arabia	2.80	136	Kazakstan	4.10
53	Turkey	2.80	136	Mozambique	4.10
53	Uganda	2.80	136	Yemen	4.10
53	Western Samoa	2.80	139	Sudan	4.20
62	Indonesia	2.85	140	Myanmar	4.30
62	Latvia	2.85	140	Rwanda	4.30
62	Malta	2.85	142	Angola	4.35
62	Paraguay	2.85	143	Azerbaijan	4.40
66	Greece	2.90	143	Tajikistan	4.40
66	Hungary	2.90	145	Turkmenistan	4.50
66	South Africa	2.90	146	Uzbekistan	4.55
69	Benin	2.95	147	Congo/Zaire	4.70
69	Ecuador	2.95	147	Iran	4.70
69	Gabon	2.95	147	Libya	4.70
69	Morocco	2.95	147	Somalia	4.70
69	Poland	2.95	147	Vietnam	4.70
74	Colombia	3.00	152	Bosnia	4.80
74	Ghana	3.00	153	Iraq	4.90
74	Lithuania	3.00	154	Cuba	5.00
77	Kenya	3.05	154	Laos	5.00
77	Slovak Republic	3.05	154	North Korea	5.00

Repressed

services attests to their real value. The government covers its huge domestic debts simply by printing more money. As a result, the currency is worth little and is not convertible on the international market.

CAPITAL FLOWS AND FOREIGN INVESTMENT
Score: 5–Stable (very high barriers)

Although North Korea's government recently claimed to recognize the importance of foreign investment, foreign investors still do not receive equal treatment under North Korean law. The government must remain a majority owner in a business, and investments are effectively banned in most industries.

BANKING
Score: 5–Stable (very high level of restrictions)

The government controls North Korea's financial system. Foreigners are barred from using banking services.

WAGE AND PRICE CONTROLS
Score: 5–Stable (very high level)

North Korea's government determines wages and prices.

PROPERTY RIGHTS
Score: 5–Stable (very low level of protection)

North Korea bans private property ownership.

REGULATION
Score: 5–Stable (very high level)

As North Korea's principal economic player, the government regulates the economy heavily.

BLACK MARKET
Score: 5–Stable (very high level of activity)

North Korea's black market is immense, and the government has imprisoned many who engage in such activity.

Korea, Republic of (South Korea)

2.30

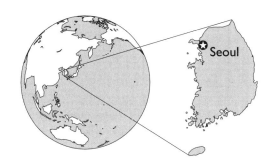

Seoul

1997 Score: **2.45**	1996 Score: **2.30**	1995 Score: **2.15**

Trade	3	Banking	2
Taxation	4	Wages and Prices	2
Government Intervention	2	Property Rights	1
Monetary Policy	2	Regulation	3
Foreign Investment	2	Black Market	2

Following the Korean War, economic liberalization became the standard in the Republic of Korea, while nationalization and collectivization were the norm in communist North Korea. In the 1960s, faced with a potential reduction in U.S. foreign aid, South Korea reformed its economy to attract foreign investment and develop export industries. As a result, it has become one of the world's fastest-growing economies. South Korea recently made its foreign investment code more transparent. Its overall score is 0.15 point better this year.

TRADE POLICY
Score: 3–Stable (moderate level of protectionism)

South Korea's average tariff rate is 7.9 percent, up from about 4 percent two years ago but down from 24.9 percent in 1980. This is due mainly to the Uruguay Round of the General Agreement on Tariffs and Trade, which permitted the government to remove some quotas on agricultural goods in exchange for tariffs. Nontariff barriers remain stringent. According to the U.S. Department of State, "U.S. exporters now experience barriers rooted in opaque and non-transparent regulations which affect licensing, inspections, type approval, marking require-ments, and other standards. Many of these technical barriers to trade are inconsistent with international norms."[1]

TAXATION
Score–Income taxation: 3+ (moderate tax rates)
Score–Corporate taxation: 4–Stable (high tax rates)
Total Taxation Score: 4+ (high tax rates)

South Korea's top income tax rate is 40 percent; the average income level is taxed at 10 percent, down from 18 percent in 1996. This makes South Korea's taxation score one-half point better this year. The top corporate income tax rate is 28 percent, although a 10 percent "resident surtax" increases it to over 35 percent. South Korea also has a 28 percent capital gains tax.

GOVERNMENT INTERVENTION IN THE ECONOMY
Score: 2–Stable (low level)

South Korea's government consumes 10.4 percent of GDP, down from 11 percent a year ago. There has been little privatization. The government remains heavily involved in such industries as banking, utilities, and services, as well as in some heavy manufacturing, but has been reducing its level of involvement in these and other areas in an effort to reduce government spending.

1	Hong Kong	1.25	77	Zambia	3.05
2	Singapore	1.30	80	Mali	3.10
3	Bahrain	1.70	80	Mongolia	3.10
4	New Zealand	1.75	80	Slovenia	3.10
5	Switzerland	1.90	83	Honduras	3.15
5	United States	1.90	83	Papua New Guinea	3.15
7	Luxembourg	1.95	85	Djibouti	3.20
7	Taiwan	1.95	85	Fiji	3.20
7	United Kingdom	1.95	85	Pakistan	3.20
10	Bahamas	2.00	88	Algeria	3.25
10	Ireland	2.00	88	Guinea	3.25
12	Australia	2.05	88	Lebanon	3.25
12	Japan	2.05	88	Mexico	3.25
14	Belgium	2.10	88	Senegal	3.25
14	Canada	2.10	88	Tanzania	3.25
14	United Arab Emirates	2.10	94	Nigeria	3.30
17	Austria	2.15	94	Romania	3.30
17	Chile	2.15	96	Brazil	3.35
17	Estonia	2.15	96	Cambodia	3.35
20	Czech Republic	2.20	96	Egypt	3.35
20	Netherlands	2.20	96	Ivory Coast	3.35
22	Denmark	2.25	96	Madagascar	3.35
22	Finland	2.25	96	Moldova	3.35
24	Germany	2.30	102	Nepal	3.40
24	Iceland	2.30	103	Cape Verde	3.44
24	South Korea	2.30	104	Armenia	3.45
27	Norway	2.35	104	Dominican Republic	3.45
28	Kuwait	2.40	104	Russia	3.45
28	Malaysia	2.40	107	Burkina Faso	3.50
28	Panama	2.40	107	Cameroon	3.50
28	Thailand	2.40	107	Lesotho	3.50
32	El Salvador	2.45	107	Nicaragua	3.50
32	Sri Lanka	2.45	107	Venezuela	3.50
32	Sweden	2.45	112	Gambia	3.60
35	France	2.50	112	Guyana	3.60
35	Italy	2.50	114	Bulgaria	3.65
35	Spain	2.50	114	Georgia	3.65
38	Trinidad and Tobago	2.55	114	Malawi	3.65
39	Argentina	2.60	117	Ethiopia	3.70
39	Barbados	2.60	117	India	3.70
39	Cyprus	2.60	117	Niger	3.70
39	Jamaica	2.60	120	Albania	3.75
39	Portugal	2.60	120	Bangladesh	3.75
44	Bolivia	2.65	120	China (PRC)	3.75
44	Oman	2.65	120	Congo	3.75
44	Philippines	2.65	120	Croatia	3.75
47	Swaziland	2.70	125	Chad	3.80
47	Uruguay	2.70	125	Mauritania	3.80
49	Botswana	2.75	125	Ukraine	3.80
49	Jordan	2.75	128	Sierra Leone	3.85
49	Namibia	2.75	129	Burundi	3.90
49	Tunisia	2.75	129	Suriname	3.90
53	Belize	2.80	129	Zimbabwe	3.90
53	Costa Rica	2.80	132	Haiti	4.00
53	Guatemala	2.80	132	Kyrgyzstan	4.00
53	Israel	2.80	132	Syria	4.00
53	Peru	2.80	135	Belarus	4.05
53	Saudi Arabia	2.80	136	Kazakstan	4.10
53	Turkey	2.80	136	Mozambique	4.10
53	Uganda	2.80	136	Yemen	4.10
53	Western Samoa	2.80	139	Sudan	4.20
62	Indonesia	2.85	140	Myanmar	4.30
62	Latvia	2.85	140	Rwanda	4.30
62	Malta	2.85	142	Angola	4.35
62	Paraguay	2.85	143	Azerbaijan	4.40
66	Greece	2.90	143	Tajikistan	4.40
66	Hungary	2.90	145	Turkmenistan	4.50
66	South Africa	2.90	145	Uzbekistan	4.55
69	Benin	2.95	147	Congo/Zaire	4.70
69	Ecuador	2.95	147	Iran	4.70
69	Gabon	2.95	147	Libya	4.70
69	Morocco	2.95	147	Somalia	4.70
69	Poland	2.95	147	Vietnam	4.70
74	Colombia	3.00	152	Bosnia	4.80
74	Ghana	3.00	153	Iraq	4.90
74	Lithuania	3.00	154	Cuba	5.00
77	Kenya	3.05	154	Laos	5.00
77	Slovak Republic	3.05	154	North Korea	5.00

Mostly Free

MONETARY POLICY
Score: 2–Stable (low level of inflation)

South Korea's average rate of inflation from 1985 to 1995 was 6.8 percent. Inflation fell to 5 percent in 1996.

CAPITAL FLOWS AND FOREIGN INVESTMENT
Score: 2+ (low barriers)

South Korea's government has relied on foreign investment to build its export economy. Foreign investments have been particularly useful in developing high-tech industries, which are heavily involved in exports. In December 1996, the government passed legislation to eliminate the possibility of variable interpretation of the foreign direct investment code, which had not always been applied systematically. Therefore, South Korea's score on this factor is one point better this year.

BANKING
Score: 2–Stable (low level of restrictions)

Foreign banks were welcome in South Korea as early as 1967. The government occasionally tries to steer capital to small businesses, but it has been removed from direct ownership of banks since the early 1990s. Local banks are permitted to underwrite, deal, and broker all kinds of securities and to invest in some real estate ventures.

WAGE AND PRICE CONTROLS
Score: 2–Stable (low level)

The market sets most prices in South Korea, although the government imposes controls on some utilities. The government also maintains stockpiles of foodstuffs that it releases into the market to raise or lower prices. South Korea has a minimum wage law, but some companies are exempt.

PROPERTY RIGHTS
Score: 1–Stable (very high level of protection)

Private property is secure in South Korea, and expropriation is very unlikely. South Korea has a stable, efficient legal system to protect private property.

REGULATION
Score: 3–Stable (moderate level)

Obtaining a business license in South Korea is simple. All businesses must be registered, but the process is efficient and not significantly burdensome. The government at times fails to publish all its regulations, and enforcement remains haphazard. Businesses can find themselves in violation of regulations they did not know existed. South Korea enforces most labor standards only on domestic firms, leaving foreign firms vulnerable to such radical labor activities as arbitrary strikes. In some cases, these activities have forced the bankruptcy of foreign firms, which then have had to flee the country without paying their employees. As a result, the government requires that foreign firms deposit three months' wages in a special account.

BLACK MARKET
Score: 2–Stable (low level of activity)

South Korea has a fairly small black market. A sizable number of employers tries to avoid the minimum wage laws, however. South Korea has stringent laws regarding intellectual property rights, and recent government crackdowns on pirated material are beginning to have an effect. Piracy of computer software, although still widespread, represents just a small portion of the economy.

NOTE
1.   U.S. Department of State, *Country Reports on Economic Policy and Trade Practices,* 1997, pp. 48–49.

Kuwait 2.40

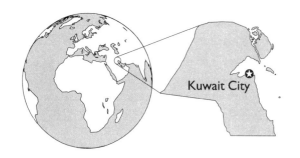

Kuwait City

1997 Score: **2.40**	1996 Score: **2.40**	1995 Score: **n/a**

Trade	2	Banking	3
Taxation	1	Wages and Prices	3
Government Intervention	4	Property Rights	1
Monetary Policy	2	Regulation	2
Foreign Investment	4	Black Market	2

Kuwait is a Persian Gulf emirate with a small and relatively open oil-rich economy. Its reserves of 94 billion barrels of crude oil make up about 10 percent of the world's total. This almost assures that Kuwait will remain affluent into the next century, absent external interference. The economy has undergone several major shocks over the past two decades, including massive government intervention in the late 1970s, the collapse of the Kuwaiti securities market in 1982, the collapse of world oil prices in the mid-1980s, and invasion by Iraq in 1990. The government continues to control oil production. Oil revenues are Kuwait's chief source of income and allow the government to keep import tariffs and taxation to a minimum.

TRADE POLICY
Score: 2–Stable (low level of protectionism)

Kuwait's average tariff rate is 4 percent. Government procurement policies cater generally to Kuwaiti firms, and nontariff barriers include strict standards on imports, especially food.

TAXATION
Score–Income taxation: 1–Stable (very low tax rates)
Score–Corporate taxation: 1–Stable (very low tax rates)
Final Taxation Score: 1–Stable (very low tax rates)

Kuwait has no income tax, corporate tax (except on some foreign firms), or other significant tax.

GOVERNMENT INTERVENTION IN THE ECONOMY
Score: 4–Stable (high level)

Government consumes 33.1 percent of Kuwait's GDP. Most GDP comes from oil production, nearly all of which is owned by the government.

MONETARY POLICY
Score: 2–Stable (low level of inflation)

Kuwait's average rate of inflation from 1989 to 1995 was about 10.5 percent. In 1996, the inflation rate was about 3.5 percent.

CAPITAL FLOWS AND FOREIGN INVESTMENT
Score: 4–Stable (high barriers)

Kuwait generally is open to some types of foreign investment, but some significant restrictions still exist. "Foreign investment...is welcome in Kuwait," according to the U.S. Department of State, "but only in select sectors as minority partners and only on terms compatible with continued Kuwaiti control of all basic economic activities."[1] Kuwaiti firms pay no corporate tax, but foreign firms must pay a corporate tax as high as 55 percent.

1	Hong Kong	1.25	77	Zambia	3.05
2	Singapore	1.30	80	Mali	3.10
3	Bahrain	1.70	80	Mongolia	3.10
4	New Zealand	1.75	80	Slovenia	3.10
5	Switzerland	1.90	83	Honduras	3.15
5	United States	1.90	83	Papua New Guinea	3.15
7	Luxembourg	1.95	85	Djibouti	3.20
7	Taiwan	1.95	85	Fiji	3.20
7	United Kingdom	1.95	85	Pakistan	3.20
10	Bahamas	2.00	88	Algeria	3.25
10	Ireland	2.00	88	Guinea	3.25
12	Australia	2.05	88	Lebanon	3.25
12	Japan	2.05	88	Mexico	3.25
14	Belgium	2.10	88	Senegal	3.25
14	Canada	2.10	88	Tanzania	3.25
14	United Arab Emirates	2.10	94	Nigeria	3.30
17	Austria	2.15	94	Romania	3.30
17	Chile	2.15	96	Brazil	3.35
17	Estonia	2.15	96	Cambodia	3.35
20	Czech Republic	2.20	96	Egypt	3.35
20	Netherlands	2.20	96	Ivory Coast	3.35
22	Denmark	2.25	96	Madagascar	3.35
22	Finland	2.25	96	Moldova	3.35
24	Germany	2.30	102	Nepal	3.40
24	Iceland	2.30	103	Cape Verde	3.44
24	South Korea	2.30	104	Armenia	3.45
27	Norway	2.35	104	Dominican Republic	3.45
28	Kuwait	2.40	104	Russia	3.45
28	Malaysia	2.40	107	Burkina Faso	3.50
28	Panama	2.40	107	Cameroon	3.50
28	Thailand	2.40	107	Lesotho	3.50
32	El Salvador	2.45	107	Nicaragua	3.50
32	Sri Lanka	2.45	107	Venezuela	3.50
32	Sweden	2.45	112	Gambia	3.60
35	France	2.50	112	Guyana	3.60
35	Italy	2.50	114	Bulgaria	3.65
35	Spain	2.50	114	Georgia	3.65
38	Trinidad and Tobago	2.55	114	Malawi	3.65
39	Argentina	2.60	117	Ethiopia	3.70
39	Barbados	2.60	117	India	3.70
39	Cyprus	2.60	117	Niger	3.70
39	Jamaica	2.60	120	Albania	3.75
39	Portugal	2.60	120	Bangladesh	3.75
44	Bolivia	2.65	120	China (PRC)	3.75
44	Oman	2.65	120	Congo	3.75
44	Philippines	2.65	120	Croatia	3.75
47	Swaziland	2.70	125	Chad	3.80
47	Uruguay	2.70	125	Mauritania	3.80
49	Botswana	2.75	125	Ukraine	3.80
49	Jordan	2.75	128	Sierra Leone	3.85
49	Namibia	2.75	129	Burundi	3.90
49	Tunisia	2.75	129	Suriname	3.90
53	Belize	2.80	129	Zimbabwe	3.90
53	Costa Rica	2.80	132	Haiti	4.00
53	Guatemala	2.80	132	Kyrgyzstan	4.00
53	Israel	2.80	132	Syria	4.00
53	Peru	2.80	135	Belarus	4.05
53	Saudi Arabia	2.80	136	Kazakstan	4.10
53	Turkey	2.80	136	Mozambique	4.10
53	Uganda	2.80	136	Yemen	4.10
53	Western Samoa	2.80	139	Sudan	4.20
62	Indonesia	2.85	140	Myanmar	4.30
62	Latvia	2.85	140	Rwanda	4.30
62	Malta	2.85	142	Angola	4.35
62	Paraguay	2.85	143	Azerbaijan	4.40
66	Greece	2.90	143	Tajikistan	4.40
66	Hungary	2.90	145	Turkmenistan	4.50
66	South Africa	2.90	146	Uzbekistan	4.55
69	Benin	2.95	147	Congo/Zaire	4.70
69	Ecuador	2.95	147	Iran	4.70
69	Gabon	2.95	147	Libya	4.70
69	Morocco	2.95	147	Somalia	4.70
69	Poland	2.95	147	Vietnam	4.70
74	Colombia	3.00	152	Bosnia	4.80
74	Ghana	3.00	153	Iraq	4.90
74	Lithuania	3.00	154	Cuba	5.00
77	Kenya	3.05	154	Laos	5.00
77	Slovak Republic	3.05	154	North Korea	5.00

Mostly Free

BANKING
Score: 3–Stable (moderate level of restrictions)

Banking in Kuwait is competitive, and banks are relatively free from government control. With the exception of investment banking, the banking system is closed to foreigners, although the government plans to increase foreign participation in the future.

WAGE AND PRICE CONTROLS
Score: 3–Stable (moderate level)

The market sets most wages and prices in Kuwait. The government continues to offer subsidies to many businesses, however, thereby distorting prices on some goods and services, like food.

PROPERTY RIGHTS
Score: 1–Stable (very high level of protection)

Private property is protected in Kuwait. The country has an efficient legal and judicial system.

REGULATION
Score: 2–Stable (low level)

Establishing a business in Kuwait is easy if the business does not intend to compete directly with state-owned concerns. Regulations are applied evenly in most cases.

BLACK MARKET
Score: 2–Stable (low level of activity)

The black market in Kuwait is confined mainly to pirated software, video and cassette recordings, and similar products. The government continues to combat violations.

NOTE

1.   U.S. Department of State, *Country Reports on Economic Policy and Trade Practices,* 1996, p. 480.

Kyrgyzstan

4.00

1997 Score: **n/a**　　　1996 Score: **n/a**　　　1995 Score: **n/a**

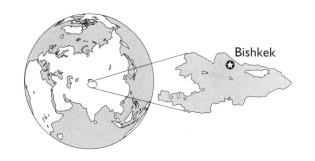

Bishkek

Trade	4	Banking	4
Taxation	4	Wages and Prices	4
Government Intervention	3	Property Rights	4
Monetary Policy	5	Regulation	4
Foreign Investment	3	Black Market	5

Kyrgyzstan became an autonomous republic of the Soviet Union in 1921 and was incorporated into the union in 1936. During some 70 years of Soviet rule, Kyrgyzstan underwent political, economic, and cultural repression, although some modernization and industrialization occurred in some urban areas of the country. Since becoming independent in 1991, Kyrgyzstan has begun to reform its economy; it is attempting to transform its centrally planned economy into a more market-based economy. Success has been sporadic, however, and the country remains hindered by an intransigent bureaucracy.

TRADE POLICY
Score: 4–Stable (high level of protectionism)

Kyrgyzstan's average tariff rate is about 10 percent. Among its nontariff barriers are corrupt customs officials who often charge arbitrary duty rates. According to the U.S. Department of Commerce, "Corruption is evident in tax and customs collection and in the enforcement of many laws and regulations and is especially noticeable in trade and in construction."[1]

TAXATION
Score–Income taxation: 4–Stable (high tax rates)
Score–Corporate taxation: 3–Stable (moderate tax rates)
Final Taxation Score: 4–Stable (high tax rates)

Kyrgyzstan has a top income tax rate of 40 percent[2] and a top marginal corporate tax rate of 30 percent. It also has a 30 percent capital gains tax and a 20 percent value-added tax.

GOVERNMENT INTERVENTION IN THE ECONOMY
Score: 3–Stable (moderate level)

Kyrgyzstan is privatizing its large state-owned sector. Government consumption as a percentage of GDP is at 23 percent.[3] The economy remains dominated by large state-owned enterprises, particularly in utilities and transportation. In 1997, however, the government passed a new law that paves the way for eventual privatization of state-owned enterprises in mining, aviation, energy, telecommunications, agriculture, and publishing. Such privatizations have yet to be completed.

MONETARY POLICY
Score: 5–Stable (very high level of inflation)

Kyrgyzstan has been plagued with hyperinflation. Although inflation was projected to be less than 35 percent in 1996, it was 42.6 percent in 1995, 278 percent in 1994, 1,209 percent in 1993, and 855 percent in 1992. Thus, although greatly reduced, inflation remains very high, both historically and by global standards.

1	Hong Kong	1.25	77	Zambia	3.05
2	Singapore	1.30	80	Mali	3.10
3	Bahrain	1.70	80	Mongolia	3.10
4	New Zealand	1.75	80	Slovenia	3.10
5	Switzerland	1.90	83	Honduras	3.15
5	United States	1.90	83	Papua New Guinea	3.15
7	Luxembourg	1.95	85	Djibouti	3.20
7	Taiwan	1.95	85	Fiji	3.20
7	United Kingdom	1.95	85	Pakistan	3.20
10	Bahamas	2.00	88	Algeria	3.25
10	Ireland	2.00	88	Guinea	3.25
12	Australia	2.05	88	Lebanon	3.25
12	Japan	2.05	88	Mexico	3.25
14	Belgium	2.10	88	Senegal	3.25
14	Canada	2.10	88	Tanzania	3.25
14	United Arab Emirates	2.10	94	Nigeria	3.30
17	Austria	2.15	94	Romania	3.30
17	Chile	2.15	96	Brazil	3.35
17	Estonia	2.15	96	Cambodia	3.35
20	Czech Republic	2.20	96	Egypt	3.35
20	Netherlands	2.20	96	Ivory Coast	3.35
22	Denmark	2.25	96	Madagascar	3.35
22	Finland	2.25	96	Moldova	3.35
24	Germany	2.30	102	Nepal	3.40
24	Iceland	2.30	103	Cape Verde	3.44
24	South Korea	2.30	104	Armenia	3.45
27	Norway	2.35	104	Dominican Republic	3.45
28	Kuwait	2.40	104	Russia	3.45
28	Malaysia	2.40	107	Burkina Faso	3.50
28	Panama	2.40	107	Cameroon	3.50
28	Thailand	2.40	107	Lesotho	3.50
32	El Salvador	2.45	107	Nicaragua	3.50
32	Sri Lanka	2.45	107	Venezuela	3.50
32	Sweden	2.45	112	Gambia	3.60
35	France	2.50	112	Guyana	3.60
35	Italy	2.50	114	Bulgaria	3.65
35	Spain	2.50	114	Georgia	3.65
38	Trinidad and Tobago	2.55	114	Malawi	3.65
39	Argentina	2.60	117	Ethiopia	3.70
39	Barbados	2.60	117	India	3.70
39	Cyprus	2.60	117	Niger	3.70
39	Jamaica	2.60	120	Albania	3.75
39	Portugal	2.60	120	Bangladesh	3.75
44	Bolivia	2.65	120	China (PRC)	3.75
44	Oman	2.65	120	Congo	3.75
44	Philippines	2.65	120	Croatia	3.75
47	Swaziland	2.70	125	Chad	3.80
47	Uruguay	2.70	125	Mauritania	3.80
49	Botswana	2.75	125	Ukraine	3.80
49	Jordan	2.75	128	Sierra Leone	3.85
49	Namibia	2.75	129	Burundi	3.90
49	Tunisia	2.75	129	Suriname	3.90
53	Belize	2.80	129	Zimbabwe	3.90
53	Costa Rica	2.80	132	Haiti	4.00
53	Guatemala	2.80	132	Kyrgyzstan	4.00
53	Israel	2.80	132	Syria	4.00
53	Peru	2.80	135	Belarus	4.05
53	Saudi Arabia	2.80	136	Kazakstan	4.10
53	Turkey	2.80	136	Mozambique	4.10
53	Uganda	2.80	136	Yemen	4.10
53	Western Samoa	2.80	139	Sudan	4.20
62	Indonesia	2.85	140	Myanmar	4.30
62	Latvia	2.85	140	Rwanda	4.30
62	Malta	2.85	142	Angola	4.35
62	Paraguay	2.85	143	Azerbaijan	4.40
66	Greece	2.90	143	Tajikistan	4.40
66	Hungary	2.90	145	Turkmenistan	4.50
66	South Africa	2.90	146	Uzbekistan	4.55
69	Benin	2.95	147	Congo/Zaire	4.70
69	Ecuador	2.95	147	Iran	4.70
69	Gabon	2.95	147	Libya	4.70
69	Morocco	2.95	147	Somalia	4.70
69	Poland	2.95	147	Vietnam	4.70
74	Colombia	3.00	152	Bosnia	4.80
74	Ghana	3.00	153	Iraq	4.90
74	Lithuania	3.00	154	Cuba	5.00
77	Kenya	3.05	154	Laos	5.00
77	Slovak Republic	3.05	154	North Korea	5.00

Repressed

Capital Flows and Foreign Investment
Score: 3–Stable (moderate barriers)

Although the government wants to promote increased foreign investment, it still maintains some barriers. Kyrgyzstan has opened most of its economy to foreign investment but forbids complete foreign ownership of mining companies and forestry. Foreigners may not own land, although they may lease it.

Banking
Score: 4–Stable (high level of restrictions)

Kyrgyzstan's banking system is not fully functional. According to the U.S. Department of Commerce, "The banking system is a private banking system supervised by a strong and independent central bank. The banking system is very weak and undercapitalized."[4] Although there are few official restrictions, the very fact that the system has yet to develop fully is a primary hindrance. Capital is scarce, lending policies usually are tightly controlled, and financial transactions are difficult. Domestic bank formation is virtually nonexistent, and the licenses of many existing banks are being revoked by the government. According to the U.S. Department of Commerce, "Four banks recently had their licenses revoked, two of them being completely insolvent former state banks."[5]

Wage and Price Controls
Score: 4–Stable (high level)

Wages and prices in Kyrgyzstan are controlled by the large number of state-owned industries. Price controls continue in such areas as agricultural products, transportation, and utilities.

Property Rights
Score: 4–Stable (low level of protection)

Kyrgyzstan's legal system does not afford private property sufficient protection. Although legal reform is a major government priority, the judiciary remains weak and corrupt. According to the U.S. Department of State, "The judicial system continues to operate under Soviet Laws and procedures.... Executive domination of the judiciary made assurances of due process problematic."[6]

Regulation
Score: 4–Stable (high level)

Establishing a business in Kyrgyzstan is a tedious and time-consuming procedure that requires individuals to overcome numerous bureaucratic barriers. According to the U.S. Department of Commerce, "Because of the state of flux, bureaucratic procedures are unclear and those in charge of implementing laws may not know what the law in fact is. This can cause a general state of confusion and lack of transparency in some issues."[7]

Black Market
Score: 5–Stable (very high level of activity)

Smuggling is rampant in Kyrgyzstan. Many imports are smuggled; according to the U.S. Department of Commerce, "Most foreign manufactured brands reportedly are smuggled."[8] Despite the existence of laws protecting intellectual property rights, there continues to be significant piracy in computer software.

Notes

1. U.S. Department of Commerce, *Country Commercial Guide,* 1997.
2. The tax on the average level of income is not available. Therefore, Kyrgyzstan is graded strictly on its top income tax rates.
3. World Bank, *World Development Report 1997.*
4. U.S. Department of Commerce, *Country Commercial Guide,* 1997.
5. *Ibid.*
6. U.S. Department of State, "Kyrgyzstan Country Report on Human Rights Practices for 1996," 1997.
7. U.S. Department of Commerce, *Country Commercial Guide,* 1997.
8. U.S. Department of Commerce, "Kyrgyzstan; Tobacco Situation," *Voluntary Report, Agworld Attaché Reports,* 1997.

Laos   5.00

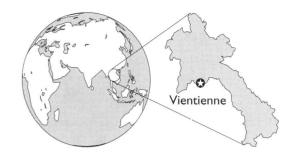

1997 Score: **5.00**	1996 Score: **5.00**	1995 Score: **n/a**

Trade	5	Banking	5
Taxation	5	Wages and Prices	5
Government Intervention	5	Property Rights	5
Monetary Policy	5	Regulation	5
Foreign Investment	5	Black Market	5

Laos, a constitutional monarchy before 1975, has one of the world's most repressed economies. It is a one-party communist state with a highly centralized, government-planned economy that is riddled with corruption and graft. The Clinton Administration recently removed a restriction on U.S. foreign aid to Laos, paving the way for the sending of U.S. development assistance to the regime. With such a highly corrupt and restricted system, however, the Laotian government is most likely to use this foreign aid to maintain the country's centrally planned economy.

TRADE POLICY
Score: 5–Stable (very high level of protectionism)

Import tariffs range from 0 percent to 200 percent, with most imports subject to a tariff of 45 percent. All imports are inspected by a corrupt customs service that applies customs duties and taxes imports arbitrarily. Officials sometimes simply confiscate imports at the border. In addition to this rampant corruption—sanctioned and supported by customs officials—trade barriers effectively bar most imports.

TAXATION
Score–Income taxation: 5–Stable (very high tax rates)
Score–Corporate taxation: 5–Stable (very high tax rates)
Final Taxation Score: 5–Stable (very high tax rates)

Because of its total control of the economy, Laos's government is able to confiscate the proceeds of all economic activity. By "owning" the fruits of economic activity, it imposes an effective rate of taxation that approaches 100 percent.

GOVERNMENT INTERVENTION IN THE ECONOMY
Score: 5–Stable (very high level)

Laos permits some restricted private economic activity, but the means of production and most of the profits gained from that production remain entirely in the hands of the state. The government owns and runs most of the country's primarily agricultural economy.

MONETARY POLICY
Score: 5–Stable (very high level of inflation)

The official average rate of inflation for Laos from 1985 to 1993 is 29.6 percent; the actual level is much higher. Because Laos has a centrally planned economy, demand usually exceeds supply for most items. In a market economy, this often leads to inflation; in centrally planned economies, it leads to shortages and rationing, which is the case with many goods and services in Laos.

1	Hong Kong	1.25	77 Zambia	3.05
2	Singapore	1.30	80 Mali	3.10
3	Bahrain	1.70	80 Mongolia	3.10
4	New Zealand	1.75	80 Slovenia	3.10
5	Switzerland	1.90	83 Honduras	3.15
5	United States	1.90	83 Papua New Guinea	3.15
7	Luxembourg	1.95	85 Djibouti	3.20
7	Taiwan	1.95	85 Fiji	3.20
7	United Kingdom	1.95	85 Pakistan	3.20
10	Bahamas	2.00	88 Algeria	3.25
10	Ireland	2.00	88 Guinea	3.25
12	Australia	2.05	88 Lebanon	3.25
12	Japan	2.05	88 Mexico	3.25
14	Belgium	2.10	88 Senegal	3.25
14	Canada	2.10	88 Tanzania	3.25
14	United Arab Emirates	2.10	94 Nigeria	3.30
17	Austria	2.15	94 Romania	3.30
17	Chile	2.15	96 Brazil	3.35
17	Estonia	2.15	96 Cambodia	3.35
20	Czech Republic	2.20	96 Egypt	3.35
20	Netherlands	2.20	96 Ivory Coast	3.35
22	Denmark	2.25	96 Madagascar	3.35
22	Finland	2.25	96 Moldova	3.35
24	Germany	2.30	102 Nepal	3.40
24	Iceland	2.30	103 Cape Verde	3.44
24	South Korea	2.30	104 Armenia	3.45
27	Norway	2.35	104 Dominican Republic	3.45
28	Kuwait	2.40	104 Russia	3.45
28	Malaysia	2.40	107 Burkina Faso	3.50
28	Panama	2.40	107 Cameroon	3.50
28	Thailand	2.40	107 Lesotho	3.50
32	El Salvador	2.45	107 Nicaragua	3.50
32	Sri Lanka	2.45	107 Venezuela	3.50
32	Sweden	2.45	112 Gambia	3.60
35	France	2.50	112 Guyana	3.60
35	Italy	2.50	114 Bulgaria	3.65
35	Spain	2.50	114 Georgia	3.65
38	Trinidad and Tobago	2.55	114 Malawi	3.65
39	Argentina	2.60	117 Ethiopia	3.70
39	Barbados	2.60	117 India	3.70
39	Cyprus	2.60	117 Niger	3.70
39	Jamaica	2.60	120 Albania	3.75
39	Portugal	2.60	120 Bangladesh	3.75
44	Bolivia	2.65	120 China (PRC)	3.75
44	Oman	2.65	120 Congo	3.75
44	Philippines	2.65	120 Croatia	3.75
47	Swaziland	2.70	125 Chad	3.80
47	Uruguay	2.70	125 Mauritania	3.80
49	Botswana	2.75	125 Ukraine	3.80
49	Jordan	2.75	128 Sierra Leone	3.85
49	Namibia	2.75	129 Burundi	3.90
49	Tunisia	2.75	129 Suriname	3.90
53	Belize	2.80	129 Zimbabwe	3.90
53	Costa Rica	2.80	132 Haiti	4.00
53	Guatemala	2.80	132 Kyrgyzstan	4.00
53	Israel	2.80	132 Syria	4.00
53	Peru	2.80	135 Belarus	4.05
53	Saudi Arabia	2.80	136 Kazakstan	4.10
53	Turkey	2.80	136 Mozambique	4.10
53	Uganda	2.80	136 Yemen	4.10
53	Western Samoa	2.80	139 Sudan	4.20
62	Indonesia	2.85	140 Myanmar	4.30
62	Latvia	2.85	140 Rwanda	4.30
62	Malta	2.85	142 Angola	4.35
62	Paraguay	2.85	143 Azerbaijan	4.40
66	Greece	2.90	143 Tajikistan	4.40
66	Hungary	2.90	145 Turkmenistan	4.50
66	South Africa	2.90	146 Uzbekistan	4.55
69	Benin	2.95	147 Congo/Zaire	4.70
69	Ecuador	2.95	147 Iran	4.70
69	Gabon	2.95	147 Libya	4.70
69	Morocco	2.95	147 Somalia	4.70
69	Poland	2.95	147 Vietnam	4.70
74	Colombia	3.00	152 Bosnia	4.80
74	Ghana	3.00	153 Iraq	4.90
74	Lithuania	3.00	154 Cuba	5.00
77	Kenya	3.05	154 Laos	5.00
77	Slovak Republic	3.05	154 North Korea	5.00

Repressed

CAPITAL FLOWS AND FOREIGN INVESTMENT
Score: 5–Stable (very high barriers)

Laos permits some foreign investment, and the government allows 100 percent foreign ownership of investments in almost all areas of the economy. But it would be a mistake to infer that this means Laos is open to foreign investment. Corruption and arbitrary government confiscation of profits through a multitude of constantly changing fees, taxes, stipends, and other charges make it nearly impossible to conduct business. Bribes to government officials are implicitly mandatory when establishing a business, and foreigners often are subject to government surveillance. Property is confiscated and foreigners are expelled on a regular basis. Although Laos does not seek actively to prevent foreign investment, its centralized, corrupt, and bureaucratic economy and one-party communist rule have had the same effect.

BANKING
Score: 5–Stable (very high level of restrictions)

Banks in Laos are owned and operated by the government, as well as influenced heavily by the state-owned central bank. There is no free-market competition in the banking industry.

WAGE AND PRICE CONTROLS
Score: 5–Stable (very high level)

The government sets virtually all wages and prices in Laos—particularly on such products as rice, sugar, cloth, and gasoline.

PROPERTY RIGHTS
Score: 5–Stable (very low level of protection)

Individuals are free to accumulate some private property, such as a home or a piece of land, but all such property is subject to expropriation, pillaging by the Vietnamese "security" forces that routinely enter Laos, extortion by corrupt local government officials, and destruction by criminal elements sanctioned by the government. The corrupt, state-controlled legal system rarely rules in favor of private citizens in complaints against the government. According to the U.S. Department of Commerce, "Laos' fledgling and evolving legal system is loosely based on the Soviet model.... The laws are not widely distributed nor are the judges sufficiently trained to ensure consistent application."[1]

REGULATION
Score: 5–Stable (very high level)

The government regulates Laos's entire economy by owning and operating all means of production. According to the U.S. Department of Commerce, "The Lao bureaucracy may be described as arcane and deliberate."[2]

BLACK MARKET
Score: 5–Stable (very high level of activity)

The black market in Laos is larger than the official or legal economy. As in other command economies, even basic economic activity is performed in the black market.

NOTES
1. U.S. Department of Commerce, "Laos—Investment Climate," *Market Research Reports,* August 15, 1996.
2. *Ibid.*

Latvia   2.85

| 1997 Score: **2.95** | 1996 Score: **3.05** | 1995 Score: **n/a** |

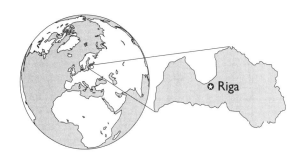

Riga

Trade	2	Banking	2
Taxation	2.5	Wages and Prices	2
Government Intervention	3	Property Rights	3
Monetary Policy	5	Regulation	3
Foreign Investment	2	Black Market	4

Latvia was an independent republic from 1918 to 1940, at which time it was annexed by the Soviet Union. Since declaring its independence in August 1991, it has liberalized its economy and made substantial progress in opening its borders to trade and investment despite some remaining roadblocks. Latvia enjoys a highly trained labor force and is home to several high-tech enterprises, as well as major ports on the Baltic Sea. After a 50 percent drop in GDP from 1991 to 1993, the economy began to recover in 1994 and has stabilized. The government, which has applied for membership in the European Union, recently reduced barriers to trade and some barriers to foreign investment and banking. It also has streamlined its court system. Recent evidence indicates, however, that the judiciary is not protecting private property rights adequately. Nevertheless, Latvia's overall score improved 0.1 point over last year.

TRADE POLICY

Score: 2+ (low level of protectionism)

Latvia's average tariff rate is less than 2 percent, down from about 10 percent in 1995. Thus, its trade policy score is two points better this year. According to the U.S. Department of State, "Latvia requires a license for the import of grain, sugar, and alcohol to protect domestic production."[1] This represents the principal nontariff barrier to trade.

TAXATION

Score–Income taxation: 2–Stable (low tax rates)
Score–Corporate taxation: 2–Stable (low tax rates)
Final Taxation Score: 2.5–Stable (moderate tax rates)

Latvia has a flat income tax rate of 25 percent and a flat corporate tax rate of 25 percent. It also has an 18 percent value-added tax and a 37 percent social payments tax.

GOVERNMENT INTERVENTION IN THE ECONOMY

Score: 3–Stable (moderate level)

Government consumes about 20.9 percent of Latvia's GDP, almost 40 percent of which is still produced by the public sector.[2] Because this is low by global standards, the public sector's portion of GDP moves Latvia's overall government intervention score into the moderate category.

MONETARY POLICY

Score: 5–Stable (very high level of inflation)

Latvia's rate of inflation was 124.5 percent in 1991, 951.2 percent in 1992, 109.2 percent in 1993, 35.9 percent in 1994, 25 percent in 1995, and 17.7 percent in 1996. Thus, even though Latvia has made tremendous progress in reducing inflation, the average annual rate since independence is still over 200 percent.

1	Hong Kong	1.25	77	Zambia	3.05
2	Singapore	1.30	80	Mali	3.10
3	Bahrain	1.70	80	Mongolia	3.10
4	New Zealand	1.75	80	Slovenia	3.10
5	Switzerland	1.90	83	Honduras	3.15
5	United States	1.90	83	Papua New Guinea	3.15
7	Luxembourg	1.95	85	Djibouti	3.20
7	Taiwan	1.95	85	Fiji	3.20
7	United Kingdom	1.95	85	Pakistan	3.20
10	Bahamas	2.00	88	Algeria	3.25
10	Ireland	2.00	88	Guinea	3.25
12	Australia	2.05	88	Lebanon	3.25
12	Japan	2.05	88	Mexico	3.25
14	Belgium	2.10	88	Senegal	3.25
14	Canada	2.10	88	Tanzania	3.25
14	United Arab Emirates	2.10	94	Nigeria	3.30
17	Austria	2.15	94	Romania	3.30
17	Chile	2.15	96	Brazil	3.35
17	Estonia	2.15	96	Cambodia	3.35
20	Czech Republic	2.20	96	Egypt	3.35
20	Netherlands	2.20	96	Ivory Coast	3.35
22	Denmark	2.25	96	Madagascar	3.35
22	Finland	2.25	96	Moldova	3.35
24	Germany	2.30	102	Nepal	3.40
24	Iceland	2.30	103	Cape Verde	3.44
24	South Korea	2.30	104	Armenia	3.45
27	Norway	2.35	104	Dominican Republic	3.45
28	Kuwait	2.40	104	Russia	3.45
28	Malaysia	2.40	107	Burkina Faso	3.50
28	Panama	2.40	107	Cameroon	3.50
28	Thailand	2.40	107	Lesotho	3.50
32	El Salvador	2.45	107	Nicaragua	3.50
32	Sri Lanka	2.45	107	Venezuela	3.50
32	Sweden	2.45	112	Gambia	3.60
35	France	2.50	112	Guyana	3.60
35	Italy	2.50	114	Bulgaria	3.65
35	Spain	2.50	114	Georgia	3.65
38	Trinidad and Tobago	2.55	114	Malawi	3.65
39	Argentina	2.60	117	Ethiopia	3.70
39	Barbados	2.60	117	India	3.70
39	Cyprus	2.60	117	Niger	3.70
39	Jamaica	2.60	120	Albania	3.75
39	Portugal	2.60	120	Bangladesh	3.75
44	Bolivia	2.65	120	China (PRC)	3.75
44	Oman	2.65	120	Congo	3.75
44	Philippines	2.65	120	Croatia	3.75
47	Swaziland	2.70	125	Chad	3.80
47	Uruguay	2.70	125	Mauritania	3.80
49	Botswana	2.75	125	Ukraine	3.80
49	Jordan	2.75	128	Sierra Leone	3.85
49	Namibia	2.75	129	Burundi	3.90
49	Tunisia	2.75	129	Suriname	3.90
53	Belize	2.80	129	Zimbabwe	3.90
53	Costa Rica	2.80	132	Haiti	4.00
53	Guatemala	2.80	132	Kyrgyzstan	4.00
53	Israel	2.80	132	Syria	4.00
53	Peru	2.80	135	Belarus	4.05
53	Saudi Arabia	2.80	136	Kazakstan	4.10
53	Turkey	2.80	136	Mozambique	4.10
53	Uganda	2.80	136	Yemen	4.10
53	Western Samoa	2.80	139	Sudan	4.20
62	Indonesia	2.85	140	Myanmar	4.30
62	Latvia	2.85	140	Rwanda	4.30
62	Malta	2.85	142	Angola	4.35
62	Paraguay	2.85	143	Azerbaijan	4.40
66	Greece	2.90	143	Tajikistan	4.40
66	Hungary	2.90	145	Turkmenistan	4.50
66	South Africa	2.90	146	Uzbekistan	4.55
69	Benin	2.95	147	Congo/Zaire	4.70
69	Ecuador	2.95	147	Iran	4.70
69	Gabon	2.95	147	Libya	4.70
69	Morocco	2.95	147	Somalia	4.70
69	Poland	2.95	147	Vietnam	4.70
74	Colombia	3.00	152	Bosnia	4.80
74	Ghana	3.00	153	Iraq	4.90
74	Lithuania	3.00	154	Cuba	5.00
77	Kenya	3.05	154	Laos	5.00
77	Slovak Republic	3.05	154	North Korea	5.00

Mostly Free

CAPITAL FLOWS AND FOREIGN INVESTMENT
Score: 2–Stable (low barriers)

There are few restrictions on investment in Latvia. Foreigners are permitted to invest in most industries but are restricted from acquiring majority shares in companies related to national defense. Investors now may own land in Latvia if there is an existing investment protection agreement between the two countries. The foreign investment code has been streamlined and updated.

BANKING
Score: 2–Stable (low level of restrictions)

Latvia's banking sector underwent significant transformation in 1995, with less competitive banks going out of business. Financial crisis in the banking industry in neighboring Russia also has caused some Latvian banks to collapse. Today, Latvia's banking system is beginning to stabilize; it is competitive and mostly free of onerous government regulation. The government has partially privatized the State Savings Bank (Krajbanka) and Unibank. The Bank of Latvia, however, must approve all foreign investments in domestic banks and all foreign bank branches.

WAGE AND PRICE CONTROLS
Score: 2–Stable (low level)

The private sector sets most wages and prices in Latvia, although the government continues to set prices on some goods and services, such as electricity, rents for government-controlled housing, and telecommunications.

PROPERTY RIGHTS
Score: 3– (moderate level of protection)

Since independence, the government has not expropriated any property. The court system is becoming more efficient, and laws are being drafted to reflect Western standards more closely. There is no indication that the government influences the legal process unduly. According to the U.S. Department of State, however, there is evidence that the "judiciary is independent but not well-trained, efficient, or free from corruption."[3] Thus, Latvia's property rights score is one point worse this year.

REGULATION
Score: 3–Stable (moderate level)

Establishing a business in Latvia is relatively easy, and many private businesses are opening. There is some corruption, and some regulations are applied unevenly. "As in other countries to emerge from the old Soviet Bloc," reports the U.S. Department of Commerce, "government bureaucracy, corruption and organized crime are the most significant hurdles to U.S. trade and investment in Latvia."[4]

BLACK MARKET
Score: 4–Stable (high level of activity)

The black market in Latvia involves mainly agricultural goods, transportation, and labor. The government estimates that black market activity is equivalent to one-third of the official economy. There is significant trafficking in pirated video tapes and motion pictures, as well as increasing black market activity in the smuggling of commodities from Russia. Some banking operations also are performed on the black market.

NOTES
1. U.S. Department of State, *Country Reports on Economic Policy and Trade Practices,* 1996, p. 224.
2. Government of Latvia, *Latvia, Country Profile,* from Latvian Embassy, Washington, D.C.
3. U.S. Department of State, "Latvia Country Report on Human Rights Practices for 1996," 1997.
4. U.S. Department of Commerce, *Country Commercial Guide,* 1997.

Lebanon   3.25

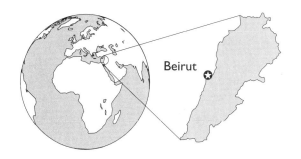

Beirut

1997 Score: **2.95**	1996 Score: **2.95**	1995 Score: **n/a**

Trade	5	Banking	2
Taxation	2.5	Wages and Prices	2
Government Intervention	2	Property Rights	3
Monetary Policy	5	Regulation	3
Foreign Investment	3	Black Market	5

After 17 years of bloody civil war, Lebanon elected Prime Minister Rafiq Hariri in 1992. Hariri embarked on an ambitious reform plan aimed at stimulating the economy. The war-torn country suffers from a shattered infrastructure, outdated utilities, and the destruction of much of Beirut, formerly one of the Arab world's foremost financial and trade centers. Hariri's reconstruction plans have opened significant opportunities to businesses, which are rushing to rebuild the country as Lebanon tries to implement a more open foreign investment regime. Parts of the Lebanese economy are among the freest in the world; most restrictions on economic freedom are the result of civil war, the lack of the rule of law, and the intimidating presence of more than 30,000 Syrian troops, who engage extensively in car theft and smuggling. Lebanon's overall score is 0.3 point worse than last year.

TRADE POLICY
Score: 5– (very high level of protectionism)

Lebanon's average tariff rate is 24.2 percent—much higher than previously thought.[1] As a result, its trade score is three points worse this year. There are few nontariff barriers, although the government does require import licenses for firearms and ammunition. The operations of the customs service are marred by some corruption and inefficiency.

TAXATION
Score–Income taxation: 2–Stable (low tax rates)
Score–Corporate taxation: 2–Stable (low tax rates)
Final Taxation Score: 2.5–Stable (moderate tax rates)

Lebanon's top income tax rate is 10 percent, with the average taxpayer in the 2 percent bracket. The top marginal corporate tax rate is 10 percent. Lebanon also has a 6 percent capital gains tax and a 12 percent social contributions tax.

GOVERNMENT INTERVENTION IN THE ECONOMY
Score: 2–Stable (low level)

Government consumes about 11.6 percent of Lebanon's GDP. It also has established a significant privatization program to reduce its role in the economy. "Lebanon enjoys a free-market economy and a strong laissez-faire commercial tradition," reports the U.S. Department of Commerce. "The government is seriously considering privatization of some public services. It has succeeded in awarding some contracts on a build/operate/transfer (BOT) basis. In 1994 it reduced the state's shares in three local medium and long term development banks to 20 percent in order to encourage private sector participation in economic reconstruction."[2]

1	Hong Kong		1.25	77	Zambia	3.05
2	Singapore		1.30	80	Mali	3.10
3	Bahrain		1.70	80	Mongolia	3.10
4	New Zealand		1.75	80	Slovenia	3.10
5	Switzerland		1.90	83	Honduras	3.15
5	United States		1.90	83	Papua New Guinea	3.15
7	Luxembourg		1.95	85	Djibouti	3.20
7	Taiwan		1.95	85	Fiji	3.20
7	United Kingdom		1.95	85	Pakistan	3.20
10	Bahamas		2.00	88	Algeria	3.25
10	Ireland		2.00	88	Guinea	3.25
12	Australia		2.05	88	Lebanon	3.25
12	Japan		2.05	88	Mexico	3.25
14	Belgium		2.10	88	Senegal	3.25
14	Canada		2.10	88	Tanzania	3.25
14	United Arab Emirates		2.10	94	Nigeria	3.30
17	Austria		2.15	94	Romania	3.30
17	Chile		2.15	96	Brazil	3.35
17	Estonia		2.15	96	Cambodia	3.35
20	Czech Republic		2.20	96	Egypt	3.35
20	Netherlands		2.20	96	Ivory Coast	3.35
22	Denmark		2.25	96	Madagascar	3.35
22	Finland		2.25	96	Moldova	3.35
24	Germany		2.30	102	Nepal	3.40
24	Iceland		2.30	103	Cape Verde	3.44
24	South Korea		2.30	104	Armenia	3.45
27	Norway		2.35	104	Dominican Republic	3.45
28	Kuwait		2.40	104	Russia	3.45
28	Malaysia		2.40	107	Burkina Faso	3.50
28	Panama		2.40	107	Cameroon	3.50
28	Thailand		2.40	107	Lesotho	3.50
32	El Salvador		2.45	107	Nicaragua	3.50
32	Sri Lanka		2.45	107	Venezuela	3.50
32	Sweden		2.45	112	Gambia	3.60
35	France		2.50	112	Guyana	3.60
35	Italy		2.50	114	Bulgaria	3.65
35	Spain		2.50	114	Georgia	3.65
38	Trinidad and Tobago		2.55	114	Malawi	3.65
39	Argentina		2.60	117	Ethiopia	3.70
39	Barbados		2.60	117	India	3.70
39	Cyprus		2.60	117	Niger	3.70
39	Jamaica		2.60	120	Albania	3.75
39	Portugal		2.60	120	Bangladesh	3.75
44	Bolivia		2.65	120	China (PRC)	3.75
44	Oman		2.65	120	Congo	3.75
44	Philippines		2.65	120	Croatia	3.75
47	Swaziland		2.70	125	Chad	3.80
47	Uruguay		2.70	125	Mauritania	3.80
49	Botswana		2.75	125	Ukraine	3.80
49	Jordan		2.75	128	Sierra Leone	3.85
49	Namibia		2.75	129	Burundi	3.90
49	Tunisia		2.75	129	Suriname	3.90
53	Belize		2.80	129	Zimbabwe	3.90
53	Costa Rica		2.80	132	Haiti	4.00
53	Guatemala		2.80	132	Kyrgyzstan	4.00
53	Israel		2.80	132	Syria	4.00
53	Peru		2.80	135	Belarus	4.05
53	Saudi Arabia		2.80	136	Kazakstan	4.10
53	Turkey		2.80	136	Mozambique	4.10
53	Uganda		2.80	136	Yemen	4.10
53	Western Samoa		2.80	139	Sudan	4.20
62	Indonesia		2.85	140	Myanmar	4.30
62	Latvia		2.85	140	Rwanda	4.30
62	Malta		2.85	142	Angola	4.35
62	Paraguay		2.85	143	Azerbaijan	4.40
66	Greece		2.90	143	Tajikistan	4.40
66	Hungary		2.90	145	Turkmenistan	4.50
66	South Africa		2.90	145	Uzbekistan	4.55
69	Benin		2.95	147	Congo/Zaire	4.70
69	Ecuador		2.95	147	Iran	4.70
69	Gabon		2.95	147	Libya	4.70
69	Morocco		2.95	147	Somalia	4.70
69	Poland		2.95	147	Vietnam	4.70
74	Colombia		3.00	152	Bosnia	4.80
74	Ghana		3.00	153	Iraq	4.90
74	Lithuania		3.00	154	Cuba	5.00
77	Kenya		3.05	154	Laos	5.00
77	Slovak Republic		3.05	154	North Korea	5.00

Mostly Unfree

MONETARY POLICY
Score: 5–Stable (very high level of inflation)

Lebanon's average rate of inflation from 1985 to 1995 was about 45.8 percent.

CAPITAL FLOWS AND FOREIGN INVESTMENT
Score: 3–Stable (moderate barriers)

According to the U.S. Department of Commerce, "Lebanon offers the most liberal investment climate in the Middle East."[3] It restricts the amount of real estate foreigners may own, is still lacking in the rule of law, and needs an efficient investment approval regime. But by global standards, the barriers to foreign investment are moderate.

BANKING
Score: 2–Stable (low level of restrictions)

Lebanon's banking system is highly competitive and saturated with private banks. There are over 70 commercial banks. Foreign banks, however, may not open wholly owned branches.

WAGE AND PRICE CONTROLS
Score: 2–Stable (low level)

The market sets most wages and prices in Lebanon with very little government involvement, although the government's consumer protection agency can establish price controls.

PROPERTY RIGHTS
Score: 3–Stable (moderate level of protection)

The most significant threats to private property are illegal activity and seizure of property by Syrian soldiers, the lack of an efficient legal system, and the inconsistent application of the rule of law. According to the U.S. Department of Commerce, "The legal system, modeled after the French system, is being studied for modernization, and new laws tend to follow international patterns. Still, court cases are not settled rapidly because of a shortage of judges and inadequate support structure."[4]

REGULATION
Score: 3–Stable (moderate level)

Establishing a business in Lebanon is easy, but corruption and crime can hinder normal business operations.

BLACK MARKET
Score: 5–Stable (very high level of activity)

Lebanon's black market includes extensive trading in pirated intellectual property like trademarks, patents, and copyrights. Many services, such as transportation and construction, also are performed in the black market.

NOTES

1. The score in this factor has changed from 2 in 1997 to 5 in 1998. Previously unavailable data provide a more accurate understanding of the country's performance. See International Monetary Fund, *Adjusting to New Realities: MENA, The Uruguay Round, and the EU-Mediterranean Initiative,* January 1997. The methodology for this factor remains the same.
2. U.S. Department of Commerce, *Country Commercial Guide,* 1997.
3. U.S. Department of Commerce, *Country Commercial Guide,* 1996.
4. *Ibid.*

Lesotho

3.50

| 1997 Score: **3.65** | 1996 Score: **3.65** | 1995 Score: **n/a** |

Trade	3	Banking	4
Taxation	4	Wages and Prices	4
Government Intervention	3	Property Rights	3
Monetary Policy	3	Regulation	4
Foreign Investment	3	Black Market	4

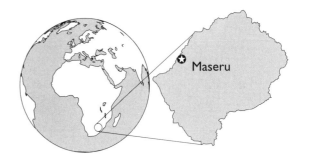

Maseru

Lesotho gained its independence from the United Kingdom in 1966. It is a constitutional monarchy, but executive power has resided with the prime minister since the 1993 constitution stripped the king of this authority. Lesotho is completely encircled by South Africa and depends on it for access to trade and employment opportunities. Employment in the South African mines, the main source of Lesotho's very high level of income from abroad, contributed 32 percent of GNP in 1994. During the 1970s and much of the 1980s, heavy restrictions were imposed on almost all economic activity. By 1990, the government had begun to consider the economic reform program that remains in place today. The economy responded with a 10.7 percent growth in GDP from 1994 to 1996. Lesotho recently reduced its barriers to trade and some taxes. As a result, its overall score is 0.15 point better this year.

TRADE POLICY

Score: 3+ (moderate level of protectionism)

The newly established Southern African Customs Union, comprised of South Africa, Botswana, Lesotho, Namibia, and Swaziland, has reduced barriers to trade. Lesotho's common average tariff rate is 12 percent, down from 17.4 percent. As a result, the country's trade score is one point better this year.

TAXATION

Score–Income taxation: 4–Stable (high tax rates)
Score–Corporate taxation: 3+ (moderate tax rates)
Final Taxation Score: 4+ (high tax rates)

Lesotho's top income tax rate is 40 percent; the average taxpayer finds himself in the 15 percent bracket. The top marginal corporate tax rate is 35 percent, down from 40 percent last year. As a result, Lesotho's total tax score is one-half point better this year. Lesotho also has a 40 percent capital gains tax and a 10 percent general services tax.

GOVERNMENT INTERVENTION IN THE ECONOMY

Score: 3–Stable (moderate level)

Government consumes about 23 percent of Lesotho's GDP, a significant portion of which is generated by the state-owned sector.

MONETARY POLICY

Score: 3–Stable (moderate level of inflation)

Lesotho's average rate of inflation from 1985 to 1995 was 13.6 percent. In 1996, inflation was 10 percent.

1	Hong Kong	1.25	77	Zambia	3.05
2	Singapore	1.30	80	Mali	3.10
3	Bahrain	1.70	80	Mongolia	3.10
4	New Zealand	1.75	80	Slovenia	3.10
5	Switzerland	1.90	83	Honduras	3.15
5	United States	1.90	83	Papua New Guinea	3.15
7	Luxembourg	1.95	85	Djibouti	3.20
7	Taiwan	1.95	85	Fiji	3.20
7	United Kingdom	1.95	85	Pakistan	3.20
10	Bahamas	2.00	88	Algeria	3.25
10	Ireland	2.00	88	Guinea	3.25
12	Australia	2.05	88	Lebanon	3.25
12	Japan	2.05	88	Mexico	3.25
14	Belgium	2.10	88	Senegal	3.25
14	Canada	2.10	88	Tanzania	3.25
14	United Arab Emirates	2.10	94	Nigeria	3.30
17	Austria	2.15	94	Romania	3.30
17	Chile	2.15	96	Brazil	3.35
17	Estonia	2.15	96	Cambodia	3.35
20	Czech Republic	2.20	96	Egypt	3.35
20	Netherlands	2.20	96	Ivory Coast	3.35
22	Denmark	2.25	96	Madagascar	3.35
22	Finland	2.25	96	Moldova	3.35
24	Germany	2.30	102	Nepal	3.40
24	Iceland	2.30	103	Cape Verde	3.44
24	South Korea	2.30	104	Armenia	3.45
27	Norway	2.35	104	Dominican Republic	3.45
28	Kuwait	2.40	104	Russia	3.45
28	Malaysia	2.40	107	Burkina Faso	3.50
28	Panama	2.40	107	Cameroon	3.50
28	Thailand	2.40	107	Lesotho	3.50
32	El Salvador	2.45	107	Nicaragua	3.50
32	Sri Lanka	2.45	107	Venezuela	3.50
32	Sweden	2.45	112	Gambia	3.60
35	France	2.50	112	Guyana	3.60
35	Italy	2.50	114	Bulgaria	3.65
35	Spain	2.50	114	Georgia	3.65
38	Trinidad and Tobago	2.55	114	Malawi	3.65
39	Argentina	2.60	117	Ethiopia	3.70
39	Barbados	2.60	117	India	3.70
39	Cyprus	2.60	117	Niger	3.70
39	Jamaica	2.60	120	Albania	3.75
39	Portugal	2.60	120	Bangladesh	3.75
44	Bolivia	2.65	120	China (PRC)	3.75
44	Oman	2.65	120	Congo	3.75
44	Philippines	2.65	120	Croatia	3.75
47	Swaziland	2.70	125	Chad	3.80
47	Uruguay	2.70	125	Mauritania	3.80
49	Botswana	2.75	125	Ukraine	3.80
49	Jordan	2.75	128	Sierra Leone	3.85
49	Namibia	2.75	129	Burundi	3.90
49	Tunisia	2.75	129	Suriname	3.90
53	Belize	2.80	129	Zimbabwe	3.90
53	Costa Rica	2.80	132	Haiti	4.00
53	Guatemala	2.80	132	Kyrgyzstan	4.00
53	Israel	2.80	132	Syria	4.00
53	Peru	2.80	135	Belarus	4.05
53	Saudi Arabia	2.80	136	Kazakstan	4.10
53	Turkey	2.80	136	Mozambique	4.10
53	Uganda	2.80	136	Yemen	4.10
53	Western Samoa	2.80	139	Sudan	4.20
62	Indonesia	2.85	140	Myanmar	4.30
62	Latvia	2.85	140	Rwanda	4.30
62	Malta	2.85	142	Angola	4.35
62	Paraguay	2.85	143	Azerbaijan	4.40
66	Greece	2.90	143	Tajikistan	4.40
66	Hungary	2.90	145	Turkmenistan	4.50
66	South Africa	2.90	146	Uzbekistan	4.55
69	Benin	2.95	147	Congo/Zaire	4.70
69	Ecuador	2.95	147	Iran	4.70
69	Gabon	2.95	147	Libya	4.70
69	Morocco	2.95	147	Somalia	4.70
69	Poland	2.95	147	Vietnam	4.70
74	Colombia	3.00	152	Bosnia	4.80
74	Ghana	3.00	153	Iraq	4.90
74	Lithuania	3.00	154	Cuba	5.00
77	Kenya	3.05	154	Laos	5.00
77	Slovak Republic	3.05	154	North Korea	5.00

Mostly Unfree

CAPITAL FLOWS AND FOREIGN INVESTMENT
Score: 3–Stable (moderate barriers)

Lesotho maintains some informal restrictions on investments in areas competing with domestic local investment. It has an established investment code but offers few incentives.

BANKING
Score: 4–Stable (high level of restrictions)

The banking system in Lesotho is heavily regulated by the government, which also owns one of the country's largest banks. According to the U.S. Department of Commerce, "There are three commercial banks in Lesotho, each targeting a distinct niche market. One of the three is wholly owned, but not operated, by the government."[1] These banks enable the government to control a large portion of the banking industry's assets.

WAGE AND PRICE CONTROLS
Score: 4–Stable (high level)

Wages and prices are affected by Lesotho's large state sector, which receives government subsidies. The government continues to set some prices on utilities, as well as on some agricultural goods.

PROPERTY RIGHTS
Score: 3–Stable (moderate level of protection)

Private property is guaranteed in Lesotho, and expropriation is unlikely. Foreigners, however, are not permitted to own land.

REGULATION
Score: 4–Stable (high level)

Establishing a business in Lesotho can be difficult if the business plans to compete directly with a state-owned company or government-sanctioned monopoly. There is some corruption.

BLACK MARKET
Score: 4–Stable (high level of activity)

Lesotho has a substantial black market, primarily in consumer goods.

NOTE
1. U.S. Department of Commerce, *Country Commercial Guide,* 1996.

Libya 4.70

Trade	5	Banking	5
Taxation	5	Wages and Prices	5
Government Intervention	5	Property Rights	5
Monetary Policy	2	Regulation	5
Foreign Investment	5	Black Market	5

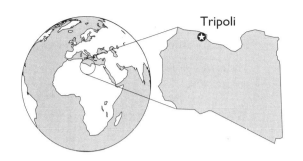

Tripoli

Libya gained its independence from Italy in 1951. Its state-dominated socialist economy depends primarily on oil revenues, which contribute almost all export earnings and about one-third of GDP. In 1992, the United Nations imposed sanctions on Libya for its support of terrorist activities. Libya's dictator, Muammar Qadhafi, has hinted at mild economic reforms, but he remains hostile to capitalism and dedicated to quasi-Marxist economic theories. Libya remains one of the world's most economically repressed countries.

TRADE POLICY
Score: 5–Stable (very high level of protectionism)

Libya's average tariff rate is over 18 percent, but tariffs represent only a small portion of the fees that importers generally must pay. If all these fees are taken into account, Libya's average tariff rate is over 34 percent.[1] The government controls almost all imports and exports, and it remains difficult to move goods and services across the border. The government also bans many imports, especially imports of goods like audio and video recordings that reflect Western culture.

TAXATION
Score–Income taxation: 5–Stable (very high tax rates)
Score–Corporate taxation: 5–Stable (very high tax rates)
Final Taxation Score: 5–Stable (very high tax rates)

Libya's government maintains its dedication to the redistribution of wealth as well as its hostility to individual wealth. Its top income tax rate is 90 percent, with the average taxpayer in the 35 percent bracket. The top marginal corporate tax rate is 60 percent. Libya also has a 60 percent capital gains tax and a *jihad* (holy war) tax of up to 4 percent of income.

GOVERNMENT INTERVENTION IN THE ECONOMY
Score: 5–Stable (very high level)

Government produces nearly all of Libya's GDP.

MONETARY POLICY
Score: 2–Stable (low level of inflation)

Libya's average rate of inflation from 1990 to 1994 was 10 percent.[2]

CAPITAL FLOWS AND FOREIGN INVESTMENT
Score: 5–Stable (very high barriers)

Libya tolerates little foreign investment. When investment is allowed, it is on a case-by-case basis.

1	Hong Kong	1.25	77	Zambia	3.05
2	Singapore	1.30	80	Mali	3.10
3	Bahrain	1.70	80	Mongolia	3.10
4	New Zealand	1.75	80	Slovenia	3.10
5	Switzerland	1.90	83	Honduras	3.15
5	United States	1.90	83	Papua New Guinea	3.15
7	Luxembourg	1.95	85	Djibouti	3.20
7	Taiwan	1.95	85	Fiji	3.20
7	United Kingdom	1.95	85	Pakistan	3.20
10	Bahamas	2.00	88	Algeria	3.25
10	Ireland	2.00	88	Guinea	3.25
12	Australia	2.05	88	Lebanon	3.25
12	Japan	2.05	88	Mexico	3.25
14	Belgium	2.10	88	Senegal	3.25
14	Canada	2.10	88	Tanzania	3.25
14	United Arab Emirates	2.10	94	Nigeria	3.30
17	Austria	2.15	94	Romania	3.30
17	Chile	2.15	96	Brazil	3.35
17	Estonia	2.15	96	Cambodia	3.35
20	Czech Republic	2.20	96	Egypt	3.35
20	Netherlands	2.20	96	Ivory Coast	3.35
22	Denmark	2.25	96	Madagascar	3.35
22	Finland	2.25	96	Moldova	3.35
24	Germany	2.30	102	Nepal	3.40
24	Iceland	2.30	103	Cape Verde	3.44
24	South Korea	2.30	104	Armenia	3.45
27	Norway	2.35	104	Dominican Republic	3.45
28	Kuwait	2.40	104	Russia	3.45
28	Malaysia	2.40	107	Burkina Faso	3.50
28	Panama	2.40	107	Cameroon	3.50
28	Thailand	2.40	107	Lesotho	3.50
32	El Salvador	2.45	107	Nicaragua	3.50
32	Sri Lanka	2.45	107	Venezuela	3.50
32	Sweden	2.45	112	Gambia	3.60
35	France	2.50	112	Guyana	3.60
35	Italy	2.50	114	Bulgaria	3.65
35	Spain	2.50	114	Georgia	3.65
38	Trinidad and Tobago	2.55	114	Malawi	3.65
39	Argentina	2.60	117	Ethiopia	3.70
39	Barbados	2.60	117	India	3.70
39	Cyprus	2.60	117	Niger	3.70
39	Jamaica	2.60	120	Albania	3.75
39	Portugal	2.60	120	Bangladesh	3.75
44	Bolivia	2.65	120	China (PRC)	3.75
44	Oman	2.65	120	Congo	3.75
44	Philippines	2.65	120	Croatia	3.75
47	Swaziland	2.70	125	Chad	3.80
47	Uruguay	2.70	125	Mauritania	3.80
49	Botswana	2.75	125	Ukraine	3.80
49	Jordan	2.75	128	Sierra Leone	3.85
49	Namibia	2.75	129	Burundi	3.90
49	Tunisia	2.75	129	Suriname	3.90
53	Belize	2.80	129	Zimbabwe	3.90
53	Costa Rica	2.80	132	Haiti	4.00
53	Guatemala	2.80	132	Kyrgyzstan	4.00
53	Israel	2.80	132	Syria	4.00
53	Peru	2.80	135	Belarus	4.05
53	Saudi Arabia	2.80	136	Kazakstan	4.10
53	Turkey	2.80	136	Mozambique	4.10
53	Uganda	2.80	136	Yemen	4.10
53	Western Samoa	2.80	139	Sudan	4.20
62	Indonesia	2.85	140	Myanmar	4.30
62	Latvia	2.85	140	Rwanda	4.30
62	Malta	2.85	142	Angola	4.35
62	Paraguay	2.85	143	Azerbaijan	4.40
66	Greece	2.90	143	Tajikistan	4.40
66	Hungary	2.90	145	Turkmenistan	4.50
66	South Africa	2.90	146	Uzbekistan	4.55
69	Benin	2.95	147	Congo/Zaire	4.70
69	Ecuador	2.95	147	Iran	4.70
69	Gabon	2.95	147	Libya	4.70
69	Morocco	2.95	147	Somalia	4.70
69	Poland	2.95	147	Vietnam	4.70
74	Colombia	3.00	152	Bosnia	4.80
74	Ghana	3.00	153	Iraq	4.90
74	Lithuania	3.00	154	Cuba	5.00
77	Kenya	3.05	154	Laos	5.00
77	Slovak Republic	3.05	154	North Korea	5.00

Repressed

BANKING
Score: 5–Stable (very high level of restrictions)

The banking system in Libya is owned entirely by the government.

WAGE AND PRICE CONTROLS
Score: 5–Stable (very high level)

The government sets most wages and prices in Libya.

PROPERTY RIGHTS
Score: 5–Stable (very low level of protection)

Private property is not legal in Libya, although there is growing tolerance of it as government officials often look the other way when individuals acquire property. According to the U.S. Department of State, "The judiciary is not independent from the government."[3]

REGULATION
Score: 5–Stable (very high level)

Establishing a business in Libya is nearly impossible. Although there is growing tolerance for some small private stores and shops, the government often makes it very difficult for private businesses to operate.

BLACK MARKET
Score: 5–Stable (very high level of activity)

The size of Libya's black market easily surpasses the size of its formal economy. Most consumer items must be smuggled into the country.

NOTES

1. The 18 percent average tariff rate is based on total revenues from tariffs as a percentage of total imports. According to the World Bank, however, if total import charges for all products are taken into account, the rate increases to 34.7 percent. See World Bank, "Open Economies Work Better," *Policy Research Working Paper* No. 1636, August 1996.
2. Figures for the average rate of inflation from 1985 to 1995, and for the rate of inflation in 1996, are not available.
3. U.S. Department of State, "Libya Country Report on Human Rights Practices for 1996," 1997.

Lithuania   3.00

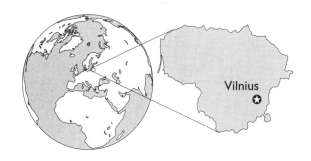

1997 Score: **3.10**		1996 Score: **3.50**		1995 Score: **n/a**
Trade	1	Banking	3
Taxation	3	Wages and Prices	3
Government Intervention	3	Property Rights	3
Monetary Policy	5	Regulation	3
Foreign Investment	2	Black Market	4

Independent from 1918 to 1940,when it was forcibly annexed by the Soviet Union, Lithuania in recent years has undergone intensive economic reform. For example, the government has instituted a privatization program and is selling off some of its state-owned enterprises. Entrenched bureaucrats, former Communist Party officials, and large state-owned monopolies, however, have slowed the process of reform. In the 1997 elections, the Nationalist Party established a majority in Parliament. Like many of its European neighbors, Lithuania relies heavily on foreign aid from the World Bank, International Monetary Fund, European Bank for Reconstruction and Development, and U.S. Agency for International Development. The government has reduced barriers to trade; thus, Lithuania's overall score is 0.1 point better this year.

TRADE POLICY
Score: 1+ (very low level of protectionism)

Lithuania has reduced its average tariff to less than 2 percent.[1] It also raises no significant nontariff barriers. As a result, its trade score this year is one point better than last year.

TAXATION
Score–Income taxation: 2–Stable (low tax rates)
Score–Corporate taxation: 3–Stable (moderate tax rates)
Final Taxation Score: 3–Stable (moderate tax rates)

Lithuania's top income tax rate is 33 percent; the average taxpayer is in the 10 percent bracket. The top marginal corporate tax rate is 29 percent. Lithuania also has an 18 percent value-added tax and a 30 percent social security tax.

GOVERNMENT INTERVENTION IN THE ECONOMY
Score: 3–Stable (moderate level)

Government consumes 21.3 percent of Lithuania's GDP. The country's large state-owned sector accounts for more than one-third of total GDP.

MONETARY POLICY
Score: 5–Stable (very high level of inflation)

Lithuania's rate of inflation was 1,163 percent in 1992, 189 percent in 1993, 45 percent in 1994, 39.6 percent in 1995, and 24.6 percent in 1996. Even though Lithuania has made great progress in reducing inflation since 1992, the rate remains very high.

CAPITAL FLOWS AND FOREIGN INVESTMENT
Score: 2–Stable (low barriers)

Lithuania has moved quickly to open its market to foreign investment, and this presents many opportunities. Foreign companies are accorded the same treatment as domestic firms. Investments in such government-owned monopolies as utilities are not permitted, however.

1	Hong Kong	1.25		77	Zambia	3.05
2	Singapore	1.30		80	Mali	3.10
3	Bahrain	1.70		80	Mongolia	3.10
4	New Zealand	1.75		80	Slovenia	3.10
5	Switzerland	1.90		83	Honduras	3.15
5	United States	1.90		83	Papua New Guinea	3.15
7	Luxembourg	1.95		85	Djibouti	3.20
7	Taiwan	1.95		85	Fiji	3.20
7	United Kingdom	1.95		85	Pakistan	3.20
10	Bahamas	2.00		88	Algeria	3.25
10	Ireland	2.00		88	Guinea	3.25
12	Australia	2.05		88	Lebanon	3.25
12	Japan	2.05		88	Mexico	3.25
14	Belgium	2.10		88	Senegal	3.25
14	Canada	2.10		88	Tanzania	3.25
14	United Arab Emirates	2.10		94	Nigeria	3.30
17	Austria	2.15		94	Romania	3.30
17	Chile	2.15		96	Brazil	3.35
17	Estonia	2.15		96	Cambodia	3.35
20	Czech Republic	2.20		96	Egypt	3.35
20	Netherlands	2.20		96	Ivory Coast	3.35
22	Denmark	2.25		96	Madagascar	3.35
22	Finland	2.25		96	Moldova	3.35
24	Germany	2.30		102	Nepal	3.40
24	Iceland	2.30		103	Cape Verde	3.44
24	South Korea	2.30		104	Armenia	3.45
27	Norway	2.35		104	Dominican Republic	3.45
28	Kuwait	2.40		104	Russia	3.45
28	Malaysia	2.40		107	Burkina Faso	3.50
28	Panama	2.40		107	Cameroon	3.50
28	Thailand	2.40		107	Lesotho	3.50
32	El Salvador	2.45		107	Nicaragua	3.50
32	Sri Lanka	2.45		107	Venezuela	3.50
32	Sweden	2.45		112	Gambia	3.60
35	France	2.50		112	Guyana	3.60
35	Italy	2.50		114	Bulgaria	3.65
35	Spain	2.50		114	Georgia	3.65
38	Trinidad and Tobago	2.55		114	Malawi	3.65
39	Argentina	2.60		117	Ethiopia	3.70
39	Barbados	2.60		117	India	3.70
39	Cyprus	2.60		117	Niger	3.70
39	Jamaica	2.60		120	Albania	3.75
39	Portugal	2.60		120	Bangladesh	3.75
44	Bolivia	2.65		120	China (PRC)	3.75
44	Oman	2.65		120	Congo	3.75
44	Philippines	2.65		120	Croatia	3.75
47	Swaziland	2.70		125	Chad	3.80
47	Uruguay	2.70		125	Mauritania	3.80
49	Botswana	2.75		125	Ukraine	3.80
49	Jordan	2.75		128	Sierra Leone	3.85
49	Namibia	2.75		129	Burundi	3.90
49	Tunisia	2.75		129	Suriname	3.90
53	Belize	2.80		129	Zimbabwe	3.90
53	Costa Rica	2.80		132	Haiti	4.00
53	Guatemala	2.80		132	Kyrgyzstan	4.00
53	Israel	2.80		132	Syria	4.00
53	Peru	2.80		135	Belarus	4.05
53	Saudi Arabia	2.80		136	Kazakstan	4.10
53	Turkey	2.80		136	Mozambique	4.10
53	Uganda	2.80		136	Yemen	4.10
53	Western Samoa	2.80		139	Sudan	4.20
62	Indonesia	2.85		140	Myanmar	4.30
62	Latvia	2.85		140	Rwanda	4.30
62	Malta	2.85		142	Angola	4.35
62	Paraguay	2.85		143	Azerbaijan	4.40
66	Greece	2.90		143	Tajikistan	4.40
66	Hungary	2.90		145	Turkmenistan	4.50
66	South Africa	2.90		146	Uzbekistan	4.55
69	Benin	2.95		147	Congo/Zaire	4.70
69	Ecuador	2.95		147	Iran	4.70
69	Gabon	2.95		147	Libya	4.70
69	Morocco	2.95		147	Somalia	4.70
69	Poland	2.95		147	Vietnam	4.70
74	Colombia	3.00		152	Bosnia	4.80
74	Ghana	3.00		153	Iraq	4.90
74	Lithuania	3.00		154	Cuba	5.00
77	Kenya	3.05		154	Laos	5.00
77	Slovak Republic	3.05		154	North Korea	5.00

Mostly Unfree

BANKING
Score: 3–Stable (moderate level of restrictions)

Legislation was passed in June 1996 aimed at creating more favorable conditions for banking in Lithuania, but its impact is not yet clear. Three large state-owned banks continue to compete directly with private banks.

WAGE AND PRICE CONTROLS
Score: 3–Stable (moderate level)

The government continues to set some wages and prices. For example, price controls remain on some agricultural products. Lithuania has a minimum wage.

PROPERTY RIGHTS
Score: 3–Stable (moderate level of protection)

A more efficient legal structure is providing better protection for private property in Lithuania. The court system, although sometimes slow, operates independently. The judiciary has yet to transform itself into a market-oriented system, however, and enforcement of contracts remains very weak.

REGULATION
Score: 3–Stable (moderate level)

Establishing a business in Lithuania is easy if the business will not compete directly with state-owned industries, and regulations are applied evenly in most cases. Lithuania has passed many new health and safety regulations that, if enforced, will prove burdensome, but these requirements are in line with those of other European countries. By general European standards, Lithuania's level of regulation is moderate.

BLACK MARKET
Score: 4–Stable (high level of activity)

The black market in Lithuania mainly involves the sale of goods and services that compete with state-owned industries. Consumer goods are sold on the black market as well. Lithuania maintains some intellectual property protection and, according to the U.S. Department of Commerce, is considering the adoption of several new laws to protect copyrights and patents. Nevertheless, the level of black market activity in pirated computer software, compact disks, and prerecorded music and video tapes is substantial.

NOTE
1. Based on total taxes on international trade as a percentage of total imports.

Luxembourg 1.95

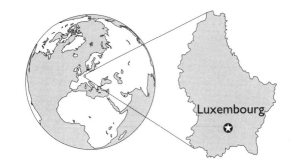

1997 Score: **2.05**	1996 Score: **1.95**	1995 Score: **n/a**

Trade	2	Banking	2
Taxation	3.5	Wages and Prices	2
Government Intervention	3	Property Rights	1
Monetary Policy	1	Regulation	2
Foreign Investment	2	Black Market	1

Luxembourg, a constitutional monarchy, was recognized as a sovereign independent state in 1839. Traditionally, Luxembourg has had an agrarian society. Throughout most of the 20th century, however, it has developed into a manufacturing and services society and one of the world's richest and most highly industrialized countries. It is a member of the European Union (EU) and has a free and thriving economic system. Luxembourg recently reduced some of its taxes, causing its overall score to improve by 0.1 point over last year's.

TRADE POLICY
Score: 2–Stable (low level of protectionism)

Luxembourg has an average tariff rate of less than 3 percent and maintains nontariff barriers common to all EU countries, including restrictions on telecommunications, television, and broadcasting as well as quotas on agricultural products like bananas.

TAXATION
Score–Income taxation: 3+ (moderate tax rates)
Score–Corporate taxation: 3–Stable (moderate tax rates)
Final Taxation Score: 3.5+ (high tax rates)

Luxembourg's top income tax rate is 51.25 percent; the average taxpayer is in the 14.54 percent bracket. The top marginal corporate tax rate is 32 percent, down from 33 percent last year, and the government has announced that it will reduce this rate further to 31 percent in 1998 and 30 percent in 1999. Because of this reduction in taxes, Luxembourg's taxation score is one point better than it was last year. Luxembourg also has a 51.25 percent capital gains tax and a 15 percent value-added tax.

GOVERNMENT INTERVENTION IN THE ECONOMY
Score: 3–Stable (moderate level)

Government consumes about 12.2 percent of Luxembourg's GDP and, despite recent attempts to privatize portions of the economy, it remains entrenched in many sectors. The government continues to own and operate the railways, as well as the mail and telephone service (known as the P&T), and either owns or is a major shareholder in companies that provide banking, electricity, air transport, and financing services.

MONETARY POLICY
Score: 1–Stable (very low level of inflation)

Luxembourg's average rate of inflation from 1985 to 1995 was 4.7 percent. In 1996, the inflation rate was 1.4 percent. For most of 1997, it has been about 2 percent.

1	Hong Kong	1.25	77	Zambia	3.05
2	Singapore	1.30	80	Mali	3.10
3	Bahrain	1.70	80	Mongolia	3.10
4	New Zealand	1.75	80	Slovenia	3.10
5	Switzerland	1.90	83	Honduras	3.15
5	United States	1.90	83	Papua New Guinea	3.15
7	Luxembourg	1.95	85	Djibouti	3.20
7	Taiwan	1.95	85	Fiji	3.20
7	United Kingdom	1.95	85	Pakistan	3.20
10	Bahamas	2.00	88	Algeria	3.25
10	Ireland	2.00	88	Guinea	3.25
12	Australia	2.05	88	Lebanon	3.25
12	Japan	2.05	88	Mexico	3.25
14	Belgium	2.10	88	Senegal	3.25
14	Canada	2.10	88	Tanzania	3.25
14	United Arab Emirates	2.10	94	Nigeria	3.30
17	Austria	2.15	94	Romania	3.30
17	Chile	2.15	96	Brazil	3.35
17	Estonia	2.15	96	Cambodia	3.35
20	Czech Republic	2.20	96	Egypt	3.35
20	Netherlands	2.20	96	Ivory Coast	3.35
22	Denmark	2.25	96	Madagascar	3.35
22	Finland	2.25	96	Moldova	3.35
24	Germany	2.30	102	Nepal	3.40
24	Iceland	2.30	103	Cape Verde	3.44
24	South Korea	2.30	104	Armenia	3.45
27	Norway	2.35	104	Dominican Republic	3.45
28	Kuwait	2.40	104	Russia	3.45
28	Malaysia	2.40	107	Burkina Faso	3.50
28	Panama	2.40	107	Cameroon	3.50
28	Thailand	2.40	107	Lesotho	3.50
32	El Salvador	2.45	107	Nicaragua	3.50
32	Sri Lanka	2.45	107	Venezuela	3.50
32	Sweden	2.45	112	Gambia	3.60
35	France	2.50	112	Guyana	3.60
35	Italy	2.50	114	Bulgaria	3.65
35	Spain	2.50	114	Georgia	3.65
38	Trinidad and Tobago	2.55	114	Malawi	3.65
39	Argentina	2.60	117	Ethiopia	3.70
39	Barbados	2.60	117	India	3.70
39	Cyprus	2.60	117	Niger	3.70
39	Jamaica	2.60	120	Albania	3.75
39	Portugal	2.60	120	Bangladesh	3.75
44	Bolivia	2.65	120	China (PRC)	3.75
44	Oman	2.65	120	Congo	3.75
44	Philippines	2.65	120	Croatia	3.75
47	Swaziland	2.70	125	Chad	3.80
47	Uruguay	2.70	125	Mauritania	3.80
49	Botswana	2.75	125	Ukraine	3.80
49	Jordan	2.75	128	Sierra Leone	3.85
49	Namibia	2.75	129	Burundi	3.90
49	Tunisia	2.75	129	Suriname	3.90
53	Belize	2.80	129	Zimbabwe	3.90
53	Costa Rica	2.80	132	Haiti	4.00
53	Guatemala	2.80	132	Kyrgyzstan	4.00
53	Israel	2.80	132	Syria	4.00
53	Peru	2.80	135	Belarus	4.05
53	Saudi Arabia	2.80	136	Kazakstan	4.10
53	Turkey	2.80	136	Mozambique	4.10
53	Uganda	2.80	136	Yemen	4.10
53	Western Samoa	2.80	139	Sudan	4.20
62	Indonesia	2.85	140	Myanmar	4.30
62	Latvia	2.85	140	Rwanda	4.30
62	Malta	2.85	142	Angola	4.35
62	Paraguay	2.85	143	Azerbaijan	4.40
66	Greece	2.90	143	Tajikistan	4.40
66	Hungary	2.90	145	Turkmenistan	4.50
66	South Africa	2.90	146	Uzbekistan	4.55
69	Benin	2.95	147	Congo/Zaire	4.70
69	Ecuador	2.95	147	Iran	4.70
69	Gabon	2.95	147	Libya	4.70
69	Morocco	2.95	147	Somalia	4.70
69	Poland	2.95	147	Vietnam	4.70
74	Colombia	3.00	152	Bosnia	4.80
74	Ghana	3.00	153	Iraq	4.90
74	Lithuania	3.00	154	Cuba	5.00
77	Kenya	3.05	154	Laos	5.00
77	Slovak Republic	3.05	154	North Korea	5.00

CAPITAL FLOWS AND FOREIGN INVESTMENT
Score: 2–Stable (low barriers)

Luxembourg has a very open foreign investment regime. Foreign and domestic businesses receive equal treatment, and there are no local content requirements. The government restricts investments that directly affect national security, however, as well as investments in some utilities.

BANKING
Score: 2–Stable (low level of restrictions)

With the exception of steel, the financial sector is probably Luxembourg's largest and most important industry, employing over 14,000 people in a country whose total population is only about 410,000. In 1990, there were over 150 foreign banks in Luxembourg. The banking system is both highly competitive and subject to little government regulation, although banks are restricted in their ability to engage in some financial services like as real estate.

WAGE AND PRICE CONTROLS
Score: 2–Stable (low level)

The market sets most wages and prices in Luxembourg. Prices also are affected by such government policies as subsidies to the state-owned sector and direct price controls on energy.

PROPERTY RIGHTS
Score: 1–Stable (very high level of protection)

Private property is safe from government expropriation in Luxembourg. The legal and judicial system is advanced and efficient. According to the U.S. Department of State, "The judiciary provides citizens with a fair and efficient judicial process."[1]

REGULATION
Score: 2–Stable (low level)

Establishing a business in Luxembourg is simple. Regulations are applied evenly in most cases, and businesses generally are free to operate with minimal intrusion from the government.

BLACK MARKET
Score: 1–Stable (very low level of activity)

The black market in Luxembourg is almost nonexistent. Protection of intellectual property is strong, and there is little piracy.

NOTE

1. U.S. Department of State, "Luxembourg Country Report on Human Rights Practices for 1996," 1997.

Madagascar

3.35

Trade	5	Banking	4
Taxation	3.5	Wages and Prices	2
Government Intervention	2	Property Rights	3
Monetary Policy	3	Regulation	3
Foreign Investment	4	Black Market	4

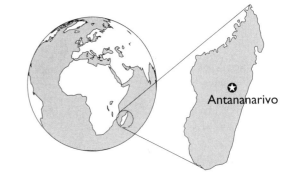

Antananarivo

Madagascar is the world's fourth largest island. It has a largely agrarian economy with rice as its largest crop. Much of its agricultural industry is state-owned, with some large plots of land held in private hands. Madagascar gained its independence from France in 1960 but enjoyed little economic growth during the rest of the decade. In 1970, the situation worsened as the government moved from a market-based economy to a command economy, resulting in -0.2 percent growth in GDP from 1980 to 1988. In 1988, the government began to institute limited economic reforms, and these led to modest economic growth of 0.7 percent from 1988 to 1993. President Albert Zafy, elected in 1993, was impeached in 1996. The December 1996 elections returned former dictator Didier Ratsiraka to power. An advocate of socialism during his 16-year rule, President Ratsiraka now claims to recognize the need for economic liberalization, although substantial change has yet to materialize. Populist political opposition has been an impediment to liberalization, but some barriers to trade have been reduced. Overall, the combination of a wavering commitment to reform and a series of devastating cyclones in 1994 has left Madagascar with a relatively stagnant economy that grew only 2 percent in 1995 and 3 percent in 1996. Madagascar recently increased its barriers to trade. As a result, its overall score is 0.1 point worse than it was last year.

TRADE POLICY

Score: 5– (very high level of protectionism)

Madagascar's average tariff rate is 27.87 percent.[1] There are no significant nontariff barriers. Because its average tariff rate is higher this year, Madagascar's trade policy score is one point worse.

TAXATION

Score–Income taxation: 3–Stable (moderate tax rates)
Score–Corporate taxation: 3–Stable (moderate tax rates)
Total Taxation Score: 3.5–Stable (high tax rates)

Madagascar's top income tax rate is 35 percent.[2] The top corporate income tax rate also is 35 percent. The government recently introduced both a 25 percent value-added tax and a 45 percent excess profits tax.

GOVERNMENT INTERVENTION IN THE ECONOMY

Score: 2–Stable (low level)

Government consumes 6.7 percent of Madagascar's GDP. Despite some progress in privatization, the state-owned sector remains large.

MONETARY POLICY

Score: 3–Stable (moderate level of inflation)

Madagascar's average annual rate of inflation from 1985 to 1995 was 17.9 percent. In 1996, the rate of inflation was around 10.5 percent.

1	Hong Kong	1.25	77	Zambia	3.05
2	Singapore	1.30	80	Mali	3.10
3	Bahrain	1.70	80	Mongolia	3.10
4	New Zealand	1.75	80	Slovenia	3.10
5	Switzerland	1.90	83	Honduras	3.15
5	United States	1.90	83	Papua New Guinea	3.15
7	Luxembourg	1.95	85	Djibouti	3.20
7	Taiwan	1.95	85	Fiji	3.20
7	United Kingdom	1.95	85	Pakistan	3.20
10	Bahamas	2.00	88	Algeria	3.25
10	Ireland	2.00	88	Guinea	3.25
12	Australia	2.05	88	Lebanon	3.25
12	Japan	2.05	88	Mexico	3.25
14	Belgium	2.10	88	Senegal	3.25
14	Canada	2.10	88	Tanzania	3.25
14	United Arab Emirates	2.10	94	Nigeria	3.30
17	Austria	2.15	94	Romania	3.30
17	Chile	2.15	96	Brazil	3.35
17	Estonia	2.15	96	Cambodia	3.35
20	Czech Republic	2.20	96	Egypt	3.35
20	Netherlands	2.20	96	Ivory Coast	3.35
22	Denmark	2.25	96	Madagascar	3.35
22	Finland	2.25	96	Moldova	3.35
24	Germany	2.30	102	Nepal	3.40
24	Iceland	2.30	103	Cape Verde	3.44
24	South Korea	2.30	104	Armenia	3.45
27	Norway	2.35	104	Dominican Republic	3.45
28	Kuwait	2.40	104	Russia	3.45
28	Malaysia	2.40	107	Burkina Faso	3.50
28	Panama	2.40	107	Cameroon	3.50
28	Thailand	2.40	107	Lesotho	3.50
32	El Salvador	2.45	107	Nicaragua	3.50
32	Sri Lanka	2.45	107	Venezuela	3.50
32	Sweden	2.45	112	Gambia	3.60
35	France	2.50	112	Guyana	3.60
35	Italy	2.50	114	Bulgaria	3.65
35	Spain	2.50	114	Georgia	3.65
38	Trinidad and Tobago	2.55	114	Malawi	3.65
39	Argentina	2.60	117	Ethiopia	3.70
39	Barbados	2.60	117	India	3.70
39	Cyprus	2.60	117	Niger	3.70
39	Jamaica	2.60	120	Albania	3.75
39	Portugal	2.60	120	Bangladesh	3.75
44	Bolivia	2.65	120	China (PRC)	3.75
44	Oman	2.65	120	Congo	3.75
44	Philippines	2.65	120	Croatia	3.75
47	Swaziland	2.70	125	Chad	3.80
47	Uruguay	2.70	125	Mauritania	3.80
49	Botswana	2.75	125	Ukraine	3.80
49	Jordan	2.75	128	Sierra Leone	3.85
49	Namibia	2.75	129	Burundi	3.90
49	Tunisia	2.75	129	Suriname	3.90
53	Belize	2.80	129	Zimbabwe	3.90
53	Costa Rica	2.80	132	Haiti	4.00
53	Guatemala	2.80	132	Kyrgyzstan	4.00
53	Israel	2.80	132	Syria	4.00
53	Peru	2.80	135	Belarus	4.05
53	Saudi Arabia	2.80	136	Kazakstan	4.10
53	Turkey	2.80	136	Mozambique	4.10
53	Uganda	2.80	136	Yemen	4.10
53	Western Samoa	2.80	139	Sudan	4.20
62	Indonesia	2.85	140	Myanmar	4.30
62	Latvia	2.85	140	Rwanda	4.30
62	Malta	2.85	142	Angola	4.35
62	Paraguay	2.85	143	Azerbaijan	4.40
66	Greece	2.90	143	Tajikistan	4.40
66	Hungary	2.90	145	Turkmenistan	4.50
66	South Africa	2.90	146	Uzbekistan	4.55
69	Benin	2.95	147	Congo/Zaire	4.70
69	Ecuador	2.95	147	Iran	4.70
69	Gabon	2.95	147	Libya	4.70
69	Morocco	2.95	147	Somalia	4.70
69	Poland	2.95	147	Vietnam	4.70
74	Colombia	3.00	152	Bosnia	4.80
74	Ghana	3.00	153	Iraq	4.90
74	Lithuania	3.00	154	Cuba	5.00
77	Kenya	3.05	154	Laos	5.00
77	Slovak Republic	3.05	154	North Korea	5.00

Mostly Unfree

CAPITAL FLOWS AND FOREIGN INVESTMENT
Score: 4–Stable (high barriers)

Madagascar has a free trade zone. Outside this zone, however, foreign investors are not treated as well as domestic investors. There are restrictions on foreign investments in the banking and insurance, energy, water, hydrocarbon production, mining, and petroleum industries; foreigners are not permitted to own land; and the bureaucratic process for establishing a new enterprise is time-consuming and not transparent. There are political considerations to be weighed, and foreign investors must demonstrate the social value of their investments.

BANKING
Score: 4–Stable (high level of restrictions)

Only five banks operate in Madagascar. Both private banking and foreign investment are limited, and the banking system remains under strict government control, particularly in such areas as credit extension. Two banks are being privatized.

WAGE AND PRICE CONTROLS
Score: 2–Stable (low level)

Most prices have been freed from government control. Administered prices for all agricultural goods except vanilla have been lifted, but there is a consumer subsidy for wheat and flour. Madagascar has a minimum wage.

PROPERTY RIGHTS
Score: 3–Stable (moderate level of protection)

Property expropriation is unlikely. The current government slowly has been settling expropriations claims dating back to the 1970s. Private property, however, does not always receive full legal protection because the legal system is sometimes inefficient. According to the U.S. Department of Commerce, "Investors in Madagascar face a legal environment in which the security of private property and the enforcement of contracts is inadequately protected by the judicial system."[3] Thus, by global standards, the level of property rights protection is moderate.

REGULATION
Score: 3–Stable (moderate level)

Madagascar's economy remains moderately regulated by the government. Obtaining business licenses and permits often involves bribery, and the bureaucracy tends to operate in a capricious manner. "In general," reports the U.S. Department of Commerce, "the Malagasy regulatory apparatus is not up to developed country standards in terms of transparency and streamlined process."[4]

BLACK MARKET
Score: 4–Stable (high level of activity)

Madagascar has a large black market because of high tariffs and government controls, although the removal of most price controls has reduced the size of the informal economy in recent years. Intellectual property rights are not fully protected; according to the U.S. Department of Commerce, "Major brand names and franchise rights are respected, but pirated copies of videotaped movies and music cassettes sell openly."[5]

NOTES
1. Based on total taxes on international trade as a percentage of total imports.
2. It was not possible to determine the tax on the average income level. Therefore, Madagascar's score is based on its top income tax rate.
3. U.S. Department of Commerce, *Country Commercial Guide*, 1997.
4. *Ibid*.
5. *Ibid*.

Malawi   3.65

Trade	5	Banking	3
Taxation	4.5	Wages and Prices	3
Government Intervention	3	Property Rights	3
Monetary Policy	4	Regulation	4
Foreign Investment	3	Black Market	4

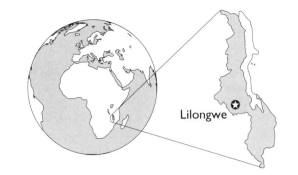

Lilongwe

Malawi gained its independence from Great Britain in 1964. During the rest of that decade and into the 1970s, it used increased agricultural production as an engine for economic growth. GDP more than doubled, with annual growth rates of 3 percent. The economy sunk into a deep recession in the 1980s, however, as drought brought widespread agricultural depression and refugees from the nearby Mozambique civil war flowed into the country. The government responded by restricting imports and spending more on social programs, thereby rapidly increasing the budget deficit and pushing the economy into depression. As a result, GDP growth was poor, averaging just 1.4 percent during the 1980s. More recently, the economy has been characterized by dramatic performance swings, including negative growth of -7.9 percent in 1992 and -12.4 percent in 1994 and positive growth of about 10 percent in 1993, 1995, and 1996. Inflation has increased over the previously measured period. As a result, Malawi's overall score this year is 0.1 point worse than it was last year.

TRADE POLICY
Score: 5–Stable (very high level of protectionism)

Malawi's average tariff rate is 15.2 percent. Nontariff barriers include strict import licenses on imports of fresh meat, gold, sugar, and military and hunting items.

TAXATION
Score–Income taxation: 4–Stable (high tax rates)
Score–Corporate taxation: 4–Stable (high tax rates)
Final Taxation Score: 4.5–Stable (very high tax rates)

The top income tax rate is 35 percent; the rate for the average income level is 0 percent. The top corporate tax rate is 38 percent. Malawi also levies municipal taxes, a border tax, and a capital gains tax.

GOVERNMENT INTERVENTION IN THE ECONOMY
Score: 3–Stable (moderate level)

Government consumes 22.7 percent of Malawi's GDP. Malawi has a large public sector that operates marketing boards for some agricultural products. These boards allow the government to confiscate crops, pay lower-than-market-value prices for them, and then export them at higher prices, keeping the profits.

MONETARY POLICY
Score: 4– (high level of inflation)

Malawi's average annual rate of inflation from 1985 to 1995 was 22 percent, up from a previous average of 18 percent. As a result, Malawi's score this year is one point worse than last year. In 1996, the rate of inflation was 12 percent.

1	Hong Kong	1.25		77	Zambia	3.05
2	Singapore	1.30		80	Mali	3.10
3	Bahrain	1.70		80	Mongolia	3.10
4	New Zealand	1.75		80	Slovenia	3.10
5	Switzerland	1.90		83	Honduras	3.15
5	United States	1.90		83	Papua New Guinea	3.15
7	Luxembourg	1.95		85	Djibouti	3.20
7	Taiwan	1.95		85	Fiji	3.20
7	United Kingdom	1.95		85	Pakistan	3.20
10	Bahamas	2.00		88	Algeria	3.25
10	Ireland	2.00		88	Guinea	3.25
12	Australia	2.05		88	Lebanon	3.25
12	Japan	2.05		88	Mexico	3.25
14	Belgium	2.10		88	Senegal	3.25
14	Canada	2.10		88	Tanzania	3.25
14	United Arab Emirates	2.10		94	Nigeria	3.30
17	Austria	2.15		94	Romania	3.30
17	Chile	2.15		96	Brazil	3.35
17	Estonia	2.15		96	Cambodia	3.35
20	Czech Republic	2.20		96	Egypt	3.35
20	Netherlands	2.20		96	Ivory Coast	3.35
22	Denmark	2.25		96	Madagascar	3.35
22	Finland	2.25		96	Moldova	3.35
24	Germany	2.30		102	Nepal	3.40
24	Iceland	2.30		103	Cape Verde	3.44
24	South Korea	2.30		104	Armenia	3.45
27	Norway	2.35		104	Dominican Republic	3.45
28	Kuwait	2.40		104	Russia	3.45
28	Malaysia	2.40		107	Burkina Faso	3.50
28	Panama	2.40		107	Cameroon	3.50
28	Thailand	2.40		107	Lesotho	3.50
32	El Salvador	2.45		107	Nicaragua	3.50
32	Sri Lanka	2.45		107	Venezuela	3.50
32	Sweden	2.45		112	Gambia	3.60
35	France	2.50		112	Guyana	3.60
35	Italy	2.50		114	Bulgaria	3.65
35	Spain	2.50		114	Georgia	3.65
38	Trinidad and Tobago	2.55		114	Malawi	3.65
39	Argentina	2.60		117	Ethiopia	3.70
39	Barbados	2.60		117	India	3.70
39	Cyprus	2.60		117	Niger	3.70
39	Jamaica	2.60		120	Albania	3.75
39	Portugal	2.60		120	Bangladesh	3.75
44	Bolivia	2.65		120	China (PRC)	3.75
44	Oman	2.65		120	Congo	3.75
44	Philippines	2.65		120	Croatia	3.75
47	Swaziland	2.70		125	Chad	3.80
47	Uruguay	2.70		125	Mauritania	3.80
49	Botswana	2.75		125	Ukraine	3.80
49	Jordan	2.75		128	Sierra Leone	3.85
49	Namibia	2.75		129	Burundi	3.90
49	Tunisia	2.75		129	Suriname	3.90
53	Belize	2.80		129	Zimbabwe	3.90
53	Costa Rica	2.80		132	Haiti	4.00
53	Guatemala	2.80		132	Kyrgyzstan	4.00
53	Israel	2.80		132	Syria	4.00
53	Peru	2.80		135	Belarus	4.05
53	Saudi Arabia	2.80		136	Kazakstan	4.10
53	Turkey	2.80		136	Mozambique	4.10
53	Uganda	2.80		136	Yemen	4.10
53	Western Samoa	2.80		139	Sudan	4.20
62	Indonesia	2.85		140	Myanmar	4.30
62	Latvia	2.85		140	Rwanda	4.30
62	Malta	2.85		142	Angola	4.35
62	Paraguay	2.85		143	Azerbaijan	4.40
66	Greece	2.90		143	Tajikistan	4.40
66	Hungary	2.90		145	Turkmenistan	4.50
66	South Africa	2.90		146	Uzbekistan	4.55
69	Benin	2.95		147	Congo/Zaire	4.70
69	Ecuador	2.95		147	Iran	4.70
69	Gabon	2.95		147	Libya	4.70
69	Morocco	2.95		147	Somalia	4.70
69	Poland	2.95		147	Vietnam	4.70
74	Colombia	3.00		152	Bosnia	4.80
74	Ghana	3.00		153	Iraq	4.90
74	Lithuania	3.00		154	Cuba	5.00
77	Kenya	3.05		154	Laos	5.00
77	Slovak Republic	3.05		154	North Korea	5.00

Mostly Unfree

CAPITAL FLOWS AND FOREIGN INVESTMENT
Score: 3–Stable (moderate barriers)

Malawi's government encourages foreign investment in industries that produce goods for export. Thus, it does not restrict foreign investment in the coffee, sugar, or tea industries. Non-citizens must obtain labor licenses to work in Malawi, and these licenses are not granted if the government determines that Malawi citizens are available and able to do the work.

BANKING
Score: 3–Stable (moderate level of restrictions)

Only a few banks in Malawi are free of government ownership. Although the government freed interest rates in 1992, it still exercises a great deal of control over the financial system. Malawi plans to allow two foreign banks to open in the near future.

WAGE AND PRICE CONTROLS
Score: 3–Stable (moderate level)

The government has lifted price controls on almost all products, although those on some food items and energy remain in effect. Malawi has a minimum wage.

PROPERTY RIGHTS
Score: 3–Stable (moderate level of protection)

Malawi has begun a huge privatization program aimed at selling its largest state-owned enterprises. Despite plans to eliminate them, however, marketing boards still control the sale of agricultural products such as corn and fertilizer. The court system is only partially independent.

REGULATION
Score: 4–Stable (high level)

Malawi's government heavily regulates the sale of such agricultural products as corn and fertilizer. It also enforces health and safety regulations erratically, causing confusion among businesses. Corruption is becoming more prevalent. According to the U.S. Department of Commerce, "There are serious but unproven allegations of corruption, particularly in official circles."[1]

BLACK MARKET
Score: 4–Stable (high level of activity)

Because Malawi's government strictly controls the importation of food, there is a huge black market in such items as eggs and poultry, which often are imported illegally. Because the government provides insufficient legal protection for intellectual property rights, there is a rather large black market in pirated computer software and recorded music and video.

NOTE

1.   U.S. Department of Commerce, "Malawi, Investment Climate," *Market Research Reports,* June 12, 1997.

Malaysia   2.40

Trade	3	Banking	3
Taxation	3	Wages and Prices	3
Government Intervention	2	Property Rights	2
Monetary Policy	1	Regulation	2
Foreign Investment	3	Black Market	2

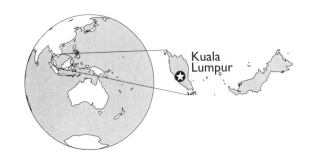

Kuala Lumpur

Malaysia gained its independence from Great Britain in 1957. In 1963, Singapore, Sarawak, and Sabah (North Borneo) joined the Federation of Malaya to form Malaysia. In 1964, Singapore withdrew to become an independent country. Although Malaysia experienced civil unrest in its early years, recent governments have moved to address the sources of ethnic and social tension and thus have enhanced political stability. Economic reforms begun in the 1970s have helped Malaysia to develop a free-market economy. Malaysia has reduced its average tariff rate. Its overall score this year is 0.2 point better than it was last year.

TRADE POLICY
Score: 3+ (moderate level of protectionism)

Malaysia's average trade-weighted tariff rate has decreased to less than 10 percent, according to the U.S. Department of State.[1] As a result, its trade policy score is two points better than last year. Nontariff barriers include import bans, licensing requirements, and strict labeling requirements.

TAXATION
Score–Income taxation: 2–Stable (low tax rates)
Score–Corporate taxation: 3–Stable (moderate tax rates)
Total Taxation Score: 3–Stable (moderate tax rates)

Malaysia's top income tax rate is 32 percent; the average income level is taxed at 7 percent. The top corporate tax is 30 percent. The sales tax is 15 percent.

GOVERNMENT INTERVENTION IN THE ECONOMY
Score: 2–Stable (low level)

Government consumes 12.7 percent of Malaysia's GDP, down from 13.5 percent one year ago. According to the U.S. Department of State, however, "While the government since 1986 has scaled back its role as a producer of goods and services, it continues to hold equity stakes in a wide range of privatized domestic companies, including telecommunications, aviation, shipping and seaport ventures."[2]

MONETARY POLICY
Score: 1–Stable (very low level of inflation)

The average annual rate of inflation in Malaysia from 1985 to 1995 was 3.3 percent. In 1996, the rate of inflation was 3.5 percent.

CAPITAL FLOWS AND FOREIGN INVESTMENT
Score: 3–Stable (moderate barriers)

Malaysia is relatively open to foreign investment. Most restrictions apply to investments in utilities and industries considered essential to national security, although the government also restricts foreign participation in some services, such as law, architecture, and banking.

1	Hong Kong	1.25	77	Zambia	3.05
2	Singapore	1.30	80	Mali	3.10
3	Bahrain	1.70	80	Mongolia	3.10
4	New Zealand	1.75	80	Slovenia	3.10
5	Switzerland	1.90	83	Honduras	3.15
5	United States	1.90	83	Papua New Guinea	3.15
7	Luxembourg	1.95	85	Djibouti	3.20
7	Taiwan	1.95	85	Fiji	3.20
7	United Kingdom	1.95	85	Pakistan	3.20
10	Bahamas	2.00	88	Algeria	3.25
10	Ireland	2.00	88	Guinea	3.25
12	Australia	2.05	88	Lebanon	3.25
12	Japan	2.05	88	Mexico	3.25
14	Belgium	2.10	88	Senegal	3.25
14	Canada	2.10	88	Tanzania	3.25
14	United Arab Emirates	2.10	94	Nigeria	3.30
17	Austria	2.15	94	Romania	3.30
17	Chile	2.15	96	Brazil	3.35
17	Estonia	2.15	96	Cambodia	3.35
20	Czech Republic	2.20	96	Egypt	3.35
20	Netherlands	2.20	96	Ivory Coast	3.35
22	Denmark	2.25	96	Madagascar	3.35
22	Finland	2.25	96	Moldova	3.35
24	Germany	2.30	102	Nepal	3.40
24	Iceland	2.30	103	Cape Verde	3.44
24	South Korea	2.30	104	Armenia	3.45
27	Norway	2.35	104	Dominican Republic	3.45
28	Kuwait	2.40	104	Russia	3.45
28	Malaysia	2.40	107	Burkina Faso	3.50
28	Panama	2.40	107	Cameroon	3.50
28	Thailand	2.40	107	Lesotho	3.50
32	El Salvador	2.45	107	Nicaragua	3.50
32	Sri Lanka	2.45	107	Venezuela	3.50
32	Sweden	2.45	112	Gambia	3.60
35	France	2.50	112	Guyana	3.60
35	Italy	2.50	114	Bulgaria	3.65
35	Spain	2.50	114	Georgia	3.65
38	Trinidad and Tobago	2.55	114	Malawi	3.65
39	Argentina	2.60	117	Ethiopia	3.70
39	Barbados	2.60	117	India	3.70
39	Cyprus	2.60	117	Niger	3.70
39	Jamaica	2.60	120	Albania	3.75
39	Portugal	2.60	120	Bangladesh	3.75
44	Bolivia	2.65	120	China (PRC)	3.75
44	Oman	2.65	120	Congo	3.75
44	Philippines	2.65	120	Croatia	3.75
47	Swaziland	2.70	125	Chad	3.80
47	Uruguay	2.70	125	Mauritania	3.80
49	Botswana	2.75	125	Ukraine	3.80
49	Jordan	2.75	128	Sierra Leone	3.85
49	Namibia	2.75	129	Burundi	3.90
49	Tunisia	2.75	129	Suriname	3.90
53	Belize	2.80	129	Zimbabwe	3.90
53	Costa Rica	2.80	132	Haiti	4.00
53	Guatemala	2.80	132	Kyrgyzstan	4.00
53	Israel	2.80	132	Syria	4.00
53	Peru	2.80	135	Belarus	4.05
53	Saudi Arabia	2.80	136	Kazakstan	4.10
53	Turkey	2.80	136	Mozambique	4.10
53	Uganda	2.80	136	Yemen	4.10
53	Western Samoa	2.80	139	Sudan	4.20
62	Indonesia	2.85	140	Myanmar	4.30
62	Latvia	2.85	140	Rwanda	4.30
62	Malta	2.85	142	Angola	4.35
62	Paraguay	2.85	143	Azerbaijan	4.40
66	Greece	2.90	143	Tajikistan	4.40
66	Hungary	2.90	145	Turkmenistan	4.50
66	South Africa	2.90	146	Uzbekistan	4.55
69	Benin	2.95	147	Congo/Zaire	4.70
69	Ecuador	2.95	147	Iran	4.70
69	Gabon	2.95	147	Libya	4.70
69	Morocco	2.95	147	Somalia	4.70
69	Poland	2.95	147	Vietnam	4.70
74	Colombia	3.00	152	Bosnia	4.80
74	Ghana	3.00	153	Iraq	4.90
74	Lithuania	3.00	154	Cuba	5.00
77	Kenya	3.05	154	Laos	5.00
77	Slovak Republic	3.05	154	North Korea	5.00

Mostly Free

BANKING
Score: 3–Stable (moderate level of restrictions)

Competition in Malaysia's banking industry is limited by government restrictions that prevent banks from providing a full range of financial services. The government also limits foreign participation in banking.

WAGE AND PRICE CONTROLS
Score: 3–Stable (moderate level)

The market determines most wages and prices in Malaysia, although the government has added price controls on key goods and maintains controls on the prices of fuel, public utilities, motor vehicles, rice, flour, sugar, and tobacco. Malaysia has a minimum wage.

PROPERTY RIGHTS
Score: 2–Stable (high level of protection)

Chances of property expropriation in Malaysia remain small. Protection of private property by the courts, however, sometimes is lax. According to some private-sector complaints, there is a "widening web of patronage and privilege between some influential politicians and private business groups."[3] This has created an incentive for the government to expropriate private property, give compensation that is less than market value for it, and then use government-owned development firms to develop it for a profit. In one recent case, the government expropriated 6,520 acres from a private company and offered compensation equal to only 25 percent of the property's market value. Such occurrences, however, represent the exception to an otherwise high level of protection of private property.

REGULATION
Score: 2–Stable (low level)

Malaysia has eliminated the majority of its most burdensome regulations. Its regulatory regime is efficient and relatively free of corruption.

BLACK MARKET
Score: 2–Stable (low level of activity)

Black market activity in Malaysia is minimal. Most services are supplied legally, and there is little incentive to engage in the black market. There is a small but growing black market in such pirated intellectual property as computer software and music and video tapes.

NOTES

1. U.S. Department of State, *Country Reports on Economic Policy and Trade Practices*, 1997, p. 54.
2. *Ibid.*, p. 53.
3. See Raphael Pura, "Property Firms' Suit Against Malaysian State Spotlights Controversial Land Acquisition Law," *Asian Wall Street Journal*, June 19, 1995, p. 1.

Mali   3.10

1997 Score: **3.10**		1996 Score: **3.10**		1995 Score: **3.50**
Trade	3	Banking	3	
Taxation	5	Wages and Prices	3	
Government Intervention	3	Property Rights	3	
Monetary Policy	1	Regulation	3	
Foreign Investment	2	Black Market	5	

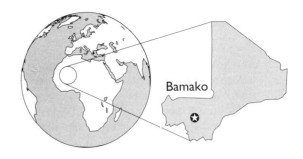

Bamako

Mali, a vast and sparsely populated country, is also one of the world's poorest with a per capita GDP of only $250 in 1995. Mali received its independence from France in 1960 and immediately adopted socialist economic policies under the leadership of President Modibo Keita. After years of state-dominated economic policy, however, it is beginning to rely more on the market for everyday economic decisions. The predominantly agrarian economy has improved recently, with GDP growing at an average of 3.6 percent from 1992 to 1996. With a vibrant democracy that includes about 45 registered political parties, Mali held its second presidential election in June 1997, reelecting President Apha Oumar Konare. The results were contested by 21 political parties but judged to be free and fair.

TRADE POLICY
Score: 3–Stable (moderate level of protectionism)

Mali's average tariff rate is about 10 percent. The government also uses a complex system of "fiscal duties" ranging from 5 percent to 30 percent.[1] Most import barriers have been lifted, although import licenses still are required. Import taxes on many goods were lowered or eliminated in 1994.

TAXATION
Score–Income taxation: 4–Stable (high tax rates)
Score–Corporate taxation: 5–Stable (very high tax rates)
Final Taxation Score: 5–Stable (very high tax rates)

Mali's top income and corporate tax rates of over 50 percent.[2] The government also levies a capital gains tax and a turnover tax.

GOVERNMENT INTERVENTION IN THE ECONOMY
Score: 3–Stable (moderate level)

Government consumes 11.2 percent of Mali's GDP. The state sector is dominant, but several state enterprises have been liquidated or privatized over the past few years.

MONETARY POLICY
Score: 1–Stable (very low level of inflation)

Mali's average annual rate of inflation from 1985 to 1995 was 4.6 percent. Inflation currently is running at 3 percent.

CAPITAL FLOWS AND FOREIGN INVESTMENT
Score: 2–Stable (low barriers)

Mali's government has an established investment code and permits investments in almost all areas. Foreign investors are offered some incentives and face few restrictions. Because of its poor economic state, Mali has received very little foreign investment to date, although there has been an upturn in recent years.

1	Hong Kong	1.25	77	Zambia	3.05
2	Singapore	1.30	80	Mali	3.10
3	Bahrain	1.70	80	Mongolia	3.10
4	New Zealand	1.75	80	Slovenia	3.10
5	Switzerland	1.90	83	Honduras	3.15
5	United States	1.90	83	Papua New Guinea	3.15
7	Luxembourg	1.95	85	Djibouti	3.20
7	Taiwan	1.95	85	Fiji	3.20
7	United Kingdom	1.95	85	Pakistan	3.20
10	Bahamas	2.00	88	Algeria	3.25
10	Ireland	2.00	88	Guinea	3.25
12	Australia	2.05	88	Lebanon	3.25
12	Japan	2.05	88	Mexico	3.25
14	Belgium	2.10	88	Senegal	3.25
14	Canada	2.10	88	Tanzania	3.25
14	United Arab Emirates	2.10	94	Nigeria	3.30
17	Austria	2.15	94	Romania	3.30
17	Chile	2.15	96	Brazil	3.35
17	Estonia	2.15	96	Cambodia	3.35
20	Czech Republic	2.20	96	Egypt	3.35
20	Netherlands	2.20	96	Ivory Coast	3.35
22	Denmark	2.25	96	Madagascar	3.35
22	Finland	2.25	96	Moldova	3.35
24	Germany	2.30	102	Nepal	3.40
24	Iceland	2.30	103	Cape Verde	3.44
24	South Korea	2.30	104	Armenia	3.45
27	Norway	2.35	104	Dominican Republic	3.45
28	Kuwait	2.40	104	Russia	3.45
28	Malaysia	2.40	107	Burkina Faso	3.50
28	Panama	2.40	107	Cameroon	3.50
28	Thailand	2.40	107	Lesotho	3.50
32	El Salvador	2.45	107	Nicaragua	3.50
32	Sri Lanka	2.45	107	Venezuela	3.50
32	Sweden	2.45	112	Gambia	3.60
35	France	2.50	112	Guyana	3.60
35	Italy	2.50	114	Bulgaria	3.65
35	Spain	2.50	114	Georgia	3.65
38	Trinidad and Tobago	2.55	114	Malawi	3.65
39	Argentina	2.60	117	Ethiopia	3.70
39	Barbados	2.60	117	India	3.70
39	Cyprus	2.60	117	Niger	3.70
39	Jamaica	2.60	120	Albania	3.75
39	Portugal	2.60	120	Bangladesh	3.75
44	Bolivia	2.65	120	China (PRC)	3.75
44	Oman	2.65	120	Congo	3.75
44	Philippines	2.65	120	Croatia	3.75
47	Swaziland	2.70	125	Chad	3.80
47	Uruguay	2.70	125	Mauritania	3.80
49	Botswana	2.75	125	Ukraine	3.80
49	Jordan	2.75	128	Sierra Leone	3.85
49	Namibia	2.75	129	Burundi	3.90
49	Tunisia	2.75	129	Suriname	3.90
53	Belize	2.80	129	Zimbabwe	3.90
53	Costa Rica	2.80	132	Haiti	4.00
53	Guatemala	2.80	132	Kyrgyzstan	4.00
53	Israel	2.80	132	Syria	4.00
53	Peru	2.80	135	Belarus	4.05
53	Saudi Arabia	2.80	136	Kazakstan	4.10
53	Turkey	2.80	136	Mozambique	4.10
53	Uganda	2.80	136	Yemen	4.10
53	Western Samoa	2.80	139	Sudan	4.20
62	Indonesia	2.85	140	Myanmar	4.30
62	Latvia	2.85	140	Rwanda	4.30
62	Malta	2.85	142	Angola	4.35
62	Paraguay	2.85	143	Azerbaijan	4.40
66	Greece	2.90	143	Tajikistan	4.40
66	Hungary	2.90	145	Turkmenistan	4.50
66	South Africa	2.90	146	Uzbekistan	4.55
69	Benin	2.95	147	Congo/Zaire	4.70
69	Ecuador	2.95	147	Iran	4.70
69	Gabon	2.95	147	Libya	4.70
69	Morocco	2.95	147	Somalia	4.70
69	Poland	2.95	147	Vietnam	4.70
74	Colombia	3.00	152	Bosnia	4.80
74	Ghana	3.00	153	Iraq	4.90
74	Lithuania	3.00	154	Cuba	5.00
77	Kenya	3.05	154	Laos	5.00
77	Slovak Republic	3.05	154	North Korea	5.00

Mostly Unfree

BANKING
Score: 3–Stable (moderate level of restrictions)

Among the most serious impediments to efficient banking in Mali are corrupt government bureaucrats, collusion by some banks to maintain high interest rates, and a generally chaotic financial system. Some restrictions have been liberalized, however. Six commercial banks, either privately owned or controlled by a majority of private-sector owners, now are permitted to invest in foreign capital markets.

WAGE AND PRICE CONTROLS
Score: 3–Stable (moderate level)

The government has lifted most price controls, but prices continue to be influenced by the government's large public sector. Mali has a minimum wage.

PROPERTY RIGHTS
Score: 3–Stable (moderate level of protection)

Property is at risk in Mali because of high crime rates and an inefficient (although generally fair) court system. Some property has been destroyed because of separatist strife in the north. Government expropriation is not likely under the current regime.

REGULATION
Score: 3–Stable (moderate level)

Regulations are applied sporadically, and government corruption increases the risk of doing business. According to the U.S. Department of Commerce, "Petty corruption is a problem."[3] Mali has simplified its business registration procedures and liberalized its commerce and labor codes over the past few years.

BLACK MARKET
Score: 5–Stable (very high level of activity)

Mali has a large black market in smuggled consumer electronics equipment like videocassette recorders. In addition, auto parts are stolen from operating cars to be resold by black marketeers, and cattle rustling is growing.

NOTES

1. Mali's average tariff rate does not include fiscal duties, which increase the rate to between 10 percent and 15 percent.
2. According to the U.S. Department of State, total taxation on income and corporate profits in Mali is over 50 percent. It was not possible to obtain the tax rate on the average income level. Therefore, Mali's score is based only on the top rate.
3. U.S. Department of Commerce, *Country Commercial Guide,* 1997.

Malta   2.85

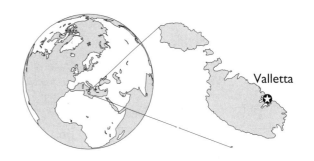

Valletta

1997 Score: **2.95**	1996 Score: **3.05**	1995 Score: **3.25**

Trade	4	Banking	3
Taxation	3.5	Wages and Prices	4
Government Intervention	2	Property Rights	2
Monetary Policy	1	Regulation	3
Foreign Investment	2	Black Market	4

Malta gained its independence from the United Kingdom in 1964. During the 1970s, socialist experiments left many businesses bankrupt. Rather than let these businesses fail, the government intervened and nationalized them, causing the budget to become bloated. Today, Malta has made progress toward free-market reform by reducing some taxes, maintaining a tight money supply, and welcoming most foreign investment. It also has managed to reduce black market activity by cracking down on smuggling. Legal protection of private property has been strengthened recently. Thus, Malta's overall score is 0.1 point better this year.

TRADE POLICY
Score: 4–Stable (high level of protectionism)

Malta's average tariff rate is 7.34 percent.[1] Some import licenses are required, especially for health and environmental products.

TAXATION
Score–Income taxation: 3–Stable (moderate tax rates)
Score–Corporate taxation: 3–Stable (moderate tax rates)
Total Taxation Score: 3.5–Stable (high tax rates)

Malta's top marginal income tax rate is 35 percent, and citizens making the average income pay 20 percent. The top corporate tax rate is 35 percent. Malta also has a 35 percent capital gains tax, a 2 percent to 7 percent stamp duty (tax on the transfer of property), and a 15 percent value-added tax.

GOVERNMENT INTERVENTION IN THE ECONOMY
Score: 2–Stable (low level)

Government consumes 21.1 percent of Malta's GDP.

MONETARY POLICY
Score: 1–Stable (very low level of inflation)

The average annual rate of inflation in Malta from 1985 to 1995 was 2.9 percent. In 1996, the rate was 3 percent.

CAPITAL FLOWS AND FOREIGN INVESTMENT
Score: 2–Stable (low barriers)

With the exception of utilities, almost all companies are open to foreign investment in Malta. There are few restrictions.

BANKING
Score: 3–Stable (moderate level of restrictions)

Most domestic banks are private, with only a few still owned by the government, and there is competition to attract customers. Foreign banks are increasing their presence.

1	Hong Kong	1.25	77	Zambia	3.05
2	Singapore	1.30	80	Mali	3.10
3	Bahrain	1.70	80	Mongolia	3.10
4	New Zealand	1.75	80	Slovenia	3.10
5	Switzerland	1.90	83	Honduras	3.15
5	United States	1.90	83	Papua New Guinea	3.15
7	Luxembourg	1.95	85	Djibouti	3.20
7	Taiwan	1.95	85	Fiji	3.20
7	United Kingdom	1.95	85	Pakistan	3.20
10	Bahamas	2.00	88	Algeria	3.25
10	Ireland	2.00	88	Guinea	3.25
12	Australia	2.05	88	Lebanon	3.25
12	Japan	2.05	88	Mexico	3.25
14	Belgium	2.10	88	Senegal	3.25
14	Canada	2.10	88	Tanzania	3.25
14	United Arab Emirates	2.10	94	Nigeria	3.30
17	Austria	2.15	94	Romania	3.30
17	Chile	2.15	96	Brazil	3.35
17	Estonia	2.15	96	Cambodia	3.35
20	Czech Republic	2.20	96	Egypt	3.35
20	Netherlands	2.20	96	Ivory Coast	3.35
22	Denmark	2.25	96	Madagascar	3.35
22	Finland	2.25	96	Moldova	3.35
24	Germany	2.30	102	Nepal	3.40
24	Iceland	2.30	103	Cape Verde	3.44
24	South Korea	2.30	104	Armenia	3.45
27	Norway	2.35	104	Dominican Republic	3.45
28	Kuwait	2.40	104	Russia	3.45
28	Malaysia	2.40	107	Burkina Faso	3.50
28	Panama	2.40	107	Cameroon	3.50
28	Thailand	2.40	107	Lesotho	3.50
32	El Salvador	2.45	107	Nicaragua	3.50
32	Sri Lanka	2.45	107	Venezuela	3.50
32	Sweden	2.45	112	Gambia	3.60
35	France	2.50	112	Guyana	3.60
35	Italy	2.50	114	Bulgaria	3.65
35	Spain	2.50	114	Georgia	3.65
38	Trinidad and Tobago	2.55	114	Malawi	3.65
39	Argentina	2.60	117	Ethiopia	3.70
39	Barbados	2.60	117	India	3.70
39	Cyprus	2.60	117	Niger	3.70
39	Jamaica	2.60	120	Albania	3.75
39	Portugal	2.60	120	Bangladesh	3.75
44	Bolivia	2.65	120	China (PRC)	3.75
44	Oman	2.65	120	Congo	3.75
44	Philippines	2.65	120	Croatia	3.75
47	Swaziland	2.70	125	Chad	3.80
47	Uruguay	2.70	125	Mauritania	3.80
49	Botswana	2.75	125	Ukraine	3.80
49	Jordan	2.75	128	Sierra Leone	3.85
49	Namibia	2.75	129	Burundi	3.90
49	Tunisia	2.75	129	Suriname	3.90
53	Belize	2.80	129	Zimbabwe	3.90
53	Costa Rica	2.80	132	Haiti	4.00
53	Guatemala	2.80	132	Kyrgyzstan	4.00
53	Israel	2.80	132	Syria	4.00
53	Peru	2.80	135	Belarus	4.05
53	Saudi Arabia	2.80	136	Kazakstan	4.10
53	Turkey	2.80	136	Mozambique	4.10
53	Uganda	2.80	136	Yemen	4.10
53	Western Samoa	2.80	139	Sudan	4.20
62	Indonesia	2.85	140	Myanmar	4.30
62	Latvia	2.85	140	Rwanda	4.30
62	Malta	2.85	142	Angola	4.35
62	Paraguay	2.85	143	Azerbaijan	4.40
66	Greece	2.90	143	Tajikistan	4.40
66	Hungary	2.90	145	Turkmenistan	4.50
66	South Africa	2.90	146	Uzbekistan	4.55
69	Benin	2.95	147	Congo/Zaire	4.70
69	Ecuador	2.95	147	Iran	4.70
69	Gabon	2.95	147	Libya	4.70
69	Morocco	2.95	147	Somalia	4.70
69	Poland	2.95	147	Vietnam	4.70
74	Colombia	3.00	152	Bosnia	4.80
74	Ghana	3.00	153	Iraq	4.90
74	Lithuania	3.00	154	Cuba	5.00
77	Kenya	3.05	154	Laos	5.00
77	Slovak Republic	3.05	154	North Korea	5.00

Mostly Free (label at left side of table)

Wage and Price Controls
Score: 4–Stable (high level)

The Department of Trade is responsible for pricing most items sold in Malta. There also is a minimum wage.

Property Rights
Score: 2+ (high level of protection)

There have been cases of government expropriation in the past, but such action is much less likely today. The judicial system has been strengthened. According to the U.S. Department of State, Malta's "Independent judiciary upholds the Constitution's protections for individual rights and freedoms.... The judiciary is independent of the executive and legislative branches."[2] There may be delays in some court cases, however. Because the protection of private property has improved significantly, Malta's property rights score is one point better this year.

Regulation
Score: 3–Stable (moderate level)

Malta has new consumer safety regulations that conform to European Union standards. Environmental regulations are enforced stringently and carry large fines. Opening a business is difficult, and licenses must be granted by many bureaucracies, including the police.

Black Market
Score: 4–Stable (high level of activity)

Malta is a major center for smuggling, and its location makes it a preferred base for black market activity. The government has cracked down on smuggling and other black market activities, however, thereby reducing them to some extent.

Notes

1. Based on taxes on international trade as a percentage of total imports.
2. U.S. Department of State, "Malta Country Report on Human Rights Practices for 1996," 1997.

Mauritania   3.80

1997 Score: **3.80**	1996 Score: **3.80**	1995 Score: **n/a**

Trade	5	Banking	5
Taxation	4	Wages and Prices	4
Government Intervention	3	Property Rights	4
Monetary Policy	2	Regulation	4
Foreign Investment	3	Black Market	4

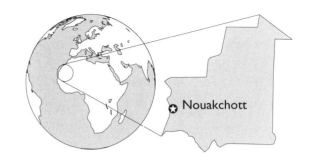

Nouakchott

Mauritania gained its independence from France in 1960. Its territory consists primarily of flat, dry plains and desert. In 1991, opposition parties were legalized and a new constitution was adopted. In 1992, President Maaouya Ould Sidi Ahmed Taya, who has ruled since 1984, won a presidential election that the U.S. Department of State characterized as "fraudulent."[1] During most of the 1980s, the government pursued a highly interventionist policy toward the economy, which consists predominantly of fishing, agriculture, and mining. In the 1990s, it has struggled to adopt a series of economic reforms. More recently, Mauritania has been praised by international groups for adhering to its economic reform agenda, which includes reducing government spending, and for improving GDP growth an average of 4.6 percent annually from 1994 to 1996. The government also has increased trade barriers, however, and the country remains a major recipient of funds from the World Bank and other donors of aid.

TRADE POLICY
Score: 5–Stable (very high level of protectionism)

Mauritania's average tariff rate is 35 percent.[2] Trade restrictions include strict labeling and inspection requirements as well as a sometimes corrupt and inefficient customs agency.

TAXATION
Score–Income taxation: 4–Stable (high tax rates)
Score–Corporate taxation: 4–Stable (high tax rates)
Final Taxation Score: 4–Stable (high tax rates)

Because top income and corporate tax rates were not available, total government revenue as a percentage of GDP (over 25 percent[3]) was used to grade Mauritania's levels of taxation.

GOVERNMENT INTERVENTION IN THE ECONOMY
Score: 3–Stable (moderate level)

Government consumes about 10 percent of Mauritania's GDP. Even though much of the economy has been privatized, the government still owns some companies, including those producing electricity and water.

MONETARY POLICY
Score: 2–Stable (low level of inflation)

Mauritania's average rate of inflation from 1985 to 1995 was 6.9 percent. In 1996, inflation was about 4.8 percent.

1	Hong Kong	1.25
2	Singapore	1.30
3	Bahrain	1.70
4	New Zealand	1.75
5	Switzerland	1.90
5	United States	1.90
7	Luxembourg	1.95
7	Taiwan	1.95
7	United Kingdom	1.95
10	Bahamas	2.00
10	Ireland	2.00
12	Australia	2.05
12	Japan	2.05
14	Belgium	2.10
14	Canada	2.10
14	United Arab Emirates	2.10
17	Austria	2.15
17	Chile	2.15
17	Estonia	2.15
20	Czech Republic	2.20
20	Netherlands	2.20
22	Denmark	2.25
22	Finland	2.25
24	Germany	2.30
24	Iceland	2.30
24	South Korea	2.30
27	Norway	2.35
28	Kuwait	2.40
28	Malaysia	2.40
28	Panama	2.40
28	Thailand	2.40
32	El Salvador	2.45
32	Sri Lanka	2.45
32	Sweden	2.45
35	France	2.50
35	Italy	2.50
35	Spain	2.50
38	Trinidad and Tobago	2.55
39	Argentina	2.60
39	Barbados	2.60
39	Cyprus	2.60
39	Jamaica	2.60
39	Portugal	2.60
44	Bolivia	2.65
44	Oman	2.65
44	Philippines	2.65
47	Swaziland	2.70
47	Uruguay	2.70
49	Botswana	2.75
49	Jordan	2.75
49	Namibia	2.75
49	Tunisia	2.75
53	Belize	2.80
53	Costa Rica	2.80
53	Guatemala	2.80
53	Israel	2.80
53	Peru	2.80
53	Saudi Arabia	2.80
53	Turkey	2.80
53	Uganda	2.80
53	Western Samoa	2.80
62	Indonesia	2.85
62	Latvia	2.85
62	Malta	2.85
62	Paraguay	2.85
66	Greece	2.90
66	Hungary	2.90
66	South Africa	2.90
69	Benin	2.95
69	Ecuador	2.95
69	Gabon	2.95
69	Morocco	2.95
69	Poland	2.95
74	Colombia	3.00
74	Ghana	3.00
74	Lithuania	3.00
77	Kenya	3.05
77	Slovak Republic	3.05

77	Zambia	3.05
80	Mali	3.10
80	Mongolia	3.10
80	Slovenia	3.10
83	Honduras	3.15
83	Papua New Guinea	3.15
85	Djibouti	3.20
85	Fiji	3.20
85	Pakistan	3.20
88	Algeria	3.25
88	Guinea	3.25
88	Lebanon	3.25
88	Mexico	3.25
88	Senegal	3.25
88	Tanzania	3.25
94	Nigeria	3.30
94	Romania	3.30
96	Brazil	3.35
96	Cambodia	3.35
96	Egypt	3.35
96	Ivory Coast	3.35
96	Madagascar	3.35
96	Moldova	3.35
102	Nepal	3.40
103	Cape Verde	3.44
104	Armenia	3.45
104	Dominican Republic	3.45
104	Russia	3.45
107	Burkina Faso	3.50
107	Cameroon	3.50
107	Lesotho	3.50
107	Nicaragua	3.50
107	Venezuela	3.50
112	Gambia	3.60
112	Guyana	3.60
114	Bulgaria	3.65
114	Georgia	3.65
114	Malawi	3.65
117	Ethiopia	3.70
117	India	3.70
117	Niger	3.70
120	Albania	3.75
120	Bangladesh	3.75
120	China (PRC)	3.75
120	Congo	3.75
120	Croatia	3.75
125	Chad	3.80
125	Mauritania	3.80
125	Ukraine	3.80
128	Sierra Leone	3.85
129	Burundi	3.90
129	Suriname	3.90
129	Zimbabwe	3.90
132	Haiti	4.00
132	Kyrgyzstan	4.00
132	Syria	4.00
135	Belarus	4.05
136	Kazakstan	4.10
136	Mozambique	4.10
136	Yemen	4.10
139	Sudan	4.20
140	Myanmar	4.30
140	Rwanda	4.30
142	Angola	4.35
143	Azerbaijan	4.40
143	Tajikistan	4.40
145	Turkmenistan	4.50
146	Uzbekistan	4.55
147	Congo/Zaire	4.70
147	Iran	4.70
147	Libya	4.70
147	Somalia	4.70
147	Vietnam	4.70
152	Bosnia	4.80
153	Iraq	4.90
154	Cuba	5.00
154	Laos	5.00
154	North Korea	5.00

Mostly Unfree

CAPITAL FLOWS AND FOREIGN INVESTMENT
Score: 3–Stable (moderate barriers)

Mauritania has passed laws to attract foreign investors. Foreign and domestic firms generally enjoy equal treatment, and there are few legal barriers. Overall, despite some problems—such as official corruption, the lack of infrastructure, and a very poor population—the new investment code has been successful in opening the economy to foreign investment.

BANKING
Score: 5–Stable (very high level of restrictions)

Some reforms are being introduced, but the banking system is still chaotic. Most banks are controlled strictly by the government, and the banking industry remains undeveloped and small. According to the U.S. Department of Commerce, "With only five commercial banks and two small credit agencies, Mauritania's banking system remains underdeveloped."[4]

WAGE AND PRICE CONTROLS
Score: 4–Stable (high level)

Wages and prices in Mauritania are controlled through subsidies to businesses, as well as to state-owned utilities like electricity.

PROPERTY RIGHTS
Score: 4–Stable (low level of protection)

Private property is not safe in Mauritania. The legal and judicial system is chaotic and sometimes corrupt. According to the U.S. Department of Commerce, "Mauritania's banks, for example, have had difficulty getting local courts to enforce a bank's right under loan agreements to seize pledged assets from local merchants."[5]

REGULATION
Score: 4–Stable (high level)

Establishing a business in Mauritania is becoming easier. Regulations, although cumbersome, are applied fairly evenly in most cases. Corrupt government bureaucrats, however, sometimes will impose arbitrary requirements on businesses. According to the U.S. Department of Commerce, "important problems remain to be resolved: improvement and development of management practices, improving transparency of government procedures, abolition of corruption within the administration, and improvement of the labor and banking laws."[6]

BLACK MARKET
Score: 4–Stable (high level of activity)

Mauritania's large informal market is confined mainly to consumer goods and entertainment products, especially computer software.

NOTES

1. U.S. Department of State, "Mauritania Country Report on Human Rights Practices for 1996," 1997, p. 1.
2. U.S. Department of Commerce, *Country Commercial Guide,* 1997.
3. This compares with about 13 percent in Japan, which has a top income tax rate of 50 percent.
4. U.S. Department of Commerce, *Country Commercial Guide,* 1997.
5. *Ibid.*
6. *Ibid.*

Mexico

3.25

1997 Score: **3.35**   1996 Score: **3.35**   1995 Score: **3.05**

Trade	3	Banking	4
Taxation	3.5	Wages and Prices	3
Government Intervention	2	Property Rights	3
Monetary Policy	5	Regulation	4
Foreign Investment	2	Black Market	3

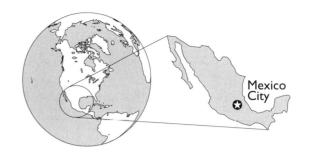

Mexico City

After decades of socialist economic policies and limited economic freedom, Mexico is well on its way toward liberalizing its market. As in other countries trying to reform their economies, many of the benefits of the free market are only beginning to take effect. Efforts to integrate the economy with those of the United States and Canada through the North American Free Trade Agreement (NAFTA) are promoting economic liberalization, but Mexico still limits economic freedom, especially with respect to trade with non-NAFTA countries, and has not reformed its political system as rapidly as it has reformed its economy. Restricted economic freedom and a lack of political openness were behind the December 1994 collapse of the peso, which caused an economic recession from which Mexico is only beginning to recover. Mexico has resumed its privatization program, however, with the result of raising its overall score by 0.1 point this year.

TRADE POLICY
Score: 3–Stable (moderate level of protectionism)

Mexico's average tariff rate is 5.1 percent.[1] Import licenses are required for 198 different products, including beans, cars and trucks, corn, dairy products, firearms, and poultry.

TAXATION
Score–Income taxation: 3–Stable (moderate tax rates)
Score–Corporate taxation: 3–Stable (moderate tax rates)
Total Taxation Score: 3.5–Stable (high tax rates)

Mexico's top marginal tax rate is 35 percent, and the average income level is taxed at 17 percent. The top corporate tax rate is 34 percent. Mexico also has a 15 percent value-added tax, a 34 percent capital gains tax, a state tax on salaries, and a resident tax.

GOVERNMENT INTERVENTION IN THE ECONOMY
Score: 2+ (low level)

Government consumes 10.4 percent of Mexico's GDP. The recent economic crisis caused Mexico's privatization program to slow in some sectors, but that trend is reversing and privatization has resumed. Mexico has privatized over 1,000 enterprises since 1986. The government also has developed plans to privatize some port facilities, airports, and railroads. As a result, Mexico's government intervention score has improved by one point this year.

MONETARY POLICY
Score: 5–Stable (very high level of inflation)

Even though Mexico has made great strides toward containing inflation since 1988, its overall record in this area has been poor. From 1985 to 1995, the average rate of inflation was 36.7 percent; in 1996, the rate of inflation was 35.2 percent.

1	Hong Kong	1.25	77	Zambia	3.05
2	Singapore	1.30	80	Mali	3.10
3	Bahrain	1.70	80	Mongolia	3.10
4	New Zealand	1.75	80	Slovenia	3.10
5	Switzerland	1.90	83	Honduras	3.15
5	United States	1.90	83	Papua New Guinea	3.15
7	Luxembourg	1.95	85	Djibouti	3.20
7	Taiwan	1.95	85	Fiji	3.20
7	United Kingdom	1.95	85	Pakistan	3.20
10	Bahamas	2.00	88	Algeria	3.25
10	Ireland	2.00	88	Guinea	3.25
12	Australia	2.05	88	Lebanon	3.25
12	Japan	2.05	88	Mexico	3.25
14	Belgium	2.10	88	Senegal	3.25
14	Canada	2.10	88	Tanzania	3.25
14	United Arab Emirates	2.10	94	Nigeria	3.30
17	Austria	2.15	94	Romania	3.30
17	Chile	2.15	96	Brazil	3.35
17	Estonia	2.15	96	Cambodia	3.35
20	Czech Republic	2.20	96	Egypt	3.35
20	Netherlands	2.20	96	Ivory Coast	3.35
22	Denmark	2.25	96	Madagascar	3.35
22	Finland	2.25	96	Moldova	3.35
24	Germany	2.30	102	Nepal	3.40
24	Iceland	2.30	103	Cape Verde	3.44
24	South Korea	2.30	104	Armenia	3.45
27	Norway	2.35	104	Dominican Republic	3.45
28	Kuwait	2.40	104	Russia	3.45
28	Malaysia	2.40	107	Burkina Faso	3.50
28	Panama	2.40	107	Cameroon	3.50
28	Thailand	2.40	107	Lesotho	3.50
32	El Salvador	2.45	107	Nicaragua	3.50
32	Sri Lanka	2.45	107	Venezuela	3.50
32	Sweden	2.45	112	Gambia	3.60
35	France	2.50	112	Guyana	3.60
35	Italy	2.50	114	Bulgaria	3.65
35	Spain	2.50	114	Georgia	3.65
38	Trinidad and Tobago	2.55	114	Malawi	3.65
39	Argentina	2.60	117	Ethiopia	3.70
39	Barbados	2.60	117	India	3.70
39	Cyprus	2.60	117	Niger	3.70
39	Jamaica	2.60	120	Albania	3.75
39	Portugal	2.60	120	Bangladesh	3.75
44	Bolivia	2.65	120	China (PRC)	3.75
44	Oman	2.65	120	Congo	3.75
44	Philippines	2.65	120	Croatia	3.75
47	Swaziland	2.70	125	Chad	3.80
47	Uruguay	2.70	125	Mauritania	3.80
49	Botswana	2.75	125	Ukraine	3.80
49	Jordan	2.75	128	Sierra Leone	3.85
49	Namibia	2.75	129	Burundi	3.90
49	Tunisia	2.75	129	Suriname	3.90
53	Belize	2.80	129	Zimbabwe	3.90
53	Costa Rica	2.80	132	Haiti	4.00
53	Guatemala	2.80	132	Kyrgyzstan	4.00
53	Israel	2.80	132	Syria	4.00
53	Peru	2.80	135	Belarus	4.05
53	Saudi Arabia	2.80	136	Kazakstan	4.10
53	Turkey	2.80	136	Mozambique	4.10
53	Uganda	2.80	136	Yemen	4.10
53	Western Samoa	2.80	139	Sudan	4.20
62	Indonesia	2.85	140	Myanmar	4.30
62	Latvia	2.85	140	Rwanda	4.30
62	Malta	2.85	142	Angola	4.35
62	Paraguay	2.85	143	Azerbaijan	4.40
66	Greece	2.90	143	Tajikistan	4.40
66	Hungary	2.90	145	Turkmenistan	4.50
66	South Africa	2.90	146	Uzbekistan	4.55
69	Benin	2.95	147	Congo/Zaire	4.70
69	Ecuador	2.95	147	Iran	4.70
69	Gabon	2.95	147	Libya	4.70
69	Morocco	2.95	147	Somalia	4.70
69	Poland	2.95	147	Vietnam	4.70
74	Colombia	3.00	152	Bosnia	4.80
74	Ghana	3.00	153	Iraq	4.90
74	Lithuania	3.00	154	Cuba	5.00
77	Kenya	3.05	154	Laos	5.00
77	Slovak Republic	3.05	154	North Korea	5.00

Mostly Unfree

CAPITAL FLOWS AND FOREIGN INVESTMENT
Score: 2–Stable (low barriers)

Mexico has reformed its foreign investment code to attract more investors, allowing for more equal treatment of foreign and domestic firms. Investors from non-NAFTA countries, however, may not own majority shares in many service industries, including banking.

BANKING
Score: 4–Stable (high level of restrictions)

Since the collapse of the Mexican peso in December 1994, the government has allowed 100 percent foreign ownership of banks, although government authorization is required for some investments. The economic situation has led the government to bail out many private banks, effectively acquiring control of many institutions, and domestic banks are prohibited from investing in real estate and industrial firms. Thus, the government remains fully entrenched in Mexico's troubled financial sector.[2] There is some corruption in the dispensing of loans to state-owned companies.

WAGE AND PRICE CONTROLS
Score: 3–Stable (moderate level)

In 1994, 60 product areas were subject to price controls; in 1995, the number decreased to 28. Some controls, such as those on milk and other foodstuffs, remain in effect. Mexico has a minimum wage with incremental cost-of-living increases.

PROPERTY RIGHTS
Score: 3–Stable (moderate level of protection)

Mexico's constitution guarantees private property, and legal protection of private property will increase as more state-owned property is privatized. Considering current levels of corruption and government-sanctioned cronyism, however, as well as the growing trade in illegal drugs, private property also faces increased risk. According to the U.S. Department of Commerce, "The Mexican judiciary has suffered from a poor career system and corruption."[3] By global standards, protection of private property is moderate.

REGULATION
Score: 4–Stable (high level)

Opening a business remains a complicated task. Each business must obtain a license or some other form of certification from numerous government agencies, including the Public Registry of Commerce, the Bureau of Statistics, federal and local tax authorities, the Mexican Social Security Institute, and the National Housing Fund. Some localities require each business to belong to a local chamber of commerce and trade association, and additional licenses may be required from the Ministry of Health and other agencies. Although Mexico is attempting to end corruption, its current regulatory environment remains an obstacle to business creation.

BLACK MARKET
Score: 3–Stable (moderate level of activity)

A black market in such transportation services as taxis and busing is prevalent in many Mexican cities, and black market labor often is available to businesses that want to skirt minimum wage laws. Some estimates put black market labor in Mexico City at over 40 percent. Mexico also is plagued with black market activity in the construction industry, and there continues to be some piracy of such intellectual property as computer software.

NOTES

1. *The World Trade and Customs Directory,* Spring 1997 (Washington, D.C.: Arrowhead International, 1997).
2. Economist Intelligence Unit, *EIU Country Reports,* 1997.
3. U.S. Department of Commerce, *Country Commercial Guide,* 1997.

Moldova

3.35

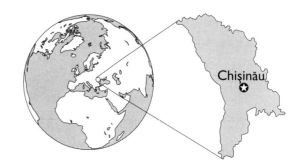

Chișinău ✪

1997 Score: **3.35**   1996 Score: **3.45**   1995 Score: **4.10**

Trade	3	Banking	3
Taxation	3.5	Wages and Prices	3
Government Intervention	3	Property Rights	3
Monetary Policy	5	Regulation	3
Foreign Investment	3	Black Market	4

Moldova, once part of Romania, gained its independence from the Soviet Union in 1991 and suffered a protracted separatist insurrection by communist, pro-Russian hard-liners. As a Soviet Socialist Republic, Moldova was a large food producer. Since independence, its economy has shrunk, unemployment has grown, and inflation has skyrocketed. The government has made some progress, however, in stabilizing the economy and laying the groundwork for the creation of a market infrastructure.

TRADE POLICY
Score: 3–Stable (moderate level of protectionism)

Moldova has an average tariff rate of around 5 percent. It also maintains nontariff barriers to trade in several areas. For example, the government imposes quotas on imports of unprocessed leather, energy products, and cereals.

TAXATION
Score–Income taxation: 3–Stable (moderate tax rates)
Score–Corporate taxation: 3-Stable (moderate tax rates)
Total Taxation Score: 3.5–Stable (high tax rates)

Moldova's top income tax rate is 50 percent; the average income level is taxed at 10 percent.[1] Moldova also has a 30 percent corporate tax and a 20 percent value-added tax.[2]

GOVERNMENT INTERVENTION IN THE ECONOMY
Score: 3–Stable (moderate level)

Government consumes 20 percent of Moldova's GDP, of which the public sector produces almost half.

MONETARY POLICY
Score: 5–Stable (very high level of inflation)

Moldova's government has made substantial progress toward reducing the hyperinflation of 1992, caused by the collapse of the ruble. The rate of inflation was 1,276 percent in 1992, 837 percent in 1993, 108 percent in 1994, 23.8 percent in 1995, and 25.5 percent in 1996. Thus, the average rate of inflation from 1991 to 1995 has been very high.

CAPITAL FLOWS AND FOREIGN INVESTMENT
Score: 3–Stable (moderate barriers)

Moldova has moved to develop foreign investment and commercial codes. Some foreign ownership of land is now legal, but 100 percent foreign ownership is not permitted. The government also prevents 100 percent foreign ownership in banking, securities and bonds, and natural resources.

1	Hong Kong	1.25	77	Zambia	3.05
2	Singapore	1.30	80	Mali	3.10
3	Bahrain	1.70	80	Mongolia	3.10
4	New Zealand	1.75	80	Slovenia	3.10
5	Switzerland	1.90	83	Honduras	3.15
5	United States	1.90	83	Papua New Guinea	3.15
7	Luxembourg	1.95	85	Djibouti	3.20
7	Taiwan	1.95	85	Fiji	3.20
7	United Kingdom	1.95	85	Pakistan	3.20
10	Bahamas	2.00	88	Algeria	3.25
10	Ireland	2.00	88	Guinea	3.25
12	Australia	2.05	88	Lebanon	3.25
12	Japan	2.05	88	Mexico	3.25
14	Belgium	2.10	88	Senegal	3.25
14	Canada	2.10	88	Tanzania	3.25
14	United Arab Emirates	2.10	94	Nigeria	3.30
17	Austria	2.15	94	Romania	3.30
17	Chile	2.15	96	Brazil	3.35
17	Estonia	2.15	96	Cambodia	3.35
20	Czech Republic	2.20	96	Egypt	3.35
20	Netherlands	2.20	96	Ivory Coast	3.35
22	Denmark	2.25	96	Madagascar	3.35
22	Finland	2.25	96	Moldova	3.35
24	Germany	2.30	102	Nepal	3.40
24	Iceland	2.30	103	Cape Verde	3.44
24	South Korea	2.30	104	Armenia	3.45
27	Norway	2.35	104	Dominican Republic	3.45
28	Kuwait	2.40	104	Russia	3.45
28	Malaysia	2.40	107	Burkina Faso	3.50
28	Panama	2.40	107	Cameroon	3.50
28	Thailand	2.40	107	Lesotho	3.50
32	El Salvador	2.45	107	Nicaragua	3.50
32	Sri Lanka	2.45	107	Venezuela	3.50
32	Sweden	2.45	112	Gambia	3.60
35	France	2.50	112	Guyana	3.60
35	Italy	2.50	114	Bulgaria	3.65
35	Spain	2.50	114	Georgia	3.65
38	Trinidad and Tobago	2.55	114	Malawi	3.65
39	Argentina	2.60	117	Ethiopia	3.70
39	Barbados	2.60	117	India	3.70
39	Cyprus	2.60	117	Niger	3.70
39	Jamaica	2.60	120	Albania	3.75
39	Portugal	2.60	120	Bangladesh	3.75
44	Bolivia	2.65	120	China (PRC)	3.75
44	Oman	2.65	120	Congo	3.75
44	Philippines	2.65	120	Croatia	3.75
47	Swaziland	2.70	125	Chad	3.80
47	Uruguay	2.70	125	Mauritania	3.80
49	Botswana	2.75	125	Ukraine	3.80
49	Jordan	2.75	128	Sierra Leone	3.85
49	Namibia	2.75	129	Burundi	3.90
49	Tunisia	2.75	129	Suriname	3.90
53	Belize	2.80	129	Zimbabwe	3.90
53	Costa Rica	2.80	132	Haiti	4.00
53	Guatemala	2.80	132	Kyrgyzstan	4.00
53	Israel	2.80	132	Syria	4.00
53	Peru	2.80	135	Belarus	4.05
53	Saudi Arabia	2.80	136	Kazakstan	4.10
53	Turkey	2.80	136	Mozambique	4.10
53	Uganda	2.80	136	Yemen	4.10
53	Western Samoa	2.80	139	Sudan	4.20
62	Indonesia	2.85	140	Myanmar	4.30
62	Latvia	2.85	140	Rwanda	4.30
62	Malta	2.85	142	Angola	4.35
62	Paraguay	2.85	143	Azerbaijan	4.40
66	Greece	2.90	143	Tajikistan	4.40
66	Hungary	2.90	145	Turkmenistan	4.50
66	South Africa	2.90	146	Uzbekistan	4.55
69	Benin	2.95	147	Congo/Zaire	4.70
69	Ecuador	2.95	147	Iran	4.70
69	Gabon	2.95	147	Libya	4.70
69	Morocco	2.95	147	Somalia	4.70
69	Poland	2.95	147	Vietnam	4.70
74	Colombia	3.00	152	Bosnia	4.80
74	Ghana	3.00	153	Iraq	4.90
74	Lithuania	3.00	154	Cuba	5.00
77	Kenya	3.05	154	Laos	5.00
77	Slovak Republic	3.05	154	North Korea	5.00

Mostly Unfree

Banking
Score: 3–Stable (moderate level of restrictions)

Although Moldova's banking system is becoming more competitive and less subject to government control, it remains underdeveloped. There are 26 private foreign banks operating in the country, but foreigners are not permitted to own 100 percent of banks and other financial institutions.

Wage and Price Controls
Score: 3–Stable (moderate level)

The market sets most prices in Moldova, but the government still controls the prices of goods produced by some state-run monopolies. Moldova has a minimum wage.

Property Rights
Score: 3–Stable (moderate level of protection)

Moldova has passed laws guaranteeing private property and strengthening the judiciary. According to the U.S. Department of Commerce, "The independence of Moldova's judiciary has increased since the 1991 dissolution of the Soviet Union, partly due to provisions for tenure designed to increase judicial independence. A series of reforms approved in 1995 have begun to be implemented, including creation of a court to deal with constitutional issues and a system of appeals courts."[3] These reforms have yet to take effect, however. The enforcement of property rights can be cumbersome and 100 percent ownership of land by foreign investors is not permitted.

Regulation
Score: 3–Stable (moderate level)

Moldova is establishing a regulatory regime that will stress environmental protection and consumer safety. Existing regulations, in addition to being burdensome, are applied haphazardly. State planning has been reduced considerably.

Black Market
Score: 4–Stable (high level of activity)

"In 1995," reports the U.S. Department of Commerce, "Moldova adopted a [law] on protection of intellectual and industrial [property]. The law and its enforcement are inadequate to curb infringements, which take place in all sectors: software, cable television, audio and video cassettes, books and other [items]."[4] This law has allowed a substantial black market to develop in these pirated items.

Notes

1. U.S. Department of Commerce, "Moldova—Economic and Trade Overview," 1997.
2. *Ibid.*
3. U.S. Department of Commerce, National Trade Data Bank and Economic Bulletin Board, products of STAT–USA.
4. U.S. Department of Commerce, "Moldova—Economic and Trade Overview," 1997.

Mongolia   3.10

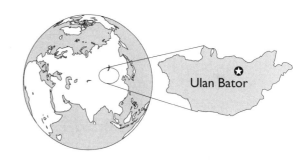

Ulan Bator

1997 Score: **3.30**	1996 Score: **3.50**	1995 Score: **3.33**

Trade	1	Banking	3
Taxation	4	Wages and Prices	3
Government Intervention	3	Property Rights	3
Monetary Policy	5	Regulation	3
Foreign Investment	3	Black Market	3

Mongolia regained its independence in 1921. Its economy remained closely linked with that of the Soviet Union, however, and it copied the Soviet model of central economic planning. After the collapse of the Soviet Union in 1991, Mongolia embarked on a program of economic liberalization; and although much remains to be done, there has been significant progress. Democratic elections were held in June 1996, and the new government agreed to accelerate the process of economic reform. Mongolia eliminated tariffs and taxes on all imports in 1997. As a result, its overall score this year is 0.2 point better than it was last year.

TRADE POLICY
Score: 1+ (very low level of protectionism)

Mongolia abolished all forms of tariffs and taxes on imports in April 1997. It is the only country with no taxes of any kind on imports. Mongolia also has streamlined its customs bureau, making it much more efficient, and there no longer are any significant nontariff barriers. As a result, its trade policy score is two points better this year.

TAXATION
Score–Income taxation: 4–Stable (high tax rates)
Score–Corporate taxation: 4–Stable (high tax rates)
Total Taxation Score: 4–Stable (high tax rates)

Mongolia has a top income tax rate of 40 percent and a top corporate tax rate of 40 percent. It also has a 10 percent sales tax.

GOVERNMENT INTERVENTION IN THE ECONOMY
Score: 3–Stable (high level)

Government consumes 25 percent of Mongolia's GDP. Although the government has undertaken a substantial privatization program, the state-owned sector remains significant and still generates almost 50 percent of GNP.

MONETARY POLICY
Score: 5–Stable (very high level of inflation)

Mongolia's rate of inflation averaged 51.6 percent during the 1985–1995 period. The inflation rate was 58 percent in 1996.

CAPITAL FLOWS AND FOREIGN INVESTMENT
Score: 3–Stable (moderate barriers)

Mongolia recently passed legislation to protect private property and foreign investments from government expropriation. New laws also provide equal treatment for Mongolian and foreign companies, and restrictions on currencies and profits have been removed. Although no industry is formally restricted, the government maintains a list of industries in which foreign investment is

1	Hong Kong	1.25		77	Zambia	3.05
2	Singapore	1.30		80	Mali	3.10
3	Bahrain	1.70		80	Mongolia	3.10
4	New Zealand	1.75		80	Slovenia	3.10
5	Switzerland	1.90		83	Honduras	3.15
5	United States	1.90		83	Papua New Guinea	3.15
7	Luxembourg	1.95		85	Djibouti	3.20
7	Taiwan	1.95		85	Fiji	3.20
7	United Kingdom	1.95		85	Pakistan	3.20
10	Bahamas	2.00		88	Algeria	3.25
10	Ireland	2.00		88	Guinea	3.25
12	Australia	2.05		88	Lebanon	3.25
12	Japan	2.05		88	Mexico	3.25
14	Belgium	2.10		88	Senegal	3.25
14	Canada	2.10		88	Tanzania	3.25
14	United Arab Emirates	2.10		94	Nigeria	3.30
17	Austria	2.15		94	Romania	3.30
17	Chile	2.15		96	Brazil	3.35
17	Estonia	2.15		96	Cambodia	3.35
20	Czech Republic	2.20		96	Egypt	3.35
20	Netherlands	2.20		96	Ivory Coast	3.35
22	Denmark	2.25		96	Madagascar	3.35
22	Finland	2.25		96	Moldova	3.35
24	Germany	2.30		102	Nepal	3.40
24	Iceland	2.30		103	Cape Verde	3.44
24	South Korea	2.30		104	Armenia	3.45
27	Norway	2.35		104	Dominican Republic	3.45
28	Kuwait	2.40		104	Russia	3.45
28	Malaysia	2.40		107	Burkina Faso	3.50
28	Panama	2.40		107	Cameroon	3.50
28	Thailand	2.40		107	Lesotho	3.50
32	El Salvador	2.45		107	Nicaragua	3.50
32	Sri Lanka	2.45		107	Venezuela	3.50
32	Sweden	2.45		112	Gambia	3.60
35	France	2.50		112	Guyana	3.60
35	Italy	2.50		114	Bulgaria	3.65
35	Spain	2.50		114	Georgia	3.65
38	Trinidad and Tobago	2.55		114	Malawi	3.65
39	Argentina	2.60		117	Ethiopia	3.70
39	Barbados	2.60		117	India	3.70
39	Cyprus	2.60		117	Niger	3.70
39	Jamaica	2.60		120	Albania	3.75
39	Portugal	2.60		120	Bangladesh	3.75
44	Bolivia	2.65		120	China (PRC)	3.75
44	Oman	2.65		120	Congo	3.75
44	Philippines	2.65		120	Croatia	3.75
47	Swaziland	2.70		125	Chad	3.80
47	Uruguay	2.70		125	Mauritania	3.80
49	Botswana	2.75		125	Ukraine	3.80
49	Jordan	2.75		128	Sierra Leone	3.85
49	Namibia	2.75		129	Burundi	3.90
49	Tunisia	2.75		129	Suriname	3.90
53	Belize	2.80		129	Zimbabwe	3.90
53	Costa Rica	2.80		132	Haiti	4.00
53	Guatemala	2.80		132	Kyrgyzstan	4.00
53	Israel	2.80		132	Syria	4.00
53	Peru	2.80		135	Belarus	4.05
53	Saudi Arabia	2.80		136	Kazakstan	4.10
53	Turkey	2.80		136	Mozambique	4.10
53	Uganda	2.80		136	Yemen	4.10
53	Western Samoa	2.80		139	Sudan	4.20
62	Indonesia	2.85		140	Myanmar	4.30
62	Latvia	2.85		140	Rwanda	4.30
62	Malta	2.85		142	Angola	4.35
62	Paraguay	2.85		143	Azerbaijan	4.40
66	Greece	2.90		143	Tajikistan	4.40
66	Hungary	2.90		145	Turkmenistan	4.50
66	South Africa	2.90		146	Uzbekistan	4.55
69	Benin	2.95		147	Congo/Zaire	4.70
69	Ecuador	2.95		147	Iran	4.70
69	Gabon	2.95		147	Libya	4.70
69	Morocco	2.95		147	Somalia	4.70
69	Poland	2.95		147	Vietnam	4.70
74	Colombia	3.00		152	Bosnia	4.80
74	Ghana	3.00		153	Iraq	4.90
74	Lithuania	3.00		154	Cuba	5.00
77	Kenya	3.05		154	Laos	5.00
77	Slovak Republic	3.05		154	North Korea	5.00

Mostly Unfree

discouraged; examples include state-owned enterprises, liquor, securities, mining, animal skins, pharmaceuticals, and chemicals. Foreigners still may not own land.

BANKING
Score: 3–Stable (moderate level of restrictions)

Even though progress has been made toward deregulating Mongolia's banks, they continue to be controlled by the government. Mongolia's banking system remains underdeveloped.

WAGE AND PRICE CONTROLS
Score: 3–Stable (moderate level)

Mongolia controls prices through a complex system of government procurement. For example, the government may buy a significant amount of a product in order to control its supply, thereby affecting the price. Noteworthy progress has been made toward liberalizing prices, however, as the government allows the market to play a more prominent role. Mongolia has a minimum wage.

PROPERTY RIGHTS
Score: 3–Stable (moderate level of protection)

Expropriation of existing private property is unlikely in Mongolia. The government has instituted new laws to protect property owners. Enforcement of laws protecting private property, however, is inefficient, and the state still holds a significant amount of land that stands little chance of being privatized in the near future.

REGULATION
Score: 3–Stable (moderate level)

The growing private sector in Mongolia, especially newly privatized companies, still is subject to significant government control. The are few official regulations, but corruption and government meddling hinder the operation of private business.

BLACK MARKET
Score: 3–Stable (moderate level of activity)

Mongolia's government buys many goods through its complex procurement program. This distorts prices for food commodities. The result is a black market for these and other government-regulated goods. There also is a moderate level of smuggling.

Morocco   2.95

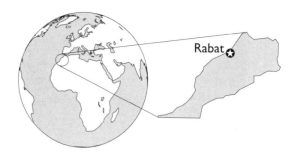

Rabat

| 1997 Score: **2.75** | 1996 Score: **2.70** | 1995 Score: **2.90** |

Trade	5	Banking	3
Taxation	3.5	Wages and Prices	3
Government Intervention	3	Property Rights	3
Monetary Policy	1	Regulation	3
Foreign Investment	2	Black Market	3

Morocco, which gained its independence from France in 1956, is a constitutional monarchy. The government of King Hassan II has imposed free-market reforms on the country's mixed economy, which has experienced slow but steady growth in recent years despite a 1995 drought. Morocco aspires to become a major manufacturing base serving markets in both Europe and Africa and is undergoing modest political liberalization along with economic modernization. Its military effort to retain control of the disputed Western Sahara, however, has been expensive and a diplomatic headache. Attempts to privatize much of the economy remain unfulfilled, and the government recently increased tariffs and decreased its level of protection of private property. As a result, Morocco's overall score is 0.2 point worse this year.

TRADE POLICY
Score: 5– (very high level of protectionism)

Morocco's average tariff rate has increased because it replaced its import quotas—used to protect many items—with tariffs. The average tariff now is around 20 percent, and there is a 10 percent to 15 percent surtax on imports.[1] For this reason, Morocco's trade policy score is one point worse this year. Bananas still are protected by nontariff barriers.

TAXATION
Score–Income taxation: 3–Stable (moderate tax rates)
Score–Corporate taxation: 3–Stable (moderate tax rates)
Total Taxation Score: 3.5–Stable (high tax rates)

Morocco's highest income tax rate is 44 percent; the average income is taxed at a rate of 0 percent. The corporation tax rate is fixed at 35 percent of profits. A value-added tax is payable at rates of 7 percent or 20 percent on sales and 7 percent on banking activities. Morocco also has a capital gains tax of 35 percent.

GOVERNMENT INTERVENTION IN THE ECONOMY
Score: 3–Stable (moderate level)

Government consumes 18.4 percent of Morocco's GDP. Under an ambitious privatization program begun in 1992, over 100 state-owned enterprises worth over $2 billion were targeted to be sold by 1995. This goal has yet to be met, although there has been steady progress. The government sold some 27 operations, including 8 hotels, in 1994. Privatization slowed in 1995 but rebounded in 1996. Morocco's government still owns substantial portions of the economy, mainly some financial institutions and steel and fertilizer companies.

MONETARY POLICY
Score: 1–Stable (very low level of inflation)

Morocco's average annual rate of inflation between 1985 and 1995 was 4.8 percent. In 1996, the rate of inflation was about 3 percent.

1	Hong Kong	1.25	77	Zambia	3.05
2	Singapore	1.30	80	Mali	3.10
3	Bahrain	1.70	80	Mongolia	3.10
4	New Zealand	1.75	80	Slovenia	3.10
5	Switzerland	1.90	83	Honduras	3.15
5	United States	1.90	83	Papua New Guinea	3.15
7	Luxembourg	1.95	85	Djibouti	3.20
7	Taiwan	1.95	85	Fiji	3.20
7	United Kingdom	1.95	85	Pakistan	3.20
10	Bahamas	2.00	88	Algeria	3.25
10	Ireland	2.00	88	Guinea	3.25
12	Australia	2.05	88	Lebanon	3.25
12	Japan	2.05	88	Mexico	3.25
14	Belgium	2.10	88	Senegal	3.25
14	Canada	2.10	88	Tanzania	3.25
14	United Arab Emirates	2.10	94	Nigeria	3.30
17	Austria	2.15	94	Romania	3.30
17	Chile	2.15	96	Brazil	3.35
17	Estonia	2.15	96	Cambodia	3.35
20	Czech Republic	2.20	96	Egypt	3.35
20	Netherlands	2.20	96	Ivory Coast	3.35
22	Denmark	2.25	96	Madagascar	3.35
22	Finland	2.25	96	Moldova	3.35
24	Germany	2.30	102	Nepal	3.40
24	Iceland	2.30	103	Cape Verde	3.44
24	South Korea	2.30	104	Armenia	3.45
27	Norway	2.35	104	Dominican Republic	3.45
28	Kuwait	2.40	104	Russia	3.45
28	Malaysia	2.40	107	Burkina Faso	3.50
28	Panama	2.40	107	Cameroon	3.50
28	Thailand	2.40	107	Lesotho	3.50
32	El Salvador	2.45	107	Nicaragua	3.50
32	Sri Lanka	2.45	107	Venezuela	3.50
32	Sweden	2.45	112	Gambia	3.60
35	France	2.50	112	Guyana	3.60
35	Italy	2.50	114	Bulgaria	3.65
35	Spain	2.50	114	Georgia	3.65
38	Trinidad and Tobago	2.55	114	Malawi	3.65
39	Argentina	2.60	117	Ethiopia	3.70
39	Barbados	2.60	117	India	3.70
39	Cyprus	2.60	117	Niger	3.70
39	Jamaica	2.60	120	Albania	3.75
39	Portugal	2.60	120	Bangladesh	3.75
44	Bolivia	2.65	120	China (PRC)	3.75
44	Oman	2.65	120	Congo	3.75
44	Philippines	2.65	120	Croatia	3.75
47	Swaziland	2.70	125	Chad	3.80
47	Uruguay	2.70	125	Mauritania	3.80
49	Botswana	2.75	125	Ukraine	3.80
49	Jordan	2.75	128	Sierra Leone	3.85
49	Namibia	2.75	129	Burundi	3.90
49	Tunisia	2.75	129	Suriname	3.90
53	Belize	2.80	129	Zimbabwe	3.90
53	Costa Rica	2.80	132	Haiti	4.00
53	Guatemala	2.80	132	Kyrgyzstan	4.00
53	Israel	2.80	132	Syria	4.00
53	Peru	2.80	135	Belarus	4.05
53	Saudi Arabia	2.80	136	Kazakstan	4.10
53	Turkey	2.80	136	Mozambique	4.10
53	Uganda	2.80	136	Yemen	4.10
53	Western Samoa	2.80	139	Sudan	4.20
62	Indonesia	2.85	140	Myanmar	4.30
62	Latvia	2.85	140	Rwanda	4.30
62	Malta	2.85	142	Angola	4.35
62	Paraguay	2.85	143	Azerbaijan	4.40
66	Greece	2.90	143	Tajikistan	4.40
66	Hungary	2.90	145	Turkmenistan	4.50
66	South Africa	2.90	146	Uzbekistan	4.55
69	Benin	2.95	147	Congo/Zaire	4.70
69	Ecuador	2.95	147	Iran	4.70
69	Gabon	2.95	147	Libya	4.70
69	Morocco	2.95	147	Somalia	4.70
69	Poland	2.95	147	Vietnam	4.70
74	Colombia	3.00	152	Bosnia	4.80
74	Ghana	3.00	153	Iraq	4.90
74	Lithuania	3.00	154	Cuba	5.00
77	Kenya	3.05	154	Laos	5.00
77	Slovak Republic	3.05	154	North Korea	5.00

Mostly Free

Capital Flows and Foreign Investment
Score: 2–Stable (low barriers)

Foreign-owned and locally owned investments are treated equally by the Moroccan government, which also permits 100 percent foreign ownership. Neither foreigners nor Moroccans may invest in industries that compete with the state's energy and water monopoly, rail and transportation services, or the mining and processing of phosphates, although the government plans to open the energy sector to private investment. Even though some foreign investors face a maze of regulations, the level of foreign investment has increased over the past several years in Morocco.

Banking
Score: 3–Stable (moderate level of restrictions)

Foreign banks may possess controlling interests in Moroccan banks. Local banks are expanding their activities to include capital market activity. Even though the government has privatized one major bank and plans to privatize another, it still owns several other financial and credit institutions. According to the U.S. Department of Commerce, "The banking system is still used by the government...as a way to channel domestic savings to finance government debt, and the banks are required to hold a part of their assets in bonds paying below market interest rates."[2]

Wage and Price Controls
Score: 3–Stable (moderate level)

Most price controls have been eliminated, although they remain on bread, cereal, milk, sugar, and other basics. The state also subsidizes these products. Even though wage and salary increases are negotiated freely between the Moroccan government and businesses, there is a minimum wage. When the Central Commission for Prices and Wages records an increase of at least 5 percent in the cost of living, the government can raise all wages and prices by decree.

Property Rights
Score: 3– (moderate level of protection)

Morocco's constitution prohibits the expropriation of private property except in special cases prescribed by law. There has been no expropriation since the early 1970s, and there are no outstanding cases of expropriation or nationalization of investments. According to the U.S. Department of State, the judicial system sometimes is "subject to corruption and Interior Minister influence."[3] As a result, Morocco's property rights score is one point worse this year.[4]

Regulation
Score: 3–Stable (moderate level)

Although establishing a business is fairly straightforward in Morocco, foreign businesses face complicated procedures and corruption. Government procedures are not always transparent, and routine business permits can be difficult to obtain, particularly from local authorities. Labor legislation makes it difficult to terminate workers.

Black Market
Score: 3–Stable (moderate level of activity)

The black market accounts for an estimated 20 percent of Morocco's GDP. There is considerable smuggling of consumer goods, as well as a lively trade in contraband. Because Morocco's laws governing intellectual property do not cover computer software, black market activity in this area is on the rise. Trademark violations, mainly in the clothing industry, also constitute a growing problem.

Notes

1. Based on total tax revenues from taxes on international transactions as a percentage of total imports.
2. U.S. Department of Commerce, *Country Commercial Guide,* 1997.
3. U.S. Department of State, "Morocco Country Report on Human Rights Practices for 1996," 1997.
4. The score in this factor has changed from 2 in 1997 to 3 in 1998. Previously unavailable data provide a more accurate understanding of the country's performance. This information is from U.S. Department of State, "Morocco Country Report on Human Rights Practices for 1996." The methodology for this factor remains the same.

Mozambique   4.10

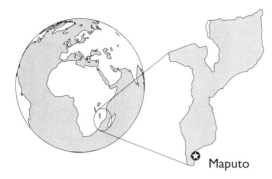

Maputo

| 1997 Score: **4.00** | 1996 Score: **4.05** | 1995 Score: **4.40** |

Trade	5	Banking	3
Taxation	4	Wages and Prices	3
Government Intervention	3	Property Rights	4
Monetary Policy	5	Regulation	5
Foreign Investment	4	Black Market	5

Mozambique won a decade-long conflict for independence from Portugal in 1975. Two years later, it became engulfed in a bloody civil war that lasted until 1992. Since then, it has been reasonably successful in building a democratic government and forging national reconciliation. Mozambique held its first multiparty democratic elections, supervised by the United Nations, in 1994. Its economy, one of the most heavily dependent on aid in the world, has been registering strong GDP growth as the government moves away from principles of Marxism that led to its previous devastation. Growth in GDP averaged 6.5 percent from 1992 to 1996; per capita GNP, however, was estimated to be only $80 in 1995 and remains quite poor. New evidence shows that the average tariff rate in Mozambique is higher than previously thought. Although the government has privatized some banks—a step that has increased competition in the banking sector—Mozambique's overall score this year is 0.1 point worse than it was last year.

TRADE POLICY
Score: 5– (very high level of protectionism)

Mozambique's tariff rates range from 0 percent to 40 percent. The U.S. Department of Commerce recently estimated that the average tariff is about 27 percent.[1] There has been some trade liberalization, including simplification of licensing procedures, but the customs service remains riddled with corruption, and the government recently has allowed private managers to manage the customs bureau. A few imports, including imports of used automobiles, are prohibited.

TAXATION
Score–Income taxation: 3–Stable (moderate tax rates)
Score–Corporate taxation: 4–Stable (high tax rates)
Total Taxation Score: 4–Stable (high tax rates)

Mozambique adjusted personal income taxes in 1995. The highest bracket is now 30 percent, up from 15 percent in 1995, and the tax on the average income is 15 percent. The top corporate income tax rate is 45 percent. Mozambique also has a 45 percent capital gains tax and a 75 percent consumption tax.

GOVERNMENT INTERVENTION IN THE ECONOMY
Score: 3–Stable (moderate level)

Government consumes 16.8 percent of Mozambique's GDP. Some 350 small enterprises have been privatized, including a brewery and cement factory that were sold to South African and Portuguese concerns, and plans for additional privatizations are on the table. In the meantime, public enterprises will continue to account for a considerable amount of the formal sector's economic output.

1	Hong Kong	1.25		77	Zambia	3.05
2	Singapore	1.30		80	Mali	3.10
3	Bahrain	1.70		80	Mongolia	3.10
4	New Zealand	1.75		80	Slovenia	3.10
5	Switzerland	1.90		83	Honduras	3.15
5	United States	1.90		83	Papua New Guinea	3.15
7	Luxembourg	1.95		85	Djibouti	3.20
7	Taiwan	1.95		85	Fiji	3.20
7	United Kingdom	1.95		85	Pakistan	3.20
10	Bahamas	2.00		88	Algeria	3.25
10	Ireland	2.00		88	Guinea	3.25
12	Australia	2.05		88	Lebanon	3.25
12	Japan	2.05		88	Mexico	3.25
14	Belgium	2.10		88	Senegal	3.25
14	Canada	2.10		88	Tanzania	3.25
14	United Arab Emirates	2.10		94	Nigeria	3.30
17	Austria	2.15		94	Romania	3.30
17	Chile	2.15		96	Brazil	3.35
17	Estonia	2.15		96	Cambodia	3.35
20	Czech Republic	2.20		96	Egypt	3.35
20	Netherlands	2.20		96	Ivory Coast	3.35
22	Denmark	2.25		96	Madagascar	3.35
22	Finland	2.25		96	Moldova	3.35
24	Germany	2.30		102	Nepal	3.40
24	Iceland	2.30		103	Cape Verde	3.44
24	South Korea	2.30		104	Armenia	3.45
27	Norway	2.35		104	Dominican Republic	3.45
28	Kuwait	2.40		104	Russia	3.45
28	Malaysia	2.40		107	Burkina Faso	3.50
28	Panama	2.40		107	Cameroon	3.50
28	Thailand	2.40		107	Lesotho	3.50
32	El Salvador	2.45		107	Nicaragua	3.50
32	Sri Lanka	2.45		107	Venezuela	3.50
32	Sweden	2.45		112	Gambia	3.60
35	France	2.50		112	Guyana	3.60
35	Italy	2.50		114	Bulgaria	3.65
35	Spain	2.50		114	Georgia	3.65
38	Trinidad and Tobago	2.55		114	Malawi	3.65
39	Argentina	2.60		117	Ethiopia	3.70
39	Barbados	2.60		117	India	3.70
39	Cyprus	2.60		117	Niger	3.70
39	Jamaica	2.60		120	Albania	3.75
39	Portugal	2.60		120	Bangladesh	3.75
44	Bolivia	2.65		120	China (PRC)	3.75
44	Oman	2.65		120	Congo	3.75
44	Philippines	2.65		120	Croatia	3.75
47	Swaziland	2.70		125	Chad	3.80
47	Uruguay	2.70		125	Mauritania	3.80
49	Botswana	2.75		125	Ukraine	3.80
49	Jordan	2.75		128	Sierra Leone	3.85
49	Namibia	2.75		129	Burundi	3.90
49	Tunisia	2.75		129	Suriname	3.90
53	Belize	2.80		129	Zimbabwe	3.90
53	Costa Rica	2.80		132	Haiti	4.00
53	Guatemala	2.80		132	Kyrgyzstan	4.00
53	Israel	2.80		132	Syria	4.00
53	Peru	2.80		135	Belarus	4.05
53	Saudi Arabia	2.80		136	Kazakstan	4.10
53	Turkey	2.80		136	Mozambique	4.10
53	Uganda	2.80		136	Yemen	4.10
53	Western Samoa	2.80		139	Sudan	4.20
62	Indonesia	2.85		140	Myanmar	4.30
62	Latvia	2.85		140	Rwanda	4.30
62	Malta	2.85		142	Angola	4.35
62	Paraguay	2.85		143	Azerbaijan	4.40
66	Greece	2.90		143	Tajikistan	4.40
66	Hungary	2.90		145	Turkmenistan	4.50
66	South Africa	2.90		146	Uzbekistan	4.55
69	Benin	2.95		147	Congo/Zaire	4.70
69	Ecuador	2.95		147	Iran	4.70
69	Gabon	2.95		147	Libya	4.70
69	Morocco	2.95		147	Somalia	4.70
69	Poland	2.95		147	Vietnam	4.70
74	Colombia	3.00		152	Bosnia	4.80
74	Ghana	3.00		153	Iraq	4.90
74	Lithuania	3.00		154	Cuba	5.00
77	Kenya	3.05		154	Laos	5.00
77	Slovak Republic	3.05		154	North Korea	5.00

Repressed

MONETARY POLICY
Score: 5–Stable (very high level of inflation)

Mozambique's average rate of inflation from 1985 to 1995 was 52.2 percent. In 1996, inflation was about 18 percent.

CAPITAL FLOWS AND FOREIGN INVESTMENT
Score: 4–Stable (high barriers)

A recent change in the investment law has improved the climate for foreign investors. Mozambique has established a one-stop shop for approval of foreign investment, and the government is granting land concessions to South African farmers in remote, underutilized areas. At the same time, however, feasibility study requirements and a corrupt government bureaucracy frustrate foreign investment, especially by small-scale investors. Infrastructure and a few other areas are off-limits to private investment. Free-trade zones were established in 1993, but their terms are not comparatively attractive. According to the U.S. Department of Commerce, "Strong deterrents to foreign investment have included political risk, corruption, bureaucratic red tape, dilapidated infrastructure, and the relatively small size of the market."[2]

BANKING
Score: 3+ (moderate level of restrictions)

Banking is dominated by state banks, although the system is being liberalized. Interest rates have been freed, and the government has privatized the Commercial Bank of Mozambique, which accounts for some 70 percent of banking assets. According to the U.S. Department of Commerce, "With the sale of BCM [Banco Commercial de Mozambique] and the entry of BIM [Banco Internacional de Mozambique], the banking system seems to have received an injection of much needed competition."[3] As a result, Mozambique's banking score is one point better this year. There still are only four private banks, however, and they remain at a disadvantage when trying to compete with the state-owned banks, in which corruption is a problem.

WAGE AND PRICE CONTROLS
Score: 3–Stable (moderate level)

The government lifted price controls on several products in 1994. Remaining price controls apply to wheat, flour, bread, rents, fuels, utilities, newspapers, transportation, and a few other services. Mozambique has a minimum wage.

PROPERTY RIGHTS
Score: 4–Stable (low level of protection)

Despite some progress in bolstering property rights, Mozambique's land tenure and property rights regime remains fairly chaotic. Technically, all land still belongs to the state, and the vast majority of housing is state-owned, although some progress has been made with residential privatization. The government recently announced that it would not make restitution for pre-independence property claims. Mozambique's underdeveloped court system is unable to protect private property adequately. According to the U.S. Department of Commerce, "The 1990 Constitution formally established an independent judiciary and specifically states that the decisions of the courts take precedence over all other authorities and individuals and must be obeyed. Nevertheless, the executive, and by extension the FRELIMO [Front for the Liberation of Mozambique] party, dominates the judiciary. In general, judges are beholden for their positions to the ruling FRELIMO party, which continues to exercise significant influence on all aspects of public life through the executive and party organs."[4]

REGULATION
Score: 5–Stable (very high level)

Mozambique's regulatory environment is characterized by rising bureaucratic corruption. Registering a company is a cumbersome and secretive process, with considerable red tape. According to the U.S. Department of Commerce, "Corruption has increased during the transition to peace, democracy and a more open economic system. Plenty of opportunity for corruption exists in the numerous and cumbersome regulations carried over from colonial days or the Marxist era which pervade the commercial regulatory system."[5]

BLACK MARKET
Score: 5–Stable (very high level of activity)

Mozambique is a center for drug trafficking and money laundering, and international crime organizations use it as a clearinghouse for black market trade between Asia and Europe. It is estimated that, because of high tariffs and corruption in the customs service, 70 percent of Mozambique's consumer goods are smuggled into the country.

NOTES

1. The score in this factor has changed from 3 in 1997 to 5 in 1998. Previously unavailable data provide a more accurate understanding of the country's performance. This average tariff rate is from a U.S. Department of Commerce, Southern Africa Office, facsimile, June 11, 1997. The methodology for this factor remains the same.
2. U.S. Department of Commerce, *Country Commercial Guide,* 1997.
3. *Ibid.*
4. *Ibid.*
5. *Ibid.*

Myanmar (formerly Burma)

4.30

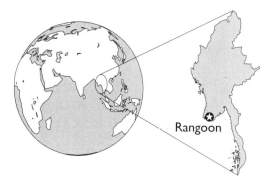

Rangoon

1997 Score: **4.30**	1996 Score: **4.30**	1995 Score: **n/a**

Trade	5	Banking	4
Taxation	3	Wages and Prices	4
Government Intervention	5	Property Rights	4
Monetary Policy	4	Regulation	5
Foreign Investment	4	Black Market	5

Burma, now known as Myanmar, gained its independence from the United Kingdom in 1948. A fragile parliamentary democracy arose but was overthrown by the military in 1962. The country then embarked on a self-imposed state of isolation. In 1974, it declared itself a "socialist republic." In 1988, an economic crisis led to some opening for foreign investment, particularly in energy and tourism, although tight controls over other sectors have kept the level of foreign investment far below that of neighboring countries. A new military government began to introduce some free market and democratic reforms, but these reforms were put on hold in 1990 after opposition parties won national elections and the regime refused to relinquish power. Today, it continues to suppress democratic opposition. Myanmar currently is seeking membership in the Association of Southeast Asian Nations.

TRADE POLICY
Score: 5–Stable (very high level of protectionism)

Myanmar's average tariff rate is over 70 percent.[1] Nontariff barriers include licenses and import bans.

TAXATION
Score–Income taxation: 2–Stable (low tax rates)
Score–Corporate taxation: 3–Stable (moderate tax rates)
Final Taxation Score: 3–Stable (moderate tax rates)

Myanmar's top income tax rate is 30 percent; the average taxpayer finds himself in the 3 percent bracket. The top marginal corporate tax rate is 30 percent. A commercial tax ranges from 0 percent to 200 percent.

GOVERNMENT INTERVENTION IN THE ECONOMY
Score: 5–Stable (very high level)

The government is privatizing several companies, but the economy remains largely state-controlled, with most GDP generated by government sources. "The number of state economic enterprises (SEEs)," reports the U.S. Department of Commerce, "fell only slightly from 1,765 in FY 90/91 to 1,675 in FY 94/95. No large SEE has been privatized, and no major privatization initiative appears imminent."[2]

MONETARY POLICY
Score: 4–Stable (high level of inflation)

Myanmar's average annual rate of inflation from 1985 to 1995 was 26.4 percent. In 1996, the rate of inflation was 16.2 percent.

1	Hong Kong	1.25	77	Zambia	3.05
2	Singapore	1.30	80	Mali	3.10
3	Bahrain	1.70	80	Mongolia	3.10
4	New Zealand	1.75	80	Slovenia	3.10
5	Switzerland	1.90	83	Honduras	3.15
5	United States	1.90	83	Papua New Guinea	3.15
7	Luxembourg	1.95	85	Djibouti	3.20
7	Taiwan	1.95	85	Fiji	3.20
7	United Kingdom	1.95	85	Pakistan	3.20
10	Bahamas	2.00	88	Algeria	3.25
10	Ireland	2.00	88	Guinea	3.25
12	Australia	2.05	88	Lebanon	3.25
12	Japan	2.05	88	Mexico	3.25
14	Belgium	2.10	88	Senegal	3.25
14	Canada	2.10	88	Tanzania	3.25
14	United Arab Emirates	2.10	94	Nigeria	3.30
17	Austria	2.15	94	Romania	3.30
17	Chile	2.15	96	Brazil	3.35
17	Estonia	2.15	96	Cambodia	3.35
20	Czech Republic	2.20	96	Egypt	3.35
20	Netherlands	2.20	96	Ivory Coast	3.35
22	Denmark	2.25	96	Madagascar	3.35
22	Finland	2.25	96	Moldova	3.35
24	Germany	2.30	102	Nepal	3.40
24	Iceland	2.30	103	Cape Verde	3.44
24	South Korea	2.30	104	Armenia	3.45
27	Norway	2.35	104	Dominican Republic	3.45
28	Kuwait	2.40	104	Russia	3.45
28	Malaysia	2.40	107	Burkina Faso	3.50
28	Panama	2.40	107	Cameroon	3.50
28	Thailand	2.40	107	Lesotho	3.50
32	El Salvador	2.45	107	Nicaragua	3.50
32	Sri Lanka	2.45	107	Venezuela	3.50
32	Sweden	2.45	112	Gambia	3.60
35	France	2.50	112	Guyana	3.60
35	Italy	2.50	114	Bulgaria	3.65
35	Spain	2.50	114	Georgia	3.65
38	Trinidad and Tobago	2.55	114	Malawi	3.65
39	Argentina	2.60	117	Ethiopia	3.70
39	Barbados	2.60	117	India	3.70
39	Cyprus	2.60	117	Niger	3.70
39	Jamaica	2.60	120	Albania	3.75
39	Portugal	2.60	120	Bangladesh	3.75
44	Bolivia	2.65	120	China (PRC)	3.75
44	Oman	2.65	120	Congo	3.75
44	Philippines	2.65	120	Croatia	3.75
47	Swaziland	2.70	125	Chad	3.80
47	Uruguay	2.70	125	Mauritania	3.80
49	Botswana	2.75	125	Ukraine	3.80
49	Jordan	2.75	128	Sierra Leone	3.85
49	Namibia	2.75	129	Burundi	3.90
49	Tunisia	2.75	129	Suriname	3.90
53	Belize	2.80	129	Zimbabwe	3.90
53	Costa Rica	2.80	132	Haiti	4.00
53	Guatemala	2.80	132	Kyrgyzstan	4.00
53	Israel	2.80	132	Syria	4.00
53	Peru	2.80	135	Belarus	4.05
53	Saudi Arabia	2.80	136	Kazakstan	4.10
53	Turkey	2.80	136	Mozambique	4.10
53	Uganda	2.80	136	Yemen	4.10
53	Western Samoa	2.80	139	Sudan	4.20
62	Indonesia	2.85	140	Myanmar	4.30
62	Latvia	2.85	140	Rwanda	4.30
62	Malta	2.85	142	Angola	4.35
62	Paraguay	2.85	143	Azerbaijan	4.40
66	Greece	2.90	143	Tajikistan	4.40
66	Hungary	2.90	145	Turkmenistan	4.50
66	South Africa	2.90	146	Uzbekistan	4.55
69	Benin	2.95	147	Congo/Zaire	4.70
69	Ecuador	2.95	147	Iran	4.70
69	Gabon	2.95	147	Libya	4.70
69	Morocco	2.95	147	Somalia	4.70
69	Poland	2.95	147	Vietnam	4.70
74	Colombia	3.00	152	Cuba	4.80
74	Ghana	3.00	153	Iraq	4.90
74	Lithuania	3.00	154	Cuba	5.00
77	Kenya	3.05	154	Laos	5.00
77	Slovak Republic	3.05	154	North Korea	5.00

Repressed

CAPITAL FLOWS AND FOREIGN INVESTMENT
Score: 4–Stable (high barriers)

Investment in Myanmar is heavily restricted. Although the government has moved to open some sectors of the economy to foreign investment, most of the economy remains closed. Foreign investors face a massive bureaucracy and extensive government corruption. Investments are approved only if they are deemed to benefit Myanmar, and only on a case-by-case basis.

BANKING
Score: 4–Stable (high level of restrictions)

The banking system in Myanmar is controlled almost entirely by the government. There is little competition, although the private banking industry is growing. According to the U.S. Department of Commerce, "At the end of FY 94/95, 82 percent of the outstanding loans of the legal banking system were to the central government, up from 79 percent two years before."[3]

WAGE AND PRICE CONTROLS
Score: 4–Stable (high level)

In many industries (such as public utilities and some agricultural goods), wages and prices are set primarily by the government. The government also controls prices through direct ownership of such industries as postal services, telecommunications, utilities, and rice. Prices are becoming more liberalized, however.

PROPERTY RIGHTS
Score: 4–Stable (low level of protection)

Private property owned by foreigners as a result of foreign investment is exempt from expropriation, but the property of Myanmar's citizens still is subject to confiscation. Government corruption makes it difficult to seek legal protection for property. The judiciary is both inefficient and subject to extensive government influence. According to the U.S. Department of Commerce, "The government continues sporadically to seize land and other property from its citizens and forcibly to relocate people. Such seizures are done without due process or transparency of purpose, and are not in accordance with international law.... Seeking protection for property rights from Burmese courts can be difficult. Although Burma has a well-developed legal system based on British law, in practice the system is undermined by corruption, unprofessional behavior on the part of some legal officials, and blatant interference in some cases by the military government."[4]

REGULATION
Score: 5–Stable (very high level)

Establishing a business in Myanmar can be time-consuming and costly. Bureaucrats are corrupt and often seek bribes, and regulations can be applied unevenly and inconsistently. According to the U.S. Department of Commerce, "Enforcement of tax, labor, health and other regulations is haphazard and can be arbitrary."[5]

BLACK MARKET
Score: 5–Stable (very high level of activity)

Myanmar's black market, mainly in consumer goods and pirated intellectual property from Western counties, continues to grow. "There is no effective protection of patents, copyrights, trademarks or any other intellectual property in Burma," reports the U.S. Department of Commerce. "A Patents and Design Act was introduced in 1945, but never brought into force.... Pirating of books, software, designs, etc., is rampant.... Civil action can be taken against misuse of a trademark, but is cumbersome and costly. Burma does not belong to any international conventions on patents, trademarks or copyrights."[6]

NOTES

1. Based on total taxes on international trade as a percentage of total imports.
2. U.S. Department of Commerce, *Country Commercial Guide*, 1997.
3. *Ibid.*
4. *Ibid.*
5. *Ibid.*
6. *Ibid.*

Namibia   2.75

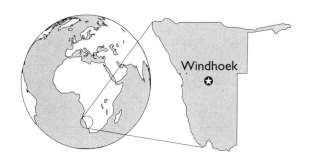

Windhoek ✪

1997 Score: **2.95**	1996 Score: **n/a**	1995 Score: **n/a**

Trade	4	Banking	2
Taxation	3.5	Wages and Prices	2
Government Intervention	4	Property Rights	2
Monetary Policy	2	Regulation	3
Foreign Investment	2	Black Market	3

Namibia was a colony of Germany prior to World War I and later became a colony of South Africa. It gained its independence in 1990 but remains closely linked with South Africa. Since becoming independent, Namibia has focused on creating a stable free-market system. The government has achieved substantial fiscal discipline and is opening the Namibian market to trade and investment. These policies have led to moderately high, but stable, levels of economic growth relative to most other countries in sub-Saharan Africa: an average of 4 percent from 1991 to 1995. Namibia has reduced some price controls and increased its crackdown on corruption, effectively reducing its regulatory burden on business. Thus, its overall score is 0.2 point better this year.

TRADE POLICY
Score: 4–Stable (high level of protectionism)

Namibia's average tariff rate is 12 percent. Namibia belongs to the Southern African Customs Union, a regional trade arrangement that also includes Botswana, Lesotho, South Africa, and Swaziland. Nontariff barriers include letters of credit that discriminate against some imports.

TAXATION
Score–Income taxation: 3–Stable (moderate tax rates)
Score–Corporate taxation: 3–Stable (moderate tax rates)
Final Taxation Score: 3.5–Stable (high tax rates)

Namibia's top income tax rate is 35 percent; the rate for the average income level is 0 percent. The top corporate tax rate is 35 percent. Namibia also imposes an 8 percent sales tax.

GOVERNMENT INTERVENTION IN THE ECONOMY
Score: 4–Stable (high level)

Government consumes about 32.2 percent of Namibia's GDP, and the public sector of the economy is substantial.

MONETARY POLICY
Score: 2–Stable (low level of inflation)

Namibia's average annual rate of inflation from 1985 to 1995 was 10.5 percent. In 1996, the rate of inflation was 8 percent.

CAPITAL FLOWS AND FOREIGN INVESTMENT
Score: 2–Stable (low barriers)

Namibia provides equal treatment for domestic and foreign firms and actively seeks foreign investment. Its modern investment code provides significant protection and incentives.

1	Hong Kong	1.25	77	Zambia	3.05
2	Singapore	1.30	80	Mali	3.10
3	Bahrain	1.70	80	Mongolia	3.10
4	New Zealand	1.75	80	Slovenia	3.10
5	Switzerland	1.90	83	Honduras	3.15
5	United States	1.90	83	Papua New Guinea	3.15
7	Luxembourg	1.95	85	Djibouti	3.20
7	Taiwan	1.95	85	Fiji	3.20
7	United Kingdom	1.95	85	Pakistan	3.20
10	Bahamas	2.00	88	Algeria	3.25
10	Ireland	2.00	88	Guinea	3.25
12	Australia	2.05	88	Lebanon	3.25
12	Japan	2.05	88	Mexico	3.25
14	Belgium	2.10	88	Senegal	3.25
14	Canada	2.10	88	Tanzania	3.25
14	United Arab Emirates	2.10	94	Nigeria	3.30
17	Austria	2.15	94	Romania	3.30
17	Chile	2.15	96	Brazil	3.35
17	Estonia	2.15	96	Cambodia	3.35
20	Czech Republic	2.20	96	Egypt	3.35
20	Netherlands	2.20	96	Ivory Coast	3.35
22	Denmark	2.25	96	Madagascar	3.35
22	Finland	2.25	96	Moldova	3.35
24	Germany	2.30	102	Nepal	3.40
24	Iceland	2.30	103	Cape Verde	3.44
24	South Korea	2.30	104	Armenia	3.45
27	Norway	2.35	104	Dominican Republic	3.45
28	Kuwait	2.40	104	Russia	3.45
28	Malaysia	2.40	107	Burkina Faso	3.50
28	Panama	2.40	107	Cameroon	3.50
28	Thailand	2.40	107	Lesotho	3.50
32	El Salvador	2.45	107	Nicaragua	3.50
32	Sri Lanka	2.45	107	Venezuela	3.50
32	Sweden	2.45	112	Gambia	3.60
35	France	2.50	112	Guyana	3.60
35	Italy	2.50	114	Bulgaria	3.65
35	Spain	2.50	114	Georgia	3.65
38	Trinidad and Tobago	2.55	114	Malawi	3.65
39	Argentina	2.60	117	Ethiopia	3.70
39	Barbados	2.60	117	India	3.70
39	Cyprus	2.60	117	Niger	3.70
39	Jamaica	2.60	120	Albania	3.75
39	Portugal	2.60	120	Bangladesh	3.75
44	Bolivia	2.65	120	China (PRC)	3.75
44	Oman	2.65	120	Congo	3.75
44	Philippines	2.65	120	Croatia	3.75
47	Swaziland	2.70	125	Chad	3.80
47	Uruguay	2.70	125	Mauritania	3.80
49	Botswana	2.75	125	Ukraine	3.80
49	Jordan	2.75	128	Sierra Leone	3.85
49	Namibia	2.75	129	Burundi	3.90
49	Tunisia	2.75	129	Suriname	3.90
53	Belize	2.80	129	Zimbabwe	3.90
53	Costa Rica	2.80	132	Haiti	4.00
53	Guatemala	2.80	132	Kyrgyzstan	4.00
53	Israel	2.80	132	Syria	4.00
53	Peru	2.80	135	Belarus	4.05
53	Saudi Arabia	2.80	136	Kazakstan	4.10
53	Turkey	2.80	136	Mozambique	4.10
53	Uganda	2.80	136	Yemen	4.10
53	Western Samoa	2.80	139	Sudan	4.20
62	Indonesia	2.85	140	Myanmar	4.30
62	Latvia	2.85	140	Rwanda	4.30
62	Malta	2.85	142	Angola	4.35
62	Paraguay	2.85	143	Azerbaijan	4.40
66	Greece	2.90	143	Tajikistan	4.40
66	Hungary	2.90	145	Turkmenistan	4.50
66	South Africa	2.90	146	Uzbekistan	4.55
69	Benin	2.95	147	Congo/Zaire	4.70
69	Ecuador	2.95	147	Iran	4.70
69	Gabon	2.95	147	Libya	4.70
69	Morocco	2.95	147	Somalia	4.70
69	Poland	2.95	147	Vietnam	4.70
74	Colombia	3.00	152	Bosnia	4.80
74	Ghana	3.00	153	Iraq	4.90
74	Lithuania	3.00	154	Cuba	5.00
77	Kenya	3.05	154	Laos	5.00
77	Slovak Republic	3.05	154	North Korea	5.00

Mostly Free

BANKING
Score: 2–Stable (low level of restrictions)

Namibia's banking system is entirely private, with minimal government intrusion or regulation. There is no deposit insurance, but commercial banks are regulated by a central bank.

WAGE AND PRICE CONTROLS
Score: 2+ (low level)

The government has abolished most price controls, and the market sets most wages and prices. As a result, Namibia's score for this factor is one point better this year. Petroleum prices still are controlled, however, and a growing "buy Namibian" movement impedes competition and raises prices on some domestically produced goods and services.

PROPERTY RIGHTS
Score: 2–Stable (high level of protection)

Namibia's legal system is efficient, fair, and independent. According to the U.S. Department of Commerce, the "judiciary is capable, if somewhat limited in number."[1] There is a shortage of lawyers, however, and the courts often become backlogged.

REGULATION
Score: 3+ (moderate level)

Namibia has begun to enforce its recent anticorruption legislation rigorously. According to the U.S. Department of Commerce, "Corruption is, thus far, the exception rather than the rule."[2] Thus, Namibia's regulation score is one point better this year. The government also has introduced new and potentially burdensome regulations on business, however, including both health and safety standards and a requirement that businesses submit an environmental impact statement for proposed new investments and construction.

BLACK MARKET
Score: 3–Stable (moderate level of activity)

Black market activity in Namibia is moderate and confined mainly to goods smuggled in from South Africa. The smuggling of gold and diamonds is a particular problem.

NOTES
1. U.S. Department of Commerce, *Country Commercial Guide,* 1997.
2. *Ibid.*

Nepal

3.40

1997 Score: **3.60**   1996 Score: **3.50**   1995 Score: **n/a**

Trade	3	Banking	4
Taxation	3	Wages and Prices	4
Government Intervention	2	Property Rights	3
Monetary Policy	2	Regulation	4
Foreign Investment	4	Black Market	5

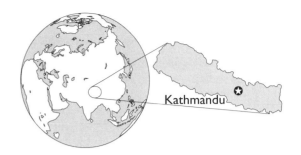

Kathmandu

From 1846 to 1951, Nepal was ruled by hereditary leaders loyal to British colonial power. In 1992, following significant unrest, it established a constitutional monarchy with a multiparty Parliament. In late 1994, the Communists gained a parliamentary plurality. Nepal's economy is mainly agricultural, and tight government controls have helped make it one of the poorest in the world. Nevertheless, there are indications that the government supports aggressive economic reform. For example, a substantial program of privatization is in place. This process has only begun, however, and much remains to be done. Nepal recently reduced some barriers to trade and cut government spending. As a result, its overall score is 0.2 point better this year.

TRADE POLICY
Score: 3+ (moderate level of protectionism)

Nepal's average tariff rate is about 9.18 percent, down from 11 percent.[1] As a result, its trade score is one point better this year. According to the U.S. Department of Commerce, however, "U.S. firms and other foreign investors have identified pervasive corruption as an obstacle to maintaining and expanding direct investment."[2] Nepal bans imports of beef.

TAXATION
Score–Income taxation: 3–Stable (moderate tax rates)
Score–Corporate taxation: 3–Stable (moderate tax rates)
Final Taxation Score: 3–Stable (moderate tax rates)

Nepal's top income tax rate is 35 percent, and government revenues equal about 14 percent of GDP.[3]

GOVERNMENT INTERVENTION IN THE ECONOMY
Score: 2+ (low level)

Government consumes about 8 percent of Nepal's GDP, down from over 11 percent a few years ago. As a result, Nepal's government intervention score is one point better this year. The public sector, however, is large; the government still owns significant portions of the national airlines, telecommunications companies, and energy companies.

MONETARY POLICY
Score: 2–Stable (low level of inflation)

Nepal's average annual rate of inflation from 1985 to 1995 was 11.6 percent. In 1996, the rate of inflation was 6.7 percent.

1	Hong Kong	1.25	77	Zambia	3.05
2	Singapore	1.30	80	Mali	3.10
3	Bahrain	1.70	80	Mongolia	3.10
4	New Zealand	1.75	80	Slovenia	3.10
5	Switzerland	1.90	83	Honduras	3.15
5	United States	1.90	83	Papua New Guinea	3.15
7	Luxembourg	1.95	85	Djibouti	3.20
7	Taiwan	1.95	85	Fiji	3.20
7	United Kingdom	1.95	85	Pakistan	3.20
10	Bahamas	2.00	88	Algeria	3.25
10	Ireland	2.00	88	Guinea	3.25
12	Australia	2.05	88	Lebanon	3.25
12	Japan	2.05	88	Mexico	3.25
14	Belgium	2.10	88	Senegal	3.25
14	Canada	2.10	88	Tanzania	3.25
14	United Arab Emirates	2.10	94	Nigeria	3.30
17	Austria	2.15	94	Romania	3.30
17	Chile	2.15	96	Brazil	3.35
17	Estonia	2.15	96	Cambodia	3.35
20	Czech Republic	2.20	96	Egypt	3.35
20	Netherlands	2.20	96	Ivory Coast	3.35
22	Denmark	2.25	96	Madagascar	3.35
22	Finland	2.25	96	Moldova	3.35
24	Germany	2.30	102	Nepal	3.40
24	Iceland	2.30	103	Cape Verde	3.44
24	South Korea	2.30	104	Armenia	3.45
27	Norway	2.35	104	Dominican Republic	3.45
28	Kuwait	2.40	104	Russia	3.45
28	Malaysia	2.40	107	Burkina Faso	3.50
28	Panama	2.40	107	Cameroon	3.50
28	Thailand	2.40	107	Lesotho	3.50
32	El Salvador	2.45	107	Nicaragua	3.50
32	Sri Lanka	2.45	107	Venezuela	3.50
32	Sweden	2.45	112	Gambia	3.60
35	France	2.50	112	Guyana	3.60
35	Italy	2.50	114	Bulgaria	3.65
35	Spain	2.50	114	Georgia	3.65
38	Trinidad and Tobago	2.55	114	Malawi	3.65
39	Argentina	2.60	117	Ethiopia	3.70
39	Barbados	2.60	117	India	3.70
39	Cyprus	2.60	117	Niger	3.70
39	Jamaica	2.60	120	Albania	3.75
39	Portugal	2.60	120	Bangladesh	3.75
44	Bolivia	2.65	120	China (PRC)	3.75
44	Oman	2.65	120	Congo	3.75
44	Philippines	2.65	120	Croatia	3.75
47	Swaziland	2.70	125	Chad	3.80
47	Uruguay	2.70	125	Mauritania	3.80
49	Botswana	2.75	125	Ukraine	3.80
49	Jordan	2.75	128	Sierra Leone	3.85
49	Namibia	2.75	129	Burundi	3.90
49	Tunisia	2.75	129	Suriname	3.90
53	Belize	2.80	129	Zimbabwe	3.90
53	Costa Rica	2.80	132	Haiti	4.00
53	Guatemala	2.80	132	Kyrgyzstan	4.00
53	Israel	2.80	132	Syria	4.00
53	Peru	2.80	135	Belarus	4.05
53	Saudi Arabia	2.80	136	Kazakstan	4.10
53	Turkey	2.80	136	Mozambique	4.10
53	Uganda	2.80	136	Yemen	4.10
53	Western Samoa	2.80	139	Sudan	4.20
62	Indonesia	2.85	140	Myanmar	4.30
62	Latvia	2.85	140	Rwanda	4.30
62	Malta	2.85	142	Angola	4.35
62	Paraguay	2.85	143	Azerbaijan	4.40
66	Greece	2.90	143	Tajikistan	4.40
66	Hungary	2.90	145	Turkmenistan	4.50
66	South Africa	2.90	146	Uzbekistan	4.55
69	Benin	2.95	147	Congo/Zaire	4.70
69	Ecuador	2.95	147	Iran	4.70
69	Gabon	2.95	147	Libya	4.70
69	Morocco	2.95	147	Somalia	4.70
69	Poland	2.95	147	Vietnam	4.70
74	Colombia	3.00	152	Bosnia	4.80
74	Ghana	3.00	153	Iraq	4.90
74	Lithuania	3.00	154	Cuba	5.00
77	Kenya	3.05	154	Laos	5.00
77	Slovak Republic	3.05	154	North Korea	5.00

Mostly Unfree

CAPITAL FLOWS AND FOREIGN INVESTMENT
Score: 4–Stable (high barriers)

Nepal has opened some of its market to foreign investment, but many investments are permitted only in the form of joint ventures, either with government-owned firms or with private companies. Bureaucratic red tape and government corruption often postpone, prolong, or terminate foreign investment initiatives.

BANKING
Score: 4–Stable (high level of restrictions)

Since 1984, Nepal has opened its banking system to foreign competition. Yet only a few banks have opened, primarily because the government prefers foreign banks to open branches through joint ventures with domestic banks. Foreign competition therefore is limited. The government owns significant shares of most banks in Nepal, although it does plan to privatize the 100 percent state-owned Rastriya Banija Bank over the next several years.

WAGE AND PRICE CONTROLS
Score: 4–Stable (high level)

Nepal controls most wages and prices through its large government-owned sector and the substantial subsidies it provides to these companies.

PROPERTY RIGHTS
Score: 3–Stable (moderate level of protection)

The main threats to private property in Nepal are crime and government corruption. Despite recent judicial reform, protection of private property by the legal and judicial system is insufficient. According to the U.S. Department of Commerce, "There is an effective means of enforcing property rights as all such transactions must be registered and property holdings cannot be transferred without following procedures. Even so, property disputes account for half of the current backlog in Nepal's court system and such cases can take years to be settled."[4] By global standards, however, the judiciary provides a moderate level of protection for private property.

REGULATION
Score: 4–Stable (high level)

Establishing a business in Nepal is difficult if the business will compete with a state-owned company. Rather than create new competition for existing state-owned companies, the government attempts to redirect private investment toward companies that are being privatized. In some cases, regulations are applied haphazardly by corrupt government bureaucracies.

BLACK MARKET
Score: 5–Stable (very high level of activity)

Nepal's black market is substantial, especially in consumer goods, labor, construction, and pirated intellectual property from Western countries. Computer software and semiconductor designs are not protected adequately, and piracy is prevalent in these areas.

NOTES

1. Based on total taxes on international trade as a percentage of total imports.
2. U.S. Department of Commerce, *Country Commercial Guide,* 1997.
3. Nepal's tax rates are unavailable. Therefore, Nepal was graded solely on total government revenues as a percentage of GDP.
4. U.S. Department of Commerce, *Country Commercial Guide,* 1997.

The Netherlands   2.20

1997 Score: **2.00**   1996 Score: **1.85**   1995 Score: **n/a**

Trade	2	Banking	1
Taxation	5	Wages and Prices	3
Government Intervention	3	Property Rights	1
Monetary Policy	1	Regulation	3
Foreign Investment	2	Black Market	1

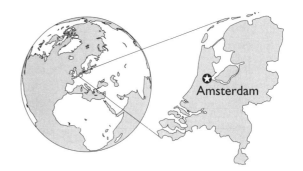

Amsterdam

The Netherlands declared its independence from Spain in 1579, although it did not become truly independent for several more years. During the 17th and 18th centuries, the Netherlands was a driving force in global trade and the establishment of colonies overseas. In the 19th century, Napoleon transformed it into the Kingdom of Holland, which lasted until independence was restored in 1815. The remainder of the 19th century saw the development of parliamentary democracy. Nazi Germany invaded and occupied the country during World War II. After the war, the Netherlands reestablished a stable government and built a solid economic system. The country maintains a large social welfare program funded by taxes that are among the world's highest, but economic freedom in other areas, such as banking and monetary policy, is far greater than in most other countries. The government recently extended price controls to pharmaceuticals and increased some regulations on business. As a result, the Netherlands' overall score this year is 0.2 point worse than it was last year.

TRADE POLICY
Score: 2–Stable (low level of protectionism)

According to the U.S. Department of State, "Dutch trade and investment policy is among the most open in the world."[1] But even though the average tariff rate is 3.6 percent, the government also maintains trade restrictions common to all members of the European Union (EU), such as restrictions on foreign participation in telecommunications systems like broadcasting.

TAXATION
Score–Income taxation: 5–Stable (very high tax rates)
Score–Corporate taxation: 4–Stable (high tax rates)
Final Taxation Score: 5–Stable (very high tax rates)

The Netherlands has a top income tax rate of 60 percent; the average taxpayer finds himself in the 6.15 percent bracket.[2] The top marginal corporate tax rate is 36 percent. The government also levies several other taxes, including a 35 percent capital gains tax and a 17.5 percent value-added tax.

GOVERNMENT INTERVENTION IN THE ECONOMY
Score: 3–Stable (moderate level)

In 1994, the government undertook a massive reduction in spending and made substantial progress in slashing its budget deficit, now about 3.3 percent of GDP. The government consumes about 14.3 percent of GDP and plays a relatively moderate role in the economy. It subsidizes private-sector research and development programs, provides funds to help some companies restructure, dominates the energy sector, and plays a large role in aviation, chemicals, steel, telecommunications, and transportation.

1	Hong Kong	1.25	77	Zambia	3.05
2	Singapore	1.30	80	Mali	3.10
3	Bahrain	1.70	80	Mongolia	3.10
4	New Zealand	1.75	80	Slovenia	3.10
5	Switzerland	1.90	83	Honduras	3.15
5	United States	1.90	83	Papua New Guinea	3.15
7	Luxembourg	1.95	85	Djibouti	3.20
7	Taiwan	1.95	85	Fiji	3.20
7	United Kingdom	1.95	85	Pakistan	3.20
10	Bahamas	2.00	88	Algeria	3.25
10	Ireland	2.00	88	Guinea	3.25
12	Australia	2.05	88	Lebanon	3.25
12	Japan	2.05	88	Mexico	3.25
14	Belgium	2.10	88	Senegal	3.25
14	Canada	2.10	88	Tanzania	3.25
14	United Arab Emirates	2.10	94	Nigeria	3.30
17	Austria	2.15	94	Romania	3.30
17	Chile	2.15	96	Brazil	3.35
17	Estonia	2.15	96	Cambodia	3.35
20	Czech Republic	2.20	96	Egypt	3.35
20	Netherlands	2.20	96	Ivory Coast	3.35
22	Denmark	2.25	96	Madagascar	3.35
22	Finland	2.25	96	Moldova	3.35
24	Germany	2.30	102	Nepal	3.40
24	Iceland	2.30	103	Cape Verde	3.44
24	South Korea	2.30	104	Armenia	3.45
27	Norway	2.35	104	Dominican Republic	3.45
28	Kuwait	2.40	104	Russia	3.45
28	Malaysia	2.40	107	Burkina Faso	3.50
28	Panama	2.40	107	Cameroon	3.50
28	Thailand	2.40	107	Lesotho	3.50
32	El Salvador	2.45	107	Nicaragua	3.50
32	Sri Lanka	2.45	107	Venezuela	3.50
32	Sweden	2.45	112	Gambia	3.60
35	France	2.50	112	Guyana	3.60
35	Italy	2.50	114	Bulgaria	3.65
35	Spain	2.50	114	Georgia	3.65
38	Trinidad and Tobago	2.55	114	Malawi	3.65
39	Argentina	2.60	117	Ethiopia	3.70
39	Barbados	2.60	117	India	3.70
39	Cyprus	2.60	117	Niger	3.70
39	Jamaica	2.60	120	Albania	3.75
39	Portugal	2.60	120	Bangladesh	3.75
44	Bolivia	2.65	120	China (PRC)	3.75
44	Oman	2.65	120	Congo	3.75
44	Philippines	2.65	120	Croatia	3.75
47	Swaziland	2.70	125	Chad	3.80
47	Uruguay	2.70	125	Mauritania	3.80
49	Botswana	2.75	125	Ukraine	3.80
49	Jordan	2.75	128	Sierra Leone	3.85
49	Namibia	2.75	129	Burundi	3.90
49	Tunisia	2.75	129	Suriname	3.90
53	Belize	2.80	129	Zimbabwe	3.90
53	Costa Rica	2.80	132	Haiti	4.00
53	Guatemala	2.80	132	Kyrgyzstan	4.00
53	Israel	2.80	132	Syria	4.00
53	Peru	2.80	135	Belarus	4.05
53	Saudi Arabia	2.80	136	Kazakstan	4.10
53	Turkey	2.80	136	Mozambique	4.10
53	Uganda	2.80	136	Yemen	4.10
53	Western Samoa	2.80	139	Sudan	4.20
62	Indonesia	2.85	140	Myanmar	4.30
62	Latvia	2.85	140	Rwanda	4.30
62	Malta	2.85	142	Angola	4.35
62	Paraguay	2.85	143	Azerbaijan	4.40
66	Greece	2.90	143	Tajikistan	4.40
66	Hungary	2.90	145	Turkmenistan	4.50
66	South Africa	2.90	146	Uzbekistan	4.55
69	Benin	2.95	147	Congo/Zaire	4.70
69	Ecuador	2.95	147	Iran	4.70
69	Gabon	2.95	147	Libya	4.70
69	Morocco	2.95	147	Somalia	4.70
69	Poland	2.95	147	Vietnam	4.70
74	Colombia	3.00	152	Bosnia	4.80
74	Ghana	3.00	153	Iraq	4.90
74	Lithuania	3.00	154	Cuba	5.00
77	Kenya	3.05	154	Laos	5.00
77	Slovak Republic	3.05	154	North Korea	5.00

Mostly Free

Monetary Policy
Score: 1–Stable (very low level of inflation)

The average rate of inflation in the Netherlands from 1985 to 1995 was 1.7 percent. In 1996, the rate of inflation was about 2.1 percent, as it has been for most of 1997 as well.

Capital Flows and Foreign Investment
Score: 2–Stable (low barriers)

There are few restrictions on investment in the Netherlands. Most restrictions apply to investment in defense-related industries, such as the manufacturing of weapons.

Banking
Score: 1–Stable (very low level of restrictions)

The Netherlands has been one of Europe's financial and banking centers for centuries, and its banking system operates freely with almost no government restriction or regulation. Banks established in the Netherlands may engage in a variety of financial services, such as buying, selling, and holding securities, insurance policies, and real estate. There are few investment restrictions imposed on banks, and most financial institutions are not subject to supervision by the central bank. There are over 80 foreign banks operating in the Netherlands today.

Wage and Price Controls
Score: 3– (moderate level)

Wages and prices in the Netherlands are set primarily by the market, although price controls on many pharmaceutical products under a law passed in June 1996 now affect some 3,000 medicines and are expected eventually to cover some 7,000 items. There is a minimum wage. Cartels, especially in the utilities area, traditionally have been sanctioned by the government; but the country's entrance into the EU has forced the government to crack down on cartels, and most are being eliminated. As a result of its increased price controls, the Netherlands' wage and price controls score is one point worse this year.

Property Rights
Score: 1–Stable (very high level of protection)

Private property in the Netherlands is safe from expropriation. The legal and judicial system is advanced, efficient, and independent.

Regulation
Score: 3– (moderate level)

Establishing a business in the Netherlands is a simple procedure, and regulations are applied evenly in most cases. While reducing some regulations in some sectors, the Netherlands recently passed laws requiring businesses to provide disability insurance, and there are increasing indications that regulations establishing minimum work weeks, mandatory leave, and separation pay for terminated workers are increasingly burdensome. As a result, the country's regulation score is one point worse this year. The government has expanded laws allowing for increased part-time work, however. With businesses free to access a larger pool of the work force, the Netherlands has one of the lowest unemployment rates in continental Europe.

Black Market
Score: 1–Stable (very low level of activity)

Because so few things are illegal in the Netherlands (even prostitution and drugs are legal), there is little incentive to engage in black market activity. Sales of pirated intellectual property are minuscule.

Notes

1. U.S. Department of State, *Country Reports on Economic Policy and Trade Practices,* 1997, p. 145.
2. This rate may increase to 37.65 percent because of a national insurance tax that can be levied on top of the lowest tax bracket. Therefore, the income tax score for the Netherlands is based on this higher rate.

New Zealand   1.75

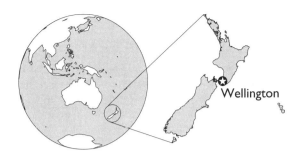
Wellington

1997 Score: **1.75**	1996 Score: **1.75**	1995 Score: **n/a**

Trade	2	Banking	1
Taxation	3.5	Wages and Prices	2
Government Intervention	2	Property Rights	1
Monetary Policy	1	Regulation	2
Foreign Investment	2	Black Market	1

New Zealand joined the British Empire in 1840, became a self-governing dominion within the empire in 1907, and achieved full independence in 1932. For the next five decades, both Labor and National Party governments pursued an economic policy of "insulationism" that included high tariffs, import licensing, foreign exchange controls, high tax rates, strict regulations, and government provision of many commercial activities; all of these elements worked to stifle the country's economic growth. After Labor's victory in 1984, the government of Prime Minister David Lange reversed course and launched what the Organization for Economic Cooperation and Development considers the most comprehensive economic liberalization program ever undertaken in a developed country. Following the National Party's triumph in the 1990 election, the government of Prime Minister Jim Bolger expanded the economic liberalization program by deregulating the labor market, balancing the budget, and cutting income tax rates. In 1993, New Zealand voted to replace its British-style "first-past-the-post" Parliament with a German-style "mixed membership" Parliament based on proportional representation. The first election under the new system was held in October 1996, but no clear winner emerged. After intensive negotiations between the parties, a coalition of the National Party and New Zealand First Party was formed. The coalition government has agreed to maintain the existing course of economic liberalization.

TRADE POLICY
Score: 2–Stable (low level of protectionism)

New Zealand's average tariff rate is about 3.2 percent.[1] In 1994, the government announced plans to eliminate all tariffs by 2004. This since has changed to the year 2000. All import licensing and other quantitative restrictions were abolished in 1992. New Zealand has a comprehensive free-trade and investment agreement with Australia and is seeking one with the United States. Most nontariff barriers to imports have been abolished, although business-run marketing boards and private associations still can impede imports, mainly in the agricultural sector.

TAXATION
Score–Income taxation: 3–Stable (moderate tax rates)
Score–Corporate taxation: 3–Stable (moderate tax rates)
Final Taxation Score: 3.5–Stable (high tax rates)

The top income tax rate in New Zealand is 33 percent, and the average income level is taxed at 21.5 percent. Other taxes include a flat 33 percent company tax, a 12.5 percent goods and services tax, a 49 percent fringe benefits tax, and a risk-based 1 percent to 8 percent levy on gross salaries and wages to pay for accident compensation insurance. New Zealand has no capital gains or estate taxes. The coalition government plans to cut the top personal income tax rate to 30 percent in 1998.

1	Hong Kong	1.25	77	Zambia	3.05
2	Singapore	1.30	80	Mali	3.10
3	Bahrain	1.70	80	Mongolia	3.10
4	New Zealand	1.75	80	Slovenia	3.10
5	Switzerland	1.90	83	Honduras	3.15
5	United States	1.90	83	Papua New Guinea	3.15
7	Luxembourg	1.95	85	Djibouti	3.20
7	Taiwan	1.95	85	Fiji	3.20
7	United Kingdom	1.95	85	Pakistan	3.20
10	Bahamas	2.00	88	Algeria	3.25
10	Ireland	2.00	88	Guinea	3.25
12	Australia	2.05	88	Lebanon	3.25
12	Japan	2.05	88	Mexico	3.25
14	Belgium	2.10	88	Senegal	3.25
14	Canada	2.10	88	Tanzania	3.25
14	United Arab Emirates	2.10	94	Nigeria	3.30
17	Austria	2.15	94	Romania	3.30
17	Chile	2.15	96	Brazil	3.35
17	Estonia	2.15	96	Cambodia	3.35
20	Czech Republic	2.20	96	Egypt	3.35
20	Netherlands	2.20	96	Ivory Coast	3.35
22	Denmark	2.25	96	Madagascar	3.35
22	Finland	2.25	96	Moldova	3.35
24	Germany	2.30	102	Nepal	3.40
24	Iceland	2.30	103	Cape Verde	3.44
24	South Korea	2.30	104	Armenia	3.45
27	Norway	2.35	104	Dominican Republic	3.45
28	Kuwait	2.40	104	Russia	3.45
28	Malaysia	2.40	107	Burkina Faso	3.50
28	Panama	2.40	107	Cameroon	3.50
28	Thailand	2.40	107	Lesotho	3.50
32	El Salvador	2.45	107	Nicaragua	3.50
32	Sri Lanka	2.45	107	Venezuela	3.50
32	Sweden	2.45	112	Gambia	3.60
35	France	2.50	112	Guyana	3.60
35	Italy	2.50	114	Bulgaria	3.65
35	Spain	2.50	114	Georgia	3.65
38	Trinidad and Tobago	2.55	114	Malawi	3.65
39	Argentina	2.60	117	Ethiopia	3.70
39	Barbados	2.60	117	India	3.70
39	Cyprus	2.60	117	Niger	3.70
39	Jamaica	2.60	120	Albania	3.75
39	Portugal	2.60	120	Bangladesh	3.75
44	Bolivia	2.65	120	China (PRC)	3.75
44	Oman	2.65	120	Congo	3.75
44	Philippines	2.65	120	Croatia	3.75
47	Swaziland	2.70	125	Chad	3.80
47	Uruguay	2.70	125	Mauritania	3.80
49	Botswana	2.75	125	Ukraine	3.80
49	Jordan	2.75	128	Sierra Leone	3.85
49	Namibia	2.75	129	Burundi	3.90
49	Tunisia	2.75	129	Suriname	3.90
53	Belize	2.80	129	Zimbabwe	3.90
53	Costa Rica	2.80	132	Haiti	4.00
53	Guatemala	2.80	132	Kyrgyzstan	4.00
53	Israel	2.80	132	Syria	4.00
53	Peru	2.80	135	Belarus	4.05
53	Saudi Arabia	2.80	136	Kazakstan	4.10
53	Turkey	2.80	136	Mozambique	4.10
53	Uganda	2.80	136	Yemen	4.10
53	Western Samoa	2.80	139	Sudan	4.20
62	Indonesia	2.85	140	Myanmar	4.30
62	Latvia	2.85	140	Rwanda	4.30
62	Malta	2.85	142	Angola	4.35
62	Paraguay	2.85	143	Azerbaijan	4.40
66	Greece	2.90	143	Tajikistan	4.40
66	Hungary	2.90	145	Turkmenistan	4.50
66	South Africa	2.90	146	Uzbekistan	4.55
69	Benin	2.95	147	Congo/Zaire	4.70
69	Ecuador	2.95	147	Iran	4.70
69	Gabon	2.95	147	Libya	4.70
69	Morocco	2.95	147	Somalia	4.70
69	Poland	2.95	147	Vietnam	4.70
74	Colombia	3.00	152	Bosnia	4.80
74	Ghana	3.00	153	Iraq	4.90
74	Lithuania	3.00	154	Cuba	5.00
77	Kenya	3.05	154	Laos	5.00
77	Slovak Republic	3.05	154	North Korea	5.00

Free (indicated alongside entries 4–7)

GOVERNMENT INTERVENTION IN THE ECONOMY
Score: 2–Stable (low level)

Government consumes 15.1 percent of New Zealand's GDP. During the 1970s and early 1980s, New Zealand had a large state-owned sector that received government subsidies. Recent privatization efforts have reduced the size of this sector, and remaining state-owned companies have been "corporatized," meaning they must operate the same way commercial companies do. The government has eliminated all subsidies to these businesses.

MONETARY POLICY
Score: 1–Stable (very low level of inflation)

New Zealand's average rate of inflation from 1985 to 1995 was 3.9 percent. In 1996, the rate of inflation was 2.3 percent. For most of 1997, it has been below 4 percent.

CAPITAL FLOWS AND FOREIGN INVESTMENT
Score: 2–Stable (low barriers)

Government approval is required for certain large direct investments and for the purchase of commercial fishing assets and rural land. New Zealand actively encourages direct foreign investment, however, and approval is routine.

BANKING
Score: 1–Stable (very low level of restrictions)

New Zealand's banking system is deregulated, and foreign banks are welcome. The Reserve Bank of New Zealand is limited to prudential supervision. The government does not impose deposit insurance on financial institutions; instead, banks provide full disclosure of their financial condition to the public.

WAGE AND PRICE CONTROLS
Score: 2–Stable (low level)

The market largely determines wages and prices. New Zealand enforces a relatively low minimum wage for most adult workers.

PROPERTY RIGHTS
Score: 1–Stable (very high level of protection)

Private property is a fundamental right in New Zealand. The legal and judicial system is efficient and provides adequate protection. Government expropriation is very unlikely.

REGULATION
Score: 2–Stable (low level)

Establishing a business in New Zealand is easy. Regulations are applied evenly and consistently, although environmental and safety regulations can be burdensome.

BLACK MARKET
Score: 1–Stable (very low level of activity)

New Zealand's negligible black market is confined to the sale of goods and services considered harmful to society, such as guns and drugs. There is virtually no black market in smuggling or pirated intellectual property.

NOTE
1. Based on total revenues from taxation on international trade as a percentage of total imports.

Nicaragua   3.50

1997 Score: **3.60**	1996 Score: **3.60**	1995 Score: **3.90**

Trade	4	Banking	3
Taxation	3	Wages and Prices	3
Government Intervention	2	Property Rights	4
Monetary Policy	5	Regulation	4
Foreign Investment	2	Black Market	5

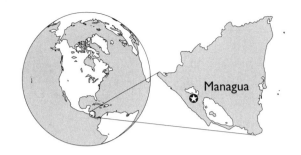

Managua

Nicaragua became an independent state in 1838. In 1979, it became a socialist economy under the Sandinista regime and, despite infusions of foreign aid, there was little economic growth. A democratic election was held in 1990, and the victor, Violeta Chamorro, promised economic reform. Progress, however, is occurring only slowly. The Sandinistas, who still hold key posts in the military and police, have blocked reforms, especially the privatization of state-owned enterprises and other nationalized sectors of the economy. Nicaragua recently reduced some tariffs. As a result, its overall score this year is 0.1 point better than it was last year.

TRADE POLICY
Score: 4+ (high level of protectionism)

Nicaragua's average tariff rate is about 10.47 percent,[1] down from almost 15 percent in 1993. As a result, its trade score is one point better this year. There are significant nontariff barriers. The U.S. Department of State reports that "Importers commonly complain of steep 'secondary' customs costs, including custom declaration form charges and consular fees. In addition, importers are required to utilize the services of licensed customs agents, adding further costs."[2] Nicaragua is becoming more open to trade than in the past, but its level of protectionism is very high when measured against global standards.

TAXATION
Score–Income taxation: 2–Stable (low tax rates)
Score–Corporate taxation: 3–Stable (moderate tax rates)
Total Taxation Score: 3–Stable (moderate tax rates)

Nicaragua's top marginal income tax rate is 30 percent, with the average income taxed at 0 percent. The top corporate tax rate also is 30 percent. Nicaragua also has a 15 percent general sales tax, a consumption tax, and a municipality tax.

GOVERNMENT INTERVENTION IN THE ECONOMY
Score: 2–Stable (low level)

Government consumes 13 percent of Nicaragua's GDP. Much of the economy has been privatized, and most of the country's GDP now is produced by the private sector.

MONETARY POLICY
Score: 5–Stable (very high level of inflation)

Nicaragua's average annual rate of inflation from 1985 to 1995 was 963.7 percent. In 1996, the rate of inflation was around 11.6 percent.

1	Hong Kong	1.25	77	Zambia	3.05
2	Singapore	1.30	80	Mali	3.10
3	Bahrain	1.70	80	Mongolia	3.10
4	New Zealand	1.75	80	Slovenia	3.10
5	Switzerland	1.90	83	Honduras	3.15
5	United States	1.90	83	Papua New Guinea	3.15
7	Luxembourg	1.95	85	Djibouti	3.20
7	Taiwan	1.95	85	Fiji	3.20
7	United Kingdom	1.95	85	Pakistan	3.20
10	Bahamas	2.00	88	Algeria	3.25
10	Ireland	2.00	88	Guinea	3.25
12	Australia	2.05	88	Lebanon	3.25
12	Japan	2.05	88	Mexico	3.25
14	Belgium	2.10	88	Senegal	3.25
14	Canada	2.10	88	Tanzania	3.25
14	United Arab Emirates	2.10	94	Nigeria	3.30
17	Austria	2.15	94	Romania	3.30
17	Chile	2.15	96	Brazil	3.35
17	Estonia	2.15	96	Cambodia	3.35
20	Czech Republic	2.20	96	Egypt	3.35
20	Netherlands	2.20	96	Ivory Coast	3.35
22	Denmark	2.25	96	Madagascar	3.35
22	Finland	2.25	96	Moldova	3.35
24	Germany	2.30	102	Nepal	3.40
24	Iceland	2.30	103	Cape Verde	3.44
24	South Korea	2.30	104	Armenia	3.45
27	Norway	2.35	104	Dominican Republic	3.45
28	Kuwait	2.40	104	Russia	3.45
28	Malaysia	2.40	107	Burkina Faso	3.50
28	Panama	2.40	107	Cameroon	3.50
28	Thailand	2.40	107	Lesotho	3.50
32	El Salvador	2.45	107	Nicaragua	3.50
32	Sri Lanka	2.45	107	Venezuela	3.50
32	Sweden	2.45	112	Gambia	3.60
35	France	2.50	112	Guyana	3.60
35	Italy	2.50	114	Bulgaria	3.65
35	Spain	2.50	114	Georgia	3.65
38	Trinidad and Tobago	2.55	114	Malawi	3.65
39	Argentina	2.60	117	Ethiopia	3.70
39	Barbados	2.60	117	India	3.70
39	Cyprus	2.60	117	Niger	3.70
39	Jamaica	2.60	120	Albania	3.75
39	Portugal	2.60	120	Bangladesh	3.75
44	Bolivia	2.65	120	China (PRC)	3.75
44	Oman	2.65	120	Congo	3.75
44	Philippines	2.65	120	Croatia	3.75
47	Swaziland	2.70	125	Chad	3.80
47	Uruguay	2.70	125	Mauritania	3.80
49	Botswana	2.75	125	Ukraine	3.80
49	Jordan	2.75	128	Sierra Leone	3.85
49	Namibia	2.75	129	Burundi	3.90
49	Tunisia	2.75	129	Suriname	3.90
53	Belize	2.80	129	Zimbabwe	3.90
53	Costa Rica	2.80	132	Haiti	4.00
53	Guatemala	2.80	132	Kyrgyzstan	4.00
53	Israel	2.80	132	Syria	4.00
53	Peru	2.80	135	Belarus	4.05
53	Saudi Arabia	2.80	136	Kazakstan	4.10
53	Turkey	2.80	136	Mozambique	4.10
53	Uganda	2.80	136	Yemen	4.10
53	Western Samoa	2.80	139	Sudan	4.20
62	Indonesia	2.85	140	Myanmar	4.30
62	Latvia	2.85	140	Rwanda	4.30
62	Malta	2.85	142	Angola	4.35
62	Paraguay	2.85	143	Azerbaijan	4.40
66	Greece	2.90	143	Tajikistan	4.40
66	Hungary	2.90	145	Turkmenistan	4.50
66	South Africa	2.90	146	Uzbekistan	4.55
69	Benin	2.95	147	Congo/Zaire	4.70
69	Ecuador	2.95	147	Iran	4.70
69	Gabon	2.95	147	Libya	4.70
69	Morocco	2.95	147	Somalia	4.70
69	Poland	2.95	147	Vietnam	4.70
74	Colombia	3.00	152	Bosnia	4.80
74	Ghana	3.00	153	Iraq	4.90
74	Lithuania	3.00	154	Cuba	5.00
77	Kenya	3.05	154	Laos	5.00
77	Slovak Republic	3.05	154	North Korea	5.00

Mostly Unfree

CAPITAL FLOWS AND FOREIGN INVESTMENT
Score: 2–Stable (low barriers)

Nicaragua has liberalized its foreign investment code to allow for 100 percent foreign ownership. Most industries are open to investment.

BANKING
Score: 3–Stable (moderate level of restrictions)

Despite some progress in ending state control, some of Nicaragua's banks remain in government hands. The government owns 3 of the 14 commercial banks now operating in Nicaragua.

WAGE AND PRICE CONTROLS
Score: 3–Stable (moderate level)

Almost all price controls have been lifted. The government still maintains a significant degree of control over some prices, however. It sets prices on petroleum products, public utilities, sugar, and locally produced soft drinks and beer. It also affects free-market pricing by purchasing "emergency stores" of such important basic foods as sugar, beans, and grain.

PROPERTY RIGHTS
Score: 4–Stable (low level of protection)

Private property is not safe in Nicaragua. Property can be confiscated by armed criminals and corrupt local governments, the court system is ill-equipped to deal with claims of confiscation, and local law enforcement remains inadequate. According to the U.S. Department of Commerce, "On the whole, the legal system is cumbersome, and enforcement of judicial determinations is uncertain and sometimes subject to political considerations."[3]

REGULATION
Score: 4–Stable (high level)

Government regulation remains a serious problem in Nicaragua. The environmental impact studies required of businesses, for example, can prevent the expansion of existing businesses and the formation of new ones. In addition, regulations are applied haphazardly, and corruption persists.

BLACK MARKET
Score: 5–Stable (very high level of activity)

Nicaragua has a large black market in several goods, including pharmaceuticals and agricultural products, and there is rampant piracy of goods from Canada, the United States, and Latin America. With unemployment rates of 40 percent, large numbers of people engage in black market activity. "Pirated videos are readily available in video rental stores nationwide, as are pirated audio cassettes," reports the U.S. Department of State. "In addition, cable television operators are known to intercept and retransmit U.S. satellite signals, a practice that continues despite a trend of negotiating contracts with U.S. sports and news satellite programmers."[4]

NOTES

1. Based on taxation of international transactions as a percentage of total imports.
2. U.S. Department of State, *Country Reports on Economic Policy and Trade Practices,* 1997, p. 283.
3. U.S. Department of Commerce, *Country Commercial Guide,* 1997.
4. U.S. Department of State, *Country Reports on Economic Policy and Trade Practices,* 1997, p. 284.

Niger   **3.70**

1997 Score: **3.70**	1996 Score: **3.70**	1995 Score: **n/a**

Trade	5	Banking	4
Taxation	4	Wages and Prices	4
Government Intervention	3	Property Rights	3
Monetary Policy	1	Regulation	4
Foreign Investment	4	Black Market	5

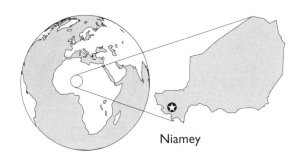

Niamey

Niger gained its independence from France in 1960 and has a long history of political instability and dictatorial governments, separated by brief periods of civilian rule. Most recently, Colonel Ibrahim Bare Mainassara led a successful coup and became president in 1996 through an election that was boycotted by opposition parties and characterized as "seriously flawed" by the U.S. Department of State.[1] Niger's economy is primarily agricultural, with more than 85 percent of the population engaged in subsistence agriculture and herding. It has averaged only 0.3 percent growth from 1980 to 1985, and per capita GDP was estimated to be only $220 in 1995. The economy remains plagued by a large public sector, a bloated bureaucracy, corruption, and an immense black market.

TRADE POLICY
Score: 5–Stable (very high level of protectionism)

Niger's average tariff rate is 18.3 percent. There are some nontariff barriers, primarily import bans and import substitution policies. Many items, such as bottled carbonated drinks, sheet metal, and soap, require special authorization from the Ministry of Commerce. According to the U.S. Department of Commerce, "This list most likely reflects measures to protect the position of well-entrenched local importers and producers."[2]

TAXATION
Score–Income taxation: 3–Stable (moderate tax rates)
Score–Corporate taxation: 4–Stable (high tax rates)
Final Taxation Score: 4–Stable (high tax rates)

Niger's top income tax rate is 60 percent; the average taxpayer finds himself in the 2 percent bracket. The top marginal corporate tax rate is 45 percent. Niger also has a value-added tax and a capital gains tax.

GOVERNMENT INTERVENTION IN THE ECONOMY
Score: 3–Stable (moderate level)

Government consumes about 14.5 percent of Niger's GDP, most of which is generated by the public sector.

MONETARY POLICY
Score: 1–Stable (very low level of inflation)

Niger's average annual rate of inflation from 1985 to 1995 was 1.3 percent. In 1996, the rate was about 11 percent.

CAPITAL FLOWS AND FOREIGN INVESTMENT
Score: 4–Stable (high barriers)

Niger provides equal treatment for domestic and foreign firms, although it also has a strict investment-review process, a hostile state-owned sector, and corruption. The bureaucracy is cumbersome and often delays investments. According

1	Hong Kong	1.25	77	Zambia	3.05
2	Singapore	1.30	80	Mali	3.10
3	Bahrain	1.70	80	Mongolia	3.10
4	New Zealand	1.75	80	Slovenia	3.10
5	Switzerland	1.90	83	Honduras	3.15
5	United States	1.90	83	Papua New Guinea	3.15
7	Luxembourg	1.95	85	Djibouti	3.20
7	Taiwan	1.95	85	Fiji	3.20
7	United Kingdom	1.95	85	Pakistan	3.20
10	Bahamas	2.00	88	Algeria	3.25
10	Ireland	2.00	88	Guinea	3.25
12	Australia	2.05	88	Lebanon	3.25
12	Japan	2.05	88	Mexico	3.25
14	Belgium	2.10	88	Senegal	3.25
14	Canada	2.10	88	Tanzania	3.25
14	United Arab Emirates	2.10	94	Nigeria	3.30
17	Austria	2.15	94	Romania	3.30
17	Chile	2.15	96	Brazil	3.35
17	Estonia	2.15	96	Cambodia	3.35
20	Czech Republic	2.20	96	Egypt	3.35
20	Netherlands	2.20	96	Ivory Coast	3.35
22	Denmark	2.25	96	Madagascar	3.35
22	Finland	2.25	96	Moldova	3.35
24	Germany	2.30	102	Nepal	3.40
24	Iceland	2.30	103	Cape Verde	3.44
24	South Korea	2.30	104	Armenia	3.45
27	Norway	2.35	104	Dominican Republic	3.45
28	Kuwait	2.40	104	Russia	3.45
28	Malaysia	2.40	107	Burkina Faso	3.50
28	Panama	2.40	107	Cameroon	3.50
28	Thailand	2.40	107	Lesotho	3.50
32	El Salvador	2.45	107	Nicaragua	3.50
32	Sri Lanka	2.45	107	Venezuela	3.50
32	Sweden	2.45	112	Gambia	3.60
35	France	2.50	112	Guyana	3.60
35	Italy	2.50	114	Bulgaria	3.65
35	Spain	2.50	114	Georgia	3.65
38	Trinidad and Tobago	2.55	114	Malawi	3.65
39	Argentina	2.60	117	Ethiopia	3.70
39	Barbados	2.60	117	India	3.70
39	Cyprus	2.60	117	Niger	3.70
39	Jamaica	2.60	120	Albania	3.75
39	Portugal	2.60	120	Bangladesh	3.75
44	Bolivia	2.65	120	China (PRC)	3.75
44	Oman	2.65	120	Congo	3.75
44	Philippines	2.65	120	Croatia	3.75
47	Swaziland	2.70	125	Chad	3.80
47	Uruguay	2.70	125	Mauritania	3.80
49	Botswana	2.75	125	Ukraine	3.80
49	Jordan	2.75	128	Sierra Leone	3.85
49	Namibia	2.75	129	Burundi	3.90
49	Tunisia	2.75	129	Suriname	3.90
53	Belize	2.80	129	Zimbabwe	3.90
53	Costa Rica	2.80	132	Haiti	4.00
53	Guatemala	2.80	132	Kyrgyzstan	4.00
53	Israel	2.80	132	Syria	4.00
53	Peru	2.80	135	Belarus	4.05
53	Saudi Arabia	2.80	136	Kazakstan	4.10
53	Turkey	2.80	136	Mozambique	4.10
53	Uganda	2.80	136	Yemen	4.10
53	Western Samoa	2.80	139	Sudan	4.20
62	Indonesia	2.85	140	Myanmar	4.30
62	Latvia	2.85	140	Rwanda	4.30
62	Malta	2.85	142	Angola	4.35
62	Paraguay	2.85	143	Azerbaijan	4.40
66	Greece	2.90	143	Tajikistan	4.40
66	Hungary	2.90	145	Turkmenistan	4.50
66	South Africa	2.90	146	Uzbekistan	4.55
69	Benin	2.95	147	Congo/Zaire	4.70
69	Ecuador	2.95	147	Iran	4.70
69	Gabon	2.95	147	Libya	4.70
69	Morocco	2.95	147	Somalia	4.70
69	Poland	2.95	147	Vietnam	4.70
74	Colombia	3.00	152	Bosnia	4.80
74	Ghana	3.00	153	Iraq	4.90
74	Lithuania	3.00	154	Cuba	5.00
77	Kenya	3.05	154	Laos	5.00
77	Slovak Republic	3.05	154	North Korea	5.00

Mostly Unfree

to the U.S. Department of Commerce, "The government now promises final authorization for an investment three months from the date of application. Nevertheless, investors should be prepared for delays caused by the process of acquiring interministerial approvals."[3]

BANKING
Score: 4–Stable (high level of restrictions)

The banking system in Niger is subject to heavy government control, although recent efforts to increase private investment have shown progress. The industry remains small, and banks generally are restricted as to the kinds of financial services they may offer. According to the U.S. Department of Commerce, "Several banks have closed in recent years. As a result, banks have stiffened lending criteria so that only the most established businesses obtain bank credit. The cost of credit is high and banks offer a limited array of financial instruments—essentially letters of credit and short- and long-term loans."[4]

WAGE AND PRICE CONTROLS
Score: 4–Stable (high level)

Wages and prices are affected by Niger's large public sector, import substitution policies, and government subsidies.

PROPERTY RIGHTS
Score: 3–Stable (moderate level of protection)

Private property in Niger is subject to expropriation, although there are few recent examples of nationalization. Niger's government is attempting to privatize many state-owned enterprises, and the legal and judicial system is becoming more efficient. According to the U.S. Department of Commerce, "Niger has a court system...to protect property and commercial rights."[5] The U.S. Department of State also reports, however, that "Family and business ties influence the lower courts and undermine their integrity. Judges sometimes fear reassignment or having their financial benefits reduced if they render a decision unfavorable to the Government."[6]

REGULATION
Score: 4–Stable (high level)

Establishing a business in Niger can be difficult. The government bureaucracy is both massive and corrupt, bribery is sometimes present, and there is embezzlement by those government officials responsible for collecting fees. According to the U.S. Department of Commerce, "Complaints have focused on occasional petty hassling by low-level officials."[7] Regulations often are applied haphazardly.

BLACK MARKET
Score: 5–Stable (very high level of activity)

The black market in Niger is larger than the formal market and growing. According to the U.S. Department of Commerce, "The economy mainly comprises subsistence agriculture and informal market activity."[8]

NOTES

1. U.S. Department of State, "Niger Country Report on Human Rights Practices for 1996," 1997.
2. U.S. Department of Commerce, *Country Commercial Guide*, 1997.
3. *Ibid.*
4. *Ibid.*
5. *Ibid.*
6. *Ibid.*
7. *Ibid.*
8. *Ibid.*

Nigeria   3.30

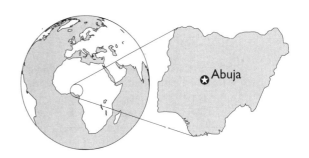

1997 Score: **3.20**	1996 Score: **3.25**	1995 Score: **3.15**

Trade	5	Banking	4
Taxation	3	Wages and Prices	2
Government Intervention	2	Property Rights	3
Monetary Policy	5	Regulation	4
Foreign Investment	2	Black Market	3

Nigeria gained its independence from the United Kingdom in 1960. It is rich in natural resources, especially oil, coal, natural gas, and fertile soil; it also has the largest population in Africa, estimated to have exceeded 110 million in 1995. Nigeria is a growing center for both the narcotics trade and international crime. In 1996, the execution of human rights activists brought international outrage. General Sani Abacha, who seized power in a 1993 coup, has announced that elections will be held in 1998. Nigeria's mixed economy has been in decline; annual per capita GNP has fallen by 75 percent since 1985, and was only $260 in 1995. Mismanagement and corruption have derailed the government's economic reform program, established in 1986, although the government has reduced taxes. Inflation has risen drastically over the past several years. As a result, Nigeria's overall score is 0.1 point worse this year.

TRADE POLICY
Score: 5–Stable (very high level of protectionism)

Despite 1995 reductions in import duties on many goods, Nigeria's average import duty is 18.3 percent. All goods are subject to additional administrative surcharges totaling 6 percent. The list of banned imports, including maize, eggs, processed wood, textiles, and used vehicles, is substantial even though the ban on wheat imports has been lifted. The customs process is burdensome.

TAXATION
Score–Income taxation: 2–Stable (low tax rates)
Score–Corporate taxation: 3–Stable (moderate tax rates)
Total Taxation Score: 3–Stable (moderate tax rates)

Nigeria's top income tax rate was lowered from 35 percent to 30 percent in 1995, and lowered again to 25 percent in 1996. The rate for the average taxpayer is 0 percent. The corporate tax rate was lowered from 35 percent to 30 percent in 1997. In 1994, the government introduced a 5 percent value-added tax, applicable to 17 categories of goods and 24 services. Nigeria also has a capital gains tax.

GOVERNMENT INTERVENTION IN THE ECONOMY
Score: 2–Stable (low level)

Government consumes 10 percent of Nigeria's GDP.[1] Privatization has stalled, and government-controlled companies, many of which are unprofitable, dominate many basic manufacturing industries.

MONETARY POLICY
Score: 5– (very high level of inflation)

Nigeria's average annual rate of inflation from 1985 to 1995 increased to 33 percent (from an average of 29.6 percent from 1985 to 1994). As a result, Nigeria's monetary policy score is one point worse this year. In 1996, the rate of inflation was 28 percent.

1	Hong Kong	1.25	77	Zambia	3.05
2	Singapore	1.30	80	Mali	3.10
3	Bahrain	1.70	80	Mongolia	3.10
4	New Zealand	1.75	80	Slovenia	3.10
5	Switzerland	1.90	83	Honduras	3.15
5	United States	1.90	83	Papua New Guinea	3.15
7	Luxembourg	1.95	85	Djibouti	3.20
7	Taiwan	1.95	85	Fiji	3.20
7	United Kingdom	1.95	85	Pakistan	3.20
10	Bahamas	2.00	88	Algeria	3.25
10	Ireland	2.00	88	Guinea	3.25
12	Australia	2.05	88	Lebanon	3.25
12	Japan	2.05	88	Mexico	3.25
14	Belgium	2.10	88	Senegal	3.25
14	Canada	2.10	88	Tanzania	3.25
14	United Arab Emirates	2.10	94	Nigeria	3.30
17	Austria	2.15	94	Romania	3.30
17	Chile	2.15	96	Brazil	3.35
17	Estonia	2.15	96	Cambodia	3.35
20	Czech Republic	2.20	96	Egypt	3.35
20	Netherlands	2.20	96	Ivory Coast	3.35
22	Denmark	2.25	96	Madagascar	3.35
22	Finland	2.25	96	Moldova	3.35
24	Germany	2.30	102	Nepal	3.40
24	Iceland	2.30	103	Cape Verde	3.44
24	South Korea	2.30	104	Armenia	3.45
27	Norway	2.35	104	Dominican Republic	3.45
28	Kuwait	2.40	104	Russia	3.45
28	Malaysia	2.40	107	Burkina Faso	3.50
28	Panama	2.40	107	Cameroon	3.50
28	Thailand	2.40	107	Lesotho	3.50
32	El Salvador	2.45	107	Nicaragua	3.50
32	Sri Lanka	2.45	107	Venezuela	3.50
32	Sweden	2.45	112	Gambia	3.60
35	France	2.50	112	Guyana	3.60
35	Italy	2.50	114	Bulgaria	3.65
35	Spain	2.50	114	Georgia	3.65
38	Trinidad and Tobago	2.55	114	Malawi	3.65
39	Argentina	2.60	117	Ethiopia	3.70
39	Barbados	2.60	117	India	3.70
39	Cyprus	2.60	117	Niger	3.70
39	Jamaica	2.60	120	Albania	3.75
39	Portugal	2.60	120	Bangladesh	3.75
44	Bolivia	2.65	120	China (PRC)	3.75
44	Oman	2.65	120	Congo	3.75
44	Philippines	2.65	120	Croatia	3.75
47	Swaziland	2.70	125	Chad	3.80
47	Uruguay	2.70	125	Mauritania	3.80
49	Botswana	2.75	125	Ukraine	3.80
49	Jordan	2.75	128	Sierra Leone	3.85
49	Namibia	2.75	129	Burundi	3.90
49	Tunisia	2.75	129	Suriname	3.90
53	Belize	2.80	129	Zimbabwe	3.90
53	Costa Rica	2.80	132	Haiti	4.00
53	Guatemala	2.80	132	Kyrgyzstan	4.00
53	Israel	2.80	132	Syria	4.00
53	Peru	2.80	135	Belarus	4.05
53	Saudi Arabia	2.80	136	Kazakstan	4.10
53	Turkey	2.80	136	Mozambique	4.10
53	Uganda	2.80	136	Yemen	4.10
53	Western Samoa	2.80	139	Sudan	4.20
62	Indonesia	2.85	140	Myanmar	4.30
62	Latvia	2.85	140	Rwanda	4.30
62	Malta	2.85	142	Angola	4.35
62	Paraguay	2.85	143	Azerbaijan	4.40
66	Greece	2.90	143	Tajikistan	4.40
66	Hungary	2.90	145	Turkmenistan	4.50
66	South Africa	2.90	146	Uzbekistan	4.55
69	Benin	2.95	147	Congo/Zaire	4.70
69	Ecuador	2.95	147	Iran	4.70
69	Gabon	2.95	147	Libya	4.70
69	Morocco	2.95	147	Somalia	4.70
69	Poland	2.95	147	Vietnam	4.70
74	Colombia	3.00	152	Bosnia	4.80
74	Ghana	3.00	153	Iraq	4.90
74	Lithuania	3.00	154	Cuba	5.00
77	Kenya	3.05	154	Laos	5.00
77	Slovak Republic	3.05	154	North Korea	5.00

Mostly Unfree

CAPITAL FLOWS AND FOREIGN INVESTMENT
Score: 2–Stable (low barriers)

In 1995, the government implemented various foreign investment reforms, including scrapping laws that mandated the employment of Nigerians. As a result, foreigners now may own 100 percent of any Nigerian enterprise. The ministry charged with approving foreign investment often acts arbitrarily, however, and there are long delays in the project-approval process. Nigeria recently has been unable to attract significant foreign investment outside the oil and gas sectors.

BANKING
Score: 4–Stable (high level of restrictions)

More than 100 domestic and foreign banks now operate branches in Nigeria, but the banking sector is doing poorly. Although 60 percent Nigerian ownership is no longer required in foreign ventures, licensing refusals are common, and the government has taken control of four large, recently privatized commercial banks. The Central Bank (which the president controls directly) fixes the discount rate, mandates lending to the agricultural and manufacturing sectors, and heavily regulates and controls the country's other banks. Private banks recently have been forced to purchase government securities.

WAGE AND PRICE CONTROLS
Score: 2–Stable (low level)

Price controls were abolished in 1987, although some products, including petroleum, are subsidized. Wages are determined by negotiations between employers and unions, and the government has the final word on wage increases. Nigeria has a minimum wage.

PROPERTY RIGHTS
Score: 3–Stable (moderate level of protection)

There is strong resistance to privatization among Nigeria's labor unions, and the enforcement of laws protecting property remains lax. According to the U.S. Department of Commerce, "The Government has taken several steps to undercut the independence and integrity of the judiciary.... [T]he Government's frequent refusal to respect court rulings also undermines the integrity of the judicial process."[2]

REGULATION
Score: 4–Stable (high level)

The process for establishing a business in Nigeria has been streamlined, although problems remain. Foreign investors must deal with bureaucratic delays, rampant corruption, and a complex web of restrictions and regulations. The U.S. Department of Commerce reports that "Nigeria offers potential investors a low-cost labor pool, abundant natural resources, and the largest domestic market in sub-Saharan Africa. However, these advantages must be weighed against Nigeria's autocratic military government, inadequate and poorly maintained infrastructure, increasing labor problems, complicated, confusing and inconsistent regulatory environment, the importance of personal ties in doing business and endemic corruption."[3] It may take several years just to acquire building permits.

BLACK MARKET
Score: 3–Stable (moderate level of activity)

High tariffs and bans on textile and agricultural imports provide incentives for smuggling in Nigeria. Government monopolies on sugar and fertilizer distribution also encourage illegal trade, and a high duty on cigarettes and luxury goods makes smuggling in these areas very lucrative. According to the Office of the United States Trade Representative, "[Import] bans are compromised by widespread smuggling."[4] The black market in pirated computer software is substantial.

NOTES

1. World Bank, *World Development Report 1997*.
2. U.S. Department of Commerce, *Country Commercial Guide*, 1997.
3. *Ibid*.
4. Office of the United States Trade Representative, *1997 National Trade Estimate Report on Foreign Trade Barriers*.

Norway   2.35

1997 Score: **2.45**   1996 Score: **2.45**   1995 Score: **n/a**

Trade	2	Banking	3
Taxation	4.5	Wages and Prices	3
Government Intervention	3	Property Rights	1
Monetary Policy	1	Regulation	3
Foreign Investment	2	Black Market	1

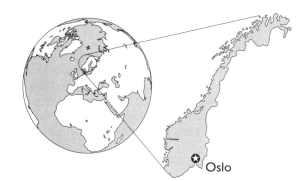

Oslo

Norway won its independence from Sweden in 1905. It remained neutral during World War I and was occupied by Nazi Germany during World War II, before which time it had an established socialized economy with generous social welfare programs. When the government was restored in 1945, new elections resulted in a powerful victory for the Labor Party, which remained in power for the next 20 years and oversaw the consolidation of the social welfare state. During the late 1950s, Norway began to pursue free trade with its neighbors, becoming a member of the European Free Trade Association in 1959. It twice has rejected full membership in the European Union (EU) but remains closely linked with the EU through the European Economic Area, which affords favorable access to the EU market for most Norwegian products. Import duties have been reduced recently. Thus, Norway's overall score is 0.1 point better this year.

TRADE POLICY
Score: 2+ (low level of protectionism)

Norway has decreased its average tariff to about 1 percent.[1] As a result, its trade score is one point better this year. Nontariff barriers include quotas and other restrictions on agricultural imports.

TAXATION
Score–Income taxation: 5–Stable (very high tax rates)
Score–Corporate taxation: 3–Stable (moderate tax rates)
Final Taxation Score: 4.5–Stable (very high tax rates)

Norway's top income tax rate is 41.7 percent, and the average taxpayer is taxed at more than 28 percent. The top marginal corporate tax rate is 28 percent. Norway also has a 28 percent capital gains tax and a 23 percent value-added tax.

GOVERNMENT INTERVENTION IN THE ECONOMY
Score: 3–Stable (moderate level)

Government consumes about 20.7 percent of Norway's GDP, almost half of which is produced by state-owned industries.

MONETARY POLICY
Score: 1–Stable (very low level of inflation)

From 1985 to 1995, Norway maintained a stable 3.1 percent rate of inflation. In 1996, the rate of inflation was 1.2 percent.

CAPITAL FLOWS AND FOREIGN INVESTMENT
Score: 2–Stable (low barriers)

Although Norway generally welcomes foreign investment, the government still maintains some restrictions on investments in telecommunications, public utilities, and industries considered vital to national security.

1	Hong Kong	1.25	77	Zambia	3.05
2	Singapore	1.30	80	Mali	3.10
3	Bahrain	1.70	80	Mongolia	3.10
4	New Zealand	1.75	80	Slovenia	3.10
5	Switzerland	1.90	83	Honduras	3.15
5	United States	1.90	83	Papua New Guinea	3.15
7	Luxembourg	1.95	85	Djibouti	3.20
7	Taiwan	1.95	85	Fiji	3.20
7	United Kingdom	1.95	85	Pakistan	3.20
10	Bahamas	2.00	88	Algeria	3.25
10	Ireland	2.00	88	Guinea	3.25
12	Australia	2.05	88	Lebanon	3.25
12	Japan	2.05	88	Mexico	3.25
14	Belgium	2.10	88	Senegal	3.25
14	Canada	2.10	88	Tanzania	3.25
14	United Arab Emirates	2.10	94	Nigeria	3.30
17	Austria	2.15	94	Romania	3.30
17	Chile	2.15	96	Brazil	3.35
17	Estonia	2.15	96	Cambodia	3.35
20	Czech Republic	2.20	96	Egypt	3.35
20	Netherlands	2.20	96	Ivory Coast	3.35
22	Denmark	2.25	96	Madagascar	3.35
22	Finland	2.25	96	Moldova	3.35
24	Germany	2.30	102	Nepal	3.40
24	Iceland	2.30	103	Cape Verde	3.44
24	South Korea	2.30	104	Armenia	3.45
27	Norway	2.35	104	Dominican Republic	3.45
28	Kuwait	2.40	104	Russia	3.45
28	Malaysia	2.40	107	Burkina Faso	3.50
28	Panama	2.40	107	Cameroon	3.50
28	Thailand	2.40	107	Lesotho	3.50
32	El Salvador	2.45	107	Nicaragua	3.50
32	Sri Lanka	2.45	107	Venezuela	3.50
32	Sweden	2.45	112	Gambia	3.60
35	France	2.50	112	Guyana	3.60
35	Italy	2.50	114	Bulgaria	3.65
35	Spain	2.50	114	Georgia	3.65
38	Trinidad and Tobago	2.55	114	Malawi	3.65
39	Argentina	2.60	117	Ethiopia	3.70
39	Barbados	2.60	117	India	3.70
39	Cyprus	2.60	117	Niger	3.70
39	Jamaica	2.60	120	Albania	3.75
39	Portugal	2.60	120	Bangladesh	3.75
44	Bolivia	2.65	120	China (PRC)	3.75
44	Oman	2.65	120	Congo	3.75
44	Philippines	2.65	120	Croatia	3.75
47	Swaziland	2.70	125	Chad	3.80
47	Uruguay	2.70	125	Mauritania	3.80
49	Botswana	2.75	125	Ukraine	3.80
49	Jordan	2.75	128	Sierra Leone	3.85
49	Namibia	2.75	129	Burundi	3.90
49	Tunisia	2.75	129	Suriname	3.90
53	Belize	2.80	129	Zimbabwe	3.90
53	Costa Rica	2.80	132	Haiti	4.00
53	Guatemala	2.80	132	Kyrgyzstan	4.00
53	Israel	2.80	132	Syria	4.00
53	Peru	2.80	135	Belarus	4.05
53	Saudi Arabia	2.80	136	Kazakstan	4.10
53	Turkey	2.80	136	Mozambique	4.10
53	Uganda	2.80	136	Yemen	4.10
53	Western Samoa	2.80	139	Sudan	4.20
62	Indonesia	2.85	140	Myanmar	4.30
62	Latvia	2.85	140	Rwanda	4.30
62	Malta	2.85	142	Angola	4.35
62	Paraguay	2.85	143	Azerbaijan	4.40
66	Greece	2.90	143	Tajikistan	4.40
66	Hungary	2.90	145	Turkmenistan	4.50
66	South Africa	2.90	146	Uzbekistan	4.55
69	Benin	2.95	147	Congo/Zaire	4.70
69	Ecuador	2.95	147	Iran	4.70
69	Gabon	2.95	147	Libya	4.70
69	Morocco	2.95	147	Somalia	4.70
69	Poland	2.95	147	Vietnam	4.70
74	Colombia	3.00	152	Bosnia	4.80
74	Ghana	3.00	153	Iraq	4.90
74	Lithuania	3.00	154	Cuba	5.00
77	Kenya	3.05	154	Laos	5.00
77	Slovak Republic	3.05	154	North Korea	5.00

Mostly Free

BANKING
Score: 3–Stable (moderate level of restrictions)

Norway's banking system is becoming more liberalized. Non-European banks are permitted to establish subsidiaries (but not branches), and Norwegian banks may engage in a variety of financial services, including the buying and selling of securities, insurance policies, real estate, and other investments. According to the U.S. Department of State, "While there has been substantial banking reform, competition in this sector still remains distorted due to government ownership of the two largest commercial banks, and the existence of specialized state banks which offer subsidized loans in certain sectors and geographic locations."[2]

WAGE AND PRICE CONTROLS
Score: 3–Stable (moderate level)

The market sets wages and prices in Norway, although the government exercises indirect control over many wages and prices through the large public sector. Large agricultural subsidies also continue to affect prices.

PROPERTY RIGHTS
Score: 1–Stable (very high level of protection)

Private property is safe from government confiscation. Norway has an efficient legal system.

REGULATION
Score: 3–Stable (moderate level)

Some of Norway's economy (especially agriculture and such service industries as telecommunications and transportation) remains heavily regulated. The government, however, also continues to reduce expenditures and privatize some businesses.

BLACK MARKET
Score: 1–Stable (very low level of activity)

Norway has a very small black market. Because it also has very strong and efficient laws concerning intellectual property rights, piracy in such products is virtually nonexistent.

NOTES

1. Based on total government taxation of international transactions as a percentage of imports.
2. U.S. Department of State, *Country Reports on Economic Policy and Trade Practices*, 1997, p. 150.

Oman   2.65

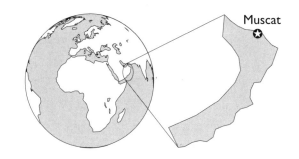

Muscat

| 1997 Score: **2.75** | 1996 Score: **2.85** | 1995 Score: **2.65** |

Trade	2	Banking	4
Taxation	3.5	Wages and Prices	3
Government Intervention	4	Property Rights	2
Monetary Policy	1	Regulation	2
Foreign Investment	3	Black Market	2

Portugal dominated the coastal areas of present-day Oman from 1507 until 1650. In the 19th century, Oman's ruling sultans cultivated close relations with Great Britain to offset outside Arab and Persian interference. Today, Oman is an absolute monarchy, although Sultan Qabas bin Said Al Said has appointed a 60-member consultative council with limited advisory powers. The economy depends heavily on oil revenues, which account for 85 percent of export earnings and about 40 percent of GDP. Oman, which did not begin to introduce free-market reforms until 1991, recently reduced its barriers to trade. As a result, its overall score has improved 0.1 point this year.

TRADE POLICY
Score: 2+ (low level of protectionism)

Oman's average tariff rate has decreased to less than 3 percent. As a result, its trade policy score is one point better this year. Nontariff barriers take the form of import licenses, which are required for all imports. According to the U.S. Department of State, "Oman's customs procedures are complex. There are complaints of sudden changes in the enforcement of regulations."[1]

TAXATION
Score–Income taxation: 1–Stable (low tax rates)
Score–Corporate taxation: 5–Stable (very high tax rates)
Total Taxation Score: 3.5–Stable (high tax rates)

Income taxes are not imposed on individuals, but the top corporate tax rate is 50 percent.[2] Oman also has a 50 percent capital gains tax, a training levy taken from non-Omani employees, and a social contributions tax.

GOVERNMENT INTERVENTION IN THE ECONOMY
Score: 4–Stable (high level)

Government consumes 27.6 percent of Oman's GDP. It also owns nearly all of the country's oil production.

MONETARY POLICY
Score: 1–Stable (very low level of inflation)

Oman's average annual rate of inflation from 1985 to 1995 was less than 1 percent. In 1996, the rate of inflation was 1 percent.

CAPITAL FLOWS AND FOREIGN INVESTMENT
Score: 3–Stable (moderate barriers)

With few exceptions, companies in Oman must be owned fully by Omanis. Foreign investment is allowed only through joint ventures and joint-stock companies. There are some tax incentives for investment.

1	Hong Kong	1.25	77	Zambia	3.05
2	Singapore	1.30	80	Mali	3.10
3	Bahrain	1.70	80	Mongolia	3.10
4	New Zealand	1.75	80	Slovenia	3.10
5	Switzerland	1.90	83	Honduras	3.15
5	United States	1.90	83	Papua New Guinea	3.15
7	Luxembourg	1.95	85	Djibouti	3.20
7	Taiwan	1.95	85	Fiji	3.20
7	United Kingdom	1.95	85	Pakistan	3.20
10	Bahamas	2.00	88	Algeria	3.25
10	Ireland	2.00	88	Guinea	3.25
12	Australia	2.05	88	Lebanon	3.25
12	Japan	2.05	88	Mexico	3.25
14	Belgium	2.10	88	Senegal	3.25
14	Canada	2.10	88	Tanzania	3.25
14	United Arab Emirates	2.10	94	Nigeria	3.30
17	Austria	2.15	94	Romania	3.30
17	Chile	2.15	96	Brazil	3.35
17	Estonia	2.15	96	Cambodia	3.35
20	Czech Republic	2.20	96	Egypt	3.35
20	Netherlands	2.20	96	Ivory Coast	3.35
22	Denmark	2.25	96	Madagascar	3.35
22	Finland	2.25	96	Moldova	3.35
24	Germany	2.30	102	Nepal	3.40
24	Iceland	2.30	103	Cape Verde	3.44
24	South Korea	2.30	104	Armenia	3.45
27	Norway	2.35	104	Dominican Republic	3.45
28	Kuwait	2.40	104	Russia	3.45
28	Malaysia	2.40	107	Burkina Faso	3.50
28	Panama	2.40	107	Cameroon	3.50
28	Thailand	2.40	107	Lesotho	3.50
32	El Salvador	2.45	107	Nicaragua	3.50
32	Sri Lanka	2.45	107	Venezuela	3.50
32	Sweden	2.45	112	Gambia	3.60
35	France	2.50	112	Guyana	3.60
35	Italy	2.50	114	Bulgaria	3.65
35	Spain	2.50	114	Georgia	3.65
38	Trinidad and Tobago	2.55	114	Malawi	3.65
39	Argentina	2.60	117	Ethiopia	3.70
39	Barbados	2.60	117	India	3.70
39	Cyprus	2.60	117	Niger	3.70
39	Jamaica	2.60	120	Albania	3.75
39	Portugal	2.60	120	Bangladesh	3.75
44	Bolivia	2.65	120	China (PRC)	3.75
44	Oman	2.65	120	Congo	3.75
44	Philippines	2.65	120	Croatia	3.75
47	Swaziland	2.70	125	Chad	3.80
47	Uruguay	2.70	125	Mauritania	3.80
49	Botswana	2.75	125	Ukraine	3.80
49	Jordan	2.75	128	Sierra Leone	3.85
49	Namibia	2.75	129	Burundi	3.90
49	Tunisia	2.75	129	Suriname	3.90
53	Belize	2.80	129	Zimbabwe	3.90
53	Costa Rica	2.80	132	Haiti	4.00
53	Guatemala	2.80	132	Kyrgyzstan	4.00
53	Israel	2.80	132	Syria	4.00
53	Peru	2.80	135	Belarus	4.05
53	Saudi Arabia	2.80	136	Kazakstan	4.10
53	Turkey	2.80	136	Mozambique	4.10
53	Uganda	2.80	136	Yemen	4.10
53	Western Samoa	2.80	139	Sudan	4.20
62	Indonesia	2.85	140	Myanmar	4.30
62	Latvia	2.85	140	Rwanda	4.30
62	Malta	2.85	142	Angola	4.35
62	Paraguay	2.85	143	Azerbaijan	4.40
66	Greece	2.90	143	Tajikistan	4.40
66	Hungary	2.90	145	Turkmenistan	4.50
66	South Africa	2.90	146	Uzbekistan	4.55
69	Benin	2.95	147	Congo/Zaire	4.70
69	Ecuador	2.95	147	Iran	4.70
69	Gabon	2.95	147	Libya	4.70
69	Morocco	2.95	147	Somalia	4.70
69	Poland	2.95	147	Vietnam	4.70
74	Colombia	3.00	152	Bosnia	4.80
74	Ghana	3.00	153	Iraq	4.90
74	Lithuania	3.00	154	Cuba	5.00
77	Kenya	3.05	154	Laos	5.00
77	Slovak Republic	3.05	154	North Korea	5.00

Mostly Free

BANKING
Score: 4–Stable (high level of restrictions)

Oman has a thriving banking sector, but competition is limited because foreigners are not permitted to open new banks.

WAGE AND PRICE CONTROLS
Score: 3–Stable (moderate level)

There are few official price controls in Oman, but the government is the main consumer of goods and services, and its purchases therefore affect prices. Oman has a minimum wage law.

PROPERTY RIGHTS
Score: 2–Stable (high level of protection)

Property expropriation is not likely. Oman's court system is efficient, and private property is well protected, although the judicial system is not completely free of government influence.

REGULATION
Score: 2–Stable (low level)

Oman's relatively straightforward regulations are applied consistently in most cases.

BLACK MARKET
Score: 2–Stable (low level of activity)

Oman has a negligible black market. There is some traffic in pirated intellectual property (primarily sound and video recordings), but the laws are strictly enforced, and black market activity in this area is minimal.

NOTES
1. U.S. Department of State, *Country Reports on Economic Policy and Trade Practices,* 1997, p. 354.
2. This rate applies to foreign-owned corporations. There is a sole proprietorship tax of up to 7.5 percent.

Pakistan   3.20

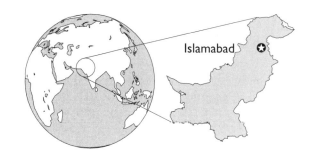

Islamabad

1997 Score: **3.10**	1996 Score: **3.05**	1995 Score: **3.15**

Trade	5	Banking	3
Taxation	4	Wages and Prices	3
Government Intervention	3	Property Rights	3
Monetary Policy	2	Regulation	4
Foreign Investment	2	Black Market	3

Since gaining its independence following the partition of the Indian subcontinent and the end of British rule in 1947, Pakistan has received huge amounts of foreign aid, much of which has been squandered, and has remained poor. In 1990, the government of Prime Minister Nawaz Sharif undertook a program of economic liberalization to increase foreign and domestic private investment, but the pace of reform slowed after Benazir Bhutto became prime minister in 1993. Terrorist attacks and political violence between warring religious and ethnic factions have destabilized Karachi, Pakistan's business center. Prime Minister Bhutto was removed from office in November 1996 under accusations of corruption, and a new government headed once again by Sharif was elected in February 1997. Inheriting an economy in deep recession, Sharif has responded by cutting some taxes and reducing some barriers to trade and investment. Protection of private property, however, has been weakened recently. As a result, Pakistan's overall score is 0.1 point worse this year.

TRADE POLICY
Score: 5–Stable (very high level of protectionism)

Pakistan's average tariff rate is 25 percent, down from 27.5 percent last year. Nontariff barriers include import licenses and fees. According to the U.S. Department of State, "Charges that customs officers demand bribes are also common."[1]

TAXATION
Score–Income taxation: 3–Stable (moderate tax rates)
Score–Corporate taxation: 4–Stable (high tax rates)
Total Taxation Score: 4–Stable (high tax rates)

Pakistan's top income tax rate is 35 percent, and the average income is taxed at about 10 percent. The top corporate income tax rate is 43 percent. Pakistan also has a 43 percent capital gains tax, a sales tax, state and local taxes, and a capital value tax that is added to certain properties like factories and automobiles.

GOVERNMENT INTERVENTION IN THE ECONOMY
Score: 3–Stable (moderate level)

Government consumes 12.1 percent of Pakistan's GDP, up from 11 percent in 1980. Although proceeding with significant privatization, it continues to own many financial institutions as well as companies in the energy and utilities, transportation, and marketing sectors.

MONETARY POLICY
Score: 2–Stable (low level of inflation)

Pakistan's average annual rate of inflation from 1985 to 1995 was 9.3 percent. The rate for 1996 was not available.

1	Hong Kong	1.25	77	Zambia	3.05
2	Singapore	1.30	80	Mali	3.10
3	Bahrain	1.70	80	Mongolia	3.10
4	New Zealand	1.75	80	Slovenia	3.10
5	Switzerland	1.90	83	Honduras	3.15
5	United States	1.90	83	Papua New Guinea	3.15
7	Luxembourg	1.95	85	Djibouti	3.20
7	Taiwan	1.95	85	Fiji	3.20
7	United Kingdom	1.95	85	Pakistan	3.20
10	Bahamas	2.00	88	Algeria	3.25
10	Ireland	2.00	88	Guinea	3.25
12	Australia	2.05	88	Lebanon	3.25
12	Japan	2.05	88	Mexico	3.25
14	Belgium	2.10	88	Senegal	3.25
14	Canada	2.10	88	Tanzania	3.25
14	United Arab Emirates	2.10	94	Nigeria	3.30
17	Austria	2.15	94	Romania	3.30
17	Chile	2.15	96	Brazil	3.35
17	Estonia	2.15	96	Cambodia	3.35
20	Czech Republic	2.20	96	Egypt	3.35
20	Netherlands	2.20	96	Ivory Coast	3.35
22	Denmark	2.25	96	Madagascar	3.35
22	Finland	2.25	96	Moldova	3.35
24	Germany	2.30	102	Nepal	3.40
24	Iceland	2.30	103	Cape Verde	3.44
24	South Korea	2.30	104	Armenia	3.45
27	Norway	2.35	104	Dominican Republic	3.45
28	Kuwait	2.40	104	Russia	3.45
28	Malaysia	2.40	107	Burkina Faso	3.50
28	Panama	2.40	107	Cameroon	3.50
28	Thailand	2.40	107	Lesotho	3.50
32	El Salvador	2.45	107	Nicaragua	3.50
32	Sri Lanka	2.45	107	Venezuela	3.50
32	Sweden	2.45	112	Gambia	3.60
35	France	2.50	112	Guyana	3.60
35	Italy	2.50	114	Bulgaria	3.65
35	Spain	2.50	114	Georgia	3.65
38	Trinidad and Tobago	2.55	114	Malawi	3.65
39	Argentina	2.60	117	Ethiopia	3.70
39	Barbados	2.60	117	India	3.70
39	Cyprus	2.60	117	Niger	3.70
39	Jamaica	2.60	120	Albania	3.75
39	Portugal	2.60	120	Bangladesh	3.75
44	Bolivia	2.65	120	China (PRC)	3.75
44	Oman	2.65	120	Congo	3.75
44	Philippines	2.65	120	Croatia	3.75
47	Swaziland	2.70	125	Colombia	3.80
47	Uruguay	2.70	125	Mauritania	3.80
49	Botswana	2.75	125	Ukraine	3.80
49	Jordan	2.75	128	Sierra Leone	3.85
49	Namibia	2.75	129	Burundi	3.90
49	Tunisia	2.75	129	Suriname	3.90
53	Belize	2.80	129	Zimbabwe	3.90
53	Costa Rica	2.80	132	Haiti	4.00
53	Guatemala	2.80	132	Kyrgyzstan	4.00
53	Israel	2.80	132	Syria	4.00
53	Peru	2.80	135	Belarus	4.05
53	Saudi Arabia	2.80	136	Kazakstan	4.10
53	Turkey	2.80	136	Mozambique	4.10
53	Uganda	2.80	136	Yemen	4.10
53	Western Samoa	2.80	139	Sudan	4.20
62	Indonesia	2.85	140	Myanmar	4.30
62	Latvia	2.85	140	Rwanda	4.30
62	Malta	2.85	142	Angola	4.35
62	Paraguay	2.85	143	Azerbaijan	4.40
66	Greece	2.90	143	Tajikistan	4.40
66	Hungary	2.90	145	Turkmenistan	4.50
66	South Africa	2.90	146	Uzbekistan	4.55
69	Benin	2.95	147	Congo/Zaire	4.70
69	Ecuador	2.95	147	Iran	4.70
69	Gabon	2.95	147	Libya	4.70
69	Morocco	2.95	147	Somalia	4.70
69	Poland	2.95	147	Vietnam	4.70
74	Colombia	3.00	152	Bosnia	4.80
74	Ghana	3.00	153	Iraq	4.90
74	Lithuania	3.00	154	Cuba	5.00
77	Kenya	3.05	154	Laos	5.00
77	Slovak Republic	3.05	154	North Korea	5.00

Mostly Unfree

CAPITAL FLOWS AND FOREIGN INVESTMENT
Score: 2–Stable (low barriers)

There are no restrictions on the amount of foreign investment in Pakistani industries. Domestic and foreign firms are treated equally. According to the U.S. Department of Commerce, "Pakistan's legal framework and economic strategy do not discriminate against potential foreign investors, but rather establish an even-handed approach."[2]

BANKING
Score: 3–Stable (moderate level of restrictions)

Foreigners are gaining more access to banks in Pakistan, although foreign banks are subject to higher taxes than domestic banks. Local banks are permitted to engage in securities and investments, but not insurance and real estate ventures. Despite recent attempts to privatize more banks, the government continues to own several banking institutions; new data show that state-owned banks control over 70 percent of total commercial bank assets. By global standards, however, the level of restrictions on banking is only moderate.

WAGE AND PRICE CONTROLS
Score: 3–Stable (moderate level)

Pakistan maintains price controls on many products. Prices are set generally on products (such as automobiles) manufactured by state-operated firms, on petroleum, and on electricity. Pakistan has a minimum wage.

PROPERTY RIGHTS
Score: 3– (moderate level of protection)

Property is protected in most cases, and expropriation is unlikely. The courts do not enforce property rights in all cases, however, and recent political strife has highlighted the government's control over the judiciary. According to the U.S. Department of State, "The Constitution provides for an independent judiciary, however, in practice, the judiciary is not independent."[3] As a result, Pakistan's property rights score is one point worse this year.

REGULATION
Score: 4–Stable (high level)

Pakistan's economy is heavily regulated, and laws like the Environmental Protection Ordinance of 1983, the Industrial Relations Ordinance of 1974, and the Factories Act often are burdensome. Corruption also remains a problem. "As in many developing countries," reports the U.S. Department of Commerce, "corruption is an unwelcome, but ubiquitous, part of the business milieu in Pakistan. Recent anecdotal reports suggest that this problem continues and that, rather than serving to facilitate transactions, the phenomenon may be having a sclerotic impact on the economy."[4]

BLACK MARKET
Score: 3–Stable (moderate level of activity)

Smuggling is encouraged by extremely high tariffs on many consumer goods. Although the black market is shrinking, illicit trade in such items as consumer electronics and recorded music is substantial. According to the U.S. Department of State, "Pakistani laws on protecting intellectual property rights (IPR) are generally adequate, but enforcement is weak, resulting in widespread piracy, especially of copyrighted materials."[5] When compared with the size of Pakistan's almost $60 billion economy, however, these activities are moderate.

NOTES

1. U.S. Department of State, *Country Reports on Economic Policy and Trade Practices,* 1997, p. 390.
2. U.S. Department of Commerce, *Country Commercial Guide,* 1997.
3. U.S. Department of State, "Pakistan Country Report on Human Rights Practices for 1996," 1997.
4. U.S. Department of Commerce, *Country Commercial Guide,* 1997.
5. U.S. Department of State, *Country Reports on Economic Policy and Trade Practices,* 1996, p. 528.

Panama   2.40

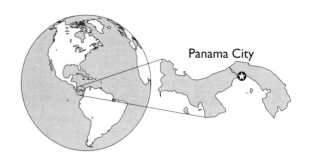
Panama City

| 1997 Score: **2.50** | 1996 Score: **2.40** | 1995 Score: **2.70** |

Trade	3	Banking	1
Taxation	3	Wages and Prices	2
Government Intervention	3	Property Rights	3
Monetary Policy	1	Regulation	3
Foreign Investment	2	Black Market	3

Panama, site of the U.S.-built Panama Canal, gained its independence from Spain in 1821 and from Colombia in 1903. It held democratic elections in May 1994. President Ernesto Perez Balladares advocates a strong policy of economic liberalization. Privatization efforts have stalled, however, leaving many businesses and utilities in government hands. Panama adopted the U.S. dollar as its official currency in 1904. This significant economic reform removed the government's ability to inflate the currency to cover government spending and is a major reason that the inflation rate is less than 3 percent and Panama has enjoyed a degree of price stability that has eluded the rest of Latin America. Panama's overall score is 0.1 point better this year.

TRADE POLICY

Score: 3+ (moderate level of protectionism)

Panama's average tariff rate is 8.73 percent, down from 10 percent last year. As a result, its trade policy score is one point better this year. Nontariff barriers, however, have been increased to include strict labeling, testing, and certification requirements, especially on poultry, pork, and beef products.

TAXATION

Score–Income taxation: 2–Stable (low tax rates)
Score–Corporate taxation: 3–Stable (moderate tax rates)
Total Taxation Score: 3–Stable (moderate tax rates)

Panama's top marginal tax rate is 30 percent, and the average income level is taxed at 0 percent. The top corporate tax rate is 30 percent, down from 35 percent in 1995. Panama also has a 10 percent capital gains tax.

GOVERNMENT INTERVENTION IN THE ECONOMY

Score: 3–Stable (moderate level)

Government consumes 15.4 percent of Panama's GDP. It also owns some telephone, electricity, and water systems, as well as some manufacturing companies.

MONETARY POLICY

Score: 1–Stable (very low level of inflation)

Panama has made its most significant progress in monetary policy, removing the government almost completely from supplying the currency. The average annual rate of inflation between 1985 and 1995 was 1.7 percent, primarily because Panama has used the U.S. dollar as its currency since 1904. This prevents the government from printing money to cover deficit spending.

1	Hong Kong	1.25	77	Zambia	3.05
2	Singapore	1.30	80	Mali	3.10
3	Bahrain	1.70	80	Mongolia	3.10
4	New Zealand	1.75	80	Slovenia	3.10
5	Switzerland	1.90	83	Honduras	3.15
5	United States	1.90	83	Papua New Guinea	3.15
7	Luxembourg	1.95	85	Djibouti	3.20
7	Taiwan	1.95	85	Fiji	3.20
7	United Kingdom	1.95	85	Pakistan	3.20
10	Bahamas	2.00	88	Algeria	3.25
10	Ireland	2.00	88	Guinea	3.25
12	Australia	2.05	88	Lebanon	3.25
12	Japan	2.05	88	Mexico	3.25
14	Belgium	2.10	88	Senegal	3.25
14	Canada	2.10	88	Tanzania	3.25
14	United Arab Emirates	2.10	94	Nigeria	3.30
17	Austria	2.15	94	Romania	3.30
17	Chile	2.15	96	Brazil	3.35
17	Estonia	2.15	96	Cambodia	3.35
20	Czech Republic	2.20	96	Egypt	3.35
20	Netherlands	2.20	96	Ivory Coast	3.35
22	Denmark	2.25	96	Madagascar	3.35
22	Finland	2.25	96	Moldova	3.35
24	Germany	2.30	102	Nepal	3.40
24	Iceland	2.30	103	Cape Verde	3.44
24	South Korea	2.30	104	Armenia	3.45
27	Norway	2.35	104	Dominican Republic	3.45
28	Kuwait	2.40	104	Russia	3.45
28	Malaysia	2.40	107	Burkina Faso	3.50
28	Panama	2.40	107	Cameroon	3.50
28	Thailand	2.40	107	Lesotho	3.50
32	El Salvador	2.45	107	Nicaragua	3.50
32	Sri Lanka	2.45	107	Venezuela	3.50
32	Sweden	2.45	112	Gambia	3.60
35	France	2.50	112	Guyana	3.60
35	Italy	2.50	114	Bulgaria	3.65
35	Spain	2.50	114	Georgia	3.65
38	Trinidad and Tobago	2.55	114	Malawi	3.65
39	Argentina	2.60	117	Ethiopia	3.70
39	Barbados	2.60	117	India	3.70
39	Cyprus	2.60	117	Niger	3.70
39	Jamaica	2.60	120	Albania	3.75
39	Portugal	2.60	120	Bangladesh	3.75
44	Bolivia	2.65	120	China (PRC)	3.75
44	Oman	2.65	120	Congo	3.75
44	Philippines	2.65	120	Croatia	3.75
47	Swaziland	2.70	125	Chad	3.80
47	Uruguay	2.70	125	Mauritania	3.80
49	Botswana	2.75	125	Ukraine	3.80
49	Jordan	2.75	128	Sierra Leone	3.85
49	Namibia	2.75	129	Burundi	3.90
49	Tunisia	2.75	129	Suriname	3.90
53	Belize	2.80	129	Zimbabwe	3.90
53	Costa Rica	2.80	132	Haiti	4.00
53	Guatemala	2.80	132	Kyrgyzstan	4.00
53	Israel	2.80	132	Syria	4.00
53	Peru	2.80	135	Belarus	4.05
53	Saudi Arabia	2.80	136	Kazakstan	4.10
53	Turkey	2.80	136	Mozambique	4.10
53	Uganda	2.80	136	Yemen	4.10
53	Western Samoa	2.80	139	Sudan	4.20
62	Indonesia	2.85	140	Myanmar	4.30
62	Latvia	2.85	140	Rwanda	4.30
62	Malta	2.85	142	Angola	4.35
62	Paraguay	2.85	143	Azerbaijan	4.40
66	Greece	2.90	143	Tajikistan	4.40
66	Hungary	2.90	145	Turkmenistan	4.50
66	South Africa	2.90	146	Uzbekistan	4.55
69	Benin	2.95	147	Congo/Zaire	4.70
69	Ecuador	2.95	147	Iran	4.70
69	Gabon	2.95	147	Libya	4.70
69	Morocco	2.95	147	Somalia	4.70
69	Poland	2.95	147	Vietnam	4.70
74	Colombia	3.00	152	Bosnia	4.80
74	Ghana	3.00	153	Iraq	4.90
74	Lithuania	3.00	154	Cuba	5.00
77	Kenya	3.05	154	Laos	5.00
77	Slovak Republic	3.05	154	North Korea	5.00

Mostly Free

CAPITAL FLOWS AND FOREIGN INVESTMENT
Score: 2–Stable (low barriers)

Most sectors of Panama's economy are open to foreign investment, although there are a few restrictions on "national interest" industries and retail activities.

BANKING
Score: 1–Stable (very low level of restrictions)

Domestic competition in banking is relatively high, and major banks from all over the world operate in Panama. Domestic banks may sell securities and real estate and make some investments, but they are not permitted to sell insurance. There are few restrictions on opening banks.

WAGE AND PRICE CONTROLS
Score: 2–Stable (low level)

The market sets most wages and prices, although the government controls the prices of a few basic foodstuffs, industrial products, medicines, public transportation, and rent. Panama also imposes minimum wages.

PROPERTY RIGHTS
Score: 3–Stable (moderate level of protection)

Property rights are constitutionally protected. The legal system in Panama is not always independent, however. According to the U.S. Department of State, "The judiciary is independent, but subject to corruption."[1]

REGULATION
Score: 3–Stable (moderate level)

Opening a business in Panama is a relatively easy process that requires obtaining a license from the Ministry of Commerce and Industry. Bureaucratic red tape remains burdensome, however, as does some corruption.

BLACK MARKET
Score: 3–Stable (moderate level of activity)

Panama has a large black market in pirated computer software and prerecorded sound and video tapes. According to the U.S. Department of State, the country continues to be a haven for black marketeers in these and other pirated intellectual properties.[2]

NOTES
1. U.S. Department of State, "Panama Country Report on Human Rights Practices for 1996," 1997.
2. U.S. Department of State, *Country Reports on Economic Policy and Trade Practices,* 1997, p. 289.

Papua New Guinea   3.15

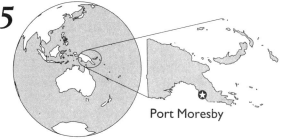

Port Moresby

1997 Score: **3.10**	1996 Score: **3.10**	1995 Score: **n/a**

Trade	5	Banking	4
Taxation	2.5	Wages and Prices	3
Government Intervention	3	Property Rights	3
Monetary Policy	1	Regulation	4
Foreign Investment	3	Black Market	3

Papua New Guinea gained its independence from Australia in 1975. Its parliamentary democracy is raucous but weak, beset by corruption, costly and overlapping local governments, and the expense of fighting a secessionist movement on the island of Bougainville. The country's high economic growth is due largely to mining, logging, and oil projects; but it also relies heavily on foreign aid. In 1994, faced with a chronic budget deficit that threatened bankruptcy, the government began to cut some trade restrictions while raising taxes and fees. In June 1996, Papua New Guinea joined the World Trade Organization, thereby obligating the government to reduce its barriers to international trade and investment and to establish laws to protect intellectual property rights. Although some taxes have been reduced, regulation of business has increased. Therefore, Papua New Guinea's overall score is 0.05 point worse this year.

TRADE POLICY
Score: 5–Stable (very high level of protectionism)

The average tariff rate for Papua New Guinea is 21.47 percent.[1] Nontariff barriers include an inefficient bureaucracy and local government requirements that tend to hamper imports of products that compete directly with domestic firms.

TAXATION
Score–Income taxation: 2+ (low tax rates)
Score–Corporate taxation: 2–Stable (low tax rates)
Final Taxation Score: 2.5+ (moderate tax rates)

Papua New Guinea's top income tax rate is 35 percent; the average taxpayer is in the 0 percent bracket, down from 10 percent. As a result, the country's overall tax score is one-half point better this year. The top marginal corporate tax rate is 25 percent. The government also levies a sales tax of varying rates.

GOVERNMENT INTERVENTION IN THE ECONOMY
Score: 3–Stable (moderate level)

Government consumes about 22.4 percent of Papua New Guinea's GDP. It also owns substantial portions of the economy, especially in the mining sector. About one-third of those employed in the formal sector work for the government.

MONETARY POLICY
Score: 1–Stable (very low level of inflation)

Papua New Guinea's average annual rate of inflation from 1985 to 1995 was 4.6 percent. In 1996, the rate of inflation was 12 percent.

1	Hong Kong	1.25	
2	Singapore	1.30	
3	Bahrain	1.70	
4	New Zealand	1.75	
5	Switzerland	1.90	
5	United States	1.90	
7	Luxembourg	1.95	
7	Taiwan	1.95	
7	United Kingdom	1.95	
10	Bahamas	2.00	
10	Ireland	2.00	
12	Australia	2.05	
12	Japan	2.05	
14	Belgium	2.10	
14	Canada	2.10	
14	United Arab Emirates	2.10	
17	Austria	2.15	
17	Chile	2.15	
17	Estonia	2.15	
20	Czech Republic	2.20	
20	Netherlands	2.20	
22	Denmark	2.25	
22	Finland	2.25	
24	Germany	2.30	
24	Iceland	2.30	
24	South Korea	2.30	
27	Norway	2.35	
28	Kuwait	2.40	
28	Malaysia	2.40	
28	Panama	2.40	
28	Thailand	2.40	
32	El Salvador	2.45	
32	Sri Lanka	2.45	
32	Sweden	2.45	
35	France	2.50	
35	Italy	2.50	
35	Spain	2.50	
38	Trinidad and Tobago	2.55	
39	Argentina	2.60	
39	Barbados	2.60	
39	Cyprus	2.60	
39	Jamaica	2.60	
39	Portugal	2.60	
44	Bolivia	2.65	
44	Oman	2.65	
44	Philippines	2.65	
47	Swaziland	2.70	
47	Uruguay	2.70	
49	Botswana	2.75	
49	Jordan	2.75	
49	Namibia	2.75	
49	Tunisia	2.75	
53	Belize	2.80	
53	Costa Rica	2.80	
53	Guatemala	2.80	
53	Israel	2.80	
53	Peru	2.80	
53	Saudi Arabia	2.80	
53	Turkey	2.80	
53	Uganda	2.80	
53	Western Samoa	2.80	
62	Indonesia	2.85	
62	Latvia	2.85	
62	Malta	2.85	
62	Paraguay	2.85	
66	Greece	2.90	
66	Hungary	2.90	
66	South Africa	2.90	
69	Benin	2.95	
69	Ecuador	2.95	
69	Gabon	2.95	
69	Morocco	2.95	
69	Poland	2.95	
74	Colombia	3.00	
74	Ghana	3.00	
74	Lithuania	3.00	
77	Kenya	3.05	
77	Slovak Republic	3.05	
77	Zambia	3.05
80	Mali	3.10
80	Mongolia	3.10
80	Slovenia	3.10
83	Honduras	3.15
83	Papua New Guinea	3.15
85	Djibouti	3.20
85	Fiji	3.20
85	Pakistan	3.20
88	Algeria	3.25
88	Guinea	3.25
88	Lebanon	3.25
88	Mexico	3.25
88	Senegal	3.25
88	Tanzania	3.25
94	Nigeria	3.30
94	Romania	3.30
96	Brazil	3.35
96	Cambodia	3.35
96	Egypt	3.35
96	Ivory Coast	3.35
96	Madagascar	3.35
96	Moldova	3.35
102	Nepal	3.40
103	Cape Verde	3.44
104	Armenia	3.45
104	Dominican Republic	3.45
104	Russia	3.45
107	Burkina Faso	3.50
107	Cameroon	3.50
107	Lesotho	3.50
107	Nicaragua	3.50
107	Venezuela	3.50
112	Gambia	3.60
112	Guyana	3.60
114	Bulgaria	3.65
114	Georgia	3.65
114	Malawi	3.65
117	Ethiopia	3.70
117	India	3.70
117	Niger	3.70
120	Albania	3.75
120	Bangladesh	3.75
120	China (PRC)	3.75
120	Congo	3.75
120	Croatia	3.75
125	Chad	3.80
125	Mauritania	3.80
125	Ukraine	3.80
128	Sierra Leone	3.85
129	Burundi	3.90
129	Suriname	3.90
129	Zimbabwe	3.90
132	Haiti	4.00
132	Kyrgyzstan	4.00
132	Syria	4.00
135	Belarus	4.05
136	Kazakstan	4.10
136	Mozambique	4.10
136	Yemen	4.10
139	Sudan	4.20
140	Myanmar	4.30
140	Rwanda	4.30
142	Angola	4.35
143	Azerbaijan	4.40
143	Tajikistan	4.40
145	Turkmenistan	4.50
146	Uzbekistan	4.55
147	Congo/Zaire	4.70
147	Iran	4.70
147	Libya	4.70
147	Somalia	4.70
147	Vietnam	4.70
152	Bosnia	4.80
153	Iraq	4.90
154	Cuba	5.00
154	Laos	5.00
154	North Korea	5.00

Mostly Unfree

CAPITAL FLOWS AND FOREIGN INVESTMENT
Score: 3–Stable (moderate barriers)

The government is opening more sectors to foreign investment, but some barriers still exist. Not all foreign companies are treated the same as domestic firms; several industrial sectors, such as mining, are closed to foreign investment; and hostility to foreign investment in the lower levels of the bureaucracy can create delays in obtaining necessary documents and meeting licensing requirements. "Though the government favors investment," reports the U.S. Department of Commerce, "many investors trying to enter the market remain frustrated with the process. Potential investors often experience difficulties and delay in obtaining necessary clearances from a cumbersome bureaucracy. Large developments are inevitably contentious and quickly become political issues, necessitating cabinet decisions. Without consensus at this level, the investor faces additional delay. Several reports in the Australian and local media have charged corruption on the part of decision-makers. Some companies have reported delays in receiving investment approvals which they believe were attributable to their refusal to pay bribes."[2]

BANKING
Score: 4–Stable (high level of restrictions)

The government exercises a great deal of influence over the banking system in Papua New Guinea. Banks are not free to engage in all types of financial services.

WAGE AND PRICE CONTROLS
Score: 3–Stable (moderate level)

Wages and prices in Papua New Guinea are set by both the private and public sectors. The government sets prices on some goods and services, such as certain foodstuffs and agricultural goods.

PROPERTY RIGHTS
Score: 3–Stable (moderate level of protection)

Private property is safe from government expropriation, and the legal and judicial system is efficient. According to the U.S. Department of Commerce, Papua New Guinea "has a Western legal system inherited primarily from Australia. The courts, which are insulated from Government interference, provide a meaningful forum in which to enforce property and contractual rights, though the country does not have a written commercial code. The insolvency act is the source of bankruptcy law and controls the dissolution of failed corporations."[3] The lack of a commercial code, however, sometimes makes enforcement of property claims costly and ineffective.

REGULATION
Score: 4– (high level)

Establishing a business in Papua New Guinea can be difficult, especially if it requires extensive contact with lower levels of the bureaucracy and with local government. The government recently increased its regulation of the economy. According to the U.S. Department of Commerce, "The government has intervened heavily in economic activity through an extensive system of licensing and approval requirements and through trade restrictions, tariffs, and price controls." Some recent laws, including health and safety regulations and strict environmental policies, are making compliance increasingly burdensome, and corruption within the bureaucracy remains a problem. According to the U.S. Department of Commerce, "The bureaucratic procedure for resolving interagency differences is cumbersome [and] bribery is assumed by the media to be rife."[4] As a result, the country's regulation score is one point worse than last year.

BLACK MARKET
Score: 3–Stable (moderate level of activity)

The black market in Papua New Guinea is confined primarily to illegal and smuggled goods, as well as to pirated video and audio cassettes.

NOTES
1. Based on total taxes on international trade as a percentage of total imports.
2. U.S. Department of Commerce, *Country Commercial Guide,* 1997.
3. *Ibid.*
4. *Ibid.*

Paraguay   2.85

| 1997 Score: **2.75** | 1996 Score: **2.65** | 1995 Score: **2.75** |

Trade	2	Banking	2
Taxation	2.5	Wages and Prices	3
Government Intervention	2	Property Rights	4
Monetary Policy	4	Regulation	3
Foreign Investment	1	Black Market	5

Asunción ⦿

Paraguay gained its independence from Spain in 1811, but did not hold its first free democratic election until May 1993. The current government of President Juan Carlos Wasmosy is attempting to control government spending, reduce customs duties and inflation, and attract foreign investment. Although its economic liberalization policies have pushed Paraguay ahead of many of its neighbors in Latin America, the country remains plagued with corruption and a repressive police force. Paraguay has decreased its level of private property protection, as a result of which its overall score this year is 0.1 point worse than it was last year.

TRADE POLICY
Score: 2–Stable (low level of protectionism)

Paraguay's average tariff rate is almost 8 percent. There are no major nontariff barriers to trade, although there are barriers to some agricultural imports like poultry.

TAXATION
Score–Income taxation: 1–Stable (very low tax rates)
Score–Corporate taxation: 3–Stable (moderate tax rates)
Total Taxation Score: 2.5–Stable (moderate tax rates)

Paraguay imposes no taxes on income derived from personal work, services provided, or professional services rendered.[1] The top corporate tax rate is 30 percent. Paraguay also has a 30 percent capital gains tax, a 10 percent value-added tax, and a 26 percent payroll tax.

GOVERNMENT INTERVENTION IN THE ECONOMY
Score: 2–Stable (low level)

Government consumes almost 7.2 percent of Paraguay's GDP, up from 6 percent in 1990. Paraguay has a successful privatization program that involves selling off its airlines and other companies. Recent moves by the legislature have slowed this process, however, and many large firms remain government-owned.

MONETARY POLICY
Score: 4–Stable (high level of inflation)

Paraguay's average annual rate of inflation from 1985 to 1995 was 24.9 percent. In 1996, the rate was 10.6 percent.

CAPITAL FLOWS AND FOREIGN INVESTMENT
Score: 1–Stable (very low barriers)

There are few restrictions on foreign investment in Paraguay. Foreign and domestic companies are treated equally, and full repatriation of capital and profits is guaranteed by law. Some exceptions include bans on investment in the cement industry and in such public utilities as electricity, telephone, and water.

1	Hong Kong	1.25	77	Zambia	3.05
2	Singapore	1.30	80	Mali	3.10
3	Bahrain	1.70	80	Mongolia	3.10
4	New Zealand	1.75	80	Slovenia	3.10
5	Switzerland	1.90	83	Honduras	3.15
5	United States	1.90	83	Papua New Guinea	3.15
7	Luxembourg	1.95	85	Djibouti	3.20
7	Taiwan	1.95	85	Fiji	3.20
7	United Kingdom	1.95	85	Pakistan	3.20
10	Bahamas	2.00	88	Algeria	3.25
10	Ireland	2.00	88	Guinea	3.25
12	Australia	2.05	88	Lebanon	3.25
12	Japan	2.05	88	Mexico	3.25
14	Belgium	2.10	88	Senegal	3.25
14	Canada	2.10	88	Tanzania	3.25
14	United Arab Emirates	2.10	94	Nigeria	3.30
17	Austria	2.15	94	Romania	3.30
17	Chile	2.15	96	Brazil	3.35
17	Estonia	2.15	96	Cambodia	3.35
20	Czech Republic	2.20	96	Egypt	3.35
20	Netherlands	2.20	96	Ivory Coast	3.35
22	Denmark	2.25	96	Madagascar	3.35
22	Finland	2.25	96	Moldova	3.35
24	Germany	2.30	102	Nepal	3.40
24	Iceland	2.30	103	Cape Verde	3.44
24	South Korea	2.30	104	Armenia	3.45
27	Norway	2.35	104	Dominican Republic	3.45
28	Kuwait	2.40	104	Russia	3.45
28	Malaysia	2.40	107	Burkina Faso	3.50
28	Panama	2.40	107	Cameroon	3.50
28	Thailand	2.40	107	Lesotho	3.50
32	El Salvador	2.45	107	Nicaragua	3.50
32	Sri Lanka	2.45	107	Venezuela	3.50
32	Sweden	2.45	112	Gambia	3.60
35	France	2.50	112	Guyana	3.60
35	Italy	2.50	114	Bulgaria	3.65
35	Spain	2.50	114	Georgia	3.65
38	Trinidad and Tobago	2.55	114	Malawi	3.65
39	Argentina	2.60	117	Ethiopia	3.70
39	Barbados	2.60	117	India	3.70
39	Cyprus	2.60	117	Niger	3.70
39	Jamaica	2.60	120	Albania	3.75
39	Portugal	2.60	120	Bangladesh	3.75
44	Bolivia	2.65	120	China (PRC)	3.75
44	Oman	2.65	120	Congo	3.75
44	Philippines	2.65	120	Croatia	3.75
47	Swaziland	2.70	125	Chad	3.80
47	Uruguay	2.70	125	Mauritania	3.80
49	Botswana	2.75	125	Ukraine	3.80
49	Jordan	2.75	128	Sierra Leone	3.85
49	Namibia	2.75	129	Burundi	3.90
49	Tunisia	2.75	129	Suriname	3.90
53	Belize	2.80	129	Zimbabwe	3.90
53	Costa Rica	2.80	132	Haiti	4.00
53	Guatemala	2.80	132	Kyrgyzstan	4.00
53	Israel	2.80	132	Syria	4.00
53	Peru	2.80	135	Belarus	4.05
53	Saudi Arabia	2.80	136	Kazakstan	4.10
53	Turkey	2.80	136	Mozambique	4.10
53	Uganda	2.80	136	Yemen	4.10
53	Western Samoa	2.80	139	Sudan	4.20
62	Indonesia	2.85	140	Myanmar	4.30
62	Latvia	2.85	140	Rwanda	4.30
62	Malta	2.85	142	Angola	4.35
62	Paraguay	2.85	143	Azerbaijan	4.40
66	Greece	2.90	143	Tajikistan	4.40
66	Hungary	2.90	145	Turkmenistan	4.50
66	South Africa	2.90	146	Uzbekistan	4.55
69	Benin	2.95	147	Congo/Zaire	4.70
69	Ecuador	2.95	147	Iran	4.70
69	Gabon	2.95	147	Libya	4.70
69	Morocco	2.95	147	Somalia	4.70
69	Poland	2.95	147	Vietnam	4.70
74	Colombia	3.00	152	Bosnia	4.80
74	Ghana	3.00	153	Iraq	4.90
74	Lithuania	3.00	154	Cuba	5.00
77	Kenya	3.05	154	Laos	5.00
77	Slovak Republic	3.05	154	North Korea	5.00

Mostly Free

BANKING
Score: 2–Stable (low level of restrictions)

Of 30 commercial banks operating in Paraguay, 17 are domestic and 13 are branches of foreign banks. Banks may engage in most financial activities, including the selling of stocks, bonds, and other securities.

WAGE AND PRICE CONTROLS
Score: 3–Stable (moderate level)

Paraguay's government controls the prices of utilities, petroleum products, pharmaceuticals, and bus fares. Paraguay also maintains a minimum wage.

PROPERTY RIGHTS
Score: 4– (low level of protection)

Expropriation of property is still possible in Paraguay. In fact, recent reports indicate a decrease in protection of private property. According to the U.S. Department of Commerce, "In many cases [government] invasions [of land] are politically motivated, with parcels of land being awarded as political bounty by local politicians. The 1992 law allowing for expropriation calls for adequate compensation, but the financial straits of the Government make this difficult"[2] There also is increasing evidence that Paraguay's judicial system has failed to protect private property rights adequately. As the U.S. Department of Commerce reports, "A complicated and sometimes non-transparent legal system makes upholding property rights difficult."[3] Paraguay's property rights score is one point worse this year.[4]

REGULATION
Score: 3–Stable (moderate level)

Paraguay's government owns and operates several industries, including public utilities and companies involved in manufacturing cement and steel. These industries are tightly regulated by government officials who oversee production levels and pricing. Environmental, consumer, labor, financial, and other regulations also are burdensome. Another problem is bureaucratic corruption; according to the U.S. Department of State, "Key obstacles to continued reform include corruption."[5]

BLACK MARKET
Score: 5–Stable (very high level of activity)

Although the government has removed most restrictions on imports, the smuggling of illegal agricultural goods and products can be lucrative. According to the U.S. Department of State, the black market in Paraguay is growing.[6] Black market activity in pirated intellectual property alone, especially pirated audio and video products, costs the United States over $100 million in losses each year.[7]

NOTES

1. Paraguay places a 30 percent tax on individuals engaged in sole proprietorship. This tax, if applied across the entire population, would be negligible.
2. U.S. Department of Commerce, *Country Commercial Guide,* 1997.
3. *Ibid.*
4. The score in this factor has changed from 3 in 1997 to 4 in 1998. Previously unavailable data provide a more accurate understanding of the country's performance. Information on property rights comes from U.S. Department of Commerce, *Country Commercial Guide,* 1997. The methodology for this factor remains the same.
5. U.S. Department of State, *Country Reports on Economic Policy and Trade Practices,* 1997, p. 292.
6. U.S. Department of State, "Paraguay Country Report on Human Rights Practices for 1996," 1997.
7. U.S. Department of State, *Country Reports on Economic Policy and Trade Practices,* 1997.

Peru   2.80

1997 Score: **2.90**	1996 Score: **3.00**	1995 Score: **3.40**

Trade	2	Banking	2
Taxation	3	Wages and Prices	2
Government Intervention	1	Property Rights	3
Monetary Policy	5	Regulation	4
Foreign Investment	2	Black Market	4

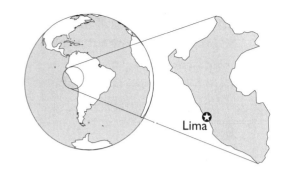

Lima

Since declaring its independence from Spain in 1821, Peru has been ruled by a succession of military governments. During the 1980s, it was among the world's most socialist and inefficient economies. Under Alberto Fujimori, who was elected president in 1990 and reelected in 1995, many important economic and trade reforms have been implemented, and subversive guerrilla activity has been virtually eliminated. Although far from achieving full liberalization, Peru has made great strides toward a free market. The government continues to privatize state-owned enterprises, and inflation is dropping. Peru recently reduced its barriers to trade. Thus, its overall score is 0.1 point better this year.

TRADE POLICY

Score: 2+ (low level of protectionism)

Peru has an average tariff rate of 9.85 percent,[1] down from 13.2 percent, and maintains few, if any, substantial nontariff barriers. Its trade score is one point better this year. "Almost all barriers to U.S. exports and direct investment have been eliminated over the past 6 years," reports the U.S. Department of State. "There are no qualitative or quantitative ceilings on imports. Import licenses have been abolished for all products except firearms, munitions, and explosives; chemical precursors (used in cocaine production); and ammonium nitrate fertilizer, which has been used as a blast enhancer for terrorist car bombs."[2]

TAXATION

Score–Income taxation: 2–Stable (low tax rates)
Score–Corporate taxation: 3–Stable (moderate tax rates)
Total Taxation Score: 3–Stable (moderate tax rates)

Peru's top income tax rate is 30 percent, and the average income is taxed at 0 percent. The corporate tax rate is a flat 30 percent. Peru also has a 30 percent capital gains tax and a sales tax.

GOVERNMENT INTERVENTION IN THE ECONOMY
Score: 1–Stable (very low level)

Government consumes only 8.2 percent of Peru's GDP. President Fujimori has succeeded in expanding the private sector while privatizing the public sector; the only areas in which the state has the primary role are education, mining, defense, and telecommunications. Many utilities are being privatized or at least opened to private investment.

MONETARY POLICY
Score: 5–Stable (very high level of inflation)

Peru's average annual rate of inflation from 1985 to 1995 was 398.5 percent, down from an average of 615.6 percent from 1985 to 1993. This decline is due primarily to progress toward controlling inflation since the early 1990s. In 1996, the rate of inflation fell to 11.8 percent. Historically, however, levels of inflation in Peru have been very high.

1	Hong Kong	1.25	77	Zambia	3.05
2	Singapore	1.30	80	Mali	3.10
3	Bahrain	1.70	80	Mongolia	3.10
4	New Zealand	1.75	80	Slovenia	3.10
5	Switzerland	1.90	83	Honduras	3.15
5	United States	1.90	83	Papua New Guinea	3.15
7	Luxembourg	1.95	85	Djibouti	3.20
7	Taiwan	1.95	85	Fiji	3.20
7	United Kingdom	1.95	85	Pakistan	3.20
10	Bahamas	2.00	88	Algeria	3.25
10	Ireland	2.00	88	Guinea	3.25
12	Australia	2.05	88	Lebanon	3.25
12	Japan	2.05	88	Mexico	3.25
14	Belgium	2.10	88	Senegal	3.25
14	Canada	2.10	88	Tanzania	3.25
14	United Arab Emirates	2.10	94	Nigeria	3.30
17	Austria	2.15	94	Romania	3.30
17	Chile	2.15	96	Brazil	3.35
17	Estonia	2.15	96	Cambodia	3.35
20	Czech Republic	2.20	96	Egypt	3.35
20	Netherlands	2.20	96	Ivory Coast	3.35
22	Denmark	2.25	96	Madagascar	3.35
22	Finland	2.25	96	Moldova	3.35
24	Germany	2.30	102	Nepal	3.40
24	Iceland	2.30	103	Cape Verde	3.44
24	South Korea	2.30	104	Armenia	3.45
27	Norway	2.35	104	Dominican Republic	3.45
28	Kuwait	2.40	104	Russia	3.45
28	Malaysia	2.40	107	Burkina Faso	3.50
28	Panama	2.40	107	Cameroon	3.50
28	Thailand	2.40	107	Lesotho	3.50
32	El Salvador	2.45	107	Nicaragua	3.50
32	Sri Lanka	2.45	107	Venezuela	3.50
32	Sweden	2.45	112	Gambia	3.60
35	France	2.50	112	Guyana	3.60
35	Italy	2.50	114	Bulgaria	3.65
35	Spain	2.50	114	Georgia	3.65
38	Trinidad and Tobago	2.55	114	Malawi	3.65
39	Argentina	2.60	117	Ethiopia	3.70
39	Barbados	2.60	117	India	3.70
39	Cyprus	2.60	117	Niger	3.70
39	Jamaica	2.60	120	Albania	3.75
39	Portugal	2.60	120	Bangladesh	3.75
44	Bolivia	2.65	120	China (PRC)	3.75
44	Oman	2.65	120	Congo	3.75
44	Philippines	2.65	120	Croatia	3.75
47	Swaziland	2.70	125	Chad	3.80
47	Uruguay	2.70	125	Mauritania	3.80
49	Botswana	2.75	125	Ukraine	3.80
49	Jordan	2.75	128	Sierra Leone	3.85
49	Namibia	2.75	129	Burundi	3.90
49	Tunisia	2.75	129	Suriname	3.90
53	Belize	2.80	129	Zimbabwe	3.90
53	Costa Rica	2.80	132	Haiti	4.00
53	Guatemala	2.80	132	Kyrgyzstan	4.00
53	Israel	2.80	132	Syria	4.00
53	Peru	2.80	135	Belarus	4.05
53	Saudi Arabia	2.80	136	Kazakstan	4.10
53	Turkey	2.80	136	Mozambique	4.10
53	Uganda	2.80	136	Yemen	4.10
53	Western Samoa	2.80	139	Sudan	4.20
62	Indonesia	2.85	140	Myanmar	4.30
62	Latvia	2.85	140	Rwanda	4.30
62	Malta	2.85	142	Angola	4.35
62	Paraguay	2.85	143	Azerbaijan	4.40
66	Greece	2.90	143	Tajikistan	4.40
66	Hungary	2.90	145	Turkmenistan	4.50
66	South Africa	2.90	146	Uzbekistan	4.55
69	Benin	2.95	147	Congo/Zaire	4.70
69	Ecuador	2.95	147	Iran	4.70
69	Gabon	2.95	147	Libya	4.70
69	Morocco	2.95	147	Somalia	4.70
69	Poland	2.95	147	Vietnam	4.70
74	Colombia	3.00	152	Bosnia	4.80
74	Ghana	3.00	153	Iraq	4.90
74	Lithuania	3.00	154	Cuba	5.00
77	Kenya	3.05	154	Laos	5.00
77	Slovak Republic	3.05	154	North Korea	5.00

Mostly Free

CAPITAL FLOWS AND FOREIGN INVESTMENT
Score: 2–Stable (low barriers)

The few restrictions imposed on foreign investment in Peru apply mainly to industries defined as vital to the national defense.

BANKING
Score: 2–Stable (low level of restrictions)

There are few restrictions on foreign banks in Peru. All banks may sell securities, real estate, and insurance policies, and all may make some investments, although they are restricted in their ability to invest in industrial firms. According to the U.S. Department of Commerce, "The Peruvian banking system has been cleaned up significantly with the liquidation of insolvent government sectoral development banks, as well as most savings and loans and cooperatives.... Peruvian law allows banks freely to take deposits and make loans in both foreign and domestic currency."[3]

WAGE AND PRICE CONTROLS
Score: 2–Stable (low level)

Most wages and prices in Peru are set by the market. The U.S. Department of State reports that "Price controls, direct subsidies and restrictions on foreign investment have been eliminated."[4] Peru maintains a minimum wage.

PROPERTY RIGHTS
Score: 3–Stable (moderate level of protection)

By global standards, private property is moderately protected in Peru; but the court system is corrupt, and it is difficult to get a fair hearing. According to the U.S. Department of Commerce, "Enforcement of property and contractual rights has generally been effective, although the Peruvian legal system is slow and inefficient. Improving the efficiency of the judicial system is a high priority of the Fujimori government."[5]

REGULATION
Score: 4–Stable (high level)

Even though the government has made significant progress in stamping out corruption, Peru remains plagued by a corrupt and inefficient bureaucracy. Obtaining a business license, although made easier in recent years, still may require bribes and can take a great deal of time. In addition, environmental regulations, which have been imposed only recently, are extremely burdensome.

BLACK MARKET
Score: 4–Stable (high level of activity)

Despite Peru's tremendous progress in reducing many black market operations (for example, in transportation), much of its labor force still operates in the informal sector. "Out of an estimated economically active population of 8 million," reports the U.S. Department of Commerce, "only about 7 percent belong to unions. Roughly two-thirds are employed in the informal sector, beyond government regulation and supervision."[6] Black market activity in the sale of pirated items from the United States and Europe is rampant.

NOTES

1. Based on taxes on international trade as a percentage of total imports.
2. U.S. Department of State, *Country Reports on Economic Policy and Trade Practices*, 1997, p. 296.
3. U.S. Department of Commerce, *Country Commercial Guide*, 1996.
4. U.S. Department of State, Country Reports on Economic Policy and Trade Practices, 1997.
5. U.S. Department of Commerce, *Country Commercial Guide*, 1996.
6. *Ibid.*

The Philippines 2.65

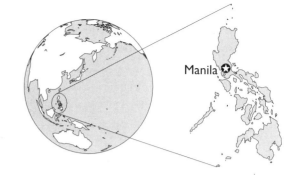

Manila

1997 Score: **2.80**	1996 Score: **2.90**	1995 Score: **3.30**

Trade	3	Banking	3
Taxation	3.5	Wages and Prices	2
Government Intervention	1	Property Rights	2
Monetary Policy	2	Regulation	3
Foreign Investment	3	Black Market	4

The Philippines became a U.S. colony in 1900. During World War II, the country was conquered by the Japanese, who remained in control until driven off by U.S. forces in 1945. On July 4, 1946, it became the independent Republic of the Philippines. The many battles fought in the Philippines during World War II destroyed much of the country's infrastructure, and the United States played a major role in reconstruction after the war. Nationalist economic policies pursued during the late 1950s and early 1960s laid the groundwork for protectionism and government interventionism, and successive administrations were plagued by ineffectiveness and corruption. Today, under the leadership of President Fidel Ramos, the Philippines is establishing a solid record of economic reform. In addition to dismantling some monopolies, opening banking to greater foreign competition, and reducing the level of regulation, the government recently managed to cut tariffs, reduce its consumption of economic output, and achieve lower levels of inflation. Because average tariff rates improved during the past year, the overall score for the Philippines also has improved by 0.15 point.

TRADE POLICY
Score: 3+ (moderate level of protectionism)

A recent law passed to reduce the tariff rate to 5 percent over the next several years has led to an average tariff rate of 12.95 percent. As a result, the Philippines' trade policy score is two points better this year. Republic Act 8179, passed in March 1996, eliminates all quantitative import restrictions on agricultural products (except rice) and replaces them with tariffs.

TAXATION
Score–Income taxation: 3– (moderate tax rates)
Score–Corporate taxation: 3–Stable (moderate tax rates)
Final Taxation Score: 3.5– (high tax rates)

The top income tax rate in the Philippines is 35 percent, and the rate for the average income level has increased to 11 percent. As a result, the Philippines' taxation score is one-half point worse this year. The top corporate tax is 35 percent. The Philippines also has a 35 percent capital gains tax and a 10 percent value-added tax.

GOVERNMENT INTERVENTION IN THE ECONOMY
Score: 1–Stable (very low level)

Government consumes 8.9 percent of GDP. Most state-owned companies are confined to utilities, and the government has made significant progress in privatizing other state-owned industries.

MONETARY POLICY
Score: 2–Stable (low level of inflation)

The average annual rate of inflation in the Philippines from 1985 to 1995 was 9.8 percent. In 1996, the rate was 8.4 percent.

1	Hong Kong	1.25	77	Zambia	3.05
2	Singapore	1.30	80	Mali	3.10
3	Bahrain	1.70	80	Mongolia	3.10
4	New Zealand	1.75	80	Slovenia	3.10
5	Switzerland	1.90	83	Honduras	3.15
5	United States	1.90	83	Papua New Guinea	3.15
7	Luxembourg	1.95	85	Djibouti	3.20
7	Taiwan	1.95	85	Fiji	3.20
7	United Kingdom	1.95	85	Pakistan	3.20
10	Bahamas	2.00	88	Algeria	3.25
10	Ireland	2.00	88	Guinea	3.25
12	Australia	2.05	88	Lebanon	3.25
12	Japan	2.05	88	Mexico	3.25
14	Belgium	2.10	88	Senegal	3.25
14	Canada	2.10	88	Tanzania	3.25
14	United Arab Emirates	2.10	94	Nigeria	3.30
17	Austria	2.15	94	Romania	3.30
17	Chile	2.15	96	Brazil	3.35
17	Estonia	2.15	96	Cambodia	3.35
20	Czech Republic	2.20	96	Egypt	3.35
20	Netherlands	2.20	96	Ivory Coast	3.35
22	Denmark	2.25	96	Madagascar	3.35
22	Finland	2.25	96	Moldova	3.35
24	Germany	2.30	102	Nepal	3.40
24	Iceland	2.30	103	Cape Verde	3.44
24	South Korea	2.30	104	Armenia	3.45
27	Norway	2.35	104	Dominican Republic	3.45
28	Kuwait	2.40	104	Russia	3.45
28	Malaysia	2.40	107	Burkina Faso	3.50
28	Panama	2.40	107	Cameroon	3.50
28	Thailand	2.40	107	Lesotho	3.50
32	El Salvador	2.45	107	Nicaragua	3.50
32	Sri Lanka	2.45	107	Venezuela	3.50
32	Sweden	2.45	112	Gambia	3.60
35	France	2.50	112	Guyana	3.60
35	Italy	2.50	114	Bulgaria	3.65
35	Spain	2.50	114	Georgia	3.65
38	Trinidad and Tobago	2.55	114	Malawi	3.65
39	Argentina	2.60	117	Ethiopia	3.70
39	Barbados	2.60	117	India	3.70
39	Cyprus	2.60	117	Niger	3.70
39	Jamaica	2.60	120	Albania	3.75
39	Portugal	2.60	120	Bangladesh	3.75
44	Bolivia	2.65	120	China (PRC)	3.75
44	Oman	2.65	120	Congo	3.75
44	Philippines	2.65	120	Croatia	3.75
47	Swaziland	2.70	125	Chad	3.80
47	Uruguay	2.70	125	Mauritania	3.80
49	Botswana	2.75	125	Ukraine	3.80
49	Jordan	2.75	128	Sierra Leone	3.85
49	Namibia	2.75	129	Burundi	3.90
49	Tunisia	2.75	129	Suriname	3.90
53	Belize	2.80	129	Zimbabwe	3.90
53	Costa Rica	2.80	132	Haiti	4.00
53	Guatemala	2.80	132	Kyrgyzstan	4.00
53	Israel	2.80	132	Syria	4.00
53	Peru	2.80	135	Belarus	4.05
53	Saudi Arabia	2.80	136	Kazakstan	4.10
53	Turkey	2.80	136	Mozambique	4.10
53	Uganda	2.80	136	Yemen	4.10
53	Western Samoa	2.80	139	Sudan	4.20
62	Indonesia	2.85	140	Myanmar	4.30
62	Latvia	2.85	140	Rwanda	4.30
62	Malta	2.85	142	Angola	4.35
62	Paraguay	2.85	143	Azerbaijan	4.40
66	Greece	2.90	143	Tajikistan	4.40
66	Hungary	2.90	145	Turkmenistan	4.50
66	South Africa	2.90	146	Uzbekistan	4.55
69	Benin	2.95	147	Congo/Zaire	4.70
69	Ecuador	2.95	147	Iran	4.70
69	Gabon	2.95	147	Libya	4.70
69	Morocco	2.95	147	Somalia	4.70
69	Poland	2.95	147	Vietnam	4.70
74	Colombia	3.00	152	Bosnia	4.80
74	Ghana	3.00	153	Iraq	4.90
74	Lithuania	3.00	154	Cuba	5.00
77	Kenya	3.05	154	Laos	5.00
77	Slovak Republic	3.05	154	North Korea	5.00

Mostly Free

CAPITAL FLOWS AND FOREIGN INVESTMENT
Score: 3–Stable (moderate barriers)

The Philippines maintains some barriers to foreign investment. Foreigners may not invest in advertising, the mass media, or public utilities, among other areas.

BANKING
Score: 3–Stable (moderate level of restrictions)

Although the government recently privatized the Philippines National Bank, the country's largest state-owned financial institution, it also continues to own shares in it. According to the U.S. Department of State, "A new law, signed in May 1994, relaxed restrictions in place since 1948. A foreign investor can enter either on a wholly owned branch basis or own up to 60 percent (up from 30 percent) of an existing domestic bank or new locally incorporated banking subsidiary."[1] Under this law, foreign banks may establish branches (but not wholly owned subsidiaries) and are limited to no more than six branches each.

WAGE AND PRICE CONTROLS
Score: 2–Stable (low level)

Although the Philippine government controls the prices of automobiles, petroleum products, electricity, water, and related utilities, most wages and prices are set by the market. The Philippines also has a minimum wage.

PROPERTY RIGHTS
Score: 2–Stable (high level of protection)

Expropriation of private property is unlikely. According to the U.S. Department of Commerce, "The Philippine judicial system can be easily accessed and the courts are known to intervene in commercial and regulatory issues. The judicial system is independent from the executive and legislative bodies and, for the most part, avoids interference from these branches."[2]

REGULATION
Score: 3–Stable (moderate level)

The Philippine government has eliminated some significantly burdensome regulations, but its regulatory regime is inconsistent, and regulations are applied haphazardly.

BLACK MARKET
Score: 4–Stable (high level of activity)

Even with an increase in the number of duty-free shops and a decline in smuggling, a substantial black market in pirated items exists in the Philippines. "Piracy of computer software is a serious problem," reports the Office of the United States Trade Representative.[3] According to the U.S. Department of State, "About 98 percent of all computer software sold is pirated. Computer shops routinely load software on machines as a free 'bonus' to entice sales.... [T]rademark counterfeiting is widespread. Many well-known international trademarks are copied, including denim jeans, designer shirts, and personal beauty and health products."[4]

NOTES

1. U.S. Department of State, *Country Reports on Economic Policy and Trade Practices,* 1997, p. 60.
2. U.S. Department of Commerce, *Country Commercial Guide,* 1997.
3. Office of the United States Trade Representative, *USTR 1997 National Trade Estimate,* p. 317.
4. U.S. Department of State, *Country Reports on Economic Policy and Trade Practices,* 1997, p. 62.

Poland 2.95

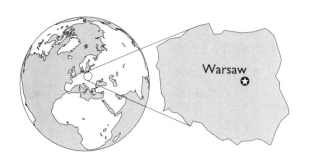

1997 Score: **3.15**	1996 Score: **3.05**	1995 Score: **3.25**

Trade	2	Banking	3
Taxation	3.5	Wages and Prices	3
Government Intervention	3	Property Rights	2
Monetary Policy	5	Regulation	3
Foreign Investment	2	Black Market	3

Poland, a former member of the Soviet-dominated Warsaw Pact, has progressed economically since the fall of the Iron Curtain. A six-party coalition led by Prime Minister Hanna Suchocka collapsed in September 1993 and was replaced by a two-party alliance of the former Communist Party and the Agrarian Party in 1994 and again in 1995. The current government of President Aleksandr Kwasniewski is committed to continuing economic reform. It has proceeded with privatization and currency stabilization. Poland has reduced its barriers to trade drastically. Thus, its overall score has improved by 0.2 point this year.

Trade Policy
Score: 2+ (low level of protectionism)

Poland reduced tariffs to an average rate of 6 percent in 1997, down from 15 percent in 1994. As a result, its trade score is two points better this year. Nontariff barriers (which in practice rarely hinder imports) include strict product standards and labeling requirements.

Taxation
Score–Income taxation: 2–Stable (low tax rates)
Score–Corporate taxation: 4–Stable (high tax rates)
Final Taxation Score: 3.5–Stable (high tax rates)

Poland's top income tax rate is 45 percent; the average income level is taxed at a rate of 0 percent. The top corporate tax rate is 38 percent, down from 40 percent in 1996. Poland also has a 38 percent capital gains tax and a 22 percent value-added tax.

Government Intervention in the Economy
Score: 3–Stable (moderate level)

Government consumes around 17.8 percent of Poland's GDP. Almost 40 percent of industrial production is generated by the state-owned sector of the economy.

Monetary Policy
Score: 5–Stable (very high level of inflation)

Poland's average annual rate of inflation between 1990 and 1994 was 147.9 percent. In 1994, the rate of inflation fell to 22 percent; in 1995, it was 23 percent; and in 1996, it was 19.1 percent. Despite this obvious progress, however, it remains very high by global standards.

Capital Flows and Foreign Investment
Score: 2–Stable (low barriers)

Domestic and foreign firms receive equal treatment under Poland's investment laws, and recent economic reforms are attracting increased foreign investment. According to the U.S. Department of State, "Poland has steadfastly pursued a policy of liberalizing trade, investment, and capital flows measures; it stands out

Mostly Free

1	Hong Kong	1.25	77	Zambia	3.05
2	Singapore	1.30	80	Mali	3.10
3	Bahrain	1.70	80	Mongolia	3.10
4	New Zealand	1.75	80	Slovenia	3.10
5	Switzerland	1.90	83	Honduras	3.15
5	United States	1.90	83	Papua New Guinea	3.15
7	Luxembourg	1.95	85	Djibouti	3.20
7	Taiwan	1.95	85	Fiji	3.20
7	United Kingdom	1.95	85	Pakistan	3.20
10	Bahamas	2.00	88	Algeria	3.25
10	Ireland	2.00	88	Guinea	3.25
12	Australia	2.05	88	Lebanon	3.25
12	Japan	2.05	88	Mexico	3.25
14	Belgium	2.10	88	Senegal	3.25
14	Canada	2.10	88	Tanzania	3.25
14	United Arab Emirates	2.10	94	Nigeria	3.30
17	Austria	2.15	94	Romania	3.30
17	Chile	2.15	96	Brazil	3.35
17	Estonia	2.15	96	Cambodia	3.35
20	Czech Republic	2.20	96	Egypt	3.35
20	Netherlands	2.20	96	Ivory Coast	3.35
22	Denmark	2.25	96	Madagascar	3.35
22	Finland	2.25	96	Moldova	3.35
24	Germany	2.30	102	Nepal	3.40
24	Iceland	2.30	103	Cape Verde	3.44
24	South Korea	2.30	104	Armenia	3.45
27	Norway	2.35	104	Dominican Republic	3.45
28	Kuwait	2.40	104	Russia	3.45
28	Malaysia	2.40	107	Burkina Faso	3.50
28	Panama	2.40	107	Cameroon	3.50
28	Thailand	2.40	107	Lesotho	3.50
32	El Salvador	2.45	107	Nicaragua	3.50
32	Sri Lanka	2.45	107	Venezuela	3.50
32	Sweden	2.45	112	Gambia	3.60
35	France	2.50	112	Guyana	3.60
35	Italy	2.50	114	Bulgaria	3.65
35	Spain	2.50	114	Georgia	3.65
38	Trinidad and Tobago	2.55	114	Malawi	3.65
39	Argentina	2.60	117	Ethiopia	3.70
39	Barbados	2.60	117	India	3.70
39	Cyprus	2.60	117	Niger	3.70
39	Jamaica	2.60	120	Albania	3.75
39	Portugal	2.60	120	Bangladesh	3.75
44	Bolivia	2.65	120	China (PRC)	3.75
44	Oman	2.65	120	Congo	3.75
44	Philippines	2.65	120	Croatia	3.75
47	Swaziland	2.70	125	Chad	3.80
47	Uruguay	2.70	125	Mauritania	3.80
49	Botswana	2.75	125	Ukraine	3.80
49	Jordan	2.75	128	Sierra Leone	3.85
49	Namibia	2.75	129	Burundi	3.90
49	Tunisia	2.75	129	Suriname	3.90
53	Belize	2.80	129	Zimbabwe	3.90
53	Costa Rica	2.80	132	Haiti	4.00
53	Guatemala	2.80	132	Kyrgyzstan	4.00
53	Israel	2.80	132	Syria	4.00
53	Peru	2.80	135	Belarus	4.05
53	Saudi Arabia	2.80	136	Kazakstan	4.10
53	Turkey	2.80	136	Mozambique	4.10
53	Uganda	2.80	136	Yemen	4.10
53	Western Samoa	2.80	139	Sudan	4.20
62	Indonesia	2.85	140	Myanmar	4.30
62	Latvia	2.85	140	Rwanda	4.30
62	Malta	2.85	142	Angola	4.35
62	Paraguay	2.85	143	Azerbaijan	4.40
66	Greece	2.90	143	Tajikistan	4.40
66	Hungary	2.90	145	Turkmenistan	4.50
66	South Africa	2.90	146	Uzbekistan	4.55
69	Benin	2.95	147	Congo/Zaire	4.70
69	Ecuador	2.95	147	Iran	4.70
69	Gabon	2.95	147	Libya	4.70
69	Morocco	2.95	147	Somalia	4.70
69	Poland	2.95	147	Vietnam	4.70
74	Colombia	3.00	152	Bosnia	4.80
74	Ghana	3.00	153	Iraq	4.90
74	Lithuania	3.00	154	Cuba	5.00
77	Kenya	3.05	154	Laos	5.00
77	Slovak Republic	3.05	154	North Korea	5.00

as one of the most successful and open transition economies."[1]

BANKING
Score: 3–Stable (moderate level of restrictions)

Poland's banking system, although becoming increasingly privatized, is still influenced by the government. Interest rates are not always set by market standards and may be driven by government budgetary concerns. This makes it more difficult for Poland's banks to provide affordable credit to needy businesses.

WAGE AND PRICE CONTROLS
Score: 3–Stable (moderate level)

Firms must gain permission from the government to raise prices on certain products (for example, fuel, transportation, and rent), and obtaining this permission may take as long as three months. Poland has a minimum wage law.

PROPERTY RIGHTS
Score: 2–Stable (high level of protection)

Private property is a constitutional right in Poland. Therefore, even though property is not always protected adequately by the courts and the legal system, expropriation is unlikely.

REGULATION
Score: 3–Stable (moderate level)

Despite some efforts at liberalization, Poland's regulatory regime remains an obstacle to the creation of new businesses. Some corruption persists, and labor, health, and safety regulations are applied randomly, creating uncertainty on the part of business owners and investors.

BLACK MARKET
Score: 3–Stable (moderate level of activity)

By global standards, Poland's black market is moderate. It also is shrinking. Although some labor, transportation, construction, and other services once were supplied routinely on the black market, an increasingly free market is reducing black market activity. Poland also has made significant progress toward protecting intellectual property, although the black market trade in computer software is growing. The U.S. Department of Commerce reports that as much as 80 percent of all computer software in Poland is pirated.[2]

NOTES
1. U.S. Department of State, *Country Reports on Economic Policy and Trade Practices,* 1997, p. 152.
2. U.S. Department of Commerce, *Country Commercial Guide,* 1997.

Portugal   2.60

1997 Score: **2.60**		1996 Score: **2.60**		1995 Score: **2.80**	
Trade	2	Banking	3		
Taxation	5	Wages and Prices	2		
Government Intervention	3	Property Rights	2		
Monetary Policy	2	Regulation	3		
Foreign Investment	2	Black Market	2		

Lisbon

Portugal has been an independent country since 1140. During the 1970s, it overthrew a dictatorship, entered a period of political chaos, and finally emerged as a constitutional republic. During the first few years following this political revolution, Portugal's government adopted socialist economic policies that were enshrined in the 1982 constitution. Economic growth sputtered. Portugal acceded to the European Union (EU) in 1986. Because of this change in policy, subsequent governments gradually liberalized the economy. In January 1996, the voters elected a Socialist Party government led by Prime Minister Jorge Sampaio. The Sampaio government is privatizing state-owned industries and cutting non–social service spending to meet the Maastricht budget deficit criteria. Today, Portugal remains burdened by a cumbersome bureaucracy, although it recently has managed to reduce inflation.

TRADE POLICY
Score: 2–Stable (low level of protectionism)

As a member of the EU, Portugal has an average tariff rate of 3.6 percent. As is common among EU members, however, it also requires import certificates for some agricultural products, and these may act as a barrier to foreign agricultural imports.

TAXATION
Score–Income taxation: 5–Stable (very high tax rates)
Score–Corporate taxation: 4–Stable (high tax rates)
Final Taxation Score: 5–Stable (very high tax rates)

Portugal's top income tax rate is 40 percent, and the average income level is taxed at 25 percent. The top corporate tax rate is 36 percent. Portugal also has a 36 percent capital gains tax, a 4 percent to 17 percent value-added tax, a 10 percent real estate tax, and a 50 percent inheritance tax.

GOVERNMENT INTERVENTION IN THE ECONOMY
Score: 3–Stable (moderate level)

Government consumes 19.4 percent of Portugal's GDP and continues to maintain major stakes in banking and the production of alcohol, cement, chemicals, food, glass, and electricity. To meet the Maastricht budget deficit criteria, however, the Socialist Party government has initiated a major privatization program.

MONETARY POLICY
Score: 2–Stable (low level of inflation)

Portugal's average annual rate of inflation from 1985 to 1995 was 11.2 percent. In 1996, the rate was 3.1 percent.

1	Hong Kong	1.25	77	Zambia	3.05
2	Singapore	1.30	80	Mali	3.10
3	Bahrain	1.70	80	Mongolia	3.10
4	New Zealand	1.75	80	Slovenia	3.10
5	Switzerland	1.90	83	Honduras	3.15
5	United States	1.90	83	Papua New Guinea	3.15
7	Luxembourg	1.95	85	Djibouti	3.20
7	Taiwan	1.95	85	Fiji	3.20
7	United Kingdom	1.95	85	Pakistan	3.20
10	Bahamas	2.00	88	Algeria	3.25
10	Ireland	2.00	88	Guinea	3.25
12	Australia	2.05	88	Lebanon	3.25
12	Japan	2.05	88	Mexico	3.25
14	Belgium	2.10	88	Senegal	3.25
14	Canada	2.10	88	Tanzania	3.25
14	United Arab Emirates	2.10	94	Nigeria	3.30
17	Austria	2.15	94	Romania	3.30
17	Chile	2.15	96	Brazil	3.35
17	Estonia	2.15	96	Cambodia	3.35
20	Czech Republic	2.20	96	Egypt	3.35
20	Netherlands	2.20	96	Ivory Coast	3.35
22	Denmark	2.25	96	Madagascar	3.35
22	Finland	2.25	96	Moldova	3.35
24	Germany	2.30	102	Nepal	3.40
24	Iceland	2.30	103	Cape Verde	3.44
24	South Korea	2.30	104	Armenia	3.45
27	Norway	2.35	104	Dominican Republic	3.45
28	Kuwait	2.40	104	Russia	3.45
28	Malaysia	2.40	107	Burkina Faso	3.50
28	Panama	2.40	107	Cameroon	3.50
28	Thailand	2.40	107	Lesotho	3.50
32	El Salvador	2.45	107	Nicaragua	3.50
32	Sri Lanka	2.45	107	Venezuela	3.50
32	Sweden	2.45	112	Gambia	3.60
35	France	2.50	112	Guyana	3.60
35	Italy	2.50	114	Bulgaria	3.65
35	Spain	2.50	114	Georgia	3.65
38	Trinidad and Tobago	2.55	114	Malawi	3.65
39	Argentina	2.60	117	Ethiopia	3.70
39	Barbados	2.60	117	India	3.70
39	Cyprus	2.60	117	Niger	3.70
39	Jamaica	2.60	120	Albania	3.75
39	Portugal	2.60	120	Bangladesh	3.75
44	Bolivia	2.65	120	China (PRC)	3.75
44	Oman	2.65	120	Congo	3.75
44	Philippines	2.65	120	Croatia	3.75
47	Swaziland	2.70	125	Chad	3.80
47	Uruguay	2.70	125	Mauritania	3.80
49	Botswana	2.75	125	Ukraine	3.80
49	Jordan	2.75	128	Sierra Leone	3.85
49	Namibia	2.75	129	Burundi	3.90
49	Tunisia	2.75	129	Suriname	3.90
53	Belize	2.80	129	Zimbabwe	3.90
53	Costa Rica	2.80	132	Haiti	4.00
53	Guatemala	2.80	132	Kyrgyzstan	4.00
53	Israel	2.80	132	Syria	4.00
53	Peru	2.80	135	Belarus	4.05
53	Saudi Arabia	2.80	136	Kazakstan	4.10
53	Turkey	2.80	136	Mozambique	4.10
53	Uganda	2.80	136	Yemen	4.10
53	Western Samoa	2.80	139	Sudan	4.20
62	Indonesia	2.85	140	Myanmar	4.30
62	Latvia	2.85	140	Rwanda	4.30
62	Malta	2.85	142	Angola	4.35
62	Paraguay	2.85	143	Azerbaijan	4.40
66	Greece	2.90	143	Tajikistan	4.40
66	Hungary	2.90	145	Turkmenistan	4.50
66	South Africa	2.90	146	Uzbekistan	4.55
69	Benin	2.95	147	Congo/Zaire	4.70
69	Ecuador	2.95	147	Iran	4.70
69	Gabon	2.95	147	Libya	4.70
69	Morocco	2.95	147	Somalia	4.70
69	Poland	2.95	147	Vietnam	4.70
74	Colombia	3.00	152	Bosnia	4.80
74	Ghana	3.00	153	Iraq	4.90
74	Lithuania	3.00	154	Cuba	5.00
77	Kenya	3.05	154	Laos	5.00
77	Slovak Republic	3.05	154	North Korea	5.00

Mostly Free

CAPITAL FLOWS AND FOREIGN INVESTMENT
Score: 2–Stable (low barriers)

Portugal has opened most of its industries to foreign investment. As a member of the EU, it treats foreign and domestic companies equally, although foreign investment is not permitted in postal carriers or in such public utilities as sewage treatment, transportation, and water services. Foreign investors may face some government opposition when investing in state-owned businesses that are being privatized.

BANKING
Score: 3–Stable (moderate level of restrictions)

As full owner of some of Portugal's large banks, including the Caixa Geral de Deposito and the Banco Fomento Exterior SA, the government plays a large role in controlling the lending practices of private banks. Because they are subsidized by the government, the state-owned banks enjoy an unfair competitive advantage against unsubsidized private banks, some of which have had to close as a result.

WAGE AND PRICE CONTROLS
Score: 2–Stable (low level)

The government eliminated almost all price controls in 1993, although the prices of electricity, water, and pharmaceutical products are still controlled. Portugal has a minimum wage.

PROPERTY RIGHTS
Score: 2–Stable (high level of protection)

Portugal is privatizing parts of its bloated state-owned sector, and citizens are increasing their purchases of shares in state-owned companies. This provides an expanding base of private property. Portugal has a relatively efficient legal system that protects property adequately in most cases. Expropriation is unlikely.

REGULATION
Score: 3–Stable (moderate level)

Despite some liberalization, the government still maintains significant regulation. As a result of Portugal's 1987 environmental protection law (the most stringent in the EU), for example, both new businesses and proposed business expansion projects must undergo cumbersome environmental impact reviews by various government bureaucracies—a hurdle that often proves too high for some businesses.

BLACK MARKET
Score: 2–Stable (low level of activity)

Portugal's black market is confined to such scarce goods as auto parts and pharmaceutical products. These scarcities are created by government-imposed price controls and trade quotas. Despite strong protection of intellectual property with stiff fines, there is black market activity in such pirated items as prerecorded music and video tapes.

Romania   3.30

1997 Score: **3.40**	1996 Score: **3.70**	1995 Score: **3.55**

Trade	2	Banking	3
Taxation	5	Wages and Prices	2
Government Intervention	3	Property Rights	4
Monetary Policy	5	Regulation	4
Foreign Investment	2	Black Market	3

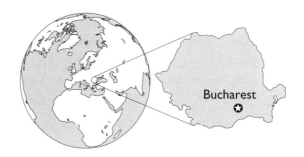

Bucharest

Romania's transition to democracy and free markets has been troubled and at times even violent. After the execution of former communist strongman Nicolae Ceausescu in 1989, Romania was ruled by the PDSR, a party controlled by former communists who were corrupt and lukewarm about free markets. Since the early 1990s, however, it has passed laws on taxation, foreign investment, and small business privatization. It also has reduced some barriers to trade. At the same time, however, the large state-owned sector continues to resist further reform. As a result of national elections held in November 1996, a coalition led by center-right President Emil Constantinescu of the Democratic Convention party came to power. Constantinescu has promised economic liberalization and reform, and developed a comprehensive program of privatization, currency stabilization, and deregulation. Money-losing enterprises are to be closed. Trade has increased, and the government has cracked down on organized crime, including the selling of pirated material in the black market. As a result, Romania's overall score is 0.1 point better this year than last year.

TRADE POLICY
Score: 2–Stable (low level of protectionism)

Romania's average tariff rate is 5.52 percent.[1] According to the U.S. Department of State, "There are no known laws that directly prejudice foreign trade or business operations [in Romania]."[2]

TAXATION
Score–Income taxation: 5–Stable (very high tax rates)
Score–Corporate taxation: 4–Stable (high tax rates)
Final Taxation Score: 5–Stable (very high tax rates)

Romania's top income tax rate is 60 percent, and the average income is taxed at 28 percent. The top corporate income tax rate is 38 percent. Romania also has a 38 percent capital gains tax and an 18 percent value-added tax.

GOVERNMENT INTERVENTION IN THE ECONOMY
Score: 3–Stable (moderately high level)

Government consumes 11 percent of Romania's GDP, most of which is produced by the public sector of the economy. Private firms and individuals make up only 5 percent of industrial output, 25 percent of construction, and 40 percent of services.

MONETARY POLICY
Score: 5–Stable (very high level of inflation)

Romania's rate of inflation was 295 percent in 1993, 61 percent in 1994, 29 percent in 1995, and 38.8 percent in 1996. Thus, the average rate of inflation since the collapse of the Soviet Empire remains very high.

1	Hong Kong	1.25	77	Zambia	3.05
2	Singapore	1.30	80	Mali	3.10
3	Bahrain	1.70	80	Mongolia	3.10
4	New Zealand	1.75	80	Slovenia	3.10
5	Switzerland	1.90	83	Honduras	3.15
5	United States	1.90	83	Papua New Guinea	3.15
7	Luxembourg	1.95	85	Djibouti	3.20
7	Taiwan	1.95	85	Fiji	3.20
7	United Kingdom	1.95	85	Pakistan	3.20
10	Bahamas	2.00	88	Algeria	3.25
10	Ireland	2.00	88	Guinea	3.25
12	Australia	2.05	88	Lebanon	3.25
12	Japan	2.05	88	Mexico	3.25
14	Belgium	2.10	88	Senegal	3.25
14	Canada	2.10	88	Tanzania	3.25
14	United Arab Emirates	2.10	94	Nigeria	3.30
17	Austria	2.15	94	Romania	3.30
17	Chile	2.15	96	Brazil	3.35
17	Estonia	2.15	96	Cambodia	3.35
20	Czech Republic	2.20	96	Egypt	3.35
20	Netherlands	2.20	96	Ivory Coast	3.35
22	Denmark	2.25	96	Madagascar	3.35
22	Finland	2.25	96	Moldova	3.35
24	Germany	2.30	102	Nepal	3.40
24	Iceland	2.30	103	Cape Verde	3.44
24	South Korea	2.30	104	Armenia	3.45
27	Norway	2.35	104	Dominican Republic	3.45
28	Kuwait	2.40	104	Russia	3.45
28	Malaysia	2.40	107	Burkina Faso	3.50
28	Panama	2.40	107	Cameroon	3.50
28	Thailand	2.40	107	Lesotho	3.50
32	El Salvador	2.45	107	Nicaragua	3.50
32	Sri Lanka	2.45	107	Venezuela	3.50
32	Sweden	2.45	112	Gambia	3.60
35	France	2.50	112	Guyana	3.60
35	Italy	2.50	114	Bulgaria	3.65
35	Spain	2.50	114	Georgia	3.65
38	Trinidad and Tobago	2.55	114	Malawi	3.65
39	Argentina	2.60	117	Ethiopia	3.70
39	Barbados	2.60	117	India	3.70
39	Cyprus	2.60	117	Niger	3.70
39	Jamaica	2.60	120	Albania	3.75
39	Portugal	2.60	120	Bangladesh	3.75
44	Bolivia	2.65	120	China (PRC)	3.75
44	Oman	2.65	120	Congo	3.75
44	Philippines	2.65	120	Croatia	3.75
47	Swaziland	2.70	125	Chad	3.80
47	Uruguay	2.70	125	Mauritania	3.80
49	Botswana	2.75	125	Ukraine	3.80
49	Jordan	2.75	128	Sierra Leone	3.85
49	Namibia	2.75	129	Burundi	3.90
49	Tunisia	2.75	129	Suriname	3.90
53	Belize	2.80	129	Zimbabwe	3.90
53	Costa Rica	2.80	132	Haiti	4.00
53	Guatemala	2.80	132	Kyrgyzstan	4.00
53	Israel	2.80	132	Syria	4.00
53	Peru	2.80	135	Belarus	4.05
53	Saudi Arabia	2.80	136	Kazakstan	4.10
53	Turkey	2.80	136	Mozambique	4.10
53	Uganda	2.80	136	Yemen	4.10
53	Western Samoa	2.80	139	Sudan	4.20
62	Indonesia	2.85	140	Myanmar	4.30
62	Latvia	2.85	140	Rwanda	4.30
62	Malta	2.85	142	Angola	4.35
62	Paraguay	2.85	143	Azerbaijan	4.40
66	Greece	2.90	143	Tajikistan	4.40
66	Hungary	2.90	145	Turkmenistan	4.50
66	South Africa	2.90	146	Uzbekistan	4.55
69	Benin	2.95	147	Congo/Zaire	4.70
69	Ecuador	2.95	147	Iran	4.70
69	Gabon	2.95	147	Libya	4.70
69	Morocco	2.95	147	Somalia	4.70
69	Poland	2.95	147	Vietnam	4.70
74	Colombia	3.00	152	Bosnia	4.80
74	Ghana	3.00	153	Iraq	4.90
74	Lithuania	3.00	154	Cuba	5.00
77	Kenya	3.05	154	Laos	5.00
77	Slovak Republic	3.05	154	North Korea	5.00

Mostly Unfree

Capital Flows and Foreign Investment
Score: 2–Stable (low barriers)

Romania maintains a fairly free market in foreign investment, and most barriers are the result of bureaucratic red tape and inefficiency. The Constantinescu government announced the attraction of foreign investment has become a top priority. According to the U.S. Department of State, "Investment barriers are few in Romania."[3]

Banking
Score: 3–Stable (moderate level of restrictions)

Although more private banks are opening in Romania, the banking environment has yet to mature. Banks are subject to strict government control. According to the U.S. Department of Commerce, "The system remains concentrated, with a relatively small number of wholly or predominately state-owned banks accounting for a substantial majority of loans and deposits."[4] Over the past seven years, however, the number of banks has grown more than fourfold, thereby increasing competition. Bank liberalization is expected to continue under the reformist government of Prime Minster Victor Ciorbea.

Wage and Price Controls
Score: 2–Stable (low level)

The market sets most prices in Romania. Exceptions include pharmaceutical products, public transportation services, and residential heat and energy supply. Romania has minimum wage laws.

Property Rights
Score: 4–Stable (low level of protection)

Romania is beginning to establish a system of property protection, but the legal system remains unable to arbitrate property rights disputes. "The judicial system," reports the U.S. Department of State, "has been subject to executive branch influence, although it is increasingly independent."[5] According to the U.S. Department of Commerce, "Property and contractual rights are recognized, but enforcement is not always effective."[6]

Regulation
Score: 4–Stable (high level)

Regulations remain subject to haphazard application. Romania has made progress in streamlining its bureaucracy, which makes it easier for businesses to obtain licenses, but the bureaucracy continues to be both cumbersome and inefficient. According to the U.S. Department of Commerce, "The Romanian government does not yet have a transparent policy to foster competition. The presence of state-owned government-subsidized enterprises in the economy is a major impediment to the efficient mobilization of capital. Cumbersome and non-transparent bureaucratic procedures are a major problem. Foreign investors point to the excessive time it takes to secure the necessary zoning permits, property titles, licenses, and utility hook-ups."[7] In addition, corruption remains endemic: "U.S. businesses have complained of corruption in all levels of government in Romania.... In some cases, demands for pay-offs by mid- to low-level officials can reach the point of harassment. Corruption in Romania can constitute an actual business risk."[8]

Black Market
Score: 3+ (moderate level of activity)

Almost half of Romania's economic activity is performed in the black market because the country's legitimate economy cannot provide basic consumer needs. Laws protecting intellectual property rights have reduced piracy in these items, however. In 1996, the U.S. Department of State reported that "Pirated copies of audio and video cassette recordings are inexpensive and sold openly."[9] Now it reports that "Pirated copies of audio and video cassette recordings are available, but not openly displayed."[10] This represents a renewed effort to crack down on sales of pirated material. As a result of this reduced activity, Romania's black market score is one point better this year.

Notes

1. Based on total taxes on international trade as a percentage of total imports.
2. U.S. Department of State, *Country Reports on Economic Policy and Trade Practices*, 1997, p. 164.
3. *Ibid.*
4. U.S. Department of Commerce, *Country Commercial Guide*, 1997.
5. U.S. Department of State, "Romania Country Report on Human Rights Practices for 1996," 1997.
6. U.S. Department of Commerce, *Country Commercial Guide*, 1997.
7. *Ibid.*
8. *Ibid.*
9. U.S. Department of State, *Country Reports on Economic Policy and Trade Practices*, 1996, p. 257.
10. U.S. Department of State, *Country Reports on Economic Policy and Trade Practices*, 1997, p. 165.

Russia   3.45

| 1997 Score: **3.65** | 1996 Score: **3.50** | 1995 Score: **3.50** |

Trade	4	Banking	2
Taxation	3.5	Wages and Prices	3
Government Intervention	3	Property Rights	3
Monetary Policy	5	Regulation	4
Foreign Investment	3	Black Market	4

Moscow

Russia, the largest of the former Soviet republics, has struggled for several years to establish democratic political institutions and a free-market economy. Significant progress has been achieved, although much needs to be done. Privatization has been disorderly, and corruption is rampant. The banking and investment systems were in disarray and millions of investors were defrauded in 1994 and 1995. The flight of Russian capital to the West has slowed considerably, although accurate estimates are not available. The result has been economic stagnation, civil unrest, coup attempts, and political polarization. At the same time, however, the orderly 1995 parliamentary and 1996 presidential elections indicate that reforms have begun to take root. Having rejected both the communists and the ultranationalists, Russia's voters generally continue to support economic reform. Russia has reduced its average tariff rate and its official government consumption rate. As a result, its overall score is 0.2 point better this year.

TRADE POLICY
Score: 4+ (high level of protectionism)

Russia's tariff rates range from 5 percent to 30 percent, with an average rate of 10.67 percent, down from 17 percent in 1994.[1] As a result, its trade score is one point better than last year. The situation may improve further with Russia's accession to the World Trade Organization, which should take place before the end of the century. Corruption is a problem in the customs services, and bribes are often necessary to bring goods into the country. According to the U.S. Department of State, "Customs regulations change frequently and often without sufficient notice...and are subject to arbitrary application."[2]

TAXATION
Score–Income taxation: 3–Stable (moderate tax rates)
Score–Corporate taxation: 3–Stable (moderate tax rates)
Final Taxation Score: 3.5–Stable (high tax rates)

Russia's top income tax rate is 35 percent, up from 30 percent last year, and the average income level is taxed at 12 percent. The top corporate income tax rate (including both federal and regional taxes) is 35 percent. Russia also has a 35 percent capital gains tax, a 20 percent value-added tax, and a social payments tax.[3]

GOVERNMENT INTERVENTION IN THE ECONOMY
Score: 3+ (moderate level)

Government officially consumes 18 percent of Russia's GDP, down from over 25 percent in the early 1990s. As a result, Russia's government intervention score is one point better this year. State-owned enterprises, however, still account for most industrial production. The government also subsidizes heavily such money-losing industries as coal mining, ferrous and nonferrous metals, and agriculture.

1	Hong Kong	1.25	77	Zambia	3.05
2	Singapore	1.30	80	Mali	3.10
3	Bahrain	1.70	80	Mongolia	3.10
4	New Zealand	1.75	80	Slovenia	3.10
5	Switzerland	1.90	83	Honduras	3.15
5	United States	1.90	83	Papua New Guinea	3.15
7	Luxembourg	1.95	85	Djibouti	3.20
7	Taiwan	1.95	85	Fiji	3.20
7	United Kingdom	1.95	85	Pakistan	3.20
10	Bahamas	2.00	88	Algeria	3.25
10	Ireland	2.00	88	Guinea	3.25
12	Australia	2.05	88	Lebanon	3.25
12	Japan	2.05	88	Mexico	3.25
14	Belgium	2.10	88	Senegal	3.25
14	Canada	2.10	88	Tanzania	3.25
14	United Arab Emirates	2.10	94	Nigeria	3.30
17	Austria	2.15	94	Romania	3.30
17	Chile	2.15	96	Brazil	3.35
17	Estonia	2.15	96	Cambodia	3.35
20	Czech Republic	2.20	96	Egypt	3.35
20	Netherlands	2.20	96	Ivory Coast	3.35
22	Denmark	2.25	96	Madagascar	3.35
22	Finland	2.25	96	Moldova	3.35
24	Germany	2.30	102	Nepal	3.40
24	Iceland	2.30	103	Cape Verde	3.44
24	South Korea	2.30	104	Armenia	3.45
27	Norway	2.35	104	Dominican Republic	3.45
28	Kuwait	2.40	104	Russia	3.45
28	Malaysia	2.40	107	Burkina Faso	3.50
28	Panama	2.40	107	Cameroon	3.50
28	Thailand	2.40	107	Lesotho	3.50
32	El Salvador	2.45	107	Nicaragua	3.50
32	Sri Lanka	2.45	107	Venezuela	3.50
32	Sweden	2.45	112	Gambia	3.60
35	France	2.50	112	Guyana	3.60
35	Italy	2.50	114	Bulgaria	3.65
35	Spain	2.50	114	Georgia	3.65
38	Trinidad and Tobago	2.55	114	Malawi	3.65
39	Argentina	2.60	117	Ethiopia	3.70
39	Barbados	2.60	117	India	3.70
39	Cyprus	2.60	117	Niger	3.70
39	Jamaica	2.60	120	Albania	3.75
39	Portugal	2.60	120	Bangladesh	3.75
44	Bolivia	2.65	120	China (PRC)	3.75
44	Oman	2.65	120	Congo	3.75
44	Philippines	2.65	120	Croatia	3.75
47	Swaziland	2.70	125	Chad	3.80
47	Uruguay	2.70	125	Mauritania	3.80
49	Botswana	2.75	125	Ukraine	3.80
49	Jordan	2.75	128	Sierra Leone	3.85
49	Namibia	2.75	129	Burundi	3.90
49	Tunisia	2.75	129	Suriname	3.90
53	Belize	2.80	129	Zimbabwe	3.90
53	Costa Rica	2.80	132	Haiti	4.00
53	Guatemala	2.80	132	Kyrgyzstan	4.00
53	Israel	2.80	132	Syria	4.00
53	Peru	2.80	135	Belarus	4.05
53	Saudi Arabia	2.80	136	Kazakstan	4.10
53	Turkey	2.80	136	Mozambique	4.10
53	Uganda	2.80	136	Yemen	4.10
53	Western Samoa	2.80	139	Sudan	4.20
62	Indonesia	2.85	140	Myanmar	4.30
62	Latvia	2.85	140	Rwanda	4.30
62	Malta	2.85	142	Angola	4.35
62	Paraguay	2.85	143	Azerbaijan	4.40
66	Greece	2.90	143	Tajikistan	4.40
66	Hungary	2.90	145	Turkmenistan	4.50
66	South Africa	2.90	146	Uzbekistan	4.55
69	Benin	2.95	147	Congo/Zaire	4.70
69	Ecuador	2.95	147	Iran	4.70
69	Gabon	2.95	147	Libya	4.70
69	Morocco	2.95	147	Somalia	4.70
69	Poland	2.95	147	Vietnam	4.70
74	Colombia	3.00	152	Bosnia	4.80
74	Ghana	3.00	153	Iraq	4.90
74	Lithuania	3.00	154	Cuba	5.00
77	Kenya	3.05	154	Laos	5.00
77	Slovak Republic	3.05	154	North Korea	5.00

Mostly Unfree

MONETARY POLICY
Score: 5–Stable (very high level of inflation)

Russia's government has achieved significant progress in bringing inflation under control. In 1992, the rate of inflation exceeded 1,300 percent. In 1993, it fell to 843 percent; in 1994, it was 203 percent; and in 1995, it was 133 percent.[4] In 1996, it fell to 26 percent. Historically, however, and despite significant progress in reducing inflation from its extremely high 1992 levels, Russia has had very high rates of inflation by global standards.

CAPITAL FLOWS AND FOREIGN INVESTMENT
Score: 3–Stable (moderate barriers)

A 1991 Russian law permits foreigners to acquire newly privatized firms and to establish wholly owned companies. By global standards, there are few legal restrictions on foreign investment; exceptions include investments in banking, securities, and insurance firms. The most significant barriers to foreign investment are legal uncertainty, crime and corruption, poor infrastructure, and political instability. "While the policy of the Russian government is to encourage foreign investment," reports the U.S. Department of Commerce, "it has had difficulties in creating a stable and attractive investment climate. Economic and political uncertainties are disincentives to companies looking for investment opportunities. Although there are no significant legal barriers to doing business in Russia, the absence of sufficiently developed civil, commercial and criminal codes is a major constraint. In addition, high and unstable taxation, a rise in violent crime, capital flight and a lag in development of local long-term capital are problems for business. Bureaucratic requirements can be confusing and burdensome to investors and bureaucratic discretion may be capricious in awarding tenders or development rights to companies."[5]

BANKING
Score: 2–Stable (low level of restrictions)

Many of Russia's state-owned banks have been privatized, and there is fierce competition in the commercial banking market. Foreign banks now operate in Russia, although they are allowed to offer only a limited range of services and most maintain only representative offices. The environment is becoming more competitive, with only limited government influence. According to the U.S. Department of Commerce, "The commercial banking system has been developing rapidly and the largest banks offer a full range of modern banking services."[6]

WAGE AND PRICE CONTROLS
Score: 3–Stable (moderate level)

Some 90 percent of all prices in Russia are set by free enterprise, with 5 percent fixed by the state and another 5 percent subject to government limits on the amount of profitability. Price controls remain on fuel and energy, grain, public transportation, medicine, and municipally owned housing rent.[7] Because the government controls much of the economy through its ownership of the public sector, however, it also exercises a high level of indirect control over wages and prices. Russia also has a minimum wage.

PROPERTY RIGHTS
Score: 3–Stable (moderate level of protection)

Although private property is guaranteed in the constitution adopted in 1993, protection remains significantly lax. The court system works poorly, and no clear and concise method for the settlement of property disputes has been developed. Moreover, protection of private property receives different levels of police attention in different localities, and both corruption and organized crime remain significant threats. According to the U.S. Department of Commerce, "Russia has a body of conflicting, overlapping and rapidly changing laws, decrees and regulations which has resulted in an ad hoc and unpredictable approach to doing business. Independent dispute resolution in Russia is difficult to obtain; the judicial system is poorly developed. Regional and local courts are not accustomed to adjudicating either commercial or international matters, and they (as well as courts in Moscow) are often subject to political pressure."[8]

REGULATION
Score: 4–Stable (high level)

Some regulations are arbitrary and unevenly enforced, and corruption in the bureaucracy remains a serious problem. According to the U.S. Department of Commerce, "Unfortunately, legal and judicial reforms have not kept pace with criminal advances. Much crime is tied to commercial activity, with one-half of all entrepreneurs in a recent survey reporting that they must pay kick-backs and protection to stay in business. Failure to make these payments can be fatal and may generally prove a disincentive to the creation of new businesses. In addition, Russia's inefficient bureaucracy is getting worse, with the result that some 85 different taxes are applied—often arbitrarily—to businesses and individuals. Businesses frequently complain about the unpredictability of these taxes."[9]

BLACK MARKET
Score: 4–Stable (high level of activity)

Despite recent moves to establish a free market, Russia's informal sector is massive even though it has shrunk considerably since 1991. Russia has not enforced its intellectual property laws, and piracy is rampant. "While the Russian government has successfully passed good laws on protection of intellectual property," reports the U.S. Department of Commerce, "enforcement of those laws has been a low priority.... Until these measures become reality...there is widespread marketing of pirated U.S. (and other) videocassettes, recordings, books, computer software, clothes and toys. Losses to manufacturers, authors and others are estimated to be in the hundreds of millions of dollars."[10] Russian organized crime has moved from such traditional activities as prostitution, drugs, and illegal arms sales to money-laundering, commodity smuggling, and bank fraud.

NOTES

1. Based on total taxes on international trade as a percentage of total imports.
2. U.S. Department of State, *Country Reports on Economic Policy and Trade Practices*, 1997, p. 168.
3. Russia has many overlapping, contradictory, and arbitrarily applied taxes. It also has varying and sometimes rapidly changing municipal and local taxes that could raise overall rates to more than 100 percent. For purposes of methodological consistency, however, only those taxes that are reported in Ernst & Young's *Worldwide Income and Corporate Tax Guides* are used here. The arbitrary application of many taxes is taken into account in the regulation factor.
4. Based on the Consumer Price Index; from U.S. Department of State, *Country Reports on Economic Policy and Trade Practices*, 1997, p. 166.
5. U.S. Department of Commerce, *Country Commercial Guide*, 1997.
6. *Ibid.*
7. Economist Intelligence Unit, *ILT Reports*, November 1996, p. 29.
8. U.S. Department of Commerce, *Country Commercial Guide*, 1997.
9. U.S. Department of Commerce, "Russia—Investment Climate," *Market Research Reports*, July 31, 1996.
10. *Ibid.*

Rwanda   4.30

Trade	5	Banking	5
Taxation	5	Wages and Prices	3
Government Intervention	4	Property Rights	5
Monetary Policy	2	Regulation	5
Foreign Investment	4	Black Market	5

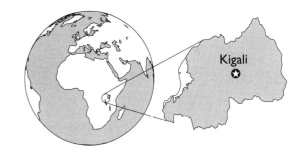

Kigali

After winning its independence from a Belgian-administered United Nations trusteeship in 1962, Rwanda almost immediately became a major recipient of foreign aid. Although proponents of foreign aid often point to Rwanda to demonstrate what they think could happen when foreign aid is cut, the facts are that Rwanda received its first foreign aid dollars from the United States in the mid-1960s and has been a major recipient ever since. Moreover, during the 1960s and 1970s, the government did nothing to establish the basis for a free market. As a result, the country has one of Africa's poorest economies (estimated per capita GNP was $180 in 1995) and remains one of the most economically repressed countries in the world. Poor economic policies and devastating internal conflicts have severely crippled Rwanda's economy, which averaged -17.3 percent growth from 1991 to 1994. In fiscal year 1997, the United States sent another $59 million in aid to Rwanda, which continues to be plagued by civil unrest, political instability, and ethnic warfare. Although the government has attempted to reduce inflation over the past several years, World Bank sources indicate that inflation has increased over historic levels. As a result, Rwanda's overall score is 0.1 point worse this year.

TRADE POLICY
Score: 5–Stable (very high level of protectionism)

Import duties in Rwanda range from 10 percent to 60 percent, and the borders are virtually closed to commerce, mainly because of civil unrest. According to the U.S. Department of State, "Violent attacks and terrorist threats against foreign aid workers have increased since mid-January 1997 and the country suffers from low-intensity insurgent attacks in all areas. Poor communication, transportation, and health services also continue to make travel in Rwanda difficult and potentially hazardous."[1]

TAXATION
Score–Income taxation: 5–Stable (very high tax rates)
Score–Corporate taxation: 5–Stable (very high tax rates)
Final Taxation Score: 5–Stable (very high tax rates)

Rwanda's central government is beginning to establish official taxation guidelines and collection services. Taxation most often takes the form, however, of private property confiscation by corrupt bureaucrats, armed insurgents, and terrorists.

GOVERNMENT INTERVENTION IN THE ECONOMY
Score: 4–Stable (very high level)

In 1993 (the most recent year for which a figure is available), government consumed 22 percent of Rwanda's GDP. Today, little economic activity occurs outside the public sector, and most private-sector economic activity occurs in the black market.

1	Hong Kong	1.25	77 Zambia	3.05
2	Singapore	1.30	80 Mali	3.10
3	Bahrain	1.70	80 Mongolia	3.10
4	New Zealand	1.75	80 Slovenia	3.10
5	Switzerland	1.90	83 Honduras	3.15
5	United States	1.90	83 Papua New Guinea	3.15
7	Luxembourg	1.95	85 Djibouti	3.20
7	Taiwan	1.95	85 Fiji	3.20
7	United Kingdom	1.95	85 Pakistan	3.20
10	Bahamas	2.00	88 Algeria	3.25
10	Ireland	2.00	88 Guinea	3.25
12	Australia	2.05	88 Lebanon	3.25
12	Japan	2.05	88 Mexico	3.25
14	Belgium	2.10	88 Senegal	3.25
14	Canada	2.10	88 Tanzania	3.25
14	United Arab Emirates	2.10	94 Nigeria	3.30
17	Austria	2.15	94 Romania	3.30
17	Chile	2.15	96 Brazil	3.35
17	Estonia	2.15	96 Cambodia	3.35
20	Czech Republic	2.20	96 Egypt	3.35
20	Netherlands	2.20	96 Ivory Coast	3.35
22	Denmark	2.25	96 Madagascar	3.35
22	Finland	2.25	96 Moldova	3.35
24	Germany	2.30	102 Nepal	3.40
24	Iceland	2.30	103 Cape Verde	3.44
24	South Korea	2.30	104 Armenia	3.45
27	Norway	2.35	104 Dominican Republic	3.45
28	Kuwait	2.40	104 Russia	3.45
28	Malaysia	2.40	107 Burkina Faso	3.50
28	Panama	2.40	107 Cameroon	3.50
28	Thailand	2.40	107 Lesotho	3.50
32	El Salvador	2.45	107 Nicaragua	3.50
32	Sri Lanka	2.45	107 Venezuela	3.50
32	Sweden	2.45	112 Gambia	3.60
35	France	2.50	112 Guyana	3.60
35	Italy	2.50	114 Bulgaria	3.65
35	Spain	2.50	114 Georgia	3.65
38	Trinidad and Tobago	2.55	114 Malawi	3.65
39	Argentina	2.60	117 Ethiopia	3.70
39	Barbados	2.60	117 India	3.70
39	Cyprus	2.60	117 Niger	3.70
39	Jamaica	2.60	120 Albania	3.75
39	Portugal	2.60	120 Bangladesh	3.75
44	Bolivia	2.65	120 China (PRC)	3.75
44	Oman	2.65	120 Congo	3.75
44	Philippines	2.65	120 Croatia	3.75
47	Swaziland	2.70	125 Chad	3.80
47	Uruguay	2.70	125 Mauritania	3.80
49	Botswana	2.75	125 Ukraine	3.80
49	Jordan	2.75	128 Sierra Leone	3.85
49	Namibia	2.75	129 Burundi	3.90
49	Tunisia	2.75	129 Suriname	3.90
53	Belize	2.80	129 Zimbabwe	3.90
53	Costa Rica	2.80	132 Haiti	4.00
53	Guatemala	2.80	132 Kyrgyzstan	4.00
53	Israel	2.80	132 Syria	4.00
53	Peru	2.80	135 Belarus	4.05
53	Saudi Arabia	2.80	136 Kazakstan	4.10
53	Turkey	2.80	136 Mozambique	4.10
53	Uganda	2.80	136 Yemen	4.10
53	Western Samoa	2.80	139 Sudan	4.20
62	Indonesia	2.85	140 Myanmar	4.30
62	Latvia	2.85	140 Rwanda	4.30
62	Malta	2.85	142 Angola	4.35
62	Paraguay	2.85	143 Azerbaijan	4.40
66	Greece	2.90	143 Tajikistan	4.40
66	Hungary	2.90	145 Turkmenistan	4.50
66	South Africa	2.90	146 Uzbekistan	4.55
69	Benin	2.95	147 Congo/Zaire	4.70
69	Ecuador	2.95	147 Iran	4.70
69	Gabon	2.95	147 Libya	4.70
69	Morocco	2.95	147 Somalia	4.70
69	Poland	2.95	147 Vietnam	4.70
74	Colombia	3.00	152 Bosnia	4.80
74	Ghana	3.00	153 Iraq	4.90
74	Lithuania	3.00	154 Cuba	5.00
77	Kenya	3.05	154 Laos	5.00
77	Slovak Republic	3.05	154 North Korea	5.00

Repressed

Monetary Policy
Score: 2– (low level of inflation)

The average annual rate of inflation from 1985 to 1995 was 10.4 percent, up from 3.7 percent. As a result, Rwanda's score is one point worse this year.

Capital Flows and Foreign Investment
Score: 4–Stable (high barriers)

Rwanda remains in economic ruin, with no clear protection of foreign investment. The most significant threats to investment continue to be armed bandits, rampant street crime, and the lack of individual freedom of movement. The government is attempting, however, to limit criminal activity, establish an up-to-date investment code, and reform its legal institutions to protect contracts.

Banking
Score: 5–Stable (very high level of restrictions)

Rwanda's banking system has collapsed, forcing banks to operate in primitive conditions. Although it is beginning to recover, the financial system remains in disarray. According to the U.S. Department of State, "The Rwandan franc is exchangeable for hard currencies in Bureaux de Change and Banks. Several Kigali Banks can handle wire transfers from U.S. banks; banks outside Kigali are slowly re-opening. Credit cards are accepted at only a few hotels in Kigali and only to settle hotel bills. Travelers should expect to handle most expenses, including air tickets, in cash."[2]

Wage and Price Controls
Score: 3–Stable (moderate level)

Wages and prices in Rwanda are set mainly by the market through barter. The government is not powerful enough to enforce laws that set prices, although there are official price controls on coffee and tea. Rwanda maintains a minimum wage.

Property Rights
Score: 5–Stable (very low level of protection)

Private property is virtually nonexistent in Rwanda, and property is subject to frequent confiscation by warring clans and corrupt government officials. According to the U.S. Department of Commerce, "Many properties were occupied by squatters after the genocide, and while the law states that such properties should be returned to the owners on their return to Rwanda, the execution of the law is proving difficult given the shortage of housing and commercial properties."[3]

Regulation
Score: 5–Stable (very high level)

Rwanda's government has yet to establish a regulatory regime for the country. Most business regulations are chaotic and subject to change, depending on which ministry is in charge of implementing them, and the jurisdictions of the various ministries often overlap.

Black Market
Score: 5–Stable (very high level of activity)

Most economic activity in Rwanda occurs in the black market.

Notes

1. U.S. Department of State Travel Advisory, 1997.
2. *Ibid.*
3. U.S. Department of Commerce, "Rwanda—Economic Overview," *Market Research Reports,* 1997.

Saudi Arabia 2.80

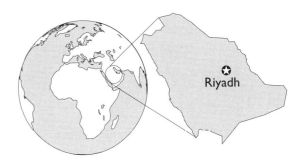

Riyadh

1997 Score: **2.80**	1996 Score: **2.90**	1995 Score: **n/a**

Trade	4	Banking	3
Taxation	4	Wages and Prices	3
Government Intervention	4	Property Rights	1
Monetary Policy	1	Regulation	2
Foreign Investment	4	Black Market	2

Saudi Arabia takes its name from the Saud family, which rose to prominence in central Arabia around 1750. The modern Saudi state was formed in 1902 under King Abdul Aziz Ibn Saud, who enlarged his holdings until uniting them as the Kingdom of Saudi Arabia in 1932. Oil was discovered in the 1930s, and large-scale production began after World War II. Saudi Arabia today has the world's largest oil reserves and, as the world's largest oil exporter, holds a dominant role within the Organization of Petroleum Exporting Countries. It also has a developing economy with a large government sector. Regulations favor Saudi businesses and often discriminate against foreigners.

TRADE POLICY
Score: 4–Stable (high level of protectionism)

Saudi Arabia's average tariff rate is about 13 percent. Nontariff barriers include strict labeling and certification requirements, import licenses, and import bans.

TAXATION
Score–Income taxation: 3–Stable (moderate tax rates)
Score–Corporate taxation: 4–Stable (high tax rates)
Final Taxation Score: 4–Stable (high tax rates)

Saudi Arabia's top income tax rate is 30 percent, and the average taxpayer is in the 10 percent bracket. The top marginal corporate tax rate is 45 percent. The government imposes several other taxes, including a 45 percent capital gains tax.

GOVERNMENT INTERVENTION IN THE ECONOMY
Score: 4–Stable (high level)

Government consumes 27 percent of Saudi Arabia's GDP; it also generates most of the country's GDP. According to the Economist Intelligence Unit, "Although the government emphasises its basic commitment to free enterprise, it maintains a monopoly role in the oil sector and a virtual monopoly in infrastructure development and the provision of most utilities and communications services."[1]

MONETARY POLICY
Score: 1–Stable (very low level of inflation)

Saudi Arabia's average rate of inflation from 1985 to 1995 was 2.7 percent. In 1996, the rate was 1 percent.

CAPITAL FLOWS AND FOREIGN INVESTMENT
Score: 4–Stable (high barriers)

Although Saudi Arabia imposes few restrictions on foreign investment and allows 100 percent foreign ownership, complete foreign ownership is uncommon in practice. The government must review and accept all investments. "It is extremely rare for the government to award a license to any 100 percent-foreign-owned operation," reports the Economist Intelligence Unit.[2] Restrictions still apply to many services, such as insurance and real estate.

1	Hong Kong	1.25	77	Zambia	3.05
2	Singapore	1.30	80	Mali	3.10
3	Bahrain	1.70	80	Mongolia	3.10
4	New Zealand	1.75	80	Slovenia	3.10
5	Switzerland	1.90	83	Honduras	3.15
5	United States	1.90	83	Papua New Guinea	3.15
7	Luxembourg	1.95	85	Djibouti	3.20
7	Taiwan	1.95	85	Fiji	3.20
7	United Kingdom	1.95	85	Pakistan	3.20
10	Bahamas	2.00	88	Algeria	3.25
10	Ireland	2.00	88	Guinea	3.25
12	Australia	2.05	88	Lebanon	3.25
12	Japan	2.05	88	Mexico	3.25
14	Belgium	2.10	88	Senegal	3.25
14	Canada	2.10	88	Tanzania	3.25
14	United Arab Emirates	2.10	94	Nigeria	3.30
17	Austria	2.15	94	Romania	3.30
17	Chile	2.15	96	Brazil	3.35
17	Estonia	2.15	96	Cambodia	3.35
20	Czech Republic	2.20	96	Egypt	3.35
20	Netherlands	2.20	96	Ivory Coast	3.35
22	Denmark	2.25	96	Madagascar	3.35
22	Finland	2.25	96	Moldova	3.35
24	Germany	2.30	102	Nepal	3.40
24	Iceland	2.30	103	Cape Verde	3.44
24	South Korea	2.30	104	Armenia	3.45
27	Norway	2.35	104	Dominican Republic	3.45
28	Kuwait	2.40	104	Russia	3.45
28	Malaysia	2.40	107	Burkina Faso	3.50
28	Panama	2.40	107	Cameroon	3.50
28	Thailand	2.40	107	Lesotho	3.50
32	El Salvador	2.45	107	Nicaragua	3.50
32	Sri Lanka	2.45	107	Venezuela	3.50
32	Sweden	2.45	112	Gambia	3.60
35	France	2.50	112	Guyana	3.60
35	Italy	2.50	114	Bulgaria	3.65
35	Spain	2.50	114	Georgia	3.65
38	Trinidad and Tobago	2.55	114	Malawi	3.65
39	Argentina	2.60	117	Ethiopia	3.70
39	Barbados	2.60	117	India	3.70
39	Cyprus	2.60	117	Niger	3.70
39	Jamaica	2.60	120	Albania	3.75
39	Portugal	2.60	120	Bangladesh	3.75
44	Bolivia	2.65	120	China (PRC)	3.75
44	Oman	2.65	120	Congo	3.75
44	Philippines	2.65	120	Croatia	3.75
47	Swaziland	2.70	125	Chad	3.80
47	Uruguay	2.70	125	Mauritania	3.80
49	Botswana	2.75	125	Ukraine	3.80
49	Jordan	2.75	128	Sierra Leone	3.85
49	Namibia	2.75	129	Burundi	3.90
49	Tunisia	2.75	129	Suriname	3.90
53	Belize	2.80	129	Zimbabwe	3.90
53	Costa Rica	2.80	132	Haiti	4.00
53	Guatemala	2.80	132	Kyrgyzstan	4.00
53	Israel	2.80	132	Syria	4.00
53	Peru	2.80	135	Belarus	4.05
53	Saudi Arabia	2.80	136	Kazakstan	4.10
53	Turkey	2.80	136	Mozambique	4.10
53	Uganda	2.80	136	Yemen	4.10
53	Western Samoa	2.80	139	Sudan	4.20
62	Indonesia	2.85	140	Myanmar	4.30
62	Latvia	2.85	140	Rwanda	4.30
62	Malta	2.85	142	Angola	4.35
62	Paraguay	2.85	143	Azerbaijan	4.40
66	Greece	2.90	143	Tajikistan	4.40
66	Hungary	2.90	145	Turkmenistan	4.50
66	South Africa	2.90	146	Uzbekistan	4.55
69	Benin	2.95	147	Congo/Zaire	4.70
69	Ecuador	2.95	147	Iran	4.70
69	Gabon	2.95	147	Libya	4.70
69	Morocco	2.95	147	Somalia	4.70
69	Poland	2.95	147	Vietnam	4.70
74	Colombia	3.00	152	Bosnia	4.80
74	Ghana	3.00	153	Iraq	4.90
74	Lithuania	3.00	154	Cuba	5.00
77	Kenya	3.05	154	Laos	5.00
77	Slovak Republic	3.05	154	North Korea	5.00

Mostly Free

BANKING
Score: 3–Stable (moderate level of restrictions)

The banking system in Saudi Arabia is competitive, and there are more than 24 commercial banks. A recent budgetary crisis, however, forced the government to finance its debt through Saudi banks; the government has resisted seeking financing from foreign banks because that would require it to release data on Saudi Arabia's financial status. The increased government pressure on commercial banks for more loans to meet this crisis has hindered the free operation of these banks. Foreign participation is limited to 40 percent ownership.

WAGE AND PRICE CONTROLS
Score: 3–Stable (moderate level)

The market sets most wages and prices in Saudi Arabia, although the government determines some prices on basic utilities. The government also subsidizes agriculture and some other enterprises. There is no minimum wage.

PROPERTY RIGHTS
Score: 1–Stable (very high level of protection)

Private property is safe from expropriation in Saudi Arabia. The legal and judicial system is both sound and efficient.

REGULATION
Score: 2–Stable (low level)

Establishing a business in Saudi Arabia is a simple process, although activities of the country's growing environmental movement could lead to increased regulation.

BLACK MARKET
Score: 2–Stable (low level of activity)

The black market in Saudi Arabia is relatively small. The government has been very successful in stamping out pirated video tapes and related copyrighted material.

NOTES
1. Economist Intelligence Unit, "Saudi Arabia," *ILT Reports*, April 1997, p. 9.
2. Economist Intelligence Unit, "Saudi Arabia," *ILT Reports*, July 1995, p. 8.

Senegal   3.25

Dakar

1997 Score: **3.25**	1996 Score: **3.40**	1995 Score: **n/a**

Trade	4	Banking	3
Taxation	4.5	Wages and Prices	4
Government Intervention	3	Property Rights	3
Monetary Policy	1	Regulation	4
Foreign Investment	3	Black Market	3

Senegal gained its independence from France in 1960. A small, semi-arid country with limited natural resources, its economy depends on trade. The largest industries are fishing, mining, and chemicals. From 1989 to 1994, economic growth was poor, with growth in GDP averaging only 0.85 percent. As a result, the government has sought to reduce spending and reform the economy. In 1995, it implemented a significant program of economic liberalization aimed at stimulating economic growth. With economic growth of 4.5 percent in both 1995 and 1996, the signs are positive that these policies are working. Senegal has reduced some barriers to trade, liberalized some prices, established a privatization program, and abolished some regulations. It also has reduced some tariffs. Nonetheless, there is increasing evidence of government influence in the judicial system. Thus, Senegal's overall score this year is the same as it was last year.

TRADE POLICY
Score: 4+ (high level of protectionism)

Senegal has adopted a flat external tariff rate of 10 percent, down from an average tariff rate of 27 percent in 1994 and over 30 percent for the 1990 to 1993 period. This reduced tariff system makes Senegal's score in this area one point better this year. Other trade restrictions include some import bans, import licenses, and strict documentation requirements. There are some complaints of limited corruption within the customs bureau.[1]

TAXATION
Score–Income taxation: 5–Stable (very high tax rates)
Score–Corporate taxation: 3–Stable (moderate tax rates)
Final Taxation Score: 4.5–Stable (very high tax rates)

Senegal's top income tax rate is 78 percent;[2] the average taxpayer finds himself in the 18 percent bracket. The top marginal corporate tax rate is 35 percent. Senegal also has a 35 percent capital gains tax and a 10 percent to 20 percent turnover tax.

GOVERNMENT INTERVENTION IN THE ECONOMY
Score: 3–Stable (moderate level)

Government consumes about 11.5 percent of Senegal's GDP. It also remains heavily involved in agriculture (although the number of private firms is increasing) and continues to control railroads, electrical production, telecommunications, and postal services.

MONETARY POLICY
Score: 1–Stable (very low level of inflation)

Senegal's average rate of inflation from 1985 to 1995 was 3.7 percent. In 1996, the rate was 3 percent.

1	Hong Kong	1.25		77	Zambia	3.05
2	Singapore	1.30		80	Mali	3.10
3	Bahrain	1.70		80	Mongolia	3.10
4	New Zealand	1.75		80	Slovenia	3.10
5	Switzerland	1.90		83	Honduras	3.15
5	United States	1.90		83	Papua New Guinea	3.15
7	Luxembourg	1.95		85	Djibouti	3.20
7	Taiwan	1.95		85	Fiji	3.20
7	United Kingdom	1.95		85	Pakistan	3.20
10	Bahamas	2.00		88	Algeria	3.25
10	Ireland	2.00		88	Guinea	3.25
12	Australia	2.05		88	Lebanon	3.25
12	Japan	2.05		88	Mexico	3.25
14	Belgium	2.10		88	Senegal	3.25
14	Canada	2.10		88	Tanzania	3.25
14	United Arab Emirates	2.10		94	Nigeria	3.30
17	Austria	2.15		94	Romania	3.30
17	Chile	2.15		96	Brazil	3.35
17	Estonia	2.15		96	Cambodia	3.35
20	Czech Republic	2.20		96	Egypt	3.35
20	Netherlands	2.20		96	Ivory Coast	3.35
22	Denmark	2.25		96	Madagascar	3.35
22	Finland	2.25		96	Moldova	3.35
24	Germany	2.30		102	Nepal	3.40
24	Iceland	2.30		103	Cape Verde	3.44
24	South Korea	2.30		104	Armenia	3.45
27	Norway	2.35		104	Dominican Republic	3.45
28	Kuwait	2.40		104	Russia	3.45
28	Malaysia	2.40		107	Burkina Faso	3.50
28	Panama	2.40		107	Cameroon	3.50
28	Thailand	2.40		107	Lesotho	3.50
32	El Salvador	2.45		107	Nicaragua	3.50
32	Sri Lanka	2.45		107	Venezuela	3.50
32	Sweden	2.45		112	Gambia	3.60
35	France	2.50		112	Guyana	3.60
35	Italy	2.50		114	Bulgaria	3.65
35	Spain	2.50		114	Georgia	3.65
38	Trinidad and Tobago	2.55		114	Malawi	3.65
39	Argentina	2.60		117	Ethiopia	3.70
39	Barbados	2.60		117	India	3.70
39	Cyprus	2.60		117	Niger	3.70
39	Jamaica	2.60		120	Albania	3.75
39	Portugal	2.60		120	Bangladesh	3.75
44	Bolivia	2.65		120	China (PRC)	3.75
44	Oman	2.65		120	Croatia	3.75
44	Philippines	2.65		125	Chad	3.80
47	Swaziland	2.70		125	Mauritania	3.80
47	Uruguay	2.70		125	Ukraine	3.80
49	Botswana	2.75		128	Sierra Leone	3.85
49	Jordan	2.75		129	Burundi	3.90
49	Namibia	2.75		129	Suriname	3.90
49	Tunisia	2.75		129	Zimbabwe	3.90
53	Belize	2.80		132	Haiti	4.00
53	Costa Rica	2.80		132	Kyrgyzstan	4.00
53	Guatemala	2.80		132	Syria	4.00
53	Israel	2.80		135	Belarus	4.05
53	Peru	2.80		136	Kazakstan	4.10
53	Saudi Arabia	2.80		136	Mozambique	4.10
53	Turkey	2.80		136	Yemen	4.10
53	Uganda	2.80		139	Sudan	4.20
53	Western Samoa	2.80		140	Myanmar	4.30
62	Indonesia	2.85		140	Rwanda	4.30
62	Latvia	2.85		142	Angola	4.35
62	Malta	2.85		143	Azerbaijan	4.40
62	Paraguay	2.85		143	Tajikistan	4.40
66	Greece	2.90		145	Turkmenistan	4.50
66	Hungary	2.90		146	Uzbekistan	4.55
66	South Africa	2.90		147	Congo/Zaire	4.70
69	Benin	2.95		147	Iran	4.70
69	Ecuador	2.95		147	Libya	4.70
69	Gabon	2.95		147	Somalia	4.70
69	Morocco	2.95		147	Vietnam	4.70
69	Poland	2.95		152	Bosnia	4.80
74	Colombia	3.00		153	Iraq	4.90
74	Ghana	3.00		154	Cuba	5.00
74	Lithuania	3.00		154	Laos	5.00
77	Kenya	3.05		154	North Korea	5.00
77	Slovak Republic	3.05				

Mostly Unfree

CAPITAL FLOWS AND FOREIGN INVESTMENT
Score: 3–Stable (moderate barriers)

Senegal does not allow foreign investment in the food and fishing industries, although 100 percent ownership is permitted in most other areas. Foreign and domestic firms are treated equally. Such industries as railroads, electricity, telecommunications, and postal services remain under state control.

BANKING
Score: 3–Stable (moderate level of restrictions)

Senegal's banking system is dominated by French banks. There is a moderate level of competition, and borrowing capital can be expensive. There is no stock market.

WAGE AND PRICE CONTROLS
Score: 4–Stable (high level)

Both by the market and the large state-owned sector set wages and prices in Senegal. The government continues to set prices on some goods and services, such as agricultural products and electricity.

PROPERTY RIGHTS
Score: 3– (moderate level of protection)

Private property in Senegal is protected by an efficient legal system, and expropriation is unlikely. But, according to the U.S. Department of State, "The judiciary is independent although subject to governmental influence and pressure."[3] Thus, Senegal's property rights protection score is one point worse this year.

REGULATION
Score: 4–Stable (high level)

Establishing a business in Senegal can be onerous if the business will compete with a state-owned enterprise. Government-sanctioned monopolies often bribe government officials to keep out new entrants. According to the U.S. Department of State, "The potential for corruption is a significant factor obstructing economic development and competitiveness in Senegal.... Credible allegations of corruption have been made concerning government procurement, dispute settlement, and regulatory and enforcement agencies. Corruption can range from large-scale customs fraud, including invoice under-valuation, to bribe taking by inspectors and public safety officials."[4]

BLACK MARKET
Score: 3–Stable (moderate level of activity)

Black market activity in Senegal is confined mainly to labor, construction, and transportation.

NOTES
1. U.S. Department of Commerce, *Country Commercial Guide,* 1997.
2. Includes a top rate of 50 percent and a mandatory proportional tax of 28 percent.
3. U.S. Department of State, "Senegal Country Report on Human Rights Practices for 1996," 1997.
4. U.S. Department of Commerce, *Country Commercial Guide,* 1997.

Sierra Leone 3.85

1997 Score: **3.85**	1996 Score: **3.75**	1995 Score: **3.75**

Trade	4	Banking	4
Taxation	4.5	Wages and Prices	3
Government Intervention	3	Property Rights	4
Monetary Policy	5	Regulation	3
Foreign Investment	3	Black Market	5

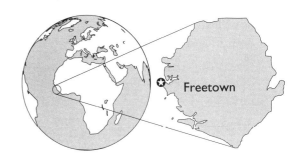

Freetown

Sierra Leone gained its independence from Great Britain in 1961. Over the next 10 years, its economy grew by 4 percent a year. Regular growth ended in the 1970s, however, when the oil crisis devastated the economy. For the past 15 years, the government has made some halfhearted efforts to reform the economy, but recovery has remained elusive, with the economy shrinking by an average of -6.3 percent from 1992 to 1994. In 1996, Sierra Leone experienced both an increase in armed banditry and the continuation of its ongoing civil and political unrest. In May 1997, a coup led by army officers toppled the government of President Ahmad Tejan Kabbah. Pressure on the rebel government to resign in favor of the democratic government it overthrew comes from Western countries that have cut off foreign aid and other West African countries that have implemented an economic blockade of Sierra Leone.

TRADE POLICY
Score: 4–Stable (high level of protectionism)

The average tariff rate for Sierra Leone is about 25 percent.[1] Nontariff barriers take the form of excessive government red tape.

TAXATION
Score–Income taxation: 3–Stable (moderate tax rates)
Score–Corporate taxation: 5–Stable (very high tax rates)
Final Taxation Score: 4.5–Stable (very high tax rates)

Sierra Leone's top income tax rate is 50 percent, with the average income taxed at 5 percent The corporate income tax rate is a flat 47.2 percent. Sierra Leone also has property taxes and a goods and services tax.

GOVERNMENT INTERVENTION IN THE ECONOMY
Score: 3–Stable (moderate level)

Government consumes 12 percent of Sierra Leone's GDP, and the large state-owned sector produces more than 30 percent of total GDP.

MONETARY POLICY
Score: 5–Stable (very high level of inflation)

Sierra Leone's average annual rate of inflation from 1985 to 1995 was 61.5 percent. In 1996, the rate was 16.6 percent.

CAPITAL FLOWS AND FOREIGN INVESTMENT
Score: 3–Stable (moderate barriers)

All investments in Sierra Leone must be approved by the government, which has established an investment code. Foreigners are not permitted to invest either in "local industries," such as cement block manufacturing or granite and sandstone excavation, or in the manufacture of certain durable consumer goods.

1	Hong Kong	1.25	77	Zambia	3.05
2	Singapore	1.30	80	Mali	3.10
3	Bahrain	1.70	80	Mongolia	3.10
4	New Zealand	1.75	80	Slovenia	3.10
5	Switzerland	1.90	83	Honduras	3.15
5	United States	1.90	83	Papua New Guinea	3.15
7	Luxembourg	1.95	85	Djibouti	3.20
7	Taiwan	1.95	85	Fiji	3.20
7	United Kingdom	1.95	85	Pakistan	3.20
10	Bahamas	2.00	88	Algeria	3.25
10	Ireland	2.00	88	Guinea	3.25
12	Australia	2.05	88	Lebanon	3.25
12	Japan	2.05	88	Mexico	3.25
14	Belgium	2.10	88	Senegal	3.25
14	Canada	2.10	88	Tanzania	3.25
14	United Arab Emirates	2.10	94	Nigeria	3.30
17	Austria	2.15	94	Romania	3.30
17	Chile	2.15	96	Brazil	3.35
17	Estonia	2.15	96	Cambodia	3.35
20	Czech Republic	2.20	96	Egypt	3.35
20	Netherlands	2.20	96	Ivory Coast	3.35
22	Denmark	2.25	96	Madagascar	3.35
22	Finland	2.25	96	Moldova	3.35
24	Germany	2.30	102	Nepal	3.40
24	Iceland	2.30	103	Cape Verde	3.44
24	South Korea	2.30	104	Armenia	3.45
27	Norway	2.35	104	Dominican Republic	3.45
28	Kuwait	2.40	104	Russia	3.45
28	Malaysia	2.40	107	Burkina Faso	3.50
28	Panama	2.40	107	Cameroon	3.50
28	Thailand	2.40	107	Lesotho	3.50
32	El Salvador	2.45	107	Nicaragua	3.50
32	Sri Lanka	2.45	107	Venezuela	3.50
32	Sweden	2.45	112	Gambia	3.60
35	France	2.50	112	Guyana	3.60
35	Italy	2.50	114	Bulgaria	3.65
35	Spain	2.50	114	Georgia	3.65
38	Trinidad and Tobago	2.55	114	Malawi	3.65
39	Argentina	2.60	117	Ethiopia	3.70
39	Barbados	2.60	117	India	3.70
39	Cyprus	2.60	117	Niger	3.70
39	Jamaica	2.60	120	Albania	3.75
39	Portugal	2.60	120	Bangladesh	3.75
44	Bolivia	2.65	120	China (PRC)	3.75
44	Oman	2.65	120	Congo	3.75
44	Philippines	2.65	120	Croatia	3.75
47	Swaziland	2.70	125	Chad	3.80
47	Uruguay	2.70	125	Mauritania	3.80
49	Botswana	2.75	125	Ukraine	3.80
49	Jordan	2.75	128	Sierra Leone	3.85
49	Namibia	2.75	129	Burundi	3.90
49	Tunisia	2.75	129	Suriname	3.90
53	Belize	2.80	129	Zimbabwe	3.90
53	Costa Rica	2.80	132	Haiti	4.00
53	Guatemala	2.80	132	Kyrgyzstan	4.00
53	Israel	2.80	132	Syria	4.00
53	Peru	2.80	135	Belarus	4.05
53	Saudi Arabia	2.80	136	Kazakstan	4.10
53	Turkey	2.80	136	Mozambique	4.10
53	Uganda	2.80	136	Yemen	4.10
53	Western Samoa	2.80	139	Sudan	4.20
62	Indonesia	2.85	140	Myanmar	4.30
62	Latvia	2.85	140	Rwanda	4.30
62	Malta	2.85	142	Angola	4.35
62	Paraguay	2.85	143	Azerbaijan	4.40
66	Greece	2.90	143	Tajikistan	4.40
66	Hungary	2.90	145	Turkmenistan	4.50
66	South Africa	2.90	146	Uzbekistan	4.55
69	Benin	2.95	147	Congo/Zaire	4.70
69	Ecuador	2.95	147	Iran	4.70
69	Gabon	2.95	147	Libya	4.70
69	Morocco	2.95	147	Somalia	4.70
69	Poland	2.95	147	Vietnam	4.70
74	Colombia	3.00	152	Bosnia	4.80
74	Ghana	3.00	153	Iraq	4.90
74	Lithuania	3.00	154	Cuba	5.00
77	Kenya	3.05	154	Laos	5.00
77	Slovak Republic	3.05	154	North Korea	5.00

Mostly Unfree

BANKING
Score: 4–Stable (high level of restrictions)

Sierra Leone's banking system is in disarray. Banks are heavily regulated, and the government sets interest rates for commercial banks.

WAGE AND PRICE CONTROLS
Score: 3–Stable (moderate level)

Price controls are imposed on certain foods. Prices also are influenced by the state-owned industries, which are subsidized by the government. Sierra Leone has no minimum wage.

PROPERTY RIGHTS
Score: 4–Stable (low level of protection)

Although private property is permitted in Sierra Leone, it also can be expropriated. An inefficient legal and law enforcement environment provides little protection. In 1996, the U.S. Department of State issued a warning on travel to Sierra Leone, mainly because of crime and corruption: "Petty crime and theft of wallets and passports are common. Requests for payments at military roadblocks are common. Robberies and burglaries of residences also occur."[2]

REGULATION
Score: 3–Stable (moderate level)

Regulations in Sierra Leone are applied haphazardly, making compliance difficult. The less-than-uniform enforcement of health and safety standards creates uncertainty among businesses.

BLACK MARKET
Score: 5–Stable (very high level of activity)

The level of black market activity in Sierra Leone is nearly as high as that of legal activity. High tariffs encourage smugglers to sell many products on the black market, and some products like coffee and rice are sold at much lower prices than in state-owned stores.

NOTES
1. Based on total taxes on international trade as a percentage of total imports.
2. U.S. Department of State, "Sierra Leone—Travel Conditions," *Market Research Reports* No. IMI960208, 1996.

Singapore 1.30

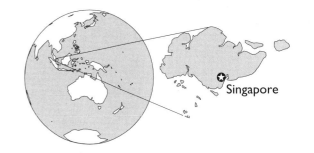
Singapore

1997 Score: **1.30**   1996 Score: **1.30**   1995 Score: **1.25**

Trade	1	Banking	2
Taxation	3	Wages and Prices	1
Government Intervention	1	Property Rights	1
Monetary Policy	1	Regulation	1
Foreign Investment	1	Black Market	1

Singapore won its independence from Malaysia in August 1965. Since that time, thanks to economic liberalization, it has been transformed into a developed country. From 1965 to 1990, Singapore enjoyed average annual growth rates of about 6.5 percent. Today, it is one of the richest countries in Asia. Singapore has made this remarkable progress by maintaining an economic environment open to trade and investment; a corruption-free, pro-business regulatory system; political stability; an efficient, strike-free labor force; and tax incentives for foreign investors.

TRADE POLICY
Score: 1–Stable (very low level of protectionism)

Singapore has an exceptionally low average tariff rate: from 0.3 percent to 0.5 percent. Nearly 96 percent of all imports enter duty-free. The government maintains straightforward labeling requirements, no import quotas, and no nontariff barriers to foreign trade. Import licenses are not required, and customs procedures are minimal. The code regulating product standards is not an impediment to trade.

TAXATION
Score–Income taxation: 2–Stable (low tax rates)
Score–Corporate taxation: 3–Stable (moderate tax rates)
Final Taxation Score: 3–Stable (moderate tax rates)

Singapore's top income tax rate is 28 percent, down from 30 percent in 1996. The average income is taxed at 8 percent. There are no taxes on capital gains. The corporate tax rate is a flat 26 percent, down from 27 percent in 1996. Singapore also has a 3 percent value-added tax, as well as a mandatory retirement fund to which employees and employers must contribute a combined 40 percent of each employee's compensation.

GOVERNMENT INTERVENTION IN THE ECONOMY
Score: 1–Stable (very low level)

Government consumed 8.9 percent of Singapore's GDP in 1996, down slightly from 9 percent in 1994. Although some critics of Singapore's economic reforms claim the government is heavily involved in the private sector, most businesses are privately owned, and direct government control of corporations is negligible.[1]

MONETARY POLICY
Score: 1–Stable (very low level of inflation)

Singapore's average annual rate of inflation from 1985 to 1995 was 3.9 percent. In 1996, the rate of inflation was 1.4 percent. For the first half of 1997, it remained below 2 percent.

1	Hong Kong	1.25	77	Zambia	3.05
2	Singapore	1.30	80	Mali	3.10
3	Bahrain	1.70	80	Mongolia	3.10
4	New Zealand	1.75	80	Slovenia	3.10
5	Switzerland	1.90	83	Honduras	3.15
5	United States	1.90	83	Papua New Guinea	3.15
7	Luxembourg	1.95	85	Djibouti	3.20
7	Taiwan	1.95	85	Fiji	3.20
7	United Kingdom	1.95	85	Pakistan	3.20
10	Bahamas	2.00	88	Algeria	3.25
10	Ireland	2.00	88	Guinea	3.25
12	Australia	2.05	88	Lebanon	3.25
12	Japan	2.05	88	Mexico	3.25
14	Belgium	2.10	88	Senegal	3.25
14	Canada	2.10	88	Tanzania	3.25
14	United Arab Emirates	2.10	94	Nigeria	3.30
17	Austria	2.15	94	Romania	3.30
17	Chile	2.15	96	Brazil	3.35
17	Estonia	2.15	96	Cambodia	3.35
20	Czech Republic	2.20	96	Egypt	3.35
20	Netherlands	2.20	96	Ivory Coast	3.35
22	Denmark	2.25	96	Madagascar	3.35
22	Finland	2.25	96	Moldova	3.35
24	Germany	2.30	102	Nepal	3.40
24	Iceland	2.30	103	Cape Verde	3.44
24	South Korea	2.30	104	Armenia	3.45
27	Norway	2.35	104	Dominican Republic	3.45
28	Kuwait	2.40	104	Russia	3.45
28	Malaysia	2.40	107	Burkina Faso	3.50
28	Panama	2.40	107	Cameroon	3.50
28	Thailand	2.40	107	Lesotho	3.50
32	El Salvador	2.45	107	Nicaragua	3.50
32	Sri Lanka	2.45	107	Venezuela	3.50
32	Sweden	2.45	112	Gambia	3.60
35	France	2.50	112	Guyana	3.60
35	Italy	2.50	114	Bulgaria	3.65
35	Spain	2.50	114	Georgia	3.65
38	Trinidad and Tobago	2.55	114	Malawi	3.65
39	Argentina	2.60	117	Ethiopia	3.70
39	Barbados	2.60	117	India	3.70
39	Cyprus	2.60	117	Niger	3.70
39	Jamaica	2.60	120	Albania	3.75
39	Portugal	2.60	120	Bangladesh	3.75
44	Bolivia	2.65	120	China (PRC)	3.75
44	Oman	2.65	120	Congo	3.75
44	Philippines	2.65	120	Croatia	3.75
47	Swaziland	2.70	125	Chad	3.80
47	Uruguay	2.70	125	Mauritania	3.80
49	Botswana	2.75	125	Ukraine	3.80
49	Jordan	2.75	128	Sierra Leone	3.85
49	Namibia	2.75	129	Burundi	3.90
49	Tunisia	2.75	129	Suriname	3.90
53	Belize	2.80	129	Zimbabwe	3.90
53	Costa Rica	2.80	132	Haiti	4.00
53	Guatemala	2.80	132	Kyrgyzstan	4.00
53	Israel	2.80	132	Syria	4.00
53	Peru	2.80	135	Belarus	4.05
53	Saudi Arabia	2.80	136	Kazakstan	4.10
53	Turkey	2.80	136	Mozambique	4.10
53	Uganda	2.80	136	Yemen	4.10
53	Western Samoa	2.80	139	Sudan	4.20
62	Indonesia	2.85	140	Myanmar	4.30
62	Latvia	2.85	140	Rwanda	4.30
62	Malta	2.85	142	Angola	4.35
62	Paraguay	2.85	143	Azerbaijan	4.40
66	Greece	2.90	143	Tajikistan	4.40
66	Hungary	2.90	145	Turkmenistan	4.50
66	South Africa	2.90	146	Uzbekistan	4.55
69	Benin	2.95	147	Congo/Zaire	4.70
69	Ecuador	2.95	147	Iran	4.70
69	Gabon	2.95	147	Libya	4.70
69	Morocco	2.95	147	Somalia	4.70
69	Poland	2.95	147	Vietnam	4.70
74	Colombia	3.00	152	Bosnia	4.80
74	Ghana	3.00	153	Iraq	4.90
74	Lithuania	3.00	154	Cuba	5.00
77	Kenya	3.05	154	Laos	5.00
77	Slovak Republic	3.05	154	North Korea	5.00

CAPITAL FLOWS AND FOREIGN INVESTMENT
Score: 1–Stable (very low barriers)

Investment laws in Singapore are clear and fair, and pose few problems for business. Foreign and domestic businesses are treated equally under the investment laws, and there are no production or local content requirements. According to the Economist Intelligence Unit, "Restrictions on equity, licensing and joint ventures are negligible."[2]

BANKING
Score: 2–Stable (low level of restrictions)

Foreign banks in Singapore are restricted as to the number of branches and automatic teller machines they may operate, mainly because of bank overcrowding. Even though it has just under 3 million people, Singapore has over 140 foreign banks—more than the number of domestic banks. All banks may participate in securities exchanges, sell insurance policies, engage in some real estate ventures, and invest in industrial firms. It is easy to form new banks.

WAGE AND PRICE CONTROLS
Score: 1–Stable (very low level)

The free market sets almost all wages and prices in Singapore. There is no minimum wage.

PROPERTY RIGHTS
Score: 1–Stable (very high level of protection)

Singapore has a solid history of protection for private property, and there is no threat of expropriation. The court system is highly efficient and strongly protects private property.

REGULATION
Score: 1–Stable (very low level)

Obtaining a business license in Singapore is easy. Government regulations are straightforward, and corruption is nonexistent. Occupational safety and health regulations are not burdensome, and there are no antitrust regulations. The government does not tolerate price gouging, however, and will act to eliminate such practices whenever they are found to exist.

BLACK MARKET
Score: 1–Stable (very low level of activity)

Singapore's black market is very small. The levels of smuggling and black market activity in pirated intellectual property are negligible.

NOTES

1. Most direct government involvement in business is restricted to shipping, real estate, construction, air transportation, and some financial services. Many of these government-owned companies have joint ventures with private firms. According to the Economist Intelligence Unit, "Few GLCs [government-linked companies] compete in sectors involving MNCs [multinational corporations] though this is gradually changing. Often, they may be involved in joint ventures." Economist Intelligence Unit, *ILT Reports, Singapore,* June 1996, p. 7.
2. *Ibid.,* p. 8.

Slovak Republic   3.05

Bratislava

1997 Score: **3.05**	1996 Score: **2.95**	1995 Score: **2.75**

Trade	3	Banking	3
Taxation	4.5	Wages and Prices	3
Government Intervention	3	Property Rights	3
Monetary Policy	2	Regulation	3
Foreign Investment	3	Black Market	3

The Slovak Republic's split from the Czech Republic in 1993 left much of its banking, experienced personnel, data analysis capability, and competitive industry across the border. In addition to struggling to transform its centrally controlled economy into a market-based economy, the Slovak Republic has had to create a democratic government. Reform has been slower in the Slovak Republic than in the Czech Republic. The government, which has made significant progress toward reducing inflation, recently increased its barriers to trade; but it also has reduced inflation. Thus, the Slovak Republic's overall score this year remains the same as last year.

TRADE POLICY
Score: 3– (moderate level of protectionism)

The Slovak Republic's average tariff rate is about 6 percent.[1] Import licensing requirements, according to the U.S. Department of State, are not burdensome: "For most of the approximately 100 groups of items in the 'general' category, obtaining a license is a formality."[2] In an attempt to curb its mounting trade deficit, however, the government recently established a requirement that importers place 20 percent of an import's value in an interest-bearing account for 180 days. This policy discourages imports. As a result, the Slovak Republic's trade policy score is one point worse this year.

TAXATION
Score–Income taxation: 4–Stable (high tax rates)
Score–Corporate taxation: 4–Stable (high tax rates)
Final Taxation Score: 4.5–Stable (high tax rates)

The Slovak Republic's top marginal income tax rate is 42 percent, with the average taxpayer subject to a rate of about 20 percent. The top corporate income tax rate is 40 percent. The Slovak Republic also has a 40 percent capital gains tax, a 23 percent value-added tax, and a 38 percent social contributions tax.

GOVERNMENT INTERVENTION IN THE ECONOMY
Score: 3–Stable (moderate level)

Government consumes 23.1 percent of the Slovak Republic's GDP. Although the private sector is the largest part of the economy, some 35 percent of GDP is produced by the state. The Slovak Republic has undergone significant privatization. Most smaller state-owned enterprises have been sold, and many of the larger ones are being privatized.

MONETARY POLICY
Score: 2+ (low level of inflation)

Since becoming independent, the Slovak Republic has had inflation rates of 10 percent in 1992, 23 percent in 1993, 13 percent in 1994, 10 percent in 1995, and 5.8 percent in 1996.[3] The average rate of inflation from 1992 to 1996 has fallen to 12 percent. Thus, the country's score in this area is one point better this year.

1	Hong Kong	1.25	77	Zambia	3.05
2	Singapore	1.30	80	Mali	3.10
3	Bahrain	1.70	80	Mongolia	3.10
4	New Zealand	1.75	80	Slovenia	3.10
5	Switzerland	1.90	83	Honduras	3.15
5	United States	1.90	83	Papua New Guinea	3.15
7	Luxembourg	1.95	85	Djibouti	3.20
7	Taiwan	1.95	85	Fiji	3.20
7	United Kingdom	1.95	85	Pakistan	3.20
10	Bahamas	2.00	88	Algeria	3.25
10	Ireland	2.00	88	Guinea	3.25
12	Australia	2.05	88	Lebanon	3.25
12	Japan	2.05	88	Mexico	3.25
14	Belgium	2.10	88	Senegal	3.25
14	Canada	2.10	88	Tanzania	3.25
14	United Arab Emirates	2.10	94	Nigeria	3.30
17	Austria	2.15	94	Romania	3.30
17	Chile	2.15	96	Brazil	3.35
17	Estonia	2.15	96	Cambodia	3.35
20	Czech Republic	2.20	96	Egypt	3.35
20	Netherlands	2.20	96	Ivory Coast	3.35
22	Denmark	2.25	96	Madagascar	3.35
22	Finland	2.25	96	Moldova	3.35
24	Germany	2.30	102	Nepal	3.40
24	Iceland	2.30	103	Cape Verde	3.44
24	South Korea	2.30	104	Armenia	3.45
27	Norway	2.35	104	Dominican Republic	3.45
28	Kuwait	2.40	104	Russia	3.45
28	Malaysia	2.40	107	Burkina Faso	3.50
28	Panama	2.40	107	Cameroon	3.50
28	Thailand	2.40	107	Lesotho	3.50
32	El Salvador	2.45	107	Nicaragua	3.50
32	Sri Lanka	2.45	107	Venezuela	3.50
32	Sweden	2.45	112	Gambia	3.60
35	France	2.50	112	Guyana	3.60
35	Italy	2.50	114	Bulgaria	3.65
35	Spain	2.50	114	Georgia	3.65
38	Trinidad and Tobago	2.55	114	Malawi	3.65
39	Argentina	2.60	117	Ethiopia	3.70
39	Barbados	2.60	117	India	3.70
39	Cyprus	2.60	117	Niger	3.70
39	Jamaica	2.60	120	Albania	3.75
39	Portugal	2.60	120	Bangladesh	3.75
44	Bolivia	2.65	120	China (PRC)	3.75
44	Oman	2.65	120	Congo	3.75
44	Philippines	2.65	120	Croatia	3.75
47	Swaziland	2.70	125	Chad	3.80
47	Uruguay	2.70	125	Mauritania	3.80
49	Botswana	2.75	125	Ukraine	3.80
49	Jordan	2.75	128	Sierra Leone	3.85
49	Namibia	2.75	129	Burundi	3.90
49	Tunisia	2.75	129	Suriname	3.90
53	Belize	2.80	129	Zimbabwe	3.90
53	Costa Rica	2.80	132	Haiti	4.00
53	Guatemala	2.80	132	Kyrgyzstan	4.00
53	Israel	2.80	132	Syria	4.00
53	Peru	2.80	135	Belarus	4.05
53	Saudi Arabia	2.80	136	Kazakstan	4.10
53	Turkey	2.80	136	Mozambique	4.10
53	Uganda	2.80	136	Yemen	4.10
53	Western Samoa	2.80	139	Sudan	4.20
62	Indonesia	2.85	140	Myanmar	4.30
62	Latvia	2.85	140	Rwanda	4.30
62	Malta	2.85	142	Angola	4.35
62	Paraguay	2.85	143	Azerbaijan	4.40
66	Greece	2.90	143	Tajikistan	4.40
66	Hungary	2.90	145	Turkmenistan	4.50
66	South Africa	2.90	146	Uzbekistan	4.55
69	Benin	2.95	147	Congo/Zaire	4.70
69	Ecuador	2.95	147	Iran	4.70
69	Gabon	2.95	147	Libya	4.70
69	Morocco	2.95	147	Somalia	4.70
69	Poland	2.95	147	Vietnam	4.70
74	Colombia	3.00	152	Bosnia	4.80
74	Ghana	3.00	153	Iraq	4.90
74	Lithuania	3.00	154	Cuba	5.00
77	Kenya	3.05	154	Laos	5.00
77	Slovak Republic	3.05	154	North Korea	5.00

Mostly Unfree

CAPITAL FLOWS AND FOREIGN INVESTMENT
Score: 3–Stable (moderate barriers)

Foreign citizens may not own land in the Slovak Republic, but there are few restrictions on foreign direct investment. Foreign and domestic firms are treated equally, and there is a well-established foreign investment code. Political instability caused by the populist government of Prime Minister Vladimir Meciar, however, has made the Slovak Republic less attractive to investors than the neighboring Czech Republic, Hungary, and Poland.

BANKING
Score: 3–Stable (moderate level of restrictions)

Permission from the Central Bank is required to open new banks, although this has become a simple formality. Of the 29 banks operating in the Slovak Republic at the end of 1994, 10 were branches of foreign banks. The banking system has yet to become completely independent of government coercion and control.

WAGE AND PRICE CONTROLS
Score: 3–Stable (moderate level)

Almost 96 percent of the Slovak Republic's price controls have been removed, although controls on the prices of some products (for example, food, fuel, electricity, and heat) remain in effect. In 1994, the government imposed some restrictions on wages in certain money-losing state-owned industries. The Slovak Republic has a minimum wage.

PROPERTY RIGHTS
Score: 3–Stable (moderate level of protection)

Expropriation is unlikely in the Slovak Republic, which has a moderately efficient and independent legal system. According to the U.S. Department of Commerce, however, "Property and contractual rights are enforced within the legal structure, but decisions may take years, thus limiting the attractiveness of the system for dispute settlement."[4]

REGULATION
Score: 3–Stable (moderate level)

The Slovak Republic has reduced its level of regulation, and most businesses do not need a license. But because political allies of the government control the remaining state-owned sector, private firms may find themselves subject to regulations that state-run firms are able to avoid.

BLACK MARKET
Score: 3–Stable (moderate level of activity)

The Slovak Republic's black market remains fairly large. About 15 percent of the working public is employed in the informal sector.[5]

NOTES

1. U.S. Department of State, *Country Reports on Economic Policy and Trade Practices,* 1996, p. 270.
2. *Ibid.,* p. 269.
3. Based on consumer price inflation.
4. U.S. Department of Commerce, *Country Commercial Guide,* 1996.
5. Economist Intelligence Unit, *EIU Country Profile, 1995–97.*

Slovenia   3.10

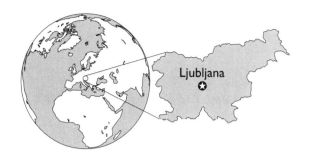

Ljubljana

1997 Score: **3.10**	1996 Score: **3.35**	1995 Score: **n/a**

Trade	4	Banking	2
Taxation	4	Wages and Prices	3
Government Intervention	3	Property Rights	2
Monetary Policy	5	Regulation	3
Foreign Investment	2	Black Market	3

Since the breakup of Yugoslavia, Slovenia has pursued an economic liberalization policy aimed at promoting international trade, attracting private investment, and privatizing the state-owned sector. The government also has made substantial progress toward curbing inflation. Yet overall progress has been relatively slow, and many hurdles still exist. Slovenia recently opened its borders to foreign investment and improved its protection of private property. The government, however, also has increased its control of some industries. As a result, Slovenia's overall score this year is the same as it was last year.

TRADE POLICY
Score: 4–Stable (high level of protectionism)

Slovenia's average tariff rate is 13 percent. Nontariff barriers take the form of quotas in textiles.

TAXATION
Score–Income taxation: 5–Stable (very high tax rates)
Score–Corporate taxation: 2–Stable (low tax rates)
Final Taxation Score: 4–Stable (high tax rates)

Slovenia's top income tax rate is 50 percent, up from 45 percent in 1995; the average taxpayer is in the 35 percent bracket. The top marginal corporate tax rate is 25 percent, down from 30 percent in 1995. Slovenia also has a 20 percent sales tax, among other additional taxes.

GOVERNMENT INTERVENTION IN THE ECONOMY
Score: 3–Stable (moderate level)

Government consumes about 20.8 percent of Slovenia's GDP, and the state sector generates a significant portion of GDP overall. The government remains heavily involved in the banking, transportation, and utility sectors.

MONETARY POLICY
Score: 5– (very high level of inflation)

Slovenia has made substantial progress toward bringing down inflation. The annual rate of inflation was 201.3 percent in 1992, 32.3 percent in 1993, 19.8 percent in 1994, and 12.6 percent in 1995. In 1996, it was 9.7 percent. Thus, from 1992 to 1996, the average rate of inflation was about 50 percent. Because 1997 is the first year that historical inflation rate figures for Slovenia have been available, however, its score this year is two points worse than last year.[1]

CAPITAL FLOWS AND FOREIGN INVESTMENT
Score: 2+ (low barriers)

Slovenia allows foreign investment in most industries, although it does require that the managing director of a business be a Slovenian national. With foreign investment continuing to increase, this does not appear to be a significant

1	Hong Kong	1.25	77	Zambia	3.05
2	Singapore	1.30	80	Mali	3.10
3	Bahrain	1.70	80	Mongolia	3.10
4	New Zealand	1.75	80	Slovenia	3.10
5	Switzerland	1.90	83	Honduras	3.15
5	United States	1.90	83	Papua New Guinea	3.15
7	Luxembourg	1.95	85	Djibouti	3.20
7	Taiwan	1.95	85	Fiji	3.20
7	United Kingdom	1.95	85	Pakistan	3.20
10	Bahamas	2.00	88	Algeria	3.25
10	Ireland	2.00	88	Guinea	3.25
12	Australia	2.05	88	Lebanon	3.25
12	Japan	2.05	88	Mexico	3.25
14	Belgium	2.10	88	Senegal	3.25
14	Canada	2.10	88	Tanzania	3.25
14	United Arab Emirates	2.10	94	Nigeria	3.30
17	Austria	2.15	94	Romania	3.30
17	Chile	2.15	96	Brazil	3.35
17	Estonia	2.15	96	Cambodia	3.35
20	Czech Republic	2.20	96	Egypt	3.35
20	Netherlands	2.20	96	Ivory Coast	3.35
22	Denmark	2.25	96	Madagascar	3.35
22	Finland	2.25	96	Moldova	3.35
24	Germany	2.30	102	Nepal	3.40
24	Iceland	2.30	103	Cape Verde	3.44
24	South Korea	2.30	104	Armenia	3.45
27	Norway	2.35	104	Dominican Republic	3.45
28	Kuwait	2.40	104	Russia	3.45
28	Malaysia	2.40	107	Burkina Faso	3.50
28	Panama	2.40	107	Cameroon	3.50
28	Thailand	2.40	107	Lesotho	3.50
32	El Salvador	2.45	107	Nicaragua	3.50
32	Sri Lanka	2.45	107	Venezuela	3.50
32	Sweden	2.45	112	Gambia	3.60
35	France	2.50	112	Guyana	3.60
35	Italy	2.50	114	Bulgaria	3.65
35	Spain	2.50	114	Georgia	3.65
38	Trinidad and Tobago	2.55	114	Malawi	3.65
39	Argentina	2.60	117	Ethiopia	3.70
39	Barbados	2.60	117	India	3.70
39	Cyprus	2.60	117	Niger	3.70
39	Jamaica	2.60	120	Albania	3.75
39	Portugal	2.60	120	Bangladesh	3.75
44	Bolivia	2.65	120	China (PRC)	3.75
44	Oman	2.65	120	Congo	3.75
44	Philippines	2.65	120	Croatia	3.75
47	Swaziland	2.70	125	Chad	3.80
47	Uruguay	2.70	125	Mauritania	3.80
49	Botswana	2.75	125	Ukraine	3.80
49	Jordan	2.75	128	Sierra Leone	3.85
49	Namibia	2.75	129	Burundi	3.90
49	Tunisia	2.75	129	Suriname	3.90
53	Belize	2.80	129	Zimbabwe	3.90
53	Costa Rica	2.80	132	Haiti	4.00
53	Guatemala	2.80	132	Kyrgyzstan	4.00
53	Israel	2.80	132	Syria	4.00
53	Peru	2.80	135	Belarus	4.05
53	Saudi Arabia	2.80	136	Kazakstan	4.10
53	Turkey	2.80	136	Mozambique	4.10
53	Uganda	2.80	136	Yemen	4.10
53	Western Samoa	2.80	139	Sudan	4.20
62	Indonesia	2.85	140	Myanmar	4.30
62	Latvia	2.85	140	Rwanda	4.30
62	Malta	2.85	142	Angola	4.35
62	Paraguay	2.85	143	Azerbaijan	4.40
66	Greece	2.90	143	Tajikistan	4.40
66	Hungary	2.90	145	Turkmenistan	4.50
66	South Africa	2.90	146	Uzbekistan	4.55
69	Benin	2.95	147	Congo/Zaire	4.70
69	Ecuador	2.95	147	Iran	4.70
69	Gabon	2.95	147	Libya	4.70
69	Morocco	2.95	147	Somalia	4.70
69	Poland	2.95	147	Vietnam	4.70
74	Colombia	3.00	152	Bosnia	4.80
74	Ghana	3.00	153	Iraq	4.90
74	Lithuania	3.00	154	Cuba	5.00
77	Kenya	3.05	154	Laos	5.00
77	Slovak Republic	3.05	154	North Korea	5.00

Mostly Unfree

barrier. In July 1997, Slovenia eliminated its law barring foreign ownership of land. Thus, its score for this factor is one point better this year.

BANKING
Score: 2–Stable (low level of restrictions)

Most government control of banking has ended. As a result, more foreign banks are opening branches in Slovenia.

WAGE AND PRICE CONTROLS
Score: 3–Stable (moderate level of wage and price controls)

The market drives wages and prices, but price controls continue on such items as electricity, gas, and telecommunications. Slovenia has a minimum wage.

PROPERTY RIGHTS
Score: 2+ (high level of protection)

Private property is guaranteed by Slovenia's constitution. The country has made significant progress toward reforming its judicial system by making it more independent and more efficient. Thus, its property rights score is one point

better this year. According to the U.S. Department of State, "The Constitution provides for an independent judiciary, and the Government respects this provision in practice.... The Constitution provides great detail for the right to a fair trial, including provisions for: Equality before the law, presumption of innocence, due process, open court proceedings, guarantees of appeal, and a prohibition against double jeopardy. These rights are respected in practice."[2]

REGULATION
Score: 3–Stable (moderate level)

Establishing a business in Slovenia is becoming easier, and the number of private businesses is growing. An entrenched and sometimes inefficient bureaucracy continues to hinder the rapid growth of a free market.

BLACK MARKET
Score: 3–Stable (moderate level of activity)

Slovenia has a large black market, primarily because of high tariffs. Black market activity also results from government control of the transportation industry. Slovenia has made significant progress toward protecting intellectual property, however, and piracy has been curtailed significantly.

NOTES

1. The score for this factor has changed from 3 in 1997 to 5 in 1998. Previously unavailable data provide a more accurate understanding of the country's performance. The methodology for this factor remains the same.
2. U.S. Department of State, "Slovenia Country Report on Human Rights Practices for 1996," 1997.

Somalia 4.70

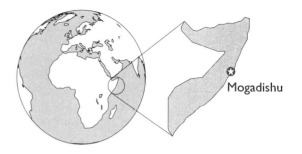

Mogadishu

1997 Score: **4.70**	1996 Score: **4.70**	1995 Score: **n/a**	

Trade	5	Banking	5
Taxation	5	Wages and Prices	3
Government Intervention	5	Property Rights	5
Monetary Policy	5	Regulation	5
Foreign Investment	4	Black Market	5

Modern-day Somalia was established in 1960 when British Somaliland gained its independence from Great Britain and joined Italian Somaliland, an Italian-administered United Nations trusteeship also granted independence that year. Its primarily agricultural economy has been devastated by civil war. There has been no central authority since the fall of Major General Muhammed Siad Barre's dictatorship in 1991. Local authority lies with regional militias, and no international recognition has been given either to the various self-proclaimed governments or to the breakaway northwest province claiming independence as the Republic of Somaliland. A group called the National Salvation Council, backed by most militia groups, was established to take the first necessary steps in establishing a democratic national government, but it faces considerable obstacles. Somalia remains one of the world's poorest countries, with an estimated per capita GNP of $110 in 1990 (the last year for which data were available). Economic prospects have improved somewhat with the signing of successive cease-fire agreements between several militia factions; but because the country still lacks both economic freedom and the rule of law, massive transfers of food aid, foreign aid, and loans and grants from the United States, Europe, and Japan have had little effect. There are indications, however, that the northern part of Somalia is attempting to establish the basis for a free-market system.

TRADE POLICY
Score: 5–Stable (very high level of protectionism)

Tariff rates play a minor role in restricting imports and exports in Somalia. The average tariff rate is over 30 percent, but the biggest impediment is the tendency of corrupt customs officials to confiscate goods for personal gain. Somalia's clan militias have destroyed what was left of a centralized customs service, although the government is trying to restore order. The U.S. Department of State warns that "looting, banditry, and all forms of violent crime are common."[1] This greatly impairs the movement of goods across Somalia's borders.

TAXATION
Score–Income taxation: 5–Stable (very high tax rates)
Score–Corporate taxation: 5–Stable (very high tax rates)
Final Taxation Score: 5–Stable (very high tax rates)

Little is left of Somalia's centralized government. The country is run primarily by warlords who operate a primitive feudal system. Taxation often takes the form of crop and private property confiscation, and it is not uncommon for citizens to be taxed by more than one group.

GOVERNMENT INTERVENTION IN THE ECONOMY
Score: 5–Stable (very high level)

Somalia has no official government and very little economic output. The entire economic system is in ruins. The level of crime, banditry, and looting—much of it carried out by warring clans and militias—makes it nearly impossible to conduct business activity.

1	Hong Kong	1.25		77	Zambia	3.05
2	Singapore	1.30		80	Mali	3.10
3	Bahrain	1.70		80	Mongolia	3.10
4	New Zealand	1.75		80	Slovenia	3.10
5	Switzerland	1.90		83	Honduras	3.15
5	United States	1.90		83	Papua New Guinea	3.15
7	Luxembourg	1.95		85	Djibouti	3.20
7	Taiwan	1.95		85	Fiji	3.20
7	United Kingdom	1.95		85	Pakistan	3.20
10	Bahamas	2.00		88	Algeria	3.25
10	Ireland	2.00		88	Guinea	3.25
12	Australia	2.05		88	Lebanon	3.25
12	Japan	2.05		88	Mexico	3.25
14	Belgium	2.10		88	Senegal	3.25
14	Canada	2.10		88	Tanzania	3.25
14	United Arab Emirates	2.10		94	Nigeria	3.30
17	Austria	2.15		94	Romania	3.30
17	Chile	2.15		96	Brazil	3.35
17	Estonia	2.15		96	Cambodia	3.35
20	Czech Republic	2.20		96	Egypt	3.35
20	Netherlands	2.20		96	Ivory Coast	3.35
22	Denmark	2.25		96	Madagascar	3.35
22	Finland	2.25		96	Moldova	3.35
24	Germany	2.30		102	Nepal	3.40
24	Iceland	2.30		103	Cape Verde	3.44
24	South Korea	2.30		104	Armenia	3.45
27	Norway	2.35		104	Dominican Republic	3.45
28	Kuwait	2.40		104	Russia	3.45
28	Malaysia	2.40		107	Burkina Faso	3.50
28	Panama	2.40		107	Cameroon	3.50
28	Thailand	2.40		107	Lesotho	3.50
32	El Salvador	2.45		107	Nicaragua	3.50
32	Sri Lanka	2.45		107	Venezuela	3.50
32	Sweden	2.45		112	Gambia	3.60
35	France	2.50		112	Guyana	3.60
35	Italy	2.50		114	Bulgaria	3.65
35	Spain	2.50		114	Georgia	3.65
38	Trinidad and Tobago	2.55		114	Malawi	3.65
39	Argentina	2.60		117	Ethiopia	3.70
39	Barbados	2.60		117	India	3.70
39	Cyprus	2.60		117	Niger	3.70
39	Jamaica	2.60		120	Albania	3.75
39	Portugal	2.60		120	Bangladesh	3.75
44	Bolivia	2.65		120	China (PRC)	3.75
44	Oman	2.65		120	Congo	3.75
44	Philippines	2.65		120	Croatia	3.75
47	Swaziland	2.70		125	Chad	3.80
47	Uruguay	2.70		125	Mauritania	3.80
49	Botswana	2.75		125	Ukraine	3.80
49	Jordan	2.75		128	Sierra Leone	3.85
49	Namibia	2.75		129	Burundi	3.90
49	Tunisia	2.75		129	Suriname	3.90
53	Belize	2.80		129	Zimbabwe	3.90
53	Costa Rica	2.80		132	Haiti	4.00
53	Guatemala	2.80		132	Kyrgyzstan	4.00
53	Israel	2.80		132	Syria	4.00
53	Peru	2.80		135	Belarus	4.05
53	Saudi Arabia	2.80		136	Kazakstan	4.10
53	Turkey	2.80		136	Mozambique	4.10
53	Uganda	2.80		136	Yemen	4.10
53	Western Samoa	2.80		139	Sudan	4.20
62	Indonesia	2.85		140	Myanmar	4.30
62	Latvia	2.85		140	Rwanda	4.30
62	Malta	2.85		142	Angola	4.35
62	Paraguay	2.85		143	Azerbaijan	4.40
66	Greece	2.90		143	Tajikistan	4.40
66	Hungary	2.90		145	Turkmenistan	4.50
66	South Africa	2.90		146	Uzbekistan	4.55
69	Benin	2.95		147	Congo/Zaire	4.70
69	Ecuador	2.95		147	Iran	4.70
69	Gabon	2.95		147	Libya	4.70
69	Morocco	2.95		147	Somalia	4.70
69	Poland	2.95		147	Vietnam	4.70
74	Colombia	3.00		152	Bosnia	4.80
74	Ghana	3.00		153	Iraq	4.90
74	Lithuania	3.00		154	Cuba	5.00
77	Kenya	3.05		154	Laos	5.00
77	Slovak Republic	3.05		154	North Korea	5.00

Repressed

MONETARY POLICY
Score: 5–Stable (very high level of inflation)

Somalia's average annual rate of inflation from 1985 to 1993 was 75.4 percent. No data for 1994, 1995, 1996, or 1997 were available.

CAPITAL FLOWS AND FOREIGN INVESTMENT
Score: 4–Stable (high barriers)

Somalia remains in economic ruins, with no clear protection of foreign investment. The most significant threat to foreign investment is continued military fighting. According to the U.S. Department of State, "Sporadic fighting among local militias continues in parts of the country. Kidnappings and other threats to foreigners occur unpredictably in virtually all regions."[2]

BANKING
Score: 5–Stable (very high level of restrictions)

Somalia's banking system has collapsed, and banks operate in primitive conditions. Most lending is performed unofficially among family members and friends, some of whom reside in other countries.

WAGE AND PRICE CONTROLS
Score: 3–Stable (moderate level)

Wages and prices in Somalia are set mainly by the market through barter. The government is not powerful enough to enforce the laws that set prices. It is not uncommon for militias to confiscate goods (particularly food) from their producers and distribute them freely to their supporters. Thus, prices often are affected by looting and theft.

PROPERTY RIGHTS
Score: 5–Stable (very low level of protection)

Private property is virtually nonexistent in Somalia, and clans and corrupt government officials often confiscate property. According to the U.S. Department of State, "There is no national government in Somalia to offer security or police protection for travelers."[3]

REGULATION
Score: 5–Stable (very high level)

Establishing a business in Somalia is nearly impossible. Meeting official requirements is beyond the ability of most entrepreneurs, so they simply operate in the black market. Corruption is rampant.

BLACK MARKET
Score: 5–Stable (very high level of activity)

Most economic activity in Somalia occurs in the black market.

NOTES

1. U.S. Department of State Travel Advisory, July 1996.
2. *Ibid.*
3. *Ibid.*

South Africa   2.90

1997 Score: **3.00**	1996 Score: **3.00**	1995 Score: **3.00**

Trade	4	Banking	3
Taxation	4	Wages and Prices	2
Government Intervention	3	Property Rights	3
Monetary Policy	3	Regulation	2
Foreign Investment	2	Black Market	3

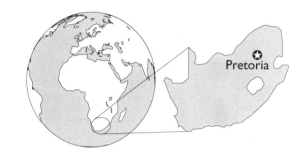

Pretoria

South Africa's transition from apartheid to nonracial democracy has gone well. The new Constitution and Bill of Rights became effective in February 1997, and the level of national reconciliation has been impressive, although some recent court and government decisions have elicited protests and riots. A key to the country's stability will be the revival of its long-depressed economy. South Africa enjoys many economic assets, including a modern industrial sector, a well-developed infrastructure, and abundant natural resources. The government over the years has maintained a great deal of control over the economy. The African National Congress, which holds the presidency and a majority in the National Assembly, seems committed to economic liberalization, fiscal austerity, and privatization, although social programs and other state interventions intended to improve the lives of previously disenfranchised black South Africans may undermine this agenda. After several years of negative growth in the early 1990s, the economy is growing at a respectable pace, averaging 2.6 percent from 1993 to 1996. South Africa recently reduced its barriers to trade. Thus, its overall score is 0.1 point better this year.

TRADE POLICY
Score: 4+ (high level of protectionism)

South Africa's average tariff rate is now 12 percent,[1] down from an average of 21 percent in 1993.[2] As a result, its trade policy score is one point better this year. According to the U.S. Department of State, "Under terms of the Import and Export Control Act of 1963, South Africa's Minister of Trade and Industry may act in the national interest to prohibit, ration, or otherwise regulate imports. In recent years, the list of restricted goods requiring import permits has been reduced, but still includes such goods as foodstuffs, clothing, fabrics, wood and paper products, refined petroleum products and chemicals."[3]

TAXATION
Score–Income taxation: 4–Stable (high tax rates)
Score–Corporate taxation: 3–Stable (moderate tax rates)
Final Taxation Score: 4–Stable (high tax rates)

South Africa has a progressive tax system, with the highest income level taxed at a rate of 45 percent and the average income level taxed at a rate of 17 percent. The corporate tax is 35 percent. South Africa also has a 14 percent value-added tax, a financial services tax, and regional taxes.

GOVERNMENT INTERVENTION IN THE ECONOMY
Score: 3–Stable (moderate level)

Government consumes 20.6 percent of South Africa's GDP, and 6 state-owned companies rank among the country's 25 largest firms. State assets include the national airline and electric utilities. The government is studying the possible "reconstruction" of state-owned enterprises.

1	Hong Kong	1.25	77	Zambia	3.05
2	Singapore	1.30	80	Mali	3.10
3	Bahrain	1.70	80	Mongolia	3.10
4	New Zealand	1.75	80	Slovenia	3.10
5	Switzerland	1.90	83	Honduras	3.15
5	United States	1.90	83	Papua New Guinea	3.15
7	Luxembourg	1.95	85	Djibouti	3.20
7	Taiwan	1.95	85	Fiji	3.20
7	United Kingdom	1.95	85	Pakistan	3.20
10	Bahamas	2.00	88	Algeria	3.25
10	Ireland	2.00	88	Guinea	3.25
12	Australia	2.05	88	Lebanon	3.25
12	Japan	2.05	88	Mexico	3.25
14	Belgium	2.10	88	Senegal	3.25
14	Canada	2.10	88	Tanzania	3.25
14	United Arab Emirates	2.10	94	Nigeria	3.30
17	Austria	2.15	94	Romania	3.30
17	Chile	2.15	96	Brazil	3.35
17	Estonia	2.15	96	Cambodia	3.35
20	Czech Republic	2.20	96	Egypt	3.35
20	Netherlands	2.20	96	Ivory Coast	3.35
22	Denmark	2.25	96	Madagascar	3.35
22	Finland	2.25	96	Moldova	3.35
24	Germany	2.30	102	Nepal	3.40
24	Iceland	2.30	103	Cape Verde	3.44
24	South Korea	2.30	104	Armenia	3.45
27	Norway	2.35	104	Dominican Republic	3.45
28	Kuwait	2.40	104	Russia	3.45
28	Malaysia	2.40	107	Burkina Faso	3.50
28	Panama	2.40	107	Cameroon	3.50
28	Thailand	2.40	107	Lesotho	3.50
32	El Salvador	2.45	107	Nicaragua	3.50
32	Sri Lanka	2.45	107	Venezuela	3.50
32	Sweden	2.45	112	Gambia	3.60
35	France	2.50	112	Guyana	3.60
35	Italy	2.50	114	Bulgaria	3.65
35	Spain	2.50	114	Georgia	3.65
38	Trinidad and Tobago	2.55	114	Malawi	3.65
39	Argentina	2.60	117	Ethiopia	3.70
39	Barbados	2.60	117	India	3.70
39	Cyprus	2.60	117	Niger	3.70
39	Jamaica	2.60	120	Albania	3.75
39	Portugal	2.60	120	Bangladesh	3.75
44	Bolivia	2.65	120	China (PRC)	3.75
44	Oman	2.65	120	Congo	3.75
44	Philippines	2.65	120	Croatia	3.75
47	Swaziland	2.70	125	Chad	3.80
47	Uruguay	2.70	125	Mauritania	3.80
49	Botswana	2.75	125	Ukraine	3.80
49	Jordan	2.75	128	Sierra Leone	3.85
49	Namibia	2.75	129	Burundi	3.90
49	Tunisia	2.75	129	Suriname	3.90
53	Belize	2.80	129	Zimbabwe	3.90
53	Costa Rica	2.80	132	Haiti	4.00
53	Guatemala	2.80	132	Kyrgyzstan	4.00
53	Israel	2.80	132	Syria	4.00
53	Peru	2.80	135	Belarus	4.05
53	Saudi Arabia	2.80	136	Kazakstan	4.10
53	Turkey	2.80	136	Mozambique	4.10
53	Uganda	2.80	136	Yemen	4.10
53	Western Samoa	2.80	139	Sudan	4.20
62	Indonesia	2.85	140	Myanmar	4.30
62	Latvia	2.85	140	Rwanda	4.30
62	Malta	2.85	142	Angola	4.35
62	Paraguay	2.85	143	Azerbaijan	4.40
66	Greece	2.90	143	Tajikistan	4.40
66	Hungary	2.90	145	Turkmenistan	4.50
66	South Africa	2.90	146	Uzbekistan	4.55
69	Benin	2.95	147	Congo/Zaire	4.70
69	Ecuador	2.95	147	Iran	4.70
69	Gabon	2.95	147	Libya	4.70
69	Morocco	2.95	147	Somalia	4.70
69	Poland	2.95	147	Vietnam	4.70
74	Colombia	3.00	152	Bosnia	4.80
74	Ghana	3.00	153	Iraq	4.90
74	Lithuania	3.00	154	Cuba	5.00
77	Kenya	3.05	154	Laos	5.00
77	Slovak Republic	3.05	154	North Korea	5.00

Mostly Free

MONETARY POLICY
Score: 3–Stable (moderate level of inflation)

South Africa's average annual rate of inflation from 1985 to 1995 was 13.7 percent. In 1996, the rate was 20.9 percent.

CAPITAL FLOWS AND FOREIGN INVESTMENT
Score: 2–Stable (low barriers)

No government approval is required for foreign investment, and foreign investors are subject to the same laws as domestic investors. In addition, there are no requirements for South African participation in management, only a few areas of the economy are reserved for South Africans, and foreign investors are free to acquire land. Foreign-controlled firms, however, are subject to domestic borrowing restrictions.

BANKING
Score: 3–Stable (moderate level of restrictions)

South Africa has a world-class financial sector. Legal restrictions that discriminate against foreign-owned financial institutions have been eliminated, and over 30 foreign banks now operate in South Africa. The banking and insurance industries, however, are tightly controlled by the Reserve Bank, with which interest-free reserve balances must be deposited. Exchange controls preclude international investment by South African financial institutions. Licenses for new banks and insurance companies are not granted readily. The new government also may pressure banks into investing in its Reconstruction and Development Program, which is designed to promote the economic advancement of black South Africans.

WAGE AND PRICE CONTROLS
Score: 2–Stable (low level)

Price controls, once pervasive, now exist only on coal, gasoline, and some utilities. There is no national minimum wage, but labor legislation currently under consideration could lead to the de facto imposition of wage controls.

PROPERTY RIGHTS
Score: 3–Stable (moderate level of protection)

No private-sector company, whether South African or foreign-controlled, has been nationalized since the 1920s. The judiciary is both professional and effective. There is the danger, however, that redistributionist policies, including the land reform program, may weaken private property rights. It also is possible that the protection of private property clause in the interim constitution will not be included in the new constitution. Squatters and crime are problems, and the state may assume control of tribal-controlled communal land.

REGULATION
Score: 2–Stable (low level)

Regulation of economic activity is minimal in South Africa. It takes only 4 to 10 days to incorporate a business, and most businesses can be started with a minimum of formalities. Licenses, required for certain activities, can be obtained with relative ease. There has been a proliferation of once-banned street vendors. The establishment of an affirmative action directorate within the Ministry of Labor is a sign that increased political pressure to practice more affirmative action in the hiring and firing of personnel can be expected.

BLACK MARKET
Score: 3–Stable (moderate level of activity)

In 1991, the government lifted legal restrictions that prevented black South Africans from owning businesses, obtaining skilled jobs, or living in major urban centers. This will reduce black market activity. There still is significant informal activity, however, in retail textiles and pirated intellectual property. Piracy accounts for as much as 70 percent of the trade in computer software.

NOTES
1. South Africa is a member of the Southern African Customs Union, which has a common external tariff of 12 percent. Other members include Botswana, Lesotho, Namibia, and Swaziland.
2. Economist Intelligence Unit, *ILT Reports, South Africa,* February 1996, p. 27.
3. U.S. Department of State, *Country Reports on Economic Policy and Trade Practices,* 1997, p. 14.

Spain   2.50

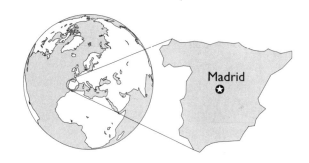

1997 Score: **2.60**	1996 Score: **2.70**	1995 Score: **2.60**

Trade	2	Banking	2
Taxation	5	Wages and Prices	3
Government Intervention	2	Property Rights	2
Monetary Policy	2	Regulation	3
Foreign Investment	2	Black Market	2

Madrid ✪

From the end of the Spanish Civil War until 1975, Spain was ruled by Francisco Franco. Following the accession of King Juan Carlos, it became a constitutional monarchy with a parliamentary government. Because of its many years of dictatorship, Spain's economy lags behind those of many of its European neighbors. Since joining the European Union (EU) in 1986, however, the government has opened the economy, removed oppressive, government-run bureaucracies from many economic decisions, and expanded the free market. In March 1996, dissatisfied with a multiyear recession and official corruption under the Socialist Party, Spain elected a new conservative government headed by Prime Minister Jose Maria Anzar of the Popular Party. The Anzar government is accelerating economic reform. As the country scrambles to meet its EU directives and liberalize large sections of its economy, it is enjoying lower unemployment and stronger economic growth. The government has liberalized the banking sector, making it more accessible to foreign investment. Anzar also has begun to liberalize Spain's highly regulated labor market to lower unemployment, and the government has pledged further privatizations. Thus, Spain's overall score is 0.1 point better this year.

TRADE POLICY
Score: 2–Stable (low level of protectionism)

Spain has an average tariff rate of about 3.6 percent. It also maintains restrictive customs procedures, strict labeling and testing requirements, and many other nontariff barriers.

TAXATION
Score–Income taxation: 5–Stable (very high tax rates)
Score–Corporate taxation: 3–Stable (moderate tax rates)
Final Taxation Score: 5–Stable (very high tax rates)

Spain's top income tax rate is 56 percent, and the average income level is taxed at 24.5 percent. The top corporate rate is 35 percent. Spain also has a 35 percent capital gains tax and a 4 percent to 16 percent value-added tax.

GOVERNMENT INTERVENTION IN THE ECONOMY
Score: 2–Stable (Low level)

Government consumes 16.2 percent of Spain's GDP, and state ownership of industry remains extensive. According to the Economist Intelligence Unit, "The government exercises monopoly control (sometimes through joint ventures with private-sector companies) over postal services and railways. State ownership remains extensive in Spanish industry, utilities, public services and transport facilities, despite a limited privatization programme pursued since the mid-1980s."[1] The Anzar government is accelerating the privatization of state-owned industries. By global standards, Spain's overall level of government intervention in the economy is low.

1	Hong Kong	1.25
2	Singapore	1.30
3	Bahrain	1.70
4	New Zealand	1.75
5	Switzerland	1.90
5	United States	1.90
7	Luxembourg	1.95
7	Taiwan	1.95
7	United Kingdom	1.95
10	Bahamas	2.00
10	Ireland	2.00
12	Australia	2.05
12	Japan	2.05
14	Belgium	2.10
14	Canada	2.10
14	United Arab Emirates	2.10
17	Austria	2.15
17	Chile	2.15
17	Estonia	2.15
20	Czech Republic	2.20
20	Netherlands	2.20
22	Denmark	2.25
22	Finland	2.25
24	Germany	2.30
24	Iceland	2.30
24	South Korea	2.30
27	Norway	2.35
28	Kuwait	2.40
28	Malaysia	2.40
28	Panama	2.40
28	Thailand	2.40
32	El Salvador	2.45
32	Sri Lanka	2.45
32	Sweden	2.45
35	France	2.50
35	Italy	2.50
35	Spain	2.50
38	Trinidad and Tobago	2.55
39	Argentina	2.60
39	Barbados	2.60
39	Cyprus	2.60
39	Jamaica	2.60
39	Portugal	2.60
44	Bolivia	2.65
44	Oman	2.65
44	Philippines	2.65
47	Swaziland	2.70
47	Uruguay	2.70
49	Botswana	2.75
49	Jordan	2.75
49	Namibia	2.75
49	Tunisia	2.75
53	Belize	2.80
53	Costa Rica	2.80
53	Guatemala	2.80
53	Israel	2.80
53	Peru	2.80
53	Saudi Arabia	2.80
53	Turkey	2.80
53	Uganda	2.80
53	Western Samoa	2.80
62	Indonesia	2.85
62	Latvia	2.85
62	Malta	2.85
62	Paraguay	2.85
66	Greece	2.90
66	Hungary	2.90
66	South Africa	2.90
69	Benin	2.95
69	Ecuador	2.95
69	Gabon	2.95
69	Morocco	2.95
69	Poland	2.95
74	Colombia	3.00
74	Ghana	3.00
74	Lithuania	3.00
77	Kenya	3.05
77	Slovak Republic	3.05

77	Zambia	3.05
80	Mali	3.10
80	Mongolia	3.10
80	Slovenia	3.10
83	Honduras	3.15
83	Papua New Guinea	3.15
85	Djibouti	3.20
85	Fiji	3.20
85	Pakistan	3.20
88	Algeria	3.25
88	Guinea	3.25
88	Lebanon	3.25
88	Mexico	3.25
88	Senegal	3.25
88	Tanzania	3.25
94	Nigeria	3.30
94	Romania	3.30
96	Brazil	3.35
96	Cambodia	3.35
96	Egypt	3.35
96	Ivory Coast	3.35
96	Madagascar	3.35
96	Moldova	3.35
102	Nepal	3.40
103	Cape Verde	3.44
104	Armenia	3.45
104	Dominican Republic	3.45
104	Russia	3.45
107	Burkina Faso	3.50
107	Cameroon	3.50
107	Lesotho	3.50
107	Nicaragua	3.50
107	Venezuela	3.50
112	Gambia	3.60
112	Guyana	3.60
114	Bulgaria	3.65
114	Georgia	3.65
114	Malawi	3.65
117	Ethiopia	3.70
117	India	3.70
117	Niger	3.70
120	Albania	3.75
120	Bangladesh	3.75
120	China (PRC)	3.75
120	Congo	3.75
120	Croatia	3.75
125	Chad	3.80
125	Mauritania	3.80
125	Ukraine	3.80
128	Sierra Leone	3.85
129	Burundi	3.90
129	Suriname	3.90
129	Zimbabwe	3.90
132	Haiti	4.00
132	Kyrgyzstan	4.00
132	Syria	4.00
135	Belarus	4.05
136	Kazakstan	4.10
136	Mozambique	4.10
136	Yemen	4.10
139	Sudan	4.20
140	Myanmar	4.30
140	Rwanda	4.30
142	Angola	4.35
143	Azerbaijan	4.40
143	Tajikistan	4.40
145	Turkmenistan	4.50
146	Uzbekistan	4.55
147	Congo/Zaire	4.70
147	Iran	4.70
147	Libya	4.70
147	Somalia	4.70
147	Vietnam	4.70
152	Bosnia	4.80
153	Iraq	4.90
154	Cuba	5.00
154	Laos	5.00
154	North Korea	5.00

Mostly Free

MONETARY POLICY
Score: 2–Stable (low level of inflation)

Spain's average annual rate of inflation from 1985 to 1995 was 6.3 percent. In 1996, the rate fell to 3.6 percent.

CAPITAL FLOWS AND FOREIGN INVESTMENT
Score: 2–Stable (low barriers)

Membership in the EU has forced the government to remove most restrictions on foreign investment. Some restrictions remain, however, in such areas as telecommunications.

BANKING
Score: 2+ (low level of restrictions)

Integration into the EU has made Spain's banking system more competitive, forcing it to accept banks from other EU members. Spain has made some progress in opening its banking system to foreign competition by removing restrictions on investments from non-EU investors. As a result, its banking score is one point better this year.

WAGE AND PRICE CONTROLS
Score: 3–Stable (moderate level)

Price controls are imposed on electricity, telephone services, rail transport, postal service, and some pharmaceutical products. Spain maintains a minimum wage.

PROPERTY RIGHTS
Score: 2–Stable (high level of protection)

Property is safe from government expropriation. Spain's legal system effectively protects private property, although the U.S. Department of State has categorized the judicial system as being occasionally "inefficient."[2]

REGULATION
Score: 3–Stable (moderate level)

The government maintains many regulations on businesses, including labor and environmental laws and regulations dealing with fringe benefits. All are moderately burdensome.

BLACK MARKET
Score: 2–Stable (low level of activity)

Spain's black market is confined mainly to pirated computer software, prerecorded music and video tapes, and illegal local cable transmissions of copyrighted movies. The government takes intellectual property infringement very seriously and has moved to enforce new laws.

NOTES
1. Economist Intelligence Unit, *ILT Reports, Spain,* 1997.
2. U.S. Department of State, "Spain Country Report on Human Rights Practices for 1996," 1997.

Sri Lanka   2.45

1997 Score: **2.45**	1996 Score: **2.65**	1995 Score: **2.80**

Trade	3	Banking	2
Taxation	3.5	Wages and Prices	1
Government Intervention	2	Property Rights	3
Monetary Policy	2	Regulation	2
Foreign Investment	3	Black Market	3

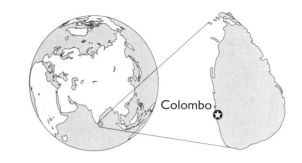

Colombo

Sri Lanka declared its independence from the United Kingdom in 1948. It adopted a new constitution in 1972, creating a republic, and began a series of economic reforms in 1977. Since 1983, civil unrest and (most recently) civil war have been a serious drain on the economy. Despite domestic turmoil, however, a new economic restructuring plan has helped fuel substantial economic growth. The government has focused on reducing trade barriers, privatizing businesses, and expanding the role of the private sector. It also has reduced trade barriers and tax levels, in addition to cracking down on government corruption.

TRADE POLICY
Score: 3–Stable (moderate level of protectionism)

Sri Lanka has a three-tiered system of 10 percent, 25 percent, and 30 percent tariffs on various imports. For some items, such as automobiles, rates range from 50 percent to 100 percent. The government also imposes a 4.5 percent defense levy, an excise tax on selected consumer and nonessential goods, and a 10 percent export-development access surcharge on a few items subject to an import duty of 45 percent or more, bringing the average tariff rate to 12 percent. There are no significant nontariff barriers.

TAXATION
Score–Income taxation: 3–Stable (moderate tax rates)
Score–Corporate taxation: 3–Stable (high tax rates)
Final Taxation Score: 3.5–Stable (high tax rates)

The top marginal income tax rate is 35 percent, with the average income level taxed at 15 percent. The top corporate income tax rate is 35 percent. Sri Lanka also has a 1 percent to 20 percent turnover tax and a social contributions tax.

GOVERNMENT INTERVENTION IN THE ECONOMY
Score: 2–Stable (low level)

Government consumes 10.5 percent of Sri Lanka's GDP, up from 8.5 percent in 1980. It also owns some sectors of the economy. While 9 of the 23 state-owned agricultural plantations have been privatized, for example, the others remain in state hands because privatization has been halted. The government also owns the telecommunications company (now undergoing privatization), some banks, the Independent Television Network, the National Paper Corporation, the National Salt Corporation, and a textile import and trading corporation.[1] Some of these enterprises may become candidates for privatization in the future.

MONETARY POLICY
Score: 2–Stable (low level of inflation)

Sri Lanka's average annual rate of inflation between 1985 and 1995 was 11.1 percent. In 1996, the rate was 15.9 percent.

1	Hong Kong	1.25	77	Zambia	3.05
2	Singapore	1.30	80	Mali	3.10
3	Bahrain	1.70	80	Mongolia	3.10
4	New Zealand	1.75	80	Slovenia	3.10
5	Switzerland	1.90	83	Honduras	3.15
5	United States	1.90	83	Papua New Guinea	3.15
7	Luxembourg	1.95	85	Djibouti	3.20
7	Taiwan	1.95	85	Fiji	3.20
7	United Kingdom	1.95	85	Pakistan	3.20
10	Bahamas	2.00	88	Algeria	3.25
10	Ireland	2.00	88	Guinea	3.25
12	Australia	2.05	88	Lebanon	3.25
12	Japan	2.05	88	Mexico	3.25
14	Belgium	2.10	88	Senegal	3.25
14	Canada	2.10	88	Tanzania	3.25
14	United Arab Emirates	2.10	94	Nigeria	3.30
17	Austria	2.15	94	Romania	3.30
17	Chile	2.15	96	Brazil	3.35
17	Estonia	2.15	96	Cambodia	3.35
20	Czech Republic	2.20	96	Egypt	3.35
20	Netherlands	2.20	96	Ivory Coast	3.35
22	Denmark	2.25	96	Madagascar	3.35
22	Finland	2.25	96	Moldova	3.35
24	Germany	2.30	102	Nepal	3.40
24	Iceland	2.30	103	Cape Verde	3.44
24	South Korea	2.30	104	Armenia	3.45
27	Norway	2.35	104	Dominican Republic	3.45
28	Kuwait	2.40	104	Russia	3.45
28	Malaysia	2.40	107	Burkina Faso	3.50
28	Panama	2.40	107	Cameroon	3.50
28	Thailand	2.40	107	Lesotho	3.50
32	El Salvador	2.45	107	Nicaragua	3.50
32	Sri Lanka	2.45	107	Venezuela	3.50
32	Sweden	2.45	112	Gambia	3.60
35	France	2.50	112	Guyana	3.60
35	Italy	2.50	114	Bulgaria	3.65
35	Spain	2.50	114	Georgia	3.65
38	Trinidad and Tobago	2.55	114	Malawi	3.65
39	Argentina	2.60	117	Ethiopia	3.70
39	Barbados	2.60	117	India	3.70
39	Cyprus	2.60	117	Niger	3.70
39	Jamaica	2.60	120	Albania	3.75
39	Portugal	2.60	120	Bangladesh	3.75
44	Bolivia	2.65	120	China (PRC)	3.75
44	Oman	2.65	120	Congo	3.75
44	Philippines	2.65	120	Croatia	3.75
47	Swaziland	2.70	125	Chad	3.80
47	Uruguay	2.70	125	Mauritania	3.80
49	Botswana	2.75	125	Ukraine	3.80
49	Jordan	2.75	128	Sierra Leone	3.85
49	Namibia	2.75	129	Burundi	3.90
49	Tunisia	2.75	129	Suriname	3.90
53	Belize	2.80	129	Zimbabwe	3.90
53	Costa Rica	2.80	132	Haiti	4.00
53	Guatemala	2.80	132	Kyrgyzstan	4.00
53	Israel	2.80	132	Syria	4.00
53	Peru	2.80	135	Belarus	4.05
53	Saudi Arabia	2.80	136	Kazakstan	4.10
53	Turkey	2.80	136	Mozambique	4.10
53	Uganda	2.80	136	Yemen	4.10
53	Western Samoa	2.80	139	Sudan	4.20
62	Indonesia	2.85	140	Myanmar	4.30
62	Latvia	2.85	140	Rwanda	4.30
62	Malta	2.85	142	Angola	4.35
62	Paraguay	2.85	143	Azerbaijan	4.40
66	Greece	2.90	143	Tajikistan	4.40
66	Hungary	2.90	145	Turkmenistan	4.50
66	South Africa	2.90	146	Uzbekistan	4.55
69	Benin	2.95	147	Congo/Zaire	4.70
69	Ecuador	2.95	147	Iran	4.70
69	Gabon	2.95	147	Libya	4.70
69	Morocco	2.95	147	Somalia	4.70
69	Poland	2.95	147	Vietnam	4.70
74	Colombia	3.00	152	Bosnia	4.80
74	Ghana	3.00	153	Iraq	4.90
74	Lithuania	3.00	154	Cuba	5.00
77	Kenya	3.05	154	Laos	5.00
77	Slovak Republic	3.05	154	North Korea	5.00

Mostly Free

CAPITAL FLOWS AND FOREIGN INVESTMENT
Score: 3–Stable (moderate barriers)

Sri Lanka generally welcomes foreign investment. Its well-defined and accessible foreign investment code treats foreign and domestic firms equally. Equity restrictions of up to 40 percent apply to some businesses, however, and foreign investment is prohibited in non-bank moneylending, pawn shops, retail trade outlets with capital investments of less than $1 million, some personal services, and coastal fishing.

BANKING
Score: 2–Stable (low level of restrictions)

Sri Lanka has over 20 commercial banks, most of them foreign-owned. The banking sector includes both private and state-owned banks, and competition has caused the industry to become increasingly efficient.

WAGE AND PRICE CONTROLS
Score: 1–Stable (very low level)

Most wages and prices in Sri Lanka are determined by the market, although there are controls on the prices of such items as foodstuffs and some energy products. A minimum wage is established by wage boards for specific sectors. Wages in other areas are determined by the market.

PROPERTY RIGHTS
Score: 3–Stable (moderate level of protection)

Sri Lanka's court system is efficient and free from government influence. Since the beginning of economic liberalization in 1977, the government has not expropriated any foreign assets. Ethnic conflict and political violence, however, still present a threat; fighting in the eastern part of the country, for example, has forced citizens to abandon their homes and businesses.[2]

REGULATION
Score: 2–Stable (low level)

Sri Lanka's bureaucracy is both efficient and stable, and the government has instituted a review board to look into complaints of corruption. There are some regulations on employee leave, health, and safety.

BLACK MARKET
Score: 3–Stable (moderate level of activity)

Sri Lanka generally has strong and efficient intellectual property rights laws, but there is a growing black market in pirated computer software, prerecorded music and video tapes, and compact disks. According to the U.S. Department of Commerce, "At present, copyright protection is not extended to computer programs, databases, and semiconductor layout designs. However, under the U.S.-Sri Lanka bilateral agreement, U.S. software producers receive copyright protection in Sri Lanka."[3]

NOTES

1. Economist Intelligence Unit, *EIU Country Report: Sri Lanka,* 2nd Quarter, 1996.
2. *Ibid.*
3. U.S. Department of Commerce, *Country Commercial Guide,* 1996.

Sudan   4.20

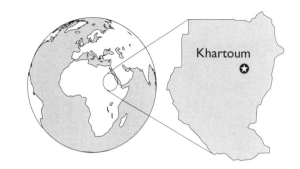

Khartoum

| 1997 Score: **4.20** | 1996 Score: **4.10** | 1995 Score: **4.22** |

Trade	5	Banking	4
Taxation	5	Wages and Prices	4
Government Intervention	3	Property Rights	4
Monetary Policy	5	Regulation	4
Foreign Investment	4	Black Market	4

Sudan gained its independence from the United Kingdom in 1956 and is Africa's largest country. In 1989, President Omar Hassan Al-Bashir's Islamic fundamentalist authoritarian regime seized power and suspended the 1985 constitution, rescinded freedom of the press, and outlawed political parties. Sudan has become increasingly isolated internationally, even among Arab countries. Egypt blames it for the attempted assassination of its president in 1995. In 1993, the U.S. Department of State declared Sudan to be a supporter of terrorism. The ruling National Islamic Front is engaged in an expensive and brutal civil war with southern Sudanese separatists, and Sudan has poor relations and border disputes with most of its neighbors. Although the government has implemented modest economic liberalization, the economy is not free and continues to deteriorate, achieving an average GDP growth of only 2.6 percent from 1993 to 1996. Government regulation and restrictions on banking have increased. Economic mismanagement and radical politics have left Sudan with few remaining foreign aid donors.

TRADE POLICY
Score: 5–Stable (very high level of protectionism)

Sudan's average tariff rate is 24 percent,[1] although some estimates put it as high as 56 percent.[2] Import and export licenses have been eliminated, although the importation of some 30 items is banned. Corruption within the customs service is rampant.

TAXATION
Score–Income taxation: 5–Stable (very high tax rates)
Score–Corporate taxation: 5–Stable (very high tax rates)
Final Taxation Score: 5–Stable (very high tax rates)

Sudan has top income and corporate tax rates of 60 percent.[3]

GOVERNMENT INTERVENTION IN THE ECONOMY
Score: 3–Stable (moderate level)

Government consumes about 17 percent of Sudan's GDP, a large portion of which is generated by the state-owned sector.

MONETARY POLICY
Score: 5–Stable (very high level of inflation)

Sudan's average annual rate of inflation from 1985 to 1995 was 63.2 percent. In 1996, the rate was 130 percent.

1	Hong Kong	1.25	77	Zambia	3.05
2	Singapore	1.30	80	Mali	3.10
3	Bahrain	1.70	80	Mongolia	3.10
4	New Zealand	1.75	80	Slovenia	3.10
5	Switzerland	1.90	83	Honduras	3.15
5	United States	1.90	83	Papua New Guinea	3.15
7	Luxembourg	1.95	85	Djibouti	3.20
7	Taiwan	1.95	85	Fiji	3.20
7	United Kingdom	1.95	85	Pakistan	3.20
10	Bahamas	2.00	88	Algeria	3.25
10	Ireland	2.00	88	Guinea	3.25
12	Australia	2.05	88	Lebanon	3.25
12	Japan	2.05	88	Mexico	3.25
14	Belgium	2.10	88	Senegal	3.25
14	Canada	2.10	88	Tanzania	3.25
14	United Arab Emirates	2.10	94	Nigeria	3.30
17	Austria	2.15	94	Romania	3.30
17	Chile	2.15	96	Brazil	3.35
17	Estonia	2.15	96	Cambodia	3.35
20	Czech Republic	2.20	96	Egypt	3.35
20	Netherlands	2.20	96	Ivory Coast	3.35
22	Denmark	2.25	96	Madagascar	3.35
22	Finland	2.25	96	Moldova	3.35
24	Germany	2.30	102	Nepal	3.40
24	Iceland	2.30	103	Cape Verde	3.44
24	South Korea	2.30	104	Armenia	3.45
27	Norway	2.35	104	Dominican Republic	3.45
28	Kuwait	2.40	104	Russia	3.45
28	Malaysia	2.40	107	Burkina Faso	3.50
28	Panama	2.40	107	Cameroon	3.50
28	Thailand	2.40	107	Lesotho	3.50
32	El Salvador	2.45	107	Nicaragua	3.50
32	Sri Lanka	2.45	107	Venezuela	3.50
32	Sweden	2.45	112	Gambia	3.60
35	France	2.50	112	Guyana	3.60
35	Italy	2.50	114	Bulgaria	3.65
35	Spain	2.50	114	Georgia	3.65
38	Trinidad and Tobago	2.55	114	Malawi	3.65
39	Argentina	2.60	117	Ethiopia	3.70
39	Barbados	2.60	117	India	3.70
39	Cyprus	2.60	117	Niger	3.70
39	Jamaica	2.60	120	Albania	3.75
39	Portugal	2.60	120	Bangladesh	3.75
44	Bolivia	2.65	120	China (PRC)	3.75
44	Oman	2.65	120	Congo	3.75
44	Philippines	2.65	120	Croatia	3.75
47	Swaziland	2.70	125	Chad	3.80
47	Uruguay	2.70	125	Mauritania	3.80
49	Botswana	2.75	125	Ukraine	3.80
49	Jordan	2.75	128	Sierra Leone	3.85
49	Namibia	2.75	129	Burundi	3.90
49	Tunisia	2.75	129	Suriname	3.90
53	Belize	2.80	129	Zimbabwe	3.90
53	Costa Rica	2.80	132	Haiti	4.00
53	Guatemala	2.80	132	Kyrgyzstan	4.00
53	Israel	2.80	132	Syria	4.00
53	Peru	2.80	135	Belarus	4.05
53	Saudi Arabia	2.80	136	Kazakstan	4.10
53	Turkey	2.80	136	Mozambique	4.10
53	Uganda	2.80	136	Yemen	4.10
53	Western Samoa	2.80	139	Sudan	4.20
62	Indonesia	2.85	140	Myanmar	4.30
62	Latvia	2.85	140	Rwanda	4.30
62	Malta	2.85	142	Angola	4.35
62	Paraguay	2.85	143	Azerbaijan	4.40
66	Greece	2.90	143	Tajikistan	4.40
66	Hungary	2.90	145	Turkmenistan	4.50
66	South Africa	2.90	146	Uzbekistan	4.55
69	Benin	2.95	147	Congo/Zaire	4.70
69	Ecuador	2.95	147	Iran	4.70
69	Gabon	2.95	147	Libya	4.70
69	Morocco	2.95	147	Somalia	4.70
69	Poland	2.95	147	Vietnam	4.70
74	Colombia	3.00	152	Bosnia	4.80
74	Ghana	3.00	153	Iraq	4.90
74	Lithuania	3.00	154	Cuba	5.00
77	Kenya	3.05	154	Laos	5.00
77	Slovak Republic	3.05	154	North Korea	5.00

Repressed

CAPITAL FLOWS AND FOREIGN INVESTMENT
Score: 4–Stable (high barriers)

Sudan's Islamic government is very sensitive to outside interference in its affairs, and this makes for an inhospitable environment for foreign investment. Foreign investment is approved on a case-by-case basis; it is not permitted in wholesale or retail companies or in the production of cotton; and bureaucratic procedures designed to encourage the employment of domestic laborers are cumbersome. There is no tax discrimination against foreign investment, but foreigners often find it nearly impossible to move about the country.

BANKING
Score: 4–Stable (high level of restrictions)

The new regime has moved to "Islamicize" Sudan's state-controlled banking system, increasing its control of economic enterprise. There is little freedom to exchange currency.

WAGE AND PRICE CONTROLS
Score: 4–Stable (high level)

Although Sudan has liberalized some prices, price controls on foodstuffs remain in effect, and many goods are subsidized. The government regulates public and private salaries. Sudan has a minimum wage.

PROPERTY RIGHTS
Score: 4–Stable (low level of protection)

There is little respect for private property in Sudan. According to the U.S. Department of State, "The judiciary is not independent and is largely subservient to the Government."[4] The wanton destruction of private property by government troops is widespread in southern Sudan, and petty crime and thievery are common.

REGULATION
Score: 4–Stable (high level)

Bureaucratic inefficiency makes business activity difficult. As is true in many developing countries, the regulatory burden in Sudan is heavy and inefficient. Businesses often find it difficult to obtain licenses to operate, and business owners may be harassed by corrupt bureaucrats. Despite a government crackdown, corruption remains a problem.

BLACK MARKET
Score: 4–Stable (high level of activity)

Rationing has led to a black market in several items, including petroleum and sugar, and the ban on some imports encourages smuggling.

NOTES

1. This figure is for 1992 to 1993 and includes a defense tax. From U.S. Department of State, Bureau of African Affairs, Office of Economic Policy.
2. World Bank, "Open Economies Work Better!" *Policy Research Working Paper* No. 1636, 1996.
3. The most recent reliable information is based on 1989 tax data from World Bank sources. There is not enough information to determine the tax rate on the average income level; thus, Sudan was graded on its top tax rate.
4. U.S. Department of State, "Sudan Country Report on Human Rights Practices for 1996," 1997.

Suriname   3.90

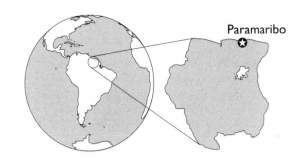

Paramaribo

1997 Score: **4.00**	1996 Score: **3.90**	1995 Score: **n/a**

Trade	5	Banking	4
Taxation	4	Wages and Prices	3
Government Intervention	3	Property Rights	3
Monetary Policy	5	Regulation	4
Foreign Investment	3	Black Market	5

Suriname gained its independence from the Netherlands in 1975. Throughout most of the 1980s, it experienced political strife, and relations between the two countries deteriorated. In 1982, the Netherlands suspended cash development grants to Suriname because of political violence; this aid was reinstated in 1988. Most aid to Suriname has been squandered and has served as the primary obstacle to economic reform. Suriname recently reduced taxes, however. As a result, its overall score this year is 0.1 point better than last year.

TRADE POLICY
Score: 5–Stable (very high level of protectionism)

"According to Ministry of Trade and Industry Officials," reports the U.S. Department of Commerce, "average import duties are between 30 and 40 percent."[1] Trade restrictions include strict import licensing and import bans.

TAXATION
Score–Income taxation: 3+ (moderate tax rates)
Score–Corporate taxation: 4+ (high tax rates)
Final Taxation Score: 4+ (high tax rates)

Suriname's top income tax rate is 50 percent, down from 60 percent in 1996, and the average taxpayer is in the 10 percent bracket. The top marginal corporate tax rate also has been reduced to a top rate of 38 percent, down from 50 percent in 1996. As a result, Suriname's overall taxation score is one point better this year. Suriname also has a 38 percent capital gains tax.

GOVERNMENT INTERVENTION IN THE ECONOMY
Score: 3–Stable (moderately high level)

Government consumes about 17 percent of Suriname's GDP, and the state sector generates a substantial amount of GDP overall.

MONETARY POLICY
Score: 5–Stable (very high level of inflation)

Suriname's average rate of inflation from 1985 to 1995 was 48.5 percent. In 1996, the rate was less than 1 percent.

CAPITAL FLOWS AND FOREIGN INVESTMENT
Score: 3–Stable (moderate barriers)

Suriname is rapidly developing a sound foreign investment climate. Because the foreign investment climate is still evolving, the appropriate ministry deals with investors on an ad hoc basis.[2]

1	Hong Kong	1.25	77	Zambia	3.05
2	Singapore	1.30	80	Mali	3.10
3	Bahrain	1.70	80	Mongolia	3.10
4	New Zealand	1.75	80	Slovenia	3.10
5	Switzerland	1.90	83	Honduras	3.15
5	United States	1.90	83	Papua New Guinea	3.15
7	Luxembourg	1.95	85	Djibouti	3.20
7	Taiwan	1.95	85	Fiji	3.20
7	United Kingdom	1.95	85	Pakistan	3.20
10	Bahamas	2.00	88	Algeria	3.25
10	Ireland	2.00	88	Guinea	3.25
12	Australia	2.05	88	Lebanon	3.25
12	Japan	2.05	88	Mexico	3.25
14	Belgium	2.10	88	Senegal	3.25
14	Canada	2.10	88	Tanzania	3.25
14	United Arab Emirates	2.10	94	Nigeria	3.30
17	Austria	2.15	94	Romania	3.30
17	Chile	2.15	96	Brazil	3.35
17	Estonia	2.15	96	Cambodia	3.35
20	Czech Republic	2.20	96	Egypt	3.35
20	Netherlands	2.20	96	Ivory Coast	3.35
22	Denmark	2.25	96	Madagascar	3.35
22	Finland	2.25	96	Moldova	3.35
24	Germany	2.30	102	Nepal	3.40
24	Iceland	2.30	103	Cape Verde	3.44
24	South Korea	2.30	104	Armenia	3.45
27	Norway	2.35	104	Dominican Republic	3.45
28	Kuwait	2.40	104	Russia	3.45
28	Malaysia	2.40	107	Burkina Faso	3.50
28	Panama	2.40	107	Cameroon	3.50
28	Thailand	2.40	107	Lesotho	3.50
32	El Salvador	2.45	107	Nicaragua	3.50
32	Sri Lanka	2.45	107	Venezuela	3.50
32	Sweden	2.45	112	Gambia	3.60
35	France	2.50	112	Guyana	3.60
35	Italy	2.50	114	Bulgaria	3.65
35	Spain	2.50	114	Georgia	3.65
38	Trinidad and Tobago	2.55	114	Malawi	3.65
39	Argentina	2.60	117	Ethiopia	3.70
39	Barbados	2.60	117	India	3.70
39	Cyprus	2.60	117	Niger	3.70
39	Jamaica	2.60	120	Albania	3.75
39	Portugal	2.60	120	Bangladesh	3.75
44	Bolivia	2.65	120	China (PRC)	3.75
44	Oman	2.65	120	Congo	3.75
44	Philippines	2.65	120	Croatia	3.75
47	Swaziland	2.70	125	Chad	3.80
47	Uruguay	2.70	125	Mauritania	3.80
49	Botswana	2.75	125	Ukraine	3.80
49	Jordan	2.75	128	Sierra Leone	3.85
49	Namibia	2.75	129	Burundi	3.90
49	Tunisia	2.75	129	Suriname	3.90
53	Belize	2.80	129	Zimbabwe	3.90
53	Costa Rica	2.80	132	Haiti	4.00
53	Guatemala	2.80	132	Kyrgyzstan	4.00
53	Israel	2.80	132	Syria	4.00
53	Peru	2.80	135	Belarus	4.05
53	Saudi Arabia	2.80	136	Kazakstan	4.10
53	Turkey	2.80	136	Mozambique	4.10
53	Uganda	2.80	136	Yemen	4.10
53	Western Samoa	2.80	139	Sudan	4.20
62	Indonesia	2.85	140	Myanmar	4.30
62	Latvia	2.85	140	Rwanda	4.30
62	Malta	2.85	142	Angola	4.35
62	Paraguay	2.85	143	Azerbaijan	4.40
66	Greece	2.90	143	Tajikistan	4.40
66	Hungary	2.90	145	Turkmenistan	4.50
66	South Africa	2.90	146	Uzbekistan	4.55
69	Benin	2.95	147	Congo/Zaire	4.70
69	Ecuador	2.95	147	Iran	4.70
69	Gabon	2.95	147	Libya	4.70
69	Morocco	2.95	147	Somalia	4.70
69	Poland	2.95	147	Vietnam	4.70
74	Colombia	3.00	152	Bosnia	4.80
74	Ghana	3.00	153	Iraq	4.90
74	Lithuania	3.00	154	Cuba	5.00
77	Kenya	3.05	154	Laos	5.00
77	Slovak Republic	3.05	154	North Korea	5.00

Mostly Unfree

BANKING
Score: 4–Stable (high level of restrictions)

Suriname's banking system is in total disarray. According to the U.S. Department of Commerce, "Suriname has an underdeveloped banking system.... Local financing of trade is basically unavailable for non-residents."[3]

WAGE AND PRICE CONTROLS
Score: 3–Stable (moderate level)

Both the market and the government set wages and prices in Suriname. The large state-owned sector continues to influence the setting of prices.

PROPERTY RIGHTS
Score: 3–Stable (moderate level of protection)

Private property is guaranteed by Suriname's constitution and protected by law. The time involved in getting a dispute resolved in the court system can be considerable, however.

REGULATION
Score: 4–Stable (high level)

Establishing a business in Suriname is generally easy, although the bureaucracy is both substantial and corrupt. According to the U.S. Department of State, "There is a high degree of state involvement and regulation."[4]

BLACK MARKET
Score: 5–Stable (very high level of activity)

Suriname has an extensive black market, primarily in pirated video and audio cassettes, computer software, and consumer goods, and there is much smuggling along the borders. According to the U.S. Department of Commerce, "With the exception of reexport of goods to eastern Guyana, and illegal smuggling to French Guiana, Suriname is not a distribution point for shipping or air cargo."[5]

NOTES

1. U.S. Department of Commerce, *Country Commercial Guide,* 1997.
2. *Ibid.*
3. *Ibid.*
4. U.S. Department of State, "Suriname Country Report on Human Rights Practices for 1996," 1997.
5. U.S. Department of Commerce, *Country Commercial Guide,* 1997.

Swaziland   2.70

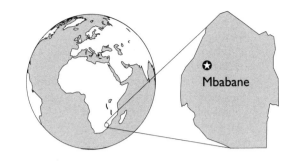

Mbabane

1997 Score: **2.80**	1996 Score: **2.90**	1995 Score: **2.90**

Trade	3	Banking	3
Taxation	3	Wages and Prices	3
Government Intervention	2	Property Rights	2
Monetary Policy	2	Regulation	3
Foreign Investment	2	Black Market	4

Swaziland gained its independence from the United Kingdom in 1968 and established a monarchy with all executive and some judicial and legislative powers resting with the king. This system of government remains in effect today. Although Swaziland traditionally has been a largely agrarian society, industry now produces 40 percent of GDP and is becoming the dominant sector of the economy. Economic growth has been reliable and positive, averaging 2.9 percent over the past five years. Swaziland has one of Africa's more free-market economies and recently reduced its barriers to foreign investment. Therefore, its overall score is 0.1 point better this year.

TRADE POLICY
Score: 3+ (moderate level of protectionism)

Swaziland is a member of the Southern African Customs Union,[1] which has an average external tariff rate of less than 12 percent. As a result, its trade policy score is one point better this year.[2] There is no evidence of any significant nontariff barriers.

TAXATION
Score–Income taxation: 2–Stable (low tax rates)
Score–Corporate taxation: 4–Stable (moderate tax rates)
Final Taxation Score: 3–Stable (moderate tax rates)

Swaziland's top income tax rate is 39 percent; there are no taxes on the average level of income. The top corporate tax rate is 37.5 percent. These are the only significant taxes.

GOVERNMENT INTERVENTION IN THE ECONOMY
Score: 2–Stable (low level)

Government consumes 23.5 percent of Swaziland's GDP. It also owns the larger public utilities, such as some transportation and telecommunications enterprises. The rest of the economy is privately owned, and the government is developing plans to privatize most remaining state-owned industries.

MONETARY POLICY
Score: 2–Stable (low level of inflation)

Swaziland's average annual rate of inflation from 1985 to 1995 was 11.7 percent. The rate for 1996 is unavailable.

CAPITAL FLOWS AND FOREIGN INVESTMENT
Score: 2–Stable (low barriers)

Foreign investment generally is encouraged, and the nationalization of foreign-owned property is prohibited by law. Foreign firms receive the same legal treatment as domestic firms. According to the U.S. Department of Commerce, "Far from discriminating against foreign participation in the country's

1	Hong Kong	1.25	77	Zambia	3.05
2	Singapore	1.30	80	Mali	3.10
3	Bahrain	1.70	80	Mongolia	3.10
4	New Zealand	1.75	80	Slovenia	3.10
5	Switzerland	1.90	83	Honduras	3.15
5	United States	1.90	83	Papua New Guinea	3.15
7	Luxembourg	1.95	85	Djibouti	3.20
7	Taiwan	1.95	85	Fiji	3.20
7	United Kingdom	1.95	85	Pakistan	3.20
10	Bahamas	2.00	88	Algeria	3.25
10	Ireland	2.00	88	Guinea	3.25
12	Australia	2.05	88	Lebanon	3.25
12	Japan	2.05	88	Mexico	3.25
14	Belgium	2.10	88	Senegal	3.25
14	Canada	2.10	88	Tanzania	3.25
14	United Arab Emirates	2.10	94	Nigeria	3.30
17	Austria	2.15	94	Romania	3.30
17	Chile	2.15	96	Brazil	3.35
17	Estonia	2.15	96	Cambodia	3.35
20	Czech Republic	2.20	96	Egypt	3.35
20	Netherlands	2.20	96	Ivory Coast	3.35
22	Denmark	2.25	96	Madagascar	3.35
22	Finland	2.25	96	Moldova	3.35
24	Germany	2.30	102	Nepal	3.40
24	Iceland	2.30	103	Cape Verde	3.44
24	South Korea	2.30	104	Armenia	3.45
27	Norway	2.35	104	Dominican Republic	3.45
28	Kuwait	2.40	104	Russia	3.45
28	Malaysia	2.40	107	Burkina Faso	3.50
28	Panama	2.40	107	Cameroon	3.50
28	Thailand	2.40	107	Lesotho	3.50
32	El Salvador	2.45	107	Nicaragua	3.50
32	Sri Lanka	2.45	107	Venezuela	3.50
32	Sweden	2.45	112	Gambia	3.60
35	France	2.50	112	Guyana	3.60
35	Italy	2.50	114	Bulgaria	3.65
35	Spain	2.50	114	Georgia	3.65
38	Trinidad and Tobago	2.55	114	Malawi	3.65
39	Argentina	2.60	117	Ethiopia	3.70
39	Barbados	2.60	117	India	3.70
39	Cyprus	2.60	117	Niger	3.70
39	Jamaica	2.60	120	Albania	3.75
39	Portugal	2.60	120	Bangladesh	3.75
44	Bolivia	2.65	120	China (PRC)	3.75
44	Oman	2.65	120	Congo	3.75
44	Philippines	2.65	120	Croatia	3.75
47	Swaziland	2.70	125	Chad	3.80
47	Uruguay	2.70	125	Mauritania	3.80
49	Botswana	2.75	125	Ukraine	3.80
49	Jordan	2.75	128	Sierra Leone	3.85
49	Namibia	2.75	129	Burundi	3.90
49	Tunisia	2.75	129	Suriname	3.90
53	Belize	2.80	129	Zimbabwe	3.90
53	Costa Rica	2.80	132	Haiti	4.00
53	Guatemala	2.80	132	Kyrgyzstan	4.00
53	Israel	2.80	132	Syria	4.00
53	Peru	2.80	135	Belarus	4.05
53	Saudi Arabia	2.80	136	Kazakstan	4.10
53	Turkey	2.80	136	Mozambique	4.10
53	Uganda	2.80	136	Yemen	4.10
53	Western Samoa	2.80	139	Sudan	4.20
62	Indonesia	2.85	140	Myanmar	4.30
62	Latvia	2.85	140	Rwanda	4.30
62	Malta	2.85	142	Angola	4.35
62	Paraguay	2.85	143	Azerbaijan	4.40
66	Greece	2.90	143	Tajikistan	4.40
66	Hungary	2.90	145	Turkmenistan	4.50
66	South Africa	2.90	146	Uzbekistan	4.55
69	Benin	2.95	147	Congo/Zaire	4.70
69	Ecuador	2.95	147	Iran	4.70
69	Gabon	2.95	147	Libya	4.70
69	Morocco	2.95	147	Somalia	4.70
69	Poland	2.95	147	Vietnam	4.70
74	Colombia	3.00	152	Bosnia	4.80
74	Ghana	3.00	153	Iraq	4.90
74	Lithuania	3.00	154	Cuba	5.00
77	Kenya	3.05	154	Laos	5.00
77	Slovak Republic	3.05	154	North Korea	5.00

Mostly Free

development, Swaziland's government has been accused of favoring expatriate business over local entrepreneurs. The Swazi government has for over a decade advanced a policy welcoming foreign investment."[3] The economy is largely open to foreign investment, with few formal barriers, and the government is trying to develop a consistent and cohesive foreign investment code.

BANKING
Score: 3–Stable (moderate level of restrictions)

Banks in Swaziland are relatively free of government control by African standards, but the government still controls the lending policies of some banks, including the Swaziland Development and Savings Bank. There also is strict government control of credit.

WAGE AND PRICE CONTROLS
Score: 3–Stable (moderate level)

Cotton, corn, milk, petroleum, energy, and tobacco products all remain subject to price controls. Swaziland has a minimum wage.

PROPERTY RIGHTS
Score: 2–Stable (high level of protection)

Property is legally protected against government expropriation, but enforcement of property rights in the court system can be weak. According to the U.S. Department of Commerce, "Swaziland has a dual legal system comprised of Roman–Dutch law and customary law. This parallel system can be confusing and has at times presented problems for foreign-owned business."[4] By global standards, however, the level of private property protection is high.

REGULATION
Score: 3–Stable (moderate level)

Swaziland has streamlined its regulatory system. The government encourages private companies to establish their own safety and health standards. Some government regulations (especially those dealing with safety conditions) are applied erratically, however, and this can lead to uncertainty and confusion.

BLACK MARKET
Score: 4–Stable (high level of activity)

Swaziland has an active black market, primarily in the supply of labor, transportation services, the construction industry, and pirated computer software. The illegal software trade is mainly the result of poor protection for intellectual property. According to the U.S. Department of Commerce, "Protection for patents, trademarks and copyrights is currently inadequate under Swazi law."[5]

NOTES

1. The Southern African Customs Union consists of Botswana, Lesotho, Namibia, Swaziland, and South Africa.
2. The score for this factor has changed from 4 in 1997 to 3 in 1998. Previously unavailable data provide a more accurate understanding of the country's performance. The methodology for this factor remains the same.
3. U.S. Department of Commerce, *Country Commercial Guide,* 1997.
4. *Ibid.*
5. *Ibid.*

Sweden 2.45

1997 Score: **2.45**	1996 Score: **2.55**	1995 Score: **2.65**

Trade	2	Banking	2
Taxation	4.5	Wages and Prices	2
Government Intervention	5	Property Rights	2
Monetary Policy	1	Regulation	3
Foreign Investment	2	Black Market	1

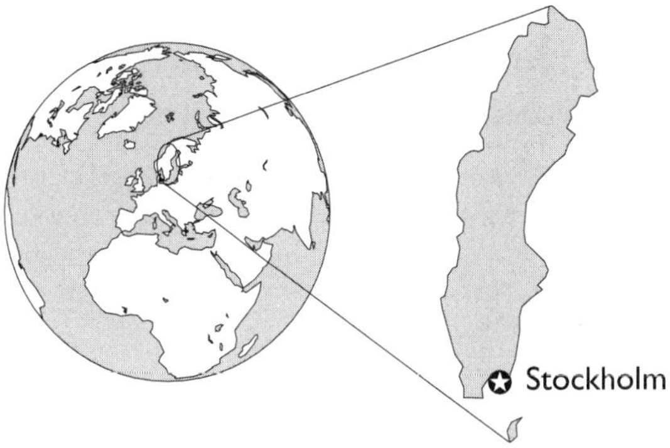

Sweden's economy has changed dramatically over the past several years. A severe recession in the 1980s exploded the myth that its cradle-to-grave welfare state could be maintained without destroying the economy. By the end of the 1980s, it was clear that high levels of government spending on social welfare, worker retraining, and unemployment compensation—to say nothing of tax rates as high as 98 percent—were leading to economic ruin. Because of the government's economic policies, GDP shrank by 4 percent from 1991 to 1993, and unemployment rose to around 8 percent in 1994. The government has been forced to abandon most of its highly interventionist economic policies and follow a more market-oriented path. Sweden joined the European Union in 1995 and has managed to reduce the rate of inflation and some of its banking regulations.

Trade Policy
Score: 2–Stable (low level of protectionism)

Sweden's tariff rates average about 2.8 percent. The government, however, maintains significant import licensing procedures for such items as agricultural goods, ferroalloys, and semi-finished iron and steel.

Taxation
Score—Income taxation: 5–Stable (very high tax rates)
Score—Corporate taxation: 3–Stable (moderate tax rates)
Final Taxation Score: 4.5–Stable (very high tax rates)

The Swedish tax burden is one of the heaviest among the world's industrialized economies: a 56 percent top income tax rate,[1] a 31 percent average income tax rate, a 28 percent top corporate tax rate, a 30 percent capital gains tax, and a 6 percent to 25 percent value-added tax.

Government Intervention in the Economy
Score: 5–Stable (very high level)

The level of government spending in Sweden has fallen from around 75 percent of GDP to about 50 percent of GDP.[2] The government is privatizing some companies; of those that employ more than 50 workers, 90 percent are privately owned.

Monetary Policy
Score: 1–Stable (very low level of inflation)

Sweden's average annual rate of inflation from 1985 to 1995 was 5.5 percent. In 1996, the rate was less than 1 percent.

1	Hong Kong	1.25	77	Zambia	3.05
2	Singapore	1.30	80	Mali	3.10
3	Bahrain	1.70	80	Mongolia	3.10
4	New Zealand	1.75	80	Slovenia	3.10
5	Switzerland	1.90	83	Honduras	3.15
5	United States	1.90	83	Papua New Guinea	3.15
7	Luxembourg	1.95	85	Djibouti	3.20
7	Taiwan	1.95	85	Fiji	3.20
7	United Kingdom	1.95	85	Pakistan	3.20
10	Bahamas	2.00	88	Algeria	3.25
10	Ireland	2.00	88	Guinea	3.25
12	Australia	2.05	88	Lebanon	3.25
12	Japan	2.05	88	Mexico	3.25
14	Belgium	2.10	88	Senegal	3.25
14	Canada	2.10	88	Tanzania	3.25
14	United Arab Emirates	2.10	94	Nigeria	3.30
17	Austria	2.15	94	Romania	3.30
17	Chile	2.15	96	Brazil	3.35
17	Estonia	2.15	96	Cambodia	3.35
20	Czech Republic	2.20	96	Egypt	3.35
20	Netherlands	2.20	96	Ivory Coast	3.35
22	Denmark	2.25	96	Madagascar	3.35
22	Finland	2.25	96	Moldova	3.35
24	Germany	2.30	102	Nepal	3.40
24	Iceland	2.30	103	Cape Verde	3.44
24	South Korea	2.30	104	Armenia	3.45
27	Norway	2.35	104	Dominican Republic	3.45
28	Kuwait	2.40	104	Russia	3.45
28	Malaysia	2.40	107	Burkina Faso	3.50
28	Panama	2.40	107	Cameroon	3.50
28	Thailand	2.40	107	Lesotho	3.50
32	El Salvador	2.45	107	Nicaragua	3.50
32	Sri Lanka	2.45	107	Venezuela	3.50
32	Sweden	2.45	112	Gambia	3.60
35	France	2.50	112	Guyana	3.60
35	Italy	2.50	114	Bulgaria	3.65
35	Spain	2.50	114	Georgia	3.65
38	Trinidad and Tobago	2.55	114	Malawi	3.65
39	Argentina	2.60	117	Ethiopia	3.70
39	Barbados	2.60	117	India	3.70
39	Cyprus	2.60	117	Niger	3.70
39	Jamaica	2.60	120	Albania	3.75
39	Portugal	2.60	120	Bangladesh	3.75
44	Bolivia	2.65	120	China (PRC)	3.75
44	Oman	2.65	120	Congo	3.75
44	Philippines	2.65	120	Croatia	3.75
47	Swaziland	2.70	125	Chad	3.80
47	Uruguay	2.70	125	Mauritania	3.80
49	Botswana	2.75	125	Ukraine	3.80
49	Jordan	2.75	128	Sierra Leone	3.85
49	Namibia	2.75	129	Burundi	3.90
49	Tunisia	2.75	129	Suriname	3.90
53	Belize	2.80	129	Zimbabwe	3.90
53	Costa Rica	2.80	132	Haiti	4.00
53	Guatemala	2.80	132	Kyrgyzstan	4.00
53	Israel	2.80	132	Syria	4.00
53	Peru	2.80	135	Belarus	4.05
53	Saudi Arabia	2.80	136	Kazakstan	4.10
53	Turkey	2.80	136	Mozambique	4.10
53	Uganda	2.80	136	Yemen	4.10
53	Western Samoa	2.80	139	Sudan	4.20
62	Indonesia	2.85	140	Myanmar	4.30
62	Latvia	2.85	140	Rwanda	4.30
62	Malta	2.85	142	Angola	4.35
62	Paraguay	2.85	143	Azerbaijan	4.40
66	Greece	2.90	143	Tajikistan	4.40
66	Hungary	2.90	145	Turkmenistan	4.50
66	South Africa	2.90	146	Uzbekistan	4.55
69	Benin	2.95	147	Congo/Zaire	4.70
69	Ecuador	2.95	147	Iran	4.70
69	Gabon	2.95	147	Libya	4.70
69	Morocco	2.95	147	Somalia	4.70
69	Poland	2.95	147	Vietnam	4.70
74	Colombia	3.00	152	Bosnia	4.80
74	Ghana	3.00	153	Iraq	4.90
74	Lithuania	3.00	154	Cuba	5.00
77	Kenya	3.05	154	Laos	5.00
77	Slovak Republic	3.05	154	North Korea	5.00

Mostly Free

CAPITAL FLOWS AND FOREIGN INVESTMENT
Score: 2–Stable (low barriers)

Sweden presents few barriers to foreign investment, but there continue to be some restrictions on foreign ownership of air transportation companies, the maritime industry, and items considered necessary during time of war, such as arms manufacturing.

BANKING
Score: 2–Stable (low level of restrictions)

With one exception, all commercial banks in Sweden are domestically owned and operated; two are owned directly by the government. Foreign banks have been permitted to establish subsidiaries and branches since 1986, but the application process remains a barrier. The government is trying to liberalize the banking system, however, so that opening new banks will become easier and banks will be able to operate more freely.

WAGE AND PRICE CONTROLS
Score: 2–Stable (low level)

The market sets most wages and prices in Sweden. There is no national minimum wage law, although the government influences wage rates by establishing a minimum wage for employees of state-owned industries. State-owned enterprises often set the prices of the products they produce.

PROPERTY RIGHTS
Score: 2–Stable (high level of protection)

There is little chance of government expropriation in Sweden today. A recently initiated, massive privatization program is returning property to the private sector, and the court system is both efficient and sound.

REGULATION
Score: 3–Stable (moderate level)

Obtaining a business license in Sweden is relatively easy. Businesses must register with the Patent and Registration Office and the appropriate tax offices. Sweden also maintains, however, a comprehensive and burdensome safety, environmental, and consumer regulatory structure. For example, the Environmental Protection Act of 1969 requires all businesses to obtain permission from the government before releasing any pollutants into the environment. In cases in which the expansion of a business may result in more pollution, a company must undergo a lengthy and sometimes extremely burdensome investigation. Businesses also must comply with many other regulatory strictures, such as a government-imposed five-week vacation.

BLACK MARKET
Score: 1–Stable (very low level of activity)

Sweden once had a rather large black market in the construction industry, but economic reforms are making it easier to exchange most goods and services legally. Sweden's protection of intellectual property is among the most efficient in the world.

NOTES

1. *Worldwide Executive Tax Guide and Directory,* 1997 edition (New York, N.Y.: Ernst & Young, 1997).
2. Based on central government expenditures; from U.S. Department of State, *Country Reports on Economic Policy and Trade Practices,* 1997, p. 178.

Switzerland (including Liechtenstein)[1]   1.90

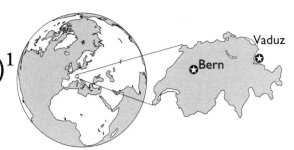

Vaduz
Bern

1997 Score: **1.90**	1996 Score: **1.80**	1995 Score: **n/a**

Trade	2	Banking	1
Taxation	3	Wages and Prices	2
Government Intervention	3	Property Rights	1
Monetary Policy	1	Regulation	3
Foreign Investment	2	Black Market	1

The Holy Roman Empire recognized Switzerland's independence in 1499. From 1798 until 1803, the country was occupied by the French under Napoleon. In 1874, it drafted a constitution that remains largely in effect today. Having maintained its neutrality throughout most of the 20th century's major international conflicts, Switzerland has become a favorite site for conventions, peace accords, and international agreements. Today, Geneva is the seat of the World Trade Organization. In 1992, the Swiss electorate voted against joining the European Economic Area (EEA), a free trade area mainly recognized between members of the European Union (EU) and other European countries that have yet to join the EU. As a result of this popular vote, Switzerland is not a member of either the EEA or the EU.

TRADE POLICY

Score: 2–Stable (low level of protectionism)

Switzerland's average tariff rate is 1.7 percent, which is lower than those of most other EU members,[2] but other trade restrictions include licensing, subsidies to the agricultural sector, and import quotas. As part of the Uruguay Round of the General Agreement on Tariffs and Trade, Switzerland has pledged to reduce its subsidies to agriculture and transform its quota system on agricultural imports into tariffs while reducing these tariffs by 30 percent by the year 2000. Although Switzerland restricts foreign participation in telecommunications, legislation currently being considered by Parliament would privatize this sector. Thus, by global standards, the level of trade protectionism is low.

TAXATION

Score–Income taxation: 1–Stable (very low tax rates)
Score–Corporate taxation: 4–Stable (high tax rates)
Final Taxation Score: 3–Stable (moderate tax rates)

Switzerland's top federal income tax rate is 11.5 percent. According to the international accounting firm of Ernst & Young, "Because of the multilayered tax system, there are no average tax rates. Taxes are calculated based on specific figures for specific cantons and municipalities. The maximum overall rate of federal income tax is 11.5 percent."[3] The top marginal corporate tax rate is 36.8 percent,[4] and a capital gains tax is levied at the regular business income rate.[5]

GOVERNMENT INTERVENTION IN THE ECONOMY

Score: 3–Stable (moderate level)

Government consumes about 14.1 percent of Switzerland's GDP and, although it has begun to privatize public corporations, it remains involved in certain parts of the economy. It owns and operates most voice transmission and telecommunications companies, for example, and its telecommunications corporation (the Postal and Telephone Authority) does not allow private competition in markets

1	Hong Kong	1.25	77	Zambia	3.05
2	Singapore	1.30	80	Mali	3.10
3	Bahrain	1.70	80	Mongolia	3.10
4	New Zealand	1.75	80	Slovenia	3.10
5	Switzerland	1.90	83	Honduras	3.15
5	United States	1.90	83	Papua New Guinea	3.15
7	Luxembourg	1.95	85	Djibouti	3.20
7	Taiwan	1.95	85	Fiji	3.20
7	United Kingdom	1.95	85	Pakistan	3.20
10	Bahamas	2.00	88	Algeria	3.25
10	Ireland	2.00	88	Guinea	3.25
12	Australia	2.05	88	Lebanon	3.25
12	Japan	2.05	88	Mexico	3.25
14	Belgium	2.10	88	Senegal	3.25
14	Canada	2.10	88	Tanzania	3.25
14	United Arab Emirates	2.10	94	Nigeria	3.30
17	Austria	2.15	94	Romania	3.30
17	Chile	2.15	96	Brazil	3.35
17	Estonia	2.15	96	Cambodia	3.35
20	Czech Republic	2.20	96	Egypt	3.35
20	Netherlands	2.20	96	Ivory Coast	3.35
22	Denmark	2.25	96	Madagascar	3.35
22	Finland	2.25	96	Moldova	3.35
24	Germany	2.30	102	Nepal	3.40
24	Iceland	2.30	103	Cape Verde	3.44
24	South Korea	2.30	104	Armenia	3.45
27	Norway	2.35	104	Dominican Republic	3.45
28	Kuwait	2.40	104	Russia	3.45
28	Malaysia	2.40	107	Burkina Faso	3.50
28	Panama	2.40	107	Cameroon	3.50
28	Thailand	2.40	107	Lesotho	3.50
32	El Salvador	2.45	107	Nicaragua	3.50
32	Sri Lanka	2.45	107	Venezuela	3.50
32	Sweden	2.45	112	Gambia	3.60
35	France	2.50	112	Guyana	3.60
35	Italy	2.50	114	Bulgaria	3.65
35	Spain	2.50	114	Georgia	3.65
38	Trinidad and Tobago	2.55	114	Malawi	3.65
39	Argentina	2.60	117	Ethiopia	3.70
39	Barbados	2.60	117	India	3.70
39	Cyprus	2.60	117	Niger	3.70
39	Jamaica	2.60	120	Albania	3.75
39	Portugal	2.60	120	Bangladesh	3.75
44	Bolivia	2.65	120	China (PRC)	3.75
44	Oman	2.65	120	Congo	3.75
44	Philippines	2.65	120	Croatia	3.75
47	Swaziland	2.70	125	Chad	3.80
47	Uruguay	2.70	125	Mauritania	3.80
49	Botswana	2.75	125	Ukraine	3.80
49	Jordan	2.75	128	Sierra Leone	3.85
49	Namibia	2.75	129	Burundi	3.90
49	Tunisia	2.75	129	Suriname	3.90
53	Belize	2.80	129	Zimbabwe	3.90
53	Costa Rica	2.80	132	Haiti	4.00
53	Guatemala	2.80	132	Kyrgyzstan	4.00
53	Israel	2.80	132	Syria	4.00
53	Peru	2.80	135	Belarus	4.05
53	Saudi Arabia	2.80	136	Kazakstan	4.10
53	Turkey	2.80	136	Mozambique	4.10
53	Uganda	2.80	136	Yemen	4.10
53	Western Samoa	2.80	139	Sudan	4.20
62	Indonesia	2.85	140	Myanmar	4.30
62	Latvia	2.85	140	Rwanda	4.30
62	Malta	2.85	142	Angola	4.35
62	Paraguay	2.85	143	Azerbaijan	4.40
66	Greece	2.90	143	Tajikistan	4.40
66	Hungary	2.90	145	Turkmenistan	4.50
66	South Africa	2.90	146	Uzbekistan	4.55
69	Benin	2.95	147	Congo/Zaire	4.70
69	Ecuador	2.95	147	Iran	4.70
69	Gabon	2.95	147	Libya	4.70
69	Morocco	2.95	147	Somalia	4.70
69	Poland	2.95	147	Vietnam	4.70
74	Colombia	3.00	152	Bosnia	4.80
74	Ghana	3.00	153	Iraq	4.90
74	Lithuania	3.00	154	Cuba	5.00
77	Kenya	3.05	154	Laos	5.00
77	Slovak Republic	3.05	154	North Korea	5.00

it controls, although the government is considering plans for privatization. Switzerland is one of the few countries with a constitution that limits the government's ability to impose economically costly policies; instead, the government must act by "emergency decrees" that are subject to public referendum. This severely limits its power to pass laws that restrict economic freedom.

MONETARY POLICY
Score: 1–Stable (very low level of inflation)

Switzerland's average annual rate of inflation from 1985 to 1995 was 3.4 percent. In 1996, the rate was about 0.8 percent.

CAPITAL FLOWS AND FOREIGN INVESTMENT
Score: 2–Stable (low barriers)

Switzerland is open to foreign investment, although it restricts investment in hydroelectric and nuclear power plants, oil pipelines, the operation of television and radio broadcasting, and transportation.

BANKING
Score: 1–Stable (very low level of restrictions)

Switzerland's banking system is one of the freest and most competitive in the world. Banks may offer a wide range of financial services with virtually no government interference.

WAGE AND PRICE CONTROLS
Score: 2–Stable (low level)

The market sets most wages and prices in Switzerland. The agricultural sector is heavily regulated and subsidized, however, and this influences the prices of agricultural goods. There is no minimum wage.

PROPERTY RIGHTS
Score: 1–Stable (very high level of protection)

From the standpoint of private property rights, Switzerland may be one of the world's safest countries. According to the U.S. Department of State, "The Constitution provides for an independent judiciary, and the Government respects this provision in practice. The judiciary provides citizens with a fair and efficient judicial process."[6]

REGULATION
Score: 3–Stable (moderate level)

Establishing a business in Switzerland is easy. Even though such industries as agriculture, television and broadcasting, and utilities are heavily regulated, regulations are applied evenly in most cases.

BLACK MARKET
Score: 1–Stable (very low level of activity)

Switzerland's black market is negligible. There is virtually no black market in pirated intellectual property. According to the U.S. Department of State, "Switzerland has one of the best regimes in the world for the protection of intellectual property, and protection is afforded equally to foreign and domestic rights holders."[7]

NOTES
1. Liechtenstein's economy is closely linked with Switzerland's.
2. This rate includes all duty-free trade.
3. *1997 Worldwide Executive Tax Guide,* Ernst & Young Web site: *http://www.ey.com/.*
4. Swiss corporate tax rates vary by canton, from 10 percent to 27 percent. This does not include an additional 9.8 percent federal tax. Thus, this figure is based on the highest canton tax and the federal tax taken together.
5. In Switzerland, capital gains are taxed as income at the regular income tax rate.
6. U.S. Department of State, "Switzerland Country Report on Human Rights Practices for 1996," 1997.
7. U.S. Department of State, *Country Reports on Economic Policy and Trade Practices,* 1997, p. 182.

Syria

4.00

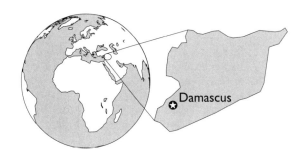

1997 Score: **4.20**	1996 Score: **4.20**	1995 Score: **n/a**

Trade	5	Banking	5
Taxation	5	Wages and Prices	4
Government Intervention	3	Property Rights	4
Monetary Policy	3	Regulation	2
Foreign Investment	4	Black Market	5

Syria gained its independence from France in 1946 and has played a leading role in Arab politics and the Arab–Israeli struggle. It was plagued by political instability and a series of military coups until General Hafez al-Assad seized power in 1970; since then, it has developed a state-dominated socialist economy and has depended heavily on foreign aid, first from the Soviet Union and more recently from the oil-rich Persian Gulf states. In 1992, the government sought to spur private and foreign investment by loosening restrictive regulations, but a swollen public sector remains an obstacle to free-market reform. The United States maintains trade sanctions against Syria because of the regime's long-standing support of terrorism. Recent studies demonstrate that corruption within the bureaucracy is having a greater impact on business. The government also has reduced inflation and cracked down on illegal smuggling, however, thereby reducing the size of the black market. As a result, Syria's overall score is 0.2 point better this year.

TRADE POLICY
Score: 5–Stable (very high level of protectionism)

Syria's average tariff rate is 24.1 percent.[1] The customs service is both onerous and confusing, and all imports require a license. According to the U.S. Department of Commerce, "Customs procedures are cumbersome, tedious, and time-consuming because of complex regulations."[2] Many imports are banned.

TAXATION
Score–Income taxation: 5–Stable (very high tax rates)
Score–Corporate taxation: 5–Stable (very high tax rates)
Final Taxation Score: 5–Stable (very high tax rates)

Syria's top income tax rate is 64 percent.[3] The top marginal corporate tax rate is over 50 percent.[4]

GOVERNMENT INTERVENTION IN THE ECONOMY
Score: 3–Stable (moderate level)

Government consumes about 25 percent of Syria's GDP, and the public sector accounts for approximately 36 percent of GDP overall.

MONETARY POLICY
Score: 3+ (moderate level of inflation)

Syria's average rate of inflation from 1985 to 1995 was 15.8 percent, down from over 22 percent from 1985 to 1993. As a result, its monetary policy score is two points better this year. In 1996, the rate of inflation was about 20 percent.

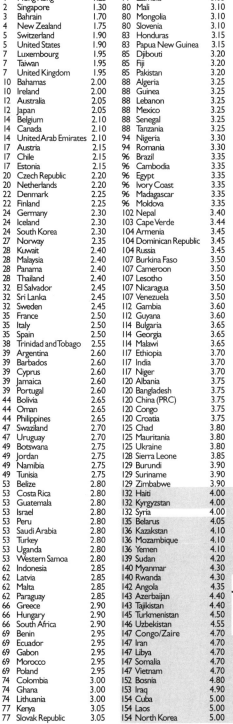

1	Hong Kong	1.25	77	Zambia	3.05
2	Singapore	1.30	80	Mali	3.10
3	Bahrain	1.70	80	Mongolia	3.10
4	New Zealand	1.75	80	Slovenia	3.10
5	Switzerland	1.90	83	Honduras	3.15
5	United States	1.90	83	Papua New Guinea	3.15
7	Luxembourg	1.95	85	Djibouti	3.20
7	Taiwan	1.95	85	Fiji	3.20
7	United Kingdom	1.95	85	Pakistan	3.20
10	Bahamas	2.00	88	Algeria	3.25
10	Ireland	2.00	88	Guinea	3.25
12	Australia	2.05	88	Lebanon	3.25
12	Japan	2.05	88	Mexico	3.25
14	Belgium	2.10	88	Senegal	3.25
14	Canada	2.10	88	Tanzania	3.25
14	United Arab Emirates	2.10	94	Nigeria	3.30
17	Austria	2.15	94	Romania	3.30
17	Chile	2.15	96	Brazil	3.35
17	Estonia	2.15	96	Cambodia	3.35
20	Czech Republic	2.20	96	Egypt	3.35
20	Netherlands	2.20	96	Ivory Coast	3.35
22	Denmark	2.25	96	Madagascar	3.35
22	Finland	2.25	96	Moldova	3.35
24	Germany	2.30	102	Nepal	3.40
24	Iceland	2.30	103	Cape Verde	3.44
24	South Korea	2.30	104	Armenia	3.45
27	Norway	2.35	104	Dominican Republic	3.45
28	Kuwait	2.40	104	Russia	3.45
28	Malaysia	2.40	107	Burkina Faso	3.50
28	Panama	2.40	107	Cameroon	3.50
28	Thailand	2.40	107	Lesotho	3.50
32	El Salvador	2.45	107	Nicaragua	3.50
32	Sri Lanka	2.45	107	Venezuela	3.50
32	Sweden	2.45	112	Gambia	3.60
35	France	2.50	112	Guyana	3.60
35	Italy	2.50	114	Bulgaria	3.65
35	Spain	2.50	114	Georgia	3.65
38	Trinidad and Tobago	2.55	114	Malawi	3.65
39	Argentina	2.60	117	Ethiopia	3.70
39	Barbados	2.60	117	India	3.70
39	Cyprus	2.60	117	Niger	3.70
39	Jamaica	2.60	120	Albania	3.75
39	Portugal	2.60	120	Bangladesh	3.75
44	Bolivia	2.65	120	China (PRC)	3.75
44	Oman	2.65	120	Congo	3.75
44	Philippines	2.65	120	Croatia	3.75
47	Swaziland	2.70	125	Chad	3.80
47	Uruguay	2.70	125	Mauritania	3.80
49	Botswana	2.75	125	Ukraine	3.80
49	Jordan	2.75	128	Sierra Leone	3.85
49	Namibia	2.75	129	Burundi	3.90
49	Tunisia	2.75	129	Suriname	3.90
53	Belize	2.80	129	Zimbabwe	3.90
53	Costa Rica	2.80	132	Haiti	4.00
53	Guatemala	2.80	132	Kyrgyzstan	4.00
53	Israel	2.80	132	Syria	4.00
53	Peru	2.80	135	Belarus	4.05
53	Saudi Arabia	2.80	136	Kazakstan	4.10
53	Turkey	2.80	136	Mozambique	4.10
53	Uganda	2.80	136	Yemen	4.10
53	Western Samoa	2.80	139	Sudan	4.20
62	Indonesia	2.85	140	Myanmar	4.30
62	Latvia	2.85	140	Rwanda	4.30
62	Malta	2.85	142	Angola	4.35
62	Paraguay	2.85	143	Azerbaijan	4.40
66	Greece	2.90	143	Tajikistan	4.40
66	Hungary	2.90	145	Turkmenistan	4.50
66	South Africa	2.90	146	Uzbekistan	4.55
69	Benin	2.95	147	Congo/Zaire	4.70
69	Ecuador	2.95	147	Iran	4.70
69	Gabon	2.95	147	Libya	4.70
69	Morocco	2.95	147	Somalia	4.70
69	Poland	2.95	147	Vietnam	4.70
74	Colombia	3.00	152	Bosnia	4.80
74	Ghana	3.00	153	Iraq	4.90
74	Lithuania	3.00	154	Cuba	5.00
77	Kenya	3.05	154	Laos	5.00
77	Slovak Republic	3.05	154	North Korea	5.00

Repressed

CAPITAL FLOWS AND FOREIGN INVESTMENT
Score: 4–Stable (high barriers)

"The Syrian government," reports the U.S. Department of Commerce, "has adopted a hesitantly positive attitude toward foreign investment in recent years. However, most representatives of foreign firms find Syria's business environment a difficult one."[5] A new foreign investment law was passed in 1991. According to the U.S. Department of Commerce, "All applications for investment under the law must be screened and vetted through the Higher Council for Investment. The Council meets at least once every two months. Membership includes the Prime Minister, and the Ministers of Economy, Agriculture, Transportation, Supply, Industry, Planning, Finance, and the Director of the Investment Bureau. No definitive criteria for approving investment is [sic] made explicit under the new law."[6]

BANKING
Score: 5–Stable (very high level of restrictions)

Syria's banking system in Syria is completely controlled by the government, which also owns all of the country's major banks. The U.S. Department of Commerce reports that "Syria's government-controlled banking system consists of five banks, the Commercial Bank of Syria, the Agricultural Cooperative Bank, the Industrial Bank, the Real Estate Bank, and the People's Credit Bank. The Central Bank of Syria oversees banking operations and manages the money supply. According to Syrian bank regulations, only the Central Bank and the Commercial Bank may engage in international transactions and hold foreign exchange deposits outside Syria. Within Syria, only the Commercial Bank may sell Syrian pounds for foreign currencies, but with only a few exceptions, one cannot sell unused Syrian pounds back to the Commercial Bank. Moreover, Law 24 of 1986 criminalizes the private exchange of foreign currencies and Syrian pounds.... Besides monopolizing the exchange of foreign currencies, the Syrian government maintains one of the last remaining fixed, multiple exchange rate systems in the world. At present the government exchanges money at six different rates."[7]

WAGE AND PRICE CONTROLS
Score: 4–Stable (high level)

Wages and prices in Syria are set mainly by the government which, according to the U.S. Department of Commerce, "retains control over 'strategic' sectors, such as oil, electricity, banking, and wheat and cotton production."[8]

PROPERTY RIGHTS
Score: 4–Stable (low level of protection)

Private property is not safe in Syria. Although the legal and judicial system recognizes the free exchange of property and some contractual agreements, private property also is subject to expropriation. "The judiciary," reports the U.S. Department of State, "is constitutionally independent, but this is not the case in the exceptional (state of emergency) security courts, which are subject to political influence."[9]

REGULATION
Score: 2–Stable (low level)

Establishing a business in Syria is easy if the business will not compete directly with the state-owned sector. The private sector is growing rapidly, and regulations often are ignored or not enforced.

BLACK MARKET
Score: 5–Stable (very high level of activity)

Syria's black market is quite large, although the smuggling of many consumer goods has prompted the government to expand its list of permitted legal imports. According to the Economist Intelligence Unit, "The strong public role in the economy and official over-valuation of the Syrian pound has led to a thriving parallel economy. Smuggling has ensured that industry has been able to obtain vital production inputs as well as a constant flow of consumer goods."[10]

NOTES

1. Based on total taxes on international trade as a percentage of total imports.
2. U.S. Department of Commerce, *Country Commercial Guide,* 1997.
3. The tax level for the average income is not available, and tax evasion is rampant.
4. Because Syria's tax system is complicated and unclear, this figure includes a host of taxes and fees and provides only a rough estimate.
5. U.S. Department of Commerce, "Syria—Investment Climate," *Market Research Reports,* May 29, 1997.
6. *Ibid.*
7. *Ibid.*
8. U.S. Department of Commerce, *Country Commercial Guide,* 1997.
9. U.S. Department of State, "Syria Country Report on Human Rights Practices for 1996," 1997.
10. Economist Intelligence Unit, *EIU Country Profile Reports,* 1996.

Tajikistan   4.40

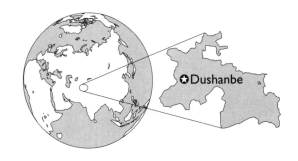

⊙Dushanbe

Trade	5	Banking	4
Taxation	5	Wages and Prices	4
Government Intervention	4	Property Rights	4
Monetary Policy	5	Regulation	4
Foreign Investment	4	Black Market	5

Subjected to continual conquest throughout much of its early history, Tajikistan became part of Ghengis Khan's Mongol Empire in the 13th century. Russia established its control in 1868 by annexing the northern part of the country. In 1916, czarist Russia attempted to enlist many Tajiks into its army. The ensuing rebellion continued throughout the Russian Revolution of 1917. The country became part of the Soviet Union in 1921 as the Turkistan Autonomous Soviet Socialist Republic, a region that included portions of present-day Kazakstan, Turkmenistan, and Uzbekistan. The area that now is Tajikistan was made autonomous in 1924 and fully incorporated into the Soviet Union in 1929. After Tajikistan gained its independence in 1991, the Soviet-era government retained control of large portions of the new government; a civil war between the pro-communists and Islamic and democratic groups ensued in 1992. The pro-communist groups eventually gained control of the country and began to persecute the Islamic and pro-democracy groups. In 1994, a cease-fire was reached, but ethnic and civil unrest continues, leaving little time for economic reform.

TRADE POLICY
Score: 5–Stable (very high level of protectionism)

The average tariff rate for Tajikistan is unavailable, primarily because of the lack of a fully functioning customs service. Although most tariffs range between 10 percent and 20 percent, customs rates charged at the border vary constantly. In addition, there is very little private trade. According to the U.S. Department of State, "The government conducts virtually all trade in Tajikistan."[1] There also is little economic freedom for individuals in the trade sector.

TAXATION
Score–Income taxation: 5–Stable (very high tax rates)
Score–Corporate taxation: 5–Stable (very high tax rates)
Final Taxation Score: 5–Stable (very high tax rates)

Tajikistan's tax system is in disarray, with redundant and overlapping taxes. According to the U.S. Department of Commerce, the government "abolished the regulation providing for exemptions for major taxes, including the profit tax, excise tax, value added tax, and customs duties."[2] Without these exemptions, businesses and individuals may be held responsible for a variety of taxes. Rates vary widely, and the collection system remains arbitrary. The government gets the bulk of its revenue from state ownership of most medium and large businesses, as well as from its ownership share (usually limited to 40 percent) of businesses that have been privatized. It also consumes much of the profit produced by these state-owned and privatized companies—in effect, taxing profits. Tajikistan also has a 20 percent value-added tax and a sales tax.

1	Hong Kong	1.25	77	Zambia	3.05
2	Singapore	1.30	80	Mali	3.10
3	Bahrain	1.70	80	Mongolia	3.10
4	New Zealand	1.75	80	Slovenia	3.10
5	Switzerland	1.90	83	Honduras	3.15
5	United States	1.90	83	Papua New Guinea	3.15
7	Luxembourg	1.95	85	Djibouti	3.20
7	Taiwan	1.95	85	Fiji	3.20
7	United Kingdom	1.95	85	Pakistan	3.20
10	Bahamas	2.00	88	Algeria	3.25
10	Ireland	2.00	88	Guinea	3.25
12	Australia	2.05	88	Lebanon	3.25
12	Japan	2.05	88	Mexico	3.25
14	Belgium	2.10	88	Senegal	3.25
14	Canada	2.10	88	Tanzania	3.25
14	United Arab Emirates	2.10	94	Nigeria	3.30
17	Austria	2.15	94	Romania	3.30
17	Chile	2.15	96	Brazil	3.35
17	Estonia	2.15	96	Cambodia	3.35
20	Czech Republic	2.20	96	Egypt	3.35
20	Netherlands	2.20	96	Ivory Coast	3.35
22	Denmark	2.25	96	Madagascar	3.35
22	Finland	2.25	96	Moldova	3.35
24	Germany	2.30	102	Nepal	3.40
24	Iceland	2.30	103	Cape Verde	3.44
24	South Korea	2.30	104	Armenia	3.45
27	Norway	2.35	104	Dominican Republic	3.45
28	Kuwait	2.40	104	Russia	3.45
28	Malaysia	2.40	107	Burkina Faso	3.50
28	Panama	2.40	107	Cameroon	3.50
28	Thailand	2.40	107	Lesotho	3.50
32	El Salvador	2.45	107	Nicaragua	3.50
32	Sri Lanka	2.45	107	Venezuela	3.50
32	Sweden	2.45	112	Gambia	3.60
35	France	2.50	112	Guyana	3.60
35	Italy	2.50	114	Bulgaria	3.65
35	Spain	2.50	114	Georgia	3.65
38	Trinidad and Tobago	2.55	114	Malawi	3.65
39	Argentina	2.60	117	Ethiopia	3.70
39	Barbados	2.60	117	India	3.70
39	Cyprus	2.60	117	Niger	3.70
39	Jamaica	2.60	120	Albania	3.75
39	Portugal	2.60	120	Bangladesh	3.75
44	Bolivia	2.65	120	China (PRC)	3.75
44	Oman	2.65	120	Congo	3.75
44	Philippines	2.65	120	Croatia	3.75
47	Swaziland	2.70	125	Chad	3.80
47	Uruguay	2.70	125	Mauritania	3.80
49	Botswana	2.75	125	Ukraine	3.80
49	Jordan	2.75	128	Sierra Leone	3.85
49	Namibia	2.75	129	Burundi	3.90
49	Tunisia	2.75	129	Suriname	3.90
53	Belize	2.80	129	Zimbabwe	3.90
53	Costa Rica	2.80	132	Haiti	4.00
53	Guatemala	2.80	132	Kyrgyzstan	4.00
53	Israel	2.80	132	Syria	4.00
53	Peru	2.80	135	Belarus	4.05
53	Saudi Arabia	2.80	136	Kazakstan	4.10
53	Turkey	2.80	136	Mozambique	4.10
53	Uganda	2.80	136	Yemen	4.10
53	Western Samoa	2.80	139	Sudan	4.20
62	Indonesia	2.85	140	Myanmar	4.30
62	Latvia	2.85	140	Rwanda	4.30
62	Malta	2.85	142	Angola	4.35
62	Paraguay	2.85	143	Azerbaijan	4.40
66	Greece	2.90	143	Tajikistan	4.40
66	Hungary	2.90	145	Turkmenistan	4.50
66	South Africa	2.90	146	Uzbekistan	4.55
69	Benin	2.95	147	Congo/Zaire	4.70
69	Ecuador	2.95	147	Iran	4.70
69	Gabon	2.95	147	Libya	4.70
69	Morocco	2.95	147	Somalia	4.70
69	Poland	2.95	147	Vietnam	4.70
74	Colombia	3.00	152	Bosnia	4.80
74	Ghana	3.00	153	Iraq	4.90
74	Lithuania	3.00	154	Cuba	5.00
77	Kenya	3.05	154	Laos	5.00
77	Slovak Republic	3.05	154	North Korea	5.00

Repressed

GOVERNMENT INTERVENTION IN THE ECONOMY
Score: 4–Stable (high level)

Tajikistan is privatizing some of its state-owned sector, but the government continues to own shares in many privatized companies. Most GDP is produced by the state-owned sector.

MONETARY POLICY
Score: 5–Stable (very high level of inflation)

Tajikistan has been plagued by hyperinflation: 1,157 percent in 1992, 2,195 percent in 1993, 452 percent in 1994, 635 percent in 1995, and 65 percent in 1996. Although inflation has fallen significantly, it remains very high, both historically and by global standards.

CAPITAL FLOWS AND FOREIGN INVESTMENT
Score: 4–Stable (high barriers)

The government has opened some of Tajikistan's economy to foreign investment and wants to promote increased investment, but the bureaucratic procedure is arbitrary and restricts many investments. According to the U.S. Department of State, "Although legislation encourages foreign investment, contradictory and unclear decrees make doing business in Tajikistan a labyrinthine process."[3]

BANKING
Score: 4-Stable (high level of restrictions)

Tajikistan's banking system is not yet fully functional. According to the U.S. Department of Commerce, "The Tajik banking sector is dominated by large specialized banks, a heritage from the state banks of the former Soviet Union. These banks—Agroprombank, Orientbank, and Tajikbankbusiness—account for over 96 percent of bank financing."[4] These three major banks are state-owned; thus, most of all the financial system's assets are state-controlled.

WAGE AND PRICE CONTROLS
Score: 4–Stable (high level)

Wages and prices in Tajikistan are controlled by the large number of state-owned enterprises. Price controls continue on such items as agricultural products, transportation, and utilities, and government subsidies to many industries continue to prohibit market pricing.

PROPERTY RIGHTS
Score: 4–Stable (low level of protection)

Private property is not sufficiently protected by the legal system. According to the U.S. Department of State, "Judicial officials at all levels of the court system are heavily influenced by both the political leadership and, in many instances, armed paramilitary groups.... Judges at the local, regional, and republic level are, for the most part, poorly trained and lack understanding of an independent judiciary.... Pressure continues to be exerted on the judicial system by local strongmen, their armed paramilitary groups, and vigilantes who operate outside of government control, sometimes leading to the dismissal of charges and dropping of cases. Bribery of prosecutors and judges is also considered to be widespread."[5]

REGULATION
Score: 4–Stable (high level)

Establishing a business is a tedious and time-consuming procedure that requires individuals to overcome numerous bureaucratic barriers. According to the U.S. Department of State, "A convoluted and corrupt bureaucracy adds to the difficulty of doing business in Tajikistan."[6]

BLACK MARKET
Score: 5–Stable (very high level of activity)

Smuggling is rampant in Tajikistan, and despite laws protecting intellectual property rights, there continues to be significant piracy in computer software. According to the U.S. Department of Commerce, "Present laws on intellectual property protection are adhered to in Tajikistan, if the cases ever get to court. However, despite a flourishing video and cassette pirating business, which no one seems to be interested in addressing, only one action, concerning published literature, was brought to court in 1996."[7]

NOTES

1. U.S. Department of State, *Country Reports on Economic Policy and Trade Practices,* 1996, p. 293.
2. U.S. Department of Commerce, "Current Status of Economic Reform in Tajikistan," June 1996.
3. U.S. Department of State, *Country Reports on Economic Policy and Trade Practices,* 1996.
4. U.S. Department of Commerce, "Banking in Tajikistan," May 1997.
5. U.S. Department of State, "Tajikistan Country Report on Human Rights Practices for 1996," 1997.
6. U.S. Department of State, *Country Reports on Economic Policy and Trade Practices,* 1996, p. 292.
7. U.S. Department of Commerce, "Intellectual Property Protection in Tajikistan," March 12, 1997.

Tanzania   3.25

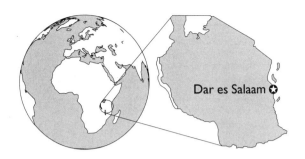

Dar es Salaam ○

1997 Score: **3.25**		1996 Score: **3.45**		1995 Score: **3.50**	
Trade	3	Banking	3
Taxation	3.5	Wages and Prices	2
Government Intervention	3	Property Rights	3
Monetary Policy	4	Regulation	4
Foreign Investment	3	Black Market	4

Tanzania was founded in 1964 from the union of Tanganyika and Zanzibar, which had gained their independence from Great Britain in 1961 and 1963, respectively. Until the late 1980s, it had a socialist economy, with nationalized industry and collectivized agriculture. It also became one of the world's poorest countries. The effects of economic mismanagement are evident still, with per capita GNP that remains among the world's lowest (estimated at $120 in 1995), despite tens of billions of dollars in foreign aid from the West. Market reforms introduced by the government of President Ali Hassan Mwinyi and continued by President Benjamin Mkapa have made limited progress toward liberalizing the economy and have led to improved growth in GDP, which averaged 3.8 percent from 1992 to 1996. Tanzania still relies heavily on foreign aid, but relations with international donors remain fragile because of the country's high levels of inflation and corruption. As noted recently by the Economist Intelligence Unit, "[A]t some stage there will have to be an amnesty [for corrupt officials in the bureaucracy] if anything is to remain of the administrative machine, so prevalent is the problem."[1]

TRADE POLICY
Score: 3–Stable (moderately high level of protectionism)

Tanzania has an average tariff rate of 8.6 percent.[2] A major nontariff barrier is the inefficient customs system. "Despite the existence of regulations and laws," reports the U.S. Department of Commerce, "the customs department is the greatest hindrance to importers throughout Tanzania. Clearance delays and extra-legal levies are commonplace when dealing with the Tanzanian Customs Department. These hindrances can cause undetermined delays when importing goods into the country and should be considered when deciding how best to bring products into the country."[3]

TAXATION
Score–Income taxation: 3–Stable (moderate tax rates)
Score–Corporate taxation: 3–Stable (moderate tax rates)
Final Taxation Score: 3.5–Stable (high tax rates)

Tanzania's highest income tax rate is 30 percent.[4] The corporate tax rate is 35 percent. Tanzania also has a sales tax of up to 30 percent.

GOVERNMENT INTERVENTION IN THE ECONOMY
Score: 3–Stable (moderate level)

Government consumes 7.7 percent of Tanzania's GDP. Although some industries have been privatized, inefficient state-owned enterprises continue to play a major role in the industrial sector, and government monopolies in agriculture still exist. Privatization has been impeded by intensifying nationalist rhetoric.

1	Hong Kong	1.25	77	Zambia	3.05
2	Singapore	1.30	80	Mali	3.10
3	Bahrain	1.70	80	Mongolia	3.10
4	New Zealand	1.75	80	Slovenia	3.10
5	Switzerland	1.90	83	Honduras	3.15
5	United States	1.90	83	Papua New Guinea	3.15
7	Luxembourg	1.95	85	Djibouti	3.20
7	Taiwan	1.95	85	Fiji	3.20
7	United Kingdom	1.95	85	Pakistan	3.20
10	Bahamas	2.00	88	Algeria	3.25
10	Ireland	2.00	88	Guinea	3.25
12	Australia	2.05	88	Lebanon	3.25
12	Japan	2.05	88	Mexico	3.25
14	Belgium	2.10	88	Senegal	3.25
14	Canada	2.10	88	Tanzania	3.25
14	United Arab Emirates	2.10	94	Nigeria	3.30
17	Austria	2.15	94	Romania	3.30
17	Chile	2.15	96	Brazil	3.35
17	Estonia	2.15	96	Cambodia	3.35
20	Czech Republic	2.20	96	Egypt	3.35
20	Netherlands	2.20	96	Ivory Coast	3.35
22	Denmark	2.25	96	Madagascar	3.35
22	Finland	2.25	96	Moldova	3.35
24	Germany	2.30	102	Nepal	3.40
24	Iceland	2.30	103	Cape Verde	3.44
24	South Korea	2.30	104	Armenia	3.45
27	Norway	2.35	104	Dominican Republic	3.45
28	Kuwait	2.40	104	Russia	3.45
28	Malaysia	2.40	107	Burkina Faso	3.50
28	Panama	2.40	107	Cameroon	3.50
28	Thailand	2.40	107	Lesotho	3.50
32	El Salvador	2.45	107	Nicaragua	3.50
32	Sri Lanka	2.45	107	Venezuela	3.50
32	Sweden	2.45	112	Gambia	3.60
35	France	2.50	112	Guyana	3.60
35	Italy	2.50	114	Bulgaria	3.65
35	Spain	2.50	114	Georgia	3.65
38	Trinidad and Tobago	2.55	114	Malawi	3.65
39	Argentina	2.60	117	Ethiopia	3.70
39	Barbados	2.60	117	India	3.70
39	Cyprus	2.60	117	Niger	3.70
39	Jamaica	2.60	120	Albania	3.75
39	Portugal	2.60	120	Bangladesh	3.75
44	Bolivia	2.65	120	China (PRC)	3.75
44	Oman	2.65	120	Congo	3.75
44	Philippines	2.65	120	Croatia	3.75
47	Swaziland	2.70	125	Chad	3.80
47	Uruguay	2.70	125	Mauritania	3.80
49	Botswana	2.75	125	Ukraine	3.80
49	Jordan	2.75	128	Sierra Leone	3.85
49	Namibia	2.75	129	Burundi	3.90
49	Tunisia	2.75	129	Suriname	3.90
53	Belize	2.80	129	Zimbabwe	3.90
53	Costa Rica	2.80	132	Haiti	4.00
53	Guatemala	2.80	132	Kyrgyzstan	4.00
53	Israel	2.80	132	Syria	4.00
53	Peru	2.80	135	Belarus	4.05
53	Saudi Arabia	2.80	136	Kazakstan	4.10
53	Turkey	2.80	136	Mozambique	4.10
53	Uganda	2.80	136	Yemen	4.10
53	Western Samoa	2.80	139	Sudan	4.20
62	Indonesia	2.85	140	Myanmar	4.30
62	Latvia	2.85	140	Rwanda	4.30
62	Malta	2.85	142	Angola	4.35
62	Paraguay	2.85	143	Azerbaijan	4.40
66	Greece	2.90	143	Tajikistan	4.40
66	Hungary	2.90	145	Turkmenistan	4.50
66	South Africa	2.90	146	Uzbekistan	4.55
69	Benin	2.95	147	Congo/Zaire	4.70
69	Ecuador	2.95	147	Iran	4.70
69	Gabon	2.95	147	Libya	4.70
69	Morocco	2.95	147	Somalia	4.70
69	Poland	2.95	147	Vietnam	4.70
74	Colombia	3.00	152	Bosnia	4.80
74	Ghana	3.00	153	Iraq	4.90
74	Lithuania	3.00	154	Cuba	5.00
77	Kenya	3.05	154	Laos	5.00
77	Slovak Republic	3.05	154	North Korea	5.00

Mostly Unfree

MONETARY POLICY
Score: 4–Stable (high level of inflation)

Tanzania's average annual rate of inflation from 1985 through 1995 was 32.3 percent. It is estimated that the current rate of inflation is 21.5 percent.

CAPITAL FLOWS AND FOREIGN INVESTMENT
Score: 3–Stable (moderate barriers)

Tanzania's new investment code has created a more favorable environment for foreign investment. A single-stop foreign investment approval office has been established, majority government participation in mining projects no is longer required, the government offers investment incentives, and there is a free trade zone on the island of Zanzibar. Bureaucratic impediments, however, include the necessity to acquire business licenses, company registrations, and other documentation from a variety of often corrupt ministries.[5] Foreign ownership of land is prohibited.

BANKING
Score: 3–Stable (moderate level of restrictions)

At least five foreign banks have opened over the past two years, and a Tanzanian-owned bank opened in 1995. These are the first private banks to take advantage of a 1991 law that allows private banking (the banking sector had been nationalized in 1967). The market now determines interest rates. Despite reforms, however, financial services still are provided largely by inefficient and corrupt state banks.[6]

WAGE AND PRICE CONTROLS
Score: 2–Stable (low level)

Most price controls have been removed in Tanzania, and the pricing of agriculture products has been liberalized. Wage controls are imposed indirectly by the government's extensive control of economic enterprise. Tanzania has a minimum wage.

PROPERTY RIGHTS
Score: 3–Stable (moderate level of protection)

No nationalization of private enterprises has taken place in Tanzania since 1973. There is a great deal of resentment, however, against individuals (particularly Asians) who have acquired privatized properties. According to the U.S. Department of State, "The Constitution provides for an independent judiciary, and in practice, the judiciary has been increasingly willing to demonstrate its independence of the government."[7] At the same time, however, "Independent observers...continue to view the judiciary as corrupt."[8] Nevertheless, the judicial system is not in disarray, and Tanzania maintains a moderate level of private property protection by global standards.

REGULATION
Score: 4–Stable (high level)

Excessive regulation is throttling the private sector in Tanzania, and corruption is rampant throughout the bureaucracy. According to the U.S. Department of Commerce, "Tanzania has in place an extensive set of policies, regulations and procedures that greatly influence trade, commerce, employment, and resource allocation. Many of these provisions are outdated and reflect conditions in the colonial era; many others reflect socialist-era circumstances and have yet to be adjusted to serve the needs of a liberal market based economy."[9]

BLACK MARKET
Score: 4–Stable (high level of activity)

Tanzania's black market is huge. High tariffs on textiles have produced a vibrant market in smuggled textiles, and the free trade zone on Zanzibar has led to the smuggling of goods to the mainland. Protection of intellectual property rights remains lax.

NOTES

1. Economist Intelligence Unit, *Country Report—Tanzania, First Quarter 1997*, p. 6.
2. Based on total taxes on international trade as a percentage of total imports.
3. U.S. Department of Commerce, *Country Commercial Guide*, 1997.
4. Tanzania's income tax score is based solely on the maximum rate.
5. U.S. Department of Commerce, *Country Commercial Guide*, 1997.
6. *Ibid.*
7. U.S. Department of State, "Tanzania Country Report on Human Rights Practices for 1996," 1997.
8. *Ibid.*
9. U.S. Department of Commerce, *Country Commercial Guide*, 1997.

Thailand   2.40

1997 Score: **2.30**	1996 Score: **2.30**	1995 Score: **2.30**

Trade	3	Banking	3
Taxation	3	Wages and Prices	3
Government Intervention	2	Property Rights	2
Monetary Policy	1	Regulation	3
Foreign Investment	2	Black Market	2

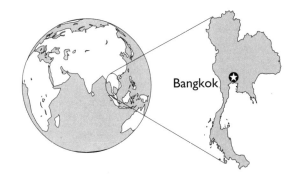

Bangkok

Thailand, a constitutional monarchy with a parliamentary government, is suffering from a major economic contraction following the government's July 1997 decision to devalue the currency in excess of 25 percent against the U.S. dollar. GDP, which grew at an annual rate of about 10 percent from 1987 to 1991, has grown by about 8 percent a year since then. This rapid growth has not been without difficulty: roads, bridges, and rail systems have failed to keep up with industrial expansion, and pockets of poverty exist in most cities. The bureaucracy has resisted the government's privatization program, and many companies remain publicly owned. Thailand has reduced some barriers to foreign investment, but also has experienced an increase in judicial corruption. Thus, its overall score is 0.1 point worse this year.

TRADE POLICY
Score: 3–Stable (moderate level of protectionism)

Thailand has an average tariff rate of 6.7 percent and maintains nontariff barriers in many areas. For example, import licenses still are required for 42 item categories, 23 of which are agricultural products. According to the Office of the United States Trade Representative, "Many importers, both Thai and foreign, charge that Customs Department procedures are a barrier to trade."[1]

TAXATION
Score–Income taxation: 2–Stable (low tax rates)
Score–Corporate taxation: 3–Stable (moderate tax rates)
Final Taxation Score: 3–Stable (moderate tax rates)

Thailand's top marginal income tax rate is 37 percent, with the average income level taxed at 5 percent. The top corporate tax rate is 30 percent. Thailand also has a 30 percent capital gains tax and a 7 percent value-added tax.

GOVERNMENT INTERVENTION IN THE ECONOMY
Score: 2– (low level)

Government consumes 9.7 percent of Thailand's GDP. Although much of Thailand's privatization is moving forward (the government, for example, recently sold off shares in its major oil refinery), recent evidence indicates that part of this program may have stalled. The number of state-owned enterprises has declined in recent years, but 58 still exist.[2] Thus, Thailand's government intervention score is one point worse this year.

MONETARY POLICY
Score: 1–Stable (very low level of inflation)

Thailand's average annual rate of inflation from 1985 to 1995 was 5 percent. In 1996, the rate of inflation was about 5.8 percent. In July 1997, the government substantially devalued its currency—an action that, among other things, can be expected to increase the rate of inflation over time.

1	Hong Kong	1.25	77	Zambia	3.05
2	Singapore	1.30	80	Mali	3.10
3	Bahrain	1.70	80	Mongolia	3.10
4	New Zealand	1.75	80	Slovenia	3.10
5	Switzerland	1.90	83	Honduras	3.15
5	United States	1.90	83	Papua New Guinea	3.15
7	Luxembourg	1.95	85	Djibouti	3.20
7	Taiwan	1.95	85	Fiji	3.20
7	United Kingdom	1.95	85	Pakistan	3.20
10	Bahamas	2.00	88	Algeria	3.25
10	Ireland	2.00	88	Guinea	3.25
12	Australia	2.05	88	Lebanon	3.25
12	Japan	2.05	88	Mexico	3.25
14	Belgium	2.10	88	Senegal	3.25
14	Canada	2.10	88	Tanzania	3.25
14	United Arab Emirates	2.10	94	Nigeria	3.30
17	Austria	2.15	94	Romania	3.30
17	Chile	2.15	96	Brazil	3.35
17	Estonia	2.15	96	Cambodia	3.35
20	Czech Republic	2.20	96	Egypt	3.35
20	Netherlands	2.20	96	Ivory Coast	3.35
22	Denmark	2.25	96	Madagascar	3.35
22	Finland	2.25	96	Moldova	3.35
24	Germany	2.30	102	Nepal	3.40
24	Iceland	2.30	103	Cape Verde	3.44
24	South Korea	2.30	104	Armenia	3.45
27	Norway	2.35	104	Dominican Republic	3.45
28	Kuwait	2.40	104	Russia	3.45
28	Malaysia	2.40	107	Burkina Faso	3.50
28	Panama	2.40	107	Cameroon	3.50
28	Thailand	2.40	107	Lesotho	3.50
32	El Salvador	2.45	107	Nicaragua	3.50
32	Sri Lanka	2.45	107	Venezuela	3.50
32	Sweden	2.45	112	Gambia	3.60
35	France	2.50	112	Guyana	3.60
35	Italy	2.50	114	Bulgaria	3.65
35	Spain	2.50	114	Georgia	3.65
38	Trinidad and Tobago	2.55	114	Malawi	3.65
39	Argentina	2.60	117	Ethiopia	3.70
39	Barbados	2.60	117	India	3.70
39	Cyprus	2.60	117	Niger	3.70
39	Jamaica	2.60	120	Albania	3.75
39	Portugal	2.60	120	Bangladesh	3.75
44	Bolivia	2.65	120	China (PRC)	3.75
44	Oman	2.65	120	Congo	3.75
44	Philippines	2.65	120	Croatia	3.75
47	Swaziland	2.70	125	Chad	3.80
47	Uruguay	2.70	125	Mauritania	3.80
49	Botswana	2.75	125	Ukraine	3.80
49	Jordan	2.75	128	Sierra Leone	3.85
49	Namibia	2.75	129	Burundi	3.90
49	Tunisia	2.75	129	Suriname	3.90
53	Belize	2.80	129	Zimbabwe	3.90
53	Costa Rica	2.80	132	Haiti	4.00
53	Guatemala	2.80	132	Kyrgyzstan	4.00
53	Israel	2.80	132	Syria	4.00
53	Peru	2.80	135	Belarus	4.05
53	Saudi Arabia	2.80	136	Kazakhstan	4.10
53	Turkey	2.80	136	Mozambique	4.10
53	Uganda	2.80	136	Yemen	4.10
53	Western Samoa	2.80	139	Sudan	4.20
62	Indonesia	2.85	140	Myanmar	4.30
62	Latvia	2.85	140	Rwanda	4.30
62	Malta	2.85	142	Angola	4.35
62	Paraguay	2.85	143	Azerbaijan	4.40
66	Greece	2.90	143	Tajikistan	4.40
66	Hungary	2.90	145	Turkmenistan	4.50
66	South Africa	2.90	146	Uzbekistan	4.55
69	Benin	2.95	147	Congo/Zaire	4.70
69	Ecuador	2.95	147	Iran	4.70
69	Gabon	2.95	147	Libya	4.70
69	Morocco	2.95	147	Somalia	4.70
69	Poland	2.95	147	Vietnam	4.70
74	Colombia	3.00	152	Bosnia	4.80
74	Ghana	3.00	153	Iraq	4.90
74	Lithuania	3.00	154	Cuba	5.00
77	Kenya	3.05	154	Laos	5.00
77	Slovak Republic	3.05	154	North Korea	5.00

Mostly Free

CAPITAL FLOWS AND FOREIGN INVESTMENT
Score: 2+ (low barriers)

There are several restrictions on foreign investment in Thailand. The government restricts foreign entry into such service areas as telecommunications and insurance, although in November 1996 it instituted a new banking law that permits increased foreign investment in this area. With this once-significant investment barrier eliminated, Thailand's score for this factor is one point better this year.

BANKING
Score: 3–Stable (moderate level of restrictions)

Foreign banks now are permitted to establish offices and engage in local currency transactions in Thailand, but restrictions on the establishment of branches by foreign banks continue. Domestic banks are prohibited from participating in some financial activities (for example, real estate ventures).

WAGE AND PRICE CONTROLS
Score: 3–Stable (moderate level)

Thailand's government imposes price controls on such items as agricultural products, matches, milk, sugar, toiletries, and vegetable oil. It also has a minimum wage.

PROPERTY RIGHTS
Score: 2– (high level of protection)

Expropriation is not likely in Thailand. The court system protects property rights adequately, although there are recent indications of corruption. According to the U.S. Department of State, "The judiciary is independent but subject to corruption.... An ingrained culture of corruption in the bureaucracy, police, and military services plagues the society."[3] The U.S. Department of Commerce reports that "Thailand has an independent judiciary that is generally effective in enforcing property and contractual rights, but in practice the legal process is slow and litigants or third parties sometimes may affect judgments through extra-legal means."[4] Thus, despite some evidence of corruption, the judiciary remains independent and the protection of property rights remains high by global standards. Because of increased corruption, however, Thailand's property rights score is one point worse this year.

REGULATION
Score: 3–Stable (moderate level)

Thailand has a large but efficient bureaucracy. Bureaucrats, however, tend to view business as exploitable and often apply taxes, fines, and charges arbitrarily. These and other actions prove moderately burdensome.

BLACK MARKET
Score: 2–Stable (low level of activity)

Thailand's black market is confined mainly to drugs and prostitution. According to the U.S. Department of State, "[C]opyright piracy of audio and video tapes and computer software remains widespread."[5]

NOTES

1. Office of the United States Trade Representative, *1997 National Trade Estimate Report on Foreign Trade Barriers*, pp. 362–363.
2. Economist Intelligence Unit, *ILT Reports*, 1996.
3. U.S. Department of State, "Thailand Country Report on Human Rights Practices for 1996," 1997.
4. U.S. Department of Commerce, *Country Commercial Guide*, 1996.
5. U.S. Department of State, *Country Reports on Economic Policy and Trade Practices*, 1996, p. 108.

Trinidad and Tobago 2.55

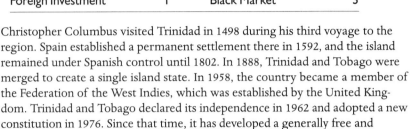

Port-of-Spain

1997 Score: **2.55**	1996 Score: **2.50**	1995 Score: **n/a**

Trade	5	Banking	2
Taxation	4.5	Wages and Prices	2
Government Intervention	2	Property Rights	1
Monetary Policy	2	Regulation	3
Foreign Investment	1	Black Market	3

Christopher Columbus visited Trinidad in 1498 during his third voyage to the region. Spain established a permanent settlement there in 1592, and the island remained under Spanish control until 1802. In 1888, Trinidad and Tobago were merged to create a single island state. In 1958, the country became a member of the Federation of the West Indies, which was established by the United Kingdom. Trinidad and Tobago declared its independence in 1962 and adopted a new constitution in 1976. Since that time, it has developed a generally free and prosperous economy.

TRADE POLICY
Score: 5–Stable (very high level of protectionism)

Trinidad and Tobago's trade liberalization law will reduce tariff rates drastically by 1998. The current average tariff rate is about 17.3 percent; but the country is a member of the Caribbean Common Market, and the government is working to bring tariffs in line with the market's common external tariff (currently between 5 percent and 20 percent for most goods). Principal nontariff barriers include strict licensing requirements for such products as chicken parts, live chickens, sugar, oil seed, and tobacco paper.

TAXATION
Score–Income taxation: 5–Stable (very high tax rates)
Score–Corporate taxation: 3–Stable (moderate tax rates)
Final Taxation Score: 4.5–Stable (very high tax rates)

Trinidad and Tobago's top income tax rate is 38 percent, and the average taxpayer finds himself in the 33 percent bracket. The top marginal corporate tax rate is 35 percent. The country also has a 35 percent capital gains tax and a 15 percent value-added tax.

GOVERNMENT INTERVENTION IN THE ECONOMY
Score: 2–Stable (low level)

Government consumes about 15.7 percent of Trinidad and Tobago's GDP and is heavily involved in various state-owned companies and industries. It owns and operates the telecommunications industry, for example, and manages the sugar industry. It also, however, is working to privatize many state-owned companies.

MONETARY POLICY
Score: 2–Stable (low level of inflation)

Trinidad and Tobago's average rate of inflation from 1985 to 1995 was 6.8 percent, up from 5.9 percent from 1985 to 1993, primarily because of high inflation in 1993 and 1994. In 1996, the rate of inflation was 3.4 percent.

1	Hong Kong	1.25	77	Zambia	3.05
2	Singapore	1.30	80	Mali	3.10
3	Bahrain	1.70	80	Mongolia	3.10
4	New Zealand	1.75	80	Slovenia	3.10
5	Switzerland	1.90	83	Honduras	3.15
5	United States	1.90	83	Papua New Guinea	3.15
7	Luxembourg	1.95	85	Djibouti	3.20
7	Taiwan	1.95	85	Fiji	3.20
7	United Kingdom	1.95	85	Pakistan	3.20
10	Bahamas	2.00	88	Algeria	3.25
10	Ireland	2.00	88	Guinea	3.25
12	Australia	2.05	88	Lebanon	3.25
12	Japan	2.05	88	Mexico	3.25
14	Belgium	2.10	88	Senegal	3.25
14	Canada	2.10	88	Tanzania	3.25
14	United Arab Emirates	2.10	94	Nigeria	3.30
17	Austria	2.15	94	Romania	3.30
17	Chile	2.15	96	Brazil	3.35
17	Estonia	2.15	96	Cambodia	3.35
20	Czech Republic	2.20	96	Egypt	3.35
20	Netherlands	2.20	96	Ivory Coast	3.35
22	Denmark	2.25	96	Madagascar	3.35
22	Finland	2.25	96	Moldova	3.35
24	Germany	2.30	102	Nepal	3.40
24	Iceland	2.30	103	Cape Verde	3.44
24	South Korea	2.30	104	Armenia	3.45
27	Norway	2.35	104	Dominican Republic	3.45
28	Kuwait	2.40	104	Russia	3.45
28	Malaysia	2.40	107	Burkina Faso	3.50
28	Panama	2.40	107	Cameroon	3.50
28	Thailand	2.40	107	Lesotho	3.50
32	El Salvador	2.45	107	Nicaragua	3.50
32	Sri Lanka	2.45	107	Venezuela	3.50
32	Sweden	2.45	112	Gambia	3.60
35	France	2.50	112	Guyana	3.60
35	Italy	2.50	114	Bulgaria	3.65
35	Spain	2.50	114	Georgia	3.65
38	Trinidad and Tobago	2.55	114	Malawi	3.65
39	Argentina	2.60	117	Ethiopia	3.70
39	Barbados	2.60	117	India	3.70
39	Cyprus	2.60	117	Niger	3.70
39	Jamaica	2.60	120	Albania	3.75
39	Portugal	2.60	120	Bangladesh	3.75
44	Bolivia	2.65	120	China (PRC)	3.75
44	Oman	2.65	120	Congo	3.75
44	Philippines	2.65	120	Croatia	3.75
47	Swaziland	2.70	125	Chad	3.80
47	Uruguay	2.70	125	Mauritania	3.80
49	Botswana	2.75	125	Ukraine	3.80
49	Jordan	2.75	128	Sierra Leone	3.85
49	Namibia	2.75	129	Burundi	3.90
49	Tunisia	2.75	129	Suriname	3.90
53	Belize	2.80	129	Zimbabwe	3.90
53	Costa Rica	2.80	132	Haiti	4.00
53	Guatemala	2.80	132	Kyrgyzstan	4.00
53	Israel	2.80	132	Syria	4.00
53	Peru	2.80	135	Belarus	4.05
53	Saudi Arabia	2.80	136	Kazakstan	4.10
53	Turkey	2.80	136	Mozambique	4.10
53	Uganda	2.80	136	Yemen	4.10
53	Western Samoa	2.80	139	Sudan	4.20
62	Indonesia	2.85	140	Myanmar	4.30
62	Latvia	2.85	140	Rwanda	4.30
62	Malta	2.85	142	Angola	4.35
62	Paraguay	2.85	143	Azerbaijan	4.40
66	Greece	2.90	143	Tajikistan	4.40
66	Hungary	2.90	145	Turkmenistan	4.50
66	South Africa	2.90	145	Uzbekistan	4.55
69	Benin	2.95	147	Congo/Zaire	4.70
69	Ecuador	2.95	147	Iran	4.70
69	Gabon	2.95	147	Libya	4.70
69	Morocco	2.95	147	Somalia	4.70
69	Poland	2.95	147	Vietnam	4.70
74	Colombia	3.00	152	Bosnia	4.80
74	Ghana	3.00	153	Iraq	4.90
74	Lithuania	3.00	154	Cuba	5.00
77	Kenya	3.05	154	Laos	5.00
77	Slovak Republic	3.05	154	North Korea	5.00

Mostly Free

Capital Flows and Foreign Investment
Score: 1–Stable (very low barriers)

There are few restrictions on foreign investment in Trinidad and Tobago. Incentives are granted in the form of tax breaks and holidays.

Banking
Score: 2–Stable (low level of restrictions)

The banking system in Trinidad and Tobago is open and competitive. Banks may be wholly owned by foreigners.

Wage and Price Controls
Score: 2–Stable (low level)

The market sets most wages and prices in Trinidad and Tobago, although the government determines prices on such goods and services as sugar, school books, and pharmaceuticals. There is no national minimum wage.

Property Rights
Score: 1–Stable (very high level of protection)

Private property is safe in Trinidad and Tobago, which has an efficient legal and judicial system. "[I]ncreased violent crime and narcotics trafficking strained the judicial system, which was severely bogged down by excessive delays," reports the U.S. Department of State,[1] but some of these delays have been lessened.

Regulation
Score: 3–Stable (moderate level)

Establishing a business in Trinidad and Tobago is a simple process, and regulations are applied evenly in most cases. Both regulations and bureaucratic red tape, however, are burdensome. Rigid environmental regulations, for example, are enforced by 28 different agencies. The government has announced a plan to create a new agency that would consolidate all environmental regulation.

Black Market
Score: 3–Stable (moderate level of activity)

Although the government has made significant strides toward cracking down on black market activity, intellectual property laws are not enforced. This has created a black market in pirated videos, computer software, recorded music, and other products. According to the U.S. Department of State, "Although the [Copyright Act of 1995] provides protection of literary, musical and artistic works, computer software, sound recordings, audio-visual works and broadcasts, it is not enforced. Video rental outlets in Trinidad and Tobago are replete with pirated videos and operate openly."[2]

Notes
1. U.S. Department of State, "Trinidad and Tobago Country Report on Human Rights Practices for 1996," 1997.
2. U.S. Department of State, *Country Reports on Economic Policy and Trade Practices,* 1997, p. 302.

Tunisia   2.75

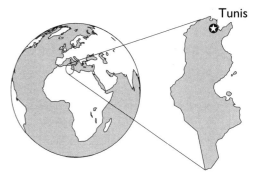

Tunis

1997 Score: **2.75**	1996 Score: **2.65**	1995 Score: **2.85**

Trade	5	Banking	2
Taxation	3.5	Wages and Prices	2
Government Intervention	3	Property Rights	3
Monetary Policy	2	Regulation	2
Foreign Investment	2	Black Market	3

Tunisia gained its independence from France in 1956. In 1964, the government nationalized all foreign-owned land, causing prolonged tension with France. In the early 1990s, after more than 30 years of unproductive socialist economic policies, Tunisia began to reform its economy. Among the results of this effort are liberalized trade, a large privatization program, and cuts in government subsidies. Tunisia remains one of the most modern, stable, and cosmopolitan countries in the Arab world.

TRADE POLICY
Score: 5–Stable (very high level of protectionism)

Tunisia has an average tariff rate of 25 percent. There are few nontariff barriers.

TAXATION
Score–Income taxation: 3–Stable (moderate tax rates)
Score–Corporate taxation: 3–Stable (moderate tax rates)
Final Taxation Score: 3.5–Stable (high tax rates)

Tunisia's top income tax rate is 35 percent, and the average income level is taxed at 15 percent. The top corporate tax rate is 35 percent. Tunisia also has a 35 percent capital gains tax, a 6 percent to 29 percent value-added tax, and a property tax.

GOVERNMENT INTERVENTION IN THE ECONOMY
Score: 3–Stable (moderate level)

Government consumes 16.2 percent of Tunisia's GDP. It also has an aggressive privatization program in place and has identified some 20 to 30 companies that are to be privatized. Several large state-owned companies continue to receive subsidies, however, and the government retains its controlling interests in cement, tobacco manufacturing, oil refining, and telecommunications.

MONETARY POLICY
Score: 2–Stable (low level of inflation)

Tunisia's average annual rate of inflation from 1985 to 1995 was 6 percent. In 1996, the rate was 6 percent.

CAPITAL FLOWS AND FOREIGN INVESTMENT
Score: 2–Stable (low barriers)

Tunisia is open to foreign investment, treats domestic firms the same as foreign firms, and offers attractive tax holidays to investors. It also prohibits the ownership of land by non-Tunisians, however.

1	Hong Kong	1.25	77	Zambia	3.05
2	Singapore	1.30	80	Mali	3.10
3	Bahrain	1.70	80	Mongolia	3.10
4	New Zealand	1.75	80	Slovenia	3.10
5	Switzerland	1.90	83	Honduras	3.15
5	United States	1.90	83	Papua New Guinea	3.15
7	Luxembourg	1.95	85	Djibouti	3.20
7	Taiwan	1.95	85	Fiji	3.20
7	United Kingdom	1.95	85	Pakistan	3.20
10	Bahamas	2.00	88	Algeria	3.25
10	Ireland	2.00	88	Guinea	3.25
12	Australia	2.05	88	Lebanon	3.25
12	Japan	2.05	88	Mexico	3.25
14	Belgium	2.10	88	Senegal	3.25
14	Canada	2.10	88	Tanzania	3.25
14	United Arab Emirates	2.10	94	Nigeria	3.30
17	Austria	2.15	94	Romania	3.30
17	Chile	2.15	96	Brazil	3.35
17	Estonia	2.15	96	Cambodia	3.35
20	Czech Republic	2.20	96	Egypt	3.35
20	Netherlands	2.20	96	Ivory Coast	3.35
22	Denmark	2.25	96	Madagascar	3.35
22	Finland	2.25	96	Moldova	3.35
24	Germany	2.30	102	Nepal	3.40
24	Iceland	2.30	103	Cape Verde	3.44
24	South Korea	2.30	104	Armenia	3.45
27	Norway	2.35	104	Dominican Republic	3.45
28	Kuwait	2.40	104	Russia	3.45
28	Malaysia	2.40	107	Burkina Faso	3.50
28	Panama	2.40	107	Cameroon	3.50
28	Thailand	2.40	107	Lesotho	3.50
32	El Salvador	2.45	107	Nicaragua	3.50
32	Sri Lanka	2.45	107	Venezuela	3.50
32	Sweden	2.45	112	Gambia	3.60
35	France	2.50	112	Guyana	3.60
35	Italy	2.50	114	Bulgaria	3.65
35	Spain	2.50	114	Georgia	3.65
38	Trinidad and Tobago	2.55	114	Malawi	3.65
39	Argentina	2.60	117	Ethiopia	3.70
39	Barbados	2.60	117	India	3.70
39	Cyprus	2.60	117	Niger	3.70
39	Jamaica	2.60	120	Albania	3.75
39	Portugal	2.60	120	Bangladesh	3.75
44	Bolivia	2.65	120	China (PRC)	3.75
44	Oman	2.65	120	Congo	3.75
44	Philippines	2.65	120	Croatia	3.75
47	Swaziland	2.70	125	Chad	3.80
47	Uruguay	2.70	125	Mauritania	3.80
49	Botswana	2.75	125	Ukraine	3.80
49	Jordan	2.75	128	Sierra Leone	3.85
49	Namibia	2.75	129	Burundi	3.90
49	Tunisia	2.75	129	Suriname	3.90
53	Belize	2.80	129	Zimbabwe	3.90
53	Costa Rica	2.80	132	Haiti	4.00
53	Guatemala	2.80	132	Kyrgyzstan	4.00
53	Israel	2.80	132	Syria	4.00
53	Peru	2.80	135	Belarus	4.05
53	Saudi Arabia	2.80	136	Kazakstan	4.10
53	Turkey	2.80	136	Mozambique	4.10
53	Uganda	2.80	136	Yemen	4.10
53	Western Samoa	2.80	139	Sudan	4.20
62	Indonesia	2.85	140	Myanmar	4.30
62	Latvia	2.85	140	Rwanda	4.30
62	Malta	2.85	142	Angola	4.35
62	Paraguay	2.85	143	Azerbaijan	4.40
66	Greece	2.90	143	Tajikistan	4.40
66	Hungary	2.90	145	Turkmenistan	4.50
66	South Africa	2.90	146	Uzbekistan	4.55
69	Benin	2.95	147	Congo/Zaire	4.70
69	Ecuador	2.95	147	Iran	4.70
69	Gabon	2.95	147	Libya	4.70
69	Morocco	2.95	147	Somalia	4.70
69	Poland	2.95	147	Vietnam	4.70
74	Colombia	3.00	152	Bosnia	4.80
74	Ghana	3.00	153	Iraq	4.90
74	Lithuania	3.00	154	Cuba	5.00
77	Kenya	3.05	154	Laos	5.00
77	Slovak Republic	3.05	154	North Korea	5.00

Mostly Free

BANKING
Score: 2–Stable (low level of restrictions)

Banks in Tunisia are becoming more independent of the government. Recent laws have eased some Central Bank regulations on foreign and domestic banks.

WAGE AND PRICE CONTROLS
Score: 2–Stable (low level)

Tunisia has a minimum wage and maintains some price controls.

PROPERTY RIGHTS
Score: 3–Stable (moderate level of protection)

Tunisia has an efficient and effective legal system. Property rights are relatively secure, although foreigners are not allowed to own land. Terrorism from Tunisia's radical Islamic fundamentalist movement, however, is a threat to private property. Most of the judiciary is part of the country's Department of Justice; therefore, the judicial system is not totally independent of the executive branch.

REGULATION
Score: 2–Stable (low level)

Tunisia has a very efficient bureaucracy. Regulations are applied fairly in most cases, although sanitary, health, and product quality regulations can be somewhat burdensome.

BLACK MARKET
Score: 3–Stable (moderate level of activity)

As Tunisia's market becomes more accessible to foreign goods, the moderately large black market is shrinking. There is some black market activity in pirated trademarks and prerecorded music and video tapes.

Turkey   2.80

1997 Score: **2.80**	1996 Score: **3.00**	1995 Score: **3.00**

Trade	2	Banking	2
Taxation	4	Wages and Prices	3
Government Intervention	2	Property Rights	2
Monetary Policy	5	Regulation	3
Foreign Investment	2	Black Market	3

Turkey became an independent state in 1923 after the collapse of the Ottoman Empire. After decades of one-party rule, a multiparty system was adopted in 1950. Turkey receives large amounts of U.S. foreign aid, which often has been used to postpone badly needed economic reforms. During the 1980s, after broad free-market reforms were instituted under Prime Minister Turgut Özal, Turkey enjoyed an economic boom. Since then, the economy has been hurt both by the United Nations economic sanctions imposed on Iraq in 1990 and by an intensifying war against Kurdish separatists in eastern Turkey. The government of former Prime Minister Tansu Çiller halfheartedly implemented a privatization program, but the June 1996 formation of a coalition government headed by Prime Minister Necmettin Erbakan, leader of the pro-Islamist Refah Party, was a major setback for economic liberalization. Although Erbakan's resignation and the formation of a secular coalition government in June 1997 have revived the prospects for free-market reform, Turkey remains hampered by a large national debt, skyrocketing inflation, huge unemployment rates, and a growing regulatory burden.

TRADE POLICY
Score: 2– (low level of protectionism)

Turkey has an average tariff rate of 5.6 percent. Its trade policy score is one point worse this year.[1] Although most import licenses have been eliminated, Turkey requires that importers obtain a certificate before selling their products in the country. This certificate is relatively easy to get, but the procedure imposes an administrative and financial burden on the importer. Beyond this, there are no significant restrictions on imports.

TAXATION
Score–Income taxation: 5–Stable (very high tax rates)
Score–Corporate taxation: 2+ (low tax rates)
Final Taxation Score: 4+ (high tax rates)

Turkey's top marginal income tax rate is 55 percent; the average income level is taxed at 25 percent. The top corporate tax rate is 25 percent, down from 45 percent in 1995.[2] As a result, Turkey's taxation score is one-half point better this year. Turkey also has a value-added tax that can reach as high as 23 percent, as well as a social contributions tax.

GOVERNMENT INTERVENTION IN THE ECONOMY
Score: 2–Stable (low level)

Government consumes about 7.6 percent of Turkey's GDP and still owns significant portions of the economy. Although Turkey has a privatization program, the government owns many companies in such areas as ports, railways, iron and steel, airports, mineral mining, airlines, petroleum, and electronics.

1	Hong Kong	1.25	77	Zambia	3.05
2	Singapore	1.30	80	Mali	3.10
3	Bahrain	1.70	80	Mongolia	3.10
4	New Zealand	1.75	80	Slovenia	3.10
5	Switzerland	1.90	83	Honduras	3.15
5	United States	1.90	83	Papua New Guinea	3.15
7	Luxembourg	1.95	85	Djibouti	3.20
7	Taiwan	1.95	85	Fiji	3.20
7	United Kingdom	1.95	85	Pakistan	3.20
10	Bahamas	2.00	88	Algeria	3.25
10	Ireland	2.00	88	Guinea	3.25
12	Australia	2.05	88	Lebanon	3.25
12	Japan	2.05	88	Mexico	3.25
14	Belgium	2.10	88	Senegal	3.25
14	Canada	2.10	88	Tanzania	3.25
14	United Arab Emirates	2.10	94	Nigeria	3.30
17	Austria	2.15	94	Romania	3.30
17	Chile	2.15	96	Brazil	3.35
17	Estonia	2.15	96	Cambodia	3.35
20	Czech Republic	2.20	96	Egypt	3.35
20	Netherlands	2.20	96	Ivory Coast	3.35
22	Denmark	2.25	96	Madagascar	3.35
22	Finland	2.25	96	Moldova	3.35
24	Germany	2.30	102	Nepal	3.40
24	Iceland	2.30	103	Cape Verde	3.44
24	South Korea	2.30	104	Armenia	3.45
27	Norway	2.35	104	Dominican Republic	3.45
28	Kuwait	2.40	104	Russia	3.45
28	Malaysia	2.40	107	Burkina Faso	3.50
28	Panama	2.40	107	Cameroon	3.50
28	Thailand	2.40	107	Lesotho	3.50
32	El Salvador	2.45	107	Nicaragua	3.50
32	Sri Lanka	2.45	107	Venezuela	3.50
32	Sweden	2.45	112	Gambia	3.60
35	France	2.50	112	Guyana	3.60
35	Italy	2.50	114	Bulgaria	3.65
35	Spain	2.50	114	Georgia	3.65
38	Trinidad and Tobago	2.55	114	Malawi	3.65
39	Argentina	2.60	117	Ethiopia	3.70
39	Barbados	2.60	117	India	3.70
39	Cyprus	2.60	117	Niger	3.70
39	Jamaica	2.60	120	Albania	3.75
39	Portugal	2.60	120	Bangladesh	3.75
44	Bolivia	2.65	120	China (PRC)	3.75
44	Oman	2.65	120	Congo	3.75
44	Philippines	2.65	120	Croatia	3.75
47	Swaziland	2.70	125	Chad	3.80
47	Uruguay	2.70	125	Mauritania	3.80
49	Botswana	2.75	125	Ukraine	3.80
49	Jordan	2.75	128	Sierra Leone	3.85
49	Namibia	2.75	129	Burundi	3.90
49	Tunisia	2.75	129	Suriname	3.90
53	Belize	2.80	129	Zimbabwe	3.90
53	Costa Rica	2.80	132	Haiti	4.00
53	Guatemala	2.80	132	Kyrgyzstan	4.00
53	Israel	2.80	132	Syria	4.00
53	Peru	2.80	135	Belarus	4.05
53	Saudi Arabia	2.80	136	Kazakstan	4.10
53	Turkey	2.80	136	Mozambique	4.10
53	Uganda	2.80	136	Yemen	4.10
53	Western Samoa	2.80	139	Sudan	4.20
62	Indonesia	2.85	140	Myanmar	4.30
62	Latvia	2.85	140	Rwanda	4.30
62	Malta	2.85	142	Angola	4.35
62	Paraguay	2.85	143	Azerbaijan	4.40
66	Greece	2.90	143	Tajikistan	4.40
66	Hungary	2.90	145	Turkmenistan	4.50
66	South Africa	2.90	146	Uzbekistan	4.55
69	Benin	2.95	147	Congo/Zaire	4.70
69	Ecuador	2.95	147	Iran	4.70
69	Gabon	2.95	147	Libya	4.70
69	Morocco	2.95	147	Somalia	4.70
69	Poland	2.95	147	Vietnam	4.70
74	Colombia	3.00	152	Bosnia	4.80
74	Ghana	3.00	153	Iraq	4.90
74	Lithuania	3.00	154	Cuba	5.00
77	Kenya	3.05	154	Laos	5.00
77	Slovak Republic	3.05	154	North Korea	5.00

Mostly Free

Monetary Policy
Score: 5–Stable (very high level of inflation)

The average annual rate of inflation in Turkey from 1985 to 1995 was 64.6 percent. In 1996, the rate was 80.4 percent.

Capital Flows and Foreign Investment
Score: 2–Stable (low barriers)

Turkey is relatively open to foreign investment, but some barriers remain. There are no limits on how much of a Turkish business a foreign investor may own, for example, but local labor groups may pressure the government not to permit full foreign ownership of some newly privatized state-owned enterprises.

Banking
Score: 2–Stable (low level of restrictions)

Banks are open to foreign ownership in Turkey, and over 20 foreign banks have been established. Although several banks are state-owned, the domestic banking market is very competitive. According to the U.S. Department of Commerce, the banking system is "still dominated by a few large state and commercial banks—some 60 percent of all assets are held by the seven largest banks."[3] By global standards, however, the level of restrictions on banking is relatively low.

Wage and Price Controls
Score: 3–Stable (moderate level)

There are few official price controls in Turkey, but prices are controlled indirectly by large state-owned corporations whose wholesale prices are controlled by the government (although the government plans to allow most of these corporations to set their own prices). Turkey has a minimum wage law.

Property Rights
Score: 2–Stable (high level of protection)

Expropriation is unlikely in Turkey. The legal system, although imperfect, protects most private property. "There are effective means for enforcing property and contractual rights in Turkey," according to the U.S. Department of Commerce. "There is no government interference in the court system. Turkey has a written and consistently applied commercial and bankruptcy law."[4] Court rulings can take several months, however.

Regulation
Score: 3–Stable (moderate level)

Turkey has reduced the size of its bureaucracy, imposed a performance evaluation test for civil servants, and centralized government economic decision making under the prime minister. Regulations are aimed at providing more freedom for businesses. Turkey has few environmental laws, but more may be added in the future. There are recent signs, however, of bribery within the bureaucracy. According to the U.S. Department of State, "Corruption has taken an economic toll and has sapped popular faith in the Government."[5]

Black Market
Score: 3–Stable (moderate level of activity)

Turkey used to have a rather large black market, especially in such foreign goods as pirated recordings and printed materials like books and magazines. The government has enacted and enforced a variety of intellectual property rights laws, however, perhaps to smooth the path to membership in the European Union. As a result, black market activity in pirated intellectual property has fallen dramatically, although significant black market activity in pirated computer software continues; some estimates place the piracy rate in computer software at 97 percent.[6]

Notes

1. The score for this factor has changed from 1 in 1997 to 2 in 1998. Previously unavailable data provide a more accurate understanding of the country's performance. The methodology for this factor remains the same.
2. This rate includes a 10 percent surtax on the corporate income tax rate of 25 percent.
3. U.S. Department of Commerce, *Country Commercial Guide,* 1997.
4. *Ibid.*
5. U.S. Department of State, "Turkey Country Report on Human Rights Practices for 1996," 1997.
6. U.S. Department of Commerce, National Trade Data Bank and Economic Bulletin Board, products of STAT–USA, 1997.

Turkmenistan 4.50

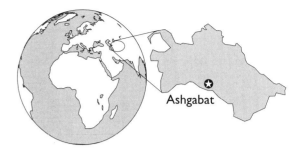

Ashgabat

1997 Score: **n/a**	1996 Score: **n/a**	1995 Score: **n/a**

Trade	5	Banking	5
Taxation	5	Wages and Prices	4
Government Intervention	4	Property Rights	4
Monetary Policy	5	Regulation	4
Foreign Investment	4	Black Market	5

The area now known as Turkmenistan has been invaded and conquered by various armies throughout its history. The region was converted to Islam by Arabs during the 7th and 8th centuries, became part of the Mongol Empire under Ghengis Khan in the 13th century, and fell to Russia in 1881. After the 1917 Bolshevik Revolution in Russia, the people revolted and enjoyed a brief period of autonomy until 1918, when the region was incorporated into the Turkistan Autonomous Soviet Socialist Republic, which included portions of present-day Kazakstan, Tajikistan, and Uzbekistan. The region became known as Turkmenistan and was fully incorporated into the Soviet Union in 1924. Turkmenistan today is predominately Sunni Muslim and Turkic-speaking. It is extremely rich in natural gas and other natural resources. Since becoming independent in 1991, Turkmenistan has been slow to change to a market-based economy. Much Soviet-era central planning continues, as does government corruption and an inefficient public bureaucracy. The government of President Saparmurad Niyazov has allowed some private-sector economic activity.

TRADE POLICY
Score: 5–Stable (very high level of protectionism)

Turkmenistan imposes official tariffs on only a few imports, like alcohol, tobacco, and some food, including fish (which has tariff rates ranging from 45 percent to over 100 percent). Instead, it uses an agency called the Commodity and Raw Materials Exchange to restrict imports. According to the U.S. Department of Commerce, "As the sole conduit for foreign trade, the CRME plays a centralized, regulatory role in Turkmenistan's economy."[1] This bureaucracy makes it difficult to get goods into and out of the country; according to the U.S. Department of Commerce, "Companies report experiencing a significant amount of 'red tape.'"[2] Some labeling requirements also hinder imports.

TAXATION
Score—Income taxation: 5–Stable (very high tax rates)
Score—Corporate taxation: 5–Stable (very high tax rates)
Final Taxation Score: 5–Stable (very high tax rates)

Turkmenistan's tax system is in disarray. Although income and corporate taxes range from 25 percent to 35 percent, there are no tax laws detailing specific rates, liability, and collection procedures. As a result, rates often are applied arbitrarily. According to the U.S. Department of Commerce, "Turkmenistan is in the process of developing its commercial and tax codes. While neither a bilateral investment treaty nor a bilateral tax treaty exists between Turkmenistan and the U.S., the former U.S.–Soviet treaty on double taxation presently applies."[3] The government also imposes a 20 percent value-added tax and various taxes on foreign exchange earnings and capital gains.

1	Hong Kong	1.25	77	Zambia	3.05
2	Singapore	1.30	80	Mali	3.10
3	Bahrain	1.70	80	Mongolia	3.10
4	New Zealand	1.75	80	Slovenia	3.10
5	Switzerland	1.90	83	Honduras	3.15
5	United States	1.90	83	Papua New Guinea	3.15
7	Luxembourg	1.95	85	Djibouti	3.20
7	Taiwan	1.95	85	Fiji	3.20
7	United Kingdom	1.95	85	Pakistan	3.20
10	Bahamas	2.00	88	Algeria	3.25
10	Ireland	2.00	88	Guinea	3.25
12	Australia	2.05	88	Lebanon	3.25
12	Japan	2.05	88	Mexico	3.25
14	Belgium	2.10	88	Senegal	3.25
14	Canada	2.10	88	Tanzania	3.25
14	United Arab Emirates	2.10	94	Nigeria	3.30
17	Austria	2.15	94	Romania	3.30
17	Chile	2.15	96	Brazil	3.35
17	Estonia	2.15	96	Cambodia	3.35
20	Czech Republic	2.20	96	Egypt	3.35
20	Netherlands	2.20	96	Ivory Coast	3.35
22	Denmark	2.25	96	Madagascar	3.35
22	Finland	2.25	96	Moldova	3.35
24	Germany	2.30	102	Nepal	3.40
24	Iceland	2.30	103	Cape Verde	3.44
24	South Korea	2.30	104	Armenia	3.45
27	Norway	2.35	104	Dominican Republic	3.45
28	Kuwait	2.40	104	Russia	3.45
28	Malaysia	2.40	107	Burkina Faso	3.50
28	Panama	2.40	107	Cameroon	3.50
28	Thailand	2.40	107	Lesotho	3.50
32	El Salvador	2.45	107	Nicaragua	3.50
32	Sri Lanka	2.45	107	Venezuela	3.50
32	Sweden	2.45	112	Gambia	3.60
35	France	2.50	112	Guyana	3.60
35	Italy	2.50	114	Bulgaria	3.65
35	Spain	2.50	114	Georgia	3.65
38	Trinidad and Tobago	2.55	114	Malawi	3.65
39	Argentina	2.60	117	Ethiopia	3.70
39	Barbados	2.60	117	India	3.70
39	Cyprus	2.60	117	Niger	3.70
39	Jamaica	2.60	120	Albania	3.75
39	Portugal	2.60	120	Bangladesh	3.75
44	Bolivia	2.65	120	China (PRC)	3.75
44	Oman	2.65	120	Congo	3.75
44	Philippines	2.65	120	Croatia	3.75
47	Swaziland	2.70	125	Chad	3.80
47	Uruguay	2.70	125	Mauritania	3.80
49	Botswana	2.75	125	Ukraine	3.80
49	Jordan	2.75	128	Sierra Leone	3.85
49	Namibia	2.75	129	Burundi	3.90
49	Tunisia	2.75	129	Suriname	3.90
53	Belize	2.80	129	Zimbabwe	3.90
53	Costa Rica	2.80	132	Haiti	4.00
53	Guatemala	2.80	132	Kyrgyzstan	4.00
53	Israel	2.80	132	Syria	4.00
53	Peru	2.80	135	Belarus	4.05
53	Saudi Arabia	2.80	136	Kazakstan	4.10
53	Turkey	2.80	136	Mozambique	4.10
53	Uganda	2.80	136	Yemen	4.10
53	Western Samoa	2.80	139	Sudan	4.20
62	Indonesia	2.85	140	Myanmar	4.30
62	Latvia	2.85	140	Rwanda	4.30
62	Malta	2.85	142	Angola	4.35
62	Paraguay	2.85	143	Azerbaijan	4.40
66	Greece	2.90	143	Tajikistan	4.40
66	Hungary	2.90	145	Turkmenistan	4.50
66	South Africa	2.90	146	Uzbekistan	4.55
69	Benin	2.95	147	Congo/Zaire	4.70
69	Ecuador	2.95	147	Iran	4.70
69	Gabon	2.95	147	Libya	4.70
69	Morocco	2.95	147	Somalia	4.70
69	Poland	2.95	147	Vietnam	4.70
74	Colombia	3.00	152	Bosnia	4.80
74	Ghana	3.00	153	Iraq	4.90
74	Lithuania	3.00	154	Cuba	5.00
77	Kenya	3.05	154	Laos	5.00
77	Slovak Republic	3.05	154	North Korea	5.00

Repressed

GOVERNMENT INTERVENTION IN THE ECONOMY
Score: 4–Stable (high level)

Turkmenistan is privatizing some of its state-owned sector, but the government still produces most GDP and continues to own significant sectors of the economy, including most utilities and cotton operations. According to the U.S. Department of Commerce, "Since the government controls access to all inputs, including parts, labor, and space, it is difficult if not impossible for domestic private enterprises to develop."[4]

MONETARY POLICY
Score: 5–Stable (very high level of inflation)

Turkmenistan has been plagued by hyperinflation: 493 percent in 1992, 3,102 percent in 1993, 2,400 percent in 1994, 775 percent in 1995, and 600 percent in 1996. Thus, even though inflation has lessened, it remains very high, both historically and by global standards.

CAPITAL FLOWS AND FOREIGN INVESTMENT
Score: 4–Stable (high barriers)

Although the government wants to promote foreign investment, Turkmenistan does not have a foreign investment code that reduces bureaucratic procedures for investments. According to the U.S. Department of Commerce, "Companies report experiencing a significant amount of 'red tape'.... [T]he President still makes the final decision in awarding a contract. Complaints of corrupt and inept practices have marred the foreign investment environment."[5] The Department also reports that "Since independence, the government has been verbally encouraging foreign investment and business, but current structures do not conform to international business norms."[6]

BANKING
Score: 5–Stable (very high level of restrictions)

Turkmenistan's banking system is not yet fully functional. According to the U.S. Department of Commerce, "The banking system in Turkmenistan consists of the State Central Bank of Turkmenistan; two state banks; the State Bank for Foreign Economic Affairs...and the State Savings Bank...and 15 commercial banks."[7] Most of these banks are state-owned, and almost all of the financial system's assets are state-controlled.

WAGE AND PRICE CONTROLS
Score: 4–Stable (high level)

Turkmenistan's large number of state-owned enterprises controls wages and prices. Price controls continue on such items as agricultural products, transportation, and utilities, and government subsidies to many industries continue to prevent market pricing of goods and services. According to the U.S. Department of State, "The government continues to control and subsidize prices for staples, medicines, housing, public transportation services, and some production costs."[8]

PROPERTY RIGHTS
Score: 4–Stable (low level of protection)

The legal system does not protect private property sufficiently. "Currently," reports the U.S. Department of Commerce, "there is no legal system in place to enforce effectively property and contractual rights."[9] According to the U.S. Department of State, "[I]n practice, the judiciary is not independent; the President's power to select and dismiss judges subordinates the judiciary to the Presidency. The court system has not been reformed since Soviet days."[10]

REGULATION
Score: 4–Stable (high level)

Establishing a business in Turkmenistan is a tedious and time-consuming procedure that requires individuals to overcome numerous bureaucratic barriers. Moreover, there is virtually no commercial code. According to the U.S. Department of Commerce, "The commercial code is unfinished, local officials are unfamiliar with Western business practices and internationally accepted norms, and business is often still a matter of personal influence and politics."[11] A recent government law regulating private business has caused new business growth to cease. According to the U.S. Department of Commerce, "As of May 1993, there were some 9,000 small businesses registered. The government subsequently issued a decree licensing private entrepreneurs and limiting price markups. This consequently had a chilling effect on the development of additional new businesses."[12] There has been recent movement toward legalizing some private production, but little progress has been made.

BLACK MARKET
Score: 5–Stable (very high level of activity)

Smuggling is rampant in Turkmenistan and, despite laws protecting intellectual property rights, significant piracy in computer software continues.

NOTES

1. U.S. Department of Commerce, "Turkmenistan–Commodity Exchange," *Market Research Reports,* January 1997.
2. U.S. Department of Commerce, "Turkmenistan: Economic and Trade Overview," September 1996.
3. *Ibid.*
4. U.S. Department of Commerce, *Country Commercial Guide,* 1997.
5. U.S. Department of Commerce, "Turkmenistan: Economic and Trade Overview," September 1996.
6. U.S. Department of Commerce, *Country Commercial Guide,* 1997.
7. U.S. Department of Commerce, "Banking in Turkmenistan," May 1997.
8. U.S. Department of State, *Country Reports on Economic Policy and Trade Practices,* 1997, p. 303.
9. U.S. Department of Commerce, *Country Commercial Guide,* 1997.
10. U.S. Department of State, "Turkmenistan Country Report on Human Rights Practices for 1996," 1997.
11. U.S. Department of Commerce, *Country Commercial Guide,* 1997.
12. U.S. Department of Commerce, "Turkmenistan: Economic and Trade Overview," September 1996.

Uganda 2.80

1997 Score: **2.90**	1996 Score: **2.83**	1995 Score: **2.94**

Trade	5	Banking	3
Taxation	4	Wages and Prices	1
Government Intervention	2	Property Rights	2
Monetary Policy	5	Regulation	2
Foreign Investment	2	Black Market	2

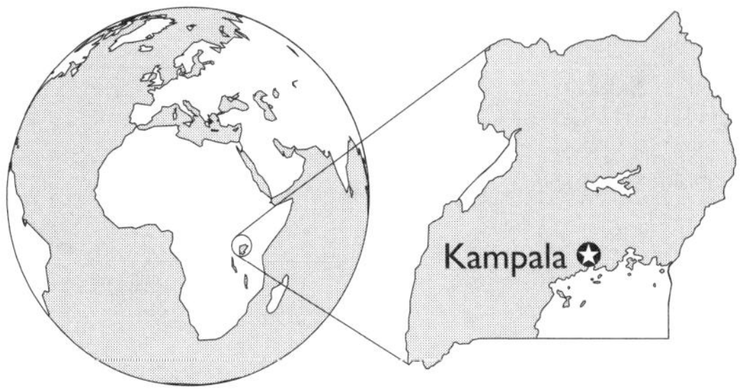

Uganda has endured civil strife and economic deterioration since gaining its independence from Great Britain in 1962. Although its 1995 constitution established a democratic system for independent elections of the president and parliament, restrictions on political parties continue, and rebel movements create instability. The decline of the economy—once one of Africa's more promising—was accelerated by government control and mismanagement. The government of President Yoweri Museveni, however, has undertaken fairly dramatic economic liberalization over the past several years. GDP grew by an average of 7.8 percent from 1992 to 1996, and it is expected that the economy will continue to grow by about 6 percent a year. Uganda also is moving toward political liberalization. Presidential and parliamentary elections were held in May 1996 for the first time in 16 years. Recent evidence indicates that trade barriers are higher than previously thought, but the government also has reduced both its intervention in the economy and its level of regulation. Thus, Uganda's overall score is 0.1 point better this year.

Trade Policy
Score: 5– (very high level of protectionism)

In 1993, Uganda lowered its highest import duty from 80 percent to 30 percent and reduced its lowest import duty from 50 percent to 10 percent. The average tariff rate is approximately 30 percent, as a result of which Uganda's trade policy score is one point worse than last year.[1] The Ministry of Commerce reserves the right to restrict the import of goods that compete with locally produced items. Beer, cigarettes, and a few other imports are banned.

Taxation
Score–Income taxation: 4–Stable (high tax rates)
Score–Corporate taxation: 3–Stable (moderate tax rates)
Final Taxation Score: 4–Stable (high tax rates)

Uganda's top income tax rate is 30 percent, with the average income level taxed at 20 percent. The corporate tax rate is 30 percent. Uganda also has a 17 percent value-added tax.

Government Intervention in the Economy
Score: 2+ (low level)

Government consumes 9.7 percent of Uganda's GDP, down from 12 percent in 1995. As a result, Uganda's government intervention score is one point better this year. The government has privatized 14 state enterprises and liquidated 11 state enterprises, including Uganda Air. Several other state-owned companies also are slated for privatization, although the government still owns the postal service, some major banking institutions, hotel chains, and similar companies.

Mostly Free

1	Hong Kong	1.25	77	Zambia	3.05
2	Singapore	1.30	80	Mali	3.10
3	Bahrain	1.70	80	Mongolia	3.10
4	New Zealand	1.75	80	Slovenia	3.10
5	Switzerland	1.90	83	Honduras	3.15
5	United States	1.90	83	Papua New Guinea	3.15
7	Luxembourg	1.95	85	Djibouti	3.20
7	Taiwan	1.95	85	Fiji	3.20
7	United Kingdom	1.95	85	Pakistan	3.20
10	Bahamas	2.00	88	Algeria	3.25
10	Ireland	2.00	88	Guinea	3.25
12	Australia	2.05	88	Lebanon	3.25
12	Japan	2.05	88	Mexico	3.25
14	Belgium	2.10	88	Senegal	3.25
14	Canada	2.10	88	Tanzania	3.25
14	United Arab Emirates	2.10	94	Nigeria	3.30
17	Austria	2.15	94	Romania	3.30
17	Chile	2.15	96	Brazil	3.35
17	Estonia	2.15	96	Cambodia	3.35
20	Czech Republic	2.20	96	Egypt	3.35
20	Netherlands	2.20	96	Ivory Coast	3.35
22	Denmark	2.25	96	Madagascar	3.35
22	Finland	2.25	96	Moldova	3.35
24	Germany	2.30	102	Nepal	3.40
24	Iceland	2.30	103	Cape Verde	3.44
24	South Korea	2.30	104	Armenia	3.45
27	Norway	2.35	104	Dominican Republic	3.45
28	Kuwait	2.40	104	Russia	3.45
28	Malaysia	2.40	107	Burkina Faso	3.50
28	Panama	2.40	107	Cameroon	3.50
28	Thailand	2.40	107	Lesotho	3.50
32	El Salvador	2.45	107	Nicaragua	3.50
32	Sri Lanka	2.45	107	Venezuela	3.50
32	Sweden	2.45	112	Gambia	3.60
35	France	2.50	112	Guyana	3.60
35	Italy	2.50	114	Bulgaria	3.65
35	Spain	2.50	114	Georgia	3.65
38	Trinidad and Tobago	2.55	114	Malawi	3.65
39	Argentina	2.60	117	Ethiopia	3.70
39	Barbados	2.60	117	India	3.70
39	Cyprus	2.60	117	Niger	3.70
39	Jamaica	2.60	120	Albania	3.75
39	Portugal	2.60	120	Bangladesh	3.75
44	Bolivia	2.65	120	China (PRC)	3.75
44	Oman	2.65	120	Congo	3.75
44	Philippines	2.65	120	Croatia	3.75
47	Swaziland	2.70	125	Chad	3.80
47	Uruguay	2.70	125	Mauritania	3.80
49	Botswana	2.75	125	Ukraine	3.80
49	Jordan	2.75	128	Sierra Leone	3.85
49	Namibia	2.75	129	Burundi	3.90
49	Tunisia	2.75	129	Suriname	3.90
53	Belize	2.80	129	Zimbabwe	3.90
53	Costa Rica	2.80	132	Haiti	4.00
53	Guatemala	2.80	132	Kyrgyzstan	4.00
53	Israel	2.80	132	Syria	4.00
53	Peru	2.80	135	Belarus	4.05
53	Saudi Arabia	2.80	136	Kazakstan	4.10
53	Turkey	2.80	136	Mozambique	4.10
53	Uganda	2.80	136	Yemen	4.10
53	Western Samoa	2.80	139	Sudan	4.20
62	Indonesia	2.85	140	Myanmar	4.30
62	Latvia	2.85	140	Rwanda	4.30
62	Malta	2.85	142	Angola	4.35
62	Paraguay	2.85	143	Azerbaijan	4.40
66	Greece	2.90	143	Tajikistan	4.40
66	Hungary	2.90	145	Turkmenistan	4.50
66	South Africa	2.90	146	Uzbekistan	4.55
69	Benin	2.95	147	Congo/Zaire	4.70
69	Ecuador	2.95	147	Iran	4.70
69	Gabon	2.95	147	Libya	4.70
69	Morocco	2.95	147	Somalia	4.70
69	Poland	2.95	147	Vietnam	4.70
74	Colombia	3.00	152	Bosnia	4.80
74	Ghana	3.00	153	Iraq	4.90
74	Lithuania	3.00	154	Cuba	5.00
77	Kenya	3.05	154	Laos	5.00
77	Slovak Republic	3.05	154	North Korea	5.00

MONETARY POLICY
Score: 5–Stable (very high level of inflation)

The Museveni government has made significant strides toward controlling Uganda's long-standing inflation problem. From 1985 to 1995, the average annual rate of inflation was 65.5 percent. In 1996, the rate was 7 percent.

CAPITAL FLOWS AND FOREIGN INVESTMENT
Score: 2–Stable (low barriers)

Uganda's government has moved to reduce foreign investment barriers. Foreign investors may own Ugandan companies in full, and foreign-owned investments are treated in a nondiscriminatory manner. There also are investment incentives, such as some tax holidays. Foreigners may not own agricultural land, however.

BANKING
Score: 3–Stable (moderate level of restrictions)

Uganda's small financial sector is dominated by several government-owned banks, although the government is trying to establish liberal banking legislation. Several foreign banks operate in Uganda, which also has many non-bank financial institutions, including 21 insurance companies.

WAGE AND PRICE CONTROLS
Score: 1–Stable (very low level)

Price controls were dismantled in January 1994, and the abolition of coffee, cotton, and other government monopolies has allowed the market to set wages and prices in these important sectors. There are over 100 private coffee trading companies. Uganda has no minimum wage.

PROPERTY RIGHTS
Score: 2–Stable (high level of protection)

The government is proceeding slowly to privatize state assets and is returning property confiscated by previous regimes. The Departed Asians Property Custodian Board has returned over 4,000 properties in the past few years. According to the U.S. Department of State, "The judiciary is generally independent, but weak; the President has extensive legal and extralegal powers."[2]

REGULATION
Score: 2+ (low level)

Uganda's government has made significant progress toward improving bureaucratic efficiency. It also has enjoyed some success in stamping out corruption. Because many state-owned businesses have undergone privatization, they have been allowed to operate relatively free of burdensome regulations on such things as established work weeks and worker and consumer health and safety standards. As a result, Uganda's regulation score is one point better this year.

BLACK MARKET
Score: 2–Stable (low level of activity)

The smuggling of cigarettes and oil is widespread in Uganda, and some electronic goods are smuggled to escape high tariffs. Black market activity has decreased as Uganda's economy has become more liberalized.

NOTES

1. The score for this factor has changed from 4 in 1997 to 5 in 1998. Previously unavailable data provide a more accurate understanding of the country's performance. The methodology for this factor remains the same.
2. U.S. Department of State, "Uganda Country Report on Human Rights Practices for 1996," 1997.

Ukraine   3.80

Kiev ●

1997 Score: **3.75**	1996 Score: **4.00**	1995 Score: **3.90**

Trade	4	Banking	4
Taxation	4	Wages and Prices	3
Government Intervention	3	Property Rights	4
Monetary Policy	5	Regulation	4
Foreign Investment	3	Black Market	4

Formerly part of the Soviet Union, Ukraine became an independent republic in 1991 but has been slow to implement economic reform. The government of President Leonid Kravchuk was composed of old communist *apparatchiki* who resisted reform. As a result, Ukraine has made less progress than Russia in reforming its economy, although some progress has been achieved since the election of President Leonid Kuchma in 1994. Kuchma moved, for example, to reduce subsidies to some state-owned industries, privatize others, and reduce barriers to trade; however, a corrupt, entrenched bureaucracy continues to stifle reform. In July 1997, Prime Minister Pavlo Lazarenko resigned under pressure from critics who claimed that the government's economic reforms harmed most Ukrainians in favor of the wealthy. The new cabinet of Prime Minister Valery Pustovoitenko and the Supreme Council (Ukraine's legislature) have forwarded an economic reform plan that includes streamlining the bureaucracy and deregulating foreign trade and domestic business activities. The government intends to cut taxes and reduce the budget, speed up the privatization of major state-owned enterprises, encourage foreign and domestic investment, and target existing social benefits to the truly needy while trimming the overall welfare burden. Whether the new cabinet with stick to this plan is not certain in view of the government's past performance. Over the past several years, the government has reduced the level of taxation that applies to a majority of taxpayers. There are recent indications, however, that the judiciary is subject to political influence. As a result, Ukraine's overall score is 0.05 point worse this year.

TRADE POLICY
Score: 4–Stable (high level of protectionism)

According to the Office of the United States Trade Representative, "Most MFN [most favored nation] tariffs in Ukraine range from zero to 30 percent."[1] The U.S. Department of Commerce reports that "Import duties vary, but generally are around 16 percent."[2] According to the U.S. Department of State, Ukraine no longer maintains any significant nontariff barriers; import licensing requirements have been eased, and now the only requirements relate to technical, safety and environmental standards, as well as efficacy standards with regard to pharmaceutical and veterinary products.[3]

TAXATION
Score–Income taxation: 4+ (high tax rates)
Score–Corporate taxation: 3–Stable (moderate tax rates)
Final Taxation Score: 4+ (high tax rates)

Ukraine's top income tax rate is 40 percent. The rate for the average income is 20 percent, down from 30 percent last year.[4] As a result, Ukraine's overall income tax score is one-half point better this year. The top corporate tax rate is 30 percent. Ukraine also has a 30 percent capital gains tax and a 20 percent value-added tax.

1	Hong Kong	1.25		77	Zambia	3.05
2	Singapore	1.30		80	Mali	3.10
3	Bahrain	1.70		80	Mongolia	3.10
4	New Zealand	1.75		80	Slovenia	3.10
5	Switzerland	1.90		83	Honduras	3.15
5	United States	1.90		83	Papua New Guinea	3.15
7	Luxembourg	1.95		85	Djibouti	3.20
7	Taiwan	1.95		85	Fiji	3.20
7	United Kingdom	1.95		85	Pakistan	3.20
10	Bahamas	2.00		88	Algeria	3.25
10	Ireland	2.00		88	Guinea	3.25
12	Australia	2.05		88	Lebanon	3.25
12	Japan	2.05		88	Mexico	3.25
14	Belgium	2.10		88	Senegal	3.25
14	Canada	2.10		88	Tanzania	3.25
14	United Arab Emirates	2.10		94	Nigeria	3.30
17	Austria	2.15		94	Romania	3.30
17	Chile	2.15		96	Brazil	3.35
17	Estonia	2.15		96	Cambodia	3.35
20	Czech Republic	2.20		96	Egypt	3.35
20	Netherlands	2.20		96	Ivory Coast	3.35
22	Denmark	2.25		96	Madagascar	3.35
22	Finland	2.25		96	Moldova	3.35
24	Germany	2.30		102	Nepal	3.40
24	Iceland	2.30		103	Cape Verde	3.44
24	South Korea	2.30		104	Armenia	3.45
27	Norway	2.35		104	Dominican Republic	3.45
28	Kuwait	2.40		104	Russia	3.45
28	Malaysia	2.40		107	Burkina Faso	3.50
28	Panama	2.40		107	Cameroon	3.50
28	Thailand	2.40		107	Lesotho	3.50
32	El Salvador	2.45		107	Nicaragua	3.50
32	Sri Lanka	2.45		107	Venezuela	3.50
32	Sweden	2.45		112	Gambia	3.60
35	France	2.50		112	Guyana	3.60
35	Italy	2.50		114	Bulgaria	3.65
35	Spain	2.50		114	Georgia	3.65
38	Trinidad and Tobago	2.55		114	Malawi	3.65
39	Argentina	2.60		117	Ethiopia	3.70
39	Barbados	2.60		117	India	3.70
39	Cyprus	2.60		117	Niger	3.70
39	Jamaica	2.60		120	Albania	3.75
39	Portugal	2.60		120	Bangladesh	3.75
44	Bolivia	2.65		120	China (PRC)	3.75
44	Oman	2.65		120	Congo	3.75
44	Philippines	2.65		120	Croatia	3.75
47	Swaziland	2.70		125	Chad	3.80
47	Uruguay	2.70		125	Mauritania	3.80
49	Botswana	2.75		125	Ukraine	3.80
49	Jordan	2.75		128	Sierra Leone	3.85
49	Namibia	2.75		129	Burundi	3.90
49	Tunisia	2.75		129	Suriname	3.90
53	Belize	2.80		129	Zimbabwe	3.90
53	Costa Rica	2.80		132	Haiti	4.00
53	Guatemala	2.80		132	Kyrgyzstan	4.00
53	Israel	2.80		132	Syria	4.00
53	Peru	2.80		135	Belarus	4.05
53	Saudi Arabia	2.80		136	Kazakstan	4.10
53	Turkey	2.80		136	Mozambique	4.10
53	Uganda	2.80		136	Yemen	4.10
53	Western Samoa	2.80		139	Sudan	4.20
62	Indonesia	2.85		140	Myanmar	4.30
62	Latvia	2.85		140	Rwanda	4.30
62	Malta	2.85		142	Angola	4.35
62	Paraguay	2.85		143	Azerbaijan	4.40
66	Greece	2.90		143	Tajikistan	4.40
66	Hungary	2.90		145	Turkmenistan	4.50
66	South Africa	2.90		146	Uzbekistan	4.55
69	Benin	2.95		147	Congo/Zaire	4.70
69	Ecuador	2.95		147	Iran	4.70
69	Gabon	2.95		147	Libya	4.70
69	Morocco	2.95		147	Somalia	4.70
69	Poland	2.95		147	Vietnam	4.70
74	Colombia	3.00		152	Bosnia	4.80
74	Ghana	3.00		153	Iraq	4.90
74	Lithuania	3.00		154	Cuba	5.00
77	Kenya	3.05		154	Laos	5.00
77	Slovak Republic	3.05		154	North Korea	5.00

Mostly Unfree

GOVERNMENT INTERVENTION IN THE ECONOMY
Score: 3–Stable (moderate level)

Government consumes 18.3 percent of Ukraine's GDP. The public sector, however, still generates most GDP overall.

MONETARY POLICY
Score: 5–Stable (very high level of inflation)

Since becoming an independent state, Ukraine has made tremendous progress toward reducing its rate of inflation: 1,310 percent in 1992, 4,735 percent in 1993, 891 percent in 1994, 377 percent in 1995, and 80 percent in 1996. As important as this progress may be, however, Ukraine's rate of inflation is still very high by global standards.[5]

CAPITAL FLOWS AND FOREIGN INVESTMENT
Score: 3–Stable (moderate barriers)

Foreign and domestic businesses are treated equally under Ukraine's foreign investment law. There are no regulatory restrictions on repatriation of capital or profits, and few restrictions on foreign ownership of businesses. Ukraine passed a new foreign investment law in 1996 that provides for a more open and stable environment than previously existed. The unpredictable application of the country's laws, widespread corruption among local and central government officials, a lack of understanding of basic economic principles by the bureaucracy, and the slow progress of reform, however, continue to deter foreign investors, who often are forced to pay bribes or kickbacks to facilitate the necessary paperwork, permits, and licenses.

BANKING
Score: 4–Stable (high level of restrictions)

Ukraine's banking environment remains in regulatory chaos, subject to heavy government intervention and the strict control of credit. Even though their number has grown, private banks remain in direct competition with government-controlled and -subsidized institutions. According to the U.S. Department of Commerce, "Ukrainian banks remain unstable and find themselves in a difficult period of transformation."[6]

WAGE AND PRICE CONTROLS
Score: 3–Stable (moderate level)

The government controls wages for jobs in Ukraine's industrial sectors. It also controls some prices, especially in housing, transportation services, and public utilities.

PROPERTY RIGHTS
Score: 4– (low level of protection)

Although its new constitution provides for the protection of private property, Ukraine has yet to establish a legal system that can enforce property rights adequately. Despite an ambitious government program to privatize large sectors of the economy, property remains subject to government expropriation, According to the U.S. Department of State, "Under the new Constitution, the judiciary is funded independently, instead of through the Ministry of Justice. However, the court system remains subject to political interference.... The judiciary is overburdened and lacks sufficient funding and staff. Long delays in trials are a problem."[7] As a result, Ukraine's property rights score is one point worse this year.

REGULATION
Score: 4–Stable (high level)

Regulations in Ukraine are applied haphazardly, posing a significant impediment to business activity. Another problem is widespread bureaucratic corruption, which limits the ability of businesses to obtain the necessary permits to conduct operations. According to the U.S. Department of Commerce, "Corruption pervades much of Ukraine's civil service and regulation system.... Conflict of interest is a poorly developed concept at this point, and many bureaucrats retain their commercial interests while in power. A complicated and non-transparent regulatory system also has encouraged petty corruption at all levels of government."[8]

BLACK MARKET
Score: 4–Stable (high level of activity)

Because the government controls large portions of Ukraine's economy, much business activity is performed in the informal sector. According to the U.S. Department of Commerce, "The World Bank estimates that the informal economy accounted for nearly half of estimated total GDP (official plus non-official economies). Some Ukrainian estimates claim that the informal sector accounts for 60 percent of Ukraine's economic activity."[9]

NOTES

1. Office of the United States Trade Representative, *1997 National Trade Estimate Report on Foreign Trade Barriers*.
2. U.S. Department of Commerce, "Ukraine: Economic and Trade Overview," March 1997.
3. U.S. Department of State, *Country Reports on Economic Policy and Trade Practices*, 1997, p. 192.
4. Ukraine recently changed the way in which it calculates income tax rates based on a complex formula that uses "multiples of the minimum nontaxable monthly wage." Because this calculation changes frequently, so do tax rate brackets. It is impossible to determine the exact rate that would apply to the average taxpayer; however, it is possible to estimate such a rate. For this analysis, the average tax rate is based on the following data: Ukraine's 1995 per capita GDP was 23,603,313 Ukrainian karbovanets (URK)—the local currency used until September 2, 1996—or roughly 1,966,942 URK per month. The monthly "nontaxable minimum wage" in 1993 was 120,000 URK. Therefore, the 1,966,942 URK monthly wage is a "multiple" of 16 of the 120,000 URK that is nontaxable. This multiple of 16 is taxed at a rate of 20 percent.
5. These figures represent consumer price inflation.
6. U.S. Department of Commerce, "Ukraine: Economic and Trade Overview," March 1997.
7. U.S. Department of State, "Ukraine Country Report on Human Rights Practices for 1996," 1997.
8. U.S. Department of Commerce, "Ukraine—Investment Climate," *Market Research Reports*, January 13, 1997.
9. *Ibid.*

United Arab Emirates   2.10

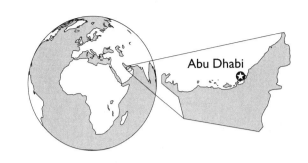
Abu Dhabi

1997 Score: **2.10**	1996 Score: **2.10**	1995 Score: **n/a**		

Trade	2	Banking	3
Taxation	1	Wages and Prices	3
Government Intervention	3	Property Rights	1
Monetary Policy	1	Regulation	2
Foreign Investment	4	Black Market	1

The United Arab Emirates (UAE) is a federation of seven emirates: Abu Dhabi, Ajman, Dubai, Fujairah, Ras al-Khaimah, Sharjah, and Umm al-Qaiwain. The individual emirates maintain considerable power over their own legal and economic affairs. Oil revenues—the single largest source of income—allow the government to keep import tariffs and taxation to a minimum. Most oil production remains in the hands of the government.

TRADE POLICY
Score: 2–Stable (low level of protectionism)

The UAE has an average tariff rate of 4.5 percent. One major nontariff barrier is the government's requirement that UAE nationals own at least 51 percent of some distributing companies not located in free-trade zones.

TAXATION
Score–Income taxation: 1–Stable (very low tax rates)
Score–Corporate taxation: 1–Stable (very low tax rates)
Final Taxation Score: 1–Stable (very low tax rates)
The UAE has no income tax, no corporate tax, and no other significant taxes.

GOVERNMENT INTERVENTION IN THE ECONOMY
Score: 3–Stable (moderate level)

Government consumes about 17.5 percent of GDP in the UAE. Much of this GDP is derived from oil, which is owned primarily by the government, which also heavily subsidizes such services as education, health care, and utilities.

MONETARY POLICY
Score: 1–Stable (very low level of inflation)

The UAE's average rate of inflation from 1990 to 1995 was about 5 percent. In 1996, the rate of inflation was about 5.2 percent, the level at which it remains today.

CAPITAL FLOWS AND FOREIGN INVESTMENT
Score: 4—Stable (high barriers)

The UAE is open to some types of foreign investment, but there are significant restrictions. "By law," reports the U.S. Department of State, "foreign companies wishing to do business in the UAE must have a UAE national sponsor, agent, or distributor.... Foreigners cannot own land or buy stocks.... Agency and distributorship laws require that a business engaged in importing and distributing a foreign-made product must be 100 percent UAE national-owned. Other businesses must be at least 51 percent owned by nationals. A 1994 law extended these

1	Hong Kong	1.25	77	Zambia	3.05
2	Singapore	1.30	80	Mali	3.10
3	Bahrain	1.70	80	Mongolia	3.10
4	New Zealand	1.75	80	Slovenia	3.10
5	Switzerland	1.90	83	Honduras	3.15
5	United States	1.90	83	Papua New Guinea	3.15
7	Luxembourg	1.95	85	Djibouti	3.20
7	Taiwan	1.95	85	Fiji	3.20
7	United Kingdom	1.95	85	Pakistan	3.20
10	Bahamas	2.00	88	Algeria	3.25
10	Ireland	2.00	88	Guinea	3.25
12	Australia	2.05	88	Lebanon	3.25
12	Japan	2.05	88	Mexico	3.25
14	Belgium	2.10	88	Senegal	3.25
14	Canada	2.10	88	Tanzania	3.25
14	United Arab Emirates	2.10	94	Nigeria	3.30
17	Austria	2.15	94	Romania	3.30
17	Chile	2.15	96	Brazil	3.35
17	Estonia	2.15	96	Cambodia	3.35
20	Czech Republic	2.20	96	Egypt	3.35
20	Netherlands	2.20	96	Ivory Coast	3.35
22	Denmark	2.25	96	Madagascar	3.35
22	Finland	2.25	96	Moldova	3.35
24	Germany	2.30	102	Nepal	3.40
24	Iceland	2.30	103	Cape Verde	3.44
24	South Korea	2.30	104	Armenia	3.45
27	Norway	2.35	104	Dominican Republic	3.45
28	Kuwait	2.40	104	Russia	3.45
28	Malaysia	2.40	107	Burkina Faso	3.50
28	Panama	2.40	107	Cameroon	3.50
28	Thailand	2.40	107	Lesotho	3.50
32	El Salvador	2.45	107	Nicaragua	3.50
32	Sri Lanka	2.45	107	Venezuela	3.50
32	Sweden	2.45	112	Gambia	3.60
35	France	2.50	112	Guyana	3.60
35	Italy	2.50	114	Bulgaria	3.65
35	Spain	2.50	114	Georgia	3.65
38	Trinidad and Tobago	2.55	114	Malawi	3.65
39	Argentina	2.60	117	Ethiopia	3.70
39	Barbados	2.60	117	India	3.70
39	Cyprus	2.60	117	Niger	3.70
39	Jamaica	2.60	120	Albania	3.75
39	Portugal	2.60	120	Bangladesh	3.75
44	Bolivia	2.65	120	China (PRC)	3.75
44	Oman	2.65	120	Congo	3.75
44	Philippines	2.65	120	Croatia	3.75
47	Swaziland	2.70	125	Chad	3.80
47	Uruguay	2.70	125	Mauritania	3.80
49	Botswana	2.75	125	Ukraine	3.80
49	Jordan	2.75	128	Sierra Leone	3.85
49	Namibia	2.75	129	Burundi	3.90
49	Tunisia	2.75	129	Suriname	3.90
53	Belize	2.80	129	Zimbabwe	3.90
53	Costa Rica	2.80	132	Haiti	4.00
53	Guatemala	2.80	132	Kyrgyzstan	4.00
53	Israel	2.80	132	Syria	4.00
53	Peru	2.80	135	Belarus	4.05
53	Saudi Arabia	2.80	136	Kazakstan	4.10
53	Turkey	2.80	136	Mozambique	4.10
53	Uganda	2.80	136	Yemen	4.10
53	Western Samoa	2.80	139	Sudan	4.20
62	Indonesia	2.85	140	Myanmar	4.30
62	Latvia	2.85	140	Rwanda	4.30
62	Malta	2.85	142	Angola	4.35
62	Paraguay	2.85	143	Azerbaijan	4.40
66	Greece	2.90	143	Tajikistan	4.40
66	Hungary	2.90	145	Turkmenistan	4.50
66	South Africa	2.90	146	Uzbekistan	4.55
69	Benin	2.95	147	Congo/Zaire	4.70
69	Ecuador	2.95	147	Iran	4.70
69	Gabon	2.95	147	Libya	4.70
69	Morocco	2.95	147	Somalia	4.70
69	Poland	2.95	147	Vietnam	4.70
74	Colombia	3.00	152	Bosnia	4.80
74	Ghana	3.00	153	Iraq	4.90
74	Lithuania	3.00	154	Cuba	5.00
77	Kenya	3.05	154	Laos	5.00
77	Slovak Republic	3.05	154	North Korea	5.00

Mostly Free

requirements to service businesses for the first time."[1] Exemptions are given to companies operating in the Jebel Ali Free Zone in Dubai. Some sectors, including oil and gas operations, petrochemicals, electricity, and water desalination, are closed to foreign investment.

BANKING
Score: 3–Stable (moderate level of restrictions)

The UAE's banking system is large and competitive. The government's largely liberal economic policies have led to a proliferation of private banks, although the government still owns some banks. The UAE has no corporate income tax, but there is a 30 percent tax on bank earnings.

WAGE AND PRICE CONTROLS
Score: 3–Stable (moderate level)

The market sets most wages and prices in the UAE. The government continues to offer subsidies to many businesses, however, and this affects the price of utilities, health care, education, and food. The government also owns many services that affect free-market pricing.

PROPERTY RIGHTS
Score: 1–Stable (very high level of protection)

Private property is protected in the UAE, which has an effective and modern legal and judicial system.

REGULATION
Score: 2–Stable (low level)

Establishing a business in the UAE is easy if the business will not compete directly with state-owned concerns. Regulations are applied evenly in most cases.

BLACK MARKET
Score: 1–Stable (very low level of activity)

The black market in the UAE is negligible. There are three laws to protect intellectual property, and the economy is virtually free of pirated material.

NOTE

1. U.S. Department of State, *Country Reports on Economic Policy and Trade Practices*, 1996, p. 372.

United Kingdom   1.95

Trade	2	Banking	2
Taxation	4.5	Wages and Prices	2
Government Intervention	2	Property Rights	1
Monetary Policy	1	Regulation	2
Foreign Investment	2	Black Market	1

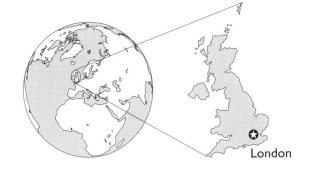

London

The United Kingdom is a constitutional monarchy with a parliamentary government that has moved from socialism to free-market capitalism. Facing near economic collapse in the 1970s, the United Kingdom turned to free-market reform under the leadership of Prime Minister Margaret Thatcher. The result was extensive market liberalization that made the economy of the United Kingdom one of the strongest in the European Union (EU). In the May 1997 elections, Labor Party candidate Tony Blair ousted the Conservative Party's John Major by a landslide, ending 18 years of Conservative Party rule. Blair ran on a campaign promise to maintain the previous administration's economic liberalization policies; specifically, he promised not to increase income taxes or alter spending plans through 1999, as established by the Conservative Party. In Labor's first budget, although Conservative spending caps were maintained and corporate income taxes were cut from 33 percent to 31 percent, tax benefits for private medical insurance were cut and a one-time windfall tax was levied on privatized utilities.

TRADE POLICY
Score: 2–Stable (low level of protectionism)

The United Kingdom's average tariff rate is 3.6 percent. Some progress has been made toward opening the United Kingdom's market to imports, but nontariff barriers still remain in air services and the energy industry.

TAXATION
Score–Income taxation: 5–Stable (very high tax rates)
Score–Corporate taxation: 3–Stable (moderate tax rates)
Final Taxation Score: 4.5–Stable (very high tax rates)

The top income tax rate in the United Kingdom is 40 percent, and the average income level is taxed at 24 percent. The top corporate tax rate is 33 percent.[1] In its first budget, Labor cut the top corporate income tax rate to 31 percent, effective April 1, 1997. The United Kingdom also has a capital gains tax and a 17.5 percent value-added tax.

GOVERNMENT INTERVENTION IN THE ECONOMY
Score: 2–Stable (low level)

Government consumes about 21.3 percent of the United Kingdom's GDP. Unlike some of its European neighbors, the United Kingdom has made progress toward privatization, a sign that the government is becoming less involved in the market. The Labor government is examining the possibility of partially privatizing London's subway and expanding the scope of private mandatory retirement savings plans.

1	Hong Kong	1.25	77	Zambia	3.05
2	Singapore	1.30	80	Mali	3.10
3	Bahrain	1.70	80	Mongolia	3.10
4	New Zealand	1.75	80	Slovenia	3.10
5	Switzerland	1.90	83	Honduras	3.15
5	United States	1.90	83	Papua New Guinea	3.15
7	Luxembourg	1.95	85	Djibouti	3.20
7	Taiwan	1.95	85	Fiji	3.20
7	United Kingdom	1.95	85	Pakistan	3.20
10	Bahamas	2.00	88	Algeria	3.25
10	Ireland	2.00	88	Guinea	3.25
12	Australia	2.05	88	Lebanon	3.25
12	Japan	2.05	88	Mexico	3.25
14	Belgium	2.10	88	Senegal	3.25
14	Canada	2.10	88	Tanzania	3.25
14	United Arab Emirates	2.10	94	Nigeria	3.30
17	Austria	2.15	94	Romania	3.30
17	Chile	2.15	96	Brazil	3.35
17	Estonia	2.15	96	Cambodia	3.35
20	Czech Republic	2.20	96	Egypt	3.35
20	Netherlands	2.20	96	Ivory Coast	3.35
22	Denmark	2.25	96	Madagascar	3.35
22	Finland	2.25	96	Moldova	3.35
24	Germany	2.30	102	Nepal	3.40
24	Iceland	2.30	103	Cape Verde	3.44
24	South Korea	2.30	104	Armenia	3.45
27	Norway	2.35	104	Dominican Republic	3.45
28	Kuwait	2.40	104	Russia	3.45
28	Malaysia	2.40	107	Burkina Faso	3.50
28	Panama	2.40	107	Cameroon	3.50
28	Thailand	2.40	107	Lesotho	3.50
32	El Salvador	2.45	107	Nicaragua	3.50
32	Sri Lanka	2.45	107	Venezuela	3.50
32	Sweden	2.45	112	Gambia	3.60
35	France	2.50	112	Guyana	3.60
35	Italy	2.50	114	Bulgaria	3.65
35	Spain	2.50	114	Georgia	3.65
38	Trinidad and Tobago	2.55	114	Malawi	3.65
39	Argentina	2.60	117	Ethiopia	3.70
39	Barbados	2.60	117	India	3.70
39	Cyprus	2.60	117	Niger	3.70
39	Jamaica	2.60	120	Albania	3.75
39	Portugal	2.60	120	Bangladesh	3.75
44	Bolivia	2.65	120	China (PRC)	3.75
44	Oman	2.65	120	Congo	3.75
44	Philippines	2.65	120	Croatia	3.75
47	Swaziland	2.70	125	Chad	3.80
47	Uruguay	2.70	125	Mauritania	3.80
49	Botswana	2.75	125	Ukraine	3.80
49	Jordan	2.75	128	Sierra Leone	3.85
49	Namibia	2.75	129	Burundi	3.90
49	Tunisia	2.75	129	Suriname	3.90
53	Belize	2.80	129	Zimbabwe	3.90
53	Costa Rica	2.80	132	Haiti	4.00
53	Guatemala	2.80	132	Kyrgyzstan	4.00
53	Israel	2.80	132	Syria	4.00
53	Peru	2.80	135	Belarus	4.05
53	Saudi Arabia	2.80	136	Kazakstan	4.10
53	Turkey	2.80	136	Mozambique	4.10
53	Uganda	2.80	136	Yemen	4.10
53	Western Samoa	2.80	139	Sudan	4.20
62	Indonesia	2.85	140	Myanmar	4.30
62	Latvia	2.85	140	Rwanda	4.30
62	Malta	2.85	142	Angola	4.35
62	Paraguay	2.85	143	Azerbaijan	4.40
66	Greece	2.90	143	Tajikistan	4.40
66	Hungary	2.90	145	Turkmenistan	4.50
66	South Africa	2.90	146	Uzbekistan	4.55
69	Benin	2.95	147	Congo/Zaire	4.70
69	Ecuador	2.95	147	Iran	4.70
69	Gabon	2.95	147	Libya	4.70
69	Morocco	2.95	147	Somalia	4.70
69	Poland	2.95	147	Vietnam	4.70
74	Colombia	3.00	152	Bosnia	4.80
74	Ghana	3.00	153	Iraq	4.90
74	Lithuania	3.00	154	Cuba	5.00
77	Kenya	3.05	154	Laos	5.00
77	Slovak Republic	3.05	154	North Korea	5.00

Free

MONETARY POLICY
Score: 1–Stable (very low level of inflation)

The United Kingdom's average annual rate of inflation from 1985 to 1995 was 5.1 percent. In 1996, the rate was 2.7 percent. The Labor government's recent grant of "operational independence" to the Bank of England should reduce the government's influence on monetary policy and lead to lower inflation rates in the future.

CAPITAL FLOWS AND FOREIGN INVESTMENT
Score: 2–Stable (low barriers)

Many non-European companies use the United Kingdom as a base for setting up businesses in Europe. The United Kingdom also is the largest recipient of U.S. and Japanese foreign investment in Europe. Despite a generally hospitable environment, however, it still restricts foreign investment in the aerospace industry and public utilities.

BANKING
Score: 2–Stable (low level of restrictions)

The United Kingdom's banking system is fairly open to competition. Privately owned banks supply most credit, and they are permitted to sell securities, insurance policies, and real estate as well as invest in industrial firms. The 1987 Banking Act, however, gives the Bank of England the right to prevent the foreign ownership of more than 15 percent of any bank in the United Kingdom.

WAGE AND PRICE CONTROLS
Score: 2–Stable (low level)

The market sets most prices in the United Kingdom, although the government caps maximum prices charged by public utilities. The government also controls the prices of some products and services, such as matches, milk, and taxi fares, and often controls rent prices for housing. Landlords are required to inform renters that they may challenge a rental increase to a "rent assessment committee" with the power to force a landlord to lower the price if it is determined to be too high. The only area currently subject to minimum wage laws is agriculture; however, the Labor government is committed to implementing a new minimum wage for all workers over 18 years of age.

PROPERTY RIGHTS
Score: 1–Stable (very high level of protection)

The government has accepted the privatizations that occurred under former prime ministers, especially Thatcher. Most of the United Kingdom's economy is private, and the court system, in addition to being efficient, provides maximum protection of private property.

REGULATION
Score: 2–Stable (low level)

Opening a business in the United Kingdom is easy. The regulatory system can be somewhat burdensome, but the United Kingdom also has done more than most other industrialized countries to reduce the level of regulation; for example, companies may self-regulate their industries: Businesses subscribe voluntarily to a code of conduct that, if violated, causes them to be penalized by consumers who see their products as shoddy. The Labor government is considering a host of regulations, however, that could decrease economic freedom. For example, it has agreed to join the EU's Social Charter, which will force employers to provide a three-month leave for a new parent, allow employees to refuse to work more than 48 hours a week, grant employees three weeks of annual paid leave, and subsidize businesses that hire workers under age 25. The government has pledged, however, not to reverse the Conservative Party's industrial relations reforms, which give the United Kingdom one of Europe's most flexible labor markets, and Prime Minister Blair has criticized other European leaders for not liberalizing their labor markets.

BLACK MARKET
Score: 1–Stable (very low level of activity)

Like those in other developed countries, the United Kingdom's black market is restricted to drugs, guns, and other illegal activities. The country's protection of intellectual property rights is among the best in the world.

NOTE

1. This rate applies to the 1996–1997 taxable year.

United States   1.90

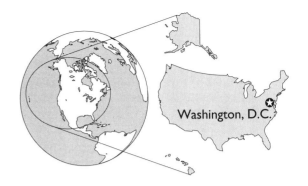

| 1997 Score: **1.90** | 1996 Score: **1.90** | 1995 Score: **1.90** |

Trade	2	Banking	2
Taxation	4	Wages and Prices	2
Government Intervention	2	Property Rights	1
Monetary Policy	1	Regulation	2
Foreign Investment	2	Black Market	1

The United States remains one of the world's most industrialized countries. It is the biggest exporter and importer of goods, has the largest economy, and enjoys the highest standard of living. It has one of the world's freest economies—but not *the* freest. Since the 1930s, a series of legislative enactments and presidential actions has reduced the level of economic freedom. Consequently, economic growth rates are lower than they otherwise would be. Significant progress was made in deregulating specific industries, such as railroads, trucking, airlines, and banking, during the two terms of President Ronald Reagan, and President Bill Clinton signed a major telecommunications deregulation law in 1996. Even though Congress and President Clinton have agreed to reduce income taxes modestly and balance the federal budget, the overall score for the United States remains unchanged.

TRADE POLICY
Score: 2–Stable (low level of protectionism)

The average U.S. tariff rate is 3.3 percent. The United States maintains trade restrictions on dairy products, animal feed, chocolate, some beers and wines, cotton, peanuts, syrups, molasses, cheese, wheat, sugar, textiles, and other items. It also is an aggressive user of unilateral trade retaliation. By global standards, however, the level of protectionism is low.

TAXATION
Score–Income taxation: 4–Stable (high tax rates)
Score–Corporate taxation: 3–Stable (moderate tax rates)
Final Taxation Score: 4–Stable (high tax rates)

The top income tax rate in the United States is 39.6 percent, and the average taxpayer is in the 15 percent bracket. The top marginal corporate tax rate is 35 percent. The United States also has state and local income taxes, state and local sales taxes, federal estate taxes, a capital gains tax, and local property taxes. The government recently reduced some taxes as part of a balanced budget agreement; the maximum rate on capital gains, for example, was reduced from 28 percent to 20 percent. None of these tax changes, however, is sufficient to affect the overall U.S. tax score.

GOVERNMENT INTERVENTION IN THE ECONOMY
Score: 2–Stable (low level)

The U.S. government consumes about 16 percent of GDP, and the recent balanced budget agreement could reduce government consumption significantly while boosting economic activity. Congress has limited government spending in programs for the first time in decades, and this, coupled with increased economic activity, has reduced slightly the overall government consumption rate— but not enough to change the overall U.S. government intervention score.

1	Hong Kong	1.25	77	Zambia	3.05
2	Singapore	1.30	80	Mali	3.10
3	Bahrain	1.70	80	Mongolia	3.10
4	New Zealand	1.75	80	Slovenia	3.10
5	Switzerland	1.90	83	Honduras	3.15
5	United States	1.90	83	Papua New Guinea	3.15
7	Luxembourg	1.95	85	Djibouti	3.20
7	Taiwan	1.95	85	Fiji	3.20
7	United Kingdom	1.95	85	Pakistan	3.20
10	Bahamas	2.00	88	Algeria	3.25
10	Ireland	2.00	88	Guinea	3.25
12	Australia	2.05	88	Lebanon	3.25
12	Japan	2.05	88	Mexico	3.25
14	Belgium	2.10	88	Senegal	3.25
14	Canada	2.10	88	Tanzania	3.25
14	United Arab Emirates	2.10	94	Nigeria	3.30
17	Austria	2.15	94	Romania	3.30
17	Chile	2.15	96	Brazil	3.35
17	Estonia	2.15	96	Cambodia	3.35
20	Czech Republic	2.20	96	Egypt	3.35
20	Netherlands	2.20	96	Ivory Coast	3.35
22	Denmark	2.25	96	Madagascar	3.35
22	Finland	2.25	96	Moldova	3.35
24	Germany	2.30	102	Nepal	3.40
24	Iceland	2.30	103	Cape Verde	3.44
24	South Korea	2.30	104	Armenia	3.45
27	Norway	2.35	104	Dominican Republic	3.45
28	Kuwait	2.40	104	Russia	3.45
28	Malaysia	2.40	107	Burkina Faso	3.50
28	Panama	2.40	107	Cameroon	3.50
28	Thailand	2.40	107	Lesotho	3.50
32	El Salvador	2.45	107	Nicaragua	3.50
32	Sri Lanka	2.45	107	Venezuela	3.50
32	Sweden	2.45	112	Gambia	3.60
35	France	2.50	112	Guyana	3.60
35	Italy	2.50	114	Bulgaria	3.65
35	Spain	2.50	114	Georgia	3.65
38	Trinidad and Tobago	2.55	114	Malawi	3.65
39	Argentina	2.60	117	Ethiopia	3.70
39	Barbados	2.60	117	India	3.70
39	Cyprus	2.60	117	Niger	3.70
39	Jamaica	2.60	120	Albania	3.75
39	Portugal	2.60	120	Bangladesh	3.75
44	Bolivia	2.65	120	China (PRC)	3.75
44	Oman	2.65	120	Congo	3.75
44	Philippines	2.65	120	Croatia	3.75
47	Swaziland	2.70	125	Chad	3.80
47	Uruguay	2.70	125	Mauritania	3.80
49	Botswana	2.75	125	Ukraine	3.80
49	Jordan	2.75	128	Sierra Leone	3.85
49	Namibia	2.75	129	Burundi	3.90
49	Tunisia	2.75	129	Suriname	3.90
53	Belize	2.80	129	Zimbabwe	3.90
53	Costa Rica	2.80	132	Haiti	4.00
53	Guatemala	2.80	132	Kyrgyzstan	4.00
53	Israel	2.80	132	Syria	4.00
53	Peru	2.80	135	Belarus	4.05
53	Saudi Arabia	2.80	136	Kazakhstan	4.10
53	Turkey	2.80	136	Mozambique	4.10
53	Uganda	2.80	136	Yemen	4.10
53	Western Samoa	2.80	139	Sudan	4.20
62	Indonesia	2.85	140	Myanmar	4.30
62	Latvia	2.85	140	Rwanda	4.30
62	Malta	2.85	142	Angola	4.35
62	Paraguay	2.85	143	Azerbaijan	4.40
66	Greece	2.90	143	Tajikistan	4.40
66	Hungary	2.90	145	Turkmenistan	4.50
66	South Africa	2.90	146	Uzbekistan	4.55
69	Benin	2.95	147	Congo/Zaire	4.70
69	Ecuador	2.95	147	Iran	4.70
69	Gabon	2.95	147	Libya	4.70
69	Morocco	2.95	147	Somalia	4.70
69	Poland	2.95	147	Vietnam	4.70
74	Colombia	3.00	152	Bosnia	4.80
74	Ghana	3.00	153	Iraq	4.90
74	Lithuania	3.00	154	Cuba	5.00
77	Kenya	3.05	154	Laos	5.00
77	Slovak Republic	3.05	154	North Korea	5.00

Monetary Policy
Score: 1–Stable (very low level of inflation)

From 1985 to 1995, the United States maintained a stable inflation rate of 3.2 percent. In 1996, the rate of inflation was 2.9 percent, and it has remained at this level for most of 1997.

Capital Flows and Foreign Investment
Score: 2–Stable (low barriers)

The United States welcomes foreign investment, which accounts for some 11.5 percent of manufacturing employment and 5.2 percent of overall employment; but it also continues to restrict foreign investment in commercial and civil aviation, some telecommunications industries, public utilities, and industries considered vital to national security.

Banking
Score: 2–Stable (low level of restrictions)

The U.S. banking system is minimally regulated by federal, state, and local governments. There are some limits on foreign banks, such as restrictions on the extent to which foreign interests may own U.S. banks. There has been some progress recently in achieving further deregulation of banking. Congress, for example, passed legislation in 1996 to permit banks to open branches across state lines—something foreign banks already were allowed to do. Other reforms currently before Congress would allow banks to engage in commercial banking, insurance, and securities underwriting services.

Wage and Price Controls
Score: 2–Stable (low level)

The market sets wages and prices in the United States, although the government continues to determine prices on some goods and services (such as peanuts and other agricultural goods) by purchasing excess production, closing borders to imports, and manipulating prices through subsidies to companies like Amtrak. The government controls prices of some dairy products by subsidizing dairy farmers. The United States also maintains a federally imposed minimum wage standard.

Property Rights
Score: 1–Stable (very high level of protection)

Private property rights are a fundamental principle of the U.S. Constitution. The legal and judicial system is efficient and provides adequate protection of private property. The likelihood of government expropriation without just compensation is low. There have been situations in which governments at various levels have been known to expropriate property without due process (for example, in cases involving suspected drug dealers or those who proposition prostitutes), however, and many environmental policies have resulted in government confiscation of property without due process. The Army Corps of Engineers sometimes has used environmental laws to infringe on the property rights of citizens.

Regulation
Score: 2–Stable (low level)

Establishing a business in the United States is easy and affordable. Regulations are applied evenly and consistently in most cases, although they also can make it more difficult for businesses to keep their doors open. Government regulation now costs American consumers about $580 billion each year. Many regulations—for example, the Americans with Disabilities Act, various civil rights regulations, environmental laws, health and product safety standards, and food and drug labeling requirements—although well-intentioned, also are onerous. Moreover, many states are adopting such regulations at much higher levels than those imposed by the federal government. For example, California has imposed regulations requiring automobile manufacturers to produce and sell electric-powered automobiles. Companies failing to do so will not be permitted to sell automobiles in the state. This increase in regulations is occurring at the local level as well. For example, San Francisco recently mandated that any firm doing business with the city must provide the same benefits to domestic partner couples that it provides to legally married couples wherever it does business throughout the world. If evidence that the increase in regulations has become a significantly greater burden on business continues to grow, the score of the United States in this area could change. By global standards, however, the level of regulation remains low.

Black Market
Score: 1—Stable (very low level of activity)

The black market in the United States is confined primarily to goods and services considered harmful to public safety, such as narcotics, prostitution, guns, and stolen goods. The level of intellectual property protection is among the highest in the world.

Uruguay   2.70

Trade	2	Banking	2
Taxation	3	Wages and Prices	2
Government Intervention	3	Property Rights	2
Monetary Policy	5	Regulation	3
Foreign Investment	2	Black Market	3

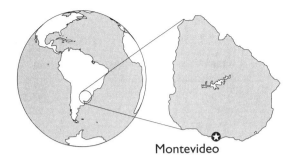

Montevideo

Uruguay, which gained its independence from Brazil in 1828, is wealthy by Latin American standards and has a relatively high level of literacy. Once a major international banking center, it experienced economic stagnation because of statist economic policies introduced in the 1960s. Today, however, Uruguay has a relatively free and open market. The government has been working to liberalize the economy and bring back respectable levels of economic growth. Recent reforms in the banking sector promote greater competition among both foreign and domestic banks, and the government has reduced its barriers to trade. Many companies in Uruguay, however, still are owned by the state.

TRADE POLICY
Score: 2–Stable (low level of protectionism)

Uruguay's average tariff rate is about 7 percent, down from 11 percent in 1992.[1] Few other restrictions on imports remain in effect. Import licenses are easy to obtain and do not restrict imports.

TAXATION
Score–Income taxation: 1–Stable (very low tax rates)
Score–Corporate taxation: 3–Stable (moderate tax rates)
Final Taxation Score: 3–Stable (moderate tax rates)

There is no income tax in Uruguay.[2] The top corporate tax rate is 30 percent. Uruguay also has a value-added tax of 23 percent, up from 22 percent in 1995, and a social security contributions tax of 37 percent to 38 percent.

GOVERNMENT INTERVENTION IN THE ECONOMY
Score: 3–Stable (moderate level)

Government consumes 12.8 percent of Uruguay's GDP, down from 14 percent in 1995, and has made significant progress in privatizing state-owned industries. Many port facilities and electricity generation plants were privatized in 1993, and the natural gas company was privatized in 1994. The government continues to play a significant role in the economy, however, and still owns many banks and financial companies, as well as the telephone company.

MONETARY POLICY
Score: 5–Stable (very high level of inflation)

Uruguay's average annual rate of inflation from 1985 to 1995 was 70.5 percent. In 1996, the rate was around 28.3 percent.

CAPITAL FLOWS AND FOREIGN INVESTMENT
Score: 2–Stable (low barriers)

Uruguay remains relatively open to foreign investment. Among the exceptions are the so-called strategic industries, which include telecommunications, transportation, banks, and the press. There are some tax incentives for foreign investment.

1	Hong Kong	1.25	77	Zambia	3.05
2	Singapore	1.30	80	Mali	3.10
3	Bahrain	1.70	80	Mongolia	3.10
4	New Zealand	1.75	80	Slovenia	3.10
5	Switzerland	1.90	83	Honduras	3.15
5	United States	1.90	83	Papua New Guinea	3.15
7	Luxembourg	1.95	85	Djibouti	3.20
7	Taiwan	1.95	85	Fiji	3.20
7	United Kingdom	1.95	85	Pakistan	3.20
10	Bahamas	2.00	88	Algeria	3.25
10	Ireland	2.00	88	Guinea	3.25
12	Australia	2.05	88	Lebanon	3.25
12	Japan	2.05	88	Mexico	3.25
14	Belgium	2.10	88	Senegal	3.25
14	Canada	2.10	88	Tanzania	3.25
14	United Arab Emirates	2.10	94	Nigeria	3.30
17	Austria	2.15	94	Romania	3.30
17	Chile	2.15	96	Brazil	3.35
17	Estonia	2.15	96	Cambodia	3.35
20	Czech Republic	2.20	96	Egypt	3.35
20	Netherlands	2.20	96	Ivory Coast	3.35
22	Denmark	2.25	96	Madagascar	3.35
22	Finland	2.25	96	Moldova	3.35
24	Germany	2.30	102	Nepal	3.40
24	Iceland	2.30	103	Cape Verde	3.44
24	South Korea	2.30	104	Armenia	3.45
27	Norway	2.35	104	Dominican Republic	3.45
28	Kuwait	2.40	104	Russia	3.45
28	Malaysia	2.40	107	Burkina Faso	3.50
28	Panama	2.40	107	Cameroon	3.50
28	Thailand	2.40	107	Lesotho	3.50
32	El Salvador	2.45	107	Nicaragua	3.50
32	Sri Lanka	2.45	107	Venezuela	3.50
32	Sweden	2.45	112	Gambia	3.60
35	France	2.50	112	Guyana	3.60
35	Italy	2.50	114	Bulgaria	3.65
35	Spain	2.50	114	Georgia	3.65
38	Trinidad and Tobago	2.55	114	Malawi	3.65
39	Argentina	2.60	117	Ethiopia	3.70
39	Barbados	2.60	117	India	3.70
39	Cyprus	2.60	117	Niger	3.70
39	Jamaica	2.60	120	Albania	3.75
39	Portugal	2.60	120	Bangladesh	3.75
44	Bolivia	2.65	120	China (PRC)	3.75
44	Oman	2.65	120	Congo	3.75
44	Philippines	2.65	120	Croatia	3.75
47	Swaziland	2.70	125	Chad	3.80
47	Uruguay	2.70	125	Mauritania	3.80
49	Botswana	2.75	125	Ukraine	3.80
49	Jordan	2.75	128	Sierra Leone	3.85
49	Namibia	2.75	129	Burundi	3.90
49	Tunisia	2.75	129	Suriname	3.90
53	Belize	2.80	129	Zimbabwe	3.90
53	Costa Rica	2.80	132	Haiti	4.00
53	Guatemala	2.80	132	Kyrgyzstan	4.00
53	Israel	2.80	132	Syria	4.00
53	Peru	2.80	135	Belarus	4.05
53	Saudi Arabia	2.80	136	Kazakstan	4.10
53	Turkey	2.80	136	Mozambique	4.10
53	Uganda	2.80	136	Yemen	4.10
53	Western Samoa	2.80	139	Sudan	4.20
62	Indonesia	2.85	140	Myanmar	4.30
62	Latvia	2.85	140	Rwanda	4.30
62	Malta	2.85	142	Angola	4.35
62	Paraguay	2.85	143	Azerbaijan	4.40
66	Greece	2.90	143	Tajikistan	4.40
66	Hungary	2.90	145	Turkmenistan	4.50
66	South Africa	2.90	146	Uzbekistan	4.55
69	Benin	2.95	147	Congo/Zaire	4.70
69	Ecuador	2.95	147	Iran	4.70
69	Gabon	2.95	147	Libya	4.70
69	Morocco	2.95	147	Somalia	4.70
69	Poland	2.95	147	Vietnam	4.70
74	Colombia	3.00	152	Bosnia	4.80
74	Ghana	3.00	153	Iraq	4.90
74	Lithuania	3.00	154	Cuba	5.00
77	Kenya	3.05	154	Laos	5.00
77	Slovak Republic	3.05	154	North Korea	5.00

Mostly Free

Banking
Score: 2–Stable (low level of restrictions)

Foreign banks are assuming a larger role in Uruguay's banking industry. Domestic banks are permitted to sell securities, but they also are prohibited from involvement in insurance, real estate, and investment transactions.

Wage and Price Controls
Score: 2–Stable (low level)

Uruguay maintains a minimum wage. The market determines most prices, although some price controls remain in effect on such items as bread, milk, alcohol, and fuels. The list of products subject to price controls changes frequently.

Property Rights
Score: 2–Stable (low level of protection)

Uruguay's court and legal system is becoming more efficient. Private property no longer is in danger of expropriation, although bureaucratic corruption often results in weak enforcement of private property laws.

Regulation
Score: 3–Stable (moderate level)

Establishing a business in Uruguay is a lengthy process. The bureaucracy is cumbersome and inefficient, and the government has yet to dismantle some of its most burdensome regulations, such as its strict environmental requirements.

Black Market
Score: 3–Stable (moderate level of activity)

Like most other Latin American countries, Uruguay has its share of black market activity. Transportation and labor, for example, are found frequently on the black market, and there is considerable black market activity in pirated computer software, video and tape recordings, and compact disks. By global standards, however, these activities remain moderate.

Notes

1. Based on total tax revenues from taxes on international transactions as a percentage of total imports.
2. There is, however, a 30 percent income tax rate for the agricultural sector. Because the agricultural sector contributes only about 8 percent of GDP, the author determined the income tax equivalent of the agricultural tax—if applied across the board to the entire population—to be less than 10 percent.

Uzbekistan   4.55

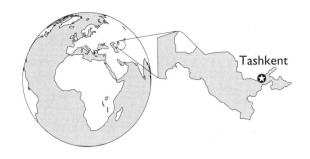
Tashkent

| 1997 Score: **n/a** | 1996 Score: **n/a** | 1995 Score: **n/a** |

Trade	5	Banking	5
Taxation	4.5	Wages and Prices	4
Government Intervention	4	Property Rights	4
Monetary Policy	5	Regulation	5
Foreign Investment	4	Black Market	5

The area now known as Uzbekistan was the site of the ancient Persian province of Sogdiana, conquered by Alexander the Great in the 4th century B.C. By the 8th century A.D., it had been conquered by the Arabs. An elaborate Turkic–Muslim civilization flourished in the principalities of Samarkand and Bukhara in the 10th through 12th centuries, and the region became part of the Mongol Empire under Ghengis Khan in the 13th century. Between 1865 and 1873, the Khorezm, Khiva, and Bukhara principalities fell under Russian control but retained a degree of autonomy. Tsarist Russia quickly extended its control over the region, leading to lingering hostilities between the Uzbeks and Russians. After the 1917 Bolshevik Revolution in Russia, the citizens revolted and continued to fight a guerrilla war against Russia into the 1920s. The area of present-day Uzbekistan became an autonomous region but was incorporated fully into the Soviet Union in 1924. Since becoming independent in 1991, Uzbekistan has seen its economy shrink by over 30 percent. Most economic reforms have been slow in coming, and resistance to continued reform flourishes. Uzbekistan is a Turkic-speaking Sunni Muslim country with a considerable ethnic Russian population in urban areas.

TRADE POLICY

Score: 5–Stable (very high level of protectionism)

Uzbekistan has an average tariff rate of about 15 percent, but the most significant barrier to trade is a regulation that requires importers to convert all currency into Uzbekistan currency. This increases actual tariff rates because the government, not the market, artificially sets the exchange rates. According to the Office of the United States Trade Representative, "[I]n October, 1996, Uzbekistan sharply curtailed convertibility of local currency into foreign exchange, making it very difficult for many U.S. companies to receive payment for exports or pay local expenses denominated in dollars. A number of firms that had supplied products to Uzbekistan have not been paid, and other [importing] firms have reduced or ceased importing because they cannot be certain they will obtain foreign exchange to honor their obligations."[1] Therefore, if these import costs are also taken into account, the effective average tariff rate is higher than 15 percent. The U.S. Department of State reports that "Customs procedures are bureaucratic, often arbitrary, and sometimes complicated by corruption."[2]

TAXATION

Score–Income taxation: 4–Stable (high tax rates)
Score–Corporate taxation: 4–Stable (high tax rates)
Final Taxation Score: 4.5–Stable (very high tax rates)

Uzbekistan's tax system is in disarray. The top income tax rate is 40 percent.[3] The top corporate tax rate is 37 percent. Uzbekistan also has a 20 percent capital gains tax, a 17 percent value-added tax, a natural resources tax, local taxes, and a 40 percent payroll tax.

1	Hong Kong	1.25	77	Zambia	3.05
2	Singapore	1.30	80	Mali	3.10
3	Bahrain	1.70	80	Mongolia	3.10
4	New Zealand	1.75	80	Slovenia	3.10
5	Switzerland	1.90	83	Honduras	3.15
5	United States	1.90	83	Papua New Guinea	3.15
7	Luxembourg	1.95	85	Djibouti	3.20
7	Taiwan	1.95	85	Fiji	3.20
7	United Kingdom	1.95	85	Pakistan	3.20
10	Bahamas	2.00	88	Algeria	3.25
10	Ireland	2.00	88	Guinea	3.25
12	Australia	2.05	88	Lebanon	3.25
12	Japan	2.05	88	Mexico	3.25
14	Belgium	2.10	88	Senegal	3.25
14	Canada	2.10	88	Tanzania	3.25
14	United Arab Emirates	2.10	94	Nigeria	3.30
17	Austria	2.15	94	Romania	3.30
17	Chile	2.15	96	Brazil	3.35
17	Estonia	2.15	96	Cambodia	3.35
20	Czech Republic	2.20	96	Egypt	3.35
20	Netherlands	2.20	96	Ivory Coast	3.35
22	Denmark	2.25	96	Madagascar	3.35
22	Finland	2.25	96	Moldova	3.35
24	Germany	2.30	102	Nepal	3.40
24	Iceland	2.30	103	Cape Verde	3.44
24	South Korea	2.30	104	Armenia	3.45
27	Norway	2.35	104	Dominican Republic	3.45
28	Kuwait	2.40	104	Russia	3.45
28	Malaysia	2.40	107	Burkina Faso	3.50
28	Panama	2.40	107	Cameroon	3.50
28	Thailand	2.40	107	Lesotho	3.50
32	El Salvador	2.45	107	Nicaragua	3.50
32	Sri Lanka	2.45	107	Venezuela	3.50
32	Sweden	2.45	112	Gambia	3.60
35	France	2.50	112	Guyana	3.60
35	Italy	2.50	114	Bulgaria	3.65
35	Spain	2.50	114	Georgia	3.65
38	Trinidad and Tobago	2.55	114	Malawi	3.65
39	Argentina	2.60	117	Ethiopia	3.70
39	Barbados	2.60	117	India	3.70
39	Cyprus	2.60	117	Niger	3.70
39	Jamaica	2.60	120	Albania	3.75
39	Portugal	2.60	120	Bangladesh	3.75
44	Bolivia	2.65	120	China (PRC)	3.75
44	Oman	2.65	120	Congo	3.75
44	Philippines	2.65	120	Croatia	3.75
47	Swaziland	2.70	125	Chad	3.80
47	Uruguay	2.70	125	Mauritania	3.80
49	Botswana	2.75	125	Ukraine	3.80
49	Jordan	2.75	128	Sierra Leone	3.85
49	Namibia	2.75	129	Burundi	3.90
49	Tunisia	2.75	129	Suriname	3.90
53	Belize	2.80	129	Zimbabwe	3.90
53	Costa Rica	2.80	132	Haiti	4.00
53	Guatemala	2.80	132	Kyrgyzstan	4.00
53	Israel	2.80	132	Syria	4.00
53	Peru	2.80	135	Belarus	4.05
53	Saudi Arabia	2.80	136	Kazakstan	4.10
53	Turkey	2.80	136	Mozambique	4.10
53	Uganda	2.80	136	Yemen	4.10
53	Western Samoa	2.80	139	Sudan	4.20
62	Indonesia	2.85	140	Myanmar	4.30
62	Latvia	2.85	140	Rwanda	4.30
62	Malta	2.85	142	Angola	4.35
62	Paraguay	2.85	143	Azerbaijan	4.40
66	Greece	2.90	143	Tajikistan	4.40
66	Hungary	2.90	145	Turkmenistan	4.50
66	South Africa	2.90	146	Uzbekistan	4.55
69	Benin	2.95	147	Congo/Zaire	4.70
69	Ecuador	2.95	147	Iran	4.70
69	Gabon	2.95	147	Libya	4.70
69	Morocco	2.95	147	Somalia	4.70
69	Poland	2.95	147	Vietnam	4.70
74	Colombia	3.00	152	Bosnia	4.80
74	Ghana	3.00	153	Iraq	4.90
74	Lithuania	3.00	154	Cuba	5.00
77	Kenya	3.05	154	Laos	5.00
77	Slovak Republic	3.05	154	North Korea	5.00

Repressed

GOVERNMENT INTERVENTION IN THE ECONOMY
Score: 4–Stable (high level)

Uzbekistan is privatizing some of its state-owned sector. The government consumption rate is over 25 percent.[4] State-owned enterprises produce almost 80 percent of GDP, and the government continues to own significant sectors of the economy, including most utilities and cotton production.

MONETARY POLICY
Score: 5–Stable (very high level of inflation)

Uzbekistan has been plagued with hyperinflation: 645 percent in 1992, 534 percent in 1993, 1,568 percent in 1994, 305 percent in 1995, and 64 percent in 1996. Thus, even though inflation has fallen, it remains very high, both historically and by global standards.

CAPITAL FLOWS AND FOREIGN INVESTMENT
Score: 4–Stable (high barriers)

Although the government wants to promote increased foreign investment, it still maintains some barriers. Uzbekistan has what appears to be a relatively free and open foreign investment code, but the U.S. Department of State reports that, "[I]n practice, negotiating and registering a joint venture is a cumbersome process which requires the approval of numerous government agencies and (usually) approval at the highest levels of the government. The registration process alone can take 3-6 months."[5] In addition, restrictions on the repatriation of profits severely hinder the ability of foreign firms to get their money out of the country. According to the U.S. Department of State, "Repatriation of funds is complicated by the cumbersome foreign exchange regulations."[6]

BANKING
Score: 5–Stable (very high level of restrictions)

Uzbekistan's banking system is not yet fully functional. According to the U.S. Department of Commerce, "As with so many other economic relationships, the collapse of the Soviet Union destroyed Uzbekistan's banking system, which had relied on central bank accounts in Moscow."[7]

WAGE AND PRICE CONTROLS
Score: 4–Stable (high level)

The large number of state-owned enterprises controls wages and prices in Uzbekistan. Price controls continue on such items as wheat, cotton, transportation, distribution, and utilities.

PROPERTY RIGHTS
Score: 4–Stable (low level of protection)

Private property does not enjoy sufficient protection under Uzbekistan's legal system. According to the U.S. Department of State, "Although the Constitution provides for an independent judicial authority, in practice the judicial branch is heavily influenced by the executive branch.... Uzbekistan continues to use the Soviet legal system."[8]

REGULATION
Score: 5–Stable (very high level)

Establishing a business in Uzbekistan is a tedious and time-consuming process that requires individuals to overcome numerous bureaucratic barriers. According to the U.S. Department of Commerce, "The bureaucratic and often inscrutable process governing the process of registering a foreign firm or joint venture in Uzbekistan is another source of frustration for those wishing to do business there."[9] The U.S. Department of State reports that "Uzbekistan inherited many production standards and environmental regulations from the former Soviet Union, but enforcement is spotty. Issuance of regulations by one government body absent coordination with other affected government organizations has caused problems for some foreign business interests."[10]

BLACK MARKET
Score: 5–Stable (very high level of activity)

Smuggling is rampant in Uzbekistan. For example, there is a large black market in tobacco. According to the U.S. Department of Commerce, "The bulk of tobacco trade involves cigarettes. Sources estimate that Uzbekistan imports 14 to 15 billion cigarettes annually, most of which are smuggled."[11] Despite laws protecting intellectual property rights, there continues to be significant piracy in computer software.

NOTES

1. Office of the United States Trade Representative, *National Trade Estimate Report on Foreign Trade Barriers,* 1997.
2. U.S. Department of State, *Country Reports on Economic Policy and Trade Practices,* 1996, p. 317.
3. The tax on the average level of income is unavailable. Thus, the income tax score is based solely on the top rate. According to the U.S. Department of State, however, "[T]he current top marginal rate of 40 percent takes effect at a relatively low level of income by Western standards." U.S. Department of State, *Country Reports on Economic Policy and Trade Practices,* 1996, p. 316.
4. World Bank, *World Development Report 1997,* and Economist Intelligence Unit, *EIU Country Report,* 1997.
5. U.S. Department of State, *Country Reports on Economic Policy and Trade Practices,* 1996, p. 317.
6. *Ibid.*
7. U.S. Department of Commerce, "Uzbekistan: Trade and Investment Overview," March 1997.
8. U.S. Department of State, "Uzbekistan Country Report on Human Rights Practices for 1996," 1997.
9. U.S. Department of Commerce, "Uzbekistan: Trade and Investment Overview," March 1997.
10. U.S. Department of State, *Country Reports on Economic Policy and Trade Practices,* 1996, p. 316.
11. U.S. Department of Commerce, "Uzbekistan: Tobacco Update; Voluntary Report," *Agworld Attaché Reports,* 1996.

Venezuela   3.50

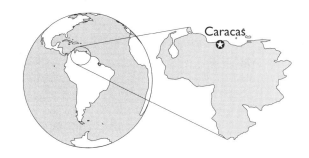

1997 Score: **3.60**	1996 Score: **3.50**	1995 Score: **3.00**

Trade	3	Banking	3
Taxation	4	Wages and Prices	3
Government Intervention	3	Property Rights	3
Monetary Policy	5	Regulation	3
Foreign Investment	3	Black Market	5

Venezuela declared its independence in 1821 and today is a multiparty electoral democracy. A cofounder, with Iraq, of the Organization of Petroleum Exporting Countries, Venezuela has an economy that relies heavily on oil exports. From 1989 to 1992, it made progress in its efforts to implement free-market reforms, but this trend began to change when President Rafael Caldera took office in February 1994. Caldera restored many state controls over the economy and ignored free-market policies. In 1996, the government signed an agreement with the International Monetary Fund following pressure from the IMF to reinstitute some degree of fiscal responsibility. The government recently reduced some barriers to trade. As a result, Venezuela's overall score is 0.1 point better this year.

TRADE POLICY
Score: 3+ (moderate level of protectionism)

The average tariff rate in Venezuela is about 9 percent, down from 10 percent in 1992.[1] For this reason, Venezuela's trade policy score is one point better this year. Nontariff barriers include special taxes designed to protect local producers and health standards designed to minimize imports of grain.

TAXATION
Score–Income taxation: 4–Stable (high tax rates)
Score–Corporate taxation: 3–Stable (moderate tax rates)
Final Taxation Score: 4–Stable (high tax rates)

Venezuela's top marginal income tax rate is 34 percent, and the average income is taxed at 16 percent. The top corporate tax rate is 34 percent. Venezuela also has a 16.5 percent to 36.5 percent value-added tax and a 34 percent capital gains tax.

GOVERNMENT INTERVENTION IN THE ECONOMY
Score: 3–Stable (moderate level)

Government consumes around 11 percent of Venezuela's GDP. According to the Economist Intelligence Unit, "The government...continues to exert considerable control over business. And although it has repeatedly stressed its commitment to selling state assets through the country's privatization program, the administration continues to enact policies that ensure the failure of state sales."[2]

MONETARY POLICY
Score: 5–Stable (very high level of inflation)

Venezuela's average annual rate of inflation from 1985 to 1995 was 37.6 percent. In 1996, the rate was 100 percent.

1	Hong Kong	1.25
2	Singapore	1.30
3	Bahrain	1.70
4	New Zealand	1.75
5	Switzerland	1.90
5	United States	1.90
7	Luxembourg	1.95
7	Taiwan	1.95
7	United Kingdom	1.95
10	Bahamas	2.00
10	Ireland	2.00
12	Australia	2.05
12	Japan	2.05
14	Belgium	2.10
14	Canada	2.10
14	United Arab Emirates	2.10
17	Austria	2.15
17	Chile	2.15
17	Estonia	2.15
20	Czech Republic	2.20
20	Netherlands	2.20
22	Denmark	2.25
22	Finland	2.25
24	Germany	2.30
24	Iceland	2.30
24	South Korea	2.30
27	Norway	2.35
28	Kuwait	2.40
28	Malaysia	2.40
28	Panama	2.40
28	Thailand	2.40
32	El Salvador	2.45
32	Sri Lanka	2.45
32	Sweden	2.45
35	France	2.50
35	Italy	2.50
35	Spain	2.50
38	Trinidad and Tobago	2.55
39	Argentina	2.60
39	Barbados	2.60
39	Cyprus	2.60
39	Jamaica	2.60
39	Portugal	2.60
44	Bolivia	2.65
44	Oman	2.65
44	Philippines	2.65
47	Swaziland	2.70
47	Uruguay	2.70
49	Botswana	2.75
49	Jordan	2.75
49	Namibia	2.75
49	Tunisia	2.75
53	Belize	2.80
53	Costa Rica	2.80
53	Guatemala	2.80
53	Israel	2.80
53	Peru	2.80
53	Saudi Arabia	2.80
53	Turkey	2.80
53	Uganda	2.80
53	Western Samoa	2.80
62	Indonesia	2.85
62	Latvia	2.85
62	Malta	2.85
62	Paraguay	2.85
66	Greece	2.90
66	Hungary	2.90
66	South Africa	2.90
69	Benin	2.95
69	Ecuador	2.95
69	Gabon	2.95
69	Morocco	2.95
69	Poland	2.95
74	Colombia	3.00
74	Ghana	3.00
74	Lithuania	3.00
77	Kenya	3.05
77	Slovak Republic	3.05

77	Zambia	3.05
80	Mali	3.10
80	Mongolia	3.10
80	Slovenia	3.10
83	Honduras	3.15
83	Papua New Guinea	3.15
85	Djibouti	3.20
85	Fiji	3.20
85	Pakistan	3.20
88	Algeria	3.25
88	Guinea	3.25
88	Lebanon	3.25
88	Mexico	3.25
88	Senegal	3.25
88	Tanzania	3.25
94	Nigeria	3.30
94	Romania	3.30
96	Brazil	3.35
96	Cambodia	3.35
96	Egypt	3.35
96	Ivory Coast	3.35
96	Madagascar	3.35
96	Moldova	3.35
102	Nepal	3.40
103	Cape Verde	3.44
104	Armenia	3.45
104	Dominican Republic	3.45
104	Russia	3.45
107	Burkina Faso	3.50
107	Cameroon	3.50
107	Lesotho	3.50
107	Nicaragua	3.50
107	Venezuela	3.50
112	Gambia	3.60
112	Guyana	3.60
114	Bulgaria	3.65
114	Georgia	3.65
114	Malawi	3.65
117	Ethiopia	3.70
117	India	3.70
117	Niger	3.70
120	Albania	3.75
120	Bangladesh	3.75
120	China (PRC)	3.75
120	Congo	3.75
120	Croatia	3.75
125	Chad	3.80
125	Mauritania	3.80
125	Ukraine	3.80
128	Sierra Leone	3.85
129	Burundi	3.90
129	Suriname	3.90
129	Zimbabwe	3.90
132	Haiti	4.00
132	Kyrgyzstan	4.00
132	Syria	4.00
135	Belarus	4.05
136	Kazakstan	4.10
136	Mozambique	4.10
136	Yemen	4.10
139	Sudan	4.20
140	Myanmar	4.30
140	Rwanda	4.30
142	Angola	4.35
143	Azerbaijan	4.40
143	Tajikistan	4.40
145	Turkmenistan	4.50
146	Uzbekistan	4.55
147	Congo/Zaire	4.70
147	Iran	4.70
147	Libya	4.70
147	Somalia	4.70
147	Vietnam	4.70
152	Bosnia	4.80
153	Iraq	4.90
154	Cuba	5.00
154	Laos	5.00
154	North Korea	5.00

Mostly Unfree

Capital Flows and Foreign Investment
Score: 3–Stable (moderate barriers)

Most industries in Venezuela are open to foreign investment, although some significant restrictions remain in effect. Foreign ownership of a few service industries, including television, radio, the Spanish-language press, and some professional services, is limited to no more than 19.9 percent.

Banking
Score: 3–Stable (moderate level of restrictions)

Although most restrictions on foreign bank branches have been removed, the government still owns about 50 percent of all banks in Venezuela. Foreign banks from countries that provide reciprocal treatment now may open 100 percent foreign-owned subsidiaries or purchase 100 percent of existing banks.

Wage and Price Controls
Score: 3–Stable (moderate level)

Venezuela maintains a minimum wage. The government has broad authority to impose price controls, such as those in effect on some basic foodstuffs, medicines, fuel, and public transportation.

Property Rights
Score: 3–Stable (moderate level of protection)

Private property is a staple of Venezuela's economy, but the government is prone to expropriation, and property is not fully protected by the court system.

Regulation
Score: 3–Stable (moderate level)

Opening a business in Venezuela is not difficult. The recent economic downturn has led to increased corruption, however, and some regulations are not applied uniformly.

Black Market
Score: 5–Stable (very high level of activity)

Venezuela's black market is active wherever prices are state-controlled (as in the transportation services sector). The black market provides about 40 percent of labor services in Caracas. Although Venezuela has established intellectual property laws, enforcement is lax and piracy in copyrighted material continues.

Notes

1. Based on total taxes on international trade as a percentage of total imports.
2. Economist Intelligence Unit, *ILT Reports,* October 1996, p. 7.

Vietnam

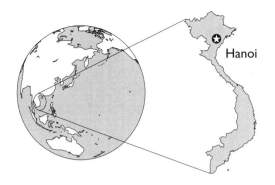

4.70

1997 Score: **4.70**	1996 Score: **4.70**	1995 Score: **4.70**

Trade	5	Banking	4
Taxation	5	Wages and Prices	4
Government Intervention	5	Property Rights	5
Monetary Policy	5	Regulation	5
Foreign Investment	4	Black Market	5

Vietnam, divided for most of its early history by warring factions, was occupied by France in the 19th century. In 1954, following its defeat at Dien Bien Phu, France agreed to withdraw from the northern part of Vietnam and moved south below the 17th parallel. The communists in the North established the Democratic Republic of Vietnam, while the non-communists in the South established the Republic of South Vietnam. After the defeat of South Vietnam in 1975, the Hanoi government established a communist system throughout all of Vietnam. In 1995, Vietnam joined the Association of Southeast Asian Nations and the Clinton Administration extended U.S. diplomatic relations to Hanoi. As a result, U.S. companies are free to invest in Vietnam. Even though the regime has begun to liberalize some areas of its centrally planned economy, Vietnam remains a communist dictatorship, and the state still owns most means of production.

TRADE POLICY
Score: 5–Stable (very high level of protectionism)

Vietnam's average tariff rate is between 15 percent to 20 percent.[1] A corrupt bureaucracy, however, creates very high barriers to imports. Many imports are confiscated by corrupt border officials. According to the Economist Intelligence Unit, "The country's most serious trade problem is smuggling, with illicit imports (not only consumer items but also some essential industrial inputs such as newsprint, steel, fertilizer, pesticides, and chemicals) amounting to the equivalent of one-fourth to one-third of the official import bill."[2]

TAXATION
Score–Income taxation: 5–Stable (very high tax rates)
Score–Corporate taxation: 5–Stable (very high tax rates)
Final Taxation Score: 5–Stable (very high tax rates)

Vietnam's top income tax rate is 60 percent, with the average income level taxed at a rate of 40 percent. The tax on foreign corporate profits is as high as 45 percent.[3] Because the economy is centrally planned and the government owns most businesses, actual tax rates are much higher than these levels suggest.

GOVERNMENT INTERVENTION IN THE ECONOMY
Score: 5–Stable (very high level)

Progress toward privatization has been anemic. The government still owns most means of production, maintains central planning, and has yet to subject the economy to the basic principles of supply and demand. The government produces almost 40 percent of GDP, up from 33 percent in 1990, and it plans to increase this level to 60 percent over the next several years.

MONETARY POLICY
Score: 5–Stable (very high level of inflation)

From 1990 to 1994, Vietnam's average annual rate of inflation was 33.2 percent. For 1995, the rate of inflation was about 8.8 percent; in 1996, it was 4.5 percent. By global standards, however, the rate of inflation remains very high.

1	Hong Kong	1.25	77	Zambia	3.05
2	Singapore	1.30	80	Mali	3.10
3	Bahrain	1.70	80	Mongolia	3.10
4	New Zealand	1.75	80	Slovenia	3.10
5	Switzerland	1.90	83	Honduras	3.15
5	United States	1.90	83	Papua New Guinea	3.15
7	Luxembourg	1.95	85	Djibouti	3.20
7	Taiwan	1.95	85	Fiji	3.20
7	United Kingdom	1.95	85	Pakistan	3.20
10	Bahamas	2.00	88	Algeria	3.25
10	Ireland	2.00	88	Guinea	3.25
12	Australia	2.05	88	Lebanon	3.25
12	Japan	2.05	88	Mexico	3.25
14	Belgium	2.10	88	Senegal	3.25
14	Canada	2.10	88	Tanzania	3.25
14	United Arab Emirates	2.10	94	Nigeria	3.30
17	Austria	2.15	94	Romania	3.30
17	Chile	2.15	96	Brazil	3.35
17	Estonia	2.15	96	Cambodia	3.35
20	Czech Republic	2.20	96	Egypt	3.35
20	Netherlands	2.20	96	Ivory Coast	3.35
22	Denmark	2.25	96	Madagascar	3.35
22	Finland	2.25	96	Moldova	3.35
24	Germany	2.30	102	Nepal	3.40
24	Iceland	2.30	103	Cape Verde	3.44
24	South Korea	2.30	104	Armenia	3.45
27	Norway	2.35	104	Dominican Republic	3.45
28	Kuwait	2.40	104	Russia	3.45
28	Malaysia	2.40	107	Burkina Faso	3.50
28	Panama	2.40	107	Cameroon	3.50
28	Thailand	2.40	107	Lesotho	3.50
32	El Salvador	2.45	107	Nicaragua	3.50
32	Sri Lanka	2.45	107	Venezuela	3.50
32	Sweden	2.45	112	Gambia	3.60
35	France	2.50	112	Guyana	3.60
35	Italy	2.50	114	Bulgaria	3.65
35	Spain	2.50	114	Georgia	3.65
38	Trinidad and Tobago	2.55	114	Malawi	3.65
39	Argentina	2.60	117	Ethiopia	3.70
39	Barbados	2.60	117	India	3.70
39	Cyprus	2.60	117	Niger	3.70
39	Jamaica	2.60	120	Albania	3.75
39	Portugal	2.60	120	Bangladesh	3.75
44	Bolivia	2.65	120	China (PRC)	3.75
44	Oman	2.65	120	Congo	3.75
44	Philippines	2.65	120	Croatia	3.75
47	Swaziland	2.70	125	Chad	3.80
47	Uruguay	2.70	125	Mauritania	3.80
49	Botswana	2.75	125	Ukraine	3.80
49	Jordan	2.75	128	Sierra Leone	3.85
49	Namibia	2.75	129	Burundi	3.90
49	Tunisia	2.75	129	Suriname	3.90
53	Belize	2.80	129	Zimbabwe	3.90
53	Costa Rica	2.80	132	Haiti	4.00
53	Guatemala	2.80	132	Kyrgyzstan	4.00
53	Israel	2.80	132	Syria	4.00
53	Peru	2.80	135	Belarus	4.05
53	Saudi Arabia	2.80	136	Kazakstan	4.10
53	Turkey	2.80	136	Mozambique	4.10
53	Uganda	2.80	136	Yemen	4.10
53	Western Samoa	2.80	139	Sudan	4.20
62	Indonesia	2.85	140	Myanmar	4.30
62	Latvia	2.85	140	Rwanda	4.30
62	Malta	2.85	142	Angola	4.35
62	Paraguay	2.85	143	Azerbaijan	4.40
66	Greece	2.90	143	Tajikistan	4.40
66	Hungary	2.90	145	Turkmenistan	4.50
66	South Africa	2.90	146	Uzbekistan	4.55
69	Benin	2.95	147	Congo/Zaire	4.70
69	Ecuador	2.95	147	Iran	4.70
69	Gabon	2.95	147	Libya	4.70
69	Morocco	2.95	147	Somalia	4.70
69	Poland	2.95	147	Vietnam	4.70
74	Colombia	3.00	152	Bosnia	4.80
74	Ghana	3.00	153	Iraq	4.90
74	Lithuania	3.00	154	Cuba	5.00
77	Kenya	3.05	154	Laos	5.00
77	Slovak Republic	3.05	154	North Korea	5.00

Repressed

CAPITAL FLOWS AND FOREIGN INVESTMENT
Score: 4–Stable (high barriers)

One of the world's few remaining communist states, Vietnam has gone farther to open its economy to foreign investment than either Cuba or North Korea. Yet much of the economy remains inaccessible to foreigners, investments still need prior government approval, and repatriation of profits remains subject to some restrictions. Even though 100 percent ownership is allowed in principle, few investments have been approved. The government heavily favors joint ventures (50–50) with foreign firms. Investments are granted on a case-by-case basis. According to the U.S. Department of Commerce, "Although the [foreign investment] license application and approval process is standardized, in practice, the process remains bureaucratic, and can be cumbersome and lengthy."[4]

BANKING
Score: 4–Stable (high level of restrictions)

Banking services are reserved almost exclusively for the government, although there have been attempts to modernize the financial system. The few private banks that do exist are heavily influenced by the government and operate at a disadvantage because of the unfair competition from large state-owned banks. The four largest banks are state-owned and control some 85 percent of all banking assets.

WAGE AND PRICE CONTROLS
Score: 4–Stable (high level)

At least 50 percent of the goods produced by Vietnamese companies are subject to some type of central planning. Vietnam has lifted price controls on some products, including steel and printing paper, but controls on the prices of electricity, water, telecommunications, and transportation services remain in effect. Many wages are set by the government.

PROPERTY RIGHTS
Score: 5–Stable (very low level of protection)

Vietnam's government is tolerant of more private ownership of property, but property still enjoys almost no legal protection. Moreover, the government does not fully permit foreign companies to seek arbitration in foreign courts; all disputes must be settled within Vietnam. The court system is subject to extensive government influence, especially when disputes arise among parties with close ties to the government. According to the U.S. Department of State, "While the Constitution provides for the independence of judges and jurors, in practice the VCP [Vietnamese Communist Party] controls the courts closely at all levels, selecting judges primarily for political reliability. Credible reports indicate the party officials, including top leaders, instruct courts on how to rule on politically important cases."[5]

REGULATION
Score: 5–Stable (very high level)

Vietnam erects many obstacles to private enterprise. According to the U.S. Department of Commerce, "Widespread official corruption and inefficient bureaucracy are blamed by Vietnam's leadership, press and citizenry, as well as by foreigners, as obstacles to continued economic growth and foreign investment."[6] The government is reducing some regulations, but it remains a major impediment to entrepreneurship and the creation of new private businesses. It establishes work weeks, forces companies to provide paid vacations and contribute to employee health and social security plans, and uses environmental regulations (the number of which is increasing) to penalize businesses.

BLACK MARKET
Score: 5–Stable (very high level of activity)

Vietnam has a large black market in such basic goods and services as foodstuffs and labor. Because of the miserable condition of the country's banks, there also is a growing black market in private financing. According to the U.S. Department of Commerce, "This lack of confidence can be seen in the fact that the public keeps as much as 45% of broad money as cash outside the banking system. Over 50% of local business transactions are conducted outside of the banking system."[7] The U.S. Department of Commerce reports that "[A]lmost all current imports, including those from the U.S., are smuggled goods. Current imports of U.S. goods are via third-country suppliers from Singapore and Thailand or smuggled."[8] Such "loan sharking" raises business costs and encourages criminal activity. Although Vietnam has passed laws protecting intellectual property, enforcement remains lax, and there is significant piracy in computer software and other items.

NOTES

1. U.S. Department of Commerce, *Country Commercial Guide,* 1997.
2. Economist Intelligence Unit, *ILT Reports, Vietnam,* April 1996, updated October 1996.
3. This is the top rate for companies without foreign-owned capital. Companies with foreign-owned capital are taxed at a top rate of 25 percent.
4. U.S. Department of Commerce, *Country Commercial Guide,* 1997.
5. U.S. Department of State, "Vietnam Report on Human Rights Practices for 1996," 1997.
6. U.S. Department of Commerce, *Country Commercial Guide,* 1997.
7. *Ibid.*
8. *Ibid.*

Western Samoa   2.80

1997 Score: **2.80**   1996 Score: **2.80**   1995 Score: **n/a**

Trade	3	Banking	3
Taxation	4	Wages and Prices	3
Government Intervention	2	Property Rights	3
Monetary Policy	2	Regulation	3
Foreign Investment	3	Black Market	2

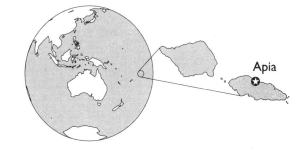

Apia

The central South Pacific island of Western Samoa gained its independence from a New Zealand–administered United Nations trusteeship in 1962. Its primarily agricultural economy is engaged chiefly in the production of coconuts, cocoa, bananas, and taro. Most consumer goods and raw materials must be imported, and this creates a chronic trade deficit.

TRADE POLICY
Score: 3–Stable (moderate level of protectionism)

Western Samoa has a 7.5 percent tariff rate for most so-called essential items and a varying tariff rate of between 5 percent and 75 percent on many consumer goods. The average rate is about 9 percent. The principal nontariff barrier is a stringent inspection process that can delay entry of some imports.

TAXATION
Score–Income taxation: 3–Stable (moderate tax rates)
Score–Corporate taxation: 4–Stable (high tax rates)
Final Taxation Score: 4–Stable (high tax rates)

Western Samoa's top income tax rate is 45 percent, with the average taxpayer in the 10 percent bracket. The top marginal corporate tax rate is 39 percent.[1] Western Samoa also has a 10 percent goods and services tax and a 10 percent to 15 percent tax on interest, royalties, and dividends.

GOVERNMENT INTERVENTION IN THE ECONOMY
Score: 2–Stable (low level)

Government consumes 17.9 percent of Western Samoa's GDP.

MONETARY POLICY
Score: 2–Stable (Low level of inflation)

Western Samoa's average annual rate of inflation from 1985 to 1995 was 10.6 percent. The rate for 1996 was not available.

CAPITAL FLOWS AND FOREIGN INVESTMENT
Score: 3–Stable (moderate barriers)

Foreigners may lease land in Western Samoa but are not permitted to own it. Permission must be granted for most investments, although registering foreign investments is becoming easier. In this respect, the government favors export industries.

BANKING
Score: 3–Stable (moderate level of restrictions)

The banking system is small. The government continues to be a joint venture partner in at least one commercial bank, the Bank of Western Samoa.

1	Hong Kong	1.25	
2	Singapore	1.30	
3	Bahrain	1.70	
4	New Zealand	1.75	
5	Switzerland	1.90	
5	United States	1.90	
7	Luxembourg	1.95	
7	Taiwan	1.95	
7	United Kingdom	1.95	
10	Bahamas	2.00	
10	Ireland	2.00	
12	Australia	2.05	
12	Japan	2.05	
14	Belgium	2.10	
14	Canada	2.10	
14	United Arab Emirates	2.10	
17	Austria	2.15	
17	Chile	2.15	
17	Estonia	2.15	
20	Czech Republic	2.20	
20	Netherlands	2.20	
22	Denmark	2.25	
22	Finland	2.25	
24	Germany	2.30	
24	Iceland	2.30	
24	South Korea	2.30	
27	Norway	2.35	
28	Kuwait	2.40	
28	Malaysia	2.40	
28	Panama	2.40	
28	Thailand	2.40	
32	El Salvador	2.45	
32	Sri Lanka	2.45	
32	Sweden	2.45	
35	France	2.50	
35	Italy	2.50	
35	Spain	2.50	
38	Trinidad and Tobago	2.55	
39	Argentina	2.60	
39	Barbados	2.60	
39	Cyprus	2.60	
39	Jamaica	2.60	
39	Portugal	2.60	
44	Bolivia	2.65	
44	Oman	2.65	
44	Philippines	2.65	
47	Swaziland	2.70	
47	Uruguay	2.70	
49	Botswana	2.75	
49	Jordan	2.75	
49	Namibia	2.75	
49	Tunisia	2.75	
53	Belize	2.80	
53	Costa Rica	2.80	
53	Guatemala	2.80	
53	Israel	2.80	
53	Peru	2.80	
53	Saudi Arabia	2.80	
53	Turkey	2.80	
53	Uganda	2.80	
53	Western Samoa	2.80	
62	Indonesia	2.85	
62	Latvia	2.85	
62	Malta	2.85	
62	Paraguay	2.85	
66	Greece	2.90	
66	Hungary	2.90	
66	South Africa	2.90	
69	Benin	2.95	
69	Ecuador	2.95	
69	Gabon	2.95	
69	Morocco	2.95	
69	Poland	2.95	
74	Colombia	3.00	
74	Ghana	3.00	
74	Lithuania	3.00	
77	Kenya	3.05	
77	Slovak Republic	3.05	
77	Zambia	3.05	
80	Mali	3.10	
80	Mongolia	3.10	
80	Slovenia	3.10	
83	Honduras	3.15	
83	Papua New Guinea	3.15	
85	Djibouti	3.20	
85	Fiji	3.20	
85	Pakistan	3.20	
88	Algeria	3.25	
88	Guinea	3.25	
88	Lebanon	3.25	
88	Mexico	3.25	
88	Senegal	3.25	
88	Tanzania	3.25	
94	Nigeria	3.30	
94	Romania	3.30	
96	Brazil	3.35	
96	Cambodia	3.35	
96	Egypt	3.35	
96	Ivory Coast	3.35	
96	Madagascar	3.35	
96	Moldova	3.35	
102	Nepal	3.40	
103	Cape Verde	3.44	
104	Armenia	3.45	
104	Dominican Republic	3.45	
104	Russia	3.45	
107	Burkina Faso	3.50	
107	Cameroon	3.50	
107	Lesotho	3.50	
107	Nicaragua	3.50	
107	Venezuela	3.50	
112	Gambia	3.60	
112	Guyana	3.60	
114	Bulgaria	3.65	
114	Georgia	3.65	
114	Malawi	3.65	
117	Ethiopia	3.70	
117	India	3.70	
117	Niger	3.70	
120	Albania	3.75	
120	Bangladesh	3.75	
120	China (PRC)	3.75	
120	Congo	3.75	
120	Croatia	3.75	
125	Chad	3.80	
125	Mauritania	3.80	
125	Ukraine	3.80	
128	Sierra Leone	3.85	
129	Burundi	3.90	
129	Suriname	3.90	
129	Zimbabwe	3.90	
132	Haiti	4.00	
132	Kyrgyzstan	4.00	
132	Syria	4.00	
135	Belarus	4.05	
136	Kazakstan	4.10	
136	Mozambique	4.10	
136	Yemen	4.10	
139	Sudan	4.20	
140	Myanmar	4.30	
140	Rwanda	4.30	
142	Angola	4.35	
143	Azerbaijan	4.40	
143	Tajikistan	4.40	
145	Turkmenistan	4.50	
146	Uzbekistan	4.55	
147	Congo/Zaire	4.70	
147	Iran	4.70	
147	Libya	4.70	
147	Somalia	4.70	
147	Vietnam	4.70	
152	Bosnia	4.80	
153	Iraq	4.90	
154	Cuba	5.00	
154	Laos	5.00	
154	North Korea	5.00	

Mostly Free

Wage and Price Controls
Score: 3–Stable (moderate level)

The market sets most wages and prices in Western Samoa, although there is a government-mandated minimum wage. The government controls some prices, mainly in the utilities sector, and also influences prices through its direct ownership of companies (for example, in the agricultural sector).

Property Rights
Score: 3–Stable (moderate level of protection)

Western Samoa's government owns large tracts of public land that are closed to business development. Most private land already has been developed.

Regulation
Score: 3–Stable (moderate level)

Establishing a business in Western Samoa is relatively easy, and regulations are applied evenly in most cases, although some regulations make it difficult for businesses to operate. The government, for example, requires all businesses to contribute 5 percent of gross earnings for each Western Samoan employee to a retirement fund, the Western Samoan National Provident Fund; it also requires that employees contribute 5 percent of their earnings to this fund. Businesses are not free to hire foreigners if there is a Western Samoan who can perform the same job.

Black Market
Score: 2–Stable (low level of activity)

Western Samoa's black market is negligible.

Note

1. This rate applies to resident-owned companies; foreign-owned companies pay a top rate of 48 percent.

Yemen

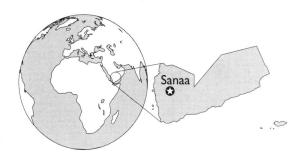

Sanaa

4.10

1997 Score: **3.90**	1996 Score: **3.75**	1995 Score: **3.75**

Trade	5	Banking	4
Taxation	3	Wages and Prices	3
Government Intervention	4	Property Rights	4
Monetary Policy	5	Regulation	4
Foreign Investment	4	Black Market	5

For centuries, Yemen was dominated by various empires, including both the Roman and the Ottoman empires. The southern part of the country became a British protectorate in 1839; the northern part was controlled by Turkey until after World War I and became fully independent in 1934. Inspired by this success, southern Yemen fought to gain its independence from the United Kingdom in 1967. Soon afterward, a Marxist government took control of southern Yemen, devastating the economy. In 1990, after two decades of political and civil chaos, North and South Yemen united. The outbreak of civil war in 1994 cut short the limited progress the country had made toward economic liberalization. Since then, there has been little economic growth. A recent increase in corruption within the bureaucracy has made foreign investment more difficult. As a result, Yemen's overall score this year is 0.2 point worse than last year.

TRADE POLICY
Score: 5–Stable (very high level of protectionism)

Tariffs in Yemen range from 5 percent to 30 percent; the average tariff is 16.2 percent. Special duties apply to some so-called luxury items; automobiles, for example, are assessed at 67 percent, and tobacco imports are assessed at a rate of 145 percent. Yemen also maintains nontariff barriers in several areas; there are import bans, for example, on pork and pork products, coffee, alcohol, and all types of fresh fruits and vegetables. There is evidence of corruption within the government bureaucracy, which also can hinder imports. According to the U.S. Department of Commerce, "Corruption and red tape within the government is endemic."[1]

TAXATION
Score–Income taxation: 2–Stable (low tax rates)
Score–Corporate taxation: 3–Stable (moderate tax rates)
Final Taxation Score: 3–Stable (moderate tax rates)

Yemen's top income tax rate is 28 percent, with the average income level taxed at 9 percent. The top corporate tax rate is 32 percent. Yemen also has a 32 percent capital gains tax and other taxes.

GOVERNMENT INTERVENTION IN THE ECONOMY
Score: 4–Stable (high level)

Government consumes 29 percent of Yemen's GDP.[2] It also generates a large portion of GDP overall.

MONETARY POLICY
Score: 5–Stable (very high level of inflation)

Yemen's average annual rate of inflation from 1990 to 1994 was 109 percent. In 1995, the rate was 65 percent; in 1996, it was 30 percent.

1	Hong Kong	1.25	77	Zambia	3.05
2	Singapore	1.30	80	Mali	3.10
3	Bahrain	1.70	80	Mongolia	3.10
4	New Zealand	1.75	80	Slovenia	3.10
5	Switzerland	1.90	83	Honduras	3.15
5	United States	1.90	83	Papua New Guinea	3.15
7	Luxembourg	1.95	85	Djibouti	3.20
7	Taiwan	1.95	85	Fiji	3.20
7	United Kingdom	1.95	85	Pakistan	3.20
10	Bahamas	2.00	88	Algeria	3.25
10	Ireland	2.00	88	Guinea	3.25
12	Australia	2.05	88	Lebanon	3.25
12	Japan	2.05	88	Mexico	3.25
14	Belgium	2.10	88	Senegal	3.25
14	Canada	2.10	88	Tanzania	3.25
14	United Arab Emirates	2.10	94	Nigeria	3.30
17	Austria	2.15	94	Romania	3.30
17	Chile	2.15	96	Brazil	3.35
17	Estonia	2.15	96	Cambodia	3.35
20	Czech Republic	2.20	96	Egypt	3.35
20	Netherlands	2.20	96	Ivory Coast	3.35
22	Denmark	2.25	96	Madagascar	3.35
22	Finland	2.25	96	Moldova	3.35
24	Germany	2.30	102	Nepal	3.40
24	Iceland	2.30	103	Cape Verde	3.44
24	South Korea	2.30	104	Armenia	3.45
27	Norway	2.35	104	Dominican Republic	3.45
28	Kuwait	2.40	104	Russia	3.45
28	Malaysia	2.40	107	Burkina Faso	3.50
28	Panama	2.40	107	Cameroon	3.50
28	Thailand	2.40	107	Lesotho	3.50
32	El Salvador	2.45	107	Nicaragua	3.50
32	Sri Lanka	2.45	107	Venezuela	3.50
32	Sweden	2.45	112	Gambia	3.60
35	France	2.50	112	Guyana	3.60
35	Italy	2.50	114	Bulgaria	3.65
35	Spain	2.50	114	Georgia	3.65
38	Trinidad and Tobago	2.55	114	Malawi	3.65
39	Argentina	2.60	117	Ethiopia	3.70
39	Barbados	2.60	117	India	3.70
39	Cyprus	2.60	117	Niger	3.70
39	Jamaica	2.60	120	Albania	3.75
39	Portugal	2.60	120	Bangladesh	3.75
44	Bolivia	2.65	120	China (PRC)	3.75
44	Oman	2.65	120	Congo	3.75
44	Philippines	2.65	120	Croatia	3.75
47	Swaziland	2.70	125	Chad	3.80
47	Uruguay	2.70	125	Mauritania	3.80
49	Botswana	2.75	125	Ukraine	3.80
49	Jordan	2.75	128	Sierra Leone	3.85
49	Namibia	2.75	129	Burundi	3.90
49	Tunisia	2.75	129	Suriname	3.90
53	Belize	2.80	129	Zimbabwe	3.90
53	Costa Rica	2.80	132	Haiti	4.00
53	Guatemala	2.80	132	Kyrgyzstan	4.00
53	Israel	2.80	132	Syria	4.00
53	Peru	2.80	135	Belarus	4.05
53	Saudi Arabia	2.80	136	Kazakstan	4.10
53	Turkey	2.80	136	Mozambique	4.10
53	Uganda	2.80	136	Yemen	4.10
53	Western Samoa	2.80	139	Sudan	4.20
62	Indonesia	2.85	140	Myanmar	4.30
62	Latvia	2.85	140	Rwanda	4.30
62	Malta	2.85	142	Angola	4.35
62	Paraguay	2.85	143	Azerbaijan	4.40
66	Greece	2.90	143	Tajikistan	4.40
66	Hungary	2.90	145	Turkmenistan	4.50
66	South Africa	2.90	146	Uzbekistan	4.55
69	Benin	2.95	147	Congo/Zaire	4.70
69	Ecuador	2.95	147	Iran	4.70
69	Gabon	2.95	147	Libya	4.70
69	Morocco	2.95	147	Somalia	4.70
69	Poland	2.95	147	Vietnam	4.70
74	Colombia	3.00	152	Bosnia	4.80
74	Ghana	3.00	153	Iraq	4.90
74	Lithuania	3.00	154	Cuba	5.00
77	Kenya	3.05	154	Laos	5.00
77	Slovak Republic	3.05	154	North Korea	5.00

Repressed

Chapter 6: The Countries

369

CAPITAL FLOWS AND FOREIGN INVESTMENT
Score: 4– (high barriers)

Although Yemen has streamlined its investment laws and procedures in an attempt to attract more foreign investment, barriers still exist. According to the U.S. Department of Commerce, "Corruption at all levels of the government inhibits investment, as does a lack of security in certain parts of the country. Foreign investors must obtain appropriate visas and work permits for themselves and expatriate staff, an often tedious process."[3] Thus, Yemen's score for this factor is two points worse this year.

BANKING
Score: 4–Stable (high level of restrictions)

Although the government plans to allow more foreign banks to operate in Yemen, not much progress has been made so far. Domestic banks remain heavily regulated, and there are only seven commercial banks. According to the U.S. Department of Commerce, "In general, international commercial banks will not confirm letters of credit issued by Yemeni commercial banks because of their low credit ratings."[4]

WAGE AND PRICE CONTROLS
Score: 3–Stable (moderate level)

Yemen's government controls some prices (part of southern Yemen's socialist legacy) but imposes no minimum wage.

PROPERTY RIGHTS
Score: 4–Stable (low level of protection)

Yemen's government has not expropriated any property since 1990. The threat of expropriation, however, still exists because of uncertain economic conditions. Terrorism is a major threat to private property, as is auto theft. According to the U.S. Department of Commerce, "Inefficiency and corruption characterize Yemen's court system. Cases often take years to be decided and usually go to the highest bidder. Often the government cannot enforce court decisions."[5]

REGULATION
Score: 4–Stable (high level)

Businesses must conduct an environmental impact study before engaging in new investments or expanding their enterprises in Yemen. Almost no investments have been turned down, but the process still causes delays. Bureaucratic inefficiency and rising corruption also remain problems. According to the U.S. Department of State, "Yemen is a poor country with an emerging market-based economy that is impeded by excessive government regulation and unchecked corruption."[6]

BLACK MARKET
Score: 5–Stable (very high level of activity)

Because of high trade barriers, smuggling essentially equals official trade in Yemen. Smuggling of some scarce items, such as certain foodstuffs, is particularly widespread. Protection of intellectual property is weak, and piracy of these products is substantial.

NOTES

1. U.S. Department of Commerce, *Country Commercial Guide,* 1997.
2. World Bank, *World Development Report 1997.*
3. U.S. Department of Commerce, *Country Commercial Guide,* 1997.
4. *Ibid.*
5. *Ibid.*
6. U.S. Department of State, "Yemen Country Report on Human Rights Practices for 1996," 1997.

Zambia   3.05

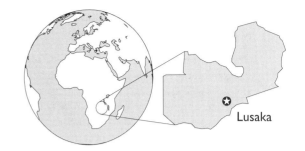

Lusaka

| 1997 Score: **2.85** | 1996 Score: **2.95** | 1995 Score: **3.05** |

Trade	3	Banking	2
Taxation	3.5	Wages and Prices	2
Government Intervention	3	Property Rights	3
Monetary Policy	5	Regulation	4
Foreign Investment	2	Black Market	3

Zambia gained its independence from Great Britain in 1964 and remained a one-party socialist state until 1989, when political opposition was legalized. It currently operates as a unitary republic under its 1996 constitution. Frederick Chiluba won reelection in 1996 (although several political parties boycotted the election) and has committed himself to revitalizing Zambia's economy. His economic liberalization agenda, however, has suffered significant setbacks. Privatization has been sluggish, the government has been tainted by corruption, and economic growth has been erratic over the past few years. The economy grew by more than 5 percent in 1993, shrank by more than 3 percent in both 1994 and 1995, and grew by more than 6 percent in 1996. In addition, both barriers to trade and the level of government consumption of the economy have increased. As a result, Zambia's overall score is 0.2 point worse than last year.

TRADE POLICY
Score: 3– (moderate level of protectionism)

Zambia's average tariff rate has risen to 7.96 percent. As a result, its trade policy score is one point worse this year. Import restrictions have eased, but resentment against an increase in South African imports has generated protectionist sentiment. Corruption in the Customs Bureau continues.

TAXATION
Score–Income taxation: 3–Stable (moderate tax rates)
Score–Corporate taxation: 3–Stable (moderate tax rates)
Final Taxation Score: 3.5–Stable (high tax rates)

Zambia's top marginal income tax rate is 35 percent, and the average taxpayer finds himself in the 15 percent bracket. In 1993, the corporate tax rate was reduced to 35 percent.[1] Zambia also imposes a 20 percent value-added tax and property transfer taxes.

GOVERNMENT INTERVENTION IN THE ECONOMY
Score: 3– (moderate level)

The government consumes 15 percent of Zambia's GDP, up from 10 percent in 1995. As a result, Zambia's score is one point worse this year. During the regime of Kenneth Kaunda, state-owned enterprises accounted for more than 50 percent of GDP, and the state sector still dominates the economy. The government, however, is considering selling off the massive state-owned copper concern.

MONETARY POLICY
Score: 5–Stable (very high level of inflation)

Zambia's average annual rate of inflation from 1985 to 1995 was 91.6 percent. Inflation currently is running at approximately 35 percent.

1	Hong Kong	1.25	77	Zambia	3.05
2	Singapore	1.30	80	Mali	3.10
3	Bahrain	1.70	80	Mongolia	3.10
4	New Zealand	1.75	80	Slovenia	3.10
5	Switzerland	1.90	83	Honduras	3.15
5	United States	1.90	83	Papua New Guinea	3.15
7	Luxembourg	1.95	85	Djibouti	3.20
7	Taiwan	1.95	85	Fiji	3.20
7	United Kingdom	1.95	85	Pakistan	3.20
10	Bahamas	2.00	88	Algeria	3.25
10	Ireland	2.00	88	Guinea	3.25
12	Australia	2.05	88	Lebanon	3.25
12	Japan	2.05	88	Mexico	3.25
14	Belgium	2.10	88	Senegal	3.25
14	Canada	2.10	88	Tanzania	3.25
14	United Arab Emirates	2.10	94	Nigeria	3.30
17	Austria	2.15	94	Romania	3.30
17	Chile	2.15	96	Brazil	3.35
17	Estonia	2.15	96	Cambodia	3.35
20	Czech Republic	2.20	96	Egypt	3.35
20	Netherlands	2.20	96	Ivory Coast	3.35
22	Denmark	2.25	96	Madagascar	3.35
22	Finland	2.25	96	Moldova	3.35
24	Germany	2.30	102	Nepal	3.40
24	Iceland	2.30	103	Cape Verde	3.44
24	South Korea	2.30	104	Armenia	3.45
27	Norway	2.35	104	Dominican Republic	3.45
28	Kuwait	2.40	104	Russia	3.45
28	Malaysia	2.40	107	Burkina Faso	3.50
28	Panama	2.40	107	Cameroon	3.50
28	Thailand	2.40	107	Lesotho	3.50
32	El Salvador	2.45	107	Nicaragua	3.50
32	Sri Lanka	2.45	107	Venezuela	3.50
32	Sweden	2.45	112	Gambia	3.60
35	France	2.50	112	Guyana	3.60
35	Italy	2.50	114	Bulgaria	3.65
35	Spain	2.50	114	Georgia	3.65
38	Trinidad and Tobago	2.55	114	Malawi	3.65
39	Argentina	2.60	117	Ethiopia	3.70
39	Barbados	2.60	117	India	3.70
39	Cyprus	2.60	117	Niger	3.70
39	Jamaica	2.60	120	Albania	3.75
39	Portugal	2.60	120	Bangladesh	3.75
44	Bolivia	2.65	120	China (PRC)	3.75
44	Oman	2.65	120	Congo	3.75
44	Philippines	2.65	120	Croatia	3.75
47	Swaziland	2.70	125	Chad	3.80
47	Uruguay	2.70	125	Mauritania	3.80
49	Botswana	2.75	125	Ukraine	3.80
49	Jordan	2.75	128	Sierra Leone	3.85
49	Namibia	2.75	129	Burundi	3.90
49	Tunisia	2.75	129	Suriname	3.90
53	Belize	2.80	129	Zimbabwe	3.90
53	Costa Rica	2.80	132	Haiti	4.00
53	Guatemala	2.80	132	Kyrgyzstan	4.00
53	Israel	2.80	132	Syria	4.00
53	Peru	2.80	135	Belarus	4.05
53	Saudi Arabia	2.80	136	Kazakstan	4.10
53	Turkey	2.80	136	Mozambique	4.10
53	Uganda	2.80	136	Yemen	4.10
53	Western Samoa	2.80	139	Sudan	4.20
62	Indonesia	2.85	140	Myanmar	4.30
62	Latvia	2.85	140	Rwanda	4.30
62	Malta	2.85	142	Angola	4.35
62	Paraguay	2.85	143	Azerbaijan	4.40
66	Greece	2.90	143	Tajikistan	4.40
66	Hungary	2.90	145	Turkmenistan	4.50
66	South Africa	2.90	146	Uzbekistan	4.55
69	Benin	2.95	147	Congo/Zaire	4.70
69	Ecuador	2.95	147	Iran	4.70
69	Gabon	2.95	147	Libya	4.70
69	Morocco	2.95	147	Somalia	4.70
69	Poland	2.95	147	Vietnam	4.70
74	Colombia	3.00	152	Bosnia	4.80
74	Ghana	3.00	153	Iraq	4.90
74	Lithuania	3.00	154	Cuba	5.00
77	Kenya	3.05	154	Laos	5.00
77	Slovak Republic	3.05	154	North Korea	5.00

Mostly Unfree

Capital Flows and Foreign Investment
Score: 2–Stable (low barriers)

The government has improved Zambia's foreign investment laws, and there is no legal discrimination between foreign and domestic investors. Few investment opportunities are off-limits, although it is uncertain whether all future privatizations will be open to foreign participation. Zambia attracts commercial farmers from South Africa and Zimbabwe. Foreign investment must be screened by an investment board, which operates quickly and efficiently.

Banking
Score: 2–Stable (low level of restrictions)

Private international and domestic banks operate in Zambia, and the market sets interest rates for loans and deposits. Merchant banking has been legalized. Zambia still has two state-owned banks, however, and the government has taken over the management of a failed major commercial bank.

Wage and Price Controls
Score: 2–Stable (low level)

Price controls have been removed in Zambia, and most subsidies have been eliminated. State subsidization of government-owned enterprises distorts the pricing system, however. There is a minimum wage.

Property Rights
Score: 3–Stable (moderate level of protection)

Former President Kenneth Kaunda's socialist regime, voted out of power in 1991, left a legacy of nationalized property. Businesses were expropriated as recently as 1989. Legislation enacted in 1993, however, provides for full compensation for newly nationalized property in convertible currency. According to the U.S. Department of Commerce, "The courts in Zambia are reasonably independent, but contractual rights and more especially property rights are weak in Zambia."[2]

Regulation
Score: 4–Stable (high level)

Acquiring a business license in Zambia involves complex procedures and delays. An investment board screens domestic investment. Corruption is a growing problem, and labor laws (including the requirement that employers provide housing to employees) are both burdensome and expensive. Residence permits are difficult to acquire.

Black Market
Score: 3–Stable (moderate level of activity)

The trade in illegal gemstones thrives because of a government monopoly, and the lack of protection for intellectual property (for example, computer software) has led to increased piracy.

Notes

1. Banking profits in excess of 1 billion Zambian kwachas are taxed at 45 percent. This one exception to an otherwise flat tax rate was judged not significant enough to earn Zambia a grade of 4, which is reserved for countries with a tax system in which the top marginal rate is between 36 percent and 45 percent.
2. U.S. Department of Commerce, *Country Commercial Guide,* 1997.

Zimbabwe   3.90

1997 Score: **3.70**	1996 Score: **3.70**	1995 Score: **3.50**

Trade	5	Banking	3
Taxation	4	Wages and Prices	3
Government Intervention	4	Property Rights	4
Monetary Policy	4	Regulation	4
Foreign Investment	4	Black Market	4

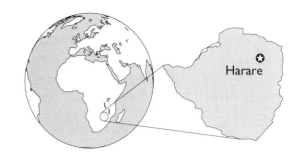

Harare

Zimbabwe gained its independence from the United Kingdom in 1980 upon its acceptance of a British-negotiated cease-fire that ended years of internal conflict between the white minority government and several black nationalist groups. Although it allows opposition parties and periodically holds elections, it is a de facto one-party state under President Robert Mugabe. Zimbabwe has one of Africa's more industrialized economies, and the government exercises considerable control over economic activity. President Mugabe has eased restrictions on foreign investment and has eliminated most price controls, but the future of market reform is uncertain because powerful elements in the government oppose liberalization. The government has made little progress toward privatization. Moreover, government spending remains too high, with a government deficit of over 10 percent of GDP (causing the International Monetary Fund to suspend aid in 1995). The government recently announced a program to confiscate the private property of whites, foreigners, and foreign-owned businesses for redistribution to the black population. It defends the right of the state to oversee and approve foreign investment ventures and partnerships between foreign and domestic businesses, and to guide the sale of privatized state companies into indigenous ownership. As a result, Zimbabwe's overall score is 0.2 point worse this year.

TRADE POLICY
Score: 5–Stable (very high level of protectionism)

The average tariff rate in Zimbabwe is 30 percent.[1] Customs procedures are complex, and concern over cheaper South African imports could lead to additional protectionist measures. Some textile and clothing imports are banned.

TAXATION
Score–Income taxation: 3–Stable (moderate tax rates)
Score–Corporate taxation: 4–Stable (high tax rates)
Final Taxation Score: 4–Stable (high tax rates)

Zimbabwe's top income tax rate is 40 percent, and the average income level is taxed at 0 percent. The top corporate income tax rate is 37.5 percent. Branches of foreign companies are subject to an additional tax of 8.4 percent. Zimbabwe also has a 10 percent to 20 percent capital gains tax and a 15 percent to 25 percent sales tax.

GOVERNMENT INTERVENTION IN THE ECONOMY
Score: 4– (high level)

Government consumes 27.2 percent of GDP, up from 19 percent. As a result, Zimbabwe's score in this area is one point worse this year. The government owns many enterprises, some of which require subsidies. These include postal, telecommunications, and broadcasting services, railroads, and the national air service, all of which are closed to private investment. The government has refused to adopt a program of privatization despite donor encouragement. According to the U.S. Department of Commerce, "The Government does not have a well-defined privatization program."[2]

1	Hong Kong	1.25		77	Zambia	3.05
2	Singapore	1.30		80	Mali	3.10
3	Bahrain	1.70		80	Mongolia	3.10
4	New Zealand	1.75		80	Slovenia	3.10
5	Switzerland	1.90		83	Honduras	3.15
5	United States	1.90		83	Papua New Guinea	3.15
7	Luxembourg	1.95		85	Djibouti	3.20
7	Taiwan	1.95		85	Fiji	3.20
7	United Kingdom	1.95		85	Pakistan	3.20
10	Bahamas	2.00		88	Algeria	3.25
10	Ireland	2.00		88	Guinea	3.25
12	Australia	2.05		88	Lebanon	3.25
12	Japan	2.05		88	Mexico	3.25
14	Belgium	2.10		88	Senegal	3.25
14	Canada	2.10		88	Tanzania	3.25
14	United Arab Emirates	2.10		94	Nigeria	3.30
17	Austria	2.15		94	Romania	3.30
17	Chile	2.15		96	Brazil	3.35
17	Estonia	2.15		96	Cambodia	3.35
20	Czech Republic	2.20		96	Egypt	3.35
20	Netherlands	2.20		96	Ivory Coast	3.35
22	Denmark	2.25		96	Madagascar	3.35
22	Finland	2.25		96	Moldova	3.35
24	Germany	2.30		102	Nepal	3.40
24	Iceland	2.30		103	Cape Verde	3.44
24	South Korea	2.30		104	Armenia	3.45
27	Norway	2.35		104	Dominican Republic	3.45
28	Kuwait	2.40		104	Russia	3.45
28	Malaysia	2.40		107	Burkina Faso	3.50
28	Panama	2.40		107	Cameroon	3.50
28	Thailand	2.40		107	Lesotho	3.50
32	El Salvador	2.45		107	Nicaragua	3.50
32	Sri Lanka	2.45		107	Venezuela	3.50
32	Sweden	2.45		112	Gambia	3.60
35	France	2.50		112	Guyana	3.60
35	Italy	2.50		114	Bulgaria	3.65
35	Spain	2.50		114	Georgia	3.65
38	Trinidad and Tobago	2.55		114	Malawi	3.65
39	Argentina	2.60		117	Ethiopia	3.70
39	Barbados	2.60		117	India	3.70
39	Cyprus	2.60		117	Niger	3.70
39	Jamaica	2.60		120	Albania	3.75
39	Portugal	2.60		120	Bangladesh	3.75
44	Bolivia	2.65		120	China (PRC)	3.75
44	Oman	2.65		120	Congo	3.75
44	Philippines	2.65		120	Croatia	3.75
47	Swaziland	2.70		125	Chad	3.80
47	Uruguay	2.70		125	Mauritania	3.80
49	Botswana	2.75		125	Ukraine	3.80
49	Jordan	2.75		128	Sierra Leone	3.85
49	Namibia	2.75		129	Burundi	3.90
49	Tunisia	2.75		129	Suriname	3.90
53	Belize	2.80		129	Zimbabwe	3.90
53	Costa Rica	2.80		132	Haiti	4.00
53	Guatemala	2.80		132	Kyrgyzstan	4.00
53	Israel	2.80		132	Syria	4.00
53	Peru	2.80		135	Belarus	4.05
53	Saudi Arabia	2.80		136	Kazakstan	4.10
53	Turkey	2.80		136	Mozambique	4.10
53	Uganda	2.80		139	Yemen	4.10
53	Western Samoa	2.80		139	Sudan	4.20
62	Indonesia	2.85		140	Myanmar	4.30
62	Latvia	2.85		140	Rwanda	4.30
62	Malta	2.85		142	Angola	4.35
62	Paraguay	2.85		143	Azerbaijan	4.40
66	Greece	2.90		143	Tajikistan	4.40
66	Hungary	2.90		145	Turkmenistan	4.50
66	South Africa	2.90		146	Uzbekistan	4.55
69	Benin	2.95		147	Congo/Zaire	4.70
69	Ecuador	2.95		147	Iran	4.70
69	Gabon	2.95		147	Libya	4.70
69	Morocco	2.95		147	Somalia	4.70
69	Poland	2.95		147	Vietnam	4.70
74	Colombia	3.00		152	Bosnia	4.80
74	Ghana	3.00		153	Iraq	4.90
74	Lithuania	3.00		154	Cuba	5.00
77	Kenya	3.05		154	Laos	5.00
77	Slovak Republic	3.05		154	North Korea	5.00

Mostly Unfree

MONETARY POLICY
Score: 4–Stable (high level of inflation)

Zimbabwe's average annual rate of inflation from 1985 to 1995 was 20.9 percent. The estimated rate for 1996 was 21.4 percent.

CAPITAL FLOWS AND FOREIGN INVESTMENT
Score: 4–Stable (high barriers)

Foreign investment regulations were liberalized substantially by a 1992 investment code. Investor incentives, including duty-free imports in some cases, have been introduced, and the Zimbabwe Stock Exchange has been opened to foreign investment. Prior government approval, however, still is required for all foreign direct investment. In 1994, the government banned foreign participation in several sectors, including much of agriculture, forestry, and transportation. As noted by the Office of the United States Trade Representative, "Notwithstanding such commitments to investment liberalization, Zimbabwe has yet to embrace the concept of national treatment or discontinue its sizable 'reserve list' of sectors that are closed to all but domestic investors and foreign investors in joint ventures with local partners."[3] In 1997, the government announced that it planned to expropriate the land owned by white foreigners and foreign corporations and redistribute it to black citizens.

BANKING
Score: 3–Stable (moderate level of restrictions)

Only a few commercial banks in Zimbabwe are foreign-owned. Foreign commercial and merchant banks are allowed majority shareholder status, but this is discouraged. Recent attempts by foreign banks to obtain operating licenses have failed. The government owns some financial institutions. Some banks, however, are becoming more independent. According to the U.S. Department of Commerce, the Central Bank "is becoming increasingly independent of government in its exercising of monetary controls and advising government on fighting inflation, including on occasion criticizing, for example, the GOZ's [Government of Zimbabwe's] lack of fiscal discipline."[4]

WAGE AND PRICE CONTROLS
Score: 3–Stable (moderate level)

Zimbabwe's government has succeeded in removing all but a few price controls, although some subsidies of food goods remain in effect. The government sets a minimum wage by employment sector, and government marketing boards continue to control exports of traditional crops.

PROPERTY RIGHTS
Score: 4– (low level of protection)

In 1992, the legislature passed a sweeping land reform bill that enables the government to force the sale of nearly half the remaining white-owned farmland and use it to establish state-owned communal farms. This legislation denies landowners due process, and its implementation has been subject to corruption. In 1997, President Mugabe announced his most comprehensive land reform proposal to confiscate more than 20.5 million acres of land owned by whites, foreigners, and foreign-owned companies. This land will be redistributed to the country's 11.5 million blacks. As a result of this expropriation of private property, Zimbabwe's property rights score is one point worse this year. According to the U.S. Department of State, "The judiciary is independent, but the Government occasionally refuses to abide by court decisions."[5]

REGULATION
Score: 4–Stable (high level)

Wages and employment in Zimbabwe are heavily regulated. Government permission is required not only to terminate an employee, for example, but also to commence virtually any commercial activity. The private sector is under increasing pressure to hire and train more Zimbabweans, and the use of foreign nationals is severely restricted. The bureaucracy lacks transparency and is highly arbitrary. According to the U.S. Department of Commerce, "Although not rampant, corruption is increasing."[6]

BLACK MARKET
Score: 4–Stable (high level of activity)

About 20 percent of Zimbabwe's GDP is in the black market, primarily because of government monopolies in such areas as transportation services.

NOTES

1. Information from the Zimbabwean Embassy, Washington, D.C., July 20, 1995. This average inflation rate is consistent with information in World Bank, "Open Economies Work Better!" *Policy Research Paper* No. 1636, August 1996.
2. U.S. Department of Commerce, *Country Commercial Guide,* 1997.
3. Office of the United States Trade Representative, *1997 National Trade Estimate Report on Foreign Trade Barriers.*
4. U.S. Department of Commerce, *Country Commercial Guide,* 1997.
5. U.S. Department of State, "Zimbabwe Country Report on Human Rights Practices for 1996," 1997.
6. U.S. Department of Commerce, *Country Commercial Guide,* 1997.

Major Works Cited

The following sources provided the basis for the country factor analyses in the 1998 *Index of Economic Freedom*. In addition, the authors and analysts of the various elements of the *Index* relied on supporting documentation and information from various government agencies and World Wide Web sites on the Internet, numerous news reports and journal articles, and official responses to inquiries. These sources are cited in each chapter where appropriate. All data and information received from government sources were verified with independent, internationally recognized nongovernmental sources as well.

Arrowhead International, *World Trade and Customs Directory*, Washington, D.C., Spring 1997.

Barro, Robert J., presentation to Heritage Foundation Roundtable on Economic Growth, June 26, 1996; copies available on request from The Heritage Foundation.

Bruno, Michael, and William Easterly, "Inflation Crises and Long-Run Growth," *Journal of Monetary Economics,* forthcoming 1997; data available through the World Bank Growth Project Web site: *http://www.worldbank.org/html/prdmg/grthweb/datasets.htm.*

Economist Intelligence Unit Limited, *EIU Country Reports,* London, 1997.

——, *Investing, Licensing and Trading Conditions Abroad (ILT Reports),* London, 1997.

Fisher, Richard D., Jr., and John T. Dori, *U.S. and Asia Statistical Handbook, 1997–1998 Edition,* Washington, D.C.: The Heritage Foundation, 1997.

Holmes, Kim R., Bryan T. Johnson, and Melanie Kirkpatrick, eds., 1997 *Index of Economic Freedom,* Washington, D.C.: The Heritage Foundation and Dow Jones & Company, Inc., 1997.

International Monetary Fund, "Adjusting to New Realities: MENA, The Uruguay Round, and the EU–Mediterranean Initiative," Working Paper WP/97/5, Washington, D.C., January 1997.

——, *Direction of Trade Statistics Yearbook,* Washington, D.C., 1996.

——, *Government Finance Statistics Yearbook,* Washington, D.C., 1996.

——, *International Financial Statistics Yearbook,* Washington, D.C., 1996.

Karatnycky, Adrian, Alexander Motyl, and Boris Shor, eds., *Nations in Transit 1997,* Freedom House, Inc., 1997.

Michalopoulos, Constantine, and David G. Tarr, *Trade Performance and Policy in the New Independent States,* Washington, D.C.: The World Bank, 1996.

Ng, Francis, and Alexander Yeats, *Open Economies Work Better!* Washington, D.C.: The World Bank, International Trade Division, August 1996.

Ricardo, David, *On the Principles of Political Economy and Taxation,* Third Edition, Piero Sraffa, ed., Cambridge: Cambridge University Press, 1951 (originally published in 1821).

Smith, Adam, *An Inquiry into the Nature and Causes of the Wealth of Nations,* R. H. Campbell and A. S. Skinner, eds., Glasgow Edition, Oxford: Oxford University Press, 1976 (originally published in 1776).

Taxation in Central and South America, Deloitte Touche Tohmatsu International, New York, 1996.

United Nations Development Programme, *Human Development Report 1997,* New York, 1997.

U.S. Department of Commerce, *Country Commercial Guides,* Washington, D.C., 1997.

——, *National Trade Data Bank and International Bulletin Board,* STAT–USA, Washington, D.C., 1997.

U.S. Department of State, *Country Reports on Economic Policy and Trade Practices,* Report Submitted to the Committee on International Relations and Committee on Ways and Means, U.S. House of Representatives, and the Committee on Foreign Relations and Committee on Finance, U.S. Senate, March 1997.

——, *Country Reports on Human Rights Practices for 1996,* released by the Bureau of Democracy, Human Rights, and Labor, January 30, 1997; available at the U.S. Department of State Web site: *http://www.state.gov/www/ind.html.*

United States Trade Representative, *1997 National Trade Estimate Report on Foreign Trade Barriers,* Washington, D.C.: U.S. Government Printing Office, 1997.

World Bank, *Statistical Handbook 1996: States of the Former USSR,* Washington, D.C., 1996.

——, *World Bank World Atlas 1997,* Washington, D.C., 1997.

——, *World Bank World Development Indicators on CD–ROM 1997,* Washington, D.C., 1997.

——, *World Bank World Development Report 1997,* Oxford University Press: The International Bank for Reconstruction and Development/ The World Bank, 1997.

Worldwide Corporate Tax Guide and Directory, Ernst & Young International, Ltd., New York, 1997.

Worldwide Executive Tax Guide and Directory, Ernst & Young International, Ltd., New York, 1997; available on the Ernst & Young Web site: *http://www1.ey.com/.*